...ONTH OF FREE READING

at

www.ForgottenBooks.com

By purchasing this book you are eligible for one month membership to ForgottenBooks.com, giving you unlimited access to our entire collection of over 1,000,000 titles via our web site and mobile apps.

To claim your free month visit:

www.forgottenbooks.com/free909685

* Offer is valid for 45 days from date of purchase. Terms and conditions apply.

English
Français
Deutsche
Italiano
Español
Português

www.forgottenbooks.com

Mythology Photography **Fiction** Fishing Christianity **Art** Cooking Essays Buddhism Freemasonry Medicine **Biology** Music **Ancient Egypt** Evolution Carpentry Physics Dance Geology **Mathematics** Fitness Shakespeare **Folklore** Yoga Marketing **Confidence** Immortality Biographies Poetry **Psychology** Witchcraft Electronics Chemistry History **Law** Accounting **Philosophy** Anthropology Alchemy Drama Quantum Mechanics Atheism Sexual Health **Ancient History** **Entrepreneurship** Languages Sport Paleontology Needlework Islam **Metaphysics** Investment Archaeology Parenting Statistics Criminology **Motivational**

Parsons St

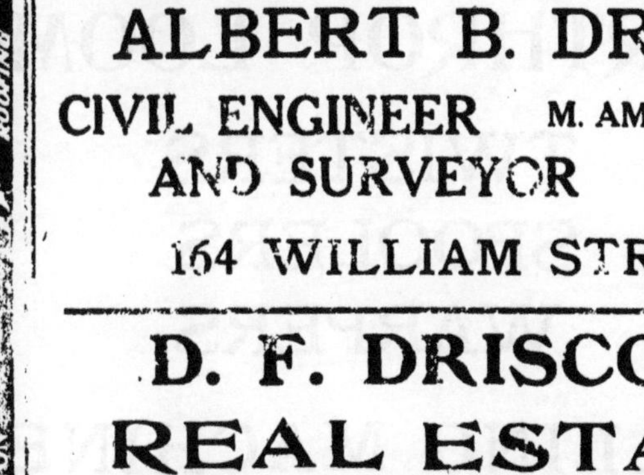

ALBERT B. DRAKE

CIVIL ENGINEER M. AM. SOC. C.

AND SURVEYOR Bell 18 Auto.

164 WILLIAM STREET

D. F. DRISCOLL

REAL ESTAT

Room 14 CLIFFORD BLDG.

Cor. Sixth and Market Sts., New Bedf

Auto. 1301 Bell 2037-2

JOHN W. PAUL HENRY H. D

PAUL & DIXON

INSURANCE THAT INSUR

Successors to

JOHN W. PAUL
SAMUEL H. COOK
HIRAM VAN CAMPEN & CO.
ROTCH & POTTER

Agency Established A. D. 1852

303 MERCHANTS BANK B
NEW BEDFORD, MAS

DAVID DUFF & SON

WHOLESALE **COAL** RETAIL

Contractors and Team

MAIN OFFICE
Merchants Bank Building, William Stre
BRANCH OFFICE, 73 Weld Street
WHARVES, Fish Island Telephone

ESTABLISHED 1884

New Bedford Steam Carpet Beating and Rug

H. M. MAINE, Prop.

CORNER NORTH AND
NORTH WATER STS.

Asphaltic ROOFING
MANUFACTURING COMPANY ROOFING AND PAVING MATERIALS 291 FRANKLIN STREET, BOSTON

NORTHROP LOOMS

TWISTERS
SPOOLERS
WARPERS

BALLING MACHINES

Reels Banding Machines

Mirror Spinning Rings

Trade Mark Registered U. S. Patent Office

Dutcher Temples

Trade Mark Registered U. S. Patent Office

Rabbeth Centrifugal Clutch Spindles

Rhoades-Chandler Separators

Moscrop Single Thread Yarn Testers

and other patented improvements in Cotton Machinery

DRAPER COMPANY

HOPEDALE, MASS.

J. D. CLOUDMAN Southern Agent
40 So. Forsyth St. Atlanta Ga.

WOOD, BRIGHTMAN & CO.

PLUMBERS

Installers of all kinds of Heating Apparatus, Steam, Hot Water and Hot Air. Manufacturers of Skylights, Cornices, Gutters, Metal Roofing and all kinds of Sheet Metal Work used on Buildings. Dealers in Pumps, Pumping Engines, Stoves, Yacht Fittings, Etc.

North Water, corner William Street

Bell 232 Automatic 1472

THOMAS F. WOOD HENRY HOWLAND

Main Office and Yard, Front Street Foot Middle

Bell 314 Automatic 1373

BRANCH OFFICES

114 WILLIAM STREET Bell 914, Auto 1053

1026 ACUSHNET AVE. Automatic 2154

We sell only the Best Grades of Coal

1825 1911

Merchants National Bank

Capital,	$1,000,000.00
Surplus,	1,000,000.00
Profits,	100,000.00

OFFICERS

HENRY C. W. MOSHER, President

H. W. TABER, Cashier

DIRECTORS

GEORGE S. HOMER	WILLIAM M. WOOD	HENRY S. KNOWLES
FRANCIS T. AKIN	OTIS N. PIERCE	JOHN W. KNOWLES
HENRY C. W. MOSHER	ELIOT D. STETSON	HENRY L. TIFFANY
	JAMES E. STANTON JR.	

Letters of credit, Travelers Cheques, and bills of exchange on all parts of the World

Safe Deposit Boxes Free to Our Customers

NEW BEDFORD

Five Cents Savings Bank

37 Purchase Street

INCORPORATED 1855

Banks Hours 9 A. M. to 1 P. M. Saturday Evenings 7 to 9

OFFICERS

LOUM SNOW, President
WALTER CLIFFORD, Vice-President
OTIS N. PIERCE, Vice-President
WILLIAM H. PITMAN, Treasurer
ANNIE E. L. BORDEN, Asst. Treasurer
GEORGE H. H. ALLEN, Clerk

TRUSTEES

Thomas Wilcox
E. Williams Hervey
Loum Snow
Otis N. Pierce
Benjamin T. Cummings
Henry C. Denison
Oliver F. Brown
Parkman M. Lund
George H. H. Allen
Walter Clifford
Robert C. P. Coggeshall
Andrew G. Pierce, Jr.
Alex. McL. Goodspeed
Francis T. Akin
George R. Stetson
Joseph Poisson
John Duff
Rufus A. Soule
Arthur L. Tucker
John H. Barrows
Henry M. Knowles
James W. Allen
Frederic Taber
William O. Devoll
William R. West
John V. Spare
Robert L. Baylies
Jireh Swift, Jr.
Homer W. Hervey
Albert R. Pierce
John H. Clifford
Joseph W. Webster
Charles M. Hussey
Benjamin Wilcox
Frank H. Gifford
J. Henry Herring
Leonard C. Lapham
Henry S. Knowles
Benjamin Baker

BOARD OF INVESTMENT

LOUM SNOW, Chairman
THOMAS WILCOX
ANDREW G. PIERCE, JR.
PARKMAN M. LUND
ARTHUR L. TUCKER
OTIS N. PIERCE
WILLIAM O. DEVOLL
WILLIAM R. WEST
JIREH SWIFT., JR.

1825 1911

Merchants National Bank

Capital,	$1,000,000.00
Surplus,	1,000,000.00
Profits,	100,000.00

OFFICERS

HENRY C. W. MOSHER, President

H. W. TABER, Cashier

DIRECTORS

GEORGE S. HOMER
FRANCIS T. AKIN
HENRY C. W. MOSHER
WILLIAM M. WOOD
OTIS N. PIERCE
ELIOT D. STETSON
JAMES E. STANTON JR.
HENRY S. KNOWLES
JOHN W. KNOWLES
HENRY L. TIFFANY

Letters of credit, Travelers Cheques, and bills of exchange on all parts of the World

Safe Deposit Boxes Free to Our Customers

NEW BEDFORD
Five Cents Savings Bank
37 Purchase Street

INCORPORATED 1855

Banks Hours 9 A. M. to 1 P. M. Saturday Evenings 7 to 9

OFFICERS

LOUM SNOW, President
WALTER CLIFFORD, Vice-President
OTIS N. PIERCE, Vice-President
WILLIAM H. PITMAN, Treasurer
ANNIE E. L. BORDEN, Asst. Treasurer
GEORGE H. H. ALLEN, Clerk

TRUSTEES

Thomas Wilcox	Francis T. Akin	Robert L. Baylies
E. Williams Hervey	George R. Stetson	Jireh Swift, Jr.
Loum Snow	Joseph Poisson	Homer W. Hervey
Otis N. Pierce	John Duff	Albert R. Pierce
Benjamin T. Cummings	Rufus A. Soule	John H. Clifford
Henry C. Denison	Arthur L. Tucker	Joseph W. Webster
Oliver F. Brown	John H. Barrows	Charles M. Hussey
Parkman M. Lund	Henry M. Knowles	Benjamin Wilcox
George H. H. Allen	James W. Allen	Frank H. Gifford
Walter Clifford	Frederic Taber	J. Henry Herring
Robert C. P. Coggeshall	William O. Devoll	Leonard C. Lapham
Andrew G. Pierce, Jr.	William R. West	Henry S. Knowles
Alex. McL. Goodspeed	John V. Spare	Benjamin Baker

BOARD OF INVESTMENT

LOUM SNOW, Chairman
THOMAS WILCOX ANDREW G. PIERCE, JR.
PARKMAN M. LUND ARTHUR L. TUCKER
OTIS N. PIERCE WILLIAM O. DEVOLL
WILLIAM R. WEST JIREH SWIFT., JR.

THE MECHANICS NATIONAL BANK

SOUTHWEST CORNER PURCHASE AND WILLIAM STREETS

CAPITAL - - $600,000

SURPLUS and UNDIVIDED PROFITS $530,000

OFFICERS

Henry H. Crapo, President — Henry C. Denison, Vice-President
E. S. Brown, Cashier — N. C. Hathaway, Asst. Cashier
George M. Kingman, Teller — Alfred Thornton, Bookkeeper

CLERKS

William C. Philips — Mabel Thornton
Louis W. Tilden — J. Herbert Smith
Earle F. Chase — Alton I. Macomber

DIRECTORS

W. W. Crapo — E. William Hervey — Henry H. Crapo
Oliver Prescott — Henry C. Denison — Andrew G. Pierce, Jr.
Thomas Wilcox — E. S. Brown — Wm. R. West
Thomas S. Hathaway — Russell Grinnell

DIRECTORS MEET WEDNESDAYS AND SATURDAYS

TUCKER, ANTHONY & CO.

Bankers and Brokers

17 PLEASANT STREET

Members of the Boston and New York Stock Exchanges
Boston Office, 53 State St. New York Office, 60 Broadway

Correspondents

Messrs. Thos. L. Manson & Co., New York
Messrs. Chas. D. Barney & Co., New York and Philadelphia

LOCAL and FALL RIVER STOCKS and BONDS BOUGHT and SOLD on COMMISSION
Benjamin A. Tripp, Manager in New Bedford

FIRST NATIONAL BANK

110 Union Street, corner South Second Street

CAPITAL	$1,000,000
SURPLUS AND UNDIVIDED PROFITS	670,000

W. P. WINSOR, President
WM. A. MACKIE, Cashier
FRANK B. CHASE, Asst. Cashier
HENRY J. PERRY, JR., Clerk
WM. F. DAMMON, Teller
HAROLD T. STURTEVANT, Bookkeeper
WM. H. TRIPP, Bookkeeper
H. McNALLY, Clerk

DIRECTORS

W. P. WINSOR
THOMAS B. TRIPP
WM. BAYLIES
THOMAS M. STETSON
EDWARD T. PIERCE
MATTHEW LUCE, JR.
GIDEON ALLEN, JR.
THOMAS A. TRIPP
HERBERT E. CUSHMAN

HAWES, TEWKSBURY & CO.

BANKERS AND BROKERS

Members Boston Stock Exchange

Masonic Building, New Bedford

Boston Office 35 Congress Street

Stocks, Bonds and Investment Securities Bought and Sold on Commission. Boxes for Rent and Valuables of Every Description received for Storage in our Fire and Burglar Proof Vaults.

NEW BEDFORD SAFE DEPOSIT AND TRUST COMPANY

61 WILLIAM STREET CORNER ACUSHNET AVENUE

CAPITAL **$200,000**

SURPLUS and Undivided Profits . **$200,000**

OFFICERS

FREDERIC TABER, President
EDMUND W. BOURNE, Cashier
WILLIAM M. THORUP, Bookkeeper HERBERT C. WILBOR, Teller

CLERKS

John F. Hatch, Jr., Asst. Teller
Albert P. Cunningham
Harry I. Gifford
Phillip D. Drew
Mark M. Gray
Charles M. Ennis
Albert D. Noel
Mary A. Swinson
Miss Josephine Swift

DIRECTORS

Rufus A. Soule
William M. Butler
Frederic H. Taber
Charles S. Paisler
Frederic Taber
Lot B. Bates
Benjamin Wilcox
William B. Gardner
Charles F. Cushing
Charles F. Wing
Edmund W. Bourne

The New Bedford Institution for Savings

INCORPORATED 1825

CORNER UNION AND FOURTH STREETS

TELEPHONE 268

Open daily from 9 A. M. and Saturday Evenings from 7 to 9 o'clock

WILLIAM W. CRAPO, President
CHARLES W. CLIFFORD, Vice-President
THOMAS B. TRIPP, Vice-President
GEORGE H. BATCHELOR, Treasurer
PHILIP E. MACY, Asst. Treasurer
EDMUND WOOD, Secretary

TRUSTEES

Charles W. Clifford
William A. Robinson
Edmund Wood
Gideon Allen, Jr.
Edward T. Pierce
Henry H. Crapo
Charles M. Taber
Gardner T. Sanford
William W. Crapo
Thomas B. Tripp
Thomas S. Hathaway
Oliver Prescott
Clarence A. Cook
Herbert E. Cushman
John W. Knowles
Benjamin Cummings
William A. Mackie
Benjamin H. Anthony
Henry C. W. Mosher
Eliot D. Stetson
David L. Parker
Charles F. Wing
Standish Bourne
Walter P. Winsor
Edward S. Brown
Henry Howland
George N. Alden
Albert W. Holmes
Henry S. Hutchinson
William A. Robinson, Jr.
Frederic H. Taber
Edmund W. Bourne
Henry L. Tiffany

BOARD OF INVESTMENT

WILLIAM W. CRAPO, Chairman
THOMAS B. TRIPP
OLIVER PRESCOTT
CLARENCE A. COOK
GIDEON ALLEN, Jr.
EDWARD T. PIERCE
THOMAS S. HATHAWAY

CONGDON, CARPENTER & CO.

Iron, Steel, Heavy Hardware and Metals

HEADQUARTERS FOR COLD ROLLED SHAFTING

Blacksmiths and Carriage Makers' Supplies
Paints, Oils and Varnishes

Agents F. W. Devoe & C. T. Reynolds Co., Lead and Zinc Paints, Colors and Brushes, Carter White Lead, Saddlery Hardware Harness, Horse Blankets, Robes and Stable Supplies, Solder Zinc, Galvanized and Black Sheet Iron, Lead Pipe, Newton Lead Traps.

LONG DISTANCE AND AUTOMATIC TELEPHONE

58 to 68 FOURTH STREET FALL RIVER

BORDEN & REMINGTON CO.

DEALERS IN

Drugs, Chemicals, Dye Stuffs and Manufacturers Supplies

Corn, Wheat and Potato Starches. Lubricating Oils of all kinds.

Bale Rope, Jute Rope and Burlaps, Cordage, also

Builders' Supplies

such as Brick, Common and Fancy, Lime and Cement, Hair, Plaster, Drain Pipe, Fire Brick, BOILER SHAPES and Clay Polished Plate Glass and Mirrors, Window Glass, Sash, Doors and Blinds

Painters' Supplies

White Leads, Oil Colors, Varnishes, Oils, Turpentine and Dryers

115 Anawan Street, Fall River, Mass.

Long Distance Telephone 426 and 427

ALLEN, SLADE & CO.

WHOLESALE GROCERS

AND DEALERS IN

Flour, Butter, Cheese, Lard, Ham, Etc.

Coffee Roasters and Spice Grinders

RECEIVERS OF

Washburn-Crosby Company's Celebrated "Gold Medal" Flour

Russell's "Regular" and

Elmore Mills Cream White Flour

NEW BEDFORD STORE AND OFFICE

1 William, corner North Water Street

FALL RIVER

18-26 and 30 Third Street

G. W. SLADE   E. B. LAKE   B. S. C. GIFFORD

A. F. CLARK F. L. SNOW F. L. HOXIE

Driscol, Church & Hall,

Wholesale Grocers

Cor. Union & First Sts., New Bedford, Mass.

ESTABLISHED 1828

Owners or exclusive wholesale distributors in this vicinity for the following well-known brands of goods:

John Alden Flour
Bridal Veil Flour
Perfection Flour
Pioneer Flour
Queen Flour
Crocker's Best Flour
Wamsutta Flour
Snow Crust Flour
John Alden Canned Goods
John Alden Molasses
John Alden Raisins
John Alden Fish Cakes
John Alden Catsup
Wamsutta Canned Goods
Wamsutta Raisins
Wamsutta Beef, in glass
Wamsutta Catsup
Moxie
Clicquot Club Beverages
Lake View Bottled Vinegar
39 Tobacco
Williams Bros. Pickles, etc.
Chippewa Salt
Sure Rising Buckwheat

ESTABLISHED 1866 INCORPORATED 1888

HOWARD BROS. MFG. CO.

—MANUFACTURERS OF—

CARD CLOTHING

Quality is our Inducement

1909

Revolving Flat Cards Clothed Complete and Superior Results Guaranteed.
(References on file from some of the largest cotton mills)
Revolving Flats Re-clothed using our own Patent End Slip. (Sole makers.)
Fillets Re-drawn. Emery Cylinders Re-covered.
Tempered Steel Twin Wire Soldered Heddles——All Sizes

A. H. HOWARD, President and Treasurer
HERBERT H. WHITHWORTH, Representative
HERBERT MIDGLEY, Supt.

44-46 VINE STREET - WORCESTER, MASS.

"Morse"

TWIST DRILLS - REAMERS - TAPS, DIES-MILLING CUTTERS, ETC.

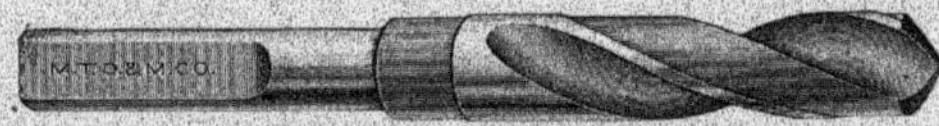

are good, reliable, accurate, serviceable tools, made so by experts. "MORSE" Tools are at work in modern shops all over the world, where the highest efficiency and greatest accurancy are demanded. Carbon and High Speed Steel.

Catalogue on request.

Morse Twist Drill & Machine Co.

New Bedford, Mass., U. S. A.

CHAS. H. SHERMAN

CARPENTER,

CONTRACTOR

and **BUILDER**

20 No. Second St.

New Bedford, Mass.

Jobbing a Specialty.

Bell Telephone Connection

ESTABLISHED 1885

THOMAS TOWNSEND

RHODE ISLAND COMB WORKS

COTTON COMBS

Made and Re-needled by the very latest improved methods

Dealer in the

Best English Cast Steel Pins and Comber needles

American, English, French and German Systems

Prompt Attention to All Repairs

157 ORANGE STREET, PROVIDENCE, R. I.

TELEPHONE CONNECTION

ESTABLISHED 1884

S. A. DUDLEY

TAUNTON, MASS.

Manufacturers of

SHUTTLES

of every description

Dudley Patent "DANDY" Spindle a Specialty

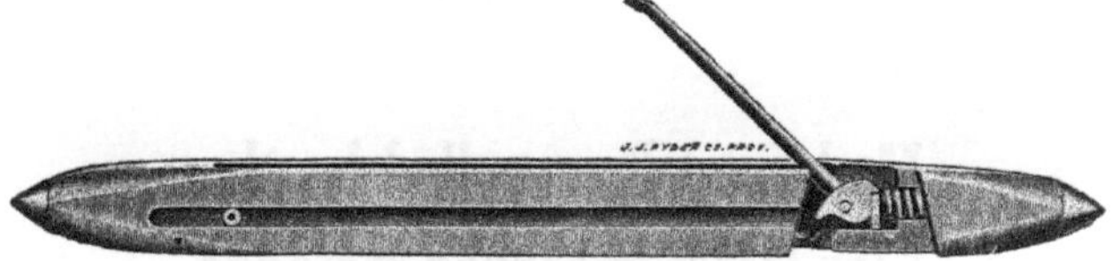

Right Hand Shuttle

"Dudley" Threader

Left Hand Shuttle

Large orders are being received for these Shuttles and they are giving PERFECT SATISFACTION.

Would be pleased to receive sample orders, which will receive my best attention.

FIRST CLASS GOODS GUARANTEED

ESTABLISHED 1885

THOMAS TOWNSEND

RHODE ISLAND COMB WORKS

COTTON COMBS

Made and Re-needled by the very latest improved methods

Dealer in the

Best English Cast Steel Pins and Comber needles

American, English, French and German Systems

Prompt Attention to All Repairs

157 ORANGE STREET, PROVIDENCE, R. I.

TELEPHONE CONNECTION

ESTABLISHED 1884

S. A. DUDLEY

TAUNTON, MASS.

Manufacturers of

SHUTTLES

of every description

Dudley Patent "DANDY" Spindle a Specialty

Right Hand Shuttle

"Dudley" Threader

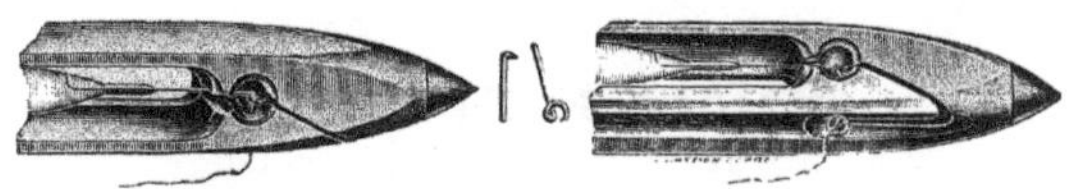

Left Hand Shuttle

Large orders are being received for these Shuttles and they are giving PERFECT SATISFACTION.

Would be pleased to receive sample orders, which will receive my best attention.

FIRST CLASS GOODS GUARANTEED

The Benjamin F. Smith Construction Co.

CONTRACTORS

AND

MILL BUILDERS

22 Mason Street, Pawtucket, R. I.

LONG DISTANCE TELEPHONE

BRANCH OFFICE

Five Cents Savings Bank Building

37 Purchase Street, New Bedford

Bell 180

ESTABLISHED 1874 INCORPORATED 1899

J. W. BISHOP COMPANY

TIMES BUILDING
NEW BEDFORD, MASS.

BOOTH MILLS, NEW BEDFORD, MASS.

CHARLES W. PRARAY
Engineer

J. W. BISHOP COMPANY
Builders

CONTRACTORS

ESTIMATES GIVEN ON ALL CLASSES OF WORK

OFFICES

New York
Providence
Boston
Worcester
New Bedford

Shops at Worcester, Mass.

C. W. LASELL, Pres. G. M. WHITIN, Treas.

THE WHITIN MACHINE WORKS

MANUFACTURERS OF

Cotton Machinery

Cards, Combing Machinery, Railway Heads,
Drawing Frames, Spinning Frames,
Twisters, Quillers, Spoolers,
Reels and Looms,
Etc., Etc.

WHITINSVILLE

Worcester County Mass.

Electric Express

Charles T. Battey, Manager

Fast, Frequent, Safe Service

The Ideal Way to Ship

TO ALL POINTS ON THE LINES OF THE

Union
New Bedford and Onset
Bay State
Providence and Fall River
Rhode Island Co.
Brockton and Plymouth

STREET RAILWAYS

For rates and other information, inquire at station.

Cor. No. Water and Elm Sts.

TELEPHONES
Bell 648
Auto. 1142

Automatic Telephone Company

OF NEW BEDFORD

41 WILLIAM STREET

AUTOMATIC TELEPHONE BUILDING

F. T. AKIN, President
L. B. BATES, Vice-President
FREDERIC H. TABER, Treasurer and Clerk
C. H. JAMES, Asst. Treasurer
W. R. BINKLEY, Supt.

DIRECTORS

F. T. Akin
F. H. Taber
F. W. Besse
Wm. C. Hawes
E. D. Sherman
L. B. Bates
Thomas Hersom
Frederic H. Taber
T. J. Moriarty

We want to Supply You with Telephone Service

We offer lowest prices. Unlimited Service. Private metalic lines. Long distance phones Modern construction and guarantee satisfaction.

Use the AUTOMATIC toll line when talking to Fall River

"CALL LONG DISTANCE"

M. STEINERT & SONS CO.

Steinert'S

PIANOS RENTED MOVED TUNED

LARGEST RETAIL PIANO HOUSE IN AMERICA
Exclusive Distributors in New England of
STEINWAY, HUME, WEBER
JEWETT, WOODBURY and OTHER
PIANOS
AND
PIANOLA PIANOS

PIANOS REBUILT REFINISHED REPAIRED

VICTORS and RECORDS

VICTROLAS and RECORDS

109 William Street

The Pairpoint Corporation

FACTORY AND SHOWROOMS

HOWLAND AND PROSPECT STS.

Showrooms open daily for
Public inspection of our line

FOUR EXCLUSIVE LINES

CUT GLASS
SILVER PLATE
ELECTRIC & GAS PORTABLES
and
BRASS GOODS

Our Goods are not THE BEST, but there are NONE BETTER.

We invite you to call and see how we make our goods, this surely will be instructive

Williston H. Collins & Co.

PAPER RULERS
BOOK BINDERS

PRINTERS

ACCOUNT BOOK MAKERS

34-36-38 N. Second St. cor. William St. NEW BEDFORD, MASS.

BOTH TELEPHONES

THOMAS HERSOM & CO.

MANUFACTURERS OF

Italian Sapone Washing Powder

Thos. Hersom & Co.'s Best— Our leading brand — Always the best

ALSO SALT WATER SOAPS

Dealers in Sperm, Neatsfoot, Palm and Castor Oils, Tallow, Grease, Rosin, Caustic Soda, Sal Soda, Potash, Etc. Also Bone Meal for Fertilizer, and Tankage Meal.

OFFICE COMMERCIAL AND FRONT STREETS

Automatic 1483 Factory foot Howard Ave. Bell 1113-2

The ACUSHNET SANITARIUM

SANITARIUM TREATMENT

Electric Light Baths
Hydro-Electric Baths
Sitz Baths
Spray and Shower Baths
Nauheim Baths
Radiodescent Light
Scotch Douche
Salt Glows
Massage—General and Facial

All Treatments given by Trained Attendants

FOR FURTHER INFORMATION ADDRESS

The Acushnet Sanitarium

Cor. Main St. and Belleville Ave. New Bedford, Mass.

Both Phones One block east of Lund's Corner

GEORGE SCHULER Established 1882 JACQUES SCHULER

SCHULER BROTHERS

MANUFACTURERS AND DEALERS IN

Fine Footwear

76 and 78 PURCHASE ST. - NEW BEDFORD

CALL FOR SHOES OF OUR MAKE BELL 1749-1

D. J. JARRY

MAKER OF

High Grade Bread

107 BOWDITCH STREE

Automatic 2089

William F. Sturtevant

Successor to E. J. Kempton

HOUSE, SHIP AND SIGN

PAINTER

Frescoing, Decorating, Graining and Paper Hanging

Whoesa e and Retail Dealer in

Paints, Colors, Oils, Glass

Putty, Picture Mouldings, Etc.

Jewett's Lead a Specialty

70 High Street, New Bedford

Connected by Telephone

A. M. RODGERS, Agent

STEAMSHIP AND RAILROAD

TICKET AGENT

Tickets to and from California, England, Ireland, Scotland, Azores, Europe, Lisbon, Gibralter, Brazil, and all parts of the world. Drafts from one pound upward all over the world. Tourists' rates a specialty.

JAMAICA VIA UNITED FRUIT CO.

Telephone Bell 1814

177 Acushnet Ave., New Bedford

CHARLES H. CHURCH

ESTABLISHED 1852

DRUGGIST

Proprietor of QUICK RELIEF, which never fails to cure NEURALGIA and RHEUMATISM. Als of the well known COLIC CURE, which, when baby has the belly ache soon makes him smile again.

122 Purchase St., corner Middle St.

Automatic 1071

Agents For Household Furnaces | Gasolene and Pumping Engines | Mill Work of all Kinds a Specialty

George J. Allen & Co.

Contractors for

High and Low Pressure Steam Piping

Plumbing, Heating and Sheet Metal Working

91-97 No. Water Street and 2-4 Elm Street

NEW BEDFORD, MASS.

F. G. HILLMAN

669 Purchase Street

New Bedford, Mass.

DEALER IN

Everything required in Textile Mills and for General Manufacturing.

ALSO

Agricultural, Automobile, Builders, Dentists, Engineers, Janitors, Machinists, Masons, Painters, Printers, and Miscellaneous Supplies.

Bolts, Brooms, Brushes, Chemicals, Crayons, Files, Glue, Hose, Commercial Metals and Minerals, Nails, Packings, Paint, Pulleys, Rope, Screws, Tools, Twine, Varnish, Waste, Wrenches, etc.

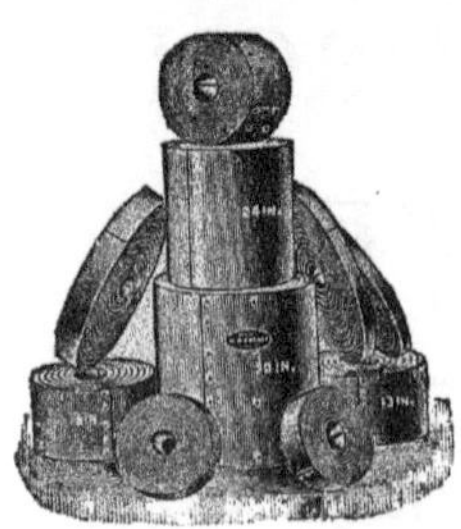

Local Representatives of

HENRY K. BARNES CO.

234-236 Devonshire Street, Boston, Mass.
(Tannery and Factory, Salem, Mass.)

High Grade LEATHER BELTING, Loom Straps, Comber Aprons and Mechanical Leather Goods.

A Large Stock of Belting on hand

Also Sole Local Representatives of

Philadelphia Grease Mfg. Co's LUBRICATING GREASES

Covel & Osborn Co.'s Cotton Banding and Braids

A. B. KENYON

REAL ESTATE

Building Lots on Easy Terms a Specialty

Suite 209-210 TIMES BUILDING, NEW BEDFORD

Bell and Automatic Telephones

CHARLES T. HERON

Real Estate Agent

114 William Street

DR. E. J. ARCAND

Surgeon Dentist

Cor. Nye St. and Acushnet Ave.

Office Hours: 9 to 12 a. m., 2 to 4 and 7 to 8 p. m.

Telephones: Auto. 2160 Bell 861-2

WILLIAM E. SPOONER

Real Estate Agent

52 Pleasant Street, Bates and Kirby Building

Opposite City Hall Telephone 1497-5

LICENSED AND BONDED

CORRESPONDENTS IN PRINCIPAL CITIES OF THE WORLD

The NATIONAL DETECTIVE AGENCY

BERNARD M. GOLDOWSKY, Gen'l Superintendent

(Formerly with Pinkerton's Detective Agency

New York, N. Y.
Brooklyn, N. Y.
Buffalo, N. Y.
Baltimore, Md.
Philadelphia, Pa.
Pittsburg, Pa.
Detroit, Mich.
Cleveland, Ohio
Cincinnati, Ohio
Kansas City, Mo.
New Orleans, La.
St. Louis, Mo.
Indianapolis, Ind.
Chicago, Ill.

San Francisco, Cali.
Los Angeles, Cali.
Denver, Colo.
Butte, Mont.
Salt Lake City, Utah
Portland, Oregon
Seattle, Wash.
Spokane, Wash.
Goldfield, Nev.
Helena, Mont.
Toronto, Canada
Montreal, Canada
Vancouver, B. C.
London, E. C. Eng.

GENERAL SECRET SERVICE

☞NO DIVORCE CASES HANDLED

Our immense success is due to the following facts, viz:

We know our profession from A to Z

We are absolutely reliable.

We can furnish highest references from leading Police Officials and the most prominent Manufacturers, Business and Professional Men in regard to our ability and standing—hence our clients can rest assured that they will not be required to pay for experiments;

And in short—

We deliver the goods

Our motto is: "THERE'S NO SUCH WORD AS FAIL."

☞WE ARE ABSOLUTELY RELIABLE

TELEPHONES

DAY Union 3924 / Broad 1205 NIGHT

W. U. T. Code Used

Cable Address

"ALERT"

Industrial Trust Co. Building, 49 Westminster St.

PROVIDENCE, R. I.

Babbitt Steam Specialty Co.

STEAM SPECIALTIES
OUR SPECIALTY

AGENTS FOR

Dodge Mfg. Co's., Line of Transmission, Scheiren Belt,
STEAM TRAPS, "Vance" "Sterling"

Famous "Durabla" High Pressure Shut Packing

"Durabla" German Gauge Glasses

We supply everything in the mechanical line.
Tell us your wants.

55-57 South Water Street - New Bedford, Mass.

MARBLE AND GRANITE MONUMENTS

J. A. POTHIER

Dealer in all kinds of

Marble and Granite Monuments and Headstones

ALL KINDS OF CEMETERY SUPPLIES

J. F. Corcoran in charge of Letter Cutting

Nothing but First Class Work

Shop, 305 Mt. Pleasant Street

Res. 183 Austin St., New Bedford, Mass.

Designs and Estimates Promptly Furnished

Tel. Automatic 2020

LETTER CUTTING ON MONUMENTS AND HEADSTONES ALREADY ERECTED IN THE CEMETERIES. BEST OF REFERENCES. J. F. CORCORAN

The 20th Century Shuttle

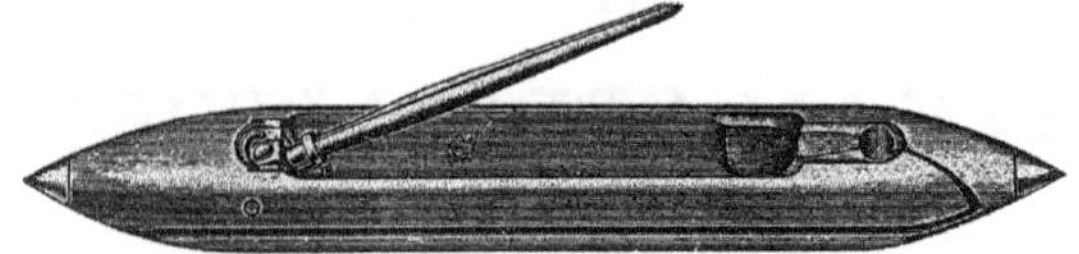

Shuttle containing our patent hand threading device, and Marble Spindle with our patent staple.

The patent staple not only prevents the top of shuttle from splitting when spindle is raised, but strengthens shuttle at the spindle end. We consider the marble spindle the most practical spindle ever invented, and when used with our patent staple greatly improves same.

Shambow Shuttle Co.

307 North Main Street

Woonsocket, R. I.

WM. F. POTTER & CO.

New Bedford, Mass.

AGENTS FOR THE FAMOUS

ONWARD FLOUR

"Best by Test"

ALSO

Ben Hur, Marvel and "Duluth Imperial" Flours

OSWEGO BRAND N. Y. State Canned Goods

DEL MONTE BRAND California Canned Fruits

Gunning Boiler and Machine Co.

BOILER MAKERS - MACHINISTS

Boilers Tested Builders of Tanks and Flues

Marine and Stationary Repairs a Specialty

Repairs Attended to Night or Day

Expert Mechanics on All Work

Estimates Cheerfully Given

All work guaranteed or no pay

Office, 67 So. Water St., New Bedford, Mass.

Bell Phone 796

The Water Supply Question

Is Your Water Supply Satisfactory and Adequate for Your Present and Future Needs?

ARTESIAN or DRIVEN WELLS will solve the water question if the conditions are favorable.

Let us know the water situation at your plant and see if we can be of assistance.

ARTESIAN AND DRIVEN WELLS
ALSO
TEST BORINGS FOR FOUNDATIONS

B. F. Smith & Co., Inc.

38 OLIVER STREET - - BOSTON, MASS.

ESTABLISHED 1878

THE

KIRSHEN PRESS

HIGH GRADE

Printers

PRINTING, ENGRAVING,
DESIGNING AND STATIONERY

WITH OUR MODERN EQUIPMENTS AND FACILITIES WE ARE ENABLED TO SERVE YOU BETTER THAN ELSEWHERE. WRITE TO US FOR ESTIMATES.

TELEPHONE 2798 FORT HILL

65 BROAD ST., BOSTON

THEOPHILE LEBEAU
REAL ESTATE
CONTRACTOR
— ALSO —
CAFE
412 No. Front St. - - New Bedford, Mass.

George Kirby, Jr., Paint Co.
Manufacturers of Motor Boat and Yacht Paints
GREEN YACHT COMPOSITE, RED YACHT COMPOSITE, OLD STYLE COPPER PAINT, NEW BEDFORD BRONZE ANTI-FOULING
Also White Lead, Zincs and Paints of all kinds for General Painters' Use.
WALL STREET Long Distance Telephone NEW BEDFORD

JOHN R. LINTON & SONS
JOHN E. LINTON
Automobile and Carriage Painting and Repairing
New Light Express, Grocery and Milk Wagons a Specialty
105 MAXFIELD STREET
Bell Telephone 773-5
Auto. Telephone 1683

Clothing on Credit
For the Family
$1.00 PER WEEK
IDEAL CREDIT CLOTHING HOUSE
7 PURCHASE ST., Cor. UNION (Over Lawton's Drug Store)

Taunton - New Bedford Copper Co.

North Front Street, New Bedford, Mass.

No. 42 Water Street, NEW YORK No. 61 Batterymarch Street, BOSTON, MASS.

YELLOW (MUNTZ) METAL SHEATHING

Dimension Sheets, Bolts and Bars, Sheathing, Slating and Boat Nails, Condenser and Supporting Plates, Piston and Pump Rods.

NAVAL BRASS NAVAL BRONZE MANGANESE BRONZE

PURE COPPER

Sheets, Bolts, Bars, Rods, Nails, Tacks, Corrugated Gaskets, etc., etc.
PRINTING ROLLERS AND SINGE PLATES FOR FINISHING TEXTILE FABRICS

Knife Switches Switch Boards Panel Boards and Cabinets

We are prepared to estimate on specifications covering Switchboards and Panel Boards of all sezes and kinds.

We will furnish sketch drawings with our estimates when called for.

Monarch Light Touch

TYPEWRITER

Is made in nine distinct models, ranging in width from 9.6 to 32.6 inches, thus covering the entire business field.

You will be interested in the special devices and special feature for

BILLING, CARD INDEXING and LOOSE LEAF WORK

Write for Descriptive Catalog.

Learn the many reasons for MONARCH superiority. Then try the MONARCH and be convinced that Monarch merit rests in the machine itself, not merely in what we tell you.

The Monarch Typewriter Company

67 MILK STREET, BOSTON

STORAGE

For All Kinds of Merchandise

DIRECT RAIL FACILITIES

STORAGE

STORAGE

Lowest Insurance Rate in Town for

COTTON and MILL PRODUCTS

Flour and Bakers Supplies

Carriages, Automobiles and Machinery

Furniture, Pianos and Trunks

New Bedford Storage Warehouse Co.

Auto. 2278 **352-378 SAWYER ST.** Bell 1240

The

New Bedford Textile School

This school offers to young men entering the cottor textile industry unsurpassed facilities for acquiring a thorough technical knowledge of the business.

Owing to the location of this school, the students attending it have the advantages of pursuing their studies in the largest manufacturing center of fine cotton goods and the fastest growing mill city in the country.

The following courses are offered by the school:

I. Cotton Manufacturing. **III. Chemistry and Dyeing**

II. Designing. **IV. Seamless Hosiery Knitting**

V. Latch Needle Underwear Knitting,

Mechanics and Shop Practice given in all courses.

Send for free catalogue. Address—

New Bedford Textile School

NEW BEDFORD, MASS.

1890 Established--21 Years in Business 1911

THE RHODE ISLAND DETECTIVE AGENCY

Frank L. Gray, Gen. Supt. C. C. Ward, Supt.

SECRET SERVICE DAY AND NIGHT

Endorsed by the Police Dept, City and State Officials

Operatives sent to all parts of the world

Phones Local and Long Distance PRIVATE LINES

Office, 395 Westminster Street
Providence, R. I.

HENRI PELLETIER

Painter and Decorator

Paper Hanging

86 HATHAWAY ST., - NEW BEDFORD

C. A. GALLIGAN

Household Furnishings

Furniture, Oil Cloth, Rugs, Stoves, Etc.

The New Galligan Building, 1516 Acushnet Avenue

COFFIN AVE. ACUSHNET AVE. PHILLIPS AVE.

NEW BEDFORD, MASS.

Established 1862

W. A. Greenough & Co.

Compilers, Printers and Publishers of

DIRECTORIES

65 BROAD STREET
BOSTON, MASS.

Telephone, Main 4415-W

CHAS. O. BRIGHTMAN

CONTRACTOR and BUILDER

Jobbing in CARPENTRY and MASONRY

Estimates Given on all Classes of Work

Member Builders' Exchange

Factory and Office, - 72 North Water Street

Residence, 82 Mill Street. Telephones: Office, 259-4; House, 1342-4, 1643-22

BOSTON STEAM AND GAS-PIPE WORKS

BRAMAN, DOW & CO.

239 to 245 CAUSEWAY STREET, corner Medford Street, BOSTON

MANUFACTURERS OF AND DEALERS IN

PLAIN AND GALVANIZED

Wrought Iron Pipe

AND FITTINGS

AND ALL GOODS USED IN CONNECTION WITH STEAM, GAS OR WATER

Contractors for Heating all kinds of Buildings with Steam or Hot Water

COTTON MACHINERY.

MASON MACHINE WORKS

CARDS, DRAWING, SPINNING, LOOMS.

TAUNTON, MASS.

Gunn, Richards & Company

TREMONT BUILDING

ENGINEERS **ACCOUNTANTS**

BOSTON

Audits **Examinations** **Scientific Management**

The founders of this firm were the first to use the terms "Production Engineering" or "Industrial Engineering" to characterize that field of engineering effort in which they, as individuals, had for years been engaged and to which so much attention is now being given on the part of the public under the title "Efficiency Engineering."

Morgan L. Cooley, C. P. A., Resident Manager, Boston

WILLIAM E. MOSHER

Florist

Floral Work a Specialty
All Kinds of Potted Plants
325 HILLMAN STREET

GREENHOUSE Bell Tel. 2601

RESIDENCE Tel. 1492-5

THE CHARLES F. WING CO.

(INCORPORATED)

Everything to Furnish a Home

The Store of Southern New England

34-38 PURCHASE STREET NEW BEDFORD, MASS.

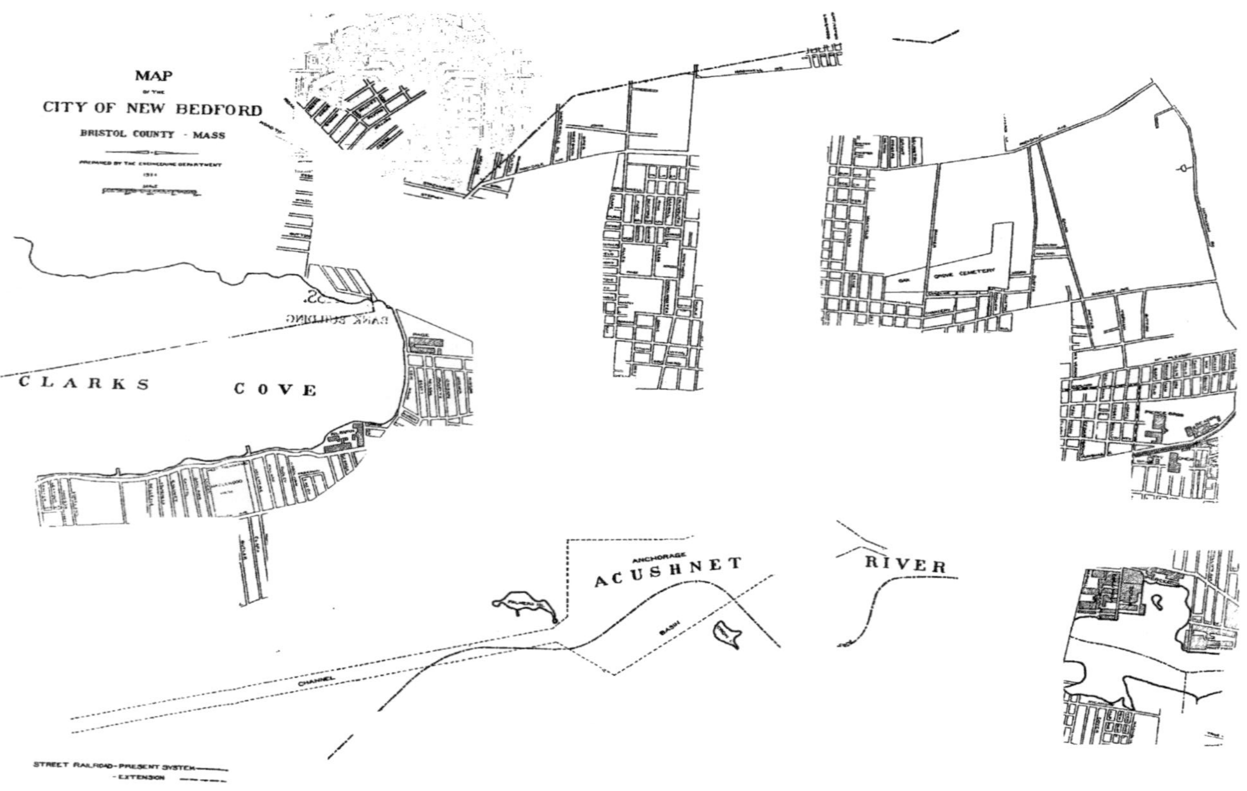

MAP
OF THE
CITY OF NEW BEDFORD
BRISTOL COUNTY - MASS
PREPARED BY THE ENGINEERING DEPARTMENT
CLARKS COVE
OAK GROVE CEMETERY
ANCHORAGE
ACUSHNET RIVER
BASIN
CHANNEL
STREET RAILROAD - PRESENT SYSTEM
- EXTENSION

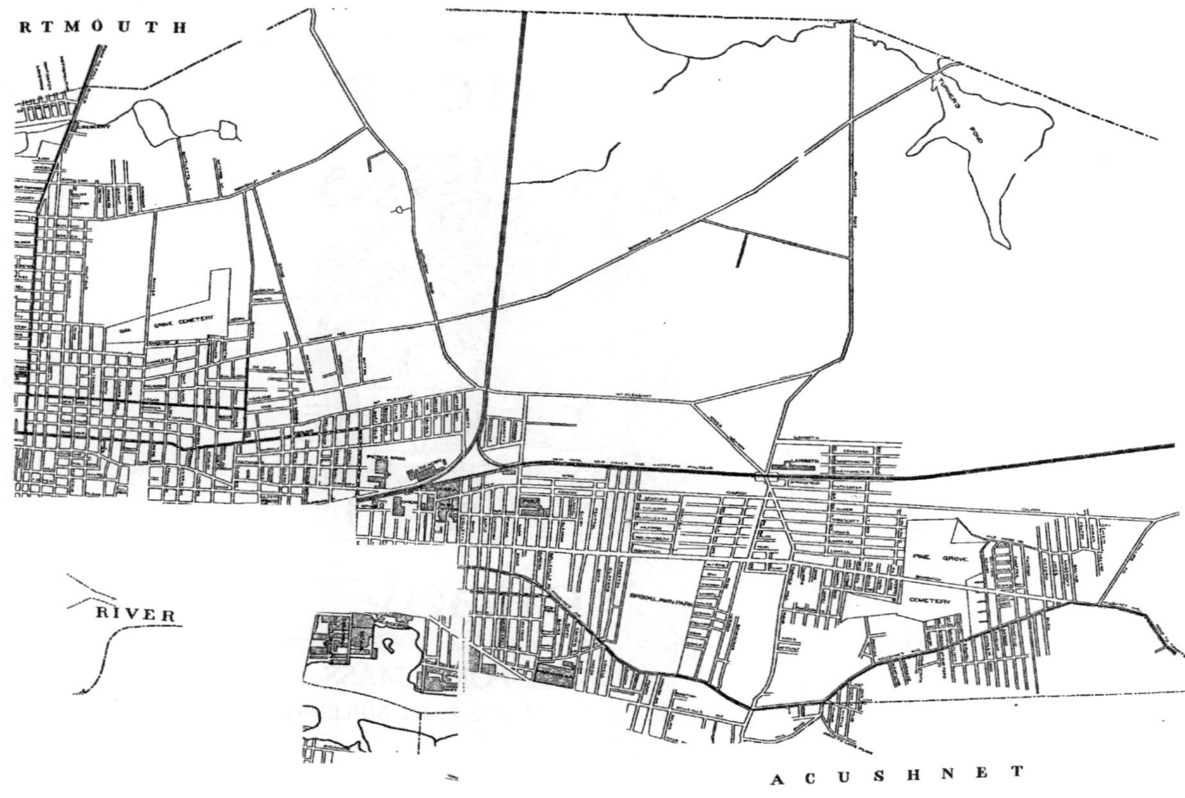
RTMOUTH
RIVER
ACUSHNET
OAK GROVE CEMETERY
PINE GROVE
CEMETERY
BROOKLAWN PARK
TURNER'S POND

BENTON'S

SCHOOL

NEW BEDFORD, MASS.

410-413 MERCHANTS BANK BUILDING

1911

AND FAIRHAVEN

DIRECTORY

— of the —

Inhabitants, Business Firms, Institutions, Manufacturing Establishments, Societies, House Directory, with Streets, Map, Etc.

No. XLIV

W. A. GREENOUGH & CO.

COMPILERS, PRINTERS AND PUBLISHERS

No. 65 Broad Street

Boston, Mass.

PRICE $4.50

Copyright by W A. Greenough & Co., 1911

TELEPHONE 1888

CHARLES W. PRARAY

Mill Engineer and Architect

Power Plants a Specialty

Rms. 302-303-304 TIMES BUILDING NEW BEDFORD

BELL 349-31 AUTO. 3334

TOURING CARS TO LET

BY HOUR OR DAY

Competent and Temperate Drivers Nice Clean and Up-to-date Cars

Sycamore St. Garage

Storing, Washing and Repairing

Supplies, Oil and Gasoline

Cole 30 Agency **Bert A. Vance, Prop.**

NEW BEDFORD, MASS.

EDWARD J. DAHILL ARTHUR C. KIRBY

DAHILL & KIRBY

CIVIL ENGINEERS AND SURVEYORS

11 CLIFFORD BUILDING
OPP. REGISTRY OF DEEDS

Auto. Phone 1237
Bell Phone 1913

NEW BEDFORD, MASS.

Chas. S. Ashley Jr., & Co.

Insurance and Real Estate

OF ALL KINDS

Cor. Pleasant and William Streets

New Bedford, Mass.

Bell Phone 2160 Auto. Phone 1696

CONTENTS

	N. Bedford	Frh'n
Abbreviations	95	
Automobile Owners	739	
Banks		*723
Blks, Bldgs, Halls, etc	86	*690
Ben P O of Elks	*669	
Business Directory	*583	*717
Cemeteries	89	*690
Census	opp 588	
Churches	*665	*722
City Government	*649	
City Offices	88	
Clubs	*672	*723
County Officers	*659	
Courts	*660	
Daughters A R	*670	
Fire Alarm	*653	*721
Fire Department	*652	*721
French Societies	*676	
General Directory	95	*691
G A of the R	*669	
House Directory	589	
Incorp Companies	*677	*723
Index to Advertisements	45	
Justices of the Peace	*680	*724
Knights of Honor	*671	
Localities of Interest	88	
Manchester Unity	*669	
Map	opp 41	
Masonic	*667	*722
Military Organizations	*672	
Notaries Public	*680	*724
Odd Fellows	*668	
Parochial Schools	*659	*722
Police Department	*652	
Post Offices	*661	*724
Private Schools	*659	
Public Libraries	*655	*722
Public Schools	*655	*722
Quarantine	89	
Railroads	*679	
Rates of Postage	*662	
Societies and Ass'ns	*673	
Sons of Veterans	*670	
Sts. Cts. Avs. Etc	49	*685
Temperance Societies	*671	
Textile Industries	*679	
Title	41	
Town Government		*721
U O R M	*670	
U S Officers, Etc	*680	
Ward Boundaries	90	
Water Company		*723
Whfs, Slips and Islands	88	*690
Women's' Releif Corps	*670	

A. W. DeWolf M. T. Vincent

DeWOLF & VINCENT

Successors to SULLINGS, KINGMAN & CO.

HARDWARE DEALERS

Paints, Oils, Brushes and Agricultural Implements

111 WILLIAM STREET - NEW BEDFORD

New England Telephone 711 Automatic Telephone 1166

Thomas O. Phillips

PAINTER AND DECORATOR

Paints, Oils, Glass and Putty **Wall Paper and Mouldings**

Graining and Paper Hanging

American and Foreign Wall Papers

First-class Work Guaranteed 167 PARK STREET

Bell Telephone

JAMES F. HOYE T. M. JAMES & CO.

INSURANCE and BONDS

Room 305, Merchants Bank Building

NEW BEDFORD

JOHN D. ELLIOT

PLUMBING in all its Branches

All Work Given Personal Attention

106 FOURTH STREET

Telephone Connection

Index to Advertisements

	Page
Acushnet Iron Co	788
Acushnet Sanitarium	24
Akin F T & Co	foot lines
Alden George N	back cover
Allen George J & Co	26
Allen Marcus M	777
Allen, Slade & Co	12
Arcand E J	27
Ashley Charles S Jr & Co	35
Ashley R R	755
Ashley William L	755
Ashton & Murphy	48
Atlas Tack Co	*683
Auger George W & Co	782
Auto Selling & Supply Co	741
Automatic Telephone Co	22
Babbitt Steam Specialty Co	29
Bacon W L	top edge
Bailey W P	766
Baker Machine Co	744
Barney B B	117
Barrett Mfg Co	front cover
Bennett Robert G	*643
Benton Charles E	map
Berger Mfg Co	753
Bertrand O	754
Bishop J W Co	19
Blair Sign & Advertising Co	754
Bolduc Azarie	780
Bonney, Folster & Co	foot lines
Borden Harry E Co	746
Borden & Remington Co	11
Bosworth W E	785
Bourgeois David	744
Braley A G & G F	*683
Braman Dow & Co	38
Briggs George L	back cover
Briggs Justus A Jr	150
Briggs William P	*604
Briggs & Beckman	785
Brightman Charles O	95
Brightman E T	610
Brightman F S Co Inc	769
Brillon Adelard	777
Brown Frederick A	778
Browne Pharmacy	back cover
Brownell C F & Co	*684
Budlong J E Press	778
Buffington Arthur E	788
Burke John P	782
Burns Detective Bureau	161
Bush Andrew M & Co	768
Caswell William T	94
Cejka George	785
Chamberlain & Silva	back cover
Chausse Aldege	772
Church Charles H	25
City Coal Co	3
Clean Wet Wash	786
Coffin Brothers	782
Coholan Jeremiah	767
Collins Williston H & Co	23
Congdon Carpenter & Co	10
Connell John Jr	774
Connor Patrick	783
Cook Brownell & Taber	189
Cook Emile A	755
Cook & McQuade	763
Cormier & Dube	776
Cornish Clifton H	778
Crapo Clifford & Prescott	199
Cronin Edward H	769
Crooker Company	754
Croshere C A	foot lines
Crossley John F	foot lines
Croteau & Wood	776
Crown Confectionery Store	783
Dahill & Kirby	42
Dantsizen John G	back cover
Davis Z B Corporation	762
Davol Clarence H	755
Delano Clarence F	767
DeMoranville D H	787
Denison Brothers Co	front edge

	Page
Desautels Hughues	760
Desautels S	758
DeWolf & Vincent	44
Dexter Lemuel LeBaron	219
Dextradeur C J	754
Dextraze C	779
Dion H P	773
Dionne Walter	752
Drake A B ft cover and bottom edge	
Draper Co	2
Driscol Church & Hall	13
Driscoll D F	front cover
Drolet & Milotte	775
Dudley S A	17
Duff David & Son	front cover
Dupuis H D & Co	757
Elliot John D	45
Faford F X	763
Fairhaven Ice Co	*684
Fairhaven Institution for Savings	*682
Fairhaven Star	758
Faunce Charles L	765
First National Bank	7
Forest F & Co	778
Foster Robert W Brass Foundry	781
Galligan C A	37
Gallop R G & Co	752
Gardiner & Milliken	262
Gauthier Joseph A	264
Gerardi V V	769
Giles & Tobey	744
Globe Dye House	foot lines
Goodspeed Alexander McL	276
Green Everett	780
Greene Fred W Jr	758
Greene & Wood	foot lines
Gregory Edward H	780
Guay Brothers	773
Gunn, Richards & Co	40
Gunning Boiler & Machine Co	31
Gurl Francis J	*643
Halliday Charles R	777
Handy Jonathan Co	766
Haskell Brothers	foot lines
Hathaway Chester F	743
Hathaway L J	771
Hathaway & Mackenzie Grain Co	opp *609
Hawes Tewksbury & Co	7
Hazard Charles B	764
Heron C T	27
Hersom Thomas & Co	24
Hervey Homer W	302
Hill Co	777
Hillman F G	26
Hirst E P Co	*629
Hitch Mayhew R	306

	Page
Holmes Albert W	back cover
Home Washing Co	786
Household Furnishing Co	94
Howard Brothers Mfg Co	14
Howard & Bullough	opp 589
Howarth Ernest	784
Howes C G Co	opp *595
Howland S D & Co	786
Hoye James F	44
Hurley C F	781
Ideal Credit Clothing House	33
James F E	back binding and 761
James T M & Co	36
Jarry Dominick J	25
Jenkins Elmir A	752
Jewett Hardware Co	784
Jones & Dodge	764
Kenney Joseph T	332
Kenyon A B	27
Kinyon's Com School	foot lines
Kirby George Jr Paint Co	33
Kirk J Frank	775
Kirshen Press	32
Lawrence J A	784
Lawton C H & H A Co	*602
Lebeau Joseph	785
Lebeau Theophile	33
Le Journal	758
Lenox Motor Car Co	742
Levesque Wilfred	787
Lilley George E	362
Linton John R & Sons	33
Loftus & Dugan	776
Loranger Theodore	763
Lowe S C Supply Co	740
Lowney & Walsh	367
MacCord William A	370
Macy J S	775
Macy Peleg S	*632
Maher Pierre	763
Maranda Donat	757
Mason J L G	774
Mason Machine Works	39
McNear George W	748
Maxfield Charles A	769
Mechanics National Bank	6
Merchants National Bank	4
Mercury Publishing Co	756
Metcalf Frank M	399
Mitchell Charles	403
Monarch Typewriter Co	34
Moore F Russell	760
Moriarty T J	49
Morse Twist Drill & Mach Co	15
Mosher William E	40
Mudge & Francis	781
Murphy C H & Son	771
Nash Road Wet Wash Laundry	789

National Bank of Fairhaven *682
National Detective Agency The 28
National Wet Wash Laundry .. 787
New Bedford Auto Co 741
New Bedford Fish Co *605
New Bedford Five Cents S Bank 5
New Bedford Ice Co 773
New Bedford Inst for Savings 9
New Bedford S D & T Co 8
New Bedford Steam Carpet Beating & Rug Co front cover
New Bedford Steam Dye House 768
New Bedford Steam Laundry ft cov
New Bedord Storage Warehouse back binding and 35
New Bedford Textile School 36
New Bedford Times 759
New York Market 772
Nicholson John G ....foot lines
North End Garage 741
North End Laundry 786
O'Neill Murray 746
Paine S S & Brother 776
Pairpoint Corp 23
Paisler & Willis 774
Palace Cafe 779
Parandelis & Dangelas 783
Parker D L & Co 746
Parker Wm C 435
Parlow & Goddard 782
Parsons Steam Laundry Co .... front cover
Paul Dixon & Cook ...front cover
Peirce W H & L F 770
Pelletier Henri 37
Perkins A W & Co 789
Perra John 766
Phillips Thomas O 44
Phoenix Garage *691
Pineault J N 761
Plummer & Jennings Grain Co . 775
Pothier Joseph A 29
Potter William F & Co 30
Prary Charles W 42
Prouteau Raoul 760
Quintin H N 767
Rankin & Arnold 780
Raymond Charles 771
Rex Monumental Works back cover
Ricard Levi 765
Richmond Charles N 94
Richmond & Co ....foot lines
Robinson Daniel 772
Robitaille Ovila 764
Rodgers Antonio M 25
Rogler Philip 772
St James Co-operative Sales ... 48
Sanford & Kelley ......front cover
Rhode Island Detective Agency 37
Sawm George F & Co 783
Schott George A 753
Schuler Bros 24
Shambow Shuttle Co 30
Shaw J E Norton 497
Sherman Albert C 770
Sherman Charles H 15
Sherman James H 767
Sherman James L 765
Sherman Peleg H ....foot lines
Sherman & McQuillan 781
Silva Henry 761
Silva M P B & Son ......foot lines
Sistare Frank B & Son 762
Slocum & Kilburn 766
Smith Bros Inc 779
Smith B F Construction Co ... 18
Sparrow Frank M 517
Spooner Wm E 27
Standard Construction Co 783
Steiger Dudgeon Co ......foot lines
Steinert M & Sons Co 23
Stetson & Stetson 521
Sturtevant Benjamin S 748
Sturtevant W F 25
Sullivan Martin H 760
Tallman Arthur S 771
Taunton-New Bedford Copper Co 34
Taylor Frank C 48
Therrien John 752
Thorpe Richard H 765
Townsend Thomas 16
Tripp Benjamin C 762
Tripp & Thorpe 764
Tucker Anthony & Co 6
Tver Rubber Co 743
Union Street Railway Co 21
Vance Bert A 42
Vaughan Harry C 555
Vaughan Undertaking Co Inc ..*643
Warren Chemical & Mfg Co opp *583
Warren's Agency back binding and 789
Washburn William R 770
Watling William 757
Watuppa Auto Co 750
Webber Lumber & Supply Co .. 761
Weihl Jacob 779
Wentworth F W Co 768
Wheaton Hiram & Sons 773
Whitin Machine Works 20
Whitinsville Spinning Ring Co opp 589
Williams George P 743
Williams John 762
Williams M A ....back cover
Wilson Henry P ....back cover
Wing C F Co The Inc 40
Wing J & W R & Co 768
Wood Brightman & Co 3
Wood-Morgan Detective Agency 753
Woodruff F T 748
Woodward Henry E 582
Wright George F 777

Long Distance Telephone 1368-1 P. O. Box 525 New Bedford

FRANK C. TAYLOR

General Contractor

For Bridges, Foundations, Wharves, Sea Walls, Concrete and Heavy Timber Construction

OFFICE, YARD AND DOCK, MIDDLE ST, FAIRHAVEN

Fifty per cent. of Selling Value for yourself or any charity you may name

Established in 1899

Over Six Thousand Dollars Distributed among Co-operative Charities in 1909-1910

ST. JAMES CO-OPERATIVE SALES

Telephone Connection 68 Linden Street, NEW BEDFORD, MASS.

ASHTON & MURPHY

Real Estate and Insurance Agents Auctioneers Appraisers

DESIRABLE PROPERTY IN ALL PARTS OF THE CITY

REAL ESTATE BOUGHT AND SOLD ON COMMISSION

1109 SO. WATER STREET

TELEPHONE BELL 707-25 TELEPHONE AUTO 2696

T. J. MORIARTY
Painting, Graining, Papering and Whitewashing
FINE WALL PAPER, PAINTERS' SUPPLIES
HARDWARE and MECHANICS' TOOLS
Street Cars Pass the Door OPEN EVENINGS
184 FOURTH STREET
Bell 220 Automatic 1083

NEW BEDFORD STREET DIRECTORY 1911

(Copyright 1911 by W A Greenough & Co)

Giving the location of each street and showing streets running from or across, with the number at intersection.

The streets of New Bedford, with few exceptions, are laid out north and south and east and west. Those running north and south number at Union street, and increase each way, with the even numbers on the east and the odd numbers on the west side. Those running east and west begin to number at the river, and increase westerly, with the even numbers on the south and the odd numbers on the north side. The letter S enclosed in parenthesis, which follows the name of any street, signifies the general bearing of such street from City Hall square. Thus School street (S) is south from City Hall square.

*Unaccepted streets.

ABBOTT (S) from 9 East French av to Ruth

ACORN (N W) from 150 Durfee to Oak Grove Cemetery

ACUSHNET AVENUE (N and S) from division to Freetown line

1	0	Division
21	20	Delano
39	40	Blackmer
55	56	Rivet
79	78	Potomska
93		Rockland
111	112	South
131	128	Grinnell
149		Tallmans lane
	158	Howland
163		Wing
	170	Griffin
185		Bedford
213		Russell
	216	Cannon
245	246	Madison
263	264	Walnut
289	288	School
305	306	Spring
	318	Old Market square
331	330	Union
	340	Barker's court
369	370	William
	386	Dover

Acushnet avenue—con
405 406 Elm
433 434 Middle
437 436 High
443 444 Kempton
455 456 Mill
473 474 North
493 494 Hillman
513 512 Maxfield
579 Campbell
587 590 Willis
623 624 Pearl
668 East pope
682 Seneca
694 Wall
712 Turner's court
716 E Merrimac
739 740 Wamsutta
827 828 Logan
858 Hicks
904 Washburn
905 906 O'Leary square
913 Weld
939 938 Kenyon
1001 982 Cedar Grove
1071 1066 Marvin
1099 1100 Coggeshall
1119 Bentley
1173 1150 Beetle
1201 1202 Sawyer
1261 1262 Holly
1301 1302 Tallman
1351 1352 Nye
1401 1400 Bullard
1441 1440 Dean
1501 1500 Coffin avenue
1533 1534 Phillips avenue
1573 1574 Collette
1601 1602 Davis
1621 1622 Earle
1647 1642 Hathaway avenue
1669 1668 Tinkham
1699 1700 Nash road
1720 Whitman
1739 0 Eugenia
1761 1762 Belleville road
1804 Bates avenue
1825 0 Central avenue
1865 0 Shaw
1878 Hatch
1898 Conduit
1900 Covell
1901 Princeton
1907 Irvington
0 Brooklynn park
1930 Hadley
1950 Duncan
1972 Ingraham
1990 Perry
2010 Howard avenue
2057 Wood
2093 Hersom
2175 Tarkiln Hill road
0 2178 Main
2176 Lund's corner
2321 2320 Mill road
0 0 Pontiac
0 0 Westland
0 0 Norwood
0 0 Monmouth
0 0 Marion avenue
0 0 Stratford
0 0 Montrose avenue
0 0 Sterling
0 0 Elliott
0 0 Kenmore
0 0 Bristol
0 0 Fairmount avenue
0 0 Maplewood
0 0 Barnum
0 0 Dewey
0 0 Osgood
0 0 Dutton
0 0 Fairfield
0 0 Lincoln
0 0 Chaffee
0 0 Tacoma
0 0 Myrtle
0 0 Glen
0 0 Victoria
0 0 Joyce
0 0 Kingcroft
0 0 Belair
0 0 Phillips road
0 0 Nye's lane
0 0 Braley road
4129 4128 Bettey lane
4232 Peckham road
0 4674 Freetown line

ADAMS (N) from 1065 County to Mt Pleasant
1 2 County
39 40 Reynolds
0 0 Myrtle
0 0 Ashland
0 0 Mt Pleasant

*ADELAIDE (N) from Marion to Kenmore avenue

ALEC (S) from 100 Grape avenue south

ALFRED (N) from Brooklawn Park to Wood

ALICE (N) from Park avenue to Tarkiln Hill road

ALLEN (S W) from 329 County west to Dartmouth line
2 1 County
68 67 Green
105 Briggs court
104 Bonney
124 Dartmouth
188 189 Cottage
0 0 Borden
234 231 Ward
255 Waverley
262 Columbia
282 283 Oak
300 Stone
318 319 Page
340 Short
354 Field
378 Clover
398 0 West
426 425 Devoll
436 Rural
437 Brigham
464 Winter
505 Brownell
537 Palmer
569 Reed
586 Rockdale avenue
0 John
0 Jacinto
0 Snow
0 0 Dartmouth line

ALLORD (S) east from 328 Brock avenue

AMES (N) from Avery northerly

ANTHONY (S W) from opposite 116 Bedford to 6 Grove

APPLETON (N) from Pine Grove to west of Bowditch

APPONEGANSETT (S) from Acushnet river to Brock avenue

AQUIDNECK (S) from East French avenue to West French avenue
0 0 East French avenue
0 0 Brock avenue
0 0 West French avenue

ARCH (W) from 386 Union to opposite 127 Arnold

ARK LANE (N) from 158 North Water to the River

ARMOUR (W) from opposite 351 Court south to Arnold
0 0 Court
0 0 Union
0 0 Arnold

ARNOLD (S W) from 413 County to near Dartmouth line
2 1 County
42 Orchard
57 Arnold place
80 79 Cottage
111 Lincoln
127 Arch
146 145 Ash (South)
163 Emerson
184 185 Chancery
212 213 Park
232 231 Atlantic
254 255 Ocean
280 279 Tremont
311 James
0 0 Rotch
360 355 Armour
0 0 Brownell
0 0 Rounds
0 0 Reed
0 0 Rockdale avenue

ARNOLD PLACE (S W) from 57 Arnold to Rotch court

ASH (NORTH) (N W) from 397 Union to 114 Sycamore
1 2 Union
17 18 Court
30 Morgan
43 42 Elm
55 56 Middle
93 92 Kempton
101 102 Mill
117 118 North
135 136 Hillman
157 158 Maxfield
169 170 Sycamore

ASH (SOUTH) (S W) from 396 Union to end of Bedford
2 1 Union
54 53 Arnold
64 63 Clinton
76 75 Maple
0 89 Hawthorn
103 Moreland terrace
108 Grove
0 129 Bedford

ASHLAND (N W) from end Summer at 31 Robeson to Nausett
0 0 Summer
0 0 Robeson
20 Hazard
32 Studley
59 60 Austin
74 Ashland place
98 Linden
108 East Durfee
111 110 Durfee
143 140 Weld
160 Ashland terrace
191 192 Clark
271 272 Peckham

Ashland—con
297 298 Coggeshall
319 320 Adams
347 350 Sawyer
371 376 Garfield
393 400 Buchanan
417 422 Fillmore
441 446 Polk
463 470 Taylor
485 0 Van Buren
503 0 Jackson
525 0 Monroe
545 0 Jefferson
567 566 Nausett
ASHLAND PLACE (N W) from Ashland next Linden to 10 Linden court
ASHLAND TERRACE (N W) from 160 Ashland easterly
ASHLEY (S) from 40 Cove to 114 David
ASHLEY LANE (S) from Brock avenue east to East French avenue C P south of David
ATLANTIC (W) from 468 Union to 141 Maple
1 2 Union
65 66 Arnold
95 96 Maple
AUSTIN (N) from 707 Purchase to Oak Grove cemetery
2 1 Purchase
24 23 Pleasant
38 Austin court
52 51 State
62 Hazard court
78 77 County
0 Linden court
144 143 Ashland
176 175 Cottage
193 Glover
222 221 Cedar
257 Richmond
280 281 Bullock
318 317 Shawmut avenue
0 0 Oak Grove cemetery
AUSTIN COURT (N) from opposite 39 Austin to 31 Hazard
AVERY (N) from Wood to Church
BABBITT (S W) from 117 Dartmouth to bey Field
2 1 Dartmouth
60 61 Field
BALL (N) from Homestead northerly
BANK (S W) from Matthew toward Rockdale avenue
BANNISTER (N) from Peckham to Coggeshall
BARKER COURT (N) from 340 Acushnet av to 17 North Second
BARNUM (N) from Acushnet avenue easterly
BARRETT (N) from Purchase west
BARTLET'S LANE from 1161 Rockdale avenue west
BATES AVENUE (N) from Healey next Belleville road to Acushnet avenue
0 Healey
71 Conduit
0 Merrill
0 0 Ernest
0 0 Acushnet avenue
0 0 Belleville avenue
BAY (S W) from 11 Dartmouth west across Cottage to opposite 32 Columbia
2 1 Dartmouth
30 29 Cottage
52 51 Borden
64 63 Ward
86 85 Columbia
BAY VIEW (S) from West French avenue easterly
BAYLIES (N) from Hersom to Wood
BEDFORD (S) from 185 Acushnet avenue to end Ash (South)
2 1 Acushnet avenue
20 19 Fourth
32 31 Fifth
50 51 South Sixth
67 Seventh
72 71 County
78 Green
100 99 Orchard
117 Anthony
124 123 Cottage
142 141 Borden
148 147 Ash (South)
236 233 Page
304 301 West
344 341 Brigham
410 407 Brownell
444 441 Palmer
476 475 Reed
BEECH (W) (Cannonville) from 815 Kempton to beyond 611 Maxfield
2 1 Kempton
12 11 Mill
24 23 North
42 41 Hillman
62 61 Maxfield
BEETLE (N) from 189 Belleville avenue to 106 Bowditch
1 Belleville avenue
12 Grandfield

	23	Bonneau court
38	37	North Front
54		Howard
70	69	Acushnet avenue
112	111	Bowditch

BEETLE LANE (E) from 158 North Water

*BELAIR (N) from Acushnet avenue to beyond Wood road

BELLEVILLE AVENUE (N) from end Kilburn to 21 Main, Lunds Corner

0		Kilburn
0	36	Washburn
61		Kenyon
91		Cedar Grove
141	140	Coggeshall
183		Beetle
215	214	Sawyer
253	252	Holly
263	264	Tallman
309	308	Nye
335		Bullard
363	364	Dean
397	396	Coffin avenue
437	438	Phillips avenue
469	470	Collette
487	488	Davis
505		Earle
0		Hope
523	0	Hathaway avenue
543		Tinkham
0		Webster court
0	570	Second
567		Nash road
573		Desautels
583		Whitman
0		Middle
	0	Riverside avenue
615		Belleville road
629		Olive
	0	Bates avenue
679		Shaw
693		Hatch
707		Covell
723		Hadley
	0	Reagan
	0	Newport
0		Duncan
0		Ingraham
	0	Brooks
763	764	Perry
779	780	Howard avenue
809	810	Sylvia
933		Main

BELLEVILLE ROAD (N) from 615 Belleville avenue beyond Whitman Mills west to the R R Germantown

2	1	Belleville avenue
0		Riverside avenue
0		Second
20		Desautels
	27	Healey
42		Hope
	47	Merrill
0		Ernest
96		Diman
	113	Brightman court
134		North Front
140	141	Acushnet avenue
0	0	Bowditch
0	0	Edison
0	0	Church
0	0	King
0	0	N Y N H & H R R

BELLEVUE (W) from Brock avenue to West French avenue

BENNETT (N) from 125 Coggeshall to Bennett Mill

BENTLEY (N) from 1119 Acushnet avenue to 100 Bowditch

BERLIN COURT (N) from 71 Church to R R

BETHEL (E) from 83 Union to 10 Elm

1	2	Union
19	20	William
45	0	Elm

BLACKBURN (N) from 297 Cedar Grove to the reservoir

BLACKMER (S) from Acushnet river westerly to 140 County

0	0	Acushnet river
106	107	South Front
124	123	South Water
138	0	South First
160	161	South Second
186	187	Acushnet avenue
0	203	County

BLANCHARD (N) from end County to Mount Pleasant opposite Sacred Heart cemetery

0	0	Purchase
0	0	County
0	0	Mount Pleasant

BOLTON (S) from Rockdale avenue to junction Fair, Hemlock and Sears

261	262	Rockdale avenue
	0	Buttonwood road
313	0	Winsper
331	0	Jenkins

Bolton—con
Howland Village
351 Sagamore
365 Sidney
379 Dunbar
391 Swift
405 Larch
425 424 Rivet
451 0 Kane
473 472 Thompson
515 516 Rockland
533 534 Fair
541 542 Sears

BONNEAU COURT (N) 204 Sawyer to 23 Beetle

BONNEY (S) from 104 Allen south to Cove road
2 1 Allen
20 Forest
34 Sherman
56 57 Grinnell
74 75 Washington
108 109 Fair
144 143 Rockland
172 171 Thompson
206 207 Rivet
246 247 Katharine
252 Windsor
0 0 Jouvette
0 0 Nelson
0 0 Cove road

BORDEN (S W) from 43 Dartmouth to 32 Grove
1 2 Dartmouth
27 26 Bay
39 38 Allen
63 62 Bedford
79 80 Grove

BOURNE (S W) from 115 Fruit to 12 Spooner
1 2 Fruit
37 38 Thompson
65 66 Spooner

BOWDITCH (N) from 35 Logan to Acushnet avenue
1 2 Logan
17 18 Weld
39 Cornell place
61 62 Cedar Grove
83 86 Coggeshall
0 100 Bentley
0 106 Beetle
125 126 Sawyer
149 150 Holly
167 168 Tallman
185 186 Nye
199 202 Bullard
219 220 Dean
239 242 Coffin avenue
259 262 Phillips avenue
277 280 Collette
291 294 Davis
307 310 Earle
323 326 Hathaway
341 342 Tinkham
0 0 Nash road
0 0 Whitman
0 Eugenia
0 0 Belleville road
0 0 Glennon
0 0 Willis avenue
0 0 Central avenue
0 0 Shaw
0 0 Clifford
0 0 Princeton
0 0 Irvington
0 0 Brooklawn avenue
0 Wood
0 0 Hersom
0 0 Park avenue
0 0 Daniel
0 0 Tarkiln Hill road
0 0 Illinois
0 0 Ohio
0 0 Jarry
0 0 Maryland
0 0 Appleton
0 0 Oregon
0 0 Florida
0 0 York
0 0 Roland
0 0 Menton
0 0 Dewey
0 0 Carson
0 0 Dutton
0 0 Chaffee
0 0 Tacoma
0 0 Victoria
0 0 Joyce
0 0 Kingcroft
0 0 Acushnet avenue

BRADFORD (N) from Coggeshall to Sawyer

BRALEY ROAD (N) from 4035 Acushnet avenue to Braley station Freetown line
0 0 Acushnet avenue
0 Phillips road
0 Braley station
0 0 Freetown line

BRANSCOMB (N) from Acushnet avenue to Waldo

BRANSCOMB AVENUE (N) from 2103 Acushnet avenue to Church

BRAWLEY (N W) from west 281 Mt Pleasant to 285 Highland

BRIDGE (E) from North Water at Middle to Fairhaven line
0 0 North Water
0 0 Fish Island
0 0 Pope's Island
0 0 Fairhaven line
BRIDGE ROAD (N) changed to Main
BRIDGE SQUARE (E) foot of Middle to Fair
BRIER (S W) from 427 Rockdale avenue
BRIGGS (S) from 365 Rivet to Fair Fair
1 2 Rivet
33 34 Thompson
77 76 Rockland
97 98 Fair
BRIGGS' COURT (S W) from 105 Allen
BRIGHAM (S W) from 439 Allen to 236 Hawthorn
0 0 Allen
0 Ryan
68 Taber
90 Priscilla
0 Plymouth
0 0 Hawthorn
*BRIGHTMAN (N) from Sylvia north
BRIGHTMAN COURT (N) from 113 Belleville road
*BRISTOL (N) from Acushnet avenue east
BROCK AVENUE (S) from 54 West French to U S land Clark's Point
2 1 West French avenue
0 Harmony
36 Ruth avenue
42 McGurk
49 Warren
66 0 George
94 85 David
102 103 Ellen
150 Mott
165 Woodlawn avenue
166 Rodney
182 181 Dudley
203 Willard
212 Frederick
219 Valentine
228 Norman
244 Clara
260 Butler
297 Lucas
328 Allord
0 0 Aquidneck
0 Bellevue
0 Marine avenue
0 0 U S land
BROCKTON (N) from Lowell west to Worcester
205 Lowell
221 228 Lawrence
241 248 Howes
267 274 Prescott
291 298 Oliver
315 322 Church
339 340 Worcester
BROOK (N) from 367 Sawyer to beyond Holly and from opposite 202 Dean to Shaw
2 1 Sawyer
25 Holly
0 0 Tallman
0 Nye
0 Bullard
0 0 Dean
120 119 Coffin avenue
138 137 Phillips avenue
156 155 Collette
170 169 Davis
186 185 Earle
202 201 Hathaway
220 219 Tinkham
238 237 Nash road
0 0 Whitman
0 0 Eugenia
0 0 Belleville road
0 0 Glennon
0 0 Laurel
0 0 Query
0 0 Central avenue
0 0 Shaw
BROOKLAWN AVENUE (N) from Church to Acushnet avenue
1 2 Acushnet avenue
255 264 Bowditch
297 292 Rochambeau
309 314 Milford
331 336 Lafayette
353 358 Maywood
375 380 Seabury
397 398 Church
BROOKS (N) from Bellevue avenue to River road
BROWNELL (W) from Grape to Hawthorn and from Arnold opposite 376 Court
1 2 Grape
23 24 Allen
53 56 Bedford
0 0 Grove
67 70 Ryan
81 84 Carroll
95 98 Plymouth
109 110 Hawthorne

Brownell—con
155 156 Maple
0 168 Clinton
183 186 Arnold
235 236 Union
253 254 Court
BUCHANAN (N W) from Myrtle to Mt Pleasant
BULLARD (N) from 335 Belleville avenue to beyond Bowditch
2 1 Belleville avenue
48 47 North Front
74 73 Acushnet avenue
122 121 Bowditch
BULLOCK (N W) from Willow at Advent church to Mt Vernon
1 2 Willow
13 14 Austin
31 West Trinity
45 46 Durfee
139 144 Mt Vernon
BUTLER (S) from East French avenue to 260 Brock avenue C P
0 0 East French avenue
0 Swan
0 Moss
0 0 Fern
0 0 Brock avenue
BUTTONWOOD (W) from end Court to 976 Kempton
0 0 Court
12 Lake
21 Kilby
44 43 Kempton
BUTTONWOOD PARK (W) end of Court
CALUMET (S) from West French avenue to Brock avenue
CAMPBELL (N) from 579 Acushnet avenue to Park opposite Oak Grove cemetery
0 5 Acushnet avenue
16 15 Purchase
24 0 Pleasant
54 53 State
70 71 County
96 97 Summer
106 107 Chestnut
112 113 Cottage
140 141 Cedar
174 173 Shawmut avenue
190 189 Chancery
200 Park
CANNON (S) from Cross to 216 Acushnet avenue
0 1 Cross
4 5 South Water
0 21 South Second
30 29 Acushnet avenue
CAPITOL (S) from West French avenue to 330 Brock avenue
*CARLISLE (N) from Bowditch street to Church street
1 2 Bowditch
30 Rochambeau
0 46 Milford
0 74 Lafayette
0 96 Maywood
0 110 Seabury
131 132 Church
*CAROLINE (N) from Parker to Durfee
1 2 Parker
0 0 Tilton
109 114 Robeson
137 142 Willow
157 162 Austin
215 216 Durfee
CARROLL (W) from Brigham to Reed
1 2 Brigham
131 138 Palmer
163 164 Reed
*CARSON (N) from Dutton avenue north
CEDAR (N W) from 95 Court to 42 Durfee
17 18 Court
33 34 Morgan
47 48 Elm
61 62 Middle
68 West High
89 90 Kempton
105 106 Mill
115 114 North
137 136 Hillman
169 174 Maxfield
187 188 Sycamore
209 210 Smith
231 230 Campbell
249 248 Willis
273 274 Parker
315 316 Locust
327 Maitland
349 350 Robeson
365 366 Willow
377 378 Austin
403 Trinity
404 Collins
417 412 Durfee
CEDAR GROVE (N) from 91 Belleville avenue
102 101 Belleville avenue
125 Cotter
152 151 North Front

177 Howard
226 225 Acushnet avenue
258 257 Bowditch
297 Blackburn
0 0 N Y N H & H R R
312 311 Purchase
344 State
366 367 County
404 405 Reynolds

CENTRAL AVENUE (N) from 1825 Acushnet avenue to N Y N H & H R R
3 2 Conduit
85 88 Acushnet
227 230 Bowditch
341 344 Edison
355 358 Church
369 370 King
0 0 N Y N H & H R R

CENTRAL WHARF (E) from 99 Front

CENTRE (E) 100 Front to 32 North Water

CHANCERY (W) from 133 Hawthorn to 206 Smith and from 180 Campbell to Robeson
1 2 Hawthorn
25 26 Maple
49 50 Clinton
57 58 Arnold
101 102 Union
121 122 Court
0 148 Morgan
159 160 Elm
178 Middle
201 202 Kempton
213 0 Mill
235 236 North
255 260 Hillman
0 274 Keene
287 288 Maxfield
307 306 Sycamore
325 326 Smith
349 350 Campbell
371 372 Willis
415 0 Parker
465 466 Tilton
0 0 Robeson

CHEPACHET (W) changed to Buttonwood

CHERRY (S) from 47 South Sixth to 394 County
0 0 South Sixth
0 Seventh
0 0 County

CHESTER (W) from Hillman north

CHESTNUT (N W) from 319 Kempton to Robeson
5 `6 Kempton
13 0 Mill
27 28 North
47 48 Hillman
69 70 Maxfield
89 90 Sycamore
109 110 Smith
131 130 Campbell
139 154 Willis
0 176 Parker
0 0 Pope
213 0 Locust
245 244 Merrimac
0 260 Robeson

CHURCH (N) from 403 Coffin avenue to Phillips road
3 4 Coffin avenue
0 0 Phillips avenue
41 Earle Court
43 44 Collette
57 60 Davis
75 78 Earle
0 100 Hathaway
0 120 Tinkham
137 138 Nash road
205 204 Belleville road
259 262 Central
277 280 Shaw
293 296 Clifford
307 310 Princeton
321 324 Irvington
0 400 Carlisle
0 466 Brooklawn
0 508 Wood
533 536 Park avenue
543 548 Tarkiln Hill road
0 0 Brockton
0 0 Lynn
0 1106 Belair
1121 1128 Kelton
1143 1150 Hamlen
0 1170 Avery
1291 1292 Phillips road

CLARA (S) from East French avenue to 242 Brock avenue

CLARK (N) from 951 Purchase to 112 Mt Pleasant
2 1 Purchase
28 27 State
48 47 County
80 81 Reynolds
100 103 Myrtle
128 129 Ashland
144 145 Mt Pleasant

CLARK'S POINT (S) south of Cove road East and West French avs

CLAY (S W) from opposite 26 Ward to 45 Oak
0 0 Ward
0 Hickory
0 Columbia
15 16 Oak

CLEVELAND (S) from 16 Cove to south of Rodney
0 0 Cove
35 36 Ruth avenue
87 92 David
113 0 Ellen
135 0 Emma
153 158 Mott
177 192 Rodney

CLIFFORD (N) from 1873 Acushnet avenue to the R R
0 0 Acushnet avenue
0 0 Bowditch
0 0 Church

CLINTON (S) from 405 County to Rockdale avenue
1 County
0 Clinton place
46 47 Orchard
88 89 Cottage
146 143 Ash (South)
182 183 Chancery
210 209 Park
) 0 Rockdale avenue

CLINTON PLACE (S) from Clinton near County

CLOVER (S W) from 95 Grape to 378 Allen

COFFIN (S E) from Akin's wharf to beyond 136 South Second
0 0 Akin's wharf
0 0 South Water
0 South First
0 0 South Second

COFFIN AVENUE (N) from Acushnet river to the R R
0 0 Acushnet river
0 67 Riverside avenue
164 165 Belleville avenue
224 223 North Front
262 263 Acushnet avenue
312 313 Bowditch
339 Coffin avenue court
357 Oneko lane
374 375 Brook
401 Church
420 Purchase
0 0 N Y N H & H R R

COFFIN AVENUE COURT (N) from 339 Coffin avenue

COGGESHALL (N) from Acushnet river at Coggeshall bridge west to Reynolds proposed to opposite 299 Mount Pleasant
0 0 Acushnet river
127 Bennett
171 Mitchell
210 209 Belleville avenue
229 Grandfield
234 Cotter
266 265 North Front
288 289 Howard
330 329 Acushnet avenue
374 373 Bowditch
385 Jean
0 0 N Y N H & H R R
434 435 Purchase
0 461 County
0 505 Reynolds
0 0 Bannister
0 0 Myrtle
0 0 Ashland
0 0 Mt Pleasant

COLLETTE (N) from Riverside av- to railroad
2 1 Riverside avenue
80 81 Belleville
172 173 North Front
218 217 Acushnet avenue
264 263 Bowditch
332 331 Brook
368 369 Church

COLLINS (N W) from 679 Cottage to 402 Cedar
1 2 Cottage
14 Glover
35 Cedar

COLUMBIA (S W) from opposite 6 Clay to 262 Allen
1 2 Clay
32 Bay
53 52 Allen

COMMERCIAL (E) from N Y N H & H R R wharf to 22 South Water
0 0 R R wharf
8 7 Front
32 35 South Water

*COMMONWEALTH (S W) from Kempton to Fairmount

CONDUIT (N) from 71 Bates avenue to Acushnet avenue
0 0 Query avenue
0 0 Central avenue
0 0 Shaw
0 0 Belleville road
0 0 Hatch
0 0 Accushnet avenue

COOK (W) from 501 Kempton to opposite 247 Mill

*COPPER (N) from Front east to river
CORNELL COURT (S) from 31 Crapo
CORNELL PLACE (N) from 39 Bowditch
COTTAGE (W) from 33 Dartmouth to 24 Durfee
1 2 Dartmouth
15 16 Bay
31 32 Allen
59 60 Bedford
81 82 Grove
91 92 Hawthorn
117 Maple
125 126 Clinton
135 136 Arnold
173 174 Union
187 188 Court
213 214 Morgan
217 218 Elm
241 242 Middle
273 272 Kempton
291 292 Mill
319 320 North
335 336 Hillman
363 364 Maxfield
385 384 Sycamore
407 408 Smith
439 440 Campbell
457 460 Willis
489 490 Parker
541 542 Locust
0 Merrimac
601 602 Robeson
621 Willow
647 648 Austin
679 Collins
701 702 Durfee
COTTER (N) from 125 Cedar Grove to 234 Cogeshall
COUNTY (W) from 63 Cove road to 1225 Purchase
21 20 Cove road
32 Cove
35 Scott
59 Nelson
69 Jouvette
85 88 Division
98 Delano
101 Mosher
113 Winsor
131 Katherine
138 Blackmer
145 Independent
161 160 Rivet
185 186 Thompson
211 216 Rockland
239 Fair
0 248 South
271 266 Washington
0 0 Washington square
279 278 Grinnell
0 South Sixth
293 Sherman
303 Forest
322 Wing
329 Allen
361 362 Bedford
378 Russell
385 Hawthorn
394 Cherry
397 396 Madison
404 Walnut
405 Clinton
413 Arnold
416 School
424 Spring
427 428 Union
443 Court
460 William
465 Morgan
479 478 Elm
485 486 Middle
504 High
513 514 Kempton
535 534 Mill
549 550 North
567 568 Hillman
591 590 Maxfield
619 616 Sycamore
635 642 Smith
661 662 Campbell
677 0 Willis
692 Pearl
North Common
695 Parker
709 710 Pope
729 Locust
726 Franklin
745 744 Merrimac
763 Robeson
781 784 Hazard
807 Studley
813 812 Austin
851 852 Linden
875 **McMurray** terrace
899 900 Weld
909 La France court
943 942 Clark
963 964 Penniman
991 990 Cedar Grove
0 0 Peckham
1043 1044 Coggeshall
1065 **Adams**
1101 0 Sawyer
0 Blanchard
0 Purchase

COURT (W) from 443 County to Buttonwood park
2 1 County
34 North Orchard
64 65 Cottage
95 Cedar
124 125 Ash (North)
145 Emerson
168 169 Chancery
198 197 Park
213 Pierce
229 Newton
255 Liberty
276 275 Tremont
306 307 James
327 Lindsey
332 Rotch
339 Jenney
356 Armour
357 Florence
376 Brownell
394 Rounds
414 413 Palmer
0 437 Reed
0 Francis
0 0 Rockdale avenue
0 Buttonwood
0 0 Buttonwood park

COVE (S) from 5 East French av to 32 County
12 0 East French avenue
0 Abbott
16 Cleveland
0 26 Roosevelt
28 Harrison avenue
42 Ashley
0 69 Harbor
70 Salisbury
0 Viall
0 McGurk
113 Morton court
0 West French avenue
137 South Water
150 0 South First
0 Stapleton
170 0 South Second
182 Margin
196 County

COVE ROAD (S) from W French av west to Dartmouth line
2 3 West French avenue
16 17 Thatcher
26 0 Shore
0 0 Stapleton
53 Margin
61 63 County
0 0 Crapo
0 Bonney
0 Orchard (S)
0 Rockdale avenue
0 0 Dartmouth line

COVELL (N) from 707 Belleville av to 1900 Acushnet av
0 0 Belleville avenue
0 0 Acushnet avenue

*COYNELA (N) from Dutton north

CRAPO (S) from 168 Grinnell to Cove road
2 1 Grinnell
8 7 Washington
16 South
26 25 Fair
31 Cornell court
42 43 Rockland
60 61 Thompson
92 93 Rivet
104 Independent
120 121 Katherine
134 Winsor
152 Mosher
162 Division
184 185 Jouvette
198 199 Nelson
212 Scott
220 221 Cove road

CROSS (S E) from Cannon to Leonard
0 Cannon
0 Pine
0 0 Leonard

DANIEL (N) from Mary to Flint

DARLING (N) from Acushent av to Ball

DARTMOUTH (S W) from 126 Allen past Rural cemetery to Dartmouth line
2 1 Allen
10 Orchard (South)
11 Bay
30 Grinnell
33 Cottage
42 Washington
43 Borden
58 Fair
61 Hickory
77 Oak
82 Rockland
88 Spooner
96 Thompson
112 Fruit
109 Weaver
114 Rilvet
117 Babbitt
124 Larch
0 Edward
128 Swift
140 Dunbar
0 Stowell

0 Sidney
0 Hollyhock
378 Sagamore
0 Matthew
0 388 Jenkins
0 416 Winsper
0 430 Schofield
0 452 Gosnold
0 0 Rockdale avenue
0 0 Dartmouth

DAVID (S) from East French av to 120 West French avenue
1 East French avenue
80 81 Cleveland
96 97 Harrison
0 99 Roosevelt
114 115 Ashley
131 Salisbury
140 141 Brook avenue
198 197 West French avenue

DAVIS (N) from Riverside avenue opposite Whitman Mills to the railroad
2 1 Riverside avenue
70 69 Belleville avenue
172 171 North Front
218 217 Acushnet avenue
0 263 Bowditch
328 329 Brook
372 373 Church
402 401 Railroad

DEAN (N) from 363 Belleville av to 1248 Purchase
36 35 Belleville avenue
80 79 North Front
108 107 Acushnet avenue
152 153 Bowditch
208 205 Brook
0 0 Quansett
238 239 Purchase

DELANO (S) from South Front at Acushnet Mill Corporation west to 96 County
2 1 South Front
20 19 South Water
38 39 First
58 57 South Second
82 81 Acushnet avenue
0 0 County

*DENNIS (S) from Brock av east

DESAUTELS (N) from 573 Belleville avenue to 22 Belleville road
0 Belleville avenue
1 Nash road
19 22 Whitman
37 40 Eugenia
53 54 Belleville road

DEVOLL (W) from Grape to 428 Allen

*DEWEY (N) from Acushnet avenue to Wood road

DeWOLFE (N W) from 91 Durfee to Mt Vernon

DIMAN (N) from Davis to 94 Belleville road
0 0 Davis
0 0 Hathaway avenue
0 0 Earle
0 0 Tinkham
0 Webster court
0 0 Nash road
0 0 Whitman
0 0 Eugenia
0 0 Belleville road

DIVISION (S) from 961 Water to 162 Crapo
6 11 South Water
20 19 First
54 55 South Second
0 0 Acushnet avenue
100 101 County
210 209 Crapo

DOVER (E) from 386 Acushnet av to 51 North Second

DRIGGS LANE (S E) from 122 S Water to Front

DUDLEY (S) from 183 Brock avenue south of Woodlawn avenue to 198 West French avenue
1 2 Brock avenue
77 78 West French avenue

DUNBAR (S W) from 379 Bolton west to 140 Dartmouth
2 1 Bolton
54 55 Hemlock
122 123 Dartmouth

DUNCAN (N) from 1950 Acushnet avenue to Kearsarge
0 0 Acushnet avenue
0 0 Kearsarge

DURFEE (N W) from 113 Ashland to opposite 1159 Rockdale avenue
2 1 Ashland
24 Cottage
25 Mt Pleasant
35 Vine
42 Cedar
49 Highland
72 65 Richmond
78 Bullock
91 DeWolfe
0 111 Shawmut avenue
150 Acorn
159 Oakland
0 0 Rockdale avenue

DURFEE COURT (N W) from 3 Myrtle to 108 Ashland
1 2 Myrtle
25 26 Ashland

*DUTTON (N) from Acushnet av to Wood road

EARLE (N) from 505 Belleville av to railroad

58 57 Belleville avenue
172 171 North Front
218 217 Acushnet avenue
264 263 Bowditch
332 331 Brook
380 381 Church
0 0 Railroad

EARLE COURT (N) from 44 Church to the railroad

EAST DURFEE (N W) from 3 Myrtle to 108 Ashland

EAST FRENCH AVENUE (S) from 12 Cove to U S land, C P

0 0 Marine avenue
0 Almshouse lane
0 Aquidneck
0 Apponegansett
0 Butler
0 Norman
0 Frederick
0 Rodney
0 Mott
0 David
0 Ruth
0 Abbott
0 0 Cove

EAST MERRIMAC (N) from 716 Acushnet avenue to the railroad

EAST POPE (N) from 668 Acushnet avenue to the river

EDISON (N) from Nash road near Bowditch to Query

1 2 Nash road
57 58 Belleville road
0 78 Glennon
123 124 Central avenue
143 144 Shaw
0 0 Query

EDNA (N) from Brooklawn park to Wood

EDWARD (S W) from beyond 127 Dartmouth to 148 Field

EIGHTH (W) from 101 Spring to 106 Elm

0 0 Spring
0 0 Union
15 14 William
32 Mechanics lane
37 36 Elm

*ELIZABETH (W) from West to Brigham

ELLEN (S) from Cleveland to Freeman

*ELLIOT (N) from Acushnet avenue east

ELM (N) from 105 N Water to 42 Ash and (W) from 135 Emerson to 48 Liberty and from 43 Florence to beyond Reed

0 0 North Water
10 Bethel
18 17 North Second
30 31 Acushnet avenue
0 0 Purchase
54 53 Pleasant
72 73 North Sixth
106 Eighth
0 115 County
131 Summer
160 161 Cottage
192 191 Cedar
200 201 Ash (North)
326 325 Emerson
342 341 Chancery
370 369 Park
388 387 Pierce
404 403 Newton
420 421 Liberty
442 441 Tremont
486 485 Lindsey
506 505 Jenney
526 525 Florence
552 551 Rounds
574 573 Palmer
598 597 Reed

EMERSON (S W) from 163 Arnold to 182 Smith

1 2 Arnold
63 62 Union
85 84 Court
135 Elm
157 Middle
187 184 Kempton
207 Mill
215 North
0 0 Hillman
0 0 Maxfield
0 0 Smith
0 0 Sycamore

EMERY (S) from Brock avenue to Freeman

EMMA (S) from Cleveland to Freeman

*ERNEST (N) from Bates to Belleville road

EUGENIA (N) from 121 Hope to Brook

0 Hope
0 Diman
0 0 North Front
0 Acushnet avenue
0 Bowditch
0 Brook

FAIR (S) from 239 County to 58 Dartmouth
2 1 County
54 59 Hall
68 69 Crapo
90 91 Bonney
104 103 Orchard (S)
128 Briggs
140 141 Bolton
142 Hemlock
145 Sears
168 165 Dartmouth
*FAIRFIELD (N) from Acushnet av east
FAIRMOUNT (W) from 693 Rockdale avenue to Jenny Lind
FAIRMOUNT AVENUE (N) from Acushnet avenue to beyond Stratford place
FARM (W) from Brigham to Brownell
FELTON (N) from Brooklawn park to Hersom
0 0 Hersom
0 0 Wood
0 0 Brooklawn park
FERN (S) from Butler south
FIELD (S W) from beyond Matthew to Rural cemetery
1 2 Rockdale avenue
83 84 Matthew
101 102 Hollyhock
119 Stowell
148 Edward
167 168 Babbitt
189 Weaver
Rural cemetery
239 0 Grape
0 0 Allen
FIFTH (S) from 212 Union to 129 Grinnell
0 1 Union
10 11 Spring
22 23 School
0 35 Walnut
44 45 Madison
68 69 Russell
86 85 Bedford
0 0 Wing
122 123 Grinnell
FILLMORE (N W) from Myrtle to Mt Pleasant
FIRST (S) from 86 Union to opposite 16 Coffin and from 44 Howland next South Water to Cove
2 1 Union
0 0 Spring
0 0 School
0 0 Walnut
0 0 Madison
172 171 Coffin
210 209 Cannon
232 231 Morgan's lane
284 283 Griffin
316 315 Howland
341 Maiden lane
382 381 Grinnell
434 433 South
524 523 Potomska
600 601 Rivet
630 635 Blackmer
688 687 Delano
724 725 Division
0 Jennings' court
822 823 Cove
FISH ISLAND (E) west end of N B & Fairhaven bridge
FLINT (N) from Tarkiln Hill road next Bowditch to Park avenue
0 0 Tarkiln Hill road
0 Daniel
0 0 Park avenue
FLORENCE (W) (CANNONVILLE) from 357 Court to 358 Maxfield
2 1 Court
25 West Morgan
43 Elm
55 Middle
98 97 Kempton
116 115 Mill
134 133 North
160 161 Hillman
0 0 Maxfield
FLORIDA (N) from Raymond to west of Bowditch
FOREST (E W) from 303 County to opposite 21 Bonney
FOSTER (N) from 169 Middle to 106 Maxfield
1 2 Middle
5 6 High
0 18 Kempton
37 38 Mill
48 North
0 60 Hillman
73 72 Maxfield
FOURTH (S) from 178 Union to 129 Rivet
0 0 Union
20 21 Spring
0 0 School
66 67 Walnut
78 81 Madison
118 117 Russell
140 141 Bedford
0 0 Wing
194 195 Grinnell
205 Washington

Fourth—con
218 217 South
246 247 Rockland
266 Potomska
227 Thompson
0 0 Rivet
FRANCIS (W) from 868 Kempton to Court
FRANKLIN (N) from 551 Purchase to 726 County
0 0 Purchase
8 7 Pleasant
0 0 State
40 39 County
FREDERICK (S) from East French avenue to 212 Brock avenue, C P
FRENCH AVENUE (S) see East and West French avenues
FRONT (N E) from Walnut at P & R coal pockets to Bridge square
0 1 Walnut
15 Merrill's wharf
0 Driggs lane
0 School
0 M V & N S S Co
54 Shepard's lane
0 N Y, N H & H Railroad
68 69 Commercial
80 81 Union
0 City wharf
85 Taber's wharf
90 Rose alley
99 Central wharf
100 101 Centre
110 Hamilton
115 Rotch square
0 Rotch's wharf
120 121 Rodman
139 Lewis wharf
146 Hazard's lane
170 Middle
0 0 Bridge square
FRUIT (W) from Bolton road to 112 Dartmouth
2 1 Bolton
32 Juniper
64 63 Hemlock
114 Mulberry
115 Bourne
132 0 Dartmouth
FULTON (S W) from Rockdale av westerly
FULTON COURT (N) from 11 Logan to 34 Hicks
GARFIELD (N W) from Myrtle to Mt Pleasant
101 102 Myrtle
145 146 Ashland
179 180 Mt Pleasant
GEORGE (S) from Brock av south of Warren to West French avenue
GIFFORD (S) from 974 South Water to the river
0 0 South Water
5 South Front
0 Harbor
GIFFORD LANE (N W) from 1107 Rockdale avenue west
GLEN (N) from 2826 Acushnet av
*GLENCOE (N) from Dutton north
GLENNON (N) from Bowditch west to Edison
GLOVER (N W) from 193 Austin to 20 Collins
*GOSNOLD (S W) from Dartmouth to Hemlock
GOULD (W) from Hawthorn to Priscilla
GRAND (N W) from 241 Shawmut avenue to Rockdale avenue
0 0 Shawmut avenue
34 Oakland
0 0 Rockdale avenue
GRANDFIELD (N) from 229 Coggeshall to 12 Beetle
GRANT (W) from next 923 Rockdale avenue to beyond Jenney Lind
GRAPE (S W) from 54 Oak to beyond Rural
2 1 Oak
16 Lewis
39 Page
78 77 Field
95 Clover
100 Alec
109 West
0 Devoll
0 Rural
GREEN (S W) from 67 Allen to 78 Bedford
GRENIER (N) from Belleville av to Acushnet av
GRIFFIN (S E) from beyond 406 S Water to 170 Acushnet avenue
6 0 South Water
18 0 South Second
26 25 Acushnet avenue
GRINNELL (S) from Acushnet river at Hastings' wharf west across County to 30 Dartmouth
0 0 Acushnet river
0 0 Prospect
60 59 South Front
68 67 South Water
76 75 First
90 91 South Second
0 0 Acushnet avenue
112 113 Fourth

129 Fifth
0 Sixth
152 151 County
168 Crapo
180 181 Bonney
198 199 Orchard (S)
240 239 Dartmouth

GRIT (S) from West French avenue near Cove road to Shore
0 0 West French avenue
0 Thatcher
0 0 Shore

GROVE (S W) from next 171 Orchard to 108 Ash (S)
1 Orchard
6 Anthony
22 21 Cottage
32 Borden
42 0 Ash (South)

HADLEY (N) from 1930 Acushnet avenue to 723 Belleville avenue
0 0 Acushnet avenue
0 Kearsarge
0 0 Belleville avenue

HALL (S) from 211 Rivet to 20 Fair
1 2 Rivet
41 40 Thompson
53 Stanton court
69 70 Rockland
111 110 Fair

HALL'S COURT (E) from 70½ William

*HAMBLIN (N) from Belleville av east to River road

HAMILTON (E) from Rotch's wharf to 48 North Water
0 0 Rotch's wharf
0 0 Front
20 17 North Water

*HAMLEN (N) from Wood road west

HAMPTON COURT (N) from 7 Logan to rear 16 Hicks

HARBOR (S) from Cove opposite Salisbury to Gifford

HARMONY (S) from 12 Social south to Brock avenue

HARRISON (S W) from opposite 22 Hickory to 23 Oak

HARRISON AVENUE (S) from 28 Cove to 98 David
0 0 Cove
0 0 Ruth
0 0 David

HATCH (N) from 693 Belleville av to 1878 Acushnet av
0 0 Acushnet avenue
0 0 Conduit
0 0 Belleville avenue

HATCH'S LANE (N) from Chancery to Shaw

HATHAWAY (N) from Riverside av to 80 Church
2 1 Riverside avenue
0 0 Bellevue avenue
0 0 Hope
62 61 Diman
82 81 Front
100 99 Acushnet avenue
130 129 Bowditch
180 179 Brook
170 171 Church

HATHAWAY CORNER (N) junction Acushnet avenue, Sylvan park and Braley road at Clifford

HATHAWAY ROAD (N W) from 453 Mt Pleasant to Smith's Mills Dartmouth line
0 0 Mt Pleasant
0 Shawmut avenue
636 Rockdale avenue
0 0 Dartmouth line

HAWES (N) from Tarkiln Hill road south to Brooklawn park
285 286 Park avenue
399 340 Tarkiln Hill road
425 426 Brockton
499 500 Lynn
567 568 Holyoke

HAWES LANE (N) from Tarkiln Hill road northerly, L C

HAWTHORN (S W) from 385 County across Rockdale avenue to Dartmouth line
2 1 County
36 37 Orchard
49 Irving
66 67 Cottage
108 109 Ash (South)
115 Hawthorn terrace
127 Chancery
162 Page
209 Tremont
236 Brigham
247 Rotch
0 Brownell
0 Palmer
0 0 Reed
0 Rockdale avenue
0 Brownell avenue
0 Dartmouth

HAWTHORN TERRACE (S W) from 115 Hawthorn near Ash (S) to 58 Maple

HAZARD (N) from 653 Purchase across County at 774 Ashland opposite the church
2 1 Purchase
28 27 Pleasant
31 Austin court
50 49 State
61 Hazard court
80 79 County
104 105 Ashland
HAZARD COURT (N) from opposite 63 Austin to opposite 60 Hazard
HAZARD'S LANE (E) from 146 Front to 90 North Water
HEALEY (N) from 13 Belleville road to Bates
HELEN (N) from Acushnet avenue to Belleville avenue
HEMLOCK (S W) from 142 Fair to Rockdale avenue
2 1 Fair
30 29 Rockland
70 69 Thompson
80 Kane
100 99 Fruit
114 113 Rivet
128 127 Larch
140 139 Swift
152 151 Dunbar
0 0 Sidney
0 0 Sagamore
0 0 Jenkins
0 0 Winsper
0 0 Schofield
0 0 Gosnold
0 Howland Village
0 0 Rockdale avenue
*HENRY (S) from Dennis north
HERSOM (N) from Acushnet river to Bowditch
1 2 Acushnet river
19 20 River road
91 92 Belleville avenue
163 166 Acushnet avenue
0 282 Felton
0 302 Vernon
0 322 Waldo
439 440 Bowditch
*HEYWOOD (N) from Dutton av north
HICKORY (S W) from 61 Dartmouth to opposite 7 Clay
0 0 Dartmouth
0 Harrison
22 Ward
0 0 Clay
HICKS (N) from 121 North Front to 858 Acushnet avenue
2 1 North Front
16r Hampton court
34 Fulton court
53 Pierce
78 79 Acushnet avenue
HIGH (N) from 125 North Second to 504 County
0 0 North Water
0 19 North Second
34 33 Acushnet avenue
48 51 Purchase
70 69 Pleasant
82 83 Foster
126 127 County
HIGHLAND (N W) from 49 Durfee and Mt Vernon to Hathaway rd
2 1 Durfee
0 0 Mt Vernon
0 Potter
150 Topham
0 Sutton
0 0 Brawley
HILL (N) from 189 Kempton to 78 Hillman
0 0 Kempton
0 0 Mill
0 0 North
61 60 Hillman
HILLMAN (N) from 278 North Water across County to beyond Jenney Lind
2 1 North Water
3 Hillman street court
24 0 North Second
28 29 Acushnet avenue
46 47 Purchase
60 59 Pleasant
64 65 Foster
75 State
78 Hill
85 Walden
97 Thomas
110 109 County
120 119 Summer
134 135 Chestnut
144 145 Cottage
154 153 Spruce
166 167 Cedar
0 0 Ash (North)
0 Emerson
218 217 Chancery
238 237 Park
270 Newton
280 279 Liberty
0 Tremont
0 Lindsey
0 Jenney
0 0 Florence
402 401 Hunter
428 427 Beech

446 445 Summit
462 461 Rockdale avenue
0 0 Jenny Lind
HILLMAN STREET COURT (N E) from 3 Hillman
HOLLY (N) from 253 Belleville av opposite Pierce Mfg Co to 25 Brook
2 1 Belleville avenue
42 41 North Front
72 71 Acushnet avenue
117 Bowditch
164 163 Brook
HOLLYHOCK (S W) from Dartmouth west to Rural cemetery
2 1 Dartmouth
28 27 Primrose
48 47 Field
0 0 Stephen
HOLY ACRE (N) between Pearl, Wamsutta and Acushnet avenue next the river
*HOLYOKE (N) from Lowell west
HOMER (N) from 63 Parker to 74 Locust
HOMESTEAD (N) from Acushnet line to 2361 Acushnet avenue
HOPE (N) from 42 Belleville road to Belleville avenue
0 0 Belleville road
0 Eugenia
0 Whitman
0 Nash road
0 Webster court
0 0 Tinkham
0 Hathaway avenue
0 Belleville avenue
HOWARD (N) from 177 Cedar Grove to 54 Beetle
1 2 Cedar Grove
27 Marvin
45 46 Coggeshall
79 80 Beetle
HOWARD AVENUE (N) from 2010 Acushnet avenue near Lund's corner to River road
2 1 Acushnet avenue
0 0 Belleville avenue
0 0 River road
HOWLAND (S E) from river beyond Prospect at P Corporation to 158 Acushnet avenue
2 3 Prospect
14 Front
30 29 South Water
42 43 First
70 71 South Second
90 91 Acushnet avenue
HOWLAND VILLAGE (S) from Bolton road at Rockdale avenue near Gosnold mill
*HOYE (N) from Dutton north
HUDSON (S) from West French av easterly
1 2 East French avenue
137 120 Brock avenue
0 174 Point
241 242 West French avenue
HUNTER (W) (CANNONVILLE) from 769 Kempton to 578 Maxfield
1 2 Kempton
13 14 Mill
27 28 North
47 48 Hillman
71 72 Maxfield
*HUNTINGTON (S W) from Commonwealth to Brownell avenue near Dartmouth line
HUSSEY (W) from Lake to Kempton
HYACINTH (S W) from 195 Rivet to 36 Thompson
ILION (W) from Buttonwood park to Kempton
ILLINOIS (N) from east of Pine Grove to Bowditch
INDEPENDENT (S W) from 145 County to 104 Crapo
INGRAHAM (N) from 1972 Acushnet avenue to Kearsarge
0 0 Acushnet avenue
0 0 Kearsarge
IRVING (S W) from 49 Hawthorn to Maple
*IRVINGTON (N) from Acushnet avenue to Church
JACINTO (S W) from Allen next St John's cemetery to Winterville rd
0 0 Allen
0 Oakland
0 Westbrook
0 0 Winterville road
JACKSON (N W) from Myrtle to Mt Pleasant
JAMES (W) from 217 Maple to North
0 0 Maple
37 36 Arnold
97 98 Union
125 124 Court
0 0 Kempton
0 0 Mill
0 0 North
JARRY (N) from east of Pine Grove to Bowditch
JEAN (N) from 373 Coggeshall to 336 Sawyer

JEFFERSON (N W) from Myrtle to Mt Pleasant
101 102 Myrtle
150 151 Ashland
185 186 Mt Pleasant

*JENKINS (S W) from Bolton to Dartmouth
1 2 Bolton
59 60 Hemlock
127 128 Dartmouth

JENNEY (W) from 339 Court to Hillman
1 2 Court
103 108 Kempton
123 128 Mill
145 150 North
173 174 Hillman

JENNINGS COURT (S) from 574 South Second to First

JENNY LIND (W) (CANNONVILLE) from Lake to Fairmount
1 2 Lake
41 42 Kempton
81 84 Hillman
117 118 Milton
145 146 Grant
163 0 Lexington
179 180 Fairmount

JOHN (S W) from Allen east of Jacinto
0 0 Hadley

JOUVETT (S) from 69 County to Bonney
0 0 County
110 0 Crapo
0 0 Bonney

JOYCE (N) from Acushnet avenue to Wood road

JUNIPER (S W) from 33 Larch to 32 Fruit
2 3 Larch
16 17 Rivet
32 33 Fruit

KANE (S) from Bolton to 80 Hemlock

KATHARINE (S) from 131 County to Orchard
0 0 County
0 0 Crapo
0 0 Bonney
0 0 Orchard

KEARSARGE (N) from 96 Perry south to Hadley
0 0 Perry
0 0 Ingraham
0 0 Duncan
0 0 Hadley

KEENE (N W) from Chancery to 159 Liberty
0 0 Chancery
0 0 Park
46 47 Liberty

*KELTON (N) from Wood road west

KEMPTON (N) from 139 N Second across County and Rockdale avenue to Dartmouth line
44 43 North Second
72 71 Acushnet avenue
102 101 Purchase
132 131 Pleasant
156 155 Foster
189 Hill
250 251 County
274 Pease court
292 291 Summer
317 Chestnut
354 349 Cottage
392 391 Cedar
424 423 Ash (North)
456 455 Emerson
476 475 Chancery
501 Cook
512 511 Park
538 Pierce
560 559 Newton
584 583 Liberty
608 Tremont
638 James
668 667 Lindsey
696 701 Jenney
724 723 Florence
706 Rounds
769 Hunter
792 Palmer
815 Beech
828 Reed
859 Summit
868 Francis
876 875 Rockdale avenue
0 Hussey
951 Mill
976 Buttonwood
0 0 Jenny Lind
1005 Watson
1180 Brownell avenue
Commonwealth avenue
1270 1273 Dartmouth line

KEMPTON'S CORNER (N) County corner Kempton

KENMORE (N) from 2891 Acushnet avenue westerly (Pine Crest)

KENYON (N) from 61 Belleville av to 956 Acushnet avenue
2 1 Belleville avenue

38 39 North Front
116 115 Acushnet avenue
KILBURN (N) from 112 North Front at Grinnell mills to beyond Belleville avenue
0 0 North Front
0 0 Belleville avenue
0 0 Acushnet river
KING (N) from Nash road next ice houses to Shaw
1 2 Nash road
58 Belleville road
0 Central
0 0 Shaw
KING'S CORNER (N) junction Weld and Acushnet avenue
KING'S HIGHWAY (N) from Mt Pleasant near Wormwell's corner to Tarkiln Hill road opposite Lambeth Rope Corporation at Acushnet station
*KINGCROFT (N) from Acushnet avenue to beyond Wood road
*LAFAYETTE (N) from Princeton to Park avenue
1 2 Princeton
19 24 Irvington
107 114 Carlisle
189 184 Brooklawn
241 246 Wood
279 280 Park avenue
LA FRANCE COURT (N W) from 909 County
LAKE (W) from Rockdale avenue to Buttonwood park
0 0 Rockdale avenue
0 Hussey
0 0 Buttonwood
0 Jenny Lind
0 0 Buttonwood park
LAMBERT (N W) from Tarkiln Hill road northerly
LANDRY (N) from Brooklawn park to Wood
LARCH (S W) from 405 Bolton to 124 Dartmouth
0 1 Bolton
33 Juniper
58 57 Hemlock
95 Mulberry
124 125 Dartmouth
*LAUREL (N) from Edison to Brook
*LAWRENCE (N) from Tarkiln Hill road to beyond Holyoke
79 80 Tarkiln Hill road
147 148 Brockton
223 224 Lynn
293 294 Holyoke

LELAND (N) from Wood road easterly
LEONARD (E) from 376 South Water to Cross
0 0 South Water
0 Cross
LEWIS (S W) from 16 Grape
LEXINGTON (W) from 943 Rockdale avenue to beyond Jenny Lind
LIBERTY (W) from 255 Court across Kempton to Smith
1 2 Union
25 24 Court
0 Morgan
50 West Elm
95 96 Kempton
97 98 Mill
0 0 North
0 0 Hillman
0 Keen
0 0 Maxfield
0 0 Smith
LINCOLN (W) from 370 Union to 112 Arnold
LINDEN (N) from 793 Purchase to 98 Ashland
2 1 Purchase
22 21 Pleasant
44 45 State
58 59 County
76 Linden court
83 Reynolds
95 Myrtle
0 109 Ashland
LINDEN COURT (N) from 76 Linden to 98 Austin
0 0 Austin
0 Ashland place
LINDSEY (W) from 327 Court across Kempton to Hillman
1 2 Court
19 20 Morgan
75 74 Kempton
0 0 Mill
0 0 North
0 0 Hillman
LOCUST (N W) from 729 County to 104 Shawmut avenue
2 1 County
32 33 Summer
50 51 Chestnut
64 65 Cottage
74 Homer
90 91 Cedar
120 121 Richmond
138 139 Shawmut avenue
LOGAN (N) from 85 North Front to 862 Purchase
0 0 North Front
0 Hampton court

Logan—con
0 Fulton court
0 Pierce
0 0 Acushnet avenue
35 Bowditch
0 0 N Y, N H & H R R
50 51 Purchase
LOMBARD (S W) from Fruit to 202 Rockland
2 1 Fruit
0 0 Thompson
71 Spooner
86 87 Rockland
*LONGWOOD (S W) from Commonwealth to Brownell avenue near Dartmouth line
*LOWELL (N) from Tarkiln Hill road to beyond Holyoke
85 86 Tarkiln Hill road
151 152 Brockton
225 226 Lynn
293 294 Holyoke
LUCAS (S) from 297 Brock avenue to West French avenue
LUND'S CORNER (N) junction Acushnet av, Tarkiln Hill road and Main
*LYNN (N) from Lowell to Worcester
MADISON (S) from 209 South Water to opposite 108 Orchard
0 0 South Water
10 9 First
16 15 South Second
24 25 Acushnet avenue
0 33 Fourth
40 39 Fifth
70 69 South Sixth
85 81 Seventh
88 87 County
100 99 Orchard
MAIDEN LANE (S) from 341 First
MAIN (N) from 2176 Acushnet av to Acushnet line
0 0 Acushnet avenue
21 Belleville avenue
40 Mill road
45 River road
0 0 Acushnet line
MAITLAND (N W) from 327 Cedar to 124 Shawmut avenue
2 1 Cedar
38 37 Richmond
68 67 Shawmut avenue
MANOMET (N) from Riverside av at Manomet Mills to Acushnet river
MAPLE (S W) from 88 Orchard to Rockdale avenue
0 0 Orchard
0 Irving court
0 0 Cottage
46 45 Ash (South)
58 Hawthorn
86 85 Chancery
117 Park
141 Atlantic
0 0 Ocean
190 191 Tremont
217 James
248 297 Rotch
356 355 Reed
382 381 Rockdale avenue
MAPLE VIEW TERRACE (S W) from 15 Tremont westerly
MAPLEWOOD (N) from Acushnet avenue to Fairmount avenue
MARGIN (S) from 53 Cove road to 182 Cove
MARINE AVENUE (S) from end East French avenue to West French avenue
MARION AVENUE (N) from Acushnet avenue westerly (Pine Crest)
MARKET (S) from 25 Pleasant to 20 North Sixth
MARKET SQUARE junction Pleasant, Market, North Sixth and William
MARVIN (N) from 27 Howard to 1066 Acushnet avenue
MARY (N) from Park avenue
0 0 Park avenue
0 Daniel
MARYLAND (N) from east of Pine Grove to west of Bowditch
MATTHEW (S W) from Dartmouth beyond Hollyhock to Rockdale av
0 0 Dartmouth
0 Primrose
0 0 Field
0 0 Stephen
0 Stackhouse
0 Bank
0 0 Rockdale avenue
MAXFIELD (N) from east of North Second across County to 876 Rockdale avenue
22 North Second
38 39 Acushnet avenue
54 55 Purchase
80 81 Pleasant
106 Foster
124 123 State
140 141 Walden
160 161 Thomas
174 171 County
202 199 Summer
222 223 Chestnut

242 243 Cottage
254 257 Spruce
286 285 Cedar
304 305 Ash (North)
326 Emerson
354 353 Chancery
378 379 Park
434 435 Liberty
0 0 Tremont
538 Florence
576 577 Hunter
610 609 Beech
628 629 Summit
652 651 Rockdale avenue

*MAYWOOD (N) Irvington to Park avenue
1 2 Irvington
87 88 Carlisle
169 170 Brooklawn avenue
223 224 Wood
261 262 Park avenue

McDONALD COURT (N) from 16 Beetle

McGURK (S) from 118 Cove to 129 Ruth
2 1 Cove
0 Social
0 0 Brock avenue
0 0 Ruth

McMURRAY TERRACE (W) from 875 County

MECHANICS LANE (N) from 71 Purchase west to 32 Eighth
0 0 Purchase
0 0 Pleasant
0 0 North Sixth
0 71 Eighth

MENTON (N) from Pine Grove cemetery west of Bowditch

*MERRILL (N) from 47 Belleville road to Bates avenue

MERRILL'S WHARF from 11 Front

MERRIMAC (N) from N Y N H & H R R across County at 774 to 560 Cottage
0 0 N Y N H & H R R
44 45 Purchase
64 65 Pleasant
77 Merrimac avenue
90 91 State
130 129 County
160 161 Summer
180 181 Chestnut
198 197 Cottage

MERRIMAC AVENUE (N) from 77 Merrimac

METCALF (N W) from Tarkiln Hill road northerly

*METROPOLITAN (S W) from Commonwealth avenue to Brownell avenue near Dartmouth line

MIDDLE (N) from 172 Front at Bridge square to opposite 57 Ash (North) and from 157 Emerson to 215 Park and from 55 Florence to 32 Rounds
0 0 Front junction Bridge sq
52 53 North Water
82 83 North Second
102 101 Acushnet avenue
130 133 Purchase
152 151 Pleasant
169 Foster
174 North Sixth
220 221 County
246 247 Summer
292 291 Cottage
305 Sullivan
328 329 Cedar
348 249 Ash (North)
370 371 Emerson
380 381 Chancery
412 413 Park
438 437 Pierce
454 453 Newton
472 471 Liberty
0 0 Tremont
0 0 James
524 523 Lindsey
554 553 Jenney
0 Florence
0 Rounds

*MILES (N) from Dewey south

*MILFORD (N) from Irvington to Park avenue
1 2 Irvington
85 86 Carlisle
163 164 Brooklawn avenue
215 216 Wood
253 254 Park avenue
325 326 Tarkiln Hill road

MILL (N) from 151 North Second across 818 Rockdale avenue to 951 Kempton Cannonville
6 7 North Second
16 15 Acushnet avenue
30 31 Purchase
44 43 Pleasant
56 57 Foster
74 75 Hill
90 91 County
120 119 Summer
132 133 Chestnut
156 151 Cottage
180 179 Cedar
188 189 Ash (North)

Mill—con
222 0 Emerson
228 227 Chancery
0 Cook
252 253 Park
286 295 Newton
312 313 Liberty
330 329 Tremont
370 371 Lindsey
390 Jenney
412 411 Florence
444 445 Hunter
476 475 Beech
0 493 Summit
518 519 Rockdale avenue
0 0 Kempton

MILL ROAD 1 (S W) Orchard to Bolton

MILL ROAD 2 (S W) Orchard to Bolton

MILL ROAD 3 (S W) Orchard to Bolton

MILL ROAD 4 (S W) Orchard to Bolton

MILL ROAD (N) from 40 Main to Acushnet avenue opposite Hersom Soap Works

MILTON (N W) from 893 Rockdale avenue to beyond Jenny Lind

MITCHELL (N) from 173 Coggeshall to 156 Sawyer

*MONMOUTH (N) from Acushnet avenue east

*MONTROSE (N) from Acushnet av

MORELAND TERRACE (S W) from 108 Ash (South) to 160 Page

MORGAN (W) from 455 County to Ash (North) opposite N B Cordage Co and from Chancery to Park
2 1 County
62 61 Cottage
90 89 Cedar
104 103 Ash (North)
0 0 Chancery
0 0 Park
212 213 Liberty
224 223 Tremont
280 279 Jenney
316 315 Sisson

MORGAN'S LANE (S E) from 343 South Water to 180 South Second

MORGAN TERRACE (S) from 60 South Sixth near Russell

MORTON COURT (S) from 113 Cove to 1026 South Water

MOSHER (S) from 101 County to 152 Crapo

*MOSS (S) from Butler south

MOTT (S) from East French avenue to Brock
2 1 East French avenue
0 0 Cleveland
136 137 Brock avenue

MT PLEASANT (N W) from Durfee opposite Cottage to junction of Plainville and Tarkiln Hill roads
49 50 Durfee
66 Weld
69 Mt Pleasant lane
112 Clark
135 Mt Vernon
186 Peckham
196 Coggeshall
216 Adams
236 Blanchard
0 Topham
0 254 Sawyer
0 300 Buchanan
0 318 Fillmore
325 Brawley
0 336 Polk
0 358 Taylor
0 368 Van Buren
0 388 Jackson
0 420 Jefferson
0 Nausett
453 Hathaway road
465 466 O C R R
0 Nashville
0 Barrett
0 Newcomb
546 Nash road
0 Kings Highway
0 Tarkiln Hill road
0 0 Wormwell's Corner

MT PLEASANT LANE (N W) from 69 Mt Pleasant to 18 Vine

MT VERNON (N W) from 135 Mt Vernon to 232 Shawmut avenue
0 0 Mt Pleasant
34 Vine
0 0 Highland
0 De Wolfe
0 0 Shawmut avenue

MULBERRY (S W) from 114 Fruit to Larch
0 0 Fruit
0 0 Rivet
0 0 Larch

MYRTLE (N W) from 95 Linden to Nausett
1 2 Linden
3 East Durfee
45 46 Weld
0 0 Clark
115 0 Peckham
0 0 Coggeshall

0 0 Adams
0 0 Sawyer
0 0 Nausett

NASH POINT (N) foot of Coffin av next to Acushnet river

NASH ROAD (N) from 567 Belleville avenue to 546 Mt Pleasant
22 21 Belleville avenue
0 27 Desautels
48 47 Hope
104 103 Diman
144 143 Front
176 175 Acushnet avenue
230 229 Bowditch
292 Brook
0 Edison
358 357 Church
0 King
0 0 Railroad
0 Purchase avenue
0 (Contemplated)
0 0 Mt Pleasant

NASHVILLE (N) from Mt Pleasant opposite Hathaway road to the railroad Germantown
0 0 Mt Pleasant
0 0 (Contemplated)
0 0 Purchase avenue
0 0 Railroad

NASHVILLE HEIGHTS (N) between Mt Pleasant station and Nash road

NAUSETT (N W) from Purchase av to Mt Pleasant

NELSON (S) from South Second n cove to Bonney

NEWCOMB (N) from Mt Pleasant next Nash road to the railroad, Germantown
0 0 Mt Pleasant
0 0 (Contemplated)
0 0 Purchase avenue
0 0 Railroad
0 0 Germantown

NEWPORT (N) from Belleville av to River road

NEWTON (W) from 485 Union to Hillman
0 0 Union
25 26 Court
71 72 Elm
125 126 Kempton
143 144 Mill
159 160 North
189 188 Hillman

NORMAN (S) from East French av to Brock avenue

NORTH (N) from 241 North Water across County to Kempton
0 0 North Water
0 0 North Second
8 9 Acushnet avenue
0 0 Purchase
38 39 Pleasant
48 49 Foster
64 65 Hill
112 0 County
0 0 Summer
142 143 Chestnut
154 155 Cottage
161 Spruce
172 173 Cedar
184 185 Ash (North)
0 0 Emerson
206 205 Chancery
220 219 Park
242 241 Newton
256 255 Liberty
0 0 Jenney
0 0 Tremont
372 271 Lindsey
338 337 Florence
358 359 Hunter
392 381 Beech
0 409 Summit
424 425 Rockdale avenue
504 503 Jenny Lind
531 532 Watson
546 557 Kempton

NORTH FRONT (E) from Wamsutta to Acushnet avenue
0 1 Wamsutta
0 24 Cooper
85 84 Logan
112 Kilburn
121 Hicks
143 144 Washburn
151 152 Kenyon
177 178 Cedar Grove
215 216 Coggeshall
247 246 Beetle
279 280 Sawyer
301 302 Holly
319 320 Tallman
337 338 Nye
353 356 Bullard
373 374 Dean
399 400 Coffin avenue
419 420 Phillips avenue
437 438 Collette
453 454 Davis
469 0 Earle
487 486 Hathaway avenue
503 504 Tinkham avenue
512 Webster court
523 524 Nash road

North Front—con
539 540 Whitman
557 558 Eugenia
571 572 Belleville road
0 0 Acushnet avenue
NORTH OAK (N) from 14 Pope
NORTH ORCHARD (W) from 327 Union to 34 Court
NORTH SECOND (E) from 111 Union to 22 Maxfield
3 4 Union
17 Barker's court
37 38 William
51 Dover
71 72 Elm
97 98 Middle
127 128 High
136 Ark lane
145 144 Kempton
151 152 Mill
183 184 North
211 212 Hillman
233 232 Maxfield
NORTH SIXTH (W) from 239 Union to 174 Middle
0 0 Union
20 Market
21 Park place
0 0 William
37 34 Mechanics lane
47 0 Elm
57 58 Middle
NORTH WATER (E) from 63 Union to foot of Willis
1 2 Union
14 Rose alley
32 Centre
48 Hamilton
55 William
62 Rodman
90 Hazard's lane
105 Elm
131 132 Middle
N B & F H bridge
159 Ark lane
183 Beetle's lane
241 North
0 278 Hillman
0 Maxfield
0 Campbell
0 Willis
NORTON COURT (N W) from 84 Parker
*NORWOOD (N) from Acushnet av east
NYE (N) from 19 Belleville avenue to beyond Bowditch
2 1 Belleville avenue
44 43 North Front
72 71 Acushnet avenue
100 99 Bowditch
NYE'S LANE (N) from Acushnet av Clifford to Acushnet
OAK (S W) from 77 Dartmouth to beyond Allen
2 1 Dartmouth
22 Oak street court
25 Harrison
45 Clay
54 Grape
114 113 Allen
OAK STREET COURT (S W) from 22 Oak
OAKLAND (N W) from 159 Durfee to 34 Grand
OCEAN (W) from Maple across Arnold at 262 to 499 Union
2 1 Maple
32 31 Arnold
80 79 Union
OHIO (N) from east of Pine Grove to Bowditch
OLD COLONY PLACE (N) from 658 Purchase
OLD MARKET SQUARE (S) from 318 Acushnet avenue to 9 South Second
OLIVE (N E) from river across 629 Belleville avenue next Belleville rd westerly
OLIVER (N) from Tarkiln Hill rd east to Park avenue
271 272 Park avenue
295 296 Tarkiln Hill road
403 404 Brockton
475 476 Lynn
ONEKO LANE (N) from 357 Coffin avenue to 298 Phillips avenue
ORCHARD (S and W) Court to Union from next 42 Arnold south to beyond 100 Bedford and from 10 Dartmouth to Clark's cove, Cove road
58 59 Arnold
74 85 Clinton
108 Madison
142 139 Hawthorn
171 Grove
210 211 Bedford
246 247 Allen
256 257 Dartmouth
302 303 Grinnell
324 323 Washington
354 353 Fair
384 383 Rockland
424 423 Thompson
464 463 Rivet
0 0 Cove road

*OSGOOD AVENUE (N) from Acushnet avenue east
*OSWALD (N) from Dutton avenue north
PAGE (S W) from opposite 39 Grape to 162 Hawthorn
17 16 Grape
65 64 Allen
135 Taber
160 Moreland terrace
185 186 Hawthorn
PALMER (W) (CANNONVILLE) from Allen to 792 Kempton
1 2 Allen
17 18 Farm
33 34 Bedford
51 52 Ryan
67 68 Carroll
85 86 Plymouth
101 102 Hawthorn
161 162 Arnold
211 210 Union
231 230 Court
257 258 Elm
299 300 Kempton
PARK AVENUE (N) from Tarkiln Hill road opposite Acushnet railroad station, east to Flint
0 0 Tarkiln Hill road
0 0 Church
0 0 Oliver
0 Prescott
0 Hawes
0 Alice
0 Mary
0 0 Bowditch
PARK (W) from 111 Maple across Arnold at 216 and Kempton at 512 to 150 Parker
31 30 Maple
51 50 Clinton
63 62 Arnold
121 122 Union
151 150 Court
0 Morgan
201 200 Elm
261 260 Kempton
281 282 Mill
301 302 North
323 324 Hillman
347 348 Keene
387 388 Sycamore
353 0 Maxfield
411 410 Smith
437 436 Campbell
461 460 Willis
501 500 Parker
PARK PLACE (S W) from 21 North Sixth
PARKER (N W) from 695 County to opposite 1003 Rockdale avenue
2 1 County
26 27 Summer
40 39 Chestnut
56 57 Cottage
63 Homer
76 77 Cedar
84 Norton court
95 Richmond
112 111 Shawmut avenue
128 127 Chancery
150 Park
0 0 Oak Grove cemetery
0 0 Rockdale avenue
PEARL (N) from east of 623 Acushnet avenue west to 692 County
2 1 Acushnet avenue
0 0 Purchase
20 21 Pleasant
28 Washington avenue
32 State
0 0 County
PEASE COURT (N W) from 274 Kempton
PECKHAM (N) from 1015 County to 186 Mt Pleasant
1 2 County
45 46 Reynolds
59 0 Bannister
83 84 Myrtle
113 114 Ashland
146 147 Mt Pleasant
PECKHAM ROAD (N) from 4228 Acushnet avenue north of Braley road to Acushnet line
PENNINMAN (N) from 975 Purchase to Mt Pleasant
2 0 Purchase
28 27 State
0 0 County
0 0 Reynolds
0 0 Myrtle
0 0 Ashland
0 0 Mt Pleasant
PERRY (N) from River road to 1990 Acushnet avenue
42 41 River road
88 87 Belleville avenue
96 Kearsarge
140 139 Acushnet avenue
PERRY NECK ROAD (N W) from Plainville Hotel to head of the river
PHILLIPS AVENUE (N) from Riverside avenue opposite Whitman Mills to Church
2 1 Riverside avenue
86 87 Belleville avenue

Phillips avenue—con
164 163 North Front
206 205 Acushnet avenue
250 251 Bowditch
298 Oneko lane
318 319 Brook
0 0 Church
PHILLIPS ROAD (N W) from Acushnet avenue beyond Mill road to Braley road near Braley's station
PIERCE (N) from 15 Logan to 52 Hicks
PIERCE (W) from 213 Court to next 526 Kempton
24 25 Court
70 71 Elm
124 125 Kempton
*PIERCE PLACE (N) from Hicks to Logan
PINE (S E) from 330 South Water to Cross
PINE GROVE (N) from 16 Tarkiln Hill road to cemetery
PLAINVILE ROAD (N W) from junction Mt Pleasant and Tarkiln Hill road to Dartmouth line
0 0 Wormwell's Corner
0 Tarkiln Hill road
0 Mt Pleasant
0 Evergreen park
0 Reed's lane
0 0 Shawmut avenue
0 0 Dartmouth line
PLEASANT (S and N) from 211 Union to 148 Weld
1 2 Union
31 Market
32 Sears court
65 64 William
85 88 Mechanics lane
103 102 Elm
121 120 Middle
139 140 High
149 148 Kempton
159 163 Mill
177 176 North
193 194 Hillman
209 210 Maxfield
223 Sycamore
257 258 Campbell
271 270 Willis
291 290 Pearl
0 0 The Common
311 310 Pope
327 326 Franklin
345 344 Merrimac
367 366 Hazard
389 390 Austin
415 414 Linden
451 452 Weld
*POINT (S) from Bay View to Hudson
POLK (N W) from Mt Pleasant to Myrtle
PONTIAC (N) from 2460 Acushnet avenue to Pine Grove cemetery
POPE (N) from 487 Purchase to Cottage
2 1 Purchase
6 5 Pleasant
11 State
0 North Oak
24 25 County
256 255 Summer
274 275 Chestnut
0 0 Cottage
POPE'S ISLAND (E) beyond Fish Island next Fairhaven line
*PORTLAND (S) from West French avenue east
POTOMSKA (S) from 95 Prospect to 266 Fourth
0 0 Prospect
52 51 South Front
62 61 South Water
76 77 **South First**
94 95 South Second
98 99 Acushnet avenue
0 125 Fourth
POTTER (N W) from 242 Shawmut avenue to Highland
PRESCOTT (N) from Tarkiln Hill road near Hawes to Park avenue
PRIMROSE (S W) from Stowell to Matthew
0 0 Stowell
0 0 Hollyhock
0 0 Matthew
*PRINCETON (N) from 1901 Acushnet avenue to railroad
*PRISCILLA (W) west to Brigham
PROSPECT (S E) from foot of Howland to Potomska
0 0 Howland
0 0 Grinnell
76 75 South
0 Rockland
96 95 Potomska
PURCHASE (N E) from 160 Union north to 420 Coffin avenue
1 2 Union
29 Sears court
47 50 William
71 Mechanics lane
99 98 Elm
121 120 Middle

153 154 High
167 166 Kempton
181 180 Mill
217 218 North
251 252 Hillman
293 294 Maxfield
383 384 Campbell
403 402 Willis
439 438 Pearl
0 495 The Common
487 Pope
545 Franklin
599 600 Merrimac
653 Hazard
658 Old Colony place
678 Wamsutta
707 Austin
785 Linden
862 Logan
891 892 Weld
949 Clark
981 Penniman
1021 1022 Cedar Grove
1099 1100 Coggeshall
1165 1166 Sawyer
1213 Blanchard
1225 County
1245 (Contemplated)
1249 Purchase avenue
0 Dean
0 0 Coffin avenue

PURCHASE AVENUE (N) from end Purchase to Nash road opposite ice houses
0 0 Purchase
0 Nausett
0 Nashville
0 Barrett
0 Newcomb

*QUANSETT (N) from Coffin avenue south

QUERY (N) from Conduit to Church
0 0 Conduit
0 0 Acushnet avenue
0 0 Bowditch
0 0 Brook
0 0 Edison
0 0 Church

REAGAN (N) from Belleville avenue opposite Hadley to Acushnet river

REED (W) (CANNONVILLE) from Allen east of Rockdale avenue to 828 Kempton
1 2 Grape
23 24 Allen
0 Bedford
0 Grove
0 86 Ryan
0 108 Carroll
0 128 Plymouth
149 148 Hawthorn
179 180 Maple
221 222 Arnold
283 284 Union
307 306 Court
353 354 Elm
405 406 Kempton

REED'S COURT (N W) from 96 Willis to Parker

REED'S LANE (N W) from Plainville road near Wormwell's Corner south to rear Evergreen park

REYNOLDS (N) from 83 Linden to beyond Sawyer
1 2 Linden
33 34 Weld
46 La France
71 70 Clark
85 84 Penniman
107 106 Cedar Grove
129 0 Peckham
147 148 Coggeshall
0 0 Adams
0 0 Sawyer

RICHMOND (N W) from 95 Parker to beyond 65 Durfee

RICKETSON (S) from East French avenue to Brock avenue
1 2 Parker
27 28 Locust
45 46 Maitland
79 0 Robeson
0 0 Willow
137 138 Austin
0 0 Trinity
0 180 Durfee

RIVER ROAD (N) from Reagan to 45 Main
0 0 Reagan
0 Newport
0 0 Brooks
0 0 Perry
100 101 Howard avenue
134 Sylvia
266 267 Main

RIVERSIDE AVENUE (N) from 67 Coffin avenue to Belleville avenue opposite Belleville road
0 0 Coffin avenue
0 Phillips avenue
0 Collette
0 Davis
0 Manomet
0 Hathaway
0 0 Belleville avenue

RIVET (S) from 398 South Front across County at 160 to 116 Dartmouth
2 1 South Front
14 13 South Water
44 43 South First
72 71 South Second
108 107 Acushnet avenue
129 Fourth
162 161 County
195 Hyacinth
211 Hall
248 239 Crapo
298 297 Bonney
318 317 Orchard (South)
365 Briggs
410 409 Bolton
444 445 Juniper
478 477 Hemlock
530 529 Mulberry
564 563 Dartmouth

ROBESON (N W) from 763 County to Oak Grove cemetery
2 1 County
22 Summer
31 Ashland
50 Chestnut
74 75 Cottage
100 99 Cedar
134 133 Richmond
160 159 Shawmut avenue
0 Chancery
214 213 Oak Grove cemetery

*ROCHAMBEAU (N) from Irvington to Park avenue
1 2 Irvington
83 84 Carlisle
161 162 Brooklawn avenue
211 212 Wood
249 250 Park avenue
333 334 Tarkiln Hill road

ROCKDALE AVENUE (W) from Cove road junction Orchard crossing Allen at 586 and across Kempton to Hathaway road
0 0 Cove road
1 2 Orchard
0 0 Oak Grove cemetery
55 54 Bolton
97 98 Hemlock
153 152 Dartmouth
0 Stephen
0 Stackhouse
369 368 Winterville road
407 Westbrook
427 Brier
499 480 Grape
494 495 Allen
597 596 Hawthorn
655 Aronld
705 Union
723 722 Court
0 Lake
803 802 Kempton
817 818 Mill
832 North
855 854 Hillman
880 Maxfield
893 Milton
923 Grant
943 Lexington
963 Fairmount
998 Parker
1069 Whittemore lane
1107 Gifford lane
1152 Durfee
1161 Bartlett lane
0 Grand
1213 Upham's lane
1389 1390 Hathaway road (Cannonville)

ROCKLAND (S) from 93 Acushnet avenue to opposite 82 Dartmouth
2 1 Acushnet avenue
18 17 Fourth
40 39 County
56 Warwick
74 75 Hall
94 95 Crapo
114 113 Bonney
130 131 Orchard (South)
150 153 Briggs
178 0 Bolton
184 185 Hemlock
202 Lombard
218 217 Dartmouth

RODMAN (E) from 120 Front to 62 North Water

RODNEY (S) from East French av to Brock avenue
1 2 East French avenue
89 90 Cleveland
131 132 Brock avenue

ROGERS (W) from Rockdale avenue to Jenny Lind
1 2 Rockdale avenue
67 68 Jenny Lind

ROOSEVELT (S) from 28 Cove to 98 David
0 0 Cove
0 0 Ruth
0 0 David

ROSE ALLEY (E) from 14 North Water to 94 Front

ROTCH (W) from 247 Hawthorn to 332 Court
1 2 Hawthorn
33 34 Maple
53 54 Clinton

73 72 Arnold
135 134 Union
155 154 Court

ROTCH COURT (S W) from 320 Union to 30 Arnold

ROTCH SQUARE (E) from 115 Front

ROUNDS (W) CANNONVILLE) from 760 Kempton to Hawthorn
2 1 Kempton
32 Middle
56 55 Elm
100 99 Court
126 125 Union
192 191 Arnold
232 231 Maple
266 265 Hawthorn

ROY (N) from Brooklawn park to Wood

RURAL (S W) from Grape at Rural cemetery to 436 Allen
1 2 Grape
27 28 Allen

RUSSELL (S) from 212 Acushnet av to 378 County
36 37 Acushnet avenue
40 37 Fourth
54 55 Fifth
64 65 South Sixth
0 0 County

RUTH (S) from East French avenue next south of Abbott to 36 Brock avenue
2 1 East French avenue
37 Abbott
52 53 Cleveland
68 69 Roosevelt
84 85 Ashley
100 101 Salisbury
117 Viall
0 McGurk
0 0 Brock avenue

RYAN (W) from Brigham to Reed
2 1 Brigham
62 63 Brownell
92 93 Palmer
122 Reed

SAGAMORE (S W) Dartmouth next beyond Hollyhock to 351 Bolton
2 Bolton
54 55 Hemlock
122 Dartmouth

SALISBURY (S) from Cove south to 130 David
0 0 Cove
36 37 Ruth
62 0 David

SAWYER (N) from Acushnet river at Bennett Mills west to Mt Pleasant
2 1 Acushnet river
156 Mitchell
174 175 Belleville avenue
204 Bonneau court
220 221 North Front
258 257 Acushnet avenue
310 311 Bowditch
336 Jean
369 Brook
0 0 Railroad
390 389 Purchase
408 407 County
440 439 Reynolds
476 475 Myrtle
518 517 Ashland
554 Mt Pleasant

*SCHOFIELD (S W) from Dartmouth to Hemlock

SCHOOL (S) from 42 Front to 416 County
2 1 Front
40 39 South Water
42 41 First
62 61 South Second
74 75 Acushnet avenue
88 87 Fourth
100 99 Fifth
108 105 Sixth
0 0 Seventh
132 133 County

SCOTT (S) from 35 County to 212 Crapo

*SEABURY (N) from Irvington to Park avenue
2 1 Irvington
90 91 Carlisle
174 175 Brooklawn avenue
226 227 Wood
266 Park avenue

SEARS (S W) from 162 Washington to 145 Fair

SEARS COURT (E) from 29 Purchase to 32 Pleasant

SECOND see south and north

SENECA (N) from 682 Acushnet avenue to N Y N H & H R R

SEVENTH (S W) from 270 Union to Cherry and 61 Bedford
2 1 Union
13 Spring
26 27 School
34 35 Walnut
52 51 Madison
0 0 Cherry
116 117 Bedford

*SEYMOUR (S) from West French easterly
2 1 East French avenue
116 117 Brock avenue
162 163 Point
226 West French avenue
SHARP (S W) from Rockdale av westerly
SHAW (N) from 79 Belleville av to R R tracks
2 1 Belleville avenue
80 81 Conduit
140 141 Acushnet avenue
308 309 Bowditch
426 Edison
444 445 Church
462 King
SHAWMUT AVENUE (N W) from 181 Smith across Plainville road to Dartmouth line
1 2 Smith
19 20 Campbell
37 36 Willis
59 60 Parker
104 Locust
121 Tilton
124 Maitland
151 152 Robeson
0 154 Willow
155 West Willow
169 170 Austin
184 West Trinity
195 196 Durfee
232 Mt Vernon
241 Grand
242 Potter
0 Topham
0 Sutton
0 0 Hathaway road
0 0 Plainville road
0 0 Dartmouth line
SHEPARD'S LANE (E) from 64 South Water to 54 Front
SHERMAN (S W) from 293 County to 34 Bonney
SHORE (S) from 26 Cove road to Grit
SHORT (S) from Grape to 340 Allen
SIDNEY (S W) from Dartmouth next beyond Dunbar to 365 Bolton
0 0 Dartmouth
0 0 Hemlock
0 0 Bolton
SISSON (W) shanged to Rounds
SIXTH see north and south
SMITH (E W) from 95 Walden across County at 642 to beyond Oak Grove cemetery to Liberty
2 5 Walden
26 27 County
39 Smith street court
64 63 Summer
86 85 Chestnut
108 107 Cottage
122 Spruce
140 139 Cedar
181 Shawmut avenue
206 Chancery
228 229 Park
0 0 Oak Grove cemetery
0 Liberty
SMITH STREET COURT (N W) from 39 Smith
*SNOW (S W) from Allen at Dartmouth line northerly
SOCIAL (S) from West French avenue south of Welcome to McGurk
2 1 McGurk
12 Harmony
40 41 West French avenue
SOULE (N) from Wood to Brooklawn Park
SOUTH (S) from Acushnet river beyond Prospect to 16 Crapo
2 1 Acushnet river
0 0 City Mfg Co's yard
0 0 Prospect
0 0 South Front
0 0 South Water
48 47 South First
0 0 South Second
64 65 Acushnet avenue
72 71 Fourth
86 87 County
124 123 Crapo
SOUTH FIRST (S) see First
SOUTH FRONT (S E) north and south from 14 Howland to 51 Potomska and from 1 Rivet to 5 Gifford
210 207 Howland
250 247 Grinnell
284 283 South
335 Potomska
0 Rivet
0 0 Blackmer
451 Delano
0 493 Gifford
SOUTH SECOND (S and E) from 112 Union to Cove
2 1 Union
24 23 Spring
48 47 School
78 77 Walnut
110 109 Madison
132 Coffin
166 165 Cannon
180 Morgan lane

222 221 Griffin
244 243 Howland
300 299 Grinnell
340 339 South
408 409 Potomska
464 463 Rivet
488 487 Blackmer
530 531 Delano
560 559 Division
574 Jennings court
622 621 Cove

SOUTH SIXTH (S) from 240 Union south to 282 County, Washington square
0 0 Union
10 11 Spring
20 21 School
34 33 Walnut
40 39 Madison
47 Cherry
60 Morgan terrace
62 61 Russell
78 73 Bedford
96 97 Wing
0 Washington square
124 125 Grinnell
0 0 County

SOUTH WATER (S and E) from 62 Union to 137 Cove
2 1 Union
22 Commercial
45 Spring
62 Shepard's lane
100 99 School
122 Driggs lane
162 161 Walnut
217 Madison
260 259 Coffin
314 315 Cannon
330 Pine
343 Morgan lane
376 Leonard
406 407 Griffin
452 451 Howland
540 541 Grinnell
600 601 South
722 721 Potomska
808 807 Rivet
850 849 Blackmer
916 915 Delano
961 Division
984 Gifford
1026 Morton court
1116 1115 Cove

SOWLE (N) from Brooklawn park to Wood

SPOONER (S W) from 71 Lombard to 88 Dartmouth
2 1 Lombard
12 Bourne
34 35 Dartmouth

SPRING (S) from 45 South Water to 424 County
2 1 South Water
8 7 First
20 19 South Second
34 33 Acushnet avenue
48 47 Fourth
64 63 Fifth
78 77 Sixth
88 87 Seventh
101 Eighth
106 107 County

SPRINGFIELD (N) from east of railroad northerly to Lynn

SPRUCE (N W) from 161 North to opposite 122 Smith
1 2 North
13 12 Hillman
19 20 Maxfield
65 64 Sycamore
75 74 Smith

STACKHOUSE (S W) from Rockdale avenue near Stephen to Matthew

STANTON COURT (S) from 53 Hall west

STAPLETON (S) from Cove road to 168 Cove

STATE (N) from 75 Hillman to 346 Cedar Grove
1 2 Hillman
51 50 Maxfield
65 66 Sycamore
89 90 Campbell
97 96 Willis
103 104 Pearl
0 0 The Common
0 0 Pope
135 124 Franklin
149 150 Merrimac
169 168 Hazard
191 190 Austin
213 212 Linden
243 244 Weld
0 0 Clark
0 0 Penniman
0 0 Cedar Grove

STEPHEN (S W) from Rockdale av near Dartmouth to Stowell
0 0 Rockdale avenue
0 0 Matthew
0 Hollyhock
0 0 Stowell

STERLING (N) from Acushnet av westerly (Pine Crest)

STONE (S W) from Allen to Grape
0 0 Dartmouth
0 0 Primrose
0 0 Field
0 Stephen

*STOWELL (S W) from Dartmouth west to Stephen
0 0 Dartmouth
0 0 Field
0 Stephen

*STRATFORD (N) from Acushnet avenue east

STUDLEY (N) from opposite 798 County to 32 Ashland

SULLIVAN (W) from 305 Middle to 15 West High

SUMMER (N W) from 131 Elm across Parker to Ashland junction Robeson
41 42 Elm
51 50 Middle
61 Summer street court
73 74 Kempton
87 88 Mill
103 104 North
119 120 Hillman
135 136 Maxfield
157 158 Sycamore
175 176 Smith
193 194 Campbell
205 206 Willis
223 224 Parker
245 246 Pope
271 270 Locust
303 304 Merrimac
318 Robeson
0 0 Ashland

SUMMER STREET COURT (W) from 61 Summer

SUMMIT (W) (CANNONVILLE) from 847 Kempton to beyond 628 Maxfield
2 1 Kempton
0 0 Mill
38 39 North
68 69 Hillman
102 103 Maxfield

SUTTON (N W) from Highland to opp 291 Shawmut avenue
2 1 Mt Pleasant
58 57 Highland
164 163 Shawmut avenue

SWAMP (N W) Cedar to Sullivan

SWAN (S) from Apponegansett to Butler
34 35 Apponegansett
134 Butler

SWIFT (S W) from 391 Bolton to 130 Dartmouth
122 121 Dartmouth
56 55 Hemlock
2 1 Bolton

SYCAMORE (N) from 229 Pleasant to Liberty
2 1 Pleasant
0 0 State
0 39 Walden
48 47 Thomas
58 0 County
0 67 Summer
74 75 Chestnut
84 85 Cottage
96 95 Spruce
106 107 Cedar
114 Ash (North)
140 141 Chancery
156 153 Park
0 0 Liberty

SYLVIA (N) from opposite 130 River road to beyond Riverside av
40 39 River road
108 107 Belleville avenue
137 Brightman
180 Acushnet avenue

SYLVIA'S COURT (S) from 79 Crapo

TABER (S W) from 135 Page to 58 Brigham
2 1 Page
54 55 West
84 Brigham

TACOMA (N) from Acushnet av to Wood

TAFT (S) from east of Brock av

TALLMAN (N) from 291 Belleville avenue opposite Pierce Mfg Co to Brook
2 1 Belleville avenue
42 43 North Front
72 71 Acushnet avenue
116 115 Bowditch
164 0 Brook

TALLMAN'S LANE (S) from 149 Acushnet avenue

TARKILN HILL ROAD (N) from 2175 Acushnet avenue at Lund's Corner to Mt Pleasant opposite Plainville road at Wormwell's Corner
13 0 Mill road
0 50 Belleville avenue
87 88 Acushnet avenue
201 0 Caswell
225 0 Yates
245 0 Metcalf
317 0 Pine Grove

0 398 Flint
421 422 Bowditch
465 Lawrence
491 494 Hawes
515 518 Prescott
541 544 Oliver
567 570 Church
596 Park avenue
593 Worcester
0 0 Railroad
0 Kings Highway
0 Mt Pleasant
0 0 Wormwell's Corner
0 0 Plainville road

TAYLOR (N W) from Myrtle to Mt Pleasant
101 102 Myrtle
145 144 Ashland
185 186 Mt Pleasant

THATCHER (S) from Grit to Cove road

THOMAS (N W) from 97 Hillman to beyond Sycamore
0 0 Hillman
0 64 Maxfield
81 0 Sycamore

THOMPSON (S) from 277 Fourth to 96 Dartmouth
2 1 Fourth
16 17 County
27 Warwick
36 Hyacinth
48 47 Hall
72 73 Crapo
92 93 Bonney
106 105 Orchard
122 123 Briggs
144 143 Bolton
170 171 Hemlock
182 181 Lombard
198 199 Bourne
216 215 Dartmouth

TILTON (W) from 121 Shawmut av to Oak Grove cemtery
0 0 Shawmut avenue
22 23 Chancery

TINKHAM (N) from Riverside av to Church
1 2 Riverside avenue
32 33Belleville avenue
48 49 Hope
102 103 Diman
142 143 Front
176 177 Acushnet avenue
230 229 Bowditch
296 295 Brooks
342 343 Church

TOPHAM (N W) from Shawmut av next to Potter to 150 Highland
0 0 Mt Pleasant
0 0 Highland
0 0 Shawmut avenue

TREMONT (W) from 191 Hawthorn across Court to 596 Kempton
1 2 Hawthorn
15 Maple View terrace
33 34 Maple
71 72 Arnold
133 134 Union
157 0 Court
191 192 Morgan
225 226 Middle
257 258 Kempton

TRINITY (N W) from 405 Cedar to Richmond

TURNER'S COURT (N) from 712 Acushnet avenue

UNION (S) from N Y N H & H R R west to Rockdale avenue
0 0 Railroad
20 19 Front
62 South Water
63 North Water
83 Bethel
86 First
112 South Second
111 North Second
142 141 Acushnet avenue
179 Purchase
178 Fourth
212 Fifth
211 Pleasant
239 North Sixth
240 South Sixth
270 Seventh
288 289 Eighth
307 County
320 Rotch court
321 North Orchard
350 351 Cottage
370 Lincoln
386 Arch
398 Ash (South)
397 Ash (North)
404 Emerson
424 423 Chancery
450 449 Park
468 Atlantic
485 Newton
488 Ocean
520 519 Tremont
546 547 James
574 573 Rotch
596 595 Armour
610 609 Brownell

Union—con
624 623 Sisson
637 Palmer
0 0 Reed
0 0 Rockdale avenue
UPHAM'S LANE (N W) from 1213 Rockdale avenue westerly near Hathaway road
VALENTINE (S) from 219 Brock avenue south of Willard to West French avenue
VAN BUREN (N W) from Myrtle to Mt Pleasant
101 102 Myrtle
145 146 Ashland
187 186 Mt Pleasant
VERNON (N) from Brooklawn Park to Hersom
VIALL (S) from Cove south to Ruth
VICTORIA (N) from Acushnet av to Wood
VINE (N W) from 35 Durfee to 4 Mt Vernon
1 2 Durfee
18 Mt Pleasant
97 98 Mt Vernon
WALDEN (N W) from 85 Hillman to 2 Smith
61 0 Hillman
0 78 Maxfield
87 88 Sycamore
95 Smith
WALDO (N) Brooklawn Park to Hersom
WALL (N) from 694 Acushnet av to Acushnet river
WALNUT (S) from Front at coal pockets west to 404 County
0 0 P & R coal pockets
0 Front
0 0 South Water
6 5 First
0 17 South Second
30 29 Acushnet avenue
40 0 Fourth
52 53 Fifth
66 65 South Sixth
76 75 Seventh
0 0 County
WALTER (W) from Hillman west to Rockdale avenue
WAMSUTTA (N) from 675 Purchase to Acushnet river at Wamsutta wharf
1 2 Purchase
0 0 N Y N H & H R R
0 0 Acushnet avenue
0 North Front
0 0 Acushnet river
WARD (S W) from 2 Hickory to beyond 234 Allen
1 2 Hickory
0 Clay
31 32 Bay
51 52 Allen
65 Waverly court
WARREN (S) from 49 Brock av to 92 West French avenue
WARWICK (S) from 27 Thompson to 56 Rockland
WASHBURN (N) from Acushnet river to 904 Acushnet avenue
0 0 Acushnet river
12 11 Belleville avenue
28 29 North Front
76 75 Acushnet avenue
WASHINGTON (S) from 205 Fourth to 42 Dartmouth
2 1 Fourth
34 35 County
96 95 Crapo
118 117 Bonney
142 141 Orchard (South)
162 Sears
196 191 Dartmouth
WASHINGTON AVENUE (N) from 28 Pearl to 33 Willis
WASHINGTON SQUARE (S) junction County South Sixth and Grinnell
WATER see north and south
WATSON (W) (Cannonville) from 1017 Kempton
WAVERLY (S W) from 101 Allen to beyond Waverly court
0 0 Allen
4 Waverly court
WAVERLY PLACE (S W) from 65 Ward to 4 Waverly
WEAVER (S W) from 109 Dartmouth to 189 Field
WEBSTER COURT (N) from Belleville avenue to 512 North Front
0 0 Belleville avenue
0 0 Hope
0 0 Diman
0 0 North Front
WELCOME (S) from West French avenue next south of Cove east
WELD (N) from 913 Acushnet av to 66 Mt Pleasant
2 1 Acushnet avenue
40 41 Weld square
64 65 Bowditch
118 117 Purchase
148 Pleasant
159 Weld avenue
170 169 State

190 191 County
226 227 Reynolds
248 247 Myrtle
276 275 Ashland
294 283 Mt Pleasant

WELD AVENUE (N) from 159 Weld to Union St Railway car houses

WELD SQUARE (N) junction Acushnet avenue

*WENDOVER (N) from Dutton to Chaffee

WEST (S W) from 109 Grape to beyond Priscilla

1 2 Grape
25 26 Allen
43 0 Bedford
59 0 Elizabeth
81 82 Taber
89 0 Priscilla

WEST ELM (W) see Elm

WEST FRENCH AVENUE (S) from Cove opposite South Water to U S land Clark's Point west side

2 1 Cove
14 0 Welcome
34 0 Social
54 0 Brock avenue
0 0 Grit
92 0 Warren
106 0 George
120 119 David
182 Woodlawn
198 Dudley
214 Willard
0 Valentine
328 Lucas
350 Oaklawn
372 Capitol
394 Calumet
416 Aquidneck
440 Bellevue
496 Almhouse lane
614 Portland
634 Hudson
654 Seymour
0 Bay View
0 Marine avenue
0 U S land

WEST HIGH (W) from 68 Cedar to 4 Sullivan

WEST MIDDLE (W) see Middle

WEST MORGAN (W) from 25 Florence

WEST TRINITY (N W) from 31 Bullock to 184 Shawmut

WEST WALL (W) changed to James

WEST WILLOW (N W) from 155 Shawmut avenue

WESTBROOK (S W) from 401 Rockdale avenue next Winterville road to Jacinto

*WESTLAND (N) from 2492 Acushnet avenue east

WESTMINSTER (N) from Edgewood to Edgeline

WHITLOW (N W) from 175 Durfee to Grand

WHITMAN (N) from Riverside av to 1720 Acushnet avenue and from east of Bowditch to Brook

14 13 Riverside avenue
24 23 Belleville avenue
28 27 Desautels
54 53 Hope
104 103 Diman
144 143 North Front
172 171 Acushnet avenue
220 219 Bowditch
276 275 Brook

WHITTEMORE LANE (N W) from 1067 Rockdale avenue east

WILLARD (S) from 203 Brock av to 206 West French av C P

WILLIAM (N) from 55 North Water to 460 County

2 1 North Water
20 19 Bethel
40 39 North Second
66 65 Acushnet avenue
70½ Halls court
92 81 Purchase
132 133 Pleasant
146 145 North Sixth
182 181 Eighth
190 191 County

WILLIS (N) from 587 Acushnet av to beyond Park

2 1 Acushnet avenue
10 9 Purchase
0 0 Pleasant
33 Washington avenue
44 43 State
60 61 County
69 Reed court
80 81 Summer
90 91 Chestnut
100 99 Cottage
120 121 Cedar
140 141 Shawmut
144 143 Chancery
0 0 Park

*WILLIS (N) from Edison to Bowditch

WILLOW (N W) from 621 Cottage to beyond Shawmut avenue
2 1 Cottage
40 39 Cedar
79 80 Richmond
95 96 Bullock
122 121 Shawmut avenue
WILSON (N W) changed to Richmond
WING (S) from 163 Acushnet avenue to 322 County
0 0 Acushnet avenue
9 0 Fourth
26 Fifth
0 South Sixth
0 0 County
WINSOR (S) from 113 County to 134 Crapo
*WINSPER (S) from Bolton to Hemlock
WINTER (S W) from 464 Allen
WINTERVILLE ROAD (S W) from Rural cemetery across Rockdale av to Dartmouth line
Rural cemetery
0 0 Rockdale avenue
Dartmouth line
WOOD (N) from 2057 Acushnet av to Church
1 2 Acushnet avenue
115 116 Felton
139 138 Vernon
159 160 Waldo
0 186 Landry
0 208 Moyuan
0 228 Roy
0 250 Alfred
277 278 Bowditch
305 306 Rochambeau
327 328 Milford
349 350 Lafayette
371 372 Maywood
391 392 Seabury
409 410 Church
WOODLAWN AVENUE (S) from 165 Brock avenue Clark's Point to 182 West French avenue
*WORCESTER (N) from Tarkiln Hill road north
1 2 Tarkiln Hill road
37 0 York
123 124 Brockton
197 198 Lynn
WORMWELL'S CORNER (N W) junction Mt Pleasant, Plainville and Tarkiln Hill roads
WORTHINGTON (N) from Edgewood to Edgeline
YATES (N) from Tarkiln Hill road northerly

BLOCKS, BUILDINGS, HALLS, ETC.

Academy Hall, Cottage cor Kempton
Acushnet Mill Corp Blocks, east of South Front near Blackmer
Albion Hall 69 Bowditch
Almshouse, Clark's Point
Andrew's Block, William corner Acushnet avenue
Arcade Building 1051 Acushnet av
Armory, Sycamore corner Pleasant
Ashley Block 739 to 745 Purchase
Ashley Hall 743 Purchase
A O H Hall 803 Purchase and 403 Rivet
Barlows Block 163 Coggeshall
Bates and Kirby's Building 46 to 52 Pleasant
Bohemian Hall 146 Bowditch
Bonaventure Hall 965 Acushnet av
Brownell Blocks, Bowditch near Coggeshall and 105 to 111 Beetle
Castle Hall 13 Fourth
Central Police Station 9 South Second
Charlmar Hall, Durfee corner Cottage
City Hall Building, Pleasant corner William
City Stables, North Ash corner Hillman
Clifford Building North Sixth corner Market
Connell Building 694 to 698 Purchase
Cook Building 80 Purchase
Co-Operative Building 510 to 516 Purchase
Cornell Block 128 to 132 Pleasant
Cornell Hall 132 Pleasant
Corson Block 21 to 25 William
County Court House 443 County
Cumberland Assn Hall 106 Union
Cummings Building 43 to 49 Purchase and 96 to 104 William
Cushing Building 34 to 36 Pleasant
Custom House, North Second corner William
Cyclone Block 260 to 262 Coggeshall
Dawson's Block 801 to 805 Purchase
Dawson's Building 641 to 645 Purchase
Dawson's Hall 803 Purchase
Dominique Hall 269 Sawyer
Douglass Block 71 Hicks
Downey Hall 403 Rivet
Duff Block 134 to 138 Pleasant

Eddy Building 185 to 187 Union
Edgerton Hall, Linden corner Purchase
Elk's Hall 88 Purchase
Emerson Building, Union corner South Sixth
Federation Hall 958 Acushnet avenue
Folsom Block 122 to 128 Purchase
Francs Tireurs Hall 70 Hicks
German Castle 244 North Front
German Red Men's Hall 69 Elm
Globe Building 348 to 362 Acushnet avenue
Grand Army Hall 132 Pleasant and 57 William
Greene Building 13-17 Pleasant
Grinnell Mfg Corp Blocks Acushnet avenue, Bowditch, Logan and Weld
Hacienda Hall 947 Acushnet avenue
Hadley's Block 879 to 885 Purchase
Hastings Building 88 to 92 Purchase
Hicks Building 65 to 71 Purchase
House of Correction and Jail, Ash between Court and Union
Howland Mill Corporation Houses, end Bolton
Jenney Hall 120 Kempton
Knights of Columbus Hall 138 Pleasant
LeBeau Building 1045-1064 Acushnet avenue
Lee Block 800 to 810 Purchase
Lewis Hall 174½ Purchase
Lowe's Block 927 to 933 and 1009 to 1019 Acushnet avenue
Lowe's Hall 1017 Acushnet avenue
Masonic Building 193 to 211 Union and 2 to 22 Pleasant
Masonic Hall, Masonic Building
Mazeppa Hall, Acushnet avenue beyond Lund's Corner
McDonald's Block 20 Beetle
Meany's Hall 955 South Water
Merchants and Mechanics Bank Building (old) 54 to 62 N Water
Merchants Bank Building 97-107 William
Mercury Building 112 and 114 Union
Merrill's Block 23 to 35 Front
Monte Pio Hall 160½ Acushnet av
National Bank of Commerce Building North Water
National Independent Guard Hall 963 Acushnet avenue
North End Guild Hall 5 Hazard
N B Five Cents Savings Bank Building 35 to 37 Purchase
N B G & E L Co Building 125 Middle
N B Institution for Savings Building 174 to 178 Union
N B V Fire Assn High corner Foster
N Y N H & H R R Depot, end of Pearl and Willis
Odd Fellow's Building 76 Pleasant
Odd Fellow's Hall 76 Pleasant
Pacific Hall 96 William
Patnaude Block 780-792 Purchase
Patnuade Hall 780 Purchase
Phelan Building 43 Delano
Poirier Building 1039 Acushnet av
Post Office Building, Acushnet av corner William
Potomska Mills Blocks, Acushnet av, South Second, Rivet and Blackmer
Public Library Building, William cor Pleasant
Query's Block 870-876 Acushnet av
Red Men's Hall 153 Union
Registry of Deeds, North Sixth cor William
Ricketson Block 182 to 192 Union
Robeson Building 41-57 William
Rotch Blocks, Bolton road
St Luke's Hospital, Page corner Allen
St Mary's Home, Kempton beyond Newton
Sherman Block 602 Purchase
Socialist Labor Hall 803 Purchase
Sons of Veterans Hall 13 Fourth
Spanish War Veterans Hall 196 Union
Standard Building, Pleasant corner Market
Temperance Hall 97 William rm 314
Temple of Honor 69 Purchase
The Arcade 1051 and 1089 Acushnet avenue
Theatre Building 249 to 253 Union
Third District Court Building, William corner North Second
Times Building 120 Purchase
Union for Good Works 12 Market
Vesta Hall 16 North Sixth
Wait Building 67 to 71 William
Wamsutta Block 659 to 675 Purchase
Wamsutta Hall 675 Purchase
Wamsutta Mill Blocks, Logan and North Front and between Hazard and Austin W P
Weaver's Hall 138 Pleasant
Webster Block 184 to 188 Purchase
Whitman Blocks, Riverside avenue Nash Point
Winslow (The) 234 to 240 Union
Winsor Block 414 to 420 North Front
Winterson's Eagle Hall, First cor Potomska
Y M C A Building, William corner Sixth

CITY OFFICES

Assessors 9 Municipal bldg
Board of Health 52 Pleasant
Cemetery Board 304 Merchant's Bank building
Chief Engineer Fire Department, Central Fire Station
Chief of Police 9 South Second
City Auditor 4 Municipal bldg
City Clerk 208 Municipal bldg
City Collector 1 Municipal bldg
City Engineer 203 Municipal bldg
City Inspectcor of Buildings 307 Municipal bldg
City Messenger 203 Municipal bldg
City Treasurer 1 Municipal bldg
Clerk of the Common Council and Committees 205 Municipal building
County Commissioners 443 Countv
Harbor Master City Wharf
Inspector of Buildings 307 Municipal bldg
Licensing Board 207 Municipal bldg
Mayor's Office 203 Municipal bldg
Overseers of the Poor 167 William
Park Commissioners 251 Union
Police Headquarters 9 South Second
Registrars of Voters 7 Municipal bldg
Sealer of Weights and Measures Mechanic's lane Odd Fellow's bldg
Soldiers Aid 210 Municipal bldg
Superintendent of Schools 166 William
Superintendent of Streets 302 Municipal building
Water Board 40 Masonic bldg
Water Registrar 40 Masonic bldg

WHARVES SLIPS AND ISLANDS

Akin's foot Coffin
Central from 99 Front
City (N and S) from Front foot Union
City Coal Co's foot Middle
Corson's Bridge square
Dennison Bros Co's off foot Hillman
Fish Island, east of Bridge square
Garfield & Proctor Coal Co's, foot Hillman
Gas Company's rear 214 South Water
Greene & Wood's, from Leonard
Hastings, from Grinnell
Hazard's from North of Rodman
Holme's foot Cannon
Howland's, from North
Lewis', from 139 Front
Merrill's from 11 Front
M V & N S S Co Front foot School
Nonquit from Front foot Commercial
Palmer's Island, opposite Grinnell
Parker's foot of Middle
Phil & Reading C & I Co, foot Walnut
Pier 9, foot School
Pope's Island, east of Fish Island
Rodman's, from Hillman
Rotch's wharf (North), Front foot Rodman
Rotch's from Front foot Rodman
Wamsutta, from Wamsutta
Wilcox & Richmond's, from North

LOCALITIES OF INTEREST IN AND ABOUT THE CITY

ACUSHNET. This is a village usualy known as the Head of the River, about three and a half miles in a northerly direction from the City Hall. The westerly part is in New Bedford and the easterly part in Acushnet. Pine Grove Cemetery is near the village. The post office is in New Bedford.

BELLEVILLE. This name was many years ago given to a spot on the bank of the Acushnet River about one mile south of the Acushnet village.

BROOKLAWN PARK. Acushnet avenue, near Howard avenue

BUTTONWOOD PARK. End Court.

CANNONVILLE. A portion of the westerly part of the city in the neighborhood of the meeting-house on the Smith's Mills road is known by this name.

CLARK'S POINT. This point forms the southerly part of the city. It has the waters of the Acushnet River on the east, and of Clark's Cove on the west. Its length is about two miles. At its southerly extremity on the river side is a large tract of land belonging to the United States at the extremity of the point is Fort Rodman. Around this point, a distance of about four miles, is a road not surpassed by any public drive in this country. It is called East and West French avenues, commencing at Cove street and follows the shore, thence along the western, southern and eastern boundaries of the point, until it terminates in the street where it has its beginning. It is eighty feet wide, smooth and level, and in its course commands a series of views of surpassing loveliness and beauty. The cove, the bay, the river, the shores, the islands, the ledges, the lighthouses, steamers and sailing craft of every description, the city on one side, its sister town of Fairhaven on the other and the noble bridge between, constitute a series of views which render a ride or a walk over this rode most delightful and attractive. The City Farm and Almshouse is located on Clark's Point.

CLIFFORD. A settlement with a post office of the same name about three miles north of Acushnet.

DOGFISH BAR. The collection of houses near the foot of Coggeshall street is often called by this name, which designates a shoal in the river near by. A bridge crosses the river at this place for Fairhaven.

GERMANTOWN. The vicinity of Church street, first settled mostly by Germans.

HOWLAND VILLAGE. End Bolton and Orchard streets S. This is a very creditable village of houses owned by the N E Cotton Yarn Co.

JESSEVILLE. Part of Mt. Pleasant and its eastern slope, near Ashland and Linden streets. Named for Jesse Reynolds, a former resident.

KENERSONVILLE. West of Purchase street, from Clark to Cedar Grove street. Named for one of the first settlers.

MOUNT PLEASANT. That portion of our city known by this name is in the northwest part, commencing at Robeson street. Here are some beautiful residences, and the view which includes the river,the harbor, the bay, and adjoining shores, villages and islands, is one of the finest in the country.

NORTH END. Purchase street north of the Common. Since 1878 has become an important business locality.

RIVERSIDE PARK. Foot of Phillips avenue next to Acushnet River.

RIVERVIEW PARK. On Acushnet avenue south of Nash road

ROCKDALE. Is about one mile north of Cannonville, on Rockdale avenue. The only quarry of any size near the city, is located here.

SHAWMUT. This is a small village located four miles northwest of City Hall.

TURNERVILLE. Vicinity of Shawmut avenue and Durfee street. Named for an early settler.

WINTERVILLE. The name given to a small collection of houses at the west of Rural cemetery on Winterville road.

QUARANTINE

Office cor County and Russell sts

The quarantine grounds are bounded as follows: Butler's flats on the south, the east shore of Clark's Point on the west, the Eleven Foot Bank on the north, and Egg Island on the east.

CEMETERIES

There are four public cemeteries in the city.

OLD CEMETERY, East side South Second street, between Griffin and Morgan lane.

THE OAK GROVE CEMETERY is in the west part of the city on the north side of Smith and Parker streets about one mile northward of the City Hall.

THE PINE GROVE CEMETERY is situated on the road leading to Tarkiln Hill, near Acushnet Village.

THE RURAL CEMETERY is in the southward part of the city, on the west side of Dartmouth street, and south side of Grape.

PRIVATE CEMTERIES

LUND'S CORNER CEMETERY, Acushnet avenue, near First Congregational Church.

PECKHAM WEST CEMETERY is in the northwest part of the city, on west side of Mt Pleasant, north of District Reservoir.

SACRED HEART CEMETERY (French) is in the northwest part of the city, on west side of Mt Pleasant north of Peckham.

ST JOHN'S CEMETERY is in the southwest part of the city on the south side of Allen street near the Dartmouth line of 1888.

ST MARY'S CEMETERY is in the west part of the city, on the north side of Kempton street at the Dartmouth line of 1888.

WARDS AND PRECINCTS

The following ward and precinct lines became effective January 1, 1907:

WARD ONE

All that portion of the city lying north and east of a line beginning at the river and drawn westerly through the centre of Linden street to the centre of Pleasant street thence northerly through the centre of Pleasant street to the centre of Weld street thence westerly through the centre of Weld street to the centre of County street thence northerly through the centre of County street to the westerly line of location of the Old Colony railroad, thence northerly and westerly by the westerly line of location of the Old Colony railroad and the southerly line of location of the Fall River branch railroad to the west line of the city, will constitute ward 1.

Precinct 1.

All that part of said ward lying north of the following described line shall be and is hereby made a voting precinct to be known as Precinct Number One: Beginning at a point in the channel of the Acushnet River formed by the extension of the centre of Deane street, thence westerly in said extended line and in the centre of Deane street to the westerly side line of location of the Fall River branch of the Old Colony railroad; thence northwesterly by said southerly line of location to the boundary line between the town of Dartmouth and the city of New Bedford.

Precinct 2.

All that part of said ward lying south of the above described line and north of the following described line shall be and is hereby made a voting precinct to be known as Precinct Number Two: Beginning at a point in the channel of the Acushnet River formed by the extension of the center line of Coggeshall street; thence westerly in said extending line and in the center of Coggeshall street to the center of County street; thence northerly in the center of County street to the westerly side of the Old Colony railroad; and thence in said westerly side line of location to intersection with the southerly line of precinct number one.

Precinct 3.

All that part of said ward lying south of the last described line of Coggeshall street to County street shall be and is hereby made a voting precinct to be known as Precinct Number Three.

WARD TWO

All that portion of the citv lying between a line drawn from the river westerly through the centre of Lindn street to the centre of Pleasant street, thence northerly through the center of Pleasant street to the center of Weld street thence westerly through the center of Weld street to the center of County street, thence northerly through the center of County street to the westerly line of location of the Old Colony railroad, thence northerly and westerly by the westerly line of location of the Old Colony railroad and the southerly line of location of the Fall River Branch railroad to the west line of the city and a line drawn from the river through the center of Pope street westerly to the center of Cottage street thence southerly through the center of Cottage street to the center of Parker street, thence westerly through the center of Parker street to the west line of the city, will constitute ward 2.

Precinct 4.

All that part of said ward lying east of the following described line shall be and is hereby made a voting precinct to be known as Precinct Number Four: Beginning at the intersection of the centre line of Pope street with the center line of County street thence northerly through the center of County street.

Precinct 5.

All that part of said ward lying west of the last described line in County street and east of the following described line shall be and is hereby made a voting precinct to be known as Precinct Number Five: Beginning at the intersection of the center line of Pope street with the center line of Cottage street, thence northerly through the center of Cottage street and of Mt Pleasant street to the southerly line of location of the Fall River Branch of the Old Colony railroad.

Precinct 6.

All that part of said ward lying west of the last described line in Cottage street and Mt Pleasant street shall be and is hereby made a voting precinct to be known as Precinct Number Six.

WARD THREE.

All that portion of the city lying between a line drawn from the river westerly through the center of Pope street to the center of Cottage street thence, southerly through the center of Cottage street to the center of Parker street, thence westerly through the center of Parker street to the west line of the city, and a line dawn from the river westerly through the center of Kempton street to the the center of Willis street, thence northerly through the center of Summer street to the center of Mill street, thence westerly through the center of Mill street to the center of Kempton street, thence westerly through the centre of Kempton street to the west line of the city will constitute ward 3.

Precinct 7.

All that part of said ward lying east of the following described line shall be and is hereby made a voting precinct to be known as Precinct Number Seven: Beginning at the intersection of the center line of Kempton street with the center line of Hill street, thence northerly through the center line of Hill street to the center line of Hillman street, thence easterly through the center line of Hillman street to the center line of State street, thence northerly through the center of State street to the centre of Willis street, thence easterly through the center of Willis street to the center of State street, thence northerly through center of State street and through extension of the same to the center of Pope street.

Precinct 8.

All that part of said ward lying west of the last described line through Hill street and State street and east of the following described line shall be and is hereby made a voting precinct to be known as Precinct Number Eight: Beginning at the intersection of the center line of Mill street, with the center line of Cottage street, thence northerly through the center of Cottage street to the center of Pope street.

Precinct 9.

All that part of said ward lying west of the last described line through Cottage street shall be and is hereby made a voting precinct to be known as Precinct Number Nine.

WARD FOUR.

All that portion of the city lying between a line drawn from the river westerly through the center of Kempton street to the center of Summer street, thence northerly through the center of Summer street to the center of Mill street thence westerly through the center of Mill street to the center of Kempton street, thence westerly through the center of Kempton street to the west line of the city and a line drawn from the river westerly through the center of School street to the center of County street, thence southerly through the center of County street to the center of Clinton street thence westerly through the center of Clinton street to the center of Park street, thence northerly through the center of Park street to the center of Arnold street, thence westerly through the center of Arnold street to the west line of the city including Fish Island and Popes Island, will constitute Ward 4.

Precinct 10.

All that part of said ward lying east of the follwing described line shall be and is hereby made a voting precinct to be known as Precinct Number Ten: Beginning at the intersection of the center line of School street with the center line of County street, thence northerly through the center of County street to the center of Kempton street.

Precinct 11.

All that part of said ward lying west of the last described line through County street and east of the following described line shall be and is hereby made a voting precinct to be known as Precinct Number Eleven: Beginning at the intersection of the center line of Clinton street with the center line of Chancery street, thence northerly through the center of Chancery street to the center of Mill street.

Precinct 12.

All that part of said ward lying west of the last described line through Chancery street shall be and is hereby made a voting precinct to be known as Precinct Number 12.

WARD FIVE.

All that portion of the city lying between a line drawn from the river westerly through the center of School street to the centre of County street, thence southerly through the center of County street, to the center of Clinton street, thence westerly through the center of Clinton street to the center of Park street, thence northerly through the center of Park street to the centre of Arnold street, thence westerly through the center of Arnold street to the west side of the city and a line drawn from the river westerly through the center of South street to the center of County street, thence southerly through the center of County street to the center of Fair street, thence westerly through the centre of Fair street to the centre of Bonney street, thence southerly through the center of Bonney street to the centre of Rockland street thence westerly through the center of Rockland street to the centre of Dartmouth street, thence northerly through the center of Dartmouth street to the center of Oak street, thence westerly through the center of Oak street to the center of Grape street, thence westerly through the center of Grape street to the center of Rockdale avenue, thence northerly through the center of Rockdale avenue to the center of Allen street, thence westerly through the center of Allen street to the west line of the city, will constitute Ward 5.

Precinct 13.

All that part of said ward lying east of the following described line shall be and is hereby made a voting precinct to be known as Precinct Number Thirteen: Beginning at the intersection of the centre line of South street with the center line of Fourth street, thence northerly through the centre of Fourth street to the center of Grinnell street, thence westerly through the center of Grinnell street to the center of Fifth street, thence northerly through the centre of Fifth street to the centre of School street.

Precinct 14.

All that part of said ward lying west of the last described line through Fourth street and Fifth street and east of the following described line shall be and is hereby made a voting precinct to be known as Precinct Number Fourteen: Beginning at the intersection of the center line of Rockland street with the center line of Orchard street, thence northerly through the center line of Orchard street to the center line of Clinton street.

Precinct 15.

All that part of said ward lying west of the last described line in Orchard street shall be and is hereby made a voting precinct to be known as Precinct Number Fifteen.

WARD SIX.

All that portion of the city lying south of a line drawn from the river westerly through the center of South street to the center of County street, thence northerly through the center of County street to the center of Fair street, thence westerly through the center of Fair street to the center of Bonney street, thence southerly through the center of Bonney street to the center of Rockland street, thence westerly through the center of Rockland street to the center of Dartmouth street, thence northerly through the center of Dartmouth street to the center of Oak street, thence westerly through the center of Oak street to the center of Grape street, thence westerly through the center of Grape street to the center of Rockdale avenue, thence northerly through the center of Rockdale avenue to the center of Allen street, thence westerly through the centre of Allen street to the west line of the city including Palmers Island, will constitute Ward 6.

Precinct 16.

All that part of said ward lying south and east of the following described line shall be and is hereby made a voting precinct to be known as Precinct Number Sixteen: Beginning at the intersection of center line of an extension of the center line of Gifford street and the channel of the Acushnet River, thence westerly in said extension and in the center of Gifford street to the center of Water street, thence northerly through the center of Water street to the center of Division street, thence westerly through the centre of Division street, to the centre of County street, thence southerly through the center of County street to Clark's Cove.

Precinct 17.

All that part of said ward lying north and west of the last described line in Gifford street, Division street and County street and east and south of the following described line shall be and is hereby made a voting precinct to be known as Precinct Number Seventeen: Beginning at the intersection of the center line of County street with the center line of Fair street, thence southerly through th center of County street to the center of Independent street, thence through the center of Independent street to the center of Crapo street, thence southerly through the center of Crapo street to Clark's Cove.

Precinct 18.

All that part of said ward lying west and north of the last described line in County street, Independent street and Crapo street, shall be and is hereby made a voting precinct to be known as Precinct Number Eighteen.

CHARLES N. RICHMOND

CONVEYANCER

Deeds, Powers, Wills, Etc.
Land Title Abstracts.
Estate Settlements.

American Bonding Company
of Baltimore.

54 PLEASANT ST., - NEW BEDFORD
Both Telephones

Everything for the Home

FURNITURE, the Latest and Best
CARPETS, in all grades :: ::
HOUSEHOLD RANGES, the World's Best
CROCKERY in full assortment

—AT—

The Household Furnishing Company

CORNER PURCHASE AND KEMPTON STREETS

Telephone, Bell 1403 Automatic 1281

ESTABLISHED 1850

CASWELL & PAINTER DECORATOR

PAINTERS SUPPLIES SHIP CHANDLERY
MARINE HARDWARE MOTOR BOAT SUPPLIES

34-38 UNION STREET Bell Telephone

CHAS. O. BRIGHTMAN
CONTRACTOR and BUILDER

JOBBING IN

CARPENTRY

— AND —

MASONRY

Estimates Given on all Classes of Work

Member Builders' Exchange

Factory and Office, 72 North Water Street

Residence, 82 Mill Street. Telephones: Office, 259-4; House, 1342-4, 1643-22

NEW BEDFORD DIRECTORY

(Copyright 1911 by W. A. Greenough & Co.)

ABBREVIATIONS USED IN THIS DIRECTORY.

Ab, above; A S M Co, Acushnet SawMills Co; agt, agent; Am, American; asst, assistant; av, avenue; b or bds, boards; bldg, building; blk, block; C P, Clark's Point; c or cor, corner; corp corporation; ct, court; dep, deputy; do, ditto; E, East; h, house; H C, House of Correction; H W C Co, Henry W Cushman Co; ins, insurance, L R Corp, Lambeth Rope Corporation; L C, Lund's Corner; mfr, manufacturer; mgr, manager; N, North; n, near; N B C Co, New Bedford Cordage Co; N B C M Corp, New Bedford Cotton Mills Corporation; N E C Y Co, New England Cotton Yarn Co; N Y, N H & H R R, New York, New Haven & Hartford Railroad; opp, opposite; pl, place; P Corp, Pairpoint Corporation; P O, Post Office; pres, president; P & R C & I Co, Philadelphia & Reading Coal & Iron Co; r, rear; rd, road; Rev, Reverend; S, South; sec, secretary; sq, square; st, street; supt, superintendent; T-N B C Co Taunton-New Bedford Copper Co; ter, terrace; treas, treasurer; U St Ry Co, Union Street Railway Co; U S A, United States Army; U S N, United States Navy; U S R, United States Revenue; W, West; whf, wharf

When the name of a corporation, factory, or firm appears immediately after the occupation, it indicates the place of business. After the name of the street, the word street is ommitted.

Abajian J oriental rugs 253 Union h 270 Pleasant

Abbott Alfred weaver h 68 Crapo

Abbott

" Emma R widow William F h 279 Cottage

" Etta M teacher Middle st school [b 67 Hillman

Abbott
" Frederick A hairdresser 82 Cedar h 76 do
" Mary Mrs rms 74 School
Abeau Joseph blacksmith bds 1022 Acushnet avenue [court
Ablinger Frank operative b 3 Hazard
Abraham Isaac operative b 250 Coggeshall [250 Coggeshall
" Joseph fruit 1484 Acushnet av h
" Joseph mill hand h 279 Coggeshall
Abrais Thomas weaver h 82 Bell rd
Abrams Alice M music teacher 86 S Second b do
" Barnard tailor 927 S Water h do
" Elizabeth widow John h 111 Grinnell
" Florence operative rms 256 Union
" Frederick J J compositor Standard h 237 Middle
" Henry S h 101 Fifth
" John E helper 185 Acushnet av bds 111 Grinnell
" Louis F driver 2193 Acushnet av
" Mary A widow William h 86 S Second
" Minnie clerk rms 256 Union
" Samuel clerk 831 S Water b 490 First [h 878 do
" William dry goods 890 S Water
" William J assessor h 67 Russell
Abramson Ike (N B Bottling Co) 32 Morton court h do
Abren Manuel laborer b 21 Rotch block 439 Bolton [lips av
Abreu Joseph fireman h 100 Phil-
Abrian Thomas mill hand h 10 Nye
Acheson James T Boston Supply Co h 695 Cottage [erson
Achorn Jasper M painter h 317 Em-
Acker William stonecutter h 95 Hathaway
Ackerman Halsey V D carriage painter 447 Kempton bds 408 Mill
" Henry J salesman h 408 Mill
" Lucy F widow Thomas J b 408 Mill
Acomb William fixer h 148 Myrtle
Acorn Wesley H agent h 49 Borden [tine
Acornley Ida V clerk bds 80 Valen-
" Mary L widow Rev John H h 80 Valentine
Acton Joseph roofer h 34 Reynolds
Acushnet Co-operative Association groceries 213 Acushnet av
" Co-operative aBkn215 Middle
ACUSHNET IRON CO (Mrs Elbert B Davis) 229 North Water See page 788
" Mill Corporation foot Delano
" Pharmacy (Oscar C Goddu) 1401 Acushnet avenue
" Post Office 42 Main
J P Bradford prop 25 Main
ACUSHNET SANITARIUM The Dr J P Bradford prop 25 Main
L C See page 24
" Saw Mills Co Frederic B Hawes president Mill road Acushnet
" Shoe Store Ira H Morse prop 889 South Water [Water h do
Adam Arthur R dentist 1111 South
" Edward carpenter h 106 Cove
" H Halford accountant Beacon Mfg Co h 85 Cottage
" Napoleon doffer b 207 Eugenia
" Philisa weaver h 207 Eugenia
Adamowicz Walenty weaver h 616 First [chase h 179 Tremont
Adams Alexander H foreman 69 Pur-
" Alice P widow Charles H h 597 County [1679 Acushnet av
" Andrew barber 413 N Front b
" Andrew J engineer bds 82 Swift
" Arthur fixer h 28 Holly
" Charles F second hand b 82 Swift
" Charles H h 535 County
" David A city employee bds 461 Bolton [do
" Ella C manager r 68 Linden h
" Emma T stenographer 33 Masonic bldg bds 196 Elm
" Express Company 14 North Sixth Acushnet R R station and Pearl st station [381 North
" George L grocer 855 Kempton h
" Halford H h 85 Cottage
" Irvin molder h 65 School
" James shoeworker b 205 Brock av
" James A foundryman h 238 Austin [h 405 Orchard (S)
" James A supt Dartmouth Mills
" John plasterer h 82 Swift
" John O bartender h 1 Clark

Steiger-Dudgeon Co.
"The WOMAN'S Store."
Tel. Bell 82 & 83, Branches connecting all depts.
" " 160 For Office only. Auto. 1211

SUMPTIONS, ASSORTMENTS AT ALL TIMES OF DEPENDABLE DRY GOODS

Adams
" John T b 371 Chancery
" Joseph weaver h 35 Briggs
" Lambert weaver h 3374 Acushnet avenue
" Lemuel D lieutenant police and court officer h 57 Fourth
" Lydia S widow Zenas H h 18 Lincoln [Merrimac
" Mary widow Peter h 30 East
" Matilda M widow John T h 196 Elm [57 Fourth
" Myra F bookkeeper 72 N Water b
" Narcisse hairdresser 413 North Front h 1679 Acushnet avenue
" Rena L clerk 855 Kempton b 381 North [h 223 Maxfield
" Stephen F salesman 41 Purchase
" William shoemaker b 1679 Acushnet avenue [avenue
" William A plasterer h 205 Brock
" William A Jr shoeworker bds 205 Brock avenue [h do
Adamsky Alfred grocer 16 Bullard
Adamson Joseph operative h 9 McMurray terrace
" Mills steam fitter h 21 Valentine
Adaroski Mike mill oprative b 184 Cedar Grove [R I
Addy Arthur removed to Pawtucket
" Benjamin loom fixer h 123 County
" Fred shoemaker rms 60 Spring
" Joshua linotype operator Standard h 261 Pope
" Joshua Jr printer b 261 Pope
" Thomas jobber h 170 Ashland
" William h 156 Durfee
Adelsohn Isaac clothing 517 South Water h 526 do [city
Adelstein Benjamin removed from
" Bernard removed from city
Adem Abdula fruit 1282 Acushnet av h 48 Davis
Adlin Abraham h 194 Cedar Grove
Adolfo Franciosi laborer b 144 Chancery [Acushnet av
Adolph E Gallot mill operative h 688
Adshead Clinton weaver b 47 Logan
" Joseph solderer h 31 Buttonwood
Affonson Filippe S insurance agent 97 William rm 310 h 75 Winsor [Water
Afonso Julio mill hand h 585 South
Aganier Hermaine Mrs mill hand bds 407 North Front
Agard Charles W superintendent P & R C & I Co foot Walnut rms 399 Union
Agnes Howard weaver h 6 McGurk
Agravia Joseph mill operative h 219 Coggeshall [ville avenue
Agrella Manuel mill hand h 184 Belle-
Aguer Walter glass cutter bds 24 Madison [Mitchell
Aguiar Manuel mill hand b 35
Aguros Charles lunch 272 Coggeshall h 31 Holly
Ahamel Albert Rev assistant pastor St Anthony's church h 1359 Acushnet avenue [Reynolds
Ahearn Michael E tool maker h 56
Ahern William mgr 155 Blackmer h 69 Crapo [Collette
Aicken Ann widow David bds 200
" Henry electrician h 200 Collette
Aiken Abbie A Mrs h 330 Cottage
" Alfred K tack maker h 19 West
" James die sinker h 231 Allen
" Maria widow James h 3 Spruce
" Samuel F foreman h 57 Cottage
" Thomas foreman h 69 Tremont
" see Akin and Aicken
Aillery Constant police h 193 Tinkham [354 Coffin avenue
" Joseph L druggist 190 Weld b
" Louis (Aillery & Susini) 78 William h 318 Union
" & Susini (Louis Aillery and Octave Susini) hairdressers 78 William [271 Palmer
Aindow Emily M clerk 185 Union b
" John H insurance 37 Purchase rm 16 h 271 Palmer [ley
Ainscough Arthur foreman b 19 Ash-
Ainsworth Alfred collector h 33 Madison [33 Madison
" Alfred Jr salesman 125 Middle b
" Isabella F Mrs h 184 Austin
" James mill operative h 228 Collette
" James weaver h 195 First
" William weaver h 47 Logan
" William T clerk Wamsutta Mill h 657 Cottage
Airey Albert weaver b 307 Collette
" John W machinist h 6 Cottage
" see Arey
Aisenstat Nathan pedlar h 114 Clark
Akerstrom Lillian F teacher Cedar Grove st school b 108 Bonney

PELEG H. SHERMAN 506 COUNTY ST.
FUNERAL DIRECTOR AND EMBALMER
OFFICE PHONES. Bell 690-13. Auto. 1305.
RESIDENCE PHONES. Bell 690-12. Auto. 1306

Akin A Horace plumber N B W W h 295 Pleasant
" Alice G E clerk h 12 Baldwin
" Charles H clerk 773 Kempton h 757 do
" Charles G (F T Akin & Co) 158 South Water h 2 Morgan ter
" Edmund G variety [illegible] cor Rockdale av h 12 Baldwin
" Francis T (F T Akin & Co) 158 South Water and president 42 William h 22 South Sixth
" Frank S inspector 125 Middle h 12 Baldwin
AKIN F T & CO (Francis T, Thomas B and Charles G Akin) painters and painters' supplies 158 South Water corner Walnut 84 Pleasant 1 North Water and 1117 Acushnet av and coal wood hay etc 158 South Water corner Walnut yard foot Griffin and 129 Cove See front lines
" Helen B h 20 Griffin [illegible]
" Josephine G widow John H h 757
" Lucy T D stenographer bds 757 Kempton
" Mary widow Alexander h 28 Hunt
" Mrs K removed to California
" Stanley G clerk P O h 47 Rotch
" Thomas B (F T Akin & Co) h N Water h 774 County
" William h 81 Liberty
" see Aiken and Allen
Akus Alhard weaver h 1980 East rd
Alandier Rene mason h 2071 Sawyer
Alber George glass cutter h 40 Russell [illegible]
Alber Joseph weaver h 273 [illegible]
Albergan Walter (Freeman & Albergan) 160 N Front h 25 Washburn [illegible]
" Stanislao bar tender h 2110 Cedar
Albert Mary A dressmaker 82 Washington h do
" Thomas Jr carpenter 210 County
" Thomas engraver h 210 County
" William J removed from city
Albee Otto clerk h 401 [illegible]
Alden Frances T laborer h 452 Park
" William F city teamster h 237 Hillman [illegible]
Alcock James office secretary [illegible]

Alcock
" James A grocer 1 Harmony h 37 Social
" Samuel died September 4 1910
" Thomas spinner h 10 Social
Alden Charles E artist 7 William h at Boston [illegible]
" Chester W plumber h at Fairhaven
ALDEN GEORGE F insurance 205 Merchants Bank bldg 57 William h 27 Arnold place See index above
" George F Jr clerk 205 Merchants Bank bldg h 27 Arnold place
Alden's Motor Boat Supply House
Alden Martin pedlar
Alfred James E removed to Fairhaven [illegible]
Aldrich Amos F conductor h 42 [illegible]
" Charles J metal [illegible] 125 Middle bds 10 Washington [illegible]
" Charles L iron moulder h 180 [illegible]
" Eliza [illegible] dealer [illegible] h 79 Bedford
" [illegible] clerk bds 79 Bedford
" Harold [illegible] Hathaway's [illegible] bds 79 Bedford [illegible]
" Mabel F shoe stitcher bds 79 Bedford
" Michael E clerk h 79 Bedford
" Oscar F police station h 79 Bedford
Alenzos John weaver h 28 Holly
Alexander Angeline F Mrs dressmaker 90 Thompson h do
" Charles A [illegible] tender h 90 Thompson
" David weaver h 22 Ashley
" Edward carpenter h 277 Brock av
" Edward E machinist h 47 [illegible]
" Florence collector 90 Thompson h 7 East Forest avenue [illegible]
" Frances widow Joseph h [illegible]
" George E machinist h 90 Thompson
" James [illegible] h 5 [illegible]
" [illegible] mill operative h 2244 Cedar Grove [illegible]
" John F [illegible] Hathaway's
" Joseph h 90 Thompson
" Joseph E died Feb 25 1910
" Lucy clerk 195 Union h 2440 Acushnet avenue
" Manuel carpenter h 277 Brock av
" Manuel Jr removed to Niagara Falls N Y [illegible]
" Manuel P grocer 673 South Water

PAINTERS' SUPPLIES
[illegible]
F. T. AKIN & COMPANY

Alexander
" Mary P widow Joseph E h 14 Acushnet avenue
" Rose Mrs h 123 Fifth
" Thomas laborer h 963 Purchase
" Thomas laborer h 202 State
" Willie clerk 361 Bowditch b 198 Pinkham [ushnet av
Alexandro Cignotti laborer h 712 Ac-
Alfama Antone laborer h r 437 South Water [ville av h 171 do
Alferes Enos D grocer 153 Belle-
" John laborer h 166 Blackmer [do
" Manuel grocer 279 Fourth h 219
Algar Reuben T h 37 Richmond
Alger Elton B fireman h 96 Clark
Alick James, cotton worker h 442 Sawyer
" Joseph B car cleaner h 122 High
" see Alleck [Cedar Grove
Alisia A Mlle phrenologist rms 382
Alix Henry weaver h 106 Beetle
" Joseph carpenter h 279 Collette
" Joseph mill operative h 225 Phillips avenue
" Nicholas mill hand b 16 Ballard
" Oscar removed from city [away
Allain Abraham carpenter h 67 Hath-
" Albert drill maker b 429 N Front
" Alphe weaver b 45 Tallman
" Andre twister b 325 North Front
" Arthur weaver b 45 Tallman
" Augustus carpenter b 98 Collette
" Clement laborer bds 19 Holly
" Cyrille fisherman b 97 Coffin av
" Cyrille removed from city
" Cyrille weaver h 128 Nash road
" Domonic mill hand h 19 Holly
" Edmonde mill hand bds 19 Holly
" Eugene A weaver h 188 Phillips avenue
" Fabian h 43 Holly [Belleville rd
" Francois mill operative b 30
" Hilaire carpenter bds 23 Holly
" Honore weaver b 325 North Front
" Laurent mill hand bds 19 Holly
" Liguore laborer bds 22 Holly
" Luca T fisherman h 97 Coffin av
" Marguerite widow Maxime h 30 Belleville road
" Meles fisherman h 45 Tallman
" Moise shoemaker h 24 Bentley
" Odillon painter 14 Jean b 325 N Front
" Placide carpenter h 429 N Front

Allain
" Samuel lineman h 137 Tallman
" Vital weaver h 8 Tallman
" see Allen [yer
Allaire Alphonse teamster h 328 Saw-
" Napoleon laundryman b 63 Holly
" Noe elevatorman b 125 Webster court
" Peter laundryman bds Tallman
Allan Laura A widow Robert h 64 Thomas [ler
Allard Alfred bricklayer bds 44 But-
" Charles removed from city
" David R city teamster h 288 Cedar Grove [Cedar Grove
" Edmonde mill operative bds 288
" Elzear weaver h 85 Dean
" Frank A died Nov 17 1910
" Gilbert brakeman b 347 N Front
" Henry driver h 129 Perry
" Henry L rope maker b 129 Perry
" Mary widow Henry h 347 North Front
" Mederic helper h 15 Washburn
" Mederic laborer b 329 N Front
" William A freight clerk foot Willis bds 62 North [ant
Allby Henry electrician h r 356 Pleas-
Alleeck John insurance agent h 135 Hathaway [h 122 High
Alleck Joseph car cleaner W St Ry Co
" see Allck
Allen Aaron S laborer h 315 Kempton [h 65 Hathaway
" Abraham carpenter U St Ry Co
" Ada A widow William C h 14 Columbia
" Ada B Mrs 732 Kempton
" Albert J bakery 36 Cove grocer 34 do h do [Kempton
" Andrew H city laborer h r 383
" Andrew T helper 55 North Water h 416 Hillman [Hathaway rd
" Anjanette widow Clark h 699
" Annie widow b 186 Grinnell
" Annie C Mrs nurse h 967 County
" Arsene wood 112 River rd h 112 do [Chestnut
" Arthur P clerk Taber Mill b 240
" Arthur S h 65 Hillman
" Asa L H pictures 228 Union h 350 Clinton
" Augustin carpenter h 232 Sawyer
" Aylesford J (Red Cross Pharmacy) h 588 Rivet

Remember to investigate our methods before taking up a business course.
Kinyon's Commercial School
Odd Fellows Bldg., Cor. William and Pleasant Sts., New Bedford, Mass.

Akin A Horace plumber N B W W b 285 Pleasant
" Alice G R clerk b 11 Babbitt
" Charles E clerk 773 Kempton b 797 do
" Charles G (F T Akin & Co) 168 South Water h 2 Morgan ter
' Ehpraim G variety Dartmouth cor Rockdale ave h 11 Babbitt
" Francis T (F T Akin & Co) 168 South Water and president 43 William h 39 South Sixth
" Frank S inspector 125 Middle b 11 Babbitt
AKIN F T & CO (Francis T, Thomas B 'and Charles G Akin) painters and painters' supplies 168 South Water corner Walnut 84 Pleasant 9 North Water and 1218 Acushnet av and coal wood hay etc 168 South Water corner Walnut yard foot Coffin and 129 Cove See foot lines
" Helen B h 26 Griffin [Kempton
" Josephine G widow John E h 797
" Lure V D stenographer bds 797 Kempton
" Mary widow Alexander h 28 High
" Orin N removed to Cuttyhunk
" Stanley G clerk P O h 45 Rotch
" Thomas B (F T Akin & Co) 9 N Water h 374 County
" William h 81 Liberty
" see Aicken and Aiken
Alax Adalard weaver h 190 Nash rd
Albardier Rene mason b 201 Sawyer
Alben George glass cutter b 40 Russell [ham
Alber Joseph weaver h 271 Tink-
Alberski Walter (Sherman & Alberski) 161 N Front h 23 Washburn [Grove
" Stanislau bar tender h 211 Cedar
Albert Mary A dressmaker 92 Washington h do
" Thomas Jr carpenter 211 County
" Ulysses engraver b 211 County
" William D removed from city
Albiez Otto clerk b 461 Coggeshall
Albro Francis T laborer b 452 Park
" William J city teamster h 237 Hillman [C A b 17 Social
Alcock James office secretary Y M

Alcock
" James A grocer 2 Harmony h 17 Social
" Samuel died September 6 1910
" Thomas spinner h 10 Social
Alden Charles E artist 7 William h at Boston [haven
" Clinton W plumber h at Fair-
ALDEN GEORGE N insurance 205 Merchant's Bank bldg 97 William h 17 Arnold place See back cover
" George N Jr clerk 205 Merchant's Bank bldg b 17 Arnold place
Alden's Motor Boat Supply House
Aldes Martin pedlar
Aldred James H removed to Fairhaven [fee
Aldrich Amos F conductor h 42 Dur-
" Charles C metar deputy 125 Middle bds 10 Washington [man
" Charles L iron molder h 155 Hill-
" Ethel pres feeder Standard b 79 Bedford
" Gladys clerk bds 79 Bedford
" Harold chief usher Hathaway's Theatre bds 79 Bedford [ford
" Mabel F shoe stitcher bds 79 Bed-
" Mildred E clerk b 79 Bedford
" Oscar F police station 5 h 79 Bedford
Alevizos John weaver h 28 Holly
Alexander Angeline G Mrs dressmaker 80 Thompson h do
" Charles A twister tender b 80 Thompson
" David weaver h 11 Ashley
" Edward carpenter b 175 Brock av
" Edward H pianist h 47 Briggs
" Florenzi collector 80 Purchase h 5 East French avenue [Rivet
" Frances widow Joseph h 208
" George K machinist b 80 Thompson
" James laborer h r 5 Wamsutta
" Jenney mill operative h 324 Cedar Grove [theatre h 208 Rivet
" John S musician Hathaway's
" Joseph h 80 Thompson
" Joseph E died Feb 25 1911
" Lucy clerk 185 Union b 141 Acushnet avenue
" Manuel carpenter h 175 Brock av
" Manuel Jr removed to Niagara Falls N Y [h 680 do
" Manuel P grocer 679 South Water

PAINTERS' SUPPLIES
Walnut, Cor. Water, 84 Pleasant St. 25 WELD SQ., 129 COVE ST.
F. T. AKIN & COMPANY

Alexander
" Mary P widow Joseph E h 14 Acushnet avenue
" Rose Mrs h 123 Fifth
" Thomas laborer h 963 Purchase
" Thomas laborer h 202 State
" Willie clerk 361 Bowditch b 198 Tinkham [ushnet av
Alexandro Cignotti laborer h 712 Ac-
Alfama Antone laborer h r 437 South Water [ville av h 171 do
Alferes Enos D grocer 153 Belle-
" John laborer h 166 Blackmer [do
" Manuel grocer 279 Fourth h 219
Algar Reuben T h 37 Richmond
Alger Elton B fireman h 98 Clark
Alick James cotton worker h 442 Sawyer
" Joseph B car cleaner h 122 High
" see Alleck [Cedar Grove
Alisia A Mlle phrenologist rms 382
Alix Henry weaver h 106 Beetle
" Joseph carpenter h 279 Collette
" Joseph mill operative h 225 Phillips avenue
" Nicholas mill hand b 16 Bullard
" Oscar removed from city [away
Allain Abraham carpenter h 67 Hath-
" Albert drill maker b 429 N Front
" Alphe weaver b 45 Tallman
" Andre twister b 325 North Front
" Arthur weaver b 45 Tallman
" Augustus carpenter b 98 Collette
" Clement laborer bds 19 Holly
" Cyrille fisherman b 97 Coffin av
" Cyrille removed from city
" Cyrille weaver h 128 Nash road
" Domonic mill hand h 19 Holly
" Edmonde mill hand bds 19 Holly
" Eugene A weaver h 183 Phillips avenue
" Fabian h 43 Holly [Belleville rd
" Francois mill operative b 30
" Hilaire carpenter bds 23 Holly
" Honore weaver b 325 North Front
" Laurent mill hand bds 19 Holly
" Ligorre laborer bds 22 Holly
" Luca T fisherman h 97 Coffin av
" Marguerite widow Maxime h 30 Belleville road
" Melos fisherman h 45 Tallman
" Moise shoemaker h 24 Bentley
" Odillon painter 14 Jean b 325 N Front
" Placide carpenter h 429 N Front

Allain
" Samuel lineman h 137 Tallman
" Vital weaver h 8 Tallman
" see Allen [yer
Allaire Alphonse teamster h 328 Saw-
" Napoleon laundryman b 63 Holly
" Noe elevatorman b 125 Webster court
" Peter laundryman bds Tallman
Allan Laura A widow Robert h 64 Thomas [ler
Allard Alfred bricklayer bds 44 But-
" Charles removed from city
" David R city teamster h 288 Cedar Grove [Cedar Grove
" Edmonde mill operative bds 288
" Elzear weaver h 85 Dean
" Frank A died Nov 17 1910
" Gilbert brakeman b 347 N Front
" Henry driver h 129 Perry
" Henry L rope maker b 129 Perry
" Mary widow Henry h 347 North Front
" Mederic helper h 15 Washburn
" Mederic laborer b 329 N Front
" William A freight clerk foot Willis bds 62 North [ant
Allby Henry electrician h r 356 Pleas-
Allcock John insurance agent h 135 Hathaway [h 122 High
Alleck Joseph car cleaner W St Ry Co
" see Alick
Allen Aaron S laborer h 315 Kempton [h 65 Hathaway
" Abraham carpenter U St Ry Co
" Ada A widow William C h 14 Columbia
" Ada B Mrs 782 Kempton
" Albert J bakery 36 Cove grocer 34 do h do [Kempton
" Andrew H city laborer h r 383
" Andrew T helper 55 North Water h 416 Hillman [Hathaway rd
" Anjanette widow Clark h 699
" Annie widow b 186 Grinnell
" Annie C Mrs nurse h 907 County
" Arsene wood 112 River rd h 112 do [Chestnut
" Arthur P clerk Taber Mill b 240
" Arthur S h 65 Hillman
" Asa L H pictures 228 Union h 350 Clinton
" Augutin carpenter h 232 Sawyer
" Aylesford J (Red Cross Pharmacy) h 533 Rivet

Remember to investigate our methods before taking up a business course.
Kinyon's Commercial School
Odd Fellows Bldg., Cor. William and Pleasant Sts., New Bedford, Mass.

Allen
" Caroline H h 147 Page
" Charles B treer h 60 Sycamore
" Charles E clerk 47 Foster h 224 North
" Charles E police h 24 Homer
" Charles E Jr teamster b 195 Smith
" Charles F traveling salesman 14 Wall h 31 Dartmouth
" Charles G shrimp Nye's wharf and janitor Central police station 127 Robeson h do
" Charles J shoe cutter h 73 Foster
" Charles J Jr clerk 125 Middle b 73 Foster
" Charles L foreman 91 North Water h 17 Jenny Lind
" Charles R removed to Cambridge
" Charles T foreman 100 Fifth h 11 Rounds [High
" Charles W driver hose 3 h 86
" Clarence E carpenter h 19 Borden
" Clark died July 23 1910
" Daniel H h Plainville road
" Daniel R laborer h 171 Smith
" David W jeweler 199 Acushnet avenue b 150 Fair
" Druscilla E Mrs h 50 North
" D Edwin proprietor The Clean Wet Wash Laundry 76 Shawmut avenue h do
" Edward supervisor h 208 Peasant [Union h 136 Chestnut
" Edward F (Allen Shoe Co) 118
" Edwin (Allen's Express Co) 149 Purchase h at Boston
" Elishup P h 78 Morgan
" Eliza M dressmaker 304 County h do [Court
" Elizabeth J stenographer b 59
" Ella F widow William H h 59 Court [ton
" Emily S Mrs removed to Taun-
" Emma C widow George C h 258 Cottage [b 21 Chestnut
" Ernest harness maker 156 Union
" Ernest A salesman b 153 Mt Pleasant
" Fannie M Mrs stenographer 125 Middle bds 68 Foster
" Fidell carpenter U St Ry Co h 43 Holly
" Florence bookkeeper b 398 Allen

Allen
" Frank G chief engineer Taber Mill h 158 Allen
" Frank H driver h 211 Smith
" Frank N, R R engineer h 23 Homer [at South Dartmouth
" Fred bookkeeper 745 Purchase h
" Frederick C laborer h 19 South Water
" Frederick E marble and granite works 18 North Second h 613 County [camore
" Frederick H city laborer b 49 Sy-
" George spinner h 398 Allen
" George C died June 17 1911
" George E (George E Allen & Co) h 79 Chestnut
" George E & Co (George E Allen) tailors and men's furnishings 120 Union
" George F bds 239 Arnold
" George H motor boat supplies h 205 Pleasant [33 Grove
" George H H clerk 100 Fifth h
" George J (George J Allen & Co) h 459 Mill
ALLEN GEORGE J & CO (George J Allen) plumbers 91 to 97 N Water See page 26
" George S driver ladder No 2 h 297 Acushnet avenue
" Gertrude F bookkeeper 140 Purchase b 304 Acushnet avenue
" Gideon Jr president 100 Fifth h 35 Grove [179 Court
" Gideon H collector 125 Middle h
" Green B foreman 100 Fifth h 118 do [Kempton
" Harry clerk 122 Purchase h 492
" Harry superintendent Wamsutta Mill h 667 Cottage [mouth
" Harry W carpenter h 29 Dart-
" Helen F widow Henry J h 69 Fourth
" Henry B painter h 550 Kempton
" Henry C farmer b 699 Hathaway road
" Henry T h 123 Bedford
" Horatio Cushing physician 11 Eighth h do [88 Newton
" Irving S clerk 386 Acushnet av b
" Isaac R tillerman ladder No 1 h 120 High
" James laborer b 570 South Water
" James H cabinet maker 36 Purchase h 68 Foster

HASKELL BROS. DEALERS IN
ICE
400 COURT STREET TELEPHONE CONNECTION NEW BEDFORD, MASS.

Allen
" James W treasurer Dartmouth Mfg Corporation and Bristol Mfg Co h 28 Lincoln [Chestnut
" Jesse harness mfr 156 Union h 21
" Jesse J rms 526 Purchase
" Jesse K bds 11 Rounds
" Jesse S harness and bicycles 92 Newton h 88 do [ton h do
" Jesse S Mrs dressmaker 88 New-
" John liquors 503 North Front h 149 Tinkham [lawn av
" John operative h 28 Wood-
" John P brick layer b 135 Bullard
" John William twister h 347 Bowditch
" Joseph motorman bds 412 Cedar
" Joseph D clerk b 258 Cottage
" Joseph H treasurer Neild Mfg Corporation h at Fairhaven
" Josephine W bookkeeper 160 Purchase b 169 Newton
" Lizzie J stenographer Whitman Mill bds 59 Court
" Louis Z machinist 8 Hazard's lane h 160 Rockland
" Lucy H bookkeeper 270 Acushnet avenue b 258 Cottage
" Lurania widow Charles h 41 Bonney [Park
" Luthan D driver 81 Front h 121
ALLEN MARCUS M painter and paper hanger 15-19 N Water b 28 Fifth See page 777
" Margaret widow John W h 203 Smith [143 Merrimac
" Margaret M widow William H b
" Maria widow James h 434 South Second [h 131 South Second
" Mary Mrs grocer 19 South Water
" Mary Mrs weaver h 666 First
" Mary A cashier 139 Union bds 11 Rounds [thorn
" Mary A widow Gilbert h 90 Haw-
" Mary E removed to Fairhaven
" Mary J widow Luke h 473 Kempton [Smith
" Mary M widow Charles M h 195
" Mary W bds 176 Pleasant
" Maud H stenographer 38 North Second bds 179 Court
" Michael operative b 63 Ruth
" Milton E shoe cutter b 309 Maxfield [b at Fairhaven
" Minnie L bookkeeper 65 William

Allen
" Mott clerk 100 William bds 150 Fair [Chestnut
" Peleg H S W machinist h 240
" Philip O machinist h 192 Shawmut avenue
" Phoebe D Mrs h 162 Campbell
" Prudence C widow James h 43 Bethel
" Ray O carpenter bds 74 Lindsey
" Robert h 56 Beetle
" Robert E captain steamer 6 h 44 Allen [10 Allen
" Robert E electrician 43 William b
" Robert organist North Congregational church h 122 David
" Roger L clerk b 60 Sycamore
" Rupert S conductor h 56 North
" Samuel head lineman 57 N Second
" Samuel R removed from city
" Sarah F h 147 Page
" Sarah F stitcher bds 74 Lindsey
" Sarah F widow William F h 74 Lindsey [old
" Sarah J widow John h 228 Arn-
" Shirley clerk 100 William
" Shoe Co (E F and George E) 118 Union
ALLEN, SLADE & CO (G W Slade, E B Lake and B S C Gifford wholesale groceries 1 William and 18, 26 and 30 Third, Fall River See page 12
" S Leroy clerk b 179 Court [av
" Thomas second hand h 32 Brock
" Thomas F h 56 Foster
" Timothy C (T C Allen & Co) h 24 Cottage
" T C & Co (T C Allen, J F Avery and A L Sylvia) cordage city pier No 2 [land terrace
" Walter S statistician h 25 More-
" Ward S fixer h 31 Dartmouth
" William A helper 144 South Water h at South Dartmouth
" William A mill operative bds 63 Ruth [68 Foster
" William A salesman 211 Union b
" William B b 150 Fair
" William H foreman h 169 Newton
" William H machinist h 907 County
" William M jeweler h 150 Fair
" William W died March 15 1911

J. F. CROSSLEY 223 MILL STREET COR EMERSON PHONE
STEAM and HOT WATER HEATING
GAS FITTING and FIXTURES

Allen
" & Booth Co wood workers 272 South Water
" & Matthews (Red Cross Pharmacy) 116 Dartmouth
" see Allan and Allain
Allen's Express Co 149 Purchase
Alletag Eugene weaver b 69 Church
" Valentine weaver h 69 Church
Alley Alfred G Jr president Consolidated Meat and Grocery Co h 53 Chestnut
" Emma S Y sewing teacher public schools bds 464 County
" Ernest V advertising manager Standard h 99 Clinton
" Robert H salesman rms 35 Fifth
Allgie Manuel laborer h 25 Griffin
Allie Horace operator h 174 State
" Rock removed from city
Allison Joseph H machinist h 888 Rockdale avenue
" Mary widow William h 76 Delano
" Norma McL mule spinner h 62 North
" William glass cutter b 76 Delano
" William removed from city
Allman Mary teacher b 288 Summer
Alma Joseph cobbler 864 Acushnet av bds 201 Coggeshall
" Joseph teamster h 255 South Second
Almedia Alberto laborer h 56 First
" Antone h 6 Warwick
" Antone mill hand h 105 Hemlock
" Antone mill operative b 435 S Water
" Augustus carpenter h 219 Allen
" Domingas shoemaker South Second corner Howland h 75 do
" Ernest B carpenter 42 Katherine h do
" Frank city laborer h 2 Walnut
" Frank driver 36 Purchase h 149 South Second
" Joaquim operative h 33 S Second
" John laborer h 28 Bourne
" John laborer h 76 Howland
" John laborer h 4 Maiden lane
" John laborer h 37 Nelson
" John laborer h 279 S Second
" John rope maker h 141 Emerson (N)
" John shoemaker h 121 Collette
" John B painter h 21 Winsor
" Joseph fisherman h 14½ Griffin

Almeida
" Joseph grocer 320 South Water h 149 South Second
" Joseph laborer h 55 Katherine
" Joseph mill hand h Rockdale av near Winterville road [do
" Juan shoe repairer 225 S Water h
" Julia Mrs removed to Fall River
" Larenco mill operative bds 96 South Second [3½ Cannon
" Louis de variety 229 S Water h
" Manuel bds 75 Howland
" Manuel mill hand h r 573 South Water
" Manuel mill operative b 59 Katharine
" Manuel operative h 389 S Second
" Manuel J barber b 148 Belleville avenue
" Manuel M barber 199 Coggeshall [h 148 Belleville av
" Manuel S drill worker h 69 Liberty
" Manuel S laborer h 207 Belleville [avenue
" Manuel S laborer h 9a Jenney
" Maria S widow Manuel S h 137 Thompson
" Marquis mill operative h 46 [School
" Mary confectionery 708 Water h 21 Windsor
" Philip laborer h 46 School
" Polly Mrs h 93 South Second
" Rose Mrs h 149 South Second
" Sebastian salesman h r 437 South Water
" Seraphim mariner h 118 South [Second
Almgren Axel glass cutter h 117½ Fifth
Almond Ellen Mrs h 20 Cove
" George weaver h r 57 Howard
" George weaver h 38 West French avenue
" James H agent 186 Purchase h [131 Rockland
" John H weaver bds 236 North Front
" Mary K teacher Abraham Lincoln school bds 288 Summer
" Nellie warper h 13 Salisbury
" Walter police inspector h 56 Hall
" William bakery 18 Harmony h 866 First
" William Jr police h 230 Allen
" William J clerk b 131 Rockland
Almy Edgar M clerk A M Corp h 81 Butler
" Edward T coachman 21 Morgan [h 126 Willis
" Edward T Jr b 126 Willis

CHARLES A. CROSHERE
38 FOURTH ST. Bell Phone 1964-23
SIGN PAINTING
GLASS LETTERING
ELECTRIC SIGNS
SHOW CARDS

Almy
" Emily M widow Benjamin R h 93 Spring [liam b 87 Hillman
" Emma M head clerk 166 Wil-
" Frederick T superintendent of carriers P O h 86 Hillman
" Gilbert F second hand b 2 Green
" Harriet M clerk 41 Purchase b 282 Palmer
" Helen R dressmaker 2 Green b do
" Horace T draughtsman 211 Merchant's Bank bldg b 16 Fifth
" James T (est) opticians 5 Purchase [Green
" Julia A widow Thomas R h 2
" Louis H clerk Standard h 282 Palmer
" Martin P died May 6 1911
" Mary Ann widow James T died
" Mary G teacher I W Benjamin school b 2 Green [Summer
" Minnie L clerk 53 William b 198
" Norman L h 21 Morgan
" Otis H h 198 Summer
" Sylvester S salesman 748 Purchase h 854 Rockdale avenue
" Thomas Rotch Jr master mechanic Sharp Mfg Co b 2 Green
" Walter C clerk 15 Hamilton b 2 Green [188 Court
" Walter T manager 5 Purchase h
" William rms 37 Purchase rm 20
" William collector 125 Middle h 20 Ash (S)
" William & Co cotton brokers 62 North Water [b 31 Holly
Aloupis Strats waiter 272 Coggeshall
Alpert David grocer 438 South Water h 526 do [h 785 do
" Isaac furniture 787 South Water
" Nathan furniture 409 South Water h do [Independence
Alphonse Anthony shoemaker h 52
" John laborer h 562 South Water
Alshaw John operative b 260 Coggeshall
Alsop Samuel master mechanic Hathaway Mfg Co h 88 Rockland
Alston George weaver bds 850 First
Altman Abram hay 75 Beetle h 8 Marvin [High
" Jacob hay 518 County h 114
" Samuel salesman b 8 Marvin

Alty Fred K motorman h 14 Willow
Alves Alexander mill operative h 180 South Second
" Anna bookkeper 1032 Acushnet avenue rms 109 Potomska
" Antone J laborer h 24 County
" Antone M mill operative h 383 Belleville avenue [Second
" Benjamin mill operative h 97 S
" Charles clerk b 383 Belleville av
" Domingo laborer h 14½ Cannon
" Frank J laborer h 109 Potomska
" George B clerk 28 Union b 15 High [h 502 Bolton
" Gutave bartender 262 Coggeshall
" Joao city laborer h 462 Maxfield
" John mill hand b 35 Mitchell
" John B salesman Anthony Swift & Co h 15 High
" Joseph fisherman h 34 South
" Joseph freight handler h 291 S Water
" Manuel clerk h 16 Cotter
" Manuel mason 39 Dartmouth h do
" Manuel mill operative h 550 South Water [& Co
" Manuel teamster Anthony Swift
" Manuel weaver h 28 County
" Manuel A weaver h 531 First
" Manuel M frame maker 25 North Second h 73 Mosher
" Mary Mrs h 12 Babbitt [land
" Mary widow Joseph A h 64 Rock-
" Silveria laborer b 103 Hemlock
Alvila Mary Mrs h 67 Delano
Amaral Antone fireman U S Ry Co power station h 322 S Front
" Antone mill hand b 103 Davis
" Antone C laborer h 17 Howland Village [97 do
" Antone P hairdresser 95 Rivet h
" Cornell P clerk Second near Potomska b 359 First [avenue
" Ernest E fisherman h 31 Acushnet
" Frank h 23 Mitchell [Winsor
" Helna widow Francisco h 90
" John mill hand h 72 Earle
" John P laborer h 31 Hathaway rd
" Joseph fisherman h rear 219 South Front
" Joseph laborer h 550 South Water
" Joseph operative h 383 Belleville avenue
" Joseph D laborer b 61 Fifth

J. G. NICHOLSON
LUMBER, SASH, DOORS and BLINDS
BOWDITCH STREET, NEW BEDFORD, MASS.

Amaral
" Joseph E mill worker h 284 South Front [Front
" Joseph P mill hand h 267 South
" Joseph S laborer h 50 Short
" Manuel fisherman h 556 South Water [eshall
" Manuel mill hand h 175 Cog-
" Manuel P hairdresser 279 Rivet h 41 Dunbar [Block
" Manuel S weaver b 9 Acushnet
" Mary h 56 Grinnell
" Nedhart third hand h 56 Briggs
" Peter h 175 Coggeshall
" Rose E widow Alfred h 125 Fair
" Walter clerk bds 50 Independent
Amarantes Januario O groceries 48 South Second h 80 Lombard
" Joseph farmer h Plainville road near Reed's lane [438 Bolton
" Manuel laborer h 10 Rotch block
Amarose Manuel bds 148 Belleville av
Ambash Max dry goods 543 South Water h 599 do
Ambrose Theodore mason h 32 Keen
American Clothing Co Inc 1029 Acushnet avenue
" Clothing Co 915 South Water
" House 1089 Acushnet avenue
" Loan Co 120 Purchase rm 203-204
" Steam Laundry (James Shanks) 659 Purchase
" Supply Co (Charles S and Herbert L Calhoon) bakers supplies 19 Commercial
" Transparol Company marine paint mfrs 405 South Water
Ames Alice bds 325 Middle
" Charles florist b 362 Pleasant
" Ethel W telephone operator 57 N Second bds 167 Summer
" Herbert helper b 325 Middle
" Herbert P laborer h 362 Pleasant
" Howard horse dealer rms 60 Spring [225 Park
" James washer 270 Acushnet av h
" Lavon T salesman h 127 Rotch
" Mary L Mrs h 83 Kempton
" Rosa widow Yorrick W h 325 Middle
" Sarah widow h 57 Crapo
" Seth K butter 128 Purchase h at Melrose [Pleasant
" Thomas P sign painter h 362
" Yorrick M died July 19 1911
Amey Harry mill fireman h 122 Clark
Amiszczyk Yusef mill hand h 16 Grandfield [49 William
Amory Ingersoll & Co cotton brokers
Amos Howard C clerk 14 N Sixth b 144 Mt Pleasant
" Stephen F clerk 14 N Sixth h 144 Mt Pleasant
Anarda Oscar blacksmith 105 Bowditch h 178 Phillips av [ly
Anctil George auto repairer b 85 Hol-
Anderly Gutave clerk 5 South Sixth h 63 Ash (N)
Anderson Addie h 210 Chancery
" Albert salesman h 88 Pierce
" Alfred hostler h 549 Union
" Arthur M clerk b 82 Pierce [mont
" Bernard chair seater h 99 Tre-
" Carl O foreman h 155 Princeton
" Charles O foreman h 151 Middle
" Claude O D rms Y M C A
" David foreman Fifth b 80 Fifth
" Edward J machinist h 154 Grinnell [Kempton
" Effe M clerk 182 Union b 517
" Francis O oiler b 82 Belleville rd
" Frank O iceman h 90 Shawmut avenue [at Fairhaven
" Frieda stenographer 12 Market b
" George E eyelet maker b 517 Kempton
" James driller h 82 Belleville road
" James W third hand b 82 Belleville road
" John glass cutter h 354 Allen
" Joseph draughtsman 3 E Pope h 111 David
" Julia Mrs removed to Middleboro
" Lars laborer h 82 Pierce
" Mabel chiropodist 71 William rm 4 bds 57 Hillman
" Robert second hand h 111 David
" Thomas overseer Bristol Mill h 207 Sawyer
" Walter operative h 350 Bowditch
" Walter operative b 540 North Front [Earle
Anderton Arthur engineer h 191
" George machinist h 151 Holly
" Herbert apprentice b 191 Earle
" James weaver h 34 Jouvett
" John weaver h 114 David
" John J carpenter h 285 Earle [av
" Joseph weaver h 27 East French
Andra Lewis laborer h 317 S Water

Steiger-Dudgeon Co.
"The WOMAN'S Store."
Tel. Bell 82 & 83, Branches connecting all depts.
" " 160 For Office only. Auto. 1211
SUMPTIONS, ASSORTMENTS AT ALL TIMES OF DEPENDABLE DRY GOODS

Andra
" Nellie Mrs h 316 South Water
" see Andrews
Andrada Antonio mill operative h 50 Howland Village [avenue
" Antonio S laborer 202 Belleville
" Francisco V driver 255 Union h 223 Brownell [Coffin av
" Guilherne A D second hand h 209
" Jesse mill hand bds 246 Cedar
" Joaquim mill hand h 49 Mitchell
" John fireman h 76 Grinnell
" John laborer h 31 Babbitt
" Joseph laborer h 152 S Second
" Joseph mill hand b 246 Cedar
" Joseph operative h 106 Potomska
" Jules yardman h 464 S Water
" Luiz mill hand h 55 Mitchell
" Manuel laborer h 246 Cedar
" Manuel laborer h 42 Division
" Manuel laborer h 429 First
" Manuel laborer h 40 North Water
" Manuel laborer h 429 South
" Manuel laborer h 191 S Water
" Manuel mill operative h 44 Howland Village
" Manuel speeder tender h 403 S Second [209 Coffin av
" Manuel yard boss Taber Mill b
" Mary Mrs h 14 Madison
" Yenocencio laborer h 15 Cotter
Andrade Manuel mill hand h 16 Howland Village [arine
" Vergino N carpenter h 59 Kath-
Andre Antonio mill hand h Jacinto
" John h 31 Babbitt
" Joseph h 116 Dartmouth [dent
" Joseph carpenter h 60 Indepen-
" Joseph chef 11 Purchase
" Joseph A (Sylvia Brothers) b 111 Larch [Larch
" Mary G widow Manuel G h 111
" see Andrews
Andreas Emma Mrs bds 198 Cedar
Andreoli John clerk h 692 Acushnet avenue [Kempton h do
Andress Benjamin A express 408
" Bradock driver h 186 Mill
" Charles clerk 88 Purchase b 370 Kempton [Water
Andrew Joseph A pool room 207 S
" Mabel G teacher Abraham Lincoln school
" Victor laborer h 31 Hazard

Andrew
" William H machinist b 81 Dunbar [67 do
Andrews Antone clerk 98 N Second b
" Antone fisherman h 501 First
" Antone mill hand h 65 Larch
" Antone removed from city
" Arthur F driver b 181 Smith
" Charles clerk b 149 Washington
" Charles elevatorman h 75 Mosher
" Charles M farmer h 1267 Rockdale avenue
" Charles O h 1092 South Water
" Clara J widow Walter b 97½ Fourth (S)
" Ebenezer F laborer h 181 Smith
" Edward C clerk 149 Washington
" Edwin H bookkeeper 132 Cottage b 6 Eighth [b 6 Eighth
" Frederick B clerk 42 Front
" Frederick W real estate h 6 Eighth
" Harry fixer h 82 Myrtle
" James E clerk 426 Kempton h 228 Smith [ant
" Jenny H Mrs provisions 426 Kempton h 175 Maple
" John C carpenter h 55 Mt Pleas-
" John D chauffeur b 43 Sycamore
" John F foreman street department h 83 Morgan
" John H baker 181 Acushnet av
" Joseph salesman 41 Purchase h 156 Hemlock
" Lizzie A Mrs nurse h 43 Cedar
" Mabel Mrs h 154 Acushnet av
" Manuel grocer h 85 Winsor
" Manuel laborer S O Co of N Y Fish Island
" Manuel A grocer 81 Acushnet avenue h 149 Washington
" Martha J W Mrs nurse h Tarkiln Hill road [55 Pierce
" S Frank driver foot North h
" Thomas L manager 426 Kempton h 175 Maple
" William F horse trader b A LaCroix's Tarkiln Hill road
" Wilson P removed to Rochester
" & Horton cotton brokers 25 North Water
" see Andra, Andre and Andrada
Angell George E paper maker b 31 Grape
" George G laborer b 88 Durfee

PELEG H. SHERMAN 506 COUNTY ST.
FUNERAL DIRECTOR AND EMBALMER
OFFICE PHONES. Bell 690-13 Auto. 1305.
RESIDENCE PHONES Bell 690-12. Auto 1306.

Angell
" Matilda A Mrs h 88 Durfee
Angelo Eva housekeeper h 40 Mosher
" Frank grocer 676 Acushnet av h do [net avenue
Angelus Soterios clerk 1150 Acush-
Angers Frederick mill hand b 56 Dean
" Joseph mill hand h 56 Dean
" Pierce mill hand bds 56 Dean
Angier Adelaide mill operative h 234 Coggeshall [532 Rivet
Anglin William H drill maker h
Anglum William laborer h 18 Trinity
Angrella John weaver h 22 Grant
Anneham Ferdinand weaver h 21 Jean
Annis Brothers (Manuel and Jrujorias) 817 South Water rms 135 Prospect. [mac
Ansay Arthur laborer h 28 E Merri-
Ansty Mary A widow Thomas b 204 Austin [Donald
Antaya Joseph shoemaker h 1 Mc-
" Paul laborer h 80 County
" Pierre motorman Electric express h 80 County [Summer
Anthinordi Dan engineer 19 Linden h
Anthony Alice G teacher piano 92 Elm h do
" Benjamin H president and treasurer E Anthony & Sons h 15 Anthony [Madison
" Celia L widow Benjamin h 98
" Charles E conductor h 47 Durfee
" Daniel A h 179 Cottage [thony
" Edmund clerk Standard b 15 An-
" Elisha D h 7 Maple
ANTHONY E & SONS Inc Benjamin H Anthony president and treasurer publishers Evening Sunday and Republican Standard Pleasant corner Market
" Florence M teacher I W Benjamin school b 7 Crapo
" George molder b 22 Dartmouth
" George S boarding officer Custom House h 14 Bay
" George W (Anthony, Guinn & Co) 396 Kempton rms do
" Guinn & Co (George W Anthony and John C Guinn) druggists 396 Kempton [Coggeshall
" John (Anthony and Gregory) 281
" Joseph bartender 717 Water
" Joseph Jr machinist h 40 Bourne

Anthony
" Joseph C bookkeeper 47 South Second b 60 Fourth [ision
" Joseph G city laborer h 193 Div-
" Laura A Mrs h 508 County
" Mamert teamster h 211 Cedar Grove
" Mark motorman h 229 State
" Maria S widow Enoch B h 150 Middle
" Martha M b 44 North
" Merrill b 179 Cottage
" M Ella L Mrs h 92 Elm
" Nathan (Tucker Anthony & Co) h at Boston [erson (S)
" Peter foreman 100 Fifth h 38 Em-
" Sophie T teacher I W Benjamin school b 14 Bay [h at Boston
" S Reed (Tucker Anthony & Co)
" Swift & Co wholesale provisions Bridge square
" William b 179 Cottage
" William grinder b 40 Bourne
" & Gregory (John Anthony, Charles Gregory) grocers 281 Coggeshall [fin
Anton Sylvest mill operative h 8 Grif-
Antoncovitch Laddius mill operative h 27 Hicks [Rockland
Antone Arthur M clerk b 160
" Joseph h 74 First
" Joseph pedlar h 160 Belleville av
" Joseph Jr fixer h 160 Rockland
" Manuel laborer h 291 Hillman
" Manuel Jr laborer N B W W h 624 South Water [ant
" Nicholas farmer h 661 Mt Pleas-
" William H laborer bds 208 Smith
Antonette Dominick laborer h 716 Acushnet avenue [ville av
Antonio Jose mill hand h 213 Belle-
" Maglorie Mrs h 6 Turner's court
Antosch Alfred operator h 173 Hathaway
Apelquist Axel K foreman bookbinder 69 Purchase h 158 Court
" Fred W student bds 158 Court
" Julius C clerk h 158 Court
Apolonsky John mill hand h 114 Nash road [Hathaway
Appleby David mill hand bds 77
April Eugene blacksmith h 186 Cove
Apsey Abbie h 61 Chancery
" Herbert J plumber b 61 Chancery
" Mary E clerk 185 Union b 61 Chancery

F. T. AKIN & CO. FORGE FACTORY FURNACE FAMILY COAL

Apsey
" Nellie bds 61 Chancery
Aque John laborer h 91 Tremont
" Leo laborer b 91 Tremont
Aradia John laborer h 507 S Second
Arado Archangelo laborer h 32 Hazard
Aralia Joaquim fireman h 385 First
" John operative h 591 First
Araujo Julio S barber 114 S Second bds 5 Walnut [ville av
" Luiz R laborer bds 202 Belle-
Arbeck Gedeon driver 380 Sawyer
" J D upholsterer 36 Purchase b 124 Collette [ams
Arbeiter Liedertafel Society 14 Ad-
Arbour Antoine carpenter h 96 Hathaway
Arcand Alphe h 168 Brock avenue
ARCAND EMILE J dentist 1356 Acushnet avenue h do office hours 9 to 12 a m, 2 to 4 and 7 to 8 p m See page 27
" George mill hand bds 35 Bullard
" Malvina Mrs mill hand h 35 Bullard [chase
" Philip stonecutter h 798 Pur-
" Victoria Mrs agent 73 William h 258 Cedar Grove [mont
Archambeault Edgar clerk h 62 Tre-
" Edmond P weaver bds 1205 Acushnet avenue
" Felix laborer bds 19 Rodney
" George weaver h 15 Katharine
" John B agent and treasurer 101 Kenyon and (R E Knapp & Co) h 163 Ashland [State
" Josephine widow Eusebe h 173
" Laura clerk 1041 Acushnet av bds 173 State
" Victor rem to Providence R I
Archand Nellie teacher h 258 Cedar Grove [ty
Archer Anna operative b 970 Coun-
" James B grocer 393 Cedar h 383 do
" Samuel spinner h 970 County
Archibald John J mill hand b 502 Bolton
" William b 502 Bolton
Arcouette Ida clerk 70 Purchase b 201 Eugenia [Phillips av
Ardelan John mill hand h 54
Ardent Walter grocer 149 N Front h do [ford Mass
Ardrey Sarah M removed to Clif-
Arendell Thomas Y carpenter h Belair road [Front
Arendt Walter grocer h 149 N
Arenville Archie spinner h 642 First
Arey Clarence W musical director h 167 Washington
" Clarinda G died April 7, 1911
" Mary A teacher James B Congdon school b 159 Washington
" Webster A asst auditor 160 Purchase h 57 Arnold
" see Airey [b 77 Davis
Argiropoulos Akalia widow Theodore
" Charles restaurant h 77 Davis
Arglanski Frank operative h 176 N Front [h 587 Purchase
Arigan Sarah A widow William J
Arkison Henry J express messenger h 889 County [Reynolds
" Marjory widow Patrick bds 14
" Michael bartender b 14 Reynolds
Arkwright John H operative h 196 Collette
Armat Artif mill hand h 42 Davis
Armfield John C fixer h 158 Collette
" John C fixer h 1 Hyacinth
Armitage Ernest third hand b 34 Sherman [man
" George B plumber bds 24 Sher-
" James h 428 Pleasant
" Thomas second hand b 34 Sherman [316 Summer
" William grocer 819 Purchase h
" William E weaver h 34 Sherman
Armour Anthony J drillmaker h 519 S Second [Front
" & Co wholesale provisions 99
Armstrong Anatole mill hand bds 154 Collette
" Angie Mrs h 96 School
" Elizabeth widow Joseph mill hand bds 74 Belleville road
" George W organist St Martin's P E church b 1½ Warwick
" Helen M telephone operator 57 N Second b 96 School
" Ivan E fireman h 34 Hilman
" Johanna widow John h 76 Myrtle
" John J stonecutter h 521 Hathaway road
" Joseph engineer h 1½ Warwick
" Robert laborer h 2½ Willis

To do things right you must be taught. Our instructors can do it.
Kinyon's Commercial School
Odd Fellows Bldg., Cor. William and Pleasant Sts., New Bedford, Mass.

Armstrong
" William H glasscutter b 76 Myrtle [141 Tremont
Arnett Edward R sub letter carrier b
" James W housekeeper police department h 75 Willis
" Robert janitor Cedar st school h 141 Tremont
" Thomas M died July 26 1910 [dar
" William N conductor h 410 Ce-
" see Arnott
Arnold Albert T teamster rms 355 Purchase [av
" Cyrus carpenter h 48 Woodlawn
" H Percy (Rankin & Arnold) 19 N Second h 26 Oak
" James third hand h 170 David
" Mahaly widow William W h 49 Parker
" Robert boilermaker h 75 Emma
" Robert Jr laborer b 75 Emma
" Stephen B clerk 639 County h 525 Cottage
" Thomas conductor h 23 Cottage
" Thomas S slasher tender h 20 La France court
Arnott George died Aug 3 1910
" Jane widow George h 12 Margin
" William E spinner h 12 Margin
" see Arnett
Arpin Ambrose mill hand bds 72 Belleville road
" Joseph doffer b 31 Bentley
" Peter carpenter h 31 Bentley
" Peter Jr back boy b 31 Bentley
Arrick Louisa M lodging h 69 Union
Arruda Anton speeder h 37 Nelson
" Anton P laborer h 136 Thompson
" Antonio carpenter h 108 Winsor
" Antonio laborer h 532 Rivet
" Antonio J operative h 16 Independent
" Frank laborer h 79 Katharine
" Frank mill hand h 149 Field
" Frank mill hand h 119 Swift
" Fortunato A carpenter 165 Rockland h 114 Grinnell
" John mill hand b 532 Rivet
" John operative h 56 Hollyhock
" John A operative h 115 Field
" Joseph removed from city
" Joseph operative h 56 Hollyhock
" Louis S laborer h 22 Hollyhock
" Manuel farmer h 391 Rockdale av
" Manuel laborer h 16 Briggs

Arruda
" Manuel P speeder tender h 426 S Water [lette
" Miguiel mill hand bds 121 Col-
Arseneau Angelina spooler b 193 N Front
" Manuel laborer bds 193 N Front
" Margaret spooler h 193 N Front
Arseneault Adele widow William b 120 Collette [man
" Amedee carpenter h 129 Whit-
" Andre laborer bds 80 Nye
" Antoine carpenter h 11 Holly
" Arthur carpenter bds 314 N Front
" Arthur gas fitter b 531 N Front
" Charles teamster h 7 Grandfield
" Emile carpenter h 159 Earle
" Emilien Mrs h 12 Nye
" Henri weaver h 10 Lucas
" Hubert laborer bds 157 Collette
" Isaac weaver h 172 Coffin av
" John weaver h 161 Cove
" Joseph fisherman h 531 N Front
" Joseph weaver b 161 Cove
" J Fred asst 7 Purchase h 104 Hemlock
" Mark carpenter h 50 Nye
" Michael removed to Fairhaven
" Napoleon teamster b 286 Davis
" Urbain P carpenter 80 Nye h do
Arsenio Manuel bartender h 530 First
" Arthur Fred musician h 173 Cedar [Park
Arthurs Ann widow Samuel h 215
Arundale James wire bender h 517 Kempton [ley
Ashburn John operative h 18 Ash-
Ashcroft Richard carpenter h 10 Linden court
Ashley Adelbert C clerk 167 Purchase h 341 Orchard (S)
" Albert fixer b 184 Davis
" Almira F widow Silas b 31 Eighth
" Andrew H student b 53 Lake
" Andrew J foreman 180 N Second h 450 Acushnet avenue
" Arthur H h 291 Palmer
" Arthur S manager 92½ Purchase h 290 Summer
" A Davis antique furniture Arcade building h 35 Eighth

Bread, Cake, Pastry
RICHMOND & COMPANY **255-257 UNION STREET**
Bell 993 Automatic 1022

Ashley
" Bettie H widow Henry T h 1789 Acushnet av [h 71 Ash (S)
" Caroline E widow Franklin M
" Charles S mayor office 203 Municipal bldg h 93 State
" Charles S Jr (Charles S Ashley Jr & Co) h 282 Hawthorn
ASHLEY CHARLES S JR & CO (Charles S Jr and R Eugene Ashley) real estate and insurance 62 Pleasant See page 43
" Clair clerk bds 82 Liberty
" Clifford W artist b 31 Eighth
" Clifton F mgr 20 Fourth b 47 S Sixth
" Clinton messenger Standard
" Courtney P chauffeur 15 Hamilton bds 47 S Sixth [way rd
" David G teamster h 672 Hatha-
" David M cutter h 87 Willis
" Edmund D artist photographer Standard h 208 Pleasant
" Edward H shoemaker h 88 Liberty
" Edwin M salesman h 44 North
" Elizabeth G widow Ellis dressmaker 375 Cedar h do
" Ellaphine h 81 State [Purchase
" Ellen M widow Daniel C b 12
" Frank H h 82 Liberty
" Frederick M dentist 30 Purchase b 111 Summer
" Freeman H b 90 David [tage
" George W carpenter h 261 Cot-
" Hannah B h 81 State
" Harriet S clerk b 7 Borden
" Helen A cashier 145 Union b 85 Bay [26 Maitland
" Horace C salesman 21 William h
" H Edward shoemaker h 88 Liberty [net av
" H Thomas police h 1791 Acush-
" Isaac L stable 12-20 Fourth h 42 S Sixth
" Isaac L Jr mgr 20 Fourth h 56 Ash (S) [58 Summer
" James C stockman 57 N Second h
" James M teamster b Thomas J Ashley's Plainville rd
" Jonathan S machinist bds 102 Acushnet avenue [Borden
" Joseph M foreman 100 Fifth h 7

Ashley
" Joshua B Jr 177 Purchase h 366 Union [342 Cottage
" Laura C bookkeeper 27 Centre h
" Leon A farmer b 26 Maitland
" Lovisa W b 90 Ashland
" Marcus teamster bds 82 Liberty
" Mary A widow William A G b 53 Lake [Maitland
" Mary E widow Bradley M b 45
" Mary I teacher J H Clifford school h 3591 Acushnet av
" Millard C mason h 4102 Acushnet avenue
" Morris D salesman b 31 Eighth
" Moses operative h 12 Locust
" Moses E H Jr clerk Bennett Mill b 12 Locust
" Nellie E teacher T A Greene school b 341 Orchard (S)
" Raymond E student b 31 Eighth
" Richard G carpenter b 375 Cedar
" Rodney F jeweler h 40 North
ASHLEY ROLAND R real estate 40 North bds 232 Pleasant See page 755
" Ruth A h 90 David
" R Eugene assessor 9 Municipal bldg and (Charles S Ashley Jr & Co) h 94 Hillman [Maitland
" Sarah E widow Horace M h 26
" Silas E carpenter h 652 Purchase
" Simeon P carpenter h 48 Oak
" Thomas J calker h Plainville rd
" Wallace mariner h 71 Fruit
" William A carpenter h 53 Lake
" William C painter h 211 Cedar
" William G electrician 141 Purchase h 48 Page [ant
" William L carpenter h 232 Pleas-
Ashline Albert H carpenter h 178 Mott [Clark
Ashton Albert loom fixer h 128
" James weaver b 94 Bowditch
" John (Ashton & Murphy) 1109 S Water h 159 Bonney [av
" John H twister h 17 E French
" Thomas S tailor 211 Union h 218 Whitman
ASHTON & MURPHY (John Ashton and William H Murphy) real estate 1109 S Water See page 48
" Walter weaver h 77 Hathaway

GLOBE DYE HOUSE 220 SHAWMUT AVE.
J. N. J. LONHOLDT, PROP. Telephone Connections Goods called for and Delivered
Down town Office, 52 Pleasant St., Room I North End Office, 1014 Acushnet Ave.

Ashworth Arthur fixer h 271 Tinkham [man h do
" Edwin picture frames 98 Tall-
" Elizabeth widow Doctor h 11 Harmony [Vernon
" Hannah widow James bds 127 Mt
" Harold clerk 120 Purchase b 127 Mt Vernon
" Harry spinner h 228 Collette
" Harry Jr chauffeur b 228 Collette [mony
" James glassworker bds 11 Har-
" James weaver h 201 Belleville rd
" James F clerk foot Willis h 99 Linden
" James W fixer h 202 Brook
" John grocer and postmaster Plainville road cor Shawmut avenue h do
" John H weaver h 128 Reynolds
" John Robert sub clerk P O h 602 Cottage [av
" Walter weaver h 23 E French
" William laborer h 50 Larch
" William A loom fixer h 26 Belleville road
Aspden James fixer h 7 Ashley
" Martin operative b 351 Bowditch
" Matilda widow b 7 Ashley
Aspin George laborer bds 94 Cleveland
" George weaver h 70 Katharine
" Joseph laborer h 345 First
" Mary b 113 Rivet [113 Rivet h do
" Mary H widow Thomas variety
" Thomas weaver b 336 Tinkham
" Thomas weaver rms 602 Purchase
Aspinall Edward toolmaker h 257 Shawmut avenue
Asselin Albert bds 125 Bates av
" Amos helper bds 125 Bates av
" Edward O laborer h 125 Bates avenue [yer
Astigey Arthur laborer h 214 Saw-
Astin Percy carpenter b 135 Bullard
Astley John C insurance agent 37 Purchase rm 23 h 31 Juniper
" John H weaver h 275 Collette
" Lawrence operative b 172 Belleville road [ville road
" Maurice operative bds 172 Belle-
" Robert removed from city
" Robert weaver h 24 Viall
" Samuel glass cutter h 484 Allen

Astley
" Thomas police station 5 h 172 Belleville road [Fourth h do
Atchison Charles M physician 94
" William B bookkeeper 55 Spring b 94 Fourth [h 344 do
Athearn Charles E fish 345 Cedar
" Ernest H clerk N B Tow Boat Co b 344 Cedar [nut
" James B electrician rms 56 Wal-
" Walter H architect 382 Cedar h do [net avenue
Atherly Gilbert teamster b 527 Acush-
" Sarah widow Thomas h 527 Acushnet avenue
Athertan Agnes operative h 13 Ruth
Atkins William mule spinner bds 27 Viall [Merrimac av
Atkinson Alice widow Joseph b 2
" Elmer b 160 David
" Ezra operative b 285 Earl
" Heaton glass worker h 28 Cove
" Herbert machinist 107 N Water h 15 Studley
" Isaiah overseer h 380 N Front
" John laborer b 163 Frederick
" Robert weaver b 72 Ruth
" Thomas weaver h 9 Viall [velt
" William mule spinner h 26 Roose-
Attaide Joseph M carpenter h 77 Taber [nut
Attridge James shipper b 133 Chest-
Atwood Andrew J polisher 362 Purchase rms 332 Pleasant
" Elizabeth removed from city
" Elmer drill worker b 249 Chestnut
" George H photo engraver Standard h 5 Green [47 Cottage
" Grace M stenographer 100 Fifth b
" Harriet S widow Joseph h 163 Campbell
" Herbert M carpenter h 47 Cottage
" James weaver h 210 Eugenia
" Mary Mrs h 25 Warren
" Mattie L clerk b 196 North
" Sidney C meat cutter 159 Purchase h 261 Pope
" Susan F widow Martin h 18 Vine
" William T tin worker h 52 Florence
" William W removed from city
" William W police h 196 North
Aube Edgar loom fixer h 23 Thatcher

GREENE & WOOD Every Kind of LUMBER AND MILL WORK
PINE STREET, off So. WATER STREET, NEW BEDFORD

Aubertin F Joseph top roll coverer 96 Mt Pleasant h do [avenue
Aubin Eugene weaver h 845 Acushnet
" Henrietta widow Joseph h 763 Purchase
" Hylas laborer b 763 Purchase
" Romeo H driver 14 N Sixth b 763 Purchase
" see St Aubin
Au Bon Marche (D L Crowley) dry goods and millinery 139 Union
Aubrey Napoleon painter h 14 Bowditch [away
Auclair Amedee weaver h 88 Hath-
" Jack chemist h 431 Mill
" Philip painter h 88 Tallman
Auctil Erase mill hand h 11 Desautels
Audette Arthur A (National Wet Wash Laundry) 281 Sawyer and (Audette & Chapdelaine) 1214 Acushnet av h 1205 do
" Arthur A weaver b 1205 Acushnet avenue
" August spinner b 55 Austin
" Clotilda Mrs b 35 Elm
" Dolphis operative h 55 Austin
" Frederick weaver h 211 Brock av
" Gilbert painter h 204 Sawyer
" Gilbert teamster b 87 Potomska
" Gilbert Jr operative b 207 Sawyer
" Godfroi weaver h 20 Nye
" Hermidas laundry man bds 1205 Acushnet avenue [ada
" Isaie removed to W Farnham Can-
" John B operative h 475 N Front
" John B weaver h 51 Dean
" Onias mill hand bds 20 Nye
" Philias carder h 158 Central av
" Silva slasher bds 60 Tallman
" Udari hairdresser h 487 N Front
" & Chapdelaine (Arthur Audette and George E Chapdelaine) lunch 1214 Acushnet avenue
Auger Asa lawyer 37 Purchase rm 25 h 310 Sawyer
" Edward carpenter h 65 Church
" Fred J bicycle repairer 228 Purchase bds 289 do
" George W (George W Auger & Co) 228 Purchase h 289 do
AUGER GEORGE W & CO (George W Auger) bicycles etc 228 Purchase See page 782
" George W Jr removed to Taunton
" William operative b 65 Church
Augers Frederick mill hand 56 Dean
August Frank at P Corporation h 307 South Second [219 Allen
Augusta Flora sewer 40 Purchase b
" Maria widow h 72 Hatch [bitt
Augustino Manuel laborer h 56 Bab-
Augusto John h 126 Fair
" Manuel operative h 175 Coggeshall [W h 400 First
Augustus Ferdinand laborer N B W
Aulisio Joseph clerk 83 Howland bds 146 Fourth [h 344 Kempton
" Marino shoe repairer 45 Ash (S)
Aumann Joseph engineer h 494 Coggeshall [h 46 Hunter
Austin Amelia J M widow John H C
" Arthur W bookkeeper 223 N Second h at S Dartmouth
" Clifford glasscutter b 327 County
" Edith A teacher Harrington school b 232 Pleasant [nolds
" Edward A machinist b 34 Rey-
" Elizabeth widow Michael h 193 Park
" Emma C clerk h 512 Kempton
" George molder bds 44 W French avenue [Cottage
" Ira B driver 92 Walden h 453
" John C hostler h 276 Middle
" Joseph dentist 163 Purchase h 66 Hillman
" Lester M clerk h 178 Fourth
" Lloyd W farmer h 305 Shawmut avenue [Franklin
" Maria L widow Benjamin h 7
" Mary E teacher High school b 512 Kempton [193 Park
" Michael C linotyper Standard b
" Percy carpenter h 135 Bullard
" Sarah widow John bds 191 Davis
" Sarah E died March 6 1911
Authier Deliasse rem to Acushnet
" F X Delos (Langlois Authier & Co) 2030 Acushnet av
AUTO SELLING & SUPPLY CO (John S Coy) 15 Fourth See page 741
AUTOMATIC TELEPHONE CO of New Bedford 41 and 43 William corner N Second See page 22
Avalia John operative h 591 First
Avaral Joacquim laborer h 219 S Front [son
Avellar Antone carpenter h 41 Edi-

BONNEY, FOLSTER & CO.,
The North End's Shopping Centre
Dry Goods and Men's Furnishings
945-947 Acushnet Ave., New Bedford, Mass.

Avellar
" Emilio fish h 273 S Second
" Florence Mrs b 94 Rockland
" Mary Mrs h 94 Rockland
Aveney Norman G asst mgr 70 Purchase rms 172 William
Averill James W stock fitter h 202 Kempton [net av
Avery Angeline widow h 31 Acush-
" James F (T C Allen & Co) city pier No 2 h 97 South
" John carder h 31 Acushnet av
" John Jr weaver h 59 Mosher
" Mary W clerk 68 Adams b 15 Chestnut
" Napoleon J salesman 50 Union
" Samuel machinist b 31 Acushnet avenue [Dartmouth
" Sevarienne H glasscutter bds 12
" William weaver h 29a Acushnet avenue [62 Ward
Avila Alfred barber 81 William bds
" Antone S operative h 440 Maxfield [ond h 75 Howland
" Antonio hairdresser 119 N Sec-
" Frank S h 266 Bonney
" Frank S Jr laborer b 266 Bonney [cond h 116 Acushnet av
" George C hairdresser 245 S Sec-
" John electrician 120 Middle b at S Dartmouth [h 88 Briggs
" John J hairdresser 74 Grinnell
" Joseph carpenter bds 137 Acushnet avenue [439 Bolton
" Joseph mill hand h 22 Rotch blk
" Joseph paper tubemaker h 145 Acushnet avenue [h 238 do
" Joseph F barber 236 S Second
" Manuel fisherman h 530 S First
" Manuel laborer h r 700 S Water
" Manuel F watchman h 85 James
" Manuel S fireman h 24 Acushnet avenue [ington
" Manuel V carpenter b 12 Wash-
" Mary Mrs h 33 Oak
" Mary widow h 12 Dartmouth
Avillar Manuel V fisherman h 115½ Fifth [pect
Ayer Charles weaver bds 53 Pros-
Ayers Frank H twister b 159 David
Ayler Louisa Mrs h 340 Middle
" Mary Ellen Mrs h 70 James
Aylward Patrick J fireman h 126 Reynolds
" Thomas fireman h 90 Kenyon
Ayotte Henry card grinder b 12 Princeton
" Paul mill hand bds 351 N Front
Azevedo John V photographer 162 County h do [176 Rounds
" Joseph J machinist 22 Fourth h
" Manuel J hostler 18 S Second h 69 Hall
" Rose H Mrs h 317 Rivet [Front
" Tomazia widow Joseph h 511 N

Baba Annie widow John h 180 Cedar Grove [Viall
Babb Joseph A elevatorman h 30
Babbitt Arthur S h 27 Robeson
" Grace I stenographer 57 N Second h at Fairhaven
" Isaac N (Babbitt Steam Specialty Co) h at Fairhaven
" Joseph M (Babbitt Steam Specialty Co) h 39 N Sixth
BABBITT STEAM SPECIALTY CO (Joseph M and Isaac N Babbitt and John A Stitt) machinery 55-57 S Water See page 29
" Susan A clerk 57 N Second b at Fairhaven
Babchick Borach junk h 76 First
Babcock Belle M Mrs bds 40 Pearl
" Charles H h 160 Fair
" Edith M Mrs h 161 Middle
" George A clerk 251 Purchase h 49 Hillman [Fourth
" Joseph C foreman 100 Fifth h 133
" Mary E widow John b 69 Fourth
Babecki Alexander laborer h 47 Washburn
Babineau August removed to Fairhaven [avenue
" Calix machinist h 1642 Acushnet
" Calixte teamster h 154 Eugenia
" Celestine carpenter h 491 North Front
" Clotilde bds 97 Coffin avenue
" Cyrille carpenter bds 20 Tallman
" Cyrille removed from city
" Dominick fisherman b 154 Eugenia
" Edward carpenter h 109 Eugenia
" Edward helper b 77 Holly
" Frank carpenter h 71 Hathaway
" Fred mill hand b 30 Belleville rd
" Fred weaver h 16 Holly
" Joseph twister b 274 N Front

Painters Supplies Wall Papers Room Mouldings Ladders
M. P. B. Silva & Son BRUSHES
157 ACUSHNET AVENUE Both Phones NEW BEDFORD

Babineau
" Neri fisherman bds 12 Tallman
" Oliver fisherman h 12 Tallman
" Peter A fisherman h 274 N Front
" see Papineau [Grove
Babola John operative h 180 Cedar
" Joseph operative 115 Cedar Grove
" Ludwig operative b 101 Collette
Bach George laborer 209 Acushnet av
" Herbert chauffeur 148 Court h 872 First
" William laborer h 25 Cannon
Bachand Arthur copperworker h 871 Purchase
" Arthur painter b 417 N Front
" Charles harness maker 247 Sawyer bds 225 Whitman [man
" Emil harness maker b 125 Whit-
" Israel weaver h 773 First
" Louis operative h 117 Bates av
" Victor weaver b 773 First
" William teamster 106 Front h 50 Kempton [net av h 1672 do
Bachman August lunch 1674 Acush-
" August F weaver h 55 Washburn
" Richard bartender h 17 Princeton
" William operative b 55 Washburn
" see Bochman
Backus George A removed from city
" George F telephone inspector b 71 Bonney [ney
" Henry D machinist b 71 Bon-
" John H assistant master mechanic N B F D h 71 Bonney
" John removed to Jersey City N JH
" Mary E widow Ansel C b 25 Mill
" Oliver C clerk bds 327 Court
" William L salesman b 71 Bonney
" William S letter carrier h 327 Court
Bacon Annie E h 18 Lincoln
" Catherine M widow David b 87 Campbell
" Edward carpenter h 203 Collette
" Joseph carder h Acushnet av bey- L C [Pleasant
" Maria K widow Grenville L h 285
BACON WILFRED L plumber 514 County h 60 Fourth See top edge
Baczek Joseph weaver h r 63 Tallman
Baddar John F teamster bds 495 Coggeshall

Badger Edward removed from city
Baganlia Manuel O laborer h 63 Prospect [Purchase
Bagley Edward plumber bds 847
" Fred E removed from city
" John H machinist h Hawes near Tarkiln Hill road [Hathaway
" Sarah A widow Richard b 124
" Sarah C widow Charles C b 362 County [Middle
Bailey Alice S widow Stephen b 343
" Alton H carpenter h 82 Rotch
" Arthur weaver b 81 Dunber
" Benjamin h 75 Hathaway [way
" Benjamin machinist h 109 Hatha-
" Elizabeth h 64 South [ham
" Gladys I bookkeeper b 53 Peck-
" Hattie S clerk 755 First b do
" James E salesman 384 Acushnet avenue h 7 Shawmut avenue
" James H copper worker b 77 Myrtle
" Jonathan loom fixer h 69 Myrtle
" Joseph blacksmith b 75 Hathaway
" Lena variety 94 Grinnell h do
" Leola C stenographer 97 William rm 303 b at Fall River
" Rachel R teacher Abraham Lincoln school b 77 Myrtle
" Ralph operative b 40 Russell
" Richard copper worker h 77 Myrtle [ham
" Richard L shipper bds 53 Peck-
" Sidney C operative b 463 Chancery [b 77 Myrtle
" Stella bookkeeper 630 Purchase
BAILEY WALTER P plumber 216 Acushnet avenue h at S Dartmouth See page 766
" William h 92 Linden
" William T electrician b 69 Myrtle
Baillargeon Arthur drill worker h 94 Nye [h 2056 do
" Louis manager 1147 Acushnet av
" Louis Mrs milliner 1077 Acushnet avenue h 2056 do
" Napolean weaver h 194 Blackmer
" Walter salesman 1147 Acushnet avenue b 2056 do
Bain Christina Mrs h 43 Katherine
" James B died April 5 1911
" Walter machinist h 48 Independent [Sixth
Bainbridge Thomas fixer h 100 South
Baines Harry doffer bds 150 Davis

Steiger-Dudgeon Co.
"The WOMAN'S Store."
Tel. Bell 82 & 83, Branches connecting all depts.
" " 160 For Office only. Auto. 1211

SUMPTIONS, ASSORTMENTS AT ALL TIMES OF DEPENDABLE DRY GOODS

Baines
" James carpenter b 7 Babbitt
" Mary housekeeper 188 Church
" Thomas bookkeeper b 150 Davis
" William clerk b 150 Davis
" William P janitor h 150 Davis
Baker Abbie M widow Russell D h 72 Foster
" Anthony bds 150 Fourth
" Benjamin 3 Merrill's wharf h 139 North [Mill rd
" Benjamin R city laborer h 19
" Carl teamster 45 Union h Fourth
" Carlton S teamtser rms 51 Spring
" Catherine H Mrs h 114 Grinnell
" Charles A drill hardener h 168 Grinnell
" Daniel W (Westby & Baker) 308 Times bldg h 60 Fifth
" Edith M Mrs h 44 Fifth
" Edward A bartender rms 25 William [14 Borden
" Edward D clerk 100 William h
" Edward Y salesman h 58 James
" Eliot C 34 N Second h at Fairhaven
" Emma E Mrs h 29 Rockland
" Emma T laundress h 36 Hillman
" Ethel A teacher I W Benjamin school b 233 Middle
" Flora B Mrs millinery 81 Hillman h do [ond b 113 Fourth
" Frank M cable splicer 57 N Sec-
" Frederick C clerk 645 County h 31 Shawmut avenue
" George L removed from city
" George O master mariner h 261 County [Pope h 221 Pope
" George W sec and treas 1 East
" Harriet C nurse h 96 Atlantic
" Henry teamster b 17 Fourth
" Hersey died Jan 3 1911
" Isadore removed to Lawrence
" James G clerk 38 N Second h at Fairhaven [net av
" John E twister h r 28 Acush-
" Joseph removed to Boston
" Joshua G Jr bookkeeper 97 Front h 26 Keene [284 Kempton
" Lillian M widow Wallace L b 284
" Lydia R dressmaker 96 Atlantic h do
" Lysander Mrs rms 493 County

BAKER MACHINE CO machinists and automobile repairing 8 Seuccca and East Pope See page 744
" Margaret G widow Ansel G h 183 Fourth [ion
" Mary E Mrs lodgings 2301 Un-
" Maurice machinst b 290 Fourth
" Sarah H widow b 83 Summer
" Sarah S widow Michael A h 82 Chestnut
" Solomon M wall papers 559 Purchase h 185 Richmond
" Tamer C died Oct 7 1910 [(N)
" Thomas O teamster h 162 Ash
" Wallace L died April 18 1911
" William engineer h 17 Bethel
" William A h 15 Washington
" William T janitor Friends Meeting House h 17 Fourth
Bakers' & Confectioners' Club 34 Pleasant [ditch
Bakewell Joseph spinner h 174 Bow-
Belanger Armand Jr laborer b 180 Sawyer
" Magloise carpenter h 142 Crapo
Balboni Charles J student bds 109 James [44 Liberty
" Ernest H sub letter carrier h
" Louis tailor 109 James h do
Balcom Mary P widow Henry L housekeeper 124 Mill [28 Clark
Balderson Joanna widow Robert h
" John H fireman h 177 Weld [ant
" Michael F teamster h 445 Pleas-
Balderstone Margaret N widow h 571 First
Baldwin Alice widow Harry h 3 Social
" Ann Mrs h 169 Rockland
" Ansel removed from city
" Benjamin clerk 393 Cedar b 76 Durfee [b 3 Social
" Benjamin T salesman 76 Purchase
" Frederick D W, U S N b 53 Hill
" Frederick W gardener b 76 Durfee [field
" George W machinist h 118 Max-
" Harold P clerk 20 Market h at Fairhaven
" Harry died Jan 1 1911
" Henrietta teacher 16 Howard b do
" Henry W gardener h 76 Durfee
" Herbert real estate b 850 First
" John conductor b 514 Purchase
" Joseph operative h 30 Rodney

PELEG H. SHERMAN 506 COUNTY ST.
FUNERAL DIRECTOR AND EMBALMER
OFFICE PHONES. Bell 690-13. Auto. 1305.
RESIDENCE PHONES. Bell 690-12. Auto. 1306.

Baldwin
" Joseph weaver b 3 Social
" Joseph T provisions 126 Cove h 81 Fair
" Lewis D asst draw tender Fairhaven bridge h 53 Hill
" Mary H Mrs h 35 Myrtle
" Thomas painter h 26 Acushnet av
" Thomas painter b 425 S Front
" Walter reedmaker h 113 Reynolds
" William laborer bds 435 S Front
Belegeno Alfred weaver b 80 Beetle
" Emilino laborer h 672 Acushnet avenue [cery
Ball Harry helper bds 189 Chan-
" Harry E cable splicer 57 N Second b 113 Fourth
" Frank warper b 12 Viall
" Joseph spinner h 156 Holly
" Tena M widow J Edward dressmaker 463 Cottage bds do
" Theophilus C overseer Kilburn Mill h 9 Social
" Thomas weaver h 90 Salisbury
" William E overseer Kilburn Mill h at Fairhaven
" William R h 11 Hunter
" William R Jr bds 11 Hunter
Balleau John laborer b 3 Seneca
" Peter laborer bds 3 Seneca
" Victoria laborer h 3 Seneca
Ballman Anna widow Julius h 446 Allen [Cedar
Balloch Caroline widow James E b 36
" James E traveling salesman h 97 Willis [Cedar
" Sarah W widow James E h 36
Ballou Ella Mrs h 85 South Sixth
Balthazar Alder machinist b 2 Cornell place
" Henri weaver b 128 Rivet
" J Arthur deputy sheriff 21 Clifford bldg b 592 First [ard
" John Baptiste clerk h 70 How-
" John B h 314 North Front
" Joseph grocer 1 Hicks h 124 N Front
" Joseph A weaver h 592 First
" Wilfred inspector h 182 Acushnet avenue [h 136 Norman
Bambardier Josephine widow Joseph
Bamber Edward removed from city
Bamford James H shoe treer h 90 Merrimac
" William shoemaker b 90 Merrimac

Bamforth Henry music teacher 199 Brock avenue h do [Washburn
Banas Walenty operative h r 42
Bancraft George painter h 11 McMurray terrace
Bancroft Abel spinner b 26 George
" Annie widow Arthur C h 812 County
" Arthur C died May 4 1911
" Bethany machinist bds 62 Vine
" Jennie A widow Julius V h 194 Pleasant
" Joel spinner h 261 Tinkham
" John spinner b 261 Tinkham
" Samuel operative h 48 Bourne
Bandarra Joseph M de hairdresser 444 South Water h 105 Fifth
" Marianno laborer h 317 S Front
Bandry Felix fireman h 152 Whitman
Banfield George iron molder 229 N Water h 619 Purchase [W High
Bankittt Sarah J widow John A h 7
Banks Carl O removed from city
" Charles machinist b 118 David
" Charles spinner h 278 Philips av
" Charles Jr spinner bds 278 Philips avenue [lantic
" Christian glass cutter h 71 At-
" John glass worker h 41 Dartmouth
" Joseph P brewery worker h 34 Reynolds [chase b 69 Park
" Lena C M bookkeeper 92½ Pur-
" Thomas fixer h 79 Bowditch
" Walter clerk b 278 Phillips av
" William operative h 79 Bowditch
Bannister Jesse h 993 County
" John W wholesale provisions 188 North Water b 194 Pleasant
" Joseph H insurance agent 41 William h 373 Cedar Grove [do
" Leonard A dentist 250 Union b
" Wilson E clerk H of C b 17 Lincoln [Hyacinth b do
Bannon Annie C dressmaker 11
" Edward T lawyer 15 Masonic bldg h 287 Summer [cinth
" James S hairdresser b 11 Hya-
" John H instructor H C b 11 Hyacinth [Hyacinth
" Lawrence A stone cutter b 11
" Mary E teacher I W Benjamin school b 264 Pleasant [b do
" Mary J dressmaker 11 Hyacinth

F. T. AKIN & CO. PAINTERS AND DECORATORS

Bannon
" Mary J widow Patrick died June 28 1911 [Pleasant lane
" Patrick F stone cutter h 5 Mt
Banoyer Leboire fixer b 845 S Water
Bant Manuel laborer h 45 Grand
Banville Aurele J driver h 94 Rodney [h 90 Fruit
Baptista Catherine C widow Antonio
" Domingo laborer h 12 Bethel
" Eugene operative b 27 Union
" John buffer b 90 Fruit [First
" John cook 62 Purchase b 421
" John hairdresser 24 Wing h do
" Manuel carpenter h 31 Page
" Manuel laborer h 86 Liberty
" Manuel steward h 49 First
Baptiste Jean laborer h r 609 Acushnet avenue [Griffin
" John clerk 133 Acushnet av h 7
" John mariner h 145 S Second
" Joseph Jr teamster Anthony Swift & Co h at Dartmouth
" Manuel doffer b 739 Water
" Manuel mill hand h 218 Rockland
" Manuel J operative h 692 S Water
" Manuel J Jr mule spinner b 692 South Water
" Maria Mrs h 739 South Water
" Peter mariner h 8½ Griffin [do
Barabe Alcide A bakery 643 First h
" Emily widow b 643 First
Baran John mill hand b 1 Riverside avenue [tailors 252 Purchase
Barash Brothers (Jacob and Samuel)
" Harris tailor h 557 Purchase
" Jacob (Barash Bros) b 557 Purchase [man
" Samuel (Barash Bros) h 29 Hill-
Barber Albert second hand h 26 Collins
" Benjamin laborer h 117 S Second
" Fred painter h 131 Tallman
" Harry operative b 148 Tallman
" Isaac engineer h 804 Purchase
" James foreman 861 Purchase
" James R weaver h 148 Myrtle
" James S cloth inspector b 478 N Front
" John spinner h 57 Beetle
" Joseph painter h 148 Tallman
" Ralph second hand h 128 Clark
" Robert changer over h 36 Myrtle
" Thomas weaver h 478 N Front
Barbieri Joseph grocer 164 Blackmer h do
" Paul weaver b 164 Blackmer
Barbosa Charles operative h 103 Mosher [Elm
Barbour Arthur J foundryman h 157
" James L machinist b 98 Larch
" Jessie M teacher High school b 29 Seventh
" John R janitor h 66 Bedford
" Peter proprietor American House 1089 Acushnet avenue h do
" Robert L police b 98 Larch
" William C carpenter h 98 Larch
" William C Jr died April 15 1910
Barboza Alfred operative h 476 Maxfield
" Antonio operative h 84 Grinnell
" Jacinthe laborer h 54 Stephen
" John laborer b 630 South Water
" Joseph laborer h 73 Washington
" Joseph operative h r 216 South Front
" Joseph operative h 484 Maxfield
" Joseph C laborer h 317 S Front
" Lawrence J mariner h 206 North
" Manuel grocer 439 Belleville av h 121 Collette
" Manuel laborer h 5 Mitchell [av
" Manuel mill hand h 204 Belleville
" Manuel operative h 103 N Front
" Mariano mill hand b 126 Dartmouth
Barcells Joseph drill worker b 61 Fifth [Grove
Barcelon Joseph weaver h 300 Cedar
Bardsley Caroline H Mrs weaver h h 175 County
" Charles loom fixer h 47 Covell
" Edwin Jr overseer Bristol Mill h 10 Warren
" James fixer b 95 Bowditch
" John weaver h 563 North Front
" John Jr weaver h 95 Bowditch
" John R loom fixer b 41 Rivet
" Lees spinner h 124 Whitman
" Ralph overseer Acushnet Mill Corp bds 101 Bonney [yer
" William operative b 332 Saw-
Bargain Clothing Co The 339 Acushnet avenue
Barger Joseph weaver b 52 Ashley
Baribeau Abbie Mrs mill hand bds 51 Tallman [Joyce st
Barie Polidor baker 238 State h

Don't dream of what you are going to do! Go and do it.
Kinyon's Short-hand School
Odd Fellows Bldg., Cor. William and Pleasant Sts., New Bedford, Mass.

Bariteau Charles painter b 246 State
" Charles second hand h 84 Whitman
" Moise teamster h 246 State
Barker Amelia Mrs h 27 Jouvette
" Amelia F widow Robert T b 290 Pleasant [Grinnell
" Emily K widow Charles W h 112
" Florence A bookkeeper 202 N Water b at South Dartmouth
" Frances widow John R h 443 Pleasant [h 238 Tremont
" Fred G lunch 224½ Union
" Harold carpenter bds 154 Whitman [est
" Helena A widow Henry h 69 For-
" Hugh fixer h 21 Independent
" Lord baker 24 Cove h do
" Margaret widow Thomas h 226 Union [857 Kempton
" Mary A H sewer 40 Purchase h
" Robert painter b 33 Lexington
" Thomas loom fixer h 118 Cove
" Thomas removed from city
" Thomas weaver h 45 Winsor
" William h 21 Independent
" William twister h 1011 County
" William C rms 95 School
" William J clerk 134 Purchase h 102 Parker
Barkers Ezra V salesman 385 Acushnet avenue [h 49 Maxfield
Barkett George teamster h 250 Cog-
" Saber operative b 250 Coggeshall
Barkley John, R R engineer h 49 Maitland
Barlow Arthur W folder b 19 Ashley
" Elizabeth Mrs h 19 Ashley
" Elizabeth D Mrs h 29 McGurk
" James h 24 Cove road
" Jesse F carpenter h 15 Chestnut
" John J operative h 234 Dean
" Lawrence C clerk b 15 Chestnut
" Peter M engineer Bennett Mill h 178 Collette
" Samuel weaver b 24 Cove road
" William h 16 Viall
" William electrician 158 Purchase
Barnaby Eugene teamster rms 602 Purchase [kiln Hill road
" Hiram dyer b Hawes near Tar-
Barnes Alice variety 78 Cove h do
" Ann Mrs h 144 Church
" Avis Mrs b 64 Mill [Cottage
" B Frank copper worker h 450

Barnes
" David gardener h 265 Middle
" Elmira K widow William H dressmaker 158 Grinnell h do
" Emily clerk 185 Union b 52 Fifth
" George shoemaker 226 Shawmut avenue h do [Grove
" Harold iron worker b 344 Cedar
" Henry machinist h 168 Belleville road
" Henry weaver b 344 Cedar Grove
" Henry physician 1416 Acushnet avenue h do
" Henry F laborer h 43 Bethel
" John tailor 136 Blackmer h do
" Joseph insurance agent 120 Purchase h 114½ Fifth
" Joseph spinner h 32 Viall
" Joseph spinner h 190 Nash road
" Melvin agent b 142 Pleasant
" Rose widow William h 35 Acushnet avenue [mut av
" Walter bricklayer h 215 Shaw-
" William T removed from city
Barnet David shoes 1219 Acushnet avenue h 88 Kenyon
" Goldie bookkeeper b 88 Kenyon
" Philip student bds 88 Kenyon
" Samuel student bds 88 Kenyon
" Thomas E laborer h 908 County
" William mill hand h 82 Dean
Barney Albert J Jr salesman 106 Front h 241 Summer

BENJ B BARNEY
COUNSELLOR AT LAW
Rooms 11 and 12 Masonic Bldg
Pleasant Street
Residence 3 North Orchard
Corner Court Street
Telephone

HASKELL BROS. DEALERS IN
ICE
400 COURT STREET TELEPHONE CONNECTION NEW BEDFORD, MASS.

Barney Benj B city solicitor 204 Municipal bldg and counsellor at law 11 and 12 Masonic bldg h 3 N Orchard
" Charles W h 38 Pearl
" Edwin L Jr assistant clerk of courts for Bristol county h 104 Ash (S)
" Lawrence H mayor's secretary rm 203 Municipal bldg b 96 State
" Mary H widow Edwin L h 96 State
" Morgan naval architect h 81 Fourth avenue
" Paul A student bds 226 Shawmut avenue
Barnum James E constable 307 Times bldg h 7 Jenny Lind
" James H salesman Anthony Swift & Co h 799 First
Barnwell Elliott overseer rms 16 Fifth
" Middleton S Rev assistant St Martin's Episcopal church b 21 S Sixth
Baron Adelard (Baron, Servais & Co) h 799 First
" Alexander driver h 409 N Front
" Alfred driver b 409 North Front
" Aloysius S weaver b 257 Coffin av
" Arthur carpenter b 88 Tallman
" Czeslaw carder b 13 Hampton ct
" Fred teamster h 409 N Front
" George T (Joseph Baron & Son) 868 Purchase b 43 Highland
" Hormidas iceman h 214 Coffin avenue
" James changer over h 1248 Rockdale av
" James weaver bds 76 Hathaway
" John S boss picker h 27 Margin
" John W operative h 16 Abbott
" John W tinsmith 28 North Water b 43 Highland
" Joseph (Joseph Baron & Son) 868 Purchase h 43 Highland
" Joseph weaver b 811 First
" Joseph & Son (Joseph and George T Baron) jewelers 868 Purchase
" Joseph L weaver h 6 Blackburn
" Lawrence weaver b 1248 Rockdale avenue
" Napoleon fixer h 811 First
" Napolean operative b 102 Whitman
" Napolean paver b 954 S Water
" Oliver carpenter h 88 Tallman
" Samuel removed to Rochester N Y

Baron
" Servais & Co (Adelard Baron & August Servais) carriage painters Acushnet av cor Sawyer
" Thomas weaver h 345 Davis
" Walter weaver rms 37 Ashley
" William driver b 409 N Front
" William machinist b 303 Tinkham
" William weaver h 4 Harmony
Barr Benjamin blacksmith h 217 Grinnell
" James H blacksmith's helper h 217 Grinnell
" John G salesman 29 Purchase b 217 Grinnell
Barre Arthur carpenter h 1781 Acushnet avenue
Barread Andrew laborer bds 658 Purchase
Barreau John R drapery foreman 36 Purchase b 223 Park
" Livien fisherman b 310 N Front
Barrell Edgar A organist Grace church and music teacher 371 County h do
Barrett Annie Mrs h 327 Tinkham
" Benjamin weaver h 30 Cove
" Catherine widow Patrick h 483 Kempton
" Colin watchman h 8 Harmony
" Colin Jr fish 1085 S Water h 1073 do
" Elizabeth widow Jeremiah b 181 Middle
" Elizabeth A dressmaker 181 Middle h do
" Ernest weaver h 12 Woodlawn av
" Fred spinner h 23 E French av
" Henry weaver h 186 State
" Irving shoemaker h 219 North
" John R salesman h 278 Cedar
" John W weaver h 155 Fair
" Katherine C clerk 147 Union b 35 Crapo
" Leo P mill hand b 63 Nash road
BARRETT MFG CO tar products 297 Franklin Boston See front cover
" Mary widow William bds 37 Phillips avenue
" Mary E widow William h 207 Brock avenue
" Patrick glass blower h 35 Crapo
" Patrick J liquors 124 Union b 483 Kempton
" Rose widow Whitney b 223 Acushnet av
" Samuel C helper b 37 Phillips av
" Thomas laborer h 973 Kempton

J. F. CROSSLEY 223 MILL STREET COR. EMERSON PHONE
STEAM and HOT WATER HEATING
GAS FITTING and FIXTURES

Barrett
" William died Feb 5 1911
" William J salesman h 181 Middle
Barrette Joseph laborer b 301 Sawyer [County
Barriteau Alfred quarryman h 884
" Alfred Jr operative b 884 County
" Arthur back boy b 884 County
" Arthur lineman U St Ry Co h 623 Acushnet avenue [niman
" Charles second hand h 8 Pen-
" Edward L machinist 8 Seneca b 623 Acushnet avenue
" Ida operative h 31 Nye
" Joseph L copper worker h 623 Acushnet avenue
" Joseph V foreman h 52 Hicks
" Victor quarryman h 288 Cedar Grove
" Wilfred laborer h 96 Ashland
" William operative b 8 Penniman
Barron Isaac meat cutter 163 Union h 53 South Second
" Stephen laborer h 251 Coggeshall
Barros Boa Centura seaman h 418 S Water
" Henry J cook h 14 Griffin
" Joao laborer h 9 Stapleton
" John mason h 169 Rockland
" Joseph bds 14 Griffin [do
" Joseph de barber 177 S Water h
" Lawrence laborer h 221 S Water
" Leando laborer h 403 S Water
" Leonora Mrs grocer 377 Hillman h do
" Manuel operative b 42 S Water
" Manuel C fireman h 103 Phillips avenue
" Mary Mrs h 27 Union
" Samuel laborer h 377 Hillman
Barrows Alice L clerk 112 William b 21 Tremont
" Allan helper b 64 Thomas
" Arthur K h 21 Tremont
" Eugene M bookkeeper (George Kirby Jr Paint Co) h 21 Tremont [Hawthorn
" Frank C postmaster P O h 215
" Frank C Jr student b 215 Hawthorn
" Fred D painter b 486 County
" Frederick S Jr salesman 6 Purchase bds 319 Acushnet av
" Frederick S Mrs h 319 Acushnet avenue

Barrows
" Harry restaurant 173 Purchase and 345 Acushnet avenue rms 205 Pleasant
" John H assistant treasurer T N B Copper Co h 64 Thomas
" John T laborer h 181 Bonney
" Joseph A second hand h 25 Lombard
" Joseph W died Feb 5 1911
" Manuel A mule spinner b 25 Lombard [Lombard
" Mary widow Joseph A bds 25
" Mary J widow E Nelson h 87 School [thorn
" Murray F salesman b 215 Haw-
" Rose Mrs grocer 179 Bonney h 181 do [school b 64 Thomas
" Sarah D teacher Phillips avenue
" Sarah M widow John N h 486 County
Barry Ann Mrs h 339 Rivet
" Clarice b 96 Elm [more
" Edmund J shoemaker h 123 Syca-
" Edward foreman 474 Acushnet av
" Eudora K teacher Acushnet av school b 186 Maxfield
" Jeremiah stone cutter h 304 Cedar
" John copper worker h 141 Cedar Grove [89 Fourth
" John D (M F Barry & Son) b
" John J porter 84 Union b 186 Maxfield [do
" John W manager 162 Union b 109
" John W removed from city
" Mable F tailoress 129 Union b 89 Fourth
" Martin fireman h 32 Richmond
" Matthew F (M F Barry & Son) tailor 129 Union h 89 Fourth
" M F & Son (Matthew F and John D Barry) tailors 129 Union
" Patrick laborer b 232 N Second
" Philip operative b 141 Cedar Grove
" Polydor baker King Croft
" Richard laborer h 186 Maxfield
" Richard laborer h 966 County
" Thayer & Co cotton 43 William
" Thomas G overseer City Mfg Co
" William W, U S N h 96 Elm
Barsalou Vital laborer h 158 Central avenue [Cedar Grove
Barselou Joseph operative h 300

CHARLES A. CROSHERE CARRIAGE AND AUTO
38 FOURTH ST. Bell Phone 1964-23 **PAINTING**

Barselou
" Laura clerk 40 Purchase b 113 Kempton [Sawyer
" Lora and Lumina operatives h 327
Barsley Jack mill hand h 332 Sawyer
Barstow Ann widow William b 101 Bonney
" Ann H bds 337 Orchard (S)
" Charles H foreman 42 Front h 175 William [337 Orchard (S)
" Charlotte L widow Ebenezer T h
" Herbert F clerk 98 Allen h 257 Maple
" William P clerk h 325 Cottage
Bartalow Josephine Mrs h 975 South Water [Acushnet av h do
Bartel Elizabeth Mrs grocer 437
Bartels Felix b 109 Hawthorn
Barthelmy Eugene E mason 254 Tinkham h do [Coggeshall
Barthiaume Cyrille C mason h 485
" Francis clerk b 485 Coggeshall
Bartholo Alipio C salesman 67 William h 402 South Front
Bartholomew James I Rev pastor County street M E church h 40 Chestnut [Cottage
Bartle Arthur W laborer h 539
Bartlett Charles H machinist h 190 Summer [William
" Clara G widow George F h 190
" Clarence H clerk 20 Market b 190 William
" Clifton W bookkeeper Dartmouth M Corporation h 2 N Orchard
" Elizabeth R dressmaker 108 Seventh b do
" Lydia M died Sept 14, 1910
" Manuel removed to Fairhaven
" Robert A clerk Acushnet Mill Corporation h 268 Palmer
" Robert W commission merchant 97 William rm 302 h 184 Cottage
" William H commission merchant h 30 Court [County
Bartley Annie M widow Martin h 688
" James (Bay State Provision Co) 878 Purchase h at Providence
" Martin died May 14 1911
" & Robert proprietors Bay State Provision Co 878 Purchase
Bartlomiej Dabroushi clerk 677 First h Scott [yer
Barton Arthur machinist h 229 Saw-
" Elizabeth died Sept 16 1910
" John J twister h 354 Earl
" Marie nurse rms 321 Union
" Oswald twister b 209 Tinkham
" Richard J twister h 349 Davis
" Wilfred F twister b 209 Tinkham
Bartow Elbert W pilot h 48 Ocean
Bartz Alexandria M removed from city [577 S Second
Basinski St Rev Polish priest h
Baskin Barnard baker h 15 Howland
" Charles M shoe repairer 980 Acushnet av h 132 N Front
" Rebecca widow Hyman h 37 Prospect
Bass Albert laborer h 11 Holly
" Archie laborer h 109 Phillips av
" Joseph h 11 Holly
" Pierre laborer bds 11 Holly
" Zacharie laborer bds 96 Davis
" see Bastarache
Bassani Peter removed from city
Bassett Albert H 2nd drill maker h 63 Durfee [fee
" Albert H 3rd machinist b 63 Dur-
" Almira D died Feb 25 1911
" Alvah H clerk 193 Purchase b 166 Mill [ushnet av
" Andrew H provisions h 2367 Ac-
" Charles M (William A Bassett Co) 193 Purchase b 166 Mill
" Ellery R electrical engineer h 160 North
" Gardner C electrical engineer b 160 North [b do
" Helen music teacher 160 North
" Irene M kindergartener Cedar st school h 166 Mill
" Irving L teamster h 384 Cottage
" Mattie S widow Charles H h 2367 Acushnet avenue
" Robert painter h 204 N Front
" Thomas E weaver h 42 Roosevelt
" Walter H manager 170 Purchase h 347 Union
" William laborer b 23 Kenyon
" William spinner h 235 Shawmut av [fish 193 Purchase
" William A Co (Charles M Bassett)

J. G. NICHOLSON
LUMBER, SASH, DOORS and BLINDS
BOWDITCH STREET, NEW BEDFORD, MASS.

Bassette Emma clerk 1009 Acushnet avenue b 1090 do [ton court
Bassinet Arthur weaver b 25 Mor-
" Edgar weaver b 25 Morton court
" Frank weaver b 25 Morton court
" Joseph laborer b 808 First
" Joseph weaver h 25 Morton court
" Louis laborer h 808 First
" Louis Jr laborer b 808 First
" see Bazinet and Bissonnette
Bastarache Aimee laborer h 17 Holly
" Simeon fisherman bds 17 Holly
" see Bass
Bastek Joseph mill hand bds 10 Nye
Bastien Aldea L clerk 40 Purchase b 179 Collette
" David b 301 Sawyer
" George news agent b 301 Sawyer
" Simeon J overseer Taber mill h 179 Collette [F b 315 Pleasant
Batchelder Florence A widow Charles
" Percy civil engineer 164 William h 29 Dartmouth
" Ward C h 111 Maple
Batchelor Fennimore G draughtsman 100 Fifth h 65 Cottage
" George H treasurer N B Institution for Savings h 193 Cottage
" Mary J widow Benjamin S h 187 Cottage
Bate William removed from city
Batelho Antonio hairdresser 257 Fourth h 188 Thompson
Bateman Charlotte Mrs housekeeper 125 David [land
" Edna T clerk 185 Union b 46 Ash-
" Estella G dressmaker 46 Ashland b do
" Thomas M Rev pastor First Primitive Methodist Church h 46 Ashland
Bates Albert spinner h 15 Mosher
" Benson C motorman h 61 Ocean
" Clarence A clerk 125 Middle b 494 County
" Edwin J h 96 Willis [man
" Eldoretta widow Orrin h 62 Hill-
" Ellen M widow Edwin A h 154 North
" James laborer h 21 E French av
" James C clerk 104 Ashland h 51 Mt Pleasant
" James R W salesman h 65 Elm

Bates
" James W (James W Bates Co) h 106 Ashland
" James W Co (James W Bates) grocers 104 Ashland
" John spinner b 76 Division
" J Clifford clerk 104 Ashland h 555 Mt Pleasant
" Kirby & Co (Frank R Kirby and Charles G Tripp) bakers and confectionery 48 Mt Pleasant
" Lonnie D manager b 71 Sycamore
" Lot B wholesale grocers 423 Acushnet av and vice president 43 William h 494 County
" Lot B Jr salesman 423 Acushnet av h 48 Summer [b 494 County
" Mary S bookkeeper 11 Commercial
" Olivia W h 22 North
" Sarah D bookkeeper 423 Acushnet avenue bds 494 County [h do
" Whitney E portraits 72 Thomas
Bath Joseph laborer h 34 Bowditch
Bathell Ernest operative h 12 Cove
Batista Manuel operative h 136 Thompson
Battey Charles T manager Electric Express h 570 Kempton
" Joseph clerk 213 Acushnet av h 53 Emerson (S) [Winsor
" William E G changer over h 44
Battistelli Fortunato clerk h 712 Acushnet avenue
Battles William A shoe findings 126 Union h 82 Morgan
Batty Samuel driver h 972 County
" Thomas laborer b 48 Washington
Baty John conductor h 72 Hathaway
" John K machinist 8 Seneca h 276 Earl
" Samuel operative bds 276 Earl
Baudette W M operative h 604 South Second
Baudoin Edmond E engraver 66 Pleasant and military instructor High school h 171 Court
Bauer Andrew drill maker h 10 Bourne
" Anna housekeeper 88 Sycamore
" Charles second hand h 1 Acushnet blks (south row) [h 30 Swift
" Charles J overseer Acushnet Mill
" Helen forelady b 225 Court
" John baker h 88 Sycamore

Steiger-Dudgeon Co.
"The WOMAN'S Store."
Tel. Bell 82 & 83, Branches connecting all depts.
" " 160 For Office only. Auto. 1211

SUMPTIONS, ASSORTMENTS AT ALL TIMES OF DEPENDABLE DRY GOODS

Bauer
" John overseer N B C M Corporation h 323 Earle
" John F loom fixer h 7 Harmony
" Joseph A eyelet maker h 411 Elm (W)
" Salome widow Henry b 225 Court
Bauldry Lyman C supt paper department P Corporation h at Fairhaven [lard
Baumann John weaver b 35 Wil-
" Rosina widow b 35 Willard
" William weaver h 35 George
Baumgartner Karl weaver b 155 Tallman [ville rd
Bausquet J B weaver h 168 Belle-
Baxendale Joseph loom fixer h 30 Howland Village
Baxter Grace b 21 South Sixth
" Mary widow h 383 Second
Bay State Chair Co (Asaph P Foster) rattan goods Prospect
" State Market Co provisions 878-882 Purchase
Bayeur Hector A grocer h 59 Cov-"
Baylies Alfred rem to Brooklyn N Y
" Arthur died Feb 8 1911
" Charles S salesman 8 Union h 2095 Acushnet avenue
" Clifford water registrar N B W W office 40 Masonic bldg b 92 Bedford [b 94 Bedford
" Edward W clerk Manoment Mill
" George H mechanician 51 Bedford h 111 Grinnell [Bedford
" John foreman 100 Fifth h 94
" Mary C widow John B h 92 Pedford [Bedford
" Robert L salesman 8 Union h 85
" Theodore B manager Hathaway's Theatre b 86 Bedford
" Wallace B salesman 23 N Water b 94 Bedford
" William flour and grain 8 Union premium department 7 Pleasant and cereals 1460 Acushnet avenue h 86 Bedford [net av
" William Jr artist rms 282 Acush-
Bayreuther John weaver h 20 Stapleton [Phillips
Bazinait Exilda widow Audultor h 101
Bazinet Edgar loom fixer h 21 Mosher
" Eli yardman h 116 W French av
" John (Margeson & Bazinet) plumbers 542 N Front h 94 Kenyon

Beacon Mfg Co cotton goods end Purchase
Beal John operative h 97 N Front
Beale Otis G foreman 38 N Second h 64 Willis
Beals Brayton helper 91 N Water
" Sadie M clerk Nonquitt bds at Acushnet [h 8 Anthony
Beaman David W supt 214 S Water
Bean Edmund E clerk 98 Allen h 46 Cottage [do
" Frank lunch 845 Purchase rms 602
Beanland Arthur steam fitter b E French avenue corner Butler
" David electrician 158 Purchase h 56 Valentine [av cor Butler
" Matthew steamfitter h E French
Bear John G shoemaker h 362 Earl
Beard Albert fireman h 119 Brock av
" John operative h 12 Marvin
" Mary J widow John D b 341 Coffin avenue [Allen
Beardsworth Alfred painter h 463
" William clerk 246 N Front h 3 Austin [Franklin
Bearse Clarence A carpenter h 7
Beatriz Frank operative bds 119 Division [sion
" Mamie S housekeeper 119 Div-
" Manuel S carpenter h 119 Division [Mrs Gibson's McGuirk st
Beattie Lawrence city employee b
Beaubien Louis teamster h 775 Purchase [149 State
Beaucaire Alfred hostler 8 Campbell h
" Frank third hand h 171 Tinkham
Beauchaine John B laborer h Milford
Beauchamp Frank clerk b 880 Purchase [53 Brock av
Beauchemin Amedee piano teacher
" Euclide died Feb 6 1911
" George R car painter b 53 Brock avenue [avenue
" Homer boss comber b 53 Brock
" L Arthur operative h 6 Warren
" Marie L clerk 419 N Front b 6 Washburn [Brock av
" Romeo painter U St Ry Co h 53
Beaudette Carrie Mrs h 975 S Water
" George draughtsman 251 Union rms 56 Walnut
" William removed from city
Beaudin Mary widow bds 56 Ashley
Beaudoin Eugene carpenter b 186 Dean

PELEG H. SHERMAN 506 COUNTY ST.
FUNERAL DIRECTOR AND EMBALMER
OFFICE PHONES. Bell 690.13 Auto 1305.
RESIDENCE PHONES. Bell 690.12. Auto. 1306.

Beaudoin
" Joseph h 194 Gendron
" Joseph h 335 Shaw
" Joseph weaver h 219½ Bowditch
" Louis carpenter h 219½ Bowditch
" Philip mason h 106 Bowditch
" Zepherin operative h 371 Pleasant
Beaudry Adore laborer h 20 Adams
" Charles laborer b 20 Adams
" Emilie h 154 Hawthorn
" Euclide Mrs mill hand h 29 Holly
" Felix fireman h 346 Cedar Grove
" John bartender 166 Coffin av h 67 Clark
" Joseph N bds 815 First
" Leon salesman 912 S Water h 12 Harmony
" Romeo removed from city
Beaulieu Anthony J canvasser bds 33 Delano
" Arthur operative bds 234 Coggeshall
" Chrysalogue granite 10 Juniper h do
" Francois spinner h 234 Coggeshall
" Henry (Fahey & Beaulieu) bds 29 Nye
" John B lather h 1 Harmony
" Joseph removed to Taunton
" Joseph slasher tender h 24 Cotter
" Joseph weaver bds 29 Nye
" Lazarre removed to Taunton
" Louis carpenter h 24 Cotter
" Louis Jr laborer h 12 Covell
" Margaret widow Henry h 33 Delano
" Napoleon overseer Nonquit Spinning Co h 29 Nye
" Ovilla spinner h 338 N Front
" Peter doffer bds 1 Clark
" Peter weaver h 20 Covell
" Philip overseer Soule Mill h 344 N Front
" Philomene widow John h 29 Nye
" Pierre teamster 1070 County h 31 Nye
" Raphael plumber h 24 Cotter
" Virginia widow Francois h 61 Bullard
Beaumont Ada W Mrs h 83 Kenyon
" Anson L clerk 98 Allen h 114 Fair
" Edward second hand Page Mfg Co

Beaumont
" Frederick E sign painter b 114 Fair
" Herbert second hand b 850 First
" Joseph W spinner h 1111 Coggeshall
" Louis laborer h 954 S Water
" Samuel spinner h 211 State
" William operative b 83 Kenyon
Beauparlant Jean B fish h 622 Maxfield
" Wilfred teamster h 8 Blackburn
Beaupre Mitchell weaver h 839 Acushnet avenue
" William removed to Quebec Canada
Beaur John baker h 88 Sagamore
Beauregard Alexander removed to Manville R I
" Alexis painter b 56 Dean
" Alfred hostler h 1183 Purchase
" Alphonse clerk 1112 Acushnet av
" Alphonse driver b 1183 Purchase
" Azaiaras baker h 75 Brock av
" Delphine widow Louis h 35 Dean
" Desire weaver h 141 Collette
" Edmonde laundryman h 199 Phillips avenue
" Frank carder h 658 First
" George barber 162 Purchase
" Hector operative h 275 N Front
" James carpenter 929 County h do
" Joseph weaver h 811 First
" Louis weaver h r 32 Acushnet av
" Lucien G barber h 366 State
" Ozias N manager 73 William h at Fairhaven
" Philip carpenter b 157 Davis
" William motorman b N Water c Elm
" Zepherin speeder tender h 211 Church
Beausang Allan L removed to Lynn
Beausoleil Joseph fisherman h 104 Cedar Grove
Beauvais Fortunat M druggist 1881-1883 Acushnet av h 60 Sylvia
" Wanton H S h 69 Fifth
Bebineau Edward plumber b 274 N Front
" Joseph carpenter b 274 N Front
" Peter fisherman h 274 N Front
Beche Joseph weaver h 431 Second
" Jules weaver b 531 S Second
Beck Edward S weaver b 16 Felton
" George W fixer h 15 Mosher
" John weaver b 16 Felton

COAL AND WOOD F. T. AKIN & COMPANY
HAY AND STRAW
WALNUT, COR. WATER, 84 PLEASANT ST., 25 WELD SQ.
129 COVE STREET WHF. FOOT OF COFFIN STREET

Beck
" Nicholas G bookkeeper 2 Rodman h 31 Cottage
" Simon weaver b 15 Mosher
" Thomas weaver b 16 Felton [way
" Thomas Jr weaver h 67 Hatha-
" William weaver h 165 Bates av
Becker Abraham tailor 146 Purchase h 275 Kempton [Cedar
" Annie E Mrs stenographer h 202
" Charles J teacher of penmanship h 202 Cedar
" Esther I bookkeeper 296 Acushnet av b 275 Kempton
" Horace removed from city
" William G removed to Holyoke
Beckett Harry operative h 67 Winsor [b 22 Nelson
Beckman Augusta widow Charles E
" Charles E (Briggs & Beckman) 35 Commercial h 243 Arnold
" Robert second hand h 22 Nelson
Beckwood Joseph helper h 33 Penniman [court
Bedan Peter operative h 17 Hampton
Bedard Eva telephone operator 57 N Second b 32 Parker
" Fabius foreman 19 Linden h at Fall River
" Firmin weaver h Hawes street
" Gaudoise blacksmith h 32 Parker
" Joseph drillworker b 40 Cove
" Lucien C Rev asst pastor St Anthony's church h 1359 Acushnet avenue
" Moise machinist b 61 Kenyon
" Oliva lunch N Front cor Coffin av h 361 Coggeshall [Bowditch
" Stanislas electricalworker h 332
" Thomas kettleman h 15 Peckham
" Wilbert operative b 330 N Front
Bedford Benjamin loom fixer bds 85 Tallman [net av
" Chester third hand b 1498 Acush-
" Chester H fixer b 92 County
" Evarado fixer h 85 Tallman
Bedlow Lucy C supervisor of drawing public schools b 20 Seventh
Bedon Joseph painter h 286 Mill
Bedord Salime second hand furniture 665 Purchase h 672 do
Bee John T fixer h 28 Winsor
Beech Leo plumber 91 N Water h 228 Tremont
Beehan Patrick laborer h 83 Larch
" William car repairer b 83 Larch
Beers Benjamin P glasscutter h 41 Dartmouth [Lake
" James C foreman 100 Fifth h 75
" Samuel W manager 172 N Water h 166 Park
Beetle Charles D boat builder East French av near Rodney h opposite do
" Charles H h 732 County
" John H surveyor h E French av near Rodney
" Ralph D teacher b J H Beetle's
" Rodolphus (estate) 8 Beetle lane
" Ruth D teacher George H Dunbar school b J H Beetle's [Liberty
Refuhs Catherine bookbinder bds 65
" Charles F baker 143 Purchase b 65 Liberty [ton
" John F shoemaker h 525 Kemp-
" William h 65 Liberty
Bega Vais mill hand bls 45 Phillips av
Begen Walter operative h 69 Linden
Begley Edward J (King & Begley) 978 Acushnet avenue h 847 Purchase [cery
" Edward J shoemaker h 150 Chan-
" Helen T removed to N Y City
" Joanna V removed to N Y City
" John shoemaker b 23 Oak
" Patrick J driver b 150 Chancery
Begue Emile weaver h 40 Roosevelt
Behonek Albert artist b 15 Bullard
" Frank removed to Dickinson N D
Beique Ernest doffer bds 351 N Front
" Eudore mill hand b 351 N Front
" Vitaline widow John h 351 N Front
Bejos Vasell mill hand b 48 Davis
Belair Henry shoemaker h 120 Collette
" Omer E (The Red Cross Shoe Co) 864 and 1494 Acushnet av b 1498 do
Beland Adolphe teamster h 275 State
" Arthur painter b 333 N Front
" Fred clerk 187 Weld b 86 Mt Pleasant [ty
" Wiliam steam fitter b 662 Coun-
Belanger Adelard loom fixer h 59 County
" Aldor painter b 319 Belleville av
" Alfred blacksmith h 170 Front

Bookkeeping, Shorthand, Typewriting, Penmanship, etc. Taught thoroughly at
Kinyon's Commercial School
Odd Fellows Bldg., Cor. William and Pleasant Sts., New Bedford, Mass.

Belanger
" Alfred chauffeur h 12 Bullard
" Alma driver h 180 Sawyer
" Armand laborer h 180 Sawyer
" Armand Jr laborer b 180 Sawyer
" Charles A clerk 806 Purchase h 66 Dean
" David S physician 125 Rivet h do
" Elizabeth widow Arthur b 871 Purchase
" Elzear speeder b 358 N Front
" Emile laborer h 155 Earle
" Emile laborer h 199 Phillips av
" Emile third hand h 86 Mott
" Felix operative b 195 N Second
" Honori weaver b 170 Rivet
" Isadore carpenter h 9 Viall
" John doffer h 125 Cove [man
" John B copperworker h 135 Whit-
" Joseph painter h 58 Covell
" Joseph second hand b 53 Ruth
" Joseph weaver bds 67 Coffin av
" Joseph weaver h 109 David
" Joseph weaver h 164 David
" Louis weaver h 92 Cove
" Louis weaver h 496 S Second
" Lucien blacksmith 454 Pleasant h 53 Hicks
" Lucien Jr operative b 358 N Front [David
" Malvina widow Archille h 109
" Michael laborer h 86 Mott [ond
" Minor A machinist h 150 N Sec-
" Oza bookkeeper b 131 Whitman
" Peter mill hand.bds 81 Davis
" Philip bds 86 Mott
" Romelard teamster b 53 Hicks
" Salut weaver b 170 Rivet
" Sifroid laborer h 170 Rivet
" Wilfred fixer h 102 Davis
Belloda Duncan hostler h 171 Cedar
Belforte Arthur bricklayer b 12 Rodney [Sawyer
Belisle Adeline Mrs weaver h 214
" Eugene mason h 28 Nye
" George carpenter b 27 Peckham
" George drillworker b 52 Fifth
" Gilbert conductor bds 28 Nye
" Henry carpenter h 109 Bullard
" Henry carpenter h r 288 Cedar Grove
" Hormidas weaver h 18 Bullard
" Napoleon carpenter h 27 Peckham [man
" Rosalie widow Joseph b 24 Tall-

Belisle
" Ulric conductor bds 28 Nye
" Victor mill hand bds 28 Nye
" Wilfred laborer h 8 Tallman
Beliveau Adelard removed from city
Bell Ann M Mrs variety 32 Dartmouth h do [land
" Ernest removed to Burnley Eng-
" Henry J operative h 455 Belleville avenue
" Joseph mill hand b 18 Holly
" Joseph H h 32 Dartmouth
" Owen porter 185 Union b 210 Brownell
" Richard hostler 50 Elm
" Robert moulder h 200 Dean
" William janitor 185 Union h 210 Brownell
Bellamy Alice Mrs h 191 Earle
" George H machinist h 244 Phillips avenue [287 N Front
Bellanger Joseph painter 14 Jean bds
" Lourice clerk 42 Weld bds do
Belleisle Alfred twister b 331 Belleville avenue [avenue
" Joseph watchman h 331 Belleville
Bellemare Leopold agent 101 Kenyon h 66 Tallman
Bellend Wilbraham mill hand h 132 Nye [Pleasant
Bellenoit Adrian J carpenter b 154 Mt
" Camille D carpenter h 42 Locust
" Edouard J clerk Cottage corner Durfee b 111 Mt Vernon
" Emille C compositor Standard b 111 Mt Vernon [Vernon
" Francis K carpenter h 111 Mt
" George E compositor Times h 145 State [164 Mt Pleasant
" Louis J carpenter 27 Bowditch h
" Victor F salesman 912 S Water h 94 Linden
Bellerose Jessie widow Louis dressmaker h 1081 County
" Joseph rms 255 North Front
" William clerk 634 First
Belliveau Ambrose b 86 Clifford
" Ambrose bds 178 Phillips avenue
" Angeline Mrs h 30 Belleville road
" Arthur fixer h 102 Eugenia
" Belonie carpenter h 180 Sawyer
" Calix laborer h 86 Clifford
" Calixte third hand b 102 Eugenia
" David mason b 429 Front

Bread, Cake, Pastry
RICHMOND & COMPANY 255-257 UNION STREET
Bell 993 Automatic 1022

Belliveau
" Ehipane carpenter b 286 N Front
" Jeffrey carpenter b 116 W French avenue
" Joseph h 189 Tinkham
" Joseph mill hand b 30 Belleville rd
" Maximillian carpenter h 159 Tinkham
" Vital teamster h 282 N Front
Bellmore Frederick H master mechanic Page Mfg Co h 596 S Second
Belmore Joseph engineer b 163 David
" Oscar H machinist h 457 Union
Belohlarvek Michael mill hand h 21 Bullard [man
Beloin Raphael weaver h 104 Tall-
Belvery Fred plumber h 531 N Front
Belyea Goerge E h 398 Orchard (S)
Benac Joseph hairdresser 1124 Acushnet avenue h 68 Kenyon
" Joseph E clerk Wamsutta Club h 9 McMurray terrace [shall
Benard John laborer rms 295 Cogge-
Bence Frederick W overseer h 104 Locust [Front
Bendaras Mariana laborer h 223 S
Bender Frank weaver h 32 Hollyhock
" Joseph pedlar h 119 Reynolds
Benedictis Anthony (Benedictis Bros) b 4 Willis
" Brothers (Anthony and Michael) shoe repairers 406 Purchase
" Michael (Benedictis Brothers) b 4 Willis [b 4 Willis
" Michael shoe repairer 105 Union
Beneducto Pasquale laborer b 692 Acushnet avenue [ney
Benevidez John blacksmith h 20 Jen-
" John laborer h 255 Allen
" Joseph carpenter h 509 River
" Joseph helper 185 Acushnet av b 255 Allen [h do
Benjamin Adonai painter 77 Bullard
" Albert b 53 Kenyon
" Archer fixer h 390 S Second
" Charles farmer h 507 Hathaway rd
" Clement carpenter h 311 Coffin av
" Donat operative h 49 Phillips av
" Egbert B clerk b 866 S First
" Flavien wood 20 Holly h do
" Frank h 815 Purchase
" Frank weaver h 815 Purchase
" Frank Jr operative bds 815 Purchase

Benjamin
" Hermidas carder h 202 County
" Hervey painter b 311 Coffin av
" Honorat clerk 1404 Acushnet av b 311 Coffin avenue [S Water
" Joseph clerk 962 S Water h 1020
" Laura sewer 185 Union b 202 County [Salisbury
" Octcave grocer 962 S Water h 48
" Olive L widow Isaac W h 50 Hill
" Ovila carder b 10 Lucas
" Philidor clerk h 48 Salisbury
" Philip laborer h 57 Kenyon
" Robert mariner h 467 S Water
" Stanislas variety 295 Rivet and pool 337 Rivet h 291 do [ton
Benn Calvin J teamster h 384 Kemp-
" Sarah widow Thomas h 7 Juniper
Bennardi Henry removed from city
Bennedetti Giuseppi rem from city
Bennett Abbie S died Oct 21 1910
" Albert spinner h 68 Hathaway
" Albert N clerk N Water corner Elm h at Fairhaven
" Annie mill hand b 90 Davis
" Arthur H supt 45 Hunter h 876 Rockdale av [183 Washington
" Charles A ticket seller R R sta h
" Charles O molder 229 N Water h 107 South [317 Middle
" Chester A driver 185 Union h
" Clifton J teamster b 317 Middle
" Department (department 1-2-3-4) N E Cotton Yarn Co 115 Coggeshall
" Edgar M toolmaker King's Highway h 135 Chestnut
" Eliza Mrs h 56 N Sixth
" Elmer E deck hand h 477 Cottage
" Elsie M teacher Harrington school b 477 Cottage
" Ernest A foreman round house h 361 Cedar [mer
" Esther widow Nelson h 141 Sum-
" Francis F paymaster Potomska Mills h 15 Fair
" Frank C mason and builder 131 Summer h do [ville av
" George M carpenter h 814 Belle-
" George T driver h 30 Potter
" Hannah E widow George W h 54 Howard avenue
" Horace S hoseman Hose 1 rms do [nolds
" James copperworker h 21 Rey-

GLOBE DYE HOUSE 220 SHAWMUT AVE.
J. N. J. LONHOLDT, PROP. Telephone Connections Goods called for and Delivered
Down town Office, 52 Pleasant St., Room 1 North End Office, 1014 Acushnet Ave.

Bennett
" Louisa A h 140 Newton
" Lulu M teacher Harrington school b 73 Forest [135 Chestnut
" Mabel E bookkeeper 645 County b
" Martha W widow Andrew h 73 Forest
" Mary A Mrs h 79 Linden
" Merton E furniture repairer 277 Purchase h 327 Cedar
" Milton carpenter b 54 Howard av
" Nellie Mrs h 482 Acushnet av
" Pamelia widow b 183 Washington
" Peter piper b 117 Bullard
" Richard H supt U St Ry Co h 31 Cottage
BENNETT ROBERT G undertaker 7 South Sixth h 57 do See advt Undertakers in Business Directory
" Rowell E carpenter h 97 Linden
" Samuel spinner h 111 S Water
" Samuel T woodworker h 105 Newton [Fifth
" Sarah R widow Jeremiah H h 57
" Stephen weaver h 9 W French av
" Susan C Mrs h 123 Kempton
" Willard B blacksmith h 2242 Acushnet avenue
" William H janitor Registry of Deeds bldg h 40 Mill
" Winfred W treas 28 N Water rms Y M C A [vue av
Benoit Agnes mill hand h 51 Belle-
" Albert painter b 325 N Front av
" Alfred F painter h 28 Linden
" Archille weaver h 198 Dean
" Arthur H (Benoit, Bourassa Co) 1249 Acushnet av h at Malden
" Bourassa Co (Arthur H Benoit and Joseph C Bourassa) clothiers 1249 Acushnet avenue
" Celina weaver h 340 N Front
" Charles H laundryman h 158 Thompson
" Clairinda h 340 N Front
" Damasse b 198 Dean
" Ernest drillworker b 131 Fourth
" Eusebe speeder h 82 Phillips av
" Henry plasterer h 735 Belleville av
" Isaac carder h 128 Rivet
" Joseph blacksmith 447 Kempton h 125 N Front

Benoit
" Joseph comber b 14 McGurk
" Joseph lineman h 218 Purchase
" Joseph Jr laborer b 125 N Front
" Joseph E agent 73 William h 131 Fourth [ton
" Joseph P blacksmith 447 Kemp-
" Josiah mason h 1017 Purchase
" Josiah teamster 35 Bowditch h 42 do
" Louis mason 407 Coggeshall h do
" May clerk 1081 Acushnet av b 27 Hicks
" Napoleon teamster h 12 Beetle
" Oliver H clerk 102 Weld h 268 do [ond
" Patrick carpenter h 516 S Sec-
" Philip P brakeman h 32 Bowditch
" Samuel G builder 188 Dean h do
" Stanislaus T jewelry 1075 Acushnet avenue and 143 Cove h 1075 County
" Victor mason h 69 Hicks
" Wilfred clerk 490 S Second h 600 do [Front
" William J brakeman bds 125 N
" William R police and (William R Benoit & Co) h 32 Bourne
" William R & Co (Perfection Wet Wash Laundry) r 28 Larch
Benson Ellen M widow John H h 83 Durfee
" Henry W helper h 46 Tremont
" John Leonard shoeworker b 82 Durfee
" Joseph H, U S N b 83 Durfee
" Martin laborer b 65 Washburn
" Mary widow Samuel h 14 Cottage [lantic
" Theophilus A chauffeur h 93 At-
Benss Autumn weaver h 57 Phillips avenue
" Joseph weaver b 57 Phillips av
Bent Alice E teacher Hosea M Knowlton school b 175 William
" John weaver h 24 Belleville rd
" Manuel laborer h 59 Crapo
" Manuel laborer h 125 Field
" Manuel Jr laborer h 55 Stowell
Bentley Arthur glassworker h 50 School [h 40 Bowditch
" Edwin L (F T Bentley & Son)

GREENE & WOOD Every Kind of LUMBER AND MILL WORK
PINE STREET, off So. WATER STREET, NEW BEDFORD

Bentley
" Edwin R foreman Adams Ex Co h 42 Hill [h 123 Fifth
" Frank T (F T Bentley & Son)
" Fred weaver b 157 Myrtle
" Fred J salesman 28 Union h 11 Homer
" F T & Son (Frank T and Edwin L Bentley) real estate agents 123 Fifth [er
" George B roll coverer h 24 Mosh-
" Hattie weaver bds 24 Mosher
" Joseph warper h 436 Orchard (S)
" Loring T h 40 Bowditch
" Mary Mrs h 620 Purchase
" Samuel E h 69 County [ty
" Samuel E 2nd student b 69 Coun-
Bento Antonio clerk h 90 Sidney
" Frank painter h 153 Acushnet av
" Manuel laborer h 69 Swift
" Manuel laborer h 46 Scott
Benton Charles Edward h 765 County
BENTON CHARLES E, PH B accountant and principal and proprietor Benton's Business School 97 William h 39 Ocean See map
" Frank mason h 257 Middle
BENTON'S BUSINESS SCHOOL Charles E Benton Ph B principal and proprietor 97 William See map
Bentson John mariner h 111 N Water [Grove
Benzel Charles laborer bds 137 Cedar
" Selma operative h 137 Cedar Grove
" William C died June 22 1911
Berard Alida clerk 1081 Acushnet av b 174 Ashland
" Frank painter 129 Eugenia h do
" Henri weaver h 799 First
" Joseph operative h 24 Ashley
" Napoleon J operative h 174 Ashland
" Napoleon J Jr (Berard & Co) druggist 274 Cedar b 174 Ashland [Second b 174 Ashland
" Rose A telephone operator 57 N
" & Co (Napoleon J Berard Jr) druggists 274 Cedar
Berenguier William twister h 118 Cove
Bergan William Frank chauffeur 87 Union h 16 Lindsey
Berger Joseph weaver h 52 Ashley
BERGER MFG CO of Mass metal ceilings 286 Devonshire Boston See page 753
Bergeron Adelard clerk 490 S Second h 180 Blackmer
" Alfred weaver h 59 County
" Arthur operative b 96 Holly
" Arthur weaver b 361 N Front
" Belino operative h 274 N Front
" Diana clerk 1105 S Water b 82½ Nye [ville av
" Edmond Jr operative b 53 Belle-
" Fortunate weaver h 71 Emma
" George A carpenter bds 145 Tallman
" Henry removed to Fairhaven
" Honore carpenter 132 Tallman h do [man
" Hormidas carpenter h 145 Tall-
" Hormidas clerk b 52 Briggs
" John laborer b 53 Belleville av
" John third hand b 76 County
" Joseph baker h 539 N Front
" Joseph driver 1070 County
" Joseph laborer h 202 State [dent
" Joseph mill hand h 48 Indepen-
" Joseph (Oliver & Joseph Bergeron) h 48 Independent
" Joseph weaver b 132 Tallman
" Ludger blacksmith h 122 Mott
" Napoleon furniture mover 114 Collette h do [ty
" Octave motorman h r 827 Coun-
" Oliver (Oliver & Joseph Bergeron) h 52 Briggs
" Oliver & Joseph (Oliver & Joseph Bergeron) provisions 188 Blackmer
" Omer carpenter h 270 Tinkham
" Onesephore boxmaker h 290 Collette
" Stanislaus laborer h 76 County
" Theodore carpenter 330 N Front h do [Merrimac
" Zepherim driver 81 Front h 60
Bergovitch Ally operative h 38 Washburn [S Water
Berkowitz Abraham blacksmith h 700
" Julius shoes 889 S Water h 105 South [h 7 Blackburn
Berman Max (N Y Upholstering Co)
Bernard Adelard D baker h 803 First [First
" Adelard D Jr machinist b 709

BONNEY, FOLSTER & CO.,
The North End's Shopping Centre
Dry Goods and Men's Furnishings
945-947 Acushnet Ave., New Bedford, Mass.

Bernard
" Albert driver b 7 McGurk
" Albert teamster h 43 Cleveland
" Albert J buyer 185 Union h 38 Buttonwood
" Arthur weaver b 194 Dean
" Clement weaver h 49 Salisbury
" Edward carpenter h 141 Phillips avenue [Gurk
" Emma widow housekeeper 7 Mc-
" Francis M president 1031 Acushnet av h 164 Brock av
" Isadore operative b 3 Marvin
" John laborer b 11 Logan
" Joseph carpenter b 36 Hazard
" Joseph weaver h 106 Beetle
" Lea Mrs variety 36 Hazard h do
" Maria widow h 45 Short [av
" Oza carpenter h 1547 Acushnet
" Robert P barber h 154 Collette
Bernardini Joseph laborer h 25 William
Bernhardt John fixer b 128 Cove
Bernier Arthur iceman h 301 Belleville road [Wilson
" Cyrille lunch 950 S Water h 73
" George fixer h 496 S Second
" George weaver h 53 Ruth
" George Jr weaver b 53 Ruth
" Henry b 31 Nye
" John fixer h 38 Ashley
" John spinner h 6 McGurk
" John E weaver b 38 Ashley
" Joseph A physician 311 Coggeshall h do [ville rd
" Placide operative b 301 Belle-
" William removed to Warren R I
Bernique Adrienne widow Joseph h 278 Nash road [road
" Lucien machinist h 47 Belleville
" Paul machinist b 278 Nash rd
Bernstein Abraham tailor 1482 Acushuet avenue h 23 Beetle
" Rose Mrs h 62 Kenyon
" Solomon shoe repairer 910 Acushuet avenue h 62 Kenyon
Bernt Frank bricklayer b 75 Clark
" Lillian bookkeeper N Water cor Elm b 75 Clark
Berong Conrad breweryworker 26 Brook h 115 Reynolds [av
Beront Fred laborer h 922 Acushnet
Berry Alfred shoemaker h 351 N Front
" Almont E removed to Fitchburg

Berry
" Annie Mrs h 101 Linden
" Chauncy I elevatorman b 161 Middle
" Daniel J machinist h 178 Kempton [road
" Horatio machinist h 336 Nash
" James driver 255 Union bds 200 Weld
" John weaver h 344 Coffin avenue
" John W bds 161 William
" Julia R Mrs h 161 Middle
" Margaret Mrs h 200 Weld
" Pedro removed from city [Fifth
" Rachel clerk 182 Union rms 63
Berthiaume Albert J brittania worker b 128 Rivet
" Emile carpenter h 9 Salisbury
" E Philip news depots 877 S Water h 23 Fair
" George died [av
" Samuel weaver b 452 Belleville
Bertholet Anias seamstress bds 64 Robeson
" August carpenter h 64 Robeson
" George student b 64 Robeson
" Julius carpenter b 64 Robeson
" Marie clerk b 64 Robeson
Bertignono George laborer h 1 Wall
Bertman Morris clothing 24 Arcade bldg [geshall
Berton John operative b 243 Cog-
" Joseph operative b 243 Coggeshall
" Levi laborer b 243 Coggeshall
" Peter died Nov 22 1910
Betram Douglas C city teamster h 332 Cottage
" Frank A glasscutter b 15 Bonney
" Frank M nurse h 15 Bonney
" John & Son (Lawrence E Bertram) roofers 59 Borden
" J Franklyn foreman 59 Borden h 202 Allen
" Lawrence E (John Bertram & Son) h 59 Borden
" Louis city teamster h 265 Cottage
" Myron H meterman 125 Middle b 15 Bonney
" Phoebe widow John h 68 Arnold
Bertrand Arthur speeder tender h 9 Nelson
" Edward barber h 862 First
" Ellen Mrs grocer 475 Belleville avenue h 90 Davis [shuet av
" John Mrs h Phillips av bey Acu-

M. P. B. Silva & Son BUILDERS
Estimates Furnished on all Kinds of Work
157 ACUSHNET AVENUE Both Phones NEW BEDFORD

Bertrand
" Joseph salesman 123 Union h 1332 Acushnet avenue
" Lorenzo waiter b 90 Davis
" Louis salesman h 90 Davis
" Louis weaver h 50 Salisbury
" Napoleon laborer h 8 Tallman
BERTRAND ONESPHORE painter 160 Bowditch h do See page 754
" Peter J teamster h 610 Purchase
" Yvonne clerk 475 Belleville av b 90 Davis
Bertuska Barbara h 47 Washburn
Beru Joseph da laborer h 929 County [vett
Berube Alfred operative h 92 Jou-
" Alfred Jr weaver b 92 Jouvett
" Antoine laborer b 186 Cove
" Antoine Rev pastor St Hyacinth's R C church h 163 County [net av
" Arelus carpenter b 1293 Acush-
" Arthur weaver h 96 Division
" Augustin h 1727 Acushnet av
" Charles watchman Acushnet Mill Corp h 94 Blackmer [av
" Daniel operative h 61 Acushnet
" Edward junk h 93 Perry
" Edward operative h 19 Nelson
" Germaine bds 163 County
" Henry C spinner h 292 Fourth
" Joseph weaver b 92 Jouvett
" Josephine widow Joseph h 63 Independent
" Jules operative h 2 Hazard ct
" Levi laborer b 94 Blackmer
" Louis carpenter h Acushnet av
" Louis P weaver b 1103 S Water
" Moise carder h 104 Jouvett
" Napoleon laborer b 186 Cove
" Ovilia widow Napoleon h 186 Cove
" Rose Mrs spinner h 80 Earle
" Simon removed from city
" Treffle Jr slubber tender h 610 S Second
" Vail third hand b 15 Nelson
" Victoria operative h 327 Sawyer
" Victoria widow Thomas h 113 Belville road
" Zenan fixer h 15 Nelson [N Front
Bervovolski Gustave operative h 176
Beserosky Harry clerk 1550 Acushnet av b 619 Purchase
Beserosky
" Lewis h 619 Purchase
" Simon clerk 740 Purchase h 78 Clark [619 Purchase
" Walter E salesman 123 Union b
" William variety 1500 Acushnet av and 740 Purchase h 76 Clark
Beserra Joseph F teamster b 269 Palmer
Besim Zaffo mill hand b 42 Davis
Bessarabian Jacob cigarett mfr 225 Coggeshall h 145 Belleville av
Besse Addie B operative bds 53 Bowditch [(S)
" Benjamin F coachman h 12 Ash
" Bertie W painter h 275 Cedar Grove [at Fairhaven
" Edward L supt 272 S Water h
" Frederick W solicitor 43 William h 281 Pleasant
" Henry W engineer h 176 Mill
" Joshua teamer 45 Weld h 53 Bowditch [Ash (S)
" Lemuel F clerk 146 Pleasant h 16
" Lott P machinist h 35 Tremont
" Millage G machinist h 207 Grinnell
" William H chauffeur b 305 Mill
Bessera Antone job team b 46 Emerson (S) [10 Viall
Bessette Adella clerk 912 S Water b
" Alcibiade weaver h 99 Holly
" Alexfort removed from city
" Alfred carpenter h 91 Hathaway
" Alfred carpenter h 153 Whitman
" Alfred machinist h 314 N Front
" Alfred M clerk 1598 Acushnet av h 79 Clark
" Alphonse machinist h 65 Kenyon
" Annie M clerk 70 Purchase b 100 Clark [av
" Arthur laborer h 922 Acushnet
" Arthur painter 18 Bullard h do
" Arthur E doffer bds 354 Cedar Grove [Tallman
" Arthur N freight checker h 131
" Augustus freight handler h 96 Holly [chase
" Azilda Mrs boarding h 880 Pur-
" Beloni machinist h 175 State [do
" Charles clerk 335 N Front b 333
" Dieudonne laborer h 186 Dean
" Donat clerk bds 10 Vaill [Bullard
" Edward clerk 357 N Front h 115½
" Edward painter 43 Hicks h do

Steiger-Dudgeon Co.
"The WOMAN'S Store."
Tel. Bell 82 & 83, Branches connecting all depts.
" " 160 For Office only. Auto. 1211

SUMPTIONS, ASSORTMENTS AT ALL TIMES OF DEPENDABLE DRY GOODS

Bessette
" Edward weaver h 53 County
" Edward L supt New Bedford Foundry & Machine Co h at Fairhaven
" Eli h 173 Collette
" Emma clerk 1009 Acushnet av rms 1090 do [yon h do
" Eulalie Mrs dressmaker 65 Ken-
" Fred clerk 1598 Acushnet av b 79 Clark [254 Cedar Grove
" George clerk 1201 Acushnet av b
" George molder 229 N Water h 525 N Front
" George H fixer h 13 Valentine
" Godfrois h 62 Phillips avenue
" Gregoire removed from city
" Hormidas operative bds 332 N Front
" Idala bookkeeper b 23 Bentley
" Jeremiah operative h 23 Bentley
" John weaver b 333 N Front
" Joseph (carpenter) rem from city
" Joseph fixer h 329 N Front
" Joseph helper 1201 Purchase
" Joseph second hand h r 11 Nye
" Joseph A weaver h 162 Whitman
" Joseph F clerk h 358 N Front
" Joseph O carpenter h 101 Holly
" Louis A groceries 61 Country h 131 Division
" L Victor clerk 28 William rms 209 Purchase [Bentley
" Maria clerk 364 Kempton b 23
" Melvina Mrs h 644 Purchase
" Michel weaver h 333 N Front
" Michel weaver h 28 Tallman
" Napoleon janitor 1448 Acushnet av h 1090 do [Grove
" Napoleon painter h 254 Cedar
" Noe laborer h 1757 Acushnet av
" Orpha widow h 49 Nelson
" Ozee operative b 43 Hicks
" Philamone widow Zephirin h 10 Viall
" Philip operative b 175 State
" Pierre removed to Fairhaven
" Rachel Mrs teacher Angel Guardian school h 254 Cedar Grove
" Rachel E clerk 40 Purchase bds 254 Cedar Grove
" Rameau plumber 915 Acushnet av rms Franklin cor Acushnet av
" Seth J clerk 100 Fifth and treas 272 S Water h 58 Arnold

Bessette
" Wilfred bds 186 Dean
" William A plumber h 201 Tinkham [State
" Zephir mgr 1066 County h 240
" Zephir second hand h r 11 Nye
Bessey Alice J Mrs h 184 North
" Allen second hand h 352 Davis
" Daniel F died Dec 16 1910 [dle
" James A pressman rms 150 Mid-
" John T whalebone cleaner 15 Hamilton rms 126 Purchase
" J Calvin master mechanic Beacon Mfg Co h 328 Coffin av
" Mabel R clerk 41 Purchase bds 184 North [Acushnet av
" Margaret widow Daniel F h 535
" William A plumber h 201 Tinkham [Belleville av
Bessick Manuel L operative h 382
Bessone Giovanni laborer h 6 Wall
Best Arthur weaver bds 76 Cove
" Caroline E asst public library b 30 Crapo [h 117 Maple
" Christopher A foreman 100 Fifth
" George butcher h 94 Rockland
" William J drillworker h 96 S Sixth [79 Morgan
Beswick Isla clerk 372 Kempton bds
" James mason h r 27 Peckham
" Thomas, U S N b r 27 Peckham
Betell Arthur spinner h 440 Pleasant
Betello John operative h 16 Cotter
Bettencourt Albert clerk 195 Court b 67 Acushnet avenue [sor
" Antone J elevatorman h 39 Win-
" Boaventura Jose furniture 147 County h 1 Independent
" Emily R bookkeeper 147 County b 200 Brock av [av
" Frank E painter h 64 Acushnet
" Joseph C laborer h 67 Acushnet avenue [fin av
" Joseph D A fireman h 194 Cof-
" Joseph J carpenter b 160 County
" Joseph M h 181 Acushnet av
" Joseph S laborer h 68 Dartmouth
" Joseph S laborer h 149 Field
" Julius drillworker b 11 Oak
" Louis porter Morris & Co b 254 S Second
" Manuel fireman b 39 Mosher
" Manuel operative h 23 Spooner
" Manuel F shoe repairer 136 Washington h 179 Grinnell

PELEG H. SHERMAN 506 COUNTY ST.
FUNERAL DIRECTOR AND EMBALMER
OFFICE PHONES. Bell 690-13. Auto. 1305.
RESIDENCE PHONES. Bell 690-12. Auto. 1306.

Bettencourt
" Manuel J laborer b 4 Washington
" Manuel S laborer h Winterville road
" Marceline operative h 11 Oak
" Maria E h 4 Washington
" Mary L clerk 182 Union bds 68 Dartmouth
" Mary I clerk 182 Union bds 68
" Mary L widow h 254 S Second
" Rose Mrs h 179 Grinnell
Betteridge Mary widow Michael F h 75 Ash (N) [ant rms 142 do
Betts George E machinist 146 Pleas-
Beveridge Ann widow John h 105 Bonney
" Hugh (Blackstone Valley Comb Works) 100 Bonney h do
" Margaret housekeeper 105 Bonney
Bezerre Frank operative h 237 Coggeshall
Bezetta John mill hand h 648 First
Bibber John S capt steamer New Hampshire h 314 Arnold
Bibbey John operative h 141 Collette [Bullard
" Joseph H mule spinner h 136
" Thomas operative h 60 Peckham
" William J mill hand h 102 Nash road [velt
Bibby Albert operative h 93 Roose-
Bibeau Albert shoemaker b 60 Bullard
" Arthur operative b 40 Bullard
" Eugene mill hand b 40 Bullard
" George mason h 103 Perry
" Maxime carpenter b 418 N Front
" Oliver operative h 40 Bullard
" Pierre fixer b 40 Bullard
Bicher Joseph h 89 Ruth
Bickford Marion E telephone operator 57 N Second b 85 Morgan
Bickustaff James mill hand h 1 Cornell place
Bielawstro Peter weaver h 203 Belleville av [lette
Bienia Josef mill hand h 101 Col-
Bienvenue Gedeon weaver h 4 Coffin avenue court
" Rudolph h 22 Ashley
Bierzerd John weaver b 475 S Front
Bigelow Alfred P motorman h 10 Penniman [net av h 46 Park
" Edward P furniture 292 Acush-
Bilawa Andrew mill hand h r 8 Beetle
Billani Antonio shoemaker h 519 Purchase [ison
Billing Andrew laborer h 72 Div-
Billings Avery D removed from city
Billington Charles variety 34 Brock av h 133 Ruth [Stapleton
" Elizabeth widow William h 32
" George slasher tender h 17 Social
" Henri twister h 124 Cove
" John fixer h Braley road
" Thomas grocer 8 Linden h 93 do
Billodeau Arthur barber h 125 Webster court [tle
" Caroline widow Louis bds 98 Bee-
" Delphine operative h 98 Beetle
" Jeremiah weaver b 395 N Front
" Joseph h 395 North Front
" Leon teamster b 166 Bates av
" Ludger weaver b 395 N Front
" Mary L operative bds 163 Weld
" Napoleon mill hand h 12 Beetle
" Wilfred laborer h 166 Bates av
Bilsborrow Alfred painter b 27 Viall
" Alice b 949 County
" John weaver b 949 County
" John J clerk h 1049 S Water
" Mary widow James h 290 Fourth
" William (Gill & Bilsborrow) 704 Purchase h 949 County
Bindas Josef weaver h 18 Hampton ct
" Stanislaus operative h 18 Fulton court [b 209 Purchase
Binette Edmond editor 101 Kenyon
Bingham Allen R foreman paper box department P Corporation h at Fairhaven [h 163 Arnold
Binkley William R supt 43 William
Binnette Lucien weaver h 412 N Front
Binns Abraham weaver h 28 Holly
" Eli twister h 105 Thompson
Birch Abraham spinner h 20 Woodlawn avenue
" Isabella Mrs h 145 Ashland
" John Edmond agent h 207 State
" Theresa A C dressmaker 207 State h do
Birchall Ellis spinner h 24 Cove
Bird Alfred spinner b 253 Cedar Grove [h 920 Belleville av
" Horace A hoseman Engine No 9
" John spinner b 51 Howland Village [berty
" Sarah E widow William h 73 Lib-
Birdsall John W weaver h 349 Davis
" Walter h 53 Ashley

PAINTERS' SUPPLIES
Walnut, Cor. Water, 84 Pleasant St. 25 WELD SQ., 129 COVE ST.
F. T. AKIN & COMPANY

Birdswell John fixer h 349 Davis
Biron Albert carpenter b 84 Clifford
" Arthur carpenter b 2471 Acushnet avenue
" Moise carpenter h 84 Clifford
" see Byron [mac av
Birtwistle Alice operative b 2 Merri-
" Christopher J clerk 185 Union b 2 Merrimac avenue
" Frank dentist 1265 Acushnet av h do [avenue
" Joseph shoemaker b 2 Merrimac
" Theresa widow James h 2 Merrimac avenue [Front
Birzadetski Louis carder h 85 North
Bisallion Adelard driver b 1191 Purchase
" Dimina teamster h 1191 Purchase
" Dimina Jr teamster b 1191 Purchase
" Joseph clerk 1071 Acushnet av
Bisbee George D died April 15 1911
" Gertrude telphone operator 57 N Second b 239 Acushnet av
" Mary widow Charles F h 239 Acushnet av [ket b 122 Middle
Bischoff Alma M bookkeeper 20 Mar-
Bisheau Frank operative h 292 Cedar Grove [eca
Bishop Arthur laborer h 154 Sen-
" Fanny Q widow Edward B b 17 Willis
" Joseph laborer b 307 Coggeshall
BISHOP J W CO (Worcester) builders and contractors 410-411 Times bldg See page 19
" Mary R Mrs h 63 Mechanics lane
" Phillip engineer b 1098 Acushnet avenue
Bisi John operative h 52 Kenyon
Bisiadecki Letan mill hand h 85 North Front [River road
Bismore Albert H city laborer h 217
Bisoski Joseph weaver h 18 Morton court [Clark
Bissett Abbie M bookkeeper bds 100
" Robert stonecutter h 100 Clark
Bisson John carpenter h Hawes
Bissonette Alcide blacksmith 13 Beetle b at Acushnet
" Arthur blacksmith h 12 Nye
" Ephraim blacksmith 13 Beetle h 21 Acushnet avenue
" Frank weaver b 25 Morton court

Bissonette
" Louisfirre blacksmith 13 Beetle b at Acushnet
" Ludger removed to Fairhaven
" Magloire F blacksmith 13 Beetle h at Acushnet
" Marcil driver h 15 Nelson
Bissot Athenaise widow Edouard h 182 Hathaway [way
" Joseph operative b 182 Hatha-
Bittar Joseph operative h 174 Clifford
Bittner Paul butcher h 15 Bullard
Bixby Miles F machinist h 340 Cottage [Belleville av
Bizzaro Manuel M operative h 171
Bjelahlavek Frank chauffeur b 348 Davis
" John mill hand h 348 Davis
Bjorngren J glasscutter b 2 Cornell court [Front
Bjurstrom Axel weaver h 259 N
Blacha Antone weaver h 39 Hicks
Black Agnes b 17 Franklin
" Alfred A cook 5 S Sixth h 293 Maxfield [ty
" Annie E widow James h 197 Coun-
" Edward J clerk 277 Cedar b 17 Frnklin
" Emma F Mrs h 4 Oak st court
" George H master mechanic Kilburn Mill h 61 Valentine
" Jacob h 237 Acushnet avenue
" Mabel R clerk b 17 Franklin
" Paul J laborer b 17 Franklin
" Peter rigger 72 Front rms at Fairhaven
" Robert H laborer h 17 Franklin
" William M engineer 8 Katharine b 17 Franklin [Cedar Grove
Blackburn Ellen operative b r 279
" George removed from city
" John weaver h 279 Cedar Grove
" Lillian widow weaver h 106 Bowditch
" Martha Mrs h 1045 County [av
" Richard laborer b 1137 Acushnet
" Robert weaver h 279 Cedar Grove
" Sarah housekeeper 279 Cedar Grove
" Thomas machinist h 366 Purchase
" Warren H machinist b 50 Bedford
" William h r 279 Cedar Grove
" William forger h 50 Bedford

There's room at the top for young men and women who can do things right.
Kinyon's Commercial School
Odd Fellows Bldg., Cor. William and Pleasant Sts., New Bedford, Mass.

Blackie Sarah A widow Charles F h 16 Grape
Blackington Albert shoemaker b 373 Cottage [entine
Blackledge Joseph fireman h 60 Val-
" Robert weaver b 246 Nash rd
Blackler Amanda M widow William G h 111 Summer [French av
Blacklock George designer bds 24 W
Blackmer Arthur L treas 223 N Second h 675 County
" Cut Glass Co 223 N Second
" C Lester removed from city
" Herbert A druggist 167 Purchase b 46 S Sixth [Abbott
Blackshaw William blacksmith h 14
Blackstone Valley Comb Works (Hugh Beveridge) 100 Bonney
Blackwell Emily J Mrs h 239 Chancery [way
Blacow Richard fixer h 110 Hatha-
" Thomas grinder h 9 Harmony
Blades Thomas fixer h 40 Woodlawn avenue
Blagdon William removed from city
Blain Amedee blacksmith 30 Bethel b 24 Nye [382½ N Front
" Dalma blacksmith 30 Bethel h
" Edmonde blacksmith 30 Bethel b 24 Nye
" Elzeard removed to Worcester
" John B weaver h 12 Nye
" Modeste carpenter h 24 Nye
Blair Hugh weaver h 100 Jouvett
" John K (Blair Sign & Advertising Co) 60 Fourth h do
BLAIR SIGN & ADVERTISING CO (John K Blair) 60 Fourth See page 754
Blais Adjutor clerk 1027 Acushnet av b 96 Holly
" Azarie carder h 162 Hathaway
" Charles hairdresser 120 Cove h 21 Acushnet av
" Ernest removed from city
" John B spinner h 198 Tinkham
" John B weaver h 971 County
" Joseph P operative h 68 Tallman
" Noe weaver h 111 Beetle
" Oscar painter b 248 Bowditch
Blaisdell A B (Blaisdell & Snyder) 956 Acushnet avenue h at Haverhill [183 Kempton
Blake Clara S clerk 166 William b
" Edward teamster h 128 Nash rd

Blake
" George A removed to Boston
" James E h 183 Kempton
" Pierce J salesman 140 Purchase rms 245 do
" Robert P removed to Boston
" Thomas laborer h 117 Tremont
" Walter P removed from city
Blakeley Albert clerk bds 154 Whitman [h 154 Whitman
" Benjamin clerk 374 Purchase
" Lewis clerk 1612 Acushnet av b 288 Earle [duit
Blakey Albert P boarding 51 Con-
Blanchard Edmond carpenter h 495 Coggeshall [geshall
" Edmond W plumber bds 495 Cog-
" Ernest blacksmith h 56 Ashley
" Felix carpenter Centre av
" Fessenden S operative rms 270 Pleasant
" Frederick roofer bds 275 State
" John B clerk h 16 Bentley
" John L laborer h 275 State
" Joseph hairdresser 81 William h 16 Tallman
" Joseph O fixer h 290 Davis
" Louis blacksmith b 56 Ashley
" Margaret widow Charles h 114 W French avenue
" Martin Jr h 39 Smith
" Philias carpenter h end Central av
" Philias iceman h 104 Whitman
" Ray L asst foreman h 17 Bonney
" Thomas machinist b 275 State
" see Blanchette [Front
Blanchette Adelard weaver h 330 N
" Albert engineer City Coal Co h 132 Bullard
" Albini carpenter h 113 Belleville road [County
" Amedee clerk 56 N Water b 140
" Amedee weaver h 113 Collette
" Celine milliner 364 Kempton and dressmaker 140 County b do
" Charles A slasher h 103 Ruth
" Elzear carpenter b 105 Bullard
" Ernest blacksmith h 56 Ashley
" Euclid student b 140 County
" Henri R clerk h 98 Kenyon
" Henry clerk 1189 Acusnet av b 98 Kenyon
" Henry janitor St Hyacinthe church h 21 Mosher
" Jean B carder b 56 Ashley

HASKELL BROS. DEALERS IN
ICE
400 COURT STREET TELEPHONE CONNECTION NEW BEDFORD, MASS.

Blanchette
" Joseph barber 1040 Acushnet av bds 4 Marvin [140 County
" Joseph bookkeeper 703 Water bds
" Louis blacksmith b 56 Ashley
" Louis N Rev assistant pastor St Ann's church h 60 Brock av
" Narcisse operative h 49 Beetle
" Narcisse Rev removed to Fall River
" Oliver h 140 County [h do
" Rose Mrs dressmaker 103 Ruth
" Stanislaus hairdresser 1040 Acushnet avenue h 4 Marvin [av
" William flagman h 1382 Acushnet
Blanchflower Franklin operative b 14 Winsor
" Frutin spinner b 41 Rivet
" James molder h 208 Thompson
" Thomas spinner h 14 Winsor
Bland Hardwell operative h 143 Holly
Blean Georgina Mrs h 110 Mott
Bleasdale James weaver h 32 Winsor
" John variety 97 County h do
" William weaver h 98 Brock av [av
Blecha Albert spinner h 251 Phillips
" Antone operative h 39 Hicks
" Charles spinner b 61 Nye
" Conrad loom fixer h 75 Clark
" Joseph grocer 120 Holly h 61 Nye
" Mary Mrs h 293 Davis
" Peter Jr doffer b 293 Davis [lard
Blechinger Charles weaver h 15 Bul-
" Joseph weaver b 15 Bullard
Blein Joseph weaver h 807 First
Blenka Yako weaver h 10 Nye [ent
Bletcher Harry laborer h 73 Independ-
Bliem Edward gardener b 41 High
" John F tailor 15 Pleasant b 41 High [b 20 Ashley
Blier Anna dressmaker 912 S Water
" Joseph contractor 26 Ashley h do
" Octave carpenter h 20 Ashley
Bliffins Frank C compositor Standard h at Fall River [b 233 Arnold
Bliss Alice E S clerk Pierce Mfg Co
" Carrie W teacher Dartmouth st school b 233 Arnold
" Charles F h 66 Parker
" D Edward salesman 830 Purchase h 69 Locust [dar
" Eliza M widow Charles h 201 Ce-

Bliss
" Ethel teacher I W Benjamin school b 233 Arnold [Arnold
" Florilla H and E Jennie h 130
" George H h 233 Arnold
" Grace E clerk Grinnell Mfg Corp b 233 Arnold
" Harold L bookkeeper Anthony Swift b 66 Parker [72 Rotch W
" Herbert W clerk 158 Purchase h
" Herman L purchasing agent T P Corporation h 65 Elm
" Rachel G widow William H housekeeper 141 Allen
" Roland H wood worker h 165 Kempton [134 Arnold
" William clerk 185 Union h
Bliven Arthur A driver 127 Union b 81 Washington [Pleasant
" George F 745 Purchase h r 359
" John E, U S A b 81 Washington
" Walter A hostler b 81 Washington
" William H h 81 Washington
Blocksage George spinner h 27 Valentine [hand h 87 Hathaway
Bloeser Jennie widow Joseph mill
Blois Albert Z manager 153 Cove h 866 First
Blomer Gustaf removed from city
Blood Annie bds 320 Court
" Winifred widow John h 320 Court
Bloom Benjamin rag picker h 30 East Merrimac
" B Moses fruit h 132 Cedar Grove
Bloomer Annie Mrs operative b 238 Sawyer
" Anthony spinner h 190 Tinkham
" William real estate h 190 Tinkham
Bloomfield Amy A widow William C h 163 Campbell
Bloomingdale Harry (Surprise Clothing Co) 156 Purchase h 52 Morgan [Mill h 92 Campbell
Blossom Alonzo W clerk Whitman
" Ansel F died August 30 1910
" Brothers (Charles) builders' supplies 159 North Second
" Charles (Blossom Brothers) h 94 Campbell [37 Buttonwood
" Frederick A foreman 111 Willis h
" Louis E clerk 10 Florence
Blouin Alfred carpenter h 172 Dean
" Germain weaver b 1205 Acushnet avenue
" Joseph operative b 209 Brook

J. F. CROSSLEY 223 MILL STREET COR. EMERSON PHONE
STEAM and HOT WATER HEATING
GAS FITTING and FIXTURES

Blouin
" Joseph weaver h 197 Belleville rd
" Jules operative h 209 Brook
" Peter weaver b 1205 Acushnet av
" Pierre operative b 209 Brook
Blount S Gilbert physician St Luke's Hospital b do. [Acushnet av
Blower Lillian operative bds 1060
" William F harness maker h 1060 Acushnet avenue
Blucas Peter (Zeses & Blucas) pool 1605 Acushnet avenue rms 162 Davis [Cedar Grove
Plume David clerk 52 Purchase b 132
" Israel shoemaker h 85 Walden
" Moses pedlar h 132 Cedar Grove
Blundell Bridget widow Anthony h 54 Liberty
" Frederick W weaver h 300 Earle
" Frederick W Jr spinner b 300 Earle [Allen
Bly Charles F M machinist h 318
" Charles M h 211 Summer
" Edward E foreman bds 318 Allen
" Edward J driver engine 5 h 104 Smith
" Harry W shipping clerk h 11 Pope
" H Percy supt bds 118 Fourth
" Leslie A inspector h 118 Fourth
" Mary nurse b 321 Union
" William H insurance 97 William rm 301 h 400 Union
" W H driver 14 North Sixth [ct
Blyraechyk Jan operative h 15 Fulton
Boardley William machinist h 290 Orchard (S) [Reynolds
Boardman Alfred loom fixer h 141
" Arthur G (Watson & Boardman) druggist 765 Kempton h 948 do
" Charles machinist h 20 Cove
" Eliza weaver h 59 Tallman
" Ernest salesman 58 Adams h 118 Locust
" Fred H apprentice b 7 Linden ct
" George h 1581 Acushnet avenue
" George E removed from city
" Harry clerk 1892 Acushnet av bds 86 Clifford
" Henry fixer h 531 South Sixth
" John W baker h 383 Cedar Grove
" Joseph A bookkeeper h 1 Warwick [Village h do
" Joseph S L variety r 29 Howland

Boardman
" Lucy E clerk Grinnell Mfg Corp b 1581 Acushnet av [Grove
" Margaret weaver h 383 Cedar
" Peter electrician h 7 Linden ct
" RobertH overseer Wamsutta Mills h 207 Weld [do
" Robert T grocer 128 County h
" William pianos 201 Acushnet av and extracts 199½ do h 205 do
" William H weaver h 14 Harmony
Bocard Louis clerk 490 S Second h 94 County [284 Cedar Grove
Bochman Albion E brewery worker h
" Amelia widow Carl G b 137 Richmond [mond
" Paul Carl glass cutter h 137 Rich-
" Paul M spinner h 36 Hazard
" see Bachman [ty
Bock Herman operative b 1054 Coun-
" Rosanna widow Frederick h 1054 County [away h 81 Davis
Bocotte William blacksmith 27 Hath-
Boczek John baker h 31 Mitchell
" Peter mill hand h 31 Mitchell
Bode Manuel F operative b 11 Margin
Boden Arthur L express 84 Walden h do [Parker
" Emma L widow Edward Jr h 48
Bodkin Anne widow Richard b 15 Bowditch [Water
Bodrick Antone seaman h 291 South
Boehler John fixer h 179 Dean
" Louise widow John Fred h 95 Tallman
" Max F drill maker h 95 Tallman
Boeneau Louis laborer h 65 Jouvett
Boetilho Christian J shoe repairer Belleville av cor Dean h 80 Davis
Bogan Isabel K removed to Springfield [Phillips av
Bogdan Sofia widow Vasalie b 57
Bogie George M weaver h 122 Rodney
" Hannah N widow Charles A operative h 83 Rockland [avenue
Bogos John mill hand b 325 Belleville
Bohan Celia clerk 182 Union b at Mattapoisett
" see Bowen [ciety 146 Bowditch
Bohemian Slavonian Benevolent So-
Boim Manuel A variety 284½ Fourth h 284 do

CHARLES A. CROSHERE
38 FOURTH ST. Bell Phone 1964-23
SIGN PAINTING
GLASS LETTERING
ELECTRIC SIGNS
SHOW CARDS

Bois Joseph weaver h 60 Bullard
" Theophile fireman h 82 Belleville road [lard
Boisclair Aime carpenter b 103 Wil-
" Antoine driver b 1191 Purchase
" Antonio painter b 103 Willard
" Arthur fish 1106 S Water bds 103 Willard [103 Willard
" Harvey clerk 1106 S Water bds
" Marion dressmaker 21 Acushnet avenue bds do [lard
" Sophia widow Joseph h 103 Wil-
" Valoire widow Adolphe h 74 Nelson [bds 968 Water
Boisey Robert auto repairer 19 Fourth
Boissoneault Calixte weaver h 106 Hemlock
" Henri variety 393 Bowditch h do
" Jacques fixer h 8 Mulberry
Boisvert Adam twister b 32 Nye
" Adelard weaver b 39 Dean
" Adelard M h 357 Bowditch
" Alexis operative h 32 Nye
" Alfred teamster h 201 Dean
" Amedee laborer b 32 Nye [evelt
" Arsene shoes 107 Ruth h 40 Roos-
" Evariste fixer h 25 Delano
" Francis weaver h 98 Collette
" Homer weaver h 909 S Water [av
" Hormidas slubber h 125 Phillips
" Mary h 96 Thompson
" Merelda clerk b 909 S Water
" Wilfred laborer b 32 Nye
Boivin Ludger teamster h 61 Nelson
" Marjoricque carpenter h 61 Nelson
Bolan Verinita widow h 6 Fulton ct
Boland Lawrence J carpenter b 161 Mill [First
Bolarinho Manuel C twister h 405
Bolduc Alphonse b 363 Coggeshall [do
" Arthur provision 65 Brock av h
BOLDUC AZARIE plumber and steam fitter 115 Bowditch h 900 Belleville av See page 780
" Celina widow Oliver h 11 Nye
" Charles carder b 103 Ruth
" Delima bookkeeper 225 Sawyer b 284 Tallman [Ruth
" Georgianna widow Charles h 103
" Hector sergeant U S A h 20 George
" Hormidas doffer b 11 Nye
" Joseph carpenter h 96 Holly
" Joseph grocer 225 Sawyer b 284 Tallman

Bolduc
" Joseph laborer bds 11 Nye
" Joseph Mrs dressmaker h 96 Holly [Tallman
" Louis fitter 115 Bowditch b 87
" Oliver died Nov 1 1910
" Phillip carpenter b 96 Holly
" Telesphore removed to Acushnet
" William h 87 Tallman [Water
Boledo Philip mariner bds 467 South
Bolek John mill hand h 1 Riverside avenue [mac
Bollea Ernisto laborer b 22 E Merri-
Bolles Annie H widow Henry C h 19 Borden
" Charles E, D D S h 108 Union
" Ella M widow Edmund H h 97 Fourth [Arnold
" Mary J widow Abraham N h 112
Bolton Alfred fixer h 331 Tinkham
" Daniel spinner h 5 Katharine
" Fergus weaver h 78 W French av
" George h 51 Potomska
" George weaver h 172 Division
" Harry baker 913 Acushnet av h 234 Dean [ter
" Henry restaurant 922 South Wa-
" Herbert plumber 87 Union b 172 Division
" Herbert weaver b 5 Katharine
" James E reserve police h 191 Earle
" John carpenter bds 171 Richmond
" John fitter h 140 Hathaway
" Lillian b 38 Cedar
" William fixer h 441 Pleasant
" Wright superintendent Hathaway Mfg Co h 96 Church
" Wright Jr machinist b 96 Church
Boman Robert P master mariner h 332 Cottage [avenue
Bombardier Alphire driver h 63 Brock
" Joseph weaver b 412 N Front
Bonanentura Parelli shoe repairer 57½ Hillman h 2 Hicks
Bond Adam removed from city
" Alex clerk 153 Cove b 104 Butler
" Francis weaver b 526 Bolton
" George h 526 Bolton
" John weaver b 526 Bolton
" Robert A machinist b 104 Butler
" Stephen H pattern maker 32 Commercial h at Fairhaven

J. G. NICHOLSON
LUMBER, SASH, DOORS and BLINDS
BOWDITCH STREET, NEW BEDFORD, MASS.

Bond
" William mule spinner h 104 Butler [Eighth
Bon Durant Robert O student b 35
Bonin Charles weaver h 940 County
" David weaver h 13 Hazard court
" David helper 125 Middle b 13 Hazard court
" Edeas eyelet maker b 13 Hazard court [Fall River
" Euclide barber 833 Purchase b at
" Nelson painter h 19 Welcome
Bonnar James M physician 173 Campbell and 186 Pleasant h do
" Mary bookkeeper 58 Adams b 173 Campbell
" see Bonner [192 do
Bonneau Adelard clerk 174 Sawyer b
" Adelard weaver h 227 State
" Adelard A student b 192 Sawyer
" Alfred weaver b 74 Division
" Alphege grocer 174 Sawyer h 192 do
" Alphege H barber b 192 Sawyer
" Alsedar poultry 3322 Acushnet avenue near Nye's lane h do
" Antonio bartender 503 N Front h 790 Purchase
" Armand clerk b 621 Cottage
" Arthur operative h 150 Highland
" Arthur painter h 385 Pleasant
" Clara widow Francois Jr b 109 Phillips avenue [Phillips av
" Euphemie widow Francois b 109
" Francis A blacksmith 1180 and 1188 Acushnet av h 187 Austin
" F Mrs boarding house 1028 Acushnet avenue
" George teamster h 215 Highland
" Henry baker h 74 Division
" Joseph second hand h 395 Belleville avenue
" Joseph B driver h 188 Austin
" Mary dressmaker 751 S Water h do
" Mary widow Jeremiah h 215 Highland [State
" Mary widow Theophile bds 227
" Narcisse A foreman 72 N Water h 621 Cottage
" Noel removed to Lewiston Maine
" Oliver carpenter h 863 Purchase
" Phileos janitor b 863 Purchase
" Philip overseer Holmes Mfg Co b 1378 Acushnet avenue

Bonneau
" Philip painter bds 215 Highland
" Phillip mill hand h 742 Belleville avenue
" Stanislas A hairdresser 912 Acushnet avenue h 346 Sawyer
" Theophile driver b 385 Pleasant
" Treffle h 435 Pleasant
" Treffle helper h 826 County
" Valentine clerk 808 Purchase b 435 Pleasant
" William tailor h 96 Jouvett
Bonnell Eli S optician 224 Purchase h 123 Maxfield
Bonner Elizabeth Mrs b 271 Union
" George H truckman U St Ry Co h 319 Cedar
" Joseph weaver h 108 Cove
" Samuel gardener b 271 Union
" see Bonnar [Bedford h do
Bonney Charles A Jr physician 67
" Charles T teacher classics High school h 343 Orchard (S)
" Elizabeth A widow Henry M h 354 County [road
" Elmer E teamster h 93 Belleville
" Fannie M widow William W h 46 Pierce
BONNEY, FOLSTER & CO (Frank S Bonney and Emile J Folster) dry goods 945-947 Acushnet av See foot lines
" Frank S (Bonney, Folster & Co) 945 Acushnet avenue h 93 Mt Pleasant [Orchard (S)
" James T leather inspector h 338
" Kate Mrs dressmaker 354 County h do [Fourth
" Marcellus P plumber b 229
" Mary E widow Charles A bds 67 Bedford
" Mary F saleslady bds 46 Pierce
" Mary M Mrs h 84 Rockland
" Nathaniel mill apprentice h 229 Fourth [R I
" Stephen K removed to Providence
" William weaver h 448 N Front
" William H painter h 354 County
" William M h 95 Hillman
" see Bunney [net av rms do
Bonnoyer Bruno tailor 1229 Acushnet
" Henry removed from city
" Liboire clerk b 992 S Water
" Theophile mason b 992 S Water
Bono Antonio laborer h 8 Wall

Steiger-Dudgeon Co.
"The WOMAN'S Store."
Tel. Bell 82 & 83, Branches connecting all depts.
" " 160 For Office only. Auto. 1211

SUMPTIONS, ASSORTMENTS AT ALL TIMES OF DEPENDABLE DRY GOODS

Bonoyer James weaver b 892 S Water
" Peter weaver h 117 Eugenia
Bonville Henry weaver h 1012 South Water [velt
Bonvoulios Levi mason h 12 Roose-
Boodry James D foreman 72 North Water h at Fairhaven
Booker Ann M Mrs b 41 Merrimac
" Joseph spinner h Shawmut av near Plainville road [avenue
" Thomas produce b 155 Shawmut
" William spinner h 34 Vine
Boomer Abram carriage trimmer 38 Fourth h at Dartmouth
" Abram Jr carriage trimmer 38 Fourth b at Dartmouth
" Ellen C widow Edwin A rms 244 Hawthorn
" Thomas h 10 Florence
" Thomas M drill maker h 351 Court
Boone Eliza C dressmaker 173 Acushnet av b do [Acushnet av
" Mary E widow William H h 173
Boorlotas James weaver b 269 Belleville avenue
Boos John laborer h 33 Washburn
Booth Almira C widow Benjamin T h 56 North [Emerson (S)
" Arthur S foreman Mercury h 13
" Charles H W clerk 159 Purchase b 139 Maxfield
" Charles L b 215 Hathaway road
" Edwin H first lieutenant steamer No 7 h 2 Vine [man
" Eliza widow William h 33 Hill-
" Elwood E foreman h 117 South
" Eva M bookkeeper 40 Purchase
" Frank fitter b 75 Bay
" Frank weaver b 51 Myrtle
" Frank A third hand b 143 North
" George machinist h 44 Fruit
" George H vice president and agent Booth Mfg Co h 52 Arnold
" James letter carrier h 51 Myrtle
" James spinner h 44 Willard
" James teamster 70 Union b Florence [school h 55 Willard
" John janitor William H Taylor
" John removed from city
" Joseph loom fixer h 25 Trinity
" Lucy A widow Zachariah b 143 North
" Mfg Co cotton goods G H Booth vice president and agent East French avenue

Booth
" Mary Mrs weaver h 178 State
" Nellie M widow Frank W h 139 Maxfield
" Rosa stitcher h 78 Hillman
" S Lizzie dressmaker 56 North b do
" Thomas second hand b 212 Weld
" William b 30 Bullock
" William third hand b 52 Arnold
" William weaver b 11 Logan
" Z Edward assistant treasurer N E C Y Co h 115 Hawthorn
Boothman Jonathan B weaver h 276 Collette
Borba John teamster h 61 Durfee
Borbetski John operative h 226 Coggeshall [b 265 Mill
Borden Albert E clerk 17 N Sixth
" Annie E L assistant treasurer N B Five Cents Savings Bank b Parker House [269 do
" Arthur H grocer 271 Cedar h
" Carlton E student b 152½ Fair
" Catherine A widow Charles M h 40 Butler C P
" Charles F h 275 County
" Charles L foreman 38 Middle h 71 Hillman
" Charles W died Jan 12 1911
" Chester K salesman 861 Kempton h 845 Rockdale avenue [tage
" Clara widow David A h 295 Cot-
" Clarence L laborer N B W W h 197 Cedar [Whitman
" Edna L Mrs stenographer h 155
" Elizabeth widow John removed to Smith's Mills
" Emma L Mrs h 34 Hillman [man
" Everett L carpenter h 155 Whit-
" Frank W operative b 39 Bullock
" Freeman M teamster b 185 Cedar
" George fixer h 28 Tallman
" George B foreman h 1285 Rockdale avenue [len b 5 Stone
" George N florist Ward corner Al-
" Gertrude assistant teacher cooking public schools b 2082 Acushnet avenue
" Gertrude F widow Joseph h 176 Smith [h 887 Rockdale av
" Gilbert B Jr inspector N B W W
" Hannah L Mrs b 197 Middle
" Harrison T coal 64 Dartmouth h 152½ Fair

PELEG H. SHERMAN 506 COUNTY ST.
FUNERAL DIRECTOR AND EMBALMER
OFFICE PHONES. Bell 690-13. Auto. 1305.
RESIDENCE PHONES. Bell 690-12. Auto. 1306.

Borden
" Harry E manager and treasurer The Harry E Borden Co 86-98 Pleasant h 11 Ash (S)
BORDEN HARRY E CO The (Harry E Borden) mill and automobile supplies and automobiles 86-98 Pleasant See page 746
" Harvey J switchboard man h 186 Arnold [124 High
" Herbert H glass smoother h
" Horace assistant superintendent street department h 15 Collins
" James boat builder h 185 Cedar
" James H Jr switchboard man 57 N Second b 21 Ash (S)
" Leander A laborer h 17 Walnut
" Lydia M Mrs b 480 Acushnet av
" Mary E h 208 Kempton
" Mary E b 2112 Acushnet avenue
" Minnie A widow Charles H h 13 Spruce
" Robert T laborer h 77 Taber
" Ruth E Mrs lodgings 3 Park pl h do [Bedford
" Sarah B widow Charles W h 42
" Stella A forewoman b 13 Spruce
" Thomas J machinist h 5 Stone
" Walter E draughtsman bds 208 Kempton [ushnet av
" Weston J canvasser h 2082 Ac-
" William bartender b 28 Tallman
" William J teamster N B Fish Co h 511 Acushnet avenue
BORDEN & REMINGTON CO dyes and chemicals 115 Annawan Fall River See page 11
Bordley Joseph W weaver h 334 Bowditch
Borgendahl Hannah Mrs h 2 Cornell
Borges Antone laborer h 99 Bellevue
" Arthur spinner h 374 S Second
" August J laborer h 68 Ward
" John laborer h 39 Grant [Bolton
" Jose N painter h 3 Rotch blk 434
" Joseph laborer h 399 Frost
" Joseph R operative h 65 Short
" Jule drill worker b 134 Fourth
" Julio teamster 37 Lombard h do
" Procopio weaver h 195 Coggeshall
Bornstein Abraham tailor h 23 Beetle
Borofsky Louis operative h 293 Austin
Borrin Mary h 61 Nelson
Borst Peter laborer h 26 Elm
Bortle Peter h 8 Bethel
" Susan A Mrs lodgings 8 Bethel
Bosok John carder h 129 Blackmer
Bosquet Oliver motorman h 883 Purchase
Bosse Emile weaver h 90 Davis
" Fabiola clerk 185 Union b 437 Purchase
Bossler Florence weaver h 142 Cove road [155 Blackmer
Boston Drug Co William Ahern mgr
" Francis R chief engineer 97 Front h 187 Pleasant
" Furniture Co 953 South Water
" Mutual Life Ins Co, John B Demers superintendent 97 William rm 311 and 141 Milk Boston
" Providence & Fall River Express Co 386 Acushnet avenue
" Specialty Shop cloaks 24 Purchase
" Supply Co (J T Acheson and E Woodland) furniture 765 Purchase [321 Union
Boswell Emma I Mrs nurse rms
" Frederick tinsmith 28 N Second h 52 Jenny Lind [land
" John glass blower h 22 Rock-
" Robert J drill worker b 22 Rockland [435 Cottage
Bosworth Almira widow William h
" Ambrose W machinist h 89 Fourth
" Calvin T (C T Bosworth & Co) h 198 County
" C T Co (Calvin T Bosworth) druggists 133 County
" Elmer J clerk 37 Purchase rm 203 rms 168 Middle [674 do
" George A builder 676 Cottage h
" George F h 170 Summer
" Joseph W carpenter 7 Leonard b 170 Summer
" Peleg h 193 Shawmut av [198 do
" Rathbone H clerk 133 County b
BOSWORTH WILLARD E refrigerator mfr 1194 Rockdale av h do See page 785
Boteilho Antone laborer h 17 Mitchell
" Antonio hairdresser h 188 Thompson
" Frank operative h 264 S Second
" John cleaner U St Ry Co h 845 South Water
" Joseph operative h 334 First
" Joseph S laborer h 23 Spooner

F. T. AKIN & CO. FORGE FACTORY FURNACE FAMILY COAL

Boteilho
" Manuel mill hand b 39 Mitchell
" Manuel operative h 581 First
" Manuel third hand h 100 Phillips avenue
" Manuel J laborer h 374 S Second
" Venus M removed from city
Botella Antone carpenter h 40 Katharine [Woodlawn av
Botham Catherine widow Joseph b 36
Bottomley Samuel collector h 24 Ash (N)
" William carder h 274 Phillips av
" William H machinist h 607 Cottage [tle
Boubeau Jean carpenter h 106 Bee-
Boucaire Frank mill hand h 171 Tinkham [Hicks
Bouchard Albert shoemaker b 19
" Archille operative b 168 N Front
" Charles machinist b 1205 Acushnet avenue
" Charles mill hand bds 15 Nye
" Edward weaver h 19 Hicks
" Eusebe weaver h 53 Hicks
" Francois Mrs h 59 Clark
" Gilbert h 117 Clark [629 Cottage
" Henry W barber 771 Purchase b
" Isadore barber h 868 S Water
" John J hairdresser 866 Purchase h 834 County
" Joseph doffer h 49 Nye
" J Alfred bartender 246 N Front b 49 Nye
" Lucien F hairdresser and towel supply 771 Purchase h 629 Cottage [59 Clark
" Mary clerk 1119 Acushnet av bds
" Telesphore baker b 53 Hicks
" William grocer 263 Coggeshall
" William teamster h 168 N Front
Boucher Adelard weaver h 23 Slocum
" Adelard weaver b 70 Eugenia
" Adeline widow Henry b 366 State
" Albert mill hand h 207 Sawyer
" Albert third hand h 917 County
" Aldase weaver b 174 Phillips av
" Alfred operative h 406 S Front
" Alice operative b 366 State
" Alice L Mrs h 137 Holly
" Andrew hairdresser 78 William h 19 Seventh
" Arthur b 88 Nye
" Arthur clerk 225 Sawyer

Boucher
" Arthur painter U St Ry Co h 56 Washburn
" Bazil operative b 344 Pleasant
" Camille weaver h 452 Belleville avenue
" Charles weaver h 968 S Water
" Clementine widow Xavier b 270 Tinkham
" David operative h 140 Tallman
" Edward doffer h 391 Bowditch
" Edward finisher h 812 Acushnet avenue
" Edward manager b 106 Ruth av
" Edward mill hand bds 126 Nash road [Cornell pl
" Edward removed from city
" Elizabeth widow Edward h 7
" Emile fixer h 149 Bullard
" Ernest operative b 88 Nye
" Ernest H manager 1029 Acushnet avenue h 137 Holly
" Eugene clerk b 70 Eugenia
" Francois operative h 88 Nye
" Fred painter b 26 Nye
" George barber 1124 Acushnet av bds 26 High [153 do
" George barber 150 Arnold rms
" George clerk 153 Cove b 8 McGurk
" George E shoeworker h 186 Cove
" Henry clerk 1275 Acushnet av b 239 State [Acushnet av
" Hilor glazier 31 Bowditch b 1812
" Isaie mill hand h 145 Bullard
" Isaie painter 38 Fourth h 936 County
" Jean B laborer h 158 Central av
" John operative h 106 Ruth
" John weaver b 67 Coffin av
" John Jr operative b 106 Ruth
" Joseph carpenter h 8 McGurk
" Joseph laborer h Central av
" Joseph laborer h 968 S Water
" Joseph removed to Norwich Conn
" Joseph teamster h 43 Union
" Joseph third hand h 38 Bullard
" Joseph wheelwright 1180 Acushnet av h 1 Weld square
" Joseph A baker 59 Bullard h 61 do [vid
" Joseph A third hand h 165 Da-
" Joseph B hairdresser h 1671 Acushnet avenue

Kinyon's Commercial School Will furnish your office help free } Odd Fellows Building COR. WILLIAM and PLEASANT STS. NEW BEDFORD, MASS.

Boucher
" Joseph E weaver b 23 Covell
" Joseph G conductor h 130 Summer [do
" Joseph I bakery 238 State h 240
" Joseph M removed to Canada
" Joseph Z (James F Hoye & Co) 305 Merchants Bank bldg and dry goods 419 N Front h 204 Davis [Bowditch
" Leon engineer city yard h 12
" Louis blacksmith 240 N Front h 70 Eugenia
" Louis painter h 26 Nye
" Louis weaver h 592 First
" Mary widow b 240 State
" Mary widow Joseph h 66 Robeson
" Michel carpenter h 88 Nye
" Napoleon tinsmith 671 Purchase rms 760 do
" Napoleon weaver h 27 Ashley
" Odila clerk 1031 Acushnet av rms 917 County [809 County
" Olivier salesman 46 Purchase h
" Oscar J clerk 1 Purchase b 1 Weld
" Peter operative b 8 McGurk
" Peter weaver h 475 S Front
" Pierre h 51 Belleville av
" Pierre operative h 88 Holly
" Pierre third hand h 343 N Front
" Roderick machinist h 968 S Wa-
" Sinai baker h 59 Clark [av
" Theophile weaver b 452 Belleville
" Victor painter b 145 Bullard
" Victor teamster h 44 Washburn
" Victor weaver h 24 Tallman
" William ball player b 12 Bowditch [6 Warren
Bouchman Arthur L boss comber h
" Paul M operative h 55 Washburn
Boudreau Andrew fisherman h 575 Belleville av
" Angus laborer b 93 Collette
" Anselme laborer h 31 Bullard
" Arthur carpenter bds 1028 Acushnet avenue
" Arthur weaver h 567 First
" Dominique carpenter 3863 Acushuet av h do [ville av
" Dominique operative h 739 Belle-
" Emille Mrs h 116 W French av
" Etienne slasher b 326 N Front

Boudreau
" Fabien h 195 Collette
" Fred carpenter b 154 Tinkham
" Fred operative h 162 Bates av
" George H bartender 133 N Front h 91 Kenyon
" Napoleon removed from city
" Simeon carpenter h 154 Tinkham
" Theophile (Egan & Boudreau) 927 S Water h 105 Rodney
Boudry Nelson steamfitter h 287 Phillips avenue [Earle
Bougela Adelard mill hand bds 88
" Joseph laborer h 20 Holly [av
Bouise Joseph fireman h 52 Bennett
Bouitts James mill hand b r 234 N Front
Boulais Alexis died July 26 1910
" Louis helper h 27 Kenyon [ard ct
Boule Alfred W operative b 6 Haz-
" Henri weaver h 6 Hazard ct
" Henry provisions 1413 Acushnet avenue h 1565 do
" Honore laborer h 444 Pleasant
" Joseph A wire boy b 6 Hazard ct
" Norbet P weaver h 131 Bullard
" Philip H pianist b 490 S Second
Boulet Adelard tinsmith 915 Acushnet avenue h 175 Eugenia
" Arthur weaver h 810 County
Bouley Amarde weaver b 204 Sawyer
" Digene weaver h 204 Sawyer
" Edmond operative h 48 Nelson
" Lulu variety 522 S Second h 490 Blackmer
Boulais Peter clerk 1091 Acushnet av b 355 Coggeshall
Boulia Leon C b 54 Fourth
Boulish Adolph weaver b 156 Tallman [Water
Bounnier Theophile mason b 855 S
" William weaver b 855 S Water
Boura Gab mill hand h 46 Mosher
Bourassa Adelard removed from city
" Adelard second hand h 176 Hathaway
" Antoine section hand b 15 Holly
" Arthur painter b 39 Dean
" Arthur twister b 616 S Second
" Donat operative h 244 Tinkham
" Eli second hand h 135 Nye
" Eva clerk b 616 S Second

Bread, Cake, Pastry
RICHMOND & COMPANY **255-257 UNION STREET**
Bell 993 Automatic 1022

Bourassa
" Hector second hand b 691 Purchase [Purchase
" Jean Baptiste Jr third hand b 691
" Jean B died Aug 21 1910
" Joseph C (Benoit Bourassa Co) 1249 Acushnet av h 1356 do
" Louis lunch 1010 S Water h 616 S Second
" Marguerite widow John B h 691 Purchase [Holly
" Marguerite widow Moise h 15
" Oliver spinner b 20 Hazard ct
" Willie weaver b 15 Holly
Bourbeau Alphonse plumber 915 Acushnet av h 4 Social
" Augustine spinner h 55 Austin
" George b 55 Austin
" George H milkman rms 1671 Acushnet avenue
" John operative h 188 State
" Joseph spinner h 87 Bowditch
" Louis driver h 8 McGurk
" William second hand h 69 Austin
Bourbo Albert C helper b 89 Butler
" Alfred D furniture 1112 Acushnet avenue h 89 Butler
" William D clerk 1112 Acushnet av h 203 Bowditch [Earle
Bourcier John H gardener h 92
Bourdeau Victor machinist b 33 Holly [ham
Bourdon Charles weaver h 151 Tink-
" Vincent speeder tender b 166 N Front
" William bartender 273 Sawyer
Bourdua Joseph blacksmith h 119 Nash road [Purchase
Bourgault Agenorse teamster h 871
" Lazar b 871 Purchase [ster ct
Bourgeois Abel operative h 131 Web-
" Adelard carpenter h 25 Adams
" Albert fisherman bds 22 Holly
" Albert weaver h 102 Eugenia
" Albini painter 91 Bullard h 137 Holly [Foster
" Amand L clerk 133 Ruth b 59
" Amanda E milliner 1039 Acushnet av b 197 Bowditch
" Amedee painter h 154 Collette
" Andrew operative b 166 Bates av
" Armond operative b 39 Tallman
" David h 59 Scott
BOURGEOIS DAVID carriage painter 105 Bowditch h 59 Scott See page 744
" Didier shoe repairer 391 N Front h 139 Earle
" Dominique removed to Charlton
" Edmonde operative b 39 Tallman
" Emile carpenter b 118 Nash rd
" Frank speeder h 20 Nye [Sawyer
" George cloth inspector b 235
" Gilbert nickel plater b 139 Earle
" Henry Mrs milliner b 125 Whitman
" Joseph T teamster h 235 Sawyer
" Louis D painter 105 Bowditch b 59 Scott
" Napoleon waxworker b 25 Adams
" Oliver A real estate agent 197 Bowditch h do
" Patrick driver h 24 Marvin
" Pierre fisherman h 39 Tallman
" Pierre laborer h 22 Holly
" Richard carpenter h 75 Nash rd
" Robert T overseer Grinnell Mfg Co 1 Kilburn [av
" Theodore laborer h 349 Belleville
" Theophilas b 102 Eugenia
" Vital operative h 22 Beetle
" William painter b 235 Sawyer
" ——— mill hand b 349 Belleville avenue
" see Burgess
Bourget Albertine bookkeeper 79 Austin b 11 Marvin
" Blanch cashier 1119 Acushnet av bds 11 Marvin [h 11 Marvin
" Joseph A bookkeeper 366 State
" Mary Mrs h 371 State [h do
" Mary Mrs dressmaker 11 Marvin
Bourgon Gustave weaver h 12 Cleveland
Bourne Edmund W cashier N B S D & T Co h 26 Arnold place
" George F tackmaker h 180 Belleville road
" George W (Bourne & Damon Co) druggist 131 Belleville road h at Fairhaven [h 75 James
" Harry R driver 386 Acushnet av
" Jonathan (Trustees estate of) 3 Merrill's wharf [enth h do
" Matilda J Mrs shirtmaker 33 Sev-
" Standish (Standish Bourne & Son) h 94 Hawthorn

GLOBE DYE HOUSE 220 SHAWMUT AVE.
J. N. J. LONHOLDT, PROP. Telephone Connections Goods called for and Delivered
Down town Office, 52 Pleasant St., Room I North End Office, 1014 Acushnet Ave.

Bourne
" Standish & Son (Standish and Williams S) auctioneers and real estate 50 N Second and storage 47-51 do
" Veneretta B h 349 Cottage
" Williams S (Standish Bourne & Son) h 150 Hawthorn [ell
Bourque Albert spinner h 58 Cov-
" Alphee spinner b 195 Phillips av
" Antoine carder h 195 Phillips av
" Arthur clerk 1174 Acushnet av h 120 Tallman
" Dennis bricklayer b 120 Collette
" Desire driver h 226 Kempton
" Eric shoeworker h 126 Nash rd
" Fidelle wood 346 N Front h do
" Henry loom fixer h 94 Kenyon
" Henry F clerk 537 N Front b 94 Kenyon
" John G laborer h 344 Pleasant
" Joseph salesman h 182 Dean
" Joseph D driver 270 Acushnet av h 226 Kempton
" Josephine clerk b 195 Phillips av
" Leda Mrs h 49 Beetle
" Onesime fisherman b 154 Eugenia
" Ovila removed to Fairhaven
" Pauline widow Ferdinand h 171 Coffin avenue
" Peter J clerk b 292 Fourth
" Philip spinner b 64 Bullard
" Philip D carpenter h 821 Purchase
" Raymond doffer b 436 N Front
" Raymond machinist h 253 Coffin avenue
" Thadde removed to Fairhaven
" Theophile twister b 346 N Front
" Wilfred carpenter h 515 N Front
" William carpenter b 118 Nash rd
" William removed from city
" William weaver h 307 N Front
" see Burke [yer
Bourret Gustave advt mgr 267 Saw-
Bousquet Adelard horse shoer 1180 Acushnet av h 226 Sawyer
" Antonio carpenter h 57 Ashley
" Desire teamster h 1 McDonald court
" George helper b 563 N Front
" Henri removed to Davenport N D
" John clerk 960 Acushnet av h 12 Bowditch

Bousquet
" John driver h 22 Beetle
" John shoemaker h 350 Bowditch
" Moses operative b 350 Bowditch
" Samuel teamster h 653 N Front
Boutelle Augusta S widow Adelbert D b 35 Ash (S) [Acushnet av
Boutellier Alexander laborer bds 1022
Bouthillette Edward mill hand h 10 Bullard [land
" Josephine mill hand h 154 Rock-
" Mastai mill hand h 104 Hemlock
" Napoleon drillworker b 154 Rockland [lips av
Boutillier Leo laborer bds 49 Phil-
Bouvier Joseph A hay h 44 Beetle
Bovyn Albert h 126 Princeton
" Arthur weaver h 271 Shaw
Bowden Fred speeder h 194 Davis
" Harry mill hand b 2 Howland Village
" Henry weaver h 23 E French av
" Percey weaver h 94 Hathaway
" Thomas slasher tender b 74 S Second [Village
" William mill hand b 18 Howland
" William weaver h 24 Mosher [po
Bowe John mule spinner h 124 Cra-
Bowen Charles A h 28 Arnold
" Charles A clerk 213 Acushnet avenue b 59 Fifth
" Charles H clerk 124 Purchase h 226 Union [Fruit
" Cornelius clerk 407 River bds 29
" David I carpenter h 76 Dean
" Earle P, U S A b 76 Dean
" Edward helper 28 N Water b 223 Grinnell
" George A painter b 223 Grinnell
" George H foreman 229 N Water h 284 Pleasant
" George S (George S Bowen & Co) h 223 Grinnell
" George S & Co (George S Bowen & Co) broom mfrs 44 Union [Okla
" Harold L removed to Chickasha
" James S h 857 Purchase
" John laborer h 954 County
" John laborer h 123 Hemlock
" John operative bds 954 County
" John W clerk h 666 Purchase
" John W laborer b 972 County
" Louis drillmaker h 229 Cedar

GREENE & WOOD Every Kind of LUMBER AND MILL WORK
PINE STREET, off So. WATER STREET, NEW BEDFORD

Bowen
" Nettie L widow Robert F art embroidery 12 Purchase h do
" Sarah E widow Charles F dry goods 227 Cedar h do
" William operative b 954 County
" see Bohan
Bowering Harry b 488 Purchase
" James removed to Cambridge
Bowers Clara dressmaker 103 Hazard b do
" Helen combmaker rms 225 Court
" Richard laborer h 24 Juniper
" Thomas h 103 Hazard
" William removed to Boston
Bowie Angela F teacher James B Congdon school h 111 Dartmouth [Lincoln
" Harold S clerk 100 Fifth h 27
" Isabelle widow Elkanah H h 2 Weaver
" James L supt b 331 Orchard (S)
" Roderick M asst foreman 474 Acushnet av [319 Cottage
" William S painter 498 County h
Bowker Ann Mrs h 128 Reynolds
" Henry weaver h 250 Brock av
" Herbert operative h 12 Cove
" Levi L h 74 Parker
" Sarah widow h 76 Willis
" Walter E drillworker b 76 Willis
" William spinner h 228 State
Bowler Joseph shoemaker 761 Purchase h 9 Linden court [ct
" Joseph Jr eyelet cutter b 9 Linden
" Samuel spinner h 72 Hathaway
" Wilfred clerk 156 Weld b 9 Linden court
Bowles Charles E carpenter h Acushnet av beyond L C [ham
" Fred M teamster b 257 Tink-
" Frederick W sawyer h 2925 Acushnet av [av beyond L C
" Henry H carpenter b Acushnet
Bowlin Michael weaver b 519 N Front
Bowman Ethel C b 47 Willis
" Clarence R piper h 343 W Morgan [133 N Second
" Edward F shipper 52 Adams b
" Frederick G bookkeeper h 19 Shawmut av [net av
" George A bartender h 170 Acush-
" George L nurse h 19 Shawmut av

Bowman
" Henry T carpenter b 263 Purchase
" Joshua B carpenter h 283 Cedar
" Lemuel shoemaker h 1 Reed's ct
" Luther C rem to Mattapoisette
" Martin M painter h 202 Blackmer
" Thomas moulder b 65 Washburn
" William B teamster h 249 Acushnet avenue
" William S spinner h 169 David
Bowser John carpenter h 97 Sidney
Boyd Eliza Mrs h 271 Pleasant
" Helen I teacher Mary B White school b 11 Fifth
" John weaver b 33 McGurk [sutta
" Lizzie Mrs operative h 5 Wam-
" Mary E b 51 Hill
" William second hand Pierce Bros Ltd b 33 McGurk [ker
" William L third hand b 43 Par-
Boyer Charles shoemaker b 241 State
" Edson insurance agent 37 Purchase rm 23 h 104 Bowditch
" Edward laborer h 241 State
" Francis B Rec pastor St Martin's Episcopal church h 172 Page
" Fred removed from city
" George brewery hand h 23 Bentley [chase
" George teamster bds 763 Pur-
" Jennie widow Peter h 54 Phillips avenue [ville av
" Joseph weaver bds 297 Belle-
" Joseph A operative b 478 Coggeshall
" Leo removed from city
" Sidney teamster h 328 Bowditch
" Victoria Mrs h 478 Coggeshall
Boyle Agnes housekeeper 972 County
" Agnes C h 971 County
" Annie F operative b 972 County
" Daniel teamster h 404 Chancery
" Elizabeth A h 40 Oak
" Elizabeth S teacher R S Ingraham school b 122 Bonney
" Emma Mrs cloth inspector b 156 Washington [Hathaway
" Francis J slasher tender h 153
" High operative b 972 County
" Hugh F overseer Soule Mill h 971 County
" James H glasscutter b 40 Oak
" John shoemaker b 108 Sycamore

BONNEY, FOLSTER & CO.,
The North End's Shopping Centre
Dry Goods and Men's Furnishings
945-947 Acushnet Ave., New Bedford, Mass.

Boyle
" John shoeworker b 1 Austin
" John H overseer h 330 Cedar Grove
" Mary operative b 972 County
" Mary speeder tender h 9 Viall
" Michael weaver h 51 Potomska
" Neil laborer h 972 County
" Patrick weaver b 804 Purchase
" Thomas C baker b 972 County
" William fireman h 113 Clark
" William J clerk 108 Cedar h 23 do [man
Boynton Clyde boxmaker b 90 Whit-
" Mary E widow William H b 499 Union
Brabeck Frank carder b 133 Bullard
Brackett Charles K bds 83 Mill
Bradbury Arthur W compositor Standard rms 15 Ash (S)
" Frank horseshoer 332 Purchase bds 52 Willow
" George machinist b 148 Sycamore
" John spinner h 1650 Acushnet av
" Rachael Mrs housekeeper 657 Cottage [velt
" Thomas operative h 22 Roose-
" Thomas overseer Wamsutta Mill h 148 Sycamore
Bradford Anna H widow Philip A b 231 River road [286 Park
" Edgar V yard man N B C Co h
" Edna H clerk b 286 Park
" G Leroy reporter Times b 174 Acushnet avenue
" Joel P prop Acushnet Sanitarium and physician 25 Main L C h 231 River rd [Acushnet av
" J Byron clerk 141 Fourth h 174
" L Alice 120 Purchase b 74 Willis
" William S clerk b 342 Union
Bradley Albert machinist h 190 Brock av
" Alfred clerk N·B W W 40 Masonic bldg h 32 Priscilla
" Arthur machinist h 81 Dunbar
" A William clerk 29 N Water b 32 Priscilla
" Charles weaver b 6 Cove road
" Edwin weaver b 597 Allen
" Elizabeth removed from city
" Emma Mrs h 104 Fifth
" Horace D salesman 19 Commercial h 26 Florence

Bradley
" James B h 20 Fifth
" Jennie removed to England
" John operative b r 60 Washburn
" John weaver b 202 Shawmut av
" Mary J widow Thomas h r 60 Washburn
" Richard elevatorman b 160 Crapo
" Robert weaver h 202 Shawmut av
" Thomas fixer b 21 Salisbury
" Thomas laborer h 21 Salisbury
" Thomas weaver bds 202 Shawmut avenue
" Thomas weaver b 597 Allen
" William b 20 Fifth [300 County
" William E collector 7 Leonard h
Bradshaw Albert fixer h 195 Brock avenue [Ashland
" Benjamin A second hand h 172
" Edwin enginer bds 88 Eugenia
" Frank M engineer Pierce Bros Ltd h 159 Myrtle [ditch
" George L asst engineer h 101 Bow-
" Herbert G clerk 66 William bds 191 Summer [av
" James weaver h 1140 Acushnet
" James T loom fixer b 191 Summer
" John H weaver b 191 Summer
" John P second hand h 86 Belleville road [genia
" Kate A widow Joseph h 88 Eu-
" Margaret A widow Charles b 289 Collette
" Richard painter b 627 Purchase
" Robert T overseer Grinnell Mfg Corp h 191 Summer
" Samuel engineer Manomet Mills h 102 Nash rd [80 Ashland
" William R clerk 368 Kempton b
Bradwell George salesman 170 Purchase h at Fairhaven
Brady Bridget E b 45 James
" Catherine V h 45 James
" James J Rev pastor St Killian's R C church h 306 Bowditch
" Joseph A glasscutter h 66 Washington
" Patrick laborer bds 77 Newton
" P Jane widow John h 74 Maxfield
" Sarah R rms 86 Court
" Thomas (N B Printing Co) 25 N Second h 55 Court
" Thomas J clerk rms 213 Middle

M. P. B. Silva & Son Paints, Oils and Glass
Sole Agents for Lucas Tinted Gloss Paints
157 ACUSHNET AVENUE Both Phones NEW BEDFORD

Brady
" Thomas Jr reporter Standard b 55 Court [shnet av
Braga Jacintho K variety 58 Acu-
" John J teamster h 70 Lindsey
" John R teamster 47 School h 88 Thompson [h 22 Hemlock
" Joseph A pressman 83 Howland
" Katherine widow John R M b 82 Crapo [Acushnet av
" Manuel teamster 45 School h
" Manuel J laborer N B W W h 219 Allen
" Manuel S mill hand h 450 First
Bragdon Chester M asst supt 37 Purchase rm 23 h at Stoughton
" Herbert L foreman 214 S Water h 111 South [Keene
Bragg Edward W blacksmith h 35
" Irman bds 35 Keene
" Milon removed from city
Bragga Frank iceman h 1194 Rockdale avenue [city
Braidwood Robert removed from
" Samuel removed from city
" William bricklayer h 23 Rodney
Brailey Susie E shipper 87 Howard av h at Acushnet
Brainerd Alexander A overseer Nashawena Mill h 234 Shawmut av
" Mabel M b 234 Shawmut av [mer
Brais Philias weaver h 130 Black-
Braislin Gibbs Rev pastor First Baptist church b 439 County
" James P clerk Page Mfg Co b 439 County
Braithwaite Mary J widow James h 513 N Front
Brakell George B moulder h 130 Fair
Braley Albert C clerk 141 Fourth h 585 Union
" Albert L sporting goods 103 Union h at Fairhaven
" Alphus A (Braley & Duckworth) h 110 High [Court
" Anthro H woodworker bds 208
" Benjamin freight clerk foot Willis h 274 Pope [do
" Charles F grocer 357 Court h 360
" Clarence E artist 25 N Second h 93 Willis
" Cyrus rms 10 Bethel
" Edward laborer h 7 Blackburn

Braley
" Eli G apprentice 107 N Water rms 180 Middle [162 Campbell
" Ella F bookkeeper 172 N Water h
" Eugene F carpenter h 166 Blackmer [land
" Eunice widow George W h 1 Ash-
" Frederick C carpenter b 1 Ashland
" Frederick J prop Sylvan Grove Stable h 4035 Acushnet av
" George clerk 36 Purchase bds 238 Chestnut [do
" George A carpenter 73 Dean h
" Herbert M inspector U St Ry Co h 39 Park
" H Bradford blacksmith 40 Spring h 30 Howard avenue
" Jasper W Jr groceries 645-647 County h 619 do
" Jessie N b 619 County
" Louise R bookkeeper 34 Pleasant b 370 Cedar [Plain
" Walton clerk 97 Front h at Long
" & Duckworth (A A Braley and G T Duckworth) grocers 81 N Second [av
Bram James mill hand h 37 Phillips
BRAMAN, DOW & CO steam and gas pipe 239-245 Causeway Boston See page 38
" Frederick A engineer h 185 Court
" George E special police h 6 Foster [Fish Co h 6 Foster
" Hattie H Mrs bookkeeper N B
" Herbert A driver r 182 N Water h 205 Brownell
" William W teamster foot North h 511 Acushnet av [Peckham
Bramhall Joseph slasher tender h 21
Bramwell Benjamin Jr spinner h 309 Earle
" Charles spinner h 561 S First
" John spinner h 24 Crapo
" Thomas spinner h 58 Blackmer
" William operative h 81 Mosher
" William N bartender h 13 McGurk [Hillman
Branceri Etta widow Paul b 70
Branchaud Adelard compositor Standard b 152 Whitman
" Edgar carpenter b 157 Davis
" Edward carpenter h 152 Whitman [man
" Homer carpenter h 155 Whit-

Steiger-Dudgeon Co.
"The WOMAN'S Store."
Tel. Bell 82 & 83, Branches connecting all depts.
" " 160 For Office only. Auto. 1211

SUMPTIONS, ASSORTMENTS AT ALL TIMES OF DEPENDABLE DRY GOODS

Branchaud
" Horace carpenter b 1690 Acushnet avenue
" Leon concrete blocks 24 Hathaway h 1690 Acushnet av
" Pierre laborer h 157 Davis
Branchini Joseph variety 8 Howland h do [Fourth
Branco Antone R laborer h 134
" Manuel de F h 56 Hollyhock
Branconnier Edward operative h 282 N Front
" Frank doffer b 282 N Front
" Joseph janitor b 282 N Front
Brand Frederick tailor 131 Union h 47 Rotch
" William H drillmaker and (Sullivan & Brand) 31 Ashland h 319 Park [Hawthorn h do
Branscomb William G physician 150
Brassard Abraham removed to Lowell
" Henri salesman 912 S Water h 1081 County
Brasseur Joseph insurance agent 110 Purchase rm 403 h 872 First
Brassi Vinano laborer h 4 Turners' court [298 Cottage
Brathwaite Alex baker 255 Union b
Braude Abraham 725 S Water h 286 S Front [geshall b do
Braudy Elizabeth clerk 248 Cog-
" Maurice clerk bds 1139 Acushnet avenue
" Samuel clothing h 119 Reynolds
" Solomon grocer 248 Coggeshall h do [92½ Purchase
Brault Eugene J advertising mgr rms
" Gilbert fixer h 53 Ruth
Braun Joseph carder h 4 Hampton ct
" Leon P organist Church of the Sacred Heart h 825 County
Braunlich Frank L removed from city
Bravo'Manuel S fisherman h 25 County [school b 215 Maxfield
Brawley Annie G principal Cedar st
" Edward L sales stable 27 Fourth h 215 Maxfield
" Maria G nurse b 215 Maxfield
" Phoebe E milliner b 215 Maxfield
" William J night watchman 50 Elm b 531 Rivet
Bray Andrew E fixer h 170 Dean
" Daniel pavingcutter b 204 Weld
Brayant Thomas weaver b 51 Bolton
Braywood Annie M Mrs hairworker 350 Purchase h do [av
" Robert brick layer b 25 E French
Brazeau Lois laborer h 909 S Water
Brazeil Thomas F machinist h 220 Phillips avenue [(W)
Brazil Antonio R laborer h 334 Elm
" Bento weaver h 274 Nash rd
" Carolyn dressmaker 79 Bedford h 273 Orchard (S)
" Manuel J fireman U St Ry Co power station h 59 Acushnet av
" Manuel T filling carrier h 110 Fifth [Fifth
" Manuel T Jr second hand bds 110
Breakell Elizabeth Mrs h 9 Austin
" George B molder h 130 Fair
" Thomas F hoseman Engine No 2 h 866 Rockdale avenue
" William H spinner h 18 Myrtle
Breau Frank h 7 Hazard court
" George fisherman h 29 Holly
" John operative b 7 Hazard court
" William fisherman h 268 N Front
Breault Aime fisherman h 32 Holly
" Albert fisherman bds b 154 Eugenia
" Aldei laborer h 190 State
" Alma clerk b 60 Sylvia
" Alphonse billiards 41 Beetle h 255 N Front
" Andre weaver b 32 Holly
" Armand mill hand b 31 Holly
" Arthur fisherman b 31 Holly
" Calixte fisherman h 97 Coffin av
" Charles laborer b 325 Belleville av
" Daniel H clerk 98 Purchase bds 22 Belleville road
" David bricklayer h 198 State
" David second hand h 203 Blackmer [avenue
" David A bricklayer b 70 Phillips
" Edmond barber 41 Beetle h 255 N Front
" Emil stone mason h 291 Sawyer
" Ernest clerk 133 Ruth b 76 Brock avenue [do
" Ferdinand mason 76 Brock av h
" George mason h 43 Howard
" Harry blacksmith b 151 Tinkham
" Henry real estate h 41 Willis
" Israel laborer h 12 Nye
" Jacob lineman h 35 Bentley
" John weaver h 183 Phillips av
" Josais laborer bds 130 River rd

PELEG H. SHERMAN 506 COUNTY ST.
FUNERAL DIRECTOR AND EMBALMER
OFFICE PHONES. Bell 690-13 Auto. 1305.
RESIDENCE PHONES. Bell 690.12. Auto. 1306.

Breault
" Joseph carpenter b 187 Earle
" Joseph carpenter rms 1332 Acushnet avenue
" Joseph laborer h 203 Sawyer
" Joseph stonecutter b 293 Sawyer
" Joseph twister b 30 Eugenia
" Julia Mrs operative b 1098 Acushnet avenue [49 Hall
" J Arthur barber 131 Purchase h
" Louis N bricklayer h 89 Austin
" Luca operative h 325 Belleville av
" Magloire laborer h 22 Belleville road [road
" Maxim stoneecutter h 130 River
" Maxime fisherman h 12 Nye
" Maxime laborer b 325 Belleville avenue
" Michele surveyor b 188 Collette
" Napoleon operative b 22 Jean
" Narcisse A police h 159 Bonney
" Octave removed to Fairhaven
" Ovid fixer b 859 S Water
" Ozee machinist b 60 Sylvia
" Philias laborer h 505 N Front
" Philias operative b 1022 Acushnet avenue
" Pierre mason h 251 State
" Wilfred fisherman h 31 Holly
" Wilfred operative b 293 Sawyer
" William carpenter b 195 Collette
" William operative b 22 Belleville road [dent
" Zephraim weaver h 73 Indepen-
Breby Joseph lumber h 1537 Acushnet avenue [burn
Bredeau Albert operative h 20 Wash-
Breder Michael bartender h 34 Washburn [ster
Breen Ellen Mrs removed to Web-
" Frank J watchman h 128 N Second [Pleasant
" George A clerk 100 William b 447
" George A compositor Standard rms 34 High
Bregaman Andre removed from city
" August removed from city
Breman Catherine widow George h 190 Maxfield [Crapo
Bremans Thomas laborer h 161
Brennan Ann widow Thomas h 161 Crapo
" Benjamin mill hand bds 126 Eugenia [av
" Bridget operative h 74 Acushnet

Brennan
" Bridget widow Edward M h 212 Smith [Maxfield
" Catherine widow George h 190
" Charles W laborer h 76 Emma
" Edward M died March 8 1911
" Elizabeth A widow Stephen b 8 George [Purchase
" Ellen M widow Patrick h 991
" Gregory operative h 57 W French avenue
" James laborer b 351 Sawyer
" James (weaver) rem from city
" John city laborer b 161 Crapo
" John died March 30 1911
" John W foreman 123 Front h 67 Clinton
" Joseph brakeman h 62 Middle
" Katherine V h 63 Sycamore
" Mary operative bds 27 Penniman
" Mary (widow Daniel) died Oct 9 1910
" Mary E operative bds 63 Ruth
" Michael H laborer h 27 Penniman
" Michael J spinner h 4 Welcome
" Peter laborer h 41 Howland Village
" Thomas clerk Times b 212 Smith
Breneke Martin chef h 123 Parker
Bresnahan Mary widow Patrick h 121 Bonney [po
Bretherton Thomas weaver h 130 Cra-
Breto Antone mill hand b 116 Phillips avenue [Purchase
Breton Adelard fisherman h 839
" Cyrille laborer h 26 Belleville av
" Felix operative h 1017 Purchase
" Ferdinand fisherman h 1017 Purchase
" Francois fisherman h 124 N Front
" Frank operative h 7 Fulton court
" Frank X laborer b 7 Fulton ct
" Henry J overseer Dartmouth Mfg Corp h 163 Bonney [net av
" John ironworker b 2891 Acush-
" Joseph carder h 23 Kenyon
" Joseph ironworker b 2891 Acushnet avenue [fin av
" Joseph slubber tender h 287 Cof-
" Philemon operative b 154 Cedar Grove [h do
" Theodore O artist 595 Purchase
Brew Joseph plumber bds 6 Oneko lane

F. T. AKIN & CO. PAINTERS AND DECORATORS

Brewer Herbert weaver b 8 George
" John weaver h 49 Bowditch
" Margaret Mrs carder b 9 Morton court [rd
" Thomas spinner h 189 Belleville
Brewster Mary Mrs operative b 219 State [ton h 328 do
Brick Harry shoe repairer 342 Kemp-
" Philip shoes 807 S Water b 79 Grinnell [79 Grinnell
" Solomon shoe repairer 33 Rivet h
Bridge Albert weaver bds 256 Weld
" Joseph electrician h 12 Woodlawn avenue [den
Bridgham Ernest G painter h 26 Bor-
Brie Frederick carpenter h 16 Viall
Brien Andre fixer h 16 Thatcher
Brier Edward laborer b 64 Tallman
" George A M (George A Brier) & Co liquors 261 Rivet h do
" Joseph laborer h 412 First
Brierley Benjamin clerk 163 Union b 81 Dunbar [av b 92 Dunbar
" Edmund tinsmith 185 Acushnet
" John mill hand h 92 Dunbar
" Joseph removed to Chile S A
Brierly Caroline widow Ernest b 15 Peckham [244½ State h do
" Elizabeth widow Samuel variety
" Ernest removed from city
" Felix tailor h 118 Potomska
" James E C S practitioner h 7 Fifth [ska h do
" Jane Mrs dressmaker 118 Potom-
" Raymond H clerk 152 N Water h 574 Kempton [ham
" Samuel slasher tender h 15 Peck-
" Thomas variety 130 County h do
" William spinner h 31 Brock av
Briggs Adeline widow F Lawrence h 150 Sycamore
" Alfred fireman b 602 Purchase
" Allen G chauffeur N B W W h 2521 Acushnet avenue
" Annie M bookkeeper rms 570 Elm
" Annie T Mrs housekeeper 69 Maple [183 Campbell
" Archie J barber 395 Kempton b
" Arthur S bookkeeper City Coal Co h 139 Chestnut
" Byron A carpenter h 115 Willis
" Carrie A widow Daniel D h 53 Bedford [dale av
" Charles A carpenter b 204 Rock-

Briggs
" Charles F h 93 School
" Charles H clerk rms 283 Union
" Chester A clerk Dartmouth M Co b 1808 Acushnet avenue
" Clifton D physician 191 Pleasant h do [570 Elm (W)
" Daisy M clerk 160 Purchase bds
" Eaton operative b 62 Roosevelt
" Elizabeth M teacher R C Ingraham school b 351 County
" Frank P operator h 370 State
" George E h 165 Fair
" George E Jr student b 165 Fair
" George K painter rms 230 Kempton
BRIGGS GEORGE L stationery etc 161 Purchase h 103 S Sixth See back cover [ton
" George W carriagemaker h 341 Maxfield
" Harriet S died Mar 20 1911
" Harry weaver b 39 Tallman
" Herbert A carpenter 204 Rockdale avenue h do
" James fixer b 439 S Front
" James operative bds 17 Margin
" James C (Briggs & Beckman) 35 Commercial h 53 Washington
" Jane widow James h 17 Margin
" Joseph weaver h 13 Salisbury

JUSTUS A BRIGGS JR
ATTORNEY AND COUNSELLOR AT LAW
18 Masonic Building
22 Pleasant Street
Telephone 1487-2
Residence 267 Hillman Street
Telephone 2139-1

Briggs Justus A Jr lawyer 18 Masonic bldg residence 267 Hillman
" J Franklin clerk 35 Commercial h 69 Fifth
" Lester W teamster h 18 Myrtle
" Lillian M Mrs h 79 Grinnell

Remember to investigate our methods before taking up a business course.
Kinyon's Commercial School
Odd Fellows Bldg., Cor. William and Pleasant Sts., New Bedford, Mass.

Briggs

" Lizzie B widow Stephen H h 351 County [204 Rockdale av
" Mabel L clerk 41 Purchase bds
" Marion asst at Public Library b 173 Acushnet avenue
" Mary E widow Elihu h 8 Borden
" Mary E widow Nathan C b 79 Locust
" Myron S driver 270 Acushnet av h 89 Washington [Elm (W)
" Otis Leonard letter carrier h 570
" Philip S carriage trimmer 173 Acushnet avenue h do [ville rd
" Prudence widow Caleb C h Plain-
" Rhoda teacher Middle st school b 18 Lincoln
" Samuel B shoecutter h 119 Parker
" Sophie E widow Henry h 127 Maple
" Susan widow David b 19 Borden
" William H conductor b 204 Rockdale avenue

BRIGGS WILLIAM P guns and locksmith 141 Purchase and inspector of wires 308 Municipal bldg h 220 Kempton See Advt Electricians in Business Directory

" William T removed to Acushnet

BRIGGS & BECKMAN (J C Briggs and C E Beckman) ship chandlery and sailmakers 31-35 Commercial See page 785

Brigham Harry P rem to Fairhaven

Bright Henry removed from city

Brightman Alfred I teamster h 119 Florence [liam h 47 State
" Arthur B meatcutter 100 Wil-
" Bros (Fred W) paint mfrs 146 Front

BRIGHTMAN CHARLES O contractor and builder 72 N Water h 82 Mill See page 95

" Charles W shoemaker b 39 Smith
" Clifford R helper 55 N Water b 157 Grinnell

BRIGHTMAN EDWARD T provisions 248 Purchase, 306 Cedar and 109 S Sixth h 72 Willis See advt Grocers in Business Directory

" Ellery E police h 130 Fruit

Brightman

" Everett M clerk 726 Kempton b 340 Cedar
" Frank C drillmaker h 251 Orchard (S)
" Frank R plumber 55 N Water h 157 Grinnell
" Franklin E chief clerk 57 N Second b 3 Park place
" Fred clerk rms 3 Park place
" Fred W (Brightman Bros h 133 Kempton
" Frederick C baker 372 Kempton h 8 Briggs court [Bedford
" Frederick S pres 127 Union h 89

BRIGHTMAN F S CO Inc news depot 127 Union See page 769

" George A h 39 Smith
" George F h 677 County
" George F woodworker 3 E Pope h 186 River road
" Harry C clerk h 68 State
" Harry S machinist b 251 Orchard (S) [h 40 Mill
" Herbert W provisions 106 Union
" Herman A officer H C h 405 Union [b do
" Ida M dressmaker 133 Kempton
" Jane A widow Jacob h 31 Sycamore
" John M teamster h 616 Union
" John Y agent h 340 Cedar
" Kenneth H (S D Howland & Co) 86 Chancery b do [Campbell
" Lawrence S city teamster h 128
" Leander clothing 55 William h 29 Madison
" Lida J Mrs h 15 Borden
" Lucy M h 613 County [Madison
" L Merton treas 127 Union h 29
" Marshall C clerk b 82 Mill
" Mary Mrs h 52 School
" Mary A widow Ellery R h 372 Cottage [b 3526 do
" Mary H clerk 3913 Acushnet av
" Noah teamster b 72 Walden
" Oliver C manager 246 Union b 82 Mill [Westport
" Omar helper 28 N Water h at
" Philip O laborer b 72 Walden
" Ralph carpenter h 647 Kempton
" Ralph plumber 54 Union h at Fairhaven
" Robert G teamster h 22 North

HASKELL BROS. DEALERS IN
ICE
400 COURT STREET TELEPHONE CONNECTION NEW BEDFORD, MASS.

Brightman
" Roswell L salesman 146 Front h 424 Union
" Sarah J widow h 50 North
" William A teamster h 72 Walden
" William C clerk 140 Union b 340 Cedar
" William O died April 4 1911
Brillion Charles carder h 92 Bowditch
" Edeas spinner h 94 Bowditch
" George teamster h 379 Coggeshall
" Joseph died Nov 29 1910 [vin
Brillode Adelard painter h r 20 Mar-
BRILLON ADELARD painter 80 Holly h 85 do See page 777
" Joseph Jr liquors 809 Purchase h 909 County
" Josephine widow b 881 County
Brimley Austin warper b 23 Warren
" John J janitor h 76 Division
" Richard engineer h 35 Jouvett
" Wilfred clerk 272 Allen b 23 Warren [Cedar Grove
Brinau Nellie widow Patrick h 274
Brindle George weaver h 319 Sawyer
" Hatton machinist h 445 Chancery
" John weaver h 23 Stapleton
" Lizzie and Sarah weavers h 13 Salisbury
" Ralph weaver h 208 Cedar Grove
" Thomas weaver b 23 Stapleton
" William P machinist h 22 Roosevelt [vis
Brindley Thomas molder bds 105 Da-
Brinley Alice weaver b 113 Division
" Elizabeth widow Peter h 113 Division
" Mary A weaver b 113 Division
Briscoe Retta M teacher Jirah Swift school b 69 Russell [side av
Brisson Jean B weaver h 5 River-
" Medix operative b 56 Clark
" Octave Mrs h 56 Clark
Bristol County House of Correction Ash (N) cor Court
" County Registry of Deeds North Sixth cor William
" Hotel Thomas Wrigley proprietor 219 Purchase [198 Coggeshall
" Mfg Corp cotton cloth mfrs
" Printing Co (James W Owen Jr) 354 Purchase [cury rms 87 Mill
Britt George W P reporter Mer-
Brittain Edward overseer Wamsutta Mill h 17 Willow [away
" Fred J blacksmith h 165 Hath-
" George H salesman h 55 Rotch av
" Joseph painter b 437 Purchase
" Margaret widow h 344 Coffin av
" Robert h 274 Pope
" Samuel C motorman b 225 Cedar
Britten James spinner h 21 Winsor
Britto Annie h 71 S Second
" Antone laborer h 94 South Water
" John variety 217 N Second h 348 South Water
" Peter waiter bds 71 South Second
" Theophilus operative h 12 Cannon
" Verissimo F longshoreman h 15 Morgan's lane [burn
Britton Albert operative h 38 Wash-
" Charles F driver 50 Elm h 363 Dartmouth [ley
" Fred mule spinner bds 10 Ash-
" Louise C widow William b 39 Hillman
Broad David bricklayer h 198 State
Broadbent Albert machinist h 5 Richmond
" Charles machinist h 53 Fair
" Charles N steam fitter h 32 Summit [avenue
" Charles T machinist b 325 Coffin
" Edwin S clerk h 25 Willow
" Eliza bookkeeper 416 Kempton b 212 Weld [b 212 Weld
" Elizabeth A clerk 368 Kempton
" Ernest W student b 196 South
" Ethel clerk P Corp b 60 Briggs
" George A spinner h 60 Briggs
" John S machine fitter b 106 South
" John T overseer Potomska Mills h 106 South
" Mary widow Thomas h 212 Weld
" Robert L mule spinner h 49 Fair
" Samuel S janitor Acushnet av school h 26 Borden
" Thomas E engineer 19 Linden h 29 Valentine
" William H overseer Hathaway Mfg Co h 200 County
" William H Jr clerk 157 Union b 200 County [er
" William S steamfitter h 15 Hom-
Broadland Ellen clerk b 101½ Fifth
" John removed to Fairhaven
" Ole blacksmith b 27 Borden
" Terry drill maker h 27 Borden

J. F. CROSSLEY 223 MILL STREET COR. EMERSON PHONE
STEAM and HOT WATER HEATING
GAS FITTING and FIXTURES

Broadmeadow Ellen bookkeeper 28 William b 97 Durfee
" George machinist h 102 Durfee
" Maximillian clerk bds 97 Durfee
" Minnie bds 102 Durfee
" Simeon h 97 Durfee
Brochu Alice milliner 51 Brock av bds 1060 Acushnet avenue
" Annie Mrs dressmaker 1279 Acushnet avenue h do [av
" Desire machinist h 1060 Acushnet
" Joseph E shoes 1275 Acushnet av h 1279 do [ant h 106 Arnold
Brock George P real estate 52 Pleas-
" Herbert N watchman h 84 Fruit
" Stephen H engineer b 84 Fruit
Brocklehurst James M doffer b 125 Rockland
" Joseph fireman h 125 Rockland
" William machinist h 288 Fourth
" William Jr operative h 128 Rivet
Broderick Katherine clerk 182 Union b 176 Fourth [away
Brodeur Aleas carpenter h 186 Hath-
" Alphonse weaver b 839 Acushnet avenue [road
" Clement machinist b 39 Belleville
" Henry barber b 27 Kenyon
" Herbert mill hand b 190 Coffin av
" Hubert clerk 1284 Acushnet av h 1280 do
" John L weaver h 67 Ruth
" Joseph agent 73 William b 111 Kempton [road
" Joseph operative h 39 Belleville
" Joseph spinner h 250 Bowditch
" Joseph J spinner b 283 Collette
" Leo bds 1280 Acushnet avenue
" Leon carpenter bds 53 Ruth
" Louis machinist h 47 Hersom
" Louis machinist h 84 Covell [av
" Napoleon weaver h 839 Acushnet
" Olivine widow Leon h 53 Ruth
" Paul weaver b 283 Collette
" Philip carpenter h 39 Belleville rd
" see Brothers [rary h 98 Fourth
Brodhead Edith H asst at public lib-
" Katherine J widow William H b 98 Fourth [net av
Brody Morris pedlar b 1139 Acush-
" Robert clerk h 94 Clark [Leonard
Brogan Alexander A carpenter b 1
" Kate widow Edward h 1 Leonard

Brogden George weaver h 25 Viall
" Harry carpenter h 163 Tinkham
" Henry carpenter b 163 Tinkham
" John operative h 12 Clark
" John W fixer b 25 Viall
Bromides John (National Ice Cream Co) 580 N Front h 124 Belleville road
Bromley Caleb machinist h 124 Crapo
" Florence A stenographer 57 N Second b 275 Hawthorn
Bronco Antone laborer h 134 Fourth
Bronshpigel Max tailor 1345 Acushnet avenue h 556 State
Brooklawn Pharmacy (F M Beauvais) 1881 Acushnet av [River rd
Brooks Abbie J widow John B h 191
" Abraham laborer h 3136 Acushnet avenue [Maple
" Andrew J drill straightener h 103
" Arthur lamp lighter b 1458 Acushnet avenue [road
" Arthur T drill maker b 191 River
" Evans mariner h 195 Bonney
" George sail maker 31 Commercial h 219 Acushnet avenue
" George H sail maker 31 Commercial b 219 Acushnet avenue
" James teamster b 22 Crapo
" James yard man h 5 Abbott
" James T glass blower h 22 Crapo
" Joseph mill hand b 46 Belleville road
" Joseph F glass cutter b 22 Crapo
" Laurence rem to Saranac Lake N Y
" Nathan B deputy sheriff h 433 Cottage [Purchase
" Susan Mrs laundress rms 527
" William J removed from city
Brophy Edward police h 441 Sawyer
" Mary C clerk 185 Union b 256 Chestnut [h 23 Oak
" Owen overseer N E C Y Co
" William H overseer Bristol Mill h 256 Chestnut [Holly
Broshek Albert R operative bds 130
" Joseph U S N b 130 Holly
" Luke removed to N Y City
" Mary widow Joseph h 130 Holly
" Peter fixer h 156 Bowditch
Broshels Albert operator 43 William
Brothers Frank steam fitter h 84 Linden
" Joseph spinner h 377 Pleasant

CHARLES A. CROSHERE CARRIAGE AND AUTO
38 FOURTH ST. Bell Phone 1964-23 PAINTING

Brotherson Frederick F janitor 57 N Second h at Fairhaven
Broughton Bracewell weaver b 257 Coffin avenue
" James weaver bds 15 Adams
" James M b 1089 Acushnet av
" John carpenter bds 15 Adams
" John weaver h 176 Bowditch
" Samuel weaver b 27 McGurk
" Thomas linotypist Stanard h Plainville road
" William weaver h 351 Sawyer
Brouillard Ernest third hand b 67 Coffin avenue [Linden
Brouillette Arthur operative b 43
" Arthur second hand b 164 Cedar
" Eleodore spinner h 67 Ruth
" George fixer b 533 S Second
" Henry clerk b 141 Cedar Grove
" Henry shuttle maker h 190 Earle
" Joseph motorman bds 164 Cedar Grove
" Moise h 164 Cedar Grove
" Moise fixer h 263 North Front
" Moise Jr clerk h 43 Linden
" Wilfred second hand b 164 Cedar Grove
" William Mrs h 533 S Second
Brousseau Absalom weaver h 138 Cedar Grove
" Cora E Mrs h 488 Acushnet av
" Henry milk 275 N Front h do
" Iseie laborer b 138 Cedar Grove
" Joseph laborer b 138 Cedar Grove
" Mary L Mrs grocer 201 Austin h do
" Napoleon piper h 50 Nye
" Oliver engineer 31 Bowditch h 201 Austin [lette
" Peter slubber tender b 150 Col-
" Thomas mason h 880 Purchase
Brown Albert D iron worker h 83 Park
" Albert N painter h 71 S Sixth
" Alexander mason h 43 Ryan
" Alice A operative b 190 North
" Alice E h 58 Campbell [ton
" Alice M stenographer b 149 New-
" Annie clerk 1026 Acushnet av b rear 94 Hathaway [8 Thompson
" Annie E bookkeeper 17 N Sixth b
" Anthony clerk b 9 Thompson
" Anthony A bartender 37 Howland bds 9 Thompson [h 117 Willis
" Arthur P shipper Bennett Mill

Brown
" Arthur R h 196 Cottage
" Austin J clerk 70 Purchase rms 172 William [av beyond L C
" Benjamin spinner h Acushnet
" Bertha S teacher Merrimac st school b 270 Pleasant
" Charles laborer h 343 Middle
" Charles B financial secretary Y M C A rms do
" Charles D shoemaker h 167 Mill
" Charles E laborer bds 78 Ash (N)
" Charles F public carriage h 197 Cedar [Willow
" Charles H engineer 97 Front h 25
" Charles W druggist 452 S Water h 111 Fifth [Rockland
" Dallas butler 379 County h 184
" Dallas Jr removed to Boston
" Daniel W (Sylvia & Brown) 25 Purchase b 25 Willow
" David laborer h 1213 Rockdale av
" David painter b 382 Cedar [do
" David E shirt mfr 83 Hillman h
" Earl C driver b 28 Maxfield
" Edward S cashier Mechanics National Bank h 405 County
" Edward S shoeworker b 4 Norton court
" Elizabeth, Mary E and Annie h 66 Penniman [Florence
" Elmer clerk 100 William b 83
" Emma E Mrs h 4 Pine
" Ernest D manager 109 William rms 175 do [78 Ash (N)
" Florence A widow William H h
" Frank drill worker h 168 Acushnet avenue
" Frank mill hand b 187 Bonney
" Frank painter h 499 Rivet
" Frank C architect b 2 Spruce
" Frank E whaling guns and lances 4 S Water rms Mansion House
BROWN FREDERICK A photographer 88 Purchase h at Fairhaven See page 778
" Frederick C paymaster P Corp b 10 High
" Frederick R treasurer Booth Mfg Co h 11 Hawthorn terrace
" F Eben clerk 4 S Water bds 103 School
" F Rudolph rms 464 County

J. G. NICHOLSON
LUMBER, SASH, DOORS and BLINDS
BOWDITCH STREET, NEW BEDFORD, MASS.

Brown
" Gabriel J drill worker bds 170 Fourth
" George operative h 190 N Front
" George teamster h 228 N Second
" George A machinist 146 Pleasant h 282 Kempton
" George A operative b 28 Howard
" George D tool makers' foreman 152 N Water h at Fairhaven
" George F Mrs h 167 Summer
" George H insurance broker 97 William rm 305 b 25 Willow
" George H T treasurer and secretary 158 Purchase b 60 Fourth
" George W janitor b 188 North
" G H clerk 100 Fifth
" Helen A Mrs h 169 Mill [Park
" Henry G horse trainer h 239
" Herbert A carpenter h 2 Spruce
" Herbert F bookkeeper h 45 Fifth
" Irving A optician 206 Union h 31 Kene
" Isaac painter 28 Elm h do
" Jacob H job wagon 31 Spring h 10 Old Market square
" James h 193 Coffin avenue [av
" James loom fixer b 976 Acushnet
" James removed from city
" James A foreman 159 N Second h 234 Allen [ton
" James E shoe worker b 334 Kemp-
" James H lawyer b 67 Merrimac
" James H shipper h 212 North
" Jessie O stenographer 84 Union b 464 County
" John rms 7 N Second
" John clerk 27 N Second
" John fireman U St Ry Co power station h at Fairhaven
" John laborer h 29 Atlantic [sq
" John laborer b 10 Old Market
" John spinner b 79 Rodney
" John C druggist 209 Coggeshall h 29 Tremont
" John C machinist h 566 Elm (W)
" John E slasher b 79 Rodney
" John F molder h 712 Kempton
" John H D janitor 391 County h 139 James [avenue
" Joseph driver b 92 Acushnet
" Joseph driver 8 Union h 275 S Second
" Joseph A weaver h 19 Bourne

Brown
" Joseph S gardener h 4 Norton ct
" Julia A M clerk 182 Union h 58 Campbell [h do
" Katherine Mrs matron Almshouse
" Kennedy weaver h 382 Cedar
" Mabel bookkeeper rms 2 Seventh
" Manuel fireman 45 School b 499 First
" Manuel laborer b 47 Hemlock
" Manuel teamster 170 Purchase h 41 Pierce [Acushnet av
" Manuel teamster 2 S Water b 92
" Manuel Jr laborer b 90 Acushnet avenue
" Manuel G h 640 S Water
" Mary sewer b 123 Crapo
" Mary widow b 28 Acushnet av
" Mary widow William b 193 Coffin avenue
" Mary Mrs h 49 Hemlock
" Mary Mrs forewoman 36 Purchase h 167 Summer
" Mary A h 1 Seventh [er 75 Willis
" Mary A J widow John housekeep-
" Mary Elizabeth librarian h 355 Cottage
" Mary F h 154 Chestnut
" Mary J Mrs h 123 Crapo
" Mary J Mrs h 439 S Front
" Melvin J physician 35 Mill h do
" Oliver F (B H Waite & Co) carpets 71 William h 139 Cottage
" Olivia Mrs h 190 North
" Paul twister b 190 Davis
" Rose C removed from city
" Sally C nurse h 58 Campbell
" Samuel A telegrapher 151 Union b 3 Lincoln [20 S Second
" Sarah widow James W lodging h
" Stephen H coachman 396 County b do
" Thomas carder h 79 Rodney
" Thomas fireman h 187 Bonney
" Thomas piper h 88 Blackmer
" Thomas twister h 28 Acushnet av
" Thomas D teamster h 259 Middle
" Thomas F supt Almshouse h do
" Walter H driver 298 Acushnet av b 56 Walnut [31 Keene
" Walter I optician 206 Union b
" Walter N driver h 106 High

Steiger-Dudgeon Co.
"The WOMAN'S Store."
Tel. Bell 82 & 83, Branches connecting all depts.
" " 160 For Office only. Auto. 1211

SUMPTIONS, ASSORTMENTS AT ALL TIMES OF DEPENDABLE DRY GOODS

Brown
" Walter S conductor h 57 Campbell [avenue
" William carpenter b 25 E French
" William clerk 1 William h 620 Union
" William librarian N End Branch Public Library and manager 1026 Acushnet av h r 94 Hathaway
" William student b r 94 Hathaway
" William weaver b 976 Acushnet avenue
" William A twister b 19 Ashley
" William G blacksmith h 50 Smith
" William G Jr blacksmith b 50 Smith
" William H drill maker h 293 Maxfield [h 84 Merrimac
" William H paint grinder 14 Wall
" William Keating painter h 149 Newton [h do
" William L G florist 101 Cedar
" William S twister h 28 Acushnet avenue
" & Co (George H T Brown) gas and electric fixtures 158 Purchase
" see Braun and Brun
Browne Frederic T (The Browne Pharmacy) 201 Union h 91 Court [bds 91 Court
" Frederic T Jr clerk 201 Union
" Harry H mgr Centre corner Main Fairhaven b 91 Court
" Henry A overseer Hathaway Mfg Co h 22 Crapo
" John slasher tender h 109 David
BROWNE PHARMACY The (F T Browne) 197 to 203 Union and Fairhaven See back cover
Brownell Adeline W widow Jirah F h 59 Mechanic's lane
" Albert F driver h 67 Chancery
" Andrew P Mrs h 133 Washington
" Benjamin S mason h 222 Shawmut avenue [mit
" Caroline widow David h 7 Sum-
" Charles E h 2 Arch
" Charles H carpenter h Plainville road [Hunter
" Charles H W tool maker h 13
" Charles T market gardener 320 Mt Pleasant h do

Brownell
" Clarence H manager Parker House h at Padanaram
" Cornelia H bds 103 Ash (N)
" David removed to Mattapoisette
" Debra widow Benjamin F h 58 Hill
" Earl C porter rms 101 Middle
" Eliza L died Nov 5 1910
" Elliot E removed to Memphis Tennessee [rence
" Elmer W meat cutter h 83 Flo-
" Elnathan C vice president (Consolidated Meat & Grocery Co) and proprietor Parker House h 69 Court [North
" Esther A widow Milton A h 155
" Florence D bds 634 Cottage
" Frederick A clerk h 114 Mill
" Frederick A driver h 335 Middle
" George A carpenter 107 Ash (N) h 103 do [h 15 Columbia
" George A pressman 350 S Second
" George H K assistant foreman Standard h 147 Hillman
" Gilbert K insurance agent h 372 Reed [Union
" Grace M widow William E h 271
" Harold R painter h 419 Kempton
" Harriet P teacher Clark street school b 161 Maxfield
" Herbert A driver b 335 Middle
" Herbert J agent h 161 Maxfield
" Herbert N painter h 88 Dartmouth
" Lena R clerk bds 155 Summer
" Lester T chauffeur 14 Ward b at Horseneck
" Mary A widow Charles H h 99 Florence [Union
" Mary L widow Stephen b 585
" Milton L operative b 147 Hillman
BROWNELL MORRIS R (Cook Brownell & Taber) 1 Masonic bldg h at Fairhaven
" Myron W clerk Parker House h 59 Hillman [North
" Olive A widow Daniel H h 185
" Samuel R h 155 Summer
" Sara V bookkeeper Old Colony Box Co b 634 Cottage [North
" Sarah L widow Charles H h 68

PELEG H. SHERMAN 506 COUNTY ST.
FUNERAL DIRECTOR AND EMBALMER
OFFICE PHONES. Bell 690-13 Auto. 1305.
RESIDENCE PHONES. Bell 690-12. Auto. 1306.

Brownell
" Sarah M widow John F matron police department h 634 Cottage [331 Cedar
" Sherod M foreman 14 Wall h
" Ulysses G (A W Perkins & Co) roofer and teaming 167 Hillman h 141 Cedar
" Walter F cashier h 47 Crapo
" William B painter 52 Oak h do
" William J mill hand h Shawmut avenue beyond Plainville road
Brownhill Alfred D glass cutter h 465 Bolton [Field
" Richard A glass cutter h 255
" Walter I glass cutter b 465 Bolton
Browning Arthur C drill maker h 351 County [580 do
" Edwin E dentist 570 Purchase h
" Lillian instructor N B Industrial school b 351 County [chase
" Lydia T widow Clark h 570 Pur-
" Thomas overseer h 253 Hillman
Brownley Phillip driver h 280 Coggeshall [Co h 58 Locust
Brownson George L foreman T-N B C
" Helen S dressmaker 58 Locust h do
Broxup John removed to Lowell
Bruce Ada G teacher H M Knowlton school b 138 Rotch
" Douglas clerk Hawes, Tewksbury & Co bds 138 Rotch
" George C insurance solicitor 24 Clifford bldg b 138 Rotch
" Gertrude A B widow George C h 138 Rotch [mouth
" James H second hand h 86 Dart-
" May U teacher Thomas R Rodman school b 138 Rotch [city
Bruckner Rudolph removed from
Brule Adelard watchman Grinnell Mill h 18 Bowditch
" Albert J plumber h 32 McGurk
" Mary widow operative h 13 Hicks
Brum Mary sewer 40 Purchase b 123 Crapo [avenue
Brumne Goao mill hand b 204 Coffin
Brun Antone wheelwright h 109 Bullard
" George weaver h 149 Bullard
" Joseph weaver h 696 Purchase
" Ovila T variety 33 Bullard h do

Brun
" Wilfred D died April 4 1911
" see Brown [Purchase
Bruneau John shoemaker rms 212
" Xavier laborer h 121 Bates av
Bruneault Felix carpenter b 19 Rodney [198 Belleville road
Brunnelle Alcide eyelet maker bds
" Arthur clerk b 97 Mt Pleasant
" Eugene weaver h 19 Thatcher
" Eugene weaver h 855 S Water
" Felix carpenter h 19 Rodney
" Joseph pool 1619 Acushnet av
" Joseph weaver h 74 Division
" Louis weaver h 642 First
" Michel h 198 Belleville road
" Oliver A millinery 8 Purchase and 129 Rivet h 97 Mt Pleasant [Sixth
" Samuel speeder tender b 43 N
Brunner Gotfreid weaver h 134 Bowditch [ushnet av
Brunnette Arthur teamster b 967 Ac-
" Gilbert mason h 434 Pleasant
" Gilbert N piper h r 115 Fifth
" Joseph A driver 122 Durfee
" Nector mason h 18 Roosevelt
" Paul weaver h 23 Viall
Bruno Benson carpenter h 128 Hicks
Brunt Albert mill hand b 1672 Acushnet avenue [den
Brush Ira B salesman h 81 Wal-
Bruso Joseph weaver b 31 Bentley
Bryan Lewis E porter h 128 Cedar
Bryant Aaron C carpenter h 721 Kempton [h 34 High
" Edward H clerk h 171 Purchase
" Eli loom fixer h 70 Hall [mer
" Elsie L music teacher b 205 Sum-
" Francis A president N B C Co h at New York
" Herbert P h 30 Seventh
" John H janitor registry of deeds h 61 Jenny Lind
" John I county commissioner Court House h at Fairhaven [County
" John W baker 92 Walden h 978
" Julia S Mrs h 493 Mill
" May teacher Phillips av school h at Fairhaven [Cottage
" Ruth M widow Israel T h 201
" Sarah widow Seth E b 51 Mt Pleasant
" Seth E Jr salesman 45 Purchase rm 2 h 51 Mt Pleasant

COAL AND WOOD F. T. AKIN & COMPANY
HAY AND STRAW
WALNUT, COR. WATER, 84 PLEASANT ST., 25 WELD SQ.
129 COVE STREET WHF. FOOT OF COFFIN STREET

Bryant
" Susan W widow Alden H clerk 28 Purchase h 436 Mill
" Victor A salesman 80 Purchase b 70 Hall
" William burnisher h 205 Summer
Bryden John W drill grinder h 347 Orchard (S)
" Samuel caretaker Fairhaven bridge h 1 Pope Island
" Walter J machinist h 73 Hathaway [ty
" William T motorman h 943 Coun-
Bryll Edward page 246½ Union b 154 S Second
" Henry h 154 S Second
" Louis operative b 154 S Second
" Matilda Mrs variety 156 S Second h 154 do
" Michael b 154 S Second [ham
" Samuel H removed to S Framing-
Bryson John dyer h 7 Salisbury
Buba John operative b 33 Delano
" Joseph weaver h 33 Delano
" Michael weaver b 33 Delano [mer
" Wladyslaw weaver h 204 Black-
Buchanan Annie widow John h 13 Harmony [er h 378 Cottage
Buchell Charles N commercial travel-
" Grace T bookkeeper 26 N Second b 378 Cottage
" Ruth B stenographer City Mfg Corporation b 378 Cottage
Buck John K removed from city
" Sophia S widow Obed b 81 Hillman
Buckles Charles weaver b 173 David
" John weaver h 173 David
Buckley Albert E machinist b 216 Shawmut avenue
" Annie Mrs h 60 Thomas
" Charles driver 10 Weaver h David
" Charles E designer h 53 Peckham
" Charles H overseer Pierce Mill h 337 Tinkham
" Cornelius freman h 117 Locust
" Daniel mule spinner h 28 George
" Elizabeth widow b 7 Reynolds
" Ella F clerk b 81 Summer
" Ellen Mrs h 52 Morton ct
" Emma C died March 22 1911
" Frank fixer h 374 N Front
" Frank second h 187 Dean

Buckley
" Frank F spinner h 189 Dean
" George elevatorman h 46 Myrtle
" Harry L clerk 17 Pleasant b 240 Collette [Shawmut av
" Henry H mule spinner h 101
" James operative h 51 Tallman
" James M spinner b 3 Winter
" John died August 15 1910
" John J fixer h 240 Collette
" John J ice 53 Howard av h do
" John P proprietor Improved Wet Wash Laundry 409 Chancery h 371 do [avenue
" John W spinner b 206 W French
" John W H loom fxer h 178 Weld
" Mary A clerk 182 Union b 117 Locust [Oil Co b 117 Locust
" Maurice Leo manager Valvoline
" Thomas electrician h 102 Ash (N)
" Thomas W instructor H of C h 96 South
" Thomas W supt 158 Purchase
" Walter clerk 874 Purchase h 273 do [b 56 Fourth
" William elevatorman 185 Union
" William Byron shoe worker b 172 William
Bucklin Ella F clerk overseers of the poor b 81 Summer
" Fred C upholsterer 27 Fifth h 144 Acushnet avenue
" Frederick C Jr mill hand b 144 Acushnet avenue
Budd John gardener h 4 Summit
" John T driver h 144 Richmond
" Stanley W shade maker 36 Purchase h 4 Summit
Budgeon Alfred clerk b 311 County
" Arthur shoemaker 64 Dartmouth h 311 County
" Marguerite E teacher Thomas Donaghy school b 311 County
" Mary A teacher Cedar Grove st school b 311 County
BUDLONG JAMES (The J E Budlong Press) 38 Middle h 54 Chestnut See page 778
" John A painter h 80 Merrimac
Buehr John weaver h 1 Cornell place
BUFFINGTON ARTHUR E mason and builder 1 Crapo h 27 do See page 788

To do things right you must be taught. Our instructors can do it.
Kinyon's Commercial School
Odd Fellows Bldg., Cor. William and Pleasant Sts., New Bedford, Mass.

Buffington
" Arthur L manager 99 Front h 60 Tremont [Fairhaven
" Henry C clerk 100 Fifth b at
" Lynton M drill maker h 418 Union [h 176 Fourth
" Oscar sampler Wamsutta Mill
Buffinton Julia A Mrs dressmaker 107 Chancery h do
" Lester G assistant bookkeeper City M Co b 107 Chancery
Buhl A Alfred forger h 49 Vine
Buist Elizabeth h 52 Smith
" Frederick carpenter h 52 Smith
Buker Milfred I teacher High school h 372 Reed [h 67 Acushnet av
Bulcoa Henry clerk 48 S Second
" Lydia clerk 997 S Water b 67 Acushnet avenue [av
" Manuel S grocer h 67 Acushnet
Bulcock Bramwell laborer h 240 Tinkham [ham
" James R operative b 240 Tink-
Bulgie Lewis labobrer b 103 Hemlock
Bulkley Edwin died Dec 29 1910
Bullard Egbert G archcitect 76 Pleasant rm 30 h 55 Chestnut
" Frank S shipper 99 Front h 343 Kempton
" John M student b 428 County
" John T physician 428 County h do
" Minnie A matron 16 Howard h do
Bullen Albert weaver b 30 Bullock
" Thomas loom fixer h 30 Bullock
Buller Joseph teamster b 535 Acushnet avenue
Bullins Robert bricklayer rms American House Arcade bldg
Bullock Sarah widow Charles h 126 Thompson [h 45 Fifth
" William J druggist 268 Fourth
Bulman Frederic carpenter 374 Orchard (S) h do [58 S Sixth
" Henry T contractor 109 Bonney h
" Lillian clerk P Corporation b 58 South Sixth [M b 37 Bonney
Bumphrey Caroline T widow James
Bumpus Charles janitor h 81 Cedar
" Frank W engineer h 12 Spruce
" George C engineer h 17 Summer
" John Q A gardener h 81 Chancery
" Mary E teacher Mary B White school b at Fairhaven

Bumpus
" Valetta E stenographer 5 Beetle lane b at Acushnet
Bunk Peter weaver b 18 Fulton ct
Bunney Joseph loom fixer h 545 Cottage [Cottage
" Walter J second hand b 545
" see Bonney [Fourth
Bunoit Arthur mill hand h 254
Bunting Adam h 116 Phillips av
" Elmer J reporter Standard rms Y M C A [Collette
Buraczenski Frank weaver h 125
" Joseph weaver h 125 Collette
Burbank Anna L stenographer 100 Fifth b 37 Madison
" Benjamin F tailor rms 60 Spring
" Christina K widow Isaac N dressmaker 37 Madison h do
" Isaac N died Jan 31 1911
" John T bookkeeper h 68 Parker
" J Frank marble worker h 42 Parker
" Nancy P Mrs lodgings 60 Spring
" William C clerk h 337 Purchase
Burbeck Edward secretary Whitman Mills h at Boston
Burcellos Joseph M glass cutter b 106 Potomska [Lind
Burcham James driver h 73 Jenny
Burchell Elmer L station agent Acushnet station h do
Burdick Annie M Mrs dry goods 1647 Acushnet av h 1430 do
" Bertha S widow Stephen h 334 Kempton [ushnet av
" Charles third hand b 1430 Ac-
" Edward L overseer Whitman Mill h 1430 Acushnet avenue
" George M fixer h 46 Ashley
" Irving F collector b 420 Union
" James collector 125 Middle b 120 Union
Burding Clifton E driver 141 Fourth b 200 Acushnet avenue
" Henry L driver 214 Purchase h 151 Rockland [Acushnet av
" Hiram E overseer 131 Court h 200
" Joseph A rope maker h 15 Morton court [net av
" William H shipper b 200 Acush-
Bureau Marceline carpenter h 300 Earl
Burgess Alice Mrs b 248 Chestnut

Bread, Cake, Pastry
RICHMOND & COMPANY 255-257 UNION STREET
Bell 993 Automatic 1022

Burgess
" Charles helper rms 41 High
" Charles E student b 68 S Sixth
" Charles W bookkeeper h 194 Davis
" Daniel W laborer h 5 McGurk
" Eva H h 134 Willis
" George F engineer Y M C A h 302 County [68 S Sixth
" George W foreman 100 Fifth h
" Harriet h 134 Willis [h 225 Earl
" James grocer 1625 Acushnet av
" Jessie W teacher Harrington school bds 62 Shawmut avenue
" John b 63 Roosevelt
" John M h 39 Foster
" Joseph fixer h 13 Princeton
" Joseph second hand h 11 Potter
" Lee removed from city
" Lucy h 134 Willis
" Maria Mrs h 60 Salisbury
" Nathan laborer h 223 Shawmut av
" Oliver W motorman h 62 Shawmut avenue [b 62 Shawmut av
" Oliver W Jr clerk Whitman Mill
" Simon weaver h 15 Katharine
" Thomas h r 827 County [Russell
" Thomas E glass cutter rms 40
" Thomas H removed from city
" Vitale mill hand h 1 McDonald ct
" William engineer b 264 Pleasant
" William W comber b 5 McGurk
" see Bourgeois
Burgiel Joseph removed from city
Burgland Samuel mariner h 10 West High
Burgo Casear cook h 371 First
" Jacques operative h 10 Bedford
Burhoe Robert D carpenter h 31 E French av
" Thomas M carpenter h 451 Rivet
" Thomas M Mrs variety 453 Rivet h 451 do
Burke Aaron photographer h 11 George [Sycamore
" Abbie widow Henry b 106
" Anne widow Myles b 37 Linden
" Arthur P clerk 43 Bedford b 38 Ash (N)
" Cecelia bookkeeper b 103 Austin
" Charles foreman Rural Cemetry h 453 Hillman
" Cyril teamster h 1 Weld square

Burke
" Edward F salesman 14 N Second h 119 South [373 Maxfield
" Ernest E grocer 546 Kempton h
" Ezelia M dressmaker 106 Sycamore h do [field
" Harold clerk 185 Union b 97 Max-
" Harry clerk b 38 Ash (N)
" Isabelle widow John h 185 Arnold
" Janet F Mrs b 652 Purchase
" John brakeman h 37 Linden
" John drillworker h 185 Arnold
" John loom fixer h 111 David
" John operative rms 1 Clark
" John E bds 38 Ash (N)
" John H laborer h 38 Ash (N)
BURKE JOHN P plumbing 903 County h 408 Cedar See page 782
" John W bricklayer b 88 Robeson
" Joseph A prop Elm Rink 302 Purchase and Elm Hotel 35 Elm also Elm Bowling Alleys 34 do h 36 do
" Marriett nurse b 782 Kempotn
" Mary operative h 219 State
" Mary widow Michael h 103 Austin . [Elm W
" Mary widow Thomas F h 364
" Michael I h 415 Pleasant
" Patrick J janitor h 32 Clark
" Richard F city laborer h 226 Chancery
" Robert (Burke & Smith) 556 Kempton h 38 Jenney
" Robert houseman 7 N Second rms do [Nash rd
" Robert metal polisher h 121
" Rose widow John h 88 Robeson
" Susan widow John b 311 Acushnet av [Water h 97 Maxfield
" Thomas metal polisher 177 N
" Thomas H clerk b 97 Maxfield
" Thomas M plumber 903 County b 103 Austin
" Walter M (Taylor & Burke) 146 Pleasant h 23 Homer
" William died Oct 9 1910
" & Smith (Robert Burke and Samuel J Smith) grocers 556 Kempton
Burkle Edward J laundryman 270 Acushnet avenue h 17 Atlantic

GLOBE DYE HOUSE 220 SHAWMUT AVE.
J. N. J. LONHOLDT, PROP. Telephone Connections Goods called for and Delivered
Down town Office, 52 Pleasant St., Room 1 North End Office, 1014 Acushnet Ave.

BURNS

DETECTIVE BUREAU

ORIGINATOR OF

THE COLLEGIAN DETECTIVE FOR WEDDINGS, RECEPTIONS, SOCIAL FUNCTIONS, ETC.

Operatives of the Highest Character and Ability

Either Sex Sent Anywhere

References from America's Leading University, Eminent Members of the Bar, Prominent Social Leaders, Bankers, Corporations, Department Stores and Police Officials.

An Absolutely Honest and Confidential Business

Write or Call for References and Rates

7th FLOOR - 1 BEACON ST.

BOSTON, MASS.

Telephones, Haymarket 249 Cambridge 183

ROBERT BURNS, - Principal

BURNS

DETECTIVE BUREAU

ORIGINATOR OF

THE COLLEGIAN DETECTIVE FOR WEDDINGS, RECEPTIONS, SOCIAL FUNCTIONS, ETC.

Operatives of the Highest Character and Ability

Either Sex Sent Anywhere

References from America's Leading University, Eminent Members of the Bar, Prominent Social Leaders, Bankers, Corporations, Department Stores and Police Officials.

An Absolutely Honest and Confidential Business

Write or Call for References and Rates

7th FLOOR - 1 BEACON ST.

BOSTON, MASS.

Telephones, Haymarket 249 Cambridge 183

ROBERT BURNS, - Principal

Burkle
" William N glasscutter h 83 Washington
Burleigh John Q died Dec 21 1910
" Richard laborer b 8 Morton ct
Burn John machinist h 67 Oak [Oak
" John Jr helper 28 N Water b 67
" John W plumber b 67 Oak
" Leonard machinist b 67 Oak
Burnes Patrick F painter h 97 Grinnell
" Robert slasher h 78 Jouvett
Burnham Charles carpenter rms 105 Elm [school b 119 Chancery
" Mabel teacher Dartmouth st
Burns Agnes Mrs h 76 Liberty
" Albert M died July 19 1911
" Andrew clerk b 69 Maple
" Annie M Mrs h 21 Richmond
" Arthur died Jan 30 1911
" Beecher loom fixer h 260 Chestnut
" Bertha C Mrs h 85 Morgan
" Bros (William A and Frank H L Burns) furniture 950 S Water
" Catherine widow Joseph operative h 219 state [215 Arnold
" Clifton J chief clerk P Corp bds
" Daniel boilermaker h 138 Hillman
BURNS DETECTIVE BUREAU 1 Beacon Boston See opposite
" Edward gardener b 69 Maple
" Elizabeth Mrs h 64 Hazard
" Frank H L (Burns Bros) b 115 Fourth [Second
" Fred clerk 745 S Water b 564 S
" Fred C electrician h 219 Acushnet avenue
" Harry L salesman b 129 Fourth
" Henry fireman h 208 State
" James slasher tender b 39 Tallman [1293 Achusnet av
" James supt Nashawena Mills b
" James F laborer b 564 S Second
" James R Rev asst pastor St Mary's R C church h 23 Robeson
" John G laborer h 514 Purchase
" John W carder h 564 S Second
" Lawrence operative b 64 Hazard
" Margaret weaver h 110 Merrimac
" Margaret A Mrs rem from city

Burns
" Mary E widow Henry E h 115 Fourth [63 Hicks
" Nellie widow Michael operative h
" Robert carder bds 24 W French avenue [215 Arnold
" Robert O salesman 182 Union h
" Robert S slasher h 38 W French
" Sarah A Mrs housekeeper 4 Bethel [257 Hillman
" Stephen J tailor 184 Purchase h
" Timothy J men's furnishings 127 Purchase h 457 Chancery
" Walter switchman h 26 Collins
" Walter H drillworker h 105 Bonney
" William laborer h 64 Hazard
" William laborer rms 282 Acushnet avenue [Fourth
" William A (Burns Bros) b 115
" William D baker h 244 State
Burpee Charles R hairdresser h 169 Elm [Bowditch
Burque Edmond car repairer h 132
Burr Jane Mrs operative h 21 Marvin
Burrell Sydney B salesman h 490 Union
Burroughs Evelyn b 75 Sycamore
Burrows May O teacher Phillips av school h at Westport Factory
" Walter L chauffeur bds 145 Newton [lawn av
" William twister h 23 Wood-
" William J chief engineer Grinnell M Corp h 303 Summer
" see Barrows
Burstein Max rabbi h 508 S Water
Burt Arthur shoemaker b 147 Rounds
" Arthur student bds 78 Morgan
" Belle W teacher Parker school b 57 Morgan
" Charles A h 197 Cottage
BURT CLARENCE EDWARD physician 298 Union rms do office hours 8 to 9 a m, 2 to 4 and 7 to 8 p m
" Edwin H machinist h 259 Weld
" Evelyn M clerk b 221 Tremont
" George A foreman 123 Front h 221 Tremont
" Hadley A machinist h 12 Lindsey
" Henry P h 355 Union [mont
" Jennie R Mrs nurse h 221 Tre-
" Joseph A carpenter h 95 Linden

GREENE & WOOD Every Kind of LUMBER AND MILL WORK
PINE STREET, off So. WATER STREET, NEW BEDFORD

Burt
" L M Mrs sewer 42 Purchase h 78 Morgan
" Nathaniel J b 78 Mt. Pleasant
" Stephen A h 145 Newton
" Wilfred G electrician h 78 Morgan
" William A letter carrier h 555 [Union
Burton Alfred laborer bds 7 Penniman
" Caroline widow Peter h 7 Penni- [man
" Edward weaver h 48 Willow
" Helen M b 113 Hillman
" James fixer bds 88 Eugenia
" John driver bds 239 Sawyer
" John L agent Nashawena Mills h 113 Hillman
" Joseph laborer bds 239 Sawyer
" Peter bricklayer h 239 Sawyer
" Wesley weaver h 1293 Acushnet avenue
" Wesley weaver h 239 Sawyer
" William A removed to Lowell
Burtt Elliott J shoe findings h 32 Crapo
Bury Adam twister h 73 Myrtle
" Alfred twister h 20 Ashley
" George weaver b 34 Bullock
" Helen Mrs rem to Pawtucket R I
" James A twister b 20 Ashley
" Richard twister h 22 Viall
" Thomas H operative h 158 Hathaway
" William E twister bds 20 Ash- [ley
Bush Andrew M (A M Bush & Co) h 77 Rotch
" Belle M Mrs shampoo specialist [77 Rotch h do
BUSH A M & CO (A M Bush and J T Champion) tailors 47 William and cleansing 19 Jenny Lind See page 768
Bushey William removed from city
Bushnell Charles F salesman 103 William h at Fairhaven
" Isaac S died Aug 27 1910
Busnengo Francesco rem from city
Busquet Antoine carpenter h 51 Ashley
Bussiere Adelard weaver h 333 Niles
" Daniel weaver b 85 Beetle
" Emilien fixer h 93 Collette
" Henry spinner b 85 Beetle
" Mary widow Paul b 85 Beetle
" Oscar weaver b 71 Brock av
" Samuel weaver h 71 Brock av
Bustrom Alexander weaver b 259 N Front
Buteau Delphine Mrs h 1279 Acush- [net av
" Joseph operative h 235 Bowditch
" Louis weaver b 1279 Acushnet av
" Thomas W weaver h 28 Tallman
Butler Alice Mrs grocer 415 Rivet h do
" Alice widow Daniel h 373 Cedar [Grove
" Arthur F boat builder h 24 Lindsey
" Bertha A bookkeeper 193 Black- [mer b at S Dartmouth
" Charles H (William P Butler & Sons) 801 S Water bds at S Dartmouth
" Daniel doffer b 115 Reynolds
" Della M stenographer 34 Masonic bldg h 66 S Sixth
" Edward watchman h 59 Clark
" Elizabeth S b 14 Emerson (S)
" George clerk 182 Union b 138 Campbell
" George private U S A 76 Pleasant rm 39 b 219 Purchase [(W)
" George H fisherman h 410 Middle
" Henry spinner h 115 Reynolds
" Herbert spinner bds 373 Cedar Grove
" Herbert F fireman h 138 Camp- [bell
" John blacksmith 8 Pine h 103 Morgan
" Mary Ann widow Richard h 212 [Nash rd
" Manuel J doffer n 100 Phillips av
" Mary J bookkeeper b 2 Sears
" Mill, Ruth cor Cleveland
" Morgan clerk rms 26 Seventh
" Nicholas b 59 Clark [Merrimac
" Obadiah supt Bristol Mill h 147
" Peter weaver b 798 First
" Robert third hand h 23 Grape
" Thomas overseer Hathaway Mfg Co h 71 Valentine
" Walter A (William P Butler & Sons) h 52 Fair
" William fixer b 71 Valentine
" William (William P Butler & Sons) h 2 Sears [Corp h at B
" William M pres N B Cotton Mills
" William P & Sons (Charles H, Walter A and William) hardware 801 S Water
Butman Sarah R died Mar 10 1911
Butterfield Frederick H music supervisor public schools h 137 Summer
" Ralph weaver h 201 Cedar Grove

BONNEY, FOLSTER & CO.,
The North End's Shopping Centre
Dry Goods and Men's Furnishings
945-947 Acushnet Ave., New Bedford, Mass.

Butterworth Edgerton spinner h 288 Earle
" Frank operative b 288 Earle
" Fred laborer h 194 Blackmer
" George copperworker h 1039 County
" George M rem to Pasadena Cal
" George M Jr rem to Pasadena Cal
" John warper h 84 Rodney
" William glassworker h 74 Fruit
" William weaver h 91 Beetle
Butts Andrew A supt 3 E Pope h at S Dartmouth [Pleasant
" Annie E widow Ellery h 218
" Charles W teamster h 102 Middle
" Daisy M teacher Parker street school h 45 Willis
" Earl carpenter h 173 Shawmut av
" Edward E sales agent 16 N Second h 463 Mill [Cedar
" Elizabeth widow Samuel A h 331
" E Maud clerk N B W W 40 Masonic bldg h 45 Willis
" Francis A bookkeeper 32 Pleasant h 22 Cottage [chard (S)
" George A drillmaker h 347 Or-
" Henry police station 5 h 14 Richmond
" Henry R fisherman h 180 Austin
" James D shirtmaker h 1 Harrison
" James D yardmaster City Mfg Corp h 1 Harrison
" John F engineer Neild M Corp h 135 Merrimac [do
" Joseph M carpenter 85 Newton h
" Martha A widow Joseph A b 85 Newton [bldg h 45 Willis
" Susan E R clerk 301 Municipal
" Thomas L bricklayer h 381 Hillman [463 Mill
" William A clerk 14 N Second b
" William F eyeletworker h 37 Lindsey [Washington
" William H D drillmaker h 87
Butz Fred William shoemaker 76 Purchase h 633 Union
" Matilda stenographer U St Ry Co b 633 Union [Mill h 117 Fair
Buzzell William O overseer Bristol
Byk Thomas weaver b 33 Delano
Byran Leon foreman h 561 Kempton
Byrne James shipper Wamsutta Mill h 219 Shawmut av [nolds
" Jane widow Patrick h 33 Rey-

Byron John removed from city
" John operative h 75 Acushnet av
" Romeo carpenter h 5 Riverside avenue
" see Biron

Cabaca John V laborer h 405 First
Cabal John S baker 654 S Water h 36 Sycamore
Caboral Luiz watchman b 23 Nelson
Cabral Amelia E h 20 Briggs
" Antone h 153 Belleville av
" Antone laborer h 73 Winsor
" Antone laborer h 86 Howland
" Antone laborer h 90 Howard
" Antone laborer h 324 S Second
" Charles carder b 93 Phillips av
" Frank operative h 73 Winsor
" Frank teamster h 249 S Second
" Jacintho cigars 79 Howland h 16 Briggs
" Joaquim mill hand h 49 Mitchell
" John fireman h 46 Scott
" John A watchman h 347 Orchard (S) [son
" John C plumber h 2 Harri-
" John De S baker h 30 Sagamore
" John M carpenter h 105 Hemlock
" John M mariner h 59 S Second
" John P mill hand h 494 Rivet
" John S operative h 237 Coggeshall
" Joseph laborer h rear 272 S Front
" Joseph mill hand h r 87 Larch
" Joseph E laborer N B W W h 11 Jenney [pendent
" Joseph L shuttlemaker h 44 Inde-
" Joseph S loom fixer b 103 Fair
" Joseph S operative h 103 Fair
" Julio J laborer h 39 Hollyhock
" Manuel laborer h 41 Winsor
" Manuel laborer h 76 Howland
" Manuel laborer h 440 S Water
" Manuel mill hand h 74 Katharine
" Manuel mill hand b 74 Belleville road [avenue
" Manuel mill hand b 204 Coffin
" Manuel operative h r 162 Cedar Grove [513 S Second
" Manuel wood 360 S Second h
" Manuel F milk h 99 Bellevue
" Manuel S third hand b 103 Fair
" Marianno A fireman h 371 S Second
" Mary Mrs b 124 High

Painters Supplies Wall Papers Room Mouldings Ladders
M. P. B. Silva & Son BRUSHES
157 ACUSHNET AVENUE Both Phones NEW BEDFORD

Cabral
" Mary widow b 30 Hollyhock
" Peter A machinist h 243 S Front
Cabrallo Jule laborer N B W W h Hemlock street
Cacho Rufino laborer h 70 Crapo
Cadaretto William h 882 S Water
Cadieux Alfred carpenter h 357 Coffin avenue
" Alida h 19 George [bury
" Alphonse carder h 46 Salisbury
" Arthur J barber h 186 Collette
" Edward driver h 56 Salisbury
" Frank carpenter h 178 Brook
" Henry loom fixer h 131 Division
" Israel carpenter h 330 Cedar Grove [Grove
" William operative b 330 Cedar
Cadinal Henry removed from city
Cadorette Antonio carpenter h 76 Brock avenue
" Eudore carpenter b 109 David
" Maxime carpenter 236 Brock av h do
Cadoza Frank P operative h 356 First
Cafferky John laborer bds 400 Elm (W) [Purchase
Cafferty Patrick J motorman h 781
Caffrey John spinner h 74 Belleville road [Grove
Cahill John H laborer h 399 Cedar
" Thomas laborer b 11 Logan
Cahouette Louis mill hand h 82 Eugenia [non
Caimbra Joseph operative h 8 Can-
Cain George J Rev asst pastor St Ann's church h 60 Brock av
Cairns James F drillworker h 36 Independent
" James T letter carrier h 46 Bay
" John porter 81 Front h 296 Austin
" John weaver h 648 Acushnet av
" Martin J clerk 124 Purchase h 55 Maxfield
" Peter weaver b 87 Potomska
" Robert carpenter h 230 Allen
Caisey Albert removed from city
" Jerry twister h 203 Bowditch
" John carpenter bds 97 Coffin av
" Sylvia Mrs removed from city
Caisse Auguste weaver b r 61 Dean
" Jude weaver h 28 Holly
" Louis weaver rms 247 N Front
" Luke fisherman b 29 Holly

Caisse
" Marciel laborer b 61 Dean
" Richard clerk 189 Belleville av h 22 Holly
" Simon carpenter h r 61 Dean
" Thomas removed to Harwich
Caizergues Louis M artist h 82 Valentine [on
Calda Emilin G Mrs h 27 Cann-
Caldecott Asa machinist h 22 Roosevelt
" Frank shoemaker rms 42 Hill
" George machinist h 151 Mt Pleasant [ant
" John operative h 151 Mt Pleas-
Calden Daniel fireman h 199 N Second
" Mary dressmaker h 349 S Water
Calderbank Leo weaver h 107 David
" Thomas weaver h 160 Brock av
Caldwell Albert F carpenter h 101 Ash (N) [h do
" Albert F Jr physician 25 Fifth
" Annie weaver h 198 Blackmer
" Blithely E telephone operator 57 N Second b at Westport [ant
" Eliza widow Seth C h 365 Pleas-
" Zachriah laborer h 5 W High
" see Colwell
Calhoon Charles S (American Supply Co) 19 Commercial h 206 Pleasant
" Herbert L (American Supply Co) 19 Commercial b 206 Pleasant
Callaghan Agnes mill hand h 204 Earle [204 Earle
" Annie and Ellen operatives bds
" James O shipper h 11 Adams
" John carder h 68 Jouvett [Weld
Callahan Charles J bricklayer h 200
" Ellen widow Daniel h 205 State
" Martin second hand b 205 State
" Mary widow James h 56 Thompson
" Michael clerk b 205 State
Callanan Francis J machinist bds 72 Oak [Oak
" John J clerk 200 Union bds 72
" Katherine clerk 198 Union b 72 Oak [Oak
" Margaret widow Thomas F h 72
Callas Peter clerk 953 Acushnet av rms 104 State
Callaso Joseph laborer b 5 Mitchell
Callery Luke clerk 145 Union b at Fall River
Calley Jessie spinner b 847 Purchase

Steiger-Dudgeon Co.
"The WOMAN'S Store."
Tel. Bell 82 & 83, Branches connecting all depts.
" " 160 For Office only. Auto. 1211

SUMPTIONS, ASSORTMENTS AT ALL TIMES OF DEPENDABLE DRY GOODS

Callow William bds 87 Clifford
Calnan Bridget widow John h 7 Campbell
" Daniel fireman h 141 Church
" Dennis laborer h 98 Merrimac
" Dennis operative h r 205 Acushnet avenue
" Jeremiah laborer h 102 Merrimac
" Michael laborer b 98 Merrimac
" Patrick J laborer h 186 Chestnut
" Timothy C clerk 812 Purchase h 429 Pleasant
" Timothy C Jr bricklayer b 429 [Pleasant
" Timothy J mill hand b 7 Campbell
Calnen Daniel A brakeman h 243 [State
" Timothy laborer h 239 State
" Timothy J student b 239 State
Calverley James W foreman h 111 Clark [away
Calvert George W weaver h 93 Hath-
Camara Adrianno da carpenter h 59 Stephen
" Joaquim M driver h 309 Austin
" Joseph P clerk 912 S Water rms 188 Purchase
" Manuel J laborer h 472 Allen
Camasbo Philomena widow Manuel h 560 Allen
Cambia Frank J oiler h 518 Rivet
" Harrison fruit h 81 Washington
" Manuel h 195 Rivet
Cambra Antone b 8 Mulberry
" Frank weaver h 398 Allen
" Frank J mill hand h 518 Rivet
" Frank J Jr mill hand b 518 Rivet
" John mill hand h 8 Grandfield
" Joseph F glassworker h 80 Sagamore
" Joseph M mill hand bds 55 Mit- [chell
" Joseph P comber h 183 Bonney
" Manuel h 8 Mulberry
" Mary housekeeper b 8 Mulberry
" Mary J dressmaker 518 Rivet b do
" Nicholas laborer h 120 Dartmouth
" Theophile picker tender h 151 County [Belleville av
Camerlin Henry H laborer h 297
Cameron Catherine E widow James h 192 Sawyer
" Charles laborer h 190 N Front
" Charles removed from city
" Charles Jr laborer b 190 N Front

Cameron
" Frank removed from city [yer
" James driver 75 Beetle b 192 Saw-
" James operative b 192 Sawyer
" James spinner h 295 Coggeshall
" James G b 15 Ash (S)
" John sausages 26 Beech h do
" Mary A widow Daniel h 60 Rockland [(S)
" Priscilla dressmaker bds 15 Ash
Camill August mariner h 356 First
Camire Charles mason h 519 N Front
" Pierre weaver b r 679 Purchase
Campbell Ademar removed from city
" Aldei iceman bds 1205 Acushnet av [school b at Fairhaven
" Elwyn G principal Middle street
" Emanuel weaver b 334 Bowditch
" Francis P letter carrier bds 9 Bonney
" Fritz H carpenter b 109 Willis
" James clerk bds 361 Coggeshall
" James removed from city
" James tailor and dry goods 11 Bonney h 9 do
" John bricklayer rms American House Arcade bldg
" John fitter b 336 Coffin avenue
" John M produce 860 Acushnet av h 361 Coggeshall [Hillman
" Joseph R teamster h rear 371
" Kenneth machinist h 134 Ashland
" Orme carpenter h 128 Rivet
" Thomas weaver b 103 Coffin av
" Thurston spinner h 395 Orchard (S) [son
" William drillworker h 32 Thomp-
Campion Mary A Mrs speeder tender h 30 Viall [Howland
Campos Joseph D laborer h rear 61
Campus Jessie widow Manuel D h 544 S Water
" Jule operative h 134 Fourth
Canaca Manuel F mariner h 85 S Second [Wellfleet
Canada Prentice A Rev removed to
Cananas John G teamster 170 Purchase rms 114 Grinnell
Canavan Alice G clerk 185 Union b 148 Shawmut avenue [Myrtle
" Ann D widow James nurse h 36
" Anna M widow Patrick H h 148 Shawmut avenue [Cottage
" Annie and Mary weavers h 624
" Edward M liquors h 920 County

PELEG H. SHERMAN 506 COUNTY ST.
FUNERAL DIRECTOR AND EMBALMER
OFFICE PHONES. Bell 690-13 Auto. 1305.
RESIDENCE PHONES. Bell 690-12. Auto. 1306.

Canavan
" John C driver b 920 County
" Mary E widow Michael h 920 County
Cann William A removed to Fall River
Cannavan Annie F bookkeeper b 427 Chancery
" Patrick housekeeper police station 3 h 427 Chancery
Canneca Manuel operative h 281 S Water
Canney Catherine b 552 County
" Ellen R physician 522 County h do
" Leonard removed to Boston
Cannon Clarence B calker bds 374 Middle
" Frank W painter h 174 Cedar
" Jerusha widow Thomas D h 15 Glover
" Lucretia C widow Edward S h 342 Union
" Margaret widow Patrick S h 77 Katherine
" Maria G widow William C h 374 Middle
Canny Annie clerk bds 416 Union
" Edward P officer H C h 416 Union
" Frank L student b 416 Union
" John E steam fitter b 416 Union
" Leonard foreman 63 Front h 506 Acushnet avenue
" see Kenney and Canney
Canos Lewis confectioner 1091 Acushet av h 355 Coggeshall
Canter Samuel pawn broker b 264 Weld
Canto Antonio seaman h 8 Morgan lane
Cantor David pedlar h 82 Kenyon
" Samuel clerk b 264 Weld
Cantwell Catherine J clerk 182 Union b 124 Bonney
" John carpenter h 124 Bonney
" John T engineer h 63 School
" Martin F propertyman Hathaway's Theatre b 62 S Second
" Michael stage hand Hathaway's Theatre b 62 S Second
Canty Timothy J foreman T P Corp h 23 Fair
Caouette Abe removed from city
" Jean B furniture 50 Delano h 52 do
" Joseph operative h 435 Pleasant
" Joseph D sheet metalworker h 275 Collette
" Joseph R clerk bds 52 Delano
" Mary h 58 Phillips avenue

Caouette
" Noe stock clerk 28 N Water h 19 Acushnet av
" Remi loom fixer h 22 Willard
" Stella teacher Phillips av school h at Fairhaven
" Wilfred clerk 50 Delano b 52 do
" see Gaouette
Caperonis Peter (Caperonis Spanoodis & Co) h 1140 Acushnet av
" Spanoodis & Co (Peter Caperonis and A E Spanoodis) restaurant 1136 Acushnet avenue
Caplar John spinner b 332 Sawyer
Caplete Bruno weaver h 331 Belleville avenue
Capra Dominick laborer h r 8 Seneca
" Frank grocer 716 Acushnet av h do
Caralaka Kosta boot black 92 Purchase
Carbonneau Stanislas weaver b 1279 Acushnet avenue
Card Bertha E clerk b 366 Cedar
" Earl laborer bds 87 Locust
" Edward B teamster h 87 Locust
" Hurlbert E shoemaker h 210 Austin
" James E motorman h 81 Thomas
" Rebecca J widow Charles H h 349 Cottage
" S Ellen widow Benjamin F variety 366 Cedar h do
" William C foreman 474 Acushnet avenue h 237 Middle
Cardin Alfred engineer Grinnell Mfg Corp h 297 N Front
" Celia housekeeper 89 Hathaway
" Eddie weaver bds 4 Welcome
" Napoleon removed from city
Cardinal Delphis laborer h 214 Coffin av
" Louise mill hand h 81 Davis
Cardo Philip insurance agent rms 20 Bethel
Cardonell Louis liquors 318 Acushnet av h 316 do
Cardoza Abel laborer bds 201 Hathaway road
" Antone E operative h 228 State
" Antonio mill hand h 202 Belleville avenue
" Antonio P laborer h 2 Shawmut avenue
" Duleterio overseer h 5 Spooner
" Eliza widow Domingo h 96 Union
" Frank cooper 350 S Second
" Frank F ropeworker h 134 Bonney
" George driver b 146 Fourth
" John M fireman h 62 Briggs

PAINTERS' SUPPLIES
Walnut, Cor. Water, 84 Pleasant St. 25 WELD SQ., 129 COVE ST.
F. T. AKIN & COMPANY

Cardoza
" Jose operative h 94 Bowditch
" Joseph laborer h r 230 S Front
" Joseph operative h 35 County
" Joseph A mill hand h 35 Mitchell
" Joseph E bakery 33 South h 19 Fair
" Joseph M operative h 61 Grinnell
" Joseph S weaver h 60 Hall
" Manuel laborer h 45 Katherine
" Manuel laborer h 21 Griffin
" Manuel laborer h 260 S Front
" Manuel mill hand h 96 Acushnet avenue
" Manuel C teamster h 4 Cannon
" Manuel E h 216 Fourth
" Manuel J mill hand h 53 Swift
" Manuel P operative h 175 Belleville avenue
" Marianno (Pacheco & Cardoza) grocers 428 N Front h 101 Phillips avenue
" Matius fireman h 289 Davis
" Zeferino helper h 201 Hathaway road
Cardozo Joaquim Rev curate St John the Baptist church h 94 S Sixth [come
Cardullo Samuel operative b 30 Wel-
Careiro Joseph carder h 23 Scott
Carew Frederick J coachman h 219 Arnold [ond
Carey Timothy doffer h 560 S Sec-
Carl Theodore operative h 131 Cedar Grove
" see Karl
Carlow David weaver h 62 Fair
Carleton Frank N foreman 34 Pleasant h at Fairhaven
" Hattie Mrs removed from city
Carlin Mary widow John b 248 Arnold [ville rd
Carling James spinner bds 88 Belle-
" Peter A engineer h 88 Belleville road
Carlsen Carl B clerk 88 Purchase h 27 Thompson
Carlson Alfred drillworker h 120 Fourth [North
" Carl molder 229 N Water h 194
" Carl Albert machinist h 230 Allen
" Christina widow John b 123 State

Carlson
" Conrad C bartender 219 Purchase rms 209 do [cery
" Daniel copperworker b 72 Chan-
" Eric drillworker rms 38 Russell
" Erick A stoker h 169 Acushnet av
" Frida h 72 Chancery
" Gustaf machinist b 169 Acushnet avenue [cery
" Ida widow Adolph bds 72 Chan-
" John removed to Providence R I
" Nils drillworker b 86 S Sixth
" Oscar clerk Greene & Wood bds 230 Allen [181 North
" Peter watchman 229 N Water h
Carlton Maude G teacher R C Ingraham school b 19 Sherman
Carman George E b 42 Hill
" John operative b 184 Davis
" Thomas fixer h 184 Davis
" William weaver h 54 Holly
Carmo Antonio P B Rev removed to Fall River [h 179 Grinnell
Carmody Catherine widow Thomas
" Frank machinist b 179 Grinnell
Carmos Amos laborer h r 207 S Front
" Henry laborer h 71 First [ter
Carney Arthur mariner b 805 S Wa-
" Daniel H teamster h 6 Jenney
" James stockman 57 N Second b 126 Shawmut avenue
" John F salesman 71 William b 805 S Water
" Joseph glassworker h 34 Oak
" Mary Mrs h 872 Purchase
" Patrick h 805 S Water
" Patrick H removed from city
" Susanna widow William H h 128 Mill [chard (S)
" William F glasscutter h 370 Or-
Carodeau Arthur freight handler h 662 Purchase
Carolan Patrick weaver h 8 Shore
Caron Achille removed to Fitchburg
" Alfred operative h 214 Sawyer
" Alphonse carder h 28 Howard
" Amedee carpenter h 214 Coffin av
" Conrad weaver b 1187 Purchase
" Damase carpenter h 792 County
" Edmund laborer h 390 S Second
" Eloie carpenter b 54 Tallman
" Ernest twister h 70 Jouvett
" Estelle clerk 1081 Acushnet av b 109 Tallman
" Girard mill hand h 54 Tallman

Don't dream of what you are going to do! Go and do it.

Kinyon's Short-hand School

Odd Fellows Bldg., Cor. William and Pleasant Sts., New Bedford, Mass.

Caron
" Henri slubber tender h 71 Jouvett
" H Ferdinand dentist 1060 Acushent av h do
" John shoemaker rms 367 Purchase
" Joseph carpenter h 109 Tallman
" Joseph laborer b 54 Tallman
" Ludger carpenter h 54 Tallman
" Ludger Jr carpenter h 156 Clifford
" Marciel weaver h 1187 Purchase
" Napoleon hairdresser 20 Harmony bds 112 Mott
" Philias decorator b 289 Coffin av
" Pierre h 26 George [Salisbury
" Renee barber 20 Harmony b 31
" Silvio carpenter 57 Dean h do
" Stanislas lather b 55 Hope [First
" William slubber tender h 803
" see Garon [boro
Carpenter Albert H W rem to Middle-
" Frank G salesman 76 Purchase h 73 Willis
" Hope A Mrs h 58 Spruce
" Lucy widow George h 9 Spring
" Mary A widow Samuel b 229 North [at Fairhaven
" Orrin B clerk U S Ry Co bds
" Philias H operative rms 807 Purchase
" Sarah E housekeeper 202 Middle
" William T rem to Providence R I
" see Charpentier
Carr Albert D hatter bds 18 Peckham
" Charles R clerk 156 Weld b 11 Studley
" Charlotte b 56 Spring [b do
" Cornelia dressmaker 68 Chancery
" David died July 22 1911
" Dorothy H stenographer 57 N Second b 46 Emerson (S)
" Edwin R plumber 55 N Water b 69 S Sixth
" Elizabeth widow David h 236 Park [31 S Ash
" Esther stenographer ft Willis b
" Hugh M boilermaker b 18 Peckham
" James laborer h 272 Fourth
" James weaver h 15 Brook
" James weaver h 108 Sycamore
" James weaver h 406 S Front
" Jane widow Thomas h 15 Brook
" John laborer b 1 North
" Joseph weaver h 442 N Front
" Katherine Mrs h 86 Hathaway

Carr
" Lizzie bookkeeper 157 Union bds 209 Summer [46 Emerson (S)
" Louise K clerk 28 Pleasant bds
" Margaret and Mary h 1 North
" Margaret Mrs h 18 Peckham
" Mary A widow James b 3 Norton court [Chancery
" Mary M widow James G h 68
" Mattie A widow nurse h 46 Emerson (S)
" Patrick laborer b 1 North
" Richard telephone operator b 11 Studley
" Robert W painter h 13 Grape
" Thomas clerk 244 N Front h 219 Church [Studley
" Thomas clerk 156 Weld bds 11
" Walter waiter 919 Acushnet av h 61 Church
" William clerk b 11 Studley
" William B collector 88 Purchase h 11 Studley [Cove
Carraher Kate widow weaver h 168
Carreau Alfred operative h 175 Eugenia
" **Elphege shoemaker b 117 Collette**
" Ernest removed to Detroit Mich
" Flavien operator h 16 Bentley
" Hormidas slasher b 16 Bentley
" Hormidas weaver h 117 Collette
" Joseph carpenter h 23 W Trinity
" Joseph third hand b 16 Bentley
" Melvina widow h 181 State
" Napoleon rem to Providence R I
" Napoleon Jr rem to Wichita Kan
" Philineas widow Alfred b 55 Merrimac [do
" Theodore bellman 435 County bds
Carreia Manuel printer 148 Bonney h 36 Katharine
Carreiro Antonio J mill hand bds 7 Bonneau ct
Carrera Seconde mason also grocer 676 Acushnet av h do [court
Caretto Antone laborer h 2 Turner's
Carrick John T motorman h 366 Earl
Carrie John J removed to Brockton
Carrier Alexander spinner h 115 Bullard
" Alfred spinner h 115½ Bullard
" Anselme h 219 Bowditch
" Arthur removed to Fairhaven
" Charles fireman h 7 Phillips av

HASKELL BROS. DEALERS IN
ICE
400 COURT STREET TELEPHONE CONNECTION NEW BEDFORD, MASS.

Carrier
" David J fixer b 61 River
" Edward h 178 Dean
" Emile pressman 47 William [Dean
" Henrietta widow Alphonse h 85
" Henry L weaver h 85 Dean
" Herbert weaver h 183 Dean
" Israel L h 519 S Second
" Joseph spinner bds 233 Sawyer
" Joseph undertaker 1220 Acushnet av h do
" Napoleon weaver b 85 Dean
" Octave fixer h 118 Potomska
" Omer baker b 178 Dean
" Omer clerk 6 W French av h 1 Harmony
" Philias insurance agent h 1 Harmony [Acushnet av
" Rudolph undertaker's asst b 1220
" Thomas operative h 57 Phillips avenue
" William operative b 37 Phillips av
Carriere Archille machinist h 127 Nye
" Jacine operative h 73 Mosher
" James spinner h 115 Bullard [av
Carriveau Ozepie painter h 53 Brock
Carroll Alice Mrs h Bank street
" Aurile widow Joseph h 65 Ward
" Charles E foreman 125 Middle bds 247 do [Arnold
" Charles M sec 127 Union h 178
" David laborer h 159 David
" Edward loom fixer h 63 County
" Edward Jr removed from city
" Eudore conductor b 65 Ward
" Frank third hand b 65 Ward
" George second hand h 125 Bates avenue [avenue
" George H apprentice b 124 Bates
" James C overseer Pierce Mfg Corp h at Fairhaven [away
" James M weaver bds 90 Hath-
" John driver 5 Mechanics lane h 44 Liberty
" John laborer h 57 S Second
" Joseph A cigarmaker 164 Union h 124 Parker
" Louis overseer Dartmouth M Corp h 2 Welcome
" Octave weaver h 55 Morton ct
" Peter H chauffeur b 2 Welcome
" Richard spinner h 178 Crapo [av
" Richard Jr spinner h 180 Brock
" Robert A removed from city

Carroll
" Rosario clerk 100 Ruth h 18 McGurk
" Sylvester driver h 84 Thompson
" Thomas spinner h 36 Winsor
" Thomas H fixer h 90 Hathaway
" Thomas P blacksmith h 48 Chancery [thorn
" William A salesman h 211 Haw-
" William E carriagemaker h 568 Kempton [ter
Carros Manuel operative h 14 Cot-
Carsley Annie W h 138 Campbell
Carson John mill hand bds 193 Dean
Carter Andrew P laborer h 36 Bowditch [N Front
" Charles helper 64 Dartmouth h 256
" Edward baker h 76 Cedar
" Edward A h 43 Rotch
" Edward H master mechanic Pierce Bros Ltd h 275 Pope
" Elizabeth C teacher William H Taylor school b 211 Park
" Elsie G Mrs h 101 Tremont
" Eseau removed to Freetown
" Estelle M teacher Harrington school [South
" Frederick W chief engineer b 114
" Grace widow John h 170 Fourth
" Henry J clerk bds 163 Pleasant
" James weaver h 150 Tallman
" John fixer h 156 David [shuet av
" John operative h 1137 Acu-
" John F glass cutter b 13 Harmony
" John J weaver h 107 Rodney
" John T overseer 131 Court h 204 Brownell [ham
" John T loom fixer h 24 Peck-
" John W laborer h 71 Cedar
" John W operative h 176 Bowditch
" Joseph E third hand b 13 Harmony [Fourth
" Margaret E bookkeeper b 170
" Marietta Mrs h 6 Bonneau ct
" Parthenia M widow Robert H h 186 Mill [h 409 Bolton
" Peter loom fixer and piano tuner
" Samuel mule spinner h 13 Harmony
" Thomas weaver h 107 Rodney
" William removed from city
" William J rigger h 275 Acushnet avenue [Acushnet av
Cartier Fabiola bookkeeper bds 1356
" Joseph gas fitter h 75 Holly

J. F. CROSSLEY 223 MILL STREET COR. EMERSON PHONE
STEAM and HOT WATER HEATING
GAS FITTING and FIXTURES

Cartier
" Marius jeweler rms 1378 Acushnet avenue [net av
" Mary widow Joseph b 1356 Acush-
Cartmell John weaver h 12 Independent
" Robert, U S N b 12 Independent
Cartwright David electrician h 11 George
" Richard plumber 185 Acushnet av h 134 Acushnet avenue
Carvalho Joao h 201 Coggeshall
" John L laborer h 573 S Water
Carvallio Antone mill hand h 680 S Water [ushnet av h 243 do
Carver David O shoe repairer 204 Ac-
" Frederick A clerk b 243 Acushnet avenue [b 243 Acushnet av
" Grace L teacher Fifth st school
" Mary Mrs bds 207 Eugenia
" Rachel Ann died
Cary Bruce cotton sampler Acushnet & Hathaway Mills h 394 Allen
" Emma V b 52 Fifth
" George W machinist h 52 Fifth
" John W manager 14 Market h 70 Ash (N) [Front
Casault Joseph weaver bds 361 N
" Ulric weaver h 361 N Front
Casavant Charles clerk 962 Acushnet avenue h 19 Bentley
" Eliza Mrs b 64 Willis
" Evangelist laborer h 20 Bullard
" Fred insurance agent 37 Purchase rm 23 bds 64 Willis
" Louis A (Casavant & Landry) grocers 1892 Acushnet avenue h 92 Covell
" Olde eyelet maker b 64 Willis
" Victor weaver h 95 Diman
" & Landry (Louis A Casavant and Joseph M Landry) grocers 1892 Acushnet avenue
Case Ada B rms 83 School
" Allen removed to Pasadena Cal
" Annie C Mrs b 729 County
" Arthur B salesman 188 N Water h 185 Pleasant [623 County
" Eliphal S widow Alexander H h
" Everett B clerk P Corp bds 98 Arnold
" George H carpenter rms 101 Middle [city
" George W T removed from

Case
" Isaac R h 625 County
" Lillian P teacher Cedar Grove st school bds 11 Fifth [Purchase
" Nellie M widow Charles A h 363
" Patience A widow Abner T h 161 Smith [Forest
" Ralph W clerk Page Mfg Co h 83
" Walter J piano tuner 99 William h 270 Pope
" Walter J Mrs b 83 School
Casey Amedee third hand b 138 Cedar Grove [803 Hathaway rd
" Charlotte T widow Edward H h
" Daniel laborer b 66 Myrtle
" Dennis weaver h 179 Weld
" Edward E clerk P O h 584 Elm
" Emma G principal Rockdale school b 803 Hathaway rd
" Fred operative b 138 Cedar Grove
" George carpenter rms 101 Middle
" Gerald carpenter b 138 Cedar Grove [803 Hathaway rd
" Henry O janitor Rockdale school
" James twister tender b 138 Cedar Grove
" John laborer b 66 Myrtle
" John T city laborer and groeer 329 Middle h do
" Joseph laborer h 27 Reynolds
" Major J boat builder h 369 Maxfield
" Manuel fisherman b 413 Kempton
" Maximillian b 138 Cedar Grove
" Michael laborer bds 112 Clark
" Robert carepnter b 156 Church
" Sylvia Mrs h 413 Kempton
" see Caissie and Caisey
Cash Charles R bell boy Parker House h 62 Middle
" Charles R piper h 790 First
" Herbert removed from city
" James P supt Hazelwood park Brock avenue h do [chase
" Winfield conductor b 596 Pur-
Cashman Thomas h 301 Cedar
Cashmere Manuel laborer h 23 Mitchell [Acushnet av
Cass Bertha M clerk 185 Union b 313
" Frank R letter carrier h 83 Hillman [h 51½ Hicks
Cassidy Albert (Cassidy & Smith)
" Albert Jr operative b 49½ Hicks
" B J collector rms Y M C A

CHARLES A. CROSHERE
38 FOURTH ST. Bell Phone 1964-23
SIGN PAINTING
GLASS LETTERING
ELECTRIC SIGNS
SHOW CARDS

Cassidy
" Charles weaver h 126 Reynolds
" John laborer h Winterville road
" John mason b 21 Peckham
" John Jr laborer b Winterville rd
" Stephen E laborer h 431 Purchase [net av
" Stephen J painter h 87 Acush-
" Thomas spinner h 110 Division
" & Smith (Albert Cassidy and James Smith) bicycles 1271 Acushnet avenue [ney
Cassin Henry J driver h 124 Bon-
Cassis Simon pedlar h 292 Cedar Grove
" William pedlar b 292 Cedar Grove
Casson Abraham K president 339 and 1029 Acushnet av h 137 Holly [av b 137 Holly
" Samuel K treasurer 339 Acushnet
Castellina Giovanni laborer h 696 Acushnet avenue
" Innocence laborer h 5 Seneca
" Joseph laborer h 8 Wall
Castenno George laborer N B W W h 2 Seneca
Caster Edward G general secretary Y M C A h 102 Arnold
Castino Etherlinda G widow John A h 82 Bay
" George F h 35 Fifth
" John A died September 23 1910
" John M roll coverer h 6 Crapo
" Louis A clerk 240 Union h 53 Merrimac
Castle Charles plumber h 6 Studley
" Fred clerk Kings highway h 236 Brock avenue [mer
" George T letter carrier h 19 Ho-
" Thomas h 80 Clark
" William operative h 76 Hathawy
Castognoli John sculptor h 109 Holly
" Joseph sculptor b 109 Holly
Castolini John laborer h 696 Acushnet avenue [Nye
Castonguay Alcide carpenter h 127
" Alphonse teamster h 159 Tallman
" Emma bds 142 Phillips av [man
" Hermenegilde plaster h 151 Tall-
" Joseph slasher bds 51 Dean
Castro Mary Mrs h 60 Independent
Caswell Addie F h 74 Kempton
" Amos R trader h 144 Mill

Caswell
" Arthur F overseer Soule Mill h 121 State [Fairhaven
" Arthur G foreman 100 Fifth h at
" Charles A police h 168 Mill
" David B inspector h 87 S Sixth
" David W teamster h 385 Cottage
" Edward T bookkeeper 34 Union h 21 Jenny Lind [Mill
" Eliza J widow William H h 64
" Emma A school stenography and typewriting 32 Masonic bldg [son
" George A conductor h 15 Emer-
" George E rodman h 69 Locust
" George F painter h 338 Pleasant
" George P engineer h 69 Locust
" Lucy C bookkeeper 2 S Water bds 79 Morgan [b 91 Robeson
" Nathaniel H blacksmith 8 Pine
" Nathaniel H Jr clerk 104 Ashland h 54 Durfee [gan
" Oscar F blacksmith h 79 Mor-
" Percy W foreman 159 Mill h 107 Robeson [Willis
" Susan widow Thomas T h 131
" Wallace C machinist h 87 Locust
" William F bookkeeper 66 Masonic bldg h 80 Bedford
CASWELL WILLIAM T painter and painters' supplies 34-38 Union h 233 Summer See page 94
Catelli Frank (Giusti & Co) 861 S Water h 25 Thompson
Cathcart Charles E engineer h 2339 Acushnet avenue [ton
" Edward B clerk rms 382 Kemp-
" William J sawyer h 13 Mill road
Catholic Union The D G Dinnigan proprietor Pleasant corner Mill
Catieux Cyrill loom fixer h 16 Roosevelt [b do
Catin Annie dressmaker 235 Fourth
" Charles solderer b 154 Grinnell
" Manuel drill maker h 154 Grinnell
" Mary L widow Manuel h 235 Fourth [Davis
Catlow Annie widow John h 344
" John fixer h 179 Dean
" John weaver b 208 Nash road
Caton Alfred plumber h 22 Reynolds
" Anthony clerk 274 Cedar b 329 South Second [Second
" Charles H salesman b 329 South

J. G. NICHOLSON
LUMBER, SASH, DOORS and BLINDS
BOWDITCH STREET, NEW BEDFORD, MASS.

Caton
" Constantina widow Bernado h 226 Rivet [dent
" Giraldo at P Corp h 56 Indepen-
" John W weaver h 26 Jouvette
" Joseph laborer b 65 Acushnet av
" Joseph sausage maker Anthony Swift & Co h at Fairhaven
" Manuel laborer h 134 N Second
" Manuel watchman h 359 Orchard (S) [Smith
" Marion D city laborer h 167
" Mary widow Joseph h 329 S Second [Fair
" Maurice W glass cutter b 139
" Olympia brittania worker h 139 Fair [Fair
" Olympia Jr glass cutter b 133
" Virginia T dressmaker 226 Rivet b do
" William cook h 25½ Howland
Catterall John overseer Dartmouth Mfg Corp h 15 Valentine
" John T operative h 20 George
" Robert laborer h 15 Willard
" William P b City farm
Catudal Joseph shoe repairer 266 Sawyer h 49 Beetle [Reynolds
Caughey James H weaver h 343
Cautherly Giles removed from city
Cavalier Evelyn nurse rms 57 Maple
" William R h 66 School
Cavanagh Edward fixer h 163 Collette
Cavanaugh Ann widow Francis h 341 Middle [Co h at New York
" Cortes W treasurer N B Cordage
" Elizabeth widow George bds 49 Chancery
" Jeremiah L Mrs h 76 Bedford
" Richard J student b 89 Bedford
" see Kavanagh
Cawley Austin machinist M T D & M Co b N Front corner Kenyon
" Austin J fireman h 584 Cottage
" Edward mule spinner b 19 Ashley
" Irene C bookkeeper 5 Pleasant b 584 Cottage [186 Division
" James janitor Rivet cor First h
" James E mill hand b 26 Howland Village
" Mary Mrs weaver h 7 E Durfee
" Mary widow Patrick b 120 Hemlock
" Michael laborer b 3 N Oak

Cawley
" Michael mule spinner h 26 Howland Village [N Front h 540 do
Caya Alphonse hairdresser 578
" Edmonde laborer h 90 Linden
" see Caille [av b 288 Cedar Grove
Cayer Alma clerk 1460 Acushnet
" Edmond removed to Acushnet
" Elmer J mason h Pontiac st
" Joseph weaver h 18 Bowditch
" Louis weaver h 190 Rivet
Cayouette Jerome shoe repairer 901 South Water h do [7 Holly
Ceborowski Bronislaw mill hand bds
" Stanley mill hand h 7 Holly
Cejka Annie widow Louis h 113 Tallman
CEJKA GEORGE tinsmith 1480 Acushnet avenue b 113 Tallman See page 785
" Peter operative b 113 Tallman
Centeio John F variety 9 Walnut h do
" Joseph clerk 9 Walnut bds do
Central Athletic Club 10 Spring
" Garage 15 Fourth
" Union Store (Inc) groceries 11 and 13 N Sixth [Davis
Cezim Ismail mill hand bds 54
" Telial mill hand h 54 Davis
Chaberik Theodore mill hand h 7 Bonneau court [lips av
Chabot Peter weaver h 49 Phil-
Chabotte Alfred mill hand h 107 Davis
" Leon carpenter b 806 First
" Napoleon loom fixer h 806 First
Chace Abram died Feb 3 1911
" Abram & Co (Walter F Chace) shipwrights 12 Merrill's wharf block mfrs 9 Front
" Albert M clerk b 133 Clinton
" Andrew P draughtsman 303 Times bldg h at Fairhaven
" Annie B widow Charles S b 315 County
" Annie M Mrs h 303 County
" Arthur H messenger 14 N Sixth h 133 Clinton [10 Borden
" Arthur M clerk 100 William h
" Bessie bookkeeper 830 Purchase h at E Freetown [b 35 Dartmouth
" Bessie E bookkeeper 48 Pleasant
" Cesime fisherman h 479 Belleville avenue
" Clarence E milk 385 Reed h do

Steiger-Dudgeon Co.
"The WOMAN'S Store."
Tel. Bell 82 & 83, Branches connecting all depts.
" " 160 For Office only. Auto. 1211

SUMPTIONS, ASSORTMENTS AT ALL TIMES OF DEPENDABLE DRY GOODS

Chace
" Ella F widow Abram h 501 Kempton [S Sixth
" Elsie M widow Walter E h 88
" Emma L Mrs h 81 North
" Frank A died Oct 24 1910
" Frank W bookkeeper h 151 Cedar
" Harry A clerk 45 School h 154 Ashland
" Horace S hostler h 128 Campbell
" Ira M Jr manager J W Bishop Co 41 Times bldg rms 8 Eighth
" Irving A, U St Ry Co h 51 Butler
" Isabel G widow Herbert F h 35 Dartmouth [Hillman
" Isabel M widow Andrew M h 277
" John P machinist h 14 Parker
" Joseph Jr h 84 S Sixth [Park
" Joseph H ship carpenter h 319
" Louis clerk 100 William b 62 Ward [Allen
" Luella A widow Arthur G h 208
" Lydia M secretary to advertising manager Standard b 85 Elm
" Mary Elizabeth h 173 Middle
" Morris C foreman h 32 Atlantic
" Phylander janitor High School h 303 County [S Dartmouth
" Robert molder 229 N Water h at
" Thomas W real estate rms 216 Middle
" T W & F W & Co (Thomas W and Frank W Chace) real estate and insurance 151 Cedar
" Walter F (Abram Chace & Co) rms 162 Clinton
" Walter F machinist h 400 Earl
" William A piper b 35 Dartmouth
" see Chase [Bowditch
Chadanais Adelard operative h 269
" Rock vocalist b 269 Bowditch
Chadbourne Fred G real estate rms 270 Pleasant [Dunbar
Chadderton Joseph H spinner h 92
Chaddonis Frank operative h r 1030 Acushnet avenue
Chadwick Arnold ice 63 Dean b do
" Charles fish 674 Purchase h 11 Studley [Hillman
" Clarissa E widow George H h 273
" Eadeauf operative b 172 Bonney
" Edward E (Chadwick & Co) h 116 North
" Elizabeth A Mrs h 186 County

Chadwick
" Elizabeth A Mrs massage 44 W French avenue h do
" Elizabeth C Mrs h 165 Kempton
" Frank B driver Engine 5 h 275 Hillman [Rockdale av
" Fred (Chadwick & Tripp) h 1267
" George F weaver h 105 Hathaway
" Hannah and Margaret h 68 Linden
" Harland C Mrs h 130 Summer
" Harry machinist b 11 Studley
" Helen R dressmaker h 83 School
" John machinist b 11 Studley
" John J glasscutter h 60 Rockland [ond
" John J second hand h 423 S Sec-
" Joseph weaver h 44 W French av
" Joseph W foreman 100 Fifth h 143 Washington [945 County
" Kay clerk 1623 Acushnet av bds
" Lewis E operative b 172 Division
" Lillie A fancy goods 58 North h do [Bonney
" Louisa A widow Robert h 172
" Luke weaver h 63 Dean
" Martha clerk 185 Union b 304 Acushnet avenue [Mill
" Mary widow William L h 117
" Mary L sailmaker 35 Commercial h 181 Grinnell [County
" Nancy W widow Solomon h 355
" Robert weaver h 44 Roosevelt
" Thomas weaver h 62 Dean
" Thomas A h 58 North [ren
" William H operative h 25 War-
" William L died Feb 1 1911
" Wright weaver h 158 Central av
" & Co (E E Chadwick) grocers 240 Union
" & Tripp (Fred Chadwick and George R Tripp) provisions 84 Cove
Chaffin Jane V Mrs h 116 Bedford
Chagarul Nick (Zavas & Co) rms 132 Bowditch [man
Chagnon Alfred spinner h 60 Tall-
" Eli weaver h 455 Coggshall
" Gelasse h 154 Tinkham
" Jovite Rev asst pastor St Joseph's R C church h 39 Ingraham
" Rosilda widow Pierre bds r 61 Dean [State
Chaille Azaire tailor 211 Union h 144

PELEG H. SHERMAN 506 COUNTY ST.
FUNERAL DIRECTOR AND EMBALMER
OFFICE PHONES. Bell 690-13 Auto. 1305.
RESIDENCE PHONES. Bell 690-12. Auto. 1306.

Chainay Aurelie widow Damase h 32 Holly [do
" Nazaire carpenter 251 Coffin av h
Chalfin Jane B widow Samuel F h 116 Bedford [net av
Chaloner Mary J Mrs h 8 Acush-
Chalupa John G laborer h 53 Crapo
Chamberlain Amerase hairdresser 2782 Acushnet av h r do
CHAMBERLAIN CHARLES E garage 156 Clinton and 148 Court and real estate 132 Cottage corner Arnold h do See back cover
" Egeus laborer h 830 County
" Erie widow John bds 166 Park
" James teamster b 43 Union
" Joseph A carpenter b 2782 Acushnet avenue [Elm
" Love P widow Andrew h 165
" Richard R collector bds 166 Park
" Sherman G motorman h 79 Pierce
Chamberlin Erwin H florist 4 Purchase h 276 Cedar
Chambers Clifton C third hand h 32 Sycamore [Court
" George A letter carrier h 59
" John weaver h 237 Tinkham
Champagne Arthur baker h 32 Acushnet avenue [1 Hazard court
" Aurore Mrs variety 36 Hazard h
" Calixte carpenter h 39 Dean
" Joseph agent 186 Purchase
" Joseph speeder b 455 Belleville avenue
" Louis carpenter h 119 Holly
" Napoleon baker 1670 County h 161 Dean
" Philip carpenter b 119 Holly
" Philip mill hand b 39 Dean
" Pierre fixer h 1 Hazard court
" Wilfred speeder rms 1378 Acushnet avenue [away
" William third hand h 211 Hath-
Champegny Joseph (Champegny & LeBlanc) h 361 Coggeshall
" & LeBlanc (Joseph Champegny and Charles I LeBlanc) shoes 1071 Acushnet avenue and 947 S Water and 123 Union
Champey Aurelle removed from city
Champigny Arthur tailor 111 Cove b 77 South
" Paul caster h 77 South

Champion John M salesman 47 William b 79 Rotch
" John T (A M Bush & Co) tailor 47 William h 79 Rotch
Champlin Mary Mrs h 174 Smith
" William D draughtsman 100 Fifth h at Fairhaven [enth
Chandler Catharine W h 21 Sev-
" Chester F bookkeeper 25 William h at Fairhaven
" Ella C kindergartener George H Dunbar school b 417 Union
" Frederick C shoemaker h 309 Austin [461 Chancery
" Herbert H collector Standard h
" Mabel W cooking teacher public schools b 233 Middle
" Robert carpenter h 206 Tinkham
" Russell apprentice Standard
Chandonet Rock machinist h 157 Collette [Bowditch
" Theodore clerk 155 Coffin av b 269
Chandonnair Alfred slasher tender h 83 Rivet [Thomas h do
Chaney Emma E dressmaker 85
" Emma J stenographer 28 N Water b 41 Keene
" Ida A h 85 Thomas [b 41 Keene
" Ralph N clerk 196 Pleasant
" Simon N W grocer 196 Pleasant h 41 Keene
Channing Edgar S clerk 358 Acushnet avenue b 68 County
" Eleanor G widow William H h 68 County [av
Chant James H weaver h 119 Brock
Chapard Horace H insurance agent h 204 Eugenia [15 Nye
Chapdelaine Alphege ball player bds
" Eva milliner b 15 Nye
" George E (Audette & Chapdelaine) lunch 1214 Acushnet av b 15 Nye
" Onesime laundryman h 15 Nye
" Onesime Jr fixer h 15 Nye
Chaplin Clarence L barber 302 Cedar h 367 Kempton [14 Salisbury
Chapman Adelbert A machinist h
" Adolphus weaver b 72 Ruth
" Charles R h 163 Pleasnat [Ruth
" Daniel overseer Butler Mill h 72
" Edward teamster b 68 Maxfield
" Elizabeth widow Reuben D h 68 Maxfield

F. T. AKIN & CO. FORGE FACTORY FURNACE FAMILY COAL

Chapman
" E T & Co (Harry M Chapman) cigars tobacco and pool 358 Acushnet avenue [h 61 S Sixth
" Harry M (E T Chapman & Co)
" Jane A widow William h 7 Ashley
" John operative h 19 E French av
" Katie Mrs bds 43 Division
" Leonora D widow Edward T h 53 Elm [city
" Margaret E Mrs removed to N Y
" Peter J operative b 68 Maxfield
" Thomas painter h 51 Short
" Thomas W operative bds 68 Maxfield [Willis
Chappell Arthur B clerk bds 21
" Esther B widow William H h 21 Willis
Chappius Adelphine h 54 Roosevelt
Chaput Adelard weaver h 70 Phillips avenue [mouth h 270 Purchase
" Joseph M blacksmith 108 Dart-
" Wilfred teamster b 270 Purchase
Charance Brandie Mrs h 64 Hicks
" Stanislas operative b 64 Hicks
Charbonneau Adelard operative h 17 Fulton court
" Adelord operative b 91 N Front
" Armand clerk 1527 Acushnet av bds 182 Dean
" Bros (John B and Joseph J) blacksmiths 454 Pleasant
" Edmonde weaver h r 162 Sawyer
" Edmonde Jr operative b r 162 Sawyer
" Eugene weaver b r 162 Sawyer
" Francois X weaver h 182 Dean
" John B (Charbonneau Bros) h 82 Myrtle
" Joseph boss comber h 59 Collette
" Joseph J (Charbonneau Bros) b 82 Myrtle
" Philip carpenter b 182 Dean [do
" Phoebe dressmaker 82 Myrtle h
" Romeo died Oct 28, 1910
" Stanislaus operative b 1279 Acushnet avenue
Charbonneaux August Mrs h 27 Hicks
" August Jr weaver b 27 Hicks
" Rock weaver b 27 Hicks
Chardonnais Frank operative h 1030 Acushnet avenue [lard
Charest Aldea mill hand b 91 Bul-

Charest
" Alic operative bds 170 N Front
" Alphonse mill hand b 41 Bullard
" Arcade removed to Canada [ham
" Athanase carpenter h 35 Ingra-
" Azilda mill hand b 91 Bullard
" Calixte blacksmith 854 Acushnet av h 32 Holly
" David h 91 Bullard
" Victor clerk 352 Kempton b 32 Holly [av
Charett Mary speeder h 47 Brock
Charette Charles C manager 75 William h at E Providence R I
" Edward laborer h 125 Cove
" Henri barber h 50 Ashley
" Henri barber 1149 Acushnet av h 162 Tinkham
" Louis weaver h 37 Ashley
" Philip speeder tender h 31 Morton court
" Theodule painter b 596 S Second
" see Sharrett
Chargaruly Nick (Zavas & Co) b 132 Bowditch [shuet av
Chariatt Louis fixer h 29 Acu-
Charity Organization Society of New Bedford 12 Market
Charlebois Daniel painter h 52 Hall
Charles Arthur weaver h 176 Hathaway [Brock av
Charnley Joseph J weaver h 187
" Lawrence molder h 146 Richmond
Charnock Robert h 883 S Water
Charpentier Albina clerk 182 Union b 69 Mt Pleasant
" Charles weaver b 361 N Front
" Edward clerk 1055 Acushnet av b 246 State
" Edward eyeletmaker b 181 State
" Eugene third hand h 1018 S Water
" George salesman b 181 State [lock
" Harmedos carpenter h 142 Bul-
" Henri C clothier 1055 Acushnet av h 12 Bentley [b 1117 do
" Henry clerk 1084 Acushnet av
" Henry weaver rms 51 Tallman
" Jean B laborer h 69 Mt Pleasant
" Joseph blacksmith h 181 State
" Joseph eyeletmaker b 181 State
" Noel H variety 905 County h 193 Weld
" Omar bartender h 427 Pleasant

Bookkeeping, Shorthand, Typewriting, Penmanship, etc. Taught thoroughly at
Kinyon's Commercial School
Odd Fellows Bldg., Cor. William and Pleasant Sts., New Bedford, Mass.

Charpentier
" Philomene laundryman bds 117 Clark [net av
" Wilfred slasher bds 876 Acush-
" William chauffeur h 185 State
" see Carpenter
Charperles James restaurant 958 S Water h 911 do [Dean
Charrette Alphonse bricklayer b 39
" Joseph laborer bds 596 S Second
" Samuel h 596 S Second
Charron Adrian weaver h 1101 County [do
" Joseph O electrician 33 Holly b
" Odina clerk 1131 Acushnet av b 80 Eugenia
" Oscar removed from city
" Ovide T student b 98½ Ruth
" Peter laborer b 2311 Acushnet av
" Philias A hostler h 98½ Ruth
" William fixer h 55 Tallman
Charroux Ambrose weaver h 642 First [Delano
" Treffle baker 945 S Water h 46
Chartier Arsene loom fixer h 286 Fourth
" Caroline Mrs h 107 Perry
" Charles O druggist W French avenue cor Cove rms 13 Viall
" Eliza A Mrs h 120 S Sixth
" Felix carpenter b 107 Perry
" Francis X bds Whitton street
" Jean B weaver h r 1527 Acushnet avenue [avenue
" John weaver h 1521 Acushnet
" Joseph rem from city [iman
" Joseph A operative h 15 Penn-
" Louis fixer h 150 Phillips av [do
" Ludger grocer 485 N Front h 483
" Marriott doffer b 122 S Sixth
" Onesime removed to Acushnet
" Rose Mrs h 159 David
Chase Ada B widow Horace F h 338 Orchard (S) [ville av
" Adolph boxmaker b 479 Belle-
" Albert carpenter b 121 Phillips avenue [chase
" Albert E teamster h 218 Purchase
" Alderick doffer b 121 Phillips av
" Alexander H mason h 28 Dartmouth
" Alice saleswoman b 15 Borden
" Allen third hand b 75 Bay

Chase
" Amy A widow Ezra b 14 Richmond [nold
" Andrew clerk 140 Union h 190 Ar-
" Andrew B master mariner h 87 Maple
" Andrew B Jr clerk 55 Spring h 105 Pine [nold
" Andrew M salesman h 192 Ar-
" Annie widow Warren E h 303 County [nold
" Archie L I motorman h 148 Ar-
" Arthur G carpenter h 8 Felton
" Arthur M clerk h 16 Borden
" Augustus E teamster h 840 Belleville avenue [299 Union
" Caroline P widow Ephraim F h
" Charles iceman h 379 Mt Pleasant [3982 Acushnet av
" Charles A teamster 26 Brook h
" Charles E painter 34 Union h 140 Mill
" Charles F carpenter and builder 24 Howard avenue h do
" Charles F instructor N B Industrial school b 113 Fourth
" Charles F machinist h 162 Allen
" Charles H farmer h Braley road
" Charlotte B stenographer 16 Masonic bldg b 43 North
" Chester W cotton broker 45 William h 68 Hillman [ton
" Clarence A painter b 804 Kemp-
" Clarence W grocer and fish 43 to 47 Bedford h 75 Bay
" Clifton E clerk 103 William rms 56 Walnut [mut av
" Collins wheelwright h 85 Shaw-
" Cora E widow Albert A nurse h 14 Richmond
" Darius teamster b 37 Hillman
" Earle D carpenter b 9 Felton
" Earle F clerk Mechanics National Bank b 299 Union [Dartmouth
" Edna L Mrs bookkeeper h 28
" Edward A farmer h 3982 Acushnet av [h at Fairhven
" Ernest S salesman 170 Purchase
" Frank B asst cashier First National Bank h 1 Morgan ter
" Fred H teamster 45 School h 282 Kempton [ville av
" Frederick E carpenter h 800 Belle-
" Frederick W carpenter h 2 Summit [h 66 Washington
" George bartender 437 S Water

Bread, Cake, Pastry
RICHMOND & COMPANY 255-257 UNION STREET
Bell 993 Automatic 1022

Chase
" George H b 41 Keene
" George H rms 371 Court
" George H teamster b 3982 Acushnet avenue [dar
" George L machinist h 413 Ce-
" George L motorman h 514 Cottage
" George M master mariner h 94 Rockland [Kempton
" Harry F foreman 255 State h 281
" Helen Mrs h 121 Phillips av
" Helen M bookkeeper 35 Commercial b 299 Union
" Henry E (Dias & Chase) 540 S Water h 148 Allen
" Henry S shoemaker h 48 State
" Henry T h 69 Summer
" Howard L Elder, Church of God h 2 Sullivan
" Isaac L b 987 Rockdale av
" Jacob W carpenter h 804 Kempton [net av
" James H shoemaker h 3982 Acush-
" Jane widow b 131 Elm
" John A clerk Acushnet Mill Corp h 373 Cottage
" John M carpenter h 27 Nye
" Joseph carpenter h 121 Phillips avenue
" Joseph P lather b 4 Watson
" Leon W drillworker h 593 Cottage
" Leroy E teamster b 2 Summit
" Lester teamster bds 473 Allen
" Lester W lather b 4 Watson
" Louis T clerk h 10 Clay
" Luella asst treas N B Theatre b Allen street [County
" Lydia C widow Nathan H h 661 County
" Lyman B laborer h 1 Pease court
" Marjory W cashier 40 Purchase b 133 Clinton
" Mary E Mrs h 567 Kempton
" Mary P stenographer 166 William b 338 Orchard (S)
" May Mrs h 236 Union
" Mellville C eyeletmaker h 221 North [way road
" Nathan P ice man h 580 Hatha-
" Nellie M clerk b 47 Mechanics lane
" Raymond police h 282 Palmer

Chase
" Raymond H operative b 318 Mt Pleasant [Fourth
" Richard D civil engineer h 59
" Robert B master mariner h 14 Richmond [mond
" Robert E drillmaker b 14 Rich-
" Robert H painter h 20 Howard avenue [Allen
" Roland F clerk 81 Front b 183
" Sarah E h 112 Arnold
" Sidney B lather h 4 Watson
" Thomas M carpenter h 7 Barrister [chase
" Walter B engineer h 496 Pur-
" Wilbur A ship carpenter h 377 Reed
" William b 27 Nye [av
" William doffer bds 121 Phillips
" William B h 43 North [Pleasant
" William F gardener h 318 Mt
" William H civil engineer 303 Municipal bldg b 162 Allen
" William R insurance 97 William rm 302 h 24 Keene
" Zebina B engineer h 99 Fruit
" see Chace
Chasseur David weaver h 102 David
Chassev Lezime C clerk yard master's office h 50 Maxfield [velt
Chatburn John weaver h 12 Roose-
Chatelle Eugene removed from city
" Mary Mrs dressmaker 1220 Acushnet av h do [net av
" Stephen chauffeur b 1220 Acush-
Chatterton Frank piper bds 24 W French avenue
CHAUSSE ALDEGE grocer 398 N Front and undertaker and livery 388 do h 396 do See page 772
" Alexina bookkeeper 398 N Front b 396 do [ditch
" Alfred clerk 11 Weld h 178 Bow-
" Alfred & Co (Alfred and Donat Chausse) liquors 1755 Acushnet avenue
" Annie widow Henry b 3 Marvin
" Antonio fixer h 186 Collette
" Blanche clerk 1039 Acushnet av h 143 Collette
" David fixer b 102 David
" Donat clerk 11 Weld h 260 do

GLOBE DYE HOUSE 220 SHAWMUT AVE.
J. N. J. LONHOLDT, PROP. Telephone Connections Goods called for and Delivered
Down town Office, 52 Pleasant St., Room 1 North End Office, 1014 Acushnet Ave.

Chausse
" Eugene harnessmaker h 396 N Front [shall
" Eugene R painter h 363 Cogge-
" George weaver b 3 Marvin
" George A operative b 117 Bullard
" Henri barber 1107 Acushnet av h 12 La France court
" Henry clerk h 3 Marvin
" Henry clerk h 170 Dean
" Joseph grocer 11 Weld h 126 Mt Pleasant [Acushnet av
" Joseph painter car barn h 862
" Joseph A physician 790 Purchase h do
" Levi weaver b 3 Marvin
" Medois operative b 3 Marvin
" Melvina Mrs clerk 1039 Acushnet avenue
" Moise teamster h 170 Dean
" Onat clerk 410 N Front h 1547 Acushnet avenue
" Ovila salesman Morris & Co h 126 Mt Pleasant [Tinkham
" Rosario clerk 398 N Front h 168
" Walter J clerk 2173 Acushnet av h 113 Nash road
" W weaver b 12 La France ct
" Xaxier bartender 1276 Acushnet avenue h 106 Bowditch [17 do
Chauvin Alphonse wood 15 Clark h
" Edward mill hand bds 196 Collette
" Fred, U S A b 17 Clark
" George carpenter rms 399 Belleville avenue [lette
" Harmedos carder b 196 Col-
" Henry W teamster b 17 Clark
" John laborer bds 17 Clark
" Joseph operative h 196 Collette
" Joseph operative h r 110 Rockland
" Paul mill hand bds 196 Collette
Chaves Joseph S fisherman h 75 Emma
Chayson Cyril laborer 57 N Second
Cheadle John watchman h 2 Durfee
Cheetham Andrew spinner h 196 Highland [shall
" Charles operative b 260 Cogge-
" Christopher loom fixer h 8 George
" James removed from city
" Thomas weaver b 111 David
" William removed to Acushnet
Chenard Avaris mechanic b 620 S First
" Ellen widow Ludger h 620 S First
Chenel Albert barber 217 Sawyer h 285 Davis [h at Boston
Chenery John A manager 27 Purchase
Chenette Emile weaver b 52 Delano
" Henry lunch 37 Rivet h 107 do
" Pierre weaver b 52 Delano
Cheney David M reporter Standard h 109 Robeson
Chenoweth Herbert A manager Comique Theatre b 83 Kenyon
Cherry George R (Cherry & Co) h 9 Orchard (N) [Providence R I
" William S (Cherry & Co) h at
" & Co (G R and W S Cherry and F Webb) cloaks and suits 40 and 42 Purchase
Chestak Carl laborer h 45 Bowditch
Chester James roller covered bds 16 Franklin
" John weaver h 443 Orchard (S)
Chevalier Edward carpenter bds 1076 County
" Oliver driver h 3 Austin ct
" Peter clerk 739 Purchase b 1076 County [ty
" Rose widow Edward h 1076 Coun-
" William carder h 1076 County
Chevrette Joseph carpenter b 1733 Acushnet avenue [Brock av
Chew Mary J widow Thomas b 205
Chiasson Cyrille lineman b 43 Holly
Chicago Furniture Co Arthur Comery manager 1228 Acushnet av
Chicoine Alme weaver b 71 Ruth
" Delia removed from city
" Esdras blacksmith 52 Dartmouth h 2 Thatcher
" Fabien teamster h 610 Purchase
" John (Chicoine & Co) h 20 Larch
" Joseph teamster h 55 Tallman
" & Co (John Chicoine) liquors 23 S Second [man
Chieppa Pasqual laborer b 319 Hill-
Child Arthur W clerk 22 Fourth h 283 Allen [Chestnut
" Elizabeth T housekeeper 95
" Joseph carpenter h 161 Richmond
" Stephen L foreman 6 Elm h 29 Fifth [29 Fifth
" Stephen L Jr porter 84 Union b
Childs Augustine F pres N B Fish Co h 51 Willis

GREENE & WOOD Every Kind of LUMBER AND MILL WORK
PINE STREET, off So. WATER STREET, NEW BEDFORD

Childs
" Charles D conductor b 331 Cedar
" Frank H salesman N B Fish Co h 25 Homer [Fourth
" Hattie B widow Josiah G h 176
" Sophia S died Mar 14 1911
Chinello Giuseppi laborer h 504 Acushet avenue [64 Borden
Chipman Elizabeth F widow Charles b
" Sands C city editor Times h 13 Bay [sutta Mill h 10 Studley
Chippendale Edward overseer Wam-
" Herbert weaver b 187 Hathaway
" Thomas J drill straightener h 5 Cottage [Belleville av
Chirigotis Anthony mill hand h 269
" Charles weaver b 269 Belleville av [ton
Chisholm Duncan removed to Bos-
" Larry lineman b 49 Sycamore
" Lawrence cable splicer 43 William b 49 Sycamore [Sixth
" Sarah A widow Elijah H h 55 N
" Thomas M loans 307 Times bldg rms 289 Purchase
Chittick Rebecca nurse h 321 Union
Chochat Andrew weaver b 204 Blackmer [Taunton
Choicener J Frank removed to
Choppin Peter carpenter h 162 Crapo
Choquette Adolphid L shipper b 1406 Acushnet avenue
" Albini died Nov 5 1910
" Alfred carpenter h 320 Davis
" Alfred mason h 189 Bowditch
" Antonio J shoemaker bds 1406 Acushnet avenue
" Charles A conductor h 206 Austin
" Clara stenographer 37 Purchase rm 15 b 89 Beetle
" Elzear H clothing 80 William h 102 Mt Pleasant
" Emery weaver h 106 David
" Eugenie clerk 1039 Acushnet av b Mt Pleasant street
" Eva clerk bds 89 Beetle
" Ferdinand J salesman 80 William b 102 Mt Pleasant
" Frank steam fitter 5 Atlantic h 50 Washburn [Weld
" Frobisher M carpenter h 177
" Henry weaver h 106 David
" Hypolite h 1406 Acushnet av
" Jean B bookkeeper 115 Bowditch h 89 Beetle

Choquette
" Leo fixer b 59 Bullard [Grove
" Louis operative h 404 Cedar
" Matılda widow Fred h 189 Bowditch
" Michael carpenter h 8 Bowditch
" Peter driver b 189 Bowditch
" Yvonne bookkeeper 80 William b 102 Mt Pleasant
Choremi Benachi & Co cotton 108 Union rm 10
Chouinard Clara h 201 Sawyer
" Ernest bds 201 Sawyer [ct
" Louis operative h 16 Hampton
Chovin Benjamin carpenter h 82 Nelson [Purchase h 68 Ocean
Christensen Henry M cutlery 190
Christian August laborer b 35 Briggs
" Joseph stonecutter h 35 Briggs
" Manuel bookkeeper b 35 Briggs
Christie Adolphus weaver h 362 Coffin av [lips av
" Alexander third hand b 62 Phil-
" Alexander weaver h 62 Phillips avenue
" Alfred (A Christie & Co) liquors 1670 Acushnet av h 206 Eugenia [1670 Acushnet av
" A & Co (Alfred Christie) liquors
" Eva milliner 1354 Acushnet av bds 62 Phillips av
" Evaline widow Alfred b 206 Eugenia [land
" George G shoemaker b 35 Ash-
" Henry weaver h 107 Coffin av
" Henry weaver bds 62 Phillips av
" Joseph machinist h 1683 Acushnet avenue
Christo Antone h 584 S Water
" Thomas mill hand h 16 Bullard
Christophe Isadore died Nov 23 1910
" Joseph laborer h 130 Robeson
Christopher Charles W painter h 63 Chancery
" Christian B mariner b 10 Collins
" Harry (Christopher & Mellen) 849 S Water b 153 Blackmer
" Joseph laborer h 30 E Merrimac
" & Mellen (Christopher Mellen and Harry Christopher) confectionery 849 S Water
Chubbuck Frank B tackmaker h 207 Chancery [ton h do
" Lurana A physician 133 Kemp-
Chumack Harriet M rem from city
" Isaac F spinner h 57 Liberty

BONNEY, FOLSTER & CO.,
The North End's Shopping Centre
Dry Goods and Men's Furnishings
945-947 Acushnet Ave., New Bedford, Mass.

Chumack
" Isaac R foreman concreter h 114 Cedar
" Leonard removed from city
" Jennet C removed from city
Church Abbie K widow Joseph E h 68 Forest
" Albert C h 76 Fourth
" Alice R widow Ephraim h 31 Shawmut avenue
" Bradford L h 110 Willis
" Charles C died
CHURCH CHARLES H druggist 122 Purchase h 46 S Sixth See page 25
" Charles R overseer b 109 Chestnut [Bourne
" Edwin W drillmaker h 32
" Eliza B bookkeeper U St Ry Co h 68 Forest [Spring
" Emma T widow William N h 102
" Ethel M b 352 Purchase
" Etta K Mrs h 352 Purchase
" Eunice S music teacher 136 Chestnut h do [at Fairhaven
" Frank H clerk 122 Purchase h
" Harriett A died Jan 27 1911
" Henry H treas Lambeth Rope Corp h at Taunton
" Horace S piper 125 Middle b 71 Arnold [at Fairhaven
" James I (Church & Hammond) h
" Lucy A h 39 North
" **Mary A and Nancy T h 9 Maple**
" Mary J h 68 Forest
" Wayne C troubleman 57 N Second h at Mattapoisett
" & Hammond (J I Church and G D Hammond) druggists 115 William
Churchill Benjamin J piper 55 N Water b 428 Kempton
" Harold S bookkeeper b 13 Eighth
" Henry C shoemaker h 23 Ashland place
" Samuel h 1171 Rockdale avenue
" Sarah E widow Isaac C b 224 North [23 Ashland pl
" Susan E clerk 474 Acushnet av b
Ciaburri James tailor h 146 Fourth
Ciborowski Stanislaus h 259 N Front
Cieurzo Paul F glass blower h 27 Clover [entine
Cinnamard James, U S A h 48 Val-
Cioper Michael weaver h 7 Salisbury
City Almshouse Thomas F Brown supt 1 E French av
CITY COAL CO Josiah Hunt treas and mgr main office and yard Front cor Middle branches 114 William, 1026 Acushnet av and 1109 S Water See page 3
" Evangelization Union 1604 Acushnet av [mfrs foot Grinnell
" Manufacturing Corporation yarn
" Mission office 755 First
" Mission Dispensary 755 First
" Mission Wood yard 1 Mill
" Stables and Work Shops Ash st
" Steam Laundry (Charles R Hathaway) 6-8 Campbell
Claer Adolphe weaver b 806 First
" Jean weaver h 806 First [Durfee
Clagg Nellie F clerk 58 Adams h 29
" see Clegg [Ruth
Claimont Hormidas painter bds 106
Clairmont Victoria h 20 McGurk
Clancy Daniel second hand h 59 Ruth
Clapp Benjamin laborer b 22 Maxfield [Myrtle
" Benjamin A Jr conductor h 18
" Charles F painter h 6 Bowditch
" George M operative b 208 Kempton [field
" Grover C conductor b 22 Max-
" Isaac N tackmaker b 22 Maxfield
" Mina clerk 1092 Acushnet av bds 6 Bowditch
Clare Emma Mrs h 154 Acushnet av
" John weaver h 48 Independent
" Mary Mrs h 350 Cedar Grove
" Michael weaver h 23 Viall
" Stephen back boy b 350 Cedar Grove
" Thomas doffer b 350 Cedar Grove
" W Henry h 191 S Second
Clark Abbot fixer h 612 S Second
" Arthur W weaver h 122 Fourth
" A Frank (Driscol, Church & Hall) wholesale grocer 84 Union h 141 Allen
" Bridget widow James h 41 Larch
" Carrie L Mrs h 53 Peckham
" Charles A motorman h 113 Austin [Grove
" Dora operative h 247 Cedar
" Edgar S shoemaker 105 Union h 14 Armour [chase
" Edward bookkeeper b 188 Pur-
" Edward spinner b 258 Coffin av

M. P. B. Silva & Son BUILDERS
Estimates Furnished on all Kinds of Work
157 ACUSHNET AVENUE Both Phones NEW BEDFORD

Clark
" Edward A engineer h 216 Middle [av
" Elisha F laborer h 90 W French
" Ellen widow Thomas b 122 Thompson
" Foust Capt V of A h Main st
" Frank laborer 350 Second
" Frederick A letter carrier b 327 Court
" Frederick L physician h 49 Fifth
" Frederick P carpenter h 11 Spruce [h 71 Hall
" George H overseer Sharp Mill
" George H Jr clerk 645 County h 123 Campbell [Fifth
" Georgia A widow Charles F b 48
" Harry W lineman 57 N Second
" Helen widow Thomas bds 122 Thompson [Court
" Henrietta widow Ulysses L h 327
" Henry weaver b 66 Brock av
" James compositor Standard h 293 Acushnet avenue
" James laborer b 41 Larch
" James weaver b 17 Austin
" Joseph operative b 41 Larch
" John weaver bds 152 Division
" John B student b 89 Robeson
" John H weaver h 251 Bowditch
" Joseph operative b 41 Larch
" J Francis Mrs b 95 Elm [land
" Louisa widow Charles h 184 Rock-
" Louise C Mrs h 358 Kempton
" Mary widow John h 217 Phillips avenue
" Mary E removed from city
" Mary J widow Elbridge G h 9 Highland
" Maud E stenographer Nashawena Mill bds 123 Campbell
" Peter F carpenter h 36 George
" Samuel real estate h 60 Parker
" Samuel R (Clark & Son) 505 S Water h 16 Ash (S)
" Terrance coachman 709 County h 89 Robeson
" Thomas laborer h 20 Division
" Walter clerk h 101 Rockland
" Willard O foreman 8 Campbell h 89 State [Ash (S)
" William (Clark & Son) bds 16
" William laborer b 41 Larch

Clark
" William J laborer h 44 Woodlawn avenue [man
" William J weaver h 123 Whit-
" & Son (Samuel R and William) plumbers and tinsmiths 503-505 S Water
Clarke Albert E driver h 147 Rounds
" A Edwin lawyer special justice 3rd district court h 183 Pleasant [James
" Charles clerk 1 William h 75
" Edward E lawyer 30 Masonic bldg h 168 Allen
" Edward T wholesale liquors 133 N Front h 188 Purchase
" Emerson J removed from city
" Frederick C (Read & Co) 141 Union h 71 North
" George W tinsmith 28 N Second h 762 County [12 Clay
" Harriet H clerk 41 Purchase bds
" John C salesman 95 Union h 30 Crapo
" Mary widow Peter h 12 Clay
" Mattie V widow Charles A h 216 Summer [h 63 Bay
" Michael gardener 71 Hawthorn
" Ronald B salesman rms Y M C A
" Thomas F gardener b 12 Clay
" William janitor I W Benjamin school h 41 Mosher
" William laborer h 1 Harmony
" William A bookkeeper P Corp h 4 Green [Kempton
" William J letter carrier h 655
Clarkson Alfred E mule spinner h 95 Willard [ton
" George mule spinner h 480 Bol-
" Sarah J Mrs h 20 Salisbury
" Wilfred weaver b 95 Willard
" William mill hand b 480 Bolton
Claudino Felicia widow John b 108 Rockland [h 199 Fourth
" Joao hairdresser 323 Acushnet av
" Joseph shoeworker 108 Rockland
" Manuel S shoemaker 120 Purchase h 143 River rd [rd
" M Chester boxmaker h 143 River
Clavner Joseph h 916 County
Clay May A clerk 185 Union b at Fairhaven [ville rd
Clayton George laborer h 184 Belle-
" John twister h r 438 Second

Steiger-Dudgeon Co.
"The WOMAN'S Store."
Tel. Bell 82 & 83, Branches connecting all depts.
" " 160 For Office only. Auto. 1211

SUMPTIONS, ASSORTMENTS AT ALL TIMES OF DEPENDABLE DRY GOODS

CLEAN WET WASH The D E Allen prop 76 Shawmut avenue See page 786
Cleary Anna A teacher Thomas R Rodman school b 245 Brownell
" Daniel laborer b 345 Coffin av
" Daniel E J stonecutter h 300 Cedar [do
" Elizabeth nurse 194 Purchase bds
" Elizabeth widow Anthony h 245 Brownell
" Elizabeth K b 245 Brownell
" James H clerk b 245 Brownell
" John F cigar mfr 183 Acushnet av h 2 Weaver
" Minnie h 4 Grape
" William E police station 5 h 193 Coffin avenue [son
" William H foreman b 124 Robe-
Clegg Charles D N steam fitter h 79 Bowditch
" Edward fixer h 96 Hathaway
" James carder b 83 Ruth
" John clerk h 105 Swift
" J Edward weaver h 23 Covell
" Ralph weaver h 289 Phillips av
" William clerk 182 Union
" see Clagg [b Bullock st
Clement Charles barber 256 Purchase
" Ephraim weaver h 69 Nelson
" Joseph driver 386 Acushnet av b 56 Dean
" Joseph teamster h 247 Bowditch
" Manuel Mrs operative h 496 Bolton
" Manuel J weaver h 50 Sherman
Clements Frank shoeworker rms 122 Middle
" Katherine S nurse b 149 Summer
Clemishaw Ernest laborer b 978 County [[978 County
" Martha J widow Walter E h
Clerc Albert weaver h 23 Viall
" Emile weaver h 23 Viall
Clerk Charles Rev asst pastor St Anthony's church h 1359 Acushnet avenue [avenue
" Henry operative bds 66 Brock
Clermont August carpenter h 132 Bullard [Bedford b do
Cleveland Alice M dressmaker 50
" Anna W asst public library b 127 Summer [Fifth
" Benjamin D master mariner h 39

Cleveland
" Cora B teacher R C Ingraham school b 105 Clinton
" Eliza Mrs h 62 Roosevelt
" Frank N driver Hose 8 h 217 Phillips avenue
" George H V D baker 14 Bedford and lunch 193 Acushnet av h 50 Bedford [105 Clinton
" Mabel W teacher High school h
" Rufus sub letter carrier h 192 Grinnell [Front
Clifford Antone fisherman h 273 S
" A Walter drillworker h 5 Richmond [er
" Benjamin H painter h 3 Spoon-
" Charles W (Crapo, Clifford & Prescott) lawyer 6 Masonic bldg h 78 Orchard
" Ellen h 3 Irving court [man
" Ernest auto washer rms 27 Hill-
" Frank tinsmith b 18 Studley
" Hattie Mrs h 236 Kempton
" John H (Crapo, Clifford & Prescott) lawyer 6 Masonic bldg b 127 Hawthorn [chase
" Marcus E plumber h 666 Pur-
" Richard laborer h 18 Studley
" Walter (Crapo, Clifford & Prescott) lawyer 6 Masonic bldg h 127 Hawthorn
Clifton Charlotte W widow Jireh W h 67 Merrimac
" Gordon removed from city
" Helen stenographer 37 Purchase rm 13 b at Marion
Clitherow Thomas watchman h 118 David [Phillips av
Clocher Alphonse printer h 15
Close John J rem to Los Angeles Cal
Clough George H clerk 65 Purchase h 991 Kempton [William
" George H police station 5 h 25
" Judson carpenter h 78 Oak
" Mildred Mrs h 192 Shawmut av
" see Clow [man
Cloutier Albert laborer b 104 Tall-
" Alexander laborer b 104 Tallman
" Antonio doffer h 174 Phillips av
" Archille operative b 104 Tallman
" Arthur P second hand h 59 Tallman [dent
" Edmond weaver h 52 Indepen-
" Ernest weaver b 59 Bullard
" Hector carpenter h 5 Hazard ct

PELEG H. SHERMAN 506 COUNTY ST.
FUNERAL DIRECTOR AND EMBALMER
OFFICE PHONES. Bell 690-13. Auto. 1305.
RESIDENCE PHONES. Bell 690-12. Auto. 1306.

Cloutier
" Isadore operative h 16 Hazard court
" James weaver h 107 Holly
" Jean B weaver h 71 Hazard ct
" Jeremiah weaver h 1 Bowditch
" Joseph removed to Worcester
" Phillibert weaver h 49 Austin
" Pierre h 104 Tallman
" Raymond awningmaker 31 Commercial b 144 Division
" Valentine weaver h 15 Hazard ct
" William driver h 103 David
Clow Helen seamstress bds 176 Smith
Club Stable Corp 34 S Second [chase
Cluett Thomas cook rms 245 Pur-
Clunie James fitter h 9 Harrison
" Robert M carder h 57 Howard
Clynes Catherine H clerk 656 Purchase b 643 do [643 do
" Dennis J clerk 143 Purchase b
" Helena M Mrs dry goods 656 Purchase h 643 do
" James J weaver h 88 Austin
" John P died May 14 1911 [chase
" Thomas J salesman h 643 Pur-
Coache Evariste carpenter h 71 Brock avenue
" Phillipe carpenter h 175 Eugenia
Coakley Edward shoemaker rms 367 Purchase
" John T optician 26 Cove h do
" Joseph salesman b 21 Centre
Coanick Melvin mill hand h 70 Nelson [Winsor
Coates David mule spinner h 89
" Ernest F laborer b 236 Union
" James weaver h 130 Holly
" John S engineer 159 N Second h 236 Union
" Samuel spinner h 58 Roosevelt
" Thomas C laborer h 161 Brook
" William weaver h 119 Reynolds
Cobb, Aldrich & Co wholesale grocers 8 Hamilton
" Atlec N driver b Hawes lane
" Bertha M operative 43 William b at Acushnet
" Carl C clerk b 5 Main
" Charles H collector rms Y M C A
" Charles W foreman W F Nye h at Fairhaven
" David A painter 379 Elm h do
" Edith H assistant public library b 5 Main L C

Cobb
" Elizabeth H assistant clerk Third District Court b 78 Bedford
" Franklin painter bds 379 Elm
" George A hardware 2172 Acushnet avenue h 5 Main L C
" George S clerk 2172 Acushnet av h Hersom
" Ira B teamster b 550 Kempton
" Ira T C drill turner h 550 Kempton
" James H laborer h Hawes lane
" John A druggist 849 Kempton b 298 Union
" John Q A gardener h 61 Beech
" John Q A Jr clerk b 61 Beech
" Phebe A widow Thomas J h 78 Bedford
" Rhoda A h 224 Chancery [cery
" Rufus B paperhanger b 224 Chan-
" Seth A removed to Marion
" William B clerk b 303 Summer
" William B painter b 224 Chancery
" William L teamster h 445 Mt Pleasant
Coblez Charley mill hand h 680 First
Coblins Robert H laborer h 310 Middle [C A
Coburn Eliott C operative rms Y M
" Thomas weaver b 297 Belleville avenue [Chestnut
Cochrane Emma T bookkeeper b 65
" Eva assistant 16 Howard b do
" Mary widow William b 82 Dean
" Samuel pattern maker b 102 State
" William J janitor Philips av school h 65 Chestnut [av
Cochshoot Herbert fixer b 8 Coffin
Cocker James operative b 30 Clark
" John spinner h 30 Clark
" Robert doffer bds 30 Clark
" William loom fixer h 67 Norman
Cocking John weaver b 172 Division
" Lawrence loom fixer h 14 Morton court
" Richard weaver b 14 Morton ct
" Robert weaver b 14 Morton ct
Cockshott Arthur J baker 39 Linden h 9 McMurray terrace
Cockshutt Alfred tinsmith 19 Linden h 175 Richmond
" John H tinsmith 745 Purchase h 128 Shawmut avenue

F. T. AKIN & CO. PAINTERS AND DECORATORS

Codaire Alphonse clerk 1404 Acushnet avenue b 207 Bowditch
" Anson weaver h 67 Coffin av
" Archille collector h 131 Whitman
" Arthur operative b 207 Bowditch
" John B operative h 207 Bowditch
" John B weaver h 84 Jouvett
" Napoleon brewery worker h 1757 Acushnet avenue [Chestnut
Codd Victoria widow Thomas b 95
Codding Jesse teamster 47 School
" Mary A widow Seth E h 8 Spruce
" William A painter b 8 Spruce
Coderre Alfred overseer h 186 Arnold
" Helen dresmaker b 186 Arnold
" Isadore weaver h 176 State
" John B laborer h 40 Acushnet av
Cody Edmond F physician 105 S Sixth h do [Grinnell
Coe Frederick P pattern maker h 207
" Isaac H Rev died Jan 17 1911
" Isaac H Jr carpenter h 124 Washington [Sears
" Walter L clerk Butler Mill b 8
" William A shipping clerk P & R C & I Co foot Walnut h 71 Mechanics lane
" William F shoe laster h 8 Sears
Coelho Antonio car cleaner U St Ry Co
" Antonio mill hand h 96 Davis [av
" Joaquim laborer b 202 Belleville
" Joseph clerk h 156 Hemlock
" Joseph operative b 96 Davis
" Leonora S widow b 156 Hemlock
Coffey James M removed to Providence R I
" James M Rev pastor St Mary's R C church h 23 Robeson
" John W glass cutter h 224 County
Coffin Arie A nurse h 157 North
" Arthur E (The A E Coffin Press) h 34 Seventh
" Arthur S (Coffin Bros) h at Chicago Ill [chase
" A E Press The printers 69 Pur-
COFFIN BROS (Walter H and Arthur S) paper box mfr 38 Middle See page 782
" George C gas light fixer h 64 State [av
" Herbert C clerk b 275 Acushnet

Coffin
" James H chief clerk Merchants National Bank b 465 County
" Milton S student b 34 Seventh
" Walter H (Coffin Bros) h 253 Acushnet av
" Williams B chauffeur b 64 State
Coffman Charles M glassworker h 211 Chestnut [Shawmut av
Coford Caroline H clerk bds 121
" J Erica widow Henry P h 121 Shawmut avenue [ton
Coggeshall Alfretta Mrs h 712 Kemp-
" Charles mariner b 217 Middle
" Charles W h 59 Hillman
" Clara L stenographer bds 483 County [Collins
" Edward H captain Engine 7 h 30
" Edward K ticket seller Hathaway's Theatre b 483 County
" George driver b 712 Kempton
" Hayden engineer h 267 Summer
" Helen R b 87 Court
" Ida T widow C Wells h 90 Elm
" James F carpenter b 86 Ashland
" Mabel A widow John L h 111 Hillman
" Mary E h 460 Acushnet av
" Mary E widow Edward L h 483 County
" Robert C P supt N B W W 40 Masonic bldg h 87 Court
" Robert H salesman 14 Wall b 483 County [1159 Rockdale av
" William A clerk 830 Purchase h
" Willis H salesman h 24 Cedar
Coggey Mary widow Tarlton b 410 Kempton [Merrimac
Coggin John F custom house h 190
Cohan Annie F widow W H bds 2 Irvington ct
Cohen Abraham h 483 S Water
" Abraham glasscutter h 230 Purchase
" Abram h 126 Fourth
" Albert h 224 Acushnet av [h do
" Albert dry goods 242 Coggeshall
" Benjamin student b 155 Holly
" Benjamin (J Cohen & Son) b 8 Marvin [1088 Acushnet av
" Bros (Morris and Kopel) clothing
" Harry driver 386 Acushnet av b 114 S Sixth
" Harry grocer 410 S Water h do

There's room at the top for young men and women who can do things right.
Kinyon's Commercial School
Odd Fellows Bldg., Cor. William and Pleasant Sts., New Bedford, Mass.

Cohen
" Hyman barber 516 S Water h do [h do
" Hyman provisions 497 S Water
" Ida widow h 114 S Sixth
" Joseph dry goods 267 S Water h 512 do · [vin
" Joseph (J Cohen & Son) h 8 Mar-
" Joseph tailor 1524 Acushnet av h do
" J & Son (Joseph and Benjamin) cloaks etc 829 Purchase
" Kopel (Cohen Bros) 1088 Acushnet av h 155 Holly
" Michael driver 386 Acushnet av b 114 S Sixth
" Morris (Cohen Bros) 1088 Acushnet av h 155 Holly
" Morris painter h 516 S Water
" Morris pedlar h 16 Howland
" Morris pedlar h 350 First
" Morris pedlar h 455 S Water
" Morris provisions 460 S Water h 455 do
" Morris second hand furniture 637 S Water h 6 Howland [av
" Nathan pedlar h 53 Belleville
" Reuben pedlar h 10 Bedford
" Samuel pedlar h 426 S Water
" Simon junk h 426 S Water
Coholan Dennis laborer b 36 Independent [dent
" James pressman bds 36 Indepen-
COHOLAN JEREMIAH plumber 703 S Water h 331 Orchard (S) See page 767
" John L overseer Taber Mill h 285 Bowditch [pendent
" Julia widow Jeremiah h 36 Inde-
Coit Clarence L bds 179 Collette
Coito Antone fireman b 10 Griffin
" Joseph laborer h 14 Cotter
Colaq Joseph mill hand b 36 Dean
Colardeau Leon glass decorator h 17 Borden [Campbell
Colbert Benton city laborer h 189
" John weaver h 279 Cedar Grove
" Mary J Mrs h 38 Bowditch [nold
Colbeth Harmon S janitor h 142 Ar-
" Marjorie M clerk b 9 Warwick
Colburn George A painter h 211 Acushnet av
" Mary E Mrs h 606 County [Hill
Colby Almira C widow Philip E h 37
" Henry T clerk b 506 Purchase
Colclough Ernest machinist h 310 Tinkham
Colcord Frederick B engineer Pierce Mfg Corp h 530 Cottage
Cole Anna E widow Charles G h 367 Purchase [N Y
" Cain P Rev removed to Brooklyn
" Carrie H Mrs h 112 Rivet
" Emma F clerk Registry of Deeds b 199 Maxfield
" Esther L Mrs teacher Phillips av school h 35 Hollyhock
" Everett W head lineman 57 N Second h 287 Court
" Harry L clerk b 35 Hollyhock
" Henrietta widow Stephen R bds 245 Tremont [rd
" James O toolmaker b 191 River
" Margaret Mrs h 19 Ashley [sion
" Susan widow William h 113 Divi-
" Theodore W granite and marble 20 William h 74 Hillman
" Theodore W Jr asst supt Pierce Mfg Corp b 74 Hillman
" Violet Mrs bds 321 Cedar
" Wilfred b 19 Ashley
" William Jr manager 213 Acushnet av h 196 Grinnell [dale av
" William T police h 1143 Rock-
Coleman Caroline E widow David B b 418 Union
" Fanny housekeeper r 235 Park
" George B laborer 144 S Water h 403 S Second
" George H h 406 Allen
" James laborer h 23 Ashley
" Louisa widow Robert h r 235 Park
" Phoebe C widow Frank b 134 Willis
Coles Ernest W J waiter b 167 Elm
" Lucy F widow Willis h 167 Elm
Colinski Samuel pedlar h 152 Acushnet avenue
Colla Tomacella laborer bds 5 Bullard
Collard Frank third hand h 60 Belleville road [otto) 67 Union
Collateral Loan Co (Barnard A Russ-
Colles Arthur C weaver h 11 Ashley
Collet Cyprien A A drugs 1567 Acushnet avenue h 1565 do
Collett Alfred King Rev pastor Primitive Methodist Church h 48 Independent
Collette Arthur painter b 203 Collette
" Fred harness maker h 12 Beetle

HASKELL BROS. DEALERS IN
ICE
400 COURT STREET TELEPHONE CONNECTION NEW BEDFORD, MASS.

Collette
" Henry bartender 416 N Front h 156 Church
" Ismahel carpenter h 203 Collette
" Joseph lineman h 188 Collette
" Napoleon removed from city
" Ulric E blacksmith 105 Bowditch and (Fredette & Collette) 1023 S Water h 192 Collette
Collier George painter rms 619 Purchase
" George A weaver h 60 Salisbury
Colligan Frank laborer b 236 Brock avenue [415 Orchard (S)
Collinge Edmund mule spinner h
" Harold mill hand b 481 Rivet
" John W spinner h 481 Rivet
" Samuel weaver bds 303 Brock av
" William doffer b 415 Orchard (S)
Collingwood Jane B b 392 Cottage
Collins Albert weaver b 19 Ashley
" Albert B registrar of deeds Court House h at Fairhaven
" Anna Mrs h 837 First
" Antone fruit h 359 Coggeshall
" Bridget widow bds 57 Fair
" Charles clerk 145 Union b 86 School [avenue
" Charles engineer b 1789 Acushnet
" Charles F shoemaker b 30 West Trinity [Mill
" Charles S clerk 7 Commercial h 75
" Cornelius laborer b 232 N Second
" Daniel J carpenter h 636 Cottage
" Edna M Mrs b 2 Pope Island
" Eugene E gardener b 192 Grinnell [Mills rms 386 Union
" Florence E Mrs clerk Wamsutta
" Florence J widow William J h 691 Cottage
" George spinner h 397 Rivet
" Gilbert N woodwork 3 E Pope h at Shawmut [Trinity
" Herbert L operative b 30 West
" Hugh J machinist h 27 Clark
" Hugh P mill hand h 120 County
" James electrician b Tarkiln Hill road
" James Jr telephone installer 57 N Second h 58 N Sixth
" James A district traffic chief 57 North Second h 170 Park
" James F plumber 145 Purchase h 17 Trinity

Collins
" John laborer b 232 N Second
" Joseph J machinst h 27 Clark
" Mary widow Patrick died 1910
" Maud Mrs h 44 Wing
" Michael J twister h 184 County
" Nicholas fruit h 359 Coggeshall
" Patrick H spinner b 336 Davis
" Sarah widow Asa B h 30 West Trinity
" Thomas laborer h 40 Independent
" Timothy P bartender 1200 Acushnet avenue h 336 Davis [Clark
" William F clerk 122 Allen b 27
" William R plumber 55 N Water h at Westport
" Williston H (Williston H Collins & Co) h 122 Clinton
COLLINS WILLISTON H & CO (W H Collins) printers and book binders 34-40 N Second See page 23
Collis Joseph weaver h 75 Emma
" Margaret widow Patrick b 75 Emma [Acushnet av
Collison Jemima mill hand bds 1264
Colomb Caroline widow Joseph h 361 North Front
" Joseph N agent h 361 N Front
Colombe Angeline widow Jere b 18 Linden [Smith
Colson Fred William painter h 164
Colte Leodor grocer h 53 Washburn
Colton Lottie Mrs b 78 Willis [ct
Colvin Ellery E piper h 4 Brightman
" Frank A hostler h 186 Smith
Colwell Annie T widow John J nurse h 251 Shawmut avenue
" Arthur F inspector N B W W b 251 Shawmut av [h 108 Pierce
" Edward H meat cutter 416 Kemp-
" George R grocer 261 Arnold h 210 Chancery [Shawmut av
" John C clerk 113 Union h 51
" Richard L clerk bds 251 Shawmut avenue [Pleasant
" Susan widow William h 63 Mt
" William clerk bds 6 Bowditch
" see Caldwell [Acushnet av
Colvar Amy A widow Sylvester b 506
" Ellen A widow Abraham L b 464 Kempton
" Frank E h 113 Campbell [den
" Frederick T carpenter h 17 Bor-
" George L painter h 145 N Second

J. F. CROSSLEY 223 MILL STREET COR. EMERSON PHONE
STEAM and HOT WATER HEATING
GAS FITTING and FIXTURES

Colyar
" Helen clerk 185 Union b 464 Union
" Nellie clerk b 464 Kempton
" Philip S teamster 36 Purchase h 170 Pleasant [bell b do
" P Meyer Mrs artist 113 Camp-
Coman George E clerk 396 Kempton b 139 Cedar [287 Coffin av
Comeau Alfred barber 397 N Front h
" Baptiste driver h 198 State
" Edward carpenter rms 847 Purchase [Otto avenue
" Henri typesetter 101 Kenyon b
" Honore weaver h 175 Phillips av
" Jean B twister h r 36 Hicks
" John laborer h 353 S Water
" Joseph h 224 Philips avenue
" Laurent H card writer 185 Union b 45 Beetle [lips av
" Leonidas musician bds 175 Phil-
" Napoleon rem to Muncton Canada
" Philip fixer h 147 Hathaway
" Philomene widow operative h 319 Belleville avenue [road
" Philomon bricklayer h 118 Nash
" Treffly weaver h 45 Beetle
" Xavier weaver b 224 Phillips av
Comery Arthur manager 1228 Acushnet avenue h 159 Tinkham
" Ernest machinist h 94 Nash road
Comey Charles M clerk A W Holmes h 56 Hill [Acushnet av
Cominsky John operative b 137
Comique Theatre 958 Acushnet av
Comire John fitter bds 257 Coffin av
Commerford Eleanor and Katharine h 634 County [Reed
Comstock Elbert A operative b 323
" Florence E b 187 Pleasant
" George H operative h 323 Reed
" Lizzie Mrs b 187 Pleasant
" Thomas W lieutenant of police station 1 h 16 Richmond
" Wilmer E machinist b 323 Reed
Conant George M tailor 131 Union h 79 Campbell [Smith
Conary Edward F engineer h 92
" George T H clerk 161 Purchase b 494 Acushnet avenue
" James F electrician b 34 Hillman
Concaicao Manuel A barber h 160 Cedar [North Second
Congdon A & Co cotton brokers 50
CONGDON CARPENTER & CO iron and steel Fall River See page 10
" Charles K manager 50 N Second h at Providence R I
" William A agent Whitman Mills h 720 County
Conlan Matthew h 195 Brock avenue
" Thomas operative b 195 Brock av
Conlin Katherine G b 69 Borden
Conlon James Rev h 593 Kempton
Conn Andrew C pressman b 141 Holly
" Samuel W weaver h 141 Holly
Connell John h 5 Wamsutta
CONNELL JOHN JR sand and gravel contractor and general teaming 350 Sawyer h do See page 774
" John J operative b 563 Acushnet avenue [net av
" Julia widow William h 563 Acush-
" Thomas h 3 Clark
" William teamster h 53 Kempton
" William J operative b 563 Acushnet avenue [Beetle
Connelly Ellen widow Patrick J h 95
" James bleacher bds 84 Rodney
" James E mule spinner h 84 Rodney
" Jennie Mrs h 90 Hathaway av
" John laborer h 49 Hemlock
" John laborer h 68 Summer
" John mill hand b 178 Belleville av
" Patrick J bookkeeper 29 Bowditch b 95 Beetle [nolds
" Patrick J engineer b 127 Rev-
Conner Isabelle widow William b 190 Brock avenue
Connick Melvin fixer h 70 Nelson
Conniff Emma L Mrs milliner 142½ Purchase h do
" John A Jr general agent 97 William rm 300 b 142½ Purchase
" see Cunniff
Connolly Albert B b 184 Ashland
" Andrew painter b 171 Richmond
" Bridget widow Patrick b r 188 Middle
" Daniel city carpenter h 370 State
" David spinner h 184 Ashland
" Francis C clerk Whitman Mills bds 370 State
" Harold joiner b 184 Ashland
" John loom fixer h 41 Vine [genia
" John W second hand h 128 Eu-

CHARLES A. CROSHERE CARRIAGE AND AUTO
38 FOURTH ST. Bell Phone 1964-23 PAINTING

Connolly
" Joseph student bds 370 State
" Matthew J card grinder h 934 County
" Paul musician h 250 Brock av
" William carpenter h 64 Parker
Connor Charles C lawyer h 580 Kempton [h 11 N Orchard
" Charles F physician 327 Union
" Daniel L laborer h 158 Summer
" Dennis student b 55 Fifth
" James weaver h 311 Collette
" Marguerite C clerk h 34 Emerson (S) [(S)
" Minnie G nurse h 34 Emerson
" Mollie bookkeeper b 55 Fifth
CONNOR PATRICK coal and wood 486 Rivet h 55 Fifth See page 783
" Samuel weaver h 429 S Front
" Stephen E clerk 94 Purchase
" Thomas laborer h 105 Beetle
" Thomas overseer Sharp Mill h 67 Dartmouth
" see O'Connor
Connors Daniel laborer h 123 S Sec-
" James J foreman 100 Fifth h 257 Maxwell [Summer
" John foreman 214 S Water h 294
" John laborer h 798 County
" John teamster 431 Rivet h do
" John weaver b 985 S Water
" John J groom 379 County h 53 Borden
" Michael elevatorman h 76 Earle
" Patrick laborer rms 263 Purchase
" Patrick stonecutter b 11 Logan
" Patrick J stoker h 559 Cottage
" Thomas b Almshouse
" Thomas overseer Bennett Mill h 284 Sawyer
" see O'Connor
Connorton Ellen T teacher William H Taylor school b 11 Fifth
Connulty Alice widow William h 64 Jouvett
" John operative b 596 Purchase
Conos John (Peters & Conos) 1295 Acushnet avenue b 355 Cogeshall
" Louis (Peters & Conos) 1091 Acushnet avenue and bootblack 1053 do b 359 Coggeshall
Conrow Lester M Rev pastor First Presbyterian church h 82 State
Conroy Michael J city laborer h 269 Mill [Grinnell
Consalves Manuel fisherman h 129
Considine Alice M widow John W (C H & H A Lawton Co) 1 Purchase h 46 Pearl
" Daniel S proprietor Weld Square Pharmacy and clerk P O sta No 1, 3 Weld h 171 Davis
" Johanna widow Michael h 175 Davis
" John W died Nov 27 1910
Consolidated Meat and Grocery Co 132 and 163 Union 64 and 143 Purchase 1141 Acushnet av and and 149 Cove [S Second
Constant Charles L M weaver b 504
" George fixer b 504 S Second
" Louis watchman h 504 S Second
Constantino Joseph laborer h 154 N Second
Continental Furniture Co (S B Sterns) 1065-1067 Acushnet av
" Wood Screw Co mfrs wood screws and screw machines 144 Front
Contois Stanislas weaver h 51 Collette [57 N Second b 29 Keene
Conway Alice T telephone operator
" Ann widow Michael h 67 S Second
" Austin Jr driver h 71 Ruth
" Edward teamster b 152 Newton
" Eugene architect rms 7 N Second
" Frank bartender 219 Purchase rms 249 do [Newton
" Frank foreman 27 Fourth h 152
" Herbert twister h 14 Cleveland
" James driver b 171 Fourth
" James laborer h 36 Bentley [h do
" James N steam fitter 470 Union
" Jane E teacher James B Congdon school b 17 Franklin
" John shoemaker b 136 N Front
" Martin J teamster h 37 Linden
" Mary Mrs h 136 N Front
" Michael A boss lineman h 152 Newton [Fourth
" Michael M burnisher h 171
" William removed from city
Cook Albert B mason h 344 North
" Alexander G mason h 344 North
" Alice P music teacher 336 Orchard (S) h do
" Ann widow James h 613 Elm
" Annie L Mrs h 25 Elm

J. G. NICHOLSON
LUMBER, SASH, DOORS and BLINDS
BOWDITCH STREET, NEW BEDFORD, MASS.

COOK, BROWNELL & TABER
Otis Seabury Cook
Morris R Brownell
Frederic H Taber
COUNSELLORS AT LAW
Masonic Building
Pleasant cor Union Street
Telephone Bell 45
Automatic 1346

Cook, Brownell & Taber (Otis Seabury Cook, Morris R Brownell and Frederic H Taber) lawyers 1 Masonic bldg
" Charles A head installer 57 N Second h 100 Campbell
" Charles E (Cook & Smith) 37 Purchase h 53 Ashland
" Charles F mason h 594 Elm (W)
" Clarence A treasurer T P Corp and vice president T N B C Co h 277 Union
" Cornelia A widow William h 75 Walnut
" Daisy M Mrs h 98 Merrimac
" D Herbert (Cook & McQuade) h 45 Maitland [Mill h 54 State
" Edward H treasurer Quissett
COOK EMILE A 1543 Acushnet av See page 755
" Ellen L widow Timothy D Jr h 100 Cottage [b 100 Campbell
" Eva J chief operator 57 N Second
" Florence E h 114 Cedar
" Francis H drill worker h 9 Beech
" Frederic B supt Masonic bldg h 253 Arnold
" George E clerk b 9 Beech
" George H captain Engine No 8 h 280 Earle [h 1212 Rockdale av
" Harrison R plumber 91 N Water
" Harry provisions 136 County h 80 Thompson
" James gardener h 25 Florence
" James teaming 124 Hemlock h do
" Jasper S insurance 97 William rm 206 h 57 N Sixth [b 1166 do
" John clerk 1162 Acushnet av

Cook
" John F clerk Nashawena Mill h 100 Oak [630 County
" John H grocer 127 Maxfield h
" Joseph clerk bds 173 Grinnell
" Lillian b 396 Middle (W)
" Mattie W Mrs furrier 57 N Sixth h do [Cotage
" Nancy C widow John S b 320
" Nellie H Mrs teacher Thompson street school h 336 Orchard (S)
" Otis P clerk 303 Merchants Bank bldg bds 100 Cottage
COOK OTIS SEABURY (Cook Brownell & Taber) 1 Madison bldg h 1 Clinton place
" Philip H mason h 10 Atlantic
" Rachel Mrs h 106 Newton
" Raymond H principal James B Congdon school h 217 Maple
" Rene widow Frank b 207 Court
" Richard H Jr tailor 326 Kempton h 171 Cedar [mer
" Ruth stenographer bds 171 Summer
" Samuel laborer h 15 Florence
" Sarah P widow Samuel H h 97 Madison [b 171 Summer
" S Ruth clerk 97 William rm 303
" Thomas W general supt of parks 251 Union h 129 Clinton
" Timothy D Jr died Dec 8 1910
" Walter S sail maker 31 Commercial h at Brockton
" William A salesman rms 344 Pleasant [dle
" William E teamster h 97 Middle
" William G assistant inspector bldgs 307 Municipal bldg h 874 Rockdale avenue [do
" William G clerk foot Willis b 114
" William S city treasurer 1 Municipal building h 48 Morgan
COOK & McQUADE (D H Cook and Patrick McQuade) masons and builders 45 Maitland See page 763
" & Smith (Charles E Cook and Abbott P Smith) real estate 37 Purchase rm 2 [b 266 Fourth
Cooke Frank T baker 125 Potomska
" Horatio B carpenter h 3 Green
" James S driver engine No 2 h 30 Buttonwood
" Robert h 266 Fourth

Steiger-Dudgeon Co.
"The WOMAN'S Store."
Tel. Bell 82 & 83, Branches connecting all depts.
" " 160 For Office only. Auto. 1211

SUMPTIONS, ASSORTMENTS AT ALL TIMES OF DEPENDABLE DRY GOODS

Cookson John F overseer Nashawena Mill b 61 Wood
Cooley Florence E clerk 41 Purchase b 2 Seventh [N Second
" Frank E employee P Corp h 119
Coombs Charles S advertising solicitor Standard h 79 Mill
" Darius laborer bds 364 Kempton
" Frank fisherman h 3 Bowditch
" Isaac bell boy b 364 Kempton
" Lucy J died Feb 1 1911
" Oakes A hostler h 364 Kempton
Coon Elizabeth C widow William S b 46 State [Rounds
" Frederick W eyelet maker h 109
" Sarah G widow George H h 242 Pleasant
" William C painter h 69 Foster
Cooney Ellen widow John h 76 Blackmer [ushnet av
Coons John S laborer bds 837 Ac-
Coop Levi overseer Dartmouth Mfg Co h 52 Lucas [ant
Cooper Arthur weaver h 426 Pleas-
" Edward operative b 27 Highland
" Ella widow Watson h 7 W High
" Harold operative h 206 Brock av
" Henry filler h 238 Rivet
" Henry spinner h 355 Pleasant
" Herbert drill inspector h 62 Ward
" Herbert operative b 27 Highland
" Herbert spinner bds 40 Winsor
" James fixer bds 105 Davis
" James machinist bds 25 Marvin
" John spinner bds 373 Cedar Grove
" John Robert weaver h 75 Nash road [321 Earle
" John W clerk N B C M Corp b
" Joseph laborer h 544 Rivet
" Lucy A widow Thomas h r 367 Kempton
" Mary widow Edgar h 116 Middle
" Sidney F stone carver h 207 Middle
" Susanna widow Fred h 444 Rivet
" Thomas weaver h 20 George
" Thomas H spinner h 114 Whitman [avenue
" William gardener b 47 Acushnet
" William laborer h 55 Fruit
" William E shipping agent and port warden h 551 Kempton
" & Brush cotton brokers 97 William
Cope John J janitor h 7 Juniper
Copeland George twister b 418 North Front
" James operative h 8 George
" Mary Mrs h 24 Roosevelt
" Percy C grocer 178 Arnold h 78 Atlantic
" Robert twister h 125 Rockland
Coppinger Frank D clerk P O b 67 Jenny Lind [Jenny Lind
" Thomas L marine engineer h 67
Corando Joseph laborer h 22 E Merrimac [Grove
Coray Joseph operative h 104 Cedar
Corbeil Fred A insurance agent 41 William b 8 Delano
" Mary Mrs operative h 8 Delano
Corbett Anna B nurse b 321 Union
" Daniel fireman h 16 Blackburn
" Elizabeth N clerk 20 Union b 300 Cedar
" Susan widow Timothy h 300 Cedar
" Thomas fireman rms 300 Acuhsnet avenue
" Timothy died August 23 1910
Corbin John B foreman h 269 Middle
Corbridge Elizabeth widow John b 96 Hathaway [h 159 Myrtle
Corcoran Charles engineer 26 Brook
" James F marble and granite b 610 County [h 89 Briggs
Cordeira Antone (Cordeira Brothers)
" Brothers (Antone and John P Corderia) lunch 108 Potomska
" Frank carder h 38 Nelson
" John mill hand b 39 Mitchell
" John ticket office 141 County and proprietor Hotel Cordeira 139 do h do
" John J carpenter h 80 Larch
" John P (Cordeira Bros) bds 89 Briggs [442 Bolton
" Jose operative h 12 Rotch block
" Joseph laborer h 85 Winsor [h do
" Louis clerk 139 and 141 County
Cordeiro Antone P real estate h 89 Briggs [ney
Cordingley James spinner h 16 Rod-
" Antone P real estate h 89 Briggs
Cordonier William telegraph operator h 1036 Acushnet avenue [Hall
Cordoza Frank F mill hand h 100 Hall
" Manuel mill hand h 45 Katharine

PELEG H. SHERMAN 506 COUNTY ST.
FUNERAL DIRECTOR AND EMBALMER
OFFICE PHONES. Bell 690-13. Auto. 1305.
RESIDENCE PHONES. Bell 690-12. Auto. 1306.

Corey Agnes widow William T h 113 Campbell [b 45 Page
" Edward V salesman 36 Purchase
" Manuel laborer h 436 Orchard (S)
" Manuel Jr mill hand b 436 Orchard (S)
" Mary A widow John h 20 Crapo
" Orlando died March 7 1911
" William S liquors 418 Kempton b 113 Campbell
" William T died 1911
" see Cory and Correia
Corish Gertrude L teacher Acushnet avenue school b 86 Mill
" Helen L teacher Sylvia A Howland school b 86 Mill
" John h 86 Mill [road
Corlett Hugh spinner h 122 River
Corley Elenore housekeeper 276 Coggeshall [yon
Cormier Albert weaver b 84 Ken-
" Alfred spinner h 274 N Front
" Andre piper b 122 Nash road
" Angelo removed from city
" Angus laborer bds 33 Tallman
" Ansemme operative h 162 Tinkham
" Anthony J carpenter h 47 Nye
" Arthur operative b 162 Tinkham
" Calixte S h 97 Collette
" Celestine carpenter h 104 Collette
" Clement weaver h 171 Coffin av
" Clement O weaver h 27 Nye
" Clovis fisherman b 97 Collette
" Daniel C hairdresser 931 S Water h 39 Independent [avenue
" David operative h 171 Coffin
" Domidile widow Theophile h 154 Hathaway [h 163 Tinkham
" Donat lineman 57 North Second
" Edgar carpenter b 103 Belleville road [Front
" Edward carpenter rms 274 North
" Edward H carpenter h 33 Tallman [Earle
" Elizabeth widow Cyrille bds 156
" Emilien fisherman h 148 Tinkham
" Emilien hairdresser 116 Union h 149 Tinkham [Front
" Eutroppe brick layer h 495 North
" Fabien D fisheman h 135 North Front [road
" Felix lineman bds 56 Belleville
" Frank fisherman b 97 Collette

Cormier
" Frank E third hand h 56 Belleville road
" Fred laborer b 45 Main [road
" Hyacinth fisherman b 56 Belleville
" John mill hand b 12 Nye
" John B lineman h 134 Nash road
" John L died June 7 1911
" Joseph barber b 97 Collette
" Joseph laborer h 80 Eugenia
" Louis bds 314 N Front
" Louis lineman h 104 Collette
" Max removed to Acushnet
" Maxim carpenter h 171 Coffin av
" Minnie operative b 63 Hathaway avenue
" Nazaire third hand h 35 Nye
" Norbert laborer bds 22 Holly
" Octave removed from city
" Odelon drill maker b 134 Nash rd
" Oliver fisherman h 65 Hathaway avenue [h 325 do
" Oliver shoe repairer 312 N Front
" Oliver weaver h 85 Dean
" Orias wood 53 Holly h 119 do
" Paul weaver h 46 Ashley [Front
" Phebee widow John L h 314 N
" Philas fisherman b 97 Collette
" Philip laborer h 3 McDonald ct
" Philip operative h 134 Nash road
" Philip removed from city
" Reuben S notary public 1893 Acushnet avenue h do [geshall
" Simeon D fisherman h 243 Cog-
" Telesphore carpenter b 33 Tallman [ville road
" Telesphore operative h 56 Belle-
" Thadde (Cormier & Dube) h 186 Dean
" Thomas laundryman b 172 Hatch
" Thomas weaver h 159 Earle
" Valentine twister b 97 Collette
" Vital removed from city
" William removed from city
CORMIER & DUBE (Thadde Cormier and Arthur Dube) painters 394 N Front See page 776
Cornelius Orrin C foreman 58 Adams h 274 Weld [Cedar
Cornell Abraham T watchman b 303
" Adeline M dressmaker 48 Cottage h do
" Albert turner h 26 Thompson
" Amos removed to Marion
" Azubah M died April 16 1911

COAL AND WOOD F. T. AKIN & COMPANY
HAY AND STRAW
WALNUT, COR. WATER, 84 PLEASANT ST., 25 WELD SQ.
129 COVE STREET WHF. FOOT OF COFFIN STREET

Cornell
" Charles C salesman 188 N Water h 74 Jenny Lind
" Charles R h 149 Allen [from city
" Clara widow Eugene removed
" Clifford E clerk b Mrs Mary A Cornell end Watson
" Edmund M sexton Oak Grove cemetery h 185 Parker [nold
" Eleanor F Mrs milliner h 248 Ar-
" Elmer driver b 124 Parker
" Emma widow George T h 13 Spruce [Highway
" Frank A wax maker h King's
" Frank N teamster h 2 Penniman
" Harriet L teacher Acushnet av school b 11 Fifth
" Herbert fixer h 48 Nelson
" John H deputy master H of C h at Smith's Mills
" Leslie painter b 248 Arnold
" Lester S clerk Merchants National Bank b 149 Allen [Watson
" Mary A widow Pardon h end
" Mary T died June 24 1911
" Mildred telephone operator 57 N Second b 74 Jenny Lind
" Milton P clerk 209 Merchants Bank bldg b Mrs Mary A Cornell's end Watson [209 Smith
" Rosanna widow William W h
" Schulyer C engineer h 303 Cedar
" Susan K widow Robert S h 118 South Sixth
" Sydney A carpenter h 114 Fair
" Sydney I blacksmith h 22 Jouvette
CORNISH CLIFTON H insurance Clifford bldg rm 12 h 609 County See page 778
Cornwell Ada B widow Edward L h 365 County
" Joseph F (Wilcox & Cornwell) cotton brokers 97 William b 365 County [Bullard
Coronus Charles shoemaker bds 60
Corr Manuel laborer h 269 S Second
Corre Joseph weaver h 872 First [sor
Correa Felix second hand h 20 Win-
Correau Damasse carpenter h 14 Cot-
" Melvina h 55 Merrimac [ter
" Modest laborer h 67 Roosevelt
Correia Alvina b 202 Belleville av
" Anibel b 202 Belleville avenue

Correia
" Anna Mrs h 115 Field
" Anton fireman U St Ry Co h 31 Stackhouse
" Antone laborer h 61 Howland
" Antone mill hand h 216 S Front
" Antone operative b r 26 Cedar Grove [house
" Antone J laborer h 31 Stack-
" Antone M mill hand h 56 Grinnell [chard (S)
" Antonio mill hand h 262 Or-
" Antonio L operative h 83 Rockland
" August operative b 563 First
" Augustine laborer h 27 Mitchell
" Christopher blacksmith h 379 S Second [Brock av
" Enocence R farmhand h end of
" Frances Mrs h 10 Winter
" Frances widow Manuel mill hand h 154 Eugenia [ville av
" Francisco operative b 127 Belle-
" Frank mill hand bds 806 Water
" Frank F mill hand h 115 Swift
" Jacintho laborer h 39 Mitchell
" Jacintho E laborer h 97 Sidney
" Joaquim A laborer h 156 Fourth
" John clerk removed to Boston
" John fireman h 12 Grandfield
" John master mariner h 49 Valentine
" John mill hand h 59 Stephen
" John operative h 5 Mitchell
" John operative h 69 Potomska
" John L shoemaker 65 Crapo h do
" John O city laborer h 73 Winsor
" Jose P operative h 125 Holly
" Joseph grocer 219 N Second h 129 South Water
" Joseph laborer h 104 Cedar Grove
" Joseph laborer h 151 Rockland
" Joseph laborer h 359 First
" Joseph mill hand h 18 Hollyhock
" Joseph mill hand h 152 Thompson
" Joseph operative h 9 Howland
" Joseph operative h 123 S Second
" Joseph A laborer h 129 N Water
" Joseph E mill hand h 145 Field
" Joseph M musician Hathaway's Theatre b 187 Bonney
" Joseph T grocer h 104 Potomska
" Jules P spinner b 125 Holly
" Louis operative h 115 Field

Kinyon's Commercial School Will furnish your office help free } **Odd Fellows Building** COR. WILLIAM and PLEASANT STS. NEW BEDFORD, MASS.

Correia
" Louis F operative h 109 Bates av
" Manuel h 16 Cotter
" Manuel h 19 Hemlock
" Manuel h 175 Belleville av [ter
" Manuel fisherman h 806 S Wa-
" Manuel laborer h 36 Katharine
" Manuel laborer h 71 Prospect
" Manuel laborer h 109 Dunbar
" Manuel laborer h 267 S Front
" Manuel laborer h 346 First
" Manuel laborer h 550 S Water
" Manuel laborer h 723 S Water
" Manuel mason's tender h 187 Bonney [dent
" Manuel mill hand 70 Indepen-
" Manuel operative h 68 Grinnell
" Manuel operative h 167 Division
" Manuel F mill hand b 178 Belleville avenue
" Manuel H salesman 16 Cotter
" Manuel J boiler maker b 66 N Second
" Manuel M mill hand h 107 Larch
" Manuel S picker tender h 107 Larch [h 45 Page
" Manuel V teamster 170 Purchase
" Mary Mrs h 9 Madison [lips av
" Mateus mill hand bds 116 Phil-
" Secon mason h 563 Acushnet av
" Theophilus mariner h 145 S Second
Correio Antone L removed from city
" Ignacio mason h 26 Elm
" Joseph mason 2 Hyacinth h do
" Joseph operative h 152 Thompson
" Manuel clerk 211 Coggeshall b 178 Belleville avenue
" Manuel farmer h 24 Grand
" Manuel operative h 82 Grinnell
" Manuel L h 143 Coffin avenue
" Portuguez newspaper 143 Acushnet avenue [sor
Correira Joseph mill hand h 85 Win-
Correll Manuel fisherman h 306 South Second [mouth h 135 do
Corrie Bartholomew J mgr 133 Dart-
Corrigan Alice T teacher Hosea M Knowlton school b 186 Summer
" Christopher fixer h 489 S Front
" John bricklayer h 1 Sutton
Corske Esidor clerk h 486 First
Corson Everett H chauffeur 22 Fourth h at Fairhaven
" Henry T druggist 639 County h 54 Campbell [Belleville rd
" Sidney W overseer rms 147
" Temple A clerk 115 William h at Fairhaven [Foster
" William E clerk 639 County b 62
Cory Albion G bookkeeper 194 N Water b 81 Merrimac [Forest
" Andrew A master mariner h 62
" Andrew T butcher h 868 Rockdale avenue [Cal
" Charles A removed to Los Angeles
" Charles S foreman 58 Adams h 150 Sycamore [Cottage
" Daniel W cashier 100 Fifth h 125
" Edgar E clerk 773 Kempton h 137 Florence
" Frank J driver 868 Rockdale av
" George A carpenter h 1 Merrimac avenue [dale av
" George G farmer h 987 Rock-
" George L machinist 8 Seneca h 393 Cottage
" Horace W b 1094 Rockdale av
" Isaac C died May 28 1911
" Isaac Niles engineer h 101 Robeson [Rockdale av
" Martha A widow Isaac C h 1094
" Michael coppersmith h 567 Acushnet avenue
" Robert A drill maker b 62 Forrest
" Sarah J widow Frederick A b 13 Jenny Lind
" see Correia and Corey [ville road
Corylo Stanislol weaver h 74 Belle-
Cosgrove Benjamin F painter h 400 Pleasant [h 158 Reynolds
" Robert F car inspector U St Ry
Cosivas John mill hand b 77 Davis
Cosmo John laborer h 65½ Prospect
" John laborer h 29 Union
Cosmos John removed to N Y City
" Joseph cook 171 Purchase rms 34 High [332 Kempton h do
" Mary Agnes Mrs clairvoyant
Cossis Simon traveling salesman b 98 Beetle
Costa Albert mill hand h 267 S Front
" Alfred C fireman h 162 Bonney
" Alvaro widow Manuel h 75 Crapo

Bread, Cake, Pastry
RICHMOND & COMPANY **255-257 UNIUN STREET**
Bell 993 Automatic 1022

Cornell
" Charles C salesm 188 N Water h 74 Jenny La
" Charles R h 149 llen [from city
" Clara widow Igene removed
" Clifford E clerk Mrs Mary A Cornell end W son
" Edmund M n Oak Grove cemetery h 18 arker [nold
" Eleanor F Mrs iliner h 248 Ar-
" Elmer driver h 4 Parker
" Emma widow orge T h 13 Spruce [Highway
" Frank A wa ker h King's
" Frank N teamst h 2 Penniman
" Harriet L tea Acushnet av school h 11 F h
" Herbert fixer h Nelson
" John H deputy aster H of C h at Smith's ls
" Leslie painter h 18 Arnold
" Lester S clerk chants National Bank h 14 Allen [Watson
" Mary A widow Pardon h end
" Mary T died Ju 24 1911
" Mildred telephon operator 57 N Second h 74 ny Land
" Milton P clerk 209 Merchants Bank bldg h s Mary A Cornell's end W on [209 Smith
" Rosanna widow William W h
" Schulyer C engi er h 303 Cedar
" Susan K widow Robert S h 118 South Sixth
" Sydney A carpe r h 114 Fair
" Sydney I blac ith h 22 Jouvette

CORNISH CLIFTO H insurance Clifford bldg rm 12 h 609 County See age 778

Cornwell Ada B wi w Edward L h 365 County
" Joseph F (Wil x & Cornwell) cotton broke 97 William b 365 County [Bullard

Coronus Charles emaker bds 60
Corr Manuel hoe h 269 S Second
Corre Joseph weave 872 First [sor
Correa Felix l and h 20 Win-
Correau Daura enter h 14 Cot-
" Melvina errimac [ter
" Modes 67 Roosevelt

Correia Al Belleville av
" Anibel eville avenue

Correia
" Anna Mrs h 115 Field
" Anton fireman U St Ry Co h 31 Stackhouse
" Antone laborer h 61 Howland
" Antone mill hand h 216 S Front
" Antone operative b r 26 Cedar Grove [house
" Antone J laborer h 31 Stack-
" Antone M mill hand h 56 Grinnell [chard (S)
" Antonio mill hand h 262 Or-
" Antonio L operative h 83 Rockland
" August operative b 563 First
" Augustine laborer h 27 Mitchell
" Christopher blacksmith h 379 S Second [Brock av
" Enocence R farmhand h end of
" Frances Mrs h 10 Winter
" Frances widow Manuel mill hand h 154 Eugenia [ville av
" Francisco operative b 127 Belle-
" Frank mill hand bds 806 Water
" Frank F mill hand h 115 Swift
" Jacintho laborer h 39 Mitchell
" Jacintho E laborer h 97 Sidney
" Joaquim A laborer h 156 Fourth
" John clerk removed to Boston
" John fireman h 12 Grandfield
" John master mariner h 49 Valentine
" John mill hand h 59 Stephen
" John operative h 5 Mitchell
" John operative h 69 Potomska
" John L shoemaker 65 Crapo h do
" John O city laborer h 73 Winsor
" Jose P operative h 125 Holly
" Joseph grocer 219 N Second h 129 South Water
" Joseph laborer h 104 Cedar Grove
" Joseph laborer h 151 Rockland
" Joseph laborer h 359 First
" Joseph mill hand h 28 Hollyhock
" Joseph mill hand h 153 Thompson
" Joseph operative h 9 Howland
" Joseph operative h 123 S Second
" Joseph A laborer h 129 N Water
" Joseph E mill hand h 145 Field
" Joseph M musician Hathaway's Theatre b 187 Bonney
" Joseph T grocer h 104
" Jules P spinner b 12
" Louis operati

Kinyon's Commercial School Or
Will furnish yo office help free

Correia
" Louis F operative h 109 Bates av
" Manuel h 16 Cotter
" Manuel h 19 Hemlock
" Manuel h 175 Belleville av [ter
" Manuel fisherman h 806 S Wa-
" Manuel laborer h 36 Katharine
" Manuel laborer h 71 Prospect
" Manuel laborer h 109 Dunbar
" Manuel laborer h 267 S Front
" Manuel laborer h 346 First
" Manuel laborer h 550 S Water
" Manuel laborer h 723 S Water
" Manuel mason's tender h 187 Bonney [dent
" Manuel mill hand 70 Indepen-
" Manuel operative h 68 Grinnell
" Manuel operative h 167 Division
" Manuel F mill hand b 178 Belleville avenue
" Manuel H salesman 16 Cotter
" Manuel J boiler maker b 66 N Second
" Manuel M mill hand h 107 Larch
" Manuel S picker tender h 107 Larch [h 45 Page
" Manuel V teamster 170 Purchase
" Mary Mrs h 9 Madison [lips av
" Mateus mill hand bds 116 Phil-
" Secon mason h 563 Acushnet av
" Theophilus mariner h 145 S Second

Correio Antone L removed from city
" Ignacio mason h 26 Elm
" Joseph mason 2 Hyacinth h do
" Joseph operative h 152 Thompson
" Manuel clerk 211 Coggeshall b 178 Belleville avenue
" Manuel farmer h 24 Grand
" Manuel operative h 82 Grinnell
" Manuel L h 143 Coffin avenue
" Portuguez newspaper 143 Acushnet avenue [sor

Correira Joseph mill hand h 85 Win-

Correll Manuel fisherman h 306 South Second [mouth h 135 do

Corrie Bartholomew J mgr 133 Dart-

Corrigan Alice T teacher Hosea M Knowlton school b 186 Summer
" Christopher fixer h 489 S Front
" John bricklayer h 1 Sutton

Corske Esidor clerk h 486 [illegible]

Corson [illegible] H chauffeur 22 Fourth h at Fairhaven
" Henry T druggist 639 County h 54 C[illegible]bell [Bellevill[illegible] rd
" Sidney overseer rms 147
" Temple [illegible] clerk 115 William h at Fairhaven [Foster
" William [illegible] clerk 639 County h 62

Cory Albert [illegible] bookkeeper 194 N Water [illegible] Merrimac [Forest
" Andre[illegible] master mariner h 62
" Andrew [illegible] butcher h 868 Rockdale avenue [Cal
" Charles [illegible] removed to Los Angeles
" Charles [illegible] foreman 58 Adams h 150 [illegible]more [Cottage
" Daniel W[illegible] cashier 100 Fifth h 125
" Edgar F[illegible] clerk 773 Kempton h 137 Florence
" Frank J [illegible]ver 868 Rockdale av
" George A [illegible]carpenter h 1 Merrimac avenue [dale av
" George [illegible] farmer h 987 Rock-
" George L [illegible]machinist 8 Seneca h 393 Cottage
" Horace W[illegible] b 1094 Rockdale av
" Isaac C [illegible] May 28 1911
" Isaac N [illegible] engineer h 101 Robeson [Rockdale av
" Martha A [illegible]widow Isaac C h 1094
" Michael [illegible]persmith h 567 Acushnet avenue
" Robert A [illegible]ll maker b 62 Forest
" Sarah J [illegible]ow Frederick A b 15 Jenny [illegible]nd
" see Corr[illegible] and Corey [[illegible]ville road

Corylo Stan[illegible] weaver h 74 Belle-

Cosgrove B[illegible] F painter h [illegible] Pleas[illegible] [h 158 [illegible]
" Robert [illegible] inspector U S [illegible]

Cosivas John [illegible] hand b 77 D[illegible] av

Cosmo John [illegible]rer h 65 [illegible] 95
" John la[illegible] h 29 Union

Cosmos John [illegible]oved to N[illegible] [illegible]ditch
" Joseph [illegible] 171 Pur[illegible] [illegible]ont h Hi[illegible] [332 [illegible] av
" Mary [illegible] [illegible]shley

Cossis Si[illegible] Bowditch Bed[illegible] [illegible]s 306 Ac-

Costa A[illegible] [illegible]haven [illegible]an h 588

Bre[illegible] [illegible]d of [illegible]BER
RICHM[illegible] [illegible]L WORK [illegible]DFORD

Costa
" Anna vest maker 144 Union b 118 Division
" Annie widow John h 932 S Water
" Antone fisherman h 305 S Front
" Antone laborer h 55 Grinnell
" Antone laborer h 76 Acushnet av
" Antone laborer h 77 Dunbar
" Antone laborer h 80 Winsor
" Antone mill hand h 73 Larch
" Antone mill hand h 145 Crapo
" Antone L fisherman h 305 South Front
" Antonio G shoe repairer 103 County h 131 Division
" Domingas operative h 78 Independent
" Elizabeth widow Frank h 104 Dartmouth
" Emily widow h 448 S Second
" Ernest painter h 429 S Water
" Fanny Mrs h 121½ Fourth
" Fernendo clerk 78 Acushnet av b 68 do
" Frank fisherman h 216 S Front
" Frank fisherman b 686 S Water
" Frank laborer h 531 S First
" Frank mill hand h 195 Division
" Frank operative h 407 S Water
" Frank removed to Fairhaven
" Fred at P Corp h 147 Rockland
" Fred mill hand h 89 Briggs
" Henrietta h 53 Rivet
" Henry insurance agent 97 William rm 310 h 107 S Second
" Henry rope worker h 335 S Water
" Jacinth fish 513 Water h 24 Crapo
" Jacintho operative h 173 Coggeshall
" Jennie Mrs h 153 Belleville av
" Joe laborer h 28 Wing
" Joe spinner bds 69 Katharine
" John laborer h 102 Middle
" John laborer h 103 Thompson
" John laborer h 276 Nash road
" John laborer h 306 S Second
" John mill hand h 391 Rivet
" John oiler h 59 Winsor
" John operative h 60 Mosher
" John operative h 514 S Second
" John plasterer h 126 Dartmouth
" John removed from city
" John second hand h 672 Purchase
" John Jr laborer b 102 Middle
" John C driver h 58 Short
" John S laborer h 323 First
" Joseph h 18 Edison

Costa
" Joseph laborer h 74 Acushnet av
" Joseph laborer h 75 Hemlock
" Joseph laborer h 531 S First
" Joseph mill hand h 27 Nelson
" Joseph mill hand h 153 Belleville avenue
" Joseph operative h 391 S Second
" Joseph operative h 631 S Water
" Joseph operative b 492 First
" Joseph twist driller h 307 S Second
" Joseph Jr variety 92½ Dartmouth h r do
" Joseph L laborer h 33 Swift
" Joseph M mill hand b 68 Grinnell
" Juan laborer b 18 Edison
" Louis weaver h 95 Bellevue
" Manuel h 456 S Water
" Manuel beamertender b 28 County
" Manuel doffer h 363 Orchard (S)
" Manuel driver h 365 First
" Manuel driver h 446 Allen
" Manuel fisherman h 9 South
" Manuel hairdresser 687 S Water h 216 South Front
" Manuel laborer h 58 Grinnell
" Manuel laborer h r 87 Prospect
" Manuel laborer h 103 Thompson
" Manuel laborer h 145 Field
" Manuel laborer h 247 S Front
" Manuel laborer h Winterville rd
" Manuel laborer b 98 Blackmer
" Manuel machinist h 260 S Front
" Manuel mill hand h 136 Thompson
" Manuel mill hand h 142 Acushnet avenue
" Manuel mill hand h 191 Belleville avenue
" Manuel mill hand h 514 S Second
" Manuel mill hand b 391 Rivet
" Manuel operative h 31 South
" Manuel operative h 396 Cedar Grove
" Manuel operative b 93 Prospect
" Manuel thirdhand h 495 First
" Manuel E master mariner h 256 County
" Manuel I laborer h 66 Middle
" Mario mill hand b 181 Coffin av
" Marion J laborer h 88 Thompson
" Marv clerk 40 Purchase b 323 First
" Mary Mrs h 12 Common
" Mary Mrs h 59 Howland

GLOBE DYE HOUSE 220 SHAWMUT AVE.
J. N. J. LONHOLDT, PROP. Telephone Connections Goods called for and Delivered
Down town Office, 52 Pleasant St., Room 1 North End Office, 1014 Acushnet Ave.

Costa
" Mary Mrs h 68 Grinnell
" Mary Mrs h 390 South Second
" Mary widow Frank h 284 Front
" Mary widow Joseph h 25 County
" Victorine fisherman h 31 County
" Victorino A removed to Boston
" see de Costa
Costaka Evangelo removed to Philadelphia Pa
" William removed to Philadelphia [Pa
Costello Edward J h 249 Chancery
" James spinner b 137 Acushnet av
" Mary Mrs speeder h 197 Weld
" Miles weaver h 76 Potomska
" Silvino shoe repairer 30a South Water h Water
" William gardener h 6 McGurk
Cota Adelaide M teacher William H Taylor school b 22 Cottage
Cote Albert carpenter b 43 Holly
" Alfred fireman b 358 N Front
" Alice clerk 1119 Acushnet av b 43 Holly
" Arcande weaver h 493 S Front
" Arthur fixer b 4 Social
" Arthur laborer h 28 Roosevelt
" Arthur removed from city
" Blanche Mrs millinery b 28 Holly
" Camille h 43 Holly [Clark
" Donat clerk 126 Bowditch h 56
" Edmond stonecutter h 87 Rivet
" Edward operative h 31 Hazard
" Emile fixer h 51 Dean
" Emile A clerk 1543 Acushnet av b 334 Bowditch
" Ernest E druggist 1972 Acushnet avenue h 39 Ingraham
" Eugene laborer h 164 Sawyer
" Eugene rem to Alberta Canada
" E laborer h 2795 Acushnet av
" Frank E h r 382 N Front
" George weaver b 310 N Front
" Hormidas driver h 36 Eugenia
" Israel fixer h 86 Davis
" John B h 310 North Front
" Joseph laborer b 87 Bowditch
" Joseph master mechanic Taber Mill h 5 Cornell place
" Joseph spinner h 93 Collette
" Joseph weaver b 47 Holly
" Joseph E removed to Acushnet
" Joseph F fixer b 101 Davis
" Joseph W driver bds 63 Dean

Cote
" Leon carpenter h 43 Holly
" Louis elevatorman b 7 Holly
" Louis removed from city
" Mary Mrs h 358 N Front
" Omer weaver b 310 N Front
" Ovilla box maker h 359 N Front
" Pierre grocer 1065 County h do
" Priscilla widow Alphonso h 186 Cove
" Remi mill hand h 3 Desautels
" Remi plumber b 43 Holly
" Reymond fixer b 43 Holly
" Sabin removed to Worcester
" Sabin Mrs clerk 1039 Acushnet avenue h 28 Holly
" Samuel weaver b 323 Tinkham
" Sinai weaver h 194 Dean
" Stanislas M grocer 76 Church h at Fairhaven
" Stanislau fixer h 125 Bates av
" Theophile fixer h 101 Davis
" Theresa R (Madam Rena) clairvoyant 135 Middle h do
" Thomas carpenter h 101 Davis
" Ulric hardware 1543 Acushnet av h 344 Bowditch
" Ulric J B clerk 1543 Acushnet av h at Fall River
" Vitel carder h 968 S Water
" Wilfred clerk 867 Purchase b 1166 Acushnet avenue
" Wilfred ice h 63 Dean
" Wilfred removed from city
" William operative h 68 Nash road
" Zepherine weaver h 65 Jouvett
Coteria Michael weaver h 819 South Water
Cotnoir Joseph L cigars 105 County h 25 Winsor
" Lewis fixer h 55 Independent
" Rose A dressmaker 55 Independent b do
Cottam Annie warper tender bds 95 Brock av
" John painter 319 Cedar h do
" John W mill hand b 41 Bowditch
" Malam bartender 572 N Front h 327 Tinkham
" Olive weaver b 95 Brock av
" Richard carpenter h 21 Ashley
" William mill hand h 41 Bowditch
Cottelle Benjamin F pianos 306 Acushnet av h at Fairhaven
Cotter Charles A lineman h 588 Cottage

GREENE & WOOD Every Kind of LUMBER AND MILL WORK
PINE STREET, off So. WATER STREET, NEW BEDFORD

Cotter
" Ellen J Mrs h 126 Bonney
" Helen M b 564 County
" James F (B P Smith & Co) 37 Delano h 18 Reynolds
" John shoemaker b 564 County
" Joseph bookkeeper rms 1332 Acushnet ave [chase h 564 County
" Katherine C bookkeeper 36 Pur-
" Patrick J mason h 31 Durfee
Cottino Louis laborer h 6 Wall
Cottle Charles P foreman 50 Elm h at Acushnet
" Evelyn A Mrs h 378 North
" Lucy widow Albert b 173 Emerson
" Percy weaver h 78 Tallman
" Zadoc A engineer h 4 Foster
Cotton James E laborer h 269 Middle
" William loom installing b 237 Collette
Cottrell Herbert C assistant shipper 16 N Second b 289 Summer
" William H Jr bookkeeper 16 N Second h 289 Summer
Couch Guy collector 170 Purchase h 119 Washington [Acushnet av
Couet Clara widow Alphonse L h 49
Coughlin Annie weaver b 351 Pleasant [niman
" Jeremiah L 3rd hand bds 24 Pen-
" John laborer rms 76 Florence
" John mason h 184 Austin
" Kate widow Timothy h 270 Austin [land
" Mary widow James b 184 Ash-
" Mary widow John h 351 Pleasant
" Mary L h 24 Penniman
" Michael Mrs died Sept 19 1910
" Rose V clerk 41 Purchase b 24 Penniman
" Timothy laborer h 991 Purchase
" Timothy mason rms 39 Mill
" Timothy W third hand b 24 Penniman [ant
" William F operative b 409 Pleas-
Coulegar John operative h 172 N Front [lard
Coulombe Arthur engineer h 91 Bul-
" Henry carpenter h 1280 Acushnet avenue [net av
" Henry Jr carpenter b 1280 Acush-
" Hermenigilde carpenter bds 178 Phillips av [lette
" Joseph clerk 78 Hicks h 269 Col-
" Oscar clerk b 269 Collette

Coulombe
" Philip carpenter h 178 Phillips avenue [man
" Virginia widow Joseph h 87 Tall-
" William carpenter b 1280 Acushnet avenue [man
" Yvone Mrs mill hand b 162 Whit-
Coulthurst John fireman h 7 Bannister [146 Davis
Counsell Henry changer over bds
" Jarvis weaver h 1631 Acushnet avenue
" John H h 1946 Acushnet av
" John H operative h 16 Covell
" Jonathan weaver h 146 Holly
" William operative b 16 Covell
Coupe Ann widow Samuel b 219 Church [net av
" Edward weaver h 1585 Acush-
" Horace clerk h 1 Warwick
" James S spinner h 15 Peckham
" John weaver h 58 Mott
" Joseph weaver b 43 Holly
" Lawrence W fixer h 350 Coffin av
" Sarah Mrs b 160 David
Courchaine Joseph laborer h 178 Phillips av
Courcy George carpenter h 68 Hatch
Cournoyer Alexis Mrs operative h 256 N Front [rd
" Edward carpenter h 47 Belleville
" Flavian blacksmith h 24 Cotter
" Henry shoeworker h 8 Tallman
" Isidore weaver h 43 Division
" Joachim weaver h 72 Division
" Levi weaver b 252 N Front
" Narcisse h 49 Division
" Oliver weaver b 330 N Front
" Paul carpenter b 88 Hathaway
" Paul operative h 25 Mosher
" Paul Jr fireman b 49 Division
" Philip carpenter b 47 Belleville rd
" pierre carpenter h end Shaw
" Pierre carpenter b 88 Hathaway
" Pierre laborer h 74 Division
Couroussi Peter (P Couroussi & Co) h 104 State
" P & Co (P Couroussi and John Rellas) confectionery 774 Purchase and 953 Acushnet av
Courroulis Peter mill hand h r 234 N Front [shall
Courry Joseph weaver h 250 Cogge-
Courtemanche Adelard fixer h 409 N Front
" Alcide painter b 128 Bates

BONNEY, FOLSTER & CO.,
The North End's Shopping Centre
Dry Goods and Men's Furnishings
945-947 Acushnet Ave., New Bedford, Mass.

Courtemanche
" Alphonse weaver h 92 Cove
" George weaver h 86 Davis
" Joseph mill hand h 125 Delano
" Napoleon bricklayer h 58 Main
" Napoleon carpenter h 190 N Front
" Paul operative h 230 State [Oak
Courtney Albert J drillworker h 68
Courtwright Frank rem from city
" Leander C glassworker h 95 S Sixth [vette
Courvelle Lucien carpenter h 17 Jou-
Coury Sahid laborer h 45 Mitchell
" William restaurant 122 Cove h 16 Cedar Grove
Cousin Victor mason h 246 Nash rd
Cousineau Emile weaver b 1205 Acushnet avenue
" Joseph weaver h 310 N Front
Coutie Manuel carpenter h 58 Howland
Coutier Exeior removed from city
Couto Frank drillmaker h 16 Griffin
Coutu Albert clerk 1023 S Water b 31 Brock avenue
" Felix weaver b 187 Dean
" Joseph carpenter h 19 George
" J Henry jeweler 1563 Acushnet avenue rms 188 Weld
" Manuel laborer h 58 Howland
" Manuel shoemaker h 142 Acushnet avenue [N Front
" Matilda Mrs mill hand bds 550
" Philias carpenter h 31 Brock av
" Romnald carpenter h 109 Eugenia
Couture Albert helper 19 Linden b Brock avenue [364 do
" Archille clerk 302 N Front h
" Arthur clerk 1510 Acushnet av rms 364 N Front
" Azaras clerk 1492 Acushnet av h 364 N Front
" Clara widow h 27 Bullard
" Edmund J weaver h r 59 Hicks
" Ernest tinsmith 185 Acushnet av h 54 Bullard
" Frank carder h 52 Hicks
" Frank weaver b 127 Coffin av
" Henry overseer Page Mfg Co h 57 Beetle
" Joseph fixer h 195 Davis [ville av
" Joseph weaver rms 395 Belle-
" Jules carpenter h 71 Ruth

Couture
" Octave bookkeeper h 1221 Acushnet avenue
" Paul E died July 12 1911
" Peter operative b 52 Hicks
" Romeo weaver h 80 Beetle [Weld
Couza Alexander loom fixer h 211
" Charles weaver b 140 Holly
" Edward weaver b 140 Holly
" Johan weaver b 59 Howard av
" Mary widow Johan h 59 Howard av
" Max fixer h 201 Davis
" Wendell second hand h 140 Holly
" William changer over b 211 Weld
" William fixer h 59 Howard av
Covell Addie R Mrs vocal teacher 14 Pope b do
" Frances G vocalist b 14 Pope
" George A Jr bookkeeper Acushnet Mill Corp h 128 School
" Harry T teamster h 804 Purchase
" Jonathan h 4 Durfee
" Lindley J clerk 193 Purchase h 171 Summer [Pope
" Lucy A widow George A b 14
" William P bookkeeper Pierce Mfg Corp h 14 Pope [lard
Covey Sherman S driver h 17 Wil-
Covil Anella W bookkeeper 28 Pleasant h 202 Maxfield
" Harriet Mrs h 202 Maxfield
" Orion E stable 33 Elm h 57 Court
Covill Arthur S machinist h 227 Acushnet avenue [nell
" Charles V teamster h 155 Grin-
" Clarence W clerk h 155 Belleville road [ford
" David F machinist h 134 Bed-
" Edward M machinist b 227 Acushet av [net av
" Frank O salesman h 1848 Acush-
" George F laborer b 506 Acushnet av [h 197 do
" H Eugene bicycles 199 Grinnell
" Paul G draughtsman 303 Municipal bldg b 134 Bedford
" Ralph drillmaker h 159 North
" Robert H L machinist b 197 Grinnell
Cowan John M drug clerk 233 Coggeshall rms 32 McGurk
" Newell T electrician h 266 Fourth
Coward Lucretia widow William h 952 Kempton

M. P. B. Silva & Son Paints, Oils and Glass
Sole Agents for Lucas Tinted Gloss Paints
157 ACUSHNET AVENUE Both Phones NEW BEDFORD

Cowden Fred chief engineer Kilburn
Mill h 13 Bay [Coffin av
Cowdley Dwight boxmaker bds 258
Cowell Margaret widow John h 28
Belleville road
" Richard removed to Fall River
" Rosanna A widow h 16 Ashley
" Thomas weaver b 16 Ashley
Cowen Charles E stage hand Hathaway's Theatre h 118 Mill
" Edward F A driver Engine No
1 h 322 Pleasant [197 Middle
" Edward K foreman 34 S Second h
" Grace H milliner b 197 Middle
" James L city laborer h 27 Maitland [dle
" Leonard T chauffeur b 197 Mid-
" Marshall L carpenter h 465 Chancery [Shawmut av
" William J quarryman h 128
Cowing Clarence E teamster h 180
Mill [Kempton h do
" Obed S carpet upholsterer 559
" William J police station 2 h 55
Foster
Cowley James T stenographer Rotch
Mill h 155 Princeton [Front
Cowling John spinner h 478 North
" Samuel iron molder h 20 Rural
Cox Charles E weaver h 78 Merrimac [mac
" Dilworth H weaver b 78 Merri-
" Edward machinist b 804 Purchase
" Eraton spinner h 30 Peckham
" James spinner b 30 Peckham
" James weaver b 11 Logan
" John weaver h 2 Irvington ct
" Joseph laborer h 117 Bates av
" Michael machinist b 804 Purchase
" Owen J clerk 64 Purchase
" William spinner b 30 Peckham
Coxen Charles H salesman 41 Purchase h 107 Chancery
" Harold M bookkeeper N B Cotton Mills Corp h 54 Pierce
Coy John S (Auto Selling & Supply
Co) 15 Fourth h 28 Ashland
Coyle Bernard third hand b 135 Reynolds [nolds
" Edward third hand h 135 Rey-
" John E weaver h 137 Reynolds
" Joseph S packer b 207 Weld
" Thomas twister b 135 Reynolds
Coyne John spinner b 7 Abbott
" Joseph spinner bds 7 Abbott

Coyne
" Michael spinner h 7 Abbott
" Patrick operative b 36 Mosher
Crabtree Frank clerk b 116 Robeson
" George removed to N Y City
" James A b 1 Social
" Jane A widow John H h 1 Social
" Sylvester joiner b 116 Robeson
" William spinner h 116 Robeson
Craft James F police h 109 Bonney
" James F Jr mill hand b 109 Bonney [ney
" John H mill hand b 119 Bon-
" Mary E widow James b 207 State
Cragen Charles H h 57 Hill
Craid Mary clerk 704 Purchase b 81
Maxfield [157 Chancery
Craig Alice clerk 18 Purchase bds
" G Edmond operative b 157 Chancery [h 670 First
" Harry freight clerk foot Willis
" Henry laborer h 43 Katharine
" John second hand h 1265 Acushnet avenue [cery
" John E W driver h 157 Chan-
" Louis waiter 233 Purchase rms
209 do [Acushnet av
" Margaret widow James bds 1265
" Mary h r 366 Purchase
" Thomas laborer h 51 Mill
" William fixer h 103 Ashland
" William H foreman h 54 Katharine [b 103 Ashland
" William L paymaster Oneko Mill
Cram Carlos M h 55 Merrimac
" George D reporter Times b 55
Merrimac [1911
Crampton Harriet E died Feb 26
" Joseph operative h r 156 Holly
Crandon Philip H Jr store keeper U
St Ry Co h 237 Hillman
Crane James weaver h 162 Division
" James weaver h r 567 First
" Patrick drillmaker h 261 Cottage
" Thomas gardener h 370 Middle
Cranshaw Thomas second hand Beacon Mfg Co h 341 Davis
Cranston Henry conductor bds 204
Weld [129 Elm
" Lydia J teacher High school h
" William W salesman 36 Purchase
h 143 Washington [Coffin av
Crapeau Oscar carpenter h 241
Crapo Albert A clerk 546 Kempton
h 610 County

Steiger-Dudgeon Co.
"The WOMAN'S Store."
Tel. Bell 82 & 83, Branches connecting all depts.
" " 160 For Office only. Auto. 1211

SUMPTIONS,
ASSORTMENTS
AT ALL TIMES
OF DEPENDABLE
DRY GOODS

Crapo
" Albert A Jr police station 5 h 71 Foster [Court
" Alexander B watchman H C h 361
" Catherine widow Francis H h 213 State [net av
" Charles H teamster h 277 Acush-

CRAPO, CLIFFORD & PRESCOTT
COUNSELLORS AT LAW
Solicitors for New Bedford Institution for Savings and New Bedford Five Cents Savings Bank
Masonic Building, Pleasant Street
New Bedford, Mass
Wm W Crapo Chas W Clifford
Walter Clifford Henry H Crapo
Oliver Prescott John H Clifford
Telephone 19

Crapo, Clifford & Prescott (William W and Henry H Crapo, Charles W, Walter and John H Clifford and Oliver Prescott) counsellors at law 6 Masonic bldg Pleasant street
" Delia Mrs weaver h 2 Cornell pl
" Ella F widow Peter h 173 Emerson (N)
" Emma nurse h 34 Desautels
" Eugene G city driver h 168 Shawmut av [av h do
" George G teaming 168 Shawmut
" George W teamster 86 Chancery h do [Summer
" Grace B sewer 185 Union bds 65
" Henry H pres U St Ry Co and Mechanics National Bank and (Crapo, Clifford & Prescott) h 81 Hawthorn
" Holder D h 226 Arnold
" Jesse F chauffeur 148 Court h 610 County
" John F clerk b 46 Mill
" Joseph E rem to San Francisco
" Lillian Mrs h 273 Mill [mer
" Mary widow George M h 65 Sum-
" Nancy B Mrs h 49 Mill
" Nicholas butcher h 34 Desautels
" Restcomb B cab driver b 383 Kempton [Desautels
" Robert C telephone operator h 22

Crapo
" Squire E painter b 63 Mechanics lane [161 Smith
" Thomas A clerk 28 William h
" Walter E salesman 45 Union h 22 Homer
" William W pres N B Institution for Savings, Acushnet Mill Corp, Wamsutta Mills, Potomska Mills and (Crapo, Clifford & Prescott) h 81 Hawthorn
Cravalho Joseph mill hand b 139 Coffin av
Craven James fixer h 561½ Cottage
" Joseph R weaver b 29 Mosher
" Matthew died Mar 14 1911 [er
" Tamer widow Mathew h 29 Mosh-
" William mill hand h 46 Front
Craw John F laborer h 26 Maitland
" Leonard H h 20 Mill [shall
" William B helper h 171 Cogge-
Crawford Robert H h 70 S Sixth
" Robert H M drillmaker bds 95 Maple
" Samuel G machinist b 23 Priscilla
Crawshaw William rem from city
" William weaver h 72 Ruth
Crear Robert G died June 23 1911
Cree James second hand h 78 Valentine
Creed Loretta M teacher I W Benjamin kindergarten school b 44 Pearl [44 Pearl
" Mark B supt Potomska Mills h
Crescent Mfg Co silks 1145 Kempton
" Tea & Butter Co 977 S Water
Crete Armand removed from city
Critchley Robert weaver h 24 Welcome [b do
Croacher Anna W physician 51 Fifth
" Frank foreman T W Croacher h 179 Orchard
" James W glazier b 51 Fifth
" Thomas lumber surveyor h 55 S Sixth. [Cross h 51 Fifth
" Thomas W lumber Leonard cor
Croasdale William H rms 347 Purchase
" William H weaver h 144 Collette
Crochetiere Albert helper Standard Oil Co h r 85 Austin
Crocker Abbie L bookkeeper 201 Union b at N Dartmouth [net av
" Charles B farmer h 2405 Acush-

PELEG H. SHERMAN 506 COUNTY ST.
FUNERAL DIRECTOR AND EMBALMER
OFFICE PHONES, Bell 690-13 Auto. 1305.
RESIDENCE PHONES, Bell 690-12. Auto. 1306.

Crocker
" Evan S tinsmith b 526 Cottage
" Herbert A teamster h 173 Emerson (N) [h 37 Campbell
" H Louise telegrapher 20 Market
" Lester D clerk U St Ry Co bds 270 Pleasant
" Parthia H h 37 Campbell [tage
" Ralph H book binder b 526 Cot-
" Sylvia G removed from city
" Thatcher B chief engineer H C h 96 Chestnut [h 118 Locust
" William H foreman foot of North
" William H yard master Holmes Mfg Co h 526 Cottage [Shore
Crockett Martha widow Esburn h 14
Crodle John laborer b 199 Dean
Crofton Patrick J granitecutter 1256 Kempton h 9 Valentine
Croke John oiler b 850 First
Croker Charles H cook rms 29 S Second [h 59 School
" Isaac restaurant 10 S Second
" Robert removed from city
Crombleholme Fred operative bds 62 Kenyon
" James operative b 23 Cotter
" Joseph spinner h 23 Cotter
Crommenschlager Jules weaver h 23 Viall [85 Bay
Crompton Edward E machinist h
" George P operative b 148 Mt Pleasant [ant
" John loom fixer h 148 Mt Pleas-
" John J grocer 101 Clark h 25 Myrtle
" Martha b 22 Collins [Pleasant
" Morris H machinist b 148 Mt
Cronan Joseph P metalworker h 3 Harrison
Crone Rachel widow William h 11 Thatcher [Water
Croney Manuel fisherman h 456 S
Cronin Alice and Catherine mill hands h 30 Viall
" Archie fixer b 869 County
" Arthur J clerk lunch cart cor Purchase and Weld b 290 Purchase
" Cornelius gardener h 3 Harrison
" Cornelius operative b 39 Bowditch
" Cornelius J h 665 County

Cronin
" Daniel W tailor 157 Union h 187 North [av
" Edward laborer b 1098 Acushnet
CRONIN EDWARD H cleansing 504 County h 44 Ash See page 769
" Edward L (William Cronin & Co) h 119 Maxfield
" John A cook b 290 Purchase
" John L conductor b 30 Viall
" Joseph A (William Cronin & Co) h 56 State [rison
" Joseph J metal turner bds 3 Har-
" Lawrence fireman Y N, N H & H R R h 140 Clark
" William & Co (E L and J A Cronin) harness mfrs 54 Elm
Cronshaw James b 201 Belleville rd
Crook Harvey weaver bds 21 Ashley
" James weaver h 162 Bates av
" Joseph weaver b 125 David
" Richard weaver h 21 Ashley
" Thomas clerk 830 Purchase h 972 County
" Thomas fixer h 234 Dean
" Thomas weaver h 25 Viall
" Thomas weaver h 125 David
" Thomas weaver h 509 S Second
" William H carpenter h 116 S Sixth
CROOKER COMPANY interior decorators 230 Weybosset Providence R I See page 754
Crooks Charles operative b 27 Highland [land
" Charles W gardener h 27 High-
" George operative b 27 Highland
Croosdale Albert died 1911
Cropper Ashworth weaver h 1547 Acushnet avenue [ton
Crosby Charles E painter h 2 Mil-
" Edgar B carpenter h 154 Sycamore [135 Hathaway av
" Edgar C clerk Manomet Mill h
" Edna clerk 70 Purchase b 154 Chancery [away
" Edward C paymaster h 135 Hath-
" Ethel clerk 70 Purchase b 154 Sycamore
" Mary h 281 Kempton
" Walter H carpenter b 154 Sycamore [shuet av
Crosetiere Louise milliner 1009 Acu-

PAINTERS' SUPPLIES
Walnut, Cor. Water, 84 Pleasant St. 25 WELD SQ., 129 COVE ST.
F. T. AKIN & COMPANY

Croshere Austin B clerk Standard b 33 Willis [33 Willis
" Blanche clerk 160 Purchase bds
CROSHERE CHARLES A carriage painter 38 Fourth h 33 Willis See foot lines
Cross Agnes Mrs h 16 Woodlawn av
" Albert h 47 Logan [chase
" Alfred shoemaker h 864 Pur-
" Alphonse barber h 156 Reynolds
" Andrew weaver b 16 Woodlawn avenue [Purchase
" Edmund mgr 66 William rms 355
" James h 4 Harmony
" James third hand b 85 Tallman
" James W pres N B Rubber Co 66 William h at Fall River
" John S Mrs removed from city
" John W operative h 65½ Durfee
" Lewis operative b 16 Woodlawn avenue [Grinnell
" Louis tinsmith 87 Union h 175
" Samuel H student b 142 Merrimac [ty
" Thomas blacksmith b 1039 Coun-
" Thomas Jr drillworker h 74 Fruit
" William clerk h 207 Weld
" William third hand b 85 Tallman
" William B lessee N B Theatre h at Brockton
" William O died Oct 31 1910
" see LaCroix
Crossley Albert chauffeur Engine No 9 h 1618 Acushnet av
" Albert spinner h 86 Briggs
" Alfred weaver h 387 Pleasant
" Charles boarding house 53 Prospect [Prospect
" Charles A blacksmith bds 53
" Douglass molder h 3 Stanton ct
" Frank plumber bds 240 Tinkham
" Fred salesman 1064 Acushnet av h 47½ Bowditch
" George weaver b r 57 Howard
" Herbert fixer h 63 Nye
" John h 7 Reynolds
CROSSLEY JOHN F & CO steam fitters 223 Mill b 7 Reynolds See foot lines
" Manuel fixer h 25 E French av
" Martha widow Taylor b 116 Hathaway [Nye
" Priscilla widow Douglass h 63
Crossman Albert laborer h 4 Blackburn

Crossman
" Annie E Mrs lodgings 48 High
" Charles M fisherman h 48 High
" Edward G (Crossman & Shepardson) grocer 111 Durfee h 322 Austin
" & Shepardson (Edward G Crossman and Donn Shepardson) grocers 111 Durfee [Clark
Crosson James F machinist h 140
Crosydale Ralph h 27 Stapleton
Croteau Adelard conductor b 20 Tallman [249 Shawmut av
" Calixte M clerk 161 Coffin av b
" Eudore h 20 Tallman
" Honore M (Croteau & Wood) 249 Shawmut av h do
CROTEAU & WOOD (H M Croteau and F H Wood) masons and plasterers 249 Shawmut av See page 776
Crothers George B P millinery 930 S Water h 369 Park
Croucher Helen M widow John E h 814 Belleville av
Crouse Arthur removed from city
Crowe James J janitor St Lawrence church h 190 Maxfield
" Michael A bartender 418 Kempton h 3 Norton
Crowell Aruna B picture frames 24 Fifth h 25 Arnold [Summer
" Elizabeth widow James A h 198
" Elizabeth N importer of photographs 20 Seventh b do [lantic
" Emma C widow Howes b 76 At-
" Ernest H mariner h 512 Purchase [Maitland
" Harry C foreman comber h 54
" Helen W widow Stephen h 20 Seventh [Woodlawn av
" Henry D piper 125 Middle h 29
" Hope E teacher Hosea M Knowlton school b 107 Sycamore
" Joseph F overseer Acushnet M Corp h 21 Social [rimac
" Lawrence J machinist b 139 Mer-
" Leander bookkeeper Bennett Mill h 21 Homer
" Mary h 154 Chestnut
" Theodore P sailmaker 35 Commercial h 187 Chancery [Fifth
" Thomas D agent 14 N Sixth b 11
Crowley Alma M stenographer 160 Purchase b 154 Maxfield

Remember to investigate our methods before taking up a business course.
Kinyon's Commercial School
Odd Fellows Bldg., Cor. William and Pleasant Sts., New Bedford, Mass.

Crowley
" Daniel J spinner b 75 Durfee
" Daniel L (Au Bon Marche) 139 Union rms 236 do
" Dennis laborer h 16 Lindsey
" Francis V inspector h 251 North
" Helen C telephone operator 151 Union b 16 Lindsey
" James F stonecutter rms 226 Purchase [field
" Jeremiah J jeweler h 154 Max-
" John clerk h 75 Durfee
" John teamster b 16 Lindsey
" John C telephone operator Postal Telegraph Co rms 401 Purchase
" John S b 83 Ruth
" Joseph L engineer Steamer No 1 h 252 Chestnut
" Julia h 475 Kempton [dar
" Lizzie C widow John J h 332 Ce-
" Mary V clerk 160 Purchase b 154 Maxfield [State
" M Joseph mgr 139 Union h 45
" Patrick H mason h 39 Bowditch
" Richard H clerk b 154 Maxfield
" Robert E clerk b 154 Maxfield
" Thomas J bartender 343 Acushnet av h 18 Willis
" Timothy b 75 Durfee
" Timothy J janitor Thomas A Greene school h 258 Acushnet avenue

CROWN CONFECTIONERY STORE Parendelis & Dangelas props 56 Purchase See page 783

Crowsdale William weaver bds 76 Cove [shuet av b Bentley st
Crowther Daniel driver 1190 Acu-
" Fred blacksmith h 63 Briggs
" John second hand h 60 Hathaway
" Mary widow James F weaver h 563 N Front [h 15 Bentley
" William bakery 1190 Acushnet av
" William Jr driver 1190 Acushnet avenue b 15 Bentley
" William H carpenter h 113 Willis
Crozman Albert teamster h 202 N Front [ond
Crudden John F lineman 57 N Sec-
" John J painter h 324 Cedar Grove
Crumley Francis V loom fixer h 68 Grape
" Eugene mason h 402 S Water
Cruz Antonio mariner h 2 Griffin

Cruz
" Dionisio laborer h 2½ Maiden lane
" Eugene mason h 402 S Water
" Joseph laborer h 8½ Griffin
" Joseph laborer h 46 School
" Joseph laborer h 272 S Front
" Joseph S mill hand h 148 Belleville avenue [shuet av h 161 do
" Manuel G notary public 159 Acu-
" Mary widow h 51 Swift
" Mary J widow h 16 Wing
" Peter cook h 412 S Water
" Philip grocer 498 Maxfield h do
Cryer Archie designer h 127 Reynolds
" David D concreter 531 Mt Pleasant h do
" James weaver h 125 Collette
" John twister h 9 Studley
" Robert third hand h 193 Dean
" Thomas back boy b 193 Dean
Csirics Rada mill hand bds 54 Phillips avenue [Bolton
Cuadros Theotonio de laborer h 507
Cuddy Helen B clerk 57 N Second b 2 Sears
" Louis W rem to Columbus Ga
" Thomas laborer h 190 W French av [Water h do
Cudish Bessie Mrs variety 700 South
" Samuel painter h 700 S Water
Cudworth Charles reedmaker b 22 Cleveland [Court
Cuff Melissa B widow Levi H h 113
Culbert Margaret J Mrs h 415 Cottage [Durfee
Culhane James R cabinetmaker b 50
" Margaret E widow Michael J h 50 Durfee
" Michael J died June 5 1911
Cullen Esther widow Matthew h 289 Earle
" James laborer b 341 Bowditch
" James F removed from city
" Joseph H second hand goods 391 Purchase h 395 do
" Mary Mrs b 26 Seventh
Culler Hyman tailor 277 Fourth bds 43 Potomska
Cullier Donat laborer b 155 Earle
Cullins Charles F shoemaker b 180 Belleville rd [ville rd
" Herbert L operative b 180 Belle-
" Sarah widow A B h 180 Belleville road [ham
Cummings Archibald bds 202 Tink-

HASKELL BROS. DEALERS IN
ICE
400 COURT STREET TELEPHONE CONNECTION NEW BEDFORD, MASS.

Cummings
" Archibald watchman b 16 Ashley
" A Emma widow Charles S h 116 Fourth [mings) h 411 County
" Benjamin (Cummings & Cum-
" Charles removed to Fairhaven
" Elmar brewery hand b 83 Kenyon [mings) h 6 Clinton pl
" Frank A (Cummings & Cum-
" James weaver h 482 Bolton
" Maria clerk 182 Union b 558 Cottage [yon
" Patrick T cooper bds 83 Ken-
" Peter twister h 359 Orchard (S)
" Peter V driver 149 Purchase h 365 Pleasant
" Thomas H laborer h 482 Bolton
" Thomas P bds 558 Cottage
" & Cummings (Benjamin and Frank A Cummings) grocers 98 to 104 William
Cummins John candymaker 1091 Acushnet av b 355 Coggeshall
Cummisky Thomas carder h 16 Briggs
Cundall Charles D druggists 44 Dartmouth h 213 Orchard
Cunha Antonio J operative h 76 Winsor [av
" Arthur operative h 113 Acushnet
" Esther presser 53 William b 95 Fourth
" Frank G laborer h 31 Swift
" Fred mill hand h 103 Thompson
" Joe mill hand h 399 S Second
" John barber 90 Allen b 522 Bolton
" John operative b 190 Bonney
" John F laborer h 197 Elm
" Manuel bookbinder h 159 Hillman
" Manuel clerk 407 Rivet h 514 do
" Manuel laborer h 263 S Second
" Manuel laborer b 190 Bonney
" Manuel operative h 58 Rivet
" Manuel operative h 129 Field
" Rosie Mrs h 190 Bonney
" Walter B salesman 170 Purchase h 333 Kempton
Cunliffe George weaver h 99 Beetle
Cunniff Edward A loom fixer h 21 Howland Village
" Edward T machinist b 21 Howland Village [land Village
" Francis A mill hand b 21 How-
" James laborer h 492 Mill

Cunniff
" John moving picture operator h 1378 Acushnet av [b 4 Jenney
" John M motion picture operator
" John H city laborer h 46 Hill
" Thomas A lawyer 4 Masonic bldg b 2 Jenney
" see Conniff
Cunningham Albert P clerk 61 William b 229 Hillman
" Annie M bookkeeper 172 N Water b 229 Hillman
" Arthur J bookkeeper N B Fish Co b 6 Green [vision
" Catherine widow James h 187 Di-
" Charles A salesman 170 Purchase h 35 Pierce [man
" Edith asst bookkeeper b 229 Hill-
" Edward J painter h 187 Cedar
" Ethel E clerk 41 Purchase b 229 Hillman [ant
" Frederick M plumber h 205 Pleas-
" George h 201 Dean
" George Jr machinist b 201 Dean
" George W engineer 48 Pleasant h 221 Hillman
" Gertrude M teacher High school b 6 Green [221 Hillman
" Harold C clerk 11 N Sixth bds
" Henry D driver h 162 Division
" Hugh A engineer h 800 First
" James paving cutter b 1089 Acushnet avenue [ington
" John J letter carrier h 23 Wash-
" John N machinist 22 Fourth h 12 McMurray terrace
" John P plumber h 229 Hillman
" John W spinner h 51 Hall
" Mary E teacher Thompson street school b 6 Green
" Patrick J janitor 246½ Union bds 187 Division
" Patrick J machinist h 6 Green
" Shirley E engineer U St Ry Co power station h 114 Willis
" Wallace E machinist h 37 Bonney
" William M operative b 51 Hall
Cure Peter mill hand h 683 First
Curley Minnie Mrs weaver h 4 Riverside avenue
" Peter weaver h 418 S Second
Curran Frank watchman U St Ry Co h 171 Weld
" John A fireman h 23 Bentley

J. F. CROSSLEY 223 MILL STREET COR. EMERSON PHONE
STEAM and HOT WATER HEATING
GAS FITTING and FIXTURES

Curran
" John H operative b 79 Prospect
" Matthew J veterinarian 50 Elm rms 53 do [pect
" Sarah widow James h 79 Pros-
" Vernon F clerk h 11 Hunter
Currie Allan B car conductor h 359 Pleasant
Curriea Joseph h 175 Belleville av
Currier Adelard actor bds 124 Rivet
" Andrew J agent Nonquitt Spinning Co b Parker House
" Anthony J painter h Oliver near Tarkiln Hill rd [County
" Charles W carriage trimmer h 359
" Joseph fixer h 118 Potomska
" Joseph W laborer b A J Currier's
" Ralph E carriage trimmer h 359 County [net av b 13 Bannister
" William V asst mgr 1031 Acush-
Curry Bros (Joseph and Jules Curry) bicycles 123 Holly
" Edward carder h 55 Potomska
" Ellen widow James b 171 Fourth
" George F carpenter h 19 Columbia
" John removed to Fairhaven
" John T letter carrier h 342 Orchard (S) [b 125 do
" Joseph (Curry Bros) 123 Holly b
" Jules (Curry Bros) 123 Holly b 125 do
" Martin laborer h 254 Earle
" Mary clerk 1119 Acushnet av b 125 Holly [av
" Mary widow Richard h 32 Brock
" Matthew weaver h 26 Willard
" May G cashier 145 Union b 19 Columbia
" Robert J painter h 69 South
" William machinist b 171 Fourth
" ——— h 101 Fifth
Curt Luciano carpenter b 103 Davis
" Silvia salesman 2 S Water rms 171 Kempton [ant
Curtis Daniel H weaver h 351 Pleas-
" Daniel J cotton grader Whitman Mill h 304 Summer [cery
" David H carpenter h 152 Chan-
" Henry clerk h 9 Lindsey
" Laura F laundress b 109 Newton
" Leonard O laundryman h 109 Newton

Curtis
" Leonard O Jr clerk 258 Purchase b 109 Newton [464 Allen
" William H lineman N B F dept h
Cushing Charles F harness mfr 34 Pleasant h 426 Union
" George H salesman 34 Pleasant h 41 Atlantic
" Joseph spinner h 49 S Second
" Waldo E engineer Soule Mill h 142 Merrimac
" William S police h 30 Sherman
Cushman Barker H bookkeeper Electric Express h at Fairhaven
" Brothers (Clarence and Harvey) grocers 141 Fourth and 726 Kempton [h 61 Forest
" Charles A manager 425 S Water
" Clarence (Cushman Bros) h 51 Russell
" Dorcas P b 396 Purchase
" Emery salesman Old Colony Box Co h 31 James [75 Campbell
" Everett M supt Holmes Mill h
" Frances R widow Henry W h 322 Arnold [Fifth
" Harvey (Cushman Bros) h 86
" Henry E at Old Colony Box Co h at Acushnet [Hawthorn
" Herbert E treas 100 Fifth h 144
" Joanna widow William H 75 Campbell
" Ruth bds 322 Arnold
" William A contract agent 57 N Second bds 75 Campbell
Cusick Rose weaver b 15 Warren
Cusson Antonio weaver h 96 Nye
" Edward weaver h 53 Hicks
" Joseph weaver h 28 Cleveland
Cutler Arthur weaver h 285 Davis
Cutting John W watchman h 111 Clark [Grove
Cygan Joseph weaver b 108 Cedar
Cypress Mary h 3 Smith st court
Cyr Alick operative b 84 Kenyon [do
" Arsene stable r 281 Sawyer h 283
" Arsene Jr driver b 283 Sawyer
" Didia h 64 Tallman
" John bds 148 Tinkham
" John twister bds 64 Tallman
" John operative h 84 Kenyon
" Levi pool 1753 Acushnet av bds 149 Tinkham
" Lucien loom fixer h 17 Jouvett

CHARLES A. CROSHERE
38 FOURTH ST. Bell Phone 1964-23
SIGN PAINTING
GLASS LETTERING
ELECTRIC SIGNS
SHOW CARDS

Dyr
" Magloire tailor 9 Arcade blk h 14 Beetle
" Oliver died Sept 30 1910
" Philias mill hand h 148 Tinkham
" Telesphore weaver b 84 Kenyon
" Zepherin removed from city
" Zephir operative h 202 State
Dyrewkopos John mill hand b rear 234 N Front [avenue
Dzaja Joseph weaver h 283 Coffin
Dzechoosk Wladyslaw weaver h 23 Acushnet avenue [ville av
Dzestic Antoni laborer h 207 Belle-
Dabaque Henry mill hand h 909 S Water [Acushnet av
Dabignon Ambrose carpenter h 1729
Dabney Manuel laborer b 180 North
" Rose Mrs h 180 North [h 8 do
Dabroosia William grocer 2 Hicks
Dacy William laborer h 442 Pleasant
Dade Isaiah C lawyer 37 Purchase rm 4 h 152 Cedar
" Julia widow John b 152 Cedar
Daffinee Eliza J widow Mannoah bds 188 Grinnell [104 Hemlock
" Harris J driver 128 Pleasant h
" John B compositor Times h 16 Fifth [nut
Daffoncea Romano laborer h 9 Wal-
Dafgord John mariner h 212 Court
" William Frank printer bds 212 Court [184 Phillips av
Dagenais Marie L widow George h
Dagesse Archand spinner b 155 Bowditch
" Ernest weaver b 155 Bowditch
" Herminie widow Arsene h 155 Bowditch
" Honore lather h 154 Nash road
" Mary grocer 47 Belleville rd h do
Daggett Almira E widow Hollis b 44 Fifth
" Eugene F carpenter b 44 Briggs
D'Aguiar Frank G opeartive h 149 Hathaway
Dahill Edward F shoe findings 667 Purchase and chief engineer fire department h 11 Robeson
" Edward J (Dahill & Kirby) b 28 Richmond
" Helen F teacher Harrington school bds 28 Richmond

Dahill
" Margaret C widow Maurice C h 28 Richmond [mond
" William B chauffeur b 28 Rich-
DAHILL & KIRBY (Edward J Dahill and Arthur C Kirby) civil engineers and surveyors 11 Clifford bldg See page 42
Dahl Anira A Mrs bookkeeper 168 S Water b 160 Grinnell
" Hannah and Mary operatives b 63 Adams
" Matilda widow h 63 Adams
Dahoney Helena L clerk Registry of Deeds b 130 Bedford
" Michael h 17 Grape
" Thomas police h 130 Bedford
" see Dohoney and Dehony
Daigle Alfred spinner h 417 N Front
" Henry mason h 4 Riverside av
" Jane widow Calixte h 107 Coffin avenue
" Luke fisherman b 107 Coffin av
" Mary widow Napoleon h 857½ First [road
" Maxime plasterer h Tarkiln Hill
" Michel weaver h 102 David
" Victorline Mrs h 68 Washburn
Daignault Joseph laborer b 182 Weld
" William plumber 1545 Acushnet avenue
Daigneault Adelard doffer h 66 Dean
" Joseph N insurance agent 97 William rm 310 h 200 Pleasant
" Treffly driver h 200 Richmond
" William apprentice bds 200 Richmond [ple
Dailey George H driver h 51 Ma-
Dainteth Harry clerk 153 Grove h 75 Brock av
Dakin John doffer b 125 Reynolds
" Sarah Mrs h 345 Middle [ham
" Thomas 2nd hand h 60 Peck-
Dalas Charlotte widow J Constant variety 36 Linden h 216 State
" J Constant died Nov 5 1910
Dalbec Albert clerk b 22 Willard
" Arthur driver h 22 Willard
" Edmond driver patrol wagon h 16 Studley
" Joseph machinist h 22 Willard
" Joseph Jr machinist h 10 Viall
" Melida carder b 15 Warren
Dale John A b 11 Fifth
" Martha Mrs h 103 Hemlock

J. G. NICHOLSON
LUMBER, SASH, DOORS and BLINDS
BOWDITCH STREET, NEW BEDFORD, MASS.

Curran
" John H operative b 79 Prospect
" Matthew J veterinarian 50 Elm rms 53 do [pect
" Sarah widow James h 79 Pros-
" Vernon F clerk h 11 Hunter
Currie Allan B car conductor h 359 Pleasant
Curriea Joseph h 175 Belleville av
Currier Adelard actor bds 124 Rivet
" Andrew J agent Nonquitt Spinning Co b Parker House
" Anthony J painter h Oliver near Tarkiln Hill rd [County
" Charles W carriage trimmer h 359
" Joseph fixer h 118 Potomska
" Joseph W laborer b A J Currier's
" Ralph E carriage trimmer b 359 County [net av b 13 Bannister
" William V asst mgr 1081 Acush-
Curry Bros (Joseph and Jules Curry) bicycles 123 Holly
" Edward carder h 55 Potomska
" Ellen widow James b 171 Fourth
" George F carpenter h 19 Columbia
" John removed to Fairhaven
" John T letter carrier h 342 Orchard (S) [b 125 do
" Joseph (Curry Bros) 123 Holly b
" Jules (Curry Bros) 123 Holly b 125 do
" Martin laborer h 284 Earle
" Mary clerk 1119 Acushnet av b 125 Holly [av
" Mary widow Richard h 32 Brock
" Matthew weaver h 26 Willard
" May G cashier 145 Union b 19 Columbia
" Robert J painter h 69 South
" William machinist b 171 Fourth
" ——— h 101 Fifth
Curt Luciano carpenter b 103 Davis
" Silvia salesman 2 S Water rms 171 Kempton [ant
Curtis Daniel H weaver h 351 Pleas-
" Daniel J cotton grader Whitman Mill h 304 Summer [cery
" David H carpenter h 152 Chan-
" Henry clerk h 9 Lindsey
" Laura F laundress b 109 Newton
" Leonard O laundryman h 109 Newton

Curtis
" Leonard O Jr clerk 253 Purchase b 109 Newton [464 Allen
" William H lineman N B F dept h
Cushing Charles F harness mfr 34 Pleasant h 426 Union
" George H salesman 34 Pleasant h 41 Atlantic
" Joseph spinner h 49 S Second
" Waldo E engineer Soule Mill h 142 Merrimac
" William S police h 30 Sherman
Cushman Barker H bookkeeper Electric Express h at Fairhaven
" Brothers (Clarence and Harvey) grocers 141 Fourth and 726 Kempton [h 61 Forest
" •Charles A manager 425 S Water
" Clarence (Cushman Bros) h 51 Russell
" Dorcas P b 396 Purchase
" Emery salesman Old Colony Box Co h 31 James [75 Campbell
" Everett M supt Holmes Mill h
" Frances R widow Henry W h 322 Arnold [Fifth
" Harvey (Cushman Bros) h 86
" Henry E at Old Colony Box Co h at Acushnet [Hawthorn
" Herbert E treas 100 Fifth h 144
" Joanna widow William H h 75 Campbell
" Ruth bds 322 Arnold
" William A contract agent 57 N Second bds 75 Campbell
Cusick Rose weaver b 15 Warren
Cusson Antonio weaver h 96 Nye
" Edward weaver h 53 Hicks
" Joseph weaver h 28 Cleveland
Cutler Arthur weaver h 285 Davis
Cutting John W watchman h 111 Clark [Grove
Cygan Joseph weaver b 108 Cedar
Cypress Mary h 3 Smith st court
Cyr Alick operative b 84 Kenyon [do
" Arsene stable r 281 Sawyer h 283
" Arsene Jr driver b 283 Sawyer
" Didia h 64 Tallman
" John bds 148 Tinkham
" John twister bds 64 Tallman
" John operative h 84 Kenyon
" Levi pool 1753 Acushnet av bds 149 Tinkham
" Lucien loom fixer h 17 Jouvett

CHARLES A. CROSHERE
38 FOURTH ST. Bell Phone 1964-23
SIGN PAINTING
GLASS LETTERING
ELECTRIC SIGNS
SHOW CARDS

Cyr
" Magloire tailor 9 Arcade blk h 14 Beetle
" Oliver died Sept 30 1910
" Philias mill hand h 148 Tinkham
" Telesphore weaver b 84 Kenyon
" Zepherin removed from city
" Zephir operative h 202 State
Cyrewkopos John mill hand b rear 234 N Front [avenue
Czaja Joseph weaver h 283 Coffin
Czechoosk Wladyslaw weaver h 23 Acushnet avenue [ville av
Czestic Antoni laborer h 207 Belle-

Dabaque Henry mill hand h 909 S Water [Acushnet av
Dabignon Ambrose carpenter h 1729
Dabney Manuel laborer b 180 North
" Rose Mrs h 180 North [h 8 do
Dabroosia William grocer 2 Hicks
Dacy William laborer h 442 Pleasant
Dade Isaiah C lawyer 37 Purchase rm 4 h 152 Cedar
" Julia widow John b 152 Cedar
Daffinee Eliza J widow Mannoah bds 188 Grinnell [104 Hemlock
" Harris J driver 128 Pleasant h
" John B compositor Times h 16 Fifth [nut
Daffoncea Romano laborer h 9 Wal-
Dafgord John mariner h 212 Court
" William Frank printer bds 212 Court [184 Phillips av
Dagenais Marie L widow George h
Dagesse Archand spinner b 155 Bowditch
" Ernest weaver b 155 Bowditch
" Herminie widow Arsene h 155 Bowditch
" Honore lather h 154 Nash road
" Mary grocer 47 Belleville rd h do
Daggett Almira E widow Hollis b 44 Fifth
" Eugene F carpenter b 44 Briggs
D'Aguiar Frank G opeartive h 149 Hathaway
Dahill Edward F shoe findings 667 Purchase and chief engineer fire department h 11 Robeson
" Edward J (Dahill & Kirby) b 28 Richmond
" Helen F teacher Harrington school bds 28 Richmond

Dahill
" Margaret C widow Maurice C h 28 Richmond [mond
" William B chauffeur b 28 Rich-
DAHILL & KIRBY (Edward J Dahill and Arthur C Kirby) civil engineers and surveyors 11 Clifford bldg See page 42
Dahl Ardra A Mrs bookkeeper 168 S Water b 160 Grinnell
" Hannah and Mary operatives b 63 Adams
" Matilda widow h 63 Adams
Dahoney Helena L clerk Registry of Deeds b 130 Bedford
" Michael h 17 Grape
" Thomas police h 130 Bedford
" see Dohoney and Dehony
Daigle Alfred spinner h 417 N Front
" Henry mason h 4 Riverside av
" Jane widow Calixte h 107 Coffin avenue
" Luke fisherman b 107 Coffin av
" Mary widow Napoleon h 857½ First [road
" Maxime plasterer h Tarkiln Hill
" Michel weaver h 102 David
" Victorline Mrs h 68 Washburn
Daignault Joseph laborer b 182 Weld
" William plumber 1545 Acushnet avenue
Daigneault Adelard doffer h 66 Dean
" Joseph N insurance agent 97 William rm 310 h 200 Pleasant
" Treffly driver h 200 Richmond
" William apprentice bds 200 Richmond [ple
Dailey George H driver h 51 Ma-
Dainteth Harry clerk 153 Grove b 75 Brock av
Dakin John doffer h 125 Reynolds
" Sarah Mrs h 345 Middle [ham
" Thomas 2nd hand h 60 Peck-
Dalas Charlotte widow J Constant variety 36 Linden h 216 State
" J Constant died Nov 5 1910
Dalbec Albert clerk b 22 Willard
" Arthur driver h 22 Willard
" Edmond driver patrol wagon h 16 Studley
" Joseph machinist h 22 Willard
" Joseph Jr machinist h 10 Viall
" Melida carder b 15 Warren
Dale John A b 11 Fifth
" Martha Mrs h 103 Hemlock

J. G. NICHOLSON
LUMBER, SASH, DOORS and BLINDS
BOWDITCH STREET, NEW BEDFORD, MASS.

Daley Adel widow Dennis h 155 Ashland
" Charles F plumber h 33 Locust
" Charles F police station 5 b 21 Reynolds
" Ellen Mrs h 200 N Front
" Ethel M teacher Thomas Donaghy school b 147 Merrimac
" Harriet widow Michael h 41 Reynolds [net av
" John operative rms 488 Acush-
" John F laborer h 433 Pleasant
" Joseph conductor h 37 Acushnet avenue [ty
" Joseph mill hand h 109 Coun-
" Joseph H clerk b 178 Davis
" Julia widow Thomas b 222 State
" J Thomas officer H C h 147 Merrimac [Tinkham
" Mary J and Elizabeth D h 218
" Michael clerk b 200 N Front
" Michael weaver b 56 Nye
" Michael E carpenter and builder 232 Collette h do
" Thomas D electrician b 37 Acushnet av [mac
" Thomas E shoemaker b 147 Merri-
" William H b 433 Pleasant
Dallaire Joseph operative h 833 Acushnet av
Dalphon Ida Mrs h 931 Acushnet av
Dalphond Jean B removed to Lowell
Dalrymple Edward E builder 189 N Water h 400 Cedar [Austin
" Mary J widow Archibald h 117
Dalton Ellen A Mrs h 18 Peckham
" Lawrence H laborer h 24 Shore
" Lennie M widow Albert b 101 Cedar
" Mary Mrs h 1098 Acushnet av
" Mary R teacher J H Clifford school b 80 Morgan [Front
Daly Ellen widow Michael h 200 N
" James clerk h 16 Thatcher
" Martin J shoemaker h 67 Foster
" Michael clerk 213 Acushnet av b 200 N Front
" see Daley and Dailey
Dalzell Frederick W carpet layer h 126 Florence
Dame Louis h 36 McGurk
" Wilfred O clerk 965 Acushnet av b 1060 do [Campbell
Dammon Arthur H clerk bds 136
" Franklin M h 136 Campbell

Dammon
" Franklin M Jr clerk b 136 Campbell [do
" Frederick A grocer 137 Smith h
" George K messenger 166 William rms 56 Walnut [chase
" Thomas H Jr clerk 630 Pur-
" William F teller First National Bank h at Fairhaven
Damon Addie H Mrs h 58 Sycamore
" Allen painter 764 Kempton h do
" Arthur C carpenter b 21 Sycamore
" Charles A b 21 Sycamore
" Clarence L steamfitter 129 Smith h 82 Robeson
" C Maude Mrs clerk b 89 Chancery
" Edward P carpenter 161 Clinton h 345 Cottage [Sycamore
" Emily H widow Samuel H h 21
" Ethel H clerk 255 Union b 764 Kempton [Cottage
" Eunice E widow Deane W h 343
" Fabien laborer bds 82 Eugenia
" Frederick E painter h 17 Willow
" Frederick H (Nichols & Damon) 103 William h 15 Arnold place
" Harriet S principal Merrimac st school b 21 Sycamore [ence
" Irville L electrician h 88 Flor-
" Luke painter b 764 Kempton
" Mabel P Mrs removed to Providence R I
" Margaret R widow Harrison F (Bourne & Damon Co) 131 Belleville road h 240 Hawthorn
D'Amoral Joseph sausage maker bds 202 Rivet
" Mary J widow h 202 Rivet
" Walter clerk 200 Rivet b 202 do
Damos Alphonse J laborer h 164 Bonney
" Joseph R carpenter h 16 Holyhock
Dana Charles E died Feb 8 1911
" Elizabeth and Alice h 8 Irving
Dandurand Armond clerk b 22 West French avenue
" Clotilde E clerk 80 Purchase bds 22 West French av [Collette
" Mary widow Peter operative h 143
" Pierre Jr (Pease & Dandurand) druggist 913 S Water h 22 W French avenue [French av
" P Hormidas clerk h 9 West

Steiger-Dudgeon Co.
"The WOMAN'S Store."
Tel. Bell 82 & 83, Branches connecting all depts.
" " 160 For Office only. Auto. 1211

SUMPTIONS, ASSORTMENTS AT ALL TIMES OF DEPENDABLE DRY GOODS

Danforth Benjamin C clerk 100 Fifth b 23 Seventh [Seventh
" Florence E widow George H h 23
" Henry W operative b 23 Seventh
" John H candy maker 48 Pleasant h at Fairhaven
Dangelas Denetrios (Parandelis & Dangelas) 56 Purchase rms 126 do [David
Daniel Domina slubber tender h 107
" Joseph weaver h 107 David
" Juan mason h 141 Hemlock
Daniels Antone P variety 135 Hemlock h 494 Rivet
" Antonio mason b 191 Collette
" John carpenter h 141 Hemlock
" Manuel P mason h 42 Rivet
" Treffle third hand h 22 Rodney
Daniou Alfred rms 604 S Second
" Arthur cane worker b 604 South Second
" Jules b 604 South Second [ond
" Pauline widow Jules b 604 S Sec-
Danis Harry pedlar h 490 S Water
" Omer mill hand b 80 Hope
" Ovid A mgr Rochambeau Club South Front [Front
Danisch John machinist b 446 North
" Theodore operative h 446 N Front
Danjoux Pauline widow h 604 S Second [Bentley
Dansereau Alderic carpenter h 32
" Joseph P Mrs h 28 Ashley
" Laurentine bookkeeper 101 Kenyon bds 148 Ashland
" Magloire shoe repairer 87 Ruth h 148 Ashland [Blackmer
" Napoleon glass cutter h 164
" Wilfred carder h 89 Hathaway
" Wilfred printer 101 Kenyon b 148 Ashland [Merrimac
Dantsizen Frank M apprentice b 111
" John C machinist b 11 Merrimac
DANTSIZEN JOHN G cabinet maker and upholsterer 214 Court h 25 Cedar See back cover
" Marion G b 125 Cedar [Merrimac
" Ophelia J widow Frank M h 111
" Rose P h 191 Elm [h 62 North
Danzell Bartlett B teamster N B W W
" Emery B hostler N B W W h 205 Court [Brownell
" James E city teamster h 241

Daprato Antonio fruit 1610 Acushnet av b 25 William [William
" Leo salesman 70 Union rms 25
D'Aragao Angello. L employer P Co h 112 Thompson
D'Aranjo Joseph laborer h 83 Crapo
Darcy Caesar machinist b 622 South Second
" Cesaire second hand N B C M Corporation h 287 Bowditch
" John J linotypist Mercury h at Fall River
" Lilly F stenographer rm 206 Municipal bldg b 115 Grinnell
" Margaret widow h 115 Grinnell
" Narcisse machinist b 279 Collette
D'Ardi Joseph laborer h 503 Acushnet avenue
Dargis Frank shoemaker h 112 Cove
" Louis P weaver b 81 Beetle
" Morris operative h 3 Marvin
Darling Alberta bookkeeper 387 Purchase h 2430 Acushnet av
" Arthur M clerk 146 Arnold b 85 Morgan [County
" Blanche R stenographer b 907
" Edgar W grocer 387 Purchase h 15 Campbell [ter
" Ella H widow Charles b 71 Fos-
" Franklin M Jr clerk Pierce Mfg Corporation h 250 Bowditch
" Walter H foreman A S M Co h 2444 Acushnet av [109 Willis
" William M clerk 387 Purchase h
Da Rosa Edward J engineer b 285 Orchard [285 Orchard (S)
" Manuel G engineer City Yard h
Darsigney Alfred removed to Lawrence
Dartmouth Cafe Club 5 S Sixth
" Club 246-248 Union
" Mfg Corporation cotton goods Cove beyond Harbor
" Pharmacy The O C Brightman proprietor 246 Union
" & Westport St Ry Co office Purchase corner William [lette
Darwell John watchman h 311 Col-
DaSilvia Jeremiah salesman 883 S Water h 36 Acushnet avenue
DeTerra Joseph I lawyer 49 William rm 10 h 26 Cove road
" Mary G Mrs h 94 Rockland
Daudelin Alider doffer b 159 Earle

PELEG H. SHERMAN 506 COUNTY ST.
FUNERAL DIRECTOR AND EMBALMER
OFFICE PHONES. Bell 690-13. Auto. 1305.
RESIDENCE PHONES. Bell 690-12. Auto. 1306.

Daudelin
" Blandina bookkeeper 1071 Acushnet avenue b 159 Earle
" Edward second hand h 159 Earle
" George operative b 161 Dean
" Henry bricklayer h 995 S Water
" Hervey laborer h 826 County
" Joseph S removed from city
Dauphinais Joseph A buyer 185 Union h 72 Park [son
Dautriel Alphonse carpenter h 15 Nel-
" Angus weaver h 82 Ruth
Davairs Joe hairdresser 131 County h 512 First [15 Smith
Davenport Abby D widow John h
" Augustus M painter h 571 Elm
" Charles M h 154 Arnold
" C M Jr clerk Page Mfg Co b 154 Arnold
" Edward D mgr h 535 N Front
" George E teamster 182 Union h 135 Sycamore
" Joseph W fixer h 161 Brook
" J Albert weaver h 24 Shore
" Machine Tool Co 90 S Sixth
" Samuel B shipper 36 Purchase h 356 Reed [h 462 Bolton
" Samuel G fireman Bennett Mill
" Walter C pressman h 420 Elm (W)
" William engineer h 98 South
" William H florist 35 Purchase h 32 Jenny Lind [Arch
" William S treas 90 S Sixth h 24
Daveny Joseph clerk 26 Wing b 305 South Second
Davey Maud L Mrs rms 74 School
David Joseph barber 236 S Second b 477 First [avenue
" Masson laborer h 656 Acushnet
" Peter dry goods 185 N Second h do [avenue
" Thomas laborer h 518 Acushnet
Davidian Albert J shoe repairing 265 Purchase h 506 Acushnet av
" Arsene shoe repairing 163 Summer h 36 Parker
" Arthur removed to Brockton
Davido Gregorio C carpenter 1 Stanton court h 65 Hall
Davidow Brothers (Mrs Sarah) jewelry and dry goods 831 S Water h 24 Crapo
" Joseph removed to Fall River

Davidow
" William clerk 831 S Water h 24 Crapo [chase h at Fairhaven
Davidson Harry B fruit 197 Pur-
" Herbert W (J Davidson & Son) b 280 Austin [280 Austin
" James (J Davidson & Son) h
" John H salesman 156 Purchase h 164 Smith
" John K clerk b 280 Austin
" J & Son (James and Herbert W) cooked meats 280 Austin
" Mark shoemaker h 379 Purchase
" Philip shoe worker b 343 S Water
" Simon dry goods 343 S Water h do [hand h 24 Belleville rd
Davie Elizabeth widow Peter mill
Davies Arthur clerk b 199 Davis
" Edward weaver h 104 Austin
" George clerk h 199 Davis
" John W drill worker b 462 Bolton
" Olive bookkeeper Manomet Mills bds 199 Davis
" Ruby E teacher Harrington school b 281 Mt Pleasant
" Thomas wood worker h 10 Washington [ington
" William C box maker b 10 Wash-
" see Davis
Davignon Alias barber 972 Acushnet avenue b 68 Kenyon
" Arthur box maker b 12 Sylvia
" Ernest S tailor 1056 Acushnet av h 1071 County
" Guillaume spinner h 53 Kenyon
" Joseph A clerk 667 Purchase h 815 do
" Marion widow Norbet h 12 Sylvia
" Napoleon weaver b 831 S Water
" Norbet mill hand h Church off Tarklin Hill road
" Stanislas hostler h 121 Webster ct
" Theodore A (North End Pharmacy) 420 North Front h 133 Phillips avenue
" Theonase removed from city
D'Avila Manuel F clerk 163 Union h 45 Lombard [Second
DaVilla Joseph clerk h 230 South
Davineau Amos slubber h 109 Rivet
Davis Alfred A janitor 162 Union h 321 Acushnet av [ushnet av
" Alfred A Jr operative b 321 Ac-
" Alice T widow Silas W h 7 Jenney

F. T. AKIN & CO. FORGE FACTORY FURNACE FAMILY COAL

Davis

" Almy W widow Moses h 361 County [Sixth
" Annie F Mrs boarding h 21 S
" Arthur C compositor 112 Union h 14 Clay
" Arthur E cutter h 58 James
" Arthur E steward House of Correction h 45 Liberty [mouth
" Carrie widow John h 102 Dart-
" Charles E contractor h 81 Walnut
" Charles E machinist h 17 Chestnut
" Charles E mason h 207 Emerson
" Charles E foreman 830 Purchase h 166 Chestnut
" Charles E Jr clerk 43 William rm 3 bds 17 Chestnut
" Charles L city laborer h 155 North
" Charles L Jr engineer h 49 Maitland [land
" Charles S engineer b 49 Mait-
" Chester E clerk E E T Co h 165 Middle
" Clara L teacher James B Congdon school b at Fairhaven
" Clarence H clerk Merchants National Bank b 33 Rounds
" Clifford weaver b 281 Mt Pleasant
" Cornelia W b 115 Summer
" C Brownell meterman 125 Middle b 184 Kemptón [Walnut
" David D clerk Kilburn Mill b 36
" Deborah B widow John dressmaker 250 Coffin av h do
" Edward G florist 191 Shawmut avenue h 195 do
" Edward L laborer b 124 High
" Edwin F shipper L R Corp h Tarkiln Hill road
" Elbert B mgr Acushnet Iron Co 229 N Water h 75 North
" Elbert B Mrs (Acushnet Iron Co) h 75 North [Morgan
" Elizabeth widow Edward S h 85
" Ellen M widow Jonathan W h 125 Hillman
" Emily C h 115 Summer
" Emily W teacher Robert C Ingraham school h 320 County
" Emma C widow Jethro C h 320 County [Thompson
" **Ernest E mule spinner bds 135**

Davis

" Esther S music teacher 8 Park place h do [253 Palmer
" Eunice clerk Holmes Mfg Co rms
" Eveline P died Nov 17 1910
" E May cashier b 17 Chestnut
" Flaver removed from city
" Frank W salesman 144 Union h 80 Morgan [Pleasant
" Franklin mill hand b 281 Mt
" Frederick W author h 71 North
" George carpenter b 9 Spring
" George laster rms 422 Purchase
" George B laborer h 439 S Orchard
" George J glass cutter h 114 Fair
" George T clerk 60 Dartmouth bds 92 Dunbar
" George T glass cutter h 155 Fair
" George W carder h 122½ Cove
" Gideon painter b 7 Jenny
" Hannah L music teacher b 22 Sycamore [Walden
" Harry C mgr 270 Kempton b 65
" Harry F carpenter 229 N Water h at North Dartmouth
" Harry S manager 120 Purchase rm 203 rms 168 Middle
" Henry weaver h 130 Ashland
" Henry O trainman b 66 N Second
" Henry S glass cutter h 135 Thompson [Works) h 27 Ocean
" Henry V (H V Davis Chemical
" Herbert painter 447 Kempton h Acushnet av corner Hillman
" Herbert Elmer salesman 41 Purchase h 74 Spruce [135 Locust
" Herbert Eugene motorman h
" H V Chemical Works (Henry V Davis) 147 Chancery [fin av
" Iona J bookkeeper b 250 Cof-
" Isabel h 171 Campbell
" Isabel widow James A h 344 Orchard (S) [Stackhouse
" Jacintho M rope worker h 49
" James h 3837 Acushnet avenue
" James farmer 735 Mt Pleasant h do
" James operative h 857½ First
" James A drill worker b 344 Orchard (S) [school b 253 Palmer
" Jane M teacher Cedar Grove st
" Jefferson (J Davis & Co) h 4 Foster
" John died Sept 24 1910

To do things right you must be taught. Our instructors can do it.

Kinyon's Commercial School

Odd Fellows Bldg., Cor. William and Pleasant Sts., New Bedford, Mass.

Davis
" John A Jr chauffeur 18 Market h 114 Rounds [rms 57 Smith
" John E blacksmith 40 Spring
" John H drill worker h 236 Maxfield
" John T weaver h 56 Salisbury
" John W clerk bds 426 Chancery
" Joseph foreman T P Corp h 36 Walnut
" Josephine Mrs b 53 Walnut
" J Herbert carriage painter 447 Kempton rms 497 Acushnet av
" J & Co (Jefferson Davis) shoes 165 Union
" Kate widow James h 93 Middle
" Katherine M widow Peter B h 78 Atlantic [cust
" Lizzie widow Elihu M h 135 Lo-
" Lulu Mrs clerk 200 Union h 114 Fair [Chestnut
" Lysander W carpenter h 106
" Mabel E teacher drawing and painting 8 Park place h do
" Mabel L bds 83 Bonney
" Mabel R nurse b 166 Chestnut
" Manuel fisherman h 226 S Front
" Manuel B h 69 Howland
" Mary h 161 Emerson (N)
" Mary bds 178 Brook
" Mary E Mrs h 162 Campbell
" Mary F widow John S h 85 Sycamore [old
" Mary I bookkeeper b 216 Arn-
" May E chiropodist 71 William rm 4 h 57 Hillman
" Merton R plumber h 12 Borden
" Nancy A widow Robert F h 33 Rounds [cery h 8 Hunter
" Nicholas S chemist 147 Chan-
" Noah B salesman 99 William h 991 Kempton [184 Kempton
" Oliver B salesman 125 Middle h
" Peter loom fixer h 54 Peckham
" Peter B died December 22 1910
" Richard J purser h 386 Union
" Richard J Mrs clerk 40 Purchase b 386 Union
" Robert weaver h 8 Acushnet av
" Robert F died March 1 1911
" Ruth M widow William G h 63 Hillman [Pleasant
" Samuel insurance agent h 281 Mt
" Susie C h 59 Foster

Davis
" Thomas h 178 Brook
" Thomas chief engineer Manomet Mills h 1305 Acusnet avenue
" Thomas E drill maker h 223 Acushnet avenue
" Thomas J h 86 Walden
" Walter weaver b 130 Ashland
" William A carpenter h 124 High
" William A city laborer City Yard
" William A piper h 52 Sherman
" William E watchman h 83 Bonney
" William F Rev pastor Pleasant St M E church h 22 Sycamore
" William F Jr student b 22 Sycamore [Tarklin Hill road
" William H clerk bds E H Davis
" William J foreman h 584 Elm
" William S timekeeper Old Colony Box Co b 80 Morgan
" William T chauffeur h 4 Smith
" William T clerk b 63 Hillman
" W F clerk 100 Fifth
" Zebina B (Z B Davis Corp) h 64 Arnold

DAVIS Z B CORP (Zebina B Davis) builders 668 Acushnet av cor E Pope See page 762
" & Hatch Spice Co (Frank E Fowler) 28 Union

DAVOL CLARENCE H insurance and real estate 23 Clifford bldg b 42 Summer See page 755

Davoll Ahira W porter h 89 Austin
" Burton G compositor Mercury h 28 Crapo [man
" Clarence J carpenter h 71 Hill-
" Edward E (R G Gallop & Co) 55 Hillman b 118 High
" Elisha carpenter h 118 High
" Joseph G h 93 Allen
" Walter E machinist b 118 High
" see Devoll [ushnet av

Dawber William spinner h 28 Ac-

Dawe Elizabeth A widow Frederick C h 907 County
" George G removed from city
" William C (W C Dawe & Co) h 159 Myrtle
" W C & Co (William C Dawe) hardware 844 Purchase [bury

Dawes William weaver h 9 Salis-

Bread, Cake, Pastry
RICHMOND & COMPANY **255-257 UNION STREET**
Bell 993 Automatic 1022

Dawnorwitz Pilot weaver h 877 S Water [h 9 Pope
Dawson Benjamin (Dawson & Son)
" Charles J spinner b 163 Shaw [lin
" Frederick A loom fixer h 3 Frank-
" George loom fixer h 163 Shaw
" George J operative b 163 Shaw
" Henry spinner b 41 Rivet
" Henry E spinner b 163 Shaw
" Herbert bottler h 543 Purchase
" Ibitson (Potomska Bowling Alleys) 705 S Water h 510 First
" Jennie widow Isaac b 9 Pope
" John spinner h 34 Robeson
" John L operative b 163 Shaw
" John T bookeeper 645 Purchase b 9 Pope [State
" Joseph (Dawson & Son) h 124
" Margaret nurse 194 Purchase b do
" Nehemiah laborer h 506 Maxfield
" Richard laborer rms 72 Maxfield
" Thomas operative b 138 Division
" Thomas roll coverer b 204 Weld
" William operative h 172 Division
" William A laborer b 163 Shaw
" William A operative b 163 State
" & Son (Benjamin and Joseph) brewers and ice mfrs 34 Brook and 645 Purchase
Day Richard laborer h 157 Elm
" Thomas E weigher D Duff & Son, Fish Island h 76 Mill
" William A light house keeper Palmer's Island h do
Days Enos E removed to Fairhaven
" Ernest shoemaker b 12 Hunter
" Joseph H painter h 12 Hunter
" William F operative b 12 Hunter
Dayton Annie E widow Luther H h 194 Summer
" George M engineer h 22 Bay
" George M Jr driver h 6 Summit
" Luther M b 22 Bay
" Luther M died May 4 1911
Deacon Jennie bookkeeper 272 South Water b 145 Hillman
" Jennie M teacher Sylvia Ann Howland school b 417 Union
" Joseph h 145 Hillman
" William inspector of plumbing 52 Pleasant h 417 Union [Swift
Deady Michael J bricklayer h 22
" Ralph apprentice b 22 Swift
Deakin Percy D clerk 474 Acushnet avenue b 143 Holly

Deakin
" William weaver b 143 Holly
Dealy Elizabeth widow Thomas h 27 Bethel
DeAmaral Corrillia widow Jason h 226 Purchase [250 Bowditch
Dean Albert E designer Neild Mill h
" A Herbert agent Cornell bldg h 217 Middle
" Frank P mason h 10 Margin
" George operative b 169 David
" George F drill worker b 15 Borden [ushnet av
" Howard B carpenter b 2389 Ac-
" Isabel S h 37 School
" James spinner bds 111 Clark
" John laborer b 8 Hazard court
" John spinner bds 111 Clark
" John H collector h 15 Borden
" Joseph G clerk Merchants National Bank rms 45 Willis
" Moses tool maker 2 Beetles lane bds 488 Acushnet avenue
" Oyster Market 17 N Second
" Ralph C b 2389 Acushnet avenue
" Roland S clerk h 4 Bonney
" Sarah P widow Aaron b 217 Middle
" Stephen weaver h 60 Peckham
" Sylvester A box maker h 2389 Acushnet avenue
" William spinner h 186 County
" William D machinist h 67 Atlantic
" William E mason h 10 Margin
Deane Cecelia A teacher I W Benjamin school b 77 Fifth
" Daniel W president 11 N Sixth h at Fairhaven
" Elmer L rodman 303 Municipal bldg b 273 Arnold
" Frank W upholstering 9 Rodman h 273 Arnold
" George R h 37 Sycamore
" Harold F upholstering 9 Rodman h at Cuttyhunk
" James police h 47 Ryan
" John oiler U St Ry Co power station h 344 Middle
" John rope carrier b 22 Roosevelt
" John G operative b 29 Ashley
" Leon C paymaster Bennett dept N E C Y Co h 281 Allen
" Peter h 22 Roosevelt

GLOBE DYE HOUSE 220 SHAWMUT AVE.
J. N. J. LONHOLDT, PROP. Telephone Connections Goods called for and Delivered
Down town Office, 52 Pleasant St., Room 1 North End Office, 1014 Acushnet Ave.

Deane
" Peter Jr rope carrier b 22 Roosevelt [Mill h 1587 Acushnet av
" Samuel L overseer Nashawena
" Thomas weaver h 30 McGurk
" Winnie E tailoress h 77 Fifth
De Arbo John laborer h 47 South
Dearborn Frank R chauffeur h 91 School
Dearden Ernest fixer b 337 Tinkham
" Frederick J loom fixer h Plainville road
" James fixer h 337 Tinkham
Deasy John mule spinner h 510 N Front
De Avelar Manuel h 45 Lombard
" Manuel J watchman h 305 Austin
De Barros Fidelle h 395 S Water
" Joseph hairdresser 177 S Water h do
" see Barros and Barrows [River
DeBeech Arthur E removed to Fall
" Charles T driver b 83 Morgan
" John janitor James B Congdon school h 482 Bolton
Debem John caulker Central wharf h 33 Wing
Deblois Joseph carpenter h 61 Dean
" Philip removed to Fairhaven
Debrosse Edmond molder h 89 Ruth
De Camp Gabriel clerk h 21 Spooner
Decate Virginia watchman h 104 Phillips avenue [Fifth
DeChaves Antonio F fireman h 108
" Isaac laborer h 201 N Second
Dechene Alfred weaver h 207 Sawyer
Decke Oscar bricklayer b 4 Rochambeau [Covell
DeCosta Domingo operative h 31
" Hector mariner h 348 S Water
" Jeffrey mariner b 5 First
" John laborer h 35 Lexington
" Joseph laborer h 54 Lindsey
" Joseph mill hand bds 63 Scott
" Joseph Jr inspector h 77 Pierce
" Lindolf laborer h 28 Grant
" Manuel operative h 64 Collette
" Manuel F drill worker b 22 Swift
" Maria widow h 12 Wing
" Marion J watchman h 22 Swift
" Mary Mrs h 440 South Water
DeCourcy Thomas F h 221 Shawmut avenue [Second
Dedads George mechanic h 501 S
Dedopoulas Brothers (Soterios & Charles) boot blacks 881 South Water [av
De Fay Joseph E twister b 113 Bates
Degagner Louis F carpenter 130 Fourth h do
De Ganger Frank h 128 Rivet
Degauff Maxim painter h 50 Phillips avenue [nell pl
DeGay Dieuonne baker rms 3 Cor-
DeGloria Maria h 74 Mosher
Degnan Katherine widow Michael h 87 Atlantic [lette
De Goff Michael painter h 117 Col-
De Gouvia Antonio C mill hand bds bds 7 Bonneau
Degrasse Charles H h 364 Kempton
Dehn Edward H stone cutter b 11 Logan [h do
" Edward W physician 23 Linden
" George R grocer 70 Cove h 23 Linden
" see Dean and Deane [Cottage
Dehoney Helen widow Thomas h 549
" John J gardener 695 County b 549 Cottage
Delacy Arthur b 8 Brock avenue
" Arthur G weaver h 32 Brock av
Delahunty Joseph glass cutter h 74 Mill
Delaire Eran fisherman h 27 Hicks
" Michael carpenter h 61 County
Delaney Thomas H engineer Kilburn Mill h 6 Acushnet avenue
Delano Annie Mrs h 14 Reynolds
" Arthur D treasurer 382 Acushnet avenue h Moreland ter [Lind
" Betsy C widow John b 58 Jenny
" Charles A removed to Tiverton
" Charles H L died Feb 24 1911
" Clark W capt steamer Kentuckian h 474 Park
" Edmund A janitor 270 Acushnet av h 1283 do
" E Flora housekeeper 11 Franklin h 176 Fourth
" Ferdinand A salesman 157 Union
" Frank R h 51 Hill
" Fred H b 88 South Sixth
" Frederick H removed to Marion
" Harvey L hairdresser h 570 South Water
" Jethro C wood 37 Crapo h do
" John F died December 19 1910

COAL AND WOOD F. T. AKIN & COMPANY
HAY AND STRAW
WALNUT, COR. WATER, 84 PLEASANT ST., 25 WELD SQ.
129 COVE STREET WHF. FOOT OF COFFIN STREET

Delano
" Julia h 20 Hawthorn [cery
" Leroy W machinist b 77 Chan-
" Lloyd S clerk h 103 Rockland
" Mary A G b 51 Hill
" Mary E Mrs h 95 Chestnut
" Nathan H h 317 Emerson (N)
" Priscilla C Mrs h 88 S Sixth
" Ralph L electrician b 77 Chancery
" Rufus B motorman h 1283 Acushnet av [399 County
" Sarah B widow Charles H L h
" Sarah E widow Harry b 51 Hill
" Seth T carpenter h 654 County
" Ursilla M widow John b 176 Fourth [Rivet h 106 do
Delarge Ferdinand shoe repairer 91
" Fred spinner b 106 Rivet
Delauriers Arthur painter h 798 Purchase [chase
Delauries Henry barber h 696 Pur-
DeLaval Melville E physician 1108 Acushnet av h do
Delcour Henry weaver h 63 Hicks
Delcourt Joseph loom fixer h 28 McGurk
Delisle Henry fixer h 357 Davis
" John A (Patnaude & Co) 1604 Acushnet av h 207 Eugenia
" Joseph A clerk 335 N Front bds 32 Holly [ty
Deller Erenne fisherman h 1060 Coun-
Deloid Charles A plumber h 96 Dunbar [Front
Delombe Arthur carpenter h 417 N
DeLonge Anna E Mrs b 32 Keen
Delour Henri weaver h 45 Hicks
De Loyd Charles A plumber 55 North Water bds Dunbar
DelPazzo Antonio baker rear 157 Coffin avenue h 157 do
" Narlie weaver b 157 Coffin av
" Vincenzo baker h 157 Coffin av
DeLude Pierre weaver b 195 Phillips avenue
Deluhe Amede laborer h 16 Hicks
" John operative b 16 Hicks
" Rose clerk 1119 Acushnet av bds 397 Bowditch
" Rudolphe harness maker 34 Pleasant bds 1205 Acushnet avenue
De Luna Isabella widow b 1 Hemlock
Delvalle Joseph porter h 277 Middle
Delwyn Amedee weaver h 947 S Water
Delyen John weaver h 32 Social
Demairo Joseph operative h 125 Division [Sawyer
Demanche Adelard operative b 322
" Edward clerk h 32 Sawyer [court
" John B second hand h 14 Hazard
" Leonidas laborer b 121 Bates av
" Louis removed from city
" Mondes toy maker b 31 Hazard
" Nap clerk h 121 Bates avenue
" Omer watchman b 31 Hazard
Demares Joseph laborer h 37 Acushnet avenue [pl
Demaris Ciserer widow bds 8 Cornell
" Alic C teamster b 134 Cedar
Demars Albert helper h 93 Perry Grove
" Arthur laborer h 211 Bowditch
" Arthur J weaver b 211 Bowditch
" George weaver h 831 Acushnet av
de Mederios Manuel Borges comber h 44 Mosher
De Mello Antone carpenter h 20 Wing
" Antone laborer h 223 Shawmut avenue
" Antone laborer b 144 S Water
" Antone operative h 310 S Second
" Antone C grocer 144 Belleville av and 88 Nash rd h 90 do
" Antone M carpenter h 78 Oak
" Antone V fireman h 924 County
" Antonio confectionery h 89 Grinnell
" Antonio grocer h 102 Mosher
" Antonio C baker h 190 Bonney
" Arthur elevatorman 36 Purchase b 99 Thompson
" August laborer h 119 Mott
" Edward time keeper h 84 Dunbar
" Fanny and Mary h 190 Bonney
" Frank mill hand h 109 Davis
" Frank C foreman h 48 Edward
" Harry C b 99 Thompson
" John laborer h 36 Thompson
" John operative h rear 20 Wing
" John C b 67 Acushnet avenue
" John C laborer N B W W h 99 Thompson [159 Allen
" John C Jr foreman N B W W h
" John R laborer h 127 Fair
" Jose R laborer N B W W h 446 Allen [ond
" Joseph foundryman h 310 S Sec-

BONNEY, FOLSTER & CO.,
The North End's Shopping Centre
Dry Goods and Men's Furnishings
945-947 Acushnet Ave., New Bedford, Mass.

De Mello
" Joseph laborer h 62 Grinnell
" Joseph operative h 17 Cotter
" Joseph U S N bds 90 Hemlock
" Joseph C clerk h 86 Nash road
" Joseph F laborer h 319 S Front
" Manuel elevatorman h 84 Earle
" Manuel operative h 310 S Second
" Manuel B mason h 59 Crapo
" Manuel C grocer 207 Bonney h 87 Rockland
" Manuel T laborer h 90 Hemlock
" Marion operative h 232 Rivet
" Mary widow Domingo S h 87 Rockland [dale av
" William, N B W W h r 230 Rock-
" William C laborer N B W W b 103 Mosher [S Second
" William laborer N B W W h 162
" William C, N B W W h 211 Acushnet avenue [net av
" William C Jr twister b 211 Acush-
" see Mello
Demers Alcide weaver b 192 Sawyer
" Alice violin teacher b 195 Davis
" Arthur weaver b 192 Sawyer
" Francis A helper h 93 Perry
" George weaver h 1 Clark
" Harmidas weaver h 7 Holly
" Hector fixer h 430 N Front
" Henry clerk 1019 Acushnet av b 195 Davis [h 200 Pleasant
" John B supt 97 William rm 311
" John G painter b 93 Perry
" Joseph shoe repairer 42 W French avenue h 31 Brock avenue
" Joseph A (P Demers & Son) 1019 Acushnet avenue h 195 Davis
" Joseph V real estate h 1871 Acushnet avenue
" Julia died Sept 5 1910
" Lavina widow Frank E h 117 Bullard [atre h 1871 Acushnet av
" Mary Mrs ticket seller Vient the-
" Melvina widow Ovilla h 192 Sawyer
" Noe weaver h 695 Purchase
" Omer weaver h 3 Hicks [Davis
" Pierre (P Demers & Son) h 195
" P & Son (Pierre and Joseph A) shoes 1019 Acushnet avenue
" Raoull clerk b 123 Bullard
" Rosaire clerk W French av cor Cove bds 2 West French av

Demers
" Ulderic fireman h 154 Cedar Grove
" see Dumas [court
Demik John weaver h 18 Morton
Deming Isador A S G Mrs h 134 State [Park h 191 Elm
De Mora Antone E hostler Court cor
" Antonio C mason h 227 Brownell
" Antonio C Jr operative b 227 Brownell
" John fireman b 227 Brownell
" Joseph baker b 227 Brownell
Demoral John laborer h rear 230 S Front [58 Sherman
DeMoranville Alton drill worker h
" Charles A teamster h 73 Foster
" Clifford S grinder h 351 Court
De MORANVILLE D HERBERT general teamster N Y N H & H Depot No 4 door and 83 Thomas h do See page 787
" Edgar L driver 83 Thomas b do
" Ella F widow Walter F h 3136 Acushnet avenue [Thomas
" Ethel M clerk 125 Middle b 83
" Frederick carpenter h 2753 Acushnet avenue
" Harold A driver b 83 Thomas
" Herbert C foreman h 81 North
" Isaac S laborer b 129 Pleasant
" James B removed to N Dartmouth
" Mary Mrs sewer 36 Purchase b 48 Newton
" Philip C b 129 Pleasant
" Stephen E laborer h 129 Pleasant
" Sydney B carpenter h 2445 Acushnet avenue opp Osgood av
" Theron G teamster h 357 Elm (W) [Oak
Dempsey Bridget widow Daniel h 45
Denault William laborer h 359 Coggeshall [h 109 Clinton
Denby Francis J commercial traveler
Deneault Alfred fisherman h 112 Phillips avenue [avenue
" Alfred mill hand b 112 Phillips
" Alfred J stone quarry h 313 Austin
" Arsene painter h 99 Perry
" David stonecutter h 11 Adams
" Delene widow h 179 State

Painters Supplies Wall Papers Room Mouldings Ladders
M. P. B. Silva & Son BRUSHES
157 ACUSHNET AVENUE Both Phones NEW BEDFORD

Deneault
" Eva telephone operator 57 N Second bds 179 State
" Henry stonecutter h 107 Durfee
" Lena widow Joseph h 221 Purchase
" Moses mason h 366 State
" Pierre h 363 Coggeshall
" Rose B Mrs dry goods 931 County h 366 State [Front
" Serville stone cutter h 326 North
" Thomas F driver bds 313 Austin
" T Arthur mason h 366 State
Deneen Daniel police sergeant sta 5 h 190 Merrimac [Whitman
Denesha David box maker bds 90
" Hubert shipper b 90 Whitman
" Theodore S carpenter h 90 Whitman [251 State
Denham Christopher operative h
" Edward h 128 School [do
" Edwin B osteopath 229 Sawyer h
" Emma Mrs h 43 N Sixth [chase
" E Thomas belt man h 535 Pur-
" George B laborer b 82 Liberty
" George H carpenter h 527 Purchase
" Joseph operative b 256 Clark
" Joseph H spinner h 126 Nash rd
" Thomas M h 363 Cottage
Denick John weaver h 18 Morton ct
Denis Philip removed from city
DENISON BROTHERS CO coal yards foot Hillman and 77 Rivet main office 32 Pleasant See front edge
" Henry C president Denison Bros Co president 382 Acushnet av and vice president Mechanics National Bank h 160 Cottage
Dennett Thomas machinist h 322 Coffin avenue [Tinkham
Dennette Edward painter h 165
Denney Wilbur glass cutter h 24 Madison [bury
Dennin William operative h 9 Salis-
Dennis Catherine C b 193 Middle
" Edith A b 193 Middle
" Henry G contractor h 193 Middle
" John N butter h 241 Court
" John R teamster 188 S Water h 21 Lexington
" John W h 574 Union
" John W (Dennis & Ellis) 6 Purchase h at Washington D C

Dennis
" Julia C clerk 160 Purchase b 11 Fairmount [mount
" Manuel R city laborer h 11 Fair-
" William R watchman h 193 Middle
" & Ellis (J W Dennis and W Ellis) Specialty Shoe Store 6 Purchase and restaurant 150 Union [Cottage
Dennison Charles shoemaker h 373
" Charles F machinist b 373 Cottage [Sycamore
" Ellen R widow Artson h 131
" Memorial City Mission Social Settlement 755 First
" Sarah A h 131 Sycamore
Denoyer Henry overseer Sharp Mill h Nelson
Denton Thomas laborer h 46 Wood
De Palteau Levi carpenter b 239 Sawyer [pher b 50 Tallman
Depault Cordelia widow Christo-
" Donat weaver h 50 Tallman
" Emile fixer h 314 N Front
" Ernest gas fitter 915 Acushnet av rms corner Tallman and Acushnet avenue
" Victor third hand h 314 N Front
Depontbriand Alpherie shoemaker h 311 North Front
DePonte Joseph operative h 303 S First [pleton
DePorto Joseph fisherman h 21 Sta-
" Joseph J twister b 21 Stapleton
" Manuel twister tender b 21 Stapleton [Fourth
Deprato Eugene fireman bds 205
" Louis fruit 983 S Water h 101 Hall [Front
Deptula Wladyslaw weaver h r 224 N
Deragon Sylva spinner h 949 County
Derby Ann Mrs variety 1051 S Water h 1049 do
" Charles A supt 194 Purchase and physician 88 do h do
" John laborer h 795 S Water
Derbyshire Joseph spinner bds 191 Dean [av
" Samuel operative h 28 W French
" Samuel scalemaker b 28 W French av [chell
DeRego Joseph operative h 35 Mit-

Steiger-Dudgeon Co.
"The WOMAN'S Store."
Tel. Bell 82 & 83, Branches connecting all depts.
" " 160 For Office only. Auto. 1211

SUMPTIONS, ASSORTMENTS AT ALL TIMES OF DEPENDABLE DRY GOODS

DeResendes Magida widow Joseph M h 54 Lombard [Walnut
Derick Otto L clerk 201 Union b 53
Deroche Arthur doffer b 214 Sawyer
" Arthur weaver h 31 Hicks
" Edmond weaver h 214 Sawyer
" Felix teamster h 167 N Front
" John painter h 944 County
" Julian operative h 111 N Front
Derocher Alphonse weaver bds 112 Mott
" Arthur loom fixer bds 112 Mott
" Camille b 112 Mott [County
DeRoches Hiliase plasterer b 1101
" Mary widow h 135 N Front
" Norbert weaver h 1101 County
" Philiase removed from city
Derosier Aldea clerk 1119 Acushnet av h 178 N Front
" Lena Mrs h 32 McGurk
" Louise clerk 1119 Acushnet av b 104 Weld [12 Beetle
Derosiers Charles bookkeeper h
" Charles M removed to Fairhaven
DeSantos Antone mill hand h 65 Acushnet av [Water
Desaroviner George laborer b 909 S
Desaulniers Clara milliner bds 24 Adams [Co h 56 Nye
" Ephraim blacksmith U St Ry
" Ernest T watchmaker 143 Cove and 1075 Acushnet av rms 120 Tallman
" Joseph driver h 171 Weld
" Joseph teamster h 431 Pleasant
" Joseph A bookkeeper h 24 Adams
" Oliver conductor b 32 Nye
Desault Edward laborer b 31 Hazard
Desautels Antoine operative h 31 Ashley
" Arthur h 20 Covell
DESAUTELS HUGHES carpenter and builder 45 Brock av h do See page 760
" Joseph spinner h 97 Perry
" Minnie Mrs h 221 Sawyer
DESAUTELS STANISLAS real estate 269 Sawyer h 1918 Acushnet avenue See page 758
Desbien Joseph weaver h 42 County
Desbiens Eli carpenter h 88 Ruth
Descelle Arcelia widow Charles bds 159 Whitman [man
Deschaine Antoine weaver h 64 Tall-

Deschaine
" Euphemie carder h 64 Tallman
" Frank lineman U St Ry Co h 688 Purchase
" Louis teamster b 929 County
" Noel fisherman bds 113 Eugenia
" Onesime weaver h 36 Jouvett
" Rose housekeeper 64 Tallman h do
" Telesphore spinner h 46 Jouvett
" Valida weaver h 64 Tallman
Descheneau Joseph lineman h 688 Purchase [Tinkham
Descheneaux Clovis helper b 193
" Oswald carpenter h 193 Tinkham
Deschenes J Alfred ticket seller R R station h 234 Austin
Des Coteau Arthur machinist h 150 Collette [b 226 State
Desforges Henriette sewer 185 Union
Deshon Thomas laborer h 82 Cedar
Desiel Eulege operative h 23 Covill
Desillets Horace operative 101 Kenyon h 1009 County [Fourth
DeSilva John F carpenter h 216
Desjardins Alcide J mgr b 125 Rivet
" Alfred driver r 28 Larch h 21 Mosher [Fair
" Amedee H mgr 889 S Water h 40
" Ancline carpenter h 190 Rivet
" Ancline 2nd carder h 96 Division
" Armand waiter 1168½ Acushnet avenue [Rivet
" Arthur clerk 889 S Water b 125
" Exliard weaver h 115½ Bullard
" Ferdinand carpenter h 125 Rivet
" Ferdinand Jr harnessmaker 34 Pleasant h 106 Rivet
" Henrietta widow Eusebe h 35 Independent
" Joseph weaver b 125 Rivet
" J Anatole interpreter overseers of poor b 190 Rivet
" Lougee weaver b 190 Rivet
" Mary widow Alphonse h 82 Independence [Second
" Paul polo instructor h 612 S
" Silva operative h 196 Rivet
Desjarlais George weaver b 359 N Front [man
Desjeunesse Jean B fixer h 154 Whit-
Deslandes Cleophis operative h 109 Brook
" Joseph weaver h 248 Rivet

PELEG H. SHERMAN 506 COUNTY ST.
FUNERAL DIRECTOR AND EMBALMER
OFFICE PHONES. Bell 690-13. Auto. 1305.
RESIDENCE PHONES. Bell 690-12. Auto. 1306.

Deslandes
" Wilfred letter carrier h 66 Robeson
Deslaurier Alphonse laborer h 383 N [N Front
" J Arthur clerk foot Willis h 74 Hicks
Deslauriers Cleophis painter h 248 Bowditch
" Ernestine M dry goods 1521 [Acushnet av h do
" Henry barber 692 Purchase b r 679 do
" Hormidas Rev pastor St Anthony's church h 1359 Acushnet av
" Nelson carpenter h 327 Sawyer
" Victor clerk b 1028 Acushnet av
" Zepherin teamster h 140 Tallman
Desmarais Alfred barber h 857 First
" Alfred died Nov 30 1910
" Amedee fixer h 968 S Water
" Arthur driver b 149 Phillips av
" Arthur weaver b 168 Cove
" Azilda widow h 27 Roosevelt
" Clorinda milliner b 149 Phillips avenue
" Damasse watchman h 2 Thatcher
" Damien mason h 535 Acushnet avenue
" Delos blacksmith b 2 Thatcher
" Frank fixer b 27 Roosevelt
" Henri weaver b 2 Thatcher
" Henry carpenter b 149 Phillips av
" Hubert weaver h 163 Holly
" Joseph fixer h 220 Church
" Joseph weaver h 149 Phillips av
" Joseph weaver b 571 S Water
" Lodias bricklayer b 15 Adams
" Lodina Mrs h 115 Dunbar
" Marcville weaver h 166 Dean
" Philip teamster b 535 Acushnet avenue
" Pierre machinist h 192 W French [avenue
" Raoul comber bds 149 Phillips av
" Rose M widow Alfred b 857 First
" Victoria removed from city
" Wilfred removed from city
" William weaver b 2 Thatcher
Desmeilier A weaver b 1145 Kempton
Desmond Annie T stenographer 301 Municipal bldg b 117 Hillman
" John F clerk rm 4 Municipal bldg h 18 Homer
" Joseph C (Power & Desmond) 67 William bds 117 Hillman
" Stephen W H died Oct 30 1910

Desmond
" Timothy J mgr Savoy Hotel 343 Acushnet av b do
" William F bookkeeper 29 Bowditch h 143 Merrimac
Desnoyer Henry overseer h 64 Nelson
" Louis carder h 581 S Second
" Wilfred weaver h 46 Salisbury
Desorcy Joseph carpenter h 47 Brock av
Desormier George weaver b 909 S [Water
" Massell clerk 860 Acushnet av b 202 State
De Sota George S operative h 159 [Rockland
Despres Alphonse A clerk 1404 Acushnet av h 1356 do
" Marcel mill hand bds 1356 Acush- [net av
DesRochers Joseph fixer h 696 First
Desroches Alfred H laborer b 168 Cove
" John B painter h 86 Nye
" Joseph molder h 871 Purchase
" Joseph weaver h 152 Whitman
" Julian weaver h 111 N Front
" Louis wood cutter bds 111 N Front
" Louis H weaver h 128 Cove
" Louis H Jr fixer h 128 Cove
" Wilfred clerk 878 Purchase h 163 Weld
Desrosier Adelard carpenter h 17 Ad- [ams
" Alice weaver h 190 Earle
" Clovis weaver h 67 Phillips av
" John B blacksmith 200 Mill h 277 Park
" Joseph weaver b 14 McGurk
" Noel carpenter h 9 Salisbury
Desrosiers Albert weaver bds 307 N Front
" Alexis h 307 N Front
" Arthur doffer b 307 N Front
" George h 370 Kempton
" Harmidas weaver b 307 N Front
" Hector twister b 307 N Front
" Henry twister tender bds 1733 Acushnet av
" Jeffrey twister tender b 1733 Acu- [shnet av
" Joseph H weaver h 307 N Front
" Joseph M fixer h 40 Bullard
" Leon h 307 N Front
" Martial baker h 92 Bowditch
" Napoleon carpenter h 1733 Acushnet avenue
" Napoleon plumber 1545 Acushnet av h at Fairhaven

F. T. AKIN & CO. PAINTERS AND DECORATORS

Desrosiers
" Wilfred twister tender b 1733 Acushnet av [Acushnet av
DesRuisseau Emil operative bds 96
" Israel b 96 Acushnet av
" James operative b 96 Acushnet av
" Joseph overseer Potomska Mills h 96 Acushnet av
" Philip spinner h 97 Austin
Dessaint Ludger weaver h 55 Hope
Dessere Wilfred loom fixer h 11 Hyacinth [mer
Dessert Anthony fixer h 154 Black-
" Joseph hairdresser 1110 S Water h 20 Viall
Dessier Conrad C dentist h 78 Ashland [23 Kenyon
Destradeau Joseph horse trader h
Destremps Louis E architect 251 Union h 124 Mt Pleasant [rd
Desuisseau Henri weaver h 18 Cove
DeTerra Andrew E spinner h 27 Viall
" Charles E laborer b 25 Salisbury
" John E machinist b 399 Rivet
" Manuel F city laborer h 1 Smith street court [b do
Deu Yee B mgr 949 Acushnet av
Devaney Ellen h 287 Cedar
Devaux Oliver weaver 49 Beetle
Dever Maurice S machinist b 41 Rivet [cipal bldg h 291 Middle
Deverell John H J watchman Muni-
Devine Bertha waitress Parker House b do
" John laborer h 99 Fruit
" John laborer h 559 S Second
" John weaver h 560 S Second
" Margaret F h 702 Acushnet av
" Mary widow h 31 Morton ct
Devito Antonio laborer h 569 Acushnet avenue [av b 360 Cedar
Devlin Bernard mgr 1518 Acushnet
" Bernard plumber b 92 Belleville road
" Catherine Mrs h 955 Purchase
" Dennis I teamster h 259 Mt Pleasant
" Francis weaver h 495 First
" Henry checker b 11 Logan
" Hugh mill hand 1649 Acushnet av
" James laborer h 92 Belleville rd
" James millworker b 495 First

Devlin
" John W electrician b 955 Purchase [chase
" Joseph H laborer bds 955 Pur-
" Owen clerk b 92 Belleville road
" Thomas G laborer b 955 Purchase
Devoll Arthur L mill hand h 306 Chancery
" Daniel T lawyer 402 Merchants Bank bldg b 18 Lincoln
" George H paper hanger h 122 Florence
" James F (Richmond & Co) baker 255 Union and 425 S Water h 5 Cottage
" Milton b 548 County [Purchase
" Pardon & Son (estate) shoes 32
" Pardon H farmer b 2924 Acushnet av [rd
" Roland G painter h Winterville
" William O treas Potomska Mills h 549 County [ion
" William O Jr reporter h 400 Un-
" see Davoll [Water
Devost Fred second hand bds 821 S
" Joseph baker h 125 Phillips av
" Oliver weaver b 49 Beetle
Dewey Robert weaver b Bowditch st
Dewhurst Charles painter h 35 Howard
" Doctor R weaver b 38 Bowditch
" Edward operative b 35 Howard
" Ernest cashier 120 Purchase rm 401 b 12 Trinity
" Frank carpenter b 12 Trinity
" George weaver h 296 Tinkham
" John laborer h 163 Tinkham
" Matthew spinner b 163 Tinkham
" Moses fixer h 64 Hathaway
" Nathaniel weaver h 12 Trinity
" Robert spinner b 48 Vine
" Robert weaver h 8 Morton court
Dewis Young beamer b 621 First
DeWitt Utley E glasscutter bds 271 Park
DeWolf Alfred W (DeWolf & Vincent) hardware 111 William h 109 Elm [Middle
" Amanda J widow William h 169
" Anna M catalóguer public library b 104 Fourth [chase
" Charles F lodgings h 380 Pur-
" Charles H teamster 45 School h 50 do [Second
" Charles O watchman h 106 S

Don't dream of what you are going to do! Go and do it.
Kinyon's Short-hand School
Odd Fellows Bldg., Cor. William and Pleasant Sts., New Bedford, Mass.

De Wolf
" Edward A officer H C b 284 Union [Second
" Edward W drillworker bds 106 S
" Gilman F salesman b 169 Middle
" Henry C machinist operative b 106 S Second
" Mary bds 10 Spruce
" Ward student b 109 Elm
DeWOLF & VINCENT (Alfred W DeWolf and Mark T Vincent) hardware cutlery and agricultural implements 111 William See page 44
Dews Henry H veterinary 73 State h do [school b 11 Franklin
Dexter Anna I teacher Merrimac st
" Arthur A clerk 1 Pleasant b 56 Campbell
" Charles E carpenter h 247 Palmer
" Charles O agent Beacon Mfg Co h 350 Union [man
" David A glasscutter h 217 Hill-
" Elizabeth nurse b 914 Belleville avenue [died Dec 24 1910
" Elizabeth (widow William P)
" George E clerk Sharp Mill bds 80 Brock av [Palmer
" George W S inspector rms 274
" Gertrude W clerk b 274 Palmer
" Henry K polisher h 365 North
" Howard N shoe sorter h 50 Campbell
" Johiah A Mrs h 148 Summer

LEMUEL LeBARON DEXTER
ATTORNEY AND COUNSELLOR AT LAW
NOTARY PUBLIC
37 Masonic Building
Pleasant corner Union Street
Bell Telephone 699-4
Residence at Mattapoisett

Dexter Lemuel LeB lawyer 37 Masonic bldg h at Mattapoisett
" Marion H teacher Jireh Swift school b 148 Summer
" Phoebe C widow Ainsworth h 56 Campbell

Dextradeur Alfred liquors 1501 Acushuet av h 869 County
" Charles operative b 62 Kenyon
DEXTRADEUR CHARLES J lathing contractor 363 N Front h do See page 754
" George mill hand b 275 N Front
" Joseph bldg mover 23 Kenyon h do
" Joseph mill hand b 275 N Front
" Mitchell weaver h 62 Kenyon
" Rebecca widow Edward h 275 N Front
" Thophile carder h 198 Tinkham
" Victor laborer h 34 Hazard
Dextras Dosithe carpenter h 100 Holly
" Gregoire operative b r 61 Dean
" Hermenegilde third hand h r 61 Dean
" Joseph weaver h 21 Washburn
" Michael h 87 Bowditch
" Philias weaver b 87 Bowditch
" Zephir carpenter b 100 Holly
Dextraze Aldea b 72 Delano
" Aldea musician b 184 Sawyer
" Arthur removed from city
DEXTRAZE CAMILLE wines and liquors 1276 Acushnet av bds 87 Bowditch See page 779
" Delphis clerk 950 First h 42 County
" Ephraim carpenter h 79 Bullard
" Joseph clerk 1413 Acushnet av b 100 Holly [42 County
" Louis (Louis Dextraze & Son) h
" Louis J (Louis Dextraze & Son) h 42 County
" Louis & Son (Louis and Louis J Dextraze) liquors 590 First
" Phillip clerk 962 Acushnet av b 87 Bowditch
Dhaze Camille machinist h 61 Dean
Diamond Charles C chauffeur bds 120 S Sixth
" James coachman h 159 Park
" Joseph H watchman h 120 S Sixth
" William C laster h 101 Morgan
Dias Albert F machinist b 129 Bonney [h 129 Bonney
" Antonio F liquors 165 S Water
" Arthur operative b 48 Parker
" Benjamin h 291 Hillman [ter
" Joaquim operative h 464 S Wa-
" Joaquim slubber tender h 536 S Water

HASKELL BROS. DEALERS IN
ICE
400 COURT STREET TELEPHONE CONNECTION NEW BEDFORD, MASS.

Dias
" John carpenter h 163 Crapo
" John carpenter b 28 County
" John F burnisher b 53 Fair
" John F (Dias & Chase) 540 S Water h 16 Crapo
" John F Mrs h 16 Griffin
" John S mill hand b 49 Larch
" Joseph clerk h 261 Rivet
" Joseph laborer h 32 Hollyhock
" Joseph laborer h 40 Katharine
" Joseph operative h 14 Cotter
" Joseph 2nd clerk The Pairpoint Corp h 47 Seventh
" Joseph F clerk h 53 Fair
" Joseph V laborer h 115½ Fifth
" Joseph V toolmaker h 33 Wing
" Josephine dressmaker 152 Allen b do
" Josephine J widow Raymond h [207 Allen
" Lionel A actor b 129 Bonney
" Louis F laborer b 201 Fourth
" Manuel farm hand Almshouse b do [435 Bolton
" Manuel laborer h 32 Rotch block
" Manuel Mrs h 317 S Water
" Margaret J school nurse b 106 South
" Marianna laundress rms 41 High
" Mark third hand h 39 Stowell
" Mary E vamper b 207 Allen
" Mary J widow Daniel S h 152 Allen
" Virginia b 207 Allen
" & Chase (John F Dias Henry E Chase) liquors 540 S Water
Diaz Flora widow Joseph A h 106 South
" Margaret J nurse b 106 South
Dibbs Thomas H harnessmaker 860 Acushnet av h 69 Hick [av
Diberg Sabar laborer h 516 Acushnet
Dichon Albini laborer h 14 McGurk
Dick Edmund barber h 16 Washburn
" William C student b 194 Arnold
Dickens Henry I teamster h 14 Topham
" James E bds 14 Topham
Dickenson Walter second hand h 362 Coffin avenue [h 43 Foster
Dickerman Helen S widow Joseph C
Dickinson Albert overseer Nashawena Mill h 160 Earle
Dickson Elijah W shoemaker 321 County h 460 Bolton

Dickson
" Frederick overseer h 11 Hickory
" William operative h 486 Rivet
DiClementi Antoni h 6 Pearl
Didier Jacques weaver h 124 County
Dictier George fixer h 55 Delano
Dietz George weaver h 19 Salisbury
Diggle Arnold milk h 239 Field
" Herbert h 125 Bonney
" John W engineer City M Co h 125 Bonney
Dignam Georgia M teacher Abraham Lincoln school b 45 Parker
Dilworth Alice widow h 190 Rivet
" James asst city clerk 208 Municipal bldg h 45 Parker
Dillingham Abraham L carrier R F D No 2 h at Acushnet
" Alberta bookkeeper 158 Purchase b at Acushnet
" Alfred B rms 64 Willis
" Anna B widow Naaman H h 177 Grinnell [deeds h 139 Maxfield
" Elizabeth J indexer registry of
" Grace W teacher Merrimac st school b 64 Willis [Acushnet
" Ruth L cashier 163 Union b at
" Walter S embalmer 7 S Sixth h 35 Emerson (S)
Dillon Mary h 19 High
" Rose Mrs h 21 Madison
Diman Ezra treas and mgr 144 Front h at Acushnet
" see Diamond and Dimond
Dimond Joseph H second mate h 153 Acushnet avenue
" Myra widow Hugh h 183 Austin
Dinelle Damien weaver h 88 Nye
Dingwell Beatrice M bookkeeper 45 Purchase rm 2 b 109 Willis
" Herbert M carpenter h 109 Willis
Dinneen Catherine and Abbe h Briggs court
Dinnigan Daniel G publisher The Catholic Union rms 127 Kempton [b 48 Davis
Dinos Assim clerk 1282 Acushnet av
Dinter Bruno weaver h 156 Holly
" Valentine Mrs h 366 Pleasant
Dion Adolph h 37 Acushnet av
" Adolph fixer h 128 Rivet
" Alfred grocer 2 Hicks h do
" Alice cashier 1119 Acushnet av b 1117 do
" Alphonse operative h 172 Rivet

J. F. CROSSLEY 223 MILL STREET COR. EMERSON PHONE
STEAM and HOT WATER HEATING
GAS FITTING and FIXTURES

Dion
" Andre removed from city
" Antoinette weaver b 172 Rivet
" Arsene weaver h r 32 Acushnet avenue
" Arthur A operative h 259 Fourth
" A John yard master Hathaway Mfg Co h 172 Rivet
" Charles weaver h 60 Cove
" Charles O organist St Hyacinth church h 163 County
" Dominic operative b 174 Hatch
" Edward laborer h 52 Hicks
" Francis weaver h 59 Ruth av
" Francois weaver h 59 Ruth
" Frank laborer h 799 S First
" George student b 78 Mt Pleasant
DION HARMIDAS P bakery 1070 County h 155 Ashland See page 773
" Henry weaver h 128 Eugenia
" Isadore helper 1100 Acushnet av b 455 Belleville av
" Jean B sec 1205 Acushnet av h 78 Mt Pleasant [Earle
" Joseph baker 59 Bullard h 179
" Joseph weaver b 60 Cove
" Joseph A weaver h 35 Ashland
" J H clerk b 17 Jouvett
" Louis laborer b 7 Salisbury
" Louis operative h 7 Salisbury
" Louis Z builder 455 Belleville av h do [net av
" Magloire carpenter h 1117 Acush-
" Marcelle A stonemason h 174 Hatch
" Mary widow h 8 Bowditch
" Napoleon weaver h 11 Penniman
" Nora widow Ernest clerk 1119 Acushnet av h 178 Bowditch
" Oliva lineman b 199 Phillips av
" Oliver wheelwrigh 222 Mill h 172 Rivet
" Pierre laborer b 194 Dean [av
" Ralph weaver b 1098 Acushnet
" Rosanna O dressmaker 1117 Acushnet av b do
" Stephen machinist h 151 Tallman
" Timothee clerk 100 Fifth h 536 Elm (W)
" Timothy waiter h 536 W Elm
" Victor B druggist 1201 Acushnet av h 1079 County [av
" Walter carpenter b 1117 Acushnet

Dion
" Walter driver 1070 County bds 78 Mt Pleasant [ant
" Walter student bds 78 Mt Pleas-
" Zephirin clerk 155 Coffin av bds 179 Earle [Fruit
Dionizio Manuel carpenter h 84
Dionne Adelie widow J Ernest h 1221 Acushnet av
" Albert carpenter b 282 Davis
" Arsene shoemaker 266 Sawyer h 80 Beetle
" Arthur weaver h 13 Vaill
" Edward laborer h 52 Hicks
" Henry weaver h 5 Jean
" Hercule loom fixer h 282 Davis
" Irene painter h 354 Coffin av
" John wood and coal 132 N Front h do
" Joseph fisherman h 21 Hicks
" Joseph foreman h 505 Bowditch
" Joseph A shoemaker 266 Sawyer b 80 Beetle
" J Ernest died Jan 8 1911 [ditch
" Laura widow J Ernest b 178 Bow-
" Peter laborer b 194 Dean
DIONNE WALTER painter and decorator 14 Jean h do See page 752
Direct Importing Co teas 80 Purchase
Deiseuette Arthur clerk bds 42 Weld
Ditchfield Frank weaver b 40 Cove
" Peter h 23 Jouvett
Dixon Annie E clerk 65 Purchase b 290 Pleasant
" Arthur removed from city
" David weaver h 26 Willard
" Frank L pressman 21 N Second b 84 State
" Grace S teacher James B Congdon school b 89 State
" Henry H (Paul & Dixon) 303 Merchants Bank bldg
" James G operative bds 15 Richmond [Reynolds
" John W grocer 214 Weld b 34
" Joseph h 34 Reynolds
" Joseph h 55 Brock av
" Mary E clerk 37 Purchase rm 16 b 15 Richmond [State
" Sarah S widow Joseph P h 84
" Thomas, U S A b 55 Brock av
" Walter h 15 Richmond
" William R died April 9 1911

CHARLES A. CROSHERE CARRIAGE AND AUTO
38 FOURTH ST. Bell Phone 1964-23 **PAINTING**

Dixwell Charles rms 283 Union
Diz Claudio removed from city
Dlouhy Charles mill hand h 89 Hathaway [b 31 Fifth
Doane Alice K bookkeeper 185 Union
" Edwin C bookkeeper 14 N Sixth b 120 Sycamore [292 Palmer
" Isaac S floorman 748 Purchase h
" Joshua G salesman h 120 Sycamore
" Myra L Mrs h 31 Fifth
" Robert N B health inspector 52 Pleasant rms 29 Fifth
" Rodman clerk b 161 William
" Ruth C bookkeeper b 31 Fifth
" Susan E bookkeeper 41 Purchase bds 83 Sycamore [Sherman
" Susan J widow Simeon h 24
" William L R clerk 8 Union h 161 William
" see Done [burn
Doante George weaver bds 50 Wash-
Dobbyn Joseph A supt money order div Post Office h 307 Court
Dobson Frank driver 386 Acushnet av h 514 Rivet
" William weaver bds 12 Viall
Docekal Adam weaver h 14 Felton
" Alois weaver h Felton street
Docker Frederick W slasher h 170 Ashland
Dodd A Margaret Mrs manicure 120 Purchase rm 206 h 70 Rockland
Dodds James police h 126 Division
" James J machinist h 120 Division
Dodge Albert glasscutter b 7 Harrison
" Annie A Mrs h 7 Harrison
" Arthur clerk b 7 Harrison
" Frederick R photo engraver Standard h 93 Park
" George J (Jones & Dodge) 202 N Water h 43 Mill
" Grace B principal Friends Academy 25 Morgan
" Harry overseer N B S Co
" Louisa A Mrs h 44 Mill
Doehla John third hand h 394 Earle
Doherty Edward P police h 270 Allen
" James C h 442 Purchase
" James J clerk b 442 Purchase
" John carder b 18 Myrtle
" John city laborer h 15 Welcome
" John (engineer) rem from city

Doherty
" John Jr city laborer b 15 Welcome
" John J h 50 Clark
" John J brakeman h 264 Weld
" John J city laborer b 15 Welcome
" Lizzie Mrs h 7 E Durfee
" Michael F city laborer b 15 Welcome
" Thomas stoker h 179 Park
" Thomas teamster h 222 N Second
Dohoney Daniel J liquors 5 N Second rms 25 William
Doige James insurance agent h 207 Brock avenue [Nye
Doiron Wilfred third hand h 37
Dolan Bridget widow b 93 Belleville road
" Daniel mill hand h 206 Brock av
" Dennis carpenter h 38 Division
" John carder h 18 Myrtle
" Patrick laborer h 865 County
" Patrick molder h 885 County
Dolecal Frank glassworker h 14 Felton [1910
Dollard Elizabeth L died Sept 2
" Ellen variety 521 Rivet b 519 do [b 588 Cottage
" Nellie F asst at Public Library
" Peter fisherman b 188 Collette
" William copy holder Standard h 193 Park
Dollery John J laborer b 41 Rivet
Dolloff Emma S h 232 Pleasant
Dombovand Harold teamster h 6 Walnut [Washburn
Dombrowski Joseph fisherman h 22
Domina Frederick W Rev pastor Penticostal church of Nazarine b 83 Atlantic [erty
" Ruth clerk 70 Purchase b 28 Lib-
Domingos Andrea laborer h 216 S Front [121 Coggeshall
" Anthony laborer 748 Purchase h
" Jacintho mariner h 81 Thompson
Domperre Alexander baker h 13 Viall
Donaghy Alex h 194 Maxfield [more
" Andrew H carpenter h 43 Syca-
" Anna J h 84 School
" Hugh L blacksmith 447 Kempton h 218 Brownell
" James J asst engineer N B F D h 89 Washington [39 Crapo
" John W captain H & L No 3 h
" Joseph salesman city pier No 2 h 194 Maxfield

J. G. NICHOLSON
LUMBER, SASH, DOORS and BLINDS
BOWDITCH STREET, NEW BEDFORD, MASS.

Donaghy
" Mary E h 84 School
" Mary L stenographer P Corp b 194 Maxfield [h 92 Thompson
" Nellie Mrs cashier 36 Purchase
" Samuel J florist 162 Ash (N) h do
" Samuel N grocer 205 Brownell b 218 do
" Samuel W treer bds 162 Ash (N)
" Thomas Jr real estate h 22 Fifth
" William ice 78 Chancery h do
Donahue Frank L clerk Bridge sq bds 38 Fifth
" James laborer b 69 Sixth
" John F operative h 207½ State
" John H mgr 69 Purchase b 82 Elm [S Sixth
" John J steward 246 Union b 69
" Joseph F cashier P & R C & P Co h 53 Campbell [State
" Thomas F copperworker h 209½
" Timothy city laborer h 133 State
" William J boilermaker b 69 S Sixth [Nye
Donaldson John mill hand h 127
" William silk dyer bds 119 David
Done Harry violin teacher 121 Austin b do [h 121 Austin
" Thomas R clerk Pierce Mfg Corp
" see Doane [h 178 Blackmer
Donley William shipper 131 Court
Donnelly Arthur insurance agent 37 Purchase rm 23 b 284 Fourth
" James electrician 141 Purchase rms 72 High [Fourth
" Jennie widow Patrick h 284
" John copperworker h 966 County
" John machinist h 172 Rivet
" John rivetmaker 8 Hazard's lane b 172 Rivet
" John weaver bds 966 County
" Joseph weaver h 1 Hyacinth
" Leo quiller bds 130 Mott
" Mary nurse rms 57 Maple
" Mary widow h 56 Middle
" Mary widow Michael b 79 Linden
" Mary E stenographer 37 Purchase rm 12 bds 835 First
" Michael F laborer b 835 First
" Mina nurse rms 57 Maple
" Peter J overseer Page Mfg Co b 169 Union [av
" Stephen foreman b 1098 Acushnet
" Timothy laborer h 835 First

Donovan Bridget widow Richard h 52 Kempton
" Daniel G roofer bds 84 Allen
" Dennis h 943 County
" James laborer b 232 N Second
" James F chauffeur b 8 Wing
" Joanna widow Patrick h 12 Wall
" John laborer h 32 Clark
" John solderer h 12 Wall
" John E salesman 382 Acushnet av h 143 Clinton [Fourth
" Margaret widow Michael J h 211
" Mary E fancy goods 133 Purchase h 150 Middle
" Matthew machinist b 12 Wall
" Matthew teamster h 32 Franklin
" Michael laborer b 12 Wall
" Patrick mason h 90 Austin [do
" Sylvester E physician 8 Wing h
" Timothy city laborer h 934 County
" Timothy laborer h 115 Thompson
" Timothy J F roll coverer h 620 Cottage
" William driver b 77 N Second
" William eyeletmaker h 934 County
Donth Joseph weaver h 179 Dean
" Robert spinner b 179 Dean
Dontigny Alfred piper 125 Middle b 79 Kenyon
" Flora dressmaker b 79 Kenyon
" Joseph plumber b 79 Kenyon
" Narcisse operative h 79 Kenyon
Doolan Catherine widow Michael h 772 County
" Patrick M removed to Fall River
" Peter weaver h 158 Reynolds
Dooley George sécond hand h 96 Linden
Doolittle Dwight T & Son lunch 1027 Acushnet av b do
" Frank (D T Doolittle & Son) 1027 Acushnet av b do
Doplaise Amedee lunch Cove c First h 54 Salisbury [Court
Doran Arthur S stonecuter bds 404
" Florence G widow William h 23 Ash (S) [138 Fourth
" James ladderman H & L No 3 b
" James P lawyer 5 Masonic bldg h 76 Bedford [h do
" Lauretta K physician 76 Bedford
" Margaret E widow William h 138 Fourth [b 138 Fourth
" Mollie K stenographer 45 School

Steiger-Dudgeon Co.
"The WOMAN'S Store."
Tel. Bell 82 & 83, Branches connecting all depts.
" " 160 For Office only. Auto. 1211

SUMPTIONS, ASSORTMENTS AT ALL TIMES OF DEPENDABLE DRY GOODS

Doran
" Samuel L coachman h 62 Chancery [91 Atlantic
" Samuel W record clerk P O h
Dore Adelard clerk 1347 Acushnet av b 132 Tallman [ter
Dorey Emma clerk bds 1183 S Wa-
" Octave widow h 1083 S Water
Dorgan Joseph operative b 587 Purchase
" Louise C stenographer b 5 Tilton
" Mary Z teacher William H Taylor school b 5 Tilton [Tilton
" Timothy J carriagemaker h 5
Dorman Allison R teacher High school h 114 Mill [ker
Dorr William A carpenter h 74 Par-
" see Dawe [State
Dorrigan James A shoemaker h 128
Dosrois Peter weaver b 226 N Second
Dostaler Abraham operative h 141 N Front
" Joseph operative b 141 N Front
" Joseph S salesman 1056 Acushnet avenue h 5 Reynolds
Doucet Joseph S salesman 1031 Acushnet av h 5 Reynolds [lette
Doucette Domicile widow b 187 Col-
" Ezra operative b 859 S Water
" George lather b 5 Bullard
" Joseph Jr doffer b 5 Reynolds
" Joseph S salesman 1056 Acushnet av h Myrtle street [Beetle
" Leo bell boy Wamsutta Club b 89
" Phebe widow George h 5 Bullard
" Terrence operative b 89 Beetle
" Wilfred mill hand b 9 Bullard
" William carpenter h 89 Beetle
Dougan Thomas clerk bds 324 Cedar Grove [ty
Douglas Beatrice cashier b 302 Coun-
" Frederick G shoemaker h 135 Chestnut
" Marie widow h 302 County
" Mildred S telephone operator 57 N Second b at Acushnet
Douglass Andrew R butler Wamsutta Club h 554 Kempton
" Beatrice B bookkeeper 64 Purchase [(W)
" Charles H chauffeur h 541 Elm
" Charles H Jr chauffeur b 541 Elm (W) [ton
" Charles Z cook rms 315 Kemp-

Douglass
" Edwin A lawyer 14 Masonic bldg h 185 Cottage
" Frederick C electrician 104 Union b 291 Middle [land
" George L motorman h 21 Mait-
" Lincoln H cook 403 Kempton h 80 Cedar
" Mary E Mrs h 291 Middle
" Murdock foreman rms 217 Purchase
" Roland C painter h 340 Allen
Doull Alexander b 173 Acushnet av
Dourte Manuel hairdresser 84 Potomska h 660 S Water
Doutreliugue John B rem to Paris France
" Reme rem to Paris France
Dow David Jr laborer h 19 Kane
" Delia M died Dec 28 1910
" James mule spinner b 840 Belleville av
" James T laborer h 503 Bolton
" Lester C machinist bds 170 Chancery
" Walter mule spinner b 19 Kane
" William A receiver 52 Adams h 170 Chancery
Dowbekin John weaver h 123 Mott
Dowd Ellen removed from city
" Frank bartender 1106 S Water h 208 W French av [chase
" Frank motorman rms 602 Pur-
" John J laborer h r 533 Acushnet avenue
" Martin warper b 206 State
" Owen J hairdresser 1039 Water h do [rms 299 Acushnet av
" Patrick cigarmaker 117 Union
" Peter H drillmaker h r 359 Pleasant [av b r 18 Mill
Dowden Charles clerk 216 Acushnet
" James h 35 Mill
Dowling James liquors 613 Acushnet av h 292 Purchase
" John fisherman rms 50 Russell
" Sarah E h 578 Cottage
Downell Wilfred clerk Wamsutta Mill b 116 Clark [rimac
Downes Pauline housekeeper 138 Mer-
Downey Abraham real estate 75 Weld b 237 Collette [249 Austin
" Agnes cashier 98 Purchase bds
" Catherine widow John J h 115 Grinnell

PELEG H. SHERMAN 506 COUNTY ST.
FUNERAL DIRECTOR AND EMBALMER
OFFICE PHONES. Bell 690-13. Auto. 1305.
RESIDENCE PHONES. Bell 690-12. Auto. 1306.

Downey
" Cornelius stoker h 29 Fruit
" Daniel police station 5 b 306 Earle [school b 7 Warwick
" Elizabeth A teacher Acushnet av
" Ellen Mrs h 868 County [ond
" Ellen widow John h 119 N Sec-
" Hannah widow Peter h 90 Parker
" Helen stenographer b 408 Orchard (S)
" James city laborer h 249 Austin
" James A student b 90 Parker
" James H chauffeur Hose 1 h 87 Washington [nolds
" Jessie widow John h 14 Rey-
" Johanna widow John h 183 State
" John died June 6 1911
" John mason h 36 Myrtle
" John B laborer b 275 Bowditch
" John J clerk b 115 Grinnell
" John L laborer h 89 Acushnet av
" John W died Aug 5 1910 [ker
" Joseph B letter carrier b 90 Par-
" Julia P died April 27 1911
" Kathryn J Mrs milliner 46 Borden h do [Merrimac
" Mark fireman 214 S Water b 102
" Mary widow Michael h 275 Bowditch [County
" Mary A widow William h 604
" Maurice liquors 407 Rivet h 408 Orchard (S)
" Maurice shoes 419 Rivet h do
" Maurice C operative b 7 Warwick
" May F clerk 41 Purchase b 115 Grinnell
" Michael laborer h 7 Warwick
" Michael laborer rms 7 N Second
" Patrick bar tender 343 Acushnet avenue h 61 Washington
" Patrick laborer b 232 N Second
" Patrick laborer h 105 Thompson
" Peter D agent b 90 Parker
" Stephen P foreman street dept b 275 Bowditch [State
" Stephen W mule spinner h 187
" Thomas loom fixer b 236 N Front
" Timothy S letter carrier Post Office b 119 N Second
" William switchman b 868 County
" William L second hand h 46 Borden [mac
" William M laborer h 102 Merri-

Downhill James loom fixer h 82 Katharine [111 Clark
" Wilfrid clerk Wamsutta Mills b
Downie Ovide A bartender h 1 Acushnet block [sett
Downing Harry E rem to Mattapoi-
" Mortimer Rev pastor St James R C church h 233 County
Downs Annie widow Benjamin b 36 McGurk [ard h 225 Court
" Benjamin F compositor Stand-
" David laborer b 16 Dudley
" Hannah Mrs removed from city
Dowse William rms 283 Union
Dowty Alexander A wood 126 County h 28 Mosher
" Charles H fireman h 156 Mill
Doyle Albert H remnants 1215 Acushnet av and 1105 S Water h 82½ Nye
" Andrew P shoemaker h 82½ Nye
" Andrew P shoemaker h 395 Orchard (S) [road
" Annie dressmaker b Tarkiln Hill
" Bryan second hand h 115 Ruth
" Byron clerk 98 Purchase b 115 Ruth [ond
" Charles moulder h 560 S Sec-
" Charles E third hand b 130 Eugenia
" Clarence C machinist b Mrs E P Doyle's Tarkiln Hill road
" Elizabeth widow Walter h 77 Merrimac
" Emma P widow John h junction Tarkiln Hill rd and Mt Pleasant
" Frederick L clerk Grinnell Mfg Co b Mrs E P Doyle's Tarkiln Hill road
" Harriet inspector b 130 Eugenia
" Henry engineer Acushnet Mill Corp h 460 Bolton
" Henry overseer Whitman Mills h 130 Eugenia
" James laborer b 144 State
" James A rms 245 Purchase
" James H engineer h 460 Bolton
" John molder 229 N Water h 194 Highland
" John pedlar h 45 Winsor
" John B comber b 130 Eugenia
" John E plumber 46 Linden h 134 Ashland [115 Ruth
" John J clerk 143 Purchase h

PAINTERS' SUPPLIES
Walnut, Cor. Water, 84 Pleasant St. 25 WELD SQ., 129 COVE ST.
F. T. AKIN & COMPANY

Doyle
" John J finisher 36 Purchase
" John T mgr 1 Pleasant b 3 Lincoln
" Joseph clerk 33 N Water b 115 Ruth av
" Joseph machinist h 3 Mt Pleasant
" Joseph P salesman 144 Union h 330 Cedar
" J Henry engineer Acushnet Mill h 460 Bolton
" Kathryn E bookkeeper 50 Union b 77 Merrimac
" Margaret widow Joseph h 4 Hazard court
" Mary E teacher Thomas A Green school b 144 State
" Mary H bookkeeper 50 Union b 77 Merrimac
" Matthew J foreman street dept h 480 Bolton
" Patrick lineman b 86 Hathaway avenue
" Patrick J h 144 State
" Patrick J variety 758 Purchase h 144 State
" Patrick M clerk 758 Purchase b 144 State
" Robert E mgr Standard Oil Co Fish Island rms 33 Seventh
" William A letter carrier h 222 County
Doyon Samuel weaver h 84 Jouvett
" Samuel weaver h 162 Hatch
" Samuel Jr weaver h 1 Gifford
" Telesphore weaver h 49 Nelson
Dozois Alexander dentist rms 209 Middle
Dragon Eudocxie widow Alphonse b 326 N Front
" Frank grocer 246 N Front h 31 Beetle
" Frank laborer b 3 Harmony
" George weaver h 15 Holly
" Joseph clerk 248 N Front h do
" Marie L mill hand h 35 Dean
" Melinda L widow Francois grocer 3 Harmony h do
" Narcisse L concreter h 16 La France court
" Olivine Mrs mill hand h 35 Dean
Draine Walter meatcutter h 176 David
DRAKE ALBERT B civil engineer and surveyor office 164 William h 121 Cottage See front cover and bottom edge

Drake
" Charles E civil engineer 164 William h 160 do
" Charles J teamster h 129 N Water
" Edward civil engineer b 121 Cottage
" Lewis E clerk 164 William b 160 do
DRAPER CO mill supplies Hopedale Mass See page 2
" Joseph laborer h 118 Cove
Dratch Benjamin dry goods h 164 Rockland
Drayton Charles H choreman h 67 Ash (N)
" Hodges W city laborer h r 509 Purchase
" James A watchman h 199 S Water
" J Arthur Jr carpenter h 226 Cottage
Drazen Harry pedlar h 472 S Water
Drefke Edward operative b 293 Austin
" Evelyne E saleslady 1056 Acushnet av b 293 Austin
Dreher Adolphus watchman h 137 Tremont
" Arthur L drillworker h 314 Court
" Clara A clerk 160 Purchase b 137 Tremont
" Walter E machinist h 147 Tremont
Drescott James A gardener h 117 Hillman
Dresner Harris removed from city
" Mary h 6 Bonneau court
" Vincent weaver h 354 Coffin av
Dresser Joseph city laborer bds 544 Cottage
Drew Alverdo A insurance agent 41 William h 13 Jenny Lind
" Arthur C supt paper mill The Pairpoint Corp h 2 Vine
" A Mabel removed to Westford
" Charles F baker h 198 Austin
" Clifford C salesman 88 Purchase h 144 Campbell
" Edmond F salesman 88 Purchase h 144 Campbell
" Edward E glasscutter bds 64 Spruce
" Elizabeth Mrs h 151 Campbell
" Frederick B clerk 108 William h 239 Cedar
" George caulker 155 Front h 70 Sycamore
" Harold B educational sec Y M C A rms do
" John T h 64 Spruce
" Moses C janitor h 239 Cedar

Bookkeeping, Shorthand, Typewriting, Penmanship, etc. Taught thoroughly at
Kinyon's Commercial School
Odd Fellows Bldg., Cor. William and Pleasant Sts., New Bedford, Mass.

Drew
" M Alice clerk 223 N Second b at Fairhaven [h 39 Locust
" Philip D bookkeeper 61 William
" Susan M widow Francis h 513 Acushnet av [39 N Sixth
" Susan M widow William W bds
" Walter A driver b 64 Spruce
" Walter M scenic artist bds 513 Acushnet av
" William M drillmaker h 6 Tilton
Drexler Conrad loom fixer h 257 Chestnut [Chestnut
" Francis widow Conrad bds 257
Drickus Margaret N widow bds 396 Middle (W)
Driesen Bridget died Mar 6 1911
" Frank third hand b 122 Nash rd
" John spinner b 122 Nash rd
" John O spinner h 122 Nash rd
Driggs Cynthia A and Margaret E h 157 Kempton [sor
Drinkwater Henry weaver h 36 Win-
Driota Josef weaver h 1 Gifford
DRISCOL, CHURCH & HALL (A Frank Clark, Fred L Snow and Frank L Hoxie) wholesale grocers 82-84 Union See page 13
Driscoll Daniel E real estate h 92 County
DRISCOLL DANIEL F auctioneer and real estate 14 Clifford bldg h 473 Cottage See front cover
" Dennis mgr h 191 Arnold
" Edward J shoemaker b 92 County
" George A chief engineer h 11 Penniman
" Joseph bricklayer b 38 Fifth
" Michael laborer h 197 Weld
" Nellie h 559 Cottage
" Patrick plumber 28 N Water b 155 Princeton av [ditch h do
" Patrick J real estate 307 Bow-
" Patrick O salesman h 475 Cottage
" Robert J b 92 County [tage
" Thomas A salesman b 475 Cot-
" Timothy J bricklayer h 147 Tremont [av
" William laborer b 2 Washington
" William A furniture mover 97 Maxfield h do
Drisdell Louis shoe repairer 2169 Acushnet av h 35 Ingraham

Drisdell
" Maximin died April 15, 1911
Driver Albert weaver h 199 Collette
" John h 54 Kempton
" William twister h 191 Davis
Drody James operative rms 1283 Acushnet av [vin
Drolet Alic weaver b 3 Marvin
" Henry weaver h 6 Bonneau ct
" Oliver (Drolet & Milotte) 109 Holly h do
DROLET & MILOTTE (Oliver Drolet and Alphonse P Milotte) painters and paper hangers 109 Holly See page 775
Drouin Alfred J slasher tender b 13 Bannister
" Alphonse musician b 212 South
Drown Edwin F fireman h 137 Mt Vernon [County
" Harriet J widow William F h 765
" Sadie M h 126 Mill [Maxfield
Drum Charles T horseshoer h 254
Drummond Andrew F laborer b 124 Cedar [ter
" Benjamin F laborer b 46 N Wa-
" Juan F B physician 124 Cedar b do [ond h 41 Bethel
" William H druggist 75 N Sec-
Drysdale John rem to Providence R I
Duane Frank b 37 Washburn
Duarte Antone laborer h 206 S Front
" John baker b 195 Coggeshall
" John mill hand h 153 Belleville avenue [ond
" John ropemaker h 152 S Sec-
" John A ropemaker h 402 S Water [375 Middle
" John L overseer 131 Court h
" Jose shoe repairer 64 Grinnell h
" Joseph mill hand h 171 Belleville avenue [Water
" Joseph A carpenter h 205 South
" Joaquin fisherman h 699 S Water
" Manuel laborer h 317 S Water
" Manuel mill hand b 139 Coffin av
" Manuel C mill hand h 178 Belleville av [618 S Water
" Manuel J barber 84 Potomska h
" Mary Ann Mrs h 27 Cannon
" Nicholas laborer h 172 S Second
" Phoebe Mrs h 349 S Water
Dube Adelard laborer h 8 Jean
" Alex weaver b 171 Weld
" Alfred operative h 194 N Front

Bread, Cake, Pastry
RICHMOND & COMPANY **255-257 UNION STREET**
Bell 993 Automatic 1022

Dube
" Alphonse fixer h 434 N Front
" Alphonse Jr weaver b 434 N Front [Front h 352 do
" Arthur (Cormier & Dube) 394 N
" Francois X second hand h 11 Jean [Front
" Harmand slasher bds 434 North
" Joseph laborer h 8 Jean
" Joseph fixer h 13 Mosher
" Louis carpenter h 171 Weld
" Napoleon machinist h 8 Jean
" Napoleon weaver b 975½ S Water
" Paul mill hand bds 16 Bentley
" Paul shaft hanger b 177 Weld
" Peter carpenter h 735 Belleville avenue [yon
" Victoria widow Remi h 68 Ken-
" Zenon pilot city roller h 4 Jean
" Zephir clerk 126 Bowditch bds 8 Jean [av
Dubera John laborer h 708 Acushnet
Dubiel Ignace weaver b 70 Delano
" Joseph weaver h 70 Delano
Dubois Albert roller coverer h 161 State [County
" Cleophas lunch 792 Purchase h 27
" Desire weaver h 93 Holly
" Dusithe weaver h 22 Jean
" Dusithe Jr weaver b 22 Jean
" Edward fixer h 80 Blackmer
" Edward third hand bds 116 W French av
" Emile weaver b 20 Ashley
" Ephrim clerk b 220 Phillips av
" Ernest carpenter h 126 Nye
" Frank weaver h 15 Holly
" George loom fixer h 22 Jean
" George weaver h 30 Ashley
" George weaver b 15 Holly
" George E second hand h 380 Pleasant
" John weaver b 52 Dean
" Joseph baker h 33 Tallman
" Joseph weaver h 16 George
" Louis weaver b 80 Blackmer
" Louis N weaver b 30 Ashley
" Napoleon carpenter h 116 West French av [Holly
" Napoleon painter 14 Jean b 82
" Napoleon weaver h 20 Salisbury
" Nicholas stonecutter h 9 Nelson
" Philiase stonecutter h Kingcroft
" Rose Mrs h 20 Ashley

Dubois
" Senial weaver h 857 First
" see Wood [Thompson
Dubord Albert carpenter h 173
Duboski Koza grocer 2 Hicks bds 8 do [195 County
Dubreuil Albert mgr 110 William b
Dubrinski Peter weaver h 55 Delano
Dubrowski Kazimier grocer h 135 N Front
Dubuis Philias removed from city
Dubuis Philias remove from city
Dubuque Arthur salesman b 119 Tallman [ditch
" Gilbert motorman bds 171 Bow-
" Henry helper 915 Acushnet av b 171 Bowditch [Tallman
" Melvina widow Adelard h 119
Duchainaux Moise laborer h 847 Acushnet av [lard
Duchaine Edward lather bds 5 Bul-
" Henry driver h 985 S Water
" Henry laborer h 93 Holly
" James h 225 Rivet
" Paul baker h 980 County
Duchaineau Napoleon third hand h 519 Acushnet av [Washburn
Ducharme Adolph loom fixer h 31
" Aldofe mill hand h 256 N Front
" Angeline Mrs b 44 Sycamore
" Arthur mill hand h 385 N Front
" Arthur weaver bds 47 Holly
" Astil operative b 74 County
" Clara died Nov 1 1910
" Edward photographer 166 Rivet h 81 Independent
" F piper h 448 Rivet
" George plumber b 178 Bowditch
" Henry weaver b 44 Sycamore
" John A removed to Richmond
" Leon h 184 Phillips av
" Louis mason 149 Phillips av h do
" Oliver b 149 Phillips av [av
" Rosanna housekeeper 184 Phillips
" Walter operative h 41 Merrimac
" Wilfred helper b 178 Bowditch
Ducheineau Mina Mrs h 31 Durfee
Duchene Frank laborer bds 59 Bullard [lard
" Joseph back boy bds 59 Bul-
" Pierre laborer h 59 Bullard [av
" Simon carpenter h 154 Phillips
Duchesneau Joseph A carpenter h Milfort street [847 do
" Wilfrid clerk 1214 Acushnet av b

GLOBE DYE HOUSE 220 SHAWMUT AVE.
J. N. J. LONHOLDT, PROP. Telephone Connections Goods called for and Delivered
Down town Office, 52 Pleasant St., Room 1 North End Office, 1014 Acushnet Ave.

Duckett Edmund fixer h 399 Pleasant
" Fred slasher b 19 Ashley
Duckworth Alexander second hand h 32 Howland Village [Cove
" Alfred repairer 14 Ward bds 44
" Ann widow Henry h 315 Davis
" Celina widow William h 52 Weld
" Franklin T driver 159 Mill b 70 do
" Frederick E clerk h 842 County
" George weaver b 351 Coggeshall
" George T (Braley & Duckworth) 81 N Second h 70 Mill
" James machinist h 60 Hall
" John weaver h 323 Earl
" John weaver b 315 Davis
" John W laborer h 33 George
" Lawrence spinner h 161 Nash rd
" Lewis weaver h 389 Bolton
" Mansfirth boarding house 65 Washburn h do [h 335 Sawyer
" Margaret Mrs speeder tender
" Robert twister h 142 Bullard
" Susan P bookkeeper 71 Union b 69 Myrtle
" Thomas painter h 27 Viall
" Thomas twister b 69 Myrtle
" Thomas weaver b 260 Cogeshall
" William H confectionery 488½ North Front h 488 do
Duclos Jules piper bds 161 Cove
" Olide weaver b 52 Delano
" Robert Jr teamster b 161 Cove
Ducuilk Stanislas operative h 167 N Front
Duddy Jennie T clerk b 82 School
" John baker 143 Purchase b 65 Fourth
" Susan h 389 Cottage [School
" Susie J clerk 48 Pleasant b 82
" William general teamster 116 S Water blacksmith 11 Walnut h 82 School [ditch
Dudevoir Arthur operative b 4 Bow-
" Evariste mason h 4 Bowditch
Dudgeon Samuel treasurer 185 Union h 119 Hillman [193 Middle
Dudley Lucy A widow Clement J h
DUDLEY S A shuttle mfr 148 Dean Taunton See page 17
Duerden Arthur weaver bds 76 Dean
" Edith A milliner 185 Union b 76 Dean [lette
" Ellen widow Jeremiah h 240 Col-

Duerden
" James removed from city
" John weaver h 17 Brock avenue
" Mary A widow William h 76 Dean
Dufault Peter ice h 81 Wood
Duff Daniel E foreman h 105 Bonney
DUFF DAVID & SON (John Duff) teaming and coal Merchants Bank bldg 105 William 73 Weld and Fish Island See front cover
" Edward steam roller pilot city yard h 2 N Oak [N Oak
" Edward J mule spinner bds 2
" Eugene laborer rms 7 N Second
" John (David Duff & Son) h 479 County [Son b 479 County
" John Jr foreman David Duff &
" Mark M asst foreman freight depot b 479 County [rill
Duffany Almeda inspector b 11 Mer-
" Celina reeler bds 11 Merrill
" Ida inspector h 11 Merrill
Dufficy Ellen housekeeper 893 County
" John city laborer h 893 County
" Joseph machinist b 239 Chestnut
" Joseph mill hand h 84 Thompson
" Patrick copper worker h 786 County
" Peter F painter h 239 Chestnut
" Richard joiner b 239 Chestnut
Duffy Alice L milliner b 60 Nye
" Arthur E deputy collector Custom House h 199 Arnold
" Catherine D dressmaker 39 Ash (S) h do [rms do
" Dora D manicure 34 Purchase
" Edward P liquors 1116 S Water h 206 W French avenue
" Francis Jr organizer h 46 Grant
" Frank spinner h 7 Bullock
" Frank O foreman Pierce Mill h 60 Nye [way
" Harold watchman h 91 Hatha-
" James C eyelet maker b 7 Bullock
" James H packer h 26 Belleville rd
" John B porter 81 Front h 168 Arnold
" John E laborer h 91 Hathaway
" John J clerk bds 73 Dudley
" John L overseer bds 60 Nye
" John P clerk b 92 Smith
" Joseph painter h 67 Coffin av
" Joseph B twister b 36 Cove

GREENE & WOOD Every Kind of LUMBER AND MILL WORK
PINE STREET, off So. WATER STREET, NEW BEDFORD

Duffy
" Mary Mrs h 36 Cove
" Mary widow John h 58 Phillips av
" Mary E M principal William H Taylor school h 199 Arnold
" Patrick steam fitter h 81 Davis
" Thomas H mgr 888 S Water b 36 Cove
" William laborer b 56 Cove
" William H clerk b 73 Dudley
" see Dufficy [bds 607 Cottage
Dufour John baker 372 Kempton
" Kate A Mrs dressmaker 607 Cottage h do
" Leon mill hand bds 607 Cottage
Dufre Rose operative h 26 Hillman
Dufresne Adam weaver b 56 Dean
" Adolph h 397 Rivet
" Alphonse removed from city
" David removed from city [ond
" Delphine D Mrs h 129 North Sec-
" Delphis P dentist 9 W French av
" Elzear removed from city
" Fred removed from city
removed from city
" Peter carpenter h 397 Rivet
" Wilfred lamp lighter h 166 Dean
Dugal Joseph teamster h 115 Nash rd
Dugally Brothers (Said and Tufitk) grocers 308 Coggeshall [Grove
" Said (Dugally Bros) h 217 Cedar
" Tufitk (Dugally Bros) b 217 Cedar Grove [Hazard
Dugan Bridget widow Thomas b 54
" Edward P salesman b 130 South Second [Clark h do
" Hugh A (Loftus & Dugan) 121
" Margaret widow h 122 Potomska
" Mary widow Michael h 130 South Second [Cedar Grove
" Thomas clerk 878 Purchase b 324
" Thomas janitor h 54 Hazard
Dugas Joseph carpenter h 207 Coffin avenue [Fairhaven
Dugdale Allen clerk 97 Front h at
" Charles H watchman h 13 Mosher
" Charles R clerk 97 Front h at Fairhaven
" Elizabeth A teacher William H Taylor school bds 14 Homer
" Francis egg tester Anthony Swift & Co b at Fairhaven
Duggan James P furniture 133 Acushnet avenue h 167 Merrimac

Duggan
" John J roofer h 633 Cottage
Duhamel Charles weaver h 151 Tallman
Duka George removed to Boston
Dukas Christophe (Stevens & Dukas) 125 Union
" Thomas removed from city
Dulin Alex carpenter h 74 Mott
" Edward carpenter h 74 Mott
Dulong Favila widow Octave h 1205 Acushnet avenue [Bowditch
Dulude Honore carpenter /bds 397
" Joseph carpenter 397 Bowditch h do
" Larry carpenter h 395 Bowditch
Duma Bactash mill hand h 54 Davis
Dumaine Arthur contractor 7 McGurk h do
" John weaver b 15 Penniman
Dumais Michael millwright h 206 Hathaway
Dumas Adelard removed to Taunton
" Albert carpenter h 60 Tallman
" Alexander weaver h 150 Collette
" Arthur hairdresser 692 Purchase h rear 679 do
" Arthur painter h 662 Purchase
" Edmond loom fixer h 130 Eugenia
" Fred F watch repairer 269 Purchase h 47 Chestnut
" George clerk h 171 Weld
" Hector back boy b 60 Tallman
" Homer fixer b 130 Eugenia
" James painter h 27 Bullard
" James painter rms 781 Purchase
" Joseph loom fixer h 18 Austin ct
" Joseph weaver h 311 N Front
" Joseph E carpenter h 429 N Front
" Leopold machinist b 60 Tallman
" Louis weaver b 429 North Front
" Marcia widow Edwin b 47 Chestnut [land
" Nelson slasher tender h 146 Rock-
" Pierre removed from city
" Raoul carpenter bds 60 Tallman
" Theodore picture operator b 429 North Front
Dumec John painter h 186 Bonney
" Peter h 186 Bonney
" Rose Mrs died Nov 13 1910
Dumianski Leopold weaver h 129 Blackmer
Dumont Ferdinand laborer h 70 Ruth
" Harriet V h 310 Kempton

BONNEY, FOLSTER & CO.,
The North End's Shopping Centre
Dry Goods and Men's Furnishings
945-947 Acushnet Ave., New Bedford, Mass.

Dumont
" Joseph weaver b 52 Delano
" Pierre operative h 186 Cove
" Thomas slasher b 70 Ruth
Dumoulin Joseph conductor h 179 Ashland [Harrison
" J Alfred clerk 62 Purchase h 8
Dun R G & Co mercantile agency 5 Beetle lane [ushnet av
Dunbar Albert A shipper h 2416 Ac-
" Alton motorman h 383 Purchase
" Jennie Mrs weaver b 117 Austin
" Sarah h 102 Middle
" William A h 41 Campbell [State
Duncan David city laborer h 198 r
" James J molder h 120 County
Dunce Emma widow h 28 Mosher
Dunham Alfred S salesman 182 Union h 435 Mill [Lindsey
" Amanda widow William G b 67
" Anna M h 248 County
" Charles H painter h 33 Babbitt
" Crawford L hardware 745 Purchase h at Fairhaven
" Ernest A nickle plater h 1430
" Florence J clerk 185 Union b at Fairhaven [h 175 Grinnell
" Frank C clerk 131 Acushnet av
" Frank S bds 175 Grinnell [Dean
" Frederic C foreman P Corp h 82
" George painter h 55 Ward
" George L master mariner h 23 Seventh [Court
" John A night officer H C h 119
" Louis C time keeper U S Ry Co h 408 Cedar [Maxfield
" Mary J widow Alfred C h 309
" Otis M clerk Wamsutta Mill h 315 Pleasant
" Samuel J removed from city
" Sarah L removed from city
" Stephen Y foreman King's Highway h 30 Richmond [Richmond
" Susan M widow Thomas S b 30
" Winthrop L clerk 84 Union h 41 Parker [h 36 Madison
" Zaccheus C clerk 201 Purchase
Dunkerley Francis Mrs h 257 Coffin avenue [Acushnet av
Dunkerly Charles motorman b 1416
" Herbert doffer b 1416 Acushnet av
" James W clerk 1290 Acushnet av h 163 Coggeshall
" John C fixer h 1416 Acushnet av

Dunkerly
" Margaret Mrs grocer 163 Coggeshall h do
Dunlap Agnes J principal Cedar Grove st school rms 258 Pleasant [ion h 237 Court
" Albert A stable 318 and 319 Un-
" Ida bds 237 Court
Dunlop James M tea and coffee 903 South Water h 905 do
Dunn Bridget widow h 276 Coggeshall
" Donald mill hand h 130 Eugenia
" Edward operative b 276 Coggeshall
" Elizabeth A b 147 James
" George A shoemaker h 77 Morgan
" James laborer bds 187 Crapo
" John h 147 James
" John weaver b 7 Juniper
" John H foreman h 126 Nye
" Patrick clerk 497 Purchase b do
" William J cable splicer 57 North Second h 113 James
" William P laborer h 147 James
Dunne William J rms 43 Fifth
Dunning Eliza S widow Henry b 73 Shawmut avenue [come
Dunton Charles weaver bds 4 Wel-
Duperry Joseph carpenter h 189 Bowditch
Duphily Etienne engineer h 12 Beetle
" Magloir grocer Clifford n Bowditch bds 52 Hicks
Dupin Eugene P city editor 267 Sawyer h 33 Viall
Duplessis Eli weaver bds 190 State
" Henriette widow Pierre h 190 State
" Joseph removed from city
Dupont Adelard bar tender 946 South Water b 1008 Acushnet av
" Antone operative h 76 Winsor
" Charles operative b 83 Crapo
" Desire weaver h 863 S Water
" Ellen widow Ignace h 1296 Acushnet avenue [net av
" Ernest plumber bds 1296 Acush-
" Ernest weaver b 11 Nye
" Eugene b 82 Eugenia
" Henry salesman h 213 Shaw
" Manuel laborer h 83 Crapo
" Manuel Jr operative b 83 Crapo
" Napoleon clerk 962 Acushnet av b 1008 do

M. P. B. Silva & Son BUILDERS
Estimates Furnished on all Kinds of Work
157 ACUSHNET AVENUE Both Phones NEW BEDFORD

Dupont
" Oliver weaver h 211 Church
" Pierre elevatorman h 125 Collette
" Elizabeth A b 1147 James
" Regina Mrs h 156 Acushnet av
" Theodore weaver h 418 N Front
" Urvano salesman b 67 Nash rd
" Valerie weaver b 143 Collette
" Zephir b 1296 Acushnet avenue
Dupre' Agnes M stenographer '185
Union bds 80 Washington
" Aleck laborer h 63 Hicks
" Antoine died June 13 1911
" Armand clerk 1023 S Water b 31
Bentley [124 Rivet
" Arsene barber Parker House h
" Arthur removed to Fairhaven
" Arthur weaver b 31 Bentley
" Ernest laborer h 70 Ruth
" Francis mason h 32 Katharine
" George clerk 1099 Acushnet av h
31 Bentley
" George shoemaker b 66 Washburn
" John laborer h 70 Ruth
" John B weaver b 165 Dean
" Joseph h 25 Nye
" Joseph laborer h 20 Lafrance ct
" Joseph weaver b 54 Holly [ington
" Joseph E section hand h 80 Wash-
" Joseph T loom fixer h 213 Fourth
" Leo weaver b 67 Coffin avenue
" Leon blacksmith 105 Bowditch h
31 Bentley [117 Clark
" Leon Jr teamer 32 Linden bds
" Louise bookkeeper 912 S Water b
80 Washington
" Mary Mrs operative h 52 Hicks
" Matilda widow David h 56 Dean
" Patrick carpenter b 188 Collette
" Peter lineman U St Ry Co rms
810 Purchase
" Peter spinner h 44 Merrimac
" Richard carpenter h 192 Collette
" Rock clerk 956 Acushnet av b 7
Bentley [ushnet av
" Susan A widow Louis b 170 Ac-
" Victor E fixer h 1073 S Water
" William laborer b 52 Hicks
" William J loom fixer b 25 Nye
Dupreu Desire carpenter b 74 Mott
Duprey William A shoe maker h 20
Reynolds
Duprie Alice F clerk b 629 Cottage
" Wilfred H h 629 Cottage [chase
Dupies Ellen widow Edward 863 Pur-

Dupuis Adam spinner h 41 Merrimac
" Adelard laborer h 19 Rodney
" Adona clerk 1351 Acushnet av
" Albenie lineman h 66 Dean
" Alcide operative h 297 Coffin av
" Arsene barber Parker House h 124
Rivet
" Arthur C shoemaker b 806 County
" Aurelie widow Oliver b 59 Bull-
ard
" Bernard removed from city [av
" Charles operative h 835 Acushnet
" Demas driver h 826 County
" Ellen widow h 863 Purchase
" Ernest E shoes 1351 Acushnet av
h 311 Coffin avenue
" Frank D driver h 826 County
DUPUIS HERMAN D (H D Dupuis
& Co) wholesale grocers 1201
Purchase h 1203 do See page
757
" Jacob laborer h 41 Merrimac
" Jean B died December 10 1910
" John B Jr slubber tender h 181
State
" Joseph clerk b 48 Salisbury
" Joseph helper 19 Linden
" Joseph operative h 803 First
" Joseph weaver h 47 Reynolds
" Joseph weaver h 871 Purchase
" Joseph A weaver h 190 Dean
" Louise widow Charles b 42 Lo-
cust
" Lucien painter h 44 Merrimac
" Michael reserve police sta 2
" Moses laborer h 78 Mott
" Omer weaver b 56 Dean
" Parmelia clerk 185 Union b at
Fairhaven [Ashland
" Patrick reserve police h 13
" Peter lineman h 814 Purchase
" Peter spinner h 44 Merrimac
" Philip carpenter h 189 Tinkham
" Romuld blacksmith h 814 Pur-
chase
" Samuel barber h 124 Rivet
" Victoria widow Jean B h 806
County [Cottage
" Wilfred H police station 5 h 629
" Wilfred M salesman 99 William
rms 172 do
Dupuy Joseph L J editor La Libeite
1205 Acushnet avenue b do
Duquet Priscilla widow Edward h
739 Belleville avenue

Steiger-Dudgeon Co.
"The WOMAN'S Store."
Tel. Bell 82 & 83, Branches connecting all depts.
" " 160 For Office only. Auto. 1211
SUMPTIONS,
ASSORTMENTS
AT ALL TIMES
OF DEPENDABLE
DRY GOODS

Duquette Anne Mrs h 514 Purchase
" Ernest weaver b 84 Blackmer
" Jeffréy fireman h 23 Bentley
" Joseph fireman h 31 Covell
" Theresa A clerk 41 Purchase bds 514 do [Belleville rd
Durand Mabel E teacher bds 125
" Thomas J blacksmith h 125 Belleville road [man
" Victorio Mrs mill hand h 16 Tall-
" Wilfred waiter b 16 Tallman
Durant Andre cable splicer 43 William h 12 Blackburn
" Charles lineman 57 N Second h 58 Bedford [ton
" Edward A student bds 199 Clin-
" Elizabeth widow George h 509 S Second [h 199 Clinton
" Firman shoe repairer 53 Chancery
" George A hostler 378 County bds 199 Clinton [129 Clark
" George L helper U St Ry Co b
" Gruide shoemaker h r 354 Purchase
" John teamster h 9 Austin court
" John W sail maker 31 Commercial h 15 **Ash (S)** [Clark
" Lawrence J police sta 5 h 129
Durfee Abram H machinist h 55 Smith
" Arthur A eyelet maker b 55 Smith
" Arthur J secretary and treasurer 182 Union h 275 County
" Charles laborer h 439 Rivet
" David S R chair seater h 55 Smith
" Edward M blacksmith 30 Bethel h 64 Foster
" George L h 87 S Sixth
" John E laborer b 151 Grinnell
" Joseph C shoemaker 151 Grinnell h do
" Kathleen C M Mrs h 238 Cedar
" William bookkeeper 182 Union h 183 Rockland [87 S Sixth
" William L driver Engine No 4 b
" William N rms 807 Purchase
Durfey Mary widow Richard T h 75 Rockland [Division
Durham Thomas operative bds 185
Durkin John J spinner h 220 State
Durocher Leo P weaver b 69 Earle
" Napoleon weaver h 69 Earle
" Napoleon Jr weaver b 69 Earle

Durrant Joseph lineman U St Ry Co h 289 Purchase
Durup Emil operative h 32 Division
Duteau Baptiste laborer h 826 County
Dutra Antonio second hand h 54 Page
" Antonio third hand h 470 First
" August at P Corp h 263 Field
" Edward clerk 446 Rivet b 99 Swift
" Ferdinand fisherman h 310 South Front
" Frances S died October 30 1910
" Francis A machinist h 105 Fifth
" Frank loom fixer h 28 Katharine
" Frank mill hand h 65 Katharine
" Henry teamster h 99 Swift
" Jose S fisherman h 211 Rivet
" Joseph A conductor b 123 Rockland
" Joseph R operative h 158 Crapo
" Manuel operative h 37 Prospect
" Manuel operative h 75 Winsor
" Manuel P operative h 7 Acushnet block
" Manuel R grocer 106 County
" Manuel R laborer h 15 Cleveland
" Mary E clerk b 123 Rockland
" Mary E Mrs h 114 Fifth
" Sergio fisherman h 109 Grinnell
" Sergio R S died June 8 1911
Dutton Alonzo variety 1666 Acushnet avenue and engineer 111 Clifford h 340 Davis [road
" Charles mason h 560 Hathaway
" Edward blacksmith h 82 Chancery
" James E baker b 21 Rural
" John wood worker h 21 Rural
" Milly H stenographer 185 Union b 82 Chancery [avenue
" William mill hand h 837 Acushnet
" William E laborer h 6 Bethel
Duval Alfred R weaver b 541 N Front
" Amedee weaver h 16 Tallman
" Arthur weaver b 16 Tallman
" Ernest watchman h 829 Acushnet avenue
" Euclide spinner h 157 Davis
" Francois carpenter h 16 Tallman
" Gene widow h 79 Nelson
" Herminie grocer 47 Belleville rd bds 121 Whitman [ditch
" Hormidas spinner h 132 Bow-
" Louis weaver b 102 Collette
" Napoleon fisherman h 16 Covell
" Napoleon watchman h 68 Tallman
" Napoleon weaver h 330 N Front

PELEG H. SHERMAN 506 COUNTY ST.
FUNERAL DIRECTOR AND EMBALMER
OFFICE PHONES. Bell 690-13 Auto. 1305.
RESIDENCE PHONES. Bell 690-12. Auto 1306.

Duval
" Napoleon Jr weaver h 199 State
" Norbert weaver h 541 N Front
" Omer salesman 106 Front
" Paul weaver h 220 Phillips av
Duvals Mary C Mrs h 371 S Water
Duxbury Abraham fixer h 90 Clark
" Albert weaver h 132 Division
" Elizabeth Mrs nurse h 13 Marvin
" Harry clerk 168 S Water b 303 Fourth [h 206 Tinkham
" Harry tinsmith 126 Acushnet av
" Herbert weaver b 208 Nash road
" John tinsmith 745 Purchase b 191 Nye [fin av
" Mary A widow Samuel h 293 Cof-
" Milton clerk b 301 Fourth
" Oliver removed from city
" Walsh weaver h 301 Fourth
" Walter weaver h 345 Sawyer
Dvorak Charles fixer b 251 Phillips av
" Mary widow Charles h 251 Phillips avenue
" Rudolph fixer b 251 Phillips av
Dwarte Manuel barber Potomska h 616 S Water [Front
Dwaszko Peter weaver h 445 South
Dwellev Andrew supt N B Storage Warehouse h at Fairhaven
" Henrietta b 17 Studley
" Leroy E overseer N B S Co rms 292 Purchase
Dwight Carl h 65 Spruce [do
" Henry L physician 156 William h
" Minerva B h 137 Fourth
Dwyer Edward watchman bds 1098 Acushnet avenue [nolds
" Ellen widow Patrick h 37 Rey-
" Fred C teamster h 17 High
" George B painter b 17 High
" James laborer h 17 Thomas [tage
" Jeremiah E shoemaker h 592 Cot-
" John bricklayer b 32 Clak
" John laborer rms 60 N Second
" Julia widow Thomas F h 592 Cottage [b do
" Lillian dressmaker 410 Kempton
" Martin J loom fixer h 296 Cedar Grove
" Mary widow John b 32 Clark
" Michael picker maker b 301 Fourth
" Patrick weaver h 53 Washburn
" Richard H mason b 37 Reynolds

Dwyer
" Robert J mason b 37 Reynolds
" Thomas E laborer b 203 Coffin av
" Thomas F grocer 600 Cottage h 332 Cedar
" Timothy spinner b 37 Reynolds
" Walter L chauffeur b 17 High
Dyer Edna H teacher R C Ingraham school rms 43 Fifth
" Ellen Mrs h 12 Salisbury
" Florence M C stenographer Page Mfg Co bds 12 Salisbury
" Florence M Dr general secretary 12 Market rms 8 Eighth [man
" Geogene widow Edward h 34 Hill-
" George C helper b 115 Durfee
" George N nurse h 193 Summer
" George W asst supt Buttonwood Park h 339 Reed [Reed
" George W Jr metal worker b 339
" John (Dyer & Co) grocer 195 Shawmut av and ice 115 Durfee h do
" John B apprentice Standard
" Joseph R roll coverer b 40 Shawmut avenue [121 Fourth
" Norman S driver Engine 6 h
" Owen molder h 301 Coffin av
" Richard K chauffeur b 121 Fourth
" Sarah E widow William H b 77 Shawmut avenue
" Stephen K overseer Hathaway Mfg Co h 129 Sycamore
" William carpenter h 187 Dean
" William H fisherman h 77 Chancery
" & Co (John Dyer) grocers 195 Shawmut av [court
Dygos Wojsiech roper h 2 Hampton
Dyring Hilma nurse b 64 Hillman
Dyson Amos H officer H of C h at Fall River
" Ann widow James h 12 Warren
" Robert boilermaker h 167 Brock avenue
" Sarah Mrs h 27 Cleveland
" Thomas mule spinner b 27 Cleveland [place
Dziuba Jozef operative h 9 Cornell

Eagan Thomas weaver bds 303 Tinkham
Eagle Express Co 45-51 School
Earle Archer B driver 270 Acushnet av rms 427 do

F. T. AKIN & CO. FORGE FACTORY FURNACE FAMILY COAL

Earle
" Frederick E (Earle, Griffin & Co) b 61 Chestnut
" Griffin & Co (Frederick E Earle and Perley Griffin) heating 57 S Water
Earley Edward C police h 21 James
" Isabel attendant b 3 Bay [Round
" James J letter carrier h 141
" Owen P bookkeeper Kennedy & Kirwin 311 S Water b 47 James [come
Earnshaw Abraham fixer h 8 Wel-
" Walter fixer bds 8 Welcome
Eastern Electric Co elctricians 22 William
" Supply Co (Hyman Romanow) dry goods 698 Purchase
Eastham James weaver h 79 Rodney
Easton Charles F Jr hairdresser 553 Kempton h 555 do
Eastwood Albert clerk 904 Acushnet avenue h 183 Bowditch
" David weaver h 98 Covell
" Edward weaver h 132 Division
" Fred carder h 202 N Front
" Hartley fixer h 581 Purchase
" James weaver b 1283 Acushnet av
" John T eyeletmaker h 88 Briggs
" Ruth widow Thomas b 88 Briggs
" Thomas laborer h 286 Coggeshall
" Thomas weaver b 286 Coggeshall
Eaton Alfred H electrician b 66 N Second [thorn b do
" Annabelle dressmaker 248 Haw-
" Chester A brakeman h 17 Franklin [36 N Second
" Clara M widow Daniel S lodging h
" Clarence W cotton broker 49 William rm 14 h at Fairhaven
" Daniel S glasscutter b 66 N Second [school b 118 Chancery
" Eliza M teacher Dartmouth street
" Harry operative b 388 Purchase
" Thomas fireman b 541 Sawyer
Eatough James spinner h 21 Salisbury [ion b 233 North
Ebel Frederick confectioner 255 Un-
Ebram Fahim mill hand b 37 Phillips av [land
Eccles George T weaver h 18 Cleve-
" Hannah widow Richard h 1618 Acushnet avenue
" James laundryman b 407 Cedar
" Thomas weaver h 407 Cedar

Eccles
" William weaver b 407 Cedar
" William weaver h 289 Collette
" see Etchells [man
Eccleston Albert E laborer b 33 Hill-
" George L engineer L R Corp h 311 Acushnet av
" Joseph engineer h 9 Jenny Lind
" Thomas second hand h 23 Peckham [dle
Edardo Antonio J laborer h 74 Mid-
Eddus James clerk h 433 Acushnet av [station rms 42 Hill
Eddy Charles V freight caller R R
" Clara widow Walter h 358 Elm
" George M h 8 Maple
" William eyeletmaker h 57 Smith
Edelstein Harris janitor h 521 S Water
Edgar John F collector h 164 North
Edge Alfred backboy b 412 Cedar
" Edward S machinist h 75 Brock avenue [883 do
" James S clerk 874 Purchase bds
" John weaver b 412 Cedar
" Peter weaver h 858 First [ter
Edger Harry G glasscutter h 49 Fos-
Edgerton John F b 6 Shawmut av
" William J real estate h 6 Shawmut av
" William J Jr h 58 N Sixth
Edinborough Horatio J hairdresser 77 Union h do
Edlin Abraham dry goods 840 Purchase h 194 Cedar Grove
Edmond John fireman b 140 Newton
Edmonson Fred C drillmaker h 32 Winsor
" John h 8 Thompson
" Rachael L stenographer Oneko Mills b 305 Austin
" Thomas S laborer h 32 Winsor
" William weaver h 137 N Front
Edwards Antonio E laborer h 77 Dunbar
" Charles F h 101 Smith
" Charles W boilermaker h 76 County [chase
" Edward shoeworker b 620 Pur-
" George J weaver h 7 Juniper
" George J Jr weaver b 7 Juniper
" Henry W bds 101 Smith
" James machinist b 620 Purchase
" John baker b 570 S Water
" John laborer h 152 S Second

There's room at the top for young men and women who can do things right.
Kinyon's Commercial School
Odd Fellows Bldg., Cor. William and Pleasant Sts., New Bedford, Mass.

Edwards
" John Mrs h 9 Viall
" Joseph T importer 112 William h 69 S Sixth [yer b do
" Lillian Mrs dressmaker 238 Say-
" Louis S clerk 143 Purchase h 379 do
" Margaret h 620 Purchase
" Mary widow h 11 Columbia
" Robert E real estate h 171 Kempton
" Ruth G b 101 Smith [chase
" Sarah A widow George b 379 Pur-
" Thomas city laborer b 620 Purchase
" Thomas dyer b 27 Viall
" William machinist h 492 N Front
Egan Arthur operative h 84 Rodney
" Frank M removed from city
" Helen Mrs h 47 Independent
" Henry oiler h 124 Cove
" James E spinner b 159 Weld
" John (Eagan & Boudreau) and Boston Furniture Co h 25 Crapo
" John spinner h 47 Independent
" John spinner h 341 Coffin av
" Robert h 193 Arnold
" Thomas ironworker h 81 Maxfield
" Thomas spinner h 47 Independent
" U Francis mill hand b 47 Independent
" & Boudreau (John Egan and Theophile Boudreau) dry goods 957 S Water [Park pl
Egenberger Edwin J hostler rms 3
Eger Oscar glassworker h 14 Crapo
Eggers George A sporting goods 10 William h 69 Tremont
" Nellie S clerk Pairpoint Corp b 39 Florence
" Selmar h 39 Florence [shnet av
Eglin Hermann weaver h 1103 Acu-
Ehret Joseph weaver h 16 Roosevelt
Eidlin Haime (N Y Upholstering Co) h 7 Blackburn [Davis
Eisenbach Englebert weaver h 337
Ekdahl Emma M widow Knut h 93 Walden [en b do
" Signe E music teacher 93 Wald-
Ekholm Bror O grinder 190 Purchase h 616 Union [av
Elas Marlik mill hand b 45 Phillips
" Louis widow b 616 Union
Elder Louise A Mrs b 410 Kempton
" Thomas loom fixer h 25 Viall
" William R linotyper bds 25 Viall
Eldred Lemuel D antiques 12 William h at Fairhaven
Eldredge Abbie A bookkeeper 38 Elm b 80 Pierce [194 Clinton
" Charles K foreman 123 Front h
" Florence L clerk 160 Purchase b 194 Clinton
" Florence P widow Howard P bookkeeper 152 N Water b 6 Sears [ham
" Harvey R boxmaker h 306 Tink-
" Josephine W stenographer New Bedford Five Cents Savings Bank b 322 Arnold
" Myra W clerk 240 Union b at Fairhaven
" Simeon B h 80 Pierce
" Thomas K machinist h 68 Mechanic's lane
" Wendell T b 194 Clinton
Eldridge Ann S widow Abram h 23 Dartmouth [Morgan
" Annah H clerk 185 Union h 70
" Chauncy G (Tucker Anthony & Co h at Boston
" Chester solderer h 100 Clifford
" Clara M Mrs lodgings 152 Purchase
" Cyrus teamster b 19 River rd
" Daniel teamster h 154 S Second
" Elsie N teacher b 244 Chestnut
" Emily M h 70 Morgan
" Frank C laborer h 152 Purchase
" Frederick E h 295 Park
" F Otis carpenter b 244 Chestnut
" Isadore F principal Dartmouth street school h 336 Orchard (S)
" James laborer b 154 S Second
" John B h 107 Fourth
" Mary J housekeeper 60 Chestnut
" Mary T money order clerk P O b 40 Parker
" Reuben removed from city
" Samuel laborer b 116 Clark
" Samuel T foreman carpenter Wamsutta Mill h 244 Chestnut
" Veranus died Sept 1 1910
" Washington A housekeeper police department h 56 Mill
" see Eldredge

HASKELL BROS. DEALERS IN
ICE
400 COURT STREET TELEPHONE CONNECTION NEW BEDFORD, MASS.

Electric Express Charles T Battey mgr N Water cor Elm
Elgeschewitz Harry shoe repairer 9 Oak h 49 Short
Elie Joseph Emmille editor 101 Kenyon [nos) h 37 North
Eliopulos Dick (Eliopulos & Pa-
" & Panos (Dick Eliopulos and Vacil Panos) fruit 82 Purchase
Eliot Ida M h 31 Clinton
Elks Home 88 Purchase
Ellenwood Annie M widow George W b 33 Richmond
Eller Mary Mrs h 58 Roosevelt
Ellershaw John W operative b 260 Coggeshall [Willis b 10 Bethel
Ellery Everett M lunch Acushnet av n
Ellington Benjamin laborer h 47 Holly
ELLIOT JOHN D plumber 106 Fourth h do See page 45
Elliott Addie H widow George W housekeeper 1176 Acushnet av
" Andrew C tailor h 601 Acushnet avenue [net av
" George W engineer b 1176 Acush-
" Isaiah shoemaker h 318 Court
" John clerk b 318 Court
Ellis Albert died February 13 1911
" Alton B painter h 3 Jenney [Bay
" Anna J widow Harvey F h 20
" Benjamin F engineer h 188 Shawmut avenue
" Betsey A widow John b 85 Bay
" Caleb L motorman h 61 Willow
" Carrie N clerk N B I for Savings b 20 Bay [avenue
" Charles B pedlar h 567 Acushnet
" Charles E wholesale cigars 48 N Water h 118 Mill
" Claude M apprentice b 177 Cedar
" Edmund weaver b 821 S Water
" Edward W operative rms 270 Pleasant
" Eliza h 267 Pope
" Florence M teacher H M Knowlton school bds 186 Summer
" Francis H sterotyper 112 Union h 18 Fifth
" Frank E shoemaker b 267 Pope
" Frank E Jr bds 267 Pope
" Frederick F linotype operator Standard h 191 Kempton
" Harry shoe maker 9 Oak h 49 Short

Ellis
" Harry C police h 296 County
" Harry L electrician h 68 Walden
" Harry R hairdresser 24 Purchase h 396 Kempton [Cedar
" Herbert B book binder bds 177
" Herbert C (Ellis & Leclair) h 89 Park
" Herbert C removed to Abington
" Herbert F removed to Abington
" Herbert W conductor h 3 Glover
" Hubert F h 66 Russell
" Isaiah S h 30 Walnut [net av
" James machinist h 1264 Acush-
" James weaver h 78 Penniman
" Joseph carpenter h 176 Allen
" Joseph W S teamster h 45 Richmond [fee h 38 do
" Julia widow John variety 36 Dur-
" Julia A teacher Merrimac street school b 73 Willis
" Katharine widow Jefferson H h 270 Middle [419 Purchase
" Margaret E widow Thomas W h
" Mary E widow Herman b 235 Maple [ushnet av
" Mary M widow Rufus K h 254 Ac-
" Mary S dresmaker 270 Middle bds do
" Richard L mariner h 150 Middle
" Robert E drill maker h 126 Bonney [do
" Samuel shoemaker 420 Purchase h
" Sara F clerk 185 Union b 68 Walden
" Thomas S engineer b 64 North
" Washington P shoemaker 348 Cedar h at Lakeside
" Wilfred I laborer h 155 Grinnell
" William A conductor b Durfee corner Wilson
" William B conductor h 177 Cedar
" William E manager 194 Union h 325 Kempton
" Winifred (Dennis & Ellis) shoes 6 Purchase h 407 Union
" W Dixon president Valvoline Oil Co h at New York
" & LeClair (Herbert C Ellis and Felix A LeClair) painters 520 County
Ellison Henry W h 56 Emerson (S)
" Walter T twister h 156 Division

J. F. CROSSLEY 223 MILL STREET COR. EMERSON PHONE
STEAM and HOT WATER HEATING
GAS FITTING and FIXTURES

Elm Hotel The Joseph A Burke proprietor 35 Elm [chase
" Rink (Joseph A Burke) 302 Pur-
Emberson Eva L stenographer 120 Purchase rm 204 b at Fair-haven [haven
" George clerk 100 Fifth h at Fair-
Embleton Mark fireman bds 317½ Hillman
" Marks laborer rms 27 Hillman
Emerson Charles P piano tuner 141 Chestnut h do
" Helen W b 115 Summer
" James A second hand h 168 Belleville road [Summer
" Robie A widow H Wilder h 115
Emery John C h 99 Bedford
" Louisa F Mrs h 130 Summer
" William M editor Fall River Evening News h 116 Cottage
Emil Charles restaurant 1492 Acushnet avenue h do
Emilio P Melo twister h 71 Mosher
Emmett John weaver h 12 Roosevelt
" Joseph weaver h 46 Roosevelt
" Ralph decorator h Plainville road near Shawmut av [chase
Emmons Alfred conductor h 1159 Pur-
Emond Frank fixer h 47 Acushnet av
Empire Clothing Co (John Morris) 88 Purchase [lette
Enault Romeo speeder b 196 Col-
Engel John manager N B Tallow Co rms 188 Purchase
England Anatole spinner h 189 State
" Carl G painter rms 287 Court
" Edward G operative h 59 Austin
" Frank baker h 78 Dudley
" George h 67 Valentine
" James G glass cutter h 122 Fourth
" James H plumber h 76 Division
" Joseph teamster h 207 Church
" Louis laborer h 189 State
" Walter operative bds 59 Austin
" William agent bds 67 Valentine
English James stable 236 Kempton b do
Engstrom Arthur O instructor N B Industrial school rms 35 Eighth
Ennis Alice G clerk 185 Union b 176 Allen [Allen
" Bessie clerk 36 Purchase b 176
" Charles M asst bookkeeper N B S D & T Co bds 7 Green

Ennis
" Charles T clerk 213 Acushnet av h 7 Green [171 Fourth
" Edward A compositor Standard h
" Elizabeth clerk b 113 Bedford
" Emma D clerk 36 Purchase b 176 Allen [Second
" George M Jr carpenter rms 7 N
" James laborer h 71 Forest
" John H painter 17 Maitland h do
" Katherine C telephone operator 57 N Second bds 278 Allen
" Lillian G clerk 36 Purchase b 176 Allen
" Mary widow Richard h 278 Allen
" M Louise clerk 182 Union b 184 Acushnet avenue [176 Allen
" Patrick H tailor's pressman h
" Patrick H Jr clerk Bennett Mill b 176 Allen [113 Bedford
" Stanislas foreman 350 S Second h
" William H laborer 350 S Second b 113 Bedford [Kempton
Eno Ernest B letter carrier h 782
Enos Antone machinist h 49 Borden
" Antone mill hand b 630 S Water
" Antone seaman h 458 S Water
" Edward florist Ward corner Allen bds 262 Allen
" Emeline widow h 630 S Water
" Frank fisherman h 132 Thompson
" Frank gardener h 262 Allen
" Frank laborer h 49 Short
" Frank laborer h 103 Fifth
" Frank laborer h 137 Coffin av
" Frank laborer bds 630 S Water
" Frank operative h 630 S Water
" Frank rope maker b 67 Acushnet avenue [avenue
" Frank Jr mill hand b 137 Coffin
" Frank S clerk bds 90 Howland
" Frank S motorman h 72 Durfee
" Fred teamster h 10 Campbell
" George clerk 349 Rivet b 347 do
" George operative h 25 Oak
" George Mrs milliner 25 Oak h do
" Joaquim laborer h 90 Howland
" John clerk 329 Rivet
" John laborer h 259 S Second
" John laborer h 396 S Second
" John laborer h 1038 Rockdale av
" John machinist b 168 Acushnet av
" John operative h 69 Short

CHARLES A. CROSHERE
38 FOURTH ST. Bell Phone 1964-23
SIGN PAINTING
GLASS LETTERING
ELECTRIC SIGNS
SHOW CARDS

Enos
" John pool 349 Rivet h 347 do
" John (Enos & Oliver) removed from city
" John E stable 83 Grinnell h do
" John E Jr plumber h 128 Fourth
" John L box maker h 130 Fair
" John W shoemaker b 23 Ash (S)
" Joseph at P Corp h 257 S Second
" Joseph clerk h 371 Rivet
" Joseph drill worker h 38 Ash (S)
" Joseph hostler 486 Rivet h 985 S Water [lage
" Joseph mason h 28 Howland Vil-
" Joseph mill hand h 328 S Water
" Joseph roofer h 13 Hall
" Joseph teamster h 985 S Second
" Joseph A grocer h 169 Rockland
" Joseph A laborer h 169 Rockland
" Joseph L solderer h 193 Chancery
" Joseph L city laborer h 23 Ash (S) [ushnet av
" Joseph M copper worker h 706 Ac-
" Joseph P grinder b 69 Howland
" Lillian milliner h 123 Fifth
" Manuel died 1911
" Manuel fireman h rear 56 Clark
" Manuel fisherman h 329 S Front
" Manuel teamster h 3 Clark
" Manuel watchman 45 School h Potomska [City
" Manuel J removed to New York
" Manuel P died 1911 [well
" Mary widow Manuel h 44 Sto-
" Mary C widow John S b 400 Orchard
" May E h 151 Grinnell
" Michael laborer h 278 S Second
" Rose widow Antone h 19 Fair
" Sylvina widow h 80 Sidney
" Verginio h 75 Rodney
Ensen Howard drill worker h 86 S Sixth [12 Spruce
Entin Samuel clerk 182 Union h
Entwistle Alice widow James b 183 Coffin avenue [b do
" Annie clerk 183 Coffin avenue
" Anthony operative h 131 Tallman
" Elizabeth grocer 183 Coffin av h do
" Ernest operative b 34 Robeson

Entwistle
" George insurance agent 41 William h 6 Oneko lane [net av
" George operative h 1602½ Acush-
" George E laborer h 1627 Acushnet avenue [den
" James copper worker h 98 Lin-
" John W weaver h 128 Bowditch
" Mary Mrs h 34 Robeson
" Thomas removed from city
" Thomas E slasher b 6 Oneko lane
" William T weaver h 68 Linden
Epstein Abraham teamster h 6 Chestnut [Coggeshall bds do
" Abram (S E Epstein & Sons) 253
" Abram teas h 6 Chestnut
" Isaac canvasser bds 57 Washburn
" Abram (S E Epstein & Sons) 253 Coggeshall h do
" Solomon & Sons (Abram and Morris) dry goods 253 Coggeshall h do
" Uel dresses and skirts 1097 and 1345 Acushnet av h 37 Washburn
Equi Mary S Mrs h 168 Smith
Erickson Bertha E telephone operator 57 N Second b 113 Acushnet av
" Brothers (Eric and Herman) grocers 39 Jenny Lind b do
" Charles master mariner h 5 Jenny Lind
" Eric grocer b 980 Kempton
" Herman carpenter b 980 Kempton
" Selma h 980 Kempton [ory
Erlandson Olaf coachman h 37 Hick-
Erlbeck Max overseer Acushnet Mill Corporation h 120 Grinnell
Erseneau Louis speeder h 106 Rivet
Escobar Antone twist drill h 94 Potomska
" Eugene A drill worker b 61 Fifth
" John F h 143 Acushnet avenue
" Manuel weaver b 19 Bourne
Escola Rocco laborer h 75 Rodney
Escolas Julien tinsmith 28 N Water
Esinhart William waver h 71 Kenyon
Espinola Antone F grocer 562 South Water h 183 Rockland
" Domingas J grocer 602 S Water h 608 do
" Manuel J laborer h 29 Hall
" Manuel J laborer h 148 Rockland
" Mary J clerk 41 Purchase b 148 Rockland

J. G. NICHOLSON
LUMBER, SASH, DOORS and BLINDS
BOWDITCH STREET, NEW BEDFORD, MASS.

Espinola
" Rauly clerk 602 S Water b 608 do
Esslinger George linotype operator Standard h 430 Union [h do
Esson Sarah dressmaker 410 Kempton
Esta Albert laborer h foot Hawes
Estaby William carder b 307 Collette
Esterbrook Leila bookkeeper b 15 Ocean [134 Willis
Estes Abby A widow Abraham bds
" Andrew L carpenter 161 Clinton h 115 Campbell [Buttonwood
" Josephine widow William H b 29
" Percy C fireman h 135 Merrimac
" William A removed to Boston
Estrella Manuel F mason h 65 Mosher
Etchells Esther Mrs h 2 Cove road
" Henry overseer Bristol Mill h 280 Sawyer
" Henry W operative h 90 Kenyon
" John W warper h 15 George
" Joseph variety 477 Rivet h do
" Nancy widow Edward h 177 Ashland
" see Eccles [French avenue
Etherington William weaver h 5 E
Ethier Arthur operative b 287 Sawyer [yer
" Charles mill hand bds 287 Saw-
" Edmonde second hand h 287 Sawyer
" Leon E doffer bds 287 Sawyer
" Omer spinner b 287 Sawyer
Etienne Emma clerk 185 Union b 60 Briggs
" Jacob sausage maker h 60 Briggs
Eubanks Frederick T clerk h 87 Mill
Eugenio Manuel laborer h 51 Sherman
Evangelidis Nicholas pedlar h 41 Bethel [maker 22 North b do
Evans Agnes A widow Frank dress-
" Albert L glass worker b Mrs C E Evans' Tarkiln Hill road
" Charlotte E widow Levi h Tarkiln Hill road [way
" Ernest motorman bds 76 Hatha-
" Flora L h Tarkiln Hill road
" James F spinner h 2 Rockland
" James W glass blower b 2 Rockland
" John glass cutter h 10 Clay
Evarts Lizzie widow h 392 Belleville avenue [cor Market
Evening Standard The Pleasant
Evers Catherine widow William h 108 Ashland [land
" John J clerk ft Willis b 108 Ash-
" William shoemaker b 108 Ashland
Ewer Rebecca D widow Joseph b 175 Maxfield
Ewing Alexander h 220 North
" Henry clerk 182 Union h 220 North [Collette
Exelson Manuel second hand h 183
Eyre Samuel granite cutter 90 Dartmouth bds at Dartmouth
Ezzemonts Egildo laborer h 628 Acushnet avenue

Faber David teamster 168 S Water
" George P carpenter b 197 County
" Jacob h 50 Washburn
Fabio William M laborer h 248 Chancery [Grinnell h do
Fachado Abel shoe repairer 135½
Faford Alphonse h 74 County
" Alphonse Jr carpenter h 19 George [b 74 County
" Anne Marie (Faford & Poitras)
" Celina (Faford & Nerbonne) b 127 Ruth
FAFORD F XAVIER contractor and builder corner W French av and Dudley h 127 Ruth See page 763
" & Nerbonne (Celina Faford and Delia Nerbonne) dry goods 49 Brock avenue
" & Poitras (Anne M Faford and Hernendine Poitras) milliners 51 Brock avenue [nut
Fagan Bernard C machinist b 36 Wal-
" Hannah widow Patrick h 216 Fourth
" John M glass blower b 216 Fourth
" Joseph pedlar h 102 Potomska
" Joseph B glass blower h 49 Hall
" Joseph P organist b 96 Washington
" Michael J h 64 W French av
" Patrick H glass blower h 96 Washington [Coffin av
Fagundes Joao V mill hand h 181
Fahey Francis laborer h 22 Bullard
" Francis (Fahey & Beaulieu) h 47 Nye [Bullard
" John B grocer 302 N Front h 126

Steiger-Dudgeon Co.
"The WOMAN'S Store."
Tel. Bell 82 & 83, Branches connecting all depts.
" " 160 For Office only. Auto. 1211

SUMPTIONS, ASSORTMENTS AT ALL TIMES OF DEPENDABLE DRY GOODS

Fahey
" Wilfred T clerk 1284 Acushnet av bds 47 Nye
" & Beaulieu (Francis Fahey and Henry Beaulieu) grocers 1284 Acushnet avenue
" see Fay
Fairbanks George L laborer b 327 County [man
" Samuel L gardener h 131 Whit-
" Samuel L shoe worker b 327 County [man
" William O gardener b 131 Whit-
Fairbrother Alice E stenographer 3 East Pope b 93 Rockland
" Edward teamster rms 116 Middle
" Nellie F h 27 Moore [Rockland
" Samuel N foreman 7 Leonard h 93
Fairchild Thomas H (White & Fairchild) 322 County h 53 Fifth
Faircliff Herbert motorman b 275 Cedar Grove [Roosevelt
Fairclough Alice widow Joseph h 66
" John T weaver h 172 Austin
" Thomas fireman h 49 Roosevelt
Fairfield Frederick head bookkeeper 36 Purchase h 188 Newton
" Louisa C Mrs b 16 Maple View terrace [h 188 Newton
" Mary E Mrs clerk 36 Purchase
Fairhaven Ferry foot Union [bury
Fairhurst John weaver h 26 Salis-
Fairweather William R piper 125 Middle h 102 David
Faisneau George E Jr clerk 185 Union h 184 Court [ral
Falcoa Daniel hairdresser h 11 Ru-
Falcon Antone G carpenter h 94 Acushnet avenue [land
" Manuel G hairdresser h 92 Rock-
Falk Rose Mrs grocer 528 S Water h do [Acushnet av h do
Fallas Hannah confectioner 1606
Fallows Richard T boss picker h 5 E French avenue
Fanning John F police Station 5 h 242 Sawyer [416 do
" William B manager 163 Union h
Fanton Charles piper 125 Middle h 322 Sawyer
Farache Manuel E b 15 Howland
Faradofski Rock operative h 51 Washburn [Coggeshall
Farage Kalil boarding house 261
Faria Antone R laborer h 73 Bates av
" Joseph h 136 Thompson [son
" Joseph E mill hand b 96 Thomp-
" Joseph M gardener h 81 Thompson
" Manuel S laborer h 11 Madison
" Rauly laborer h 544 Rivet
Farinha Manuel T laborer h 7 Bonneau court [road
Farland Adelard weaver h 18 Cove
" Arthur weaver h 773 First [Hotel
Farley Alferie E clerk b Weld square
" George operative h 13 Princeton
" George spinner b 2 Hicks
" Joseph spinner b 198 Tinkham
" Louis b 198 Tinkham [Tinkham
" Nathalie widow Isadore h 198
" Thomas motorman h 411 Pleasant
Farmer Clifford M wiring inspector 125 Middle h 11 Homer
" Mable S Mrs dressmaker b 109 Fourth
Farnardes Rosslina removed from city
Farnham Charles H W clerk 87 Union b 30 Keene [Keene
" Ezra G engineer Quissett Mill h 30
" Flora E Mrs corsets 30 Keene h do [h 9 Borden
" Jerome B engineer 1145 Kempton
" Lydia P widow George W b 36 Madison
Farnsworth Fred weaver h 299 Brook
Farr William foreman 6 Elm h 107 Chestnut [ushnet av
Farrady Annie widow h 851 Ac-
" Hannah J waitress 968 Acushnet avenue b 9 Mt Pleasant lane
" James weaver h 22 George [Earle
" Mary widow Isaac weaver h 84
Farran Joseph mill hand h 71 Fruit
Farrar Edward overseer h 80 Katharine [h 46 State
" William F ticket agent R R depot
Farras Assad (Farras & Joseph) h 3 McDonald court
" & Joseph (A Farras & B Joseph) grocers 283 Coggeshall [ond
Farrell Daniel shoemaker h 64 S Sec-
" Dora E widow William b 31 Walnut
" Elizabeth Mrs h 9 Viall
" Ellen widow John b 19 Welcome
" Francis B shoemaker b 114 Rockland [Parker House
" George E manager Bennett Mill b

PELEG H. SHERMAN 506 COUNTY ST.
FUNERAL DIRECTOR AND EMBALMER
OFFICE PHONES. Bell 690-13. Auto. 1305.
RESIDENCE PHONES. Bell 690-12. Auto. 1306.

Farrell
" James F helper b 19 Welcome
" James H laborer h 138 Division
" James J fixer h 19 Welcome
" John clerk h 509 Rivet
" John J piper b 19 Welcome
" Katherine Mrs h 76 W French av
" Michael mason b 81 Summer
" Timothy S mason h 114 Rockland
" William P tailor 157 Union h 351 Elm (W)
" see O'Farrell
Farrelly Patrick laborer h 142 Crapo
Farren Mary Mrs h 126 Thompson
" Roger weaver h 4 Cove road
Farrer Edward H third hand bds 80 Katharine [Weld
Farrington Thomas weaver b 207
Farrow Sarah E Mrs weaver h 194 Nash road [son h 49 Larch
Farry Antone R clerk 126 Thomp-
Fartado Joaquim fisherman h 528 S Water
Farwell Rebecca died Dec 29 1910
Fass Otto baker h 199 N Front
Fatimia Fred hostler h 916 County
Fatulli Peter confectionery 123 Fourth h 101 Hall [County
Faucher Hector shoe maker h 917
Faulkner Ernest L poultry h 868 Hathaway road
" George B baggage master R R depot h 906 Hathaway road
" Jonathan D fisherman h 136 Willis [h 72 Smith
Faunce Albert M foreman 158 Mill
" Annie P widow b 299 County
FAUNCE CHARLES L contractor and builder 138 N Second h 13 Pope See page 765
" Phoebe B widow Loum H h 95 High
Fauteux Henry canvasser h 439 Mill
" Henry A mason h 154 Whitman
Favor Charles engineer rms 72 Foster
" David teamster h 100 Nelson
Favreau Archille clerk 267 Coggeshall h 72 Kenyon [Grove
" Joseph teamster h 253 Cedar
" Joseph F clerk h 320 Pleasant
Fawcett George L h 119 Brock av
" Isaac mule spinner h 263 Phillips avenue
" Joseph died January 15 1911

Fawcett
" Phoebe and Jane h 993 County
" Sarah Mrs h 134 Division
" William second hand h 137 Thompson
" see Fossett [ond
Fay Edward F teamster b 125 N Sec-
" Emma Mrs h 10 Winsor
" Harry painter b 7 Blackburn
" James L liquors 962 Acushnet av h 42 Pearl
" John H police b 401 Orchard (S)
" Joseph E instructor H of C h 21 Emerson (S) [h 125 do
" Laurence P manager 27 N Second
" Mary E died July 19 1911
" Miles E spare engineer N B F D bds 401 Orchard (S)
" Patrick H watchman h 401 Orchard (S)
" Roger T liquors 25-27 N Second h 58 Pierce
" Thomas lieut of police h 17 Bay
" Thomas J teamster b 125 N Second [avenue
" William barber h 241 Coffin
" see Fahey [Phillips av
Fazackerly William weaver h 282
Fealteau Louis operative h 70 Washburn [h 242 Maxfield
Fearing Fannie J widow William H
" F Mildred b 242 Maxfield
" Sherman T clerk 125 Purchase b 242 Maxfield
Feather J Arthur designer Acushnet Mills Corporation h 5 Arch
Featherston John steam fitter h 311 Pleasant
" Patrick h 32 Larch
Febeo Fred fixer h 675 First
" Joe fireman h 675 First
Fecteau Arthur tailor 912 S Water h 81 Independent
" Henry operative h 333 Bowditch
Feegan James removed to Dartmouth
" James Jr removed to Dartmouth
Feeley Edward shoe worker b 98 Nye
" Edward J painter h 364 Pleasant
" John laborer h 188 Division
" John weaver h 28 r Acushnet av
" Thomas H mgr 120 Purchase rms 158 Middle [364 Pleasant
" William J clerk 115 William h

F. T. AKIN & CO. PAINTERS AND DECORATORS

Feenan Alice G teacher Hosea M Knowlton school b 156 Chestnut [wood
" Bernard C carpenter h 15 Button-
Feeney John card grinder h 34 Hemlock
" Mary Mrs waitress h 25 William
" Thomas slubber tender b 34 Hemlock [niman
" William copper worker h 61 Pen-
Fegarsky Benjamin tailor b 7 Beetle
" Louis pedlar h 7 Beetle
" Samuel pedlar h 7 Beetle
Feingold Abraham furniture 399 S Water h 428 do
" Philip carpenter h 15 Howland
Feldgen Francis H laborer h 1213 Rockdale avenue
" Herman J h 1213 Rockdale av
Feldon Richard (Lonsdale & Feldon) 1081 S Water h do
Felecia Christiana died Aug 14 1910
Felecianno John grocer 261 Allen h 267 do
" John Jr mgr 189 Allen h 191 do
" Manuel clerk b 267 Allen
" Mary dressmaker 267 Allen h do
" Nellie V Mrs grocer 189 Allen h 191 do
" Olympia milliner b 267 Allen
Felix Anthony W hostler h 81 Newton
" Harry laborer rms 7 Marvin
Fell William weaver h 10 Linden ct
Fellows Richard T carder h 5 Abbott
Fells Manuel laborer h 56 Grinnell
Felton Alexander S janitor h 19 Bonney
" Harry Rev pastor Howard M E church rms 257 Palmer [ard
" James baker 175 Dean b 139 Bull-
" Robert J mason h 12 Potter
Fender Elizabeth widow James h 21 Ashland place
" John operative h 130 Crapo
Fennell Albert glass cutter rms 300 Acushnet avenue
Fenney Collins operative rms 140 N Second [Parker
Fenton James P supt 185 Union h 29
" Thomas laborer h 85 Hathaway
" William H operative h 135 Bullard [chase
Feran Frank operative rms 434 Pur-
Ferat Hoso laborer h 191 Belleville av

Fereira Constance h 356 S Water
Ferguson Alexander drill maker h 19 Atlantic [do
" Andrew G orderly 194 Purchase b
" Daniel weaver b 273 Coggeshall
" Daniel H inspector of school property 166 William h 563 Union
" David teaming 98 Park h do
" Edith M stenographer 37 Masonic bldg b 49 State
" Fergus overseer Whitman Mill
" George B shoemaker b 49 State
" George T physical director Y M C A h 473 Cottage
" James assistant supt h 49 State
" James operative b 133 Reynolds
" James A shoemaker b 49 State
" James M plumber's apprentice b 421 Union [h at Mattapoisete
" James N clerk N Water cor Elm
" Joseph coachman 81 Hawthorn h 450 Union
" Robert student b 421 Union
" Robert teamster b 98 Park
" Samuel J coachman 385 County h 421 Union
" Thomas laborer h 189 North
" William engineer H C h 855 Rockdale avenue
" William variety 67 Cedar h do
Ferland Celestine pattern maker h 109 Locust
" Leon laborer h 407 N Front
" L Philip clerk 410 N Front h 25 Bentley [Water
Fermine Florentine laborer h 417 S
Fern Samuel operative h 199 Davis
Fernandes Alfred grocer 360 S Water h 218 Acushnet avenue
" Amos grocer 11 S Water h do
" Annie Mrs h 505 S Water
" Antone laborer h 485 Hathaway road [court
" Antone operative h 7 La France
" Antone rope maker b 474 Union
" Antone Jr rope maker b 474 Union
" Antonio removed from city
" Antonio A grocer 200 Rivet h 202 do [(S)
" Antonio J laborer h 292 Orchard
" Charles A clerk 322 County b 292 Orchard (S)

Kinyon's Commercial School Will furnish your office help free
Odd Fellows Building COR. WILLIAM and PLEASANT STS. NEW BEDFORD, MASS.

Fernandes
" Ernest h 42 Katharine
" Eugene laborer h 48 Hemlock
" Frank laborer h 3 Wall
" Frank weaver h 522 Bolton
" Frank A (M A & F A Fernandes) h 16 Clay
" Frank H clerk 98 Allen 239 Field
" Frank J h 41 Cottage
" Fred rivet maker 8 Hazards lane bds at Dartmouth
" Henry weaver h 271 Phillips av
" John carder h 56 Clark [(S)
" John glass cutter b 292 Orchard
" John B laborer h 9 Madison
" Joseph laborer h 45 Short
" Joseph A police h 229 Brock av
" Joseph H clerk h 383 S Second
" Joseph J operative h 103 Fair
" Leander laborer h 73 S Second
" Louis laborer b 73 S Second
" Manuel mill hand h 17 Bullard
" Manuel mill hand h 136 Thompson
" Manuel Mrs h 2 Blackburn
" Manuel A (M A & F A Fernandes) h 129 Division
" Mary G widow h 48 Hemlock
" M A & F A (Manuel A and Frank A) shoes 126 Dartmouth
" Neva freight handler h 56 First
Fernandez Anton laborer h 3 Wall
Fernley John A supt Butler Mills h 203 Hawthorn [Willis
Ferns John P letter carrier h 84
" Joseph h 270 Pope
Ferraira Mariano laborer 320 S Second [yon
Ferreau Archille operative h 72 Ken-
" Manuel P laborer h 15 Cotter
Ferreia Antone P laborer h 73 Bates avenue [ska
" Jacinth mill hand h 101 Potom-
" Joseph spinner h 29 Winsor
Ferreira Antone clerk 25 Lombard h 379 Second
" Antone cook b 307 S Front
" Antone laborer h 233 S Front
" Antonio mill hand h 39 Dunbar
" Eugene barber 42 Elm b 20 Mill road [ville av
" Francisco G carder h 202 Belle-
" Frank operative h 186 Division
" Frank V mill hand h 46 South

Ferreira
" Jacinth laborer h 137 Field
" Jacinth mariner h 7 Bethel
" Jacques shoemaker h 45 Howland Village
" James operative h 174 S Second
" John mill hand h 41 Dunbar
" John teamster 2 S Water h 9 Rotch block 438 Bolton
" John P clerk 562 S Water
" Jose operative h 12 Rotch blk 438 Bolton [438 Bolton
" Jose D operative h 11 Rotch blk
" Joseph died Aug 1 1910
" Joseph mill hand h 686 S Water
" Joseph mill hand b 46 Howland Village
" Joseph painter h 335 S Water
" Joseph L teamster h 263 S Second
" Joseph P laborer h 310 S Front
" Jule M operative h 39 Mitchell
" Julio fish 67 Howland h at Fairhaven
" Manuel carpenter h 13 Rural
" Manuel carder h 125 Fair
" Manuel laborer h 5 Mitchell
" Manuel laborer h 143 Field
" Manuel laborer h 202 Belleville av
" Manuel laborer h 868 County
" Manuel laborer h 912 County
" Manuel mill hand h 397 Rivet [av
" Manuel operative h 125 Belleville
" Manuel variety 240 S Second h do
" Manuel G mill hand b 7 Bonneau court
" Manuel J teamster h 85 Prospect
" Manuel M operative h 494 Rivet
" Mary Mrs h 1 E Durfee [way
" Mary widow Fank h 208 Hatha-
" Victorine laborer h 76 Katharine
Ferren Laverna Mrs b 39 Fifth [ham
Ferriere Adam V agent h 210 Tink-
Ferrigos Frank removed from city
Ferris Antone laborer h 73 Prospect
" Ethel clerk Gosnold Mills Co
" John carder bds 621 First
" Joseph variety 155 County h do
" Manuel hairdresser Parker House h 198 Grinnell [N Second
" Manuel laborer N B W W h 128
Ferro Anthony driver 36 Purchase
Ferron Joseph clerk 41 Bentley h 23 Holly [way
Feser Kasper operative h 157 Hatha-

Bread, Cake, Pastry
RICHMOND & COMPANY **255-257 UNION STREET**
Bell 993 Automatic 1022

Fezette Felix C fixer h 301 Coffin av
Fialho Frank C carpenter h 325 S Front
" Manuel F weaver h 459 Bolton
" Manuel V h 32 South
Fiatta Manuel V mill hand h 32 South [Water h 81 Elm
Fichtenmayer George tinsmith 28 N
" Martin P horseshoer 326 S Water h 272 Dartmouth [88 Sycamore
" Otto blacksmith 326 S Water h
Fidler Arthur J tinsmith b 496 Bolton
" Margaret widow Arthur J h 496 Bolton [burn
Fiebeger Anton weaver h 14 Wash-
Field Ada L clerk b 55 State
" Anna L bookkeeper b 55 State
" Charles W teamster h 7 Willis
" Edward H janitor Merrimac st school h 286 Pleasant
" Gilbert weaver b 129 Eugenia
" Godfrey bds 129 Eugenia
" Henry h 55 State
" John teamster b 51 Bolton
" Leonard B laborer h 339 Pleasant
" Lynn A compositor Standard h 2 Foster
" see Fields
Fielden John died June 12 1910
" Joseph twister b 24 Welcome
Fieldin Martha S widow John h 31 Social
Fielding Amelia Mrs h 6 McGurk
" Mercer loom fixer h 59 Fruit
" Rachel Mrs weaver h 32 Franklin
" R Carl upholsterer 71 William b 382 Maxfield
" Thomas weaver b 158 Hathaway
" William variety 208 Cedar h 120 Parker [ond
Fields Joseph C laborer h 141 S Sec-
" William E jobber b 275 Acushnet avenue
Fife Michael laborer h r 21 Washburn
Figarsky Benjamin b 7 Beetle
Figg Benjamin laborer b 135 Bullard
Figueiredo Edward J wood 425 S Second h 422 do [226 Brownell
" Joseph S tailor 83 Howland h
" Manuel laborer h 56 Hollyhock
Filiault Alex weaver h 740 Purchase
Fillioult Alex mill hand h 742 Belleville avenue [Front h do
Filochowski John grocer 197 North

Finch Albert fixer h 27 Viall [av
" Albert weaver h 847 Acushnet
" Arthur spinner h 109 Mott
" Ernest loom fixer h 113 Mott
" Mary Mrs h 201 Cedar Grove
" Pakinson removed from ctiy
" William laborer h 184 Phillips av
Findeisen Oscar E steam fitter h 14 Rural [Clark
Findlay Thomas S time keeper h 129
Fine Max locksmith 39 S Second h 37 Prospect
Finger Alex h r 648 Acushnet av
" Frank weaver b 50 Washburn
" Sigmund h 1132 Acushnet av
Fink George weaver h 199 Dean
Finkelstein Israel h 23 Beetle
" Samuel pedlar h 19 Cotter
Finkle Harry pedlar h 206 S Front
Finklestein Gertrude widow Edward grocer 521 S Water h do
Finlan Dennis h 109 Smith
" Hugh Mrs h 3 Clark
Finley John W weaver h 19 Austin
" Patrick laborer h 164 Bonney
" Theresa A Mrs dressmaker 46 W French av h do [av
" Thomas F laborer h 46 W French
Finlon Hugh weaver h 788 County
" James died June 6 1910
" Patrick weaver b 788 County
Finn James J glass cutter h 226 Park
" John T painter b 211 Chestnut
" Michael inspector Wamsutta Mill h 211 Chestnut
Finnegan John T jeweler 1109 Acushnet av bds Parker House
" Thomas mill worker b 90 Clark
" Patrick J jewelry 1109 Acushnet avenue bds Parker House
Finnell Grace M teacher Cedar Grove school b 27 Locust
" James H clerk h 616 Cottage
" John H assessor 9 Municipal bldg h 311 Bowditch [Elm
" John N clerk 124 Purchase h 17
" Stephen L clerk 645 Purchase h 27 Locust [coln
" Thomas officer H C h 17 Lin-
Finnerty James engineer h 378 Middle (W) [County
" Johanna widow Patrick h 877
" John clerk b 878 County [ham
" Michael removed to S Framing-

GLOBE DYE HOUSE
220 SHAWMUT AVE.
J. N. J. LONHOLDT, PROP. Telephone Connections Goods called for and Delivered
Down town Office, 52 Pleasant St., Room 1 North End Office, 1014 Acushnet Ave.

Finnerty
" Michael J engineer h 150 Chancery [ty
" Patrick J brakeman h 878 Coun-
Finni Charles D h 328 Acushnet av
" Charles D Jr driver h 59 Fifth
" Dominick fruit Union corner Purchase h 573 Kempton
" Ernesto A clerk 58 N Second b 328 Acushnet av [av b 328 do
" Joseph N dentist 1105 Acushnet
" Paul motorman h 12 Atlantic
Firme Henrique O (New Bedford Stained Glass and Window Co) 164 County h 29½ Acushnet av
First Church of Christ Scientist 36 Pleasant
FIRST NATIONAL BANK Walter P Winsor president William A Mackie cashier 110 Union See page 7
Firth Leonard removed to Baltic Conn
" Samuel third hand h 72 Ruth
Fischer Antone carpenter b 487 Coggeshall
Fish Addie Mrs b 140 Mill
" Alice W b 144 Summer
" Andrew J tailor 52 Pleasant h 279 Palmer [land Ohio
" Andrew J Jr removed to Cleve-
" Benjamin b rear 338 Kempton
" Benjamin F bds 133 Cedar
" Betsey T widow Ansel F h 619 County [fin av h do
" Bourgoyne stocking mfr 254 Cof-
" Catherine E removed to Hartford Conn [ond
" Fred Walter piper h 64 S Sec-
" Frederick C shoemaker h 37 Atlantic [more
" Frederick R driver b 57 Syca-
" Frederick R supt glass dept T P Corp h 68 Borden [mer
" Grafton D B student b 279 Pal-
" Harold B chauffeur b 144 Summer
" Harriet widow L Nelson h 144 Summer
" James weaver b 117 Austin
" John loom fixer h 730 S Water
" Loranus C grocer 59½ Sycamore h 57 do [h 417 Union
" Lucy B teacher Middle st school
" Luther weaver bds 64 Ruth

Fish
" Rebecca widow James h 28 Dartmouth
" Richard weaver b 602 Purchase
" Thomas H sausage maker h 858 First [avenue
" William weaver h 13 E French
Fisher Arthur E yard foreman City Coal Co h 179 Tremont
" Basil V clerk N B Five Cents Savings Bank b 458 Mill [Mill
" Belle S widow Hervey L h 458
" Charles spinner h 33 Desautels
" Charles C salesman 2 S Water h 143 North
" Charles L assistant recording teller Merchants National Bank bds 458 Mill [h at Fall River
" Edward L president 2 S Water
" Elisha H salesman h 411 Union
" Elizabeth C widow Matthew h 71 S Sixth
" E L Co Inc wholesale produce and fruit 2 S Water
" Frank operative h 139 Division
" Frank M conductor N Y, N H & H h 105 Sycamore
" Frederick brakeman h 247 State
" George D removed from city
" George E laborer h 993 S Water
" George L fisherman h 97 Middle
" Gustave clerk 674 Acushnet av b do [h do
" Herbert L carpenter 101 Chestnut
" John operative b 336 Coffin av
" Joseph laborer bds 116 Division
" Leon C student b 6 Franklin
" Lydia laundress rms 366 Purchase
" Max Emil baker 97 Allen h 99 Brigham [b 143 North
" Merton C lawyer 37 Masonic bldg
" Michael engineer h 1061 County
" Paul L clerk 240 Union b 6 Franklin [R I
" Richard removed to Central Falls
" Richard A janitor City Coal Co h 8 Spruce [ushnet av h do
" Sarah widow Louis grocer 674 Ac-
" Sidney S teamster 36 Purchase h 6 Franklin
" Thomas laborer bds 33 McGurk
" Walter C helper 28 N Water h 72 Jenny Lind

GREENE & WOOD Every Kind of LUMBER AND MILL WORK
PINE STREET, off So. WATER STREET, NEW BEDFORD

Fisher
" William H flagman h 116 Willis
" see Fischer [Water
Fishman Hyman mill hand h 371 S
Fiske Alice agent N B Children's Aid Society 12 Market b 175 Mill
Fissette Euclide blacksmith b 126 Princeton [ton
" Louis blacksmith h 126 Prince-
" Ulric machinist b 126 Princeton
" Wilfred blacksmith 105 Bowditch h 102 Beetle
Fitch Addie Mrs b 35 Elm [do
" Horace A electrician 109 Union b
Fitchiney Mary h 51 James
Fitting Anthony painter h 5 Felton
" David back boy b 5 Felton
Fitton Edward spinner h 33 George
" Frederick laborer b 270 Coggeshall
" John comber tender b 371 State
" Robert doffer b 270 Coggeshall
" Sarah Mrs b 177 Weld
" Thomas laborer h 270 Coggeshall
" William overseer Dartmouth Mfg Corp h 68 Crapo [rimac
Fitts Ethel M stenographer b 160 Mer-
" James S h 160 Merrimac
" Winfield S b 31 Keene
Fitzgerald Edward h 35 Morton ct
" Edward Jr speeder b 35 Morton court
" Ellen weaver h 955 Purchase
" James eyelet maker b 146 Davis
" James P conductor h 143 Willis
" Jennie F clerk 185 Union b 1650 Acushnet avenue
" John watchman h 46 Reynolds
" Martin Rev h 233 County
" Patrick J watchman h 146 Davis
" Robert shoe worker h 305 Mill
" William spinner b 336 Coffin av
" William F lunch 102 Union h 70½ William [ond h 240 Middle
" William L special agent 57 N Sec-
Fitzpatrick Daniel removed from city
" Ellen widow of Thomas h 113 Hathaway
" John bellman 435 County b do
" Mary weaver h 46 W French av
" Michael spinner h 128 Nash road
" Patrick removed from city
Fitzsimmons Ann nurse h 219 State

Fitzsimmons
" Nicholas H bricklayer h 87 Ashland [ditch h 106 Princeton
Fivett Louis blacksmith 105 Bow-
" Wilfred blacksmith 105 Bowditch h 102 Beetle
Flagg Maurice I removed to Minneapolis Minnesota [Warwick
" William D driver Engine 1 h 5
Flaherty Alonzo laborer b 15 S Second [Fifth
" Bridget clerk 139 Union bds 112
" Ellen widow Matthew h 189 Chancery
" Fannie h 100 S Second
" James H laborer b 15 S Second
" John laborer bds 112 Fifth
" John teamster h 28 Spring
" John E clerk b 105 Fifth
" John J laborer bds 189 Chancery
" Lena A clerk b 189 Chancery
" Morgan laborer b 65 Washburn
" Thomas laborer h 15 S Second
" Thomas Jr laborer b 15 S Second
" Willard C h 13 Spring
Flanagan James laborer h 33 McGurk
" John J driver 123 Fourth b 12 Clark
" John J fireman h 118 Fruit
" Katherine and Alice weavers h 98 Austin
" William laborer h 12 Clark
Flanders Cyrus H fruit 17 Commercial h 69 Fourth
" Elihu W salesman b 69 Fourth
" Ella G Mrs h 573 Kempton [av
Flannery Annie weaver h 8 Acushnet
" Michael laborer h 10 Acushnet av
" Michael lunch 106 Weld h 8 Clark
Flarez John Francis Jr carpenter bds 335 Orchard (S)
" John F h 335 Orchard (S)
Fleetwood Charles h 124 Cedar
Fleischer Jacob I tailor 356 Acushnet avenue h 236 do
Fleischmann Co The yeast 38 Elm
Fleish Samuel clerk h 303 Middle
Fleming Anna widow Richard h 696 Acushnet avenue [Middle (W)
" Caroline widow George bds 396
" Fred laborer h 417 Hillman
" John clerk 43 Bedford rms do
" Joseph F salesman 14 N Second bds 50 Fifth [ny Lind
" Lillian S widow Joseph h 138 Jen-

BONNEY, FOLSTER & CO.,
The North End's Shopping Centre
Dry Goods and Men's Furnishings
945-947 Acushnet Ave., New Bedford, Mass.

Fleming
" Owen A weaver b 138 Jenny Lind
Fletcher Alfred A weaver h 426 Pleasant
" Ann R h 114 Seventh [man
" Annie widow Edward h 124 Whit-
" John spinner b 52 Morton ct
" Louis J cable splicer 57 N Second b 113 Fourth
" Mary A widow James b 28 Maxfield [50 Page
" Mary E widow James T h
" Percy I clerk 100 Fifth b at Fairhaven
" Peter operative h 28 Tallman
" Ralph W fixer b 30 Sherman
" Susan R died Nov 5 1910
" Thomas operative h 51 Salisbury
" William H fitter h 139 Bullard
Fleury Adelard fixer h 27 Bullard
" Arthur operative b 199 Phillips avenue [avenue b do
" Celestine dressmaker 199 Phillips
" Elizabeth widow Celestine bds 199 Phillips av
" Henry painter b 112 Mott
" Laurent Mrs h 13 Hicks [av
" Thomas carpenter h 199 Phillips
" Thomas Jr removed to Montreal Canada [34 Pearl
Flint Burt W supt Times bldg h
" Daniel B b 34 Pearl
Flood Bartholomew b 110 County
" Bartholomew 2nd joiner b 110 County [from city
" James (229 Brock av) removed
" James drillmaker h 274 Allen
" James weaver b 1283 Acushnet av
" John loom fixer h 110 County
" John Jr spinner b 110 County
" L Daniel woodworker b 159 Newton
" May Mrs h 13 Bannister
" Thomas fireman b 8 Tallman
" Thomas weaver b 51 Bolton
Florence Garry baker 166 Purchase rms 366 do
Florent Adolph carpenter h 253 Sawyear [av b 253 Sawyer
" Annette milliner 1077 Acushnet
" Hector plumber 1545 Acushnet av h 236 Collette
" Isadore laborer 108 River rd
" Joseph laborer h 108 River rd
" Uldric iceman h 3 Jean
Flores John laborer h 77 Fruit
Floria John mill hand b 195 Belleville av [av
" Manuel mill hand h 195 Belleville
Floris Manuel J fisherman h 22 Swift [175 Shawmut av
Flower William G diemaker h
Flowers Charles weaver h 390 Purchase [lane b 330 Earle
Flue Michael baker 55 Mechanics
Fluegel Christopher machinist b 438 S Second
" Katherine died April 23, 1910
Flynn Daniel foreman rms 290 Pleasant [net av
" Francis M Mrs bds 1737 Acush-
" John stonecutter h 112 Clark
" John A h 175 Fourth
" John E shoemaker b 112 Clark
" John T drillworker b 280 Earle
" Mary E F bookkeeper 1100 Acushnet av b 112 Clark [shnet av
" William glassworker h 138 Acu-
" William H officer House of Correction h 1093 Rockdale av
" William L boilermaker h 198 Arnold
" William L machinist h 50 Pierce
Fogarty Emma F nurse 158 Allen
" Mary A widow Edmond h 22 Hall
" Mary E h 158 Allen
" Philip E painter 22 Hall b do
" Thomas glassblower h 158 Allen
Fogg Harry machinist h 31 Jouvett
Foisy Albert clerk h 18 Jean
" Alphonse weaver h 543 Acushnet avenue [nolds
" Edward J conductor h 113 Rey-
" Gustaf removed from city
" Hormidas removed from city
" Joseph clerk 380 Sawyer h 237 Coffin av [81 Park
" Joseph H salesman 185 Union h
" Prosper hay 380-382 Sawyer h r 1085 County
" Prosper Jr clerk h 249 State
Foley Catherine M widow James h 6 Austin court [N Y
" Charles A rem to Morris Heights
" Edmund police h 168 Allen
" Edward clerk 47 School b 18 Jean
" Edward F brakeman h 24 Penniman
" James shoemaker b 295 Cedar
" James teamer b 52 School
" James A weaver h 197 Tinkham

M. P. B. Silva & Son Paints, Oils and Glass
Sole Agents for Lucas Tinted Gloss Paints
157 ACUSHNET AVENUE Both Phones NEW BEDFORD

Foley:
" James J laborer h 101 Linden
" Johanna widow John b 18 Jean
" John granite Court c Jenney h 408 Court
" John laborer 1081 Acushnet av rms 1293 do
" John plumber b 375 Kempton
" John F laborer b 101 Linden
" John M graniteworker c Jenney and Court h 408 Court
" Joseph eyeletmaker b 101 Lindden [Bullock
" Katharyn widow Michael h 22
" Martin B mgr Anthony swift & Co h 43 Florence [N Front
" Mary widow weaver rms 346
" Michael J graniteworker b 408 Court
" Patrick J laborer h 772 County
" Thomas b 18 Jean
" Thomas operative b 59 Tallman
" Timothy laborer h 1053 County
" William plumber h 25 Reynolds
" William F removed from city
" William F variety 341 Sawyer h 18 Jean
Folger Charles E bookkeeper b 61 Hillman [75 Chestnut
" David B grocer 140-142 Union h
" Frank S h 48 Thompson
" Frank S Jr second hand h 48 Thompson [Hillman
" Susan R widow Charles F h 61
Folkes Mary widow h 27 Cleveland
Folsom Frances A h 126 Purchase
" Irod J B conductor h 60 Mt Pleasant
" Simeon h 126 Purchase
Folster Adelard baker b 251 Phillips av [b 267 Bowditch
" Clarence U clerk 945 Acushnet av
" Elmire widow George h 251 Phillips av [b 251 Phillips av
" Emile J (Bonney Folster & Co)
Fonce Manuel laborer h 216 S Front
Fonseca Antone M fisherman h 453 Belleville av [h 60 Briggs
" Frank P shoemaker 76 Purchase
" John operative h 356 S Water
" Joseph N operative h 248 Bowditch [mer
" Manuel operative h 68 Black-
" Philip C fisherman h 136 Irvington

Fontaine Andre D druggist 1115 S Water b 73 Independent [rd
" Edward carpenter h 110 Nash
" Edward piper 125 Middle [vis
" Fernando mill hand bds 154 Da-
" Gustave, U S A h 357 Bowditch
" Henry second hand h 118 Mott
" Hermidas fixer h 34 Acushnet av
" John B laborer h 118 Nash rd
" Leon weaver bds 118 Nash rd
" Louis salesman b 20 Covell
" Lucie b 73 Independent
" L J Oscar music teacher 177 Bowditch h do [vis
" Olivine Mrs mill hand h 154 Da-
" Ovilla weaver h 24 Warren
" Peter bartender b 221 Purchase
" Phillias clerk 326 Bowditch bds 296 Sawyer
" Pierre wholesale liquors 870 Acushet av h 821 Purchase
" Theodore weaver b 587 First
" William bartender 46½ Howland h do
" William weaver h 326 N Front
" see Lafontaine [h 171 Bowditch
Fonteaneau Alfred driver 238 State
" Amanda widow Antoine h 63 Austin [net block
Fontes Antone fisherman b 8 Acush-
" Joseph fisherman b 8 Acushnet block
" Joseph R fisherman b 408 First
" Tony R fisherman b 468 First
" Vitriano R laborer h 8 Acushnet block [ond
Foote Antone cook h 137 S Sec-
" Mary widow George weaver h 323 Earle [74 Willis
" Warren C mgr 57 N Second h
" W Cleveland mgr h 74 Willis
Footman Carrie E principal Phillips avenue school b 70 Morgan
Foran John J salesman 125 Middle h 174 Ashland [chase
Forand Alciade machinist b 703 Pur-
" Alice C clerk b 703 Purchase
" Alfred master mechanic Wamsutta h 703 Purchase
" Alfred J machinist h 438 Pleasant [lawn av
" Francois X weaver h 32 Wood-

Steiger-Dudgeon Co.
"The WOMAN'S Store."
Tel. Bell 82 & 83, Branches connecting all depts.
" " 160 For Office only. Auto. 1211

SUMPTIONS, ASSORTMENTS AT ALL TIMES OF DEPENDABLE DRY GOODS

Forand
" George student b 1108 Acushnet av [av h 1108 do
" Henry dry goods 1235 Acushnet
" Hormidas weaver b 430 N Front
" Jean A salesman 1064 Acushnet av h 81 Bullard
" Joseph C joiner h 68 Summer
" Joseph F card grinder h 826 County [av
" Laura housekeeper 1108 Acushnet
" Moses clerk 1273 Acushnet av b 1108 do
" Oliver fixer h 98 Beetle
" Paul L loom fixer h 128 Mott
" Peter loom fixer h 475 Rivet
" Regina rem to Providence R I
" Rosa A clerk b 703 Purchase
" Rosalie widow Denis h 430 N Front
" Rose L clerk b 1108 Acushnet av
" Telesphore weaver b 430 N Front
" Wilfred mill hand b 1108 Acushnet avenue
Forant Desire h 88 Nelson
" Joseph spinner h 45 Brock av
" Stanislas drill worker b 88 Nelson [83 Summer
Forbes Arthur W clerk 123 Front h
" Edward carpenter h 115½ Bullard
" Edward H manager 114 William h 3 Ash (N) [Hillman b do
" Florence E music teacher 67
" James R carriage painter 33 Elm h 38 Mill [Co h 299 Chancery
" Joseph C foreman Denison Bros
" Thomas operative b 371 S Second
" Thomas H captain steamer No 5 h 120 Chestnut [net av
Forcier John painter b 1280 Acush-
" Joseph motorman h 37 Linden
" Paul cook h 1280 Acushnet av
" Victor clerk 497 Purchase h 44 Washburn
" see Fortier
Ford Albert b 154 Cedar Grove
" Alexander twister b 19 Brock av
" Alfred reporter Times rms 298 Union
" Cecil weaver b 30 Bolton road
" Edwin H fixer h 76 Lombard
" Everett E bookkeeper b 67 Willis
" N Ernest salesman 36 Purchase h 67 Willis
" Patrick weaver h 29 Hall
Fordham Louisa widow Joseph T h 80 Potomska [yon
Forehand Robert laborer h 23 Ken-
Foreman Walter H removed from city
Forest Felix (Felix Forest & Co) 1041 Acushnet av h at Pottersville
FOREST FELIX & CO (Felix Forest) musical instruments and stationery 1041 Acushnet av See page 778
Forester Annie Mrs h 218 Purchase
Forge Sylvester second hand h 31 Nye
Forgue Edward carder h 623 Acushnet avenue
" George W weaver b 874 County
" Henry A weaver h 874 County
" Joseph operative b 53 Kenyon
" Joseph J fitter h 303 Sawyer
" Joshua weaver h 53 Reynolds
" Rose widow Pierre b 618 Cottage
" William laborer h 53 Kenyon
Forham Louisa widow h 100 Potomska
Forman Jacob stitcher and dry goods 426 S Water h 465 Rivet
" Reuben shoemaker 7 Purchase h 465 Rivet
" Samuel laborer h 426 S Water
Forrest James H clerk 1200 Acushnet avenue h 138 Davis
" John conductor b 290 Purchase
" John weaver h 46 Larch
" Richard second hand h 138 Holly
" Richard Jr machinst's helper b 138 Holly [Thompson
" Susanna widow William h 81
" William weaver h 441 Orchard (S)
Forrester Annie h 218 Purchase
" Eugenie L music teacher h 22 Salisbury [Purchase
" Joseph salesman 211 Union b 300
Forsblom Claus F bricklayer h r 140 State [chase h 35 Smith
Forsyth Alexander salesman 43 Pur-
" Margaret widow Andrew b 37 Jenny Lind
" William A district foreman 57 N Second h 567 Kempton [land
Fort Albert bookkeeper h 133 Ash-
" Albert electrician h 133 Ashland
" Harry twister b 133 Ashland
" Joshua twister h 348 Coffin av

PELEG H. SHERMAN 506 COUNTY ST.
FUNERAL DIRECTOR AND EMBALMER
OFFICE PHONES. Bell 690-13. Auto. 1305. RESIDENCE PHONES. Bell 690-12. Auto. 1306.

Fortes Joseph F operative h 8 Cannon [ditch
Fortier Adelard carpenter b 387 Bow
" Adolph weaver b 151 Tinkham
" Alvina Mrs weaver b 27 Bullard
" Ami carpenter b 93 Holly
" Armand quiller h 59 Ellen
" Arthur operative h 85 Beetle
" Cleophas checker h 505 Coggeshall
" Cyprien Manuel removed from city [ditch
" Frederick third hand b 387 Bow-
" Godfrois h 387 Bowditch [shall
" Henry A checker b 505 Cogge-
" Hormidas doffer b 387 Bowditch
" Julia Mrs h 12 Beetle
" Leon plasterer h 874 Acushnet av
" Ludger weaver h 89 Collette
" Rodelpha weaver b 93 Holly
" Rosalba widow Alphonse bds 136 Norman
" Rose D Mrs h 93 Holly
" Theodore weaver h 131 Bullard
" see Forcier [ushnet av
Fortin Adjutor operative h 1149 Ac-
" Albina removed from city [net av
" Alfred real estate b 1205 Acush-
" Alphonse weaver h 1103 S Water
" Amedee laborer h r 863 Purchase
" Azeline dry goods 17 Weld h 20 Ashland
" Charles teamer 163 Coggeshall
" Clara clerk 1285 Acushnet av b 1205 do
" Daniel C h 20 Ashland
" Emile weaver h 139 Bullard
" Eugene weaver b 206 Church [av
" Eva dressmaker b 1205 Acushnet
" Ferdinand h 192 Sawyer
" George twister b 1221 Acushnet avenue [Front h 88 Holly
" Henri mfr blood pudding 173 N
" Henry fireman Parker House
" Henry laborer h 88 Holly
" Ivan C Rev rector St James Episcopal church h 716 County
" Joseph driver h 74 Hicks
" Julien E physician 1205 Acushnet avenue h do
" Justin spinner h 872 Acushnet av
" Philas weaver h 86 Clifford [yon
" Phillip shoe operator h 87 Ken-
" Pierre blacksmith b 346 N Front

Fortin
" Placide third hand b 301 Belleville road
" Samuel weaver h 248 Bowditch
" Sophia widow Octave h 255 Shaw
" Toussaint slasher h 1221 Acushnet avenue [Orchard (S)
Fortnam William E electrician h 414
Fortuna Santi boarding house 86 N Second [Coffin avenue
Fortune Edward mill hand bds 204
" Henry removed to Westport
" Joseph mill hand h 204 Coffin av
Fosbry Mary E press feeder Standard rms 186 Fourth [net av
Foss Charles teamster b 2331 Acush-
Fossett Charles S salesman 16 N Second h 463 Cottage
" see Fawcett [avenue
Foster Antone carder h 103 Phillips
" Asah P (Bay State Chair Co) Prospect and Antique furniture 38 N Water h at Fairhaven [school b 22 Robesson
" Bessie K teacher Harrington
" Charles warper h 84 Rodney
" Charles J machinist h 342 Bowditch [North
" Charles O cotton broker bds 79
" Constantia widow Joseph B h 92 Potomska
" Ella J widow Walter H b 85 Oak
" E Edwin physician 271 Union h 217 Orchard
" George removed to Houstin Texas
" Henry teamster h 234 S Front
" Henry S machinist h 22 Robeson
" Isabella Mrs h 74 Hathaway road
" James mill hand h 64 Division
" John h 140 Dartmouth
" John iron molder h 509 Purchase
" John B machinist h 132 Dartmouth
" Joseph A stable 430 Purchase h 428 do [South
" Joseph B letter carrier h 104
" Manuel operative h 48 Nelson
" Mary widow George h 428 Kempton
" Mary Mrs h 201 Austin
" Nancy C money order clerk P O rms 8 Eighth [b 55 Bonney
" Nellie L teacher Dartmouth st school

COAL AND WOOD F. T. AKIN & COMPANY
HAY AND STRAW
WALNUT, COR. WATER, 84 PLEASANT ST., 25 WELD SQ.
129 COVE STREET WHF. FOOT OF COFFIN STREET

Foster
" Robert W prop R W Foster Brass Foundry 115 N Water h at Fairhaven
FOSTER R W BRASS FOUNDRY Robert W Foster prop 115 N Water See page 781
" William engineer h 85 Jouvett
" William gas fitter 125 Middle h 478 Union [Dartmouth
" William O second hand b 140
Fostiak Basil weaver b 11 Merrill
Fothergill John E spinner h 1767 Acushnet avenue [Howland Village
Foulds Arthur mill hand bds 24
" Fred mill hand b 24 Howland Village [Independent
Fountain Adeline widow Andre h 73
" Andre clerk b 73 Independent
" Arthur plumber's apprentice b 73 Independent
" Napoleon fixer h Hawes
" Ovila electrician b 73 Independent
" William operative b 137 Acushnet avenue
Fountaine Olivine Mrs h 154 Davis
Fouquette Arthur laborer b 2½ Willis
" Delia Mrs h 2½ Willis
" Joseph operative h 162 Whitman
" Theodore laborer N B W W b 2½ Willis [av h Rivet
Fournier Adelard clerk 15 W French
" Albert operative h 228 Collette
" Aldie drill maker h 28 **Margin**
" Alphonse clerk b 310 N Front
" Charles spinner h 314 N Front
" Charles E wood worker 31 Bowditch h 301 Earle
" Edmond loom fixer h 8 Viall
" Eli weaver h 233 Sawyer
" Elzear carpenter 253 Coffin av
" Frank wood worker **h 12 La-** France court
" George carpenter h 194 N Front
" George mason h 53 Salisbury
" Girouard weaver b 23 Sawyer
" Henry h 1279 Acushnet avenue
" Henry J wood worker 31 Bowditch h 148 Tallman [ond
" Herbert Z plumber h 608 S Sec-
" Joseph second hand h 37 Scott
" Joseph second hand h 126 Nye
" Joseph weaver b 48 Morton ct
" Joseph weaver b 772 S First

Fournier
" J Leo clerk 166 Brock av h 119 Mott
" Michael weaver b 233 Sawyer
" Moses painter h 132 Nye
" Napoleon teamster b 310 N Front
" Napoleon J carpenter 577 S Second h do
" Pierre sash maker h 184 Austin
" Silvio fixer h 189 Earle
" Theodore concreter h 190 Rivet
" Timothy laborer h 48 Morton ct
" Wilfred U motorman b 608 S Second [chase h 959 County
Foutter Robert R bartender 887 Pur-
Fowden Albert Mrs operative h 306 Tinkham av [chase b 16 North
Fowkes Alfred E tinsmith 745 Pur-
" Henry T tinsmith 745 Purchase h 16 North [bds 123 State
Fowler Alice operator 31 Commercial
" Annie Mrs b 208 Weld
" Austin J plumber 1545 Acushnet avenue b 65 Mt Pleasant
" Edward S watchman 350 S Second h 12 Walnut
" Frank E (Davis & Hatch Spice Co) 28 Union h 42 Foster
" Harry insurance agent 37 Purchase rm 23 b 88 Walden
" Howard W bill poster b 8 High (W) [ant
" James loom fixer h 65 Mt Pleas-
" John spinner bds 26 Roosevelt
" Mary F widow Peter h 13 Jenney
" Nathan fixer h 244 Phillips av
" Philip clerk 410 N Front
" Ruth milliner b 270 Weld
" Walter insurance agent 37 Purchase rm 23 h 140 Shawmut av
" William assistant superintendent 120 Purchase h 270 Weld
" William sergeant police station 5 h 88 Walden [chase h 266 do
Fox Benjamin upholsterer 264 Pur-
" James F removed from city
" John grocer 293 Coggeshall h 964 Acushnet avenue
" Mary widow James h 199 Davis
" Mary E widow George S h 98 Elm
" Max junk 135 S Water h 487 Acushnet avenue [ska
Foy John L spinner bds 55 Potom-
" Joseph spinner b 17 Thatcher
" Joseph A removed to Newport R I

Remember to investigate our methods before taking up a business course.

Kinyon's Commercial School

Odd Fellows Bldg., Cor. William and Pleasant Sts., New Bedford, Mass.

Foy
" Margaret widow Lawrence h 55 Potomska
" Patrick rms 781 Purchase
" Patrick weaver h 32 Mosher
" Patrick T clerk 182 Union h 114 Park
" Thomas spinner bds 55 Potomska
Foye John operative h 10 Hazard ct
" Joseph spinner h 993 S Water
Fradipetro Alfred clerk b 20 Woodlawn avenue [avenue
" Pasqualle tailor h 20 Woodlawn
Fraga Angelo L clerk P O h 86 Briggs
" Constantino M drill worker h 115 Bonney
" John J shoemaker 32 Cove h do
" John M watchman h 432 Allen
" Joseph M at P Corp h 112 Fifth
" Manuel laborer h 104 Acushnet avenue [First
Fragosa Antone clerk bds 477 South
" Antone M printer h 477 S First
" Carlos M laborer h r 33 Wing
Franades Frank laborer h r 5 Wamsutta [174 Mt Pleasant
France Samuel C mgr 1 William h
" see LaFrance [Cedar
Francis Annie L Mrs nurse h 344
" Annie L Mrs h 14½ Griffin
" Anthony S liquors 165 S Water and 2c Walnut
" Anthony S Mrs h 289 Acushnet avenue [avenue
" Antone laborer b 233 Acushnet
" Antone weaver h 31 Grit
" Antone E bartender 37 Howland h 21 Hall
" Antone M machinist h 133 Willis
" Antonio F (A F Francis & Co) 77 Grinnell h 354 Orchard (S)
" Arthur student b 100 Hawthorn
" Arthur T compositor Times b 18 Myrtle [(W)
" Arthur W student b 404 Middle
" Aurora h 19 Fair
" A F & Co (Antonio F Francis) wines and liquors 77 Grinnell
" A M Mrs dressmaker 133 Willis h do [net av
" Charles drill maker b 137 Acush-
" Charles fisherman b 76 Oak
" Charles J retired h 184 Coffin av

Francis
" Charles J Jr (Mudge & Francis) h 83 Forest [h 494 Maxfield
" Clement carpenter 111 Willis h
" Domingo teamster h 234 S Front
" Edward vamper h 70 Spruce
" Edward D fisherman h 303 South Front [ton
" Edward D shoemaker h 86 Kemp-
" Ellen widow Barnaby H boarding h 469 Acushnet av [145 Bonney
" Francisco T clerk 41 Purchase b
" Frank clerk b 98 Dartmouth
" Frank oiler h 76 Oak
" Frank harness maker h 148 Bonney [av h 4 Stanton ct
" Frank E assistant 173½ Acushnet
" Frank E salesman 129 Cove h 67 Grape [Water h 255 S Second
" Frank J (Francis & Rose) 599 S
" Frank V machinist h 15 Griffin
" Frank W treasurer 164 Union h 21 Fifth
" Frederick J clerk h 63 Briggs
" F W Cigar & Tobacco Co The 164 Union
" George fireman b 50 Alpine
" Georgiana widow bds 70 Spruce
" Harry A shoemaker h 86 Kempton
" Horace weaver h 53 Ruth
" James A laborer h 67 Hathaway
" James P accountant 27 Masonic bldg h 100 Hawthorn [land
" James T real estate h 130 Ash-
" John laborer b 75 Winsor
" John laborer 350 S Second h 271 South Front
" John B laborer h 1081 County
" John B Jr insurance and real estate 97 William rm 212 h 81 Howland [rms 184 Bonney
" John G clerk 1104 Acushnet av
" John H cigarmaker 164 Union h 2 Jenney
" Joseph h 4 Stanton court
" Joseph carpenter h 1 Mulberry
" Joseph carpenter h 55 Babbitt
" Joseph clerk 1020 S Water bds 255 South Second [h 83 do
" Joseph driver 386 Acushnet av
" Joseph laborer h 16 Howland
" Joseph laborer h 317 Hillman
" Joseph laborer h 450 First
" Joseph operative h 92 Potomska

HASKELL BROS. DEALERS IN
ICE
400 COURT STREET TELEPHONE CONNECTION NEW BEDFORD, MASS.

Francis
" Joseph shoe repairer 105 Union h 544 South Water
" Joseph third hand h 468 Rivet
" Joseph D laborer b 929 County
" Joseph F h 271 County
" Joseph F Jr student b 271 County
" Joseph M mill hand h 149 Hathaway
" Manuel carpenter h 98 Dartmouth
" Manuel fireman 97 Front h 74 Acushnet avenue
" Manuel fisherman h 13 Rivet
" Manuel fisherman h 58 Grinnell
" Manuel painter and paper hanger 404 Middle (W) h do
" Manuel teamster h 232 S Front
" Manuel teamster h 523 Acushnet avenue [145 Bonney
" Manuel B laborer N B W W h
" Manuel V Portugese banjos 6½ Griffin bds do [Grinnell
" Margaret widow Manuel J h 91
" Mary dressmaker b 76 Oak
" Mary Mrs mill hand b 125 Fair
" Mary widow Daniel h 21 Katharine
" Mary widow John E h 3 De Wolfe
" Mary widow Manuel J h 257 S Second
" Mary A Mrs h 27 Hillman
" Mary D Mrs h 271 S Front
" Mary P Mrs h 81 Howland
" Michael T h 18 Myrtle
" Philomena widow Manuel A midwife h 55 Katharine
" Rose Mrs h 45 Bethel
" Ruel S iceman h 495 Union
" Sarah W widow Joseph C boarding 109 Fourth
" Theodore hostler 50 Elm
" Thomas H laborer h 170 S Second
" Vincent clerk 27 Masonic bldg b 107 South [tle
" Walter H second hand h 94 Bee-
" Wellington A clerk 164 Union h 66 State [South
" William clerk 98 Allen b 115
" William fisherman b 58 Grinnell
" William teamster bds 450 First
" William H watchman 144 South Water h 615 Acushnet av

Francis
" William J clerk 185 Union b 255 South Second [ditch
" William W twister h 341 Bow-
" & Rose (Frank J Francis and Joseph Rose), liquors 599 S Water [South Sixth
Franciscan Missionary of Mary 98
Francisco Antone laborer b 16 Cannon
" John city laborer h 16 Cannon
" Manuel laborer h 16 Cannon
" William city laborer b 16 Cannon
Francotte Francis Jr glass cutter h 4 Social [sutta
Franedes Antone teamster h 52 Wam-
Franiczyk P mill hand h 91 S Front
Frank Charles mill hand h 552 Rivet
" Joao grocer 197 Coggeshall h do
" Joseph operative bds 97 Rivet
" Peter cook Almshouse bds do
" William L painter rms 54 Maxfield [h 24 Elm
Frankel Jacob grocer 69 N Second
Franklin Alice Mrs housekeeper 129 Austin [h 1737 Acushnet av
" Edwin overseer Whitman Mills
" Horace eyelet maker b 60 James
" Manuel h 60 James
" Sarah Mrs rms 508 County
" William fireman h 566 First
" William removed from city
Franks John hay h 88 Walden
Frano Joseph clerk cor Acushnet and River [Acushnet avenue
Frappied Albena Mrs spinner h 1655
Fraser David motorman h 2834 Acushnet avenue
" Della Mrs h 74 South Second
" Edward painter 24 N Water
" George overseer Oneko Mills h 1671 Acushnet avenue
" John operative h 7 Fulton ct
" John W hostler 689 County rms 32 Hillman
" Margaret nurse Almshouse b do
Frasier Adeline M bookkeeper b 10 Bay
" Antone F laborer h 42 Sherman
" Elizabeth E Mrs h 130 Chestnut
" John laborer h Stackhouse
" John E driver h 402 Pleasant
" John W clerk P O b 89 S Sixth
" Joseph foreman h 33 Katharine
" Joseph Jr laborer h 107 Cove rd

J. F. CROSSLEY 223 MILL STREET COR. EMERSON PHONE
STEAM and HOT WATER HEATING
GAS FITTING and FIXTURES

Frasier
" Joseph A physician 210 Union h 2 Fifth [avenue
" Manuel city laborer h 83 Howard
" Manuel laborer b Stackhouse
" Manuel F laborer b 42 Sherman
" Mary h 191 N Second
" Mary I bds 42 Sherman
" Thomas electrician rms 60 Spring
Fratado Joseph mill hand h 59 Crapo
" Manuel clerk 262 Coggeshall h 178 Belleville avenue [Front
Frates Adeline Mrs h 257 South
" Amelia widow John J h 352 County
" Antone back boy b 207 S Front
" Antone driver h 146 Holly
" Antone laborer h 14½ Griffin
" Antone laborer h 79 Ash (N)
" Antone laborer 269 S Second
" Antone seaman h 12 Griffin [land
" Antonio watchman h 163 Rock-
" Arthur driver h 146 Holly [net av
" Augustus steam fitter b 71 Acush-
" Candido laborer h 22 Grant
" Caton grinder h 47 Babbitt
" Constantine teamster Acushnet Saw Mills Co h Tarkiln Hill rd
" Delia Mrs clerk 1031 Acushnet h 217 Phillips avenue
" Domingos laborer h 45 Mitchell
" Emanuel laborer h 238 Rivet
" Francisco A at P Corp h 176 Thompson [Rockland
" Frank driver 108 Grape h 218
" Frank laborer h 218 Rockland
" Frank shoeworker h 647 Mt Pleasant [ushnet av h do
" Frank A harness maker 154 Ac-
" Harry M machinist h 408 Middle (W) [Middle (W) h do
" Harry M Mrs dressmaker 408
" Henry laborer h 41 Howland
" Isabel Mrs h r 284 S Second [dent
" Joaquim carpenter h 51 Indepen-
" Joe fireman h 4 Maiden lane
" John city teamster h 34 Lindsey
" John clerk b 352 County [Bolton
" John laborer h 34 Rotch block 435
" John mill hand b 7 Bonneau ct
" John mill hand b 163 Rockland
" John M watchman h 432 Allen
" Joseph driver 62 Dartmouth b 33 Babbitt [net av
" Joseph glass worker b 71 Acush-

Frates
" Joseph laborer h 81 Cove road
" Joseph laborer h 739 Belleville av
" Joseph mill hand h 55 Mitchell
" Joseph mill hand h 132 Thompson
" Joseph stage mgr 958 Acushnet av bds 352 County
" Joseph weaver h 21 Crapo
" Joseph D grocer 77 Dartmouth h
" Joseph F collector b 45 Oak
" Joseph G b 352 County [1 Oak
" Joseph L laborer h 15½ Cannon
" Justin mill hand b 213 Belleville avenue
" Louis mason h 121 Hathaway [av
" Manuel box maker b 137 Acushnet
" Manuel concrete worker h 235 S Second [dent
" Manuel fisherman h 51 Indepen-
" Manuel grocer 145 Belleville av h 122 Belleville av
" Manuel mill hand h 72 Hatch
" Manuel operative h 67 Rivet
" Manuel operative h 93 Grinnell
" Manuel operative h 235 S Second
" Manuel rope worker h r 207 South Front [ville av
" Manuel F laborer bds 202 Belle-
" Manuel J third hand h 109 N Second [ville avenue
" Manuel M operative h 123 Belle-
" Manuel R laborer N B W W h 1 Stanton court
" Mary Mrs h 638 South Water
" Mary widow h 87 Rockland
" Mary A Mrs h 291 S Second
" Raulino laborer h 213½ S Front
" Virginio Mrs h 20 Winsor
" William S engineer Old Colony Box Co h 217 Philips avenue
" see Freitas and Fraits
Frawley Catherine Mrs b 329 Cottage
" David E eyelet maker b 115 Cedar
" Edward F wood turner h 329 Cottage [b 847 Purchase
" Elizabeth clerk 1081 Acushnet av
" George S mason h 187 Mill
" Joseph furniture mover 847 Purchase h do [bldg b 115 Cedar
" Mary H stenographer 4 Masonic
" Rose M widow Elias h 115 Cedar
" William J clerk P O b 115 Cedar
Frayes John operative h 52 Rivet
Frazer Joseph laborer h 81 Cove rd
Frazier August laborer h 385 First

CHARLES A. CROSHERE **CARRIAGE AND AUTO**
38 FOURTH ST. **Bell Phone 1964-23** **PAINTING**

Frazier
" Manuel shoe repairer 427 S Water h do
Frechette Arthur driver h 73 Nelson
" August elevatorman h 16 Hicks
" Charles clerk 65 Brock avenue
" Charles driver h 73 Nelson [av
" Edward operative h 28 Howard
" Elzear died 1911
" George spinner h 43 Hicks
" Harry operative b 1296 Acushnet avenue [Front
" Henry third hand h 492 North
" Joseph spinner h 16 Hicks
" Oliva clerk 1285 Acushnet av h 76 Beetle
" Phoebe widow h 73 Nelson
" Phillipe carpenter b 84 Blackmer
" Pierre spinner h 541 Purchase
" Simeon second hand b 330 North Front
" Theodore carder h 160 Ashland
Frederic Arthur S treer b 110 Ash (N) [Ash (N)
" Frances M widow George H h 110
" Guy F treer b 110 Ash (N)
" Ransom teamster 70 Union h 315 Chancery [Oak
Frederick Adolph J decorator h 103
Fredette Aldos weaver b 60 Nye
" Alfred clerk 1147 Acushnet av h 126 Holly [Nye
" Edmond F salesman 43 Weld h 60
" Edward laborer h 109 Eugenia
" Eli operative h 342 Bowditch
" Ernest N clerk bds 60 Nye
" Francis H driver b 42 Merrimac
" Frank A weaver b 10 Nye
" Frank H driver 270 Acushnet av h 101 Hall
" Fred operative h 101 Hall
" George driver h 53 Emerson (S)
" George A engineer h 196 Earle
" Hormidas J provisions h 213 Brownell
" John mill hand h 235 N Front
" John P stage hand Hathaway's Theatre h 121 Hathaway
" Joseph helper 36 Purchase h 109 Brook
" Joseph C h 10 Nye
" Joseph C engineer h 90 Whitman
" Joseph H helper 36 Purchase h 71 Chancery

Fredette
" Joseph H teamster h 109 Brook
" Leo operative b 287 Sawyer
" Louis carpenter rms 3 Park place
" Louis machinist h 287 Sawyer
" Louis N (Fredette & Collette) h 20 Viall [yer
" Matilda widow John B h 301 Saw-
" Napoleon engineer bds 10 Nye
" Paul engineer bds 10 Nye
" Pierre finisher b 13 Princeton
" Samuel D freight handler h 42 Merrimac [213 Brownell
" Walter D clerk 188 N Water bds
" William H engineer h 332 Sawyer
" William V drill maker b 287 Sawyer
" & Collette (Louis N Fredette and Ulric E Collette) hardware 1023-1025 S Water [Cedar
Freedom Emma L widow John h 83
" Flossie M music teacher 83 Cedar b do [Merrimac
Freelove Chester A roll coverer h 77
Freeman Andrew rms 212 Purchase
" Arthur carpenter b 51 Tallman
" Charles coaster h 63 S Second
" Chester L, R R engineer h 91 Willis [ond
" Joseph operative h 180 South Sec-
" Mary A died Oct 19 1910
" Tristram M driver b r 269 Middle
" Valintine teamster h 180 S Second
" William N chauffeur h 555 Kempton [Kempton h do
" William N Mrs dressmaker 555
" Willianna widow David S h r 269 Middle [h 1159 Purchase
Fregeau Edward painter 24 N Water 1159 Purchase
" Frank operative h 76 Hicks
" John variety 64 Hicks h 63 do
" Joseph operative b 189 Bowditch
" Joseph twister h 41 Capitol
Freierman Isadore tailor 40 Purchase b 292 Cedar Grove [ville av
Freitas Antone laborer h 383 Belle-
" Antone mill hand b 191 Belleville avenue
" Antone painter b 71 Acushnet av
" Antone J clerk 1147 Acushnet av bds 304 Davis
" Antonio J h 131 County

J. G. NICHOLSON
LUMBER, SASH, DOORS and BLINDS
BOWDITCH STREET, NEW BEDFORD, MASS.

Freitas
" Augustine barber h 4 Rotch blk 434 Bolton [avenue
" Augustus laborer b 71 Acushnet
" Frank J electrician h Lewis [land
" Fred F speeder tender h 10 Cleve-
" George J clerk bds Lewis
" John drill worker h 193 Austin
" Joseph E clerk b 71 Acushnet av
" Joseph M mill hand h 304 Davis
" Lena widow b 9 Morton court
" Manuel mill hand h 136 Thompson
" Manuel police h 46 Willard
" Manuel G laborer h 204 Belleville avenue [net avenue
" Mary widow Manuel h 71 Acush-
" Rudolpho S weaver b 96 Davis
" see Frates
Fremon Fred spinner h 57 Winsor
French Arthur W teacher 27 Arnold bds do [bell
" Fred E laundryman b 170 Camp-
" James third hand b 57 Merrimac
" John A linotype operator Mercury h 170 Campbell [son (N)
" Lena widow Joseph h 173 Emer-
" Mary A Mrs h 111 Acushnet av
" Mary H teacher Cedar Grove st school bds 64 Willis
" Roy M telephone inspector 57 N Second h 208 Tremont [rimac
" William J mule spinner h 57 Mer-
Frendes John weaver h 53 Winsor
Frennette Alfred clerk 415 N Front b 1650 Acushnet avenue
" Emile clerk 415 N Front b 1650 Acushnet avenue
" Fred clerk b 1650 Acushnet av
" Jean mill hand bds 203 Sawyer
" John clerk 415 N Front h 1650 Acushnet av [Acushnet av
" John B grocer 415 N Front h 1650
" J Charles photographer 1 Arcade bldg 1650 Acushnet av [net av
" Roseanna milliner b 1650 Acush-
" Ulbald weaver h 82 Independent
" Wilfred clerk 415 N Front b 1650 Acushnet avenue
" Wilfred overseer Nonquit Spinning Co h 1602½ Acushnet av
" Wincelas clerk b 82 Independent
Freundschuh Martin shoemaker 41 Bedford h 64 Mechanics lane
Frew Mary W weaver h 89 Winsor
Frey Catherine widow Charles h 50 Pierce
" Charles died January 9 1911
" Charles Jr grocer 386 Kempton h 10 Beech
" Frank glass cutter h 92 Rockland
" Fred W linotype operator Standard bds 50 Pierce
Fricker Alexander G eyelet maker h 420 Elm (W)
" Oscar G manager 1049 Acushnet avenue h 99 Hazard [Second
Friedberg William pedlar h 274 S
Friedman Albert M clerk 57 N Second bds 1043 S Water
" I (Friedman's Ladies & Gents Furnishings) h 1043 S Water
" Joseph clerk 182 Union b 29 Fifth
" L J (Friedman's Ladies & Gents Furnishings) h 1043 S Water
Friedman's Ladies & Gents Furnishings (L J and I Friedman) 1043 S Water
Frieh Eugene spinner h 330 Earl
Frietas Anton J clerk b 912 County
" Joseph M mill worker h 912 County
Frifield Martha widow Max grocer 512 S Water do
" Max died January 23 1911
Frigeault Alfred clerk b 84 Nye
" Octave clerk 1174 Acushnet av h 84 Nye [Nye
" Octave Jr clerk 225 Sawyer b 84
Frink Howard W reed maker b 113 Reynolds [h 251 do
Frissell Amasa R hostler 255 State
Frizzell James B master mariner h 43 Locust
" Leah teacher Harrington school
Frohmater Katherine widow Christopher h 127 Ruth [Front
Froment Noe laborer h 407 North
Frommell Martin H photographer 80 Purchase [b 356 County
Frost Annie L widow Rev Samuel T
" Bertram bookkeeper b 368 County
" Carrie M teacher William H Taylor school b 245 Palmer
" Ellen widow William h 25 Fair
" Estella W bookkeeper 7 S Sixth b at N Dartmouth [Kempton
" Gertrude M Mrs clerk h 118
" Henry operative bds 24 Clark
" Herbert F Mrs h 368 County

PELEG H. SHERMAN 506 COUNTY ST.
FUNERAL DIRECTOR AND EMBALMER
OFFICE PHONES. Bell 690-13 Auto. 1305.
RESIDENCE PHONES. Bell 690-12. Auto. 1306.

Frost
" Lewis A electrician 27 William
" William A engineer b 319 County
Frye Charles Jr grocer h 10 Beech
Fryer Sidney fixer h 328 Sawyer
Fucazak Woyciech mill hand h 399 Belleville avenue [Front
Fuette Charles carpenter h 358 North
Fullen John F clerk 962 Acushnet av h 136 Nye [388 Reed
Fuller Abby L widow Benjamin F b
" Addie B Mrs h 347 Purchase
" Antonio mariner h 5 First
" Arthur B clerk U St Ry rms 290 Purchase
" Austin C antiques 18 N Water h 16 Maple View terrace
" Avis widow John F b 51 Borden
" Edward A clerk 125 Middle h 518 Cottage [ton
" Eugene B city laborer h 462 Bol-
" Frank D assistant treasurer 1145 Kempton b 46 Borden [nut
" Frank N blacksmith b 126 Chest-
" Frederick S public accountant 37 Purchase rm 7 h 36 Seventh
" George T painter h 388 Reed
" Hannah H widow Jonathan A b 34 Grape [Chestnut
" Harry L blacksmith 16 First b 126
" John H carpenter h 46 Borden
" John Y president 41 Purchase h 3 Arch [Smith
" Mary A widow Benjamin bds 146
" Matilda Mrs h 498 S Second
" Maurice clerk 1 William rms 21 Fifth
" Nancy B h 56 Spring
" Nelson T horse shoer 16 First h 162 Chestnut
" N Bryon bookkeeper 352 Sawyer rms 1293 Acushnet av
" Thomas H charcoal and coke 214 S Water and r 182 N Water h 71 Sycamore
" William H watchman h 32 Wing
" William H Jr drill maker b 32 Wing
" William O painter h 159 Rockland
" Willis S foreman 100 Fifth h 51 Borden [Bonney
Funans Frank drill straightener h 150
" Mary I widow John h 21 Babbitt
" see Furnans
Furbey James blacksmith h 546 Rivet
Furbush William F reporter Times
Furlong Annie widow Thomas J h 181 Summer
" Joseph engineer h 290 Sawyer
" Mary clerk h 119 Shawmut av
" Matthew T died
Furnans Brothers (J E and J R Furnans) clothing 144 to 148 Union and 351 South Water
" Ernest W clerk 144 Union b 317 Pleasant [Dartmouth
" John E (Furnans Bros) h at S
" Joseph R (Furnans Bros) h 317 Pleasant [rms 96 Union
Furness Frederick clerk 52 Purchase
" Peter S piper bds 16 Harmony
" Richard weaver h 165 Bates av
" William second hand h 137 Reynolds [Merrimac
Furtack Mary widow Frank h 28 E
Furtado Alfred operative h 62 Blackmer
" Annie Mrs h 71 Smith [mouth
" Anthony S operative h 67 Dart-
" Antone laborer h 79 Cove road
" Antone J operative b 387 Belleville avenue
" Antone M fisherman h 17 Mitchell
" Antonio S laborer h 42 Grape
" Candido third hand b 387 Belleville avenue
" Charles laborer h 429 First
" David mill hand h 281 S Second
" Frank fisherman h 531 First
" Frank operative h 259 S Second
" Frank operative h 439 Belleville avenue
" Frank S clerk b 48 Briggs
" George P engineer b 153 Hemlock
" Jacintho S gardener h 16 Bourne
" Joaquim laborer h 469 First
" John operative h 278 Tinkham
" John S operative h 48 Briggs
" John S Jr overseer Gosnold Mills Co h 47 Briggs
" Jose operative h 5 Mitchell
" Joseph fisherman h 56 Grinnell
" Joseph third hand h 387 Belleville avenue [Front
" Joseph Jr fisherman h 325 South
" Joseph C laborer h 14 Cotter
" Joseph S mill hand b 48 Briggs
" Kate widow Joseph h 332 S Front

PAINTERS' SUPPLIES
Walnut, Cor. Water, 84 Pleasant St. 25 WELD SQ., 129 COVE ST.
F. T. AKIN & COMPANY

Furtado
" Manuel carder h 178 Belleville av
" Manuel carder h r 272 S Front
" Manuel mill hand h 10 Grandfield [avenue
" Manuel mill hand h 178 Belleville
" Manuel operative h 331 First
" Manuel operative b 387 Belleville avenue [ville av
" Manuel Jr operative b 178 Belle-
" Manuel F laborer h 121 Ash (N)
" Manuel J laborer h 245 Tinkham
" Maria mill hand bds 18 Holly
" Mary Mrs h 41 Dunbar [nell
Furtaites Joseph laborer h 56 Grin-
Fury Bartholmew P salesman rms 315 Pleasant
" Emma Mrs h 514 Cottage
" Mary E teacher H M Knowlton school bds 514 Cottage

Gabriault Moise fireman h 475 North Front [fee
Gabriel Manuel C farmer h 210 Dur-
" Samuel E driver 8 Campbell h 463 Cottage [124 Belleville rd
Gacess Anton clerk 580 N Front bds
Gachet Leon weaver h 47 Ashley
Gadbois Arthur weaver h 357 Davis
" George weaver h 247 N Front
" George Jr operative b 247 North Front
" Napoleon weaver b 247 N Front
" Pierre electrician b 247 N Front
Gadboury Charles P Rev pastor Church of the Sacred Heart h 27 Ashland [yer
Gadreau Joseph teamster h 285 Saw-
Gadu Adelard removed to Fairhaven
Gaeng Fred clerk 1103 Acushnet av b 115½ Bullard [lard
" Paulina widow Fred h 115½ Bul-
Gaetz Walter J superintendent h 299 Chancery [81 Maple
Gaffney Ethel V clerk 23 Purchase b
" Lydia E widow Edwin J h 81 Maple
" Mabel L clerk b 81 Maple
Gage Clara C M principal Mary B White school b 162 Summer
" John A weaver h 188 Division
" Joseph N harness mfr 144 Pleasant h 162 Summer [av
Gagne Alfred carpenter h 207 Coffin

Gagne
" Alfred weaver h 57 Nelson
" Arthur loom fixer h 103 Jouvett
" Edward cable splicer 57 N Second b 113 Fourth [Dean
" Hermenigilde blacksmith h 198
" Jeremiah carpenter h Princeton avenue
" Jeremiah laborer h end Princeton
" John loom fixer h end Princeton
" Joseph helper 745 Purchase
" Leon clerk 265 Sawyer b 872 Acushnet avenue
" Norbet carpenter b end Princeton
" Paul foreman 32 Linden h 13 LaFrance court
" Theophile third hand h 109 Nash road [h do
" Ulric photographer 551 N Front
" William W removed from city
Gagner Gideon mason b 68 Nash rd
" Joseph mill hand b 1149 Acushnet avenue
" Joseph V salesman b 411 Rivet
Gagneu Phoebe h 910 S Water
Gagnon Agathe widow Joseph h 39 Independent
" Alexander operative h 57 Kenyon
" Amedee carpenter b 7 Phillips av
" Amedee weaver h 107 Rivet
" Arthur removed to Canada
" Arthur E (Gagnon & Son) 301 N Front h 306 do
" Clovis laborer h 51 Dean
" Donat died Sept 30 1910
" Emile teamster b 91 Holly [dent
" Eugene operative b 39 Indepen-
" Fabien weaver h 182 Dean
" Francis removed to Fairhaven
" Frank (Gagnon & Son) 301 North Front h 306 do
" Henry weaver h 52 Dean
" Joseph bartender h 93 Collette
" Joseph carpenter h 16 Tallman
" Joseph carpenter h 68 Tallman
" Joseph clerk h 798 Purchase
" Joseph clerk 870 Acushnet av rms 93 Collette
" Joseph fixer b 32 Bowditch
" Joseph loom fixer h 19 Nelson
" Joseph operative b 193 Bowditch
" Joseph removed to Fairhaven
" Joseph A weaver h 292 Fourth
" Joseph B removed to Boston

To do things right you must be taught. Our instructors can do it.
Kinyon's Commercial School
Odd Fellows Bldg., Cor. William and Pleasant Sts., New Bedford, Mass.

Gagnon
" Julia widow Joseph h 154 Eugenia
" Louis G carpenter h 193 Bowditch
" Luc weaver h 30 Willard
" Ludger operative b 15 Phillips av
" Marie Mrs weaver h 91 Holly
" Napoleon weaver b 330 N Front
" Octave carpenter h 7 Phillips av
" Oscar operative b 15 Phillips av
" Pascal h 194 Belleville av [Ashley
" Pauline widow Napoleon h 53
" Peter J fixer h 186 Dean
" Pierre h 15 Phillips avenue [av
" Pierre Jr operative b 15 Phillips
" Ralph carpenter h 114 Collette
" Sylfred foreman b 154 Eugenia
" Wilfred teamster b 883 Purchase
" William proprietor The Acushnet Cigar Mfr rms 20 Arcade
" & Son (Frank and Arthur E Gagnon) liquors 301 N Front
Gaida John laborer h 24 Morton ct
Gaillois Arthur fixer h 288 Cedar Grove [Mill
Gainville John H blacksmith h 264
" Walter J checker h 488 Maxfield
" William E clerk h r 367 Kempton
Gajewski Valentine mill hand h 7 Rotch block 438 Bolton
Galanska Louis fixer h 659 First
Gale Charles A shoemaker b 27 James
" Clara M bds 233 Middle
" Howard C R Rev pastor First Universalist church h 27 James
" Mary J widow George H h 4 N Oak [pect
Galego Manuel C laborer h 87 Pros-
Galfey Josephine bds 406 Union
Galipeau Henry L weaver h 8 Hicks
" Rose B widow Joseph h 20 Roosevelt
" Victor hostler h 434 Pleasant
Gallagher Bernard baker b 7 Thatcher
" Bernard operative h 23 Cleveland
" Charles H operative h 154 Belleville road
" Ellen weaver h 89 Potomska
" Hugh filler carrier h 157 Crapo
" James laborer h 4 Wamsutta
" J Stanley clerk 201 Union b 567 Kempton [geshall
" Lawrence city foreman h 137 Cog-
" Michael laborer b 33 McGurk

Gallagher
" Neil tailor 89 Fifth h 107 South Sixth
" Thomas operative h 210 Division
" William laborer h 7 Thatcher
Gallant Albert clerk b 326 Coffin av
" Albini h 93 Hathaway [do
" Alfred wood 103 Belleville rd h
" Amaug bds 150 Phillips avenue
" Arthur helper b 102 Eugenia
" Benjamin driver 36 Purchase
" Chrysostone carpenter h end Clifford
" Delia h 71 Peckham
" Edward blacksmith h 286 Davis
" Edward A blacksmith h 150 Phillips avenue
" Eucher teamster h 102 Eugenia
" Fanny h 543 Acushnet avenue
" George boiler maker b 102 Eugenia [avenue
" Hyacinth operative h 326 Coffin
" Isadore laborer h 3 Hillman st ct
" John mill hand h 221 N Front
" Moise driver h 180 State
" Philip clerk 962 Acushnet av h 137 Holly [Front
" Raymond shoemaker h 282 North
" Sylvian operative h 54 Phillips av
" Wilfred laborer h 96 Davis
Galley Truman A ex messenger h 371 Chancery [Mill
Galligan Alice widow Patrick h 78
" Charles clerk b 355 Pleasant
GALLIGAN CHARLES A oil cloth and carpets 1516 and 1522 Acushnet av h 36 Pearl See page 37
" Edward W grocer 70 Washington bds do [70 Washington
" James A shipper Page Mfg Co b
" James B laborer h 461 Bolton
" Jane widow James h 19 Austin
" John E clerk 111 Durfee b 62 do
" John H clerk Anthony Swift & Co bds 70 Washington [495 do
" John H furniture 497 Purchase h
" John H helper 36 Purchase h 62 Durfee
" Katie A dressmaker 78 Mill b do
" Margaret widow Patrick h 355 Pleasant [b 355 Pleasant
" Patrick J clerk 1516 Acushnet av
" Terrence F h 70 Washington

Bread, Cake, Pastry
RICHMOND & COMPANY **255-257 UNIUN STREET**
Bell 993 Automatic 1022

Galligan
" Thomas driver 47 School h 200 Elm
" Thomas F clerk b 70 Washington
" T Clinton clerk 70 Washington b do [lips av
Gallipeau Donat painter h 199 Phil-
" Stanislas weaver h 287 Rivet
" Stanislas Mrs dressmaker 287 Rivet h do [Co
" Victor hostler Anthony Swift &
Gallison Israel conductor b 264 Pleasant [Union
Gallivan Marie Mrs nurse rms 321
Gallo Adolph operative h 686 Acushnet avenue [h 153 Smith
Gallop Richard G (R G Gallop & Co)
GALLOP R G & CO (Richard G Gallop and Edward E Davoll) painters 55 Hillman See page 752
Galloway Annie E widow John h 16 W High
" James loom fixer h 949 County
Galoska Michel mill hand h 399 Belleville avenue [S Second
Galph Joseph operative h rear 238
Galpin John L farmer h 1360 Rockdale avenue [Shawmut av
Galvin Ellen E widow Timothy b 148
" Frank J clerk b 148 Shawmut av
" Louise B clerk 185 Union b 148 Shawmut avenue
" Margaret Mrs b 98 Covell [ion
" Mary E widow Daniel h 298 Un-
" Millett rope maker h 406 S Water
" William spinner h 98 Covell
Gamache Aldei clerk 1075 Acushnet av b 1225 do
" Alfred weaver bds 122½ Cove
" Celina Mrs h 16 Viall
" Didas spinner h 88 Hathaway
" Edward weaver b 122½ Cove
" Eugene weaver h 55 Phillips av
" Euzeb weaver h 122½ Cove [Holly
" Flavian baker 1070 County h 88
" Fred weaver h 399 Belleville av
" Joseph carpenter h 1225 Acushnet avenue
" Joseph iceman bds 57 Dean
" Joseph weaver b 1205 Acushnet avenue [ushnet av
" Joseph Jr operative bds 1225 Ac-
" Marcille washer h 57 Dean

Gamache
" Oliver janitor b 57 Dean
" Ozias fixer b 8 Cove road [net av
" Thomas carpenter h 2471 Acush-
" Vital mill hand h 211 Whitman
" Wilfred third hand b 1225 Acushnet avenue [net av
" William carpenter b 1225 Acush-
Gamage William F driver h 56 Parker
Gamansky Rosa Mrs grocer 480 S Water h do [ell
Gamble Edward J spinner h 25 Stow-
" James helper b 25 Stowell [mouth
" William H mill hand h 92½ Dart-
Gamboa Frank A operative b 77 Dunbar
" Mary S Mrs h 77 Dunbar
Gammage William F driver 36 Purchase h 56 Parker [325 N Front
Gammond Alfred third hand bds
Gammons Abbie K Mrs h 38 Russell
" Amantha B widow Edgar H h 337 Hathaway road
" Charles A clerk h 257 Tinkham
" Edgar H Jr farmer b 337 Hathaway road [man
" Edwin A shoemaker h 129 Hill-
" Ephraim T Jr shoemaker h 230 Kempton [b 46 Myrtle
" Frank M motorman Electric Ex
" Helen M widow Samuel P b 337 Hathaway road [Maxfield
" Jennie M widow Lester h 202
" Roswell K carpenter h 38 Russell
" Susie T widow Edwin h 46 Myrtle
Ganger Hermengilde blacksmith h 198 Dean
Gangne Leon waiter rms r 20 Marvin
Gangnier Gedeon mason h 68 Nash rd
Gann Abbie Mrs h 86 First
Gannon John operative b 869 County
" Patrick h 869 County
" Patrick J operative h 182 State
" William weaver h 269 Coggeshall
Ganson Edwin machinist h 45 Katharine
" Joseph laborer b 22 Cleveland
" Mary widow Edwin h 8 Bonney
Ganter Maxwell Rev assistant pastor St Martins Episcopal church b 21 South Sixth [County
Gaouette Desire second hand h 827
" Louis operative bds 82 Eugenia
" Ludger overseer h 352 Davis

GLOBE DYE HOUSE 220 SHAWMUT AVE.
J. N. J. LONHOLDT, PROP. Telephone Connections Goods called for and Delivered
Down town Office, 52 Pleasant St., Room 1 North End Office, 1014 Acushnet Ave.

Gaouette
" Napoleon clerk h 26 Nye
" see Goyette
Garand Pierre laborer h 74 County
Garant Ambrose removed to Fairhaven
" Charles spinner h 282 Tinkham
" Thomas spinner bds 282 Tinkham
Garceau Hector spinner h 113 Bullard
Garcia Ellen fitter 40 Purchase b 239 Field
" Frank J h 97 Hall
" Frederick laborer h 41 Union
" Joseph V grocer 121 Dartmouth h 109 do [880 do
Gardeka Peter clerk 878 Purchase b
Gardiner Francis D removed from city
" George N (Gardiner & Milliken) 3 Masonic bldg h at Fairhaven
" Sarah E widow Samuel W rem from city

GARDINER & MILLIKEN
Attorneys at Law
Notaries Public
3 Masonic Building
Corner Pleasant & Union Streets

Gardiner & Milliken (George N Gardiner and Allen W Milliken) lawyer 3 Masonic bldg[chase
Gardner Alexander meats h 1129 Pur-
" Archer C watchmaker 2 Purchase h 807 Kempton
" Arnold C treasurer Manomet Mills h 76 Bedford
" Arthur slubber tender h 85 Beetle
" Charles E h 38 Beech
" Charles E eyeletter h 3½ Green
" Charles E (Gardner & Gray) 861 Kempton h 360 Reed
" Charles H overseer Manomet Mills h 201 Pleasant
" Corinne H widow Herbert B h 132 Washington [ton
" Daniel B mason rms 367 Kemp-
" David spinner h 360 Pleasant

Gardner
" Elizabeth A Mrs h 19 Cleveland
" Enoch weaver h 23 Salisbury
" Frederick A (New Bedford Welding Co) 177 N Water h 54 Emerson (S) [ton
" Frederick T hostler h 514 Kemp-
" Frederick W machinist b 82 Dartmouth
" George h 140 Fourth
" George A clerk h 131 Chestnut
" George O supt 72 N Water h 181 Maple
" George W motorman h 137 Locust
" Grace B teacher Harrington school b 29 Dartmouth
" Hannah C widow O P b 360 Reed
" Harold plumber b Dartmouth
" James laborer h 261 Tinkham
" Jane E asst at public library bds 319 Union
" Jane M h 46 Campbell
" Jerome D W paymaster Whitman Mills b 131 Chestnut
" Lawrence E hostler b 360 Reed
" Lucy accountant b 132 Washington [Hawthorn
" Mary E widow Charles b 211
" Oliver H instructor N B Industrial school h 48 North
" Ralph R grinder b 201 Pleasant
" Sarah A Mrs rms 37 Foster [(S)
" Walter mill hand h 400 Orchard
" Walter weaver h.167 David
" Wilfred shoemaker b 85 Beetle
" Wiliam B treasurer Nashawena Mills h 124 Hawthorn
" & Gray (Charles E Gardner and John R Gray) sales stable 861 Kempton
" see Gardiner [man
Garfield & Proctor Coal Co foot Hill-
Gargan Catharine widow John b 269 Coggeshall [203 Collette
" John overseer Manomet Mills h
" Thomas spinner b 269 Coggeshall
Gariepy Louis carpenter h 1016 Acushnet avenue
Garland Bernard T h 152 Florence
" Daniel J painter b 152 Florence
" Fanny b 545 Acushnet avenue
" John H painter rms 1 Pease ct
" Sadie A b 545 Acushnet avenue

GREENE & WOOD Every Kind of LUMBER AND MILL WORK
PINE STREET, off So. WATER STREET, NEW BEDFORD

Garlick George lunch room 762 Purchase h 275 Phillips avenue
" William T weaver h 213 Weld
Garlington Edward warper h 117 Mott
" James shoemaker b 77 Fruit
" James spinner b 122 David
" James Jr third hand h 122 David
" John operative h 222 County
" John twister b 133 Ruth avenue
" Mary Mrs weaver h 77 Fruit
Garneau Ernest weaver b 968 S Water [h 367 Kempton
Garnes Celia College Mrs hairdresser
" James H hostler 50 Elm h 367 Kempton [h do
Garon Louis S baker 37 Acushnet av
Garrant Joseph painter 22 Lucas h do
Garrard Lewis weaver b 28 Cove
Garriety John spinner b 621 First
Garrity James spinner b 33 McGurk
" Martin spinner b 877 S Water
" Patrick spinner b 877 S Water
" Patrick F undertaker 149 Blackmer rms do
" Thomas laborer h 38 W French av
" William weaver h 144 Tallman
Garrow Charles spinner b 187 Earle
" Josephine Mrs h 10 Campbell
Garry Arthur mill hand h 109 Bullard [ard b 271 Austin
Garside Alston H reporter Stand-
" Arthur weaver h 183 Bowditch
" Eliza J Mrs h 114 David
" George H weaver weaver bds 418 N Front [David
" Joshua W mill hand bds 114
Garstan James weaver b 38 Bowditch
Garthly Margaret M stenographer Kilburn Mill b 11 Borden
" William bookkeeper 167 Hillman h 11 Borden
Gartland Albert musician b 322 Sawyer [school b 9 Washington
" Emma L principal Thompson st
Gartside James weaver h 21 Scott
" William oiler h 3 Winter [Dean
Garvenyski John box maker h 36
Garvey Austin weaver h 282 Davis
" James mason b 257 Cedar Grove
" John fireman h 362 Coffin av
" John J operaitve b 362 Coffin av
" John J section hand h 63 Independent [dent
" Joseph T mill hand b 63 Indepen-

Garvey
" Marion R scalp specialist 305 Times bldg b 493 County
" Rose A stenographer 36 Purchase bds 63 Independent [avenue
" Thomas P weaver b 362 Coffin
" William operative b 362 Coffin av
Garvin Ettenne shoemaker bds 320 Davis
" Ettenne Jr barber h 320 Davis
" George F painter bds 165 Weld
" James overseer h 95 Oak
" Margaret widow Thomas h 165 Weld [chase
Gasby John conductor rms 602 Pur-
Gaschka William glass decorator h 129 Clark [ville av
Gasket James mill hand b 178 Belle-
Gaspa Antone laborer h 518 Rivet
Gaspar Manuel operative h 283 Fourth
Gasperella Henry laborer h 28 Maxfield [man
Gasse Alfred third hand b 519 Tall-
" Alice widow Tancred h 14 Holly
" Alphonse teamster h 159 Tallman
" Antone weaver h 276 Collette
" John operative b 159 Tallman
" Marguerite teacher b 20 Viall
" Raoul teamster h 159 Tallman
" Tancred died Feb 18 1911
Gasser Thaubant weaver h 21 Jean
Gast Paul A mgr 1099 Acushnet av h 33 Cedar
Gatenby Crawford electrician 33 N Water h 310 Orchard (S)
" James S police h 79 Robeson
" Jeanette widow John h 310 Orchard (S)
" John (Gatenby & Swift) 33 North Water h 126 Division [Court
" William S hoseman Hose 1 h 208
" & Swift (John Gatenby and Obed N Swift) electricians 33 North Water [Middle
Gates Samuel A boat repairer h 212
" William B warper h 16 Clay
Gatie Henry b 101 Bonney [land
" Henry W carpenter b 154 Rock-
" Joseph weaver h 101 Bonney
" William J foreman 100 Bonney h 21 do [Myrtle
Gatley Joseph mule spinner h 69

BONNEY, FOLSTER & CO.,
The North End's Shopping Centre
Dry Goods and Men's Furnishings
945-947 Acushnet Ave., New Bedford, Mass.

Gaubin Etienni hairdresser 1496 Acushnet avenue [Tallman
Gaucher Alphonse carpenter h 134
" Arthur weaver h 27 Ashley
" Calixte operative b 182 Dean
" Elphege constable 37 Purchase rm 17 h 357 Bowditch
" Felix carpenter b 157 Davis
" Hormidas operative h 91 Bullard
" Mary widow John B b 159 Bowditch [Davis
" Melina widow Harmedas h 157
Gaudette A Alcide removed from city
" Edgar carpenter b 33 Holly
" John D machinist h 23 Tallman
" Joseph grocer 555 N Front h 125 Eugenia [lette
" J Arthur letter carrier h 188 Col-
" J Maxime clerk 1360 Acushnet av h 361 N Front
" Leonard twister b 33 Tallman
" Levi weaver h 126 Cedar Grove
" Ludger overseer Wamsutta Mills h 8 Austin
" Napoleon removed from city
" Narcisse weaver b 287 N Front
" Thomas laborer h 113 Eugenia
Gaudreau Adelard fixer h 61 Covell
" Antoine laborer b 81 Wood
" Joseph barber 113 Cove h cor First and Cove
" Joseph driver h 287 N Front
" Joseph foreman h 1142 Acushnet avenue [First h 673 First
" Joseph X pool and lunch 634
" Marie J dry goods 1890 Acushnet avenue h do [ville road
" Philip mule spinner b 39 Belle-
" see Goudreau
Gaughan John T mason h 7 Willis
" Thomas E barber 1673 Acushnet av h 15 Bowditch [Nash rd
Gaugnier Omer mill hand bds 68
Gaum Mary widow John b 367 Chancery [Riverside av
Gaumond Mederic mill hand h 4
Gaumont Herculan sexton St Ann's church h 58 Salisbury
Gaunt Clough rem to Enfield
Gauthier Adelard teamster h 88 Hathaway
" Adelard weaver b 644 Purchase
" Adeline widow Severe b 86 Belleville rd [ville rd
" Adella Mrs boarding h 61 Belle-

Gauthier
" Adrian Rev asst pastor St Hyacinth's church h 163 County
" Alfred barber b 82 Ruth av
" Amedee weaver b 207 Bowditch
" Aristide J carpenter h 125 Whitman [av
" Arthur doffer b 609 Acushnet
" Arthur twister b 616 S Second
" Arthur weaver h 27 Ashley
" Clovis weaver bds 157 Davis
" Delphas cabinetmaker h 130 Robeson
" Dennis clerk bds 125 Whitman
" Dolor copperworker h 207½ State
" D Hormidas furniture 867-873 Purchase b 40 Linden [chase
" Emma Mrs waitress h 760 Pur-
" Ephraim designer b 125 Whitman
" Frank fixer h 71 Hathaway
" George laborer h 86 Belleville rd
" George H teamster 188 N Water
" Gorgiana dressmaker 40 Linden b do [ville rd
" Hector meatcutter h 61 Belle-
" Henri weaver h 82 Ruth av
" Henry clerk 1347 Acushnet av h 77 Davis
" Henry operative b 157 Davis
" Henry Mrs boarding house 77 Davis [land
" James beamer tender h 18 Cleve-
" Joseph grocer 634 Acushnet av h do
" Joseph removed from city
" Joseph weaver h 206 Cedar Grove

JOSEPH A GAUTHIER
ATTORNEY AT LAW
Notary Public
Justice of the Peace
Room 15
Five Cents Savings Bank Building
37 Purchase Street
Telephone Connection
Residence 1405 Acushnet avenue

Painters Supplies Wall Papers Room Mouldings Ladders
M. P. B. Silva & Son BRUSHES
157 ACUSHNET AVENUE Both Phones NEW BEDFORD

Gauthier Joseph A lawyer 37 Purchase rm 15 h 1405 Acushnet avenue [shnet avenue
" Joseph E carpenter h 343 Acu-
" Ludger weaver b 82 Ruth av
" Marie C clerk 40 Purchase b 25 Fair
" Michel clerk rms 130 Weld
" Napoleon barber 617 Acushnet av h 609 do
" Napoleon carpenter h 81 Davis
" Octave carpenter h 157 Davis av
" Olivier copperworker h 198 State
" Olivier oiler h 29 Roosevelt
" Paul removed from city
" Pierre h 40 Linden
" Rene doffer bds 157 Davis
" Sidonie clerk 40 Purchase b 25 Fair [Tallman
Gauthreau Lawrence carpenter h 126
Gautrault Adolphe spinner b 105 Bullard
Gautreau Alphee lineman 57 N Second h 209 Bowditch
" Julia housekeeper 359 N Front
" Madaline Mrs mill hand b 23 Holly [7 N Second
" Thomas lineman 43 William rms
Gautreault Charles mill hand h 105 Bullard [Collette
Gauvin Adelbert carpenter h 141
" Albert carpenter h 141 Collette
" Emile removed to Brockton
" Ernest fixer h 1060 Acushnet av
" Ernest operative h 1060 Acushnet av [ditch h 324 Davis
" Etienne shoe repairer 206 Bow-
" Louis weaver h end Clifford
" Onesime carpenter h 82 Eugenia
" Prudent carpenter h 112 Collette
" Tranquil carpenter h 209 Bowditch [State
Gavaghan John coppersmith h 219
Gaw Cooper editor Sunday Standard h 54 Fifth [dependent
Gawthrope James F weaver h 61 In-
" W Robert weaver b 61 Independent
Gay Bertha M asst chief operator 57 N Second b 36 Parker
" Dorothy clerk 474 Acushnet av b at Acushnet
" Douglas E carpenter h 432 Court
" Elmer B (Taber & Gay) 421 Purchase h at S Dartmouth

Gay
" George F carpenter 248 Palmer
" George W carpenter 115 Chancery h do [b 36 Parker
" Georgia clerk 474 Acushnet av
" Harry M carpenter b 115 Chancery [Cottage
" Julia A widow Horace H h 265
" Margaret H clerk 8 Hamilton b 125 Campbell [125 Campbell
" Samuel R foreman 27 Centre h
" Theophilus carpenter h 36 Parker [av h do
" T Franklin carpenter 72 Shawmut
" see Guay [Purchase
Gaynor Edward shoemaker rms 212
Gayton Dora b 267 Cottage [Cove
Geary Albert Victor electrician b 88
" Edward h 200 Earle [Cove
" Elizabeth I widow George b 88
" Ernest clerk 393 Cedar bds 57 Willow [av b 57 Willow
" George W mgr 353 Acushnet
" Harvey b 200 Earle
" James H rem to Portland Me
" John E clerk 352 Acushnet av b 57 Willow
" Peter bartender 98 Cove h 88 do
" Richard card grinder b 483 N Front [h 57 Willow
" Richard liquors 353 Acushnet av
" Richard sawyer b 200 Earle
" Susan C teacher b 39 Mill road
" Thomas J laborer h 346 Purchase
" Walter fitter b 57 Willow
" Walter removed to Portland Me
Geddis Garfield clerk h 242 Sawyer
" George C, R R engineer h 183 Ashland [Hazard
" George C Jr R R fireman h 105
" Joseph A clerk 358 Acushnet av rms 290 Purchase
" Martha A Mrs 242 Sawyer
" William J removed to Athol
" William R engineer N B E Co h 133 Chestnut [Co h 474 Park
Gedley Charles R treas N B Textile
Gee Amos overseer h 188 Washington
" Edward spinner b 570 S Second
" John weaver b 303 Tinkham
Ge Gatt Harriet B widow h 51 Mill road [shnet av
Gegatt James R laborer b 1982 Acu-
" Lewis C farmer b 51 Mill rd

Steiger-Dudgeon Co.
"The WOMAN'S Store."
Tel. Bell 82 & 83, Branches connecting all depts.
" " 160 For Office only. Auto. 1211

SUMPTIONS, ASSORTMENTS AT ALL TIMES OF DEPENDABLE DRY GOODS

Geier Vincent operative h 264 Brock avenue [69 Mill
Geils Frederick H letter carrier h
" Gerrett died Dec 31 1910
" Gerrett Jr (Stetson & Stetson) lawyer 34 Masonic bldg h 526 Cottage [Austin
Geldard Arthur W musician b 184
Gelder Edward janitor Washington Club h do [Village
" Richard laborer b 39 Howland
" William H laborer h 39 Howland Village [Park
Gellette Charles E carpenter h 126
" Charles W keeper the Common h 113 Willis [h 54 Bullard
Gelinas Aime clerk 107 Bowditch h
" Aristide C W clerk h 31 Bullard
" Cariste weaver h 28 Nye
" Clement spinner h 142 Phillips av
" Donat driver 107 Bowditch bds 128 do
" Elzear spinner b 806 First
" Hector rem to Yamachiche Canada [av
" Joseph slasher b 1205 Acushnet
" Leon rem to Yamachiche Canada
" Marorique shoemaker h 806 First
" Napoleon weaver b 13 Valentine
" Omer spinner b 128 Bowditch
" Onesime bookkeeper 107 Bowditch h 128 do
" Ovide clerk h 202 County
Gem Wet Wash Laundry John A Jardine prop 15 Katharine
Genard Joseph fixer h 33 Holly
Genaw Angus painter h 4 Social
Gendion Cyrille carder h 21 Morton court
Gendreau Marie nurse b 42 Locust
" Marie J clerk b 42 Locust
" Roual bricklayer b 42 Locust
Gendron Charles machinist h 240 Tinkham [Grove
" Charles painter h rear 126 Cedar
" Fergenon carpenter h 172 Hatch
" George D special police b 333 N Front [h 213 Bowditch
" George E chief inspector police
" George H weaver h 23 Ashley
" Hugo A mgr 1071 Acushnet av h 129 Holly
" Joseph teamster h 63 Brock av
" Joseph A barber b 129 Holly
" Joseph E dry goods h 82 Nye

Gendron
" Joseph S tailor h 863 Purchase
" J Emile dry goods 1115-1119 Acushnet av h 82 Nye [Grove
" Olivera painter b r 126 Cedar
" Ozebelle weaver h 63 Hicks
" Wallace baker's helper 1653 Acushnet avenue b 206 Tinkham
Genensky Harry salesman 847 S Water b 20 George
" Jacob clerk 851 Acushnet av b 88 Kenyon [George
" Jacob clerk 847 S Water b 20
" Jacob real estate b 69 Russell
" Philip clothing 847 S Water h 20 George
" Rena widow Wolf pawn broker 851 Acushnet av b 88 Kenyon
" Samuel real estate 69 Russell h do
General Accident Fire and Life Assurance Corp Ltd 97 William rm 300
Genereux Eugene shoes and repairing 1107 S Water h 20 McGurk [liam h 71 Brock av
" Eugene Jr shoe repairer 103 Wil-
" Urgelle mgr b 20 McGurk
Generoux Edmond fixer h 150 Collette [bury
" William H carpenter h 58 Salis-
Genest James musician b 121 Cedar
Gent Arthur fixer h 26 Roosevelt
Gentilhomme Pierre weaver h 276 Collette
Geoghegan William G Rev pastor Unitarian church h 47 S Sixth
George Antone M laborer h 185 S Front [Pleasant
" Charles L engineer b 163 Mt
" Ethel clerk 1100 Acushnet av b 11 Bowditch [av rms do
" James bootblack 1504 Acushnet
" Joseph painter h 11 Bowditch
" Joseph F at P Corp b 53 Short
" Smith h 19 George
" Thomas H bell boy Parker House b 153 Elm [157 S Second
" William H laborer 144 S Water b
Geotta Peter painter 421 First h do
Gerad Napoleon laborer h 109 Sawyer
Geraia Antone h 510 S Second
" John speeder b 510 S Second

PELEG H. SHERMAN 506 COUNTY ST.
FUNERAL DIRECTOR AND EMBALMER
OFFICE PHONES. Bell 690-12. Auto. 1305.
RESIDENCE PHONES. Bell 690-12. Auto. 1306.

Gerardi Anthony weaver 1145 Kempton b 36 Eighth [Eighth
" Anthony D silk weaver bds 36
" Julia A b 36 Eighth
GERARDI V VINCENT ladies' tailor and dressmaker 36 Eighth h do See page 769
Gerin Henry grocer 187 Weld h 86 Mt Pleasant [ty
" Mary L widow Joseph h 662 Coun-
" see Guerin [away
Germain Mary weaver h 154 Hath-
Germano Vincenzo watchman h 75 Ash (N) [Shawmut av
Gero Edward F letter carrier h 172
" Frank weaver h r 22 Washburn
" Henry P machinist b 108 Sycamore
" Joseph H b 108 Sycamore
" Mary widow Henry b 172 Shawmut avenue
Gerold Otto rem to Providence R I
Gerome Jose operative h 25 County
Geron Henry grocer 187 Weld h 86 Mt Pleasant [ly
Geroude Everiste twister b 119 Hol-
Geroux George operative h 99 N Front
Gerrard Louis weaver h 28 Cove
" William variety 625 First h 637 do [177 Summer
Gerraughty Bridget widow Martin h
" Martin J bartender 48 Kempton b 177 Summer [b do
" Mary E dressmaker 177 Summer
" William H bartender h 177 Summer [Clark
Gerstein Hyman salesman h 78
" Morris pedlar h 225 Acushnet av
Gersten Israel provisions h 75 Kenyon
" Sadie bookkeeper 213 Acushnet av b 75 Kenyon [Holly
Gervais Antonio boxmaker bds 103
" Edgar slasher tender b 103 Holly
" Ernest plumber b 563 N Front
" Ludger boarding house 19 Hicks
" Ludger third hand h 210 Brook
" Oliver boxmaker h 103 Holly
" Rosario slasher helper b 103 Holly
" Thomas fixer h 50 Blackmer
" William H speeder tender h 19 George [chell
Gervcia Joseph mill hand b 35 Mit-
Getchell Charles F h 317 Kempton
" Gertrude M Mrs h 38 Cedar

Geyer Frank baker b 249 Bowditch
" Henry baker 11 Purchase h 249 Bowditch
Ghiloni John removed from city
" Peter removed from city
Gianetto Giovanni laborer h 12 Viall
Giard Bernard laborer b 135 Dartmouth
" Guito mill hand h 5 Mitchell
Giasson Francois carpenter h 247 N Front
" Zephir lunch b 247 N Front
Gibbons Jeffrey weaver h 147 State
" John J dentist 560 County b do
" Margaret widow Patrick h 560 County
" Margaret M teacher Thomas A Green school b 560 County
" William F h 178½ Arnold
Gibbs Alberta W Mrs b 189 Maxfield [bldg b 30 Howard av
" Charles E elevatorman Times
" Charles H bds 847 Purchase
" Elizabeth F died Nov 22 1910
" Elizabeth M widow John L bds 32 Shawmut av
" Ellen M died Feb 13 1911 [Mill
" Florence L music teacher b 90
" George F h 25 Hunter
" Harriet bds 331 Cedar
" Harry overseer Beacon Mfg Co b 258 Coffin avenue
" Henry painter b 613 Acushnet av
" Howard M real estate 114 Rotch h do [Pleasant
" Jennie W widow Lot H h 176
" John Lothrop died May 8 1911
" John L supervisor of buildings Old Colony division h 27 Sycamore
" John W twister h 209 Tinkham
" Joseph L supt of public buildings 307 Municipal bldg h 71 Fourth
" J Edward bookkeeper Times 120 Purchase h at Acushnet
" Lucinda C widow William H H h 59 Shawmut av [av h do
" L Henry teaming 467 Acushnet
" Mabel W bookkeeper 141 Fourth b 25 Hunter [Newton
" Maud clerk 185 Union b 101
" Nathan S h 101 Newton
" Nathaniel F police b 101 Newton
" Ralph fireman b 2746 Acushnet av

F. T. AKIN & CO. FORGE FACTORY FURNACE FAMILY COAL

Gibbs
" R Manning h 98 Clinton
" William A framemaker 200 Union h 181 Fourth [shnet av
" William J provisions 2914 Acu-
" William J Jr porter 84 Union h 436 Orchard (S) [mut av
" William L driver h 155 Shaw-
" Zipporah widow George W h 42 Durfee
Gibeault Albert painter b 42 Davis
Gibson Agnew B carpenter h 19 Ocean [chase b do
" Bertha M S milliner 205 Pur-
" Frank b 19 Ocean
" James fixer h 33 McGurk
" John (Haskins & Gibson) real estate 66 Pleasant b 19 Ocean
" John W spinner h 155 Durfee
" Nancy widow Samuel S h 3883 Acushnet av [Purchase
" Nellie E widow Harry F h 205
" Patrick J weaver h 112 Cove
" Priscilla widow Abraham h 49 Roosevelt
" Thomas H weaver h 103 Ruth
" William E clerk 98 Purchase h 8 Warwick
" William J hostler 50 Elm h 153 do [Yates
Gicard Murilda milliner bds 113
Gidley Albion R furniture packer 36 Purchase h 155 Elm [474 Park
" Charles R treas N B Textile Co h
" Chester F carpenter h 606 County
" Cyrus J jewelry 23 Purchase h 141 Merrimac
" Elijah B salesman h 14 Cottage
" Harriet C widow Joseph b 421 Union
" James G gardener h 81 Cedar
" John C h 236 Maxfield
" Joseph R carpenter h 3 Bay
" Louis sizer Bennett Mill h 242 Maxfield [Mill h 42 Campbell
" William H bookkeeper Kilburn
" William J rem to Dartmouth
Gidney Cora Mrs operative h 122 Middle [Second
Giegoire John B furniture h 604 S
Gifford Abram surveyor h 355 Court
" Alden M shipper N E C Y Co depts 7 and 8 b 19 Emerson (S)
" Alfred M h 63 State

Gifford
" Alfred M driver h 94 Maxfield
" Alice nurse rms 321 Union
" Alma clerk h 909 County
" Almira teacher b 57 Morgan
" Almy F h 35 Eighth [ton b do
" Annie G dressmaker 176 Kemp-
" Annie L bookkeeper 43 Purchase
" Azuba A clerk 159 Mill h 146 Hillman
" Benjamin S C (Allen, Slade & Co) 1 William h at Fall River
" Bradford F clerk City Mfg Co b 24 Allen [gan
" Carrie E widow Noah h 57 Mor-
" Catherine P widow Sylvanus h 38 Reynolds
" Charles A clerk h 130 Mill
" Charles C police lieutenant Station 3 h 151 North
" Charles Henry h 26 Walnut
" Charles Humphrey died Dec 26 1910 [nell
" Charles M machinist h 156 Grin-
" Charles T W farmer h 291 Shawmut av
" Christopher C b 5 Cottage
" Clara A widow Charles H b 385 Reed [Pleasant
" Collins S M farm hand h 73 Mt
" Daniel H clerk 146 North h 118 Maxfield
" David H carpenter b 389 Reed
" David L carpenter b 83 Kempton
" Edgar B painter h 279 Cedar
" Edgar H clerk 97 Front h 26 Rounds
" Edith nurse rms 321 Union
" Edith B widow Charles H h 31 Madison [av
" Edward operative b 173 Shawmut
" Edward H clerk b 146 Hillman
" Edward H clerk 100 Fifth b 136 Campbell
" Edward H laborer h 125 Willis
" Edward S Jr bds 94 Allen
" Edward W, R R inspector h 185 Richmond [enth
" Elizabeth widow Eli h 29 Sev-
" Elliott W clerk 100 Fifth b 65 Clinton
" Elmer E clerk h 909 County
" Emily widow Samuel T b 137 Chestnut [Emerson (S)
" Emily A widow George P h 19

Don't dream of what you are going to do! Go and do it.
Kinyon's Short-hand School
Odd Fellows Bldg., Cor. William and Pleasant Sts., New Bedford, Mass.

Gifford
" Emma J widow Edward S h 94 Allen
" Ernest stereotyper apprentice Standard h 400 Elm (W)
" Esther widow William h 57 Foster
" Ethel I Mrs bookkeeper 127 Union h Summer
" Etta N housekeeper 355 Court
" Eugene T lather b 17 Chestnut
" Florence L Mrs piano teacher 57 Foster h do
" Frank F slubber tender h 370 Cedar
" Frank H cotton broker 17 Hamilton h 280 County
" Frank W carpenter b 74 School
" Fred C eyeletter h 227 North
" Frederick shoemaker b 94 Maxfield
" George clerk 140 Union bds 227 North
" George waiter 62 Purchase rms 25 William
" George E clerk h 125 Ash (N)
" George H carpenter b 2543 Acushnet av
" George M driver h 17 Bonney
" George P Jr clerk 182 Union b 19 Emerson (S)
" George R bds 1212 Rockdale av
" George S B motorman h 22 Richmond
" George W R clerk b 227 North
" Giles A inspector U St Ry h 37 Keene
" Hannah C h 786 Belleville av
" Harold A b 227 North
" Harry A (Gifford & Magee) h 256 Hillman
" Harry I asst bookkeeper N B S D & T Co b r 252½ Hillman
" Harry W eyeletmaker bds 405 Cottage
" Herbert C asst foreman N B W h 75 Maxfield
" James N real estate 200 Merchants Bank bldg h at Fairhaven
" Jennie widow Stephen C h 117 Shawmut av
" Jesse h 301 County
" John A clerk City M Co h 94 Allen
" John C b 490 Acushnet av
" John F foreman h 226 Mill
" John F sexton Pine Grove cemetery h 118 Perry
" John H fireman h 176 Kempton

Gifford
" John I yard master Rotch Mill h 72 Larch
" John W at P Co h 101 Durfee
" Joseph A door keeper N B Theatre bds 54 Fifth
" Joseph T machinist b 613 Acushnet av
" Julia C teacher Middle st school h 32 Bedford
" Leonora M music teacher 19 Emerson (S) b do
" Lewis h 389 Cedar
" Lewis R wood and coal 348 North h do
" Lillian clerk h 47 Locust
" Luther H electrician h 197 Weld
" Luther R driver 8 Campbell h 49 Smith
" Lydia B widow Gideon h 291 Pleasant
" Margaret A died Aug 25 1910
" Mary Mrs h 244 Hawthorn
" Mary A widow William S h 32 Bedford
" Mary C dressmaker 375 Kempton h do
" May A clerk 185 Union b 274 Pope
" Maynard B foreman b 226 Mill
" Melvina widow Edward W bds 50 Russell
" Nellie A widow Obed F h 8 Hawes lane
" Obed F died January 11 1911
" Pardon B reporter Mercury h 101 Morgan
" Phedora F widow Charles nurse h 2453 Acushnet av
" Ralph A student b 57 Morgan
" Ray E twist drill b 301 County
" Rebecca W h 295 Shawmut av
" Richmond A clerk rms 101 Cedar
" Richmond L salesman 386 Acushnet av h 29 Seventh
" Robert B h 135 Cottage
" Rose C widow James F b 63 Foster
" Ruth A widow William h 117 Cedar
" Sadie F clerk 41 Purchase b 146 Hillman
" Samuel F inspector U St Ry Co h rear 77 Linden
" Sarah housekeeper 371 Court
" Sarah A h 124 Bedford
" Sarah A housekeeper 29 Seventh
" Sarah F died April 25 1911
" Sarah L widow Peli h 244 Hawthorn
" Sidney teamster h 218 Purchase
" Sumner E (S E Gifford Auto Co) b r 77 Linden
" Susan B stenographer P Corp b 32 Bedford

HASKELL BROS. DEALERS IN
ICE
400 COURT STREET TELEPHONE CONNECTION NEW BEDFORD, MASS.

Gifford
" Susan W rms 84 Court
" S E Auto Co (Sumner E Gifford) 131-139 Pleasant [389 Cedar
" Thomas clerk Pierce Mfg Corp b
" Thomas J (Thomas J Gifford & Co) plumbers 650 Cottage h 65 Ashland [209 h 44 State
" T Merritt clerk 120 Purchase rm
" William 2nd carpenter h 17 Chestnut [cial h at Dartmouth
" William A sail maker 31 Commer-
" William D h 83 Locust
" William F clerk 144 S Water bds 116 North South [Acushnet av
" William H carpet cleaner b 304
" William H gardener h 117 Cedar
" William H laborer h 397 Cedar
" William L second hand b 389 Cedar [Water h 57 Foster
" William O bookkeeper 188 North
" William S painter h 446 Pleasant
" William T second hand h Shawmut av beyond Plainville road
" & Magee (Harry A Gifford and Robert S Magee) bakers 214 Purchase [County
Gignac Benjamin loom fixer h 51
" Ojeda perfumer 129 Hillman h do
Giguere Adelard carder b 267 Bowditch
" Aime doffer h 54 Bullard
" Alphonse painter h 88 Holly
" Damien hod carrier b 125 Phillips avenue [Hathaway
" Dolphis clerk 161 Coffin av b 127
" Henry weaver h 6 Riverside av
" John B operative h 125 Phillips avenue
" Joseph weaver h 269 Bowditch
" Odelon carder h 127 Hathaway
" Olivier druggist 161 Coffin av and (O Giguere & Co) h 127 Hathaway
" O & Co (Oliver Giguere and Charles E McMurray) druggists 1669 Acushnet avenue
" William weaver b 125 Phillips av
Gilbert Arthur painter b 74 Division
" Arthur F principal Parker street school
" Charles carpenter h 110 Blackmer
" Charles cook h 137 S Water
" Charles laborer h 954 S Water

Gilbert
" Edward laborer h r 198 State
" Edward A dentist 60 Purchase b 314 Acushnet avenue
" James weaver h 123 Ruth
" Marie R V Mrs h 7 Cleveland
" Nancy Mrs h 16 Ashley
" Walter J clerk 100 Fifth h 205 Maple
" see Guilbeaut
Gilcher Charles removed from city
Gilchrist John machinist h 17 Marvin [nolds
" Margaret widow John h 27 Rey-
Gildard Annie h 512 Acushnet avenue
Gildea Edward J spinner h 1530 Acushnet avenue [h do
" Mary Mrs teas 1530 Acushnet av
Gile John F master mechanic City Mfg Corp h 47 Dartmouth
Giles Isaac W (Giles & Tobey) h 90 Mill
" Walter electrician h 7 Abbott
GILES & TOBEY (Isaac W Giles and Charles W Tobey) auto repairs 44 Middle See page 744
" see Geils [avenue
Gilg John weaver bds 638 Acushnet
Gilham Ann Mrs h 10 Warren
Gilholm John golfer b 31 Sycamore
Gilkey Eben S awning maker 35 Commercial h 111 Maxfield
Gill Albert spinner h 24 Peckham
" Charles speeder tender h 72 Belleville road [Hathaway
" Elizabeth widow James h 72
" Francis T removed from city
" Harry machinist h 195 Brock av
" James baker 704 Purchase h 356 Cedar Grove [avenue
" James spinner h 175 Phillips
" John S pattern maker h 30 Dudley
" Manuel E weaver h 8 Independent
" Severa rms 35 Fifth
" Severin farmer h 175 Durfee
" Vianna widow John E h 2 Richmond
" & Bilsborrow (James Gill and William Bilsborrow) bakers 704 Purchase [atre h 8½ Nye
Gilleney John H manager Viens the-
Gillespie Andrew M overseer Holmes Mfg Co b 25 Viall
" Charles city employee b 2 N Oak

J. F. CROSSLEY 223 MILL STREET COR. EMERSON PHONE
STEAM and HOT WATER HEATING
GAS FITTING and FIXTURES

Gillespie
" Eugene teamster b 2 N Oak
" John R laborer b 2 N Oak
" Lillian piano teacher 9 Jean b do
" Oliver fireman h 9 Jean [N Oak
" Robert foreman st department h 2
Gillett George b 9 Studley [Studley
" James W clerk 878 Purchase h 9
" John weaver b 25 Viall
" Richard weaver b 25 Viall [Mill
Gillette Frank E eyelet maker h 286
Gillibrand John second hand h 186 Hathaway [ond
Gillick John H engineer h 162 S Sec-
" Lawrence carpenter h 78 James
Gillis Lawrence A clerk 270 Acushnet av h 37 Hickory [Weld
" Robert baker 372 Kempton h 256
Gillow Joseph gardener h 694 First
Gillum Ernest laborer h 179 Mill
" Ernest E drill worker h 150 Fourth
" George H drill worker b 179 Mill
" Ida clerk 70 Purchase b 149 Mill
" William clerk 178 Arnold b 179 Mill [ter
Gilman Albert helper 28 North Wa-
" Alfred drill worker b 40 Russell
" Augustus drill worker b 40 Russell [Grinnell
" Carrie E widow Joseph h 169
" Frank E foreman 100 Fifth h 80 Oak [Russell
" H Augustus drill worker b 40
" Joseph C clerk 13 N Sixth b 169 Grinnell [ant
" Thomas R accountant h 389 Pleas-
Gilmartin Charles W dentist 910 S Water b 32 Rockland
" Katharine T clerk 125 Middle b 32 Rockland
" Michael W glass cutter h 32 Rockland [Second
Gilmette Jack cook bds 101 South
Gilmore Alfred lunch 835½ S Water rms Blackmer cor Second
" Arthur barber 835 S Water h 856 S First
" Charles carder h 7 Bentley
" Delia A dressmaker 12 Spruce h do [ushnet av h 125 Nash rd
" Edmund T hairdresser 1673 Ac-
" Frederick spinner b 7 Bentley

Gilmore
" Harry clerk b 7 Bentley [ton
" Helen G milliner b 156 Washing-
" James warper h 874 County
" Jane E principal I W Benjamin school b 245 Acushnet av
" John mason h 162 Nash rd
" John mill hand h 121 Nash rd
" John P overseer h 454 Sawyer
" Levy hairdresser 397 N Front rms 51 Tallman [Washington
" Margaret A inspector bds 152
" Percy shoemaker h 193 Cedar
" Richard ice and furniture mover 18 Stapleton h do
" Richard Jr weaver b 18 Stapleton
" Robert J teamster h Rockdale av near Mill [Washington
" Thomas overseer N B S Co h 156
" William laborer h 156 Washington [Grove
" William C spinner h 356 Cedar
" William H steam fitter h 156 Washington
Gilmour Arthur W hairdresser 835 South Water h 856 First
" James b 534 N Front [Cedar
" James coachman 731 County h 23
" Patrick barber h 534 N Front
Gilston John W overseer Pierce Mfg Corp h 43 Parker [ville av
Gimer Frank mill hand b 399 Belle-
Gingras Arthur driver 106 Front bds 131 Nye
" Delphas weaver h 15 Holly
" Henry removed from city
" Lorenzo J weaver b 115 Bullard
" Philip fixer h 115 Bullard
" Rene h 131 Nye [Holy h do
" Stephaine Mrs dressmaker 15
Ginn John mill hand b 48 Davis
Ginnochio Amanda E Mrs h 43 State
" Emiline M telephone operator 57 N Second b 43 State
" John B liquors 131 N Water h 425 Acushnet avenue [ond
Ginsburg Max salesman h 72 S Sec-
" Rebecca Mrs h 12 Cannon
" Samuel butcher h 279 Kempton
Giotski Lawrence laborer h 26 Washburn [E Merrimac
Giovanni Monticane laborer h 20
" Spadssa laborer h 67 Acushnet av
Giraca Antone h 5 Penniman [ditch
Girard Abraham fisherman h 1 Bow-

CHARLES A. CROSHERE
38 FOURTH ST. Bell Phone 1964-23
SIGN PAINTING
GLASS LETTERING
ELECTRIC SIGNS
SHOW CARDS

Girard
" Agnes widow h 872 Acushnet av
" Albert spinner h 19 Holly
" Alphonse slasher b 211 Whitman
" Elmer spinner h 491 N Front
" Eugenia milliner and dry goods 1239 Acushnet av h 14 Linden
" Eusebe fixer b 178 Collette
" Francois X foreman h 178 Collette
" Francois X loom fixer h 39 Ashley
" John B weaver h 872 Acushnet avenue
" Louis collector b 91 Bullard
" Napoleon carpenter h 67 Hathaway
" Oliver h 1 Riverside avenue
" Paul N express h 358 Coffin av
" Pierre operative b 58 Covell
" Toussant carpenter h 211 Whitman
" Valmore weaver h 178 Collette
" Vital undertaker 14 Linden h do
" Wilfred P fireman b 58 Covell
Girardo Domenico laborer h 274 Cedar Grove
Girouard Aldege weaver b 608 S Second
" Aldege weaver b 1205 Acushnet avenue
" Alphee weaver b 119 Holly
" Aurore clerk bds 23 First
" Claudia back boy b 119 Holly
" Elie weaver h 162 Bowditch
" Fred overseer Oneko Millh 119 Holly
" Hector carpenter b 119 Holly
" Joseph weaver b 608 S Second
" Levi carpenter b 174 Phillips av
" Melace B removed to Leominster
" Michel fisherman h 5 Bullard
" Napoleon operative h 109 Beetle
" Ovila pool b 232 Acushnet av
Giroux Alphege glass worker b 831 S Water
" Aristides removed from city
" Egesipe baker h 215 Coffin av
" George weaver h 2 Hicks
" John shoemaker h 60 Nye
" Louis removed from city
" Peter laborer h 70 Phillips av
" Pierre carpenter h 553 N Front
" see Gero
Girrioer Thomas F removed to Brooklyn N Y
Girvan Douglas J clerk h 84 Thompson
Giusti Ceasar (Giusti & Co) rms 86 N Second
" John (Giusti & Co) h 38 McGurk
" & Co (John and Caesar Giusti and Frank Catelli) bakers 861 South Water [h 46 do
Gladding Wanton M supt 100 Fifth
Glådu Adelard teamster h 105 Davis
" Arthur weaver h 492 Bowditch
" Damien weaver h 492 Bowditch
" Dammin lodging 19 N Sixth
" Frank C painter h 669 First
" George clerk b 22 W French av
" George clerk b 193 Dean
" Henri shipper b 27 County
" Henry weaver b 211 Coffin av
" Jean B h 669 First
" Joseph weaver h 22 W French avenue
" Napoleon weaver h 211 Coffin av
" Stanislas loom fixer h 11 Ashley
Glaser Ferdinand clerk 1130 Acushnet avenue h 362 Earle
" Martin P mill hand b 362 Earle
Glasgow Albert C removed from city
" Francis J compositor Times h 118 Shawmut av
" William J Jr business mgr Times [h 252 Summer
Glass Charles F painter h 133 Chestnut
" Mitchel weaver h 154 Hathaway
Glasse Clarissa C widow Walter R h 324 Cedar
Glasser John weaver h 18 Clark
Gleason Ann M teacher James B Congdon school b James Gleason
" Arthur electrician b 519 Rivet
" Colin weaver h 229 Brook
" Ellen died Sept 7 1910
" George gardener h 74 Park
" George F clerk 163 Union b 74 Park
" Helen C teacher William H Taylor school b James Gleason's
" Helena M milliner 185 Union bds 519 Rivet
" Henry engraver b 519 Rivet
" James h Clara near E French av
" James W clerk h 276 Fourth
" John J bartender 283 S Second b Clara

Steiger-Dudgeon Co.
"The WOMAN'S Store."
Tel. Bell 82 & 83, Branches connecting all depts.
" " 160 For Office only. Auto. 1211

SUMPTIONS, ASSORTMENTS AT ALL TIMES OF DEPENDABLE DRY GOODS

Gleason
" Joseph student b James Gleason's
Clara [don school b Clara
" Margaret teacher James B Cong-
" Timothy J clerk 688 Kempton b
74 Park
" Timothy J engineer b 4 N Oak
" William E machinist h 519 Rivet
Gleckman Wolf furniture 577 South
Water h 589 do [land Village
Gledhill Simeon mill hand h 1 How-
Gleek Abraham shoe repairer 123
Potomska h 57 Grinnell
Glennon Charles L operative b 56
Locust
" Dennis A shoes 241 Purchase bds
74 Locust [545 Cottage
" Edward salesman 22 William bds
" John E h 74 Locust
" John F cotton sampler Quissett
Mill b 691 County [74 County
" Joseph R supt Quissett Mill h
" Matthew T president N B Textile
Co h 545 Cottage
" Michael J overseer Wamsutta
Mill h 56 Locust [691 County
" Thomas F agent Quissett Mill h
" William F police h 84 Newton
Glick Abraham shoemaker h 57 Grin-
nell [burn
Glinsky Felex dry goods h 22 Wash-
Glista Frank h 110 Newton
" Joseph shoemaker b 110 Newton
Globe Credit Co clothing 140-142
Purchase
GLOBE DYE HOUSE (J N J Lon-
holdt) 220 Shawmut av and
1014 Acushnet avenue office 52
Pleasant rm 1 See foot lines
Gloria Mary E widow h 252 Bonney
Glosh Frank operative h 6 Coffin av
court [Union bds 146 State
Glover Ethel M asst bookkeeper 185
" Rebecca died May 21 1911
Glowaski John clerk 159 N Front h
43 Washburn
" Joseph shoe repairer and variety
16 Hicks h do [Hathaway
Glynn Michael S mill hand h 87½
Gobeille Anna milliner b 45 Tallman
" Anthony twister b 137 Phillips av
" Henry fixer b 137 Phillips av
" Joseph fisherman h 137 Phillips
avenue [Phillips avenue
" Joseph Jr clerk 420 N Front b 137
" Odino mason b 155 Bowditch
Gobeille Anna milliner b 45 Tallman
" Arthur carder h 49 Phillips av
" Bartholomew carpenter h 45 Tall-
man [avenue
" Emma Mrs milliner h 195 Phillips
" John C carpenter b 45 Tallman
" Joseph carpenter h 195 Phillips
avenue
" Thomas carpenter b 45 Tallman
Gobell John J clerk foot Willis h
551 Kempton
Goddard Alvano C (Parlow & God-
dard) 97 William rm 206 h at
Fairhaven
" Emery (Kingcroft Iron Foundry)
h 2891 Acushnet avenue
" James R engineer Steamer No 7 h
679 Cottage [tage
" Sarah widow William b 679 Cot-
Goddu Oscar C (Acushnet Pharmacy)
1401 Acushnet av h 87 Bullard
Goddune Edward C L meter inspector
125 Middle h 224 Allen [man
Godere Arthur teamster b 64 Tall-
" Delor teamster b 64 Tallman
" Paul laborer h 64 Tallman
" Paul Jr teamster b 64 Tallman
" William fixer h 172 State
Godfrey Charles A M died Sept 20
1910 [Seventh
" Chester S clerk 100 Fifth b 26
" Eugene H stable 35 Hillman h 37
do
" Foster removed from city
" James O clerk 368 Kempton h
457 Cottage
" Seth W officer H C h 429 Union
" Willard E clerk 702 Purchase rms
249 do [avenue
Godin Arthur laborer h 127 Coffin
" Ephraim driver 659 Purchase
" Ephraim mill hand b 39 Dean
" Ephraim removed from city
" Frank removed from city
" Joseph hairdresser 1601 Acush-
net avenue h 259 Weld
" John laborer h 135 N Front

J. G. NICHOLSON
LUMBER, SASH, DOORS and BLINDS
BOWDITCH STREET, NEW BEDFORD, MASS.

Godreau Rodolphe advertising agent 101 Kenyon h 158 Bates av
Godwin Isabell widow Edward h rear 330 Cedar Grove
" see Goodwin [h 317 do
Goewey Charles R grocer 327 Davis
Goff Charles F carpenter h 152 North
" George H h 38 Cedar
" Lucy P died January 27 1911
" Michael weaver h 68 Jouvett
" Sarah widow Charles H h 101 Cedar
Gogais Henry twister b 39 Tallman
Gogan Fred fisherman b 132 Whitman
" Harry fisherman b 132 Whitman
" John carpenter h 132 Whitman
Goggin Delia widow Michael h 264 Pleasant
" John F deputy collector Custom House h 190 Merrimac
" John W h 48 Newton
" Lena E housework New Bedford Tuberculocis Sanitarium Acushnet av Clifford Mass
" Walter J teacher High school bds 35 Eighth [Hatch
Goguen Adele widow Odelon h 172
" Arthur twister b 16 Holly
" Henry mill hand h 39 Tallman
" Joseph removed to Somerville
" Joseph twister h 257 Sawyer
" Odelon died Aug 24 1910
" Philias carpenter h 16 Holly
" Philias mill hand b 148 Tinkham
" Philip doffer b 207 Sawyer
" Stephen fisherman h 51 Collette
" Telexphore teamster b 172 Hatch
Gois Manuel shoemaker h 323 First
Golasz Alex operative h 191 N Front
Goldberg Alex real estate h 106 Beetle
" Harry milliner h 127 Nye [Cove
" Harry shoes 277 Fourth h 118½
" Michael removed from city
" Morris shoes 733 S Water h 118 Acushnet avenue
" Phillip pedlar h 486 First
" Samuel shoe repairer 22 Wing h 26 do [h do
Golden Annie variety 841 S Water
" Mary widow John h 5 Spooner
Goldfarb Wolf junk collector h 280 Cedar Grove [nolds
Goldis Samuel real estate h 61 Rey-
Goldrick Eugene driver b 184 Shawmut av [35 Howland Village
" James H plumber 55 N Water h
" J Frank shoe worker h 184 Shawmut avenue [Second
Goldstein Barnard junk bds 429 S
" Bouet pedlar h 434 S Second
" David clerk h 515 N Front
" Harris pedlar h 84 Washington
" Harry blacksmith h 434 S Second
" Henry fruit h 84 Washington
" Israel driver 70 Union b 995 S Water [do
" Leon variety 1104 S Water h 995
" Max produce h 9 Cannon
" Moses dry goods and clothing 33-35 Weld h 88 Kenyon
" Samuel blacksmith 431 S Second h 434 do [Washington
" Samuel clerk 739 Water b 84
" William pedlar h 279 Coggeshall
Goldthrop Alexander laborer h 10 Trinity
" John J spinner h 10 Trinity
Goldthwaite Bradley D h 370 Cedar
Goldys Samuel real estate 61 Reynolds h do [S Second
Golezynski Yosef operative h 558
Golin Albert h r 259 N Front
" Peter teamster h 98 Beetle
" Vilon operative h 20 Washburn
Gomes Alves laborer h 9 S Water
" Annie widow h 7 Bethel
" Antone laborer h 45 Adams
" Antone mariner h 322 S Water
" Antone F laborer h 262 Fourth
" Benjamin laborer h 466 Maxfield
" Caesar laborer h 11 Morgans lane
" Emily widow h 59 Acushnet av
" Fannie Mrs h 206 S Front
" Frank laborer h 121 Dartmouth
" Frank laborer h 117 S Second
" Henrique grocer 138 Belleville av h 1201 Coggeshall
" Henry laborer h 52 Middle
" Henry steward h 7 Bethel
" Isaac laborer h 62 S Water
" Isaac laborer h 559 Acushnet av
" James operative bds 326 First
" Jennie Mrs h 8 Morgans lane [ter
" Jennie widow Antone h 63 S Wa-
" John laborer h 19 Bullard
" John laborer h 22 Bourne
" John mariner h 316 First

Steiger-Dudgeon Co.
"The WOMAN'S Store."
Tel. Bell 82 & 83, Branches connecting all depts.
" " 160 For Office only. Auto. 1211
SUMPTIONS, ASSORTMENTS AT ALL TIMES OF DEPENDABLE DRY GOODS

Gomes
" John pool 107 S Second
" John variety h 92 Acushnet av
" John A hairdresser 10 N Second h at Lakeville [Village
" John D mill hand h 36 Howland
" John F painter h 49 Katharine
" John G operative h 44 Hemlock
" Joseph laborer h 47 First
" Joseph laborer h 63 S Second
" Joseph laborer h 317 S Water
" Joseph J operative h 5 Walnut
" Joseph S fisherman h 57 Cove rd
" Joseph S weaver h 60 Mosher
" Joseph laborer h 63 S Second
" Josephine h 94 S Second
" Jule h 22 Bourne
" Justa widow h 438 S Water
" Louis laborer h 317 S Water
" Manuel barber 114 S Second h do
" Manuel laborer h 87 S Second
" Manuel laborer h 179 Belleville av
" Manuel mariner h 422 S Water
" Manuel seaman h 148 S Second
" Manuel weaver h 142 Division
" Manuel A grocer 129 S Water rms do
" Manuel F died Oct 20 1911
" Manuel J farmer h Aquidneck
" Martin A clerk 351 S Water h 10 Griffin
" Mary Mrs h 46 School [Madison
" Michael shipping agent h 20
" Michael yard master 295 Phillips av h Main near Mill rd L C
" Paul laborer h 63 First
" Peter laborer h 26 Elm [Bolton
" Sabina R widow Manuel F h 530
" Saverino laborer h 72 Crapo
" William F teamster 99 Front h 22 Babbitt [ton h 464 do
Gomley John A bakery 468 Kemp-
" Lizzie L and Susan E b 196 Elm
" see Gormley [h 15 Fulton court
Gonet Charles driver 215 Coggeshall
" Jan weaver h r 259 N Front
" Kaval teamster h 15 Fulton ct
" L Walter operative h 108 Phillips avenue [Elm
Gongleux Louis glass cutter h 428
Gonneville Adelard L clerk 1141 Acushnet av h 1042 do
" Adrian weaver b 92 Holly
" Andrew clerk h 109 Locust

Gonneville
" Eli clerk 959 Acushnet av h 301 Sawyer
" Emile weaver bds 92 Holly
" Felix grocer 936 County h 12 La France court [109 Locust
" Joseph A clerk 100 William bds
" Louis A removed from city
" Wilfred E weaver h 92 Holly
Gonsalves Alvira clerk 70 Purchase b 194 Park [rd
" Anna widow John h Winterville
" Antone fisherman h 17 Bullard
" Antone laborer h 14 Bethel
" Antone laborer b 49 Hemlock
" Antone laborer h 522 Maxfield
" Antone operative h 62 Middle
" Antonio farmer h 723 Allen
" Antonio weaver h 75 Mosher
" Antonio M (A M Gonsalves & Son) h 25 Stowell
" August laborer h 244 Acushnet av
" A M & Son (A M and F M Gonsalves) hairdressers 136 Dartmouth
" Caesar city laborer h 39 Stephen
" Constantine laborer h 381 S Second
" Domingos fish 211 Coggeshall
" Eustis clerk b 194 Park [nell
" Fernandes blacksmith h 75 Grin-
" Flora Mrs h 139 Perry
" Frank carpenter h 10 Juniper
" Frank laborer h 32 Clark
" Frank A Jr buffer h 56 Babbitt
" Frank J mason 30 Dartmouth h do [Son) b 25 Stowell
" Frank M (A M Gonsalves &
" Fred h 71 First
" Januario laborer b 49 Hemlock
" Jerome janitor public library h 63 Spruce
" Joaquim laborer h 48 Babbitt
" John city emp h 49 Hemlock
" John helper 64 Dartmouth b 28 Rotch block 439 Bolton
" John mill hand b 28 Rotch block 439 Bolton
" John removed to Fairhaven [av
" John mill hand h 218 Acushnet
" John operative h 202 Belleville avenue [mouth
" John F operative bds 30 Dart-
" John J weaver h 75 Delano
" Jose steward h 194 Park

PELEG H. SHERMAN 506 COUNTY ST.
FUNERAL DIRECTOR AND EMBALMER
OFFICE PHONES. Bell 690-13. Auto. 1305.
RESIDENCE PHONES. Bell 690-12. Auto. 1306.

Gonsalves
" Joseph clerk h 335 S Front
" Joseph cooper h 5 Harrison
" Joseph laborer h 31 S Second
" Joseph laborer h 126 Dartmouth
" Joseph market gardener 5 Jenney h do [mouth
" Joseph operative h 121 Dart-
" Joseph operative h 12 Babbitt
" Joseph plasterer h 126 Dartmouth [24 1911
" Joseph (Winterville rd) died June
" Joseph M laborer b 40 N Water
" Joseph N removed from city
" Justin grocer 186 Belleville av h 179 do [av h 203 do
" Justin hairdresser 201 Belleville
" Lottie Mrs h 18 Cannon
" Manuel barber 201 Belleville av h 90 Sawyer
" Manuel M laborer b 40 N Water
" Martin M lunch 189 S Water h 40 N Water
" Nicholas painter h 27 Stackhouse
" Olympia Mrs h 10 Morgan's lane
" Rose Mrs h 141 S Water
" Theatonil barber h 76 Sidney
" William laborer b 11 Oak
Goodby Henry weaver h 945 County [County
Goodfellow Charles weaver h 864
" John A b 1045 County [way
" Joshua H spinner h 122 Hatha-
" Samuel A overseer Taber Mill h 116 Hathaway [Hathaway
Goodhue Noe carpenter bds 153
" Thomas carpenter h 206 Hathaway
Gooding Charles H h 365 North
" Charles H Jr conductor h 225 Cedar [b 132 Willis
" Clinton S clerk City Coal Co
" Gertude P teacher Harrington school b 132 Willis [132 Willis
" Leon L tinsmith 28 N Water bds
" Robert A carpenter h 132 Willis
Goodinson Martha widow Joe h 131 Fair [ton h 383 do
Goodman Bessie clerk 384 Kemp-
" Charles (Barnett & Goodman Inc) h 16 Clay [ton h 383 do
" Esther Mrs dry goods 384 Kemp-
" Ethel bookkeeper 97 William rm 407 b 383 Kempton [475 do
" Hyman clothing 321 S Water h

Goodman
" Julius clothing 475 S Water h 472 do
" Louis mgr 384 Kempton h 382 do
Goodovitch Charles grocer 42 Washburn h 47 do
Goodreau Delor contractor 9 Beetle and teaming 27 Hathaway h at Acushnet
" Zephir teamster h 9 Beetle
Goodrich Addie F Mrs h 83 Kempton [Vt
" William G rem to Morrisville

GOODSPEED ALEXANDER McL Counsellor at Law, U S Commissioner, Examiner of Titles for the Court of Land Registration, Notary Public 37 Purchase Street rm 13 b 20 Seventh Street

Goodwin Albert janitor h 180 Mid-
272 Davis
" Albert janitor h 180 Middle
" Charles drillmaker rms 35 Fifth
" Dexter B salesman 16 N Second b 180 Middle
" John laborer b 644 Purchase
" John F weaver b 24 Independent
" John J weaver h 24 Independent
" Thomas R laborer h 175 Eugenia
" Walter waiter 62 Purchase b 24 Independent
" see Godwin [ton
Gordon Abraham tailor h 286 Kemp-
" Anna M widow Cassius h 298 Cottage [Green
" Caroline widow Jabez A h 5
" Carrie R widow Thomas P b 15 Hawthorn ter
" Celestine Mrs b 485 County
" Eliza housekeeper 24 Howard
" Fred weaver b 67 Coffin av
" Harry laborer h 329 S Second
" Helen M h 11 Franklin
" James J painter h 50 Durfee

F. T. AKIN & CO. PAINTERS AND DECORATORS

Gordon
" James J Jr painter h 175 Richmond [Sherman
" James W twister tender bds 53
" John R page public library b 53 Sherman
" Joseph third hand b 11 Logan
" Kate weaver h 198 Blackmer
" Morris tailor h 72 S Second
" Patrick laborer h 963 Purchase
" Percy Rev rector Grace church h 372 County
" Peter driver h 24 Elm
" Richmond asst mgr 17 Pleasant h 15 Hawthorn ter
" Thomas P died Sept 22 1910
" Walter S treas Consolidated Meat & Grocery Co h 692 County
" William clerk h 53 Sherman
" William foreman 100 Fifth h 449 Union
" William painter b 28 Howard
" see Godin [Acushnet av
Gore James H machinist h 1264
" Robert spinner h 1264 Acushnet av
Gorham Adeline R h 203 Pleasant
" Carrie P widow Jabez A h 5 Green [Green
" Fred R salesman 99 William b 5
" James H mgr Hallet & Davis Piano Co 99-101 William h 86 Morgan
" Mark h 14 Studley
" Michael J steward h 38 Robeson
" Robert S mgr h 79 Morgan
" Walter F removed to Taunton
Gorka Zofia grocer 190 Church h do
Gorman Edward operative h 258 Tinkham
" Joseph electrician b 122 Thompson [Thompson
" Joseph helper U St Ry Co h 122
" Mary variety 65 County h do
Gormley Georgianna N widow William rms 87 School [ton
Gorner Arthur motorman b 32 Staple-
" Catherine widow Henry h 75 Brock av [Stapleton
" Doctor tinsmith 159 Cove h 32
" Henry S clerk h 59 Willow
" James S painter 713 Kempton h 33 Lexington [Reynolds
" John tinsmith 87 Union h 25
Gorsetsa Wolkas operative h 61 Washburn [North
Gorton Mary J widow Nathan D h 9
" Samuel yclerk 1099 Acushnet av h 13 Bannister
" Timothy weaver h 7 Cleveland
" William fixer h 42 Salisbury
Gosciminsky Henry H painter b 763 Purchase [ald ct
Gosda Joseph mill hand b 2 McDon-
Goshein Milton clerk 740 Purchase b 22 Beetle [h 22 do
" Rebecca Mrs grocer 28 Beetle
Goskovitch John carder h r 60 Washburn [Middle
Goslin Minnie widow William h 94
Gosnold Mills Co cotton goods mfrs Orchard (S) cor Cove rd
Goss Richard W student b 47 Chancery [cery
" Robert A coachman h 47 Chan-
Gosseler George fixer h 116 W French av [Front
Gosselin Albert weaver bds 330 N
" Alfred barber 81 William h 1073 Water [Whitman
" Annie widow Telesphore b 122
" Arthur weaver h 32 Penniman
" Auguste P (Lemlin & Gesselin) h 190 Division [av
" Delphis spinner h 195 Phillips
" Edward driver b 107 Holly
" Eusebe barber 116 Union h 60 State
" Ferdinand third hand h 212 State [1733 Acushnet av
" Gilbert overseer Taber Mill bds
" Henry teamster h 107 Holly
" Hormidas brakeman b 107 Holly
" Joseph operative b 9 Hazard ct
" Joseph I glasscutter b 60 State
" Julia widow Joseph h 182 Weld
" J Henry h 182 Weld
" Moise job team 107 Holly h do
" Napoleon carpenter bds 330 N Front
" Napoleon mill hand h 7 Holly
" Peter h 53 County
" Richard Z spinner b 182 Weld
" Samuel operative h 122 Whitman
" Samuel Jr operative b 122 Whitman
" Thomas spinner b 9 Hazard ct
" Xavier laborer h 9 Hazard ct

Bookkeeping, Shorthand, Typewriting, Penmanship, etc. Taught thoroughly at
Kinyon's Commercial School
Odd Fellows Bldg., Cor. William and Pleasant Sts., New Bedford, Mass.

Gotlieb Isaac dry goods 776 Purchase h 229 State
Goudin Alexander laborer b 1507 Acushnet av [Sawyer
Goudit Adelard clerk 41 Bentley b
Goudreau August iceman h 287 N Front
" Ferdinand weaver h 37 Ashley
" Fred operative b 39 Dean
" Gustave weaver h 88 Ruth
" Ida widow Samuel h 392 Belleville av
" Joseph H hairdresser 113 Cove
" Joseph J clerk b 81 Wood [chase
" Napoleon laborer h 863 rear Pur-
" William doffer b 392 Belleville av
" Zephio painter h 211 Church
Goulart Adeline sewer 40 Purchase b 32 Acushnet av [Page
" Antone F laborer N B W W h 55
" Antonio hairdresser 586 S Water h 142 Fair [19 Elizabeth
" Arthur asst janitor 246½ Union h
" Charles driver b 44 Crapo
" Domingos S helper 185 Acushnet av h 44 Crapo [Village
" Joaquim laborer h 15 Howland
" Joseph S fireman h 110 Rockland
" Manuel fish 207 Coggeshall h Belleville av [ond
" Manuel operative h 326 S Sec-
" Manuel photographer 110 S Sixth h do [nell
" Manuel second hand h 55 Grin-
" Manuel F laborer h 22 Hemlock
" Manuel V operative h 382 Belleville av [son
" Marianna widow h 136 Thomp-
" Michael scrubber h 55 Grinnell
" Roza L mill hand b 181 Coffin av
Gould Albini fisherman h 93 Collette
" Mary L widow James h 180 State [Purchase b 174 State
" Patrick T shoe repairer 766
" Pollet T copperworker b 180 State
" Theodore helper b 180 State
Goulding Alice A teacher Harrington school b 260 Hillman [Hillman
" Cornelius T city teamster b 260
" Frances R bookkeeper 250 Purchase b 260 Hillman [net av
" James S machinist h 490 Acush-
" James S surveyor b 260 Hillman

Goulding
" Julia E clerk 185 Union b 260 Hillman
" Michael J foreman city blacksmith shop h 260 Hillman
Goulet Adelard carpenter b 53 Ruth
" Adeline widow Joseph h 35 Dean
" Alfred doffer h 189 Earle
" Alfred mill hand bds 63 Dean
" Anatole weaver h 168 N Front
" Charles eyeletmaker b 35 Dean
" Cyril elevatorman h 72 Belleville road [do
" Edward barber 33 Linden b 35
" Fred foreman 238 State h 1011 County
" George H barber h 35 Linden
" John carpenter h 5 Bonneau ct
" Joseph A weaver h 207 Bowditch
" Louis laborer h 63 Dean
" Matthew R fisherman h 62 Sherman
" Philip third hand h 95 Diman
" Regina widow George millinery 35½ Linden h 35 do
" Samuel third hand h 52 Dean
" Wilfred carpenter b 63 Dean
" William J barber b 35 Linden
Gourley John pavingcutter h 40 Orchard
Gousie Michael laborer h 229 State
Govang James J shoemaker h 293 Belleville av
Govera John laborer h 55 Mitchell
Govin Joseph copperworker h 235 N Front
Govisky Frank h 539 S Second
Govoni Angelo tackmaker h 820 Kempton [way
Gow John operative h 173 Hatha-
" Robert teamster b 173 Hathaway
Goyer Dona operative h 104 Jouvett
" Donase teamster h 104 Jouvett
" Sabin h 26 Nelson
Goyette Alexis fixer h 28 Tallman
" Antoine carpenter h 55 County
" Antoine weaver h 47 Reynolds
" Benjamin fireman h 16 Clark
" Donat teamster 27 Bowditch h Kenyon street [Bowditch
" Emile clerk 507 N Front bds 344
" Florence widow Marcel bds 352 N Front [city
" Joseph (36 Hicks) removed from
" Joseph farmer h 4 Kenyon
" Joseph operative h 84 Kenyon

Bread, Cake, Pastry
RICHMOND & COMPANY 255-257 UNION STREET
Bell 993 Automatic 1022

Goyette
" Joseph Jr operative b 84 Kenyon
" Malvina widow Gotfroid boarding house 20 Covell [ditch
" Walter machinist h 132 Bow-
" William weaver h 540 N Front
" see Gaouette [land
Grace Antone drillmaker b 88 Rock-
" Antone hostler h 51 South
" Emily J widow Joseph h 53 Short
" Henry G second hand h 202 Park
" John laborer h 545 Acushnet av
" Joseph M mgr 781 S Water h 233 Palmer [9-10 h 70 Hall
" Manuel overseer N E C Y Co dept
" Manuel twister h 218 Fourth
" Manuel A city laborer h 102 Ash (N)
" Manuel S pool 538 S Water h 525 do
" Vincent J student b 233 Palmer
Gracia Albertina dressmaker bds 71 Dartmouth
" Anna widow b 55 Page
" Antone mgr Idle Hour Theatre h 106 Potomska [lane
" Antonio operative h 3 Maiden
" Antonio operative h 107 Larch
" Antonio operative b 150 Acushnet av [land h 178 Rockland
" Antonio B baker Bolton c Rock-
" Caesar carpenter b 71 Dartmouth
" Charles operative h 150 Acushnet av [shuet av
" Charles V mill hand h 150 Acu-
" Emily Mrs removed to Fairhaven
" Etelvina clerk b 239 Field [Fair
" Frank clerk 659 S Water h 42
" Frank laborer h 30 Hollyhock
" Frank pool 75 Potomska h 83 Acushnet av [mouth
" Frank A carpenter h 71 Dart-
" John clerk 16 Briggs h 150 Acushnet av
" John cook h 137 S Second
" John laborer h 8 Cannon
" John laborer h 51 Swift
" John laborer h 419 First
" John operative h 69 Potomska
" John M operative h 69 West
" John V driver 126 Thompson b 16 Briggs
" Joseph drillmaker h 47 Borden
" Joseph machinist b 9 Briggs ct

Gracia
" Joseph operative b 150 Acushnet av
" Joseph S painter h 55 Briggs
" Louis baker h Sylvia ct
" Manuel laborer h 8 Weaver
" Manuel mill hand h 75 Mosher
" Manuel E painter h 46 Katharine
" Manuel E removed to Fairhaven
" Manuel S machinist h 9 Briggs court [53 Briggs
" Marguerita S widow Manuel S h
" Maria widow John b 69 Potomska
" Marianna Mrs h 56 Briggs
" Mary Mrs h 109 County
" Mary widow h 84 Washington
" Victor teamster 99 Front
" see Garcia [Cedar Grove
Graciae Joseph operative h rear 162
Gracie Elizabeth M died May 21 1911
" Frank S carpenter b 90 First
" Irene R buttonholemaker h 379 Cottage
Grad John chauffeur 22 Fourth b 7 N Second [Acushnet av
Grade Frank F drillmaker h 63
" John F Jr hostler 430 Purchase h 66 Summer [rine
" Joseph de Freitas h 59 Katha-
Grady Eliza boarding house 47 Logan
" John chauffeur rms 7 N Second
" John slasher tender b 74 Church
Graham Anna widow John h 131 Cedar Grove
" Charles laborer b 46 Reynolds
" George J second hand h 1069 County [cial b 9 Harmony
" Herbert awningmaker 31 Commer-
" James weaver h 26 George
" Jane F widow John T h 82 Court
" John laborer h 9 Harmony
" Mary Mrs h 71 Rivet
" Raven painter b 9 Harmony
" Wallace teamster b 9 Harmony
" William loom fixer h 59 Willard
" William weaver h 168 Austin
Graner Frank glassblower h 354 Orchard (S)
Grant Alice M teacher Plainville school b Plainville road
" Charles h 330 Brock av
" George P police station 5 h 190 Shawmut av
" Louise W Mrs h 111 County
" Mary J Mrs h 355 Cottage

GLOBE DYE HOUSE 220 SHAWMUT AVE.
J. N. J. LONHOLDT, PROP. Telephone Connections Goods called for and Delivered
Down town Office, 52 Pleasant St., Room 1 North End Office, 1014 Acushnet Ave.

Grant
" Nettie E h 190 Shawmut av
" Richard laborer h 195 Bonney
" Terrence watchman h 113 Allen
" Virginia widow James housekeeper 432 Kempton
" William h 72 Durfee [Purchase
" W T Co department store 65-69
Gratto Samuel H machinist 146 Pleasant b 952 Kempton
Gratton Joseph grocer 538 N Front h 540 do [Acushnet av h do
Gravalides Andrew bootblack 1407
Gravel Alderic holstler 57 Holly h 105 Beetle [shnet av
" Alexina Mrs milliner 1245 Acu-
" Alfred M overseer h 39 Austin
" Arthur H dentist 1043 Acushnet avenue
" Edmond driver 57 Holly b 59 do
" Exilme R stable 57 Holly h 59 do
" Octave carder h 170 Hatch
Gravelle Alfred M overseer Wamsutta Mill b 39 Austin
" Frank watchman b 67 Coffin av
" Napoleon card grinder b 435 Pleasant
" Napoleon laborer h 228 N Second
" Omer carder h 75 Kenyon
Graves Fred C physician 256 Union h 17 Campbell
" Henry superintendent Knowles Loom Reed Works rms 52 Walnut [S Dartmouth
" Thomas P clerk 240 Union h at
" see Greaves
Graville Donet third hand b 75 Kenyon [field
Gray Albert L driver b 94 Max-
" Annie A Mrs h 69 Summer
" Archibald carder b 29 McGurk
" Belle T b 22 Grape
" Bertram manager 128 Purchase h 499 Union [ion h do
" Bertram Mrs millinery 499 Un-
" Catherine widow Frank h 287 Arnold [Bowditch
" Catherine widow Robert L h 183
" Charles A Jr paper hanger h 427 Purchase
" Charles E foreman Old Colony Box Co b 74 Church
" Clara Mrs presser 53 William h 106 Acushnet avenue

Gray
" Edna clerk b 69 Summer
" Edward B (Gray's Band and Orchestra) b 288 Palmer
" Edward B principal H M Knowlton school h 759 County
" Ellen M widow James h 80 Mill
" Everett H repairman 131 Pleasant bds 42 Hill
" Francis H laborer h 168 Emerson
" George F Jr motorman h 126 Ashland [427 Purchase
" Georgianna C widow Charles A b
" Gideon F grocer 46 Parker h 44 do
" Harry M conductor h 38 Pierce
" Helen telephone operator 57 N Second b 183 Bowditch
" Henrietta h 102 Middle
" Henry A musician h 288 Palmer
" Henry C pianist b 28 Palmer [lis
" Irene P widow Edward b 73 Wil-
" James weaver h 28 Margin
" James F rms 106 Oak [Grinnell
" James H foreman carpenter h 202
" John R (Gardner & Gray) 861 Kempton h 88 Florence
" Marion clerk 160 Purchase b at Acushnet [202 Grinnell
" Mark Morton clerk 61 William b
" Mary A widow Daniel h 29 McGurk [kiln Hill rd
" Philip master mariner h Tar-
" Robert third hand b 29 McGurk
" Ross mill hand h 106 Acushnet av
Gray's Band and Orchestra (Edward B Gray) 5 S Sixth
Great Atlantic and Pacific Tea Co The 98 Purchase [fin av
Greaves Joseph weaver h 183 Cof-
" Walter W weaver h 38 Ashley
Green Albert J operative b 284 Sawyer
" Alexander h 86 Clark
" Alfred operative h 19 Ruth
" Benjamin laborer b 315 Earle
" Clark horse trainer h 41 School
" Etta H Mrs h 211 Smith
GREEN EVERETT sheet metal work 185 Acushnet av h 21 Bay See page 780
" Harry fixer h 42 Roosevelt
" Henry spinner b 284 Sawyer

GREENE & WOOD Every Kind of **LUMBER** AND MILL WORK
PINE STREET, off So. WATER STREET, NEW BEDFORD

Green
" Herbert insurance agent 41 William h 259 Bowditch [Elm
" Ida M clerk 65 Purchase rms 81
" Israel furniture 567 Purchase h 565 do
" James h 284 Sawyer
" James W spinner h 290 Sawyer
" John clerk 43 Bedford
" Mary widow Henry b 396 Middle W [avenue
" Mary E weaver h 13 East French
" Matthew L music teacher h 22 North
" Mitchell pedlar h 27 Mitchell
" Richard operative h 52 Hall
" Richard weaver h 254 Cedar Grove
" Sarah weaver h 13 E French av
" Spencer h 254 Cedar Grove
" Thomas shoemaker h 40 Cove
" Thomas weaver h 126 Crapo
" Thomas F laborer h 438 Pleasant
" William fixer h 32 Brook
" William laborer h 44 Adams
" William R laborer h 8 Walnut
" William T presser 144 S Water h 118 Fruit
" see Green
Greene Amos clerk b 703 Kempton
" Annie M widow Charles H h 126 Fair
" Arthur operative b 59 Bdford
" Carrie Mrs bookkeeper b 6 Harrison
" Charles E tillerman Ladder No 3 h 205 County
" Emma F nurse b 205 County
" Ethel M clerk b 126 Fair
" Francis B died April 8 1911
" Frank A C capt Central Fire station rms do
GREENE FRED W JR auctioneer 21 Clifford bldg and sec Board of Trade h 65 Russell See page 758
" George D ice 703 Kempton h do
" Helen K clerk 65 Purchase b 126 Fair
" Horatio D Mrs h 108 Bonney
" Isabella F widow William K bds 179 Fourth [do
" John E clerk 43 Bedford b 59
" John H h 259 Acushnet av

Greene
" Joseph fixer h 134 County
" Joseph F painter h 10 Spruce
" Lucy P widow Augustus A h 245 Acushnet av [do
" Marshall S mason 233 Rivet h
" N Herbert driver Hose Wagon Engine 6 h 59 Bedford
" N Herbert Jr driver b 59 Bedford
" Sarah L h 24 Pearl
" Sydney weaver b 41 Rivet
" Thomas removed to Fall River
" Thomas E foreman 50 Elm h 131 Summer
" T P Ernest dentist 208 Times bldg h 35 Buttonwood [South
" William M machinist h 118
GREENE & WOOD (George R and Edmund Wood) lumber and planing mill Pine near S Water See foot lines
" see Green
Greenfield John h 341 Collette
Greenhalge Alice widow Thomas h 270 Coggeshall
" Fred W weaver h 23 Salisbury
" John second hand h 74 Washington
" Joseph spinner b 322 Bowditch
" Robert spinner h 322 Bowditch
Greenhalgh Charles A operative h 159 Durfee
" James b 322 Bowditch
" James brakeman h 28 Winslow
" Martha widow William H h 163 Jenny Lind [av
" Wallace spinner h 350 Coffin av
" Walter machinist h 59 Willow
" Willard E carpenter 163 Jenny Lind b do [Briggs
Greenleaf Mark E plumber bds 44
" Mark L carpenter h 44 Briggs
" Rhoda S bookkeeper b 44 Briggs
Greenough John fireman h 2 Linden court
" Joseph L clerk h 64 Bay
" William H clerk 243 Purchase rms 106 S Sixth [S Water
Greenstein Barnard barrels h 569
" Louis tailor h 208 Acushnet av
Greenstone Morris P hay 551 S Water h 9 Howland
Greenup Ernest W died Oct 6 1910

BONNEY, FOLSTER & CO.,
The North End's Shopping Centre
Dry Goods and Men's Furnishings
945-947 Acushnet Ave., New Bedford, Mass.

Greenup
" Isaac W clerk 645 Pleasant h 446 do [h 542 Purchase
Greenwell George insurance agent
Greenwood Alice widow John b 26 George
" Andrew h 361 Davis
" Arthur cook b 4 Smith
" Arthur mill hand b 157 Davis
" Benjamin collector 36 Purchase h 71 Hathaway
" Catherine Mrs removed from city
" Dan weaver h 186 Hathaway
" Daniel removed from city
" Fred driver 10 Weaver h 62 Roosevelt [velt
" Frederick operative h 62 Roose-
" Howarth slasher h 14 Viall
" James wireman b 77 Jouvett
" James T glasscutter b 118 David
" John h 103 South
" John (59 Durfee) rem from city
" Joseph loomfixer h 11 Austin ct
" Mabel bookkeeper 770 Purchase h 400 Pleasant
" Mary Mrs b 19 Ashley
" Mary E Mrs h 55 Maitland
" Ovila mill hand b 157 Davis
" Ray head waitress Parker House b do
" Robert weaver h 296 Earle
" Samuel confectionery 1268 Acushnet av h do
" Walter driver h 335 Sawyer
" Walter rem to Burnley Eng
" Walter spinner h 118 David
" William liquors 98 Cove h 12 Viall
" William H bartender h 400 Pleasant [400 Pleasant
" William H Jr clerk 51 Hicks bds
" see Boisvert [h at Fairhaven
Greenya Robert S clerk 57 N Second
Greer George h 342 Middle
" George A pressman 47 William b 342 Middle
" Jeanette teacher Harrington school b 148 Rotch
" John watchman h 148 Rotch
" Sarah Mrs h 134 Division
Gregg Madeline A teacher Cedar st school b 41 Parker
Gregoire Alfred rem from city
" Edward rem to Weir
" Frank operative b 40 Mosher

Gregoire
" Joaquim fisherman h 69 Potomska
" John B hardware and furniture 924 and 928 S Water h 604 S Second [h 74 Nelson
" Napoleon hairdresser 145 Cove
" Napoleon stone mason 159 Tallman h do [h 608 S Second
" Philias janitor Ingraham school
" Seraphim J fisherman h 40 Mosher
" Simon concreter h 55 County
" Wilfred clerk 924 S Water b 604 Second [Dartmouth
Gregoria Antonio mill hand h 123
Gregorio Bernardino shoe repairer h 550 First [rms 356 do
Gregory Agil clerk 254 Coggeshall
" Charles (Anthony & Gregory) h 355 Coggeshall
GREGORY EDWARD H plumber 880 S Water h 878 do See page 780
" Frank glasscutter h 15 Marvin
" George h 3 E Durfee court
" Harry lunch 881 Purchase
" James glasscutter b r 292 Davis
" James mule spinner h 62 Vine
" James K fixer h 21 Peckham
" James K (281 Mt Pleasant) rem from city [ditch
" Jane A widow John h 95 Bow-
" John Jr weaver h 311 Coggeshall
" John B twister h 71 Jouvett
" John C weaver h 21 Ashley
" Joseph b r 292 Davis
" Joseph M weaver b r 292 Davis
" Joshua weaver h 257 Austin
" Margaret Mrs (Gregory Plumbing Co) h 1547 Acushnet av
" Plumbing Co (Mrs Margaret Gregory and Samuel Howarth) 1545 Acushnet av
" Robert weaver h 3 Oakland
" Thomas mgr Gregory Plumbing Co) 1545 Acushnet av h 1547 do
" William police h 292 Davis
" William weaver h r 438 S Second
" see Gregoire [man
Gregson Albert weaver b 85 Tall-
" Harry shoemaker h 18 Roosevelt
" James b 85 Tallman [man
" John twister tender b 145 Tall-

M. P. B. Silva & Son BUILDERS
Estimates Furnished on all Kinds of Work
157 ACUSHNET AVENUE Both Phones NEW BEDFORD

Gregson
" Louis foreman 100 Fifth h 33 Dartmouth [man
" Mathias mill hand h 145 Tall-
" Robinson blacksmith h 8 Harrison
" Wilfred machinist b 8 Harrison
Grenache Alice Mrs pianist 958 Acushnet av b 132 Bowditch
" J E machinist operator 958 Acushnet av h 132 Bowditch
Grenada Annie widow h 250 Fourth
Grenier Armur J tailor 40 Purchase h 44 Sycamore
" Cyprien laborer b 241 N Front
" Edgar O tailor 1014 Acushnet av h 347 Purchase
" Elphage b 241 N Front
" Emil chauffeur b 195 County
" Francis X builder 448 Sawyer h do [net blk
" George mill hand h 11 Acush-
" Honore carpenter b 442 Sawyer
" Hormidas carpenter h 60 Cove
" Joseph removed to Swanton Vt
" Ovila weaver h 195 County
" Rudolph weaver h end Princeton
" Simeon h 31 Ashley [tin
Grenon Andre third hand h 45 Aus-
Gresino Manuel mill hand h 53 Crapo [lock
Gresser Adolph driver b 40 Hem-
" John h 40 Hemlock [at Fairhaven
Greto Frank fireman Bennett Mill
Grew Caroline A housekeeper 198 Pleasant [ond
" Charles laborer rms 20 S Sec-
" David farmer h 215 Hathaway rd [av
" David Jr teamster h 120 Shawmut
" Everett clerk b 215 Hathaway rd
" George city laborer h 91 Robeson
" John W city teamster h 463 Chancery [field
" Mary widow Salem T h 243 Max-
" Susan E milliner 243 Maxfield b do [Dartmouth h 21 Page
Grewcock James W granitecutter 90
Grey Albert L clerk b 94 Maxfield
" Annie A Mrs clerk 41 Purchase h 69 Summer
Grierson Richard twister h 101 Nye
Grieve Jessie K nurse b 43 Shawmut av [b 43 Shawmut av
" Mary F state teacher of blind
" William W gas fitter h 186 Fourth [chard (S)
Grieves Alfred twister b 440 Or-
Griffin Arthur D died Dec 29 1910
" Charles G photographer 71 William h 126 Park
" Charles J laborer h 51 Spring
" Enoch piano player 269 Sawyer h Kenyon street [Chestnut
" Eva J widow Perley M h 61
" Felix card grinder h 232 Collette
" Florence C b 106 South
" Fred operative b 178 Crapo [road
" George L rope maker b 55 Mill
" James mill hand b 232 Collette
" James operative h 178 Crapo [rd
" James H box maker b 55 Mill
" Joel plumber b 61 Chestnut
" John laborer h 55 Mill road
" John Jr teamster b 55 Mill road
" John F shoemaker h 512 Acushnet avenue
" John T fireman h 31 Social
" Joseph E mill hand b 232 Collette
" Michael J foreman h 507 Bowditch [net av
" Nora widow James h 487 Acush-
" Patrick machinist h 195 Rivet
" Perley (Earle, Griffin & Co) 57 South Water b 61 Chestnut
" Samuel asst cook 435 County
" William H box maker b 55 Mill rd
Griffith Anna I city mission visitor 755 First [91 Kenyon
" Enoch pianist National Theatre b
Griffiths Charles engineer h 71 Nash road [lawn av
" Herbert brick layer h 41 Wood-
" James F (Warren's Agency) 1063 South Water h 35 Grape
Griggs Isaac porter h 180 Emerson
Grigware Joseph N overseer Acushnet Mill Corp h 53 Briggs [come
Grillo Dominick operative b 30 Wel-
" Joseph operative b 30 Welcome
Grime Elizabeth Mrs h 29 Holly
" Thomas designer h 59 Clifford
Grimes John J third hand h 182 State [away
" Michael H laborer h 95 Hath-
Grimki Ada B laundry 57 Liberty

Steiger-Dudgeon Co.
"The WOMAN'S Store."
Tel. Bell 82 & 83, Branches connecting all depts.
" " 160 For Office only. Auto. 1211

SUMPTIONS, ASSORTMENTS AT ALL TIMES OF DEPENDABLE DRY GOODS

Grimshaw Aaron weaver h 6 Austin
" Alice Mrs h 708 First [chase h do
" Bertha Mrs millinery 14 Pur-
" Clara clerk 70 Purchase b 314 Park
" David laborer b 78 Linden
" Elizabeth J Mrs h 95 Brock av
" Francis T weaver h 324 Earle
" Fred P clerk Parker House h 14 Purchase
" John T h 314 Park
" Joseph W h 204 Davis
" Philip piper b 14 Purchase
" Robert weaver b 95 Brock av
" Thomas furniture 874 S Water h do
" Thomas weaver b 75 Durfee
" William J weaver h 332 Coffin av
Grindrod Albert laborer h 34 McGurk
" Henry furniture mover 215 Shawmut av h do [Fairhaven
" Joseph hostler 630 Purchase h at
" Leonard clerk 63 Purchase h at Fairhaven
" Samuel weaver b 34 McGurk
" Thomas spinner b 34 McGurk
" William fixer b 260 Coggeshall
Grinnell Abraham carpenter rms 282 Acushnet avenue
" Amy A Mrs nurse h 324 Cedar
" Arthur G artist 89 Hawthorn h do [Newton
" Charles H 2nd carpenter h 184
" Daniel H laborer b 23 Woodlawn avenue [man
" Franklin machinist h 158 Tall-
" Frederick Mrs h 379 County
" Jenny G widow Edmund h 6 Maple [thorn
" Lydia widow Joseph G h 89 Haw-
" Mary R h 76 Cottage
" Mfg Corp 1 Kilburn cor N Front
" Richard S motorman h 133 Reynolds
Griswold Walter B molder h 71 Ruth
Groblecki John operative h 8 Fulton court [Fifth h do
Grocshinsky Herman physician 48
Groebe George janitor h 272 Middle
" Henry rope worker b 272 Middle
Grogan Catherine weaver h 893 County [Pleasant
" Winifred widow Patrick h r 441
Grohde Frank fish h 1187 Rockdale av
Grosl Frank weaver h 6 Coffin av court [Cedar
Gross Tobias tailor 157 Union h 111
Grossi Antonio laborer h 418 Purchase [do
" Emilia J variety 434 Purchase h
Grotel John weaver b 199 Dean
Grotsch William overseer Acushnet Mill Corp b 76 Division
Groton Anton removed from city
Groulx Alcide operative h 109 Nash road [ton
Grovell Herbert laborer h 384 Kemp-
Grover Arthur W jeweler h 74 Fourth
" Louis E salesman h 177 Fourth
Groves Benjamin C engineer Engine No 5 b 6 Foster
" Jennie F Mrs dressmaker 69 Mechanics lane h do
" Lydia widow h 54 Durfee [(S)
" Mary widow Perry G h 57 Ash
" Milly Mrs h 302 Coggeshall
" William H b 6 Foster [Washburn
Growatski John operative h 61
Grumbt Elizabeth milliner 8 Purchase b 106 Washington
" Herman h 106 Washington
Grundy clerk Mansion House [ant
" James engineer h 112 Mt Pleas-
" John weaver b 301 Fourth
" Joseph weaver h 448 Sawyer
" Samuel drillmaker h 336 Coffin avenue
Grunwold Nicholas rem from city
Guard George W brakeman h 350 Cedar [ton
Guarm James laborer rms 367 Kemp-
Guay Ambrose weaver h 4 Austin ct
" Arthur (Guay Bros) 846 Acushnet av h 189 Bowditch
GUAY BROS (Arthur, Herva and Ralph) hay and grain 846-848 Acushnet av See page 773
" Henry operative b 1406 Acushnet av
" Herva (Guay Bros) 846 Acushnet av b 61 Kenyon
" Peter grain h 61 Kenyon
" Pierre carpenter h 61 Kenyon
" Ralph (Guay Bros) 846 Acushnet av bds 61 Kenyon [shnet av
" William machinist b 1406 Acu-
" & Harpin wood and coal 846 Acushnet av
" see Gay

PELEG H. SHERMAN 506 COUNTY ST.
FUNERAL DIRECTOR AND EMBALMER
OFFICE PHONES. Bell 690.13. Auto. 1305.
RESIDENCE PHONES. Bell 690-12. Auto. 1306.

Guba Emily widow William bds 21 Homer
" Frank glass decorator h 56 Bourne
" Frank Jr plumber h 56 Bourne
" Louis clerk 246 Union b 56 Bourne
Gubinville Charles furniture 961 Acushnet av h 158 Mt Pleasant
Gudgeon James H fireman bds 60 [Beetle
" John coachman h 59 Bay
" Joseph second hand b 60 Beetle
" Mary widow William h 60 Beetle
" Nellie Mrs millinery 86 Cove h 5 Shore
" Simon loom fixer h 5 Shore
Guenette Joseph H foreman h 16 La France court
Guerette Elzear loom fixer h 604 [S Second
Guerin George N hairdresser 329 Kempton h 333 do
" John fixer h 9 Division
" John operative b 285 Purchase
" Wilfred hairdresser 285 Purchase h do
" see Gerin
Guerreiro Antonio M h 510 S Sec- [ond
Guertin Arthur clerk 878 Purchase h 10 Blackburn
" Azilda Mrs h 107 Davis
" Cleophas variety 1974 Acushnet [av h do
" Frank clerk h 4 Blackburn
" Joseph, U S A b 107 Davis
" Napoleon carpenter h 926 S Water
" Remi operative h 531 N Front
Guest Ethel clerk 185 Union b 6 Ocean
" George H weaver h 19 Winsor
Guevemont Louis meatcutter b 32 McGurk
Guilbeault Arele widow Henry h 131 [Nye
" Joseph weaver b 395 N Front
" Milina Mrs h 15 Penniman
" Moise weaver b. 395 N Front
" Ora waitress rms 493 County
" Paul laborer h 395 N Front
" Philomenne laborer h 59 Hicks
" Thomas twister b 395 N Front
Guilbert Eugene clerk 888 Purchase b 133 Clark
Guild Albert blacksmith 30 Bethel b [168 Summer
" George F carpet layer 36 Purchase h 150 Mill [at Fairhaven
Guilford Frank F tailor 144 Union h
Guillett Archille operative bds 130 Nye
" Arthur teamster 1 William h 151
" Arthur (Guillett Bros) h 124 Nye
" Bros (Theodule and Arthur) grocers 1347 Acushnet av
" Delphis bartender 1276 Acushnet av h 874 do
" Ernest clerk 1347 Acushnet av [b 130 Nye
" Hercule clerk 1138 Acushnet av b 130 Nye
" Nobert wood 107 Coffin av h do
" Odie clerk 407 Rivet h 339 do
" Theodule (Guillett Bros) h 130 Nye
Guillette Delphis laundryman h 107 [Bates av
Guilmette Alfred driver 12 School h 492 N Front
Guimaraes J A Santos jewelry 162 [Hathaway h do
Guimond Eugene clerk 507 N Front rms 1415 Acushnet av
Guimont Charles mason h 31 Cleve- [land
" Ernest weaver b 872 First
Guinet A Pocsch widow Pierre dressmaker 187 North h do
Guinn Alfred G clerk h 319 Middle
" A Fisher vocalist b 319 Middle
" John C (Anthony, Guinn & Co) 396 Kempton h 155 Cedar
" Josephine V h 176 Smith
" see Gwynn
Gullio Manuel C mill hand h r 87 [Prospect
Gumbleton Edmund P painter b 137 Acushnet av
Gundberg Robert gardener h 39 Hem- [lock
Gunderson Carl electrician h 41 Page
" Emile A glass blower h 31 Grape
" Flora assistant cashier 41 Purchase b 128 Bonney
" Fred glass worker b 81 Fair
" Fritjof galss blower h 101½ Fifth
" Hjalmer glass blower h 128 Bonney
" Lillian clerk P Corp b 81 Fair
" Martin glass cutter b 31 Grape
" Regina widow Martin b 99 Fair
" Robert glass blower h 99 Fair
" Sarah widow Sigurd h 81 Fair
Gunn Frank E mgr 1027 Acushnet av b do
" Harold N clerk N Water cor Elm [h at Fairhaven
GUNN, RICHARDS & CO engineers Tremont bldg Boston See page 40

COAL AND WOOD F. T. AKIN & COMPANY
HAY AND STRAW
WALNUT, COR. WATER, 84 PLEASANT ST., 25 WELD SQ.
129 COVE STREET WHF. FOOT OF COFFIN STREET

Gunning Andrew pres (Gunning Boiler & Machine Co) 67 S Water h 42 Atlantic [Atlantic
" Andrew J boiler maker bds 42
GUNNING BOILER AND MACHINE CO 67 S Water See page 31
" James boilermaker b 42 Atlantic
" John J boilermaker h 358 Elm
GURL FRANCIS J monumental works Sawyer cor Ashland h 63 Adams See advt opp Undertakers Business Directory
" James W carpenter h Sawyer n Mt Pleasant [Pleasant
" Joseph H city teamster b 260 Mt
" Mary Ann widow Michael h 1643 Acushnet avenue
" Mary F h 260 Mt Pleasant
Gurney Frank A clerk 141 Fourth h 235 Maple [Acushnet av
" Franklin J (A S M Co A) h 4026
" Jessie shoeworker b 127 Grinnell
" John clerk 13 N Sixth h 79 Fifth
" Julia M widow Henry A h 57 North
" Oliver S horseshoer h 79 Fifth
" William A carrier No 1 R F D h at Acushnet
Gurry Annie Mrs h 1013 Purchase
Gussaume August weaver h 103 Ruth
Gustafson Annie C widow August h 155 Maple
" Carl O grocer 46 Keene h do
Guthrie Annie M clerk b 179 Washington [Washington
" Harold B clerk 98 Allen b 179
" Walter W metal turner h 179 Washington [rms 62 Foster
Guy Joseph G salesman 46 Purchase
Guyer Frank baker 439 Purchase bds 249 Bowditch
Gwozdz Jan weaver h 101 Collette
" Stanislau operative h 115 Cedar Grove [ton b 174 Smith
Gwynn Charles A clerk 352 Kemp-
" Viola removed to Boston
" see Guinn

Haag Mary E nurse b 127 Summer
Habicht Andrew M P metal turner b 40 Liberty

Habicht
" Frank A job printer 21 N Second h 49 Emerson (S)
" Frank E compositor 21 N Second h 155 Maple [sell h do
" George L ladies' tailor 73 Rus-
" Henry P machinist b 40 Liberty
" Marguerite E bookkeeper 35 Commercial b 73 Russell
" William H machinist h 40 Liberty
Hacker John iron molder b 619 Purchase [Grove
Hackett Bernard carder b 167 Cedar
" Clifford E drill worker h 63 Bay
" Hattie housekeeper 465 Union
" Hugh J spinner h 167 Cedar Grove [at Fairhaven
" Marguerite M mgr 996 Purchase h
Hacking Harry operative h 33 Penniman
" Harry L laborer b 371 State
" Henry H weaver h 371 State
" James T bookkeeper 18 Market b 371 State
" Mark weaver h 811 County
Haddocks John G barber 24 Purchase h 96 Cedar [Kempton
" Richard A gas maker h 324
Hadfield Alexander baker 175 Dean h 177 do [Second
" Arthur tinner 514 County b 7 N
" Charles city laborer h 98 Willis
" George spinner b 260 Coggeshall
" George A florist b 226 Park
" James bds 291 Collette
" James spinner bds 31 McGurk
" John Mrs b 31 McGurk [h do
" Martha dressmaker 291 Collette
" Walter E carder h 31 McGurk
Hadley Amos W insurance agent h 77 Clinton [Fairhaven
" Caroline B clerk 100 Fifth b at
" Emma A widow Jacob B b 81 Summer
" Eugene J lawyer b 42 Campbell
" Hannah M widow George T h 89 Chancery [77 Clinton
" Helen L teacher High school h
" Miles S timekeeper P Corp rms 249 Acushnet av [Kempton
" Susan E widow Frank R b 157
Hadson William weaver b 96 Cove
Haffards Sophia b 51 Russell

There's room at the top for young men and women who can do things right.
Kinyon's Commercial School
Odd Fellows Bldg., Cor. William and Pleasant Sts., New Bedford, Mass.

Hafford Albert E overseer Oneko Mill h 193 Dean [shnet av
" Charles A salesman h 1808 Acu-
" Eloise A h 84 Spring [Pleasant
" Maria A widow Benjamin h 332
" Stephen Jr police b 73 State
" Willard B carpenter h 39 Hillman
Hafner A widow h 483 N Front
Hageloh George farmer h 3699 Acushnet av
Hagen John F stenographer Neild M Corp b at Fairhaven
Haggas Charles H operative h 167 Brock av
Haggerty Alice E clerk b 23 Valentine [h 23 Valentine
" Jeremiah T captain Hose No 4
" John agent 186 Purchase
" John second hand h 306 Earle [av
" Patrick third hand b 217 Phillips
" Thomas J musician b 27 Robeson
" Timothy motorman b 174 Fourth
" William J fireman h 27 Robeson
Haggle Xavier weaver h 1132 Acushnet av
Hague John W weaver h 106 David
" Samuel machinist 8 Seneca h 563 Cottage [h do
Hahn Gustaf grocer 47 Washburn
" Henry grocer 277 State h 34 Penniman
" Philip real estate h 2 Washburn
Haigh Jenet B widow Alan h 107 Butler
" William J twister h 1031 County
Haight Kenneth V mill hand b 32 James
" Louis H metal working instructor N B Industrial school h 32 James [av
Hainault Emery fixer h 19 Phillips
" Henry weaver b 19 Phillips av
" Joseph weaver h 121 Phillips av
" Leon operative b 19 Phillips av
" Prexea widow Moses bds 350 Sawyer [827 do
Hait Morris tailor 619 Purchase h
Hajkoc Alex mill hand h 819 S Water [shnet av
Haldru Samuel plumber b 1283 Acu-
Hale George C physician 635 County h do
Halenan Mary J h 67 Merrimac
Hales Arthur J pay master N E C Y Co depts 7 and 8 h 49 Howland Village
Haley Katherine teacher Thomas R Rodman school rms 156 Chestnut
Hali Yasha mill hand b 54 Davis
Halin Camille fixer b 165 Dean
" John B h 165 Dean
" Julius fixer b 165 Dean
" Ovid E overseer b 165 Dean [rd
Halkyard John spinner h 94 Nash
Hall Andrew fireman h 515 N Front
" Anna E widow Sylvanus M h 327 Pleasant
" Benjamin rem to Edgartown
" Bessie Mrs rem to Edgartown
" Charles A b 327 Pleasant
" Edward H clerk b 850 First
" Elizabeth widow George rms 27 Hillman
" Emma R bds 327 Pleasant
" Ernest H spinner h 18 Myrtle
" Frank operative h 69 Katharine
" Fred C overseer Kilburn Mill rms 92½ Purchase
" George b 440 N Front
" Gilbert N h 397 County [Robeson
" Harry mgr 437 Purchase b 82
" Hubert twister h 24 Winsor
" James rem to N Y city
" Jesse F dist mgr 57 N Second h at Fairhaven
" John h 47 Fruit
" John iron molder 229 N Water
" John molder h 7½ Cornell place
" John molder h 1053 County
" John weaver h 106 Rivet [av
" John Jr operative h 44 W French
" Joseph P foreman G & P Coal Co h 1 North
" Joseph R janitor b 74 Parker
" Julius removed from city
" Lewis conductor b 185 Weld
" Louis operative h 185 Weld
" Mabel Mrs h 331 Orchard (S)
" Margaret widow William H h 440 N Front
" Marie h 141 S Water
" Mary E Mrs h 450 Second
" Mary F Mrs bds 15 Cannon
" Morris F removed to Edgartown
" Richard bookkeeper h 480 Union
" Robert meter reader 125 Middle h 386 Cedar

HASKELL BROS. DEALERS IN
ICE
400 COURT STREET TELEPHONE CONNECTION NEW BEDFORD, MASS.

Hall
" Robert spinner h 122 Thompson
" Sarah widow b 18 Myrtle
" Thomas baker 959 Acushnet av h 165 Bates av [168 Arnold
" Thomas coachman 103 Spring h
" Thomas Jr baker b 161 Bates av
" William asst assessor h 271 Weld
" William conductor h r 226 State
" William Jr h 138 Hillman
" William J salesman h 82 Robeson [vid
Halle Joseph machinist h 99 Da-
Hallet Agnes L b 180 Grinnell
" Angelica T widow Francis h 180 Grinnell
" Francis purchasing agent Bennett Mill b 180 Grinnell [liam
" & Davis Piano Co 99-101 Wil-
HALLIDAY CHARLES R (Hill Co) 257 Union h 7 Park place See page 777
" William A asst supt 37 Purchase rm 23 h 80 Willis [away
Halligan John T laborer h 158 Hath-
Hallikens George cook rms 34 High
Halliwell Duke weaver h 15 Cleveland
" James weaver b 137 Thompson
" John mule spinner h 26 George
" Mary Mrs h 32 Mott
" S widow b 81 Thompson
Halloran James F grinder h 47 Reynolds [Front
" Johanna widow John h 446 N
" Mary J h 46 Sycamore
" Patrick J carpenter b 446 N Front [Second h 44 Grant
Hallowell James F pressman 350 S
" William O foreman U St Ry Co h 625 Purchase [Collette
Hallworth Elisha weaver h 303
" Frederick operative b 175 Eugenia [285 Earle
" Herbert H clerk 100 Fifth h
" John B weaver h 62 Independent
" Vernon bookkeeper b 303 Collette [man
Halma Frank weaver h 144 Tall-
Halsall Harry machinery erector h 59 Willow
" James fixer h 321 Coffin av
Hamblin Amanda widow Thatcher E h 81 Bedford [ford
" Emma A bookkeeper b 81 Bed-

Hamblin
" Mary F stenographer 131 Court b 81 Bedford
Hambly Albert R groceries 40 Main b 36 do [N Dartmouth
" Avis C bookkeeper 6 Elm h at
" Byron B foreman machinist 272 S Water h 367 Reed
" Inez W clerk Kilburn Mill h at Smith Mills [ton
" William H mason h 770 Kemp-
" W Clifton glasscutter bds 770 Kempton [Baths h at Chelsea
Hamburg Harry mgr Ideal Turkish
Hamel Albert twister b 82 Holly
" Dennis carpenter b 659 First
" Donat machinist h 109 Collette
" Flavien plumber 915 Acushnet av h 85 Bullard [ly
" Henry barber 19 Hicks h 75 Hol-
" Henry laborer b 8 Tallman
" Hermenegilde operative h 5 Bonneau court [av
" Joseph carpenter b 137 Acushnet
" Joseph fixer b 103 Coffin av
" Joseph joiner h 71 Emma
" Joseph loom fixer h 402 S Front
" Joseph weaver h 82 Holly
" Jousaint plumber h 5 Bonneau ct
" Napoleon weaver b 304 Davis
" Philip L machinist h 304 Davis
" William D foreman 915 Acushnet av h 119 Tallman
Hamer Edwin weaver b 81 Mosher
" James R A elevatorman Standard b 490 Union
" John spinner h 276 Davis
" John T piano tuner h 72 Dean
" Lewis painter h 85 Tallman
" Lewis Jr fixer b 85 Tallman
" Nicholas spinner b 276 Davis
" William A news press foreman Standard h 490 Union
Hames Mary F widow William h 55 Durfee [ton
Hamilton Anna Mrs h 358 Kemp-
" George b 311 Arnold
" Herbert B veterinary and inspector of milk and animals 134 Pleasant h 79 Hillman
" Ralph awningmaker 31 Commercial h 311 Arnold [h 379 do
" Samuel variety 377 Coggeshall h
" Walter I principal Thomas Donaghy school h 39 Buttonwood

J. F. CROSSLEY 223 MILL STREET COR. EMERSON PHONE
STEAM and HOT WATER HEATING
GAS FITTING and FIXTURES

Hamilton
" William W mgr 13 Pleasant h 27 Ashland place [more
Hamlen Carleton LeB b 101 Sycamore
" Walter G (N B Printing Co) 25 North Second h 101 Sycamore
Hamlet Thomas loom fixer h 43 Reynolds [bldg rms 207 Middle
Hamlin Frank M clerk 40 Masonic
" Jefferson teamster rms 150 North Second
" see Hamblin [452 Park
Hammer Lena B widow Fred M h
" Nella O stenographer 37 Purchase rm 28 b 452 Park [Hathaway
Hammerer Eugene weaver b 115
" Francois weaver b 115 Hathaway
" Julius weaver h 115 Hathaway
Hammerle Elizabeth widow Conzabert h 18 Clark
Hammersley Raymond J corporal U S A h 10 Lucas
Hammersmith George Jr laborer h 1045 County [1049 County
" Joseph G bartender 14 Adams b
Hammett Elizabeth B Mrs clerk 185 Union bds 130 Florence
" Harold M clerk Bennett Mill rms 8 Eighth [112 Pierce
" Seth B tinsmith 28 N Second h
" Valmoure A mason h 106 Ash (N)
Hammill Margaret Mrs b 62 Hatch
" Margaret widow William b 310 Earle
Hammond Chester A laborer b 126 Perry [h 2 Smith
" Chester B draughtsman 100 Fifth
" Chester M carpenter b 323 Park
" Clemont S carpenter b C E Lawrence's Tarkiln Hill road
" Corinne M clerk b 136 Newton
" C & Son (Edgar B) architects 179 N Water [h 66 North
" Edgar B (C Hammond & Son)
" Edward shoecutter b C E Lawrence's Tarkiln Hill road
" Elizabeth widow James M h 47 Thompson [Ash (S)
" Ellis D salesman 70 Union h 56
" Emery W farmer b 3253 Acushnet avenue [Mill
" Emma L widow Henry F h 79

Hammond
" Ernest P picture framer 24 Fifth b 47 Thompson [h 79 Mill
" Francis T architect 179 N Water
" Francis W died March 17 1911
" Fred painter b 25 Cannon
" George A carpenter h 126 Perry
" George D (Church & Hammond) 115 William h at Fairhaven
" Hanna G teacher I W Benjamin school bds 55 Fifth
" Henry F died July 24 1910
" Henry W drill maker h 22 Oak
" Herbert h 1082 Acushnet avenue
" Herbert grocer h 113 Austin
" Herbert M carpenter h 323 Park
" Herbert S Jr aprentice 55 N Water b 136 Newton
" John weaver b 19 David [net av
" John N carpenter h 2941 Acush-
" Marietta asst register of deeds Court House b 86 Court
" Myra A clerk 123 Front b 66 S Sixth [319 Cottage
" Oscar S carpenter 177 N Water h
" Ruby A widow Job E h 3253 Acushnet avenue [Elm
" Sarah A widow William b 196
" Sumner B carpenter h 4 Durfee
" Thomas E brittannia worker b 47 Thompson
Hampson Fred weaver h 255 Shaw
" James spinner b 131 David
" Joseph overseer Pierce Mfg Corp h 112 Mt Pleasant
" Joseph spinner h 131 David
" Paul grocer 133 David h 131 do
" Thomas weaver h 131 David
" William O laborer h 94 Hathaway [lane
Hampton James operative h 12 Oneko
" Thomas H weaver b 315 Earle
Hancock George H spinner h 124 Whitman
" James T pedlar h Phillips av
" John William weaver h 208 Weld
" Oscar H watch repairer 20 Purchase h at Mattapoisett
" Samuel A died Feb 9 1911
" Samuel A Jr rem to Fitchburg
" Samuel A Mrs variety 273 Rivet b 79 Crapo
" Sarah widow b Phillips road

CHARLES A. CROSHERE CARRIAGE AND AUTO
38 FOURTH ST. Bell Phone 1964-23 **PAINTING**

Hand Samuel L building mover h 2 Irvington ct
" William spinner h 326 Sawyer
" William H b 464 County
" William H Jr naval architect 108 Union rm 4 h 22 Arch
Handfield Ovilina Mrs h 86 Clifford
Handford Ann S widow James b 602 Cottage
" John E W spinner h 274 Sawyer
" Joseph H chairman assessors 9 Municipal bldg h 349 Clinton
" Samuel removed from city
Handley Fred engineer bds 88 Cove
" John H freight clerk foot Willis b 270 Pleasant
Handrahan Frank removed to Providence R I
Handron John laborer h 236 Brock avenue
Handy Elizabeth H widow Jonathan h 482 County
" George shoemaker h 197 Chestnut
" John T h 286 Orchard (S)
" John T Jr rem to Philadelphia Pa
HANDY JONATHAN CO C A Jewett mgr iron and steel 28-30 William See page 766
" Leon S asst foreman compositor Standard h 225 Grinnell
" Mary A widow h 87 S Sixth
" Mary A J laundress h 545 Acushnet avenue
" Thomas laborer h 5 Clark
" Thomas laborer h 7 Clark
Haney William G (Tripp & Haney) Mechanics lane h at Fairhaven
Hanger Damase weaver h 37 Scott
Hankerson James florist b 151 Campbell
" James Jr machinist h 93 Walden
" Thomas N coll h 117 High
Hanley Daniel T laborer h 39 Thompson
" Frank mill hand b 10 Howland Village
" James twister tender b 31 McGurk
" John h 10 Howland Village
" John clerk 98 Purcase b 587 First
" Kate widow Jeremiah h 39 Bowditch
" Patrick died Feb 26 1911
Hanlon Eliza h 301 Coggeshall
" Katherine and Julia h 77 Merrimac
Hanna Frank A bookkeeper 100 S Water h 196 Washington

Hanna
" John T Jr bookkeeper Greene & Wood h 64 Arnold
" Martha L bookkeeper 200 Union h at Fairhaven
" William A steward N B Yacht Club h 69 Summer
Hannibal Daniel F freight handler h 141 S Water
Hannigan John spinner h 56 Valentine
" Thomas J master mechanic Soule Mill h 310 Summer
Hannon John laborer bds 291 Hanman
" Sarah F nurse b 94 Fourth
Hanrahan Catherine widow Patrick b 460 Sawyer
" Charles E second hand h 290 Davis
Hansen Karin Mrs h 71 Bates av
" Nils P yachtman h 177 Allen
Hanslick Kasper weaver h 156 Bowditch
Hanson Axel G glasscutter h 46 Hill
" Clinton R bookkeeper 106 Front
" George P master mechanic Butler Mills h 11 Warren
" John master mariner h 100 Dartmouth
" Joseph P machinist h 1938 Acushnet avenue
" Martha L bookkeeper 100 Fifth bds 288 Palmer
Haran James spinner b 258 Coffin av
" John F mgr h 143 Reynolds
" Luke T police Sta 5 h 90 Walden
" May clerk 70 Purchase b 90 Walden
Harbec Mary L Mrs h 210 Ehigenia
Harbeck Adelard upholsterer h 91 Hathaway
" Dieudunne clerk h 28 Adams
" Henry B clerk h 124 Rivet
Hardacre John weaver h 13 E French av
" Martha widow Joseph h r 26 Cove
" Richard weaver b r 26 Cove
" Thomas weaver b r 26 Cove
Harden Anthony F agent h 461 Bolton
" Joaquina widow Joseph F b 88 Briggs
" Joseph F assistant superintendent 120 Purchase rm 403 h 15 Oak
Harder Fred M shipper h 316 Davis
Hardicourt R J J weaver b 509 S Second
Harding Charles E machinist h 567 Kempton
" Charles L president Whitman Mills h at Dedham

J. G. NICHOLSON
LUMBER, SASH, DOORS and BLINDS
BOWDITCH STREET, NEW BEDFORD, MASS.

Harding
" Frank machinist h 112 County
" James police h 85 Robeson
" James G h 62 State
" John H h 43 Arch [ville av
" Phillip E teamster h 914 Belle-
" Rebecca S widow Wilbur F b 152 Smith [ton
Hardman Herbert folder h 34 Staple-
" James E operative h 234 Dean
" James F folder b 34 Stapleton
" Joseph second hand h 38 Ashley
" Sarah L widow Samuel bds 52
" Thomas spinner b 135 Bullard
Hardwick George T collector 125 Middle h 151 Hillman
Hardy Albert spinner h 159 Ashland
" Charles E bookkeeper 133 Union h 140 Summer [Whitman
" Charles H furniture mover h 127
" Curtis baker h 51 Emerson (S)
" Elen M Mrs nurse bds 140 Summer
" Joseph weaver h 85 Holly
" Joseph Jr foreman 272 S Water h 29 Clover [Maple
" Robert H clerk 293 Purchase h 51
" Sarah L widow Samuel bds 52 Grape [h 291 do
Hargrave John P plumber 293 Rivet
Hargraves Alexander Y weaver h 30 Salisbury
" Arthur fixer h 16 Welcome [land
" Elizabeth widow John h 145 Ash-
" George H weaver h 179 Earle
" James nurse b 242 Sawyer
" James spinner h 135 Bullard
" James weaver b 16 Welcome
" James E joiner b 28 Myrtle
" James F shoemaker h 342 Cottage
" John loom fixer h 100 Clifford
" John weaver h 123 Hathaway
" John weaver bds 296 Tinkham
" Jonathan weaver h 328 Sawyer
" Joseph millman h 127 Summer
" Joseph weaver b 171 Bonney
" Letitia M h 171 Bonney [Sawyer
" Linda M clerk 185 Union bds 328
" Margaret J widow Edmund h 29 Myrtle
" Richard weaver b 38 Bowditch
" Richard weaver b 183 Coffin av
" Thomas copper worker h 303 Tinkham

Hargraves
" Thomas fixer h 37 Bullock
Hargreaves John J weaver h 31 Tinkham
" Robert (Hargreaves & Marshall) liquors 407 Kempton h 154 Newton
" & Marshall (Robert Hargreaves and Fred Marshall) liquors 407 Kempton
Harkins John b 186 Elm [ushnet av
Harlain Richard machinist h 72 Ac-
Harley Cornelius chief engineer Bennett Mill b 43 Beetle
Harlow Bertha Mrs b 58 Sycamore
" Elmer E master mechanic 131 Court h 162 Arnold
" George A h 160 Mill
" Henry painter h 417 Union
" Mary E h 10 Bethel
Harney John J overseer City Mfg Co h 158 Thompson
" Joseph machinist h 557 First
" Lawrence liquors 821 S Water h 62 Independent [Thompson
" Raymond R mill hand bds 158
" Robert fixer h 498 S Second
Harnish William J overseer 1145 Kempton h 59 Willard
Harnois Pierre C millman h 2469 Acushnet avenue [Morgan
Harper Ella sewer 40 Purchase b 78
" Harry helper h 215 Park
" Herbert (Harper's X L Mfg Co) h 95 Walden
" James laborer h 171 Cedar [way
" Joseph S machinist h 169 Hatha-
" Sarah E widow Richard h 204 Cedar
Harper's X L Mfg Co extracts 5 Willis [h 10 Willis
Harpin Arthur hairdresser 42-44 Elm
" Oscar (Guay & Harpin) coal and wood h 258 Cedar Grove
Harps Alice G widow William W h 237 Maxfield [30 Collins
" Edward F billiards 224 Cedar h
Harriman Arthur N compositor Standard h 256 Field
" Henry P painter h 173 Smith
" William A variety and real estate 165 Brock av h 165½ do

Steiger-Dudgeon Co.
"The WOMAN'S Store."
Tel. Bell 82 & 83, Branches connecting all depts.
" " 160 For Office only. Auto. 1211

SUMPTIONS,
ASSORTMENTS
AT ALL TIMES
OF DEPENDABLE
DRY GOODS

Harring James J asst supt Bennett dept N E C Y Co h at Fairhaven
Harrington Adaliza H Mrs h 369 Cottage [nolds
" Arthur bookkeeper b 17 Rey-
" Charles E operative b 320 Pleasant [court
" Charles T gardener b 2 Oak st
" Daniel comber b 90 Rockland
" Daniel A tinsmith h 168 Merrimac
" Daniel A wholesale liquors 591 Acushnet av h 3 Willis
" Daniel D section hand h 561 Acushnet av [b 62 Shawmut av
" Daniel F driver 16 N Second
" Daniel F police station 5 h 44 Bowditch [net av
" Daniel H clerk h 1737 Acush-
" Dennis died Feb 14 1911
" Dennis P died Mar 12 1911
" Edward b 320 Pleasant
" Edward J clerk 45 Linden b 62 Shawmut av
" Edward S clerk h 133 State
" Ellen widow William H h 174 Fourth
" Ellen A widow Cornelius h 285 Summer [174 Fourth
" Frank G salesman 157 Union h
" Frederick G glasscutter h 15 Marvin [port
" George removed to Newbury-
" Hannah W widow h 185 Fourth
" James mill hand b 285 Summer
" James teamster h 320 Pleasant
" Jeremiah copperworker h 946 County [nister
" Jeremiah copperworker h 7 Ban-
" Jeremiah M section boss h 82 Myrtle
" John machinist rms 20 Bethel
" John A Jr city laborer h 2 Oak street court [(N)
" John F supt Texas Co h 4 Oak
" John H tinsmith h 17 Reynolds
" John S clerk 73 Weld h 62 Shawmut av [av
" John S Jr laborer b 62 Shawmut
" Joseph clerk 904 Acushnet av b 44 Bowditch
" Joseph P salesman 591 Acushnet av rms 292 Purchase
" Julia widow John died 1911

Harrington
" Kathryn R dressmaker 940 County b do
" Leo spinner b 285 Summer
" Louise A bookkeeper 113 Union b 62 Shawmut av
" Margaret E h 409 Pleasant
" Margaret M b 14 North [Fourth
" Mary widow William h 174
" Mary A widow Timothy H h 16 Franklin [North
" Mary E clerk 185 Union bds 24
" Maurice laborer h 66 Myrtle
" Michael farmer h 44 Bowditch
" Michael F florist's asst 327 Coffin av b 940 County
" Nellie clerk 1100 Acushnet av b 44 Bowditch
" Peter J shoemaker b 24 North
" Peter M teamster h 24 North
" Susan T widow Peter E h 207 State
" Timothy h 46 Reynolds
" Timothy laborer b 113 S Second
" Timothy laborer bds 940 County
" Timothy section hand b 561 Acushnet av [285 Summer
" William A presman Standard b
Harris Abbie S widow William G h 308 Chancery
" Arthur B driver h 308 Chancery
" Clara clerk 70 Purchase b 238 County
" David laborer h 287 Bowditch
" Edward teamster h 14 W High
" Edward A shoemaker h 78 Locust [State
" Elliott B clerk 103 Union h 64
" Frank W carpenter b 88 Ruth
" Fred weaver b 183 Coffin av
" George F driver 14 N Sixth b 308 Chancery
" Ida Mrs h 5 Morgan's lane [h do
" James restaurant 250 Coggeshall
" John helper b 850 First
" Julius clerk 1602 Acushnet av b 3 Beetle [Conn
" Reuben removed to New London
" Susan widow George b 38 Myrtle
Harrison Albert (Harrison & Scowcroft) h 22 Warren
" Alexander car repairer U St Ry Co h 13 Jean [(S)
" Ann widow James h 440 Orchard
" Benedict J book binder 38 N Second h 32 Social

PELEG H. SHERMAN 506 COUNTY ST.
FUNERAL DIRECTOR AND EMBALMER
OFFICE PHONES. Bell 690-12. Auto. 1305.
RESIDENCE PHONES. Bell 690-12. Auto. 1306.

Harrison
" Bridget Mrs h 666 First [do
" Charles H driver 50 Elm h 187
" Christopher laborer b 275 Acushuet av
" Edward carpenter h 20 Roosevelt
" Esther widow Thomas b 124 Cove
" Fannie widow John M h 65 Howard
" George b 186 Smith [tle
" George H loom fixer h 65 Myr-
" Herbert M clerk 133 County b 108 Division
" James spinner b 32 Katharine
" James H weaver h 443 Pleasant
" James S tinsmith 87 Union h 156 Bowditch
" John carpenter h 128 Reynolds
" John clerk b 1073 S Water
" John grocer 85 County h at S Dartmouth [Whitman
" John overseer Soule Mill h 318
" John plumber h 69 Hicks
" John spinner h 74 Hathaway
" John weaver h 72 Brock av
" John weaver h 212 Hathaway
" John W spinner h 218 Whitman
" Joseph spinner h 116 Hathaway
" Kimball B removed to Middleboro
" Leo laborer b 212 Hathaway
" Margaret widow William bds 44 Salisbury [vision
" Raymond H machinist b 108 Di-
" Richard weaver h 62 Roosevelt
" Robert machinist b 65 Howard
" Samuel shoes 43 Rivet h 108 Division
" Thomas operative b 24 Welcome
" Thomas weaver h 15 Abbott
" Thomas H removed from city
" William spinner b 440 Orchard (S) [267 Weld
" William H clerk 57 N Second h
" Wright weaver b 301 Fourth
" & Scowcroft (Albert Harrison and Mrs Maud Scowcroft) bakers 51½ Brock av
Harrop William supt N E C Y Co depts 7 and 8 h 530 Bolton
Harrup Albert loom fixer h 159 Crapo
Hart A V pianos 104 Weld rms 216 Bullock [N Sixth
" Carlton P clerk 19 N Water b 56

Hart
" Caroline W widow John C h 16 Columbia [lips av
" Charles B second hand h 278 Phil-
" Edith D bookkeeper 160 Purchase b 16 Columbia
" Edward H draughtsman 3 E Pope b 308 County
" Emmie S Mrs h 56 N Sixth
" Frank J shoemaker b 77 Newton
" Frank W carpenter b 120 High
" George S b 34 Bonney [Franklin
" Gilbert J master mariner h 29
" Harry laborer h 275 Middle
" Helen widow Robert b 120 Hemlock
" Henry meatcutter b 435 County
" Herbert W laborer b 120 High
" James eyeletter h James
" John laborer h 435 S Water
" Lolis teamster b 2740 Acushnet av [shnet av
" Lydia A widow Lewis h 545 Acu-
" Mary A widow William h 340 Court
" Mary L stenographer 97 William rm 206 b 940 County
" Matthew J sec Weaver's Union 138 Pleasant h 32 Thompson
" Micheal bartender Mansion House rms 7 N Second
" Moses A T removed to Fall River
" Oliver h 13 S Water [Newton
" Patrick porter 84 Union h 77
" Robert J shipper b 120 Hemlock
" Samuel C Jr h 35 Lincoln [lock
" Thomas J city emp h 120 Hem-
" William J boilermaker h 20 Acushnet av
Hartel Adolph weaver h 4 Bowditch
Hartford Bertha T Mrs h 276 Kempton
Hartley Albert shoe repairer 1679 Acushnet av h 143 Holly
" Edgar operative b 70 Linden
" Elizabeth Mrs bakery 911 S Water h 874 S Water
" James twister h 98 Covell
" James watchman h 183 County
" John engineer Wamsutta Mills h 116 Clark
" John H insurance agent 27 Purchase rm 23 h 70 Linden
" Joseph weaver h 23 Cleveland
" Levi sub letter carrier h Plainville road

PAINTERS' SUPPLIES
Walnut, Cor. Water, 84 Pleasant St. 25 WELD SQ., 129 COVE ST.
F. T. AKIN & COMPANY

Hartley
" Mark spinner h 474 Coggeshall
" Mary Ann Mrs h 20 Welcome
" Ralph weaver h 59 Howard
" Richard driver 645 Purchase h 133 Ruth av
" Robert fixer h 246 Nash rd
" Robert operative b 23 Cleveland
" Robert weaver h 107 Rodney
" Thomas chief engineer Wamsutta Mills h 127 Reynolds
" Thomas weaver h 235 Sawyer
" Thomas weaver b 15 McGurk
" Thomas Jr weaver b 235 Sawyer
" Walter weaver b 303 Tinkham
" Wellington weaver h 10 McGurk
" Wilfred weaver h 55 Brock av
Hartman Bozena Mrs furniture 1004 Acushnet av h 1008 do
" Charles weaver b 19 Washburn
" Frank G weaver b 19 Washburn
" George weaver h 19 Washburn
Hartwell H M removed from city
Harte John weaver b 19 Ashley
" John M letter carrier b 96 Washington
" Mary J Mrs h 69 Winsor [ton
" Richard spinner h 96 Washing-
" Richard spinner h 335 Bowditch
" see Hervey [vis
Harwood Albert fixer bds 290 Da-
" Charles h 468 Union
" Eliza widow John h 53 Ash (N)
" Isabelle teacher T A Greene school b 53 Ash (N)
" James weaver h 36 Linden
" John R clerk Beacon Mfg Co b 53 Ash (N)
" Michael filling man b 301 Fourth
" Samuel operative h 81 Mosher
" Thomas machinist h 132 Tallman
" William S clerk 131 Court b 53 Ash (N)
Haskell Allen W salesman 21 William h 985 Kempton
" Arthur teamster h 349 Coffin av
HASKELL BROS (Isaac F Jr and Edward B Haskell) ice dealers 400 Court See foot lines
" Clifton L removed to Fairhaven
" Edward B (Haskell Bros) 400 Court h 488 Middle
" Edward P special deputy collector Custom House h 369 County

Haskell
" Edward S (Madison Kennels) 70 Madison h at Fairhaven
" Ethel widow Solomon h 321 Cedar
" Frank C removed to Fairhaven
" Franklin H (Haskell Press) 555 Purchase h 557 do
" Frederick P operative h 39 Hazel
" Frederick P Jr baker b 365 Pleasant [Mills h 470 County
" George M bookkeeper Wamsutta
" Isaac F Jr (Haskel Bros) 400 Court h do [557 do
" J Burton agent 555 Purchase h
" Louisa B widow Edward h 345 Union [Purchase
" Press (Franklin H Haskell) 555
Haskins Amanda L widow Charles L b 474 County
" Charles A hoseman Engine No 9 h 2588 Acushnet av [Purchase
" Clara J widow George S h 237
" Eben F h 38 Foster
" Elmore P (Haskins & Gibson) h 95 Chestnut [Purchase
" George W carriage painter h 527
" Henry A motorman h 19 Mill rd
" Herbert K real estate 87 Chestnut h do [erson (N)
" Isaiah washer 50 Elm h 161 Em-
" James L capt S F E No 1 h 536 Purchase
" Job T watchman h 203 River rd
" Martha h 416 County
" Mary A Mrs h 383 Kempton
" Ruth F bookbinder 117 Union h 39 High
" Susan F b 87 Chestnut
" Sylvia S Mrs h 107 Sycamore
" William H salesman 358 Acushnet avenue h at Acushnet
" & Gibson (Elmore P Haskins and John Gibson) real estate 66 Pleasant [yer
Haslam Herbert doffer h 436 Saw-
" John bar tender 69 Bowditch h 434 Sawyer
" John weaver h 436 Sawyer [city
" John (200 Collette) removed from
" Marion K teacher Thomas A Green bds 159 Washington
" Thomas doffer b 436 Sawyer

Kinyon's Commercial School Will furnish your office help free } Odd Fellows Building COR. WILLIAM and PLEASANT STS. NEW BEDFORD, MASS.

Hassey Ellis laborer h 577 Acushnet avenue [Phillips av
Hasson Husan mill hand bds 45
Hastings Charles H R R conductor h 248 Pleasant
" Edith b 140 Cottage
" Nathaniel carpenter h 190 North
" Russell P removed to Palo Alto California
Haswell Ernest R clerk Bennett Mill b 672 Kempton [222 Pleasant
Hatch Amelia B widow George E h
" Annie E widow Philip janitress Plainville school h Plainville road
" Charles W painter b 36 James
" Clifford laborer b 113 Belleville
" Clifton N third hand h 210 Chestnut
" Francis M h 16 Studley
" Frank W asst supt 131 Court h 36 James
" George E clerk P O h 275 Acushnet avenue [Franklin
" Ida E widow Joseph W b 27
" John F h 193 Pleasant
" John F Jr asst teller N B S D & T Co bds 193 Pleasant
" Joshua J carpenter h 500 Cottage
" Mary E housekeeper 52 Bowditch
" Mercy Mrs boarding 24 High
" Roland A salesman b 24 High
" Seth h 24 High
" Stephen A clerk h 389 Bolton
" Thomas W teamster Gosnold Mills Co h 108 Sidney
" William E president N B Textile school h 83 Ash (S)
Hatfield George operative b 260 Coggeshall [ton
" George tack maker h 805 Kempton
" Isaiah boss comber h 155 Belleville road [805 Kempton
" James J salesman 109 William h
Hathaway Abraham G clerk 271 Cedar h 124 Willis
" Albert G city laborer h 318 Park
" Allan G teamster b Rockdale n
" Alvira widow James C h 721 Kempton [345 Reed
" Andrew B florist 146 Court rms
" Andrew E proprietor Hathaway's Theatre and bill poster 90 Purchase h 120 Mill

Hathaway
" Anna L widow James H h Tarkiln Hill road L C [50 Mill
" Annie M bookkeeper 71 William h
" Bertha C teacher Thomas A Greene school b 43 Ocean
" Braddock B clerk 350 Acushnet av b 62 Campbell
" Braddock D clerk 516 Purchase b 14 Franklin [ker
" Bradford A carpenter h 74 Parker
" Caroline W h 6 Park place
" Celia Mrs housekeeper 190 Campbell h 445 Chancery [Franklin
" Charles B drill grinder bds 14
" Charles H farmer h 390 Union
" Charles P foreman compositor Times h 78 Park
" Charles R clerk 1 Municipal bldg and prop Hathaway's Laundry 6 to 8 Campbell b 18 do
HATHAWAY CHESTER F machinist and auto repairer 107 N Water b 36 Maxfield See page 743 [ty
" Chester M carpenter h 54 Liberty
" Clara E widow John W h 877 Hathaway rd
" Clara O Mrs h 68 State [North
" Clarence W clerk 185 Union b 369
" Clifford M student b 877 Hathaway rd [Middle
" Clifton L clerk 145 Union b 209
" Dallas B operative h 6 Warren
" David L (D L Hathaway & Son) h 498 Cottage
" Dudley C h 43 Ocean
" D L & Son (David L and Jethro H) carpenters 27 Centre
" Edward E b 318 Park
" Edward R (Peoples' Credit Co) 80 Purchase h 351 County
" Elizabeth stenographer 7 Commercial b 360 Reed
" Elizabeth B bds 258 Pleasant
" Elizabeth B Mrs clerk city clerk's office h 360 Reed
" Emma E h 32 Bonney
" Emma R b 233 Middle
" Ethel bookkeeper 15 Fourth b 22 Sycamore [chase
" E Frank glasscutter h 863 Purchase
" Florence C housekeeper 14 Franklin [est
" Frank W drillmaker h 61 Forest

Bread, Cake, Pastry
RICHMOND & COMPANY 255-257 UNION STREET
Bell 993 Automatic 1022

Hathaway

" Franklin B building mover 570 Elm (W) h do [C h 108 Court
" Franklin L keeper and master H
" Franklin L Jr overseer Manomet Mill and (Peoples' Credit Co) 80 Purchase h 45 Fifth
" Fred B glassworker b 358 Orchard (S)
" Fred E machinist h 83 Walden
" Fred L painter h 66 Dartmouth
" Frederick A sailmaker 35 Commercial h 257 Maxfield
" George B foreman h 8 Ash (S)
" George O brakeman h 395 Cedar
" Hannah E widow rms 3 Park pl
" Harriet widow William h 45 Pierce
" Harry R painter b 209 Middle
" Henry C cook b 62 Campbell
" Henry C, U S shipping commissioner and auctioneer 350 Acushuet av h 62 Campbell
" Henry L janitor Dartmouth st school h 117 Bonney [way rd
" Henry W farmer h 210 Hatha-
" Herbert A removed from city
" Hollis student b Mrs A Hathaway's Tarkiln Hill road [ton
" Horace M carpenter h 721 Kemp-
" Horatio Mrs h 385 County [h do
" Ida F dressmaker 257 Maxfield
" Isabel M h 411 Union
" James H h 198 Middle [bell
" James L accountant h 89 Camp-
" James S b 124 Willis
" James W machinist h 32 Bonney
" Jethro H (D L Hathaway & Son) h 498 Cottage [Franklin
" John B clerk 100 Fifth bds 14
" John B salesman 8 Hamilton h at Assonet
" John D physician 388 County h do
" John M boxmaker h 910 Belleville av
" John M resident mgr Hathaway's Theatre h 323 Cottage
" John T carriage painter 7-9 Elm h 32 Sycamore
" Joseph S ice 369 North h do
" Joseph T b 101 Sycamore

HATHAWAY LEONARD J carriage mfr 7-9 Elm h 36 Maxfield See page 771

Hathaway

" Leonard J Jr civil engineer 303 Municipal bldg h 3906 Acushnet av
" Louisa A h 149 Elm [421 do
" Lucy E bookkeeper 140 Union b
" Lucy P h 345 Reed
" Mabel L clerk 160 Purchase b 65 Summer [b 390 Union
" Mabel L teacher Cedar st school
" Mfg Co cotton goods S Front n Gifford [526 Purchase
" Martha L widow Freeman R b
" Mary J widow Warren A h 330 Hathaway road
" Mary R Mrs h 359 Orchard (S)
" Merton L probation officer h 87 Court [av
" Milfred K driver b 77 Shawmut
" Nancy widow James S bds 236 Pleasant
" Nathan C asst cashier Mechanics National Bank h 120 Mill
" Nathaniel office 26 Masonic bldg h at Germantown Penn
" Nellie C shoeworker b 72 State
" Nelson F teamster rms 73 Elm
" Pheobe D widow Richmond B h 14 Franklin [vile road
" Rebecca F housekeeper 180 Belle-
" Ruth E asst matron H C h 108 Court
" Samuel (American Transparol Co) 405 S Water h 47 Crapo
" Samuel B h 21 Fifth [h do
" Sarah L dressmaker 41 Union
" Savory C salesman 56 N Water b 26 Seventh
" Sidney N teamster h 101 Middle
" Susan E h 154 Chestnut [h do
" Susan M millinery 78 Hillman
" Thomas S president Hathaway Mfg Co office 24 Masonic bldg h 385 County
" Wallace G clerk P O b 46 Pierce
" Walter D bicycles and records 132 Purchase h 77 Shawmut av
" Walter F salesman 123 Purchase h 421 Union [Summer
" William E clerk Bennett Mill b 65
" William E president and treas The Hathaway & Mackenzie Grain Co h 411 Cedar
" William F (Hathaway & Co) 516 Purchase h 526 do

GLOBE DYE HOUSE 220 SHAWMUT AVE.
J. N. J. LONHOLDT, PROP. Telephone Connections Goods called for and Delivered
Down town Office, 52 Pleasant St., Room 1 North End Office, 1014 Acushnet Ave.

Hathaway
" William F painter h 148 Cedar
" William H laborer h 4 Jenney
" William J machinist h 106 Hemlock
" & Co (William F Hathaway) wooden ware 516 Purchase
HATHAWAY & MACKENZIE GRAIN CO The William E Hathaway president and treas 748 Purchase See opp Grain in Business Directory
Hathaway's Laundry (Charles R Hathaway) 6-8 Campbell
" Theatre 90 Purchase [28 Fifth
Hatherley Ida M boarding house
Hatton Charles J supt St Mary's Cemetery h at Dartmouth
" John C mill hand h 77 Hathaway
Haughey Hugh fireman Parker House bds 414 Purchase [Pope
" Isabel clerk 182 Union rms 270
" see Hoye [Merrimac
Haurlen John A fisherman h 106
Havacen Catherine clerk 185 Union b 209 State [h 1 Kilburn
Havard D H Mrs dressmaker 92 Weld
" Ella B photographer 92 Weld b 581 Purchase [chase
" Emerson machinist h 596 Pur-
" Joseph photographer 92½ Purchase h 581 do
" Raymond A b 581 Puchase
Haverstock Elizabeth E Mrs h 2 Seventh
Havey Ulderic weaver h 182 Dean
Hawes A Clifford h 7 Park place
" Everett teamster 26 Brook h 126 Tallman
" Frederic B president and Corp clerk Acushnet Saw Mills Co h 2831 Acushnet avenue
" George W second hand h 2355 Acushnet avenue [ushnet av
" Harry C glass cutter h 2339 Ac-
" Helen W bookeeper Leonard cor Cross b 60 Sycamore
" John C driver h 18 Bullock
" Lester E chauffeur h 155 Rotch
" Lydia widow William b 60 Sycamore
" Mary h 99 Maple

Hawes
" Mary W widow Jonathan C h 2143 Acushnet av
" Roy meterman 125 Middle [h do
" Sarah B music teacher 7 Park pl
" Susie P h 7 Park place
HAWES, TEWKSBURY & CO (William C Hawes and John W Tewksbury) bankers and brokers Masonic bldg See page 7
" Walter H glass cutter h 2247 Acushnet avenue
" William died Nov 8 1910
" William C (Hawes, Tewksbury & Co) Masonic bldg h 163 Hawthorn [ham
Hawkins Ezekiel teamster b 193 Tink-
" Samuel quiller b 167 Brock av
" William H, R R engineer h 290 Summer [Jouvette
Hawkshaw Thomas P laborer b 64
Hawkswell Lucy widow William weaver h 136 Tallman [fin av
Hawley William fixer bds 258 Cof-
Haworth Albert third hand b 70 Penniman
" Dennis musician h 333 Arnold
" Emily widow George E b 36 Hazard [446 Rivet h 52 Briggs
" Fred (James Haworth & Sons)
" George clerk 878 Purchase b 1060 Acushnet avenue [man
" George H slasher bds 70 Penni-
" Harold weaver b 51 Myrtle
" Henry conductor rms 602 Purchase
" James & Sons (Fred and William J) grocers 446 Rivet h 448 do
" James W spinner b 70 Penniman
" John fixer h 70 Penniman
" William clerk 446 Rivet h 80 Swift
" William weaver h 401 Pleasant
" William weaver h 975 Kempton
" William J (James Haworth & Sons) 446 Rivet h 80 Oak
Hayden Abram L police h 63 Pierce
" Edward D clerk city yard h 120 Cedar [Fairhaven
" Ernest J mgr 7 Purchase h at
" Frank T janitor Standard rms 43 William [len
" George D draughtsman h 318 Al-

GREENE & WOOD Every Kind of LUMBER AND MILL WORK
PINE STREET, off So. WATER STREET, NEW BEDFORD

Hayden
" John W third hand h 16 Hazard court [511 County
" Michael J traveling salesman h
" Myra h 30 Durfee [h 171 Smith
" William H janitor public schools
Haydock Harry weaver b 307 Collette
" John drillworker h 28 Cleveland
" Joseph J weaver h 156 Brock av
" Thomas P weaver h r 288 Cedar Grove
" William removed from city
Hayes Annie clerk 1081 Acushnet av b 479 Belleville av
" Annie J stenographer 97 William
" Annie M variety 138 Thompson b 117 Washington
" Austin J waiter b 117 Washington [h 6 Waverley
" Charles hairdresser 482 S Second
" Clinton N clerk 65 William bds 50 Walnut
" David K h 223 Maxfield
" Edward machinist b 74 Church
" Elizabeth G primary asst public schools b 1 Park place
" Eudora nurse h 36 Hillman
" Eugene J asst engineer Sharp Mill b 117 Washington
" Eugene S engineer Rotch Mill h 117 Washington [b 50 Walnut
" Grenville H salesman 65 William
" Ira R overseer Whitman Mills h at Fairhaven [90 Rockland
" James P foreman Rotch Mill h
" Johanna K h 59 Hill
" John fireman h 115 Thompson
" John F hostler h 362 Pleasant
" John H shoecutter rms 187 Purchase [479 Belleville av
" Julia widow Thomas weaver h
" Lemuel W engineer h 69 Sycamore [Co h 6 Waverly
" Lewis C designer Dartmouth Mfg
" Norman P hardware 65 William h 50 Walnut [187 Purchase
" Patrick piper 125 Middle rms
" Patrick spinner h 58 Blackmer
" Robert S student b 117 Washington
" Stephen W physician 61 Orchard h do [ton
" Walter E clerk b 117 Washing-
" see Heyes and Heys [h 193 Dean
Hayford Albert E master mechanic
" Wilbur E machinist h 13 Hall
Hayhurst Richard presser h 30 Salisbury
" William twister h 29 Mosher
Haynes John H h 181 Mill
" Richard meter inspector 125 Middle b 24 Ash (N) [thorn
Hayward Caleb A mfr h 126 Haw-
" Caleb A Jr b 126 Hawthorn
" Carl F engineer h 21 Peckham
" Carrie E Mrs nurse h 143 North
" Emily W widow John C bds 104 Ash (N) [h at Fairhaven
" Frederick J clerk 31 Commercial
" Gordon chauffeur 87 Howard b 143 North
" John J laborer h 585 Acushnet av
" Richard teamster b 585 Acushnet avenue [chase h 64 Park
Haywood Frederick J mgr 40 Pur-
Hayworth William seaman b 190 Acushnet av
HAZARD CHARLES B carpenter and builder 69 Wood h do See page 764
" Charles T mgr 445 S Water h 198 Allen [Allen
" Charles T Jr glasscutter b 198
" Cotton Co 62 N Second
" Lizzie R h 85 Hillman
" Louis A (L E Milliken & Co) 96 Allen h 37 do
" Mary J Mrs variety 445 S Water h 198 Allen
" Susan M died Oct 25 1910
" Verona D widow Henry C h 68 North [Water
Hazell Charles W mariner b 199 S
Hazzard Angenette widow James B h 59 Hill [Pleasant b 59 Hill
" Alton L bicycles, paints etc 136
" Edward V auto and carriage painter 1 Spring h 5 Arch
" Herbert J N weaver b 59 Hill
Head Arthur S drillmaker h 95 Grinnell
" Dennis A doffer b 146 Davis
" Edgar E police h 179 Tremont
" James T cyanide maker 147 Chancery h 30 Ash (S)
" John apprentice b 146 Davis
Headley Phineas C cotton broker 56 N Water h at Fairhaven
Heald James spinner h 240 Collette

BONNEY, FOLSTER & CO.,
The North End's Shopping Centre
Dry Goods and Men's Furnishings
945-947 Acushnet Ave., New Bedford, Mass.

Healey Aquilla E overseer Page Mfg Co h 1 Weaver
" Edward H clerk 240 Union bds [94 Fourth
" Emma M clerk 185 Union b 1 Weaver
" Frank T clerk 2 Union h 36 [George
" George P electrician 33 N Water h 235 Park
" Herbert mill hand h 96 Dunbar
" John h 78 Jouvette
" John insurance agent 120 Purchase rm 403 bds Cove
" Lillian M clerk b 1 Weaver
" Martin C (M C Healey & Co) h 154 Merrimac
" Mary A widow Peter J h 120 [Belleville rd
" M C & Co (Martin C Haley) druggists Cottage cor Durfee
" Patrick F hairdresser 416 Purchase h 414 do
" Peter weaver h 6 Thompson
" Sabra widow Edwin h 9 Washing- [ton
" Theobald M collector Standard h 120 Belleville road
" William H loom fixer b 1 Weav- [er
" William J spinner b 120 Belleville road
Healy Alton W clerk 457 Kempton b [194 Chancery
" Bertha C cashier 200 Union b 194 Chancery
" Edwin J spinner h 90 Tallman
" Grace E clerk b 1680 Acushnet av
" Harrison T physician 1680 Acushnet avenue b do
" Herbert E clerk Dartmouth Mfg Co bds 194 Chancery
" John C antique furniture h 194 Chancery
" Mary J widow Thomas h 98 Nye
" Nannie M operative h 212 Middle
" Thomas F shoes and real estate 1084 Acushnet av h 1680 do
" Thomas F Jr clerk 215 Purchase bds 1680 Acushnet avenue
" William mill hand b 204 Davis
Heap Adelaide E widow William H h 141 Chestnut
" Anne widow Thomas W h 643 [Purchase
" Charles F overseer Potomska Mill h 63 Rotch
" Harry fixer b 374 N Front
" Holden A weaver h 399 Pleasant
" James E baler b 46 Roosevelt

Heap
" John A fixer h 159 Shawmut av
" John A weaver h 40 Roosevelt
" John R weaver h 19 Brock av
" J Odgen loom fixer h 12 Studley
" Leonard driver 645 Purchase bds 643 do
" Richard fixer h 374 N Front
" Samuel shoemaker 76 Purchase b 46 Roosevelt
" William cabinet maker bds 399 [Pleasant
Hearne Anne widow James h 186 Hathaway
" Annie Mrs h 190 Davis
" Ernest H h 623 County
" Thomas spinner b 280 Tinkham
Heath George R clerk 51 William b 271 Acushnet avenue
" John M lineman 57 N Second h 61 [Walden
" Julia clerk 198 Union b at Fairhaven
" Margaret Mrs boarding h 232 N [Second
" William spinner h 232 N Second
Heatley Thomas E supt Taber Mill rms Y M C A
Heaton Herbert machinist bds 13 [Cleveland
" John weaver h 52 Ashley
" Thomas fireman b 451 Sawyer
" William engineer h 13 Cleveland
Heaver Margaret M bookkeeper bds 113 County
" Peter F molder 229 N Water h 10 [Atlantic
" Thomas A second hand h 113 County
Hebblewaite Catherine E widow Ed- [ward h 215 Weld
Hebden Stephen weaver h 60 Hathaway
Hebert Adelard grocer h 10 McMur- [ray terrace
" Adelard C driver h 188 Weld
" Adolph mill hand b 139 Earle
" Albini weaver h 149 Tinkham
" Alphonse spinner h 68 Division
" Alphonse G jeweler 1080 Acushnet av h 110 Hathaway
" Arthur painter bds 32 Nye
" Arthur teamster h 478 Coggeshall
" August box maker b 32 Holly
" B Fabiola removed from city
" Calixte weaver h 533 S Second
" Charles h 389 Pleasant
" Charles teamster h r 211 Bowditch
" Charles weaver h 71 Eugenia
" Delphis mill hand b 188 Collette
" Ernest operative h 66 Dean

M. P. B. Silva & Son Paints, Oils and Glass
Sole Agents for Lucas Tinted Gloss Paints
157 ACUSHNET AVENUE Both Phones NEW BEDFORD

Hebert
" Eugene D, U St Ry Co h 56 Nye
" Eva milliner 129 Rivet b 61 Acushnet avenue
" Frank teamster h 65 Hatch [do
" Henry clerk 1162 Acushnet av b
" Henry operative h 23 Holly
" Hormidas teamster h 232 State
" Jaques weaver b 166 Bates av
" Joseph blacksmith 854 Acushnet av b 1028 do
" Joseph clerk bds 56 Nye
" Joseph fisherman h 3 Riverside avenue [ham
" Joseph mill hand bds 148 Tink-
" Joseph weaver h 166 Nash rd
" Joseph weaver h 183 Collette
" Joseph Jr weaver b 183 Collette
" Joseph P carpenter h 506 Purchase
" Josephine Mrs h 56 Nye [lette
" Julie A widow Peter bds 143 Col-
" Louis carpenter h 226 N Second
" Margaret widow John h 92 Nye
" Mary widow Sylvian b 109 Phillips av
" Napoleon chauffeur h 12 Beetle
" Olive widow Simeon h 166 Bates avenue
" Pierre fixer h 55 Tallman
" Pierre third hand h 75 Jean
" Sylvian fisherman h 148 Tinkham [Hathaway
" Theodore slasher tender h 186
" William fisherman h 82 Phillips avenue
" William weaver b 55 Tallman
" see Hibbert
Heck Joseph weaver h 161 Hathaway
Hedge George H (Hedge-Lewis Mfg Co) h 136 Clinton
" James weaver b 883 Purchase
" -Lewis Mfg Co (George H Hedge and A W Lewis) button mfrs 6 Elm [Front h 32 Shawmut av
Hedges Clifford J machinist 42
Hegele Ernest machinist 8 Seneca h 561 Cottage [Woodlawn av
Heggas Charles plasterer bds 12
Heighton Margaret J hairdresser 72 Summer h do
Heights George W h 25 Hillman
Heilmann August weaver h 319 Sawyer [Pleasant
Heineman M & Co cloth brokers 60
Heise Albert R clerk U St Ry Co h at Fairhaven [Arnold
Heisel Christian H bricklayer h 194
Hellowell Albert operative b 122 Mott
" Fred weaver h 126 Mott
" Seline Mrs h 122 Mott
Hellyer Albert E apprentice b 573 Purchase [Cedar
" Eva widow J George Jr h 290
" James G plumbing 571 Purchase h 573 do
" J George Jr died Apr 23 1911
" Thomas A plumber b 573 Purchase
Helm John variety h 622 First
Helman Tyna teacher High school b 56 S Sixth [Water
Helme Charles A laborer h 205 S
" Mattie Mrs h 312 Acushnet av
" Minnie F Mrs h 345 Middle
" Robert G driver 36 Purchase h 28 Spring [net av
" Schuyler chauffeur b 312 Acu-
Hemenway James teamster 486 Rivet h 197 do
" Joseph carpenter h 207 Rivet
" Martha A died Aug 17 1910
Hemmings James W C insurance agt 120 Purchase rm 403 h 29 Salisbury
Hemston James weaver b 76 Cove
Henaumont Andrew joiner h 2 Jean
Henchey ——— editor b 464 County
Henderson Adam C linotype operator Standard h 484 Mill
" Elizabeth h 40 Hazard
" George O clothing cleaner 404 Kempton [School
" George H cook 5 S Sixth rms 96
" Mary Mrs caretaker 36 Purchase h 96 Cedar
" Minnie F Mrs h 345 Middle
" Robert S mule spinner h 10 Social [Cedar
" Susannah A widow William h 96
" Thomas spinner h 38 Willard
Hendra William designer Dartmouth Mfg Corp h 169 David
Hendricks John weaver h 126 Thompson [Independent
Hendriques Antonio E weaver h 60
" Joseph M driver h 119 Mott
Henk Christina Mrs housekeeper 306 Bowditch

Steiger-Dudgeon Co.
"The WOMAN'S Store."
Tel. Bell 82 & 83, Branches connecting all depts.
" " 160 For Office only. Auto. 1211

SUMPTIONS, ASSORTMENTS AT ALL TIMES OF DEPENDABLE DRY GOODS

Henk
" Mary stenographer 6 Masonic bldg b 306 Bowditch
Henke K William advertising agent h 135 Whitman [ville av
Henley Elzear weaver h 297 Belle-
" Hermenegilde weaver b 162 Whitman
" John W clerk b 587 First
" Theodore weaver b 297 Belleville avenue [ditch
Henner Eugene blacksmith h 7 Bow-
" Gilbert blacksmith h 25 Salisbury
" Inez widow John B h 97 Austin
" Noe blacksmith's helper h 103 Ruth
" see Hanna [shuet av b 5 Cottage
Hennessey Edward driver 298 Acu-
" John laborer b 34 Willis
" John J gardener 196 Hawthorn h 184 Chancery
" John L dentist 74 Purchase rms do [b 34 Willis
" Mary E bookkeeper 159 Purchase
" Mary G stenographer rms 29 Seventh
" Timothy h 34 Willis
Hennigan Thomas J master mechanic h 310 Summer
" William machinist b 310 Summer
" Winifred died April 19 1910
Henning Nora A Mrs dressmaker 390 Acushnet av h do
" William A hairdresser 336 Acushet av h 390 do
Henoumont Andre weaver b 2 Jean
Henrikson Harry C machinist 55 N Water h at Padanaram [bitt
Henriques Joseph M clerk h 22 Bab-
" Severino hairdresser 236 S Second h 477 First [Belleville av
Henriquez Francisco G laborer b 148
Henroy Frank slasher tender b 1089 Acushnet av
Henry Calixte fixer h 301 Davis
" Frank operative b 68 Hillman
" James operative h 858 First
" James weaver h 9 Morton ct
" Jerre clerk 301 Davis
" Patrick mason h 51 Sherman
" Tanjore T machinist h 194 Chancery
" Thomas blacksmith h 91 County
" Wilfred fireman h 244 Tinkham
" William died Mar 26 1911

Henry
" William overseer Dartmouth M Co b 200 Brock av [Maxfield
" William porter 14 N Sixth b 54
" William teamster U St Ry Co h 777 Purchase
" William C h 287 Bowditch
" William S hostler rms 12 W High
Henser Joseph operative h 24 Rotch blk 423 Bolton [Acushnet av
Henshaw Andrew picker boss h 1642
" William weaver h 205 Highland
Henson Daniel overseer h 336 Coffin avenue
Henthorn James h 195 Rivet
Hentis Vital weaver h 346 Sawyer
Henwood William A laborer h 226 Cottage
Henzl Joseph operative h 69 Hicks
Heptonstall Frederick boss grinder h 138 Davis [ditch h do
Heran Frederick janitor 144 Bow-
Herbert Arthur painter rms 32 Nye avenue
" Joseph speeder b 23 Austin
" Philip weaver b 59 Hicks
" William M hostler 388 N Front h 50 Kenyon
Herbolt William H blacksmith 144 N Water h at Fairhaven [burn
Herlihy Agnes and Jane h 56 Wash-
" Mary E teacher J H Clifford school b 54 Washburn [(W)
" Mary F widow Thadeus h 338 Elm
" Patrick granite works 54 Washburn h do [Water h 50 Fifth
Herman Abraham clothing 493 S
" David M h 76 First
" Israel pedlar h 366 S Second
" Joseph (Herman & Levine) 498 S Water h do [mut av
" Julius F drillmaker h 327 Shaw-
" Morris junk collector h 9 Howland
" Samuel clerk b 50 Fifth
" Samuel L h 129 Bedford
" & Levine (Joseph Herman and Hyman Levine) provisions 498 S Water
Hermann Paul removed from city
Hern Frank H mgr 156 Clinton bds 122½ Cove [et
Hernan Eugene weaver h 172 Riv-
Herold Rose cashier 1 Purchase b 1086 County
" Wolfgang h 1086 County

PELEG H. SHERMAN 506 COUNTY ST.
FUNERAL DIRECTOR AND EMBALMER
OFFICE PHONES. Bell 690-13. Auto 1305. RESIDENCE PHONES. Bell 690-12. Auto. 1306.

HERON CHARLES T real estate 114 William b 63 State Tel Bell 1728 Auto 1053 See page 27
" James T janitor Thompson street school b 63 State
" William E grinder h 55 Foster
Heroo Minnie M Mrs h 27 Cannon
Heroux Georgiana Mrs h 236 Acushnet [Purchase
" Joseph checker R R depot h 746
Herring J Henry representative R G Dun & Co Beetle lane h 684 County
Herrity Edward removed from city
" James removed from city
" John pool b 203 Weld
" Joseph drillworker b 203 Weld
Herron Edward laborer b 31 Howland Village [sell
" George D glasscutter h 40 Rus-
" James laborer b 31 Howland Village [Howland Village
" John J foreman st dept h 31
" William, U S N b 39 Howland Village [S b 174 Mt Pleasant
Hersey Caroline M widow William
" Charles F Rev city missionary office 755 First h do
Hersom Thomas (Thomas Hersom & Co) 11 Commercial h at Acushnet
HERSOM THOMAS & CO (Thomas and Thomas Hersom Jr) soap mfrs Howard av office 11 Commercial See page 24
" Thomas Jr (Thomas Hersom & Co) 11 Commercial h at Acushnet [ton
Herstoff Abraham pedlar h 59 Kemp-
" Albert fruit h 12 Atlantic
" Benjamin shoemaker b 494 Acushnet av [net av
" Kate widow Jacob h 494 Acush-
" Samuel fruit h 238 Chestnut
Hervey E Williams h 191 Hawthorn
" Harry R clerk b 99 South

HOMER W HERVEY
COUNSELLOR AT LAW
Merchants Bank Building
Rooms 405-406
97 William Street, New Bedford
Residence 189 Maple Street
Corner Tremont Street
Telephone Connections

Hervey Homer W lawyer 97 William rms 405-406 h 189 Maple
" James W h 578 County
" Mary A widow Roger boarding h 99 South [211 Grinnell
" Willard F foreman 100 Fifth h
" see Harvey
Herzog Adolph fixer h 234 Dean
" Augustus weaver h 253 Tinkham av
" Caroline died April 6 1910
" Emil plumber 1545 Acushnet av bds 354 Coffin av
" Frank h 41 Austin [Vine
" Frank collector 125 Middle h 75
" Frederick fixer b 41 Austin
" Godfried weaver h 354 Coffin av
" Herman shoemaker b 354 Coffin av [av
" William, U S N bds 254 Coffin
Hesford Ben overseer Wamsutta Mill h 18 Jean
" Ellis spinner h 360 Pleasant
" Henry mule spinner h 82 Penniman
" James spinner h 402 Sawyer
" John operative b 55 Howard
" Susan Mrs mill hand h 55 Howard
Hesketh Samuel laborer h 474 Coggeshall [First
Hesmondhalgh Edward weaver b 850
Hess Christian J bookkeeper 301 Municipal bldg h 4449 Acushnet av [347 do
Hesse Emil artist 189 Purchase rms

F. T. AKIN & CO. FORCE FACTORY FURNACE FAMILY COAL

Hetherington Edward weaver h 313 Earle
Hetherston John removed from city
Hettinger Adam laborer h 3 Social
" Fred mule spinner h 29 Viall
" John clerk b 3 Social
" Joseph provisions 34 W French av h 29 Viall
" William spinner h 29 Viall [av
Hetu Albert weaver bds 67 Coffin
" Angelina widow Henri bds 31 Covell [man
" Antoine carpenter h 110 Whit-
" Henry weaver h 4228 Acushnet avenue [vis
" Marie Mrs operative h 81 Da-
" Octave fixer b 127 Coffin av
" Octave fixer b 455 Belleville av
" Orey operative b 110 Whitman
Hetzel Frank overseer N B C Co b 457 Union
Heuberger Charles gardener Ward c Allen bds 41 Dartmouth [ct
" Helmuth weaver h 8 Coffin av
" Ludwig weaver h 289 Bowditch
Hevev Isaie weaver h 194 Dean
" Ulderic weaver h 182 Dean
Hewins Benjamin E roll coverer b 762 County [do
" George C engineer 100 Fifth h 84
" Mary widow Luther G Jr h 762 County
" Sarah H h 111 Merrimac
Hewitt Catherine widow John h 24 McGurk [Campbell
" Charles E shoe trimmer h 115
" Edward fisherman b 24 McGurk
" Frederick H student bds 115 Campbell
" James bridgeworker b 24 McGurk
" Matilda widow Thomas h 16 Harmony
" Michael removed from city
" Thomas fisherman h 24 McGurk
" William operative h 22 Dunbar
Hey Frank clerk 1518 Acushnet av h 120 Tallman
Heyer Myra C stenographer 3 Masonic bldg h 406 Union
" Rebecca K widow Andrew h 62 Parker
Heyes Annie Mrs h 94 Dartmouth
" Eli second hand h 231 Brock av
" Frederick L supt Nashawena Mill h 1325 Acushnet av

Heyes
" John shoemaker b 94 Dartmouth
" Thomas fixer h 125 David
" Thomas mill hand h 126 Whitman
" William overseer Gosnold Mill h 14 Valentine [Smith
Heyliger Robert G conductor h 224
Heys Benjamin weaver h 9 Stapleton
" Cavig brakeman h 285 Bowditch
" Matthew h 1765 Acushnet av
" Robert compositor 112 Union h 327 Tinkham
" Thomas loom fixer h 125 David
" William machinist b 1325 Acushnet av
" see Hayes [ton
Heywood John S operative h 8 Til-
" Thomas laborer h 83 Purchase
Heyworth Daniel bottler 151 Field h do
" Robert laborer h 159 Tinkham
Hezek Joseph operative h 69 Hicks
Hibbard George salesman 36 Purchase h 163 Clinton
" Harry Jr clerk b 488 Purchase
" John E framemaker 200 Union h 163 Clinton [488 Purchase
" Katherine E widow Joshua E h
Hibbert Malcolm operative h 30 Rodney [h 279 Collette
Hibbs Isaac M overseer Taber Mill
Hickey Bridget L widow John h 56 Rockland [land
" Elizabeth M milliner b 56 Rock-
" James laborer h 390 Cedar
" James Jr shoemaker b 390 Cedar
" John doffer b 800 County
" John lineman b 390 Cedar
" Michael A painter 151 Blackmer h 56 Rockland
" Patrick laborer h 800 County
" Peter mill hand b 14 Howland Village
" Thomas laborer b 800 County
" Thomas mill hand b 14 Howland Village
" William removed to Brockton
Hicks Alexander salesman b 98 Hillman
" Anna R widow b 208 Kempton
" Belle B bds 98 Hillman
" Caroline E h 625 County [cery
" Catherine housekeeper 117 Chan-
" Charlotte h 44 North [Chancery
" Clara widow Herbert E h 25
" Edward E h 98 Hillman

Remember to investigate our methods before taking up a business course.
Kinyon's Commercial School
Odd Fellows Bldg., Cor. William and Pleasant Sts., New Bedford, Mass.

Hicks
" Edward H reporter Mercury b 98 Hillman
" Granville P h 85 Elm
" Herbert E died Mar 8 1911
" Isaac C h 117 Chancery [net av
" James stableman b 148 Acushnet av
" Louise E teacher Parker street school b 98 Hillman [ant
" Margaret widow h 447½ Pleas-
" Mary widow William h 75 Ash (S)
" Mary L artist bds 75 Ash (S)
" Robert driver 70 Union b 148 Acushnet av [nut
" Sarah widow John J h 68 Wal-
" William H foreman 11 Walnut h 148 Acushnet av [Acushnet av
" William H J glassworker b 148
" William J checker h 141 Davis
" William J drillmaker b 75 Ash (S)
Higginbotham Eli yard overseer h 156 Brock av [av
" Harold operative bds 156 Brock
Higginbottom Cephas preserves h 156 Hemlock
" Clara bookkeeper 156 Hemlock
" Edward removed from city
" George removed from city
" John A weaver b 47 Holly
" Thomas salesman h 513 N Front
" William E removed from city
Higgins Amelia F bds 98 Elm
" Benjamin F died Feb 25 1911
" Bernard O clerk b 58 Jenny Lind
" Carrie L Mrs h 33 Willis
" Catherine widow Thomas h 367 Chancery
" Daniel Mrs h 7 Jenney
" Daniel F operative h 6 Harmony
" Edward O plumbing 361 North h 58 Jenny Lind [Middle
" Edward T clock repairer rms 96
" Frederick operative h 217 Tinkham
" George clerk rms 71 Foster
" George H drillworker h 17 West
" Gladys F clerk 185 Union b 33 Willis
" Herbert grinder b 804 County
" James H grinder h 162 Thompson
" James H Jr glasscutter bds 162 Thompson

Higgins
" John laborer h 8 Harmony
" John painter h 110 David
" John Jr spinner h 963 Purchase
" John E spinner h 364 Pleasant
" Mary widow Benjamin F h 771 Kempton
" Patrick laborer h 804 County
" Robert driver 14 N Sixth
" Thomas P clerk 403 Purchase b 33 Willis [cery
" William drillmaker h 77 Chan-
Higginson Elizabeth A widow Joseph h 119 David
" James machinist h 685 Cottage
" George weaver b 46 Larch
" William loom fixer h 48 Washington
Higham Charles E (William M Higham & Co) 403 Purchase b 61 Locust [70 Willis
" Clifford W clerk 212 Union bds
" Emma C stenographer Pierce Mfg Co b 61 Locust
" Hiram h 197 Summer
" James weaver h 59 Covell
" James H b 41 Fifth
" John fixer b 19 Ashley [Parker
" Mary Ann widow Hiram h 120
" Samuel foreman painter and license commissioner h 61 Locust
" Thomas spinner h 50 Larch
" William M (William M Higham & Co) h 70 Willis
" William M & Co (William M and Charles E Higham) druggists 212 Union and 403 Purchase [Rockland
Higton Nancy widow John h 74
Hildman Edward J glasscutter h 69 Hall
" Peter glasscutter h 31 Clover
Hildridge Samuel laborer b 118 Clark
Hill Albert R carpenter h 259 Arnold [205 Washington
" Alonzo B drummer 269 Sawyer b
" Arthur painter b 1098 Acushnet av
" A B musician b 205 Fourth
" Christ H glasscutter h 4 Warwick
HILL CO (Charles R Halliday) sign painters 257 Union See page 777

HASKELL BROS. DEALERS IN
ICE
400 COURT STREET TELEPHONE CONNECTION NEW BEDFORD, MASS.

Hill
" Daniel laborer b 1098 Acushnet av
" Edward painter 19 N Water rms 299 Acushnet av [ty h do
" Frances (Pink House) 464 Coun-
" Frank watchman rms 249 Purchase [av
" George musician h 437 Acushnet
" George M h 13 Cannon
" Henrietta (Pink House) 464 County h do [tic
" Henry M musician rms 83 Atlan-
" Herbert D third hand b 56 Vine
" Isabella C h 138 Bedford
" James slasher b 19 Ashley
" Jane widow Robert h 451 Sawyer
" John J carpenter h 159 Arnold
" Katherine Mrs dressmaker 67 Parker h do [Brock av
" Mary, Isabella and Ada h 98
" Peter A barber h 76 Rodney
" Ralph weaver h 43 Katharine
" Robert second hand h 154 Davis
" Sarah J Mrs h 24 Ashley
" Stephen R janitor 92½ Purchase b 464 County
" Thomas molder b 13 McGurk
" Thomas mule spinner h 44 Woodlawn av
" Thompson h 163 William
" William overseer Soule Mill h 56 Vine [Smith
Hillegass Lewis S machinist bds 77
Hiller George L Jr piper 28 N Water h at Fairhaven [ington
Hillman Alexander H h 52 Wash-
" Alexander H 2nd janitor h 217 Cedar [Savings b 81 Mill
" Alice M stenographer N B I for
" Benjamin painter h 101 Maxfield
" Charles B Jr bookkeeper h 152 Fourth [81 Mill
" Charlotte N widow Thomas R h
" Clarinda T widow Charles B h 152 Fourth
" Daniel T bookkeeper Potomska Mills h 141 Summer [Pleasant
" Emma B widow Getbro b 228
" Francis W painter b 148 Maxfield
HILLMAN FREDERIC G mill supplies 669 Purchase h 231 Pope See page 26
" Henry T musician b 148 Maxfield

Hillman
" Lucy E nurse h 152 Fourth
" Mary L h 81 Mill
" Robert combmaker 22 Fourth
" Robert T, R R conductor h 148 Maxfield [field
" William E operative h 440 Max-
Hilt Mary Mrs canvasser rms 91 Walden [b 414 Cedar
Hilton Elizabeth clerk 185 Union
" Elizabeth(widow John) rem from city
" Ethel M teacher Hosea M Knowlton school b 437 Union [rd
" James mule spinner bds Phillips
" John mule spinner h 263 Phillips avenue
" John second hand h Phillips rd
" Joseph teamster h 121 Field
" Richard carpenter h 12 Ashley
" Ruth G clerk b 414 Cedar [sant
" Samuel copperworker b 447 Plea-
" Thomas E fixer h 414 Cedar
" William spinner b 69 Winsor
Himes Arthur C clerk Bennett Mill b 116 South
" Elizabeth F h 229 Court
" John R drillmaker h 116 South
" Sarah widow Charles b 320 County [Welcome
Hinchcliff George spinner h 24
Hinchcliffe Humphrey weaver h 271 Weld [dard
Hinchey James H copy writer Stan-
Hinckley Amelia S widow George rms 1 Park place [h 173 Fourth
" Benjamin job pressman Standard
" Edna W teacher Merrimac street school b 270 Pleasant
" Everett H insructor N B Textile school h 488 Union
" Mary R died Dec 25 1910
" Sarah B widow Seth h 34 Bonney
" see Hinkley
Hindle Arthur bricklayer b 191 Dean
" Edmund designer Pierce Mfg Corp h 248 Chestnut
" Edward I student b 63 Parker
" Elizabeth H housekeeper 147 Maxfield
" George bricklayer b 191 Dean
" James W painter 10 Homer h 63 Parker
" John fixer b 307 Collette
" John overseer Beacon Mfg Co h 183 Ashland av

J. F. CROSSLEY 223 MILL STREET COR. EMERSON PHONE
STEAM and HOT WATER HEATING
GAS FITTING and FIXTURES

Hindle
" John twister h 12 Potter
" Joseph liquors Acushnet av c Elm h 139 Locust
" Joseph weaver b 259 Bowditch
" Mary widow Thomas h 27 Reynolds [ham
" Mary J Mrs weaver h 261 Tink-
" Robert E weaver h 34 Stapleton
" Sarah J died Aug 25 1910
" Ward machinist h 67 Ruth
" William weaver h 169 Hathaway
" William T clerk 387 Purchase h 22 Homer [Acushnet av
Hindley Benjamin J machinist h 1982
" Joseph comber h 48 Woodlawn avenue
" Josiah warper b 257 Austin
" Robert L laborer h 257 Austin
Hinds Fred C boxmaker h 157 Chancery
" John driver b 163 Emerson (N)
" William H laborer h 302 Middle
Hines Addie widow Henry S h 2 Topham [ion h do
" Catherine M dressmaker 404 Un-
" Michael bartender rms 129 Pleasant
" Patrick J electrician h 2 Durfee
" see Hynes [court
Hinkley William clerk h 20 Hazard
" William B, U S immigrant inspector Custom House h 57 Clinton [18 Clark
Hirschman Apolona widow John h
Hirshlag Antone fixer h 399 Earle
Hirst Bessie G clerk 28 N Water b 14 Homer [Fairhaven
" Eben P pres 28-32 N Water h at
HIRST E P CO plumbing heating and ventilating engineers 28-32 N Water See advt Plumbers in Business Directory
" Foster weaver h 55 Potomska
" Herbert W grocer 630 Purchase h 14 Homer [b 14 Homer
" Jesse B clerk N B I for Savings
" Lois widow Matthew H h 14 Homer
" Matthew H died July 1 1911
" see Hurst
Hirth Emile J clerk h 183 Park
" Mary music teacher 183 Park b do [b 99 Bedford
Hiscox Edward F clerk 100 Fifth

Hiscox
" Emma widow William b 99 Bedford
" Mary h 16 Grape [Elm
Hitch Frank B cotton sampler b 105
" Mary widow Ansel S h 76 Maxfield [105 Elm
" Mary F teacher High school b

MAYHEW R HITCH
Attorney and Counsellor at Law
Notary Public
37 Masonic Building
Pleasant cor Union Street
Residence 119 Mill Street
New Bedford, Mass
Telephone Bell 699-4

Hitch Mayhew R lawyer 37 Masonic bldg h 119 Mill [Elm
" Melancie F widow Joshua C h 105
" Otis L carpets and awnings 76 William h 109 Chestnut [man
Hitchcock C Bert fixer b 134 Tall-
" Walter S L pipe fitter b 191 Davis [1588 Acushnet av
" William C overseer Oneko Mills h
" William G janitor h 191 Davis
Hitt Mary M widow Howard F boarding h 299 County [Mott
Hittenhine William W quiller h 130
Hjelm Carl V copperworker h 325 Austin
Hlebus Frank weaver h 110 Mott
Hoard Charles E city teamster h 228 Chancery
Hobin John fixer h 367 Pleasant
" Thomas weaver bds 812 County
Hobson J Henry fixer h 38 Stowell
Hodgdon Edward J jeweler 45 Purchase rm 2 h at Haverhill
Hodgeson William weaver b 77 Hathaway
Hodgins John J twister b 19 Division
" William spinner h 19 Division
Hodgkins George H (G H Hodgkins & Co h at Boston

CHARLES A. CROSHERE
38 FOURTH ST. **Bell Phone 1964-23**
SIGN PAINTING
GLASS LETTERING
ELECTRIC SIGNS
SHOW CARDS

Hodgkins
" G & Co (George H Hodgkins and Mrs A Beatrice Lowther) investments 71 William
" L M Mrs h 54 Fourth
Hodgsen William weaver h 98 Kenyon [Conn
Hodkinson Thomas rem to Taftville
" William blacksmith b 27 Margin
Hodkowski Edmont mill hand h 9 Bullard [h do
Hodsdon Villa matron 208 County
Hodson Clarence E drillmaker h 73 Myrtle
" Edward J insurance agent 37 Purchase rm 23 h 10 Clay
" Frederick J second hand h 139 Bullard [land Village
" George watchmaker h 25 How-
" Richard loom fixer h 14 Cleveland
" William drillmaker h 73 Myrtle
Hodziewich George grocer 32 Delano h 106 Rivet
" George Jr painter b 106 Rivet
Hoefle Peter died Nov 27 1910
Hofe Chester T salesman 194 Union b 29 Fifth [Fifth
" Sarah J widow Nicholas h 29
Hoffman John shoe repairer 165 Hathaway h do [shuet av
" Martin mill hand bds 1672 Acu-
" Theodore C traveling salesman h 52 Russell
Hoffmire Arthur E rem to N Adams
Hogan Abbie nurse h 2 Harrison
" James removed to N Y city
" John weaver b 67 Coffin av
" Martin fireman h 51 Potomska
" Mary h 88 Austin [court
" Mary widow Thomas h 44 Morton
" Thomas carpenter h 103 Austin
" William laborer h 8 Viall
" see Horgan [away
Hogarth David molder h 85 Hath-
" Edward mill hand b 85 Hathaway
" John weaver b 85 Hathaway
" William mill hand b 85 Hathaway
Hogg William weaver h 124 Holly
Hoglund Albertina widow Gustaf b 65 Ocean
Hois Anna M asst bookkeeper 17 N Sixth b 207 Kempton

Hois
" Joseph carpenter h 207 Kempton
Holberton Rena A widow Lewis h 64 North
Holbrook Mary A died Mar 21 1911
Holcomb Adeline S widow Henry h 298 County [Hillman
" Annie E widow Munroe h 124
" Charles R h 324 Cottage
" Clark William (N B Boiler & Machine Co) 42 Front h 115 Mill [Cottage
" Elizabeth M widow Roland h 324
" Henry A h 66 Fourth [Cove
Holcroft George clerk 87 Ruth b 96
" John Henry weaver b 96 Cove
" Sarah Mrs variety 87 Ruth b 96 Cove
Holden Ada R teacher James B Congdon school b 16 Cottage
" Alice speeder b 59 Tallman
" Arthur J (Oneko Woolen Mills) h at Bennington Vt
" Charles weaver b 188 Bell rd
" Charles H (C H Holden & Co) h 337 Cedar
" C H & Co (Charles H Holden) wholesale provisions 45-49 Union
" Edward mill hand b 533 Rivet
" Frank bookkeeper b 310 Tinkham
" George A carpenter h 166 Durfee
" George H salesman 45 Main h 31 Maitland
" Harry painter b 40 Woodlawn
" Henry weaver h 432 Pleasant
" Isabella widow Thomas bds 187 Hathaway
" James weaver b 189 Dean
" James E baker 861 Purchase h r 70 Linden
" James H weaver b 833 County
" James W copperworker h 189 Dean
" James W weaver h 290 Collette
" John died [ville rd
" John A real estate h 176 Belle-
" John H mill hand bds 533 Rivet
" John H mule spinner h 533 Rivet
" John William stonecutter b 40 Woodlawn
" John W weaver b 422 Pleasant
" Joseph concreter b 176 Belleville road

J. G. NICHOLSON
LUMBER, SASH, DOORS and BLINDS
BOWDITCH STREET, NEW BEDFORD, MASS.

Holden
" Joseph glasscutter b 189 Dean
" Joseph painter bds 158 Crapo
" Joseph A weaver h 293 Coffin av
" Julian L fitter b 924 Belleville av
" Kate widow Edward H variety 93 First h do
" Leonard & Co (A J Holden and C W Leonard) props Oneko Woolen Mills end Purchase
" Margaret h 872 Acushnet av
" Mary widow weaver b 1264 Acushnet av
" Philip weaver b 290 Collette
" Samuel plumber 91 N Water b Pleasant street
" Sarah widow h 66 Independent
" Sarah Jane widow William (Counsell & Holden) 1956 Acushnet av h 1946 do
" Theresa matron Hathaway's Theatre b 1946 Acushnet av
" Thomas overseer h 197 Bowditch
" Thomas spinner b 34 McGurk
" Thomas weaver b 158 Crapo
" Thomas H conductor b 432 Pleasant [way
" Thomas W weaver h 187 Hatha-
" Walter removed to Atlanta Ga
" William C weaver h 62 Rossevelt
Holderness Joseph weaver h 18 Myrtle [Belleville rd
Holding Charles loom fixer h 188
" Mary widow Joseph b 188 Belleville road [lips av
Holdridge Oscar E fixer h 37 Phil-
Holdsworth Herbert W electrical worker bds Tarkiln Hill road n Lunds corner
" Leonard N electrical worker b Tarkiln Hill road n L C [rd
" Norman watchman h Tarkiln Hill
Holgate Anna E stenographer Gosnold Mills Co b 99 County
" Eliza widow William F dry goods 99 County h do
" Joseph b 99 County
Holland Charles rms 7 N Second
" Charles H driver 14 N Sixth bds 269 Fourth [net av
" Charles H teamster b 535 Acush-
" Isaac F engineer tug Hart h 34 Keene
" John fireman h 111 Ash
" Joseph weaver h 178 Belleville av

Holland
" William H weaver h 269 Fourth
Holleran Michael wire worker 43 William rms 32 Elm
Holliday Robert fixer h 264 Fourth
Hollihan John clerk 739 Purchase h 25 Homer [79 Richmond
" John H dentist 5 Arcade bldg h
" Martin fixer b 59 Brock avenue
" Michael fixer h 59 Brock av
" William P removed to Providence R I [William b 67 Howard
Hollingsworth George pressman 47
" Hartley spinner h 211 Weld
" John spinner b 208 Nash road
" John H carder h 67 Howard
Hollis Elizabeth housekeeper 29 Mosher [Tremont
Holloway Arod B police h 145
" Etta M clerk 40 Masonic bldg b 245 Tremont
" J Thomas laborer h r 235 Park
" J Thomas Jr laborer b r 235 Park
Holly Drug Co (Arthur L Walsh) 1263 Acushnet av [Second
Hollywood Frank laborer h 229 North
" Frank Jr teamster h 229 N Second [135 Chestnut
" Henry A variety 251 Summer b
" John laborer b 229 N Second
" Michael warper b 195 N Second
Holm Charles mariner h 166 North
Holmans Thomas C janitor George H Dunbar school h 66 Cottage
HOLMES ALBERT W coal and wood 201 Purchase and Holmes wharf foot of Cannon h 5 Clinton place See back cover
" Alfred supt Nonquitt Spinning Co h 1767 Acushnet avenue
" Alice Mrs removed from city
" Andrew weaver b 28 Reynolds
" Annie Mrs h 271 Acushnet av
" Charles cab maker h 45 Ashley
" Charles H carpenter b 45 Ashley
" Charles M agent and treasurer Holmes Mfg Co h 4 N Orchard
" Clarence E musician h 186 Arnold [h do
" C E Mrs dressmaker 186 Arnold
" Edward W lawyer 37 Purchase rm 5 bds 661 County
" Ellis W h 402 Union
" Ezra officer H C h 661 County

Steiger-Dudgeon Co.
"The WOMAN'S Store."
Tel. Bell 82 & 83, Branches connecting all depts.
" " 160 For Office only. Auto. 1211

SUMPTIONS, ASSORTMENTS AT ALL TIMES OF DEPENDABLE DRY GOODS

Holmes
" Frank C foreman U St Ry Co h 79 Locust
" Harry weaver b 119 David
" James slater b 59 Bullard
" John boss comber h 15 Cleveland
" John J hostler h 127 Cedar
" John P vice pres N B Fish Co Merrills wharf h 47 Willis
" John W paint grinder 14 Wall h 28 Reynolds
" Joseph mariner h 273 S Front
" Joseph B baker 439 Purchase h 661 County
" Lillian F Mrs b 180 Allen
" Mfg Co cotton yarns E French avenue cor Mott
" Philip C clerk Grinnell Mfg Corp b 661 County [b 103 Sycamore
" S Agnes teacher Parker st school
" William A bds 166 Washington
" William S mill hand h 531 Rivet
" William W h 166 Washington
Holmquist Ellen O teacher Parker st school b at Fairhaven [County
Holmstrom John operative h 175½
" Peter twister b 275½ County
Hologgotis Constantine operative h 28 Linden
Holt Albert weaver h r 51 Dean
" Ellen widow William h 315 Coffin avenue
" Fred loom fixer h 21 Crapo
" Frederick doffer b 315 Coffin av
" Fredrick L wire chief h 42 Park
" Frederick W fixer h 447½ Pleasant
" George R weaver h 395 Orchard (S) [Orchard (S)
" George R Jr clerk 182 Union b 395
" James loom fixer h 30 Felton
" James W fixer h 53 Merrimac
" James W weaver b 46 Roosevelt
" John fixer h 99 Brock avenue
" John C fixer h 336 Sawyer
" Mary h 24 Mosher
" Robert weaver h 223 N Front
" Rose housekeeper 4 Wamsutta
" Samuel designing principal N B T school h 39 Shawmut avenue
" Samuel laborer b 307 Collette
" Samuel (132 Nye) removed from city
" William removed from city
" William weaver b 39 Shawmut av

Holt
" William Jr h 1547 Acushnet av
HOME WASHING CO (Eliphalet A Tripp) 111 Myrtle See page 786
Homer Esther C Mrs housekeeper 164 Middle
" Frederick A office city pier No 2 rms 117 High
" George fisherman h 37 Maxfield
" George S pres 152 N Water office city pier No 2 h 38 Grove
" Thomas spinner h 20 Peckham
Homshaw Frank carder b 208 Weld
Honeker Daniel baker h 512 Purchase [Davis
" Fred foreman 439 Purchase h 353
Honneman Joseph W operative b 542 Purchase [chase
" Victor E N baker b 596 Pur-
Hood Matthew T slubber tender h 74 Myrtle
" Warren machinist rms 66 School
" William operative h 17 Weld
" see Houde
Hook Gilman E mason 21 Columbia and (Sturtevant & Hook) h 21 Columbia [bia
" Walter E bookkeeper b 21 Colum-
Hooper George R cashier foot Willis h 143 State [nold
" Nathan master mariner h 142 Ar-
Hope John H weaver h 839 S Water
" Katherine I teacher b 23 Woodlawn av [lawn av
" Robert I machinist h 23 Wood-
Hopgood Richard b 138 Division
Hopkins Arnold C drill inspector h 128 Cottage [lette
" Bernard operative h 283 Col-
" Clifton baker 92 William h 35 Smith
" Henry C artesian wells 23 N Water rms 56 Walnut
" Ivan baker rms 366 Purchase
" Ivy G manicure 76 Pleasant rm 25 rms do
" James carder b 71 Rivet
" James F salesman rms 40 Russell
" L M Miss stenographer Sharp Mill [tage h do
" Margaret E dressmaker 48 Cot-
" Thomas b 71 Rivet
" Thomas Jr carder b 71 Rivet

PELEG H. SHERMAN 506 COUNTY ST.
FUNERAL DIRECTOR AND EMBALMER
OFFICE PHONES. Bell 690-13. Auto. 1305.
RESIDENCE PHONES. Bell 690-12. Auto. 1306.

Hopkinson Annie E widow Wood h 236 County
" Arthur clerk b 109 Chestnut
" James removed from city
" Sadie M stenographer U St Ry Co b 236 County [68 Hathaway
Hopwood John freight handler bds
" Richard spinner h 2 Welch
Horacek Johan weaver h 203 Dean
Horan Dominick laborer h 19 Viall
" James carpenter b 65 Howard
" Mary A teacher I W Benjamin school b 19 Viall [S Water
Horenstein Haskell operative h 505
" Max barber 336 Acushnet av h 291 S Second [net av
" Philip second hand h 90 Acush-
" Samuel mgr 348 Acushnet av b 291 S Second [land
Horn Joseph weaver h 9 Cleveland
Hornby Edward E operative bds 1159 Purchase
" Richard W h 1159 Purchase
" Thomas operative h 592 Cottage
" Wallace clerk h 680 Purchase
" Wilfred operative b 1159 Purchase [Corp h 34 Wood
Horne Albert H overseer Neild M
" Benjamin weaver h 199 Bowditch
Horner Charles R operative h 67 Howard [h 272 Davis
Hornshaw Emma widow William E
" Frank comber b 272 Davis
" William fitter b 272 Davis
Horovitz David painter h 714 Acushnet av
Horr Benjamin F h 100 State
" Isabel F stenographer b 100 State
Horricks James eyeletworker b 625 Purchase [Orchard (S)
Horrocks Henry operative h 416
" William weaver b 183 David
Horsfall Amos loom picker mfr 64 Katharine h do [Jouvett
" Ernest loom picker maker h 60
" George weaver b 105 Davis
" Joseph A loom picker maker 64 Katharine h 70 do
Horsfield John E dry goods 1500 Acushet av h 2112 do
Hortense Mme 931 Acushnet av
Horton Charles M foreman 100 S Water h 169 River rd [chase
" Dexter copperworker b 644 Pur-

Horton
" Eliphalet C floor man 100 S Water b Walnut c Fifth
" Eliphalet M police h 437 Mill
" Hector mason b 644 Purchase
" Lawrence motorman h 426 Pleasant
" Printing Co 258 Purchase
Horvitz Abraham b 77 South
" Abraham J crockery 541 S Water h 146 Acushnet av
" Ezra at 106 Dartmouth h 77 South [106 Dartmouth
" Grain Co (Morris Horvitz) grain
" Isaac pedlar h 146 Acushnet av
" Israel salesman 64 Union b 16 Washington [Washington
" Jacob A salesman 64 Union b 16
" Jacob A shoes 883 S Water h 101 South [av b 16 Washington
" Julius A manager 1131 Acushnet
" Louis bds 77 South [South
" Morris (Horvitz Grain Co) h 77
" Rose Mrs h 3 McDonald court
" Samuel junk b 372 S Second
" Samuel shoes 64 Union and 1131 Acushnet av h 16 Washington
" see Hurvitz and Hurwitz [ditch
Hosker Edward fireman h 47 Bow-
Hosmer William H clerk Bennett Mill h 100 Mt Pleasant
Hosp Joseph weaver h 6 Roosevelt
Hotte Albani (Hotte Brothers) b 195 County
" Alfred packer b 57 Kenyon
" Alphonse painter h 57 Kenyon
" Arthur clerk 48 Rivet bds 195 County [cers 48 Rivet
" Bros (Philomon and Albini) gro-
" Cesaire h 195 County [ty
" George clerk 48 Rivet b 191 Coun-
" Leonide clerk 48 Rivet h 191 County [Ruth
" Philemon (Hotte Brothers) h 106
" William clerk 48 Rivet h 195 County [av h do
Houde Alphonse J grocer 314 Coffin
" Frank X loom fixer h 52 Briggs
" Isadore F clerk 961 Acushnet av b 135 N Front
" Joseph S died June 21 1911
" Mary widow Marcel b 7 Holly
" Theodore slasher h 326 N Front
" Theodore slasher h 326 N Front

F. T. AKIN & CO. PAINTERS AND DECORATORS

Hough Garry de Neuville physician 542 County h do
" George A managing editor Standard h 85 Campbell [ant
" Henry weaver h 531 Mt Pleas-
" Lydia W widow George T h 95 Elm [Co) bds 86 Elm
Hougham George H (G H Hougham
" G H Co (George H Hougham) loans 76 Pleasant rm 20
Houghton Albert insurance agent 120 Purchase rm 403 b 9 Grandfield
" Albert tinsmith h 103 Holly
" Albert tinsmith b 211 Collette
" Edward engineer h 42 Page
" George carpenter b 27 Salisbury
" Harold clerk b 211 Collette
" Henry laborer h 9 Grandfield
" James mill hand h 20 Briggs
" James second hand h Winterville road corner Rockdale avenue
" James spinner h 292 Cedar Grove
" John weaver h 211 Collette
" John weaver b 244 Phillips av
" John Jr mill hand b 211 Collette
" Manuel weaver h 418 N Front
" Nellie Mrs nurse Almshouse b do
" Richard agent h 6 Warren
" Robert weaver h 38 Hollyhock
" Robert weaver h 313 Earle
Houldsworth Matthew spinner h 57 Beetle [avenue
Houle Adelard fixer h 1293 Acushnet
" Anselme elevatorman h 201 Sawyer
" Arsene fixer h 582 First
" Arthur carpenter h 145 Coggeshall
" Arthur laborer 2795 Acushnet av
" Damase widow Israel h 103 Clifford
" Dolor A carpenter h 187 Collette
" Edmond carpenter h 303 Collette
" Edmond weaver h 103 Clifford
" Ernest weaver b 201 Sawyer
" Francis X carpenter h 226 State
" Frank weaver h 582 First
" Henri (H Houle & Son) shoe repairers 786 Purchase rms 188 Weld
" Henri & Son (Henri and W L Houle) shoe workers 786 Purchase [Acushnet avenue
" Henry milk h Bristol av off 2746
" Henry removed from city

Houle
" Hormidas weaver b 103 Clifford
" Jeanette operator 31 Commercial bds 125 Division
" Joseph weaver b 201 Sawyer
" Joseph O collector 43 William h 293 North Front [h do
" Leonidas builder 21 Whitman
" Lionel clerk 945 Acushnet av b 187 Collette
" Narcisse weaver h 2 Riverside av
" Philip fixer bds 52 Delano
" Romeo barber h 10 Nye [yer
" Sinai mill hand bds 201 Saw-
" Thomas removed to Canada
" Wilbert S salesman 170 Purchase bds 81 Chestnut
" Wilfred L (H Houle & Son) 786 Purchase h 75 Thomas
" Zacharie barber 81 William h 16 Central avenue [State
Hourihan Timothy gardener h 218
HOUSEHOLD FURNISHING CO W H Bassett mgr 170-174 Purchase See page 94
Houselhof Hugo baker 1233 Acushnet avenue h 101 Holly
Houserman Fred weaver h 324 Earle
Houston Edmond A clerk 70 William bds at Acushnet
" James designer bds 117 Eugenia
" William F teamster h 62 Kenyon
Houth Joseph glass blower h 131 Rockland
Houtman John W porter h 157 Elm
" Louise E Mrs b 84 Ash (N)
" Peter J janitor h 142 Chancery
" Robert H choreman h 52 Cedar
Howard Addie clerk P Corp b E Fairhaven [ushnet av
" Alfred K fireman h 2476 Ac-
" Arthur F window dresser 185 Union h 121 Locust
" Benjamin h 173 Campbell
" Benjamin operative h 10 Abbott
" Betsey J widow Abner h 342 Pleasant
HOWARD BROS MFG CO card clothing 44-46 Vine Worcester Mass See page 14
" David hairdresser h 51 Salisbury
" David operative h 51 Salisbury
" Edward painter h 100 Campbell
" Elmer C clerk Anthony Swift & Co rms 149 Middle

To do things right you must be taught. Our instructors can do it.
Kinyon's Commercial School
Odd Fellows Bldg., Cor. William and Pleasant Sts., New Bedford, Mass.

Howard
" Elma R troubleman 57 N Second b at N Dartmouth [shnet av
" Everett L provisions h 2904 Acu-
" Frances M bds 6 McGurk
" Frank C linotype operator Times h 97 Locust [nold
" George E drillmaker h 182 Ar-
" George W hostler b 96 Union
" Hannah widow Edward F h 500 Acushnet av [Mosher
" Hannah widow William h 59
" Henry laborer b 6 McGurk
" Henry machinist h 60 State
" Henry Jr paymaster Wamsutta Mills h 20 Arch [at Fairhaven
" Henry T clerk Beacon Mfg Co b
" Isaac H b 570 County
" Jacob h 100 Parker
" James laborer h 27 Salisbury
" James S h 4 Pope Island
" Jessie I nurse b 22 Arnold pl
" Leslie A cigars 570 County h do
" Louise F telephone operator 57 N Second b at Fairhaven
" Marie S teacher b 53 Fifth
" M Frances clerk 182 Union b 342 Pleasant
" Richard laborer h 173 David
" Robert piper b 45 Winsor
" Robert twister h 60 Briggs
" Sarah widow Andrew h 1280 Acushnet av
" Susan E rms 181 Middle
" Thomas machinist b 27 Roosevelt
" William T overseer h 182 Cove

HOWARD & BULLOUGH AMERICAN MACHINE CO Ltd cotton machinery Pawtucket R I See advt end of General Directory

Howarth Albert machinist h 862 First
" Alice widow James h 481 Rivet
" Arthur operative h 47 Bowditch
" Edward laborer b 230 Rockdale avenue
" Ellen widow William Jr h 53 Fruit [County h do
" Elsie P Mrs dressmaker 865

HOWARTH ERNEST electrical contractor 120 Middle b 53 Fruit See page 784
" Frederick clerk b 112 Thompson
" George weaver h 230 Rockdale av

Howarth
" George E slubber h 286 Coggeshall
" Hiram boarding 67 School
" Irene nurse 194 Purcase b do
" James operative h 27 Cleveland
" James weaver b 7 Juniper
" James weaver h 59 Roosevelt
" James E twister h 219 Rivet
" James E weaver h 130 Mott
" James H removed from city
" Joseph loom fixer h 865 County
" J Wesley stockman 57 N Second h 101 Newton [230 Rockdale av
" Margaret A widow Edmund bds
" Maria widow Thomas h 112 Thompson
" Richard city laborer h 56 Beetle
" Richard weaver h 18 Viall
" Robert carpenter h 81 Dunbar
" Robert weaver h 25 Reynolds
" Samuel (Gregory Plumbing Co) 1545 Acushnet av h at Dorchester [av
" Thomas weaver b 38 W French
" Walter motorman rms 279 Pleasant [1911
" William (15 Lexington av) died
" William twister b 975 Kempton
" see Haworth [Phillips rd

Howe Anna H widow Stephen A bds
" Benjamin F bookkeeper Acushnet Saw Mills Co h end Phillips road
" Benjamin F draughtsman 303 Municipal bldg b 109 Campbell
" Charles A h 109 Campbell
" George C boxmaker h end Phillips road
" Walter b 31 Brock av

Howell George clerk b 1060 Acushnet av [net av
" John operative bds 1060 Acush-

Howes Carrie H Mrs h 102 Newton
" Charles M foreman b 75 Lindsey

HOWES C G CO cleansers Allston Mass See opposite Cleansers in Business Directory
" Francis N truant officer h 107 Sycamore [sey
" Frank LeB engineer h 75 Lind-
" George H Rev pastor Unity Home h 64 Borden
" Loretta nurse 321 Union rms do
" Phoebe D cashier h 73 Foster

Bread, Cake, Pastry
RICHMOND & COMPANY **255-257 UNION STREET**
Bell 993 Automatic 1022

Howland Abby B widow Philip h 69 Mechanics lane [Rockdale av
" Abner A laborer h rear 1267
" Abraham H weigher h 5 Campbell [er h do
" Abraham P ice cream 10 Weav-
" Ada D teacher William H Taylor school b at S Dartmouth
" Alfred G bit grinder h 496 Acushnet av
" Alice Russell h 149 Hawthorn
" Annie C widow Hubert M h 731 County
" Annie M Mrs h 47 Hemlock
" Arthur R glasscutter h 116 S Sixth [ant h 170 do
" Austin T picture framer 52 Pleas-
" Barker C physician 96 William rms 12-14 h 81 School
" Beriah E clerk Standard h 233 Shawmut av [233 Shawmut av
" Beriah G salesman 98 Purchase h
" Beulah clerk 97 William rm 301 b 297 County [Russell
" Carrie widow Jonathan Jr h 54
" Carrie E widow Henry T h 136 Cedar [134 Fourth
" Charles A laborer 144 S Water h
" Charles F R clerk 55 William rms 28 Fifth
" Charles S receiving teller Merchants National Bank h 89 Chestnut [297 County
" Charlotte A B widow Isaac C b
" Clara C widow William H h 291 Acushnet avenue
" Clifford oiler b 249 Acushnet av
" Cora E telephone operator 57 N Second b 47 Hemlock [305 do
" Daniel W tailor 303 Maxfield h
" David W h 219 Kempton
" Edgar F (Ezra F Howland & Son and Howland & Sampson) h 181 Grinnell
" Edna B teacher Harrington school b 233 Shawmut avenue
" Ednora E h 71 Fourth
" Edward S died Feb 21 1911
" Elizabeth J widow Samuel R b 48 Walnut
" Elizabeth K h 95 Madison
" Ezra farmer h 284 Union

Howland
" Ezra F (Ezra F Howland & Son) h 84 Forest
" Ezra F & Son (Ezra F and Edgar F) spar mfrs Front next Merrill's wharf
" Florence telephone operator 57 N Second b 496 Acushnet avenue
" Fred T pressman Standard b 165 Middle
" Frederick A Jr painter h 23 Bay
" George farmer b 284 Union
" George F h 297 County
" George L variety 122 Campbell and painter 124 do h do
" George W cotton inspector b 105 Butler
" Gertrude S h 63 Hillman
" Hannah widow Elihu h 45 Morgan
" Harriet S widow Edward h 249 Acushnet avenue [47 Hemlock
" Harry A clerk 60 Shawmut av b
" Hattie P Mrs florist 473 Allen h do
" Henry (Wood Brightman & Co) 55 N Water h 280 Pleasant
" Henry B jewelry 26-28 Purchase h 61 Russell
" Herbert P clerk Nonquit Spinning Co h 345 Orchard (S)
" Horatio K b 95 Madison
" Hotel 51 Howland Village
" Humphrey D master mariner h 85 Bay [Chancery
" Ida M widow Ernest L h 192
" Isaac C h 35 Tremont
" James F engineer h 177 Newton
" James H frame maker b 66 N Second
" John J h 74 North
" John S salesman h 70 Borden
" Jonathan Jr died March 13 1911
" Julia A h 32 Bedford
" Julian fitter 24 Fifth b 924 Belleville avenue [48 North
" Laura T clerk city clerk's office b
" Louise R teacher Jireh Swift school bds 233 Shawmut av
" Lysand F Jr chauffeur h 2 Pease court [pital b do
" Mabel dietician St Luke's Hos-
" Mabel M Mrs telephoner 185 Union b 7 Shawmut avenue

GLOBE DYE HOUSE 220 SHAWMUT AVE.
J. N. J. LONHOLDT, PROP. Telephone Connections Goods called for and Delivered
Down town Office, 52 Pleasant St., Room 1 North End Office, 1014 Acushnet Ave.

Howland
" Maria L widow Ebenezer h 171 Campbell [Chancery
" Mary A widow Joseph B b 191
" Mary J widow A C h 924 Belleville avenue
" Mary T Mrs h 45 Morgan
" Myron P draughtsman 97 William rm 401 h 22 Keene
" Nicholas E express agent 149 Purchase h 274 Pleasant
" Nora F Mrs h 56 Spring [Forest
" Norris P clerk 55 N Water h 66
" Orloff R carpenter h 181 James
" Paul Jr job printer 20 Wall h 91 State
" Philip G laborer h 75 Cedar
" Robert A shuttle maker b 91 State [School
" Sarah C widow James T bds 87
" Sarah C widow William W h 291 Acushnet avenue [Cedar
" Sarah F widow Edward S h 129
" Sarah M seamstress h 70 Oak
" Stanley T b 25 West Arch
" Stephen D (S D Howland & Co) 86 Chancery b do [Willis
" Susan M widow Thomas D h 93
" Sylvia G died Feb 17 1911
HOWLAND S D & CO (Stephen D Howland and Kenneth H Brightman) coat apron and towel supply 86 Chancery See page 786
" Thomas H salesman h 171 Grinnell
" Walter S Mrs h 105 Butler
" William A E police h 473 Allen
" William F drill polisher 100 Fifth h 349 Court
" William G watchman b 64 Fifth
" William P mfr potato chips 262 Orchard (S) h do [North
" Winthrop O glass cutter h 181
" & Sampson (Edgar F Howland and Isaac D Sampson) riggers 27 Front
Howley John spinner b 258 Coffin av
" Thomas weaver h 15 Marvin
Howman Hillery weaver h 156 David
Howson Angus operative b 96 Cove
" Leonard baker h 119 Brock av
" Margaret E Mrs b 25 Cleveland
" Walter weaver b 301 Fourth

Howson
" William spinner b 38 Bowditch
Hoxie Edward A prop New York Market 251 Purchase h 4409 Acushnet av
" Frank C patternmaker 272 S Water h 155 Washington
" Frank L (Driscol, Church & Hall) 84 Union h 139 Clinton
" Harold L clerk 84 Union h 90 High
" John R removed from city
" Mirabel N clerk b 155 Washington [ney
" William glassworker h 122 Bon-
" William R variety and bicycles 88 Allen b 55 Bonney
Hoye Annie L housekeeper 72 Atlantic [land
" Frederick J foreman b 79 Rock-
" Ida B cashier 912 S Water b 79 Rockland
" James F (James F Hoye & Co) 305 Merchants Bank bldg 97 William h 15 Pope
HOYE JAMES F & CO (James F Hoye and Joseph Z Boucher) insurance 305 Merchants Bank bldg See page 44
" Martin B foreman h 72 Atlantic
" Sarah widow Bernard h 358 Cedar [land
" Thomas F foreman h 79 Rock-
" see Haughey [h 24 Independent
Hoyes Bridget, Mary Ann and Kate
Hoyle Ernest died Dec 22 1910
" John E chief engineer Dartmouth Mills h 176 Cove
" John H weaver h 71 Merrimac
" John T operative b 13 Austin
" J Stephen floor walker 185 Union b 71 Merrimac
" Mary A Mrs h 249 Purchase
" Richard helper 28 N Water b 176 Cove [Merrimac
" William J buyer 182 Union b 71
" William J loom fixer h 13 Austin [Walnut
Hoyt James H ship carpenter h 8
" William D optician 5 Purchase h 511 Union
Huard Alexander H hairdresser 33 Elm h 790 Purchase
" Alfred clerk N Front cor Coffin av h 36 Hicks [b 790 Purchase
" Archie clerk 1567 Acushnet av

GREENE & WOOD Every Kind of LUMBER AND MILL WORK
PINE STREET, off So. WATER STREET, NEW BEDFORD

Huard
" Ducidie Mrs removed from city
" Joseph asst engineer h 16 Washburn [89 Newton
Hubbard Benjamin F carpenter h
" B Franklin bds 89 Newton
" Catherine widow Patrick h 25 Cottage [nut
" Catherine dressmaker b 25 Chest-
" Ellen widow James b 25 Chestnut
" Joseph N teamster b 24 Elm
" Manley R painter U St Ry Co h 162 Davis
" Sarah E Mrs h 1 Pease court
Hubbenett Betsey J widow Isaac variety 147 Crapo h do
Huber Andreas spinner h 324 Earle
" Frank brewer b 57 Washburn
Huberdeau Adilord gardener h 42 Page [Tinkham
Huberger Carl Frederick fixer h 271
Hubert Alexis carpenter h 301 Tinkham [do
" Oliver driver 281 Sawyer h 336
Huckins Melissa C Mrs b 199 Pleasant [Cedar
Hudler Martha widow Frank b 157
Hudner Michael T provisions 145 Union h at Fall River
Hudon Joseph E hairdresser 150 Arnold h 56 Ash (S)
" Victor loom fixer h 79 Nelson
Hudson Ellen widow John b 77 Hathaway
" James teamster h 190 Nash rd
" Mary S Mrs h 147 Smith
" Thomas weaver h 297 Fourth
" Thomas J steam fitter h 74 School
" William E twister h 108 Cove
" William H weaver b 77 Hathaway [Penniman
Huebner Gustav operative h 34
Huette Emile weaver h 775 First
" Louis weaver b 41 Rivet
Huggins Leon M reporter Standard h 17 Bay [net av h 101 Holly
Hughes Arthur J mgr 929 Acush-
" Bridget grocer 929 Acushnet av h 101 Hollis
" Edward removed to Fall River
" Edward L clerk 1592 Acushnet av h 353 Davis [132 Hathaway
" Hiram clerk 1592 Acushnet av h

Hughes
" James M lineman 43 William h 162 Nash road
" Oswald H laborer h 201 Eugenia
" Thomas H papermaker h 31 Grape
" Wilfred twister b 201 Eugenia
" William laborer h 201 Eugenia
Hull Wallace G driver 83 Thomas h 225 N Second
Hulme Thomas fitter h 74 Hathaway
" see Hume [et
Hulton Chadwick spinner h 506 Riv-
" Elizabeth A widow Joseph h 27 Bourne
Hume E Maude h 366 County
" Ida Mrs h 182 Arnold
Humphrey Daniel J day housekeeper police station 2 h 212 Fourth
" Harry J fish 253 Purchase h 456 Mill [h 807 Kempton
" Horace L watchmaker 2 Purchase
" James L died Sept 14 1910
" James L Jr wholesale butter 95-97 Front h 2 Clinton place
" John floorwalker 40 Purchase b 21 Fifth [Shawmut av
" Margaret M widow Daniel b 43
" Samuel yarn packer b 850 First
" William floor walker 40 Purchase b 21 Fifth [dale av
" William H salesman h 860 Rock-
Humphries George painter bds 688 Purchase [Acushnet av
Hunniman Bertram C clerk bds 1140
Hunt Albert E city laborer h 144 Division
" Carrie J teacher H M Knowlton school h 147 Maxfield [h do
" Charles R physician 474 County
" Clifford E receiving teller N B I for Savings h 13 Arch
" Edward W tailor 137 Union h 96 Willis
" Edwin fisherman h 518 Kempton
" Edwin laborer h 290 Middle
" Fred florist's assistant 327 Coffin av b 110 Hathaway
" Fred E gardener h 244 Tinkham
" Frederick W b 47 Hillman
" Grace E clerk High school b 147 Maxfield
" Hannah B h 33 Sherman
" Ivah M clerk 394 Merchants Bank bldg b 30 Chestnut
" James laborer b 644 Purchase

BONNEY, FOLSTER & CO.,
The North End's Shopping Centre
Dry Goods and Men's Furnishings
945-947 Acushnet Ave., New Bedford, Mass.

Hunt
" James H drillworker b 71 Hall
" Jessie nurse rms 256 Union
" Josiah treas City Coal Co h 165 Maple
" Julia A masseuse h 30 Chestnut
" Myra L seamstress h 499 Purchase
" Patrick overseer h 203 Weld
" Raymond Z clerk b 30 Chestnut
" Robert weaver h 119 Hathaway
" Walter S gas fitter 125 Middle h 109 South
" William carpenter h 216 Fourth
" William J carpenter h 216 Fourth
Hunter Ellen dressmaker 55 N Sixth b do [County
" Florence A clerk 201 Union b 175
" Henry D liquors 56 Weld h 54 do [County
" Isabella widow George W h 175
" Janet sub teacher public schools b 55 N Sixth
" Joseph laborer bds 7 Cornell pl
" Lillian G teacher Harrington school b 162 Campbell
" Lucy M cashier b 175 County
" Margaret widow Charles E operative h 7 Holly [tle ct
" Michael painter 14 Jean h 1 Bee-
" William h 155 Tallman
" William weaver b 236 N Front
" William H Jr evangelist h 173 County
" William J operative h 155 Tallman [Adams
Huntington Arthur operative h 13
Huntoon Ernest foreman Old Colony Box Co h Whitman [av b do
Huot Rudolph clerk 1972 Acushnet
Hurd Antoine h r 30 Allen
" Edward weaver b 41 Rivet
" Elizabeth widow Oliver h 561 Acushnet av [nell
" Frank grocer 26 Wing b 186 Grin-
" George L teamster b 561 Acushnet av
" Joseph teamster h 37 Maxfield
" William T driver b 561 Acushnet avenue
" see Huard [62 Ashland
Hurel Gustave editor 267 Sawyer h
Hurl Joseph copperworker h 610 Purchase [232 Sawyer
Hurley Agnes C clerk 185 Union b

Hurley
" Andrew C lunch 15 S Water h 392 Acushnet av
" Bessie h 2 Linden ct [chase
" Charlotte seamstress b 367 Pur-
" Cornelius laborer b 2 Washington av
HURLEY CORNELIUS F roofer 90 Beetle h 169 Merrimac See page 781 [b 43 Beetle
" C James engineer Bennett Mills
" Elizabeth J teacher William H Taylor school b 232 Sawyer
" Ellen A teacher Parker st school b 45 Smith
" Frances clerk b 232 Sawyer
" Hannah widow h 45 Smith
" James blacksmith 16 First rms 25 Mill
" Jeremiah laborer b 559 Cottage
" Michael J conductor h 172 Austin
" Michael J (McCarthy & Hurley) 346 Acushnet av h 49 Larch
" Patrick h 232 Sawyer [dar Grove
" Thomas F stone mason h 383 Ce-
" William H car starter U St Ry Co h 22 Borden [Water
" & Brady Co cotton brokers 62 N
" see Herlihy [chase h 41 Morgan
Hurll Charles W optician 23 Pur-
" Daniel brakeman h 109 Austin
" George P optician 23 Purchase h 240 Maxfield [land
Hurst George T spinner h 12 Cleve-
" John spinner h 13 Clark
" see Hirst
Hurwitz Ezekiel h 243 Acushnet av
" Levi pedlar h 86 Grinnell
" Samuel clothing 789 S Water h 592 S First
Hushon John spinner h 16 Division
" Thomas spinner h 84 Mosher
Hussey Caroline M B widow Peter h 190 Summer [Cottage
" Cabrels H helper 159 Mill h 309
" Charles M agent 133 Union h Moreland terrace [ving
" Elizabeth R widow George h 1 Irving
" Emily M b 1 Irving [46 State
" Fonshonetta H widow Frederick h
" George student b Moreland ter
" Vesta E nurse rms 149 Summer
" Wallace student rms Y M C A
Huston William h 155 Cottage

Painters Supplies Wall Papers Room Mouldings Ladders
M. P. B. Silva & Son BRUSHES
157 ACUSHNET AVENUE Both Phones NEW BEDFORD

Hutchings David wood Mosher near County h 214 Fourth [Fourth
" Walter clerk 14 N Second b 214
Hutchins Caroline A widow Stephen J h 316 Pleasant [h 15 Warren
Hutchinson Clarence A electrician
" Edith teacher Cedar Grove street school bds 116 Austin
" George (Robert Hutchinson & Son) and provisions 537 N Front h 550 do
" Henry S (H S Hutchinson & Co) and The R Beetle Estate h 59 Campbell
" H S & Co (Henry S Hutchinson) stationery 198-200 Union
" James F oiler U St Ry Co power station h 213 Chestnut [Boston
" Joseph loom fixer removed to
" Joseph machinist h 14 Beetle
" Louis J clerk 201 Union h 249 Arnold
" Robert b 116 Austin [116 Austin
" Robert C cigars 836 Purchase h
" Sarah J clerk b 116 Austin
" William machinist b 116 Austin
Hutt Harry C clerk 1 Purchase rms 1 Park place [avenue
Hutton John operative h 21 E French
Huxford Charles D h 51 Mt Pleasant
Hyde John A loom fixer b 92 County
" Josephine h 92 County
" Mary A widow George h 1285 Rockdale av [ushnet av h do
" Rose widow Jacob grocer 714 Ac-
Hyerpe Carl glass cutter bds 275½ County
Hyland John laborer h 20 George
" Michael stonecutter rms 781 Purchase [cutine
Hynes Edward A police h 60 Val-
" George laborer b 153 Arnold
" John laborer h 153 Arnold
" J Harry gardener b 153 Arnold
" Michael steam fitter b 63 Ash (N)
" Thomas W variety 79 Acushnet avenue h do
" William machinist b 153 Arnold
" see Hines

Ibertson Walter operative b 907 County [Village
Iddon Harry weaver h 9 Howland
Ide Smith M h 50 Page
IDEAL CREDIT CLOTHING HOUSE 7 Purchase See page 33
" Turkish Baths, N Front near Beetle
" Wet Wash Laundry 270 Kempton
Idle Hour Theatre 62 Acushnet av
Ilsley Ernest F plumber h 32 Ashley
Iltis Ernest operative h 34 Bentley
Imbrecht Jean weaver b 271 Shaw
Improved Wet Wash Laundry (John P Buckley) 409 Chancery
Ingalls Susan A Mrs h 74 Willis
Ingham Harry weaver h 42 Roosevelt
" John R mill hand h 86 Hathaway
" William h 52 Holly [man
Ingleson Thomas spinner h 118 Whit-
Ingram John operative b 79 Bowditch
Inman Grace D teacher Thomas Donaghy school b 11 Fifth
" Harry C conductor rms 6 Franklin [Franklin
" Rebecca H widow Edward rms 6
Inne Albert third hand h 101 Nye
" Louis operative h 190 Nash rd
International Correspondence Schools N B Agency 23 Clifford bldg
Intershaw Frank operative bds 103 Holly
Iredale William weaver h 32 Cove
Ireland James weaver b 1283 Acushnet av [av
" Louis weaver bds 1283 Acushnet
Irish Charles S h 270 Pleasant
" George O dentist 34 Purchase h at Fairhaven [W French av
Ironfield Joseph bricklayer h 116
Irons Benjamin C teamster 65 William
" Caroline Mrs b 10 W High
Ironside George operative h 15 Bentley [sion
Irvin Jeremiah loom fixer h 4 Divi-
Irving Catherine widow John J h 93 Willis
" James machinist b 93 Willis
" Lucile C teacher Abraham Lincoln school b 93 Willis
Irwin Eliza B widow Rev John h 76 County
" Emily b 716 County
" Gertrude nurse rms 321 Union
" Henry police h 60 Kenyon
" Henry Jr b 60 Kenyon
" James machinist h 320 Davis

Steiger-Dudgeon Co.
"The WOMAN'S Store."
Tel. Bell 82 & 83, Branches connecting all depts.
" " 160 For Office only. Auto. 1211
SUMPTIONS, ASSORTMENTS AT ALL TIMES OF DEPENDABLE DRY GOODS

Irwin
" James yard master Bennett Mill h 33 Cedar
" James A carpenter h 68 Pierce
" Ralph clerk 36 Purchase b 68 Pierce
" William weaver b 60 Kenyon
Isabell Arthur slasher h 1406 Acushnet av
" Arthur J third hand b 1406 Acu-[shnet av
" Eugene slasher h 60 Tallman
" Eustache hairdresser 1148 Acushnet av h 1733 do
" Frank W caulker b 36 Ash (S)
" George carpenter h 148 Central avenue
" Maria mill hand b 511 N Front
" Ovide printer b 1406 Acushnet av
" Philip spinner h 86 Mott [rd
Ise Victor mill hand h 126 Nash
Isherwood Alfred J clerk P O h 129 Ausitn [Cottage
" Alice M clerk 41 Purchase b 637
" Allisen A student b 129 Austin
" Arthur weaver b 135 Nye
" Elizabeth widow h 74 Penniman
" Harry weaver b 135 Nye
" Hilda M clerk Purchase b 637 Cottage [av
" James H fixer h 233 Acushnet
" James H Mrs boarding house 233 Acushnet av
" John bottler 69 Winsor h do
" John clerk h 637 Cottage
" John Jr student b 69 Winsor
" John A overseer Page Mfg Co h 850 First
" John H fixer h 287 Cedar
" John J weaver b 74 Penniman
" Nancy weaver b 128 Clark [pl
" Ralph R fireman b 26 Ashland
" Reuben weaver h 32 Myrtle
" Roland E sub letter carrier h 26 Ashland place [av
" Thomas weaver b 216 Shawmut
" Walter stonecutter h 778 Purchase
" William weaver b 74 Penniman
" William H fixer h 135 Nye
" William L bottler 69 Winsor b do
Isteva Joseph mill hand h 173 Coggeshall
Ivers Ella F h 448 County [Tallman
Ivey James A police station 5 h 154
" James A Jr sailor b 154 Tallman
Jabot John weaver h 845 Acushnet avenue [avenue
" Ludger weaver h 837 Acushnet
Jabott Hormidas lunch 265 Sawyer h 332 Sawyer [Cedar Grove
" Joseph clerk 265 Sawyer h 164
" Simon operative h 39 Hicks
Jabotte Alfred laborer b 107 Davis
" Alfred Jr laborer b 107 Davis
" Pierre laborer b 49 Phillips av
Jachemowicz William grocer h 47 Washburn [land Village
Jacinth Antone mill hand h 42 How-
" John h 71 Rockland
" John laborer h 71 Grape
" Jose laborer h 23 Mitchell
" Joseph at P Corp h 522 Bolton
" Joseph mill hand b 511 N Front
" Manuel laborer h 400 Orchard (S)
" Mary widow b 400 Orchard (S)
Jacintho Antone laborer h 20 E Merrimac
" Antone laborer h 21 Mitchell
" Antone laborer h r 154 N Second
" Frank fireman h 389 Rockdale av
" John gardener h Winterville rd cor Rockdale av
" Joseph farmer h Jacinto street
" Joseph operative b Winterville rd cor Rockdale av
" Joseph operative h 71 Rockland
" Manuel laborer h 36 Thompson
" Rose widow h 170 Division
" Tony painter b 71 Rockland
" William E helper 170 Purchase h Winterville rd cor Rockdale av
Jack Cornelius C machinist b 94 Allen [Bedford
" Rosetta widow Alexander h 25
Jackman Lucia asst 208 County bds do [Hamilton ct
Jackouvlitch John operative h 4
Jackson Abraham fixer h 194 Nash road
" Albert H shoemaker 170 Cedar h 157 Emerson (N) [av
" Alfred P fireman h 345 Coffin
" Ambrose F shademaker 36 Purchase b 89 Acushnet av
" Aurelia died April 3 1911
" Catherine Mrs h 89 Acushnet av
" Cynthia V h 294 Court
" Edgar M L variety 840 Kempton h 31 Summit [Maxfield
" Edgar W tailor 85 Cedar h 640
" Eliza A Mrs b 18 Ashley

PELEG H. SHERMAN 506 COUNTY ST.
FUNERAL DIRECTOR AND EMBALMER
OFFICE PHONES. Bell 690-13. Auto. 1305.
RESIDENCE PHONES. Bell 690-12. Auto. 1306.

Jackson
" Elizabeth widow Alfred B h 389 Hillman
" Ernest weaver h 522 Bolton
" Fergus removed from city
" Frank driver h 36 Jouvett
" Fred loom fixer h r 5 E French av
" Fred loom fixer h 137 Ashland
" Frederick P fireman h 7 Abbott
" George clerk 36 Purchase h 97 Fourth
" Harry grocer 96 Brock av h do
" Harry mill hand b 448 Rivet
" Herbert M clerk 1 Municipal bldg bds 1 Bedford
" Ivy weaver b 194 Nash road
" James overseer Gosnold Mills Co
" James E master mechanic Nonquitt Spinning Co h 93 Potomska
" James E mining engineer h 69 Russell [h 19 Hemlock
" James E overseer Gosnold Mill
" John bartender h 162 S Second
" John mule spiner h 48 Rivet
" John oiler h 26 Crapo
" John operative h 175 Richmond
" John B grocer 876 S Water h 878 do
" John P weaver h 26 Cleveland
" John R compositor b 369 Cottage
" Joseph removed from city
" Leonard operative b 59 Covell
" Manuel carpenter b 161 S Second
" Manuel laborer h 470 First
" Margaret widow h 93 Potomska
" Martha widow John h r 5 East French avenue [198 do
" Mary Alice variety 200 Smith h
" Richard helper 55 N Water h 95 Willis [ard h 99 Fair
" Robert linotype operator Stand-
" Robert weaver h 22 Collins [po
' Samuel mule spinner h 163 Cra-
" Sylvia h 148 Bedford
" T Williams music teacher 597 Maxfield h do
" William shoemaker b 362 Pleasant
" William J second hand b 369 Cottage [chase h do
Jacob Joseph dry goods 410 Pur-
" Julian laborer h 908 County
" Lewis operative h 87 Clifford
Jacobs Ellsworth C reserve police h 213 Middle [School
Jacobson Carl screw maker bds 96
" Joseph (Yamins & Jacobson) 701 S Water h 486 First
" Joseph M rabbi Hebrew Synagogue h 86 Grinnell [ette
Jacques Achille operative h 52 Col-
" Clara widow Simeon operative h 113 Tallman
' Eli removed from city [26 Bullard
" Elsie widow Simeon mill hand b
" Frank bds 908 County
" George spineer b 113 Tallman
" Joseph E mason h 298 Cedar
" Leopold carpenter b 52 Collette
" Victor lather b 52 Collette
" Victor weaver h 367 Sawyer
Jagedrieziski Jan operative h 16 Fulton court [h 76 Fourth
Jahn H August florist 290 Brock av
Jaillet Andre R carpenter and builder 51 Tallman h do
" Eustache fisherman h 118 Nash rd
" Jean B carpenter h 51 Tallman
Jalbert Frank X mechanical dentist 301 Times bldg h 224 Arnold
" Hormidas caterer b r 164 Cedar Grove
" Joseph fixer h 164 Cedar Grove
" Joseph operative b 56 Clark
" Louis carpenter h 157 Collette
" Louis clerk b r 164 Cedar Grove
" Malvina widow George h 56 Clark
" Simon weaver bds r 164 Cedar Grove [Bullard
Jamaba William copper worker h 141
James Agnes M teacher R C Ingraham school rms 39 Fifth
" Alfrd F engineer h 101 Maxfield
" Alfred S insurance rm 201 Merchants Bank bldg h 123 Clinton
" Alonzo J teamster bds 113 Court
" Arthur J laundry man 270 Acushnet avenue b 50 Cedar
" Bessie P widow Henry G seamstress 185 Union b 113 Court
" Clarence H asst treasurer 43 William h 181 Fourth
" Everett E operative b 45 Myrtle

COAL AND WOOD HAY AND STRAW
F. T. AKIN & COMPANY
WALNUT, COR. WATER, 84 PLEASANT ST., 25 WELD SQ.
129 COVE STREET WHF. FOOT OF COFFIN STREET

JAMES FRANKLIN E carpenter and builder 169 Clinton h 71 Arnold See back binding and page 761
" Henry B carpenter 169 Clinton h 21 Arch [dale av h do
" Henry E locksmith 1213 Rock-
" Herbert L carpenter h 45 Myrtle
" John operative b 103 Holly
" Joseph weaver h 309 Earle
" Martha J widow h 50 Cedar
" Percy C plumber 55 N Water h 133 Arnold
" Robert joiner b 203 Collette
" Susan F widow b 32 Bonney
" Thomas M & Co insurance 305 Merchants Bank bldg 97 William
" William E bookkeeper N B I for Savings h 80 Willis
Jameson Frederick piper h 129 Maxfield [den
" Harry A electrician h 43 Lin-
" John H light trimmer h 9 Mt Pleasant lane
" Sarah Mrs nurse h 426 Rivet
Jamieson Elmer operative b 52 Walnut [52 Walnut
" Humphrey I master mariner h
" Mark L master mariner bds 622 County [net av b 33 Hicks
Janak Jerome restaurant 919 Acush-
" Lydia widow Peter b 137 Cedar Grove [33 do
" Raimund variety 33 Hicks h r
Janell Catherine widow Charles F b 439 Union [Merrimac
" Henry F foreman st dept h 170
Janes Clyde N overseer Acushnet Mill Corp rms 35 Eighth
Janicoblas Marinos barber 306 Coggeshall [64 Pierce
Jansen Clara M widow Halvor M h
Janson C Alexander clerk 1301 Acushnet av b 103 Coffin av
" John M removed to Taunton
" Joseph C real estate h 103 Coffin av [net av h 119 Bullard
" Raymond druggist 1301 Acush-
Janvrin Emily widow Frank h 153 Florence
Jardin Manuel hairdresser 199 Coggeshall h 148 Belleville av
" Manuel mill hand h 90 Nash rd
Jardine John A (Gem Wet Wash Laundry) 18 Katharine h 15 do
Jardini Manuel operative h 90 Nash road [rms 93 School
Jarmain Charles cashier 99 Front
Jaros Peter furniture mover h 22 Washburn
Jarry Delphis fixer h 265 N Front
JARRY DOMINICK J bakery 107 Bowditch h 109 do See page 25
" Edmire widow Julien b 88 Earle
" Frederick overseer Butler Mill h 49 Nye
" Henry weaver b 24 Nye
" Jean B carder h 88 Earle
" John weaver h 25 Nye
" Odilon h 51 Nye
" P Damien (Pease & Dandurand) 913 S Water. h 102 Brock av
" Thomas fixer b 265 N Front
Jarvais Jerry mill hand h 270 Tinkham [ond
Jarvis Edward speeder h 511 S Sec-
" Ernest laborer b 563 N Front
Jasmin Oclide D clerk 929 Acushnet av h r 874 County
Jason Alonzo V master mechanic 51 Bedford h 111 Seventh
" Alonzo V Jr plumber h 74 Spruce
" Antone laborer h 152 Thompson
" Chester H electrician b 111 Seventh [b 111 Seventh
" Cora M teacher Harrington school
" Dora M teacher Harrington school b 111 Seventh
" Ethel M bookkeeper 133 Acushnet av b 146 do
" Frank E carpenter h 305 Allen
" Fred L carpenter h 62 Bedford
" George mill hand b 14 Acushnet avenue [111 Seventh
" Harry H electrician 100 Fifth b
" John A hairdresser 533 S Water h 30 Thompson
" Joseph at P Corp b 125 Fair
" Joseph mill hand h 400 First
" Manuel operative h 62 Briggs
" Margaret Mrs sewer 40 Purchase b 120 Grinnell [111 Seventh
" May B teacher First st school b
" William weaver h 125 Fair
Jata Jan mill hand b 108 Phillips av

Don't dream of what you are going to do! Go and do it.
Kinyon's Short-hand School
Odd Fellows Bldg., Cor. William and Pleasant Sts., New Bedford, Mass.

Jay Elizabeth L dressmaker 95 School h do [shnet av h do
Jean Arthur L dentist 1462 Acu-
" Cedulie mill hand b 10 Bullard
" Eva L clerk Registry of Deeds b 1035 Acushnet av
" Jean B (George H York & Co) insurance and real estate h 1305 Acushnet av
" Louis (Read & Co) 141 Union h 662 County [isbury
Jeannenot Alphonse weaver b 17 Sal-
Jefferson Edmond baker b 162 State
" John T blacksmith h 162 State
" Joseph P driver 285 Acushnet av h 197 Elm
" Paul teamster rms 422 Purchase
Jeffrey Arthur millwright h 49 Thompson
" Emil speeder tender b 87 Rivet
" Ephraim student b 87 Rivet
" Robert baker b 87 Rivet [Rivet
" Xavier engineer city yard h 87
Jeffries Peter T machinist h 203 Eugenia [h 176 do
Jeglinski Frank grocer 159 N Front
Jemery Edward mill hand b 98 Collette [Orchard (S)
Jemphrev Robert mill hand b 374
Jenard Joseph fixer h 14 Holly
Jenckes William H supt Nonquitt Spinning Co rms 248 Pleasant
Jendreau Siffroid T h 3 Desautels
Jenesky Jake student h 88 Kenyon
" Rena widow h 88 Kenyon
Jenison Anna E clerk T N B C Co b 190 Kempton [190 Kempton
" F Myra clerk Wamsutta Mill b
" Joseph G carpenter h 190 Kempton [Union b 73 Liberty
Jenkins Ella F Mrs seamstress 185
JENKINS ELMIR A painter 431 Acushnet av h 63 Mill See page 752
" Emily E widow William h 189 Park
" Frank paving cutter h 28 Reynolds [428 Chancery
" Frank M optician 64 Pleasant h
" Harry E driver 437 Purchase bds 189 Park [I
" H Elton removed to Providence R

Jenkins
" Lester I linotype operator Times bds 63 Mill
" Nellie M widow James h 48 Cedar
" Samuel H clerk 6 W French av h 48 Briggs [Pleasant
" Thomas H gardener h 281 Mt
" Walter glass cutter h 156 Fourth
" William G machinist b 189 Park
" William L supt Bennett Mill h 115 Coggeshall [Collette
Jenkinson William spinner h 279
Jenks Albert T clerk 98 Allen h 96 Bonney [(W)
" Andrew F chauffeur h 537 Elm
" Elizabeth H Mrs dressmaker 96 Bonney h do
" Florence M teacher R C Ingraham school b 96 Bonney [er
" George E drill maker b 121 Park-
" William supt rms 248 Pleasant
" William M clerk 152 Arnold h 121 Parker [rms 148 Maxfield
Jenness Peter H mgr 82 Purchase
Jenney Alice E Mrs teacher H A Kempton school h 43 Locust
" Asa W freight conductor h 89 Shawmut avenue
" Benjamin F h 43 Arch
" Bertha E teacher Thompson street school b 65 Fifth
" Charles engineer h 89 Potomska
" Charles B machinist h 291 Middle
" Charles C machinist h 37 Bay
" Charles W shoemaker h 180 Austin [h 65 Fifth
" Clara B widow Clarence T
" Clarence P machinist h 43 Locust
" Edmund R boats to let foot Grinnell b 174 Fourth [fee
" Edward copper worker h 67 Dur-
" Eliza widow Lyman L rms 43 Fifth
" Elsie bds 37 Bay
" Emily E widow Charles H b 119 Court [net av h 30 Walnut
" Ethel W Mrs variety 264 Acush-
" Eunice widow Nathaniel h 1811 Acushnet avenue [180 Austin
" Eva H bookkeeper 140 Purchase b
" Fannie L Mrs h 29 Durfee
" Frances C Mrs h 234 Allen
" George shipping clerk 81 Front h at Fairhaven [116 Chestnut
" Georgianna widow Frederick h

HASKELL BROS. DEALERS IN
ICE
400 COURT STREET TELEPHONE CONNECTION NEW BEDFORD, MASS.

Jenney
" Harrison S clerk 100 Fifth b 170 Grinnell [Campbell
" Harry C supt E E T & Co h 17
" Henry P real estate 1799 Acushnet av h do [Grinnell
" H A Miss clerk 10 Fifth b 170
" Irving H foreman 100 Fifth h 7 Clay
" John teamster b 48 Parker
" John B W screw maker b 62 Bedford [h at Fairhaven
" Joseph J cooper Standard Oil Co
" Julia A widow Edward P A b 326 Cedar
" Lenora C clerk P Corp b 65 Fifth
" Lester W (Perry, Jenney & Potter) 57 William h at Mattapoisett
" Louis machinist h 129 Perry
" Lydia P stenographer b 37 Bay
" Mary A widow Jeptha h 40 Hazard
" Mary A widow John P h 556 County [Kempton
" Mary E widow Perry P h 151
" May B widow Zachariah F h 65 Summer [field
" Nathan G bookkeeper h 233 Max-
" Nathaniel H h 1811 Acushnet av
" Perry P & Son (Walter A Jenney) hardware 146 Pleasant
" Phoebe A widow Pardon W h 62 Bedford [Chestnut
" Susan A widow Ezra T h 69
" Walter A (Perry P Jenney & Son) h 151 Kempton
" Walter F grocer 138 Washington h 95 do [170 Grinnell
" William A clerk 57 N Second b
" William B h 174 Grinnell
" William S clerk 2177 Acushnet av h at Acushnet
" William S marine supplies Merrills wharf h 30 Walnut
" William T bookkeeper 84 Union h 170 Grinnell
Jennings Addie H widow William A furniture mover 73 Shawmut avenue h do
" Anna L h 74 Sycamore
" Arthur driver 47 School h 26 Peckham [467 Mill
" Arthur H salesman 97 Front h

Jennings
" Bernard driver 149 Purchase b 61 Merrimac [len
" Betsey widow Joseph I h 81 Al-
" Charles E h 12 Reynolds
" Charles F carpenter h 152 North
" Charles H janitor h 324 Kempton [h 38 Beech
" Charles S driver 270 Acushnet av
" Clark H salesman 97 Front h 357 Reed [av b 570 Purchase
" Constant L grocer 1645 Acushnet
" Cora widow Frederick b 283 Cedar
" David mason h 190 Campbell
" David P h 71 Rotch
" Edward F removed from city
" Edward H mgr 22 William h 300 Allen [court
" Edward R teamster b 1 Jennings
" Ellen widow Alfred h 105 Hathaway [h 676 County
" Ernest A vice pres 36 Purchase
" Ethel L stenographer 1 Masonic bldg b 304 County [mac
" Francis shoeworker b 61 Merri-
" Frank C clerk b 81 Allen
" Frank E machinist h 45 Bay [ct
" Frank M machinist h 1 Jennings
" Frederick T clerk b 304 County
" Frederick W shipper 182 Union h 304 County [h 215 Fourth
" George L foreman 350 S Second
" Gerald second hand h 49 Acushnet av
" Gilbert M mason h 75 Forest
" Gilbert M Jr asst inspector buildings 307 Municipal bldg h 459 Allen [Reed
" Harrie B clerk 84 Union h 349
" James oiler h 61 Merrimac
" James P 3rd hand h 366 Cedar Grove [Rockland
" Jireh P drill inspector h r 52
" John decorator rms 60 N Second
" John W watchman h 300 Allen
" Latham T mason h 104 Ash (N)
" Lewis S died Mar 2 1911
" Lucy T Mrs clerk 3 Pleasant h 304 County
" L Alexander h 55 Park
" Mabelle W 304 County
" Martin operative h 131 Tallman

J. F. CROSSLEY 223 MILL STREET COR. EMERSON PHONE
STEAM and HOT WATER HEATING
GAS FITTING and FIXTURES

Jennings
" Minnie H dressmaker b 145 Kempton
" Nathan J foreman h 23 Sycamore
" Perry L clerk 218 Union b 71 Rotch
" Ralph A clerk Denison Bros Co [h 220 Brownell
" Samuel W foreman machinist 42 Front h 111 Florence
" Sophia W widow Stephen W h 145 Kempton
" Stephen W clerk bds 145 Kempton
" Thomas laborer rms 32 Elm
" William A died May 2 1911
" William E clerk 165 Purchase h 33 Parker
" William H machinist h 33 Parker
" William H treas 100 S Water h 116 Cottage
Jensky Antony mill hand h 1 Hampton court
Jepson Alfred fixer h 67 Dean
" Anna widow James H b 67 Dean
" Frank weaver h 311 Coffin av
" George E drillmaker h 311 Summer
" James W dressmaker b 126 Eugenia
" J Willis foreman 100 Fifth h 197 Campbell
Jereau Omar shoemaker b 125 N Front
Jermaine Gibbs mill hand h 27 Washburn
Jernegan Walter S physician 28 Fifth bds do
Jerome Antone laborer h Winterville road
" Joseph mill hand h 658 S Water
Jerrauld Maurice removed to Providence R I
Jesse Joseph laborer rms 66 N Second
Jessie Manuel overseer Gosnold Mills Co h 287 Rivet
Jesuit Norman weaver rms 54 Holly
Jesus Henry J cook h 7 Bethel
" Joaquim grocer 99 Potomska h 104 do
" John A painter b 71 Delano
" Maria A widow August h 109 Davis
" Philemon h 162 Cedar Grove
" Vincent removed to Dartmouth
Jette Alfred W removed from city
" Joseph carder h 109 Brook
" Napoleon mgr 485 N Front h 188 Weld
" Peter teamster 27 Bowditch b 889 Purchase
Jewell Clement operative b 86 Beetle
Jewett Charles A mgr (Jonathan Handy Co) 28 William h 80 Bay
JEWETT HARDWARE CO (William N Jewett) 108 Middle and 415 Acushnet avenue See page 784
" Nelson E machinist h 313 Orchard (S)
" William N (Jewett Hardware Co) 108 Middle h 220 Grinnell
Jilo Cosmo C laborer h 103 Thompson
Jirasco Frank weaver h 174 Bowditch
Joaquim Joseph P weaver h 22 Acushnet av
Joaquina Mary widow h r 308 S Front
Jobin Edbt widow h 485 S Front
Jock John painter b 63 Mechanics lane
" Joseph E brakeman h 543 Acushnet av
Jodoin John fixer h 48 Nelson
" Joseph weaver h 20 La France court
" Matilda dressmaker bds 53 Reynolds
" Napoleon carder b 53 Reynolds
" Phileas fixer h 51 Tallman
" Phileas Jr weaver b 51 Tallman
" Rosanna widow Joseph h 53 Reynolds
Johanson Oscar shade maker 170 Purchase b 8 Shawmut av
John George laborer h 5 Hillman st ct
" Hancock Mutual Life Insurance Co Times bldg rms 401-407
" Joseph laborer b 126 Cedar Grove
" Manuel driver 368 Acushnet av h South Water
Johns Annie L widow George h 130 Purchase
" Charles A glass cutter h 64 Mechanics lane
" William A waiter h 58 Hazard
Johnsen Oscar E janitor N B T school h 121 Sycamore
Johnson Albert C drill worker h 16 Bedford
" Albert G paper ruler b 283 Court
" Albert J porter Parker House h 157 Cedar
" Albert L eyelet painter h 188 Elm
" Albert M drill worker h 4 Waverly
" Albion C foreman st dept h 46 Page
" Alex spinner h 344 Pleasant
" Alfred J janitor h 204 Arnold
" Alvin carpenter rms 279 Pleasant

CHARLES A. CROSHERE CARRIAGE AND AUTO
38 FOURTH ST. Bell Phone 1964-23 **PAINTING**

Johnson
" Andrew H electrician h 430 Pleasant [Front
" Andrew W weaver h 236 North
" Annie F widow William P h 124 Collette
" Arthur bds 228 Smith
" Arthur blacksmith b 748 First
" Arthur mill hand b 75 Hathaway
" Arthur teamster rms 7 N Second
" Benjamin S driver 16 N Second b 268 Arnold [Arnold
" Benjamin W eyelet maker h 268
" Bertha A clerk Registry of Deeds b 8 Franklin [Dartmouth
" Carl grinder 190 Purchase b 41
" Carl razor maker b 72 Chancery
" Carl tool maker h 41 Bank
" Carl A carpet upholsterer 170 Purchase h 8 Shawmut avenue
" Caroline widow E Oscar h 36 Keene [ushnet av
" Carrie T widow Beriah b 289 Ac-
" Charles painter h 62 Summer
" Charles A gardener b 219 Arnold
" Charles A machinist h 129 Bonney
" Charles C painter 201 Park h do
" Charles L drill worker b 50 S Second [net avenue
" Charles P carpenter h 489 Acush-
" Charles W engraver b 320 Union
" Charles W inspector h 105 Tremont [ushnet av
" Chester H glass cutter b 289 Ac-
" Edgar F wood worker h 143 Cedar
" Edmund gardener h 92 Robeson
" Edward shoemaker b 268 Arnold
" Edward C clerk 98 Purchase b 36 Keene [159 Bowditch
" Edward W molder 229 N Water h
" Edwin spinner h 8 Franklin [tle
" Edwin R pipe coverer h 76 Myr-
" Emery hostler b 105 Tremont
" Emil A gardener h 32 Liberty
" Erick St J physician 271 Union rms do
" Ernest carder h 87 Hathaway
" Ernie J molder b 159 Bowditch
" Frances E Mrs h 395 Hillman
" Francis H driver h 222 State
" Francis O gardener h 69 Park
" Frank E drill maker b 36 Keene
" Fred shoemaker h 338 Pleasant

Johnson
" George operative h 75 Hathaway [lawn av
" George second hand h 40 Wood-
" George waiter rms 7 N Second
" George A telephone operator Hawes Tewksbury & Co h at Fairhaven
" Gilford second hand h 1 Baylies
" Grace L nurse bds 201 Park
" Gustave A machinist h 113 Bonney [230 Union
" Harold waiter Parker House rms
" Harry driver b 404 Pleasant
" Harry police station 5 h 43 Adams [h 239 Cedar
" Harry B clerk 60 Shawmut av
" Henry L driver city yard h 544 Cottage
" Horace C pilot h 75 Locust
" Horatio H waiter 224½ Union b 320 do [ant
" James W operative b 344 Pleas-
" Jennie h 83 Atlantic
" John h 53 Locust
" John driver b 1537 Acushnet av
" John laborer h 359 Coggeshall
" John third hand h 16 Covell
" John A gardener 427 County h 220 Union
" John A machinist b 96 S Sixth
" John A Jr chauffeur 163 Hawthorn h 17 Atlantic
" John F teamster 64 Dartmouth **h 9 Spooner** [Front
" Joseph cementworker h 505 N
" Joseph E molder 229 N Water
" Joseph S chair reseater 28 Crapo h do [Florence
" Josephine widow William T h 127
" Joshua B city chauffeur h 217 Smith [h 133 Cedar
" Laura Mrs clerk 347 Kempton
" Laura L dressmaker 50 Mill b do
" Leonard supt Page Mfg Co h 15 Tremont [Ward
" Leonard E clerk 98 Allen h 62
" Levi R foreman h 39 Locust
" Lillian A telephone operator 57 N Second b 62 Summer
" Lizzie widow Willis b 157 Chancery [ker
" Luen M motorman b 102 Par-
" Maria K widow Charles h 100 Morgan

J. G. NICHOLSON
LUMBER, SASH, DOORS and BLINDS
BOWDITCH STREET, NEW BEDFORD, MASS.

Johnson
" Martin oiler h 50 S Second
" Martin removed from city
" Mary widow James h 219 Arnold
" Mary widow William b 43 Adams
" Mary F Mrs chiropodist 161 Middle h do
" Myra A compositor 38 N Second b 100 Morgan
" Nancy M teacher Thompson st school b 544 Cottage
" Nancy M widow Charles J h 544 Cottage
" Nathan T machinist b 28 Crapo
" Nellie h 56 First
" Onslow C wireman U St Ry Co h r 893 County
" Ophelia widow Charles h r 269 Middle
" Oscar clerk 68 Adams b Keen st
" Oscar L head lineman 57 N Second h 97 James
" Petrina widow Carl b 35 Myrtle
" P H Mrs removed to Fall River
" Robert bookkeeper b 27 E French av
" Robert carpenter b 7 Babbitt
" Robert laborer h 516 Maxfield
" Robert I switchman h 2 Hillman street court
" Samuel laborer h 49 Roosevelt
" Samuel F machinist b 81 Myrtle
" Sarah C widow William H h 208 Smith
" Severance operative h 99 N Front
" Spiros clerk 1091 Acushnet av b 359 Coggeshall
" Sylvia A S h 520 Maxfield
" Thomas drillworker b 211 S Second
" Thomas glassworker h 88 Belleville rd
" Thomas H drillworker h 211 S Second
" Thomas P boxmaker h 367 Earle
" Uriah F gardener 325 Hillman b 268 Arnold
" Walter W clerk Mer Nat Bank b 75 Locust
" William gardener 178 Hawthorn b 219 Arnold
" William operative h 15 Bentley
" William B artist h 207 Middle
" William H spinner h 60 Howard
" William T died Jan 17 1911
Johnston Kate E widow Harry E h 20 Jenney
Jolicoeur Emily widow Peter bds 94 County
" Louis painter h 18 Linden
Joly Alfred carpenter h 113 Eugenia
" David carpenter h 954 S Water
" Gilbert carpenter h 954 S Water
" Stanislas laborer h 39 Dean
" Victor carpenter b 954 S Water
Jones Abner I foreman 18 Market rms 6 Dover
" Adelaide I widow Alexander h 29 Summit
" Albert engineer h 44 Mt Vernon
" Alexander J (A Jones & Co) h 88 Briggs
" Anna widow David C h 31 Fifth
" Annie P music teacher 31 Fifth b do
" Arthur weaver h 47½ Bowditch
" Arthur H capt of police 9 S Second h 49 Morgan
" Arthur W conductor b 131 Clark
" A & Co (Alexander J Jones) plumbers 15 Division
" Belle M bookkeeper 1112 Acushnet av
" Benjamin porter 84 Union h 11 Chestnut
" Benjamin W gardener h 67 Shawmut av
" Carolyn S teacher Sylvia Ann Howland school b 49 Morgan
" Cecelia h 71 S Second
" Charles teamster rms 110 Middle
" Charles E baker h 194 Arnold
" Charles F toymaker h 15 Mill
" Charles F F cashier 125 Middle h 64 Borden
" Charles L teamster h 615 Elm
" Charles W (Jones & Dodge) h 66 Mill
" Clarence E musician h 50 Ash (N)
" Clarence S painter b 417 Hillman
" Edward T teamster h 523 Acushnet av
" Edward W driver 65 William b 269 Middle
" Edward W Mrs h 189 Elm
" Elliot F hostler h 76 Maxfield
" Ernest clerk general delivery P O h 121 Austin
" E Frank variety 382 Kempton rms do
" Francis F student b 64 Borden
" Fred porter 81 Front h 6 Bethel
" Frederick N laborer h 16 W High
" George barber rms 167 Cedar
" George mill hand rms 15 Glover
" George E operative h 204 Nash road
" George H musician b 48 Oak

Steiger-Dudgeon Co.
"The WOMAN'S Store."
Tel. Bell 82 & 83, Branches connecting all depts.
" " 160 For Office only. Auto. 1211

SUMPTIONS, ASSORTMENTS AT ALL TIMES OF DEPENDABLE DRY GOODS

Jones
" Herbert F laborer 144 S Water h 77 Fruit
" Herbert L h 67 S Sixth
" Herbert O asst cashier 120 Purchase rm 403 b 91 School
" Ida roller coverer b 19 Homer
" Isabella I dressmaker 185 Union b 319 Maxfield [29 Potter
" James H supt Wamsutta Mill h
" Jane Mrs housekeeper 154 Tinkham b do [(W)
" John B teamster b 380 Middle
" John C b 179 Ashland [53 Cedar
" John H clerk 28 Purchase rms
" Jonathan insurance agent 37 Purchase rm 23 h 179 Ashland [401 h 122 Bedford
" J Edwin supt 120 Purchase rm
" J Robert weaver b 83 Dunbar
" Lavinia widow Thomas H h 53 Cedar [305 Middle
" Mary E widow William H h
" Mary L widow Edward C h 396 County
" Patrick A removed from city
" Philip horses 13 Elm h 15 do
" Philip E glasscutter h 48 Oak
" Philip H salesman 145 Arnold b 48 Oak
" Richard oiler bds 12 Cleveland
" Sarah A widow Benjamin bds 6 Jenney
" Sarah E housekeeper 35 Eighth
" Selina widow John h 83 Dunbar
" Susan R Mrs bds 486 Cottage
" Thomas engineer wax works h 6 Felton
" Thomas painter h 441 Rivet
" William millinery 956 S Water h 33 Buttonwood
" William plumber h 319 Sawyer
" William teamster Anthony Swift & Co h Cottage street
" William C b 164 North
JONES & DODGE (C W Jones and George J Dodge) carpenters 202 North Water See page 764
Jongleux Louis glasscutter h 428 Elm (W) [Blackburn
Jordan Andrew stonecutter h 11
" Flora I b 200 Elm
" Harry fireman h 67 Emma
" Henry machinist h 55 Potomska

Jordan
" John laborer rms 282 Cottage
" John B fixer h 38 W French av
" Joseph E driver 70 Union h 37 Maxfield
" Josephine h 437 Acushnet av
" Lawrence A operative b 163 Emerson (N) [Emerson (N)
" Lawrence F city laborer h 163
" Margaret widow David h 153 Hathaway [shnet av
" Michael J brick layer h 658 Acu-
" Ruby E clerk 68 Cove b 66 do
" Sarah E H Mrs clerk 185 Union h at Fairhaven [Chestnut
" William S horseshoer h 239
Jordanis Joseph laborer b 106 Whitman
" Philip fixer h 106 Whitman
Jose Frank operative h 390½ S Second [field
Joseph Aaron C painter h 488 Max-
" Anna Mrs b 464 S Second
" Antonio laborer h 42 Thompson
" Antonio seaman h 95 First
" Bertha clerk 182 Union bds 8 Spooner [Cedar Grove
" B (Farras & Joseph) h 216
" Charles drillmaker h 97 S Sixth
" Charles fish 108 Larch h 112 do
" Frank bartender 166 Coffin av h 241 S Front [194 Bonney
" Fred C clerk 187 Acushnet av b
" Frederick silver caster h 194 Bonney [Front
" George fruit 11 Cotter h 176 N
" Helen (John & Helen Joseph) 666 S Water h 664 do
" Henry tailor b 280 Allen
" Ira S laborer h 456 Maxfield
" John b 16 Richmond
" John (John & Helen Joseph) 666 S Water h 664 do
" John laborer h 173 Florence
" John teamster h 184 Thompson
" John & Helen grocers 666 S Water
" John Jr clerk 666 S Water b do
" John E clerk 131 Acushnet av h 97 S Sixth
" Manuel conductor b 206 Rockland
" Manuel laborer h 71 Delano
" Manuel laborer h 79 Hemlock
" Mary widow h 30 Kane [Fourth
" Mary B widow Manuel h 213

PELEG H. SHERMAN 506 COUNTY ST.
FUNERAL DIRECTOR AND EMBALMER
OFFICE PHONES. Bell 690-12. Auto. 1305.
RESIDENCE PHONES. Bell 690-12. Auto. 1306.

Jordan
" Mary W widow Manuel h 280 Allen [83 Crapo
" Nassar (N Joseph & Bros) h
" N & Bros (Nassar & Peter) dry goods 259 Rivet [Crapo
" Peter (N Joseph & Bros) h 83
" Peter grocer h 250 Coggeshall
" Peter weaver h 53 Ashley [chase
Joubert Charles laborer b 863 Pur-
" Frederick teamster h 23 Highland
Jourdain Anna E widow Anthony G Jr dressmaker 279 Arnold h do [10 h 279 Arnold
" Edwin B lawyer 49 William rm
" John fixer h 125 Cove
" Kate P B Mrs hairworker 6½ Fifth h do [232 Acushnet av
Jouvette May clerk 70 Purchase bds
" Sarah E D h 119 Fifth
" Thomas L shipping clerk h 232 Acushnet av [92 Earle
Jouvin Charles chimney builder bds
" George mason h 92 Earle
" Joseph doffer b 184 Sawyer
" Jules third hand b 92 Earle
Jowett Ivy clerk 474 Acushnet av b 69 Walden
" Ralph comb fixer h 69 Walden
Joyal Azilda mill hand b 20 Holly
Joyce John E clerk 184 Fourth bds 95 County [den
" John T car conductor h r 77 Lin-
" Mary Mrs speeder tender h 476 S Second
" Michael spinner h 95 County
" Michael A clerk bds 95 County
" Patrick spinner h 204 N Front
" Patrick J liquors 98 S Water h 187 Crapo [Mt Pleasant
Jubenville Blanche clerk, bds 152
" Charles furniture 961 Acushnet av h 152 Mt Pleasant
" Damien speeder b 60 Tallman
Judd Emery S freight and passenger agent foot Willis h 94 Hillman
" James W second hand h 51 Norman [h 184 Campbell
Judge John F engineer 303 Purchase
" Louise clerk b 184 Campbell
Judson Abbie widow George J h 603 Cottage [Village
" Barrett loom fixer h 22 Howland

Judson
" Bros (Howard G and David W) carpenters and builders 50 Locust [Locust
" David W (Judson Bros) h 50
" Delia M b 50 Locust [mut av
" Edwin T drillmaker h 232 Shaw-
" Ezra A carpenter h 107 Durfee
" Frank A carpenter 18 W Willow h do
" George J died Dec 19 1910
" George W carpenter b 109 Willis
" Howard G (Judson Bros) carpenter 50 Locust h at Padanaram
Jukes Wilfred weaver h 15 Ruth
Jules Frank mill hand h 672 S Water
Julia Maglina widow h 103 Acushnet av
Julien Alice h 254 Purchase
" Matthew C Rev pastor Trinitarian Congregational church h 37 Fifth
Jump James spinner h 31 Juniper
Junier James weaver b 70 Acushnet avenue [shnet avenue
" Leonard boss comber h 70 Acu-
" William weaver b 70 Acushnet avenue [47 Washburn
Jurczykowski Kostonti operative h
Jussaume Aime b 269 Coggeshall
" Alderic weaver h 18 Washburn
" Arthur weaver b 18 Washburn
" Dennis weaver h 18 Washburn
" Joseph clerk 305 N Front h 269 Coggeshall
" Oliva clerk bds 18 Washburn
" Oliva provisions 305 N Front b 171 Bowditch
Justly Manuel S machinist h 91 Durfee [lette
Jutras Simeon mill hand rms 89 Col-
Jymm William shoemaker 76 Purchase

Kabels Lesannio removed from city
Kahler Carl A H mgr 23 Clifford bldg rms 175 William
Kaliff Albert salesman b 8 Delano
" Jacob mgr h 8 Delano [shnet av
Kalinsky Samuel pedlar h 152 Acu-
Kalisch Antone drillmaker h 146 Bullard
" Frank clerk b 136 Nye
" John weaver h 136 Nye

PAINTERS' SUPPLIES
Walnut, Cor. Water, 84 Pleasant St. 25 WELD SQ., 129 COVE ST.
F. T. AKIN & COMPANY

Kalish Cotilda clerk 48 Pleasant h 1264 Acushnet av [av
" Mary mill hand h 1264 Acushnet
" Peter h 63 Holly
Kalısz Mikolaiz bartender h 189 N Front [Belleville av
Kalita Michel mill hand bds 325
Kallınger Henry weaver h 17 Princeton av [Davis
Kamber Sahule mill hand bds 54
Kamel George laborer h 5 Campbell
Kamionek Tomon operative h 197 N Front [Water rms 271 Union
Kammerer Edward P cotton 29 N
Kane Catherine and Margaret h 244 State [Borden
" Charles florist 49 Cottage b 32
" Charles H h 32 Borden
" Eugene F shoemaker h 40 Vine
" Felix driver 100 S Water h 193 Chancery
" George weaver b 820 First
" Helen C b 275 County
" Helen E h 397 Union [lette
" James L second hand b 237 Col-
" James T mason h 77 Fifth
" James V second hand h 67 Lindsey [Co h 530 Cottage
" James W foreman T-N B Copper
" John A weaver b 89 Austin
" John B weaver h 820 S First
" John H asst foreman T-N B Copper Co h 58 Locust
" Lester A teamster h 384 Cottage
" Margaret widow John h 3 Waverly
" Martin laborer b 3 Waverly
" Michael porter rms 96 Middle
" Patrick bartender b 86 Myrtle
" Philip weaver b 820 First
" Sarah C h 127 Grinnell
" Thomas L laborer h 237 Collette
" William P baker b 32 Borden
Kansinski Stanislaus operative h 11 Clark
Kanuse Franklin h 141 Church
Kaplan Abraham dry goods 731 S Water h 490 First
" Abraham Mrs shoe repairer 148 Thompson h 500 S Water
" Davids waiter b 327 S Water
" Jacob removed from city

Kaplan
" Joseph shoes 463 and 327 S Water h do [do
" Morris clerk 463 S Water b 327
" Samuel pedlar h 486 First
" William J h 490 First
Kapler Stephen weaver b 156 Holly
Kapopovolos Apostelos fruit h 359 Coggeshall [ard
Karand Louis operative h 24 How-
Karcher Abbie widow Herman b 179 Fourth
" Frederick h 22 Dartmouth
" Frederick Jr police h 35 Hollyhock [Fourth
" Herman L glasscutter h 179
Karelcas Charles fruit h 361 Coggeshall [man
Kares Venzel weaver h 136 Tall-
Karfer Voycher carder h 20 Washburn [Phillips av
Karkowcki Joseph mill hand h 108
Karl Annie removed to Boston
" Frederick shoemaker h 21 Homer
" Hironimus shoemaker h 568 Union
" Joseph driver b 58 Pierce
" Walburga widow Joseph b 58 Pierce [cial
Karmarch Walenty weaver h 8 So-
Karmous Basil h 112 Phillips av
" Pasquale mason b 112 Phillips av
Karsem Husam mill hand b 54 Davis
Karsez Adam weaver h 529 S Second [av
Kasab Giril weaver h 57 Phillips
Kasinski Ignace operative h 7 Clark
" Stanislaus operative h 11 Clark
Kasmire Charles P h 359 County
" George F dept mgr 36 Purchase h at Freetown
" Philip S shoemaker b 359 County
Kataszewski Florien h 159 Cedar Grove
Kateon Margaret I teacher Abraham Lincoln school b 437 Union
Katsarakis Theodorus hairdresser 251 Coggeshall and 1744 Acushnet av h 1042 do
Katzman Philip junk 94 Front h 332 S Second
Kaula Theresa died April 19 1911
Kava Felix operative h r 46 Washburn [1010
Kavanagh Cecile R died Nov 30

Bookkeeping, Shorthand, Typewriting, Penmanship, etc. Taught thoroughly at
Kinyon's Commercial School
Odd Fellows Bldg., Cor. William and Pleasant Sts., New Bedford, Mass.

Kavanagh
" Grace telephone operator 57 N Second b 335 Pleasant
" Patrick teamster h 5 North
" Susan h 293 County
" Thomas F telegraph operator R R depot h 335 Pleasant
Kavanaugh Joseph M compositor Pleasant cor Mill b 224 Pleasant [224 Pleasant
" Leo F compositor Standard bds
" Martin F dancing teacher 96 William h 224 Pleasant
Kay Ada h 303 Brock av
" Charles teamster h 20 Peckham
" James spinner h 1031 County
" Margaret widow James h r 336 Davis
" Mary Mrs h 65 Kenyon
" Thomas spinner b 118 Hathaway
" see Key [road
Kaye Joseph carder b 147 Belleville
" Sarah A Mrs h 118 Hathaway
Kazinski Isidore operative h 23 Nye
Keach Horace W florist b 240 Chancery [cery
" Thomas R spinner h 240 Chan-
Kean Charles H clerk h 135 Willis
" Elizabeth M clerk 160 Purchase b 259 Weld
" Frederick fixer h 156 Division
Keane Albert W sporting editor Times h 127 Florence
" John F h 259 Weld
" John W laborer h 41 Wing
" William F linotype operator Times h 127 Florence
" see Kane and Keene [ton
Kearney Michael polisher h 465 Bol-
" Valentine student b 256 Cedar Grove [Grove
" William watchman h 265 Cedar
Kearns Thomas H cigars 218 Union
Kearsley William pres and general mgr N B Waste Co 58 Middle h at Acushnet [h 9 Warwick
Keating Margaret E and Nancy T
" Peter laborer h 273 S Front
" Thomas teamster 229 N Water rms 188 Elm [273 S Front
" Timothy P clerk 721 S Water b
Keavy Michael clerk 145 Union h 38 Borden
Keches George boot black 58 Pleasant [35 Acushnet av
Keck Conradina widow Leonard h
Keefe Martin laborer h 280 Cedar Grove [Maxfield
Keeble Charles shuttlemaker h 123
Keehn Herman died April 24 1911
" Phebe baker 913 Acushnet av h 300 Cedar Grove
" Robert b 300 Cedar Grove
" see Keene and Keen
Keelan Henry removed from city
" Mary Mrs weaver b 44 Salisbury
" Ruth Mrs h 187 Brock av
" Samuel carpenter b 187 Brock av
Keelty John copperworker h 65 Howard [457 Cottage
Keen Ann G widow Washington h
" Charles F cabinetmaker 17 Centre h 370 Cottage
" Charles F carpenter h 79 Locust
" Elizabeth C widow Franklin h 67 Parker [370 Cottage
" Etta M bookkeeper 11 N Sixth b
" Joseph W shoemaker b 237 Maxfield
" Leonard Jr h 39 Parker
" Sarah L clerk 160 Purchase bds 370 Cottage [237 Maxfield
" Tabathy G widow Obadiah h
" see Keene, Keehn and Keane
Keenan Ellen widow William h 150 Merrimac
" Thomas operative b 241 State
" Thomas watchman h 241 State
Keene Horace M engineer 45 School h 403 Cottage [net av h do
" Margaret fancy goods 69 Acush-
" see Keen, Kehn and Keane
Keeney Mary R Mrs h 33 Fifth
Keighley Walter plasterer h 87 Fruit
Keil Anna widow Frank H bds 75 Clark [County
" William A Mrs weaver h 954
Kein Mary A widow Andrew b 568 Union
Keith Allen P supt of public schools 166 William h 20 Locust
" Anna F bookkeeper 87 Union rms 29 Sycamore [school b 8 Ward
" Annie R teacher G H Dunbar
" Charles F Mrs dressmaker 55 Walnut b do
" Charles H baker 11 and 437 Purchase h at Brockton [60 Fifth
" Clayton E mgr 11 Purchase rms

Bread, Cake, Pastry
RICHMOND & COMPANY 255-257 UNION STREET
Bell 993 Automatic 1022

Keith
" Frederick A Jr salesman 36 Purchase h 77 Pierce
" Lucy K widow h 161 Maxfield
" Luke T foreman 8 Seneca h 6 Franklin
" Mary H died Mar 16 1911
" Otis M clerk 45 School h 139 North [(S)
" Peter C gardener h 35 Emerson
" William gardener h 8 Ward
" William H clerk 100 Fifth b 8 Ward [S Co b 300 Purchase
Kelleher Alice stenographer N B
" Daniel J (N B Printing Co) 25 N Second b 201 Pleasant
" Florence A b 300 Purchase
" Hubert S clerk 215 Purchase b 300 do
" John M druggist 513 County and 215 Purchase b 300 do [chase
" Mary A widow Daniel h 300 Pur-
" Oscar D mgr 315 County b 300 Purchase [h 215 Coffin av
" Thomas W bartender 503 N Front
Kelley Abbie M b 243 Maxfield
" Albert J eyeletworker h 564 County
" Anderson W mgr William F Nye Fish Island h at Fairhaven
" Andrew J cooper h r 112 Grinnell
" Arthur M electrician b 72 State
" Charles E cashier 14 N Sixth h 54 Tremont [net av
" Charles E laborer b 636 Acu-
" Charles H laborer h 208 Kempton
" Charles S (Sanford & Kelley) banker 20 Market h 270 Union [h 110 Cottage
" Charles S Jr clerk 20 Market
" Cynthia A widow Henry F h 267 Cottage
" Edmund F teamster h 72 State
" Edward M painter h 176 Cedar
" Elizabeth Mrs b 74 Washington
" Elizabeth widow Edward b 136 Newton [ton
" Frank C carpenter b 550 Kemp-
" Frank H clerk 37 Purchase rm 12 h at Fairhaven
" Gertrude F teacher Harrington school b 101 Chestnut

Kelley
" Grace D clerk 14 N Sixth b 54 Tremont [State
" Hanora widow Thomas C h 191
" Henry W carpenter b 55½ Fifth
" Henry W carpenter b 112 Grinnell
" Herbert N skiver h 243 Maxfield [Park
" Irving B eyeletmaker bds 271
" Isabella C T widow George S h 242 Acushnet av
" James fixer h 297 Austin
" James weaver h 2 Acushnet blk
" James F foreman h 394 Elm (W)
" James H painter h 702 Acushnet av
" James S Jr watch repairer 1109 Acushnet av h 101 Chestnut
" James S Mrs dressmaker 101 Chestnut h do [Kempton
" John I clerk 85 Elm rms 59
" John T at P Corp h 280 Earle
" John William liquors 243-247 Purchase h 117 Fourth
" Joseph corporal U S A 76 Pleasant rm 39 b 219 Purchase
" Lewis glasscutter h 246 Fourth
" Lillian M Mrs h 46 Thompson
" L Auburt job pressman Standard h 83 School [cery
" Michael J machinist b 192 Chan-
" Minnie F bookkeeper b 54 Tremont
" Patrick laborer h 19 Welcome
" Patrick J clerk b 19 Welcome
" Peter laborer h 445½ Pleasant
" Richard weaver b 88 Cove
" Ruth F bookkeeper 185 Union b 101 Chestnut [Crapo
" Theresa sewer 40 Purchase b 32
" Thomas h 397 Pleasant
" Thomas laborer h 152 Division
" Thomas teamster h 577 Cottage
" Thomas E spinner b 297 Acu-
" Thomas E spinner b 297 Austin
" William weaver b 32 Hollv
" William E bookkeeper 358 Acushuet av b 158 Grinnell
" William L conductor h 297 Cedar
" William L jewelry 2 Purchase h 478 County
" see Kelly
Kellock John R removed from city
Kelly Herbert laborer b 346 Purchase

GLOBE DYE HOUSE 220 SHAWMUT AVE.
J. N. J. LONHOLDT, PROP. Telephone Connections Goods called for and Delivered
Down town Office, 52 Pleasant St., Room 1 North End Office, 1014 Acushnet Ave.

Kelly
" John spinner h 208 Davis
" John weaver b 32 Tallman
" Katherine widow Dennis W h 379 Cedar
" Leonard laborer b 346 Purchase
" Patrick fixer h 32 Tallman
" Sarah widow Jeremiah h 346 Purchase
" Thomas lineman 43 William b 208 Davis [h 22 Pope av
" William mgr 1081 Acushnet av h
" William H clerk 1592 Acushnet av b 208 Davis [Penniman
" William H top roll coverer h 21
" William L conductor b 32 Tallman
" see Kelley
Kelter Grusca welter h 106 Rivet
Kemnitzer Frank weaver h 6 Linden court [avenue
Kemp Ernest fixer h 44 W French
Kempton Louisa E widow Manasch E h 208 Thompson
" Lydia A widow William h 38 Bay
" Susan H widow David B h 553 County
Kendall Edith V Mrs public stenographer 97 William rm 210 b at Fairhaven [av
" John jeweler bds 1637 Acushnet
" Thomas H fixer h 71 Dartmouth
Kendra Wojech mill hand h 325 Belleville av
Kendrick Allen T carpenter 161 Clinton h 159 Arnold
" Belmont W cabinetmaker 36 Purchase h 491 Middle (W)
" Robert E glasscutter h 286 Mill
" Stanley clerk Hawes, Tewksbury & Co h at Fairhaven
Kenealy James H clerk 214 Purchase h 249 Arnold
" John city laborer h 23 North
Kennedy Albert insurance agent 37 Purchase rm 23 h 449 Orchard (S)
" Alfred J fixer h 19 W Trinity
" Amanda Mrs h 162 North
" Annie C widow William A h 25 Cottage [French av h n do
" Archibald D nurse Almshouse E
" Arthur A chauffeur 99 William b 122 Bonney [Bonney
" Augustus M glassworker h 101

Kennedy
" Charles plumber 745 Purchase h 17 Austin [Court
" Charles F time keeper h 396
" Edward glassworker h 59 Grinnell
" Edward J driver rms 73 Elm
" Francis M dentist 139 Purchase h 369 Cottage
" Frank J glasscutter b 17 Austin
" George H time keeper b 305 Arnold [Palmer
" George S salesman 99 Front h 290
" Isabel M clerk 182 Union b 122 Bonney [Church
" James slasher tender **h 74**
" John spinner h 17 Austin
" John watchman h 122 Bonney
" John G foreman 100 Fifth h 86 Park [mut av
" Joseph P blacksmith h 124 Shaw-
" Joseph P (Kennedy & Kirwin) h 15 Sherman
" Mary A teacher Thomas Donaghy school b 11 Fifth [nell
" Nancy widow Edward h 59 Grin-
" Patrick police h 144 Bedford
" Patrick foreman 167 N Second and confectionery 57 W French av h do [thorn h 305 Arnold
" Thomas coachman 181 Haw-
" Thomas F clerk 140 Union bds 122 Bonney
" Thomas S b 305 Arnold
" William gardener 163 Hawthorn b 319 Union
" & Kirwin (Joseph P Kennedy and Henry H Kirwin) paper and twine and roofing 311 S Water
Kennelty Joseph C supt 37 Purchase rm 23 h 190 Clinton
Kenney Agnes F inspector bds 178 Fourth [son
" Edward D Jr fireman h 42 Robe-
" Edward W clerk 645 County b 42 Robeson [mut av
" Garret M quarryman b 250 Shaw-
" George H painter h 465 Union
" Henry laborer rms 7 N Second
" James laborer h 415 Cedar
" James laborer b 49 Rivet
" John motorman h 38 Robeson
" John teamster h 33 Penniman
" John F salesman b 42 Robeson

GREENE & WOOD Every Kind of LUMBER AND MILL WORK
PINE STREET, off So. WATER STREET, NEW BEDFORD

JOSEPH T KENNEY
ATTORNEY AND COUNSELLOR
AT LAW
Room 203
Merchants Bank Building
97 William Street
Residence 479 County Street

Kenny Joseph T lawyer 97 William rm 203 h 479 County
" Mary Mrs h 57 Ash (S)
" Mary widow John b 109 Austin
" Patrick housekeeper police station 2 h 178 Fourth [avenue
" Thomas D farmer h 250 Shawmut
" William D milk 250 Shawmut av bds do
" see Kinney and Canny
Kent Amanda A widow William J h Aquidneck
" George L Mrs h 108 Norman
" Mary E Mrs h 410 Cedar
" Mary S teacher h 157 Purchase
" Myra J h 157 Purchase [349 Park
" Percy L clerk Potomska Mills h
" Phillip W operative b Aquidneck
" Sarah widow George E h 349 Park [ditch
Kenten Henry weaver h 328 Bow-
" Thomas weaver b 365 Coffin av
Kenworthy Bramley maihinist h 299 Collette
" Harry A insurance agent 120 Purchase rm 403 h 161 Richmond
" Joseph operative h 18 Mill
" William clerk b 161 Richmond
KENYON ALBERT B real estate 209 Times bldg h 90 Hillman See page 27
" Arthur carpenter b 208 Brock av
" Arthur weaver b 90 Austin
" Benjamin W overseer Holmes Mfg Co h 94 Belleville road
" Eli weaver h 90 Austin
" Elizabeth h 26 Shore
" Elizabeth and Emma h 26 Cove
" Harold clerk rms 42 Hill

Kenyon
" Harry operative b 125 Webster court [436 Rivet
" Harry steam fitter 91 N Water h
" Harry A driver h 9 Willis
" Henry doffer b 38 Myrtle
" Henry spinner h 125 Webster ct
" James fireman h 9 E French av
" James operative h 38 Myrtle
" James mill hand h 96 Division
" John weaver h 155 Earle
" John weaver b 96 Division
" John W machinist h 204 Austin
" Joseph A removed to Waltham
" Louis A weaver h 57 Salisbury
" Marjorie Mrs weaver h 7 East Durfee
" Polly operative h 98 Brock av
" Robert H h 1757 Acushnet avenue
" Rosali Mrs housekeeper 36 Purchase h 435 Mill
" Sarah Mrs bds 158 Reynolds
" Theodore F provisions 152 Arnold rms 435 Mill
" Thomas removed from city
" Thomas weaver h 208 Brock av
" Vina Mrs variety 210 Brock av h 208 do
" Walter weaver b 90 Austin
" Walter A carder b 291 Collette
" William A assistant engineer Page Mfg Co h 109 David
Kern Henry A h 216 Grinnell
" John engineer h 23 Bentley [ford
" Maria L widow Charles h 83 Bed-
" William E h 216 Grinnell
" William E Jr treasurer Taber Mill h 216 Grinnell [French av
Kerney Peter carpenter b 23 East
Kerns Mary M Mrs h 239 County
Keroack Alphonse clerk h 30 Jouvett
" Joseph h 125 Cove [h 47 Park
Kerr Louis R asst treas Butler Mill
" Nathaniel B treas Butler Mill h 43 Seventh
Kerrem Jafer mill hand b 54 Davis
Kerrigan Hubert J tool maker h 889 Rockdale avenue
" Michael J laborer h 316 Davis
Kersec Adam laborer h 533 S Second [chase h 100 Pierce
Kershaw Albert A clerk 169 Pur-
" Annie Mrs h 38 Foster
" Elias H h 62 Bonney

BONNEY, FOLSTER & CO.,
The North End's Shopping Centre
Dry Goods and Men's Furnishings
945-947 Acushnet Ave., New Bedford, Mass.

Kershaw
" George operative h 12 Cleveland
" James B drill worker h 22 Ash (N)
" James W weaver h 69 Mosher
" Ralph clerk 97 Front b 24 Mosher
" Squire oiler h 12 Cleveland
" Thomas changer over h 154 Tallman [Front
Kersner Moses laborer h 511 North
Kervack Yvonne stenographer b 125 Cove
Kerwin George P overseer Beacon Mfg Co b 257 Cedar Grove
" William J supt Beacon Mfg Co h 90 Dean [h at Providence
Kessler Joseph (Zalkind & Kessler)
Kesterbaum Emanuel crockery 801 Water h 893 do [Eugenia
Kettell Mary Mrs mill hand b 130
Kettewell Ruth Mrs h 26 Acushnet av
Key Albert operative b 281 Davis
" Charles loom fixer h 281 Davis
" Joseph second hand h 147 Belleville road
" Mary A operative h 281 Davis
" Walter fixer h 281 Davis
" see Kay
Keyes George gardener h 60 Park
" John packer b 281 Davis
" Lewis E (Keyes & Woodland) 108 Cedar h 67 Hillman
" & Woodland (Lewis E Keyes and Robert E Woodland) provisions 108 Cedar
Kidd James Mrs h 260 Coggeshall
Kider Charles T manager 2 S Water h 6 Ocean [County
Kiel Grace widow Charles S h 1057
" Margaretta widow Joseph b 1057 County [ville av
Kielka Antoni operative b 19 Belle-
Kiernan James tack maker h 18 Richmond
" Thomas watchman b 162 North
Kilanowich Annie widow Thomas spinner h 27 Hicks
Kilbride James Mrs h 288 Fourth
" James third hand b 288 Fourth
" John J spinner h 213 Fourth
Kilburn Charles A carder h 567 Elm (W) [place
" Clara S widow Edward h 1 Park

Kilburn
" Clifford (Pierce & Kilburn) bds 264 County
" Frank J machinist h 264 County
" Harriet E widow Hiram b 96 Bedford
" Hiram laborer bds 7 Jenney
" Hiram W gardener b 88 Linden
" John E h 240 Fourth
" Mills, W French av
Kilcoin John F shoemaker b 467 Cottage [tage
" Joseph glasscutter bds 467 Cot-
" Luke mason b 467 Cottage
" Luke J mason h 467 Cottage
Killeen Celia widow John T h 64 Jouvett
Killigrew Edward L (W H Killigrew & Co) h 657 County
" Edward L Jr student bds 657 County [b 657 County
" Elizabeth M sewer 185 Union
" George F clerk 357 Acushnet av b 482 do [school b 657 County
" Helen E teacher Harrington
" Mary widow Daniel h 482 Acushnet av [b 657 County
" Mary L teacher Parker st school
" William H (W H Killigrew & Co) h 237 Summer
" W H & Co) W H and E L) liquors 357 Acushnet av
Killoran James H linotype operator N B Times h at Fall River
Kilmartin James shoemaker b 17 Hazard court [court
" John W laborer bds 17 Hazard
" Mary h 176 State
" Michael carder h 20 Division
" Michael died Nov 8 1910
" Sarah Ann widow M William h 17 Hazard court
" see Gilmartin [64 Mosher
Kilpatrick Margaret widow Robert h
" William A teamster h 56 Mosher
Kilshaw Ellen Mrs grocer 62 Ruth h do
" George weaver h 74 Roosevelt
" Richard weaver h 62 Ruth
" Thomas weaver h 34 Jouvett
Kimball Elizabeth widow Lewis b 80 Newton [h do
" Emma B Mrs nurse 57 Bedford
" Emma F widow William h 185 Elm

M. P. B. Silva & Son BUILDERS
Estimates Furnished on all Kinds of Work
157 ACUSHNET AVENUE Both Phones NEW BEDFORD

Kimball
" Harry H asst master mechanic 51 Bedford h 57 do
" John mgr 1100 Acushnet av
" Laura S Mrs h 202 Kempton
" Mary C widow Horatio N h 309 Cottage
" William baker h 73 Linden
" William A driver h 254 Purchase
Kimber Joseph S overseer N B Cotton Mills Corp h 243 Shawmut avenue
King Alexander b 105 Fourth
" Alfred A removed to Fairhaven
" Alfred M real estate and painter 77 Rivet b 21 Independent [ty
" Ambrose S operative h 184 Coun-
" Anthony clerk 827 S Water
" Antone operative h 65 Short
" Antone S laborer h 60 Howland
" Antonio operative h 232 Rivet
" Antonio Jr operative b 232 Rivet
" Benjamin F conductor h 690 Cottage
" Benjamin F Jr h 204 Brownell
" Brayton W h 267 Cottage
" Burgess T city painter h 585 Elm
" Caroline F Mrs matron 180 Allen h do [Purchase
" Catherine L widow Cyrus b 388
" Charles E h 242 Summer
" Charles E real estate and painter 77 Rivet b 21 Independent
" Charles J machinist h 24 Ward
" Charles S twister b 299 S Front
" Clifford b 95 Rodney
" Dental Co 24 Purchase
" Edward A died Dec 13 1910
" Edward J shoeworker h 171 Brock av
" Edwin R teacher manual training public schools h 156 Chestnut [ley
" Ellen widow Thomas h 14 Ash-
" Ellen G clerk 48 Pleasant b 97 Hall
" Elsie b 690 Cottage [305 Middle
" Emma J widow William H h
" Eva D bookkeeper 143 Purchase b 690 Cottage [Front
" Frances widow Antonio h 307 S
" Frank C lather h 388 Purchase
" Frank W piano tuner h 95 Bonney

King
" Fred S brakeman h 61 Reynolds
" Fred W rem to Providence R I
" George J shoemaker b 388 Purchase
" Hannibal mule spinner h 23 Oak
" Harry removed to Middleboro
" Henry B blacksmith 139 Pleasant b 154 Mill [County
" Henry F copperworker h 940
" Herbert clerk h 96 Cedar
" Herbert R asst 201 Union b 690 Cottage
" Hiram R removed from city
" Horace E b 156 Grinnell
" Horace W weaver b 2 Austin ct
" Ida M widow Henry L h 122 Shawmut av
" Ina G roll coverer b 690 Cottage
" Isaiah porter h 67 Ash (N)
" John h 52 Willow
" John fireman h 44 Winsor
" John gardener b 150 Chancery
" John H asst 206 Union bds 3 Lincoln [land Village
" John J third hand h 12 How-
" John S stockman 57 N Second h 397 Union
" Joseph clerk rms 230 Union
" Joseph fireman h 65 Mosher
" Joseph laborer b 299 S Front
" Joseph mill hand h 42 Edward
" Joseph F yard foreman Potomska Mill h 122 Fair
" Laura M teacher Thomas Donaghy school b at Fairhaven
" Lydia widow Edward A h 480 Mt Pleasant
" Manuel drillworker h 17 Griffin
" Manuel gardener rms 76 Cedar
" Manuel mill hand h 48 Stephen
" Manuel mill hand h 641 S Water
" Manuel F engineer h 58 Sherman
" Manuel F Jr engineer h 47 Babbitt
" Marietta millinery 7 Purchase b 305 Middle [b 95 Willis
" Marion R stenographer 123 Front
" Martin teamster b 52 School
" Mary Mrs h 299 S Front
" Mary widow Joseph J h 74 Katharine [234 Allen
" Mary A widow Alexander W b
" Mary E widow William J h 21 Independent [b 89 High
" Nora P Mrs clerk 65 Purchase

Steiger-Dudgeon Co.
"The WOMAN'S Store."
Tel. Bell 82 & 83, Branches connecting all depts.
" " 160 For Office only. Auto. 1211

SUMPTIONS, ASSORTMENTS AT ALL TIMES OF DEPENDABLE DRY GOODS

King
" Oren A chauffeur b 152 Mill
" Patrick J loom fixer h 35 Crapo
" Peter Joe carpenter h 74 Independent [lis
" Philip R city carpenter h 95 Wil-
" Reuben T asst janitor h 136 Bedford
" Robert B foreman h 389 Reed
" Roland E clerk Bennett Mill b 61 Reynolds [ton
" Rosa widow Joseph b 728 Kemp-
" Samuel bricklayer h 27 Nash rd
" Sarah P rem from city [Hall
" Theresa widow Thomas L h 97
" Thomas Jr removed from city
" Walter shoe repairer 204 Brock av h 71 Emma [Elm
" Walter L carriage trimmer b 585
" Warren A chauffeur 148 Court rms 3 Lincoln [son
" William loom fixer h 43 Thomp-
" William weaver b 450 First
" William F copperworker b 272 Weld [Bowditch
" William H gas fixtures h 185
" William H H S driver S F E No 7 h 272 Weld
" William S watchman h 74 South
" William S Jr clerk b 74 South
" & Begley gas fitters 978 Acushnet av [4 Welcome
Kingcard James real estate bds
Kingcroft Iron Foundry (Emery Goddard) 2891 Acushnet av
Kinkman George F Mrs h 159 Cottage
" George M paying teller Mechanics Nat Bank h 120 School
Kingsley Frances H teacher High school b 50 S Sixth [av
" Howard weaver h 1462 Acushnet
" Nelson M b 261 Cottage
" Robert mule spinner b 168 Acushnet av
Kinney Edward D yard foreman Wamsutta Mill h 526 Purchase
" John spinner b 1054 County
" Mary widow John R h 90 Nash road
" Robert H spinner h 1054 County
" William operative b 1054 County
" see Kenney [Bolton
Kinniery Peter P machinist h 462
Kinyon William H (Kinyon & Russell) 76 Pleasant rm 21 h at Pawtucket R I
" & Russell (William H Kinyon and Herbert C Russell) props Kinyon's Commercial School 76 Pleasant rms 21-24
KINYON'S COMMERCIAL SCHOOL (Kinyon & Russell props) 76 Pleasant rms 21 to 24 See foot lines
Kipp David R chauffeur h 388 Allen
Kirby Albert C deputy sheriff h 33 S Sixth [Purchase
" Andrew F foreman 54 Elm h 212
" Arthur C (Dahill & Kirby) 11 Clifford bldg b 54 Ashland
" Benjamin H h 37 Dartmouth
" Caroline E bookkeeper rms 35 Eighth [ant b 227 Arnold
" Charles E harnessmaker 144 Plea-
" Edward A h 227 Arnold
" Frank B letter carrier h 21 Buttonwood
" Frank R (Bates, Kirby & Co) 48 Pleasant h 150 Cottage
" George Jr pres George Kirby Jr Paint Co h 672 County
KIRBY GEORGE JR PAINT CO paint mfrs 14-20 Wall See page 33
" George A treas George Kirby Jr Paint Co h 54 Ashland
" George F clerk George Kirby Jr Paint Co h 25 Tremont [b do
" Holder C physician 33 S Sixth
" Lydia L widow George h 343 Purchase [chase
" Thomas C teamster b 340 Pur-
" Wilfred S b 33 S Sixth
" William A h 173 Middle
" William P machinist h 92 Washington [Franklin
Kirk Eveline widow John h 27
" Helen J teacher Sylvia Ann Howland school b 27 Franklin
" Joseph h 215 Weld
KIRK J FRANK hay grain and straw 370-374 Purchase h 94 State See page 775
Kirkham Anna M widow b 95 Brock avenue [Front
" Mary widow operative h 426 N

PELEG H. SHERMAN 506 COUNTY ST.
FUNERAL DIRECTOR AND EMBALMER
OFFICE PHONES. Bell 690-13. Auto. 1305.
RESIDENCE PHONES. Bell 690-12. Auto. 1306.

Kirkham
" Thomas overseer Dartmouth M Corp h 95 Brock avenue [pl
Kirouach Louis teamster h 3 Cornell
Kirschbaum Ernest T clerk U St Ry Co b 226 North
" William G agent board health 52 Pleasant h 226 North
Kirwin Edwin at P Corp h 246 Brownell [Grove
" George W designer b 257 Cedar
" Henry H (Kennedy & Kirwin) 31 S Water b 101 S Sixth
" Mary J dressmaker 101 S Sixth bds do [school b 101 S Sixth
" Sarah E principal Acushnet av
" Walter J clerk b 101 S Sixth
Kisbert George weaver b 172 Bonney
" John h 172 Bonney [ant b do
Kiser Edward hostler 101 Mt Pleas-
Kispert John weaver b 10 McGurk
Kitchen James conductor h 29 Myrtle
Kite Elizabeth Mrs b 31 McGurk
Kittredge Frank R salesman b 67 Fourth
" William operative b 172 Dean
Kleeb Leonard Jr master mechanic Gosnold Mills rms 68 S Sixth
Klein Robert weaver h 485 Coggeshall [ushnet av rms 312 do
Klobedanz Fred A clerk 324 Ac-
Knapp Antone shoemaker h 389 Davis
" Gertrude M clerk b 299 Palmer
" Lina L insurance 10 Masonic bldg b 161 William [299 Palmer
" Robert E (R E Knapp & Co) h
" R E & Co (R E Knapp and J B Archambeault) insurance 13 Masonic bldg [Brock avenue
Knapton Charles A overseer h 63
Knechtel Herman K glass decorator h 53 Grape [lantic
Kniffen J Lewis foreman h 75 At-
Kniffin Sidney K cable splicer 57 N Second b 189 Chancery [Willis
Knight Albert F mill hand bds 87
" Alice B teacher Clark st school b 50 Locust
" David fixer h 117 Eugenia
" Ella R Mrs h 50 Locust [Ashland
" Jesse A agent Manomet Mill h 77
" John electrician b 292 Palmer
" John glass cutter b 41 Dartmouth
" Louise B bds 87 Willis

Knight
" Nathan J h 94 Pierce [Willis
" Sarah E widow Alfred F h 87
" Stantis E milliner b 87 Willis
Knoblich John laborer b 176 State
Knott Elizabeth widow John b 71 Dartmouth
" James E h 5 Linden ct [av h do
" Thomas real estate 1683 Acushnet
Knowe Charles mason h 67 Foster
Knowles Abraham h 281 Bowditch
" Annie widow Thomas H h 402 County [ington
" Arthur glass cutter h 19 Wash-
" Arthur weaver h 29 Mosher
" Caroline M widow Daniel M h 362 Union
" Charles S wax mfrs and electrical goods King's Highway h 11 Moreland terrace
" Cuthbert plumber b 23 Peckham
" Edward O cotton broker 15 Clifford bldg bds 556 County
" Foster glass cutter b 137 Acushnet avenue
" George B removed to Taunton
" Henry M merchant 37 Purchase rm 30 h 178 Hawthorn
" Henry M 2nd bookkeeper 37 Purchase rm 30 h at Fairhaven
" Henry S lawyer 97 William rm 301 bds 112 Cottage
" Hubert baker h 50 Page
" Hughie removed to Fall River
" Isabelle Mrs weaver h 30 Rodney
" James H weaver h 283 Collette
" John P Jr Mrs h 485 County
" John glasscutter b 137 Acushnet avenue
" John W laborer h 69 Diman
" John W treas Page Mfg Co h 88 Orchard (S)
" Joseph rem to Providence R I
" Joseph F clerk Acushnet Mills Corp h 181 Hawthorn
" Lewis W removed to Boston
" Loom Reed Works (William H Knowles) loom reed mfrs Myrtle c Penniman [County
" Mary J widow Joseph C h 729
" Nathan weaver h 29 McGurk
" Richard weaver h 187 Hathaway
" Richard L lawyer 6 Masonic bldg b 11 Moreland ter [thorn
" Robert W student bds 178 Haw-

F. T. AKIN & CO. FORGE FACTORY FURNACE FAMILY COAL

Knowles
" Rupert shoemaker b 57 Salisbury
" Sarah A widow John P 2nd h 120 Bedford [ter
" Thomas C clerk b 11 Moreland
" Thomas E steam fiter h 866 First
" Thomas P stoves 635 Purchase h 637 do [ditch
" William glasscutter h 174 Bow-
" William insurance agent 120 Purchase rm 403 h 191 Belleville road
" William weaver h 54 Roosevelt
" William H (Knowles Loom Reed Works) h 143 Cottage
Knowlton Grace A teacher Acushnet av school b 258 Pleasant
Knox Elijah H laborer b 183 Campbell [bell
" William J clerk P O h 183 Camp-
Kobeck Joseph weaver h 21 Bullard
Kobes Richard designer h 123 Hathaway
Kobza Charles weaver h 92 Tallman
" Clodia clerk 1119 Acushnet av b 92 Tallman [Tallman
" Rupert clerk N B W W bds 92
Kocolinakis Michael waiter 251 Coggeshall h do
Koeber Wenzel weaver h 81 Church
Koehler Azubah N widow Paul R h 59 Fifth
" Edna W H teacher Jirell Swift school b at Shawmut
Koenig Edmund weaver h 61 Rivet
Koffman Louis fruit 41 Mitchell h do [Durfee
Kohn Frank T case hardener h 2
Kokofski Michal weaver h 52 Kenyon
Kokowski John carder h 8 Fulton ct
Kolaczuck John tonic bds 11 Holly
Kolapo Stephen clerk 1141 Acushnet avenue b 10 Beetle
Kolasz William weaver h 109 Mott
Koleck Michael operative h 69 Hicks
Kolifas Harry laborer h 46 Scott
Kollock Helen M widow Lemuel M h 27 Lincoln
Kolnig Antonette h 46 Scott
Kolodziev Peter grocer h 648 First
Kolouch Joseph weaver h 101 Nye
Kolouck Mike operative h r 42 Washburn
Kondakos Peter weaver b 269 Belleville av [Front h 21 Washburn
Konstance Wolin bartender 161 N
Konvalinka Joseph weaver h 103 Holly [geshall
Kopacki Frank operative h 461 Cog-
Koplitzski Frank mill hand h 18 Grandfield [shuet av h do
Korobkin Benjamin grocer 504 Acu-
" Harry clerk 52 Purchase b 504 Acushnet av
" Israel bds 504 Acushnet av
Koroski John weaver h 358 Earle
Kosera Andrew operative h 9 Fulton court
" Jan operative h 9 Fulton court
Koshelba Albert carder h r 159 David [vin
Kosiba Andrew operative h 16 Mar-
Koss Alexander h 34 McGurk
Koster Anna b 225 North
" Charles W clerk foot Willis h 225 North [225 North
" Edna M bookkeeper 252 Cedar b
" Emma M boxmaker b 225 North
" Jacob grocer 252 Cedar h 225 North
Kosto Peter operative h 69 Hicks
Kouble Frank weaver h 19 Bentley
Kounday Joseph laborer h 10 Hampton court
Koupar Aso fruit h 359 Coggeshall
Kourafas Peter mill hand h 6 Bonneau court [rms do
Koury James fruit 1092 Acushnet av
Kovstylov Frank baker 43 Washburn h do [Nye
Kozochzka Stanislaw mill hand b 11
Kozorek William F photographer 921 Acushnet av h 100 Kenyon
Krafka William operative b 2 Weld av [Rockland b 45 Crapo
Kraihanzel Charles clerk Crapo cor
" Frank b 100 Rockland
" Joseph F grocer Crapo cor Rockland h 100 Rockland [man
" Joseph F Jr weaver h 135 Tall-
" Louis glassworker bds 100 Rockland [Cove rd
Krakowska Peter operative h 26
Kral Frank spinner h 21 Bullard
" Mavcel operative h 5 Fulton ct
" Sixmont mill hand b 21 Bullard
Kramer Abraham painter h 1 McDonald court
" Abraham Mrs dry goods 234 N Front h 1 McDonald court

There's room at the top for young men and women who can do things right.
Kinyon's Commercial School
Odd Fellows Bldg., Cor. William and Pleasant Sts., New Bedford, Mass.

Kramer
" Aly rubber Ideal Turkish Baths h do
Kranzler Harry L clerk 4 Purchase b 531 Acushnet av
" Mates second hand goods 533 Acushnet av and grocer 505 do h 531 do [1046 County
Krapf Albert H breweryworker h
Kratachville Antone laborer h 449 S Front [chase
Krause Arthur electrician 158 Pur-
" Otto shoemaker h Braley rd
Krauss John carpenter h 106 Oak
Kravetz Hyman shoe repairer 597 Purchase h 230 State
Krebs Barbara widow Michael b 217 Grinnell [nell
" Charles M glassworker b 217 Grin-
" Michael F molder T P Corp bds 217 Grinnell [217 Grinnell
" William H foreman T P Corp b
Krenmager Joseph weaver h 11 Welcome
Krenoff Hyman confectionery 497 S Water h Prospect cor Holland
Krone Frederick weaver b 67 Coffin avenue [ond b 136 Blackmer
Kronplad Elmert stockman 57 N Sec-
Krouzek Wenzel died Feb 19 1911
" William machinist h 291 Phillips avenue [ter h do
Krudvird Abraham baker 480 S Wa-
Kruger Louis meatcutter 188 Water h 433 Acushnet av [Cedar
Krumbholz George A weaver h 363
Krupa Stanley mill hand b 7 Bonneau court [lips av
Krupka John weaver h r 260 Phil-
" Joseph fixer b r 260 Phillips av
Kruse Lawrence carpenter h 82 School [dar Grove
Kubacki Antone operative h 108 Ce-
Kubat Anthony cleaner 229 N Water rms 51 Spring [Reynolds
Kubicek Vincent machinist h 125
Kubu Vac operative h 69 Hicks
Kucefski Roman grocer 42 Washburn h r 42 do [Ruth
Kucharski Andrew weaver h 82
Kuckera Jan spinner b 9 Fulton ct
" Piotz operative h 12 Fulton ct
Kudajewski Brouislaw clerk 878 Purchase h at Oxford
Kuechler Bros (Richard M and Kurt R Kuechler) sausage mfrs 337 S Second [Second
" Kurt R (Kuechler Bros) h 337 S
" Paul janitor h 3687 Acushnet av
" Richard M (Kuechler Bros) h 102 South [Front h 172 do
Kulaczeuoski John bartender 161 N
Kulick Jacob weaver h 15 Grandfield
Kuligo John grocer 181 N Front h 172 do
Kulik Peter weaver h 15 Washburn
Kulon K baker h 649 First
Kulpa John weaver h 305 Earle
Kulpinski Casmere operative h 27 Kenyon
Kuntz Alfred drillturner h 115 Ruth
" Arnold weaver b 443 Coggeshall
" Leo weaver h 443 Coggeshall
" Otter operative b 443 Coggeshall
Kuplisky Samuel weaver h 57 Grinnell
Kurgan Jan weaver h 121 Collette
Kussi Wenzel weaver h 341 Coggeshall [15 Bullard
Kuthan Charles clerk 52 Purchase b
" John weaver h 15 Bullard
" Louis operative b 15 Bullard
Kwiatskowski Stanislaw grocer 232 N Front h 180 Cedar Grove
" Veitenity carder bds 180 Cedar Grove [(N)
Kydd William foundryman h 72 Ash

Labadie Alphee stinner b 102 Collette
" Clovis operative h 102 Collette
" Treffle spinner b 102 Collette
Labarge Adelard weaver h r 85 Austin [ator h 22 McGurk
LaBarre Alfred moving picture oper-
" Alfred Jr trap drummer bds 22 McGurk [ushnet av
" Josephine widow Octave h 545 Ac-
LaBarte Aime carpenter b 165 David
Labau Napoleon fixer h 80 County
Labbe Albert mill hand b 49 Phillips avenue
" Albertine Mrs removed from city
" Jeffrey operative b 49 Phillips av
" Ludger painter h 195 Phillips av
" Peter D laborer h 49 Phillips av
LaBel Toefil h 36 Jouvette [av
LaBella Joseph spinner h 362 Coffin
LaBelle Charles spinner h 154 Davis

HASKELL BROS. DEALERS IN
ICE
400 COURT STREET TELEPHONE CONNECTION NEW BEDFORD, MASS.

LaBelle
" Frank second hand b 391 Bowditch
" Joseph photographer rms 41 High
" Walter weaver b 154 Davis
Labelle Arthur laborer h 163 Weld
" David h 507 South Second
Laberge Oliver slasher tender h 14 Studley [701 do
Laberge John clerk 702 Purchase b
" Manuel laborer h 701 Purchase
" M Ernestine clerk 40 Purchase b 110 Shawmut av [Water
Labombard Nelson laborer h 1101 S
Labonne Georgé h 159 Whitman
LaBonte Aime operative h 857 First
" Albert operative h 213 State
" Alfred operative b 131 N Front
" Alfred operative b 811 First
" Alfred teamster 810 Purchase
" Ambroise fixer h 35 Bentley [vid
" Anna widow Napoleon h 105 Da-
" David carpenter h 315 Sawyer
" Delia widow Adolphus bds 345 Coffin avenue
" Eli teamster h 291 Sawyer
" Eli E mgr Viens Theatre b 291 Sawyer
" Eliza Mrs weaver b 4 Social
" Fedora clerk 40 Purchase b 213 State
" Fred operative b 131 N Front
" Gideon weaver b 52 Ashley
" Hector operative b 345 Coffin av
" Joseph b 52 Hicks
" Joseph teamster b 54 Holly
" Napoleon operative b 165 David
" Nestor carder h 22 Jean
" Noe weaver h 64 Jouvett [Front
Labonti Joseph operative h 247 N
LaBossiere Alfred weaver b 241 N Front [lane
" Charles plumber h 66 Mechanics
" Charles O weaver b 215 Highland
" Joseph operative b 241 N Front
" Oliver painter h 241 N Front
" Philias barber b 241 N Front
" Philip painter 394 N Front bds Beetle [man
Labrade Levi machinist h 84 Whit-
Labradora Antonio laborer h r 142 Belleville avenue
Labrec O carder b 975 S Water
LaBrecque Aristide weaver h 189 Bowditch
" Joseph loom fixer h 64 Hicks
" Joseph teamster h 204 Sawyer
" Ovilia spinner h 194 Belleville av
" Pierre grocer 79 Belleville road h 56 do [ditch
LaBrie Elizabeth folder h 319½ Bow-
" Joseph M laborer h 1 Clark
Labrie A Donat carpenter h 148 Central avenue
" Edmund shoemaker h 50 Hillman
LaBrode Henry H contractor 54 Maitland h do [b 16 Willow
" Leo draughtsman 251 Union
Labrode Alder second hand h 382 Pleasant [low
" Alice widow Harmidas h 16 Wil-
" Henry C designer b 16 Willow
" Irene stenographer Lambeth Rope Co bds 16 Willow [h 247 State
" Joseph A clerk 1501 Acushnet av
" Nora M stenographer Bennett Mill bds 16 Willow
LaCasse Armidos type setter 101 Kenyon b 1415 Acushnet avenue
" Edmond A weaver h 310 N Front
Lace William corporal U S A h 293 Brock avenue [net av
Lacerda Joseph P weaver h 22 Acush-
Lacerte Hormidas helper 166 Belleville avenue bds do [First
Lacey Michael J paper worker h 473
" Philip laborer h 15 E Durfee
Lach Frank J insurance agent 120 Purchase rm 403 h 1026 South Water [lips avenue
Lachance Edward mason h 225 Phil-
" Emile R removed from city
" Honore weaver h 174 Phillips av
" Peter carpenter h 617 First
LaChance Francis carpenter b 225 Phillips avenue
LaChappelle Adelard designer Grinnell Mfg Corp h 94 Beetle
" Arthemese widow Luke h 63 County
" Azilda widow Eli h 81 Beetle
" Delphis laborer h 3 Riverside av
" Levi J loom fixer h 41 Ashley
" Levi L changer over b 41 Ashley
" Lily widow Hormidas b 3 Riverside av [George
Lacharite William carpenter h 71

J. F. CROSSLEY 223 MILL STREET COR. EMERSON PHONE
STEAM and HOT WATER HEATING
GAS FITTING and FIXTURES

Lacharite
" William Jr carpenter b 71 George
Lacherites Albert teamster 423 Acushnet av b 19 Mill [kiln Hill rd
Lackemacher Christopher h Tar-
" William machinist b C Lackemacher's Tarkiln Hill road
Lackey Bridget widow William h 3 Austin court [Court
Lackie George A coachman h 294
Laclair Charles third hand h r 291 Sawyer [genia
Lacombe Almon mill hand b 82 Eu-
" Macelin doffer h 60 Belleville rd
" Victoria Mrs operative h 1 Blackburn [b 24 Bentley
Lacomte Firmin driver 1070 County
" Joseph mill hand b 36 Bentley
LaCose Napoleon bricklayer bds 871 Purchase [Second
Lacourse Alphonse carder h 622 S
" Homere barber 835 S Water b cor Second and Cove
" Ulric machinist h 10 Juniper
Lacouture Felix shoemaker b 1142 Acushnet av
LaCroix Armand grocer 2177 Acushnet av h Tarkiln Hill rd
" Armina widow Joseph h 22 Jean
" Arthur spinner b 22 Jean
" David boss grinder h 26 Nye
" George painter b 359 Bowditch
" George D shoes 1138 Acushnet av h 225 Bowditch
" John carpenter h 27 Ashley
" Leo clerk b 26 Nye [lette
" Marie widow Firman h 195 Col-
" Mary Mrs operative h 66 Washburn
" Napoleon laborer h 27 Washburn
" Pierre grocer 261 Bowditch h 359 do [Coffin av
" P Aldege clerk 201 Union h 297
" Ramuald third hand b 1205 Acushnet av [b 26 Nye
" Wilfred J lunch 1278 Acushnet av
" Willie clerk 361 Bowditch h 218 Whitman [Purchase
LaCross Mary Mrs spinner bds 871
Ladere Manuel C clerk b 178 Belleville av [kiln Hill rd h do
Ladieu Henry J sausagemaker Tar-
Ladino Lewis fireman h 85 Grinnell
" Manuel carpenter h 256 Field
Ladue Henry mgr 186 Purchase h 188 do [man
LaFaille George helper b 150 Tall-
" Henry weaver h 76 Beetle
" Jean B laborer h 150 Tallman
" Reme bds 118 Mott
" Wilfred laborer b 150 Tallman
Lafavor Joseph weaver h 721 First
Lafferiere Adam spinner h 268 Tinkham [ham
" Albert mill hand bds 268 Tink-
" Edward medicines h 79 Clark
" Joseph carpenter h 268 Tinkham
" Napoleon operative b 268 Tinkham [Ashland pl
Lafferty Andrew A engineer h 26
" Edward clerk b 159 Weld [Weld
" Harry clerk 630 Purchase b 159
" Isabella Mrs h 159 Weld
" Jennie boarding house 41 Rivet
" John A bartender h 191 Bonney
" Owen foreman shipper T P Corp
" William P laborer b 111 Fourth
Laflamme Alfred b 47 Holly
" Alfred carpenter h 3 Bowditch
" Arthur weaver b 47 Holly
" Charlotte removed from city
" Cyrille carpenter b 47 Holly
" Delor removed from city
" Joseph weaver h 47 Holly
" Joseph Jr fixer h 27 Nye
" Mary L widow Philias h 364 Coffin av
" Napoleon carpenter h 179 Weld
" Patrick carpenter b 132 Bowditch
" Philias clerk b 364 Coffin av
" Philip carpenter h 177 David
" Philip clerk 201 Union b 365 Coffin av
Lafleur Albert weaver h 92 Ruth
" Ferdinand insurance agent 37 Purchase rm 23 h 13 Princeton avenue
" Henry weaver bds 311 N Front
" Hermenigilde carpenter 103 Brock av h do
" John weaver b 945 S Water
" John B weaver h 186 Davis
" John B Jr laborer h 311 N Front
" Louis h 50 Ashley [Ruth
" Octavia widow Theophile bds 92
" Oliver carpenter b 92 Ruth
" Zenon prop Whitman House 67 Coffin av h do
Lafoie John operative h 13 Hicks

CHARLES A. CROSHERE
38 FOURTH ST. Bell Phone 1964-23
SIGN PAINTING
GLASS LETTERING
ELECTRIC SIGNS
SHOW CARDS

LaFond Lucien clerk 215 Coggeshall h 19 Bentley
LaFontaine Braiding Co (Louis G and George LaFontaine and Thomas Pennington) braid and tape mfrs 85 and 87 Whitman
" Ephraim horseshoer b 346 N Front [h 78 Eugenia
" George (LaFontaine Braiding Co)
" Louis G (LaFontaine Braiding Co) h 87 Whitman
" Philip clerk b 346 N Front
" Thomas carder h 373 Bowditch
" see Fontaine [h 32 Nye
LaForest George Jr painter 14 Jean
" Oscar I clerk 420 N Front b at Fall River [b 290 Purchase
" Romeo asst engineer Bennett Mill
LaFranaye Amide carpenter h 52 Mosher [69 Covell
LaFrance Aduaran boilermaker h
" Aldei (LaFrance Bros) h 204 Nash road [h 6 Trinity
" Alphonse L shoemaker 105 Union
" Armoza clerk 182 Union bds 6 Trinity
" Arthur weaver b 168 Tinkham
" Beatrice clerk 185 Union bds 6 Trinity
" Bros (Philias, Joseph A, Jeremie and Aldei) grocers 79 Austin and props N B Packing Co 224 Cedar Grove
" Cyprien painter b 461 Sawyer
" Edward I shoecutter h 90 Robeson [ia
" Ferdinand driver h 88 Eugen-
" George carpenter h 50 Ashley
" Henry mule spinner b 461 Sawyer
" Hormidas mason h 85 Austin
" Irene M hairworker 96 Purchase b 85 Austin [Austin
" Jeremie (LaFrance Bros) h 81
" Joseph h 81 Austin
" Joseph farmer h 643 Purchase
" Joseph laundry 111 Clifford h 461 Sawyer
" Joseph painter b Weld sq Hotel
" Joseph Jr clerk h 1064 County
" Joseph A (LaFrance Bros) h 825 County
" Joseph R gas fitter b 6 Trinity

LaFrance
" Lidora clerk 185 Union b 6 Trinity
" Lucien Mrs h 7 Salisbury
" Peter gasfitter b 6 Trinity
" Philias (LaFrance Bros h 825 County
" Philips painter b 461 Sawyer
" Philiza slasher tender h 89 Robeson [16 LaFrance ct
" Rose A clerk 1049 Acushnet av b
" Simon slasher tender h 126 Bowditch
" Thomas back boy b 461 Sawyer
" Vincent mason 348 Sawyer h do
LaFrancis Marian waitress b 343 Kempton [Mott
Lafrenais Albert carpenter h 74
" Alphonse third hand h 55 Willard
" Henry bricklayer h 56 Cove
" Hermengilde carpenter h 73 Capitol
" Ovide carpenter b 73 Capitol
Legard Nathan h Austin street
Lagasse Adolph P undertaker 201 Blackmer h 199 do [man
" Alfred cabinetmaker b 81 Hill-
" Arsene mason b 52 Delano
" Delphis carpenter b 27 Acushnet av
" Frobe J (Lussier & Lagasse) druggist 125 Rivet h 23 Independent [Blackmer h 119 Ruth
" George A J asst undertaker 201
" Henry shoemaker h 135 Nash rd
" Idala A carpenter h 21 Acushnet av [27 Acushnet av
" Isadore window framemaker h
" Louis fireman h 418 N Front
" Napoleon carpenter b 27 Acushnet av
" Pierre teamster h 60 Cove
Lagesse Henry furniture mover h 164 N Front
" Joseph laborer h 839 Purchase
Lagras Joseph shoemaker b 131 N Front [240 Phillips av
Lagrenade Augustin carpenter bds
" Joseph carpenter h 240 Phillips avenue [ty
Lague Adelard carpenter h 827 Coun-
" Alfred loom fixer h 459 Bolton
" Alpherie contractor 63 Ruth h do
" Clovis carpenter h 226 State

J. G. NICHOLSON
LUMBER, SASH, DOORS and BLINDS
BOWDITCH STREET, NEW BEDFORD, MASS.

Lague
" Edmond loom fixer h 205 Hathaway
" Ernest carpenter b 773 First
" Henry operative bds 773 First
" Joseph b 2030 Acushnet av
" Joseph operative h 248 Bowditch
" Joseph weaver h 9 Kearsarge
" Joseph Jr carpenter h 907 County
" Joseph A weaver bds 9 Kearsarge
" Jules third hand h 287 Coffin av
" Rose widow Godfrey h 126 Perry
" Wilfred carpenter b 773 First
" Xavier weaver h 773 First
Lahaie Hilas rem to Douville Canada
LaHaye Robert h 143 County
Lahood Shaker variety h 642 Purchase
" Yafath pedlar h 520 Acushnet av
Laine Alpherie barber b 68 Dean
" Furman weaver h 1 Riverside av
Laivmonere Peter yard foreman Nonquitt Spinning Co h 47 Covell
Lajeunesse Edouard weaver h 4 Welcome
" Edward grocer 15 W French av h 13 do
" Edward teamster h 106 Whitman
" Edward Jr clerk 15 W French av b 13 do
" Emma Mrs weaver b 12 Roosevelt
" Francois weaver h 829 Acushnet avenue
" Henry clerk bds 13 W French av
" Joseph weaver b 968 S Water
" Michel variety 8½ McGurk h 8 do
" Nathalie Mrs h 968 S Water
LaJoie Elsie widow Narcisse h 27 Kenyon
" Isaie weaver h 109 N Front
Lajoie Charles mill hand h 20 Bentley
" Georgianna Mrs housekeeper 1108 Acushnet av
" Lamous weaver h 166 N Front
" Rose dressmaker 1031 Acushnet avenue b 1108 do
" William brewery worker h 141 Holly
Lajoy Amende mechanic h 21 Jean
Lake Clara B h 22 Maxfield
" Deborah A Mrs h 348 North
" E B (Allen Slade & Co) 1 William h at Fall River
" Fred operative b 58 Lindsey
" Frederick mill hand b 348 North
" George A machinist b 348 North

Lake
" Joseph eyelet maker b 28 Washburn
" Leon, laborer h 240 Chancery
" William teamster h 28 Washburn
" William A h 188 Shawmut av
Laliberte Adelard lather h 99 Jouvette
" Antonio insurance agent 120 Purchase rm 403 h 67 Hathaway
" Archie spinner b 16 Jean
" Charles machinist h 16 Jean
" Dominique operative b 411 North Front
" Edward salesman 46 Purchase h at Fall River
" Elie Mrs b 16 Jean
" Felix h 5 Gifford
" Hyacinthe h 411 N Front
" Irinie carpenter h 49 Phillips av
" Jeffrey laborer h 807 First
" Joseph operative h 14 Bowditch
" Louisa Mrs h 25 Madison
" Ludger h 50 Hillman
" Ludger carpenter b 33 Tallman
" Ludger mason b 29 Ashley
" Michele insurance 67 Ruth h do
" Patrick machinist b 16 Jean
" Rudolph lather b 95 Scott
Laliberty Adam weaver h 81 Independent
Lally Patrick machinist h 83 Winsor
Lalumiere Mathilda mill hand h 340 North Front
Lamarche Existe fireman h 1187 Purchase
" Jean M clerk b 9 Bowditch
" Margaret widow Xavier died Oct 4 1910
" Mary Mrs h 141 Collette
" Mederic weaver b 910 S Water
" Noel mill hand h 14 Austin ct
" Prosper clerk h 307 Coggeshall
Lamarine Adelard engineer Union St Ry Co power station b 5 North
" Adelia widow Joseph h 5 North
" Arthur b 5 North
" Benjamin A engineer h 38 Foster
" Emma lodging h 41 High
" Enos tinsmith 26 N Second h at Dartmouth
Lamarre Luc weaver h 70 Nelson
Lamb Albert S carpenter h 1458 Acushnet avenue
" Ann widow Robert h 1 Farwell

Steiger-Dudgeon Co.
"The WOMAN'S Store."
Tel. Bell 82 & 83, Branches connecting all depts.
" " 160 For Office only. Auto. 1211

SUMPTIONS, ASSORTMENTS AT ALL TIMES OF DEPENDABLE DRY GOODS

Lamb
" Arthur B installer 57 N Second bds 406 Union
" Ernest second hand h 23 Bourne
" Eugene W h 85 Campbell
" John weaver h 353 Coggeshall
" Mary S clerk b 406 Union
" Percival LeRoy bookkeeper Nonquitt Spinning Co h 52 Washington [Maxfield
" Susan E widow Charles H h 54
" William G janitor Library bldg h 406 Union [S Water
Lamba Manuel D mill hand bds 505
Lambalot Augustina Mrs h 723 First
" Celestine laborer h 723 First
" Emile changer over h 39 Roosevelt
Lambert Alonzo weaver h 857 First
" Amanda clerk 304 N Front b 306 do [306 do
" Amos restaurant 304 N Front h
" Charles weaver h 70 Ruth av
" Edmond A granite cutter end Robeson h at Acushnet
" Emma clerk 1500 Acushnet avenue bds 306 North Front
" Frank carpenter 50 Tallman h do
" Frank weaver h 80 Beetle
" Henry T weaver h 20 Warren
" James machinist h 187 David
" Jams machinist h 187 David
" John machinist h 113 Bates av
" Joseph carpenter h 735 Belleville avenue
" Joseph painter b 211 Brock av
" Louis A bartender 62 Purchase h 248 Rivet [av
" Ludger teamster h 174 Phillips
" Mark clerk 1625 Acushnet av b 258 Coffin avenue [Fourth
" Peter hoseman Hose 3 h 129
" Rosilda O clerk 185 Union b 306 North Front
" William A fixer h 45 Brock av
Lambeth Rope Corp Tarkiln Hill rd
Lamelin Joseph foreman bds 385 N Front [net av
Lamiele Joseph weaver h 40 Acush-
Lamielle Edmond weaver h 20 Roosevelt [Coggeshall
Lamond Alphonse operative b 478
Lamontagne Alphe barber h 52 Ashley [court
" George J B weaver h 129 Webster
" Janvier stonecutter b 30 Ashley
" Joseph weaver b 26 George
" Peter weaver h 12 Division
" Pierre loom fixer h 74 Nelson
Lamontague Joseph loom fixer h 74 Nelson
Lamore Joseph A pool 949 Acushnet av h 164 Tinkham
" William J removed from city
Lamothe Aldei clerk 1404 Acushnet av b 356 do [h do
" Alexander physician 519 N Front
" Alfred weaver b 1060 Acushnet avenue [Davis
" Benjamin police Station 4 h 208
" Edward A real estate h 294 Sawyer
" Ernest clerk bds 18 Roosevelt
" Francis X stonecutter h 162 Davis
" Frank b 132 Bullard
" Joseph h 1060 Acushnet av
" Joseph hairdresser 111 Union h 334 Pleasant [av
" Joseph slubbertender h 287 Coffin
" Joseph slubber h 132 Bullard
" Joseph weaver h 815 First
" Mary L widow b 25 Ashley
" Michael laborer h 18 Roosevelt
" Nazaire mill hand b 1356 Acushnet av [Coffin av
Lamoureux Edward weaver bds 289
" Gaspard druggist 1104 Acushnet av h 81 Mt Pleasant [tol
" Hermengilde operative h 73 Capi-
" J Charles clerk h 226 Kempton
" Mathilda widow Charles h 33 Viall
" Stanislaus A druggist 1598 Acushnet av and physician 211 Collette h do [Front
Lampara Peter weaver h 329 N
Lamprey Lloyd C cable splicer 57 N Second h 105 Pierce
Lampros Peter clerk 774 Purchase
Lamy Henry lineman N B F D h 76 Mill [Fourth
Lanagan Catherine A Mrs h 113
" Edward S clerk 177 Purchase h 78 Willis
" Esther F clerk b 113 Fourth
" George fisherman b 12 Stone
" James T laborer h 10 Stone

PELEG H. SHERMAN 506 COUNTY ST.
FUNERAL DIRECTOR AND EMBALMER
OFFICE PHONES. Bell 690-13. Auto. 1305.
RESIDENCE PHONES. Bell 690-12. Auto. 1306.

Lanagan
" John driver 45 School h 191 Washington [chase b 10 Stone
" John Frederick salesman 6 Pur-
" Lemuel T clerk 177 Purchase h at Fairhaven [b 113 Fourth
" Leonard installer 57 N Second
" Levi clerk 163 Union h at Fairhaven
" Thomas laborer h Alec street
" William H drill grinder h 12 Stone
" see Lannigan [Earle
Lancaster John loom fixer h 188
" John M clerk b 111 Rockland
" William weaver b 850 First
Land Enos fireman h 8 Griffin
" Laura Mrs variety 153 County h do [b 15 Chestnut
Landers Edna M clerk 160 Purchase
" Elmer plumber 211 Coffin av h at Acushnet [Chestnut
" Emily E clerk 160 Purchase b 15
" Frank H glasscutter h 446 Chancery [man
" Joseph E bookkeeper h 125 Hill-
" Sarah V b 125 Hillman
Landerville Albina J clerk b 612 S Second [S Second
" Arthur clerk 912 S Water b 612
" Donat weaver b 859 S Water
" Elzear filler h 612 S Second
Landre Emma Sally h 98 Fourth
Landress Ephraim A h 40 Parker
Landreville Albini third hand b 295 N Front [Hillman
Landrie Charles F machinist h 28
Landry Albert carpenter b 224 Phillips av
" Ambrose carpenter h 109 Nash rd
" Amedee weaver b 29 Nye [Dean
" Arthur grocer 335 N Front h 85
" Auto Co (Joseph E Landry) 335 N Front
" Daniel carpenter h 340 Coffin av
" Daniel Jr operative b 340 Coffin avenue
" David laborer h 190 Davis
" Delphine widow Lawrence h 347 N Front
" Edward fisherman b 15 Beetle
" Edward laborer h 417 N Front
" Edward mill hand bds 150 Phillips av
" Fabian Mrs h 826 County

Landry
" Frank carder b 1028 Acushnet av
" George clerk 1527 Acushnet av b 224 Phillips av
" George fixer b 29 Nye
" George E removed from city
" Herman carpenter h 297 Earle
" Herman mill hand b 150 Phillips avenue
" Israel operative b 131 Tallman
" Joseph slasher b 871 Purchase
" Joseph E (Landry Auto Co) h 54 Bullard
" Joseph M (Casavant & Landry) grocers 1892 Acushnet av h 92 Covell
" Lawrence died May 20 1910
" Louis B carpenter h 224 Phillips avenue [Coggeshall
" Maggie widow Benjamin h 478
" Napoleon operative h 24 Clark
" Oliver weaver h 68 Dean
" Onesimer fixer h 224 Phillips av
" Peter carpenter h 13 Bates av
" Peter operative b 340 Coffin av
" Pierre carpenter 54 Bullard h do
" William removed from city
Landy William operative h 200 Brock avenue [110 Cedar
Lane Charles W cook 224½ Union bds
" Rosa A Mrs baker 221 Park h do
" Samuel machinist h 212 Nash rd
" Willard N job foreman Mercury h 261 Palmer [Thompson
Lang Andrew P wood worker h 178
" Charles baker bds 11 Clark
" Charles F fixer b 11 Clark
" Charles J baker 372 Kempton bds 324 Cedar Grove
" Eleonora Mrs h 11 Clark
" Francis A shoes 1059 Acushnet av h 864 County
" Frank clerk City Mfg Corp
" Fred baker 372 Kempton
" Henry second hand h 79 Linden
" Julius weaver h 475 Coggeshall
" William baker bds 11 Clark
" William H operative h 858 First
Langdon Raymond J clerk Times b 1530 Acushnet av
Lange Albert carpenter b 546 N Front
" Arthur removed to Pawtucket R I
" John G h 253 Fourth
" Joseph h 546 N Front

F. T. AKIN & CO. PAINTERS AND DECORATORS

Lange
" Rozinna Mrs b 461 Sawyer
Langelier Alfred third hand h 21 Washburn [burn
" Ferdinand overseer h 21 Wash-
" Henry nightman 388 N Front b 21 Washburn [avenue
" Jean B carpenter b 149 Phillips
" Ovilla doffer b 21 Washburn
Langevin Absolom clerk 398 N Front bds 113 Collette
" Adelard operative b 113 Collette
" Albini carpenter h 70 Phillips av
" Emile plumber h 101 Phillips av
" Frederick weaver h 19 Acushnet avenue [254 Tinkham
" Henry A grocer 326 Bowditch h
" Hormidas laborer h 203 Eugenia
" Hormidas weaver h 15 Phillips av
" Joseph grocer 357 N Front h 1296 Acushnet av [avenue
" Louis speeder tender h 171 Coffin
" Ludge carpenter h 113 Collette
" Roderick clerk 357 N Front bds 1296 Acushnet avenue
Langfield Joseph J chauffeur 125 Middle h 268 Weld
" Walter piper bds 268 Weld
Langhorn Ernest b 310 Tinkham [ham
" Frederick **loom fixer h** 310 Tink-
" Walter E conductor b 109 Fourth
Langill James T carpenter h 340 Court [avenue
Langis Alfred carder h 220 Phillips
Langley Joseph V overseer b 43 Beetle
" Margaret **Mrs** h 45 Maxfield
Langl Adelard (Langlois & Roy) 934 S Water b 90 Brock av
" Adrien doffer b 325 N Front
" Alder molder b 325 N Front
" Antonio clerk b 121 Hathaway
" Armas weaver h 154 Cedar Grove
" Arthias loom fixer h 154 Cedar Grove [Weld
" Arthur clerk 806 Purchase h 171
" Arthur painter b 121 Hathaway
" Arthur J weaver h 154 Cedar Grove
" Authier & Co (Joseph Langlois and F X Delos Authier) carpenters and builders 2030 Acushnet av [Collette
" Crosby clerk 267 Coggeshall h 196

Langlois
" David clerk 79 Austin h 198 State [N Front
" Delphis driver 12 School h 339
" Delphis hairdresser h 417 N Front
" Edouard died Feb 12 1911 [av
" Edward Mrs rms 1332 Acushnet
" Emery weaver h 229 State
" Eugene weaver b 89 Mosher
" Henri glassworker h 2603 Acushnet av
" Joseph boarding house 815 Fifth
" Joseph doffer b 121 Hathaway
" Joseph (Langlois, Authier & Co) 2030 Acushnet av h do
" Joseph wheelwright h 121 Hathaway [Grove
" Leonados weaver bds 154 Cedar
" Moise carpenter h 127 Coffin av
" Oliva clerk 225 Sawyer h 194 Belleville av [121 Hathaway
" Rosario helper 211 Coffin av b
" Silas barber h 616 S Second
" Simeon removed from city
" Virginia A widow Arthur dressmaker 325 N Front h do
" & Roy (Adelard Langlois and Zoel Roy) bakers 945 S Water
Langshaw Albert C h 219 Hawthorn
" Edward E asst supt Dartmouth Mills h 212 County [171 Butler
" Hatton supt Dartmouth Mills h
" John P h 234 County
" Walter H pres and agent Bristol Mfg Co and Dartmouth Mills h 152 Cottage [b 152 Cottage
" Walter S clerk Dartmouth Mills
Langton John weaver h 24 Cove
Languedoc Arthur laborer b 531 S Second
" Clement bricklayer b 76 County
" Clement mason 531 S Second h do
" Oliver weaver h 76 County
Languirand Henry operative bds 64 Mosher
" Levi loom fixer h 64 Mosher
" William carpenter b 64 Mosher
Lanier Arthur spinner b 892 S Water
" Treffle slasher h 892 S Water
Lanous Alexandria h 6 McGurk

Kinyon's Commercial School Will furnish your office help free — **Odd Fellows Building COR. WILLIAM and PLEASANT STS. NEW BEDFORD, MASS.**

Lanous
" Arthur operative h 24 Ashley
" Christopher weaver b 6 McGurk
" Frank laborer b 6 McGurk
" Jereme operative b 6 McGurk
" John operative b 49 Salisbury
" Joseph weaver h 18 Ashley
Lanphear Charles E engineer h 63 Mill [63 Mill
" Charles I teamster 97 Front bds
Lansing Frances A widow David b 396 Middle [ter
Lansky Jacob pedlar b 614 S Water
" Julius fruit 614 S Water b do
" Louis produce 494 S Water h do
" Samuel fruit r 60 Howland h do
Lantagne Adolph doffer b 86 Davis
Lantain Oliver operative h 138 Cedar Grove [sion
Lanthier Ludger plumber h 32 Division
Lao Manuel T grocer 145 Belleville av
LaPage Emile carpenter h 86 Hathaway [ty
Lapage Joseph mason h 936 County
LaPalne Joseph rem to Fall River
" Mary widow John B h 19 Hicks
" Odile widow Joseph h 24 Tallman
" Oscar operative b 24 Tallman
" Wilfred weaver h 195 Collette
Lapan Levi teamster h 194 Cedar
Lapan Levi teamster h 194 Cedar Grove [County
" Louis clerk 770 Purchase b 1064
Laperiere Archie operative bds 125 Nash road
" Louis operative h 125 Nash rd
LaPerle Joseph weaver h 135 N Front
Lapham Edney A clerk 62 Purchase h 30 Liberty
" Frederick brakeman b 116 Willis
" George A janitor h 23 Vine
" George H brakeman h 366 Pleasant [dar
" George W gardener h 323 Cedar
" Joshua G watchman Custom House h 48 Walnut
" Leonard C treas Nonquitt Spinning Co h 36 Madison
" Sophia milliner h 48 Walnut
LaPierre Alexander fisherman b 101 Coffin av [av
" Edmond weaver h 190 Coffin
" Elizabeth clerk b 190 Coffin av
" Eusebe boilermaker b 50 School

LaPierre
" Fred stonecutter h 558 Hathaway road
" Hugo operative h 64 Hicks
" Joseph lamp lighter h 31 Beetle
" Louis mill hand b 302 Coggeshall
" Louis removed from city
" Lucien laborer b 190 Coffin av
" Theodore driver foot North
LaPlante Albini widow Ulric h 196 Collette
" David third hand b 57 Merrimac
" Olivina Mrs variety 132 Bullard h do [Belleville av h 16 Bullard
" Philias (Laplante Bros) wood 279
Laplante Albert lather b 63 Hicks
" Albert (Laplante Bros) h 59 Collette
" Alphonse lather h 807 Purchase
" Amos baker 704 Purchase
" Brothers (Philias and Albert) wood 279 Belleville av
" Charles carpenter h 72 Tallman
" Georgiana Mrs h 286 Davis
" Joseph h 53 Belleville avenue
" Joseph lather b 807 Purchase
" Joseph mills 242 Nash rd h do
" Pierre (Vigneault & Laplante) 273 Sawyer h 223 Bowditch
" Wilfred mill hand h 135 Whitman
" see Plante [avenue
Lapoint Joseph fixer b 1537 Acushnet
Lapointe Alphonse operative b 16 Bentley
" Aime baker h 486 Coggeshall
" Ambroise carder h 25 Ashley
" Charles machinist rms 20 S Second [h do
" Dora Mrs variety 543 N Front
" Emily A died Feb 5 1911
" Evette Mrs clerk 40 Purchase bds 1537 Acushnet av
" Felix fixer h 543 N Front
" Firman spinner h 16 Hicks
" Frank conductor h 143 Collette
" Hormidas spinner b 16 Hicks
" Isadore baker and grocer 488 Coggeshall h do
" Joseph carder h 25 Katharine
" Joseph carpenter b 193 Bowditch
" Joseph fisherman h 16 Bentley
" Joseph slubber h 31 Morton
" Joseph spinner b 16 Hicks

Bread, Cake, Pastry
RICHMOND & COMPANY 255-257 UNION STREET
Bell 993 Automatic 1022

Lapointe
" J Oscar insurance agent 37 Purchase h 73 Independent
" Lair operative b 22 McGurk
" Napoleon carpenter h 5 McGurk
" Narcisse clerk 100 Ruth h 38 McGurk
" Philias spinner h 486 Coggeshall
" Philip copper worker b 16 Hicks
" Pierre sexton St Anthony's church h 193 Bowditch
" Pierre D broom mfr 190 Chestnut h 55 Hope
Lapolla Joseph grocer and bicycle repairer 543 Purchase h 4 Franklin
Laporte Alexander weaver h 93 [Hathaway
" Arthur fireman h 36 Hicks
" Arthur Jr bartender b 36 Hicks
" Camille fireman h 282 Davis
" Edmond clerk 590 First
" Edmond laborer h 178 River rd
" Edmonde baker 913 Acushnet av h r 36 Hicks
" Joseph h rear 36 Hicks
" Leonide waiter b 36 Hicks
" Philiman widow of Ferdinand b 154 Cedar Grove
" Sophie widow Zephir h 8 Marvin
Laprade Louisa Mrs mill hand h 319 Tinkham
Lapre John carpenter h 126 Clara
" Louis herbalist h 815 First
Laprie Joseph carpenter h 126 Clara
" Joseph weaver h 803 First
Laranger Joseph laborer b 941 S Water
Larch Fred agent h 1026 S Water
Lardner Joseph drill maker h 59 Sherman
Lareau Adalord carder h 188 Weld
" Emile fixer b 1103 S Water
" Ferdinand hairdresser Wamsutta Club h 140 State
" Henri insurance agent 37 Purchase rm 23
" Josephine Mrs bds 188 Weld
" Theodore second hand h 19 Holly
" see LaRue
Lariviere Adolphus weaver h 102 Ruth
" Arthur hostler 388 N Front h 386 [do
" Augustin weaver h 86 Davis

Lariviere
" Cyril barber 87 William b 1 Ashland [avenue
" Emily mill hand h 70 Phillips
" Henry S clerk 1516 Acushnet av h 429 North Front
" Joseph laborer b 70 Phillips av
" Joseph weaver b 163 David
" Joseph P carpenter h 50 Nye
" Louis wood yard 145 Coggeshall b 145 do
" Ludger weaver h 97 Collette
" Octave laborer h 128 Cove
" Octave weaver h 109 Nash road
" Rose mill hand h 70 Phillips av
Lark Charles laborer h 140 Newton
Larkin Agnes nurse h 50 Thompson
" Catherine T variety 11 W French av b 50 Thompson
" C May stenographer P Corp b 75½ Atlantic
" Edward J painter h 75½ Atlantic
" Elizabeth h 50 Thompson
" Sarah J variety 50½ Thompson h [50 do
Larma John carpenter h 380 Dartmouth
" Sarah J Mrs variety 380 Dart- [mouth h do
Larner James J died Dec 11 1910
" Jeanette M widow James J h 49 S Second
" John laborer 214 S Water b 17 [Walnut
" Thomas laborer h 17 Walnut
LaRoche Olive widow Joseph h 134 Nash road
" Thomas baker h 2 Tilton
Larochelle Alfred blacksmith 162 N Front h 346 do
" Alphonse painter b 1103 S Water
" Damase furniture mover h 4 Delano
" Edmond grocer 41 Bentley h 302 [Sawyer
" Edward painter b 4 Delano
" James h 17 Ashley
" Jean B blacksmith h 975 South [Water
" Jean B Jr weaver b 975 S Water
" Napoleon second hand h 25 Morton court
" Stephen speeder tender h 4 Del- [ano
" Telesphore stonecutter h 479 S Front
" William carder b 4 Delano
Larocque Alfred H paymaster b 86 S Sixth
" Edward operative h 81 Indepen- [dent

GLOBE DYE HOUSE 220 SHAWMUT AVE.
J. N. J. LONHOLDT, PROP. Telephone Connections Goods called for and Delivered
Down town Office, 52 Pleasant St., Room 1 North End Office, 1014 Acushnet Ave.

Larocque
" Henry beamer b 90 Brock av
" Henri died Jan 15 1911
" Henry operative b 81 Independent
" Hermine widow Henry h 86 S Sixth
" Lucy widow Joseph dressmaker 412 N Front h do
" Narcisse second hand b 125 Tallman
" Napoleon operative h 78 Independent
" Oliver operative b 81 Independent
" Ovide barber b 29 Ashley
" Wilfred drillworker b 81 Independent
" see Rock
LaRose Arthur weaver h 92 Holly
" Henry weaver h 78 Tallman
Larose Emeline clerk b 92 Holly
Larrabee Birdie Mrs rem to Providence R I
Larriabbee Alcide weaver h 79 Nelson
Larrivee Cyrill S barber h 1 Ashland
Larson Hans fisherman rms 8 Bethel
" Matilda cook h 206 Park
" Robert Rev h 69 Ocean
LaRue Alhena widow spinner bds 20 Bentley
" Diascor died Feb 20 1911
" Emma shoeworker rms 92 High
" Eugene clerk 41 Bentley b 202 Tinkham av
" Isadore mill hand h 35 Independent
" Timothy operative h 65 Kenyon
" Victoria widow Alderic b 70 Phillips av
" Wilfred mill hand bds 35 Independent
Lasell Herbert F laborer b 43 Sycamore
Lassey Harry painter bds 194 Davis
" Joseph mill hand h 194 Davis
Lassow Hyman tailor 40 Purchase b 107 Fifth
Latham Beatrice weaver b 27 Margin
" Emma bds 64 South
" Jane Mrs h 27 Margin
" John compositor b 27 Margin
" John laborer b 210 Division
" Margaret widow Thomas E h 210 Division
" Robert fixer h 131 Tallman
" Thomas gardener h 482 Bolton
Latimer Doralice widow John mill hand h 384 N Front
" James carder b 1 Blackburn

Latimer
" Robert blacksmith h 1 Blackburn
Latour Desire rem to Montreal Can
" Joseph carpenter b 391 Bowditch
Latraverse Amedos operative bds 20 Nye
" Louis weaver h 86 Davis
" Omer laborer b 20 Nye
" Paul laborer h 20 Nye
Lattimore Louis mill hand h 307 Coggeshall
Latulippe Louis baker 1070 County
Latusik Joseph carder h 3 Hampton court
" Leon picker b 3 Hampton court
Laube Adolph died June 17 1911
" Arnold weaver h 181 Bowditch
" Bertha widow Adolph h 181 Bowditch
" Oscar removed to Boston
Laudino Lewis fireman 26 Brook
Lauer John weaver h 82 Phillips av
Lauermann Charles weaver h 9 Oneko lane
" Henry spinner b 9 Oneko lane
" Joseph spinner b 9 Oneko lane
" Rudolph back boy bds 9 Oneko lane
Laughlin Annie weaver h 36 Hazard
" Frank variety 9 Weld h 1620 Acushnet av
" James laborer h 312 Court
" John J laborer h 124 Collette
" Margaret widow John bds 124 Collette
" Thomas laborer h 222 State
" William T clerk 9 Municipal bldg h 74 Chestnut
" see Loughlin
Laurendeau Emile mill hand h 492 N Front
" Ernest machinist b 531 N Front
" Hiliare h 531 N Front
Laurenz Pasquale laborer b 32 Hazard
Laurient Oliver painter h 118 Dartmouth
Lauzon Adaline widow Thomas h 152 Whitman
Lavalle Adelard laborer h 17 Beetle
" Alexander fixer h 10 Salisbury
" Arthur painter 1351 Acushnet av b 311 Coffin av
" Charles mill hand h 115 Bullard
" Damase weaver h 17 Beetle
" Edward b 306 N Front
" Edward weaver h 721 First
" Edward B millwright h 723 First

GREENE & WOOD Every Kind of LUMBER AND MILL WORK
PINE STREET, off So. WATER STREET, NEW BEDFORD

Lavalle
" Emile clerk 11 Weld b 311 Coffin av
" Frank laborer b 311 Coffin av
" Fred weaver b 86 Davis
" Georgiana clerk 1081 Acushnet av b 1 Weld square [av
" Henry A rms 1142 Acushnet av
" John conductor rms 86 N Second
" Joseph speeder tender h 311 Coffin av
" Joseph weaver h 16 George
" Leonora clerk 40 Purchase b 17 Clark
" Louis weaver b 311 Coffin av
" Omer fixer h 82 Phillips av
" Peter spinner h 1 Weld
" Thomas fixer h 99 David
" Victor J motorman b 274 Pleasant
Lavallee Victoria widow h 587 First
Lavalley Alexis J mason h 88 Nelson
Lavault Louis baker h 859 S Water
Laverdiere Achille operative h 115½ Bullard [Pleasant
Lavers Joseph W watchman h 238
Laverty Emma E bds 4 Pine
Lavetto Peter laborer h 5 Seneca
Lavigne Albert weaver h 31 Ashley
" Athanase machinist h 18 Cove rd
" Henry weaver h 72 Division
" Joseph laborer b 8 Tallman
" Omer weaver h 12 Nye
Lavimoniere Peter yard foreman Nonquitt Mill h 190 Earle
Laviolette Alice F b 85 Walden
" Eudger insurance agent 37 Purchase rm 23 h 85 Walden
" Matilda widow Rudolph bds 85 Walden [geshall
Lavivieri Pierre weaver b 145 Cog-
Lavueque Frank machinist 117 Bowditch
LaVoie Joseph carpenter h 56 Ashley
Lavoie Albert W rem to Taunton
" Alfred carder h 23 Thatcher
" Anna widow Jean h 33 Viall
" Charles weaver b 101 Holly
" Eador shoemaker h 89 Austin
" Edmund weaver b 101 Holly
" Eliza widow Neal h r 5 Campbell [man
" Esdras J blacksmith h 137 Tall-
" Frank carder b 101 Holly
" Fred shoemaker rms 7 N Second
" George weaver b 33 Viall

Lavoie
" Henri barber 285 Purchase h 69 Merrimac
" John operative b 131 N Front
" John painter h 1 Ashland
" John B weaver h 434 Pleasant
" Joseph h 122 Mott [b do
" Josephine dressmaker 117 Ruth
" Louis grocer 109 Davis h do
" Louis weaver h 117 Ruth
" Ludger operative b 23 Thatcher
" Peter D weaver h 161 Cove
" Philip carpenter h 17 N Water
" Remi fixer h 57 Rivet
" William bartender Parker House b r 5 Campbell [ditch
Law Abram lunchman b 210 Austin
" Alice M clerk 185 Purchase b 314 Allen [Crapo
" Arthur carriage painter h 33
" Arthur O helper b 210 Austin
" Edwin L mgr h 191 Washington
" Emma bookkeeper b 314 Allen
" George mason h 255 N Front
" Jesse mgr h 314 Allen
" Jesse Jr drillmaker b 314 Allen
" John spinner h 210 Tinkham
" Samuel lunch Spring cor S Second h 210 Austin
" Sarah widow Young housekeeper 1547 Acushnet av
" William instructor N B Industrial school rms 179 William
Lawes Annie J widow Walter h 38 Summit [tle
Lawless Walter J operative h 95 Bee-
" William stonecutter b 33 Reynolds
Lawlor John F granite 1256 Kempton h 77 Fifth
Lawrence Alice J principal Clark st school b 351 County [lette
" Anthony second hand b 157 Col-
" Anthony watchman b 153 Mt Pleasant
" Anthony P clerk b 61 Bedford
" Antone carpenter Clifford h do
" Antone spinner h 44 Independent [Kempton
" Charles H driver 255 Union b 171
" Charles L second hand h 50 Princeton [net av
" Chester bootblack b 282 Acush-

BONNEY, FOLSTER & CO.,
The North End's Shopping Centre
Dry Goods and Men's Furnishings
945-947 Acushnet Ave., New Bedford, Mass.

Lawrence
" Clara S stenographer Standard b 61 Bedford [kiln Hill rd L C
" Clarence E machinist h Tar-
" Cyrus T h 329 Cedar
" David E wholesale produce and fruit 39 Union h 90 Bedford
" Dennis W switchman h 30 Locust
" Edward A died July 7 1911
" Edward I janitor H A Kempton school h 49 Emerson (S) [Hill
" Edward P wholesale cigars h 61
" Ellen A bookkeeper 226 N Water b 3531 Acushnet av
" Frank removed from city
" George H (John H Lawrence & Son) h 50 Rotch [Dartmouth
" George R sergeant police h 68
" George W mason h 3842 Acushnet av [Princeton
" George W Jr yardman b 50
" Henry C letter carrier Clifford P O h 3531 Acushnet av
" Herbert C drillmaker h 281 Fourth [ushnet av
" Herbert W teamster h 2588 Acu-
" James T laborer h 45 Adams
" James W h 630 County
" John operative b 77 Taber
" John spinner h 487 N Front
" John D teamster h 61 Bedford
" John E glasscutter h 224 State
" John H (John H Lawrence & Son) h 66 Parker
" John H & Son (John H and Geo H) top roll coverers 167 N Second
" John J weaver h end Clifford
" Joseph drillmaker h 190 Bonney
" Joseph operative h 248 S Second
" Joseph teamster Morris & Co h 202 Purchase
LAWRENCE JOSEPH A hardware 1032-1034 Acushnet av h 195 Earle See page 784
" Joseph F operative b 806 S Water
" Joseph F painter b 79 Prospect
" Joseph H blacksmith N B W W h 171 Kempton [Bedford
" Lucy A cook 435 County h 61
" Manuel bartender 233 S Second
" Manuel laborer h 93 Nelson
" Manuel laborer b 350 S Second
" Manuel mill hand h 166 Grinnell

Lawrence
" Manuel A Jr glass blower h 173 Fourth [Shawmut av
" Mary D widow James A h 159
" Matthew laborer h 158 Fair
" Maude A bookkeepr 185 Union b 45 Bonney [lette
" Minnie Mrs spinner h 157 Col-
" Peter mill hand b 487 N Front
" Sarah C widow Charles E h 283 Union [ney
" Thomas A machinist h 45 Bon-
" Thomas W h 248 Cedar
" Walter machinist h 249 Austin
" William T engineer h Tarkiln Hill road
" see Lorenz [First
Lawson Andrew coal shoveler h 72
" J Thomas weaver h 95 Beetle
" Lizzie died 1910
Lawton Abram C salesman 188 N Water h 40 Hunter
" Albert C clerk Merchants National Bank b 179 Austin
" Albert W driver h 23 Walnut
" Asaph T salesman 2 Water b 70 Mill [h 40 Hunter
" A Chester salesman 188 N Water
" Benjamin sailmaker h 60 Chestnut
" Charles F supt of streets 301 Municipal bldg h 12 Maple View terrace
" Charles H Mrs h 89 Elm
" Charles W provisions 773 Kempton h 404 Mill [County
" Clara P widow Horace h 491
" Clarence E janitor h 66 Willow
LAWTON C H & H A CO (Joseph W Nicklas and Mrs Alice M Considine) druggists 1 and 3 and 52 Purchase and 113 Union See advt Druggists in Business Directory
" Edwin B plumber b 327 Court
" George clerk h 105 Fifth
" Harry C mill hand b 12 Maple View ter [chase h 179 Austin
" Henry C blacksmith 332 Pur-
" Hettie H lodging h 187 Purchase
" James weaver h 59 Elm
" Joseph M h 397 Cottage
" Lawrence clerk 219 Purchase bds 527 do [State
" Mary M widow Perry G h 87

M. P. B. Silva & Son Paints, Oils and Glass
Sole Agents for Lucas Tinted Gloss Paints
157 ACUSHNET AVENUE Both Phones NEW BEDFORD

Lawton
" Richard E engineer h 87 Hathaway [h 103 Chestnut
" Robert T coremaker 229 N Water
" Russell S h 112 Dartmouth
" Theodore E h 70 Mill
" William P h 198 Kempton
Laycock Florence clerk 11 Myrtle b 7 Ashland ter
" Frederick weaver b 850 First
" John W clerk b 7 Ashland ter
" Robinson weaver h 36 Larch
" Thomas T men's furnishings 939 Weld h 7 Ashland ter [ty
" William conductor h 1086 Coun-
Layfield James spinner h 51 Wood
" James A waiter 62 Purchase b 51 Wood
Layland John J weaver h 67 Dean
" William loom fixer h 163 Holly
Layton Agnes E clerk b 257 Acushnet av [Acushnet av
" Agnes M widow John S h 257
" John S died Feb 4 1911 [av
" John W operative b 257 Acushnet
" Joseph chef 62 Purchase rms 58 S Second [do
Lazaro John grocer 78 First h 74
Leach Eliza widow James L h 10 Studley
" Harry J died July 12 1911
" Joseph H h 53 Bowditch
" Lucy S teacher Clark st school b 163 Maxfield [Hillman
" Sarah A widow George C h 143
" William H H salesman 1 William h 75 Sycamore [163 Maxfield
" William W salesman 198 Union b
" W Carleton clerk b 14 Studley
Leadbeater Ellen widow John bds 1159 Purchase [Liberty
Leahy Mary A widow Thomas h 50
" Mary H bookbinder b 50 Liberty
" Michael J mgr 182 Union h at Fall River [Thomas
" William T police Station 5 b 60
Leake Joseph E weaver b 163 Tinkham [Bonney
Leal Hilda P bookkeeper bds 121
" John G salesman bds 121 Bonney
" John J florist 191 Shawmut av b 207 Durfee [Rivet
" Louise widow Frank G h 518

Leal
" Manuel J laborer Standard Oil Co h 207 Durfee
" Mary Mrs b 14 Thompson
" Rose housekeeper 230 Bonney
" Theresa P widow John h 121 Bonney
" William bds 121 Bonney
" William electrician b 207 Durfee
Leaming Emily B and Florence L h 41 North
" Stanley L student b 41 North
Leandro Antone J operative h 55 Mitchell [ter
" Joaquim mill hand h 692½ S Wa-
" Manuel J laborer h 55 Mitchell
Lear Frank drill worker h 81 Howland [ion
Leary Abbie tailoress rms 256 Un-
" Charles E drill worker b 75 Oak
" Chrystom J physician 415 Pleasant h do [Harrison
" Cornelius J engineer P Corp h 2
" Dennis drill worker h 99 Beetle
" Dennis shoemaker b 35 Ashland
" Dennis Jr blacksmith 100 Pleasant h 35 Ashland [b 75 Oak
" Edith A stenographer 251 Union
" Edward painter h 75 Oak
" Edward Jr drill worker b 75 Oak
" Henry drill worker b 75 Oak
" Humphrey laborer h 205 Austin
" John h 8 Robeson [Kempton
" John tailor 76 William h 56
" Margaret L clerk b 17 Bullock
" Margaret T b 396 Middle (W)
" Mary A widow Daniel b 213 Cottage [French av
" Mary J widow John D h 15 E
" Michael laborer h 85 Park
" Michael M copper worker h 432 Pleasant
" M Henry operative b 205 Austin
" Rose clerk b 17 Bullock [land
" Timothy city laborer b 35 Ash-
" William foreman h 17 Bullock
" William machinist b 1022 Acushnet avenue
" see O'Leary
Leatherbarrow Robert weaver h 335 Sawyer [113½ Hathaway
Leathers H Ellen widow Robert b

Steiger-Dudgeon Co.
"The WOMAN'S Store."
Tel. Bell 82 & 83, Branches connecting all depts.
" " 160 For Office only. Auto. 1211

SUMPTIONS, ASSORTMENTS AT ALL TIMES OF DEPENDABLE DRY GOODS

Leathers
" Herbert fireman h 113½ Hathaway [chase
" Mary J Mrs lodgings 384 Pur-
Leaver Albert E elevatorman h 126 Eugenia [French av
" Benjamin second man bds 32 W
Leavitt Carrie M teacher William H Taylor school rms 16 Fifth
" Charles L carpenter h r 297 Cedar [Co
" Clarence D clerk Gosnold Mills
" John W laborer b r 297 Cedar
" Louis changer over h 104 Collette
" Milton H packer b 23 Homer
" Minnie T Mrs clerk 49 William rm 4 h 60 Washington
" M Abbie sewer 40 Purchase b 57 Bedford [nell
" Ralph B clerk P O h 163 Grin-
LeBaron Alonzo T foreman 123 Front h 77 Fourth [Ohio
" Harrison D removed to Oxford
" Philip C clerk 294 Purchase rms do
Lebeau Adelard weaver h 12 Beetle
" Alex shoe repairer 864 Acushnet av h 1498 do
" Alexander (The Red Cross Shoe Co) 1494 Acushnet av h 1498 do [do
" Alfred painter 183 Phillips av h
" Archille operative bds 6 Hicks
" Bruno fixer h 43 Ashley
" David A manager 1351 Acushnet avenue bds 276 Earle
" Delphis weaver h 16 Stapleton
" Emanuel weaver h 176 Cedar Grove
" Eusebe spinner h 426 N Front
" Guillaume loom fixer h 55 County
" Henri weaver h 36 McGurk
" Joseph clerk h 79 Bullard
" Joseph clerk b 410 N Front
" Joseph mason b 131 Webster ct
LEBEAU JOSEPH painter and paper hanger 141 Collette h do See page 785
" Louis third hand h 80 Eugenia
" Mary Mrs weaver h 658 First
" Moise h 6 Hicks
" Napoleon loom fixer h 71 Ruth
" Oliver fitter h 139 Hathaway

Lebeau
" Oliver weaver b 176 Cedar Grove
" Ovila weaver b 1498 Acushnet av
" Peter removed from city
" Prudent Mrs h 1060 Acushnet av
" Remi weaver h 12 Hazard ct
" Solime clerk 410 N Front h 150 Phillips avenue
" Speridion motorman h 90 Linden
LEBEAU THEOPHILE real estate 410½ N Front and liquors 416 do h 185 Phillips av See page 33
" Theophile Jr student b 185 Phillips avenue
" Wilfred weaver h 82 Nelson
" William operative b 194 Dean
" Xavier teamster b 703 Purchase
LeBeauf Alexina b 106 Beetle
LeBel Edward h 38 Ashley
" George second hand b 36 Jouvett
" Gregoire weaver h 2784 Acushnet avenue
" Teofil h 36 Jouvett
LeBell Harry removed from city
" Harry O hay and grain 171 Dean h do
" Joseph removed from city
LeBert Etienne laborer h 382½ N Front [fin av
LeBlanc Adelin fisherman b 101 Cof-
" Alfred overseer h 166 Bates av
" Alfris carpenter h 154 Belleville road [avenue
" Alphe second hand h 214 Coffin
" Alyre carpenter b 172 Hatch
" Antoine weaver h 282 N Front
" Aurella widow Charles h 164 Holly [yer
" Benjamin fisherman h 184 Saw-
" Cecile widow Eustache h 369 chase [ville av
" Charles mill hand h 319 Belle-
" Charles spinner b 164 Holly
" Charles I (Champegny & LeBlanc) h 149 Bullard [av
" Cleophas fisherman b 101 Coffin
" Damilde widow James h 120 Collette
" Daniel carpenter h 120 Collette
" Dominique mill hand h 456 Belleville av
" Edgar helper b 871 Purchase
" Edmund painter h 311 N Front

PELEG H. SHERMAN 506 COUNTY ST.
FUNERAL DIRECTOR AND EMBALMER
OFFICE PHONES. Bell 690-13. Auto. 1305.
RESIDENCE PHONES. Bell 690-12. Auto. 1306.

LeBlanc
" Edward carpenter b 268 N Front
" Ernest fixer h 52 Collette
" Ernest laborer rem to Fitchburg
" Evariste clerk b 195 Phillips av
" Ferdinand B clerk 1516 Acushnet av h 105 Collette
" Fidele lather b 237 Coffin av
" Fidele twister b 456 Belleville av
" Frank mill hand h 409 N Front
" Fred carpenter h 141 Bullard
" George h 101 Coffin av
" George operative b 164 Holly
" George rem to Vancouver B C
" Gregoire carpenter h 268 N Front
" Hubert second hand h 1176 Acushnet av
" Isaie mill hand h 342 N Front
" Israel twister b 456 Belleville av
" Jacob carpenter h 164 Tinkham
" Jacques removed from city
" James S died April 13 1911
" Jeffrey W P clerk 398 N Front h 201 Coffin av
" Jennie E dressmaker 369 Purchase h do
" John artist 456 Belleville av b do
" John A operative b 7 Salisbury
" Joseph h 162 Bates av
" Joseph engineer h 132 Bullard
" Joseph fisherman h 18 Holly
" Joseph fisherman b 477 N Front
" Joseph (fisherman) rem from city
" Joseph laborer h r 198 State
" Joseph spinner b 164 Holly
" Joseph twister b 871 Purchase
" Joseph weaver h 1103 S Water
" Julia widow Henry h 417 N Front
" Lea dressmaker 268 N Front b do
" Louis clerk h 446 N Front
" Maggie clerk 1100 Acushnet av rms 241 N Front
" Magloire fisherman h 291 Belleville av
" Marcellin fisherman h 286 N Front
" Marie widow Maxime h 65 Penniman
" Martin foreman h 20 Tallman
" Maurice carpenter h 66 Dean
" Maximillian fisherman h 101 Coffin av
" Michel mill hand h 352 N Front
" Minnie clerk 1081 Acushnet av b 417 N Front
" Narcisse loom fixer h 104 Bowditch
" Napoleon carder h 66 Dean

LeBlanc
" Napoleon mill hand h 213 Belleville av
" Olive widow Paul bds 148 Tinkham
" Olivier removed to Fairhaven
" Ovide removed from city
" Patrick laborer b 65 Penniman
" Patrick shoemaker b 221 N Front
" Paul carder b 644 Purchase
" Paul fisherman h 11 Holly
" Philip carpenter h 164 Tinkham
" Pierre operative h 164 Holly
" Pierre stonecutter b 325 N Front
" Regina hairdresser 174½ Purchase h 369 do
" Samuel carpenter b 158 Tinkham
" Samuel rem to Moncton N B
" Theophile laborer h 871 Purchase
" Theophile B b 515 N Front
" Theophile L clerk 867 Purchase h 781 do
" William carpenter b 331 Belleville av
" see White
LeBoeuf Alexander carpenter h 47 Brock av
" Alida mill hand h 286 N Front
" Alphonse fruit h 83 Brock av
" Alphonse weaver h 9 Bullard
" Dana E weaver h 10 McGurk
" Esther Mrs fruit 27 Delano h 83 Brock av
" Ida weaver h 275 N Front
" Louis loom fixer h 345 Davis
" Valerie Mrs grocer 345 Davis h do
Lebranche Edrias rem from city
Lebrun Bernard weaver h 142 Phillips av
" Joseph weaver h 1086 S Water
LeChance Emile laborer h 690 First
L'Echo Publishing Co 101 Kenyon
Leck Carrie W Mrs h 43 Bethel
LeClair Adelard carder h 495 Coggeshall
" Adelard clerk 100 Ruth bds 27 Ashley
" Adelard A weaver b r 831 S Water
" Adolphus blacksmith h 209 State
" Albert painter h 289 Coffin av
" Amalda Mrs mill hand h 31 Nash rd
" Arthur teamster h 107 Beetle
" August laborer N B W W h r 36 Hicks
" Charles third hand h 187 Hathaway
" Delia Mrs mill hand h 330 N Front
" Delia widow Montague b 254 Mt Pleasant

COAL AND WOOD F. T. AKIN & COMPANY
HAY AND STRAW
WALNUT, COR. WATER, 84 PLEASANT ST., 25 WELD SQ.
129 COVE STREET WHF. FOOT OF COFFIN STREET

LeClair
" Donat steam fitter h 289 Coffin av
" Edmond weaver b 27 Ashley
" Eugene weaver h 49 Salisbury
" Felix weaver b 49 Salisbury
" Felix A (Ellis & LeClair) 520 County h 25 Richmond
" Fred carpenter b 53 Brock av
" Harry N removed to Norwood
" Heloise widow Victor boarding 289 Coffin av h do
" Henry carder h 114 David
" Honore carpenter h 31 Nash road
" John city employer h 111 Cedar
" Joseph painter b 289 Coffin av
" Joseph spinner b 1205 Acushnet avenue
" Joseph weaver h 27 Ashley
" Joseph O bricklayer h 56 Nye
" Julius laborer b 8 Pearl
" Louis weaver b 27 Ashley
" Mildred M clerk 160 Purchase b at Fairhaven [Dean
" Misael clerk 225 Sawyer h 56
" Onesime weaver b 1022 Acushnet avenue
" Ulric bds 52 Delano
" William hairdresser 116 Union h 71Merrimac [ham
" William loom fixer h 241 Tink-
LeClaire James loom fixer h 86 Robeson
" Ovela weaver h 13 Princeton av
Lecocq John B weaver h 344 Davis
Lecompte Azaire carpenter h 24 Bentley [Bentley
" Firman driver 1070 County b 24
Lecourse Alphonse operative h 622 S Second [av h do
Lecuyer Hector tailor 1140 Acushnet
" Joseph S insurance agent 120 Purchase rm 403 h 162 Tinkham [court
Leddy James P weaver h 2 Hazard
Lederman Abram shoemaker h r 559 Purchase [Coffin avenue
Ledoux Alphonse carpenter h 251
" Cora h 36 Independent
" David weaver b 162 Whitman
" Henri A roll coverer b 36 Independent [Front
" Hormidas mill hand h 541 North

Ledoux
" Hormidas slubber tender rms 418
" Joseph spinner h 274 N Front
" Matilda widow Anthony h 36 Independent
" Omer weaver b 1191 Purchase
" Peter operative h 111 Tallman
" Philip L U S N b 36 Independent
" Pierre elevatorman h 33 Holly
" Rose Mrs h 59 Elm
" Victor loom fixer h 1191 Purchase
Leduc Damase insurance agent 120 Purchase h Tarkiln Hill road
" Damase mill hand h 183 Collette
" Delima dry goods 1291 Acushnet avenue b 1293 do
" Joseph weaver b 504 S Second
" Margaret widow Damase lodging h 1293 Acushnet av
" Osease weaver h 477 S Front
" Philodore N grocer County cor Sawyer h do
" Pierre A insurance agent 41 William h 373 Bowditch
" Theodore drill worker b 27 Clark
Lee Agnes and Elizabeth L h 288 Summer
" Annie removed to Syracuse N Y
" Arthur C driver h 30 Mill
" Benjamin W clerk 1499 Acushnet avenue [Second h 131 Elm
" Bessie telephone operator 57 N
" Charles C letter carrier h 115 Sycamore [amore h do
" C C Mrs hairdressing 115 Syc-
" Daniel removed from city
" Emma L widow Allen L h 5 Spruce [75 Mill
" Ernest W optician 5 Purchase b
" Frank F grocer 145 County h 18 Mosher [ty
" Hannah widow Cyrus h 619 Coun-
" Harold spinner h 208 Nash rd
" Ida V h 172 Emerson (N)
" James molder b 65 Washburn
" James spinner h 154 Ashland
" John Albert foreman 123 Front h 96 Morgan [pendent
" Joseph F drill maker h 56 Inde-
" Mary Mrs h 103 Holly
" Mary A h 49 Hall
" Mary A teacher James B Congdon school bds 71 Arnold

Remember to investigate our methods before taking up a business course.
Kinyon's Commercial School
Odd Fellows Bldg., Cor. William and Pleasant Sts., New Bedford, Mass.

Lee
" Mary E clerk 1100 Acushnet av bds 103 Holly
" Samuel T variety 1100 Acushnet av 973 S Water and 314 to 318 Coggeshall h 87 Ashland [Mill
" Sarah E widow William M h 75
" William A overseer rms 35 Eighth
Leeman John spinner h 92 County
Leeming Henry engineer Engine 6 h 23 Crapo [rd
" Isabella widow Thomas b 71 Nash
" Robert laborer h 71 Nash rd
Leen Philip kitchen furnishings 451 S Water bds 456 do [33 Fair
" Philip Jr shoes 449 S Water h
" Samuel D kitchen furnishings 153 Purchase h 72 S Sixth
Lees Albert motor inspector 125 Middle h 53 Woodlawn av
" Annie R stenographer 97 William rm 305 b 475 Rivet
" Edmund b 191 Brock av
" Frances widow h 20 Reynolds
" Fred packer b 52 Winsor
" George C rem to Easton Pa
" James bookkeeper 424 S Second h 191 Brock av
" Jane widow John h 165 Bates av
" John second hand b 165 Bates av
" John spinner h 52 Winsor
" Lewis shipper Rotch dept N E C Y Co b 475 Rivet
" Percy spinner h 14 Salisbury
" Samuel baker 959 Acushnet av h 157 Bates av [cher
" Walter second hand h 23 That-
" William K overseer Rotch dept N E C Y Co h 475 Rivet
Lefebvre Aldeia clerk 912 S Water b 170 Rivet
" Alfred weaver h 289 Coffin av
" Clothile widow Alexis h 170 Rivet
" Edgar P H carder b 170 Rivet
" Eugene A removed from city
" John B slubber tender h 173 State
" Joseph weaver h 721 S First
" Napoleon laborer b 364 Coffin av
" Pierre A. carpenter h 364 Coffin avenue
" Rose Mrs h 28 Nye
" Rudolph weaver b 190 Dean
Leffingwell Helen R teacher James B Congdon school b 108 Bonney [vell
Lefort Theophile weaver h 27 Co-
LeFrancois Calixte clerk 1162 Acushnet av h 8 Austin court
" Edward carpenter h 369 N Front
" Emile carpenter 160 Bowditch h do [Front
" Marceline widow Jules b 361 N
Lefrancois Albert weaver b 8 Austin court [ley
Legault Ferdinand fixer h 30 Ash-
" Omer weaver b 8 Cove rd
" Romeo A painter b 8 Cove road
" Rosanna widow Felix h 8 Cove rd.
Legendre Ovid second hand b 968 S Water [lard
Leger Alcide carpenter b 38 Bul-
" Alfred carpenter h 192 Collette
" Alfred doffer b 12 Tallman
" Dennis fisherman h 38 Bullard
" Frank laborer b 113 Nash rd
" Frank removed to Rumford Me
" Frank M carpenter h 338 N Front
" Henry machinist b 149 Tinkham
" Joseph carpenter h 73 Hathaway
" Joseph insurance agent 120 Purchase rm 403 b 104 Collette
" Joseph mill hand b 148 Tinkham
" Joshua steam fitter b 20 Tallman
" Jude laborer h 12 Tallman
" Mary card grinder h 12 Nye
" Olive widow Victor b 28 Holly
" Philip foreman h 49 Howard av
" Pierre carpenter h 104 Davis
" Placide A mill hand h 113 Nash road [Front
" Stanislaus mill hand h 383 N
" William J clerk 1645 Acushnet av b 104 Davis [vis
Legere Aime carpenter h 190 Da-
" Albert laborer h 99 Perry
" Ferdinand operative b 332 Bowditch [Collette
" Joseph J insurance agent h 104
" Ludger mill hand h 332 Bowditch
" Mark mill hand h 12 Nye
" Philias carpenter h 99 Perry
" Reuben machinist b 190 Davis
Lehner Annie widow Joseph h 1061 County
" Joseph operative b 349 Coffin av
" Konrad shoemaker h 349 Coffin av [Tallman
Leigh Benjamin W bartender b 137

HASKELL BROS. DEALERS IN
ICE
400 COURT STREET TELEPHONE CONNECTION NEW BEDFORD, MASS.

Leigh
" John bicycles 321 Rivet h do
" John tailor 346 Purchase h do
" Thomas bicycle repairer 321 Rivet h 440 Orchard (S)
" see Lee [Mill
Leighton Edward G chauffeur h 126
" Harry operative b 271 Austin
" John D mariner h 14½ Griffin
" Joseph cook h 57 School
" Manuel fish 523 S Water
" Marion R h 27 Cannon
" Robert fixer h 301 Earle
Leistritz Paul R twister h 447 Pleasant
Leitao Henrique laborer N B W W
Leite Annie F widow Manuel F h 69 Short
" Jose insurance agent 120 Purchase rm 403 b 124 County
" Louis jeweler h 281 S Second
" Manuel F operative h 69 Short
" Manuel P shoemaker h 65 Independent
" Marian mill hand b 50 Dean
Le JOURNAL Gustave Hurel editor 267 Sawyer See page 758
Lekovisky Morris fisherman h 159 Cedar Grove [Weld
Lelaidier Armand operative bds 260
" August painter b 260 Weld
" Helmina widow h 260 Weld
" Jules died April 18 1911
Lelanne George barber 833 Purchase rms Acushnet cor Hicks
Lelievre Gustave fixer h 101 Davis
" Henry clerk 555 N Front h 184 Phillips av [Hemlock
Lema Antone M operative h 44
" John F city laborer h 214 S Front
" Joseph laborer h 526 Rivet
" Mary Mrs removed to Fairhaven
Lemaire Alphonse third hand h 99 Bowditch [rd
" Alphonse mill hand b 68 Nash
" Amelia widow Calixte h 279 Coggeshall [shall
" Andre operative bds 279 Cogge-
" Antoine painter h 1230 Acushnet avenue
" Arthur weaver b 53 Rivet
" Aurore dressmaker b 249 State
" Baptiste painter h 6 Front cor Holly
" Charles operative h 268 N Front

Lemaire
" Charles teamster h 363 Coggeshall
" Charles Jr painter h 268 N Front
" Edward driver 13 N Sixth b 166 N Front
" Florence died Sept 18 1910
" Frank painter h 475 N Front
" Frank roofer h 86 Nye
" Frank teamster h 159 Coggeshall
" Frederick baker and wood 249 State h do [State
" Frederick Jr teamster bds 249
" Henri teamster h 9 Bentley
" John weaver b 67 Coffin av
" Joseph carpenter h 279 Coggeshall
" Joseph driver b 249 State [av
" Joseph operative h 109 Phillips
" Joseph operative h 272 Davis
" Joseph roofer b 16 Holly
" Joseph teamster h 34 Bentley
" Joseph fixer h r 64 Hazard
" Joseph Mrs removed from city
" Ludovic printer 101 Kenyon
" Magloire carpenter h 307 Coggeshall
" Obert roofer b 16 Holly
" Peter driver 19 S Second h 7 N Second
" Peter painter h 297 N Front
" Rose widow Napoleon h 25 Thompson
" Seraphin carder h 68 Nash rd
" Stanislas removed from city
" Theophile laborer h 16 Holly
Lemarche Alex carpenter b 721 First
Lemarcher Rene operative h 14 Salisbury
LeMay Elizabeth Mrs weaver h 369 Coggeshall [ton av
Lemay Francis painter h 13 Prince-
" Joseph fixer h 190 Earle
" Louis weaver h 293 Earle
" Napoleon rem to Providence R I
" Wilfred speeder h r 679 Purchase
Lemerise Albert T milk 116 Phillips av b do
" Arthur G business college rms 11 and 12 Arcade bldg h 352 N Front
" Edmond mill hand b 113 Collette
" Emile carpenter b 116 Phillips av
" Joseph carpenter h 116 Phillips av
" Oliver teamster h 101 Phillips av

J. F. CROSSLEY 223 MILL STREET COR. EMERSON PHONE
STEAM and HOT WATER HEATING
GAS FITTING and FIXTURES

Lemerise
" William mill hand b 113 Collette
Lemery Arcade loom fixer h 178 Collette [N Second
Lemieux Alfred steam fitter h 212
" Alfred weaver b 100 Tallman
" Armanda widow Armis h 86 Hathaway [av
" Charles Rev bds 1415 Acushnet
" Daniel cigarmaker 117 Union
" Elzear removed to Dartmouth
" Ernest weaver h 100 Tallman
" Euclid weaver h 811 First
" Fred roll coverer h 28 Tallman
" Fred R overseer Pierce Bros Ltd
" George removed from city
" John P (J P Lemieux Co) 329 N Front h do
" Joseph clerk 1099 Acushnet av b 135 N Front
" Joseph hairdresser 2172 Acushnet avenue h 103 Perry
" Joseph (4 Social) rem from city
" Joseph (109 Bowditch) removed from city [h 301 Coffin av
" Joseph E painter 329 North Front
" J P Co (John P Lemieux) painters 329 North Front
" Louis removed from city
" Oliver weaver h 5 Bowditch
" Oscar removed from city
" Oscar stonecutter h 15 Adams
" Ovila carpenter b 86 Hathaway
" Raphael overseer h 101 Bowditch
" Thomas oiler h 1415 Acushnet av
" Victor helper h 402 Pleasant
" William removed from city
" Zephir weaver h 226 Sawyer
Lemire Alexander spinner h 6 Penniman
" Eugene operative h 150 Tallman
" Louis teamster h 1191 Purchase
" Philip operative h 10 Penniman
" Philip Jr operative b 10 Penniman [man
" Romeo millwright h 131 Tall-
" Wilbram fixer h 186 Collette
Lemlin Philip carpenter h 96 Division
" William J (Lemlin & Gosselin) bds 190 Division
" & Gosselin (William J Lemlin and Lengert P Gosselin) hardware 7 W French av [burn
LeMoine Paul carpenter h 32 Wash-
Lemoine Clement laster h 883 Purchase
" Edouard laborer h 47 Holly
" Jerry clerk 537 N Front rms 135 Nash road [shall
" Joseph teamster h 159 Cogge-
Lemond Wilfred carpenter h 478 Coggeshall
Lemos Alfred E painter h 139 Fair
" Alfred M clerk b 368 Allen
" Antone lamplighter h Hawes n Tarkiln Hill road
" Antone M fish h 368 Allen
" Antonio M driver S F E No 8 h 176 Davis
" Frank K hairdresser Parker House h 5 Tallman lane
" Frank S (Vetorino & Lemos) farmer 1379 Rockdale av h do
" Frederick carpenter b 45 Butler
" James L driver 374 Purchase h 267 Pope [Bowditch
" John clerk 878 Purchase bds 289
" John conductor h 419 S Second
" John laborer h 510 Acushnet av
" John A foreman 19 S Second h 28 Elm [mouth
" John E switchman h 53 Dart-
" John M motorman h 289 Bowditch
" Joseph hairdresser 137 Grinnell h 91 Durfee
" Manuel mill hand h 52 Swift
" Manuel J operative h 237 Tinkham
" Manuel S farmer Almshouse b do
" Walter M steamship agent 73 Howland h at Fairhaven
" William J driver 47 School h 57 do [Cedar
Lemunyon Frederick C baker h 117
" Susan widow John b 26 Florence
" see Leymunion
Lengnick Alfred C removed from city
Lenhart Adolph died April 14 1911
" Annie widow b 50 Sherman
" Elnora clerk 48 Pleasant h 264 Weld
" Frank weaver h 284 Cedar Grove
" Frank P inspector h 50 Sherman
" George operative b 284 Cedar Grove [Second b 50 Sherman
" Lillian A stenographer 57 North
" Mary widow Adolph h 264 Weld

CHARLES A. CROSHERE CARRIAGE AND AUTO
38 FOURTH ST. Bell Phone 1964-23 PAINTING

Lenhart
" Mary widow Frank h 398 Earle
" Rose h 150 Field
" Rudolph bds 398 Earle [Grove
" William operative bds 284 Cedar
Lennon Hugh H salesman 50 Union bds 367 Pleasant
LENOX MOTOR CAR CO Inc 3368 Washington Jamaica Plain Mass See page 739
Lent Manuel F weaver b 134 Bonney
" Mary widow h 134 Bonney
Lenz Joseph B glass cutter h 107 Willis [yer
Leoder Courtois salesman h 109 Saw-
Leonard Andrew city laborer h 83 County [County
" Charles pressman Times h 830
" Charles A motorman h 226 State
" Charles W (Oneko Woolen Mills) end Purchase h at Newtonville
" Daniel B died March 13 1911
" Daniel B Mrs h 74 Butler
" Edmond tailor b 107 Holly [mac
" Ellen widow Martin h 41 Merri-
" Frank G spinner h 161 Nash rd
" Gertrude H sewing teacher public schools bds 26 Seventh
" Hannah F h 110 Newton
" Herbert C machinist b 357 Reed
" John F laborer h 100 Hall
" John W traveling salesman h 3572 Acushnet avenue
" Jose F h 96 Hall
" Joseph cook b 98 Union
" Juliet P (Oxford Shop) 97 William rm 403 h at Fairhaven
" Lawrence asst steward rms 7 N Second [h do
" Mary A dressmaker 30 Bonney
" Mary B b 26 Seventh
" Mary F Mrs h 170 Rounds
" Mary M teacher Harrington school b 96 Oak [h do
" Milton H physician 83 Ash (S)
" Patrick laborer h 295 Cedar
" Paul C traveling salesman b 3572 Acushnet av
" Peter laborer b 137 Acushnet av
" Roland A asst assessor h 26 Seventh [Elm
" William H G brick layer h 5
" William J carpenter h 96 Hathaway
Leonare Philimon tailor h 107 Holly
Leonardo Joseph F shoe repairing 10 Dartmouth h 96 Hall [Front
LePage Come blacksmith h 252 N
" Ernest mason h 13 Ruth
" Hormidas doffer b 43 Union
" Joseph weaver h 311 Coffin av
" William fixer h 99 David
LePalme Alice Mrs housekeeper 60 Brock av [hand h 1064 County
Lepan Angelina widow Levi mill
" Louis machinist b 1064 County
Lepine Flavien second hand h 96 Division
" Henry carder h 857 First
" James spinner h 8 Welcome
" Moses B weaver h 180 State
Lepire Edward weaver b 84 Blackmer
" John Jr weaver h 23 Viall [mer
" Julia widow Batiste h 84 Black-
" Narcisse rem from city
Lerch John bricklayer h 87 Clifford
" Julius gardener h 31 High
Lereau Henry insurance agent b 289 Coffin av
Lermond Jennie nurse b 15 Mill
Leroux Adelard mill hand b 171 Coffin av
" Omer mill hand h 171 Coffin av
Leschna Gasper shoemaker h 167 Division
Lesieur George rem from city
" Helen Mrs mill hand h 187 Collette [lette
" Henry mill hand bds 187 Col
L'Esperance Ralph clerk rms 25 William [Belleville av
Lessard Frank mill hand rms 392
" Harvey inspector 43 William bds 229 Sawyer
" John H b 7 Ashland ter
" Joseph spinner b 187 Earle
" Lewie operative b 7 Ashland ter
" Mary widow Lewie h 7 Ashland ter [Front h 229 Sawyer
" Thomas confectionery 250 North
" Thomas doffer b 187 Earle
Lestage Felix carpenter h 44 Adams
Lester James restaurant 403 Kempton b 404 Maxfield [Water
Letarte Alfred upholsterer b 968 S
" Palmer weaver b 968 S Water
" Peter weaver h 968 S Water
Letendre Adelard weaver h 219½ Bowditch
" Donat weaver h 330 N Front

J. G. NICHOLSON
LUMBER, SASH, DOORS and BLINDS
BOWDITCH STREET, NEW BEDFORD, MASS.

Letendre
" Edmond weaver b 1280 Acushnet av
" Israel rem to Monville R I
" Israel twister h 287 Coffin av
" Noel fixer h 160 Earle
" Wilfred weaver b 1280 Acushnet av [vis
Lethbridge Walter fixer h 296 Da-
L'Etoile Marjorique carpenter h 297 Coffin av [Bentley
Letourneau Alfred carpenter h 25
" Charles clerk h 361 N Front
" Donat repairman U St Ry Co 784 Purchase
" Elezard mill hand h 59 Scott
" Francois machinist h 835 Acushnet av [835 Acushnet av
" Frank repairman U St Ry Co h
" Gabriel mill hand h 129 Eugenia
" Hector back boy b 142 Phillips avenue [Eugenia
" Hermenegilde mill hand b 129
" Hormidas second hand h 48 Nelson
" Hormidas second hand h 115 Ruth [av
" Joseph operative bds 142 Phillips
" Narcisse h 142 Phillips av
Leuchsenring Laura widow Robert b 149 Armour
" Robert machinist h 149 Armour
Leupold Adam weaver h 173 Hathaway [way
" Everett spinner bds 173 Hatha-
Leva James laborer h 20 Woodlawn av [Tinkham
Levalley Albert J spinner h 258
" Charles F watchman h 274 Phillips av [lips av
" Charles F Jr laborer b 274 Phil-
" Emma Mrs carder b 201 Eugenia
" Frank A mgr 62 N Water h at Fall River [ant
" Victor C motorman b 274 Pleas-
" William spinner b 274 Phillips av
" see Lavalle [tel h do
Levasseur Alex prop Weld sq Ho-
" Alex operative h 57 N Front
" Alfred real estate h 124 Rivet
" Antoine weaver h 47 Acushnet av
" David clerk h 229 Mt Pleasant
" Ernest engineer h 113 Bowditch

Levasseur
" Evelyn clerk 185 Union b 111 S Water
" Exear weaver h 530 N Front
" Fred painter b 55 Hope
" Hector weaver h 525 N Front
" Joseph clerk 17 Weld rms Purchase
" Ludger A conductor b 106 Ruth
" Paul carpenter h 122 Nash rd
" Pierre weaver h 106 Ruth
" Rose clerk 1039 Acushnet av h 477 North Front [den
Leveille Alfred real estate h 77 Lin-
Levenson Max furniture 600 S Water h do [French av
Lever Benjamin carder bds 32 West
" John laborer b 190 Tinkham
Levesque Adolor carpenter 1220 Acushnet av h do [vis
" Alexander elevatorman h 107 Da-
" Alfred clerk h 207 Eugenia
" Alfred machinist h 147 Tallman
" Alfred plumber b 194 Phillips av
" Alphonse second hand h 147 Hathaway
" Antoine machinist b 12 Bullard
" Arsene J hardware 1360 Acushnet avenue h 170 Dean [Grove
" Arthur operative b 154 Cedar
" August loom fixer b 214 Sawyer
" Clarina widow Telesphore h 60 Belleville road
" Dora spinner h 954 S Water [av
" Etienne carpenter h 194 Phillips
" Eva clerk bds 56 Nye
" Fred clerk 145 Union b Eugenia
" George blacksmith U St Ry Co h 56 Nye
" Hormidas laborer h 9 Campbell
" John teamster h 16 Beetle
" Joseph machinist 117 Bowditch h 192 Phillips avenue
" Joseph spinner h 18 Holly
" Omer carpenter h 319 Belleville avenue [Grove
" Panteleon N weaver h 288 Cedar
" Philias removed to Boston
" Philip third hand h 214 Coffin av
" Philip H overseer Page Mfg Co h 148 Rockland
" Telesphore died Dec 22 1910
" Theodore (1065 County) died December 23 1910

Steiger-Dudgeon Co.
"The WOMAN'S Store."
Tel. Bell 82 & 83, Branches connecting all depts.
" " 160 For Office only. Auto. 1211
SUMPTIONS, ASSORTMENTS AT ALL TIMES OF DEPENDABLE DRY GOODS

Levesque
" Theodore joiner b 194 Phillips av
" Theodore laborer h 154 Cedar Grove
LEVESQUE WILFRED plumbing 211 Coffin av b 194 Phillips av See page 787
Levin Bessie Mrs h 138 Acushnet av
" Charles clerk 266 Coggeshall b 270 do [270 do
" Folk dry goods 266 Coggeshall h
" Hyman butcher h 169 Acushnet avenue
" Jacob clerk yard master's office railroad depot h 19 Cotter
" Nathan baths 24 Howland h do
" Nathan real estate h 82 Grinnell
Levine Brothers (Meyer and Harry) 725 Water
" Carl F glass cutter b 121½ Fourth
" Harry salesman 934 South Water h 8 Delano
" Meyer clothing 725 and 834 S Water h 932 do
" Samuel salesman 934 S Water h 8 Delano [bds 8 Delano
" Sarah bookkeeper 394 S Water
Levins Eliza speeder h 827 County
" Lawrence J jeweler 975 Kempton h do
" Henry J laborer h 975 Kempton
Levique Philomone widow Theodore h 1065 County [Coggeshall
Levovsky Israel clerk 67 Union b 225
" Louis poultry h 642 S Water
Levy Abraham provisions 916 South Water b 72 S Sixth
" Abraham A h 289 County
" Anna clerk 900 S Water b 289 County
" Asher H h 577 First [Bullard
" Clara D clerk 182 Union b 113
" Fanny Mrs h 557 First
" James removed to Newport R I
" Maurice A mgr 915 S Water bds 557 First [Sixth
" Max clerk 97 N Second h 72 S
" Vaiax baker 642 First
" William crockery 900 S Water h 28 McGurk
" William W clerk 156 Purchase h 224 Acushnet avenue
Lewcanis Thomas baker 55 Clark
Lewin Charles variety 1087 Acushnet avenue h 247 Cedar Grove
" Charles Jr clerk 1087 Acushnet av b 247 Cedar Grove
" Joseph helper 514 County b 247 Cedar Grove [way
" Thomas operative h 157 Hathaway
" Thomas F clerk h 247 Cedar
" Thomas F weaver h 1082 County
" Winnie T clerk 84 Union b 247 Cedar Grove
Lewis Albert h 32 Social
" Albert laborer b 270 Middle
" Albert W (Hedge-Lewis Mfg Co) 6 Elm h at Westport [Sixth
" Alexander fisherman h 122 South
" Alfred weaver bds 200 Earle
" Anthony S repairman 248 Union h 57 Taber
" Antone barber h 16 Wing [av
" Antone hairdresser 323 Acushnet
" Burton A salesman Anthony Swift & Co h 638 County
" Carlton C b 76 Walnut
" Daniel operative h r 198 State
" Dexter W clerk h 75 Willis
" Don C reporter Times b 76 Walnut [h 3 Clinton pl
" Edgar R merchant 15 Hamilton
" Edward D died 1911 [shnet av
" Edward F farm hand h 4215 Acu-
" Eliza A widow Joseph D h 64 Russell
" Ella F widow Henry h 285 Park
" Ellen widow William h 28 Ashland
" Emily Mrs b 84 Fruit [ty
" Fanny widow Manuel h 131 Coun-
" Frank bartender 437 S Water h 161 Acushnet av
" Frank A lieutenant Central Fire Station h 207 Court [ond
" Frank E carpenter h 63 N Sec-
" Frank F salesman h 27 Hillman
" Frederic grocer 124 S Sixth h 122 do [ton
" Frederick C salesman 8 Hamil-
" George iron melter 229 N Water h at Freetown [h do
" George F physician 76 Walnut
" George H b 4215 Acushnet av
" George H whalebone cleaner 15 Hamilton h 519 Acushnet av

PELEG H. SHERMAN 506 COUNTY ST.
FUNERAL DIRECTOR AND EMBALMER
OFFICE PHONES. Bell 690-12. Auto. 1305
RESIDENCE PHONES. Bell 690-12. Auto. 1306.

Lewis

" Gertrude E asst bookkeeper 100 William b 28 Ashland [Forest
" Harold P master mariner h 68
" Harry driver 8 Campbell h 169 State
" Henry H teamster h 137 Perry
" Herbert poolroom 1074 S Water h 32 Social
" Hugh H compositor Standard h 382 Acushnet av
" James choreman b 26 S Sixth
" Job removed from city
" John died Mar 13 1911
" John fisherman h 297 S Front
" John lather b 82 William
" John variety 124 S Sixth h 122 do
" Joseph candymaker h 223 Smith
" Joseph helper 48 Pleasant
" Joseph loom fixer h 16 Cove
" Joseph H, U S A h 231 Brock av
" Joseph S Jr piper h 574 Union
" J Joseph rectifier Smith Bros h 54 Durfee [av
" Leonard weaver b 24 W French
" Lila B bookkeeper N B Textile school b 64 Russell [Mill
" Lucretia widow William h 112
" Lucy Mrs lodgings 82 William h do
" Manuel city laborer h 53 Swift
" Manuel laborer b 391 Rivet
" Marjory teacher James B Congdon school b 71 Russell
" Marshall F supt 131 Court h 71 Rusell [Fairhaven
" Mary sewer 40 Purchase b at
" Mary A widow Elijah b 96 Madison
" Mary E Mrs h Alec street
" Mary J clerk 120 S Sixth b 122 do [State
" Matilda widow Joshua h 169
" Nellie widow Jesse h 101½ Fifth
" Percy R clerk 131 Court b 71 Russell [land
" Sadie clerk 100 William b 28 Ash-
" Samuel pedlar h 19 Bentley
" Thomas weaver h 200 Earle
" Walter shoemaker h 161 Middle
" Walter J hairdresser h 8 W High
" William laborer b 258 Coffin av
" William spinner b 307 Collette
" William teamster rms 1 Mill

Lewis

" William A telegrapher 17 Pleasant h at Fairhaven
" William W whale bone cleaner h 143 Cedar
" see Luiz and Louis

Leymunion Mary W teacher Fifth street school h 112 Arnold
Leyton Antonio N laborer h 175 S Water
" Henry N laborer h 2a Walnut
L'Heureux Alberic painter b 60 Tallman
" Albert M plater b 2 Cornell pl
" Antoinette cashier 123 Union b 60 Tallman [av
" Charles spinner b 9 W French
" Edward spinner b 9 W French avenue
" Euclide operative h 807 First
" Eudore mill hand b 60 Tallman
" Job barber 33 Elm
" John h 582 First [Cornell pl
" Joseph barber 833 Purhase h 2
" Joseph loom fixer h 154 Eugenia
" Julia removed to Westboro
" Napoleon weaver b 154 Eugenia
" Omer weaver h 60 Tallman
" Ovila weaver b 60 Tallman
" Stanislaus tinsmith h 82 Holly
" William weaver h 799 First
L'Homme Alphonse weaver bds 60 Bullard
" Alphonse E clerk b 59 Collette
" Celina Mrs b 59 Collette
" Hormidas woodworker 3 E Pope h 245 State
" Napoleon h 10 Blackburn
Libby Louis P boxmaker h 74 Church
Liberty Damino laborer h 4 Clark
Liddell Alexander K clerk h 59 Bay
Lider Esther clerk 23 Weld bds 30 Bowditch
" Harry reporter Times 120 Purchase b 30 Bowditch [ditch
" Jacob variety 23 Weld h 30 Bow-
" Michael plumber b 30 Bowditch
Liedholm Elsie Mrs h 169 Campbell
Lienard Ademour tailor 1014 Acushnet av b Holly street
" Philomon tailor h 107 Holly
Lightbody William K rem to Boston
Lightbown Elizabeth widow William h 44 Briggs
" Hugh H weaver h 98 Linden

PAINTERS' SUPPLIES
Walnut, Cor. Water, 84 Pleasant St. 25 WELD SQ., 129 COVE ST.
F. T. AKIN & COMPANY

Lightfoot Charles porter b 192 Elm
" Elizabeth widow Charles h 192 Elm
" Susan housekeeper 192 Elm
Liljequist David glassblower h 51 Tremont [h at Fairhaven
Lilley Alice teacher Fifth st school
" Charles linotype operator Standard b at Fairhaven

GEORGE E LILLEY
ATTORNEY AND COUNSELLOR AT LAW
37 Purchase Street Room 17
Residence 77 Thomas Street

Lilley George E lawyer 37 Purchase rm 17 bds 77 Thomas
" Mary E widow Dr William h 77 Thomas [mac
Lilly Albert weaver bds 80 Merri-
" Wilbur A engineer h 17 Lucas
Lima Anthony M Jr clerk 400 Kempton h 410 Maxfield [shnet av
" Antone clerk 71 Howland b Acu-
" Antone laborer h 260 S Second
" Antone mill hand h 72 Blackmer
" Antone C driver h 64 Acushnet avenue
" Antone M laborer h 73 Liberty
" Frances T widow Manuel h 61 Acushnet av
" Frank laborer h 2 Mulberry
" Frank operative h 28 Wing
" John operative h 595 S Water
" John laborer h 12 Bethel
" John laborer h 65½ Prospect
" John operative h 272 S Front
" John teamster h 14 Highland
" John F mill hand h 16 Rotch blk 442 Bolton
" John L conductor h 20 Briggs
" Joseph operative h 382 Belleville avenue
" Joseph operative b r 435 S Water [thaway
" Joseph speeder tender h 87½ Ha-
" Joseph weaver h 9 Stapleton

Lima
" Joseph A ship keeper h 564 S Water
" Joseph M (New York Furniture Store) 180 Acushnet av and dentist 83 Fifth h do
" Manuel carder h 56 Hollyhock
" Manuel mill hand h 23 Mitchell
" Manuel B clerk 170 Purchase h at Fairhaven
" Manuel J died Jan 8 1911
" Manuel L laborer h 103 Dunbar
" Manuel P laborer h 21 Margin
" Marcelina operative h 134 Bonney [do
" Mary A dressmaker 63 Fifth h
" Seraphim E laborer h 104 Acushnet av
" William clerk b 73 Liberty
" see Lema [at Fairhaven
Lincoln Amy L clerk 185 Union bds
" Arthur F conductor N Y, N H & H R R b 286 Pleasant
" Bessie P bookkeeper 160 Purchase b at Fairhaven [land
" Charles A conductor h 40 High-
" Charles J clerk W F Nye Fish Island h 299 County [Middle
" Clifton H clerk 17 N Sixth h 180
" Frank N clerk h 37 Bay
" Helen H bookkeeper 160 Purchase b 299 County [mond
" Mary A widow John b 2 Rich-
" Mary E rms 35 Eighth [Spruce
" William H drillmaker h 72
Lincourt Fred blacksmith h 79 Cedar
Lindberg Claus A master mechanic Holmes Mfg Co h 167 Davis
Lindblom John H glasscutter h 202 Rockland
Lindeh Hannah h 83 Atlantic
Linden Arthur engineer Hathaway M Corp h 17 Spruce
" Helen J h 17 Spruce
" Robert removed to Boston
" Thomas mule spinner h 174 Ashland [av
Lindey John laborer b 1122 Acushnet
Lindgren Olaf carpet upholsterer 36 Purchase h 287 Court
Lindley Charles spinner h 144 Richmond [nia
" James W third hand h 130 Euge-
Lindsay Elizabeth S bookkeeper 70 Union b 436 Allen
" Margaret W b 67 Russell

To do things right you must be taught. Our instructors can do it.
Kinyon's Commercial School
Odd Fellows Bldg., Cor. William and Pleasant Sts., New Bedford, Mass.

Lindsay
" Mary widow William A h 436 Allen [Park
" Robert supt 214 S Water h 291
" William A h 436 Allen
" William A Jr salesman 70 Union bds 436 Allen
" see Lindsey [Phillips av
Lindsey Albert carpenter bds 154
" Henry carpenter b 211 County
Linfield H Delbert government inspector b 69 Fifth [dar Grove
Linhares Antone fisherman b 108 Ce-
" John h 126 Fourth
" Jose fisherman h 108 Cedar Grove
Linnehan Peter D driver h 490 Acushnet av [Acushnet av
Linney Charles F watchman h 1105
Linscott Willis B clerk 103 Union b 11 Fifth [man
Linton Cordelia E Mrs b 125 Hill-
" John E (J R Linton & Sons) h 107 Maxfield
" Joseph P clerk h 143 Parker
LINTON J R & SONS (John E Linton) auto and carriage painters and wagon mfrs 105 Maxfield See page 33
" Mary A widow John R b 107 Maxfield
Lipman Abraham (Lipman Bros) rms 64 Russell [tailors 45 Purchase
" Brothers (Abraham and Samuel)
" Harry shoes 943 S Water h 4 Dean
" Samuel (Lipman Bros) h 483 Acushnet avenue [field
Lipnick Hyman pedlar h 10 Grand-
Lipschitz Joseph reporter Times bds 101 Parker [Parker
" Samuel tailor 239 Purchase h 101
Lipsett Lauchlin A inspector 100 Fifth [b 397 Cedar Grove
Lipson Eddie clerk 967 Acushnet av
" Joseph tailor 139 Cove rms 238 County
" Meyer shoes 1101 S Water h do
" Morris H shoes 967 Acushnet av h 397 Cedar Grove
Lisboa Joseph S carpenter h 58 Short
Lisbon Joseph C shoemaker h 55 James
Lister William J weaver h 126 David
Lita Howard G removed from city
Little Abby H b 464 County [Front
" Alexander weaver bds 236 North
" Arnold stage hand b 513 N Front
" Charles H laborer h 143 James
" Francis laborer h 189 Fourth
" Frank A removed to S Dartmouth
" Herbert operative b 35 Howard
" James A roofer h 164 Durfee
" Mabel L widow Edward E dressmaker 1 Cottage h do
" Mark operative bds 35 Howard
" Mary h 35 Howard
" Mary b 137 Hawthorn
" Mary Mrs h 35 Howard
" Matthew operative b 53 Swift
" Matthias operative b 35 Howard
" Sara W nurse 12 Market h at Marion [lips av
" William second hand h 193 Phil-
Littlefair James loom fixer h 36 George [Russell
Littlefield Herbert glass cutter b 40
Littler Arthur spinner b 32 Brook
" Ernest teamster b 32 Brook
" Harry operative b 32 Brook
" Henry weigher h 32 Brook
" John steamfitter b 32 Brook
Littlewood Thomas letter carrier h 117 Dartmouth
Livesey Albert actor b 29 Welcome
" Clarence removed from city
" Ellen widow William h 25 Viall
" Francis spinner h 182 County
" George weaver h 16 Cove
" James loom fixer h 29 Welcome
" James painter b 118 Cove
" James twister b 36 Winsor
" James weaver h 152 David
" James H loom fixer h 256 Weld
" John clerk h 43 Ashley
" John mill hand h 7 Babbitt [Cal
" John T removed to Los Angeles
" Martin weaver h 115 Hathaway
" Richard weaver h 197 Tinkham
" Richard weaver b 115 Hathaway
" Robert weaver b 36 Tiknham
" Ulderic weaver b 182 Dean
Livesley Isaac Jr h 13 Studley [mer
" Simeon B machinist h 218 Sum-
Livingston Janet M teacher Thomas Donaghy school b 45 Dartmouth

Bread, Cake, Pastry
RICHMOND & COMPANY **255-257 UNION STREET**
Bell 993 Automatic 1022

Livingston
" Mary F teacher I W Benjamin school bds 49 Dartmouth
Livingstone Joseph bricklayer h 273 Weld [ley
Lizotte Armand operative b 24 Bent-
" Arthur laborer b 178 State
" Bruno B loom fixer h 29 Ashley
" Bunio bds 22 Roosevelt
" Celia Mrs h 20 Bentley
" Charles carpenter h 27 Ingraham
" Daniel operative b 198 State
" Emile weaver b 20 Bentley
" Eugene weaver b 242 State
" Frank mill hand bds 14 Bowditch
" Henry shoemaker b 1142 Acushnet avenue
" Joseph driver h 132 Bullard
" Joseph laborer b 20 Bentley
" Joseph mill hand h 351 N Front
" Joseph teamster h 159 Tallman
" Melvina Mrs h 178 State
" Michael operative h 24 Bentley
" Thomas weaver h 22 Roosevelt
" Wilfred weaver b 24 Bentley
Lloyd Tom baker h 1054 County
" Tom Jr spinner h 1056 County
" William teamster h 121 Cedar
" William teamster b 24 High
Lobdell Charles H supt of delivery P O h 130 Clinton
" George W rms 169 Union
Lobo Joseph N laborer h 72 Sycamore
" Louis C laborer b 72 Sycamore
" Manuel G hairdresser 259 Purchase h 242 Pleasant
Locherhell Levi fixer h 910 S Water
Locke Lansing B rem from city
Lockwood C Augusta nurse h 57 Maple [rms 940 County
" Frank L chauffeur 57 N Second
Lodge Bridget widow William h 908 County
Loey Samuel fixer h 812 First [vett
Lofthouse William weaver h 43 Jou-
Loftus Annie h 451 County
" Antony (Lofus & Dugan) 121 Clark h 859 Rockdale av
" Bernard laborer b 451 Pleasant
" Bridget widow Thomas h 9 Valentine
" Mary A h 36 Woodlawn av
" Patrick F removed from city

Loftus
" Thomas A h 236 Brock av.
LOFTUS & DUGAN (Antony Loftus and Hugh A Dugan) contractors etc 121 Clark See page 776
Logwood Burt E dentist 25 Purchase h do [Chancery
" Ellen widow Burt E rms 235
Loiseau Cleophas R slasher h 141 Bullard
Loiselle John B fixer b 92 Ruth
" Joseph mill hand h 3 Desautels
L'Oiselle Adelard rem from city
" Charles H operative h 202 Tinkham
" Edgar removed from city [ham
" Henry section hand h 202 Tink-
" Lea widow Eugene rem from city
" Philip carpenter h 399 Belleville av [lips av
" Sophia widow John B h 101 Phil-
Lomas Elizabeth h 44 Roosevelt
" Harold back boy b 6 Felton
" John W butcher h 31 Jouvett
" William back boy b 6 Felton
" William J spinner h 6 Felton
Lomba Andrew h 30 Acushnet av
" Anthony bicycle repairer 249 Union b 30 Acushnet av
" Antone J removed to Onset
" Henry ropemaker h 9 Cannon
" Henry stable 30 Acushnet av h 21 Lombard
" Isabella Mrs h 14 Griffin
" John cook h 137 S Second
" Joseph operative h 316 S Water
" Kate Mrs h 379 S Water
" Manuel J laborer h 68 Brigham
" Mary Mrs h 247 State [chase
Lompos John spinner h 410 Pur-
London Myers stitcher rms 170 North
Lonergan Andrew b 198 Austin
" Richard laborer h 198 Austin
" Simon P Rev asst pastor Church of the Sacred Heart h 27 Ashland
Long Arthur L instructor Swain Free school h at Brockton
" Catherine widow Richard h 185 County [Second
" Edgar A driver 45 School h 49 S
" Fred teamster b 24 Marvin
" George motorman h 344 Cedar Grove

GLOBE DYE HOUSE 220 SHAWMUT AVE.
J. N. J. LONHOLDT, PROP. Telephone Connections Goods called for and Delivered
Down town Office, 52 Pleasant St., Room 1 North End Office, 1014 Acushnet Ave.

Long
" Henry H removed from city
" Rhoda Mrs b 314 Acushnet av
" Richard F laborer b 185 County
" R H Waldorf Shoe 75 William
" Sarah H widow George R h 512 County
" William H machinist h 858 First
Longchamp Ernest automobile repairer b 193 Bowditch
Longden Isaac b 101 Rockland
" James spinner h 54 Maitland
" John carder b 62 Roosevelt
" Thomas carder b 54 Maitland
Longfield Ellsworth M tinsmith 55 N Water h 34 Liberty
" Joseph S tinsmith 55 N Water h 52 Shawmut av [av
" Olive K milliner b 52 Shawmut
Longill Jacob b 63 Oak
" William H W foreman 235 N Water h 23 Crapo [Fifth
Longley Herbert E machinist h 76
Longpre Joseph Z yard foreman 27 Bowditch h 24 Myrtle
" Pierre driller h 102 Whitman
Longtin Melvin A weaver h 197 Rivet
" Wilfred weaver h 591 First
Longton Antoni woodcutter h 124 N Front
" Edmund operative b 124 N Front
" Thomas laborer b 105 Davis
Longuey Arfon clerk 42 Weld b do
Longworth William R weaver h 8 Cove road
Lonholdt John N J (Globe Dye House) 52 Pleasant rm 1 h 220 Shawmut av
Lonsdale Maria widow William nurse h 58 Shawmut av
" Thomas laborer b 58 Shawmut av [h 143 Holly
" Thomas shoe repairer 158 Union
" William operative b 143 Holly
Lonza Joseph removed from city
Look Francis sawyer h 340 Purchase
" George E harness maker 34 Pleasant h 1 Shawmut avenue
" Hiram W h 176 Kempton [137 do
" Walter A clerk 318 Acushnet av b 137 do [avenue
Loose-Wiles Biscuit 383-385 Acushnet

Lopes Adelino hostler b 202 Belleville av [Walnut
" Albert hostler 486 Rivet b 19
" Anthony operative b 62 S Second
" Antonio h 104 Rockland [av
" Antonio blacksmith h 16 Central
" Antonio mariner h 285 S Water
" Berginni speeder tender h 9 Howland
" Caesar operative h 18 Cannon
" Enos P clerk h 68 Acushnet av
" Frank h 242 S Front
" Frank mariner h 29 S Second
" Frank R operative h 56 Nelson
" Isaac laborer b 29 S Second
" Joaquim P provisions 78 Acushnet av h 52 Rockland [Lambert
" John clerk 448 S Water b 30
" John teamster h 50 Mill
" John third hand h 30 Lombard
" John weaver b 450 First
" Joseph laborer h 30 Spring
" Joseph mariner b 28 Elm [Village
" Joseph mill hand bds 16 Howland
" Joseph removed from city
" Jule boilermaker h 96 S Second
" Julia Mrs h 395 S Water
" J P grocer 78 Acushnet av h 52 Rockland
" Levana Mrs h 10 Griffin
" Manuel mariner h 53 Short
" Manuel mill hand h 187 Bonney
" Manuel operative b 16 Howland Village
" Manuel speeder h 235 Rivet
" Manuel R laborer h 30 Lombard
" Manuel R mill hand h 109 Fruit
" Manuel R mill hand h 173 Thompson [ond
" Marianna laborer h 201 N Sec.
" Matthew mill hand h 355 First
" Messiline operative b 62 S Second
" Peter mariner h 14½ Cannon
" Sylvester variety 3 Walnut h 71 First [Phillips av
Loranger Adelard carpenter h 234
" Antonio carpenter b 234 Phillips avenue
" Peter driver h 99½ Linden
LORANGER THEODORE carpenter 238 Phillips av h do See page 763
" Victor A teamster h 8 Bowditch

GREENE & WOOD Every Kind of **LUMBER** AND MILL WORK
PINE STREET, off So. WATER STREET, NEW BEDFORD

Lord Albert machinist b 105 Davis
" Ann Mrs h 435 S Front [lin
" Clarence drill maker b 15 Frank-
" Edgar treasurer Acushnet and N B Co-operative Banks 125 Middle h 403 Union [Franklin
" Elizabeth widow Joseph h 15
" Ernest clerk b 271 Coggeshall
" Frank carpenter b 866 Purchase
" George H music teacher 399 Pleasant h do
" Henry mill hand b 289 Davis
" James h 866 Purchase
" James mill hand h 162 Nash rd
" James mill hand h 255 N Front
" James weaver h 332 Bowditch
" John variety 297 Coggeshall h 295 do [Co h 175 Newton
" John W overseer Gosnold Mills
" Joseph weaver h 494 Coggeshall
" Moise lather h 289 Davis
" Mortimon electrician b 1 Weaver
" Peter electrical contractor 104 Union h 20 Acorn
" Susan H widow Foster h 228 Ar-
" Thomas yard master Quissett Mill h 415 Orchard (S)
" Thomas spinner h 171 Weld
" Thomas Jr electrician h 305 S Second [ville rd
" William card grinder h 88 Belle-
" William Ogden physician 864 Purchase h do
Loreau Ferdinand barber h 140 State
Lorek Joseph bricklayer h 87 Clifford
Lorenz Antonio farmer h 137 Field
" Domingas laborer h 35 S Front
" John mill hand b 19 Bullard
" Manuel mill hand h 181 Coffin av
" Manuel G city laborer h 240 S Front [State
Lorette Wilfrid carpenter h 207½
Loring Florence L teacher Thomas Donaghy school rms 19 Sherman
" Jessie widow Antonio h 59 School
" John clerk bds 59 School
" Joseph J fisherman h 146 Acushnet avenue [av h do
" Mary J dressmaker 146 Acushnet
Lorning Thurston private U S A 76 Pleasant rm 39 b 219 Purchase
Lorraine Frederick teas and coffees 22 Purchase and 1110 Acushnet avenue h 43 Fifth [Bullard
Lortie Geremie mill hand h 131
" Joseph b 131 Bullard [h 52 Vine
Losette Antone baker 273 Kempton
Loshink Frank h 10 McGurk
Losianno Antone porter h 34 Richmond [201 Kempton
Lothrop Mary F and Annie W h
Loughlin Frank variety 9 Weld bds 1620 Acushnet avenue
" Jessie clerk 303 Municipal bldg b 228 Pleasant
" Kate Mrs h 1620 Acushnet av
" Martin spinner h 53 Howard
" Mary clerk b 1620 Acushnet av
" Patrick removed to Pontiac R I
" William clerk b 1620 Acushnet avenue [Howard
" William H clerk 97 Front bds 53
" see Laughlin
Lougnez Eva Mrs h 16 Warren
Louis Manuel teamster h 119 Division
" Thomas W barber 240 Cedar h 113 James
" see Lewis and Luiz
Louise Doule operative h 69 Hicks
Lovatt Frederick C h 459 Allen
Lovejoy Elizabeth F died Mar 13 1911 [97½ Fourth
" Elizabeth M widow George W h
" Mary clerk 182 Union b 97½ Fourth [fin av
" Thomas J florist's asst 327 Cof-
Lovelace William agent 73 William b 44 Mill
Lowandowski Wladyslaw mill hand b 325 Belleville av
Lowden Susan B Mrs b 67 Fourth
Lowe Abner D h 132 Mill
" Charles T overseer Page Mfg Co b 170 Shawmut av
" Edith M bds 350 Cottage
" Florence widow Samuel J h 74 Chancery
" George h 92 Covell
" George operative h 53 Howard
" James weaver h 289 Coffin av
" James A machine operator b 303 Acushnet av
" John salesman h 286 Summer
" John H died July 2 1911 [tage
" John H Jr collector b 350 Cot-

BONNEY, FOLSTER & CO.,
The North End's Shopping Centre
Dry Goods and Men's Furnishings
945-947 Acushnet Ave., New Bedford, Mass.

Lowe
" Margaret C h 63 Ash (S) [tage
" Mary A widow John H h 350 Cot-
" Mary J widow John J h 303 Acushnet av
" Philip C combermaker 22 Fourth bds 35 Ash (S)
" Samuel city teamster h 285 Cedar
" Samuel C driver b 285 Cedar
" Samuel J deputy inspector h 205 Pleasant
" Samuel J died Jan 12 1911
" Stephen A salesman 24 Pleasant h 35 Ash (S)
" Stephen C pres 87-91 Union and 22 Fourth h at W Newton
LOWE S C SUPPLY CO mill supplies plumbing hardware etc 87 Union and automobile garage 22 Fourth Always open See page 740
" Thomas C plumber 87 Union h 170 Shawmut av
Lowell Fannie C Mrs C S practitioner 8 Borden h do [av
Lower John weaver h 82 Phillips
Lowles George boxmaker b Tarkiln Hill road n L C [ard
Lownds Squire spinner h 31 Haz-
" Thomas slasher h 10 Harmony
Lowney Catherine widow John J h 1498 Acushnet av
" Catherine F nurse 1498 Acushnet av b do [shnet av
" Daniel S machinist b 1498 Acu-
" Dennis J physician 1498 Acushnet av h do
" John laborer h 379 Cedar
" John B (Lowney & Walsh) lawyer h 558 Cottage [h do
" John H plumber 540 N Front
" John H plumber 915 Acushnet av b 152 Whitman [man
" Patrick H blacksmith h 418 Hill-
" Timothy h 220 State

LOWNEY & WALSH
ATTORNEYS AT LAW
John B Lowney Joseph Walsh
Justice of the Peace, Notary Public
Room 2 Masonic Building
New Bedford, Mass
Telephone Connection

Lowney & Walsh (John B Lowney and Joseph Walsh) lawyers 2 Masonic bldg [Parker
Lowrie Edward P shoemaker h 117
" George H (Wood & Lowrie) 50 Union h 48 State
Lowther Alice W teacher Thomas R Rodman school b 253 Mill
" A Beatrice Mrs (G H Hodgkins & Co) 71 William b at Boston
" Carrie clerk 97 William rm 303 b 36 Ash (N)
" George H police h 253 Mill
" George M drillworker b 36 Ash (N) [36 Ash (N)
" Mitchell H foreman N B C Co h
" Olive music teacher 253 Mill b do
" William H drillmaker b 36 Ash (N) [sher
Lovnds James city employee b 15 Mo-
Lubera Andra operative h 25 Belleville av [ville av
" Stanislaus carder h 25 Belle-
Luby John E engineer h 447 Coggeshall [shall
" Katherine clerk bds 451 Cogge-
" Michael J glasscutter h 57 Bay
Lucardi Gildo mason h 241 Tremont
" Giraldo died Sept 14 1910
" Mary widow Giraldo h 210 Court
Lucas Arthur M draughtsman 3 E Pope h 240 Tremont
" Edna A b 55 Court
" Elizabeth R widow Henry K W h 95 Bedford
" Etta C h 95 Hillman [h do
" Everett A carpenter 206 James
" Harry weaver h 71 Brock av

Painters Supplies Wall Papers Room Mouldings Ladders
M. P. B. Silva & Son BRUSHES
157 ACUSHNET AVENUE Both Phones NEW BEDFORD

Lucas
" Isabella widow Augustus E h 55 Court [Ashland
" James A clerk 52 Purchase b 28
" Jaspar L carpenter b 206 James
" John changer over h 22 George
" John laborer h 499 Rivet
" Manuel operative h 20 Rotch blk 439 Bolton
" Manuel S clerk h 181 County
" Mary D b 292 Palmer
" Norman C conductor h 36 Linden
" Shoe Co 43 Purchase
" Squire H H h 112 High
" William F engineer b 14 Fair
Lucchesi Luigi fruit 884 Purchase h 396 Cedar Grove
Luce Arthur G business mgr Mercury 112 Union h 346 Cottage
" Arthur R drill inspector b 195 Arnold
" Charles T (Powers & Luce) 37 Purchase rm 3 rms 37 Morgan
" Frederick C real estate 130 Willis h do
" George A carpenter b 29 Willis
" Ida E clerk 185 Union rms 39 Fifth
" Jeremiah L h 24 Cedar
" John E Jr weigher h 164 Grinnell
" Josephine W Mrs h 493 County
" Mary H Mrs h 133 Perry
" Robert H Capt boarding house 11 Fifth [Maxfield
" Sarah R widow Hervey E h 111
" Thomas h 550 County
" Thomas E clerk 426 Kempton h 144 Campbell [nold
" Walter A letter carrier h 195 Ar-
" Walter A L clerk 163 Union bds 139 Campbell [Campbell
" William T fish 131 Smith h 139
" William T Jr clerk 387 Purchase h 290 do [Thatcher
Luchraft William third hand h 5
Lucier John bds 329 N Front
" Louis operative b 86 Mott
" see Lussier
Luiz Antone operative h 912 County
" Antonio laborer h 269 Orchard (S)
" Antonio laborer h 429 S Water
" Frank laborer h 83 Crapo

Luiz
" Frank operative h 227 S Front
" John coal passer U St Ry Co power station b 83 Crapo
" John G boarding h 18 Hall [sher
" John G Jr electrician b 85 Mo-
" Jose M G spinner h 81 Sidney
" Jose M G spinner h 198 Bonney
" Joseph laborer h 93 Prospect
" Manuel laborer h r 47 Howland
" Manuel C engineer U St Ry Co power station h 68 Hall
" see Lewis
Lumba Henry stable h 459 Bolton
Lumbard Charles E carpenter and builder 19 Bethel h at Fairhaven [Fairhaven
" Ralph E clerk 100 Fifth b at
Lumbert Harriet E widow John b 258 Elm (W)
" Hiram T janitor Sylvia Ann Howland school h 185 Maxfield
" John died Sept 19 1910
Lumiansky Barnard (B Lumiansky & Son) 871 S Water h do
" B & Son (Barnard & Maurice S) clothing 871-873 S Water
" David student b 873 S Water
" Harry salesman 871 S Water b do
" Helen teacher Harrington school b 873 S Water
" Maurice S (B Lumiansky & Son) h at Boston
Luminiello Antonio variety 153½ Coffin avenue h 157 do
Lund Henry weaver h 306 Earl
" James h 306 Earle [mut av
" Maria widow Martin h 1 Shaw-
" Parkman M h 252 Pleasant
" William C b 252 Pleasant
Lunday Annie Mrs speeder tender h 280 Tinkham
" Thomas operative b 280 Tinkham
Lundin Gustaf designer h 174 Clifford
Lundy Anthony laborer b 302 Coggeshall
" John operative h 55 Howard
" Richard operative b 1098 Acushnet av
Lunn Harry loom fixer h 70 Linden
Lupo Emanuel D restaurant 363 Acushnet avenue and 154 Purchase rms 36 N Sixth

Steiger-Dudgeon Co.
"The WOMAN'S Store."
Tel. Bell 82 & 83, Branches connecting all depts.
" " 160 For Office only. Auto. 1211

SUMPTIONS, ASSORTMENTS AT ALL TIMES OF DEPENDABLE DRY GOODS

Lupton John H shipper h 51 Florence
Luscomb Abraham R laborer h r 119 Sycamore
" Frederick W traveling salesman h 318 Arnold
" George E telephone operator h 139 Chestnut [h 245 Cedar
" Isabella teacher Clark st School
Lussier Alexis operative h 206 Church
" Althea teamster h 437 Purchase
" Archie carpenter b 203 Bowditch
" Arthur operative h 171 Tinkham
" Azarie carpenter b 142 Bullard
" Bros (Gaudiace and Elzear) grocers 166 Brock av
" Clement M (Lussier & Lagasse) 125 Rivet h 167 County
" Cleophas laborer h Lowell off Tarkin Hill rd [ditch
" Delimina widow Elie h 203 Bow-
" Elzear (Lussier Bros) h at Fall River [Bowditch h do
" Exilia widow Achille grocer 201
" Frederick carder h 141 Tallman
" Gaudiace (Lussier Bros) h at Fall River
" Henry carpenter b 203 Bowditch
" Homer R weaver h 291 N Front
" Isaie weaver h 104 Tallman [man
" Joseph H operative h 125 Tall-
" Louis h 51 County
" Napoleon hypnotist b 94 Rodney
" Narcisse b 171 Tinkham
" N Rosalphee druggist 1189 Acushnet avenue h 350 Sawyer
" Roderick carpenter b 203 Bowditch [N Front
" Virginia widow Alexander h 358
" & Lagasse (C M Lussier and F J Lagasse) druggists 125 Rivet
" see Lucier
Luther Hale R clerk rms 91 School
" J Arthur G salesman 65 William h 420 Union [avenue
Lutz August glass blower h 258 Brock
" Frank bookkeeper b 258 Brock av
Lyman Anthony M clerk h 410 Maxfield [Congdon b 106 South
Lynch Catherine F teacher James B
" Daniel F fisherman h 4 Willis
" Edward G cable splicer 57 N Second b 113 Fourth

Lynch
" James overseer Bennett Mill h 346 Sawyer [tage
" Jeremiah blacksmith b 577 Cot-
" John laborer b 4035 Acushnet av
" John removed from city
" John W b 346 Sawyer
" John W painter h 234 Austin
" Patrick F engineer b 577 Cottage
" Selina died August 7 1910
" Simon F overseer N E C Y Co dept 9-10 h 193 Weld [way rd
" William H iceman h 270 Hatha-
" Zoeth bookkeeper b 346 Sawyer
Lyndon Thomas removed from city
Lyng Frederick J clerk 124 Union h 138 S Second [Second
" Mary widow Frederick h 138 S
" William H supt D Duff & Son h 25 Willis
Lynn Allen weaver b 26 George
Lyon Annie B teacher James B Congdon School b 16 Fifth
" John spinner h 305 Tinkham
" Mary A widow William h 297 Cottage
Lyonnais Raoul clerk b 10 Viall
Lyons Bridget widow Edward S h 33 Reynolds
" Dennis laborer h 375 Cedar
" Edward bartender 416 N Front h 193 Bowditch
" Edward coachman h 50 Chancery
" Edward driver b 63 Robeson
" Edward spinner b 11 Fulton ct
" Edward Jr clerk 57 N Second b 50 Chancery
" Hugh J shoemaker b 64 Spruce
" James operative b 11 Fulton ct
" John foreman N B Storage Warehouse
" John iron worker 11 Fulton ct
" John laborer h 44 Reynolds
" John weaver b 850 First
" Joseph P asst pastor St Lawrence R C Church h 110 Summer
" Patrick steward b 11 Fulton ct
" Patrick J clerk h 11 Fulton ct
" Peter city laborer h 64 Spruce
" Thomas H manager 4 N Second h 63 Robeson

PELEG H. SHERMAN 506 COUNTY ST.
FUNERAL DIRECTOR AND EMBALMER
OFFICE PHONES. Bell 690-13. Auto. 1305.
RESIDENCE PHONES. Bell 690-12. Auto. 1306.

Mabbott Elizabeth widow John b 133 Ashland [house b do
MacAdams Katharine B nurse Almes-
Macaulay Archibald plumber and sheet metal work 138 Blackmer b 167 Allen
" Daniel M apprentice b 167 Allen
" George inspector b 167 Allen
" James F machinist b 167 Allen
" Walter S machinist h 167 Allen
" Walter S Jr molder b 167 Allen
MacAuliffe John laborer 350 S Second

WILLIAM A MacCORD
Attorney and Counsellor at Law
Notary Public, Justice of the Peace
Commissioner for Quebec
Room 5
Five Cents Savings Bank Building
New Bedford, Mass.
Telephones: Bell 1987
Automatic 1467
Residence Bell 1559-4
Residence 744 County St

MacCord William A lawyer Five Cents Savings Bank building rm 5 h 744 County
MacDonald Nathaniel S manager Postal Tel Co rms 29 Seventh
" Nellie C nurse bds 119 Acushnet avenue [Morgan
Macdonald Charles A nurse rms 41
" Ethel telephone operator 57 N Second b 123 Maxfield
" Michael laborer h 480 S Second
Macedo Antonio mill hand h 28 Rotch block 439 Bolton
" Frank C died Feb 26 1911
" Frank S machinist h 466 Union
" Frederick hackman h 263 Philips avenue
" John S mill hand b 30 Sagamore
" Louis V teamster 106 Front h 53 Short [Front
" Mado widow Frank h 319 So

Macedo
" Manuel S weaver b 53 Swift
Macek Joseph weaver h 9 Bullard
Macerel John B operative h 211 Coffin av [Elm
Macfarlane Archibald operative h 73
" Flora M weaver b 130 Division
" Joseph A nurse Almshouse b do
McGregor William carpenter h 91 James [County
Machado Alfred operative h 928
" Annie F widow Antonio F h 123 County [Dartmouth
" Antone city employee h 128
" Antonio weaver h 17 Hall
" Antonio deC laborer h 74 Independent
" Antonio b 25 Hall
" Antonio Jr weaver h 25 Hall
" Bernardo J bricklayer h 55 Page
" Casimer S laborer h 23 Juniper
" Frank laborer b 381 Coggeshall
" Frank removed from city
" Frank teamster 2 S Water b 661 do
" Frank S operative h 43 Hemlock
" Fred laborer h 285 S Second
" Gertrude Mrs h 18 Hollyhock
" Herbert hairdresser h 125 Dartmouth [435 Bolton
" Frank operative 33 Rotch block
" John drill worker b 108 Fifth
" John laborer h 105 N Second
" John laborer h 912 County
" John mill hand 381 Coggeshall
" John operative h Bliss cor Stockhouse [435 Bolton
" John operative h 33 Rotch block
" John F cigar maker 164 Union h 11 Columbia
" John S city laborer h 118 Parker
" John S clerk 2c Walnut h 62 South
" Joseph h 71 Acushnet avenue
" Joseph city laborer h 42 Edward
" Joseph laborer h 119 Rivet [Rivet
" Joseph oiler street dept h 208
" Joseph B drill worker b 55 Page
" Joseph S clerk 659 S Water h 661 do
" Manuel carder h 2 Jennings ct
" Manuel laborer h 479 Frost
" Manuel operative h 7 Beetle
" Manuel operative h 108 Fifth

F. T. AKIN & CO. FORGE FACTORY FURNACE FAMILY COAL

Machado
" Manuel (16 Independent) removed to Dartmouth
" Manuel G carpenter h 62 Lindsey
" Manuel G Jr shipper h 44 Lindsey
" Manuel L clerk b 175 Coggeshall
" Manuel M laborer h 181 County
" see Marshall [ditch
Machon John A weaver b 28 Bow-
" William weaver h 28 Bowditch
Macia William H foreman Lambeth Rope Corp h Bowditch cor Tarkiln Hill rd
Maciel Antone da S laborer N B W W h 120 Locust [lantic
" Arthur B glass cutter. b 19 At-
" Joseph J laborer b 11 Margin
" Joseph S laborer h 321 Arnold
" Manuel laborer b 49 Hemlock
" Theresa B Mrs h 19 Atlantic
" William J smoker 99 Front h at S Dartmouth [shall
Macier Joseph operative h 304 Cogge-
Maciolsk Charles photographer 234 N Front h do
MacIsaac Edward photo engraver Standard [at Fairhaven
Mack Edna B clerk 160 Purchase b
" Elizabeth B nurse rms 25 Sycamore
" Helen L b 419 Purchase
" Joseph H died Nov 22 1910
" Lottie widow Joseph H bds 399 Belleville av [Fairhaven
" Thomas C clerk 100 Fifth b at
" Thomas E clerk 100 Fifth h at Fairhaven [Bedford
Mackay Donald K drill worker h 16
" Edna M clerk 182 Union b 16 Bedford [Bedford
" John A salesman 182 Union b 16
" John D carpenter b 219 Arnold
" John H clerk 100 William h 1643 Acushnet avenue
" John H painter 81 Oak h do
" Lavinia clerk 182 Union bds 16 Bedford [171 Maple h do
" Malcomb A carpenter and builder
" Murdoch coachman h 54 Rotch
" see Mackay
MacKelvey Ethel L b 8 Eighth
" Mary E Mrs h 8 Eighth

MacKenzie Angus W motorman h 603 Cottage [h 435 Cottage
" Daniel A carpenter 445 Kempton
" Daniel O carpenter b 435 Cottage
" Donald clerk b 15 Bonney
" Frank A removed from city
" Frank E carpenter 445 Kempton b 435 Cottage [435 Cottage
" Oliver carpenter 445 Kempton b
" Sadie Mrs h 463 Union
" William drill worker h 200 Tremont [rms 44 Fifth
Mackie Henry L supt 41 William
" James H salesman 358 Acushnet av b 53 Elm [h 49 Dartmouth
" Wallace A compositor N B Times
" William A cashier First National h 77 Walnut
MacKinstry Albert B police h 85 Robeson [ville avenue
Macklem Albert painter b 456 Belle-
Mackler Joseph confectionery 179½ Belleville av h 383 S Water
MacLane Ellen Mrs prop Scranton House 7 N Second h do
" Henry H painter h 7 N Second
MacLeod Angus h 36 Woodlawn av
" Credit Co (Everett B MacLeod) clothing 92½ Purchase
" Everett B (MacLeod Credit Co) and (Ward Six Furniture Co) h at Fairhaven
MacNeil Alexander surveyor h 319 Tinkham avenue
Macoliza John operative h 23 Cotter
Macomber Aba A widow Thomas W h 38 Mill
" Alice J b 326 Cottage
" Alice W bookkeeper 120 Purchase b 105 Durfee
" Alton I clerk Mechanics National Bank h 84 Florence
" Andrew A checker b 105 Durfee
" August C student b 74 State
" Calista E widow William E h 19 Sherman [Forest
" Caroline E widow Homer B h 66
" Charles F (Dean's Oyster Market) 17 N Second h 81 Cedar
" Charlotte M clerk 24 Purchase b 54 Fourth [Acushnet
" Clara Mrs agent 73 William h at
" Edward carpenter h 29 Rounds
" Edward C h 126 Ashland

Don't dream of what you are going to do! Go and do it.
Kinyon's Short-hand School
Odd Fellows Bldg., Cor. William and Pleasant Sts., New Bedford, Mass.

Macomber
" Ella widow Caleb h 84 Florence
" Eunice M widow Sylvanus A h 54 Fourth
" George E ice cream manufacturer 159 Mill h 311 Park [County
" George P copper worker h 774
" George T real estate 326 Cottage h do [55 Grape
" George W teamster b 56 Linden
" Harold S plumber 28 N Second h h 55 Grape
" Harry T died 1911
" Hattie R Mrs h 209 Middle
" Hillard M foreman ft Walnut h 355 Reed
" James A carpenter h 105 Durfee
" James S weigher city stone crusher h 42 Rounds
" Jesse M gardener h 286 Cedar
" John H b 15 Bethel
" Leonard K b 492 Kempton
" Lizzie B telephone operator 57 N Second b 66 Forest
" Louis C salesman b 54 Fourth
" May W Mrs housekeeper 496 Purchase
" Melvin J h 161 North
" Merie Whitridge stenographer Wamsutta Mills b 38 Mill
" Pardon A clerk 364 Merchants Bank bldg h 201 Kempton
" William B h 74 State
" William B janitor 435 County b 115 Cedar [av
" William B lodgings 299 Acushnet
" William C clerk 43 Purchase h 176 Mill [ville avenue
Macot Amidas blacksmith h 331 Belle-
MacPhail Walter S bookkeeper Smith Bros h 304 Summer
MacQuarrie James foreman U S Ry Co h 131 Clark
Macreading Annie L principal Thomas Greene school h 33 Bonney [school h 33 Bonney
" Lydia A Mrs teacher Fifth street
" Mary S b 33 Bonney
Macy Andrew assistant superintendent Soule Mill b 22 Parker
" Arthur W watch repairer 2 Purchase h 161 Grinnell [net av
" Edward operative b 1028 Acush-

Macy
" Edward J weaver b 301 Davis
" Edwin B 111 Hawthorn [Clinton
" Frank E letter collector h 203
" Frank H assistant treas Pierce Bros Ltd h 95 Court
" Frederick B treasurer and secretary Soule Mill h 22 Parker
" George painter h 154 Hathaway
" George I overseer Grinnell Manufacturing Co h 633 County
" George T fixer b 531 N Front
" Herbert E salesman 211 Union h 115 Park [Parker
" Herbert F clerk 212 Union b 22
MACY JOHN S express and stable 21 S Second bds 33 High See page 775
" J Roland assistant superintendent 123 Front h 74 Bay
" Louis W bookkeeper 659 S Water h 257 Maple [Bay h do
" Louise R Mrs practitioner 74
" Maria widow Frederick h 234 Acushnet avenue
MACY PELEG S real estate 78 Smith h do See advt Real Estate in Business Directory
" Peter J loom fixer h 301 Davis
" Philip E assistant treasurer N B I for Savings h 111 Hawthorn
" Roland furniture repairer 11 Bedford h 1 Green
" Thomas W bookkeeper 55 N Water h 111 Hawthorn
" Wendell furniture repairer 11 Bedford h 48 Borden
" Willard B salesman 211 Union b 203 Clinton [do
" William C dentist 17 Seventh h
Madden John F electrician h 46 W French avenue
" Mary A Mrs h 1036 Acushnet av
" Patrick E teamster 98 Front b 500 Acushnet av
" William H foreman 98 Front h 167 Smith [High
Maddox Clifton C chauffeur b 10 W
" Isaac D Rev h 10 W High [shall
" Joseph city laborer b 381 Coggeshall
Madeiros Joe h 18 Wing [Pleasant
Madigan Thomas operative h 411
Madison Benjamin foreman 152 N Water h 245 Palmer

HASKELL BROS. DEALERS IN
ICE
400 COURT STREET TELEPHONE CONNECTION NEW BEDFORD, MASS.

Madison
" May P Mrs clerk 41 Purchase h 97 Tremont [ton h 97 James
" Samuel T gas fitting 312 Kemp-
Madruga Joseph B laborer N B W W h 552 Rivet [First
" Mary P widow Manuel h 550
" Samuel mill hand h 51 Babbitt
" Samuel V laborer h 4 Spooner
Magalheis Antonio clerk 146 Belleville avenue [County
Magauhey Thomas E machinist b 889
Magee Andrew laborer h 60 Hazard
" George A driver b 60 Hazard [H
" Henry foreman to Manchester N
" Joseph foreman Old Colony Box Co h 211 Hathaway
" Robert S (Gifford & Magee) 214 Purchase h 126 Ash (N) [ard
" William R city laborer b 60 Haz-
" see McGee [ond
Magellen Frank steward h 230 S Sec-
Magnan Aristide Rev assistant pastor St Anthony's Church h 1359 Acushnet av [Acushnet av
Magnant Aglae dressmaker b 1142
" Armand J carpenter h 13 Edison
" Arthur B carpenter h 144 Church
" Edmond H clerk 1669 Acushnet av b 178 Bowditch
" Edward clerk 77 Austin h 108 Locust [Bowditch
" Fred bartender 273 Sawyer h 132
" Fred stitcher b 6 Cornell pl
" George molder 229 N Water bds 6 Cornell pl
" Henri carpenter b 13 Edison
" Henry (J Magnant & Son) h 273 Coggeshall
" Herman carpenter b 16 Bowditch
" Henry operative removed to Lowell [ditch
" Hormidas carpenter h 178 Bow-
" Isaie manager h 39 Austin
" John spinner h 16 Bowditch
" John Jr spinner h 16 Bowditch
" Joseph (J Magnant & Son) h 273 Coggeshall
" J & Son (Joseph and Henry) furniture 275 Coggeshall
" Louis h 104 Tallman
" Louis doffer b 13 Edison

Magnant
" Louis Jr fish 277 Coggeshall h 82 Penniman
" Magloire spinner h 6 Cornell pl
" Mizael weaver h 346 N Front
" Peter weaver b 1142 Acushnet av
" Rose B milliner 1009 and 1013 Acushnet av b 346 Sawyer
" Sophie widow Elie h 1142 Acushnet av
" Tobal carpenter b 178 Bowditch
Magnett Emma B widow Benjamin C h 184 Acushnet av
" James H janitor First National Bank h 54 Bedford
" Mary H teacher George H Dunbar school b 54 Bedford
Magoon Minnie Mrs bottler h 269 Purchase [Mill
Magrath Edward F shoemaker h 228
" see McGrath [North
Mague Frank A eyelet maker h 216
" Henry F clerk b 216 North
Maguire Dennis comber tender b 9 Morton ct
" Edward carder h 178 Crapo
" Edward J operative b 9 Morton ct
" James operative b 670 Frost
" James Jr harness maker h 62 S Second
" John F overseer h 9 Morton ct
" John F Jr carder b 9 Morton ct
" John W operative b 288c Grove
" Martin operative h 159 Crapo
" Mary Mrs operative b 162 State
" Robert weaver h 288c Grove
" Stephen laborer b 66 Middle
" Thomas b 12 Hazard ct
" Thomas foreman b Maxfield
" Thomas operative h 670 Frost
" see McGuire
Mahan Marie h 25 McGurk
" William doffer b 25 McGurk
Mahaney Earle auto repairer 22 Fourth [Front
Maher Elzear weaver b 358 North
" Emma Mrs weaver h 15 Beetle
" Eugene weaver b 358 N Front
" George died Feb 22 1911
" Henry weaver h 27 Bullard [av
" Joseph carpenter h 181 Belleville

J. F. CROSSLEY 223 MILL STREET COR. EMERSON PHONE
STEAM and HOT WATER HEATING
GAS FITTING and FIXTURES

MAHER PIERRE mason 358 North Front h do See page 763
" see Marr [av h 99 Holly
Maheu Ludger jeweler 1021 Acushnet
Mahon Dennis h 81 Myrtle
" Dennis J helper Standard Oil Co b 81 Myrtle
" George A brakeman h 56 Linden
" George W inspector U St Ry Co h 30 Willow [tle
" John J hoseman Hose 2 b 81 Myr-
" Patrick foreman of S O Co of N Y h 12 High
" Lizzie and Theresa h 49 Windsor
" William clerk b 99 South
" see Mann
Mahoney Catherine A widow Michael h 431 Pleasant
" David gas fitter b 90 Rockland
" Dennis laborer N B W W h 10 Willis
" Dennis F treer h 62 Jenny Lind
" Dennis J janitor Public Library h 480 Bolton [328 Cedar
" Edward T druggist 45 Linden b
" Francis A clerk 849 Kempton b 508 Cottage [Cottage
" Fred G clerk 45 Linden b 508
" Hanorah widow Patrick h 21 State [Princeton
" Helen L clerk 65 William b 155
" James H lieutenant hose 2 h 96 Clark
" Jeremiah laborer h 5 Middle [len
" Jeremiah F coal passer h 84 Al-
" John laborer h 585 Acushnet av
" John F student b 164 Chestnut
" John H plumbing 957 County h 959 do [tage
" Joseph A city laborer b 508 Cot-
" Julia widow Michael h 1416 Acushnet avenue
" Margaret operative h 4 Clark
" Mary A widow Timothy E h 508 Cottage [Tinkham
" Matilda widow Jeremiah M h 218
" Michael engineer h 155 Princeton
" Michael J spinner b 431 Pleasant
" Patrick F removed to Boston
" Patrick H city laborer h 596 Cottage [Mill h 164 Chestnut
" Patrick J overseer Wamsutta
" William S clerk 508 Cottage
Maia Archille operative h 107 Beetle
Maiden James T Jr conductor h 1007 Purchase
Mailhot Adelphis hairdresser 1408 Acushnet av b 91 Hathaway
" Agnes widow Peter h 91 Hathaway
" Alfred carpenter h 164 Tinkham
Maillette Albert carpenter b 24 Tallman
" Alphe carpenter h 153 Collette
" Elas weaver b 103 Belleville rd
" J Baptiste laborer h 103 Belleville rd
" Placide carpenter h 24 Tallman
" see Maillotte and Mayotte
Maillotte Albert clerk 201 Union b 75 Kenyon
" Alphonse weaver h 75 Kenyon
" Arthur mule spinner b 75 Kenyon
" Elsie nurse rms 75 Kenyon
Mailloux Cyrille loom fixer h 137 River rd
" Cyrille wood 53 Nelson h 60 do
" Dionne cigar maker b 164 Cedar
" Domino rem to Woonsocket R I
" Ernest painter b 202 State
" Louis rem to Woonsocket R I
" Lydia clerk 912 S Water b 604 S Second
" Mary Mrs dry goods 1239 Acushnet av h 187 Phillips av
" Paul operative h 206 Cedar Grove
" Peter chauffeur h 35 Nye
" Pierre laborer h 202 State [Grove
" Prosper carpenter h 208 Cedar
" William h 208 Cedar Grove
" Zepherin chair maker h 604 S Second
Mailot Frank operative b 23 Cotter
Maimaris Demetrios fruit 32 Pleasant h 51 Spring
Main David adjutant Salvation Army 279 Acushnet av h do [Front
Maino Amato third hand h 546 N
Maine Henry M (N B Steam Carpet Beating and Rug Co) h 1 Morgan [535 Kempton
" Ice Cream Co (George Peterson)
Mainville Alexander laborer h 99 Holly
" Alfred laborer b 99 Holly

CHARLES A. CROSHERE
38 FOURTH ST. Bell Phone 1964-23
SIGN PAINTING
GLASS LETTERING
ELECTRIC SIGNS
SHOW CARDS

Mainville
" William mill hand h 99 Holly
Majndle Antonnette widow Louis h 130 Tallman
" Charles spinner b 130 Tallman
" Louis weaver b 130 Tallman
" William spinner h 130 Tallman
Major Treffle loom fixer h 274 Nash rd
" Wilfred spinner b 278 Phillips av
Maker Almira J operator b 239 Arnold
" Alonzo A clerk b 175 Durfee
" Charlotte A widow George W h 96 Maxfield
" Eliza A Mrs h 239 Arnold
" Sylvanus engineer St Luke's Hospital h at Fairhaven [net av
Makin Alfred operative h 36 Acush-
" Ann widow b 36 Acushnet av
" Harry machinist h 28 Rockland
" Isaac overseer h 99 Brock av
" Robert weaver b 137 Acushnet av
" William operative h 438 S Second
Maley Elizabeth widow Michael J h 95 Ashland
" James E b 95 Ashland [land
" Thomas J mill hand b 95 Ash-
" William J second hand b 95 Ashland [Tallman
Malige Rose widow Baptiste h 141
Malkowcke Felix box maker bds 11 Holly [land
Malley Patrick D foreman h 70 Rock-
Mallick Lewis tailor h 114 S Sixth
Malliet Cora E Mrs removed to Fairhaven [97 William rm 306
Malloch John & Co cotton buyers
Malmedie Carrie E widow Charles H bds 133 Fourth
" Charles H Jr foreman 100 Fifth h 208 Grinnell
Malo Blanche A' operative 57 N Second b 345 Sawyer
" Prime fixer h 345 Sawyer
Maloine Antonio laborer 696 Acushnet av [Davis
Malone Ellen B widow Peter b 277
" George salesman 341 Acushnet av h 80 Merrimac
" John weaver h 27 McGurk
" John T fixer h 277 Davis
" William weaver h 178 Brook
Maloney George carpenter h 316 Pleasant [rd
" James T laborer b 46 Belleville
" Lawrence mule spinner bds 4 Social [ville rd
" Lawrence operative h r 61 Belle-
" Mathias P laborer h 46 Belleville rd [Allen
" Nellie clerk 182 Union b 230
" Thomas mill hand bds 46 Belleville rd [Social
" Thomas J machine operator b 4
Malonson Frank A (M Malonson & Son) h 259 Mt Pleasant
" Mary & Son (Frank A) market gardeners 255 Mt Pleasant h 259 do
Maloy James E drill worker h 131 Sycamore [Chestnut
Malyan Richard J carpenter h 197
Manchester Alton shoemaker b 174 Ashland [b 90 Robeson
" Alvah J bookkeeper 36 Purchase
" Annie B widow Adoniram b 45 Rotch [ence
" Benjamin A teamster b 130 Flor-
" Charles H baggage master h Tarkiln Hill rd [mut av
" Charles H carpenter h 122 Shaw-
" Cora Mrs h 118 Durfee
" Cora E widow H G h 90 Robeson
" Damon D driver rms 379 Cottage
" Edward E shoemaker h 29 Bullock
" Emily F widow Harry L h 227 Chancery
" Fred rem to Dartmouth
" Fred F laborer 137 Richmond
" Frederick J drill worker h 21 Cottage
" Henry engineer rms 152 Purchase
" Herbert A clerk 688 Kempton h 59 Jenny Lind
" Hezekiah A foreman machinist 100 Fifth h 90 Elm
" James B painter h 201 Cedar
" James C clerk h 174 Maxfield
" James H grocer 688 Kempton h 690 do [do
" John A fish 274 Kempton b 690
" John B housekeeper police station 3 rms 51 Emerson (S)
" Lillian M Mrs b 296½ Acushnet av [Cottage
" Maria N widow Thomas h 342

J. G. NICHOLSON
LUMBER, SASH, DOORS and BLINDS
BOWDITCH STREET, NEW BEDFORD, MASS.

Manchester
" Mary A widow L D b 136 River road
" Mary H widow Phineas B h 130 Florence [lock
" Merrick S shoemaker b 29 Bul-
" Nathaniel D motorman bds 29 Durfee [h 379 Cottage
" Philander F salesman 65 William
" Ruel D clerk 1061 Acushnet av h 90 Robeson [ion
" Ruth A widow Calvin h 419 Un-
" Stephen F h Tarklin Hill rd [tin
" Stephen F shoemaker h 204 Aus-
" Theodore N conductor h 29 Durfee
" Wilfred F coachman b 72 Spruce
" William F drill maker h 39 Chestnut [Sycamore h do
Mandell Augustus H physician 25
" George E clerk 100 Fifth h 11 Maple View terrace
" see Mendell
Mandeville Alexie chauffeur h 50 Nye [Nye
" Elizabeth widow George h 63
" Felix carpenter b 63 Nye
" George carpenter b 63 Nye
" George helper 1545 Acushnet av b 43 Dean
" Lea music teacher 204 Davis b do
" Noe operative h 28 Nye
" Pierre clerk 1070 County b 43 Dean [292 Allen
Mandly Antonio J master mariner h
" Harold T electrician b 292 Allen
" Henry master mariner h 277 Palmer
" Leon A helper h 205 Acushnet av
" William carpenter b 277 Palmer
" see Manley [Water
Manery James weaver bds 1046 S
Manghan James spinner h 72 Ruth
" William spinner h 76 Cove [ditch
Mangnant John spinner h 16 Bow-
Mangold S George weaver h 1 Blackburn [vision
Mangum Joseph operative h 110 Di-
Manha Frank A city laborer h 199 Allen
Maniette Marie clerk b 82 Pierce
Mankin Louis pedlar h 868 County
Manley Martin laborer b 53 S Second
" M Alice widow Thomas h 67 Dean
" Thomas A spinner b 67 Dean
Mann Joseph twister b 383 Coggeshall [wife h 185 S Second
" Margaret A widow James H mid-
" Marion L teacher R C Ingraham School b 70 Hillman
" Mary widow Henry E h 95 High
" Thomas plumber 91 N Water b 271 Pleasant [h 84 Mill
" William W dentist 174½ Purchase
Manning Florence F Mrs h 60 N Second [Sixth
" Francis J boss comber b 96 S
" Frank clerk P O b 213 Court
" James h 213 Court
" James L clerk b 213 Court
" Jane widow Peter h 96 S Sixth
" Joseph S police h 191 Chancery
" Michael laborer h 42 Ash (N)
" Nellie housekeeper h 233 County
" Richard copper refiner T N B Copper Co h 57 Reynolds
" Sylvester overseer City Manufacturing Co h 3 Warwick [Myrtle
" Timothy copper worker h 66
" William H removed from city
" William T tinsmith h 124 Bonney
Mannion James F engineer h 250 Summer
" James H spinner h 51 Austin
Manny Adam weaver h 87 Clifford
" Aldoh clerk 739 Purchase b 1 Kilburn [Kilburn
" Alfred grocer 126 N Front b 1
" Domenique spinner h 1 Kilburn
" Harry grocer 200 Belleville av h r 43 Beetle
" Josephat carpenter h 211 Collette
" see Meny
Manomet Mills, Riverside av corner Manomet [fee
Manseau John D salesman h 30 Dur-
" Joseph clerk 1131 Acushnet av h 391 Bowditch [Purchase
Mansfield Dennis city laborer h 509
" Kenneth rms 464 County
Mansion House J F McAdams prop 93 to 109 Union
Mansley Fred spinner b 15 Adams
" Walter weaver h 15 Adams
" William elevatorman h 83 Crapo

Steiger-Dudgeon Co.
"The WOMAN'S Store."
Tel. Bell 82 & 83, Branches connecting all depts.
" " 160 For Office only. Auto. 1211

SUMPTIONS, ASSORTMENTS AT ALL TIMES OF DEPENDABLE DRY GOODS

Manstie B agent 186 Purchase
Mansur Frank foreman 100 Fifth h 38 Liberty
Manter Bessie N dressmaker 22 Cedar b do
" M Augusta Mrs h 22 Cedar
Manuel David dry goods h 238 County
" Mary widow Frank h r 161 Smith
" William R herb specialist h 99 Tremont
Manufacturers Supply Co Arthur D Delano treas mill supplies and hardware 382 Acushnet av
Manville Samuel carpenter h 61 Bullard
Maranda Azilda widow Misel h 385 Front
MARANDA DONAT real estate and variety 393 N Front h 387 do See page 757
" Joseph ropemaker h 86 Liberty
" Ovila carpenter h 241 Coffin av
Maranha Jose operative h 868 County
Marble Abbie S b 274 Pleasant
" Annie widow John h 113 Sycamore
" A Ethel bookkeeper 191 Cedar b 113 Sycamore
" Charles H woodworker rms 69 Mechanics lane
Marceau Arthur clerk b 62 Foster
Marcelino Frank J laborer N B W W
Marcelli Antonio laborer h 15 First
March Richard H blacksmith 11 Front h 201 Davis
Marchado Urbano hairdresser 271 Rivet h Dartmouth street
Marchal Emile weaver h 16 Salisbury
" Xavier weaver b 16 Salisbury
Marchand Delisica carpenter bds 9 Bentley
" Frank carpenter h 9 Bentley
" Fred salesman b 28 Bentley
" John A carpenter h 28 Bentley
" Joseph weaver b 28 Bentley
" Samuel operative b 9 Bentley
" Zephir operative b 28 Bentley
Marchant Cynthia C widow asst matron H of C b 195 Cottage
" Everett L lawyer 97 William rm 203 rms Y M C A
Marchessault Aldei driver 238 State h 367 Pleasant
" Annias telephone operator b 1149 Acushnet av
" Arthur carpenter b 225 Bowditch

Marchessault
" Celinda widow Elaire b 87 Bullard
" Charles E steam fitter h 50 Hazard
" Emma widow Alcide h 367 Pleasant
" Eugene clerk 335 N Front h 301 Coffin av
" Henri tinsmith h 240 Phillips av
" John B A removed to Chicago Ill
" Joseph carder h rear 164 Cedar Grove
" Louis clerk 1404 Acushnet av h 87 Bullard
" Minnie E bookkeeper 40 Purchase h 181 Summer
" Roderique removed from city
" William died Dec 1 1910
Marchi Joseph clerk 153 Cove h 280 Fourth
Marciel William laborer b 321 Arnold
Marcielle Ida M Mrs b 179 Mill
Marcille Adelard decorator 1119 Acushnet av b 917 County
" Leon chauffeur b 917 County
" Melvina widow Joseph h 917 County
Marcotte Albert insurance agent 37 Purchase rm 23 rms 292 do
" Alfred teamster b 883 Purchase
" Arthur carder h 166 N Front
" Dennis spinner b 68 Dean
" Henry painter h Tarkiln Hill rd
" Hormidas h 235 N Front
" Ida widow Frank h 118 South
" Joseph doffer h r 68 Dean
" Joseph hostler 50 Elm
" Leo oil 68 Dean b do
" Olivier weaver b 118 South
" Omer helper h 235 N Front
" Severe Mrs h 68 Dean
Marcourele Antoine speeder tender h 92 Earle
" Frank rem to Providence R I
" John B b r 679 Purchase
Marcoux Alfred weaver h 815 First
" Arcade grocer 61 County h 85 Jouvette
" Arthur L clerk 513 County bds 205 Pleasant
" Didace laborer b 949 County
" Eusebe laborer b 6 Coffin av ct
" Henry speeder h 65 Acushnet av
Marder Albert salesman b 611 Purchase
" James driver 14 N Sixth b 611 Purchase

PELEG H. SHERMAN 506 COUNTY ST.
FUNERAL DIRECTOR AND EMBALMER
OFFICE PHONES. Bell 690-13. Auto. 1305.
RESIDENCE PHONES. Bell 690-12. Auto. 1306.

Marder
" Max grocer 607 Purchase h 611 do [do
" Robert clerk 607 Purchase b 611
Margeson Ernest (Margeson & Bazinet) plumber 542 N Front h 62 Myrtle [h 200 Dean
" Harry plumber 1545 Acushnet av
" James weaver bds 38 Bowditch
" Moses weaver b 26 George
" Richard plumber h 22 Cleveland
" Thomas operative h 299 Brook
" Thomas operative b 11 Logan
" William carder h 26 Salisbury
" William fireman h 282 Phillips av
" & Bazinet (Ernest Margeson and John Bazinet) plumbers 542 N Front [ley
Marginson William spinner h 14 Ash-
Margolis Barnard G student b 209 Acushnet av
" Isaac (Star Clothing Co) 1262 Acushnet av h 1264 do
" Simon Rabbi h 209 Acushnet av
Maria Annie h 139 Coffin av
" Antone carpenter h 59 Crapo
Marin Philip laborer h 27 Ashley
Marinelle Charles laborer h 11 Abbott
Mariners' Home 15 Bethel, Rev Charles S Thurber chaplain and agent [Sawyer
Marinis Peter auto repairer h 239
Marino John laborer h 708 Acushnet av
Marinoff Samuel pedlar h 80 First
Marion Antoine h 91 Bullard
" Eva mill hand b 492 N Front
Markey George A granite end Robeson h 142 Florence
" George E (George E Markey & Co) 233 S Second h at Providence R I [ond
" George E & Co liquors 233 S Sec-
Markham Maude widow Leander G h 138 Fourth
Markmen John janitor h 159 Elm
Markowitz Samuel 739 S Water b 169 Acushnet av
Marks Antone S operative h 15 Fair
" Antonio mule spinner h 28 Bourne
" Frank operative h 23 Spooner
" Frank painter h 464 S Water

Marks
" Frank S overseer Rotch dept N E C Y Co h 19 Spooner
" John S metalworker h 200 Brock avenue [er
" John S mill hand h 23 Spoon-
" Joseph carpenter h 272 S Water
" Joseph carpenter b 289 Fourth
" Mary Mrs b 64 Mosher
" Tracy glasscutter h 116 S Sixth
" William S decorator b 200 Brock avenue
Marl John fisherman h 87 Prospect
Marland Harry machinist b 106 Bowditch
" John janitor h 315 Davis
" Septimus fireman h 84 Merrimac
Marleau Edward weaver h 109 Phillips av
Marley Anna M stenographer 301 Municipal bldg b 103 Chestnut
" John F foreman h 103 Chestnut
" John T salesman h 27 Borden
Marlow Louis bottler b 48 High
Marmonti Eugene plumber b 231 North [ond
Maroon Joseph pedlar h 216 N Sec-
" Thomas pedlar h 218 N Second
Marotte Amede carpenter h 1129 Purchase [Maxfield
Marquand James special police h 71
Marques John helper h 559 S Second
" Joseph weaver h 410 S Front
" Joseph S laborer h 4 Tallman's lane [ond b 477 First
" Manuel de S barber 236 S Sec-
Marquis Nina B Mrs h 614 County
" Paul machinist h 54 Blackmer
" William weaver h 25 Delano
Marr John third hand h 260 Coggeshall
" Margaret L h 19 Cannon [Smith
" Mary V widow William J h 209
" see Maher [Washburn
Marrick Thomas operative h 33
Marriner Jessie removed from city
Marriott Edward spinner b 257 Tinkham
" Nathaniel A Rev pastor Union Baptist church h 7 Spruce
Marrotte Felix W superintendent Wamsutta Club h 403 Cottage

F. T. AKIN & CO. PAINTERS AND DECORATORS

Marrotte
" Francis carpenter h 1 Washington avenue [chard (S)
" John C O carpenter b 416 Or-
" see Merritt [Crapo
Marsala Philip S operative h 59
Marsden Albert weaver h 964 Acushnet avenue [av
" Alfred spinner h 3506 Acushnet
" David weaver b 32 Viall
" Edwin twister b 107 David
" Elias teamster h r 69 Linden
" Emma h 39 N Sixth
" Fred collector h 57 W French av
" Frederick A salesman 37 Purchase rm 19
" George b 52 Swift [net av
" George physician h 1579 Acush-
" Harry weaver b 108 Blackmer
" James spinner h 187 Davis
" Jeremiah liquors 687 Purchase h 11 Studley [h do
" John T bakery 1653 Acushnet av
" Joseph spinner b 187 Davis
" Lawrence weaver b 40 Cove
" Margaret weaver h 52 Swift
" Robert clerk h 32 Viall
" Robert loom fixer h 389 Bolton
" William F weaver b 8 George
" William H (David McGill & Co) 193 Blackmer h 189 Blackmer
Marsh Alphonso L teamster N B W W h 483 Acushnet avenue
" Eva milliner 8 Purchase bds at Fairhaven [Weld
" Harry L insurance agent h 185
" Henry overseer Pierce Brothers Ltd h 59 Howard [Oak
" Henry traveling salesman h 30
" Herbert laborer b 871 Purchase
" Herbert operative b 40 Highland
" James (Ricard & Marsh) liquors 410 N Front h 241 Coffin av
" Joseph mill hand h 100 Clifford
" Joseph spinner h 49 Acushnet av
" Joseph weaver b 574 S Second
" Sarah J widow Henry h 315 Coffin avenue [Y M C A
" Thomas R machine erector rms
Marshall Albert R machinist h 914 Belleville avenue
" Antone fish h 368 Allen [av
" Antone mill hand h 75 Acushnet

Marshall
" Antone stone worker h 396 S Second
" Antone A (Richards & Marshall) grocer 44 Howland h 7 Stone
" Antonio mill hand h 104 Dartmouth [Rockland
" Augusta clerk 182 Union bds 159
" Barbara widow dressmaker 108 Rockland h do [h 28 Holly
" Bella clerk 1100 Acushnet avenue
" Carrie widow Manuel b 37 Court
" Catherine Mrs b 525 Cottage
" Charles (Marshall & Co) 106 Front h 460 County [153 Smith
" Charles E driver 160 N Water h
" Earl C presman Standard h 426 Chancery
" Eli operative h 162 Division
" Ellis electrician b 199 Brock av
" Frank furniture 89 Howland bds 120 S Sixth [ct
" Frank H gate tender h 8 Hazard
" Frank J died January 3 1911
" Fred drill worker h 107 Fifth
" Fred (Hargreaves & Marshall) liquors 407 Kempton h 54 Katharine
" F mill hand h 13 Hall
" Hannah widow Smith b 21 Reynolds [av h 213 Cottage
" Henry J plumber 126 Acushnet
" Jack barber rms 171 Grinnell
" James liquors 1200 Acushnet av h 21 Reynolds
" James supt Oneko Woolen Mills
" James weaver h 205 Brock av
" Jane widow John h 1848 Acushnet avenue
" John h 154 Rockland
" John hostler h 487 S Water
" John washer 50 Elm
" John B operative h 159 Rockland
" Joseph laborer h 208 Rivet
" Joseph laborer h 371 S Second
" Joseph oiler b 181 Bonney
" Joseph S carpenter h 130 Blackmer [103½ South
" Joseph T clerk 659 S Water h
" Laura widow Hiram h 426 Chancery
" Louis laborer h 262 S Second
" Manuel carpenter h 141 Hemlock

Bookkeeping, Shorthand, Typewriting, Penmanship, etc. Taught thoroughly at
Kinyon's Commercial School
Odd Fellows Bldg., Cor. William and Pleasant Sts., New Bedford, Mass.

Marshall
" Manuel helper 36 Purchase b 44 Lindsey
" Manuel operative h 1081 County
" Manuel C operative b 103 Thompson [Front
" Manuel F carpenter h 492 South
" Manuel F died Nov 21 1910
" Manuel P liquors 437 S Water h 175 Fourth
" Margaret J teacher Cedar Grove st school b 1848 Acushnet av
" Mary Mrs h 104 Fifth
" Mary E Mrs millinery 460 County h do
" Palmira clerk rms 383 Purchase
" Peter farmer h 597 Allen
" Phebe Mrs h 69 Howland
" Ralph H clerk 66 Pleasant b 426 Chancery [215 S Front
" Rita A widow Manuel F h
" Sarah J died April 4 1911
" Smith chauffeur b 21 Reynolds
" Squire weaver h 110 David
" Thomas R watchman h 810 Belleville av [Chancery
" William M Bennett Mill h 426
" William T gilder h 82 Chancery
" & Co (Charles Marshall) wholesale provisions 106 Front
" see Machado [Beech
Marsland George operative bds 40
" John J shoemaker h 23 Kenyon
" Joseph h 147 Holly
Marston J H Chester advertising solicitor Times h at Fairhaven
" Mary widow Charles h 603 Maxfield [ty
Martel Albert H mason h 1085 Coun-
" Albini S (A S & E D Martel) h 1356 Acushnet av [N Front
" Alphonsine widow Xavier b 314
" Alfred doffer h 198 State
" A S & E D (Albini S and Eleanor D) milliners 1354 Acushnet avenue
" Edward removed from city
" Emanuel teamster h 29 Bullard
" Eugene operative b 1016 Acushnet av [1016 Acushnet av
" George tinsmith 671 Purchase b
" Henry operative b 1016 Acushnet avenue
" Honore carpenter h 202 Brook

Martel
" Imelda B clerk 40 Purchase bds 1354 Acushnet av
" Joseph carpenter h 163 David
" Joseph machinist h 7 Phillips av
" Lena (A S & E D Martel) h 1356 Acushnet av
" Mary mill hand b 35 Dean
" Prosper fixer h 268 Tinkham
" Teles barber h 77 Jouvett
*Martin Adam b 63 Washburn
" Albert J officer H C h 92 High
" Albert N removed to Lawrence
" Alonzo laborer h 125 Cove
" Anthony T painter h 62 Ward
" Antone h 398 Orchard (S)
" Antone operative h 54 Blackmer
" Antonio mill hand b 28 Rotch block 439 Bolton
" Arthur collector h 131 Whitman
" Arthur mill hand bds 45 Phillips av [Front
" Arthur L operative bds 307 S
" Calixte weaver h 2 Riverside av
" Carrie A stenographer bds 181 Washington
" Charles driver h 63 Washburn
" Charles H janitor h 181½ Mill
" Christopher weaver h 163 Frederick
" Clovis carpenter b 149 Tinkham
" Cyrill mill hand bds 495 N Front
" David mason h 156 Tallman
" Delor fisherman h 712 S Water
" Delors third hand b 50 Nye
" Edmond machinist b 96 Nye
" Edward machinist h 96 Nye
" Edward H proofreader Standard h 203 Purchase
" Emerie grocer 126 N Front and 31 Washburn h do
" Emile weaver h 22 Salisbury
" Emily widow Peter h 232 Arnold
" Ettienne carpenter h 49 Acushnet av
" Euclide weaver b 127 Whitman
" Eugene weaver h 493 S Second
" E Fanny widow Henry O h 181 Washingotn
" Ferdinand L cook h 213 S Front
" Francisco mill hand h 421 First
" Frank drillworker h 181 Acushnet av
" Frank operative h 204 Crapo
" Fred carpenter b 8 Tallman

Bread, Cake, Pastry
RICHMOND & COMPANY 255-257 UNIUN STREET
Bell 993 Automatic 1022

Martin
" Frederick W insurance agent 41 William h 6 Ash (S)
" George F clerk 409 Rivet rms 91 School
" George M removed from city
" Gertrude widow h 912 County
" Gregore seaman h 445 S Water
" Henry mill hand b 81 Davis
" Henry weaver h 50 Nye
" Henry weaver h 152 Tallman
" Henry weaver h 926 S Water
" Isabel widow Peter h 170 S Second
" Isabella Mrs died March 11 1911
" James carder h 18 Viall
" John clerk h 88 Potomska
" John mill hand b 60 Bullard
" John operative h 495 N Front
" John teamster h 88 Potomska
" John weaver b 926 S Water
" John H glasscutter b 232 Arnold
" John L clerk 100 Fifth h 42 Dartmouth [h 57 Bay
" John L insurance agt 41 William
" John P motorman h 72 Swift
" Joseph h 359 N Front
" Joseph baker 537 First h 550 do
" Joseph died June 23 1911
" Joseph steward h 15 S Second
" Joseph P shoe repairer 455 Rivet h 457 do [liam h 663 Kempton
" Joseph S photographer 49 Wil-
" Josephine widow Pierre h 553 N Front
" Levi laborer b 495 N Front [ty
" Lewis C roll coverer h 827 Coun-
" Luiz S laborer h 35 Mitchell
" Manuel laborer h 188 Thompson
" Manuel laborer h 440 S Water
" Manuel mill hand h 39 Mitchell
" Manuel mill hand b 148 Belleville av
" Manuel weaver h 50 Katharine
" Manuel F city laborer h Winterville road
" Manuel F laborer h 45 Grant
" Manuel J hairdresser 86 Union h 5 First
" Maria widow John h 4 Crapo
" Marianna hairdresser 6 Fifth h 29 South
" Mary Mrs h 531 N Front
" Mary Mrs weaver h 2 Bethel

Martin
" Mary E teacher Abraham Lincoln school b 67 Mill [341 First
" Mary O Mrs bookkeeper bds
" Michael laborer h 20 Division
" Napoleon grocer 175 N Front h 141 Cedar Grove
" Olivia S corsets 2 Seventh rms do
" Peter mariner h 4 Walnut [av
" Peter second hand h 45 Phillips
" Philebert carpenter h 20 Central av [chase b 232 Arnold
" Rebecca A bookkeeper 170 Pur-
" Richard h 926 S Water
" Robert cable splicer 57 N Second b 232 Arnold
" Robert weaver h 9 E French av
" Samuel D carpenter 5 Bullard h do
" Sarah J Mrs b 64 Division
" Thomas bookkeeper 188 N Water b 87 Maple [ond
" Thomas weaver h 566 S Sec-
" Thomas B motorman h 204 Weld
" Victor clerk 126 N Front h 31 Washburn
" Victor motorman h 139 Earle
" Walter mason h 160 Earle
" William clerk b 341 First
" William mason h 50 Richmond
" William shoe repairer r 1136 Acushnet av [mer
" William O carpenter h 209 Sum-
" & Manny grocers 126 N Front
" see Martine and Martyn
Martine John D (New Bedford Reed Co) 189 N Water h 138 Maxfield
" Manuel D (New Bedford Reed Co) 189 N Water h 67 Mill
Marting Manuel speeder tender b 96 S Second
" Pedros hostler b 96 S Second
" Roman operative b 96 S Second
Martins Frank sexton St John the Baptist church h 10 Bay
Marts Sophia E died July 31 1910
Martyn Elfrida b 97 Fourth
" John teamster 559 S Second
" Martin h 99 Fourth
" William C Rev rem to Newton
Marvel Aaron sub letter carrier bds 45 Mosher
" George glassworker h 26 Cove
" James loom fixer h 45 Mosher

GLOBE DYE HOUSE 220 SHAWMUT AVE.
J. N. J. LONHOLDT, PROP. Telephone Connections Goods called for and Delivered
Down town Office, 52 Pleasant St., Room 1 North End Office, 1014 Acushnet Ave.

Marvel
" James W mule spinner h 12 Woodland
" John burnisher h 100 South
" Robert weaver h 25 Marvin
" Sumner E teacher High school b 98 Arnold [ter
Marvine Andrew carpenter h 49 Fos-
Marwan Antone weaver h 187 David
" John h 153 Hathaway [son
Masalina Frank J laborer h 36 Edi-
Masaninoff Samuel junk h 455 S Water
Maseau Noel weaver h 166 N Front
Mashow George A ship carpenter rms 282 Acushnet av
Mason Albert G treas Whitman Mill h at Mattapoisette
" Charles rms 781 Purchase
" Clara V widow Edward H b 17 Seventh [b 53 Willis
" Clarence W clerk Beacon Mfg Co
" Daniel weaver h 21 Grape
" Dennis S clerk 70 Union h 155 Shawmut av [496 Acushnet av
" Ernest plumber 91 N Water bds
" Fannie M widow George J h 163 Mt Pleasant [h 32 Parker
" Frank carpenter U St Ry Co h
" George spinner h 55 Durfee
" George N laborer h 113 James
" George N Mrs dressmaker 113 James h do [Kempton
" George W shoeworker h 113
" Harold O clerk b 245 Palmer
" Henry clerk 82 Purchase rms 488 Acushnet av [av
" Henry M engineer h 496 Acushnet
" Henry W chief police 9 S Second h 53 Willis
" John clerk b 224 Rivet
" John fireman h 56 Belleville rd
" John laborer h 226 Rivet
MASON JOHN L G mason 51-53 Foster h 53 North See page 774
" Joseph laborer h 129 Tallman
MASON MACHINE WORKS Taunton Mass See page 39
" Margaret E buyer b 526 Cottage
" Mary h 12 Viall [b 526 Cottage
" Mary F dressmaker 79 Bedford
" Reuben carpenter b 159 Shawmut av
" Richard weaver h 64 Hathaway

Mason
" Ruth b 504 Elm
" William mason h 44 Richmond
" William F changer over h 10 Social [ance 23 Clifford bldg
Massachusetts Accident Co insur-
" Civil Service office 52 Pleasant.
" Society for the Prevention of Cruelty to Children 12 Market
Masse Arthur fixer h 55 Clifford
" Honorat J drug clerk 1201 Acushnet av h 1081 County
" Hormidas tailor 131 Union h 260 Summer
" Joseph restaurant 61 Delano h 525 S Second [Village
" Ovide second hand h 8 Howland
" Raphael clerk b 201 Bowditch
" Rock weaver h 384 N Front
" R A clerk b 201 Bowditch
Massette Giovanni laborer h 192 N Front [rd
Massola Edward mill hand b 67 Nash
" Gabriel h 67 Nash rd [man
Masson Charles doffer b 129 Tall-
" Godfrey clerk 185 Union b 32 Parker [Mills h 108 Willis
" James M agent Oneko Woolen
" Joseph weaver h 129 Tallman
" Louis weaver b 47 Ashley
Mastera Frank milk 3697 Acushnet avenue near Clifford P O h do
" John farmer h 3691 Acushnet av near Clifford P O [Phillips av
Mates Antonio mill hand bds 101
" William removed from city
Mather Arthur H overseer Dartmouth Mfg Corp h 117 Butler
" James operative b 72 Hathaway
" John weaver h 207 Weld
" Joseph H operative b 365 Pleasant [Chancery
" Lucy A widow Joseph h 103
" Robert H bartender 678 Purchase h 365 Pleasant [Cal
" Walter removed to Los Angeles
Matherin Joseph removed from city
Mathews Manuel laborer h 80 Katherine
" William operative h 96 Hall
Mathewson Caroline widow Daniel b 27 Robeson [av
" Charles carpenter b 469 Acushnet
" John H motorman h 52 Willow

GREENE & WOOD Every Kind of LUMBER AND MILL WORK
PINE STREET, off So. WATER STREET, NEW BEDFORD

Mathieu Alfred operative b 131 North Front
" Emil weaver h 16 Roosevelt
" Frank L bartender Parker House h 32 Social
" George fixer bds 50 Nye
" Hormidas laborer h 60 Cove
" Joseph P laborer h 11 Clark
" Michel Mrs 100 Mt Pleasant
" Rock P weaver b 232 Acushnet av
" William H laborer h 608 S Second
Mathild Albert sausage maker Anthony Swift & Co b 63 N Second
Mathurin Hyacinthe h 187 Earle
" Paul mill hand b 187 Earle
Matise Manuel carder h 47 Thompson
Matt Edward janitor 14 Adams h do
Mattas A tailor bds 19 Fair
" Leonora tailoress b 19 Fair
" Mary widow Manuel F h 19 Fair
Matters Walter L glass worker h 76 Swift [Hollyhock
Matteus Jacintho carpenter h 32
Matthews Abram H city laborer h 33 High [ray ter
" Albert F conductor h 16 McMur-
" Alfred (Allen & Matthews) h 239 Field [ington
" Charles J solderer h 184 Wash-
" Etta widow Thomas h 2 Warwick
" Flora M clerk 111 William h 117 Hillman [ney
" Flora M stenographer b 55 Bon-
" Frank W compositor Standard h at Fairhaven [78 Penniman
" Fred T overseer Potomska Mill h
" Henry G metal spinner h 129 Bonney [av h 46 Fair
" Henry T foreman 474 Acushnet
" James H lunch 240 Purchase h 9 Campbell
" John B hostler h 20 La France ct
" John W glass cutter h 163 Purchase
" Joseph operative h 21 Griffin
" Leonard C teamster 170 Purchase bds 226 do
" Louis brakeman h 199 Smith
" Mary widow Antone h 239 Field
" Mary R widow Robert h 33 Fair
" Lawrence carpenter h 15 West
" Robert weaver b 132 Nye

Matthews
" Robert T decorator h 23 Dartmouth [h Fair
" William foreman 474 Acushnet av
" William P operative b 40 Winsor
Mattici Marsilio waiter 62 Purchase rms 104 Morgan
Mattocks William weaver h 212 Weld
Mattos Antone C carder h 7 Beetle
" Charles bootblack 1053 Acushnet avenue b 314 Coggeshall
" Jose laborer h 54 Katharine
" Manuel machinist h 80 Katharine
" Mary dressmaker h 12 Wing
" Mary F widow Manuel F b 108 Rockland
Mattson Charles P fisherman h Fern
Matz Hyman tailor h 35 Prospect
Maudley George awning maker 31 Commercial b 144 Division [ley
Maudsley Thomas laborer b 21 Ash-
" William loom fixer h 183 David
Maule William laborer h 18 Howland Village
Mauran William L president Booth Mfg Co h at Providence R I
Maurer John weaver h 249 Tinkham
Maurice Alfred spinner h 119 Phillips avenue
" Manuel operative h 222 N Front
Mauricio Manuel fisherman h 17 Mitchell [tage
Maw George draughtsman b 329 Cot-
" John molder h 124 Cove
Maxcy Mabel E Mrs h 15 Mill
" Marion S teamster h 280 Cedar
" Melvin E doffer bds 83 Dunbar
" Sydney operative h 200 Cedar Grove
" William J teamster b 280 Cedar
Maxfield Arthur helper 55 N Water
" Asha widow William H h 137 Chestnut
MAXFIELD CHARLES A plumbing stoves etc 26 N Second h at Fairhaven See page 769
" Charles T gardener b 225 N Second
" Edmund F h 236 Pleasant
" Fredrick T bookkeeper 24 N Water h 67 Hillman [415 Park
" George F clerk 111 William h

BONNEY, FOLSTER & CO.,
The North End's Shopping Centre
Dry Goods and Men's Furnishings
945-947 Acushnet Ave., New Bedford, Mass.

Maxfield
" Helen T teacher Parker st school b 16 Fifth [b 137 Chestnut
" Ida B clerk 207 Municipal bldg
" J Henry iron molder h 152 Fair
" Maria E dressmaker 137 Chestnut bds do [Library b 137 Chestnut
" Minerva F librarians' sec Public
" Walter S laborer 139 Front rms 263 Acushnet av [ics lane
" William H painter h 49 Mechan-
Maxie Marvin teamster h 280 Cedar
Maxim Agatha widow George W b 30 Hill
" Agatha L electric needle specialist 568 County b do [ington
" Agnes E dressmaker b 67 Wash-
" Charles W A machinist b 155 Campbell
" George D shoemaker h 30 Hill
" Henry C foreman 100 Fifth h 201 Austin
May Frederic W dyer h 637 Union
" John P died December 1 1910
" Mary widow Thomas h 89 Mosher
" Michael F gardener h 154 Rotch
" Thomas spinner b 89 Mosher
" William H doffer b 89 Mosher
Mayall Alfred mule spinner h 862 First [lips av
Mayer Gotthot operative h 297 Phil-
" Napoleon operative h 352 North Front [dle
Mayhew Abner gardener h 374 Mid-
" Alfred operative bds 208 Cedar Grove
" Allen G fisherman h 166 Mill
" see Mailloux
Maymon George removed from city
Maynard Charles engineer 281 Sawyer b 1205 Acushnet avenue
" Charles laundry man b 1205 Acushnet avenue
" Charles painter h 132 Tallman
" Docithe weaver h 292 Fourth
" Domitild widow Paul h 1205 Acushnet avenue
" Edward D engineer h 359 North
" Ernest fireman b 333 N Front
" Fred removed from city
" Fred weaver h 46 Belleville road
" George L clerk h 160 County
" George N clerk 878 Purchase

Maynard
" Henry Jr fixer h 36 George
" John M loom fixer h 177 Weld
" Joseph D weaver h 1009 County
" Josephine widow Theophile h 159 Whitman [Acushnet av
" Laura D clerk 40 Purchase h 1205
" Mederic F contractor h 810 Belleville avenue
" Paul H died September 18 1910
" Peter steamfitter b 44 Beetle
" Rose clerk 185 Union b 808 First
" Rose A Mrs h 1 Austin ct
Mayo Asbury A painter 34 Union h 117 Sycamore [State
Mayob Sarah J widow John h 163
Mayor Daniel shoes 1559 Acushnet av h 60 Beetle
Mayot Edward quiller h 161 Cove
Mazza Dominick laborer h 11 Abbott
" Leon laborer h 11 Abbott
McAdams James F prop Mansion House 109 Union h do
McAfee Bros (William M Thomas D and James R McAfee) furniture movers 41 Spring
" Emma A teacher Hosea M Knowlton school h 114 Chancery
" Helen A Mrs bookkeeper 170 Purchase b 48 Ash (S)
" Ida A assistant editor Standard h 114 Chancery [136 High
" James lunch 44 Acushnet av h
" James R (McAfee Brothers) 41 Spring h at Mattapoisett
" John K clerk b 48 Ash (S)
" Mary Mrs h 195 N Second
" Robert W clerk 63 Union h 119 Kempton [Spring h 106 High
" Thomas D (McAfee Brothers) 41
" William M (McAfee Brothers) 41 Spring h 313 Acushnet av [(S)
" William T drill maker h 48 Ash
McAllister John J H physician 210 County h do [avenue h do
" Joseph Mrs grocer 31 E French
" Joseph weaver h 31 E French av
" William C H boiler maker h 205 Fourth [Sixth
McAloon Edward F rigger h 112 S
" Frederick J b 217 Purchase
McAlpine Allan plumbing 339 Kempton h 335 do

M. P. B. Silva & Son BUILDERS
Estimates Furnished on all Kinds of Work
157 ACUSHNET AVENUE Both Phones NEW BEDFORD

McAlpine
" James twister h 133 Ashland
" James Jr twister b 133 Ashland
" John loom fixer h 133 Ashland
" John weaver h 236 Brock av
" Robert T plumber b 335 Kempton
McArdle Francis piper 28 N Water
" Frank plumber b 137 Acushnet avenue
" Frank watchman h 219 Rivet
McAulay Michael E motorman h 184 Summer [Fourth
McAuliffe Cornelius machinist b 272
" Daniel bowling 40 Delano h 699 S First [school h 48 Newton
" Dennis J janitor Harrington
" John J letter carrier h 134 Chestnut [Chestnut
" John J Jr second hand b 134
" John P city laborer b 48 Newton
" Leo F clothes cleaner 45 Hunter h 290 Palmer
" Mary F teacher Harrington school b 48 Newton
" Thomas W clerk P O b 48 Newton
McAvoy Andrew J W assistant postmaster P O h 206 Pleasant
" Charles A fish 633 First b 25 Welcome [48 Rockland
" Daniel V hairdresser 47 Delano h
" Elizabeth M dressmaker 206 Pleasant b do
" Ellen M died Nov 6 1910
" Francis A drill maker b 25 Welcome [avenue
" Henry A clerk h 4125 Acushnet
" James died 1911
" Jane Mrs h 25 Welcome [come
" John J clerk 633 First b 25 Wel-
" Joseph A clerk 633 First bds 25 Welcome [ant b do
" Martha A dressmaker 206 Pleas-
McBay Charles L police lieutenant h 9 Smith [Second b 9 Smith
" Irene I telephone operator 57 N
" Mary J widow b 19 Howland Village [Page
McBride Annie widow Anthony h 42
" John E linotype operator Standard h 168 Fourth [127 Park
" William machinist Standard h
" William M machinist h 121 Park
McCabe Bernard C clerk 645 County h 26 Liberty [ney
" Elizabeth widow Hugh h 191 Bon-
" Hugh F warper tender b 191 Bonney
" John weaver h 658 First
" Laura C teacher Dartmouth st school b 49 Dartmouth
" Michael L driver h 146 Cedar
McCaffery James bricklayer h 273 Fourth
McCafferty Annie Mrs b 301 Fourth
" James clerk 613 Acushnet av bds 367 Purchase [ter
McCall John spinner h 16 McMurray
McCann Ann widow George L b 4 Smith st ct
" Catherine h 4 Smith st ct
" Edward J piper b 159 Coggeshall
" Frank C carder h 203 Coffin av
" George operative b 200 N Front
" James L removed from city
" John fireman h 39 Reynolds
" Kate mill hand h 199 Davis
" Philip operative rms 158 Middle
" Phillip overseer Kilburn Mill rms 92½ Purchase
" William insurance agent 35 Arcade h 200 N Front
" W Thomas operative b 200 North Front
McCardell Robert driver 14 N Sixth h 461 Court [Katharine
McCarthy Catherine widow John h 36
" Catherine dresmaker 192 Chancery h do
" Charles carder h 147 Holly
" Cornelius J tinsmith 55 N Water bds 9 Waverly
" Dora nurse b 9 Smith
" Edward bricklayer h 168 Austin
" Edward iron worker bds 934 County
" Edward helper 10 Spring [ty
" Edward J shoemaker b 934 Coun-
" Florence E teamster h 499 Union
" Fred removed from city
" George shoemaker rms 50 Maxfield [h 457 Cottage
" George H plumber 55 N Water
" Hannah widow Michael h 449 Pleasant
" Helen T dressmaker b 51 Locust
" Henry machinist h 445 Pleasant

Steiger-Dudgeon Co.
"The WOMAN'S Store."
Tel. Bell 82 & 83, Branches connecting all depts.
" " 160 For Office only. Auto. 1211

SUMPTIONS, ASSORTMENTS AT ALL TIMES OF DEPENDABLE DRY GOODS

McCarthy
" Henry teamster h 3 Hillman st pl
" James operative rms 96 Middle
" James L third hand h 9 Willow
" James M engineer 214 S Water h 102 Oak
" Jeremiah copper worker b 46 Reynolds
" Jeremiah died March 12 1911
" Jeremiah police sergeant bds 27 Clark
" Jeremiah J (McCarthy & Hurley) 346 Acushnet av h 240 Fourth
" Jeremiah P operative h 125 Campbell
" John laborer h 29 Clark
" John laborer h 73 Dean
" John laborer b 39 Bowditch
" John spinner h 70 Jouvett
" John H mason b 19 Spruce
" John J laborer b 47 Holly
" John J removed to Taunton
" Julia bookkeeper 156 Weld bds 449 Pleasant
" Julia widow Patrick h 84 County
" Margaret widow Edward h 934 County
" Martin spinner h 51 Locust
" Mary h 16 Rodney [Spruce
" Mary widow Jeremiah h 19
" Michael laborer bds 39 Bowditch
" Michael machinist b 449 Pleasant
" Michael C laborer h 151 Holly
" Michael E plumber h 82 Dartmouth
" Michael J gardener h 9 Waverly
" Michael J laborer h 3 N Oak
" Mortimer died June 19 1910
" Patrick weaver b 64 Ruth
" Patrick J shoemaker b 19 Spruce
" Peter J carpenter b 9 Waverly
" Stella teacher Hosea M Knowlton school bds 79 Bay
" Thomas J doffer b 884 County
" William operative h 159 Crapo
" William spinner h 68 Crapo
" see McCarty [h 945 County
McCartney Thomas grocer 35 Parker
" William city laborer h 872 Purchase [chase
" William Jr machinist b 872 Pur-
McCarty A Gertrude stenographer 15 Clifford bldg bds 178 Davis

McCarty
" Bernard F supt Manomet Mills h 178 Davis [Hazard
" C Henry foreman 258 State b 87
" Daniel b 87 Hazard
" Daniel S removed to Indianapolis
" George died Nov 6 1910 [av
" John city W W b 1098 Acushnet
" Julia widow John h 87 Hazard
" J Edward foreman 258 State bds 87 Hazard
" Mary h 38 Durfee
" Mortimer general teamster 258 State h 87 Hazard
" Stephen J laborer h 38 Fair [Fair
" William H glass polisher h 38
" see McCarthy
McCaskie George spinner b 90 Nash
" William spinner b 90 Nash rd
McCauley Edward J laborer h 100 Fruit [Kempton
" Gertrude shoeworker bds 715
" James A electrician's apprentice bds 715 Kempton
" John W Mrs h 715 Kempton
" Thomas F driver 423 Acushnet avenue h 102 Middle
McClarence John removed from city
McClung Robert actor h 153 Grinnell
McClure Donald teamster h 11 Beetle
" George teaming 82 Tallman h 81 Beetle
" Joseph operative b 81 Beetle
" William teamster b 81 Beetle
" William F manager 151 Union h 561 do [b 282 Bowditch
" William F overseer Neild M Corp
McClurenon John clerk b 25 Marion
McClurg Milo removed from city
" William H operative h 53 Howard [h 2½ Willis
McClusky Catherine widow William
" Henry bookkeeper 34 Brook h 290 Pleasant
" James laborer b 137 Acushnet av
McCombes Alice Mrs h 186 Division
" George J weaver b 186 Division
" John operative b 186 Divison
" Thomas loom fixer b 24 Independent [Davis
McConnell James bartender h 138
McConville Bernard weaver b 489 S Front [Grove
" Edward laborer h 203 Cedar

PELEG H. SHERMAN 506 COUNTY ST.
FUNERAL DIRECTOR AND EMBALMER
OFFICE PHONES. Bell 690-13 Auto 1305.
RESIDENCE PHONES. Bell 690-12. Auto. 1306.

McConville
" George salesman Anthony Swift & Co b 201 Cedar Grove [Fifth
" Henry F grocer 329 County h 119
" John laborer h 36 Independent
McCormac John J teamster 1 William h 127 Kempton [sey
McCormack John laborer h 37 Lind-
" John twister h 170 Hatch [isbury
McCormick Michael twister b 9 Sal-
" Patrick weaver h 28 Penniman
" Rose h 46 Sycamore
" William laborer h 100 Cleveland
McCown Catherine widow Reese A h 78 Merrimac [h 281 Hillman
McCoy Edmund blacksmith's helper
" Helen teacher Middle st school rms 24 S Sixth
" Patrick H died March 18 1911
" Thomas F agent b 79 Forest
McCraken Louis C insurance agent 37 Purchase rm 23 h at Fairhaven [ty
McCready Reed engineer h 629 Coun-
McCreary Robert removed from city
McCrillis Frank A foreman h 115 Maxfield [ushnet av
McCrohan Daniel L mason b 2138 Ac-
" James P student b 2138 Acushnet avenue
" John police b 2138 Acushnet av
" Timothy mason h 2138 Acushnet avenue [net av
" Timothy F mason b 2138 Acush-
McCue Jane widow William h 110 Ashley [640 County
" John granite mfr 6-12 Smith h
" Thomas weaver h 22 Salisbury
" Walter joiner b 10 Ashley
" see McHugh
McCulley Nathaniel E foreman 111 Willis h 20 Richmond
McCulloch Alice M bookkeeper 144 Union bds 445 Mt Pleasant
" George H shoemaker h 72 Mt Pleasant
" John T removed from city
" Mary widow Robert bds 72 Mt Pleasant [City
" Mary F removed to New York
" William P removed from city
McCullough Frank machinist h 87 Hathaway

McCullough
" Helena h 300 Purchase
" John junk 98 and 100 Front h 38 S Sixth [Sixth
" John 3rd clerk 98 Front b 38 S
" Loretta telephone operator 57 N Second bds 33 Atlantic
" Mary E stenographer Whitman Mills bds 33 Atlantic
" Patrick J watchman N B W W h 33 Atlantic
" Sarah h 300 Purchase
McCurdy Amy h 30 Maitland [561 do
McCure N R asst mgr 151 Union b
McCusker James shoemaker rms 401 Purchase [rms 298 Union
" John P salesman Morris & Co
McDaniel Sarah A widow William W h 160 Ashland [Mill h 98 State
McDavitt William L overseer Pierce
McDermott Antoine removed to St John Canada
" Charles laborer h 451 Pleasant
" Charles W fish 39 Weld and 1518 Acushnet av h 360 Cedar
" Ducele bds 2 Irvington court
" Edward clerk b 358 Cedar
" Edward laborer b 451 Pleasant
" Henry rem to St John Canada
" James watchman h 358 Cedar
" John mill hand b 89 Hathaway
" John B removed from city
" John H painter h 7 Warwick
" John L apprentice b 45 Smith
" Joseph D salesman 1262 Acushnet av h 288 Earle
" Mary h 111 Park
" Mary A teacher Dartmouth street school bds 45 Smith
" Michael janitor h 45 Smith
" Owen carder h 190 Tinkham
" Patrick laborer b 150 Chancery
" Patrick H removed to Boston
" Thomas removed from city
" Thomas F clerk 39 Weld rms 360 Cedar
" William removed from city
McDiarmid Anna B removed from
McDonald Agnes clerk 185 Union b 119 Acushnet avenue [Second
" Alexander carpenter rms 92 S
" Annie Mrs h 202 N Front

COAL AND WOOD F. T. AKIN & COMPANY
HAY AND STRAW
WALNUT, COR. WATER, 84 PLEASANT ST., 25 WELD SQ.
129 COVE STREET WHF. FOOT OF COFFIN STREET

McDonald
" Arthur ladderman Hook & Ladder
No 2 h 75 Clark [av
" Christie widow Alex h 118 Bates
" Daniel J police Station 5 b 300
Cedar [geshall
" Edward R iron worker b 475 Cog-
" Francis spinner h 282 Phillips av
" [illegible]e bookkeeper b 123 Max-
well
" Henry J spinner h 149 Bonney
" Henry J undertaker h 205 Fourth
" Hugh J died July 2 1911
" Isabelle widow Hugh J h 195 S
Second [Second
" Isabelle F clerk P O h 195 South
" James butter 381 Cedar h 144
Merrimac [ond
" James card grinder h 596 S Sec-
" James removed from city
" James spinner b 79 Bowditch
" James teamster h 9 W High
" Jeremiah spinner h 385 Orchard
(S) [ushnet av
" Joanna widow John J h 119 Ac-
" John laborer b 107 Willis
" John laborer b 701 First
" John laborer rms 152 Purchase
" John operative b 118 Bates av
" John C brakeman b r 359 Pleas-
ant [Bonney
" John E hoseman Hose 4 b 149
" John H driver N B F D b 385
Orchard (S)
" Katherine R h 475 Coggeshall
" Luke removed from city
" Margaret Mrs b 362 County
" Martin boss comber Rotch Mill h
18 Swift
" Mary Mrs h 86 Mott
" Mary A h 26 Ash (N) [Front
" Mary J widow Edward h 519 N
" Michael twister b 985 S Water
" Murdock carpenter h 59 James
" Neil bricklayer bds 1089 Acush-
net avenue [ska
" Patrick J laborer h 109 Potom-
" Rhoda mill hand b 62 Deane
" Ronald C salesman h 123 Max-
field
" Sadie Mrs h 122 Maxfield
" Stephen mill hand b 519 N Front
" Thomas laborer h 45 Winsor

McDonald
" Thomas operative h 16 Covell
" Thomas operative b 90 Hatha-
way av
" William F driver H & L No 1 b
385 Orchard (S)
" Winnifred Mrs h 70 Earle
" see Macdonald
McDonnell Annie h 277 Orchard (S)
" Annie F widow Patrick h 48
Smith [dar
" Bridget widow Patrick h 334 Ce-
" Francis laborer h 18 Stapleton
" Francis J janitor Custom House
rms 245 Purchase
" James teas 144 Merrimac h do
" John F clerk h 116 Rivet
" John J removed from city
" Michael grocer 372 Cedar b 334
do [81 Fair
McDonough George T operative b
" Michael Vincent Rev assistant
pastor St Kilian's R C church
h 306 Bowditch
McDuff Albert rem to Pawtucket R I
" Alphege died May 18 1911
" John B spinner b 147 Tallman
" Joseph spinner h 147 Tallman
McEmmons Charles E rem to Dart-
mouth
McEnnis Robert police h 98 Parker
McEwen George engineer N B C Co
h 36 Cedar [h 42 Mt Vernon
" Robert P rope maker 140 Durfee
McFadden George H & Bros Agency
cotton merchants 29 N Water
" Maria widow James h 193 Weld
" Peter J variety b 193 Weld
McFarland Annie M widow Albert b
263 Purchase
" Archie G b 73 Allen
" Catherine widow h 1046 S Water
" David J belt maker h 1046 S
Water
" Earl teamster h 102 Middle
" George carpenter b 41 Rivet
" James machinist b 1046 S Water
" Samuel laborer h 696 First
" Thomas clerk b 1046 S Water
McFarlane David J belt maker h
1046 S Water
" Robert glass cutter b 111 Fourth
" Thomas laborer b 1046 S Water
" William b 111 Fourth

There's room at the top for young men and women who can do things right.

Kinyon's Commercial School

Odd Fellows Bldg., Cor. William and Pleasant Sts., New Bedford, Mass.

McFarlin Adelaide J teacher Thos R Rodman school h 272 Cottage
" Albert C mgr 71 Spruce b do
" Archer weaver rms 17 Weld sq
" Charles roll coverer b 78 Park
" Ellen E h 272 Cottage
" James job wagon 71 Spruce h do
McFerguson John teamster rms 116 Middle [chase
McGarigle Edward laborer h 700 Pur-
" Edward F clerk 368 Kempton h 700 Purchase [net av
" Emma Mrs boarding 303 Acush-
McGarrity Charles F mule spinner h 63 Ruth [Warren
McGaughey Thomas E machinist h 6
McGee Andrew G driver h 188 Division
" Ann h 147 Mill [126 Holly
" Douglass L assistant assessor h
" Ferdinand D machinist h 36 Dartmouth
" James laborer h 461 Bolton
" John J third hand b 177 State
" Josephine Mrs dressmaker 7 Bentley h do
" Romeo helper b 7 Bentley
" see Magee
McGill David agent Cunard Steamers 193 Blackmer
" David (David McGill Co.) 193 Blackmer h at Fairhaven
" David Co (David McGill and Willam H Marsden) wholesale confectionery 193 Blackmer
" George mason rms 277 Middle
" John H confectionery h 207 Court
McGinness Mary widow Thomas b 11 Adams
" William b 11 Adams
McGinnis Mary widow Thomas b 245 Brownell
McGladory John loom fixer h 21 Hall
McGlennon Susan widow h 19 Mill
McGlynn Edward city laborer b 3½ N Oak
" James laborer b 3½ N Oak
" John city teamster h 3½ N Oak
" Patrick laborer h 3 N Oak
" Thomas operative b 3½ N Oak
" Thomas F teamster N B Fish Co b 567 Acushnet av [av
" Thomas J laborer h 567 Acushnet
McGoff Dennis h 351 Sawyer [345 do
" James E plumber 339 Sawyer h

McGoff
" Kate Mrs weaver h 188 Church
McGonigle Charles W lunch 1484 Acushnet av h do [land
McGorian William clerk b 103 Ash-
McGough Michael ropemaker h 457 Union
" Peter J foreman b 382 Maxfield
McGovern James weaver h 41 Valentine [67 Mill
McGowan Arthur R reedmaker h
" Bertha M clerk 185 Union bds 2 Spruce
" Edward weaver h 183 David
" Edward J steam fitter b 36 George [ant b 197 Mill
" Frank M horseshoer 100 Pleas-
" Harry P blacksmith 100 Pleasant h 197 Mill
" Joseph h 32 Rounds
" Joseph weaver h 26 Shaw
" Patrick laborer h 452 S Second
" Thomas A h 2 Spruce
" Thomas A Jr stereotyper Standard h at Fairhaven
" William weaver b 183 David
McGrath Charles overseer Rotch Mill h Thompson
" Edward F spinner h 383 Pleasant
" Edward J operative b 242 State
" James J laborer h 383 Pleasant
" James S stonecutter h 100 Clark
" Jane Mrs h 91 County
" John laborer b 12 Austin
" John laborer b 257 Cedar Grove
" John B doffer b 383 Pleasant
" John Jr laborer b 12 Austin
" John P operative b 242 State
" Joseph operative b 242 State
" Michael h 242 State
" Michael J city laborer h 355 Elm
" Michael laborer b 12 Austin
" Thomas F removed from city
" Thomas L laborer b 383 Pleasant
" William pedlar h 658 Acushnet av
" see Magrath [Kempton
McGreevy John electrician bds 475
" John F hairdresser 39½ Rivet b 14 Howland Village [ton
" Michael ropemaker h 475 Kemp-
" Thomas E mule spinner h 14 Howland Village
" Thomas E Jr mill hand b 14 Howland Village

HASKELL BROS. DEALERS IN
ICE
400 COURT STREET TELEPHONE CONNECTION NEW BEDFORD, MASS.

McGregor Carolyn widow William boarding house h 134 Tallman
" Cornelius J glasscutter h 114½ Fifth
" Hugh weaver h 49 Katharine
" John glassworker b 238 Acushnet av
" Loretta clerk 139 Union bds 238 [Acushnet av
" Peter J glassworker h 238 Acushnet av
McGuigan Hugh J shipper 311 S [Water b 64 School
McGuiggan Patrick F laborer h 8 Hazard court
McGuinness A Katharine Mrs millinery 10 Purchase h 35 Mt Vernon
" Benjamin F fixer h 33 Fair
" Bernard A clerk U St Ry Co h 12 Lindsey
" Bridget widow bds 11 Adams
" Catherine A teacher Thompson st school b 33 Fair
" George operative b 1137 Acushnet [av
" James E mgr b 33 Fair
" James J drillworker b 405 Orchard (S)
" John F mgr 10 Purchase h 35 Mt [Vernon
" Joseph laborer h 405 Orchard (S)
" Joseph second hand h 18 Jean
" see McEnnis
McGuire Bernard painter h 80 First
" Ernest eyeletmaker b 447 Pleasant
" John overseer Mfg Corp h 354 [Earle
" John W laborer h 34 Bowditch
" Patrick operative h 53 Katherine
" Robert weaver h r 280 Cedar Grove
" see Maguire
McGurk Catherine widow John h [42 Ward
"Charles J city auditor 4 Municipal bldg and (Tracy Rosenberg & McGurk) h 79 Rockland
McGurty Mary E widow Farrell h 108 Sycamore
McHaffey Mary supt N B Tuberculosis Hospital h do
McHale James third hand b 162 Hatch
" Philip third hand b 162 Hatch
" William third hand b 162 Hatch
McHugh Edward h 30 McGurk
" James A grocer 904 Acushnet av h 94 Kenyon
" Michael mason h 112 Thompson

McHugh
" William A overseer Gosnold Mill h 106 Thompson
" see McCue
McIntosh James operative b 1098 [Acushnet av
" Mary stenographer Butler Mills b 55½ Fifth
McIntyre Katherine E fitter 40 Pur- [chase b 3 Spruce
" Mark H tailor 15 Pleasant h 69 Willis
" Mattie Mrs oil packer h 86 High
" Robert A rodman 303 Municipal bldg b 69 Willis
McIsaac Angus carpenter bds 213 [Court
" Annie E clerk b 213 Court
" Annie E widow Daniel clerk 185 Union h 213 Court
" Edward S engraver b 212 Court
" John E died April 24 1911
" Nora widow John E h 271 Pleasant
McKay Edward laborer bds 185 [Weld
" Felix weaver h 595 Purchase
" Franklin operative b 185 Weld
" James loom fixer bds 43 Ruth
" John loom fixer b 236 N Front
" John operative h 666 S First
" John T police Station 5 h 191 Davis
" John second hand h 185 Weld
" Mary widow James boarding house 236 N Front
" William carpenter h 228 Arnold
" William weaver b 170 David
McKee Margaret widow h 1440 S Second
McKelvie Sarah widow Anthony bds [120 Rodney
McKenna Charles A clerk h 449 Pleasant
" Charles H shoemaker h 384 North
" Elizabeth A supervisor 57 N Second b 80 Rockland
" Frank laborer h 31 Valentine
" James glassblower h 80 Rockland
" James J dentist 149 Bowditch b 80 Rockland
" James J twister b 31 Valentine
" John fireman h 14 Viall
" John H shoemaker h 230 Kemp- [ton
" John P salesman 385 Acushnet av b 50 S Second
" Mary widow Patrick b 499 Pleas- [ant
" Mary G milliner 185 Union bds 80 Rockland

J. F. CROSSLEY 223 MILL STREET COR. EMERSON PHONE
STEAM and HOT WATER HEATING
GAS FITTING and FIXTURES

McKenna
" Sarah L teacher Harrington school b 80 Rockland
" William F florist b 31 Valentine
McKenzie Catherine widow Thomas bds 188 Coffin avenue
" Frank R drillworker b 167 North
" James A overseer Pierre Bros Ltd h 297 Davis
" Mary E nurse rms 321 Union
" Patrick piper h 188 Coffin av
" Robert h 47 Ocean
" Robert Jr laundryman bds 47 Ocean
" Stephen W shoemaker h 164 Purchase
" Thomas master mariner h 167 North
" see MacKenzie
McKiernan Hanora widow John h 44 Ash (S)
" James E mgr 21 Purchase rms 158 Middle
" James F clerk 12 School h 399 Elm (W)
" Martin J mason b 44 Ash (S)
" Michael F overseer Manomet Mills h 58 Park
" William laborer b 58 Park
McKillop Ellen Mrs h 156 Reynolds
McKim Charles H h 156 Elm
" Charles H Jr b 156 Elm
" George F driver b 156 Elm
" Lewis boxmaker rms 43 Foster
" Samuel teamster h r 35 Smith
McKinley Robert G waiter h 102 State
McKinnon Daniel A wood turner h 100 High
" Donald removed to Taunton
McKowen Edward F insurance agent h r 228 State
" John brakeman b r 228 State
McLachlan Richard L mariner h 63 N Second
McLaughlin Bridget h 53 Mosher
" Frank engineer h 112 S Sixth
" James clerk h 212 Nash road
" James F field engineer 57 N Second h 295 Palmer
" James T loom fixer h 165 David
" Joseph laborer b 33 Reynolds
" Mary Mrs h 7 Austin court
" Matthew weaver b 8 Shore
McLean George J variety h 101 Ashland
" James laborer h 295 Cedar
" John loom fixer h 28 Linden

McLean
" Joseph baker 59 Bullard h 448 N Front
" Matthew weaver bds 101 Ashland
" Michael b 101 Ashland
" Odila clerk 40 Purchase b 448 N Front
McLee Thomas steamfitter h 219 State
McLellan Florence widow Archibald b 135 Bullard
" John weaver h 79 Nash road
McLeod Alexander carpenter h 52 Rounds
" Angus W rem to Vancouver B C
" Catherine widow John C h r 37 Washburn
" Charles city employee h 276 Purchase
" Daniel A apprentice b 68 Park
" Donald A removed from city
" Florence Mrs nurse h 77 Maple
" Jane widow Norman h 446 Pleasant
" Jeanette widow John h 68 Park
" John A carpenter h 77 Maple
" John Charles removed to Vancouver B C
" Norman E electrician b 446 Pleasant
" Robert clerk h 120 Division
" Samuel D police h 20 Keen
McLaughlin Frederick weaver h 68 Jouvett
McLauthlin Frank A pianos h 100 Malvern road
McLynch Patrick spinner h 90 Hathaway
McMahon Andrew P clerk bds 184 Austin
" Annie widow William h 128 Bonney
" Eliza E hairdresser 97 William rm 309 rms do
" Franklin laborer h 12 Clark
" Henry weaver h 3 Wamsutta
" James janitor 46 Purchase h 12 Rounds
" John mill hand b 247 N Front
" John operative b 2 Cove road
" John H operative b 48 Independent
" Owen coachman h 36 Borden
" Robert grocer 417 Allen h do
" William clerk 70 Purchase bds 99 South
" William H clerk 129 Cove h 35 Morton ct
McMann Annie widow Edward h 224 Pleasant
" Edward C glass cutter bds 224 Pleasant

CHARLES A. CROSHERE CARRIAGE AND AUTU
38 FOURTH ST. Bell Phone 1964-23 PAINTING

McMann
" Francis stone cutter rms 1098 Acushnet av [Mills h 156 Davis
" Hugh chief engineer Whitman
" Michael mason b 344 Cedar
McManus Bernard carpenter h 886 County [h 118 Fair
" Edward overseer Gosnold Mills
" Ella nurse rms 107 Chestnut
" John glass worker b 122 Potomska
" John A druggist 122 Allen h 124 do
" John L foreman h 212 Rockland
" John T plumber 46 Linden b 886 County
" Julia widow h 122 Potomska
" Phillip operative b 122 Potomska
" Thomas fitter h 110 Nash road
McMay John H weaver h 109 Hathaway [203 Coffin avenue
McMenamin Margaret mill hand h
" Mary h 203 Coffin av [lette
McMillan Annie mill hand h 188 Col-
" Harriet mill hand h 188 Collette
" James A shoemaker b 98 Park
" Robert machinist h 101 Austin
McMullen Abbott D teaming 10 Spring h Spring cor First
" Abbott D Jr driver 47 School b 4 Cornell court [Orchard (S)
" James F window dresser h 266
" James H bookkeeper 10 Spring h 36 Atlantic
" John E teamster h 113 Kempton
" Sidney furniture mover h 358 Coffin avenue
McMurray Charles E (O Giguere & Co) 1669 Acushnet av h 213 Shaw
" David H carpenter b 373 Purchase
" William h 373 Purchase [County
McNaboe Ann widow Thomas h 83
McNair Samuel operative h 117 Mott
McNally Ethel M clerk 185 Union b 110 Merrimac [Merrimac
" George salesman 38 Elm b 110
" Henry J clerk 182 Union h 109 South [b 110 Merrimac
" Hervey clerk First Nationl Bank
" Johnson weaver h 110 Merrimac
McNamara Edward toy maker b 20 Holly

McNamara
" Florence L teacher George H Dunbar school bds 103 Fair
" John L Rev asst pastor St James R C church h 233 County
" Mary and Martha h 130 Crapo
McNamee Harry glass cutter h 318 Park
" John weaver h 33 McGurk [nell
" John H glass blower h 117 Grin-
" John J bookkeeper b 117 Grinnell
" Michael painter b 482 Cottage
McNaughton James H overseer Gosnold Mills [velt
McNealy James weaver h 62 Roose-
" James A oiler b 62 Roosevelt
" John bricklayer b 62 Roosevelt
McNEAR GEORGE W automobile accessories 26-30 Cambria Boston See page 748
McNeil Daniel waiter h 153 Acushnet avenue
" Sandy box maker h 341 Tinkham
" Sylvester weaver b 103 Hazard
" William glass cutter b 153 Acushnet avenue [Smith
McNeill Sarah widow George h 152
McNichols James second hand h 32 McGurk
McNulty Agnes fitter h 63 Forest
" Bridget F milliner b 115 Fourth
" Dennis painter h 160 Durfee
" Francis H stevadore P & R C & I Co h 161 Mill [ond b 161 Mill
" Frank A contract agent 57 N Sec-
" James C cigar maker 164 Union h 75 Shawmut avenue [wick
" James H letter carrier h 2 War-
" John bicycle repairer 844 Purchase bds 463 Mt Pleasant
" John A b 101 Ashland
" John F clerk N Water corner Elm bds 160 Durfee
" John H carpenter b 161 Mill
" Joseph driver bds 160 Durfee
" Joseph salesman 36 Purchase b 463 Mt Pleasant [Cedar
" Margaret I music teacher bds 360
" Michael J station agent Mount Pleasant h 463 do [Ashland
" Peter R R section foreman h 101

J. G. NICHOLSON
LUMBER, SASH, DOORS and BLINDS
BOWDITCH STREET, NEW BEDFORD, MASS.

McNulty
" Thomas supt N E C Y Co department 9 and 10 h 360 Cedar [ant
" Thomas P laborer b 465 Mt Pleas-
" William H laborer b 160 Durfee
" Winifred died Mar 26 1911
McPeak Thomas overseer Wamsutta Mill h 12 Studley
McPhee Agnes T teacher Thomas R Rodman school b 131 Summer
" Albert mill hand b 30 Belleville road [Second b 43 Sycamore
" Frances telephone operator 57 N
McPherson Susan A Mrs h 81 State
McQuade Bridget widow Frank h r 60 Washburn [burn
" Frank mill hand b r 60 Wash-
" John B doffer b 510 N Front
" Joseph teamster h 486 Rivet
" Owen laborer h 510 N Front
" Patrick (Cook & McQuaid) 45 Maitland h 108 Locust
" William helper b 510 N Front
McQuilkin James eyeletmaker h 449 Orchard (S)
" John h 451 Orchard (S)
" John Jr hoseman Hose 2 b 451 Orchard (S)
McQuillan Charles J clerk 268 Fourth h 174 Washington [do
" Edwin J dentist 218 Fourth bds
" Patrick J h 218 Fourth
" Peter F (Sherman & McQuillan) 250 Purchase h 66 Mill
McSally James joiner h r 188 State
" Patrick section hand h r 198 State
McVey Samuel carpenter h 23 Priscilla [Maitland
McVicker James H foreman h 39
" John R weaver h 363 Coggeshall
" Seth T laborer h 221 Shawmut av
McWeeney James twist driller h 80 S Sixth [Crapo
McWhinnie Edward engineer h 34
" James steam fitter h 80 S Sixth
" Robert overseer Wamsutta Mill h 317 Davis [gon h 163 Park
Meade James G driver patrol wa-
Meadeiros John teamster h 326 S Second [son
Meader John drillmaker h 30 Thomp-
Meagher Grace E clerk 65 Purchase b 304 Acushnet av

Meagher
" Henry bartender Parker House h 401 Purchase [h 224 Mill
" John J foreman N B Tallow Co
" William T clerk 106 Union h 304 Acushnet av [Middle
" William T Jr drillmaker h 101
Meakin James D salesman 3 E Pope h 14 Winsor
" see Meekin
Meal Fred operative h 457 Sawyer
" John agent Philanthropic Burial Society h r 124 Whitman
" Lewis drillworker h 283 Rivet
Mealey Edward mule spinner h 53 Mosher
" Thomas doffer b 53 Mosher
Meaney Annie h 60 High
" Daniel laborer b 8 Dover
" Dennis laborer rms 20 Bethel
" Edward shoemaker h 128 Summer [ver
" Ellen E widow James P h 8 Do-
" Hannah E widow John J teacher Thompson street school h 174 Washington [Dover
" James P apprentice 55 Spring b 8
" Mary variety 212½ Fourth h 64 Division [po
" Mary widow Thomas J h 25 Cra-
" Rose M teacher Parker st school b 128 Summer
Meany Patrick H salesman 140 Purchase h 64 Division [do
Meats Edith nurse 321 Union rms
Mebame John T laborer h 108 Cedar
Mecado Frank V clerk h 108 Sycamore
Mechaber Amos salesman 849 Purchase b 171 Merrimac
" Eddy dry goods h 83 Kenyon
" Hyman (R Mechaber & Son) h 87 Kenyon [Merrimac
" Louis clerk 849 Purchase b 171
" Louis salesman 1050 Acushnet av b 83 Kenyon [b 83 Kenyon
" Rachmiel (R Mechaber & Son)
" R & Son (Rachmiel and Hyman) dry goods 1050 Acushnet av
" Simon clothing 849 Purchase h 171 Merrimac
MECHANICS NATIONAL BANK The Edward S Brown cashier 47 Purchase c William See page 6

Steiger-Dudgeon Co.
"The WOMAN'S Store."
Tel. Bell 82 & 83, Branches connecting all depts.
" " 160 For Office only. Auto. 1211

SUMPTIONS, ASSORTMENTS AT ALL TIMES OF DEPENDABLE DRY GOODS

Mecido Anton speeder h 25 Katharine
Mecier Eugene clerk b 199 Blackmer
" Joseph weaver h 199 Blackmer
Medeiros Agusto mill hand h 39 Mitchell
" Angelo grocer 226 Coggeshall h 180 Belleville avenue
" Annie Mrs h 418 First
" Antone h r 187 Bonney
" Antone carder h 16 Cotter
" Antone farmer b 439 Belleville av
" Antone laborer h 55 Katharine
" Antone mill hand h 3 Mitchell
" Antone mill hand b 96 Thompson
" Antone speeder h 49 Rivet
" Antone twister h 12 Hyacinth
" Antone J removd from city
" Antone L clerk 71 Howland b 408 South First
" Antone S laborer h 36 Sagamore
" Antone S laborer h 95 Prospect
" Antonio laborer h 22 Hollyhock
" Antonio laborer h 23 Scott
" Antonio J h 167 Division
" Antonio S h 50 Katharine
" August laborer h 262 S Front
" August laborer h 679 S Water
" Brothers (Angelo and Eunize) grocers and fish market 222 and 226 Coggeshall
" Charles P laborer h 423 Bowditch
" Calogero painter h 51 Mill
" Daniel mill hand h 195 Coggeshall
" Domingas A roofer h 173 Thompson
" Emily Mrs h 98 Blackmer
" Ernest S foreman Snell & Simpson h 131 Mt Vernon
" Eunize (Medeiros Brothers) grocers 222 and 226 Coggeshall h Cotter
" Francis P grocer 130 Dartmouth h 132 do
" Frencisco laborer h 63 Scott
" Francisco J laborer h 68 Blackmer
" Frank laborer h 85 Cove road
" Frank laborer h 421 Allen
" Frank mill hand h 55 Stowell
" Frank mill hand h 391 Rivet
" Frank mill hand h 706 S Water
" Frank mill hand b 222 N Front
" Frank weaver h 405 First
" Frenk B painter h 377 S Second
" Frank E fireman h 30 Dartmouth

Medeiros
" Frank L rope maker h 80 Sidney
" Frank P laborer h 76 Winsor
" Jacintho mill hand b 50 Dean
" Jacintho E mill hand h 39 Stowell
" Jacintho F operative h 212 South Front
" Joacquim laborer h 289 S Second
" John barber 621 S Water h 623 do
" John fisherman h 153 Belleville avenue
" John hairdresser 393 Rivet
" John insurance agent h 30 Thompson
" John laborer h 75 Crapo
" John mill hand b 13 Mitchell
" John operative h 260 S Front
" John operative h 552 Rivet
" John teamster h 72 Howland
" John weaver h 74 Mosher
" John weaver b 211 Rivet
" John E mill hand b 222 N Front
" John F clerk 601 Water
" John J elevatorman h 16 Rodney
" John J laborer h 58 Rivet
" John L laborer b 16 Rodney
" John S weaver b 50 Katharine
" John V driver h 97 Bellevue
" John V grocer 448 S Water h 135 Fourth
" Jose D shoe repairer 64 Grinnell h 240 S Front
" Joseph carpenter h 359 Orchard (S)
" Joseph clerk 71 Howland b 80 Mosher
" Joseph fisherman h 472 S Second
" Joseph laborer h 31 Acushnet av
" Joseph laborer h 461 Bolton
" Joseph laborer h 618 S Water
" Joseph laborer b 128 N Second
" Joseph laborer b 148 Tallman
" Joseph mill hand h 48 Howland Village
" Joseph mill hand h 213 Bellville av
" Joseph mill hand b 418 First
" Joseph operative h 39 Mitchell
" Joseph operative h 71 Davis
" Joseph operative h 65 Independent
" Joseph operative b 127 Belleville avenue
" Joseph operative h 278 S Second
" Joseph operative b 127 Belleville avenue
" Joseph operative b 244 Acushnet avenue
" Joseph third hand h 423 Bowditch

PELEG H. SHERMAN 506 COUNTY ST.
FUNERAL DIRECTOR AND EMBALMER
OFFICE PHONES. Bell 690-13. Auto. 1305.
RESIDENCE PHONES. Bell 690-12. Auto. 1306.

Medeiros
" Joseph C shoe repairer h 31 Acushnet avenue [Front
" Joseph D shoemaker h 268 South
" Joseph D shoe repairer h 240 S Front
" Joseph F carpenter b 69 Swift
" Joseph J operative h 103 Acushnet avenue
" Joseph S carder h 65 Delano
" Joseph V laborer h 783 S Water
" Jule laborer h 58 Grinnell
" Manuel h 123 Hemlock
" Manuel doffer h 53 Winsor
" Manuel fish 135 Crapo h 83 do
" Manuel helper b 105 Hemlock
" Manuel laborer h 8 Rotch block 438 Bolton
" Manuel laborer h 18 Griffin
" Manuel laborer h 27 Bullard
" Manuel laborer h 42 Thompson
" Manuel laborer h 70 Winsor
" Manuel laborer h 83 Crapo
" Manuel laborer h 273 S Front
" Manuel laborer h 293 Fourth
" Manuel laborer h 431 First
" Manuel laborer h 536 S Water
" Manuel laborer b 59 Lombard
" Manuel laborer b 423 Bowditch
" Manuel mill hand h 71 Prospect
" Manuel mill hand h 195 Coggeshall
" Manuel mill hand h 236 S Front
" Manuel third hand b 418 First
" Manuel wood h 314 S Second
" Manuel B laborer h r 609 Acushnet avenue [h 134 Fourth
" Manuel E car cleaner U St Ry Co
" Manuel F weaver h 206 Rockland
" Manuel G watchman h 63 Delano
" Manuel R h 23 Nelson
" Manuel R laborer h 45 Nelson
" Manuel S mason h 43 Hemlock
" Manuel S mill hand h 86 Nash rd
" Manuel S ropemaker h 378 Middle (W) [Independent
" Marianno barber 5 Bedford h 44
" Marianno laborer h 176 Thompson
" Marion mill hand b 71 Prospect
" Mary Mrs sewer 40 Purchase b 244 Acushnet av
" Mary widow h 80 Sagamore

Medeiros
" Paulineo h 429 Second
" Paulineo operative h 49 Katharine
" Peter operative b 72 Earle
" Raul h 69 Swift
" Rosa widow h 59 Lombard [ant
" Vergino laborer h 640 Mt Pleas-
" William laborer h 1 Maiden lane
Mederville George rem from city
Medina John weaver h 318 S Front
" Manuel B third hand h 70 Acushnet av
Meehan Daniel police h 62 Foster
" James salesman b 3 Cornell court
" James trackman h 715 Kempton
" John molder h 3 Cornell court
Meekin Hugh mule spinner h 141 Division
" Patrick removed from city
Meeking James spinner h 118 Hathaway
Megan James F fitter h 172 Ashland
Meikle Chester F engineer b 45 Foster [ter h do
" Emma E Mrs dressmaker 45 Fos-
" George D electrician 214 S Water h 45 Foster
" G Stanley student b 45 Foster
Mein Frederick K foreman shipper 100 Fifth h 29 Bonney [Elm
" James B clerk 41 Purchase b 107
Mekolaczk Joseph weaver h 11 Holly
Melancon Alfred carpenter b 179 Bowditch
" Dennis h 487 N Front
" Eugene barber h 79 Nelson
" Leger third hand h 38 Sherman [av
" Maxime fisherman h 141 Phillips
" Nelson clerk 1071 Acushnet av h 179 Bowditch [ditch
" Patrick carpenter h 179 Bow-
Melanson Abel weaver b 487 N Front
" Adelin teamster b 487 N Front
" Eugene E barber 771 Purchase h 79 Nelson
" George carpenter h 194 Highland
" Raphael operative h 787 N Front
" Thomas laborer h 67 Penniman
Melia Frank A J cashier 385 Acushnet av rms 290 Pleasant
" Michael J steam fitter b 116 Hathaway
" Thomas spinner h 46 Ashley

PAINTERS' SUPPLIES
Walnut, Cor. Water, 84 Pleasant St. 25 WELD SQ., 129 COVE ST.
F. T. AKIN & COMPANY

Melland Joseph machinist h 21 Morton court
Mellen Christopher (Christopher & Mellen) 849 S Water h at Bristol R I
Melling Ellen died July 1911
" Frederick (Melling & Sons) h 211 Brock av [Mott
" Herbert (Melling & Sons) h 130
" Jennie h 91 Merrimac [Mott
" Walter (Melling & Sons) h 130
" & Sons (Walter, Herbert and Frederick Melling) bakers 977 S Water [Second
Mello Alexandre painter h 273 S
" Antone insurance agent 120 Purchase rm 403 h 16 Katharine
" Antone laborer h 150 Field
" Antone mill hand h 308 S Front
" Antone operative h 47 South
" Antone operative h 112 Bates av
" Antone C driver 64 Dartmouth h Crapo street [av h 90 Nash rd
" Antone C grocer 144 Belleville
" Antone F slubber tender h 9 Acushnet block [field
" Antone S mill hand h 12 Grand-
" Antonio mill hand h 222 N Front
" Antonio operative h 30 South
" Antonio operative h 194 Bonney
" Antonio B chauffeur N B W W h 58 Short [land
" Antonio G operative h 66 Rock-
" Antonio J laborer h 38 Hollyhock
" Antonio R laborer h 179 Division [av
" Antonio T laborer h 148 Belleville
" August operative h 54 Woodlawn
" Bent B fireman h 20 Margin
" Bros (Manuel E and Seraphin) grocers 176 Rockland [County
" Camille E grocer 61 Crapo b 169
" Domingos weaver b 100 Phillips avenue
" Francisco h 201 Coggeshall [ter
" Francisco mill hand h 595 S Wa-
" Frank laborer h 178 Rockland
" Frank mill hand h 53 Winsor
" Frank C laborer h 53 Winsor
" Frank S clerk 781 S Water h 261 Rivet
" Jacinth laborer h 505 Rivet
" Jennie widow Samuel h 439 Belleville av [Hollyhock
" John barber 137 Dartmouth h 38

Mello
" John fisherman h 216 S Front
" John laborer h 97 Acushnet av
" John laborer h 216 S Front
" John mill hand h 114 Larch
" John operative h 723 S Water
" John spinner h 10 Coffin av ct
" John B grocer 66 Howland h 86 do [b 112 Bates av
" John D clerk 1249 Acushnet av
" John E clerk 176 Rockland b 65 Independent [S Water
" John P clerk 80 Potomska h 697
" Joseph blacksmith 326 S Water b 868 do
" Joseph doffer b 80 Earle
" Joseph fisherman h 1 Margin
" Joseph fisherman h 44 Sherman
" Joseph laborer h 68 Dartmouth
" Joseph laborer h 646 S Water
" Joseph mill hand h 204 Coffin av [av
" Joseph mill hand b 104 Phillips
" Joseph operative h 39 Stowell
" Joseph operative h 608 S Second
" Joseph painter h 288 S Second
" Joseph C clerk 144 Belleville av h 86 Nash road [h 193 do
" Joseph E druggist 195 Court
" Joseph M mill hand b r 19 Nye
" Joseph S freight handler h 507 Bolton [nell
" Lichandre plasterer h 75 Grin-
" Louise widow h 77 Delano
" Manuel breweryworker h 207 S Front
" Manuel carpenter h 396 S Second
" Manuel city laborer h 30 Juniper
" Manuel clerk h 8 Spooner
" Manuel clerk h 405 Orchard (S)
" Manuel fish 221 Rivet h 238 do
" Manuel fisherman h 472 First
" Manuel grocer cor S Second and Delano h 510 S Second
" Manuel hostler b 66 Rockland
" Manuel mill hand h 25 Mitchell
" Manuel mill hand h 80 Sidney
" Manuel mill hand h 137 Coffin av
" Manuel mill hand h 505 Rivet
" Manuel mill hand b 17 Howland Village [avenue
" Manuel mill hand b 104 Phillips
" Manuel operative h 188 Belleville avenue
" Manuel operative h 12 Stackhouse

Kinyon's Commercial School Will furnish your office help free
Odd Fellows Building COR. WILLIAM and PLEASANT STS. NEW BEDFORD, MASS.

Mello
" Manuel operative h 399 First
" Manuel B removed from city
" Manuel C mill hand b 139 Coffin av
" Manuel C mill hand b 153 Belleville av
" Manuel E (Mello Bros) h 8 Spooner
" Manuel F clerk 165 S Water h 405 Orchard (S)
" Manuel J operative h 537 First
" Manuel M mill hand h r 19 Nye
" Manuel P twister h 16 Independent
" Manuel Santos painter h 98 Thompson
" Manuel S laborer h 43 Hall
" Manuel S operative h 33 Winsor
" Marceline P operative h 109 Grinnell
" Mary mill hand h 18 Swift
" Mary Mrs h 49 Short
" Mary Mrs h 170 Division
" Mary Mrs h 269 S Second
" Philomena mill hand h 18 Swift
" Rose widow Manuel h 17 Bullard
" Rose widow Manuel h 104 Phillips av
" Seraphin (Mello Bros) bds 178 Rockland
" Seraphin operative h 22 Hollyhock
" Severino P grocer 80 Potomska h 82 do
" Victor fireman h 203 County
" Victor laborer h 407 First
" see DeMello
Mellor Alfred R student b 1276 Rockdale av
" Arthur spinner h 29½ Acushnet avenue
" Charles E carpenter b 1276 Rockdale avenue
" Dennis F weaver h 189 Belleville road
" Frank H carriage painter and ice 1272 Rockdale av h 1248 do
" John A packer b 147 Tallman
" John E operative b 81 Mosher
" John E removed from city
" Leonard H overseer Booth M Corp h 181 Newton
" Marriott W mill hand b 120 S Sixth
" Sarah widow John h 1276 Rockdale av
Melody Anthony J overseer h 116 Fruit
" Mary clerk b 116 Fruit
" William mule spinner h 73 Fruit
Meltzer Morris pedlar h 268 Acushnet av
" Samuel pedlar h 9 Bedford
Meminger Leslie T asst mgr 65 Purchase rms 56 Walnut
Memit Arsm mill hand b 54 Davis
Menager Simeon rem to Fitchburg
" Thomas rem from city
Menard Alberic J overseer h 280 Earle
" Alec carpenter h 960 S Water
" Alexander weaver h 292 Fourth
" A L bds 280 Earle
" Clovis hairdresser 870 S Water h do
" Edmonde weaver b 239 Sawyer
" Edward operative b 808 First
" Emily Mrs milliner b 808 First
" Ernest fireman h 73 Hathaway
" Ernest shoeworker b 292 Fourth
" Frank clerk 1413 Acushnet av h 326 N Front
" Henry mill hand bds 7 Phillips av
" Henry spinner h 808 First
" Joseph fixer h 21 Mosher
" Jules clerk 326 Bowditch
" Norbert slasher h 325 N Front
" Wilfred baker h 12 Bowditch
" William L salesman 39 Union h 194 Nash road
" see Maynard
Mendanca Mary widow h 244 Rivet
Mendell Benjamin W carpenter h 84 Parker
" Charles H fireman h 412 Middle (W)
" David P harnessmaker 646 Purchase h 125 Shawmut av
" David T carpenter h 456 Chancery
" James sawyer b 259 Acushnet av
" Jennie C clerk 97 William rm 212 h at Mattapoisett
" see Mandell
Mendelson Abram (A Mendelson & Son) h 1149 Acushnet av
" A & Son (Abram and Hymen) clothing 1135 Acushnet av
" Harry clerk b 1149 Acushnet av
" Hymen (A Mendelson & Son) h 116 Clark
Mendes Constancia L dressmaker b 73 Dartmouth
" Frank E operative h 926 County
" John R operative b 16 Howland Village
" Joseph R mill hand h 16 Howland Village
" Manuel M carpenter h 73 Dartmouth
" Manuel R laborer h 36 Howland Village

Bread, Cake, Pastry
RICHMOND & COMPANY 255-257 UNION STREET
Bell 993 Automatic 1022

Mendez Jacintho concreter h 345 Middle [h 121 Willis
" John C chauffeur 98 Pleasant
Mendoza Anna D widow Antoni B h 58 Sherman
" Antone operative h 502 S First
" Antone J clerk 721 S Water b 502 S First
" Annie B widow h 131 Fair
" Barbara J widow John h 191 Arnold [thorn b do
" Frank V coachman 196 Haw-
" Fred laborer h 624 First
" John clerk b 35 Bolton
" John mill hand b 148 Belleville av
" John mill hand b 191 Belleville av
" John shoemaker h 19 Cleveland
" John speeder tender b 19 Cleveland
" Joseph laborer h 441 Orchard (S)
" Joseph M laborer h 80 Windsor
" Joseph M mill hand h 67 Prospect
" Manuel operative h 365 First
" Manuel A mason 35 Stowell h do
" Manuel E carpenter h 143 Crapo
" Mary Mrs h 441 Orchard (S)
" Mary operative h 35 Rotch blk 435 Bolton [ney
" Mary widow Frank bds 115 Bon-
" Maurice eyeletmaker b 96 School
" Philip mill hand b 441 Hemlock
Menelis Loma pedlar h 138 Acushnet avenue [ond
Menes Antone driver b 161 S Sec-
" Antone laborer h 235 Fourth
" Francisco laborer h 11 Margin
" Joseph fisherman h 21 Stapleton
" Joseph laborer h 323 S Front
" Joseph operative h 177 David
" Louis operative h 666 S Water
" Manuel grocer 322 S Second h 320 do
" Manuel laborer h 65½ Prospect
" Manuel laborer h 66 Acushnet av
" Manuel mill hand bds rear 19 Nye
" Manuel A mill hand b 77 Davis
" Manuel J laborer h 55 Prospect
" Mary Mrs h 55 Howland
" Mary Mrs sewer 40 Purchase b 147 Rockland [ter
" Michael operative h 664 S Wa-
" Michael operative b 666 S Water
Menez Frank laborer h 472 S Second
Menezes Joseph operative h 195 Bonney
" Joseph operative h 147 Rockland
" Manuel F laborer b 202 Belleville avenue [Nelson
Mengeau Hermidas carpenter h 9
Menies John fisherman h 19 Cotter
" Marianno laborer h 66 Grinnell
Mentella Joseph fireman b 439 Belleville av [arine
Menton Fred F laborer b 58 Kath-
" Joseph overseer City Mfg Co b 58 Katharine
" Patrick laborer h 58 Katharine
Menzer Joseph B saelsman h 71 Locust
Meny Ernest h 239 Sawyer
" Frederick twister h 239 Sawyer
" see Manny [Rockland
Mercer Alexander B shipper h 206
" Eliza widow b 63 Roosevelt
" Fred weaver h 184 Davis
" George W cable splicer 57 N Second b 113 Fourth
" John h 49 Bowditch
" John machinist b 206 Rockland
" John N drillworker h 192 Division
" Randle R doffer b 206 Rockland
" Richard piper b 206 Rockland
Merchant Ambrose F lieutenant Engine 9 h 814 Belleville av
" Maria Mrs h 34 Durfee
" Walter H Jr engineer Engine 4 h 61 Bay
Merchants Club 128 Union
" Law Exchange The Inc 97 William rm 312
MERCHANTS NATIONAL BANK William corner Purchase H C W Mosher president H W Taber cashier See page 4
Mercier Ernest weaver h 366 Earle
" Ernest rem to Montreal Canada
" Frank weaver h 109 Nash road
" William laborer N B W W h 184 Davis
" see Messier
MERCURY PUBLISHING CO publishers Mercury and job printing 112 and 114 Union See page 756
Merideth William spinner h 55 Independent
Merrick Emma J h 129 Hillman

GLOBE DYE HOUSE 220 SHAWMUT AVE.
J. N. J. LONHOLDT, PROP. Telephone Connections Goods called for and Delivered
Down Town Office, 52 Pleasant St., Room 1 North End Office, 1014 Acushnet Ave.

Merrick
" Josephine A assistant public library bds 129 Hillman
" Matthew bleacher h 79 Rodney
Merrihew Irving H (Dean's Oyster Market) 17 N Second b 60 Spring
Merrill Converse clerk b 132 School
" George B Mrs h 132 School
" Lulu M (Vienna Hair and Corset Shop) 96 Purchase h at Providence [chase
" William H teamster h 347 Pur-
Merrill's Wharf Benjamin Baker agent 3 Merrill's wharf [11
Merrimack Loan Co 96 William rm
Merritt Frank T motorman h 366 Purchase
" see Marrotte [Robeson
Merrow Charles A motorman h 107
Merry Elizabeth E widow William H h 73 S Sixth
Meskreiewski Toni operative h 18 Washburn [Bonney
Mesquita Frank S carpenter h 181
Messenger Christopher baker 439 Purchase h 125 Tallman
Messier Admire widow Joseph mill hand h 184 Phillips avenue
" Alexander J salesman 293 Purchase h 125 Tallman
" Amos operative b 184 Phillips av
" Arthur J H machine operator 101 Kenyon b 140 Bullard
" August hairdresser h 20 Tallman
" Augustine hairdresser 50 Weld h 20 Falmouth [131 Reynolds
" Bertha clerk 474 Acushnet av b
" Edward weaver b 81 Mosher
" Eliza widow Charles h 328 Bowditch
" Ernest teamster h 9 Blackburn
" Henry J operative b 499 Coggeshall
" Homer clerk b 184 Phillips av
" Homer helper 19 Linden b Bullard [near Bowditch
" Hormidas weaver h Princeton
" Joseph laborer b 328 Bowditch
" Joseph A loom fixer h 434 North Front [rms 315 Sawyer
" Louis shoe repairer 141 Bowditch
" Oscar painter b 328 Bowditch

Messier
" Oscar salesman 1201 Purchase h 239 Sawyer [499 Coggeshall
" Oswald P grocer 134 Reynolds h
" Ozias mill hand b 26 Bullard
" Pierre laborer b 70 Howard
" Treffle third hand h 140 Bullard
" William fixer h 49 Howard
" see Mercier [away
Messner Frank weaver h 169 Hath-
Mestan Agnes widow Joseph h 862 Acushnet avenue [144 Tallman
Metcalf Arthur pressman Mercury b
" Elizabeth widow Joseph h 330 Brock avenue

FRANK M METCALF
Civil Engineer and Surveyor
211 Merchants Bank Building
Auto Telephone 1276
Bell Telephone 431-2
Residence 72 Spring Street
Bell Telephone 767-5

Metcalf Frank civil engineer and surveyor 211 Merchants Bank bldg h 72 Spring [road
" George S planer h 191 Belleville
" Harold removed to Milwaukee Wisconsin
" James baker b r 36 Linden
" James A overseer b 1035 County
" James E laborer h 16 Ashley
" James E overseer City Mfg Corp h 52 Fair
" Jesse mason h Tarkiln Hill road
" John weaver b 301 Fourth
" Matthias laborer h 144 Tallman
Methe Adhemar grocer 75 County h 17 Jouvett
" George A clerk b 189 Tinkham
" Mary milliner 1009 Acushnet av b 189 Tinkham avenue
" Narcisse h 70 Jouvett
" Oliva grocer 1681 Acushnet av h 189 Tinkham [189 Tinkham
" Rose milliner 1039 Acushnet av b

GREENE & WOOD Every Kind of LUMBER AND MILL WORK
PINE STREET, off So. WATER STREET, NEW BEDFORD

Methia Alfred weaver b 16 Roosevelt
" Emille weaver h 16 Roosevelt
" Raymond operative h 22 Ashley
Methot Cammille carpenter b 147 Hathaway
" Elzear carpenter b 147 Hathaway
" Joseph A agent 73 William h 52 Collette
" Leonce carpenter b 147 Hathaway
" Louis removed from city
" Raoul carpenter b 52 Collette
Metise John fixer b 98 Blackmer
Metivier Adelard barber h 10 Bowditch [city
" Joseph carpenter removed from
" Joseph third hand h 82 Kenyon
" Joseph weaver h 16 Roosevelt
" Michael operative h 242 Nash rd
Metras Lucien weaven b 207 Sawyer
" Medore laborer h 4 Cornell pl
" Napoleon weaver h 65 Jouvett
Metropolitan Life Insurance Co of N Y 37 Purchase rm 23
Mette Henry Rev pastor St John German Lutheran church h 296 Kempton [Kempton
" Henry clerk 8 Hamilton bds 296
Metthe Augustus driver 12 School h 366 State
" David h 223 State
" George J clerk 41 Bentley b 35 do
" Joseph G h 109 Bowditch
" Oliver painter b 223 State
" Pierre painter h 35 Bentley
" Wilfred clerk 223 State b do
Meunier Alphonse fixer h 101 Holly
" Honoreus iceman h 26 Bullard
" Philip removed from city [ly
Meury Pauline widow John b 85 Hol-
Mevins Henry boarding 39 Tallman
Meyer August painter b 95 Tallman
" Edward weaver h 37 Ashley
" George b 145 Kempton
" Louis conductor h 135 Maxfield
" Thomas N carpenter h 48 Smith
Mezrole Barb widow bds 126 Bullard [blk 439 Bolton
" Mial Joseph mill hand h 19 Rotch
Michael John mill hand h 72 Belleville road [Second
Michaels Frank A laborer h 149 S
Michaud Alfred boarding house 880 Purchase [Water
" Damase boarding house 948 S

Michaud
" Damase clerk 147 Union b 948 S Water
" Fred weaver b 102 Davis
" George A salesman 956 Acushnet av b 202 State
" Honore fixer h 30 Nye
" Ignace E salesman 211 Union h 633 County
" John carpenter h 30 Welcome
" Joseph carder h 45 Tallman
" Joseph jeweler 1307 Acushnet av rms 119 Bullard [h 102 Davis
" Sophia widow Napoleon operative
" Thomas laborer h 30 Welcome
Michelfelder Carl mgr Casino Theatre 882 Purchase h at N Y city
Michelsen B Frank music teacher b 38 Durfee
" John h 38 Durfee [Acushnet av
Michelson Charles shoeworker h 208
" Henry F carder h 26 Adams [son
Michon Arthur weaver h 30 Thomp-
" Frank removed from city
" Hector A operative h 272 Davis
Mickell Antone city employee h 281 Fourth
" Frederick h 154 Chestnut
Mickelson Joseph junk h 12 Salisbury
" Sam pedlar h 20 S Second
Mickenofski Edward operative h 193 N Front
Mickett Oliver carpenter h 550 N Front [burn
Mickoy John operative h 34 Wash-
Miclo August weaver h 103 David
Middlebrook Fred weaver h 28 Reynolds [Davis
Middleton George E steam fiter h 161
" Harry weaver b 39 Roosevelt
" James h 39 Roosevelt [39 Fifth
" James E mgr 24 Purchase rms
" John fixer h 98 Brock av
" Samuel weaver h 69 Norman
" William fixer h 23 Woodlawn av
Midgley William overseer Beacon Mfg Co h 112 Clark
Miett Joseph Rev rem from city
Miggins George H h 7 Spruce
Miguel Fernando painter h 26 Hall
" John laborer h 17 Ash (S) [Short
" Manuel laborer N B W W h 51
" Manuel milk 99 Field h do
" Manuel K clerk h 37 Columbia
Mikati Nagip fruit 258 Coggeshall h do

BONNEY, FOLSTER & CO.,
The North End's Shopping Centre
Dry Goods and Men's Furnishings
945-947 Acushnet Ave., New Bedford, Mass.

Mikati
" Nijab (Tufik Mikati & Bro) 274 Coggeshall rms 13 Crawford
" Tufik & Bro (Nijab and Tufik) grocers 274 Coggeshall
Mikolajczyk Josef mill hand h 11 Holly [come
Milberger John laborer h 29 Wel-
Miler Joseph laborer b 63 Nash rd
" Joseph mill hand h 63 Nash rd
" William fireman b 63 Nash rd
Miles Alice A widow Henry h 57 Ash (N) [Second
Milette Ada widow Joseph h 218 N
" Napoleon fireman b 218 N Second
" Victor operative b 218 N Second
Miller Abraham pedlar h 493 S Water
" Addie G Mrs treas N B Theatre 249 Union h 54 Fifth
" Albert E machinist Whitman Mill h 127 Hathaway
" Alice nurse b 242 Maxfield
" Almeda E Mrs housekeeper 88 S Sixth
" Archie R glasscutter h 210 Allen
" Arthur A weaver b 79 County
" Arthur F 43 Weld rms Clark's point
" August weaver b 10 McGurk
" Catherine boarding 111 Fourth
" Charles M sales agent 38 Elm h 54 Fifth
" David pedlar h 17 Cannon
" David A laborer h 111 Fourth
" Delmont A troubleman 57 North Second h 32 Florence
" Elas C Rev pastor North Baptist church h 167 Ashland [Austin
" Elizabeth widow Joseph h 193
" Elizabeth and Mary A operatives h 25 Marvin
" Emma M Mrs h 167 Cedar
" Eugene engineer W F Nye Fish Island h at Fairhaven
" Francis operative b 5 Franklin
" George spinner b 850 First
" George A bartender h 28 Lindsey
" George E watchmaker and optician 24 Brock av b 154 Rockland
" Granville A barber b 185 Elm
" Hannah H died January 8 1911
" Harriet L chiropodist 42 Summer h do

Miller
" Heiman junk h 11 Morgans lane
" Herbert A contractor 232 Grinnell h do
" James operative h 131 Reynolds
" Jennie Mrs h 20 Rodney
" John city laborer b 59 Mosher
" John laborer h 5 Franklin [lage
" John laborer b 51 Howland Vil-
" John operative h 218 Whitman
" John Jr laborer b 5 Franklin
" John A operative h 155 Tallman
" John F engineer Almshouse b do
" John J police h 117 Fair
" John T engineer h 157 Fair
" John T grinder h 8 George
" Joseph b 301 Davis
" Joseph laborer h 42 Washburn
" Josephine M nurse rms 321 Union
" Mary and Agnes web drawers h 969 County [tine
" Percy mule spinner h 13 Valen-
" Samuel rope maker h 164 Emerson
" Thomas mule spinner b 8 George
" Thomas spinner h 68 Crapo
" Walter B supt Nashawena Mill h 277 Earle
" William h 79 County
" William weaver h 164 State
" William H master mechanic Whitman Mill h 289 Summer [ty
" William J operative b 139 Coun-
" William M paymaster Pierce Mfg Corp b 1011 County
" see Mellor [ton
Millett Harry D clerk h 62½ Washing-
Millette Albert clerk 161 Cove b 596 South Second
" Augustin weaver h 10 Austin ct
" Damase weaver b 75 Brock av
" Delor slasher tender h 180 Blackmer
" Emery mill hand h 82 Eugenia
" Frank motorman h 29 Bullard
" Frank weaver h 14 McGurk
" Fred weaver h 592 First
" George teamster b 195 N Second
" George R electrician h 83 Ruth
" Henri weaver h 53 Rivet
" Henry weaver h r 91 County
" John second hand h 195 N Second
" Joseph weaver h 103 David

M. P. B. Silva & Son Paints, Oils and Glass
Sole Agents for Lucas Tinted Gloss Paints
157 ACUSHNET AVENUE Both Phones NEW BEDFORD

Millette
" Louis brakeman h 184 Middle
" Louis driver 50 Elm [Fifth
" Louise clerk 40 Purchase b 123
" Napoleon third hand b 135 Nye
" Peter driver h 135 Nash road
" Pierre clerk b 135 Nash road [do
" Pierre driver 244 N Front h 247
" Piere driver 244 N Front h 274 do
" Remi weaver h 107 Perry
" Victor clerk 404 Purchase bds 2 Hillman [Plainville road
" Xavier teamster h Shawmut av n
Milligan George N machinist h 134 Tallman
" James operative h 138 Holly
" Thomas machinist b 138 Holly
Milliken Alfred S student b 39 Sycamore
" Allen W (Gardiner & Milliken) lawyer 3 Masonic bldg bds 8 Lincoln
" Chales A salesman b 22 S Sixth
" Eben C baker 166 Purchase h 94 Elm [amore
" Frank baker 92 Walden h 39 Syc-
" Frank A lawyer 33 Masonic bldg h 8 Lincoln
" Grace artist Merrill's Wharf bds 22 South Sixth [Pleasant
" Harriet J widow Edward R h 287
" Helen K Mrs h 22 South Sixth
" Lewis E (L E Milliken & Co) h 73 Hillman
" Lewis E & Co (Lewis E Milliken, Edward C Mosher and Louis A Hazard) Ideal Cash Store groceries and provisions 98-104 Allen
Millray Frederick W carpetner h 112 Mott [lette
Mills Adam mill hand bds 307 Col-
" Aadmson E machinist h 21 Valentine [h at Fall River
" Albert A billiards 82 Purchase
" Asa A pres 182 Union h at Fall River [Mills h 124 Hathaway
" Benjamin B engineer Whitman
" Edward piper's helper 125 Middle h 259 Fourth
" Ethel B A teacher Harrington school b 131 Merrimac
" Ezra clerk b 137 Acushnet av

Mills
" George baker h 969 County [av
" George operative b 137 Acushnet
" George weaver b 161 Brook
" Jane Mrs boarding house 137 Acushnet av
" John rem to Providence R I
" John J weaver h 856 First
" Susie S widow John M h 65 Foster [481 do
" Thomas hairdresser 489 Rivet h
" William E shipper 16 N Second
" William J insurance agent h 101 Merrimac [lard
Millward James W laborer h 147 Bul-
Milne Annie M housekeeper Parker House
Milnes Elizabeth A widow George W variety 170 Thompson h do
" George W died Mar 8 1911 [av
Milot Alcide weaver rms 121 Phillips
" Elphege weaver rms 162 Davis
Milotte Albert baker h 1077 County
" Alphonse P (Drolet & Milotte) h 17 Reynolds [872 Purchase
" J Alphonse clerk 185 Union h
" Napoleon painter 20 Nye h do
Minard Henry laborer b 53 Prospect
Miner Howard E operative h 115 David [142 Acushnet av
Mingo Willmay R widow Charles h
Minier Ethel M sub teacher public school b 137 Florence
" E Frank foreman 54 Union h 137 Florence [McDonald ct
Minkofski Wladyslaw mill hand h 2
Minney George H teamster h 177 Dean [Front
Mono Albert third hand h 546 N
Minor Charles S driver Morris & Co h 842 County
" Henry S b 286 Palmer
Minsky Isaac Rev Kenyon street synagogue h 132 Cedar Grove
Minstrell Gertrude A laundress rms 72 Maxfield [rms 367 Kempton
Minton Frank hairdresser 133 Smith
Miour Edmonde fixer h 29 Roosevelt
" Ephraim harnessmaker 247 Sawyer b 207 do
Miranda Angelina sewer 40 Purchase b 152 Thompson
" Antone laborer h 198 Bonney
" John carpenter h 416 Orchard (S)
" Jose S grocer 229 Coggeshall h 188 Belleville av

Steiger-Dudgeon Co.
"The WOMAN'S Store."
Tel. Bell 82 & 83, Branches connecting all depts.
" " 160 For Office only. Auto. 1211

SUMPTIONS, ASSORTMENTS AT ALL TIMES OF DEPENDABLE DRY GOODS

Miranda
" Joseph h 536 S Water
" Manuel A laborer b 570 S Water
" Manuel F laborer h 443 Orchard (S)
Miron Gilbert fixer b 11 Ashley
" Manuel weaver b 11 Ashley
Mirsky Israel junk 500 S Water h do
Mishar Bar Mrs h 180 Cedar Grove
Mishelly Margaret widow Hugh h 636 Acushnet av
Misier Edward weaver b 1028 Acushnet av
Misiolsk Albert mill hand h 36 Rotch blk 435 Bolton
Miskell James H supt Greene & Wood h 2 Green
" John laborer rms 309 Kempton
" Joseph B salesman Greene & Wood b 2 Green
Mitchel Joseph laborer b 16 Howland
Mitchell Alexander helper b 137 Acushet av
" Alfred G engineer h r 5 Campbell
" Catherine widow John b 14 Howland Village

CHARLES MITCHELL
successor to
RAYMOND & MITCHELL
Attorney and Counsellor at Law
Notary Public
Rooms 16-17 Masonic Building
Pleasant Street, New Bedford
Telephones: Bell 1487-1
Residence 1026-3

Mitchell Charles lawyer 16-17 Masonic bldg h 20 Maple View terrace
" Charles F operative h 10 Hazard
" David engineer h 331 Rivet
" David H h 241 Shawmut av
" Edward h 182 Weld
" Edwin h 89 Austin
" Edwin Jr conductor h 909 County
" Elizabeth widow Dennis h 16 Salisbury
" George A h 283 Cottage

Mitchell
" George E spinner b 16 Salisbury
" George W salesman Anthony Swift & Co h at Fairhaven
" Georgianna widow Daniel D h 133 North Second
" Grover C clerk 2 Union h 386 do
" Hannah Mrs clerk h 386 Union
" Harry bricklayer h 137 Perry
" Harry E chief clerk foot Willis h 114 do
" Hezekiah laborer bds 28 Summit
" Jacob N teamster b 28 Summit
" James W carpenter h 188 Middle
" Jane A widow James h 378 Maxfield
" John died Oct 31 1910
" John steam fitter 19 Linden h at Fall River
" John E laborer h 15 Jenney
" John J second hand h 69 Hazard
" Joseph dry goods 694 Purchase h 696 do
" Joseph P Jr shoemaker 730 Kempton h 362 do
" Lavelia V h 107 Elm
" Louis removed from city
" Marion E, Victoria, Winifred and Florence h 215 Acushnet av
" Mary seamstress b 168 Arnold
" Mary widow Antonio S h 101 Phillips avenue
" Michael ice cream maker 535 Kempton rms 50 Liberty
" Nehemiah waiter b 89 Austin
" Patrick F operative h 51 Howland Village
" Robert milk 241 Shawmut av b do
" Robert J screw maker b 89 Austin
" Sereno G instructor N B Textile school h 56 Ash (S)
" Shirley G clerk 81 Front h at Fairhaven
" Stephen driver 535 Kempton rms 50 Liberty
" The Tailor 27 Purchase
" Thomas foreman h r 260 Phillips avenue
" Walter lawyer b 241 Shawmut av
" William fixer b 49 Bowditch
" William P police h 51 Dartmouth
Mitron Joseph loom fixer h 102 Bowditch
Miville Ernest second hand h 206 Tinkham
Miz Andre mill hand h 26 Rotch blk 439 Bolton
Moanter Charlie weaver b 50 Washburn

PELEG H. SHERMAN 506 COUNTY ST.
FUNERAL DIRECTOR AND EMBALMER
OFFICE PHONES. Bell 690-13. Auto. 1305.
RESIDENCE PHONES. Bell 690-12. Auto. 1306.

Millette
" Louis brakeman h 184 Middle
" Louis driver 50 Elm [Fifth
" Louise clerk 40 Purchse b 123
" Napoleon third hand h 135 Nye
" Peter driver h 135 Nas road
" Pierre clerk b 135 Nas road [do
" Pierre driver 244 N Fnt h 247
" Piere driver 244 N Fro h 274 do
" Remi weaver h 107 Pery
" Victor clerk 404 Purchase bds 2 Hillman [Plainville road
" Xavier teamster h Shawmut av n
Milligan George N machinist h 134 Tallman
" James operative h 13 Holly
" Thomas machinist b 1 Holly
Milliken Alfred S student b 39 Sycamore
" Allen W (Gardiner & Milliken) lawyer 3 Masonic bldg bds 8 Lincoln
" Chales A salesman b 2 S Sixth
" Eben C baker 166 Purchase h 94 Elm [amore
" Frank baker 92 Wald h 39 Syc-
" Frank A lawyer 33 Masonic bldg h 8 Lincoln
" Grace artist Merrill's Wharf bds 22 South Sixth [Pleasant
" Harriet J widow Edward R h 287
" Helen K Mrs h 22 South Sixth
" Lewis E (L E Milliken & Co) h 73 Hillman
" Lewis E & Co (Lewis E Milliken, Edward C Mosher and Louis A Hazard) Ideal Cash Store groceries and provisions 98-104 Allen
Millray Frederick W car tuer h 112 Mott [lette
Mills Adam mill hand h 307 Col-
" Aadmson E machinist h 21 Valentine [h a Fall River
" Albert A billiards . Purchase
" Asa A pres 182 Union h at Fall River [Mills h 1: Hathaway
" Benjamin B engineer Whitman
" Edward piper's helper 125 Middle h 259 Fourth
" Ethel B A teacher Harrington school b 131 Merrimac
" Ezra clerk b 137 Acushnet av

Mills
" George baker h 969 County [av
" George operative b 137 Acushnet
" George weaver b 161 Brook
" Jane Mrs boarding house 137 Acushnet av
" John rem to Providence R I
" John J weaver h 856 First
" Susie S widow John M h 65 Foster [481 do
" Thomas hairdresser 489 Rivet h
" William E shipper 16 N Second
" William J insurance agent h 101 Merrimac [lard
Millward James W laborer h 147 Bul-
Milne Annie M housekeeper Parker House
Milnes Elizabeth A widow George W variety 170 Thompson h do
" George W died Mar 8 1911 [av
Milot Alcide weaver rms 121 Phillips
" Elphege weaver rms 162 Davis
Milotte Albert baker h 1077 County
" Alphonse P (Drolet & Milotte) h 17 Reynolds [872 Purchase
" J Alphonse clerk 185 Union h
" Napoleon painter 20 Nye h do
Minard Henry laborer b 53 Prospect
Miner Howard E operative h 115 David [142 Acushnet av
Mingo Willmay R widow Charles h
Minier Ethel M sub teacher public school b 137 Florence
" E Frank foreman 54 Union h 137 Florence [McDonald ct
Minkofski Wladyslaw mill hand h 2
Minney George H teamster h 177 Dean [Front
Mono Albert third hand h 546 N
Minor Charles S driver Morris & Co h 842 County
" Henry S b 286 Palmer
Minsky Isaac Rev Kenyon street synagogue h 132 Cedar Grove
Minstrell Gertrude A laundress rms 72 Maxfield [rms 367 Kempton
Minton Frank hairdresser 133 Smith
Miour Edmonde fixer h 29 Roosevelt
" Ephraim harnessmaker 247 Sawyer b 207 do
Miranda Angelina sewer 40 Purchase b 152 Thompson
" Antone laborer h 198 Bonney
" John carpenter h 416 Orchard (S)
" Jose S grocer 229 Coggeshall h 188 Belleville av

Steiger-Dudgeon Co.
"The WOMAN'S Store."
Tel. Bell 82 & 83, Branch connecting all depts.
" " 160 For Office only. Auto. 1211
SUMPTIONS, ASSORTMENTS AT ALL T... OF DEP...

Miranda
" Joseph h 536 S Water
" Manuel A laborer b 570 S Water
" Manuel F laborer h 443 Orchard (S)
Miron Gilbert fixer b 11 Ashley
" Manuel weaver b 11 Ashley
Mirsky Israel junk 500 S Water h do
Mishar Bar Mrs h 180 Cedar Grove
Mishelly Margaret widow Hugh h 636 Acushnet av [shnet av
Misier Edward weaver b 1028 Acu-
Misiolsk Albert mill hand h 36 Rotch blk 435 Bolton
Miskell James H supt Greene & Wood h 2 Green
" John laborer rms 309 Kempton
" Joseph B salesman Greene & Wood b 2 Green [land
Mitchel Joseph laborer b 16 How-
Mitchell Alexander helper b 137 Acushnet av [bell
" Alfred G engineer h r 5 Camp-
" Catherine widow John b 14 Howland Village

CHARLES MITCHELL
successor to
RAYMOND & MITCHELL
Attorney and Counsellor at Law
Notary Public
Rooms 16-17 Masonic Building
Pleasant Street, New Bedford
Telephones: Bell 1487-1
Residence 1026-3

Mitchell Charles lawyer 16-17 Masonic bldg h 20 Maple View terrace [court
" Charles F operative h 10 Hazard
" David engineer h 331 Rivet
" **David H h 241 Shawmut av**
" **Edward h 182 Weld**
" Edwin h 89 Austin
" Edwin Jr conductor h 909 County
" Elizabeth widow Dennis h 16 Salisbury
" Georg

Mitchell
" George E spinner b 16 Salisbury
" George W salesman Anthony Swi & Co h at Fairhaven
" Georgiana widow Daniel D h 133 Nor Second
" Grover C clerk 2 Union h 386 do
" Hanna Mrs clerk h 386 Union
" Harry bricklayer h 137 Perry
" Harry chief clerk foot Willis h 13
" Hezekiah laborer bds 28 Summit
" Jacob teamster b 28 Summit
" James W carpenter h 188 Middle
" Jane widow James h 378 Maxfield
" John died Oct 31 1910 [Fall River
" John steam fitter 19 Linden h at
" John laborer h 15 Jenney
" John J second hand h 69 Hazard
" Joseph dry goods 694 Purchase h 696 [Kempton h 362 do
" Joseph P Jr shoemaker 730
" Lavelia W h 107 Elm
" Louis moved from city
" Marion E, Victoria, Winifred and Florence h 215 Acushnet av
" Mary seamstress b 168 Arnold
" Mary widow Antonio S h 101 Phillips avenue
" Michael ice cream maker 535 Kempton rms 50 Liberty
" Nehemiah waiter b 89 Austin
" Patrick operative h 51 Howland Village
" Robert milk 241 Shawmut av b do
" Robert screw maker b 89 Austin
" Sereno instructor N B Textile sch h 56 Ash (S)
" Shirley F clerk 81 Front h at Fairhaven [50 Liberty
" Stephen driver 535 Kempton rms
" The Tailor 27 Purchase [avenue
" Thomas foreman h r 260 Phillips
" Walter drawyer b 241 Shawmut av
" William mixer b 49 Bowditch
" William P police h 51 Dartmouth
Mitron Joseph loom fixer h 102 Bowditch [Tinkham
Miville Ernest second hand h 206
Miz Andrew mill hand h 26 Rotch blk 439 Bolton [burn

Modesto Manuel R clerk 130 Dartmouth b 132 do [Coffin av
Moessinger Christian E baker 322
Moffet Thomas weaver h 30 Welcome
Moffett David G salesman 38 N Second rms 53 Walnut [avenue
Moffit Arcade weaver h 455 Belleville
Moharam Tarlep mill hand b 42 Davis
Moher Patrick J overseer Nashawena Mill h 189 Belleville road
Mohr & Fenderl cotton buyers 97 William rm 306 [ton
Moister Andrew mason b 83 Kemp-
Moll John operative h 363 Earle
Molleo Edward machinist b 239 Acushnet avenue [Acushnet av
" George D porter 164 Union h 239
Molleur Mary widow Emile b 82 Myrtle [away
Molloy Edward spinner h 124 Hath-
Molway Josephine M h 52 Fifth
" Philip machinist bds 92 High
Momarquette Joseph carpenter h 127 Whitman [son
Mombleau Cyrille teamster h 100 Nel-
" David tinsmith b 16 Bowditch
" Edward driver b 100 Nelson
Monaghan Bryan paver h 277 Park
" James F foreman h 304 Acushnet avenue
Monahan James died Dec 12 1910
" Jennie widow James h 23 Peckham
" Neil F clerk h 130 Bedford
Monarch Margaret Mrs h 133 Grinnell [nell b do
" Mina E teacher painting 133 Grin-
MONARCH TYPEWRITER CO 67 Milk Boston See page 34
Monblow David tinsmith 1480 Acushnet av h 16 Bowditch
Moncrief Martha widow Robert John h 42 Hazard [mac
" William A student bds 142 Merri-
" William T grocer 44 Hazard h 142 Merrimac
Moncrieff J Chester (Moncrieff & Co) bds American House
" & Co (J C Moncrieff) eye sight specialists 7 Arcade block and 861 S Water [N Front
Mondeau Edward laborer bds 329
" Peter laborer b 329 N Front

Mondeau
" Rock laborer h 329 N Front
Mondon William speeder tender h 44 Merrimac
Mondville Oliver died June 16 1910
Monest C helper 1201 Purchase
Monette Augustus teamster h r 11 Penniman
" Augustus teamster b 311 N Front
" Donat doffer b 311 N Front
" Donat painter h 50 Tallman
" Elzear weaver h 311 N Front
" Napoleon painter b 50 Tallman
" Wilfred painter b 311 N Front
" William weaver b 311 N Front
Mongeau Joseph carpenter h 77 Jouvett
" Louis carpenter h 95 Jouvett
Mongeron Albert weaver h 59 County
Moniz Anthony carpenter h 198 Rockland
" Antone laborer h 363 Dartmouth
" Antone weaver h 197 Coggeshall
" Antone weaver h 17 Mitchell
" Antone J boat builder h 82 Thompson
" Antonio laborer h 203 Hathaway
" Claudina widow Manuel h 44 Stowell
" Frank operative h 19 Nye
" Frank weaver h 129 Division
" Henry operative b 82 Thompson
" John mill hand h 419 S Second
" John operative h 3 Cannon
" John B grocer 133 Crapo h do
" Joseph laborer h 143 Field
" Joseph operative b 19 Nye
" Manuel laborer h 147 Rockland
" Manuel machinist h 178 Belleville avenue [field
" Manuel mill hand h 12 Grand-
" Manuel mill hand h 17 Mitchell
" Manuel operative h 38 Hollyhock
" Manuel M drillworker b 262 Orchard (S) [hock
" Manuel S operative h 45 Holly-
" William machinist h 157 Collette
Monjeau Joseph carpenter h 77 Jouvett
" Louis carpenter 61 County h do
" Louis J carpenter h 95 Jouvett
Monjohn Thomas H hairdresser 54 Ash (S) h 121 Cedar
Monk John weaver b 418 N Front
Monnier John weaver b 501 S Second

F. T. AKIN & CO. FORGE FACTORY FURNACE FAMILY COAL

Monroe Frederic S public stenographer 49 William rm 6 b 474 Kempton
" see Munroe [County
Mont Amanda widow George h r 91
" Charles weaver h 286 Fourth
" Frank teamster 423 Acushnet av h 19 Mill [h 160 Crapo
" Walter teamster 423 Acushnet av
" Welsford weaver b r 91 County
Montague Manuel S operative h 25 County [James
" Mary W widow N Lyman h 28
Monteiro Alfred laborer h 356 S Water
" Antone h 48 Thompson
" Antone mariner h 418 S Water
" Domingos laborer h 53 First
" Gregory laborer h 23 Walnut
" Honorat freight handler bds 56 First
" James laborer h 41 Union
" John mariner h 285 S Water
" Jose insurance agent 120 Purchase rm 403 b 123 County
" Manuel clerk b 23 Walnut [First
" Manuel freight handler bds 56
" Marcellino J removed from city
" Marthinho S farm hand h 53 First
" Mary Ann h 85 First [sor
Montgomery Annie weaver h 89 Win-
Montigney Antoine fixer h 123 Ruth
Montmaquette Archie rem to St Hyacinth
" Arthur rem from city
Montminy Amanda millinery 1535 Acushnet av and 865 S Water b 905 do [h 193 Arnold
" Telesphore V salesman 182 Union
Montpetit Alfred carpenter h 210 Eugenia [do
Montro Ernest barber 387 S Water b
Montrond Leopoldo hairdresesr and pool 387 S Water h do [do
Monty Anseline weaver h 872 First
" Arsene weaver b 402 S Front
" Aurelia widow Francis h 13 Hicks
" Blanche clerk b 6 Washburn
" Frank stable 6 Washburn h do
" Frank weaver b 89 Collette
" Hector teamster b 6 Washburn
" Lillian Mrs h 371 Hillman
" Nicholas operative h 73 First

Monty
" Philip hairdresser 662 Purchase h 18 Washburn [18 Washburn
" Philip Jr barber 662 Purchase h
" Thomas laborer h 402 S Front
" Thomas Jr quiller h 773 First
" Vloy mill hand bds 402 S Front
" William W barber h 32 Bentley
Monville George plumber's helper b 43 Dean
" Narcisse h 43 Dean
" Oliver laborer h 37 Bullard
" Pierre bookkeeper b 43 Dean
Moody Charles P rem to Charlotte N C
" Frank J third hand b 36 Dartmouth [mouth
" Frank P operative h 36 Dart-
Moon John died Dec 12 1910
Moonan Michael bartender h 178 Mill
Mooney James E insurance agent 37 Purchase rm 23 b 95 Fourth
" Martin J teamer W F Nye h at Fairhaven
" Owen painter b 360 Cedar
" Robert A clerk foot Willis b 59 Elm [ton
Moore Albert engineer h 328 Kemp-
" Alexander h 130 Crapo
" Alexander Jr driver h 27 Bourne
" Bertha Louise b 231 S Second
" Cecelia milliner b 96 Oak
" Charles baker h 156 Church
" Charles blacksmith h 103 Morgan
" Eldad E carpenter h 96 Tremont
" Florence E teacher J H Clifford school b 227 Pope
MOORE F RUSSELL carpenter and builder 96 Tremont h do See page 760 [b 227 Pope
" Helen F teacher Phillips av school
" Horatio laborer b 10 Old Market sq [Atlantic
" Isabella widow Alexander h 82
" James blacksmith b 137 Acushnet av
" James D machinist b 105 Park
" James E bookkeeper 105 William h 87 Campbell
" James F Mrs prop Hotel Gazette 231 S Second h do
" James J builder 125 Oak h do
" James J clerk U St Ry Co h 109 Robeson [Robeson
" James J police Station 5 h 109

Remember to investigate our methods before taking up a business course.
Kinyon's Commercial School
Odd Fellows Bldg., Cor. William and Pleasant Sts., New Bedford, Mass.

Moore
" James T drillworker b 137 Acushnet av
" James T glassblower b 54 First
" John drillworker b 96 Oak
" John H carriage painter 50 Elm h 65 Mt Pleasant
" John P insurance agent 120 Purchase rm 403 h 227 Pope
" J Edward bookkeeper Anthony Swift & Co b Pope street
" Kate teacher Harrington school b 105 Park
" Lewis b 4 Rockland
" Lewis janitor h 238 North
" L Katherine Mrs h 95 N Second
" Margaret widow b 10 Studley
" Mary E widow Albert W b 52 Weld
" May E Mrs h 618 Cottage
" Moses shoemaker 4 Fifth h 101 Park [lette
" Nancy widow William b 307 Col-
" Nathan died Dec 23 1910
" Robert H carpenter h 161 Davis
" Robert J shoe repairer 4 Fifth h 105 Park
" Robert W laborer h 137 Ashland
" Russell b 96 Tremont
" Stephen R stenographer bds 282 Bowditch [chase
" Thomas eyeletmaker h 535 Pur-
" Thomas helper b 156 Church
" William laborer h 96 Oak
" William J h 4 Rockland
" William J janitor Y M C A bldg h 112 Bonney [282 Bowditch
" William R engineer S F E No 8 h
Moorehouse Martha Mrs b 157 Collette [Rounds
Moores John E letter carrier h 38
" Joseph brakeman h 970 County
" Mabel R cashier 100 William b 38 Rounds [Bowditch
Moorhouse Daniel A weaver bds 366
" James h 366 Bowditch
Moots Jerry carpenter h 92 Cove
Moquin Albert barber 1526 Acushnet av
" Albert R driver b 380 Pleasant
" Edward speeder tender h r 4 Hicks [av h 16 Hicks
" Henri hairdresser 1526 Acushnet
" Joseph twister b 88 Hathaway
" Julian operative h 150 Collette

Moquin
" Julien laborer N B W W h 596 Purchase [nia
" Louis wood planer h 113 Euge-
" Luc drillmaker h 326 Coffin av
Mora Augustine C grocer 146 Belleville av
" Manuel laborer h 201 Fourth
" Manuel operative h 201 Fourth
Morak Thomas operative h 16 Marvin
Morach Stanley mill hand h 1085 S Water
Moraes Joseph J asst supt 97 William rm 310 h 274 Orchard (S)
Moran Andrew city laborer h 8 Felton [Front
" Edward A salesman h 297 N
" Edward F blacksmith h 24 Dartmouth [cery
" Ellen widow Cornelius h 61 Chan-
" James plasterer h 242 Nash rd
" James spinner b 12 Potter
" James spinner b 21 Marvin
" John bricklayer b 67 Clark
" John laborer h 94 Clark
" John loom fixer h 7 Harmony
" John mule spinner b 509 Purchase
" Joseph teamster h 276 Purchase
" Margaret variety 773 S Water h do [445 Pleasant
" Mary widow Henry operative h
" Michael spinner h 140 Bullard
" Michael weaver h 67 Clark
" William L pres Booth Mfg Co h at Providence R I
" see Morin [Austin
Morancy Andrew J clerk bds 306
" Bertram A proof reader Mercury b 306 Austin
" John clerk b 32 County
" Leo laborer h 32 County
" Leo Jr laborer b 32 County
" Mary E Mrs h 198 Cedar
" William J motorman h 306 Austin [Blackmer
Morcier Antone glassworker h 131
Morde Albert clerk P O bds 32 Keene
" Carl E assistant foreman T P Corporation h 204 Tremont
Moreau Charles speeder tender b 299 Tinkham
" David drill maker b 299 Tinkham
" Delphise elevatorman h 84 Jouvett

HASKELL BROS. DEALERS IN
ICE
400 COURT STREET TELEPHONE CONNECTION NEW BEDFORD, MASS.

Moreau
" Delphise J driver h 213 Austin
" Delphise J Jr clerk 381 Cedar b 84 Jouvett
" Emile carpenter b 182 Dean [vett
" Eugene clerk 381 Cedar b 84 Jou-
" Frank picker h 299 Tinkham
" John comber h 100 Holly
" Joseph clerk b Bullard street
" Joseph laborer h Milford
" Jule twister bds 100 Holly
" Julia E sewer 185 Union bds 100 Holly
" Levi laborer b 402 Pleasant
" Paul mason h 34 Bullard
" Paul E weaver b 34 Bullard
" Ralph clerk 537 N Front h 103 Belleville road
" Richard twister b 100 Holly
" Thomas laborer 350 S Second
" Wilbert painter b 299 Tinkham
Moreis Manuel mill hand h 34 South
Morelander Charles D driver 47 William [Ash (N)
Morelli Luigi fruit 98 Union h 5
Morency Andrew J clerk 44 Dartmouth
" John clerk h 32 County
" Joseph manager h 186 Dean
" Joseph P grocer 167 Cove b 1075 South Water
Morey John loom fixer h 15 Willard
Morgado John M laborer h 137 Rockland
" Manuel L watch repairer 157½ Acushnet av h 574 S Water
" Manuel M laborer h 363 Orchard
Morgan Albert fireman h 328 Kempton
" Annie operative h 31 Bullard
" Arthur spinner h 4 Marvin
" Charles W baker 255 Union h 168 North [net av
" Darby stonecutter b 1028 Acush-
" David A seaman b 168 North
" Elias S baker 255 Union h 73 S Second [Fourth
" Elizabeth A widow John F h 136½
" F Helen bookkeeper b 136½ Fourth
" James operative h 4 Marvin
" John laborer h 38 Bowditch

Morgan
" Noah W master mariner h 168 North
" Rufus F motormon h 86 Clark
" Thomas third hand h 114 Nash rd
" Walter drill maker h 397 Earle
" William overseer Beacon Mfg Co
" William shoemaker h 15 Cannon
" William T overseer Oncko Mill h 109 Clark [Ruth
Moriarty Delia Mrs boarding 83
" Edward L manager 15 Fourth b 38 Fifth
" John laborer h 55 Prospect
" John third hand b 102 Bowditch
" John E undertaker 149 Blackmer h 133 Fourth
" John H laborer h 963 Purchase
" Joseph T shoe lace mfr h 74 Rockland
" Patrick laborer b 55 Prospect
" Patrick tailor 134 Blackmer b do
" Rossa clerk 184 Fourth h 186 do
" Sarah widow Edward h 38 Fifth
" Thomas E second hand h 279 Hillman
MORIARTY TIMOTHY J paints hardware etc 184 Fourth h 115 Division See page 49
" Una R stenographer 71 William rm 2 b 74 Rockland
Morie William h 1103 S Water [lard
Morin Agnes widow Joseph h 147 Bul-
" Albert painter b 81 Holly
" Alexander hostler b 64 Bullard
" Antoine h 10 Cleveland
" Antoine Jr machine operator b 10 Cleveland [bury
" Charles loom fixer h 50 Salis-
" Clemence widow Charles b 31 Nash road
" Cyril spinner h 196 Earle
" Delphis weaver h 530 N Front
" Edward carpenter b 135 Bullard
" Elzear painter 80 Holly h 81 do
" Emerance widow Thomas h 64 Bullard
" Etienne weaver h 20 La France ct
" George plater bds 81 Holly
" John weaver h 21 Morton ct
" John B laborer h 411 Rivet
" Joseph fixer h 190 Coffin avenue
" Joseph operative b 90 Davis
" Louis carpenter h 1026 S Water

J. F. CROSSLEY 223 MILL STREET COR. EMERSON PHONE
STEAM and HOT WATER HEATING
GAS FITTING and FIXTURES

Morin
" Louis fixer h 28 McGurk
" Louis shoemaker h 15 Penniman
" Louis weaver h 93 Hathaway [tle
" Napoleon second hand h 12 Bee-
" Napoleon speeder h 812 First
" Napoleon G barber b 857½ First
" Pierre fixer h 282 N Front
" Pierre Jr spinner b 282 N Front
" Thomas furniture mover 190 Coffin av h do [81 Holly
" Wilfred janitor Dominick Hall b
" Wilfred operative h 147 Bullard
Morley Grace Mrs h 696 Purchase
" William S weaver h 141 Reynolds
Mornsky Zerick tailor 820 Acushnet av h do [ond
Morosse Alfred painter b 490 S Sec-
" Constanty weaver b 563 First
" Henry clerk b 490 S Second
" William H painter h 490 S Second [nell pl
Morreau Arthur baker rms 3 Cor-
" Georgianna widow Henry h 310 N Front [Belleville av
Morreia Manuel S mill hand h 171
Morrell Frank cook h 131 S Second
" Frank E conductor b 455 Coggeshall
" Joseph weaver h 32 Social [Front
" Maria Mrs operative h 339 N
" Victor laborer rms 202 State
" William W repairman U St Ry Co b 339 N Front
Morresette Eusibe h 882 S Water
Morrey Alice widow James h 28 Cottage [tage
" Joseph H drillworker b 28 Cot-
Morrice Charles H painter h 273 Coggeshall
" Frank fireman h 139 Coffin av
" Joseph mill hand b 139 Coffin av
Morrill Arthur blacksmith h 565 Purchase
" Arthur E steam fitter h 85 Park
" Bert glassworker rms 299 Acushnet av
" Charles teamster 748 Purchase
" Edward teamster b 41 Covell
" Francis J driver 285 Acusnhet av
" George teamster 27 Bowditch b 760 Purchase
" Lucia D milliner b 216 Cedar
" Mary Mrs h 760 Purchase

Morrill
" Sadie widow Henry h 118 Dartmouth [Cedar
" William B mgr 157 Union h 216
" see Morrell
Morris Amos laborer h 177 Thompson [son
" Angelo E weaver h 80 Thomp-
" Annie and Nellie weavers h 321 Earle [Thomas
" Annie P widow Veta E h 81
" Antone fisherman h 84 Earle
" Antone laborer h 55 School
" Antone J fireman h 105 Bullard
" Antonio mill hand h 143 Coffin av
" Antonio C engineer 168 S Water h 208 Rockland [Thomas
" Charles P clerk 100 Fifth b 81
" Edward spinner h 21 Marvin
" Edward spinner b 85 Tallman
" Elizabeth B widow John N b 320 County [net av
" Frank mill hand h 2623 Acush-
" Frank J cooper h 46 Bonney
" Frank J teamster N B Fish Co h 467 Acushnet av [ney
" Frank J Jr machinist b 46 Bon-
" George J drillworker h 131 Fair
" Henry barber 5 Bedford bds 2 Stanton court
" **Henry bartender h 6 Warren [yer**
" James second hand h 245 Saw-
" James weaver b 38 Bowditch
" James R weaver h 54 Peckham
" John (Empire Clothing Co) 88 Purchase h 235 Pope [Pleasant
" John engineer 3 E Pope h 440
" John Jr machinist 8 Seneca b 440 Pleasant
" John J grinder h 163 Rockland
" John J salesman 127 Purchase b 81 Thomas
" John P L laborer b 340 Allen
" Joseph laborer h 13 Abbott
" Joseph operative h 74 Middle
" Joseph weaver b 850 First
" Joseph E janitor 69 Bowditch h do [len
" Joseph F city paver h 340 Al-
" Joseph F laborer h 45 Borden
" Joseph M laborer h 15½ Griffin
" Josephine widow Emanuel h 417 First
" Manuel cook h 101 S Second

CHARLES A. CROSHERE
38 FOURTH ST. Bell Phone 1964-23
SIGN PAINTING
GLASS LETTERING
ELECTRIC SIGNS
SHOW CARDS

Morris
" Manuel mill hand h 222 N Front
" Manuel F spinner h Winterville road cor Rockdale av
" Mary Mrs h 208 Rockland
" Mary widow Antone h 331 First
" Mary widow b 15 S Second
" Philip H machinist h 341 Bowditch [h 60 Bay
" Samuel asst janitor Court House
" William barber h 280 Coggeshall
" William clerk 212 Union bds 81 Thompson [av
" William mill hand h 479 Belleville
" William spinner b 280 Coggeshall
" William F laborer h 49 Acushnet avenue [sq
" & Co wholesale provisions Bridge
" see de Mora
Morrison Angus L rem to Boston
" Catherine operative h r 33 S Second [sutta Mill h 250 Chestnut
" Charles A asst bookkeeper Wam-
" Clara removed to Boston
" George machinist b r 25 Smith
" James weaver h 115 David
" James A stage hand Hathaway's Theatre b r 33 S Second
" John beamer b 115 David
" John operative b 280 Coggeshall
" Joseph P chauffeur h 42 Emerson (S) [170 Rivet
" Marie L widow Alexander O h
" Minnie h r 33 S Second
" Napoleon operative b 170 Rivet
" Richard F clerk Potomska Mills h 33 Atlantic
" Thomas janitor Mary B White school h 79 Forest
" Thomas A linotype operator 112 Union h 48 Richmond
" Wilfred H died August 14 1910
" William weaver h 280 Coggeshall
" William weaver b 115 David
" William G compositor 112 Union bds 79 Forest
Morrissette Albert fixer h 12 Rodney
" Edmonde laborer h 61 Kenyon
" Edward operative b 61 Kenyon
" Eusebe weaver h 882 S Water
" George cook b 290 Purchase
" Mary widow John b 61 Kenyon
Morrissey David H salesman b 54 S Second [avenue
" Dennis F mariner b 70 Acushnet
" Ellen widow William h 54 S Second
" Frank J clerk b 54 S Second
" Harry J stage manager Hathaway's Theatre b 54 S Second
" John H molder b 54 S Second
" Rose widow Dennis h 70 Acushnet avenue [ond
" William James clerk b 54 S Sec-
" William John actor b 54 S Second
Morrois Philemon carpenter b 32 Holly [net av
Morrow Arthur driver rms 872 Acush-
" Arthur laborer 1070 County bds 3 Cornell place [Mosher
" Frank J speeder tender h 73
" Harry machinist b 26 Roosevelt
" Jennie Mrs h 389 Acushnet av
" Wilbert clerk h 299 Tinkham av
" William spinner h 26 Roosevelt
" see Moreau and Merrow
Morse Albert S Jr salesman 423 Acushnet avenue h 450 do
" Alfred R Jr piper 55 N Water rms 477 Acushnet avenue
" Ansel C machinist h 38 Bay
" Arthur fisherman h E French av near Rodney [son
" Carleton D student b 37 Madi-
" Charles M salesman 1 William h 106 Front [Stowell
" Chester E piper 55 N Water b 38
" Emma F widow William R h 229 Fourth [net av
" Everett C box mfr h 2481 Acush-
" Frank S painter b 87 Parker
" Frederick C plumber 91 N Water h 47 Hillman [ion
" Frederick H shoemaker h 394 Un-
" Frederick J butler h 1 Sullivan
" George laborer W F Nye h at Fairhaven
" George F teamster h 41 Covell
" Hendrick W master mariner h 401 S Water
" Henry A h 87 Parker [chase
" Henry A 2nd painter h 355 Pur-
" James C teamster h 2405 Acushnet avenue
" John V b 29 Fifth

J. G. NICHOLSON
LUMBER, SASH, DOORS and BLINDS
BOWDITCH STREET, NEW BEDFORD, MASS.

Morse
" Julia A V music teacher 205 Park h do [ton D C
" Leonard F removed to Washing-
" Leonard H gardener 729 County b do [Cedar
" Leonard H Jr shoemaker h 283
" Lucy J bookkeeper 98 Allen b 47 Cottage [son
" Malcolm W salesman b 37 Madi-
" Milo L salesman b 39 Valentine
" Sarah E cook h 205 Park
MORSE TWIST DRILL AND MACHINE CO 100 Fifth See page 15
" Willard H dry goods 1049½ Acushnet av h 37 Madison
" William weaver h 39 Valentine
" William H chauffeur 22 Fourth h 728 Kempton
" William J teamster h 57 School
" William R died June 27 1911
Morsette George operative h 9 Bowditch [43 Bay h do
Morsey John J carpenter and builder
Mort Gertrude widow Harry P h 204 Nash road
" Harry P died June 9 1911
Morton Edwin F mason h Phillips rd
" Elbridge G removed to Fairhaven
" Frank P farmer h 4299 Acushnet avenue [av
" George H spinner h 63 Acushnet
" Josiah clerk 141 Purchase b 220 Kempton [h 97 Hillman
" Walter P clerk city treas office
" Walter S driver h 474 Coggeshall
Moseley William H Rev pastor First P M E church h 42 Columbia
Moser Wilhelm weaver h 95 Tallman
Moses Peter laborer h 518 Acushnet avenue
Mosher Albert E police h 11 Jenny Lind [mouth
" Albert G carpenter h 35 Dart-
" Brycia E teacher 27 Arnold pl b do [chanic's lane
" Charles A carpenter rms 69 Me-
" Charles A decorator h 766 Kempton
" Charles E E principal Mosher Home Preparatory school 29 Arnold pl h do [h do
" Charles H ice 1372 Rockdale av

Mosher
" Charles M carpenter h 445 Chancery
" Chauncy R instrumentman 303 Municipal bldg h at Dartmouth
" Crawford N drillworker h 94½ Dartmouth [bard
" David A shoecutter h 54 Lom-
" Edward C (L E Milliken & Co) 98 Allen h 4 Bonney
" Emily C b 41 Bonney
" Eudora F widow Allen h 151 Fair
" Frank A with Hawes Tewksbury & Co b 277 Union
" Frank T carpenter 161 Clinton h 216 Rockland [nold
" Frank W machinist h 216 Ar-
" Frederick E driver Hose 4 h 156 Brock av [av
" Frederick P clerk b 156 Brock
" George B farm hand h 702 Hathaway road [ton
" George F chauffeur b 663 Kemp-
" Harry A carpenter h 92 Brigham
" Henry A solderer h 111 Smith
" Henry C W pres Merchants National Bank h 465 County
" Henry M foreman h 205 County
" Henry S silversmith b 172 Acushnet av
" Herbert F clerk b 104 Sycamore
" Hetty C housekeeper 10 Florence
" James T engineer h 41 Wing
" Lester master mariner h 69 Vine
" Lillie H widow William J b 104 Sycamore
" Lizzie S b 10 Spruce
" Loren N h 96 Dartmouth
" Luthan W painter h 80 Florence
" Margaret E clerk P Corp b 41 Wing [Purchase h 168 Austin
" Mary A Mrs charpet sewer 36
" Mary E chiropodist 24 Purchase rms do [Kempton
" Mary K widow Joseph R b 804
" M A checker 14 N Sixth
" Nathaleen doffer b 77 N Second
" Orrin machinist 8 Hazard's lane b 96 Dartmouth
" Thomas driver 55 Mechanic's lane b 96 Dartmouth
" Viola G b 104 Sycamore
" Walter E mill hand b 606 Cottage
" Willard L asst 80 Pleasant h 71 Fourth [tage
" Willard P mariner h 283 Cot-

Steiger-Dudgeon Co.
"The WOMAN'S Store."
Tel. Bell 82 & 83, Branches connecting all depts.
" " 160 For Office only. Auto. 1211

SUMPTIONS, ASSORTMENTS AT ALL TIMES OF DEPENDABLE DRY GOODS

MOSHER WILLIAM E florist 325 Hillman h 232 North See page 40
" William S farmer h 2057 Acushnet av
Mosie Abdo dry goods and remnants 424 N Front h r do
Moss Charles P overseer Acushnet Mill Corp h 32 Ashley
" Edward weaver h 33 George
" George h 109 Division
" George operative h 172 Austin
" George Jr machinist bds 425 S Front
" John weaver b 64 Ruth
" John weaver b 172 Austin
" John weaver b 301 Fourth
" William weaver h 39 Valentine
Mossie Alfred rem to Worcester
" Joseph carpenter h 3 Harmony
Mossis Abdod mill hand h 7 Grandfield
Mother Maria do Sagrado Corocao directoress 98 S Sixth h do
Motil Joseph operative h 24 Howard [Fourth
Mott Cassius B carpenter h 134
" Gertrude Mrs grocer 1612 Acushet av h 204 Nash rd
Motta Antone barber 252 Coggeshall h 145 Belleville av
" Antonio real estate 151 Hemlock h 153 do [b 924 County
" Frank clerk 439 Belleville av
" Frank laborer h 83 Crapo
" Hattie E Mrs h 382 Kempton
" John carpenter h Tarkiln Hill rd
" Joseph operative h 127 Belleville avenue [av
" Joseph F laborer h 96 Acushnet
Mouchiesienn John clerk 817 S Water rms 135 Prospect [Eng
Moulson Harry S rem to Bradford
Moult James boarding house 11 Logan [Union h 56 Hill
Moulton Augustus G bookkeeper 133
" Fred F h 213 Summer [mer
" George L D salesman b 213 Sum-
" Joel H inspector U St Ry h 3 Glover [aghy school b 56 Hill
" Mabelle A teacher Thomas Don-
" Sadie M teacher First st school b 213 Summer
" William fireman b 1 Sutton
Mount Pleasant Banding Co Hathaway road n Mount Pleasant
Mountain Mary Mrs h 596 Cottage
Moura Antone mill hand h 55 Mitchell
Mower John mill hand h 192 Division
Mowry Ann widow Daniel C h 99 Willis [Willis
" Annie A clerk 40 Purchase b 99
" Daniel C died Jan 15 1911 [Fair
" George W card grinder h 152
Moxham Thomas mason h 156 Division [net av
Moy Toy Co restaurant 354 Acush-
Moyer Charles glass cutter h 80 South Sixth
" Joseph H watchman h 51 Bonney
" Ralph inspector b 51 Bonney
Moynan Charles S letter carrier h 236 Union [Maxfield
" Martha W widow Robert h 382
" Mary F stenographer b 382 Maxfield [382 Maxfield
" W Robert helper U St Ry Co b
Mrkvicka Vincent weaver h 13 Felton
Mroz Konstanti carder h 8 Social
Mudge William H (Mudge & Francis) h 378 Allen
MUDGE & FRANCIS (William H Mudge and Charles Francis Jr) plumbers 157 Acushnet av See page 781
Muhl Joseph weaver h 69 Diman
Muir Philip mill hand h 2 McDonald court [man
" Telesphor mill hand b 132 Tall-
Mulberry Harry plumber b 359 Pleasant
" James L machinist b 359 Pleasant
" William H clerk h 359 Pleasant
Mulcahey Edward laborer b 33 McGurk
" Edward Jr weaver b 33 McGurk
" Frank L loom fixer h 130½ Summer [Warren
Muldoon Edward J rarpenter b 25
Mulholland Alice M widow John h 375 Pleasant [ant
" Charles Q H driver bds 375 Pleas-
" James F spinner b 375 Pleasant
" Mary bds 147 Mill [Thompson
Mulkearn Martin teamster h 47
" Martin J shoemaker b 47 Thompson
" Peter shoemaker b 47 Thompson

PELEG H. SHERMAN 506 COUNTY ST.
FUNERAL DIRECTOR AND EMBALMER
OFFICE PHONES. Bell 690-13. Auto. 1305.
RESIDENCE PHONES. Bell 690-12. Auto. 1306.

Mulkearns James died May 10 1911
" James A doffer bds 417 Rivet
" John L clerk b 417 Rivet
" Mary E widow James h 417 Rivet
" William M mill hand b 417 Rivet
Mullaley Edward F rodman 303 Municipal bldg b 126 Eugenia [1911
" Margaret widow Thomas died
Mullaney Bridget P widow Michael h 69 South
" Charles ice b 34 Crapo
" Francis laborer h 34 Crapo
" James W engineer h 121 Fifth
" John F clerk b 69 South
" Joseph helper b 34 Crapo
" L Edward machinist b 69 South
" Michael died March 1 1911
" Michael J machinist b 69 South
" Thomas A operative h 170 Washington
" Thomas spinner h 86 Mosher
" Thomas F turner 111 Willis h 28 Shawmut av [Mosher
Mullarkey Edward spinner h 87
" Joseph spinner h 415 Orchard (S)
Mullen Harold clerk 329 Rivet h at Dartmouth
" James grocer 171 Division h do
" James Jr mule spinner h 210 Division
" Margaret Mrs removed from city
" Mary and Eliza h 210 Division
" Patrick J spinner h Hawes near Tarkiln Hill road
" Thomas operative b 210 Division
" William clerk 329 Rivet b 331 do
" William fireman h 2 Weld av
" William H drill worker rms 129 Acushnet avenue [French av
Muller Antone weaver h 150 West
Mulligan George mason h 301 Coggeshall [shall
" Thomas mill hand b 269 Cogge-
Mullin James variety 171 Division h do [do
" William clerk 329 Rivet bds 331
Mullins Daniel fisherman b 303 Sawyer [115 Butler
" Doran L electrician 120 Middle b
" Enoch police h 115 Butler
" Jeremiah laborer b 138 Bowditch

Mullins
" Joanna E widow Dennis b 1650 Acushnet avenue [avenue
" John watchman h 44 Bowditch
" Joseph F weaver h 1650 Acushnet
" Timothy F fisherman h 27 Rodney
" see Mullen [away
Mulloy Edward spinner h 124 Hath-
Mulroy Francis machinist b 36 Hazel
" Thomas laborer h 36 Hazel [Front
Mulvey Bernard J plasterer h 550 N
" Thomas apprentice b 550 N Front
Munds Andrew fixer h 67 Clark
" Andrew laborer h r 251 Coggeshall [Co h Brock avenue
Mungall John overseer Holmes Mfg
Munn James supt weaving Whitman Mills h 191 Collette
Munroe Arthur D piper 125 Middle h 163 Pleasant [avenue
" Charles C painter h 32 Acushnet
" Cynthia W widow Joseph P G h 32 Acushnet avenue
" Florian weaver b 751 S Water
" Helen widow Richard h 47 Bowditch
" John junk 300 Middle h do
" John overseer N B S Co h 15 Morton court
" John spinner h 85 Mosher
" Joseph plumber h 32 W French av
" Joseph B painter h 16 Willow
" Phillip fixer h 751 Water
" Robert C laborer h 107 Cedar
" see Monroe
Munsey Alice C principal R C Ingraham school h 39 Arch
" George W Jr lawyer 24 Clifford bldg h 461 Mill [County
Munzing Louis C laborer h 1053
Muontrand Leo hairdresser 387 S Water
Murach Joseph picker h 428 S Front
" Peter weaver b 428 S Front
" Stephen weaver b 428 S Front
Murberg Andrew mason b 263 Acushnet av [lette
Murden Roseanna Mrs h 276 Col-
Murdoch Guy L treas 16 Elm h 268 Hawthorn [William
" Paul H clerk foot Willis b 156
Murdock Frederick J tool grinder h 10 Devoll [High
" Sarah M Mrs lodging house 72

F. T. AKIN & CO. PAINTERS AND DECORATORS

Murdy Robert H police h 12 Spooner [N Front
Mureria John laborer bds rear 162
Murgatroyd Abraham carpenter h 13 Ruth
" John died Sept 25 1910
Murkland Annie L teacher R C Ingraham school b 55 Walnut
" James H asst supt bldg 307 Municipal bldg h 55 Walnut
Murnin Arthur J moulder bds 390 Pleasant [ant
" Bernard gardener h 390 Pleas-
Murphy Agnes C b 15 Pope
" Alfred F plumber 87 Union b 167 Grinnell [Rockland
" Alice S widow Robert h 111
" Andrew clerk 438 Purchase h 304 Cedar [mouth
" Angela widow Henry b 111 Dart-
" Ann widow John h 133 N Second
" Annie widow Cornelius J h 220 Summer [dar h do
" Annie Mrs dressmaker 304 Ce-
" Barbara widow Henry h 2 Pope
" Catherine widow Jeremiah h 863 County [ion b 32 Crapo
" Catherine F bookkeeper 163 Un-
" Catherine M widow Timothy J h 167 Grinnell
" Catherine T Mrs h 25 William
" Charles laborer b 10 Old Market square
" Charles F bellman 435 County b 498 Bolton [b 71 Park
" Charles W plumber 28 N Water
" Clara M Mrs h 42 N Sixth
" Cornelius D liquors 166 Coffin av rms 119 Kempton
" Cornelius H (C H Murphy & Son) h 314 County
" C Henry Jr (C H Murphy & Son) h 431 Mill
MURPHY C H & SON (Cornelius H and C Henry) stable 40 and 42 Fourth See page 771
" Daniel F blacksmith h 208 Nash road
" Daniel F carpenter h 273 Cedar
" Daniel J conductor h 274 Pope
" Daniel T shoemaker b 116 Robeson
" David W foreman h 224 North
" Dennis J compositor Standard h 184 Middle

Murphy
" Edward h 32 Crapo
" Edward drawtender h 112 Fourth
" Edward reserve police h 5 Reynolds [Purchase rms do
" Edward D asst undertaker 235
" Edward F clerk 59 Linden h 168 Austin [do
" Edward H painter 112 Fourth h
" Edward L reporter Times h 87 Elm [niman
" Elizabeth widow David h 66 Pen-
" Elizabeth A stenographer 57 N Second h 29 Keene
" Elizabeth F Mrs dressmaker 53 Kempton h do
" Elizabeth U bookkeeper 132 Union b 314 County
" Florence A clerk 307 Municipal bldg b 133 N Second
" Francis A police h 285 Cedar
" Frank A clerk b 167 Grinnell
" Frank E sales 94 Union b 498 Bolton [County
" Frank T clerk 58 Linden b 721
" Fred E stableman 42 Fourth h 55 Ward [Smith
" Frederick M brakeman h 181
" George F b 209 Cedar Grove [ty
" Helna M bookkeeper b 314 Coun-
" Isabel F stenographer 34 Masonic bldg b 275½ County
" James laborer h 136 Blackmer
" James student b 66 Penniman
" James A druggist 409 Rivet b 314 County
" James C piper h 284 Fourth
" James F plumber 87 Union h 167 Grinnell
" James H died June 28 1911
" James P laborer h 218 N Second
" Jane A teacher G H Dunbar school h 301 Arnold
" Jennie h 275 Cedar Grove
" Jeremiah clerk b 133 N Second
" Johanna widow William J b 834 County
" John h 209 Cedar Grove
" John copper worker b 66 Penniman [Winsor
" John engineer Parker House h 64
" John laborer h 92 Oak [Glover
" John repairman U St Ry Co h 15
" John roofer b 39 Bowditch

To do things right you must be taught. Our instructors can do it.
Kinyon's Commercial School
Odd Fellows Bldg., Cor. William and Pleasant Sts., New Bedford, Mass.

Murphy
" John speeder tender b 93 Tallman
" John E clerk b 209 Cedar Grove
" John F news stand R R Depot h at Boston
" John H blacksmith h 32 Crapo
" John H janitor Parker st school h 184 Ashland
" John J laborer h 301 Arnold
" John W warper b 863 County
" Joseph A testman 57 N Second b 167 Grinnell [Chancery
" Joseph T mgr 42 Front h 31
" Lawrence J clerk 1 Pleasant h 15 Ash (S)
" Lillie Mrs h 275½ County
" Lucy M stenographer 96 William rm 11 b 111 Rockland
" Luke weaver h 138 Davis
" Margaret widow Arthur H h 1 Reeds ct[school b 184 Ashland
" Margaret T C teacher Middle st
" Mary Mrs b 53 Hillman
" Mary widow Patrick h 24 Independent
" Mary widow Peter h 93 Tallman
" Mary A clerk 160 Purchase b 419 Chancery [al b do
" Mary A nurse St Luke's Hospit-
" Mary E forwoman 47 William b 301 Arnold
" Maurice J telegrapher Acushnet av n William rms 188 Purchase [ond
" Michael gardener rms 66 N Sec-
" Michael J Mrs h 71 Park
" Myra G Mrs h 286 Mill
" Nellie E supervisor 57 N Second b 208 Nash rd [Bolton
" Nellie M widow Dennis E b 498
" Owen engineer b 350 S Second
" Patrick engineer h 350 Elm
" Patrick gardener h 419 Chancery
" Patrick laborer b 259 N Front
" Patrick H clerk 1130 Acushnet av b 209 Cedar Grove [92 Oak
" Paul V lino operator Standard b
" Peter bricklayer h 134 Tallman
" Philip F glass worker h 50 Short
" Philip J removed to St Louis Mo
" Richard J drill maker b 1 Reeds court
" Richard J operative h 103 Austin

Murphy
" Samuel clerk h 883 S Water
" Thomas A carpenter h 332 Cedar
" Thomas E steamfitter b 53 Kempton [721 County
" Thomas J grocer 58 Linden h
" Thomas J installer 57 N Second b 220 Summer
" Timothy J undertaker 235 Purchase rms 69 S Sixth [Oak
" Ursula M clerk 182 Union b 92
" Victoria widow John dressmaker Arcade rm 25 b 206 Hathaway
" William E R R car inspector h 275½ County
" William H (Ashton & Murphy) 1109 S Water h 111 Rockland

Murray Agnes E clerk 68 Adams b 526 Kempton
" Amelia A teacher H A Kempton school b 246 Hillman[h 483 do
" Anthony J liquors 376 Kempton
" Charles laborer h 14 Abbott
" Edward agent b 112 Bonney
" Frances G teacher Harrington school b 104 Austin
" Frank G storekeeper 57 N Second
" Frank J watchman h 10 McMurray ter [burn
" George F machinist h 52 Wash-
" George H motorman h 184 Ashland [Bonney
" Hannah M widow John W h 112
" Hugh second hand b 507 Bowditch
" Hugh A doffer b 203 Tinkham
" James J weaver h 126 Whitman
" James T ad writer Standard h 18 Emerson (S)
" Joanna widow John b 406 Allen
" John F second hand h 1098 Acushnet av
" John J laborer h 204 Weld
" John J weaver b 7 Austin ct
" John P doffer b r 203 Tinkham
" John W carpenter b 294 Cedar
" Joseph h 291 S Second
" Joseph C capt tugboat J T Sherman h 246 Hillman
" Joseph D clerk Holmes Mfg Co h 2 E Durfee [ham
" Joseph P joiner b r 203 Tink-
" Katherine Mrs speeder h 622 Purchase [45 Dartmouth
" Lauchlan W foreman 100 Fifth h

Bread, Cake, Pastry
RICHMOND & COMPANY 255-257 UNION STREET
Bell 993 Automatic 1022

Murray
" Margaret A widow Jeremiah matron 396 Middle (W) b do
" Margaret E widow Hugh h r 203 Tinkham
" Mary Mrs h 81 Maxfield
" Mary Mrs bakery 292 Cedar av h 294 do [Chancery
" Michael J clerk 124 Union h 205
" Patrick laborer b 307 Collette
" Patrick weaver h 7 Austin ct
" Peter fireman h 104 Austin
" Thomas mill hand h 23 Howland Village
" Thomas mill hand b 95 Dunbar
" Thomas weaver h 59 Willard
" Thomas F carder h 46 Robeson
" Thomas J spinner h 95 Dunbar
" Thomas P laborer h 294 Cedar
" William b 46 Robeson [Robeson
" William A boss comber b 46
" William B grinder h 7 Devoll
" William C copper 350 S Second h 216 Rockland
" William E clerk 904 Acushnet av b 203 Tinkham [mer
" William F overseer h 294 Sum-
" William J clerk h 806 Rockdale avenue
" Winifred G Mrs b 526 Kempton
Murty Thomas operative h 192 Division [W French av
Musgrave Frederick spinner bds 24
Muspratt Annie J h 87½ S Sixth
" John compositor b 87½ S Sixth
Myer John weaver h 126 Tallman
" Wilfred carpenter b 815 First
Myers Albert F buyer 185 Union h 665 County
" George overseer Bennett Mill variety 319 Bowditch h 128 Hathaway
" Michael H laborer h 315 Middle
" Sarah R seamstress b 315 Middle
" Wiloughy O mat board gilder 92 Newton rms at Fairhaven
Myerson Isaac rem to N Y city
Mylotte Edward teamster h 222 N Second [N Second
Myrick Chester L carpenter h 520
" Ellen J bookkeeper 38 N Second b 43 Fifth [Eighth
" Emma C widow Walter h 13

Nadeau Arthur teamster b 31 Bentley
" Delia widow John h 48 Davis
" George operative b 31 Bentley
" John B weaver h 19 Peckham
" Joseph loom fixer h 239 Sawyer
" Joseph Jr weaver b 239 Sawyer
" Joseph C slasher h 1030 Acushnet av
" Napoleon mason h 74 Division
" Oscar blacksmith h 178 Phillips avenue [Bentley
" Victorine widow John B h 31
Naden Smith fixer b 336 Tinkham
Naegele August laborer h 104 Sidney [Water
Nagueira Joseph operative h 723
Naiman Hosheia plasterer h 34 Penniman [mony
Nairn Mary J widow h 8 Har-
Nall Albert clerk b 113 Fourth
Nannery Joseph h 148 Hillman
Nano Brahim mill hand h 45 Phillips av [b 343 Purchase
Nansett Laura laundress 435 County
" Mary A Mrs h 343 Purchase
Napoleon Louis speeder h 21 Acushnet av [mer
Nareimento Anna Mrs h 72 Black-
Nardini Giovanni fruit Union cor Pleasant b 274 Mill [State
Nary Alice Mrs demonstrator h 163
" William weaver h 12 Independent
Nascimento Antonio mill hand b 36 Howland Village
Nash Clara J widow Thomas N h 1715 Acushnet av
NASH ROAD WET WASH LAUNDRY Joseph C Roy prop 95 Nash road See page 787
Nashawena Mills Co William B Gardner treas Belleville av opposite Belleville rd
Naski Zeska laborer h 666 First
Nason Edna E teacher Hosea M Knowlton school b 74 Sycamore [ond
National Biscuit Co 14-16 N Sec-
" Cash Register Co 37 Purchase rm 19
NATIONAL DETECTIVE AGENCY The 49 Westminster Providence R I See page 28

GLOBE DYE HOUSE 220 SHAWMUT AVE.
J. N. J. LONHOLDT, PROP. Telephone Connections Goods called for and Delivered
Down town Office. 52 Pleasant St., Room 1 North End Office, 1014 Acushnet Ave.

National
" Ice Cream Co (John Bromides and Athan Sanopulus) 580 N Front [Sawyer
" Theatre (Joseph Tabbas) 269
NATIONAL WET WASH LAUNDRY CO Audette & Chapdelaine props 281 Sawyer See page 787
Nault Calixte police Station 5 h 300 Sawyer
" Joseph P died May 30 1911
" Louis teamster h 300 Sawyer
" Louis weaver h 80 Hope
" Marcel mill hand b 80 Hope
" Octave h 153 N Front
" Omer mill hand b 80 Hope
" Philias weaver b 80 Hope
" Pierre Mrs h 300 Sawyer
" Pierre N died June 12 1911
" Pierre N Jr clerk 36 Purchase b 300 Sawyer [Front
" Telesphore operative bds 135 N
Navasey James W second hand h 103 Hazard
Navinsky Nathan tailor 593 Purchase h 45 Bowditch [Hillman
Naylor Charles F salesman h 32
" Smith plumber h 22 Roosevelt
" Susie M Mrs bookkeeper 1031 Acushnet av h 32 Hillman
Nedeau Joseph G woodcutter h rear 1030 Acushnet av
Neagus Albert C shipper h 112 Willis [man
" Charles E shoemaker b 157 Hill-
" Clarence clerk b 157 Hillman
" Edward C mason h 157 Hillman
" Edward C Jr driver b 157 Hillman
" George spinner h 300 Sawyer
" Hugh B piper h 439 Allen
" Inez E stenographer 87 Union b at N Dartmouth
" John P engineer 350 S Second h 166 Washington
" Melvin E ticket collector Hathaway's Theatre rms 60 Mechanic's lane
" see Negus [h 56 Ash (S)
Neal Charles A dentist 155 Union
" Frank weaver b 211 Hathaway
" John A bookkeeper 47 School h 643 County
" John A spinner h 46 Ashley
Neale George H paving cutter h 71 Emma [man
Nealey William painter b 217 Hill-
Neary Annie E b 285 Middle [Middle
" Bridget M widow Michael b 285
" John R fixer b 5 Cornell pl
" Stephen F second hand h 5 Cornell place
Needham Alfred spinner h 44 Fruit
" John W laborer h 16 Rodney
" Joseph laborer h 16 Marvin
Neenan Edward clerk 821 S Water h 10 Acushnet av [sion
" Mary widow John h 136 Divi-
" Thomas laborer h 631 First
Neglia Tony laborer h 30 Welcome
Negus Alonzo laborer 144 S Water h at Dartmouth
" Elmer J paymaster Union St Ry Co Purchase cor William b at Smith Mills [Florence
" Herbert E driver 50 Elm h 124
" Ida T stenographer 6 Masonic bldg h at Clifford
" Lewis D F electric trimmer 125 Middle h 228 Pleasant
" Mahala S T widow Ira S Nat Cor L of the G A R h 155 Campbell [dle h 343 Cedar
" Southworth P meterman 125 Mid-
" see Neagus
Neil Warren bricklayer rms Y M C A
Neild Charles L machinist b 51 State
" Eli supt Booth Mill h 12 Bentley [h 371 Bowditch
" Ernest overseer Neild M Corp
" Frank I supt Neild M Corp h 54 State [State
" John agent Neild M Corp h 51
" John draftsamn b 12 Bentley
" Mfg Corp silk mfrs Nash rd cor Brooks
" see Nield
Neill Margaret Mrs h 6 McGurk
Nelson Anders glasworker b 2 Cornell court [sor
" Annie widow James h 113 Win-
" Bessie M Mrs cashier 97 William rm 310 h 1 Hemlock
" Bros (Walter H and Fred S) masons 316 S Second
" Carl upholsterer 9 Rodman rms 129 Fourth [ry b 67 James
" Carl A linotpye operator Mercu-
" Daniel E mason b 99 South
" Edward removed to Boston

GREENE & WOOD Every Kind of LUMBER AND MILL WORK
PINE STREET, off So. WATER STREET, NEW BEDFORD

Nelson
" Emma widow Nicholas h 309 Kempton [place
" Francis H patternmaker b 5 Park
" Frank drillworker h 154 Thompson [Robeson
" Frank machinist 15 Fourth h 91
" Frank L foreman 57 N Second h 39 Pierce [amore
" Frank W teamster b 114 Syc-
" Frederick S (Nelson Bros) h 43 Sherman
" Henry J weaver h 146 Collette
" Hilda M W telephone operator 57 N Second b 3 Kilburn
" Hulda W widow Nels E h 9 Ocean [dar n Parker
" Ida clerk 48 Pleasant b Ce-
" Irene teacher b 9 Ocean
" Isaac laborer h 864 Purchase
" Ivar V glasscutter h r 58 Bedford [146 Collette
" James tinsmith 745 Purchase b
" James weaver h 3 Kilburn
" James Jr clerk P O h 3 Kilburn
" John laborer h 67 James
" John F conductor h 230 Sawyer
" Joseph laborer h 80 Sagamore
" Joseph Jr watchman b 80 Sagamore [b 91 Robeson
" Joseph A cigarmaker 164 Union
" Margaret Mrs h 343 Middle
" Martin S fireman Engine No 5 h 59 Thomas [Kempton
" Mary E clerk 48 Pleasant b 340
" Mason E teamster h 1 Harmony
" McLena widow Hugh h 560 Hathaway rd [Ocean
" Oliver E reporter Standard b 9
" Peter h 5 Park place
" Peter W fixer h 16 Dudley
" Richard b 104 Fifth
" Robert twister b 128 Bonney
" Ruth J bookkeeper C S Knowles b 10 Borden
" Samuel J asst foreman 474 Acushnet av h 1 Hemlock
" Stella clerk b 43 Sherman
" Theresa widow Thomas h 91 Robeson [rms 384 Purchase
" Walter B foreman C S Knowles
" Walter H (Nelson Bros) h 10 Borden
" William carpenter h 58 Bedford
" William foreman rms 2 Seventh

Nelson
" William weaver h 119 Brock av
" William O fireman h 69 Ash (S)
" William N Mason 46 Oak h do
" William W physician 384 Kempton h do [fin av
Nemec Charles brakeman h 353 Cof-
" Christine widow Frank h 353 Coffin av
" Norbert fixer h 361 Davis
" Wenzel brakeman h 193 Dean
Nerbonne Alfred lunch h 54 Ash (N)
" Delia (Faford & Nerbonne) 49 Brock av b 127 Ruth [Cottage
" H Arthur barber 152 Union b 615
" Joseph lunch cart Purchase cor Weld h 64 Newton [net av
" Joseph operative h 868 Acush-
" Melissa widow Benonie bds 127 Ruth
" Pierre lunch 233 Purchase and Acushnet av c Barker's court h at Watertown [615 Cottage
" William hairdresser 152 Union h
" Zephirine inspector b 615 Cottage
Nesbet James Jr second hand b 168 Cove [h do
Nesbett Norman B dentist 331 Union
" Ralph W clerk Kilburn Mill h 27 Sycamore
Nesmith Bessie L teacher Abraham Lincoln school b 245 Palmer
Netcher George F h 211 Kempton
" Helen E b 211 Kempton
Neto John M laborer h 59 Kempton
" Joseph operative h 322 S Front
Netto Antonio M died April 11 1911
" Frances widow Antonio M h 128 Dartmouth [chase
Neveaux Joseph weaver h 843 Pur-
" Joseph A weaver b 843 Purchase
Neves Andre watchmaker 509 S Water h r 63 Grinnell [1910
" Antone G DeS Rev died Nov 11
" Antonio Mrs h 83 Washington
" Augustus third hand h 101 Potomska
" Fortunato Rev h 94 S Sixth
" Frank telephone operator 45 Purchase rm 4 b 21 Crapo
" John S weaver h 83 Winsor
" Joseph bottler 277 S Second b 61 Fifth
" Joseph fireman h 238 S Second

BONNEY, FOLSTER & CO.,
The North End's Shopping Centre
Dry Goods and Men's Furnishings
945-947 Acushnet Ave., New Bedford, Mass.

Neves
" Joseph R real estate h 82 Independent [Babbitt
" Manuel A hairdresser 1 Oak h 51
" Manuel A Jr operative b 51 Babbitt
" Manuel G h 6 Lindsey
Neville Catherine clerk 70 Purchase b 382 North
" James W foreman h 382 North
" Mary widow Daniel H h 487 Acushnet av
" Samuel spinner h 130 Crapo
" Thomas weaver b 52 Winsor
Nevins James weaver b 67 Coffin av
New Bedford Art Studio 25 Purchase
NEW BEDFORD AUTO CO G L Murdoch treas 16 Elm See page 741
" Bedford Board of Fire Underwriters 37 Purchase rm 27
" Bedford Board of Trade 97 William rm 202
" Bedford Boiler & Machine Co (Clark W Holcomb) 42 Front
" Bedford Bottling Co (Ike Abrahamson soda waters 32 Morton court
" Bedford Box & Shook Co Princeton av near Railroad
" Bedford Children's Aid Society 12 Market [Middle
" Bedford Co-operative Bank 125
" Bedford Cordage Co 131 Court
" Bedford Cotton Mills Corp 295 Phillips av [ion
" Bedford Daily Mercury 112 Un-
" Bedford Day Nursery 16 Howard and 298 County [Second
" Bedford Despatch Express 4 N
" Bedford Dry Goods Co 182 to 190 Union
" Bedford Eagle Bottling Co r 234½ N Front [Purchase
" Bedford Emergency Hospital 194
" Bedford Extractor Co fertilizer works Shawmut av beyond Hathaway road
NEW BEDFORD FISH CO Inc City pier No 4 and end Merrill's wharf See advt Fish in Business Directory
NEW BEDFORD FIVE CENTS SAVINGS BANK 37 Purchase See page 5
" Bedford Foundry & Machine Co 272 S Water
" Bedford Free Public Library Pleasant between William and Market [den) 43 Weld
" Bedford Furniture Co (F M Wee-
" Bedford Gas and Edison Light Co 125 Middle works 214 S Water [Middle (W)
" Bedford Home for Aged 396
NEW BEDFORD ICE CO George H Paul treas office and depot 12 School See page 773
" Bedford Industrial School 87 N Water
NEW BEDFORD INSTITUTION FOR SAVINGS George H Batchelor treas 174-178 Union See page 9
" Bedford Loan Co 37 Purchase rm 25
" Bedford Martha's Vineyard & Nantucket Steamboat Co C G Whiton agent 7 Commercial
" Bedford Packing Co (LaFrance Bros) beef 222 Cedar Grove
" Bedford Paper & Supply Co (Jacob H Robinson) 71-73 Union
" Bedford Printing Co (W G Hamlen T Brady and D J Kelleher) 25 N Second
" Bedford Public Warehouse School cor Water
" Bedford Pumping Station c Purchase and Cedar Grove
" Bedford Reed Co (J D and M D Martine) mfrs reeds and slasher combs 189 N Water
" Bedford Reform and Relief Association 180 Allen
" Bedford Rubber Co (James W Cross pres) rubber goods and oil clothing 66 William
NEW BEDFORD SAFE DEPOSIT & TRUST CO The 61 William See page 8
" Bedford Shuttle Co A G Seabury mgr 6 Elm
" Bedford Specialty Co wholesale grocers cor N Front and Kenyon Archambeault Arthur prop h 64 Kenyon

Painters Supplies Wall Papers Room Mouldings Ladders
M. P. B. Silva & Son BRUSHES
157 ACUSHNET AVENUE Both Phones **NEW BEDFORD**

New
" Bedford Stained Glass & Crystal Window Co (H O Firme) 164 County
NEW BEDFORD STEAM CARPET BEATING AND RUG CO (H M Maine) North cor N Water See front cover
NEW BEDFORD STEAM DYE HOUSE William E Smith prop 53 William works 45 Hunter See page 768
NEW BEDFORD STEAM LAUNDRY F G Tripp prop 128 and 130 Pleasant See front cover
NEW BEDFORD STORAGE WAREHOUSE CO 352-378 Sawyer See back binding and page 35
" Bedford Tallow Co r 182 N Water
" Bedford Textile Co (C R Gidley treas) textile banding 1 E Pope
NEW BEDFORD TEXTILE SCHOOL 303-331 Purchase See page 36
" Bedford Theatre 249-253 Union
NEW BEDFORD TIMES Charles G Wood publisher Times bldg 120 Purchase See page 759
" Bedford Tow Boat Co Merrill's wharf [ter
" Bedford V F A High cor Fos-
" Bedford Waste Co J L Dexter treas cotton waste 58 Middle
" Bedford Water Works office 40 Masonic bldg repair shop 213 N Water
" Bedford Welding Co (Frederick A Gardner 177 N Water
" Bedford Yacht Club Fairhaven bridge [chase cor William
" Bedford & Onset St Ry Co Pur-
" England Comb Works (Vera & Curry props) 120 S Sixth
" England Cotton Yarn Co (Bennett dept 1-2-3-4) 115 Coggeshall (Rotch dept 7-8) Orchard (S) beyond Rivet (N B Spinning Co dept 9-10) North near N Water
" England Navigation Co The office 2 Union [Purchase
" Process Gas & Supply Co 211
" York Cloak Store 1097 Acushnet avenue

New
" York Furniture Store (Joseph M Lima) 180 Acushnet av
NEW YORK MARKET (E A Hoxie) 251 Purchase See page 772
" York, N H & H R R depot foot Pearl freight office foot Willis ferry foot Union N Y freight office 2 do
" York Upholstering Co (Max Berman and Haime Eidlin) 757 Purchase [George
Newby Jabez second hand h 17
Newcastle Lena M teacher High school rms 175 William
Newcomb Ada widow William J h 18 Mill [chase
" James card grinder h 1183 Pur-
" John removed to Milwaukee Wis
" Mary widow William b 23 Oak
" William J died Feb 23 1911
Newel Mary L died Nov 23 1910
Newell Annie S widow b 57 North
" John fitter b 336 Coffin avenue
Newhall Louise M teacher Hosea M Knowlton school rms 232 Pleasant [Cottage
Newman Anthony confectioner h 592
" Charles overseer Wamsutta Mill h 255 Chestnut
" Charles weaver h 27 Austin
" Otto W awning maker 126 Arnold h do
" see Neuman
Newmark Boris watch maker 79 William h 125 Belleville av
Newsham Charles J removed to San Francisco Cal
" Enoch bds 9 Acorn
" John operative h 213 Belleville av
" Joseph spinner h 155 Earle
" Robert spinner h 9 Acorn
" Sarah widow James h 27 Clark
Newton Archie variety 142 Davis h do [school h 390 Union
" Cora A principal Harrington
" Henry mill hand h 117 Eugenia
" Isaac laborer h 49 Beech
" James W weaver h 12 Cleveland
" Joseph third hand h 3 Acushnet block
" Samuel clerk h 21 Marvin
" Thomas weaver h 113 Austin [av
" William weaver h 23 Woodlawn

Steiger-Dudgeon Co.
"The WOMAN'S Store."
Tel. Bell 82 & 83, Branches connecting all depts.
" " 160 For Office only. Auto. 1211

SUMPTIONS, ASSORTMENTS AT ALL TIMES OF DEPENDABLE DRY GOODS

Newton
" William J bds 98 Brock avenue
Neyland Harry A artist h 66 Russell
Nicholas Daniel shoemaker 413 S Water h 412 First [(S)
" Philomena widow h 398 Orchard
Nichols Andrew F shoe cutter h 39 Bullock [land h do
" Andrew J shoe repairer 96 Ash-
" Charles M shoemaker rms 133 Kempton
" Clifton laborer h 34 Vine
" Francis h 113 Bedford
" Georgia Mrs clerk b 34 Bonney
" Grace U kindergarten T A Greene school bds 57 State [Vine
" Harry G clerk 819 Purchase h 24
" Henry W supt New Bedford Textile school h 57 State
" John J laborer h 128 Ash (N)
" Joseph M bds 4 Walnut [vin
" Joseph W painter h r 20 Mar-
" Leander P (Nichols & Damon) h 49 North
" Manuel carder h 480 S Second
" Rebecca L nurse b 17 Richmond
" Sarah A died Oct 2 1910 [42 Hill
" Walter R clerk 14 N Sixth rms
" & Damon (L P Nichols and F H Damon) shoes 103 William
Nicholson Edward F treas Union St Ry Co h 433 Cottage [lard
" Isabelle widow Miles h 136 Bul-
" John cloth presser h 48 Winsor
" John pedlar h 450 First
" John third hand b 9 Ashley
" John B bds 433 Cottage
NICHOLSON JOHN G lumber 27-35 Bowditch h 115 Hillman See foot lines
" John J machinist h 130 Norman
" Joseph lunch 423 Rivet b 436 do
" Michael third hand b 126 Eugenia
" Thomas mill hand b 154 Whitman
" Thomas operative h 12 Ashley
Nickerson Abbie F widow Maranda R h 137 Kempton [155 Hillman
" Alberto S cleaner 229 N Water h
" Alice E clerk bds 115 Cedar
" Charles E removed from city
" Charles F police h 290 Pleasant
" Dean B teamster Standard Oil Co h at Fairhaven

Nickerson
" Elmer operative bds 6 Jenney
" Frank E chauffeur h 38 Walnut
" Frederick U h 404 Court [mouth
" George S removed to S Dart-
" Gilbert K clerk h 318 Pleasant
" Hattie T bottler W F Frye bds 137 Kempton
" James foreman b 290 Purchase
" John operative b 24 Peckham
" Joseph A fisherman h 114 Grinnell
" Mary J widow George bds 75 Kempton [Jenney
" Minnie L widow Charles E h 6
" Rena D Mrs clerk 73 William h 170 Pleasant
" Sylvanus E freight handler Electric Express b 114 Grinnell
" Thomas died Jan 5 1911
" William J physician 164 Middle h
" William W shoemaker h 262 Cottage
Nicklas Frank J h 23 Fair
" John oiler h 75 Clark
" John J driver 68 Adams h 379 Coggeshall
" Joseph W (C H & H A Lawton Co) 113 Union h 109 Hawthorn
" see Nicholas
Nickerson James loom fixer h 24 Peckham [burn
Nicola Ademand laborer b 8 Black-
" Kitas mill hand b 54 Davis
" Vanziel mill hand h 11 Nye
Nicolol Deom laborer h 8 Blackburn
Nicolos Gligor mill hand b 16 Bullard
Nicolou Mary h 70 Forest
Niech Antone operative h 259 Belleville av [Bullard
Niedzwiechi Joseph operative h 132
Nield Charles mill hand h 1537 Acushnet av
" Ellis mill hand b 31 Juniper
" William A physician 62 Fifth h do [ton ct
Nietch Clemens laborer h 17 Hamp-
Nightingale Joseph weaver h 28 Woodlawn av
" Margaret Mrs b 14 Cleveland
" Robert weaver h 25 Social [cial
" William operative bds 25 So-
Nil Francois motorman b 59 Clark
Niles William fixer h 76 Cove

PELEG H. SHERMAN 506 COUNTY ST.
FUNERAL DIRECTOR AND EMBALMER
OFFICE PHONES. Bell 690-13. Auto. 1305.
RESIDENCE PHONES. Bell 690-12. Auto. 1306.

Niles
" William H carpenter h 606 Cottage [Co h 380 Court
Nilson John A engineer Page Mfg
" Nils carpenter b 72 Chancery
Ninze Manuel laborer h 390½ S Second [Front
Niquette Oliver carpenter h 550 N
Nisbet Ernest joiner b 13 Ashley
" James third hand h 13 Ashley
" James Jr second hand b 168 Cove
" William clerk 765 Purchase h 25 Winsor [shnet av
Nisbett George spinner h 63 Acu-
" Robert mill hand h 65 Acushnet avenue
" William joiner h 25 Winsor
" see Nesbett [chase h 557 do
Nisson Herman shoe repairer 517 Pur-
" Louis grocer 474 S Water h do
Nistele Charles E clerk 1103 Acushnet av h 485 Coggeshall
Nixon Alfred J physician 84 Acushnet av h do
Noblits George clerk b 30 George
Noble Catherine Mrs corsets and hair goods 1049 Acushnet av h 110 Hathaway
" Herbert weaver h 31 Viall
" Isaac C fitter h 110 Hathaway
" Jane E bakery 68 Cove h 66 do
" John W loom fixer h 89 Dunbar
" Joseph hairdresser 711 Kempton h 140 Florence
" Thomas b 66 Cove [vid
Noblet Alfred machinist h 170 Da-
" George clerk h 30 George
Noel Albert clerk 195 Fourth h 113 do [195 Bowditch
" Albert E clerk 57 N Second bds
" Blanch spinner b 86 Davis
" Desire weaver h 2 Jean
" Joseph removed to Fall River
" Nelson real estate h 195 Bowditch
" Philomen mill hand b 86 Davis
" Samuel barber 78 William h at Dartmouth
Nofftz Richard E florist 106 William and 961 Kempton h 969 do
Noia Frank carpenter b 79 County
" Henry clerk b 79 County
" Manuel C laborer 144 S Water h at Fairhaven
" Manuel L h 79 County

Noia
" Manuel L grocer 135 Rockland h 137 do
" see Noyer [Chancery
Nokelski Martin glasscutter h 62
Nolan Andrew laborer b 22 Holly
" Francis screwmaker b 158 Nash road
" Henry laborer b 22 Holly [ty
" Henry twister tender b 958 Coun-
" Henry weaver h 447 First
" James tailor h 158 Nash road
" James J druggist 862 Purchase b 958 County [22 Holly
" Jane widow Alex boarding house
" Joseph operative b 958 County
" Margaret M widow John h 40 Cove
" Mary J housekeeper 958 County
" Philip screwmaker b 158 Nash road
" Samuel painter h 958 County
" see Nowlan
Noland Bessie M teacher I W Benjamin school b at Fairhaven
Nolet Joseph A salesman 80 William h 90 Robeson [av
" Samuel teamster h 833 Acushnet
Nolin Benjamin weaver h 229 Sawyer
" Donat lather b 36 Hicks
" Edward weaver b 229 Sawyer
" Elodie Mrs h 36 Hicks
" Fabien fisherman b 14 Beetle
" Honorine carpenter b 180 Davis
" Joseph third hand h 146 Bullard
" Joseph Jr clerk 92½ Purchase h 268 Weld
" Louis weaver h 287 N Front
" Napoleon h 131 N Front
" Napoleon A second hand b 146 Bullard [Front
" N Mrs boarding house 131 N
" Ovedus carpenter h 180 Davis
" Pierre carpenter 180 Davis h do
Nonquitt Spinning Co Andrew J Currier agent Belleville av n Hatch [Weld
Noon Ellen widow Martin h 182
" Fernando ropemaker h 258 S Second
" James mill hand h 23 Beetle
" John T laborer b 182 Weld
" Martin laborer b 182 Weld

COAL AND WOOD F. T. AKIN & COMPANY
HAY AND STRAW
WALNUT, COR. WATER, 84 PLEASANT ST., 25 WELD SQ.
129 COVE STREET WHF. FOOT OF COFFIN STREET

Noonan Anna widow John b 1140 Acushnet av [yer
" Dennis E produce h 447 Saw-
" Edward assistant mgr 140 Purchase b 139 Merrimac
" John city laborer b 68 Hazard
" John T h 68 Hazard
" Joseph doffer h 4 Wamsutta
" Luke V cable splicer 57 N Second bds 113 Fourth
" Mary h 68 Hazard [Merrimac
" Mary J widow Edward D h 139
" Michael bottler b 4 Wamsutta
" Thomas park police h 165 Bates avenue
" Thomas J machinist h 173 Allen
Nooning Belle F bookkeeper 32 Pleasant bds 127 Summer [Morgan
" Hannah H widow William B h 86
Nooth William E laborer h 53 Cedar
Norcross John driver h 389 Bolton
" Lucius helper 28 N Water
" Olivia H teacher William H Taylor school b 84 School [len
Nordmark August carpenter h 410 Al-
Noreau Wilfred operative b r 63 Tallman
Norlander Albert machinist Prospect near Howland bds 322 Austin
" Charles h 169 Shawmut av
" Charles D teamster h 328 Austin
Normand Philip weaver h 24 Warren
" Narcisse machinist h 1 Rotch blk 434 Bolton
" Wilfred engineer h 163 David
Normandeau Alfred machinist b 578 Mt Pleasant [578 Mt Pleasant
" Arthur clerk 1081 Acushnet av h
" Fred U lamplighter h 578 Mt Pleasant [578 Mt Pleasant
" Mary D tailoress 46 Purchase b
" Octave b 578 Mt Pleasant
Normandin Ademor A fish 248 Sawyer h 235 do
" Adline h 50 Ashley
" Alcide clerk b 28 Holly
" Alfred J clerk 598 Purchase b do
" Alphonse (A Normandin & Co) and physician 37 Purchase rm 9 h 18 Linden
" A & Co (Alphonse Normandin and Hilaire Therrien) druggists 122 North Front

Normandin
" Camile h 10 Cornell place
" Cordelia milliner h 54 Holly
" Emile removed to Woonsocket R I
" Francois X h 28 Holly
" Frank fireman S B brewery h 167 Cedar Grove
" Fred laborer h 59 King
" John b 10 Cornell place
" Joseph clerk b 164 Cedar Grove
" Joseph weaver h 54 Holly
" Joseph E grocer 1404 Acushnet av b 10 Cornell place
" Leo operative b 164 Cedar Grove
" Louis Z physician 584 Purchase and druggist 598 do h 586 do
" Narcisse h 164 Cedar Grove
" Nelson weaver b 164 Cedar Grove
" Romeo J clerk 598 Purchase h 596 do
" Romeo P carpenter b 28 Holly
Normile James weaver h 134 Division
" Thomas weaver h 161 Division
" William P janitor N B Textile school b 6 Cove road
Norris Albert W laborer h 23 Woodlawn avenue
" Alfred laborer h 90 Austin
" Edward machinist h 19 Hazard ct
" Edward weaver h 13 Salisbury
" George B spinner h 188 Belleville road
" James weaver 59 Willow
" Joseph spinner b 43 Highland
" Joseph A linotype operator
" Standard h 113 Grinnell [erine
" Mary widow John b 43 Kath-
" Robert laborer b 25 Bolton road
" Thomas B mgr 84 Pleasant h 33 Keene [ter
" Thomas W weaver h 5 Ashland
" William employee P Co h 10 Harmony
" William N restaurant 171 Purchase h 325 Kempton [Second
Norse H A sign painter rms 7 North
North End Day Nursery 16 Howard
NORTH END GARAGE (A E Perron) 115 and 117 Bowditch See page 741
" End Hardware and Furniture Co (Manuel L Sylvia) 1147 Acushnet avenue

Don't dream of what you are going to do! Go and do it.
Kinyon's Short-hand School
Odd Fellows Bldg., Cor. William and Pleasant Sts., New Bedford, Mass.

NORTH END LAUNDRY CO 1066 County See page 786
" End Loan Association 1307 Acushnet avenue
" End Pharmacy (T A Davignon) [420 N Front
" End Public Market 838 Purchase
" End Wet Wash Laundry Zephir Bessette manager 1066 County
" George spinner b 850 First
Northcott John W principal Abraham Lincoln school h 8 Robeson
Norton Alidia h 163 Coggeshall
" Annie widow E E bds 66 Willow
" Ansel A B salesman 6 Purchase h 46 Atlantic
" Catherine E stenographer 108 Union b 277 Park
" Catherine L widow Patrick h 526 [Kempton
" Catherine M clerk b 186 Elm
" Charles F driver h 55 Maitland
" Charles H gas fitter h 30 Cove
" Cynthia widow William T h 833 Kempton
" Eliza Mrs h 460 Bolton
" George P teamster h 981 Pur- [chase
" George W glass engraver b 25 Mill
" James clerk bds 277 Park
" James mill hand h 99 Bowditch
" James E drillmaker b 186 Elm
" James F clerk 132 Union b 277 Park
" James H laborer h 186 Elm
" John bds 1137 Acushnet av
" John mule spinner h 457 Sawyer
" John J operative b 457 Sawyer
" Joseph gasfitter bds 30 Cove
" Joseph J gas fitter 115 Cove h do
" Lewis rms 352 Purchase
" Mary E widow William O h 25 [Mill
" Michael laborer h 570 First
" Michael J overseer N B Cotton Mills Corp h 460 Sawyer
" Patrick laborer b 277 Park
" Patrick J pressman Mercury b 186 Elm
" Thomas E foreman 100 Fifth b 61 [Washington
" Thomas J foreman street dept h 52 Locust
" Thomas L boxfitter h 126 River [rd
Norwood Alexander twister h 102 Ruth
" Hamilton molder 229 N Water [h 99 Willard
" James teamster h 56 Cove
" John laborer h 24 Juniper
" Malcolm twister h 513 N Front
" William twister h 857½ First
Nosek Enos operative h 10 Fulton
Notter Julia B widow John h 522 County
Nourse Charles C driver Standard Oil [Co h 198 Rockland
Novick Abraham S tailor 263 Acushnet av h do
Novinsky David laborer b 45 Bow- [ditch
" Nathan tailor h 45 Bowditch
" Zelis dyer 920 Acushnet av h 908 do
Nowakowski Michael operative h 259 [N Front
Nowell Joseph C h 12 Lincoln
" Leonard bowling 1497 Acushnet av h 254 Tinkham
" Samuel J h 51 Seventh
Nowlan Amede fisherman b 11 Holly
" Fabian fisherman b 23 Holly
Noyer George W variety 77 County b do
" John C hairdresser 137 Grinnell [h 189 Fourth
" Ventura C drillworker h 53 Oak
Noyes Benjamin C h r 77 Linden
Nudd Alice T sec St Luke's Hospital b 31 Ash (S)
" Frederick D asst undertaker 506 County h 31 Ash (S)
Nulman Herman I tailor 139 Purchase h do
Nulty John painter b 63 Forest
Nune James mill hand b 37 Phillips avenue
Nunes Antone laborer 144 S Water h [334 S Front
" Antone F carpenter b 61 Bedford
" Antonio mill hand b 36 Howland Village
" Antonio C laborer h 36 Jenney
" George J drillworker h 358 Orchard (S)
" Joaquim removed from city
" John laborer h r 435 S Water
" John S weaver h 457 Rivet
" Joseph b 148 Belleville av
" Joseph F mill hand h 248 Bow- [ditch
" Joseph S carpenter h 3 Devoll
" Manuel operative h 2 Rotch blk 434 Bolton
" Manuel A Jr mill hand bds 36 [Howland Village

HASKELL BROS. DEALERS IN
ICE
400 COURT STREET TELEPHONE CONNECTION NEW BEDFORD, MASS.

Nunes
" Manuel B carpenter h 175 Division
" Mary h 614 S Water [Second
" Mary C widow Joseph h 329 S
" Mary J widow Manuel J h 64 Washington [lock
" M Clarence carpenter h 28 Bul-
" Paul S laborer N B W W h 58 Grinnell
Nure Harchif mill hand b 54 Davis
" James mill hand h 54 Davis
Nurses Home 321 Union
Nuttall Burt fitter h 1627 Acushnet avenue [road
" Fielding laborer b 56 Belleville
" Edward weaver b 850 First
" George fireman h 150 Nash rd
" James H druggist 146 Arnold h 43 Willis [ditch
" Jane widow William h 156 Bow-
" Wilfred weaver h 351 Sawyer
" William weaver b 156 Tallman
" William weaver h 156 Tallman
Nutter Arthur weaver h 188 Austin
" Joseph weaver h 105 Davis
" Simeon weaver b 38 Bowditch
Nye Annie L C Mrs h 189 Maxfield
" Clark D painter 34 Union h 64 Foster [Purchase
" Dora widow George H h 212
" Edna L telephone operator 57 N Second b 66 Smith
" Ernest B clerk h 340 Kempton
" Evelynn D housekeeper 360 Court
" Fred M clerk 146 Arnold b 324 Park
" Frederick L grocer 156 North rms 111 Summer [23 Arnold pl
" George H supt of cemeteries h
" Isabel M Mrs h 324 Park
" Jane W widow Clement D h 9 Anthony
" Joseph K pres W F Nye estate Fish Island h at Fairhaven
" Lester B shoemaker b 66 Smith
" Mary B milliner b 325 Kempton
" Meribah W widow Franklin b 31 Parker [Smith
" Orlando I clerk 185 Union h 66
" Pemberton H ship agent 2 city pier rms 37 Morgan [County
" Susan C widow Thomas Jr h 709
" Walter D rem from city [land
" William F estate oils Fish Is-

Nye
" William T stereotyper Times h 121 Shawmut av [Fourth
Nyman Ego glassblower h 121½

Oakes Norman W tinsmith 55 N Water h 61 Hill [School
" Rachel T widow John bds 83
" Robert removed from city
Oates Hugh helper b 233 Sawyer
" John F overseer Beacon Mfg Co h 42 Locust [shall
Oatner Henry cooper h 487 Cogge-
Ober Harlan F special agent 12 Market rms Y M C A [rd
Oblonski John mill hand h 114 Nash
O'Brien Addie nurse rms 321 Union
" Anastacia widow Owen h 9 Harrison [b 7 Priscilla
" Annie E stenographer Times
" Annie J h 588 Cottage
" Bridget widow John h 305 Cedar
" Daniel N overseer Potomska Mills h 109 Bonney [do
" Daniel P physician 330 Union h
" Daniel S hairdresser h 41 Arch
" Dennis shoemaker rms 72 High
" Ellen widow h 841 S Water
" Ellen widow William h 113 Hathaway [h 95 S Sixth
" Frank J meter tester 125 Middle
" F Thomas overseer Manomet Mills b 6 Hicks
" George L laborer b 116 Rivet
" James coachman h 7 Priscilla
" James insurance b 191 Bonney
" James teamster bds 920 County
" James J clerk 214 Union h 29 Cedar
" John blacksmith h 30 Locust
" John moving and jobbing h 44 Washburn
" John shoemaker b 30 Locust
" John stoker h 186 Chestnut [av
" John E engineer h 165 Shawmut
" John H clerk 240 Union b 132 State
" John J (rigger) died 1911
" John J teamster h 133 Jenny Lind [den h 101 Robeson
" John N wood and coal 32 Lin-
" John N Jr clerk Times b 101 Robeson
" Joseph shoemaker b 30 Locust
" Joseph F machinist b 116 Rivet

J. F. CROSSLEY 223 MILL STREET COR. EMERSON PHONE
STEAM and HOT WATER HEATING
GAS FITTING and FIXTURES

O'Brien
" Joseph J sexton St James church h 152 Acushnet av
" Mabel B nurse b 321 Union
" Margaret V electrolysis 230 Davis b do [way
" Mary comb tender b 113 Hatha-
" Mary widow Bernard h 116 Rivet
" Mary widow Dennis h 135 Hathaway
" Mary widow Michael b 95 S Sixth
" Mary widow Robert H h 184 State
" Mary L h 305 Cedar
" May L music teacher b 116 Rivet
" Michael foreman h 734 Kempton
" Michael laborer N B W W h 920 County
" Patrick foreman h 76 Florence
" Patrick H laborer 602 Cottage
" Patrick H liquors 438 Purchase h 132 State
" Patrick J shoemaker b 30 Locust
" Robert H laborer b 184 State
" Sanford awningmaker 31 Commercial b 219 Acushnet av
" Thomas laborer h 8 Clark
" Thomas B student b 101 Robeson
" Thomas F overseer b 43 Beetle
" Timothy laborer b 11 Logan
" Timothy F lawyer 71 William b 54 Fourth
" Timothy J clerk 438 Purchase h 11 Reynolds [field
" Timothy J shoemaker h 190 Max-
" Timothy J watchman h 230 Davis
" William spinner h 178 Weld
" William F city laborer b 799 Water [Sixth
" William J meter maker h 95 S
" William A student b 30 Locust
Obue Adelard slasher b 59 Bullard
O'Callahan Nellie J cashier 132 Union bds 11 Adams
O'Connell Catherine teacher Acushnet av school b 35 Fifth
" Dennis h 35 Mosher
" James operative b 35 Mosher
" John A musician b 461 Union
" John F second hand h 141 Division
" John J third hand b 207½ State

O'Connell
" John P glass worker h 370 Orchard (S)
" Joseph F musician h 461 Union
" Joseph F Jr leader orchestra Hathaway's Theatre h 99 Pierce
" Thomas machinist b 15 Morton ct
O'Connor Dennis J ice 431 Rivet b do
" Elizabtth died Jan 18 1911
" Frank J clerk 217 Purchase b do
" James brakeman h 15 Franklin
" James copper worker b 168 Tinkham
" James grinder h 129 Grinnell
" Jeremiah tailor b 177 Fourth
" Jeremiah E P insurance agent 37 Purchase rm 23 h 125 Parker
" Jeremiah J supt h 18 Parker
" John laborer 100 S Water b 177 Fourth [Rivet
" John L clerk 184 Fourth b 431
" John T spinner h 1005 Acushnet av [lor school b 431 Rivet
" Mary E teacher William H Tay-
" Michael operative b 178 Belleville avenue [et
" Patrick H physician B b 431 Riv-
" Thomas J A clerk 10 William h 60 Washington [Water
Odams Louisa Mrs h 221 South
Oddy Benjamin weaver b 146 Holly
" John weaver h 152 Tallman
" Thomas weaver h 146 Holly
Oden John H barber b 186 Mill
O'Donnell Annie V bookkeeper 702 Purchase b 213 Austin
" Annie V stenographer 105 William b 32 Maitland
" Bridget A h 85 S Second
" Edward J proprietor Plymouth House 245 Purchase h do
" James laborer h 57 Prospect
" John fireman b 301 Fourth
" John mariner h 32 Maitland
" Margaret and Mary h 159 Weld
" Michael shoemaker h 57 Prospect
" Owen city laborer h 570 S Water
" Patrick b 57 Prospect
" Patrick fireman h 213 Austin
" Patrick weaver h 748 First
" Thomas packer h 55 Potomska
" William engineer h 191 N Second
" William waiter h 577 Cottage

CHARLES A. CROSHERE CARRIAGE AND AUTO
38 FOURTH ST. Bell Phone 1964-23 PAINTING

Oesting Edward A real estate h 36 Jenny Lind
" F William h 689 County [County
" F William Jr third hand b 689
" Gertrude clerk b 22 Rockland
" Katherine widow Paul h 22 Rockland
" Mary E bds 698 County
" Paul J engraver b 22 Rockland
Offley Arlington L rope worker b 169 Elm
" Charles A waiter h 195 Smith
" Charles E barber 150 Purchase b 319 Elm
" George W laborer h 820 Kempton
" John K H cook h 110 Cedar
" John R Rev (Offley & Son) h 169 Elm [Elm
" John W (Offley & Son) h 169
" & Son (John R and John W) hairdressers 150 Purchase
Ogara Albert weaver b 648 First
" Joseph operative b 12 Washburn
" Lawrence weaver b 1 Rivet
" Peter weaver h 12 Washburn
" Thomas teaming 12 Washburn h do [Grove
Ogarro John operative h 108 Cedar
Ogden Abraham operative h 209 Durfee [Phillips av
" Arthur R clerk 2 Union h 278
" Ernest W clerk h 47 Lombard
" Fred third hand b 6 Oneko lane
" George C fixer h 289 Collette
" James H clerk 819 Purchase b 447 Pleasant
" John h 10 Studley
" Joseph carpenter b 606 Cottage
" Richard operative b 16 Abbott
" Robinson mule spinner h 544 Rivet
" Rose housekeeper b 12 Pope
" Thomas bartender 1501 Acushnet av b 57 Beetle [av
" Timothy twister b 1637 Acushnet
" William clerk h 278 Phillips av
" William laborer h 447 Pleasant
Ogera Louis weaver h 23 Acushnet av
Ogie Eli B weaver h 39 Roosevelt
Ogof Zwad oprative h 226 Coggeshall
O'Grady James carder h 39 Ingraham
" James operative h 69 Vine

O'Grady
" Stephen spinner b 69 Vine [h do
" Thomas bakers' supplies 69 Vine
O'Hara Edward operative h 1 Clark
" John P salesman 165 Union b 25 Richmond [mond
" Mary widow John h 25 Rich-
" Thomas F mgr 32 Purchase h 599 Cottage
" William J treer b 25 Richmond
O'Hare James removed to Worcester
" James W plasterer h 63 Clark
O'Hearn John F laborer b 13 Abbott
" Mary widow Patrick h 71 Hall
" Michael operative b 71 Hall
" Thomas weaver rms 215 Coffin av
" William real estate h 13 Abbott
Ohlson Gustave paper hanger rms 419 Purchase [N Y
Ohm William C rem to Rochester
Ohnesorge William weaver h 249 Tinkham [250 S Second
O'Independent A C Vieira publisher
O'Kane Elizabeth widow James b 46
O'Keefe Anastasia b 88 Mill
" Edmund h 88 Mill [Mill
" John A salesman 99 William b 88
" see Keefe
Okiski Antone weaver h 39 Rivet
Old Colony Box Co Nash road cor Church [N Water
" Dartmouth Historical Society 37
Oldfield Abraham weaver h 18 Viall
" Frank jeweler 987 S Water h at Fairhaven
" Frederick machinist b 138 State
" Samuel F fitter b 138 State
" William fixer h 1 Hyacinth
" William weaver h 138 State
Oldham Arnold rem from city
" Fred rem from city
" George overseer Grinnell Mfg Co h 149 Myrtle
" Harold rem from city
" John Rev pastor Wesley Methodist Episcopal church h 283 Bowditch [h 149 Myrtle
" Joseph overseer Pierce Mfg Corp
" Lily bookkeeper 1623 Acushnet av b 283 Bowditch
" Shaw removed from city
O'Leary Daniel b 935 Acushnet av
" Ellen widow Richard h 63 Clark
" Eugene operative h r 198 State
" Helen stenographer b 9 Stone

J. G. NICHOLSON
LUMBER, SASH, DOORS and BLINDS
BOWDITCH STREET, NEW BEDFORD, MASS.

O'Leary
" Henry coachman 379 County h 9 Stone
" Joseph clerk b 935 Acushnet av
" Mary E bookkeeper b 9 Stone
" Patrick breweryworker 26 Brook
" Patrick liquors 925 Acushnet av h 935 do
" Sophia telephone operator 57 N Second b 935 Acushnet av
" Thomas laborer h 700 Purchase
" Wesley A director N B Industrial school rms 371 County
" see Leary [thaway
Oleiveria A M watchman h 212 Ha-
Olejas John operative h 5 Fulton ct
Olevitz Alexander operative h 106 Cove
" John weaver h 8 Social
" Joseph weaver h 819 S Water
Oliveira Antone driver h 263 S Second [av
" Antone E operative b 139 Coffin
" Antonio operative b 120 Dartmouth
" Caton weaver h r 309 S Front
" Frank laborer h 18 Griffin
" Frank mill hand h 114 Larch
" Joaquim R laborer N B W W
" Joaquim Santos publisher 143 Acushnet av h do
" John weaver b 121 Collette
" John S painter b 208 Fourth
" Jose carder h 21 Mitchell [av
" Jose E laborer h 387 Belleville
" Joseph operative h 371 S First
" Joseph painter h 298 Fourth
" Joseph clerk 439 Belleville av h 121 Collette
" Luiz S weaver h 64 Collette
" Mary widow Francisco h 120 Dartmouth
" Victorino (Oliveira & Rebello) 175 Sawyer h 202 Belleville av
" & Rebello (Victorino Oliveira and Frank Rebello) grocers 175 Sawyer [Nye
Oliver Abbie S widow Joseph b 12
" Andrew J teamster 1 William h 859 Kempton
" Annie h 149 Elm
" Annie widow h 82 Crapo
" Antone laborer h 79 Grinnell
" Antone mill hand h 212 Hathaway

Oliver
" Antonio Jr b 75 Crapo
" Avelina A variety 485 S Water h 505 do [High
" Charlotte A widow Albert b 24
" Clara Mrs h 267 S Second
" Clara widow h 86 Howland
" Clarence W harness cleaner 50 Elm h 305 Maxfield
" Dennis mill hand h 265 S Front
" Emma L widow Richard W h 198 Smith
" Enos operative h 417 First
" Frank driver h 10 Weaver
" Frank farmer Almshouse b do
" Frank farmer h 1038 Rockdale av
" Frank J grocer 341 First h do
" Frank J Jr clerk b 341 First
" Fred E laborer h 123 Cedar
" Garrison L janitor h 80 Cedar
" George collector 7 Purchase h 152 Bonney [(W)
" Hubert elevatorman b 390 Elm
" Jacinth removed from city
" James H painter h Hudson
" Joaquim S provisions 113 S Second h 18 Madison
" John laborer h 486 S Water
" John mill hand h 104 Thompson
" John ship carpenter h 428 Kempton
" John A removed to Nantucket
" John B deputy sheriff 37 Purchase rm 28 h 297 Cottage
" John F police h 390 Elm (W)
" John F shipper removed to Boston
" Joseph h 265 South Front
" Joseph laborer h 75 Crapo
" Joseph laborer h 19 E French av
" Joseph weaver h 600 S Second
" Joseph M clerk Purchase cor Elm h 12 Nye
" Julius P drill maker h 75 Crapo
" Lawrence J engineer h 165 Grinnell [bard
" Manuel clerk 163 Union h 45 Lom-
" Manuel laborer h 2 Waverly pl
" Manuel J clerk b 341 First
" Marcelino drill scourer h 169 Fourth [ly
" Mary clerk 139 Union b 4 Waver-

Steiger-Dudgeon Co.
"The WOMAN'S Store."
Tel. Bell 82 & 83, Branches connecting all depts.
" " 160 For Office only. Auto. 1211

SUMPTIONS, ASSORTMENTS AT ALL TIMES OF DEPENDABLE DRY GOODS

Oliver
" Mary widow h 152 Bonney
" Mary widow h 435 S Water
" Mary widow Frank P h 154 Thompson [Front
" Michael mill hand b 546 North
" Onesime removed from city
" Pedro operative h 46 Scott
" Seraphin operative h 14 Bourne
" Samuel U manager Ward 6 Furniture Co 1020 S Water h 300 County
" William twister h 19 E French av
Oliveria Mary widow h 57 Acushnet avenue [Eighth
Olivier Frederick P carder bds 14
" George L (G L Olivier Co) h 14 Eighth [net av
" G L Co liquors 384-386 Acush-
" Israel weaver h 389 Bolton
" Kenneth S clerk 386 Acushnet av b 14 Eighth
" Louis H bds 62 Foster
" Manuel mill hand h 13 Mitchell
Olmsted Henry drill worker rms 56 Walnut
Olsen Erick G drill maker b 44 Fifth
" Harry foreman h 59 Pierce
" John auto repairer 22 Fourth h 22 Mill
" John Mrs died May 26 1911
Olson Axel glass cutter h 68 Ward
" Carl J removed from city
" Charles W removed to Gloucester
" Ingal carpenter h 847 Rockdale avenue [avenue
" John A carpenter b 847 Rockdale
" Nils paper hanger h 204 Brownell
" Olaf steam fitter 91 N Water bds 248 Rivet [dale av
" Victor E carpenter b 847 Rock-
Olsson Carl J carpenter h 166 Clinton
Olstein Annie B widow John L b 117 Hillman [117 Hillman
" John H janitor Court House bds
O'Malley Agnes M teacher Parker street school b 103 Hazard
" John laborer h 103 Hazard
" John machinist h 272 Fourth
" Katherine M teacher Parker st annex school b 103 Hazard
" Margaret widow h 49 Winsor

O'Malley
" Matthew fireman 350 S Second h 104 Mosher
" Michael drill worker h 38 Ash (S)
" Patrick operative h 17 Beetle
" Patrick spinner h 210 Coffin av
" Patrick H laborer h 8 Pearl
" Thomas laborer h 29 Winsor
" Thomas laborer h 49 Winsor
" Thomas laborer h 575 Acushnet avenue
" Thomas F operative b 575 Acushnet avenue [h 63 School
" William special police 62 Union
Oman Charles A foreman 144 South Water h 54 Allen
" Charles E second hand b 54 Allen
" James D salesman 185 Union h 2430 Acushnet avenue [Allen
" Mabel J clerk 160 Purchase b 54
" Nena P stenographer 144 S Water rm 23 b 54 Allen
O'Meara Morgan h 256 Hillman
Omerod Edward weaver b 19 Ashley
" James shoemaker h 1039 County
Omey Allie W bookkeeper 42 Front h at Fairhaven
" Elizabeth E teacher Middle st school b 63 Thomas [David
" Ellen I widow Alexander h 90
O'Neil Anna clerk 1081 Acushnet b 100 Clark
" Charles B removed to Fall River
" Clara M teacher Harrington school bds 34 Emerson (S)
" Daniel piper b 25 McGurk
" Dennis h 104 Locust
" Edward W glasscutter h 111 Bonney [Emerson (S)
" Eleanor clerk 7 Pleasant b 34
" Hannah widow Dennis h 138 Bowditch
" James fixer b 358 Coffin av
" James laborer h 223 N Front
" James A carpenter b 64 Russell
" John fireman h 237 State
" John glasscutter b 111 Bonney
" John laborer h 46 Reynolds
" John H clerk 977 Acushnet av b 25 Trinity [h 25 Trinity
" John H inspector U St Ry Co
" John H track master Evergreen park h Plainville rd [Trinity
" John H Jr yarn inspector b 25

PELEG H. SHERMAN 506 COUNTY ST.
FUNERAL DIRECTOR AND EMBALMER
OFFICE PHONES. Bell 690-13. Auto. 1305.
RESIDENCE PHONES. Bell 690-12. Auto. 1306.

O'Neil
" John V plumber b 87 Atlantic
" Michael fixer 27 Peckham
" Patrick laborer h 14 Highland
" William H foreman 8 Union h 34 Emerson (S) [geshall
" William H Jr clerk h 461 Cog-
O'Neill John laborer b 521 Hathaway road
" John E clerk h 256 Union
" Katherine E (Mrs James F Powers) millinery 262 Union
" Margaret widow William H h 57 Locust
O'NEILL MURRAY automobile repairing and garage 55-57 Spring rms 38 Walnut See page 746
" Nora Z cashier 67 William b 104 Locust
" Thomas F liquors 215 and 221 Coggeshall h 196 Hawthorn
Oneko Woolen Mills Holden Leonard & Co) dress goods end Purchase
Oniski Andrew weaver h 110 Mott
Onley Charles H tailor 340 Acushnet av h 147 Smith [Willis
" John A clothes cleaner bds 121
" William G hairdresser 57 Smith h 121 Willis
Onofrio Angelo D fruit 263 Purchase h 501 Acushnet av
Oothout George M insurance agent 41 William b 72 Dean
" William J mgr Crescent Mfg Co h 73 Lake [vett
Openshaw Edward spinner h 31 Jou-
" George b 31 Jouvett
" James toymaker h 130 Division
" William porter b 233 Acushnet av
Orcutt Charles N carpenter bds 118 High [High
" Elcy clerk 36 Purchase bds 118
" James shoemaker h 53 Hillman
" Nelson L builder h 118 High
" Susan E B Mrs nurse h 118 High
O'Reilly Joseph L barber h 6 Blackburn [chase
Orient Distributing Co teas 60 Pur-
O'Riley Myles operative b 131 Whitman
" Robert operative b 131 Whitman

Ormerod William weaver h 120 Division [Clark
Ormonde Bernard M operative h r 56
" Joaquim M operative h r 56 Clark
" John R laborer N B W W
O'Rourke Annie widow h 579 First
" James h 185 Division
" James Jr weaver b 185 Division
" John weaver b 185 Division
" William H asst supt 120 Purchase rm 403 h 1 Cornell court
" see Rourke
Orr Harry H operative h 17 Ashley
" James slasher tender h 4 Harmony
Orrell William H rem from city
Orzechowski Walter weaver h 2 Weld avenue [Roosevelt
Osbaldestom Alfred spinner bds 58
" Edward weaver h 3 Abbott
" Sidney spinner h 58 Roosevelt
Osborne Edward D physician 37 S Second h do
" John D laborer h 188 Elm
" Mary widow Richard h 163 Emerson (N)
" Michael J city laborer h 84 Walden [ville rd
" Murtys E shoemaker h 198 Belle-
" Patrick V (Rae & Osborne) b 163 Emerson (N) [ton
" Richard gardener h 317 Kemp-
Osgood Edward A clerk 28 William h 740 Kempton [Kempton
" Ida J widow William S b 755
" Ruth A widow Christopher A h 74 Lindsey
" William S Jr driver 270 Acushnet av h 755 Kempton
O'Shea Joanna widow Thomas h 215 Grinnell
" Patrick T groom b 215 Grinnell
Ossibach Edward weaver h 136 Bullard [ney
Osswald John K clerk h 126 Bon-
" Thomas weaver h 5 Stanton ct
" Thomas Jr weaver b 5 Stanton court [36 Jouvett
Ostignay Emily widow Adelard h
" Pierre salesman h 83 Rivet [yer
Ostiguay Arthur laborer h 214 Saw-
Ostler Edward carpenter h 30 Dudley

PAINTERS' SUPPLIES
Walnut, Cor. Water, 84 Pleasant St. 25 WELD SQ., 129 COVE ST.
F. T. AKIN & COMPANY

Ostroff Sam hairdresser 461 S Water h 455 do [Acushnet av
Ostrofsky Abram shoemaker b 567
" Annie Mrs h 567 Acushnet av
" Charles laborer b 567 Acushnet av [av
" David laborer b 567 Acushnet
" Philip student b 567 Acushnet avenue [dence R I
O'Sullivan Jeremiah rem to Provi-
" John B rem to Providence R I
" see Sullivan
Otheman Bartholomew h 4 Sears
" John salesman b 129 Clinton
" Mary violin teacher 4 Sears b do
Otins Jose A laborer h 71 Mosher
Otis Dexter L clerk 377 Cedar b 156 Merrimac
" Edmund G h 10 Eighth
" Edward F druggist 377 Cedar h 156 Merrimac [rimac
" Ethel F stenographer b 156 Mer-
" George student b 10 Eighth
" John rem from city
" Thomas student b 10 Eighth
Otter Rene spinner rms 1 Weld sq
Ottiwell Sarah D librarian High school h 184 Kempton
Ouillette Alphonse carpenter b 268 N Front
" Andre fixer h 117 Bates av
" Antoine carpenter h 15 Nye
" Armand carpenter b 1205 Acushnet av
" August second hand h 582 First
" Clement spinner h 38 Bullard
" Delima widow John h 59 Bullard
" Ephriam carpenter b 1205 Acushnet av [Nye
" Eugene driver 1070 County b 15
" Felix operative b 107 Perry
" Felix spinner h 329 N Front
" Florence tailor 1014 Acushnet av b Holly street [rd
" Frank weaver h 56 Belleville
" George fixer b 195 Davis
" John fixer h 141 Church
" Joseph operative h 63 Tallman
" Napoleon rem to Fall River
" Pierre weaver b 67 Coffin av
" Thomas carpenter h 178 Dean
" Thomas machinist h 4 Blackburn
Ouimette Alexandrina clerk b 90 Brock av
" Antoine speeder b 121 Bates av

Ouimette
" Armand removed from city
" Arthur baker b 643 First
" Arthur slasher h 85 Beetle
" Delima widow Louis h 1117 Acushnet avenue [Delano
" Delphine grocer 690 First h 46
" Delphis furniture 639 First rms 32 Salisbury
" Delphis laborer h 359 Bowditch
" Edmond h 665 Purchase
" Ernest clerk 104 Cove h 7 Viall
" Eugene rem from city [av
" Eugene painter b 1117 Acushnet
" Felix bricklayer b 186 Dean
" Francois b 384 N Front
" George operative h 94 Beetle
" Horace clerk b 187 Phillips av
" Joseph watchman h 457 Coggeshall
" Joseph died Aug 13 1910
" Joseph Jr laborer b 457 Coggeshall [Phillips av
" Josephine widow Alexander h 187
" Ludger provisions 104 Cove h 7 Viall
" Napoleon bricklayer h 186 Dean
" Napoleon clerk 912 S Water h 66 Brock av [1911
" Napoleon (fixer) died June 10
" Narcisse bricklayer b 186 Dean
" Nellie widow Ludger bookkeeper 104 Cove b 63 Brock av
" Onesphore slasher tender b 85 Beetle [chase h do
" Phoebe Mrs furniture 665 Pur-
" Pierre slasher tender b 158 Salisbury [b 457 Coggeshall
" Victor bottler 878 Acushnet av
" Yvonne clerk 185 Union b 187 Phillips av [geshall
Oulawski Louis mill hand h 381 Cog-
Ould Thomas G carpenter h 63 Adams [dar Grove
Oullery Annie housekeeper 137 Ce-
Ouoriere Boulangeri baker 642 First
Ousey Mary Mrs h 449 Orchard (S)
Ousley Arthur fixer h 195 Collette
Outlaw Walter C janitor Purchase
" William h 197 Emerson
Owen Alfred grocer 89 Fruit h do
" Alfred spinner h 27 Viall
" Bert mill hand b 89 First [do
" James W physician 76 Beetle h
" James W Jr (Bristol Printing Co) 354 Purchase h 358 do

Bookkeeping, Shorthand, Typewriting, Penmanship, etc. Taught thoroughly at
Kinyon's Commercial School
Odd Fellows Bldg., Cor. William and Pleasant Sts., New Bedford, Mass.

Owen
" John operative b 5 Cornell pl
" Joseph operative h 5 Cornell pl
" Martha rms 45 North
Owens Amelia Mrs h 390 Kempton
" Michael J Rev asst pastor St Lawrence R C church h 110 Summer [Conn
" Thomas removed to Bridgeport
Oxford Shop (Juliet P Leonard) embroidery 97 William rm 403
Oxnard Henry E Rev pastor First Congregational church Lunds Corner h 2135 Acushnet av
Ozga Sylvester operative h 19 Hampton court

Pache John laborer h 104 Fifth [ond
Pacheco Alfred laborer h 154 N Sec-
" Antone h 93 Phillips av
" Antone laborer h 389 S Second
" Antone mason h 22 Dunbar
" Antone mill hand h 410 S Front
" Antone mill hand b 50 Dean
" Antone operative h 5 Warwick
" Antone operative h 264 S Front
" Antone operative h 266 S Second
" Antonio laborer h 7 South [av
" Charles mill hand b 153 Belleville
" Francis operative h 9 South
" Frank fireman U St Ry Co power station h 377 S Second
" Frank laborer h 22 Griffin
" Frank J bartender b 241 S Front
" Guilherme M grocer 263 Coggeshall h 22 Bullard
" Jacinth operative h 313 S Second
" James mill hand b 125 Holly
" Joaquim laborer h 641 S Water
" John laborer h 1 Hillman
" John mill hand h 100 Phillips av
" John operative h 8 Felton
" John J (Pacheco & Cardoza) h 101 Phillips avenue
" John J laborer h 241 S Front
" Joseph clerk b 16 Stapleton
" Joseph fish 689 S Water h 244 Rivet
" Joseph laborer b 295 S Front
" Joseph mill hand b 50 Dean
" Joseph mill hand h 23 Mitchell
" Joseph operative h 46 South
" Joseph operative h 96 Thompson

Pacheco
" Joseph shoe repairer 1478 Acushnet av h 80 Potomska [ond
" Joseph twist drill h 284 S Sec-
" Joseph wood 485 First h do
" Louis laborer h 570 S Water
" Manuel carder h 148 Tallman
" Manuel grocer 679 S Water h 680 South Water [32 Nelson
" Manuel hairdresser 275 Rivet h
" Manuel laborer h 15 Cotter
" Manuel laborer h 195 Division
" Manuel laborer h 236 S Front
" Manuel mason h 475 First
" Manuel mill hand h 180 Belleville avenue [ville av
" Manuel mill hand h 383 Belle-
" Manuel painter b 544 Rivet
" Manuel Jr mill hand 680 S Water
" Manuel C helper h 18 Babbitt
" Manuel J drill worker h 243 S Front [ville av
" Manuel L mill hand h 382 Belle-
" Manuel V mill hand b 381 Coggeshall
" Mariano laborer h 16 Stapleton
" Mariano removed to Fairhaven
" & Cardozo (John J Pacheco and Marianno Cardoza) grocers 428 North Front [Maxfield
Packard Arthur F shoemaker h 96
" Ellen H h 261 Middle
" Hannah widow George W b 207 State [field
" Mary G widow Frank b 96 Max-
" Minnie A clerk 41 Purchase b at Fairhaven
" William J spinner h 207 State
Packer Joseph H watchman rms 91 School [96 Newton bds do
Paddack Fannie C music teacher
" William C h 96 Newton
Padelford Bertha F stenographer 43 William b 450 Cottage
" Charles h 5 Bay [h 105 Allen
" Fred boarding stable 5 Briggs ct
" William removed to Taunton
Paes Antone clerk b 97 Acushnet av
" Antone clerk h 446 S Second
" Antone C operative h 30 County
" Frank M insurance agent 97 William rm 310 h 97 Acushnet av

Bread, Cake, Pastry
RICHMOND & COMPANY **255-257 UNION STREET**
Bell 993 Automatic 1022

Paes
" Vasco G janitor Luzitano Club 100 Acushnet av h 190 Cove [ter
Page Albert operative bds 751 S Wa-
" Albert J molder b 95 Fourth
" Alfred operative h 19 George
" Alice died Jan 26 1911
" Charles G upholsterer 36 Purchase h 950 Kempton
" James C foreman Greene & Wood h 236 Acushnet avenue
" Lillian E teacher Jireh Swift school h at Fairhaven
" Mfg Co cotton goods mfrs Cove road corner Bonney
" Martin C sawyer b 95 Fourth
" Oliver plumber h 361 N Front
" see LePage [Front
Pageotte Alphonse fixer h 448 North
" Joseph E third hand h 139 Hathaway
Pager Amanda M h 25 Hillman
Paige George W wagon man police department h 34 James
" James H h 9 Mill road
" Maurice W mgr 385 Acushnet av h 49 Willis [liam h at Onset
" William H piano tuner 109 Wil-
Pailthorpe Albert E stonecutter h 584 Cottage
Painchaud J R prop Standard Construction Co h 283 Sawyer
Paine Alvin H eyeletmaker h 55 Hill
" Andrew D mgr 62 N Water h 173 Court
" Arthur carpenter b 35 Smith
" Carleton C carpenter h 75 Locust
" Charles H carpenter h 131 Fair
" Frances E widow Samuel S h 345 Pleasant [h 137 Summer
" George W (S S Paine & Bro)
" Hillard H mason 247 Palmer h do [Lind
" Israel N carpenter h 2 Jenny
" Mary A widow Noah b 24 Sherman [Fourth
" M Ella widow Benoni R h 246
" Olin S (S S Paine & Bro) h 87 State
PAINE S S & BRO (George W and Olin S) lime bricks cement etc 139 Front See page 776

Paine
" Thomas upohlsterer 36 Purchase b 151 County
" see Payne
PAIRPOINT CORP The cut glass mfrs and plated ware Prospect c Howland See page 23
Pais Antonio operative h 30 County
" Carlos h 190 Cove
" Gilbert operative b 190 Cove
" Joseph slubber b 190 Cove [Cove
" Vasco da Gama slubber h 190
Paisler Charles S (Paisler & Willis) 160 N Water h 81 Summer
PAISLER & WILLIS (Charles S Paisler and William H Willis) lime and bricks 160 N Water See page 774
Paisley John H overseer Hathaway M Co h 14 Crapo [Swift
Paiva Francisco T laborer h 51
" Frank M jobing 51 South h do
" Luiz C mill hand h 180 Belleville avenue
" Manuel F carder h 29 Katharine
" Seraphino C mill hand bds 175 Coggeshall
" Venancio fireman U St Ry Co power station h 208 S Front
PALACE CAFE Harry Barrows prop 173 Purchase See page 779
Palacz John farmer h Plainville rd n Shawmut av [h 43 Liberty
Pallatroni Antonio clerk 64 Purchase
" Antonio fruit 114 Purchase h 43 Liberty
" Joseph laborer h 226 Court
" Louis porter 170 Purchase b 43 Liberty [court
Palme Fred fireman h 8 Coffin av
" Joseph grocer 1120 Acushnet av h 1917 do
" Otto clerk b 58 Washburn
" Theresa widow Frank b 8 Coffin av court [av
" William weaver bds 364 Coffin
Palmeira Jacintho mill hand h 175 Coggeshall [h 65 Forest
Palmer Amanda M widow Henry F
" Annie S teacher James B Congdon school b 89 State
" Arthur G painter b 65 Forest
" Carl F student b 12 Ward
" Clifford D drillworker b 1005 Kempton [ton
" Earl operative bds 1005 Kemp-

GLOBE DYE HOUSE 220 SHAWMUT AVE.
J. N. J. LONHOLDT, PROP. Telephone Connections Goods called for and Delivered
Down town Office, 52 Pleasant St., Room 1 North End Office, 1014 Acushnet Ave.

Palmer
" Ephraim C real estate 66 Pleasant h at N Dartmouth
" Foster operative b 1005 Kempton
" Fred W watchmaker 2 Purchase h 12 Ward [len
" Frederick A shipper h 709 Al-
" Frederick H clerk 239 Purchase h 18 Jenny Lind
" George E b 336 S Second
" George P machinist h 22 Collins
" Harry removed to Boston
" Jennie stenographer 12 Market h at Fairhaven [at Fairhaven
" John molder 229 N Water h
" John M clerk A M Corp h at Fairhaven
" John P watchman h 85 Church
" Loretta widow George S h 336 S Second
" Mary D died Nov 10 1910
" Mary J widow William H employment office 345 Orchard (S) b do [Cedar
" Susie widow Henry C nurse h 343
Palnaude Elinor h 54 Rivet
Panoi Alphonse rem from city
Panos Vacil (Eliopulos & Panos) 82 Purchase h 37 North
Paoni Angelo mill hand h 12 Wall
Papa Antony variety 2784 Acushnet av h r do [av b 113 Bullard
" William clerk 1295 Acushnet
Papaioannou Peter grocer 310 Coggeshall h do
Papas Andrew h 172 Dean
" George laborer bds 157 Coffin av
" John mill hand h 12 Nye
" Louis mill hand b 12 Nye [ant
Papillion Henri spinner b 381 Pleas-
" Joseph weaver h 381 Pleasant
Papineau Oscar fireman h 418 N Front
" see Babineau [Washburn
Paquet Ashimer operative h 45
Paquette Amelia Mrs h 8 Pearl
" Charles fixer h 45 Ashley
" Damase weaver b 400 S Second
" Delphine clerk 1604 Acushnet av b 454 Sawyer [at Acushnet
" Henry clerk 2012 Acushnet av h
" Jean B real estate agt rm 29 Arcade bldg h 373 Bowditch
" John carpenter h 363 Pleasant
" Joseph carpenter h 105 Beetle

Paquette
" Joseph conductor rms 602 Purchase
" Joseph O real estate rm 29 Arcade bldg h 123 Hathaway
" J Simon pressman 53 William h 618 Cottage [yer
" Louis A shoe repairer h 454 Saw-
" Louis J collector 43 William h 81 Independent
" Oda Mrs dry goods 2147 Acushnet av h at Acushnet
" Philomene Mrs b 13 Princeton
" Pierre painter h 400 S Second
" Rudolph clerk 103 Rivet b 45 Ashley [h at Acushnet
" Serville grocer 2012 Acushnet av
Paquin Adolphus laborer h 28 Tallman [net av
" Alvia operative b 1225 Acush-
" Dieudonne carpenter h 1225 Acushnet av
" Ernest carpenter h 418 N Front
" Ferdinand operative h 268 N Front
" Henry overseer h 136 Holly
" Joseph painter b 207 Bowditch
" Joseph A electrician 1539 Acushnet av b 1225 do
" J Ubalde physician 1304 Acushnet av h 1306 do
" Ludger rem from city
" Ludger teamster b 929 County
" Peter carpenter b 1690 Acushnet av [h 59 Tallman
" Raoul E clerk 1347 Acushnet av
" Valtheas salesman h 159 Whitman
" Victor salesman 222 Cedar Grove
Paradis Adelard laborer b 264 Mt Pleasant [Water
" Arsene second hand bds 968 S
" Cecil h 86 Clifford [av h 68 Dean
" Gaudiose clerk 1162 Acushnet
" George gardener h 264 Mt Pleasant
" Henry fixer h 283 Coffin av
" Hervie spinner h 311 Coggeshall
" John twister tender h 56 Cove
" Joseph second hand h 28 Margin
" Levi weaver b 311 Coggeshall
" Paul weaver b 311 Coggeshall
" Peter laborer h 12 Division
" Velmor machinist b 109 Bowditch

GREENE & WOOD Every Kind of LUMBER AND MILL WORK
PINE STREET, off So. WATER STREET, NEW BEDFORD

Parandelis Nicholas K (Parandelis & Dangelas) 56 Purchase rms 126 do [do
" Peter clerk 56 Purchase rms 126
" & Dangelas (Nicholas K Parandelis and Demetrios Dangelas props Crown Confectionery Store 56 Purchase and 342 Acushnet av [lard
Paratore Vincenzo laborer h 5 Bul-
Parcello Gabriel mill hand b 546 N Front [b at Fairhaven
Pardee Bertha T cashier 185 Union
" Timothy B reporter 5 Beetle lane rms 271 Union [h do
Pare Alveres provisions 28 Salisbury
" Ovid weaver b 18 Cove road
Parent Albert rem to Saskachewan Canada
" Alfred carpenter b 477 N Front
" Alphonse supt h 73 Hathaway
" Andre bds 118 Bates av
" Arthur fixer b 1225 Acushnet av
" Arthur weaver h 811 First
" Delphis weaver h 92 Nelson
" Ephraim removed from city
" Flemine widow b 131 Nye
" George operative h 477 N Front
" George Jr rem to Saskachewan Canada
" Heliodore h 118 Bates av
" Henry weaver h 13 Bowditch
" Joseph F driver h 36 Hicks
" Leon spinner b 477 N Front
" Louis spinner h 98 Collette
" Michel drillworker h 164 Brock avenue [604 Second
" Omer J salesman 924 S Water b
" Pierre fixer h 492 N Front
" Willard fixer b 13 Bowditch
Parenti Louis tailor 157 Union h 87 Pierce [1031 Acushnet av
Paris Store Co ladies' outfitters
Pariseau Archie operative b 50 Tallman
" Arthur removed from city
" Joseph rem from city [Oak
Park Lucy H widow Oliver P b 26
" Luke weaver h 18 Abbott
" Sarah A Mrs b 74 Willis
" Thomas weaver h 25 Cleveland
Parker Angeline C widow Henry D h 106 Cedar
" Anna nurse rms 321 Union
" Arthur L clerk h 169 Shawmut av

Parker
" Arthur L Mrs music teacher 169 Shawmut avenue h do [road
" Avery O carpenter h Tarkiln Hill
" Carrie A Mrs b 46 S Sixth
" Charles E clerk 28 William h at Dartmouth [do
" Charles F bricklayer 45 Grand h
" Charles R mason b 59 Richmond
" Daniel H carpenter h 20 Howard avenue [h 188 Cottage
" David L (D L Parker & Co)
PARKER DAVID L & CO (David L Parker) automobiles 14-18 Market See page 746
" Dora D sewing teacher (public schools b 161 Maxfield [er
" Eliza widow George H h 40 Park-
" Frank operative h 868 Acushnet avenue
" Franklin B clerk h 378 Cottage
" George H overseer h 129 Ruth
" George J farmer h 2228 Acushnet avenue [dle
" George W accountant h 188 Mid-
" Henry J overseer h 91 Brock av
" Henry W physician 13 S Sixth rms do [5 Morgan terrace
" Herbert brew master 26 Brook h
" Herbert weaver b 850 First
" Herman clerk 201 Union b Tarkiln Hill road [Purchase
" House, E C Brownell prop 110
" Jacob S b 5 Morgan terrace
" James N secetary and treasurer 36 Purchase h 73 North
" John laborer h 15 Margin
" John C deputy chief 9 S Second h 255 North
" John F painter h 924 Belleville av
" John H collector 125 Middle h 130 Liberty [75 Clark
" John H engineer 214 S Water h
" John W second hand h 126 Nye
" Laura B instructor N B Industrial school b 5 Morgan terrace
" Lawrence H rms Y M C A
" Leander V blacksmith 174 Shawmut av h 27 W Trinity
" Margaret weaver h 152 Division
" Oscar speeder tender b 619 Purchase
" Stephen E laborer b 29 Durfee

BONNEY, FOLSTER & CO.,
The North End's Shopping Centre
Dry Goods and Men's Furnishings
945-947 Acushnet Ave., New Bedford, Mass.

Parker
" S Lilla widow Ward R h 284 Union [Bedford
" Theron R clerk 98 Allen bds 57
" Thomas weaver h 56 Mosher
" Wallace R salesman 38 Elm b 43 Sycamore [188 Cottage
" Ward M salesman 18 Market b

WILLIAM C PARKER
Attorney at Law
29 and 30 Masonic Building
Cor Union and Pleasant Streets
Telephone Bell 1523-5
Bell 699-5 Automatic 1419
Residence 156 Cottage Street
Telephone Bell 1523-5

Parker William C lawyer 29-30 Masonic bldg h 156 Cottage
" William L G city teamster h 59 Richmond
Parkes John picker tender h 15 Margin [Front
" William glass worker h 333 South
Parkin Robert teamster h 95 Linden
Parkins William G brewery worker h 1049 County
Parkinson Alfred quiller bds 40 Cove
" Benjamin molder 229 N Water b 307 Collette
" Edmund driver h 830 County
" Elizabeth widow b 5 Abbott
" George watchman Manomet Mills h 147 Belleville road
" Henry weaver h 972 County [rd
" Ida widow William Jr b 190 Nash
" James carpenter b 204 Dean
" James machinist b 19 Ashley
" James weaver h 59 Covell
" John hairdresser 1126 Acushnet avenue h 1132 do
" John weaver h 8 Woodlawn av
" John W laborer b 41 Covell
" Joseph twister b 850 First
" Joseph weaver h 27 Cleveland
" Joseph weaver h 104 Clifford

Parkinson
" Joseph weaver b 850 First
" Richard removed from city [av
" Richard weaver h 205 Shawmut
" Thomas died May 30 1911
" Thomas laborer h 233 N Second
" Thomas H h 11 McMurray ter
" Thomas H second hand h 51 Peckham
" Thomas T painter h 137 Tallman
" Vincent weaver b 22 Cleveland
" Whiltaker weaver b 850 First
" Wilfred copper worker h 102 Davis [h 204 Dean
" William bartender 678 Purchase
" William glass cutter b 561½ Cottage [avenue
" William weaver h 8 Woodlawn
" William Jr died May 30 1911
Parks Michael operative b 197 Weld
Parlau John fisherman h 20 Belleville avenue [do
Parlin Ralph B osteopath 124 Mill h
Parlow Caroline S h 85 Thomas
" Evelyn L stenographer 3 Merrills wharf h 87 S Sixth
" Henry B (Parlow & Goddard) 206 Merchants Bank bldg h 287 Palmer
" Loring T capt Engine No 2 h 763 Kempton
PARLOW & GODDARD (Henry B Parlow and Alvano C Goddard) insurance 206 Merchants Bank bldg See page 782
Parmentier Jules weaver h 198 Dean
Parmento Mary widow Jose h 21 Hall
Parr Charles A clerk 416 Kempton h 874 County
" Elmina H Mrs h 483 Union
Parris Elizabeth rem from city
" George teamster h 10 Campbell
" George teamster h 217 Cedar Grove
" Ralph C machinist h 260 Weld
Parry Arthur J mechanic h 188 Chancery
" Eliza widow John b 1 Harrison
" Frank R pressman Standard b 188 Chancery [son
" John T drillmaker h 1 Harrison
" Louis A machinist b 188 Chancery
" Manuel B laborer h 327 Second

M. P. B. Silva & Son BUILDERS
Estimates Furnished on all Kinds of Work
157 ACUSHNET AVENUE Both Phones NEW BEDFORD

Parry
" William R teamster h 6 Spruce
" William R Jr clerk 308 Times bldg b 6 Spruce
" see Perry
Parry's Orchestra 188 Chancery
Parson Bertram laundry b 237 Collette [Maitland
Parsons Charles drillmaker h 21
" Elizabeth C widow Walter h 6 Sears [Pearl
" Emeline widow William C h 40
" Howard W machinist b 20 Fifth
" Louis J Jr picture frames 4 Beetle lane h 79 Bay
" Sarah R rem to Provincetown
PARSONS STEAM LAUNDRY CO The (E W Russell and E A Wheaton) 270 Acushnet av See front cover
" Thomas L real estate 131 Elm h do [amore
" Walter H mgr 97 Front h 59 Syc-
" William F clerk h 55 Brock av
" W Frances M stenographer 100 Fifth b 6 Sears [Myrtle
Partington Arthur gardener b 73
" Frank fixer h 303 Collette [av
" George weaver b 137 Acushnet
" Walter driver 8 Campbell h 90 Merrimac
Paryse John laborer b 15 Nye
Pasell Francis H h 257 Mt Pleasant
" George W foreman h 57 Shawmut av
Pasho Antone fireman b 26 Alpine
Pass Henry mill hand b 274 Nash rd
Paste Dominick laborer h 672 Acushnet av
Pastime Theatre 955 S Water
Patistas Charles grocer 241 Coggeshall h r 251 do
" George grocer 241 Coggeshall h r 251 do [Acushnet av
" John pool 245 Coggeshall h
Patnaude Adelard clerk 888 Purchase b 162 Hatch [Washburn
" Adjuten driver 107 Bowditch h 31
" Alphonse conductor h 31 Washburn
" Arthur plumber b 39 Dean
" Arthur weaver h 103 Bowditch
" Augutor baker h 24 Washburn
" Clida machinist b 1191 Purchase
" Delima widow Samuel h 39 Dean

Patnaude
" Edmond drillworker b 221 Cedar Grove
" Eugene weaver h 35 Dean
" Frank carpenter h Church beyond Tarkiln Hill road [man
" Gedeon D weaver h 127 Whit-
" Henry painter b 39 Dean
" Henry J butter h 1133 Acushnet avenue [yer
" Hormidas carpenter h 442 Saw-
" John Baptiste janitor h 162 Hatch
" John B motorman h 211 State
" Joseph carpenter b 337 Earle
" J Arthur clerk h 328 Sawyer
" J Henry clerk 1347 Acushnet av h 1602½ do [274 Sawyer
" Moise foreman U St Ry Co h
" Napoleon laborer h 187 State
" Oliver teamster rms 92 S Second
" Rose clerk b 1077 County
" Rose A Mrs (Patnaude & Co) dry goods 1604 Acushnet av h 1602½ do
" Samuel died April 7 1911
" Silvia driver h 11 Jean
" Solomon salesman 1065 Acushnet av h 221 Cedar Grove
" Theodore machinist b 1077 County [dar Grove
" Theodore operative bds 221 Ce-
" William removed from city
" & Co (Mrs Rose A Patnaude and John A Delisle) dry goods 1604 Acushnet av [shall
Patropoulas Christus h 279 Cogge-
Patry Dela harnessmaker h 285 Pleasant [ditch
Patsy Emanuel fireman h 350 Bow-
Patt Lester D overseer Acushnet Mill Corp h 44 Allen
Patten Annie M stenographer 12 Market b at Marion
" George weaver h 371 State [ett
Patterson Alice Z removed to Ever-
" Charles G police h 84 Florence
" Douglas bridge builder h 155 Purchase
" Francis designer b 183 Coffin av
" Franklin P R salesman Anthony Swift & Co b 78 Fifth
" Ida widow John rms 8 Franklin

Steiger-Dudgeon Co.
"The WOMAN'S Store."
Tel. Bell 82 & 83, Branches connecting all depts.
" " 160 For Office only. Auto. 1211

SUMPTIONS, ASSORTMENTS AT ALL TIMES OF DEPENDABLE DRY GOODS

Patterson
" William operative h 1005 Kempton [S Sixth
Paul Albina seamstress 185 Union 85
" Antone mill hand h 603 Water
" Charles shipper rms 27 Fifth
" Charles silver plater h 398 First
" Charles A driver h 85 S Sixth
" Charles F died August 9 1910
" Enos C operative h 26 Thompson
" Florence E assistant editorial department Standard bds 85 South Sixth
" Frank h 128 Acushnet avenue
" George F died 1911
" George H treasurer New Bedford Ice Co 12 School h 94 Fourth
" John W (Paul & Dixon) 303 Merchants Bank bldg h 71 Morgan
" Manuel laborer h 284 S Front
" Manuel J laborer h 263 S Second
" Napoleon twister b 47 Belleville road [man's lane
" Stephen K cone cutter h 4 Tall-
" Sylvester letter carrier h 25 Emerson (S)
PAUL & DIXON (John W Paul and Henry H Dixon) successors to John W Paul, Samuel H Cook and Rotch & Potter insurance 303 Merchants Bank bldg See front cover
Paulding Emma A nurse 97 William rm 307
" Herbert operative h 176 Grinnell
" Herbert R foreman h 176 Grinnell
" John B heel mfr 176 Grinnell h do
" John J supt C S Knowles h 4 Smith
Paulino Candido h 114 Thompson
" Manuel operative h 64 Rockland
Paull Alice T teacher Middle street school bds at Fairhaven
" Edward L driver h 66 Summer
" James molder 229 N Water h at Fairhaven [Belleville av
Paulo Gironimo mill hand bds 202
" Manuel laborer b 103 Hemlock
" Manuel B laborer h 61 Covell
" Nunes laborer b 103 Hemlock
Pava Manuel fisherman b 162 Cedar Grove [mouth h 84 Dunbar
Pavao John C blacksmith 108 Dart-
Pavonia John S operative h 44 Hemlock [avenue
Payette Arthur painter b 199 Phillips
" Fred O electrical contractor 1539 Acushnet av h 1547 do
" Honore clerk 1539 Acushnet av h 199 Phillips avenue [do
" Honore grocer 80 Tallman h 78
" Louis watchman h 12 Nye
" Remie J real estate agent h 93 Tallman
" William A undertaker end Purchase h 1757 Acushnet avenue
Payne Alice telephone operator 57 N Second b 151 County
" Charles F cook h 153 Elm
" Edith L Mrs sewer 40 Purchase h 301 Maxfield [ond
" Francis T engineer h 157 S Sec-
" James M pressman Standard h 301 Maxfield [11 1911
" Matilda widow Henry J died July
" Thomas P (Ster Optical Co) 224 Purchase h 151 County
" see Paine [rms 16 Fifth
Payson A Edward mgr Morris & Co
Payton Ernest third hand h 337 Sawyer
" James loom fixer h 89 Mosher
Peabody Francis R h 15 Maple View terrace [lane
" Frank S clerk b 69 Mechanics
Peach Henry S clerk h 290 Acushnet avenue
Peake John W oils h 129 Mt Pleasant
Pearce Anna Belle teacher at Chatham bds 81 Bay
" Annie E teacher Mary B White school bds 370 Cottage
" Edward physician 44 Fifth h do
" G Girdwood student b 18 Seventh
" George R salesman h 18 Seventh
" John Rev pastor Fourth st M E church h 81 Bay
" Jane A widow Daniel h 189 Dean
" Orin A machinist h 45 Foster
" Thirza D b 370 Cottage
" see Peirce and Pierce [chase
Pearsall John upholsterer 36 Pur-
Pearson Alfred weaver h 284 Collette

PELEG H. SHERMAN 506 COUNTY ST.
FUNERAL DIRECTOR AND EMBALMER
OFFICE PHONES. Bell 690-13. Auto. 1305.
RESIDENCE PHONES. Bell 690-12. Auto. 1306.

Pearson
" Annice widow Robert h 284 Collette [av h 37 Collette
" Bert K elevatorman 270 Acushnet
" Daniel weaver b 189 Dean
" Edward weaver b 284 Collette
" Fred bricklayer h 140 Bullard
" George beamer h 59 Ellen
" James twister h 19 George
" Jane A widow Daniel h 189 Dean
" John painter h 174 Kempton
" Joseph weaver b 948 S Water
" Octave rem from city
" Thomas G weaver h 115 Dartmouth [33 Crapo
" William overseer Butler Mill h
Pease Benjamin P engineer h 34 Grape
" Briden student b 182 Fourth
" Chester C clerk Whitman Mills rms Y M C A
" C H & Co (Fred A Pease) wholesale produce 94 Union
" Elizabeth K h 493 County
" Francis M h 60 Cove road
" Frank R druggist 977 Acushnet h 973 do [Union
" Frank W (F W Pease Co) h 236
" Fred A (C H Pease & Co) 94 Union h at Fairhaven
" F W Co wholesale fruit Union cor N Water [County
" James E dentist 1 Bedford b 658
" Johanna M widow Peleg h 180 Fourth
" Lillian stitcher b 119 Chancery
" Louis mariner h 1 Leonard
" Lucinda C widow James H h 658 County [ty
" Manuel M laborer h 912 Coun-
" Manuel O farmer Almshouse b do [kery 46 Thompson h do
" Otis W dancing teacher and ba-
" Rodney W clerk 977 Acushnet av b 973 do [Kempton
" Ursula A widow David h 525
" Zephania W editor Mercury h 182 Fourth
" & Dandurand (P Dandurand and P D Jarry) druggists 913 S Water [dar Grove
Pechoto Antonio fisherman h 108 Ce-
Peck Albion S window dresser 40 Purchase h 132 Fruit

Peck
" Charles H offiicer House of Correction h at Smith's Mills
" Elizabeth T asst 30 Purchase bds 10 Collins
" Frank removed from city
" Frank weaver b 89 Hathaway
" Herbert N boss carpenter Whitman Mills h 56 Locust [Collins
" Hervey B clerk 100 Fifth h 10
" Walter B driver 14 N Sixth h 28 Shawmut av [av
" Walter C student b 28 Shawmut
" William bricklayer b 290 Collette
Peckham Curtis student b R B Peckham off 3136 Acushnet av
" Elizabeth A art goods 85 Fourth h do [Second b 92 S Second
" Ellen C telephone operator 57 N
" Ellery L carpenter 3 Beetle lane h do [Sherman
" Emily F widow Samuel W h 28
" Emma widow Frank h 35 McGurk
" Frank B clerk 17 N Sixth h 117 Court
" George H teamster foot Coffin av h at Fairhaven [ond
" George W foreman h 92 S Sec-
" Georgianna dressmaker 127 Cedar b do [h 92 S Second
" Herbert D mechanical toy maker
" James P died June 23 1911
" John painter b 6 Jenney
" John P bds 82 Liberty [av
" Lewis farmer b r 3136 Acushnet
" Mirtie widow James P h 30 Main
" Reuben B mason h r 3136 Acushet av [233 Cedar
" Rhoda E widow William R h
" Roy agent b r 3136 Acushnet av
" Susan A widow Samuel h 127 Cedar [N Front
Pecrar John mill hand h r 259
Pedro Antone milk h 413 Maxfield
" Frank salesman 509 S Water h 63 Grinnell [len
" George E iron dresser h 206 Al-
" George W laborer rms 61 Chancery
" Jerome J carpenter h 94 Fruit
" John Jr wood 166 Belleville av h do
" Joseph clerk h 229 S Front
" Joseph clerk h 272 S Front
" Joseph loom fixer h 1058 S Water

F. T. AKIN & CO. FORGE FACTORY FURNACE FAMILY COAL

Pedro
" Juan V laborer h 644 Mt Pleasant
" Manuel machinist h 12 Warren
" Manuel mill hand h 53 Mitchell
" Manuel operative h 20 Belleville avenue [chase
" Manuel operative h 1187 Pur-
" Michael student bds 63 Grinnell
" Ruth widow Frank b 36 Borden
" Susan widow John H h 219 North
" William operative h 36 Borden
Pedrozo Alfred L A student bds 12 Washington [Washington
" Manuel A mgr 133 Union h 12
Peel Florence Mrs h 7 E Durfee
" Robinson slasher h 161 Richmond
Peers James weaver b 320 Pleasant
" Samuel weaver h 321 Pleasant
" William weaver h 320 Pleasant
Peets Charles H engineer h 25 Grand
" John E stereotyper Standard b 198 Belleville road [dar
" William H machinist h 413 Ce-
" William H silver plater bds 248 Arnold
Pegg William mule spinner h 98 Covvell [209 Pleasant
Peirce Ada L bookkeeper 50 Elm b
" Amanda E widow Charles M Jr h 731 County
" Andrew h 165 Kempton
" Annie F widow Andrew B b 41 Campbell
" Asa C h 42 Fifth
" Bessie P principal H A Kempton school b 97 Willis
" Charles W died Dec 19 1910
" Clifford O piano tuner rms 300 Acushnet avenue [av
" Clifford O Mrs h 100 Acushnet
" Cynthia M Mrs h 304 Kempton
" Cyrena A widow Stephen D h 41 Fifth [h 202 Clinton
" C Clifford bookkeeper Soule Mill
" Easton Y florist 49 Cottage h do
" Edward M bds 32 Borden
" Ellen widow Charles W b 22 Dartmouth
" Ellery h 97 Willis
" Estelle C Mrs h 320 Cottage
" Fred clerk b 63 N Second [do
" George piano tuner 7 Homer h
" George Jr driver Engine 7 h 120 Robeson

Peirce
" Gertrude B teacher Harrington school b 116 Sycamore
" Herbert S furniture 659-661 S Water h 64 Fifth
" Joanna P widow Abraham W h 191 Kempton [231 Allen
" Joseph V florist 49 Cottage h
" J H (estate) L F Peirce mgr wood 425 Kempton
" Leland C insurance 10 Masonic bldg h 61 Hillman
" Lewis F (W H & L F Peirce) and mgr 425 Kempton b 304 do [school b 22 Dartmouth
" Lizzie A teacher G H Dunbar
" Lydia M widow John b 53 North
" Rebecca R Mrs h 72 Summer
" Stephen D Jr automobiles 99 William h 85 Chancery
" Sumner captain steamer S C Hart h 116 Sycamore
" Walter H (W H & L F Peirce) 304 Kempton b do
" William L drill maker h 33 High
" William P florist 232 Union and greenhouse 172 Elm h 217 Cottage [Mfg Co h 157 Maxfield
" Windsor C overseer Hathaway
PEIRCE W H & L F (Walter H and Lewis F) livery boarding and sales stable 304 Kempton See page 770
" & Kilburn (Charles E Peirce and Clifford Kilburn) builders foot Leonard
" see Pierce and Pearce
Pejko Martin grocer 13 Hicks h do
Peland James weaver h 32 Bourne
" Narcisse weaver h 775 First
Pelardy Joseph laborer h 225 State
Pelczar Annie widow Stanislaw h Plainville road
" Stanislaw died June 30 1911
" Walter farmer h Plainville road corner Shawmut avenue
Pelerin Aristides removed from city
Pelisier Zenon weaver h 54 Blackmer
Pell John F M hairdresser 86 Ashland b 10 Trinity
" Percey weaver b 341 Coggeshall
" Walter D laborer h 82 Cedar

There's room at the top for young men and women who can do things right.
Kinyon's Commercial School
Odd Fellows Bldg., Cor. William and Pleasant Sts., New Bedford, Mass.

Pell
" William overseer Pierce Brothers Ltd h 341 Coggeshall [net av
Pellant Joseph Mrs b 1791 Acush-
Pellend Henry carpenter h 73 Nelson
Pellerin Zennon operative h 194 Blackmer [man
Pelletier Adrian doffer bds 64 Tall-
" Albert janitor b 106 Tallman
" Albert painter b 90 Nye
" Alfred bricklayer b 27 Covell [av
" Alfred laborer h 2740 Acushnet
" Alfred loom fixer h 91 Jouvett
" Antoine h 936 County
" Armand barber b 119 Tallman
" Arthur grocer 490 S Second and pianos 94 County h do [road
" Arthur mill hand b 109 Nash
" Arthur painter h 921 County [do
" Arthur Mrs variety 921 County h
" Cleopas spinner h 119 Tallman
" Damase carder h 283 Shaw
" Eli laborer b 119 Tallman
" Ernest driver 1201 Purchase b 1203 do [b 160 Bowditch
" Ernest hack driver 57 Holly b
" Hector h 193 Bowditch
PELLETIER HENRI painter 86 Hathaway h do See page 37
" Hermenigilde b 127 Nye
" John B laborer bds 27 Covell
" John G operative bds 90 Nye
" Joseph blacksmith h 27 Covell
" Joseph box maker h 363 Coggeshall
" Joseph driver b 24 Nash road
" Joseph glass worker b 363 Coggeshall
" Joseph grocer h 244 Tinkham
" Joseph laborer b 119 Tallman
" Joseph molder 229 N Water h 33 Holly [h do
" Joseph Mrs dressmaker 33 Holly
" Joseph P agent 73 William h 106 Tallman
" Leo weaver b 64 Tallman
" Leon painter 110 Tallman h do
" Leon teamster h 301 Dàvis
" Levoie barber 111 Union bds 216 Sawyer [rd
" Lorenzo carpenter h 150 Nash
" Louis teamster h 49 Salisbury
" Luke teamster b 936 County

Pelletier
" Odilon died 1911
" Omer washer b 39 Tallman
" Omer weaver b 127 Nye
" Peter boxmaker h 27 Covell
" Peter Jr carpenter b 27 Covell
" Philias weaver b 1406 Acushnet avenue
" Phillip baker h 102 Beetle
" Phillip speeder h 70 Phillips av
" Raymond weaver b 49 Salisbury
" Rozario carpenter b 106 Tallman
" Valerie widow Euclid h 90 Nye
" Victor operative h 237 Coffin av
" ——— Mrs h 683 First
Pells Lloyd G hostler 50 Elm h 514 Kempton [geshall
Pelnara Antone mill hand h 369 Cog-
Peloquin Aime laborer h 11 Cleveland [b 87 Rivet
" Amelia clerk 1077 Acushnet av
" Charles mason h 90 Nye
" George painter b 1117 Acushnet av [man
" Louis second hand bds 125 Tall-
" Octave carpenter h 52 Collette
" Uldric shoeworker rms 90 Robeson [Weld h 101 Bullard
" Zepherine I Mrs milliner 98
Peltier Anna clerk 40 Purchase b 160 Bowditch [rms do
" Isabel H clairvoyant 24 Purchase
" Joseph mill hand h 387 Bowditch
" Napoleon operative h 15 Logan
" Philip baker h 102 Beetle
Pelv Wojciech weaver h 620 First
Pemberton Albert clerk h 367 Earle
" Charles T fixer h 180 Brock av
" George A insurance agent h 157 Richmond
" Levi A fixer h 199 Collette
Pementel Peter clerk 67 Howland bds 108 Sycamore [Maitland
Pender Edward F glasscutter h 30
" George W clerk 240 Union b 22 Atlantic [tic
" William gardener h 22 Atlan-
Pendergast Patrick copperworker b 21 Penniman [Viall
Pendlebury Thomas yardman bds 27
Pendleton Amelia Mrs housekeeper 64 Sears [Hospital b do
Penix John F physician St Luke's
Pennell Annie L Mrs bds 191 S Second

HASKELL BROS. DEALERS IN
ICE
400 COURT STREET TELEPHONE CONNECTION NEW BEDFORD, MASS.

Pennell
" John hostler h r 775 Purchase
" Joseph stonemason h r 41 Merrimac
" Joseph N carder b r 41 Merri- [mac
Penney B Frank news comp foreman Standard h 14 Locust [h do
" Edward F plumber 266 County
" Emma nurse h 12 Spruce
" Joseph H h 573 Kempton
" William E student b 14 Locust
Penniman Sarah H died Oct 17 1910
Pennington Frank weaver h 37 Howland Village
" Joseph tinsmith h 109 County
" Thomas (La Fontaine Braiding Co) 85 Whitman h at Lowell
" see Pinnington
Penny Joseph H rem from city
Pentleton David teamster h 40 Adams
" George R carpenter bds 40 Ad- [ams
Penton Frank stitcher bds 8 Thompson
People's Credit Co (Edward R and Franklin L Hathaway Jr) clothing 80 Purchase [mony
Pepin Adelard carpenter b 3 Har-
" Camille carpenter b 170 Hatch
" Donat carpenter h 271 Shaw
" Edward carpenter b 170 Hatch
" Edward operative b 170 Hatch
" Elzear clerk 555 N Front h 109 Eugenia [side av
" Ernest mill hand h 6 River-
" Gasper baker h 59 Ruth
" Gustave carpenter b 170 Hatch
" Hilaire clerk h 109 Eugenia
" John B carpenter h 154 Nash rd
" Mary L widow Joseph h 102 Collette [Cove h 31 Viall
" Omer J clerk W French av cor
" Rudolph carpenter b 105 Davis
" Sarah widow George E h 99 Potomska [Nelson
Pepp Querino G operative h 40
" Querino G Mrs variety 40 Nelson h do [Hampton ct
Perboiller Michael mill hand h 1
Percival Ruth h 72 School
Percy Edwin L died Feb 8 1911
" Elizabeth widow Charles h 28 Summit
" Emma W nurse b 403 Elm

Percy
" Samuel A picture frames 362 Purchase h 274 Pleasant
" Thomas job wagon Spring cor First h 403 Elm (W) [ter
Pereira Antone mason h 630 S Wa-
" Antonio L laborer 58 Howland
" August mason b 630 S Water
" Francisco (Pereira & Santana) h 8 Beetle
" John L weaver h 32 Nelson
" Manuel B photographer rear 63 Grinnell h do [h 126 Arnold
" Manuel E watchman city yard
" Michael mason b 630 S Water
" Raul M printer h 21 Spooner
" Seraphim J h 191 S Water
" & Santana (Francisco Pereira and Manuel Santana) grocers 195 Belleville av
Perfection Wet Wash Laundry (Wm R Benoit & Co) rear 28 Larch
Perisier Alma operative h 60 Tallman
Perkins Anna D widow Andrew W h 141 Cedar
PERKINS A W & CO (John A Perkins and U G Brownell) concreting slate and gravel roofing and teaming 167 Hillman See page 789
" Gertrude L stenographer Standard b 68 Spruce
" Harold A sampler Holmes Manufacturing Co b 55 Walnut
" Harry H removed to Dartmouth
" Harry T shipper 385 Acushnet av b at Fairhaven
" Jerome D died Oct 16 1910
" John A (A W Perkins & Co) h 68 Spruce [22 Rounds
" Justin C inspector N B W W b
" Luella G teacher Harrington school b 68 Spruce [Rounds
" Mira J widow William H h 22
" Roy H chauffeur b 275 Palmer
" R Archer electrician h 275 Palmer [Walden
" Verona H widow Jerome D h 81
" see Paquin [108 do
Perlin Adam grocer 108 Blackmer h
Permette Paul weaver h 23 Cleveland
Pernelet Ernest J weaver h 1671 Acushnet av
Peroni Angelo weaver h 319 Hillman

J. F. CROSSLEY 223 MILL STREET COR. EMERSON PHONE
STEAM and HOT WATER HEATING
GAS FITTING and FIXTURES

Perra Arthur helper 19 Linden b 183 Bowditch [ditch
" Delia widow John B h 195 Bow-
PERRA JOHN steamfitter 19 Linden h 183 Bowditch See page 766
" John B died April 15 1911
Perras Alphonse rem to Worcester
" Eli clerk h 359 N Front
" Joseph chauffeur b 359 N Front
" Louis physician 359 N Front b do
" Vital mason h 359 N Front
" Wilber removed to Worcester
Perreault Adolphe weaver h 3 Bannister
" Alphonse h 25 Bentley [Bowditch
" Dennis overseer Butler Mill h 335
" Euclid machinist b 3 Bannister
" Fred clerk 1099 Acushnet av b 3 Bannister av
" George weaver h 68 Hatch
" George weaver h 235 N Front
" Joseph weaver b 26 Reynolds
" Josepr wood and coal Division cor Second h 92 Jouvett
" Ludger loom fixer b 26 Reynolds
" Moise loom fixer h 26 Reynolds
Perreira Antone laborer h 4 Acushnet block
" Antone laborer h 229 S Front
" Frank operative h 79 Thompson
" John mill hand h 13 Mitchell
" John operative h 4 Griffin
" John L mill hand h 32 Nelson
" Joseph A carpenter h 90 Sidney
" Jule clerk b 195 Coggeshall
" Manuel fisherman b 17 Bullard
" Miguel mill hand b 195 Belleville av [h 970 Acushnet av
Perrenod Albert (A Perrenod & Co)
" A & Co (Albert Perrenod) jewelers and opticians 970 Acushnet av [ant h 71 Orchard
Perrier Albert C J dentist 5 Pleas-
" Amedee weaver h 187 Dean
" Joseph rem to Providence R I
" Numa L mechanical dentist 5 Pleasant b do
Perrin Angelin Mrs b 91 Kenyon [av
" Austin spinner b 1225 Acushnet
" Frank doffer b 1225 Acushnet av
" Helen widow John h 1225 Acushnet av [av
" Herbert joiner b 1225 Acushnet

Perrin
" John E second hand h 256 Cedar Grove
" Sylvester clerk b 91 Kenyon
" see Parent
Perrington Daniel laborer h 46 Fruit
Perron Adeline A b 22 Salisbury
" Arthur prop N End Garage 117 Bowditch h 113 do [364 do
" Cordelia dry goods 354 N Front b
" Frank fixer h 42 County [do
" Gelina grocer 350 N Front h 364
" Oscar clerk 350 N Front b 364 do
" Rouel weaver b 42 County
Perroni Peter barber h 275 Kempton
Perry Albert wax worker h 32 Penniman
" Albert weaver h 7 Waverly
" Alexander G auto repairer 55 Spring h 84 Rockland [dale av
" Alfred A apprentice b 1130 Rock-
" Alice L assistant editorial dept Standard b 93 Bedford [75 Mill
" Alonzo F tinsmith 54 Union b
" Andrew operative h 35 Prospect
" Anna G nurse b 93 Bedford
" Annie Mrs h 232 Rivet
" Annie widow h 283 S Second
" Anthony carpenter b 536 W Elm
" Anthony clerk 295 Purchase h at Fairhaven
" Antone fireman h 19 Nye [do
" Antone grocer 65 Grinnell h 67
" Antone mason b 630 S Water
" Antone tubeworker h 31 Page
" Antone F fisherman h 270 Field
" Antone J carpenter b 1130 Rockdale av
" Antone J seaman b 27 Cannon
" Antone R carpenter h 24 Ward
" Antonio E grocer 124 Thompson h 13 Briggs
" Antonio E insurance agent 97 William rm 310 h at Fairhaven [son b 13 Briggs
" Antonio E Jr clerk 124 Thomp-
" August city laborer h 22 Griffin
" August mason b 630 S Water
" Augustine operative h 56 Babbitt
" Benjamin driver h 32 Penniman
" Bernard A glasscutter bds 596 Union [erty
" Burton L steamfitter h 88 Lib-

CHARLES A. CROSHERE
38 FOURTH ST. Bell Phone 1964-23
SIGN PAINTING
GLASS LETTERING
ELECTRIC SIGNS
SHOW CARDS

Perry
" Calixte h 525 N Front [net av
" Charles operative h 218 Acush-
" Charles operative h 58 S Second
" Charles C teamster b 96 Middle
" Charles V motorman rms 610 Purchase [Front
" Clara widow Joseph h r 219 S
" Cyril chauffeur b 525 N Front
" Ebenezer S (Ebenezer S Perry & Son) h 199 Maxfield
" Ebenezer S & Son (Ebenezer S and Everett W Perry) real estate 136 Pleasant
" Edith S Mrs h 91 School
" Edward C commercial traveler b 78 Walden
" Edward E machinist b 54 Oak
" Elijah L laborer b 306 Court
" Elsie stenographer foot of North b 671 County
" Emil weaver h 21 Morton court
" Emily A widow Charles H stenographer Manomet Mills b 28 Crapo [b 1009 County
" Estelle bookkeeper 878 Purchase
" Eugene laborer h 306 Court
" Everett W (Ebenezer S Perry & Son) h 199 Maxfield
" Francis Mrs h 96 Howland
" Frank b 84 Rockland
" Frank carpenter h 104 Thompson
" Frank driver h 325 Cedar
" Frank driver 8 Campbell b 232 Acushnet av [Fayette
" Frank insurance solicitor h 131
" Frank laborer 144 S Water
" Frank mill hand h 19 Nye
" Frank motorman h 559 S Water
" Frank second hand h 97 Grinnell
" Frank teamster h 70 Rockland
" Frank J h 30 Thompson
" Frank T carpenter h 509 County
" Fred second hand h 12 McGurk
" Freeman A painter b 159 Arnold
" French h 126 Perry
" George clerk 36 Purchase b Page street [isbury
" George speeder tender h 49 Sal-
" George second hand h 21 Hall
" George Sylvia laborer h 113 Rounds
" George S paying teller Merchants National Bank h 63 Clinton
" George W h 70 Spruce

Perry
" Grace B stenographer 37 Purchase rm 2 h at Fairhaven
" Grace R Mrs mill hand b 151 Fair [Howard av
" Helen S cashier 157 Union b 64
" Henry mariner h 338 S Front
" Henry operative h 48 Edward
" Henry operative h 356 S Water
" Henry variety and bicycles 269 Rivet h 271 do
" Henry C grocer h 671 County
" Henry C Jr third hand b 671 County
" Henry J painter h 93 Bedford
" Henry J Jr clerk First National Bank b 93 Bedford [field
" Hugh A shoemaker h 148 Max-
" Jenney & Potter (William B Perry, Lester W Jenney and George H Potter) lawyers 57 William
" Jesse speeder h 37 Nelson
" Joaquim fisherman h 399 First
" John clerk 271 Rivet b 75 Hemlock
" John hostler h 66 Ward
" John operative h 129 S Second
" John A watchman h 596 Union
" John A Jr clerk b 596 Union
" John B died Feb 14 1911
" John B clerk 162 Acushnet av b 327 S Second [Thompson
" John E shoes 111 Rivet h 126
" John J laborer h 715 S Water
" John M painter h 270 Field
" John R salesman 32 Purchase b 96 Spring
" John S h 490 County
" John T caulker h 109 Potomska
" John T died Mar 4 1911
" Jose laborer h 51 Short
" Joseph cabinetmaker 287 South Water h do [158 Coggeshall
" Joseph clerk 144 Belleville av h
" Joseph clerk h 6 Thompson
" Joseph cook h 30 Hollyhock
" Joseph drill worker h 55 Page
" Joseph fisherman h 54 Grinnell
" Joseph laborer h 45 Short
" Joseph laborer h 154 Thompson
" Joseph laborer h 395 S Water
" Joseph laborer h 422 S Second
" Joseph laborer h 413 Kempton
" Joseph mill hand h 391 Rivet

J. G. NICHOLSON
LUMBER, SASH, DOORS and BLINDS
BOWDITCH STREET, NEW BEDFORD, MASS.

Perry
" Joseph shoes 107 County h 75 Hemlock
" Joseph teamster h 109 Davis
" Joseph weaver h 775 First
" Joseph (r 219 S Front) died June 21 1911
" Joseph B laborer h 1 Hemlock
" Joseph C salesman h 265 County
" Joseph D laborer h 391 S Second
" Joseph E boss comber h 67 Dartmouth
" Joseph F carpenter h 973 Kempton
" Joseph G fireman h 76 Grinnell
" Joseph J cigarmaker h 87 Briggs
" Joseph M carpenter rms Y M C A
" Joseph Ricardo builder 60 Borden h do
" Joseph R operative h 259 S Second
" Joseph S salesman 180 Acushnet av h 6 Thompson
" Laura clerk 182 Union b 75 Hemlock
" Laurence S lawyer 97 William rm 312 h 105 Summer
" Lawrence E third hand h 60 James
" Leander lather h 136 River rd
" Louisa E h 64 Washington
" Louisa H b 74 Sycamore
" Luiz laborer h 48 Hemlock
" Lydia A widow Orren G h 213 Chancery
" Manuel baker h 484 Maxfield
" Manuel clerk 67 Howland b 86 do
" Manuel cook bds 255 N Second
" Manuel farmer Almshouse b do
" Manuel gardener h 126 Shawmut avenue
" Manuel inspector U St Ry Co h 1009 County
" Manuel laborer h 68 Swift
" Manuel laborer h 212 N Second
" Manuel laborer h 389 Rockdale avenue
" Manuel mason h 373 S Second
" Manuel mill hand h 93 Phillips av
" Manuel operative h 24 County
" Manuel operative h 107 Cove rd
" Manuel patternmaker h 193 Court
" Manuel second hand h 177 Thompson
" Manuel B laborer h 327 S Second
" Manuel D machinist h 92 Grinnell
" Manuel Enos phonographs 605 S Water h 54 Oak

Perry
" Manuel F h 15 Clay
" Manuel F h 32 South
" Manuel J h 65 Katharine
" Manuel J laborer h 407 First
" Manuel J mason h 27 Bourne
" Manuel N carpenter h 412 First
" Manuel P druggist 91 Grinnell h 199 Fourth
" Manuel R carpenter h 54 Borden
" Manuel S engineer st dept h 183 Thompson
" Manuel S laborer h 103 Hemlock
" Manuel S shoemaker h 103 Hemlock
" Manuel T driver h 49 Fair
" Manuel V mariner h 303 S Front
" Margaret widow Joseph h 3 Hillman st ct
" Maria V widow seamstress bds 73 Dartmouth
" Martha Mrs clerk 36 Purchase b 60 Fourth
" Mary Mrs h 17 Cannon
" Mary Mrs h 275 State
" Mary Mrs h 434 S Second
" Mary widow h 371 S Second
" Mary widow Frank h 245 Tinkham
" Mary widow John B h 494 Acushnet av
" Mary C Mrs dressmaker 183 Thompson h do
" Mary C Mrs millinery 535 S Water h 265 County
" Mary C widow Franklin E h 177 Allen
" Mary C widow Solomon T b 77 North (W)
" Mary E widow Antonio h 566 Elm
" Mary H h 323 Cottage
" Mary M widow A H h 66 Willow av
" Matthew baker h 41 Woodlawn
" Michael laborer b 630 S Water
" Narcisse h r 863 Purchase
" Nellie widow Joseph h 14 Cannon
" Nicholas clerk 721 Water b 155 S Second
" Oscar carpenter b 296 Sawyer
" Raul compositor h 21 Spooner
" Samuel laborer h 494 S Water
" Samuel H traveling salesman h 111 Hillman
" Stephen painter rms 273 Cottage
" Stephen D h 201 Court
" Stephen D dentist 132 Pleasant b 62 Thomas

Steiger-Dudgeon Co.
"The WOMAN'S Store."
Tel. Bell 82 & 83, Branches connecting all depts.
" " 160 For Office only. Auto. 1211

SUMPTIONS, ASSORTMENTS AT ALL TIMES OF DEPENDABLE DRY GOODS

Perry
" Stephen J operative h 117½ Fifth
" Susan F widow William D h 55 Howard avenue [Union
" Susan R widow Arthur E h 319
" Thomas M machinist h 30 Main
" Walter A h 25 William
" Walter E removed from city
" William b 29 South
" William A provisions 159 Purchase h 78 Walden
" William B (Perry, Jenney & Potter) 57 William h 62 Thomas
" William E removed to Hyannis
" William H h 106 S Seventh
" William H carriage painter h 1130 Rockdale av [Rockdale av
" William T eyeletmaker h 1071
" Winifred teacher Harrington school b 111 Hillman
" see Parry, Perreira and Praeda
Perryman William spinner h 85 Holly
Persin Desire mill hand b 2 Jean
" Gustave mill hand bds 2 Jean
Perville Emile weaver h r 36 Hicks
Pesheau Frank blacksmith 944 County [ond h do
Peter David dry goods 98 S Sec-
" John laborer h 216 S Front
" Joseph laborer h 41 Cleveland
" Joseph white washer h r 154 N Second
" Manuel elevatorman h 17 Griffin
Peterhoff Michael baker h 43 Washburn [sutta
Peterino Emilio weaver h 3 Wam-
Peters Albert G eyelet maker b 15 E Durfee [rimac
" Albert H letter carrier h 172 Mer-
" Allen W clerk 41 Purchase h 89 Shawmut av [112 North
" Ambrose J shipsmith 11 Front b
" Anthony D coachman 378 County h 17 Columbia
" Archibald R clerk 14 N Sixth h 125 Shawmut avenue
" Avis G widow Joseph A removed to Gay Head [at Fairhaven
" Charles E blacksmith 11 Front h
" Edward died June 21 1911 [land
" Eliza widow Richard h 16 Mait-

Peters
" Elizabeth widow James H h 15 E Durfee
" Frank H Rev pastor North Christian church h 65 Chestnut
" Frank J died March 16 1911
" Frank L seaman b 47 Howland
" George A sub letter carrier b 172 Merrimac
" James T laborer h 15 E Durfee
" Johnanna Mrs h 112 North
" Lyman E hostler h 329 Middle
" Manuel mill hand h 96 Hall [rd
" Manuel J farmer h 702 Hathaway
" Mary widow Frank variety 47 Howland h do [Grinnell
" Nancy S widow John H h 156
" Richard H gardener h 305 Austin
" Stephen (Peters & Conos) 1091 Acushnet av h at Lawrence
" William laborer b 98 Blackmer
" William H clerk 126 Union b 68 Cedar
" William J clerk h 16 Maitland
" William L dentist 185 Purchase h at Fairhaven
" & Conos (Stephen Peters and John Conos) confectionery 1295 Acushnet avenue [Smith
Peterson Andrew T steam fitter h 153
" Aurilla P widow Zephaniah W h 434 Cottage [man h do
" Charles A B physician 90 Hill-
" Doris widow George h 66 School
" George (Maine Ice Cream Co) 535 Kempton b 522 County
" George W insurance agent 41 William b 434 Cottage
" John A drill worker h 65 Ocean
" Klaus blower b 2 Cornell ct
" Lawrence operative h r 228 State
" Matilda widow Alfred h 121½ Fourth [av
" Nils glass cutter b 137 Acushnet
" Peter conductor h 130 Mill [ditch
Pitijean Gustave weaver h 95 Bow-
Petipas Henry spinner b 105 Collette
" William fisherman h 105 Collette
Petit Alex A druggist 888 Purchase and milliner 1245 Acushnet av h 133 Clark
" Alexander spinner h 436 S Front
" Joseph weaver h 388 Pleasant

PELEG H. SHERMAN 506 COUNTY ST.
FUNERAL DIRECTOR AND EMBALMER
OFFICE PHONES. Bell 690-13. Auto. 1305.
RESIDENCE PHONES. Bell 690-12. Auto. 1306.

Petit
" Rose bookkeeper 20 N Second b at Fall River
Petitjean Xavier removed from city
" Xavier F operative h 299 Tinkham
Petre Joseph h 53 Ashley
Petropoulos Chrut clerk 310 Coggeshall h 279 do [all
Pettey James A third hand h 26 Vi-
" John I roll coverer h 14 Willow
Petviska Jusaf mill hand h 5 Hampton ct
Petzold Frank salesman b 49 Fair
" Frank G weaver h 49 Fair
Pfaffenzeller Joseph J printer 134 Pleasant h 205 Tinkham
Pfeninger Albert fixer h 11 Welcome
Pflug Michael baker h 330 Earle
Phaneuf Amos fisherman b 16 Washburn [dependent av
" David (Phanuef & Son) h 23 In-
" Edward (Phaneuf & Son) h 55 Crapo
" Euclide operative h 28 Roosevelt
" Frank painter h 216 Sawyer
" Frank J fixer h 102 Beetle
" Henri molder 229 N Water b 102 Beetle
" Henry weaver h 275 N Front
" Isaac driver b 23 Independent
" Jean B removed to Fall River
" John helper h 883 Purchase
" Joseph h 342 Bowditch
" Leo bds 102 Beetle
" Paul weaver h 52 Dean
" Peter spinner b 357 Davis
" Philias h 16 Washburn [dent
" Sylvane clerk bds 23 Indepen-
" Victor weaver h 24 Nye
" & Son (David and Edward) hay and grain 188 Rivet
Phelan Alice C clerk 40 Purchase b 78 Mill
" Ann and Mary E h 238 Middle
" Charles F clerk Mansion House b 238 Middle [b 78 Mill
" Eugene F bookkeeper Smith Bros
" James liquors 894 S Water b 57 Fair [Ashland
" James J clerk 685 First h 26
" John E laborer h 78 Mill
" John J eyeletter b 78 Mill

Phelan
" John J Rev pastor Immanuel Baptist church h 718 County
" Joseph clerk Oneko Mill b 112 South [Middle
" Katherine C dressmaker h 238
" Mary clerk 40 Purchase b 78 Mill [South
" Michael liquors 685 First h 112
" Thomas machinist b 78 Mill
Pheland Clara Mrs h 271 Hillman
" Gertude M clerk b 271 Hillman
Phelps Isaac W claim adjustor U St Ry Co h 299 Summer
" Isaac W Jr b 299 Summer
Phenix Arthur clerk h 69 Merrimac
" Charles grocer 292 Sawyer h 257 Tinkham
" Hector laborer b 149 State
" Philip grocer b 149 State
" Virginia Mrs h 87 Fruit
Phife George bellman 435 County b do [Iron Co foot Walnut
Philadelphia and Reading Coal &
Philie Edmonde weaver b 110 Whitman
Philip Jacinth laborer h 408 First
Philippi Jacob foreman h 291 Fourth [461 Coggeshall
Philla Fannie widow Heinrich h
" Joseph clerk b 461 Coggeshall
Phillips Allen L hoseman Hose 2 h 127 Mt Vernon
" Anna speeder h 73 Hathaway
" Bessie widow b 71 Maxfield
" Charles B grocer Plainville road n Shawmut av h do
" Charles F h 268 Arnold [ter
" Elizabeth J Mrs h 18 McMurray
" Elmer E foreman 474 Acushnet av h 71 Maxfield
" Ferdinand farmer h 380 Hillman
" Frank B watch repairer b 126 Perry [ditch
" Fred A brick layer h 235 Bow-
" George E fish h 232 Tremont
" George R notary public and treas Board of Trade 37 Purchase rm 2 h 97 Elm
" George W removed to Wilton
" Henry T janitor Fifth st school h 311 County [mond
" Lydia A widow nurse h 17 Rich-
" Mabel F clerk 474 Acushnet av b 167 Park [way
" Margaret mill hand h 73 Hatha-

F. T. AKIN & CO. PAINTERS AND DECORATORS

Phillips
" Margaret E teacher R C Ingraham school b 268 Arnold
" Mary I bookkeeper b 268 Arnold
" Seth died Dec 27 1910
PHILLIPS THOMAS O painter 167 Park h do See page 44
" William drillmaker h 256 Fourth
" William C asst teller Mechanics National Bank h 97 Elm
" William R joiner b 289 Collette
" W Carleton clerk 20 Market b 10 Studley [D h 58 Arnold
Phinney Annie M R widow Nathan
" Charles E police h 235 North
" George H salesman h 28 Dartmouth [Fourth
" Harry E clerk 140 Union h 181
" Henry H eyeletmaker h 28 Jenny Lind
" Lydia A h 221 Pleasant
" Martha G widow Stephen C b 181 Fourth [Acushnet av
" Mildred M stenographer b 215
" N D (estate) men's furnishings 194 Union [ton
" W Earle salesman b 130 Clin-
" Zenas H carpenter 215 Acushnet av h do
Pias Manuel laborer h 14 Bethel
Picand Manuel C laborer h 48 Edward [Fair
Picanso Joseph B carpenter h 58
" Manuel J operative h 101 Hall
Picard Almira widow Pierre h 1137 Acushnet av
" Annie Mrs bds 11 George
" Arsene loom fixer h 183 County
" Arthur removed from city
" Arthur teamster 1070 County b at Acushnet [av
" August twister b 137 Acushnet
" Calixte weaver h 178 Dean
" Glorian bookkeeper b 1137 Acushnet avenue [Acushnet av
" Horace clerk 225 Sawyer b 1137
" Jeanette clerk 1031 Acushnet av rms 1137 do
" John driver b 1137 Acushnet av
" Joseph fixer h 5 Abbott
" Merelda b 1137 Acushnet avenue
" M Jeanette b 1137 Acushnet av
" Rene driver 281 Sawyer b 1137 Acushnet avenue

Piche Alexina Mrs b 20 Austin ct
" Ernest weaver b 917 S Water [ley
" Joseph grocer 100 Ruth h 26 Ash-
" Joseph plumber 915 Acushnet av
" Lola bookkeeper 100 Ruth b 26 Ashley
Picher Joseph h 115 Hathaway
" Joseph Jr plumber 915 Acushnet av bds 115 Hathaway
Pichette E Antonio tailor 185 Union h 226 State
Pickens George h 149 Summer [ony
Pickering Elizabeth Mrs h 4 Harm-
" Rosa A widow weaver h 52 Swift
" William engineer b 23 Howland Village
" William H spinner h 284 Weld
Pickett Forrest A box maker b 341 Tinkham
" Thomas P spinner h 350 Cedar
Pickles Charles H overseer Oneko Woolen Mills h 178 Dean
" William mill hand b 171 Weld
" William printer 258 Purchase bds 285 Middle [Holly
Pickup Elizabeth widow Henry b 47
" Michael spinner h 296 Tinkham
" Samuel laborer h 47 Holy [lette
" Thomas K machinist h 289 Col-
Pidgeon Adelard carpenter h 60 Belleville road
" Alex weaver h 121 Hope
" Edmund weaver h 872 First
" Rose weaver b 141 Collett
" Samuel weaver h 74 Eugenia
" Zoe widow h 15 Bowditch
Piekielniak Wojciech operative h 8 Fulton ct
Pielho Paul laborer h 564 Purchase
Pieraccini Frank fruit b 394 Maxfield
" Frank Jr fruit 392 Kempton bds 394 Maxfield
" John W h 390 Maxfield
" Peter fruit h 974 County
" Raphael polime h 394 Maxfield
Pierce Albert R supt Pierce Mfg Co h 4 Clinton place [Fourth
" Almena M Mrs housekeeper 137
" Almira F h 201 Middle
" Andrew chef bds 203 Smith
" Andrew G Jr treas Pierce Mfg Co president P Corp and Pierce Brothers Ltd h 99 Madison
" Andrew G Mrs h 103 Spring

Kinyon's Commercial School Will furnish your office help free } Odd Fellows Building COR. WILLIAM and PLEASANT STS. NEW BEDFORD, MASS.

Pierce
" Andrew M bar tender b 56 Bedford [Bedford
" Annie E widow Frank M h 56
" Arabelle widow Henry b 173 Park
" Arthur M pressman 112 Union h at S Dartmouth
" Arthur V physician 99 Elm h do
" Austin C second hand h 56 Ashley
" Austin L glass cutter h 543 South Water
" Bros Ltd Purchase junc County
" Charles machine operator b 226 River road [field
" Charles A machinist h 254 Max-
" Charles C clerk b 25 Lincoln
" Cahrles C driver h 371 Hillman
" Charles E carpenter h 25 Lincoln
" Charles E job foreman Standard h 62 Thomas [b 59 Spruce
" Charles E teamster 111 William
" Charles F porter 111 William h 59 Spruce
" Charles W mason b 201 Middle
" Clara h 17 Robeson
" Clarence A clerk Green and Wood rms 118 Chancery
" Clarence H upholsterer 36 Purchase h 118 Chancery
" Clifton B asst supt U St Ry Co h 37 Keene [343 W Morgan
" Clifton D clerk 45 William bds
" Crawford S died Oct died 14 1910
" Curtis M student b 26 S Sixth
" Cynthia T music teacher b 312 Pleasant [117 Shawmut av
" David H foreman Manomet Mill h
" Edward E clerk P O h 343 West Morgan [gan
" Edward T designer b 343 W Mor-
" Edward T pres Pierce Mfg Corp treas Wamsutta Mills and Pierce Bros Ltd h 74 Hawthorn
" Edward T Jr student b 74 Hawthorn
" Eli W died Oct 2 1910 [S Sixth
" Elizabeth widow A Martin h 26
" Flizabeth h 201 Middle
" Elmer A mason h 400 Maxfield
" Elvira C Mrs millinery 543 S Water h do
" Erastus C laborer h 51 Mill
" Erskine H h 61 Cottage

Pierce
" Everett C chief engineer Holmes Mfg Co h 116 South
" Frank kettleman b 38 Reynolds
" Frank E agent h 147 Elm
" Franklin O grinder h 17 Buttonwood [h 65 Maple
" Fred J watchmaker 29 Purchase
" Frederick E dentist 97 William rm 207 b 147 Elm
" George Jr hoseman Engine 7 h 120 Robeson [ton
" George F teamster h 525 Kemp-
" George L mason b 201 Middle
" Hannah widow Anthony bds 17 Robeson [Chancery
" Harold Eustice student bds 119
" Harriet widow h 119 Fifth
" Jason F janitor Jireh Swift school h 226 River road [ant
" Jennie widow George b 312 Pleas-
" Judith C widow Otis h 1 Spruce
" Julia R widow Oliver h 30 Chestnut
" Lillian Moulton Mrs chiropodist 163 Purchase h 37 Keene
" Lydia M widow John b 53 North
" Mfg Corp Belleville av cor Sawyer [ker
" Nathaniel E conductor h 90 Par-
" Orin F compositor b 71 Walden
" Otis N pres Grinnell Mfg Corp h 98 Cottage [North
" Phoebe A widow Josiah h 194
" Ruth W teacher Harrington school b 17 Buttonwood
" S Emma housekeeper 16 Spruce
" William bds 56 Bedford
" William E upholsterer 36 Purchase h 119 Chancery
" William G laborer h 4 Crapo
" William L machinist b 15 Shawmut av
" see Pearce and Peirce [Ellen
Pierson George H ball warping h 59
Pies Joseph weaver h 305 Earle
Piet Arthur carder b 189 Hathaway
Pietras Joseph h 52 Dean
Pifko Alexandra bootblack 71 Washburn b 904 Acushnet av
Pigeon Enoch fixer h 12 Bullard
Pike Elida Mrs h 1 Austin court
" George A clerk 159 Purchase h 116 Rounds
" John oiler h Whitlow [land
" John W glasscutter h 75 Rock-

Bread, Cake, Pastry
RICHMOND & COMPANY **255-257 UNION STREET**
Bell 993 Automatic 1022

Pike
" Joseph B F b 211 Durfee
" Lucy A widow Andrew J h 62 Lindsey [h end Oak st ct
" Nelson L sexton Rural cemetery
" Rosa widow Joseph B F h 211 Durfee
" Victor driver b 24 Grant
Pilaire Emile weaver h 105 David
Pilders Morris shoe repairer 1027 S Water h 801 do [neau ct
Pilkington George twister h 6 Bon-
" George weaver h 98 Covell
" James laborer h 9 Abbott [way
" John third hand h 116 Hatha-
" Thomas weaver h 48 Willard
Pilling George twister h 13 W French avenue [avenue
" John R fireman h 1458 Acushnet
" William weaver h 14 Cleveland
Pimblett John W weaver h 251 Bowditch [Belleville av
Pimental Antone mill hand h 180
" Antone shoemaker 145 Dartmouth h 152 Swift
" Daniel hostler b 379 S Second
" Ferdinand mill hand h 88 Thompson [417 do
" Francisco shoemaker 421 Rivet h
" Francisco Jr clerk b 417 Rivet
" Frank mgr 337 Rivet b 417 do
" Honorato mason h 255 Field
" Joseph clerk 261 Rivet [ville av
" Joseph mill hand b 439 Belle-
" Joseph weaver b 417 Rivet
" Louis laborer h 692 S Water
" Manuel laborer bds 109 Bates av
" Manuel mill hand h 137 Field
" Manuel J hairdresser h 109 Bates avenue
" Marie widow h 45 Katharine
" Mary A widow Manuel A h 379 S Second
" Mary J widow h 137 Rockland
" Samuel hostler b 379 S Second
" Virginio shoemaker h 70 S Second
Pina Annie Mrs h 46 School
" Antone laborer h 162 S Second
" Antonio laborer h 88 First
" August cook h 7 Bethel [ter
" Benjamin mariner h 421 S Wa-
" Carlos T laborer h 142 Chancery
" Fidel laborer h 199 N Second
" Gaudencis died Nov 26 1910

Pina
" Gentil cook h 3 Sullivan
" Isolina widow Gaudest h r 476 Maxfield
" John laborer h 57 Prospect
" John teamster h 317 Middle
" John F variety 487 S Water h do
" Joseph b 3 Mitchell
" Joseph laborer h 2 Walnut
" Louisa Mrs grocer 201 N Second h 199 do
" Manuel operative h 353 S Water
" Manuel F laborer h 356 S Water
" Manuel S carpenter h 69 West
" Mene Mrs h 107 S Second
" Philomina Mrs variety 264 Middle h 3 Sullivan
" Raulin laborer h 466 S Water
" Rufina laborer h 27 Union
" Vetrine mariner h 401 S Water
Pinard Arthur slasher b 203 Sawyer
Pinault Joseph mill hand h 103 Davis
" Joseph A electrical worker b 206 Chestnut
" Vivian T helper b 206 Chestnut
" Zepherin R mgr 96 William rm 11 h 36 North [Front
Pinda Manuel C operative h 210 S
Pindleberry Greenwood stopper b 109 Division [County
Pineau James asst engineer bds 831
" John fireman b 880 Purchase
" Peter engineer Grinnell Mfg Co h 831 County
PINEAULT JOSEPH N carpenter and builder 682 Purchase h 206 Chestnut See page 761
" M Laura Mrs h 206 Chestnut
Pinel Joseph laborer h 11 Jean
Pinell Adelard boss grinder h 219 Sawyer [Orchard (S)
Pinha Philomena G widow h 274
Pinheiro Jose operative h 3 Maiden lane
Pink House (Henrietta and Frances Hill) boarding house 464 County
Pinkham Arthur D b 257 Middle
" H Lester removed from city
" Isabelle F Mrs h 257 Middle
" Mary widow George operative h 242 State [86 Davis
Pinnard Harmidas mill hand bds

GLOBE DYE HOUSE 220 SHAWMUT AVE.
J. N. J. LONHOLDT, PROP. Telephone Connections Goods called for and Delivered
Down town Office, 52 Pleasant St., Room 1 North End Office, 1014 Acushnet Ave.

Pinnell Adelard carder h 219 Sawyer
Pinner Alfred third hand h 309 Davis
" William comber tender h 309 Davis
" William Jr spinner b 309 Davis
Pinnington John J tinsmith 87 Union h 71 Jouvett
" Joseph tinsmith 87 Union bds [Jouvett
" Richard plumber 28 N Water b 71 Jouvette
Pino Frank weaver b 407 Purchase
" John weaver b 407 Purchase [man
Pinpore Joseph mill hand h 131 Whit-
Pinto James L insurance agent 97 William rm 310 h 14 Howland
" John A laborer h 356 S Water
Pintov Paul tailor 29 Walnut h 268 Acushnet avenue
Pion Arthur operative h 182 Weld
Piorascinc Gioconde variety 951 Acushnet av h 974 County
Piper Augustus D shoemaker h 204 Chancery
" Benjamin fixer b 337 Tinkham
" Cornelius B janitor Municipal bldg bds 383 Purchase
" Cornelius B Mrs hairdresser 383 Purchase b do [49 Florence
" David M janitor Municipal bldg h
" J Arthur Mrs h 68 Cedar
" J Arthur Jr chauffeur b 68 Cedar
" Sarah A widow Augutus D h 383 Purchase
" William A cook b 68 Cedar
Piplow Mary J died Dec 10 1910
Pippin Wilfred removed from city
Pirmentel Fernando operative h 88 Thompson [272 Kempton
Pirroni Peter (Pirroni & Schiolino) b
" & Schiolino (Peter Pirroni and Goetano Schiolino) hairdressers 352 Acushnet avenue
Pisi Albert laborer h 563 First [burn
Pisowcrvk John brewer h 60 Wash-
Pitman Ethel L book sewer b 16 Atlantic [117 Campbell
" George N janitor 37 Purchase h
" Lucy J widow Henry L h 16 Atlantic
" William treasurer N B Five Cents Savings Bank h 60 Chestnut
" see Pittman
Pitt Joseph weaver h 4 Welcome
Pitta Joao Carlos da Silva physician 43 Allen h 57 do
" John Jr student b 57 Allen
Pittl Anna clerk 185 Union b 1230 Acushnet avenue
" Augustus h 1230 Acushnet avenue
" Charles supt 12 Arcade h 1230 Acushnet av [Acushnet av
" Otto F driver 12 School bds 1230
" Rudolph operative b 1230 Acushnet avenue [Foster
Pittman Augusta W bookkeeper h 37
Pittsley Bradford T carpenter b 174 Kempton
" Elmer farmer h 3217 Acushnet av
" Herbert B drillmaker h 396 Court
" Hervey W quarryman h 558 Hathaway rd [kiln Hill rd
" Lydia A widow Howard h Tar-
" L Ralph farm hand b William B Pittsley's
" William B h Braley rd
Piva Frank laborer h 31 South
" John laborer h 84 Dunbar
" Joseph laborer h 49 Rivet
" Joseph mill hand h 50 Dean
" Manuel laborer b 17 Bullard
" Manuel speeder tender h 147 Rockland
" Marie Mrs h 391 Rivet
" Marie Mrs h 617 First
Pives Domingas Mrs h 93 S Second
" Hermina A Mrs h 129 S Second
" John operative b 93 S Second
Place Charles H milk 2949 Acushnet av h do
" Frank student b 211 County
" Joseph A police h 211 County
Plant Charles spinner h 67 Roosevelt
" Elzear musical instruments 929 S Water h Fall River
" Ernest laborer h 107 David
" John W weaver b 67 Roosevelt
Plante Alexander weaver h 35 Dean
" Archille weaver b 84 Kenyon
" Eliza widow h 84 Kenyon
" Eugene carpenter h 32 Social
" Francois X insurance agent 120 Purchase rm 403 h 51 Tallman [yer
" Gedeon second hand h 440 Saw-

GREENE & WOOD Every Kind of LUMBER AND MILL WORK
PINE STREET, off So. WATER STREET, NEW BEDFORD

Plante
" George carder b 1028 Acushnet avenue
" John G operative h 41 Adams
" Joseph plumber h 24 Adams
" Joseph weaver b 103 N Front
" Louis clerk 946 S Water h 19 Nelson
" Stanislas carder h 202 State
" see LaPlante [31 Covell
Plantier Edith widow Alexander bds
" Edward machinist b 1191 Purchase
" Nelson machinist b 31 Covell
Platt Alyn H machinist h 99 Brock avenue [b 109 Campbell
" Charles H overseer Gosnold Mill
" James C Jr operative bds 109 Campbell
" James W died Nov 25 1911
" James W Jr b 392 Sawyer [ond
" John lunch 110 Rivet h 519 Sec-
" Joseph laborer h 105 Beetle
" Margaret P bookkeeper 109 William bds 109 Campbell
" Mary E carder b 21 Ashley
" Mary E Mrs h 109 Campbell
" Samuel painter b 172 Cove
" Sarah J widow James W h 332 Sawyer
" William machinist h 86 Mott
Plaze Antoni operative h 199 N Front
Pleil Joseph weaver b 179 Dean
Pleso Jose Pacheco molder h 74 Grape [596 Purchase
Plomondon Delina widow operative h
" Joaquim carpenter h 216 State
Plotnick Samuel fruit pedlar h 426 S Water
Ploude Peter wrestler b 159 Tallman
" Silvio carpenter h 112 Mott
Plouffe Diogene weaver h 96 Jouvett
" Diogene Mrs dressmaker 96 Jouvett h do
" Emile rem from city [184 Sawyer
" Francois pool 236 Purchase h
" Joseph carpenter b 659 First
" Omer spinner h 123 Belleville av
" Pierre laborer h 130 Weld [way
Plummer Albert weaver h 85 Hatha-
" Daniel carpenter b 837 First
" Elizabeth Mrs b 21 S Sixth
" Frank O treas 158 Purchase h at Greene R I

Plummer
" Horace M h 29 Willis [h do
" Leander A artist 148 Hawthorn
" Leander A Jr cotton broker 15 Hamilton b 148 Hawthorn
" Millard F solderer h 194 Summer
" Walter E asst engineer b 29 Willis
PLUMMER & JENNINGS GRAIN CO flour grain and hay 100 S Water See page 775
Plyer Ophelia E widow Harry G b 180 Grinnell
Plymouth Club 21 Masonic bldg
" House (Edward J O'Donnell) 245 Purchase [ren
Podgorski Anton weaver h 16 War-
Podliz Stanislaus operative h 87 N Front
Poettich Henry operative h 127 Nye
Point Antonio J C painter h 105 Fifth
Pointe John laborer h 53 Windsor
Poirier Aime J clerk b 28 Bentley
" Alfred weaver b 446 Belleville av
" Amanda Mrs died Jan 20 1911
" Andrew motorman b r 61 Dean
" Andrew second hand h 95 Hathaway [yer
" Antoine A watchman h 226 Saw-
" Areos clerk 1131 Acushnet av b 446 Belleville av
" Armand weaver b 396 N Front
" Armand C druggist 2173 Acushnet av h 254 Cedar Grove
" Arsene blacksmith h 28 Bentley
" Arthur clerk 1174 Acushnet av b 226 Sawyer [av
" Arthur operative b 446 Belleville
" Basil fisherman h 446 Belleville av [357 North
" Belonie hairdresser 111 Union h
" Charles A provisions 1174 Acushnet av h 113 Holly
" Charles R millinery 1039 Acushnet av and 970 S Water h 254 Cedar Grove
" Cyprian doffer b 109 Collette
" C R Mrs millinery 1039 Acushnet av h 254 Cedar Grove
" David painter b 213 Nash rd
" Delphis builder 23 Rodney h do
" Donat carpenter rms 1332 Acushnet av
" Edward carpenter h 109 Collette

BONNEY, FOLSTER & CO.,
The North End's Shopping Centre
Dry Goods and Men's Furnishings
945-947 Acushnet Ave., New Bedford, Mass.

Poirier
" Euphemie widow Cajutan h rear 61 Dean [Locust
" Felix clerk 62 Purchase h 123
" F Regis carpenter b 23 Rodney
" Henry carpenter rem from city
" Henry 2nd hand h 16 Salisbury
" Hervey clerk 1437 Acushnet av bds 109 Collette
" Isidore carpenter h 396 N Front
" Joseph baker 2161 Acushnet av h 2237 do [b do
" Joseph laborer 320 Mt Pleasant
" Joseph weaver h 32 Division
" Jules removed from city
" Louis h 2237 Acushnet av
" Louis weaver h 57 Rivet
" Marcel teamster b r 61 Dean
" Marie Mrs h 99 David
" Michel slasher tender h 910 S Water
" Noel shoemaker h 101 Phillips av
" Odilon operative h 213 Nash rd
" Philias removed to Arctic Centre R I
" Philip carpenter h 213 Nash rd
" Richard h 183 Philips av
" Sigfroid operative h 310 Sawyer
" Thomas electrician b 1280 Acushnet av
" Valmore weaver b 396 N Front
Poisson Alfred L (Poisson Bros) 1064 Acushnet av h 99 Mt Pleasant
" Arthur box maker b 236 Collette
" Arthur millhand b 100 Haley
" Bros (Joseph and Alfred L) clothing and dry goods 1056 and 1064 Acushnet av
" Gedeon (G & L Poisson) 912 S Water h 54 S Sixth
" G & L (Gedeon and Ludger Poisson) clothing 912 S Water
" Gedeon operative b 100 Holly
" George operative b 100 Holly
" Joseph carpenter rem from city
" Joseph (Poisson Bros) h 99 Mt Pleasant
" Laurent h 54 Court
" Ludger plumber b 236 Collette
" Ludger (G & L Poisson) h 34 S Sixth
" Napoleon operative b 100 Holly
" Napoleon J overseer N B C M Corp h 391 Bowditch
" Paul doffer b 391 Bowditch

Poisson
" Pierre weaver b 1280 Acushnet av
" Wallace third hand b 391 Bowditch [9 W French av
" William clerk 1115 S Water b
Poitras Alphonse carpenter rms 399 Belleville av [net av
" Ambroise laborer h 1901 Acush-
" Damasse carpenter h 184 Phillips av [b 40 Independent
" Hermendine (Faford & Poitras)
" Hormidas furniture mover 235 N Front h do [net av
" Joseph conductor h 1901 Acush-
" Joseph operative h 23 Austin
" Napoleon weaver h 40 Independent [Grove
" Victoria widow h 104 Cedar
Pokrywaka Mary operative h rear 42 Washburn [burn
Polak Frank operative h r 42 Wash-
Polan John fisherman h r 162 Cedar Grove
Polar Frank weaver b 305 Earl
Polardy Joseph operative h 24 Ashley
Polchlopek Antone operative h 43 Washburn
Poliquin H Clara millinery h 778 Purchase [Belleville road
Pollard Annie widow William bds 28
" C B Mrs clerk U St Ry Co rms 161 William [Fourth
" Ella A widow Andrew C h 48
" Emma G nurse b 174 Acushnet av
" Hartley clerk 125 Middle h 21 Reynolds
" John H weaver b 833 County
" Matthew fixer h 60 Salisbury
" Walter operative b 25 Reynolds
" William h 28 Belleville road
Pollitt Fred spinner h 28 Holly
" George spinner h 90 Hathaway
" James T mill hand h 327 County
" James W sawyer b 87 Hathaway
" Joseph operative h 45 Maxfield
" Mary widow James H h 87 Hathaway [h 54 Kempton
Pollock Albert H molder 229 N Water
" Carl operative b 97 Locust
" Edward A drill worker b 156 Grinnell [school h 171 Mill
" Frederick O janitor Cedar Grove
" Harry glass cutter b 97 Locust
" John H janitor third dist court bldg h 97 Locust

M. P. B. Silva & Son Paints, Oils and Glass
Sole Agents for Lucas Tinted Gloss Paints
157 ACUSHNET AVENUE Both Phones NEW BEDFORD

Polonsky Maurice h 474 S Water
" Maurice pedler h 63 Clark
Polveran Ernest laborer h 712 Acushnet av
Polycarpo David F clerk h 21 Crapo
" Miguel F compositor h 63 Crapo
Pomber Antone grocer 114½ Acushnet av h 114 do [Whitman
Pombriend Armand doffer b 135
" Oscar shipper b 135 Whitman
" Remi carpenter h 132 Tallman
Pomeroy Emma h 203 Purchase
Pomfort Mary widow operative h 55 Howard
" Thomas weaver h 55 Howard
Poncelot Jane Mrs h 366 Cedar Grove
" Joseph weaver h 350 Cedar Grove
Ponta Urbano clerk 781 Water bds Nash rd [77 Davis
Ponte Antone P driver 39 Union bds
" Antone P grocer 359 First h do
" Antone P laborer h 29 South
" Domingos mill hand h 17 Mitchell
" Frank laborer h 333 First
" Frank M laborer h 291½ S Second
" Frank Perry h 29 South
" Joao G laborer h 202 Belleville av
" John fisherman h 94 Potomska
" John laborer h r 235 Park
" Joseph laborer h 10 Griffin
" Joseph mill hand h 303 S Front
" Joseph Perry h 151 Rockland
" Manuel mill hand h 30 Briggs
" Manuel G laborer h 202 Belleville av
" Manuel P clerk h 77 Davis
" Vergino (Ponte & Andrews) 91 Grinnell h 87 do
" & Andrews (V T Ponte and Manuel Andrews) grocers 91 Grinnell Now red ink
Pool Mabel L asst at south branch library h County cor Mill
Poole Ada W widow George H h 49 Sycamore [non
" Albert K teamster h 124 Mt Ver-
" Arthur T teamster h Plainville rd near Evergreen park
" Charles G laborer h 124 Mt Vernon [at N Dartmouth
" Erford W estimator 3 E Pope h
" Florence A teacher Thomas R Rodman school b 35 Jenny Lind

Poole
" Frank B supt Mt Pleasant Banding Co h Plainville rd n Reed's lane
" George A b 82 Forest
" Harry W conductor h 341 North
" John E asst supt h Plainville rd near Reed's lane
" John L (L W Poole & Son) carpenter 42 Spring h 91 Pierce
" Lindsay W (L W Poole & Son) 42 Spring h at N Dartmouth
" L W & Son (Lindsay W and John L Poole) carpenters 42 Spring
" Philip S farmer h Plainville rd
" Willard G foreman city carpenter h 232 Shawmut av [ton
Poley Arthur J Mrs removed to Bos-
Pontes Frank farm hand h 46 School
Poor Bros (George R and Lewis F Poor) jewelry 20 Purchase
" George R (Poor Bros) 20 Purchase h 77 Fourth
" Lewis F (Poor Bros) 20 Purchase h at Fairhaven
Pope Abner P h 63 Thomas
" Frank L h 103 S Sixth
" F Lewin Jr driver 270 Acushnet av h 46 Summer
" George W clerk Dartmouth Mfg Corp b 103 S Sixth [Fairhaven
" Harry L clerk 100 Fifth h at
" Sarah L widow John G W h 27 Walnut
Poper George W clerk b 103 S Sixth
Popielasc Anthony grocer h 205 N Front [Cedar Grove
Popopek Joseph operative h 212
Popple Zebedee A clerk 70 Cove rms 9 Salisbury [net av
Porrier Joseph baker h 2237 Acush-
Porter Charles H removed from city
" Charles H instructor N B Textile school h 343 Maxfield [ham
" Elmer E box maker b 323 Tink-
" James operative b 90 Clark
" James P clerk P O h 123 Locust
Porth Frederick P glass cutter h 21 Griffin
Portnoy Isaac second hand goods 212 Coggeshall h 127 Belleville av
" Israel clerk 212 Coggeshall b 127 Belleville av
" Simon J watch repairer 246 Coggeshall h 202 Belleville av

Steiger-Dudgeon Co.
"The WOMAN'S Store."
Tel. Bell 82 & 83, Branches connecting all depts.
" " 160 For Office only. Auto. 1211
SUMPTIONS, ASSORTMENTS AT ALL TIMES OF DEPENDABLE DRY GOODS

Portugal Joaquim F mill hand h 75 Nash rd [av
Posch Fritz operative b 297 Belleville
" Lawrence weaver h 1105 Acushnet av [av
" Leopold operative h 297 Belleville
" Leopold Jr operative b 297 Belleville av [Belleville av
" Leopold Jr mill operative b 297
Pospisil Edward spinner h 89 Hathaway
" Joseph weaver h 89 Hathaway
" Joseph Jr mill hand b 89 Hathaway [pendent
Post Antone spinner h 78 Inde-
" Benjamin washer 6 Campbell
" Benjamin J driver b 326 Middle
" Carrie b 326 Middle [as
" Frank glass decorator h 82 Thom-
" Harry W butler b 326 Middle
" John W waiter h 326 Middle
" Leon C removed from city
" Mary E widow William C b 97 South
" Office Acushnet av c William
Postal Telegraph-Cable Co N S MacDonald mgr Acushnet av cor William [net av
Potello August mason h 151 Acush-
Pothier Alexander horse trainer h 11 Bowditch [h 90 Nye
" Edmond D president 101 Kenyon
" Edward liquors 946 S Water h 52 Fair
" Edward mill hand b 11 Bowditch
" Ernest packer 36 Purchase
" Hormidas doffer b 37 Bullard
POTHIER JOSEPH A monumental works 305 Mt Pleasant h 183 Austin See page 29
" Joseph C physician 245 Fourth h 274 do
" Napoleon clerk rms 11 Bowditch
" Octave h 37 Bullard
" Ovide spinner h 8 Cornell place
" Saul spinner h 78 Tallman
" Wilfred machinist b 37 Bullard
" see Potter
Potliz Josef mill hand h 85 N Front
Potnier Napoleon shoe repairer 66 Washburn h do
Potomska Bowling Alleys (Charles T Smith) 705 S Water [S Water
" Mills Corp cotton goods mfrs 774

Potter Abner trainer New Bedford Driving Club Plainville rd b do
" Albert A fish 400 Kempton h 277 Hillman [do
" Alberto L clerk 60 Dartmouth h
" Alice widow William F h 1 Anthony [Hill
" Almira widow Isaiah A h 55
" Anna C stenographer 100 Fifth h at S Dartmouth
" Benjamin h 826 County
" Charles C b 40 Butler
" Charles F h 350 Allen
" Charles W H h 47 Chestnut
" Clarence M machinist h 52 Fruit
" Edward E F bookkeeper 125 Middle h 100 Summer [C A
" Edwin J civil engineer rms Y M
" Edwin L grocer 60 Dartmouth h 9 Cottage [87 Briggs
" Edwin L Jr clerk 60 Dartmouth h
" Eleanor widow Horace bds 85 Shawmut av
" Eliza widow b 535 N Front
" Fred box maker h 11 Philips av
" Ernest A machinist h 201 Belleville rd [Emerson (N)
" Fred M clerk 100 Fifth h 317
" George H (Perry Jenney & Potter) 57 William h at Smith Mills [nut
" Grace M music teacher b 48 Wal-
" Harriet S widow Sylvanus B b 39 North
" Helen L stenographer 2 Masonic bldg h at N Dartmouth
" Hiram J treas Old Colony Box Co h at Boston
" Isaac E painter 96 Pierce h do
" James L weaver b 17 Holly
" James W coachman b 508 County
" James W oiler h 17 Holly
" James Y plumber h 69 Crapo
" Jennie L stenographer 57 William b at Smith's Mills [Arch
" John W mgr 830 Purchase h 37
" Lester A clerk Mer Nat Bank b 325 Cedar [do
" Lester F physician 278 Union h
" Lucy T stenographer 36 Purchase b at S Dartmouth [Fifth
" Mary A widow Edward L b 20
" Mary K widow Frederick S h 143 Hawthorn [son
" Milton drill worker h 317 Emer-

PELEG H. SHERMAN 506 COUNTY ST.
FUNERAL DIRECTOR AND EMBALMER
OFFICE PHONES. Bell 690-13. Auto. 1305. RESIDENCE PHONES. Bell 690-12. Auto. 1306.

Potter
" Nellie C stenographer 200 Union b 43 Foster [Hillman
" Robert bartender 887 Purchase h
" Robert W steamfitter h 85 Hillman [h 325 Cedar
" Sadie A bookkeeper 748 Purchase
" Sarah M B widow Andrew H h 100 Madison
" Stephen R h 333 Union [ant
" Thomas boilermaker h 443 Pleas-
" Thomas A salesman h 325 Cedar
" Thomas E boilermaker b 34 High
" Thomas E Jr liquors 887 Purchase h 34 High
" Walter F overseer Holmes Mfg Co h 266 Pope [more
" Walter S watchman h 85 Syca-
" William B clerk 193 Purchase rms 33 High
" William Frank (William F Potter & Co) h 27 Arnold pl
POTTER WILLIAM F & CO (William Frank Potter) wholesale grocers 81-85 Front and 3-11 Union See page 30
" William G physician 546 County h do [mut av
" William H brakeman h 85 Shaw-
Potts Annie M dressmaker 253 Union h 248 Hawthorn
" Jean nurse b 248 Hawthorn
" Lydia widow Zion h 57 Ash (N)
Potvin Albert J buyer h 285 Allen
" Abina milliner bds 102 Ruth av
" Alphonse F tailor 174 Cedar h do
" Blanche L fitter 40 Purchase b 174 Cedar
" Edmond loom fixer h 31 Hicks
" Edmond operative h 31 Hicks
" Eugene boiler maker h 30 Ashley
" Francis operative b 102 Ruth
" Joseph laborer h 28 Nelson
" J Edmond Rev pastor Holy Rosary R C church h 68 Bowditch
" Mary widow Louis h 102 Ruth
" Napoleon carder h 102 Ruth
Pouchard Atude weaver h 4 Kenyon
Poudrier Alexander driver b 198 State
" Arthur driver h 198 State
Poulette Cleophas carpenter h 201 Sawyer
" George carpenter h 289 Coffin av
" Louis carpenter 154 Collette h do
Poulin Albert F builder 90 Nye
" Arthur J bookkeeper h 966 Kem
" Arthur J bookkeeper h 966 Kempton
" Charles A bookkeeper b 210 do
" Francois X h 88 Holly
" Joseph M clerk 538 N Front h 75 Holly [90 Nye b do
" Louise and Amazelie dressmakers
" Philbert builder 82 Holly h do
" Wilfred A carpenter b 417 N Front
" ——laborer b 275 N Front
Poulos Stegos fruit 1150 Acushnet av
Pounder Matthew weaver b 27 Viall
Poutre Henri laborer h 36 Bentley
Povong Antone S laborer h 233 S Front [h 219 Acushnet av
Powell George E clerk 125 Middle
" Isaac waiter rms 282 Cottage
" John W shearer h 274 Philips av
" Mary A Mrs b 219 Acushnet av
" Stanislaw operative b 143 Bullard
Power Annie widow William h 439 Rivet [rms 181 Middle
" George H (Power & Desmond)
" & Desmond (George H Power and Joseph C Desmond) clothing and men's furnishings 67 to 69 William
Powers Alfred carder h 239 Sawyer
" Annie widow William b 239 Sawyer [b 262 Allen
" Bartholomew clerk 145 Arnold
" Edward J foreman h 507 Bowditch [ning Co
" Edwin overseer Nonquitt Spin-
" Edwin B engineer h 70 Walden
" George W removed from city
" Isaac waiter rms 305 Middle
" James h 96 Jouvette
" James rms 168 Middle
" James driver b 384 Cottage
" James wood 64 Winsor h do
" James F master mechanic Pierce Mfg Co h 138 Merrimac
" James F Mrs (Katherine E O'Neill) millinery 262 Union h 138 Merrimac
" James T harness maker 860 Acushnet av b 374 N Front
" John operative b 374 N Front
" John operative h 3 Hazard ct
" John J (Powers & Luce) 37 Purchase rm 3 h 6 Brightman ct

COAL AND WOOD F. T. AKIN & COMPANY
HAY AND STRAW WALNUT, COR. WATER, 84 PLEASANT ST., 25 WELD SQ. 129 COVE STREET WHF. FOOT OF COFFIN STREET

Powers
" Joseph brass worker b 528 County [Trinity
" Lawrence H wheelwright h 18
" Margaret widow John H operative h 374 N Front [Allen
" Mary E clerk 185 Union b 262
" Mary E widow Richard h 12 Morton ct [sor
" Michael wood cutter b 64 Win-
" Michael J drill worker b 262 Allen
" Patrick gardener h 262 Allen
" Patrick H glass cutter h 150 Tallman
" Patrick H glass cutter b 262 Allen
" Peeris laborer h 144 Division
" Philip A driver h 528 County
" Richard Jr weaver b 12 Morton court [h at Fall River
" Robert W automobiles 99 William
" Telsford awning maker 31 Commercial b 15 Ash (S)
" Walter driver 159 Mill b 32 Rockland [man ct
" William J hostler b 6 Bright-
" & Luce (John J Powers and Charles T Luce) real estate 37 Purchase rm 3 [Howard
Poymola Stanley operative bds 20
Prada James mill worker h 147 Acushnet av [fin av
Praeda Antone laborer h 143 Cof-
" Antone M teamster 8 Union h 235 Fourth
" Frank mill hand b 139 Coffin av
" Joseph h 75½ Hemlock
" Joseph Jr operative h 75 Hemlock [Acushnet av
" Joseph R drill worker bds 147
" Manuel mill hand h 10 Acushnet block [ville av
" Manuel mill hand h 181 Belle-
" Manuel operative h 70 Winsor
" Manuel J operative h 2½ Hyacinth
" Mary widow Antone h 147 Acushnet av [net av
" Seraphin fireman h 4228 Acush-
" see Perry
Prairie Arcade weaver h 1176 Acushnet av [Middle
Prang W Edw cartoonist rms 158
PRARAY CHARLES W architect and mill eng 302 Times bldg h 167 Davis See page 42

Pratt Charles A physician 60 Orchard h do [do
" David D physician 319 Union b
" George S adv dist b 635 County
" Herbert C salesman 94 Union h 120 High [141 Summer
" Isaiah P foreman E E T Co h
" James E carder h 344 Coffin av
" John L removed to Fairhaven
" Leon weaver h 407 N Front
" Sarah F teacher Thomas Donaghy school b 106 Fourth
" Walter F student b 141 Summer
Pray Roland G theatrical mgr h 250 Coffin av [burn
Prebe Arthur ladderman h 32 Wash-
Prefontaine Philip clerk 1285 Acushnet av b 346 N Front
Preimoure Mary Mrs mill hand h 369 Coggeshall [fin av
Prejsner Joseph weaver h 283 Cof-
Preneau Delphis weaver b 203 Sawyer
" Hermenegilde h 203 Sawyer
" John B teamster h 2 DeWolfe
" Marie widow Charles h 112 Collette
" Wilfred doffer b 203 Sawyer
Prentiss Annie I widow Frank L h 72 Durfee
" Chester L removed to Mansfield
" Clara M music teacher 72 Durfee b do [Acushnet av
Prescott Albert mill hand bds 137
" Charles D physician 176 William and 108 Ash (S) h do
" Henry D physician 176 William b 108 Ash (S)
" Mary E Mrs b 161 Maxfield
" Mary R h 401 County
" Oliver (Crapo, Clifford & Prescott) lawyer 6 Masonic bldg h at Dartmouth
" Thomas weaver h 18 Cleveland
Presnor Frank operative h 39 Washburn
" John operative h 33 Washburn
Press Charles mule spinner bds 339 Rivet
" Edward removed to E Hampton
" Ernest operative b r 205 Acushnet av [av
" Lottie C Mrs h r 205 Acushnet
Preston Christopher spinner b 190 Wash rd

Remember to investigate our methods before taking up a business course.
Kinyon's Commercial School
Odd Fellows Bldg., Cor. William and Pleasant Sts., New Bedford, Mass.

Preston
" George weaver h 12 Cove
" Harry weaver h 7 Cleveland
" Henry W variety 1502 Acushnet av h 296 Tinkham
" John weaver b 70 Hathaway
" Roger copper worker h 102 Davis
" Walter F stage carpenter N B Theatre h 418 Union
Prevost Grace H Mrs b 98 Merrimac
" Joseph weaver h 68 Delano
" Moise D real estate 307 Times bldg h 78 S Sixth
" Philip teamster h 1012 S Water
Priaulx Peter gardener h 177 Arnold
Price Catherine Mrs h 153 Mt Pleasant
" Charles R treas 125 Middle h 16 Arnold pl
" Edmund T student b 16 Arnold pl
" Edward driver b 153 Mt Pleasant
" Henrietta h 91 James
" James teamster h 156 Cedar Grove
" John J joiner h 20 La France ct
" Manuel M operative b 868 County
" Mary S widow George H h 38 Campbell
" Ralph clerk 42 Front h at Fairhaven
" William H barber bds 60 Babbitt
" William F hostler b 2588 Acushnet av
Pries John cook h 7 Griffin
Priestly George h 28 Parker
Prifogle Edward police h 33 Durfee
Progoda Annie Mrs h 22 Cedar Grove
Prihoda Adolph weaver b 152 Tallman
" Franz weaver h 152 Tallman
" Franz Jr weaver b 152 Tallman
Prince Alfred mach oper 101 Kenyon h Nye
" Annie h 833 S Second
" Edmonde mill hand bds 106 Whitman
" Joseph barber h 153 Blackmer
Prior John mach h 8 Welcome
Pripa Joseph operative h 49 Rivet
Proctor Arthur weaver bds 206 Brook
" Edwin clerk bds 10 Harmony
" Henry weaver b 217 Phillips av
" Richard clerk 84 Pleasant b 10 Harmony
" Robert clerk 1200 Acushnet av
" Robert weaver h 166 Wash rd

Proctor
" Robert W weaver b 46 Ashley
" William removed from city
Prospect House Mrs L Lewis 82 William
Protin Leon mill hand bds 201 Sawyer
Proudfoot Harry weaver h 25 Mosher
Proulx Andrew third hand h 357 Bowditch
" George L laborer b 333 Shawmut av
" Hector A painter h 760 Purchase
" Henry operative h 373 Pleasant
" Henry J undertaker 45 Logan h do
" Joseph A weaver h 396 N Front
" Louis painter h 39 Roosevelt
" Peter F driver 235 State b 45 Logan
" Theophile eyeletter h 333 Shawmut av
PROUTEAU RAOUL contractor 82 Phillips av h do See page 760
Prouty Alfred W salesman 109 William rms 209 Middle
" Iris instructor N B Industrial school b 26 Seventh
" Iris G teacher rms 35 Eighth
" Sarah E Mrs b 3 Beetle lane
Provencher Achille box maker h 480 Coggeshall
" Dennis weaver b 162 Tinkham
" Dorilla clerk 1100 Acushnet av b 480 Coggeshall
" Fiada operative b 383 N Front
" Hormidas weaver h 383 N Front
" Philip weaver b 196 Collette
Provost Alfred baker 55 Mechanics lane b 178 Bowditch
" Arthur painter removed to Southbridge
" Arthur removed to Southbridge
" Arthur weaver b 384 Pleasant
" Austin foreman h 881 County
" De Forest jockey h 51 Nye
" Joseph fisherman h 28 Cleveland
" Joseph fixer removed from city
" Joseph H freight handler h 147 State
" Philip chauffeur Hose 2 bds 324 Cedar Grove
" Similien loom fixer h 384 Pleasant av
Prown Frank fireman b 52 Bennett
Prudeau Andrew removed from city
Prudential Ins Co (The) of America 41 William
Prue Peter F foreman 223 State bds 45 Logan

HASKELL BROS. DEALERS IN
ICE
400 COURT STREET TELEPHONE CONNECTION NEW BEDFORD, MASS.

Pruistas Ignaci weaver h 59 Washburn [Bowditch
Prunneau Nelson operative h 2
Prutcher Hannah W widow Charles J b 339 Reed
Przastek John operative h rear 46 Washburn [ton ct
Przbyla Wladyslaw weaver h 17 Ful-
Przyszewski Wladyslaw mill hand h 251 Coggeshall
Public Library William c Pleasant branches 20 Bowditch and Blackmer cor S Water
Puchala Paul milk Shawmut av n Plainville rd h do [Purchase
Puckering Frank motorman rms 602
Puerwinski John operative h 132 Cedar Grove [Sullivan
Pugh Isabella widow John A h 7
Puhamel Existe operative h 66 Washburn
Pullen Elizabeth weaver h 13 Salis-
Punch John mill hand h 157 Hathaway [Acushnet av
Punts August shoeworker h 29a
Puntschuh John F loom fixer h 125 Reynolds
Pupos John operative h 7 Marvin
Purcell James buffer h 78 Thomas
" John J loom fixer h 1631 Acushnet av [av
Puritan Laundry Co 298 Acushnet
" Lunch 1027 Acushnet av
" Tea & Coffee Co (Albert P White) 169 Campbell
Purrington Abbie music teacher 87 Mill h at Mattapoisett
" Charles H agt Fairhaven ferry rms 23 North [old
" Edward E glass cutter b 147 Arn-
" Frank H advt 107 Summer h do
" John G gardener h 147 Arnold
" Mary A Mrs died Dec 18 1910
" Oliver B Rev curate Grace church b 93 State [(S)
" William F die maker h 21 Ash
Purtkieurk Auty h 487 S Front
Pusere Peter agt h 931 Acushnet av
Putchlopek Frank operative h 193 N Front
Putnam Arthur C chief engineer Nashawena Mill [Kempton
" Edward R shoe cutter bds 119
" Elsie M teacher Thomas Donaghy school b 11 Fifth

Putnam
" Harry shoemaker b 119 Kempton
" Mary E widow Wilbur A h 119 Kempton
" Ralph M asst undertaker 594 Purchase bds 45 Willis
Putz Albert draftsman b 18 William
" Annie Mrs laundress h 18 William
" Henry salesman b 122 Middle
" Maria widow Gustave H, C lodging 122 Middle
Pye Alfred weaver h 14 Viall
" John B operative h 811 County
" John S h 1082 Acushnet av
" John T removed from city
Pyne Catherine widow James h 64 Bullard
" William J painter b 64 Bullard
Pyteraf Michal operative h 212 Cedar Grove
Pytraf Lawrynz carder h 9 Jean

Quackinbush Emeline widow Charles rms 18 Seventh
Quail Hugh driver h 92 Jouvett
" James bottler h 144 Division
" Mary A cloth inspector b 44 Salisbury [bury
" Nora cloth inspector b 44 Salis-
Quapp John carpenter h 83 Topham
Quaresma Manuel F h 161 Acushnet avenue
Quartarone Rosario operative h 4 Willis
Queen Harry kitchen furnishings 1075 S Water h 238 Acushnet av [do
" Henry real estate 125½ Fourth h
" James canvasser h 200 Acushnet av [do
" Louis optician 238 Acushnet av h
" Max removed to Providence R I
" Samuel comb maker 22 Fourth b 238 Acushnet av
Quenipel Benjamin Jr farmer 40 Main
Query Alphonse J wines and liquors 876 Acushnet av h 1814 do
" Ernest H & Co druggists 352 Kempton and 1759 Acushnet av b 81 Beetle [51 Nye
" Joseph clerk 876 Acushnet av h
" Paul h 81 Beetle
Quesko Olie E b 574 Kempton
" William cook h 574 Kempton

J. F. CROSSLEY 223 MILL STREET COR. EMERSON PHONE
STEAM and HOT WATER HEATING
GAS FITTING and FIXTURES

Quesko
" William H clerk 726 Kempton h 38 Round [Tinkham
Quigley Thomas F second hand h 203½
Quill Charles A fireman h 229 State
" Edward S mill hand b 229 State
" John overseer b 39 Bowditch
" Joseph operative b 39 Bowditch
" Timothy laborer h 569 Acushnet av
Quimby Arthur barber 302 Cedar rms 437 Purchase [Summer
" Cordelia M widow Ezra h 135
Quinham John W removed from city
" William E removed from city
Quinlan John R drill worker b 255 Weld [Water
" Matthew asst assessor h 877 S
" Thomas J spinner h 255 Weld
Quinn Edward laborer h 237 State
" John foreman h 481 Rivet
" John twister b 39 Bowditch
" John A sub letter carrier h r 70 Linden
" Joseph twister b 39 Bowditch
" Joseph P carder b 30 Acushnet av [net av
" Margaret widow Peter h 30
" Mark third hand h 134 County
" Martin oiler b 89 Mosher
" Michael h 64 Nelson
" Michael foreman 474 Acushnet av h 94 Durfee
" Michael real estate h 28 Stapleton
" Patrick foreman h 51 Valentine
" Robert carder b 30 Acushnet av
" Thomas egg candler 97 Front b 30 Acushnet av [110 Fruit
" Thomas engineer Butler Mill h
" Thomas operative b 217 Tinkham
" Thomas J painter h 324 Cedar
Quinnan Catherine F widow John h 215 Weld [Weld
" Lucy S clerk 185 Union b 215
" Thomas F spinner h 11 Adams
Quinnin George H clerk b 175 Sawyer
" Mary A widow Thomas h 175 Sawyer [av
" Thomas died Mar 22 1911
Quintal John mill hand b 116 Phillips
Quinten Ernest weaver b 1145 Kempton
" Edgar weaver h 1145 Kempton
Quintin Alfred iceman b 525 N Front
" Arsene fixer b 600 S Second

Quintin
" Arthur painter b 533 S Second
" Ernest clerk b 525 N Front
" Ernest mill hand b 14 Beetle
" Etienne city teamster h 1086 S Water
QUINTIN HERMENEGILDE N hardware 1223 Acushnet av b 99 Holly See page 767
" Hermidos h 81 Mosher
" Joseph b 148 Belleville av
" Joseph car cleaner U St Ry Co h
" Joseph carder h 225 Phillips av
" Joseph laborer h 478 Coggeshall
" Joseph weaver h 195 Phillips av
" Louis eyelet maker b 28 Washburn [S Second
" Marceline widow Amedee h 533
" Mary Mrs h 600 S Second
" Pierre h 120 Acushnet av
" Theodore O clerk 1223 Acushnet av h 99 Holly [Richmond
" Stanislas tailor 46 Purchase h 157
" Vitalis card grinder h 293 Coffin av [40 Elm
" Wilfred driver 215 Coggeshall h
" Zephir grocer 189 Belleville av h 525 N Front
" Zotique weaver h 107 Coffin av
Quintino Manuel laborer b 8 Beetle
Quirk George M teamster Standard Oil Co h at Fairhaven
" Grace widow William boarding house 1098 Acushnet av
" James carpenter b 95 Tremont
" John V fixer h 176 Coffin av
" Joseph laborer b 95 Tremont [do
" Louise G matron 194 Purchase b
" Nellie F clerk b 95 Tremont
" Margaret J h 95 Tremont [net av
" Richard operative b 1098 Acush-
" Samuel W spinner h 395 N Front
" William died April 3 1911
Quirt Joseph operative h 14 Cotter
Quissett Mill cotton mfrs Grinnell

Rabeilo Antone operative h 102 Mosher [ville av
" Frank S operative h 125 Belle-
" Innocence operative h 31 Margin
" Joseph laborer b 31 Margin
" Manuel laborer h 104 Mosher
Rabenovet Z Samuel salesman 934 S Water b 932 do [Water
Rabideau Joseph shoemaker h 926 S

CHARLES A. CROSHERE CARRIAGE AND AUTO
38 FOURTH ST. Bell Phone 1964-23 PAINTING

Rabideau
" Nory removed to Fairhaven
Rabidovitch Annie widow Joseph h 458 S Water
" Sam clerk b 458 S Water
" Samuel (Resevitz & Rabidovitch) 315 S Water b 458 do
Rably Joseph hostler 486 Rivet h 31 Margin [net av h 1176 do
Racette Alphonse clerk 1347 Acush-
" Anselme removed to Fitchburg
" Louis operative b 20 Salisbury
" Roch weaver h 20 Salisbury
" Victor rem to Wallington Conn
Racicot Arthur tinsmith 19 Linden h 94 Nye [Bullard h do
" Elie S cigar manufacturer 101
" Henry contractor h 82½ Nye
Racine Benoni picker tender h 20 Holly
" Charles weaver b 20 Holly
" George carpenter h 411 Rivet
" Jules hairdresser 1210 Acushnet av h 291 N Front
" Oscar weaver b 411 Rivet
" Osias fixer h 43 Holly
Rack Charles carpenter h 93 N Front
Radcliffe Charles second hand h r 874 County
" Wilfred lunch and second hand store 400 Purchase h 388 do
" see Ratcliffe
Radix Manuel mill hand h 35 Rotch block 435 Bolton
Rae Edward J (Rae & Osborne) 27 Fifth h at Fairhaven
" & Osborne (Edward J Rae and Patrick V Osborne) furniture repairers 27 Fifth
Rafel Joseph fisherman h 32 South
Raffael Manuel carpenter h 28 Bourne
" see Raphael
Rafferty Mary E h 102 State [rd
Rafuce Vernon M laborer b 2 Cove
Ragin Harry Hebrew teacher h 600 S Water
Ragori Victoria laborer h 4 Wall
Railton James agent h 1058 S Water
Rainey Henry operative h 101 Potomska
Rainford Alfred died Dec 29 1910
" Alfred E letter carrier h 114 Sycamore [Rockdale
" Mary A widow Alfred bds 1276
Rainville Albert h 203 Sawyer
" Alfred N carpenter h 269 Coggeshall [60 Bullard
" Armand blacksmith 30 Bethel b
" Arthur machinist b 11 Nye
" Domina carpenter h 154 Belleville rd
" Felix carpenter h 11 Nye [av
" George mill hand h 194 Belleville
" George twister h 52 Phillips av
" Joseph farmer h Plainville rd
" Joseph G farmer h Plainville rd
" L Frederick clerk 1592 Acushnet av h 257 Tinkham [60 Bullard
" Peter S clerk 1347 Acushnet av h
" Philbert O musician h 148 Arnold [Co b 257 Tinkham
" Philip E clerk Old Colony Box
" Wilfred L carpenter h 60 Bullard
" William manager rms 273 Cottage
" Zacher J removed from city
Raistrich Frederick machinist h 211 Hathaway [mony
Ralph James operative b 14 Har-
Ralston William H clerk Potomska Mills b 15 Richmond
Ramalhete Joaquim P agent 73 William h 77 Hemlock
" John T carder h 20 Cove rd
Ramanon Hyman shoes 842 Purchase h 111 Clark [b 19 Walnut
Rames John F clerk 286 Acushnet av
Ramford James weaver h 159 David
Ramon Joseph M laborer h 247 S Front [12 Green
Ramos Annie S widow Joseph S h
" Antone rope worker h 407 S Water
" Arthur carpenter h 81 Sidney
" Carall laborer h 85 S Second
" Francisco Mrs h 85 S Second
" Frank mill hand h 97 S Second
" Frank operative b 19 Walnut
" John cook h 412 S Water
" John laborer h 435 S Water
" John weaver h 67 Rivet
" Joseph removed from city [Green
" Joseph S silver worker b 12
" Manuel grocer h 8 Morgan lane
" Manuel laborer h 19 Walnut[(S)
" Manuel laborer h 269 Orchard
" Manuel B laborer h 28 County
" Manuel J operative h 85 Mosher
" Matthew seaman h 62 S Second
" Maurice driver b 19 Walnut

J. G. NICHOLSON
LUMBER, SASH, DOORS and BLINDS
BOWDITCH STREET, NEW BEDFORD, MASS.

Ramos
" Nicola mariner h 412 S Water
Ramsbottom Archibald weaver b 105 Davis [Margin
" Caleb E janitor 755 First h 16
" Charles G clerk 141 Purchase b 16 Margin [Davis
" Frances widow Jonathan bds 141
" Francis molder h 50 Princeton
" John W music teacher b 16 Margin
Ramsdell Frank E Rev pastor North Cong church h 446 County
" Charlotte housekeeper 69 Sycamore [446 County
" Theodore reporter Standard b
Ramsden Albert S driver 270 Acushnet av h 46 Atlantic [place
" George A operative b 15 Ashland
" John h 15 Ashland
" John rms 22 Warren
" Thomas W music teacher 682 Cottage h do [van
Ramsey Edric rope maker h 2 Sulli-
Ramshead Joseph slasher h 34 Howland Village [Dartmouth
Ranagan Isaac B tube worker h 27
Rancourt Joseph weaver h 22 Nelson
Randall Edgar F cabinetmaker h 81 Hillman
" George E painter h 11 Phillips av
" George W carpenter 13 Cottage h do [fee
" Georgianna widow h r 102 Dur-
" Harriet H widow Theodore E h 14 Emerson (S)
" Hattie K clerk b 13 Cottage
" Ida h 5 Franklin [h 305 do
" James A variety 307 Acushnet av
" Philip C foreman 226 N Water h 22 Grape
" Sarah S died Jan 25 1911 [av
" William mill hand h 140 Acushnet
" William F mechanical toymaker h r 144 N Second
Ranicar A spinner h 150 Hathaway
Rankin Thomas carder h 15 Ashley
" William weaver h 107 Rockland
" William E machinist bds 107 Rockland
" William H (Rankin & Arnold) 19 N Second rms 93 School

RANKIN & ARNOLD (William H Rankin and H Percy Arnold) machinists 19 N Second See page 780
Ransom Frances H dressmaker 592 Kempton h do
" Mary S Mrs Rev pastor Home Gospel Mission h 334 Kempton
Rapa Laurant weaver h 9 Blackburn
Raphael Felix hairdresser 407 Purchase h 10 Willis
" Frank J carpenter N B W W h 16 Richmond
" Jesse painter h 203 Division
" Joseph fisherman h 575 S Water
" Martin laborer h 2 Maiden lane
" William S plumber N B W W h 18 Richmond [mouth
Raposa Angelo mill hand b 104 Dart-
" Antone clerk b 365 First
" Antoine comber h 45 Nelson
" Augustine mill hand h 27 Swift
" John F 263 Coggeshall h 81 Field
" Joseph operative h 277 S Front
" Joseph Jr fireman h 63 James
" Manuel laborer h 13 Rivet
" Manuel laborer h 55 Howland
" Manuel laborer h 422 S Second
" Manuel operative h 99 Field
" Manuel C mill hand h 27 Swift
" & Co (John F Raposa and Gustave Alves) liquors 263 Coggeshall [ond
Rapoza Antone laborer h 191 S Sec-
" Antone laborer h 365 First
" Jacintho laborer h 55 Mitchell
" Jacken mill hand h 775 Water
" Joseph laborer h 205 N Second
" Joseph operative b 93 Prospect
" Manuel foundryman h 54 Page
" Manuel mill hand b 54 Lombard
" Manuel operative h 45 Mitchell
" Manuel (23 Mitchell) rem to Fall River
" Mary widow Antone h 411 First
" M C & Co grocers 133 Dartmouth
Rappolo Anton labored h 12 Wall
Rasmussen Hans twist driller h 116 Acushnet av
Rasscette Alice salesman b 127 State
" Archie operative b 127 State
" Edmond laborer b 127 State
" Emil laborer b 127 State

Steiger-Dudgeon Co.
"The WOMAN'S Store."
Tel. Bell 82 & 83, Branches connecting all depts.
" " 160 For Office only. Auto. 1211

SUMPTIONS, ASSORTMENTS AT ALL TIMES OF DEPENDABLE DRY GOODS

Rasscette
" Louis blacksmith 2171 Acushnet av h 127 State [Bowditch
Ratchford Michael weaver h 343
Ratcliff Charles operative h 16 Cleveland
Ratcliffe Daniel farmer h 133 State
" Harry overseer Grinnell Mfg Corp h 2529 Acushnet av
" John weaver b 850 First
" John weaver h 13 Marvin
" Myers sweeper rms 282 Acushnet avenue [yer
" Ralph copperworker h 448 Saw-
" William clerk h 45 Vine
" see Radcliffe [150 Fourth
Rathburn Abbie G widow Elisha h
Rathe Joseph carpenter h 86 Clifford
Ratte Arthur clerk h 61 Bullard
Rau Gustavus L special police h 36 Buttonwood [ham
Raulet Jules operative h 85 Top-
Raulino Antonio J variety 104½ Thompson h 106 do [Thompson
" Arthur J cloth presser bds 106
" Claudino J teamster 45 Union
Raulins Oliver J laborer h 65 Independent
Ravich Simon physician r 153 Acushnet av h do [Bonney
Rawcliffe Anthony machinist h 15
" Arthur machinist h 86 Dartmouth
" Fred weaver h 126 Crapo
" Percy clerk 100 Fifth b 15 Bonney [27 Willard
" Thomas inspector N B W W h
" Walter machinist h 32 Lindsey
Rawlins Anthony J overseer Acushnet Mill Corp h 35 McGurk
" Arthur J mill hand h 192 Washington
Rawson Alfred weaver h 297 Coffin avenue [av
" Charles twister h 240 Phillips
" Joseph weaver b 16 Ashley
Rawstron John T weaver h 1637 Acushnet av
" Mary J widow Thomas h 17 Scott
" see Rostron [school b 50 Locust
Ray Annie S teacher Clark street
" Archie rem from city [Larch
" Diana S widow Charles M h 65
" Harry L asst foreman h 205 Brock av

Ray
" Isabella Mrs h 131 State
" John drillworker h 265 Middle
" John B overseer Taber Mill h 6 Harrison [ond
" Joseph J weaver h 519 S Sec-
" Thomas glasscutter b 370 Orchard (S)
Raymond Abbie bds 151 Grinnell
" Alfred O letter carrier b 28 McGurk
" Alphonse weaver b 28 McGurk
" Annie W widow Arthur W lodgings 188 Purchase [geshall
" Anthony S salesman h 361 Cog-
" Benjamin D chauffeur bds 188 Purchase
" B Frank b 228 Pleasant [Smith
" Calvin Jr driver 14 N Sixth h 104
RAYMOND CHARLES stable 396 Cottage h 83 Sycamore See page 771
" Charles E plumber h 15 Homer
" Edward police h 347 Rivet
" Ellen widow Joseph b 235 Bowditch
" Frances bds 182 Arnold
" Frank laborer b 104 Acushnet av
" George D loom fixer h 28 McGurk
" George E overseer h 18 Studley
" Henry L loom fixer h 163 Bonney [h 163 Bonney
" Henry W hairdresser 405 Rivet
" Hiram E police h 149 Central av
" Joseph cook 131 S Second
" Joseph operative h 177 N Front
" Joseph M laborer h 247 S Front
" Joseph photographer 897 S Water h 907 do [Morgan lane
" Manuel grocer 339 S Water h 8
" Mary widow h 235 Fourth
" Mary S died June 14 1911
" Paul operative h 32 Woodlawn avenue [h 256 Summer
" Thomas A clerk G & P Coal Co
" Walter T clerk 5 Purchase b 104 Smith
" Wilfred painter b 163 Bonney
" Willard F grocer 62 Spruce h 58 do [Fifth
" William D master mariner h 25
Raymundo Manuel M laborer h 76 Sidney [lard
Rayner Edward spinner h 26 Wil-

PELEG H. SHERMAN 506 COUNTY ST.
FUNERAL DIRECTOR AND EMBALMER
OFFICE PHONES. Bell 690-13. Auto. 1305.
RESIDENCE PHONES. Bell 690-12. Auto. 1306.

Rayner
" John W joiner b 26 Willard
" Joseph clerk 446 Rivet b 26 Willard
" Thomas conductor h 276 Earle
Rayno Orra widow John bds 86 Belleville road
" William weaver h 86 Belleville [rd
Rays Rose P widow h 60 Howland
Razario Jule seaman h 152 S Second
Raze Antoni ropeworker h 141 Emerson (N)
Razoux Henry A chiropodist 74 Purchase h at Fairhaven
Rea Manuel J deck hand h 115½ [Fifth
Read Charles W 340 Acushnet av h 442 County
" Clara A and Ella H h 404 Coun- [ty
" Cynthia A widow Joseph R h 404 County
" Everett P b 11 Lincoln
" Ferdinand S supt Taunton-New Bedford Copper Co h 111 Campbell
" George P Jr carpenter h 327 [Cedar
" James weaver b 158 Hathaway
" John teamster h 182 Weld
" Joseph M cotton broker 62 N Water h 5 Lincoln
" Sanford K metal spinner h 104 South
" William weaver h 369 Cogge- [shall
" William Alexander h 695 County
" William F h 11 Lincoln
" William T clerk 100 Fifth h 4 Arch
" W Kempton clerk Kilbury Mill [h 157 Page
" & Co (Louis, Jean and Frederick C Clark) men's furnishings 141 Union
" see Reed and Reid
Ready Philip F chauffeur h 11 West
Reagan John O salesman h 701 First
" Nellie widow Jeremiah h 60 Washburn
" Richard laborer b 60 Washburn
" see O'Reagan
Real Emilo grocer 688 Acushnet av [h do
" F h 182 Weld
Reanoud Frank bartender h 76 Hicks
Reardon Agnes clerk 182 Union b 60 Liberty
" Hannah housekeeper 60 Liberty
" James gardener h 60 Liberty
" James laborer b 232 N Second

Reardon
" Johanna widow Patrick h 106 Merrimac
" John shoemaker rms 148 Max- [field
" John teamster h 81 Liberty
" Mary widow David h 25 McGurk
" Patrick H clerk 809 Purchase b 106 Merrimac
" Patrick H laborer h 10 Hazard ct
" Patrick P laborer h 247 Mill
" Thomas F gardener h 63 Ash (N)
Reaume Leo loom fixer h 6 McGurk
Rebello Angelo watchman h 30 South
" Frank (Oliveira & Rebello) grocer 175 Sawyer h 16 Cotter
" Manuel E operative h 103 Davis
" Manuel P clerk b 102 Mosher
Rebinan Gotthilf baker 362 Earle
Reca Frank S carpenter and hardware 84 Dartmouth h 82 do
" John F clerk 246 Union bds 82 Dartmouth
" Lillian M clerk 41 Purchase bds [82 Dartmouth
Recardo Virginia carder h 41 Mosher
Reckords George C motorman rms r 893 County
Red Cross Pharmacy (Allen & Matthews) 116 Dartmouth
" Cross Shoe Co The (Alexander Leabeau and Omer E Belair) shoe repairing 864 Acushnet avenue
Reddy Ann widow h 16 Morton ct
" James clerk 104 Cove b 96 do
" James weaver b 16 Morton ct
" J Patrick operative h 228 State
" Mary widow John b 152 Washington
" Michael weaver b 16 Morton ct
" Michael J weaver h 96 Cove
" Michael J Jr machinist b 96 Cove
" Patrick operative h 131 State
" Sarah F teacher Thomas Donaghy school h 152 Washington
" see Ruddy
Redfearn Dixon photo supplies 853 S Water and 933 Acushnet av h 931 do
Redfern Ella F Mrs h 6 Dover
" Joseph A repairman 18 Market h 6 Dover
" Mark machinist h 170 Ashland
" Thomas rem to Rochester N Y
Redfield Charles O glasscutter h 48 Grape

PAINTERS' SUPPLIES
Walnut, Cor. Water, 84 Pleasant St. 25 WELD SQ., 129 COVE ST.
F. T. AKIN & COMPANY

Redfield
" Charles T b 48 Grape
Redman Hall 963 Acushnet av
" Joseph W spinner h 66 Phillips avenue [French avenue
" Winsor B machinist h 114 W
Redpath William J clerk 240 Union h 744 County
Reece Fred weaver h 43 Reynolds
" Herbert weaver h 37 Reynolds
Reed Albert operative b 1007 Rockdale avenue
" Arthur F conductor b 62 North
" Bertha D music teacher 103 Sycamore b do
" Charles A ice 36 Dartmouth h do
" Charles H machinist h 179 Arnold [dale av
" Charles T teaming h 1007 Rock-
" Clara Mrs operative 31 Commercial h 24 High [88 Chancery
" Clarence W salesman 8 Union h
" Clifford E teamster h 289 Earle
" Edmond A clerk 1 Municipal bldg h 88 Washington
" Edward B clerk h 89 High
" Edwin J master mariner h 12 Borden
" Ethel A teacher George H Dunbar annex school b 246 Fourth
" Fannie W Mrs b 20 Crapo
" Fanny Mrs bds 273 Mill
" Frank L carpenter h 81 Lake
" Fred b Howard Pittsley's Tarkiln Hill road
" Frederick teamster h 85 Austin
" Frederick A drillworker b 77 Taber [shnet av
" Frederick A fireman b 1498 Acu-
" Frederick M mechanical engineer 100 Fifth rms 117 Fourth
" Frederick R laborer h 340 Kempton
" George H bottler h Hawes lane
" George E driver h 327 Shawmut avenue
" Grace Mrs h 292 Middle
" Harriet h 289 Acushnet av
" Henrietta T widow Eli W h Tarkiln Hill road by the pond
" Hollis M blacksmith h 120 Robeson
" Horace H cook h 326 Middle
" Isaac carpenter h Tarkiln Hill rd

Reed
" James loom fixer h 216 Shawmut avenue
" James A h 246 Fourth
" James E photographer 7 Purchase h 172 Arnold [ton
" Jirah F drillworker b 340 Kemp-
" Jeptha watchman h 133 Willis
" John H laborer h 712 Kempton
" Jonathan W chief engineer 214 S Water h 83 Atlantic [len
" Leander driver 2 Union h 394 Al-
" Leander M helper b 64½ Dartmouth [Water h 851 Kempton
" Leonard R iron melter 229 N
" Leslie S installer 57 N Second
" Lottie M clerk 41 Purchase b 23 Seventh [Elm
" Lyman K stonecutter h 149
" Lydon A clerk 36 Purchase b 340 Kempton
" Marion piper h 64½ Dartmouth
" Marion S piper 125 Middle h 9 Spooner
" Mary widow Frank B h 353 Park
" Matilda widow Joseph h 101 Campbell
" Minnie A clerk 41 Purchase b at N Dartmouth [avenue
" Percy B laborer b 987 Rockdale
" Philip A carpenter b 48 Cedar
" Pheobe M Mrs h 54 First
" Rebecca E Mrs h 163 Mt Pleasant
" Richard A watchman h 80 Oak
" Roland slasher tender h 34 Stapleton [103 Sycamore
" Ruth H widow Benjamin F H b
" Thomas F salesman 188 N Water h 18 Hunter
" Wallace assistant superintendent Oneko Woolen Mills h 1462 Acushnet av
" Willard chauffeur b 77 Taber
" Willard H h 56 Kempton
" William slasher h 208 Weld
" William H foreman cooper 144 S Water h 244 Arnold [lane
" William P farm foreman h Hawes
" see Read and Reid [genia
Reedy James third hand b 128 Eu-
" John mill hand b 128 Eugenia [ter
" Joseph conductor h 11 McMurray
Reel John teamster h 182 Weld
Reeves Albert weaver b 14 McGurk

To do things right you must be taught. Our instructors can do it.
Kinyon's Commercial School
Odd Fellows Bldg., Cor. William and Pleasant Sts., New Bedford, Mass.

Reeves
" Aime weaver h 187 Earle
" Franklin T removed from city
" Harry carpenter 2 Watson
" J Napoleon insurance agent 120 Purchase rm 403 h 200 Collette
" Levi laborer h 14 McGurk
" Samuel baker h 20 George
" Wilfred J removed from city
Refhuss George F upholsterer 36 Purchase [dle h 51 Maitland
Refuse Robert G meter man 125 Mid-
" Robert T horse shoer 391 Acushnet av h 45 Richmond
Regados Joseph mill hand h 201 Coggeshall [ond
Regan Andrew laborer b 232 N Sec-
" Charles laborer h 30 Juniper
" Dennis laborer h 541 Rivet
" John removed from city
" John W operative h 44 Roosevelt
" Mary widow John b 59 Roosevelt
" Michael desk editor Times h at Fall River
" Patrick laborer bds 531 Rivet
Regetto Peter salesman 67 William b 86 N Second
Regis Theophile painter h 50 Nye
Rego Angelo mill hand b 109 Davis
" Antone bds 3 Mitchell
" Antone laborer h 383 S Second
" Antone mill hand b 80 Davis
" Antone F spinner h 153 Belleville
" Frank interpretor 299 Acushnet avenue
" Frank laborer h 107 Perry
" John weaver b 396 S Second
" Joseph fisherman h 20 County
" Joseph fisherman h 396 S Second
" Joseph hairdresser 332 Coggeshall h 35 Mitchell
" Manuel operative h 514 S Second
" Max mill hand b 109 Davis
Reichwein William mgr rms 16 Fifth
Reid Clara roll coverer b 16 Willow
" Frank A foreman 77 Rivet h 68 Oak
" John laborer h 28 Acushnet av
" John laborer h 1122 Acushnet av
" Margaret widow Benjamin h 16 Willow
" Nelson glass cutter h 100 S Sixth

Reid
" Rebecca Mrs b 57 Cottage
" Robert sexton St Martins Episcopal church h 178 Blackmer
" Robert F linotype operator Standard h 453 Cottage [av
" Samuel weaver b 1122 Acushnet
" William clerk 47 Foster b 68 Oak
" see Read and Reed
Reidell Clifford teacher Swain Free school h at Marion
Reidemann Alphonse pressman 185 Union h 348 Coffin avenue
Reidy Annie widow b 19 Ruth
" David mule spinner h 10 Warren
" Margaret h 19 Ruth
Reil Frank E removed to N Y City
Reilly Agnes G stenographer 97 William rm 205 h 144 Cedar
" Elizabeth operative h 155 Tallman
" Florence M druggist 396 Union h do [Providence R I
" Frank L hats 21 Purchase h at
" George removed to Fall River
" George W removed from city
" James died May 24 1911
" Joseph C died June 23 1911
" Martin A fitter b 76 W French av
" Nancy L physician b 396 Union
" Richard laborer b 155 Tallman
" William removed to Fall River
" see Riley
Reinieche Edward weaver h 29 Ashley
" Edward J removed from city
" Emile weaver h 40 Roosevelt
" Jules weaver h 17 Salisbury
Reis Antone J Jr farmer b 571 Allen
" Antonio farmer h 571 Allen
" Antonio operative h 141 Emerson (N) [Rotch blk 439 Bolton
" Joaquim De mill hand h 27
" Joseph h 12 Babbitt
" Manuel city laborer h 33 Swift
" Manuel operative h 67 Independent
" Nellie Mrs h 10 Griffin
Riesch Frank insurance agent h 15 Washburn
Reiter John W musician h 185 North
Reizendes Victorino operative h 25 Hall [104 State
Rellas John (P Couroussi & Co) h

HASKELL BROS. DEALERS IN
ICE
400 COURT STREET TELEPHONE CONNECTION NEW BEDFORD, MASS.

Remi Adaline widow Dominick h 178 Bowditch
" Henry operative h 47 Ashley
Remick Edgar painter rms 300 Acushnet avenue [Middle
Remier Charles R salesman rms 158
Remillard Emile tailor 1014 Acushnet av b 179 Bowditch [Bowditch
" Joel tailor 1014 Acushnet av h 179
" Napoleon carder b 96 Holly
" Narcisse laborer h 96 Holly
" Oscar teamster h 809 County
" Richard clerk 79 Austin h 434 Pleasant
" Rosalie dressmaker 85 Rivet h do
Remington Charles S teamster b 615 Acushnet avenue [h 11 Spruce
" Emerald A painter 347 Kempton
" Emma A h 221 Middle
" Frank L police station 5 h 73 Linden [h 117 Robeson
" Holden asst supt Brooklawn park
" Holden student rms 1 Ash (N)
" Lucy J bds 67 Fifth
" Walter H B city clerk office 208 Municipal bldg h 1 Ash (N)
" William S h 68 Fifth
Remus Joseph hairdresser h 91 Berkley [Bowditch
Remy Adeline widow Dominie h 178
Rena Madame (Therena R Cote) clairvoyant h 135 Middle
Rene Adam clerk 1401 Acushnet av bds 1405 do [h 55 Pierce
Renehan Thomas bartender 214 Union
Renaud Arthur weaver b 67 Coffin av
" Frank clerk h 76 Hicks
" Leon carpenter h 124 Collette
" Napoleon capenter h 302 Sawyer
" Victor weaver b 975 S Water
Renault Eugene shoe repairer 1053 County h 1060 do [av
Renee Ami weaver h 1405 Acushnet
Renihan Thomas bar tender h 53 Pierce
Rennerfelt Charles H h 117½ Fifth
Renex Annie W Mrs nurse h 83 Mt Pleasant
" Belle nurse b 83 Mt Pleasant
" Charles T chauffeur b 83 Mt Pleasant [sant
" George E salesman b 83 Mt Plea-
Repeta Louis removed from city
Repmun Gotthilf baker b 362 Earle
Resevitz Abram H (Resevitz & Rabinovitz) 315 S Water b 21 Morgan's lane
" Louis removed to Brockton
" & Rabinovitz (Abram H Resevitz and Samuel Rabinovitz) furniture 315 S Water [State
Rettinger Lawrence C baker h 172
Reul Henry weaver b 50 Washburn
" John fixer bds 128 Eugenia
" Leopoldine widow George h 50 Washburn [av
Reusch Joseph doffer b 287 Phillips
" Leopold shoe repairer r 287 Phillips av h do
Revalion Herbert I baker 437 Purchase h 338 Kempton [man
Revallion William clerk h 375 Hill-
Rex Fred J b 183 Allen [h 92 do
" Harry W foreman 90 Dartmouth
" John granite cutter 90 Dartmouth h 160 Fair
REX MONUMENTAL WORKS 90 Dartmouth See back cover
" Samuel T prop Rex Monumental Works 90 Dartmouth h 183 Allen
Rexford Chester P asst claim adjuster U St Ry Co Purchase cor William h 106 School
" George P foreman inspector 100 Fifth h 78 do
Reynolds Albert rope maker h Plainville road [tor h 243 Chestnut
" Alonzo F foreman R R car inspec-
" Benjamin b 76 Durfee [av
" Charles D laborer b 2331 Acush-
" Daniel weaver b 111 Fourth
" Edward h 62 Washburn
" Edward wood h 3277 Acushnet av
" Edward A piper b 394 Elm (W)
" Edward G h 210 Pleasant
" Elias H carpenter h 28 Sylvia
" Emma L clerk b 2331 Acushnet avenue
" Emma rem to Acushnet
" Everett clerk b 111 Fourth
" Franklin S laborer b r 900 Belleville av
" Fred clerk 43 Bedford [rd
" Frederick engineer b 174 River
" Frederick W supt Whitman Mills h 53 Fourth

J. F. CROSSLEY 223 MILL STREET COR. EMERSON PHONE
STEAM and HOT WATER HEATING
GAS FITTING and FIXTURES

Reynolds
" George H mfr circulation dept Standard h 88 Park [av
" Grace E clerk b 2331 Acushnet
" Harry clerk 403 Kempton rms 325 do [Mill
" Helen W clerk 185 Union bds 56
" Herbert C plumber 46 Wing h 53 Fifth [North
" Howard N gas fitter bds 178
" James mule spinner b 111 Fourth
" James F teamster h 2331 Acushnet av [dle h at Acushnet
" Jeanette M bookkeeper 125 Mid-
" John designer Whitman Mill Co h 23 Welcome
" John salesman h 12 Crapo
" John watchman h 227 State
" John weaver h 27 E French av
" Joseph A fireman b 12 Rounds
" Joseph B blacksmith h 56 Mill
" Lillian Mrs clerk 40 Purchase b 140 Acushnet av
" Llewellyn B rem to Smith Mills
" Luella F clerk 200 Union b 243 Chestnut [ond b 54 Allen
" Mabel A supervisor 57 N Sec-
" Mary E stenographer 474 Acushnet av b 181 Summer
" Maxwell removed from city
" Nettie L Mrs dressmaker 56 Mill h do [Fourth
" Rebecca C widow George bds 53
" Thomas clerk 70 Cove bds Social [h at Fall River
" Thomas F plumber 28 N Water
" Willard E roll coverer h 141 Tallman [son
" William watchman b 90 Robe-
" William D salesman 70 Union h 178 North [178 North
" William S teamster 70 Union b
Rezendes Albert bookkeeper bds 41 Briggs
" Antone mill hand h 50 Dean
" Antone operative h 10 Oneko lane
" Antone D operative h 8 Oneko lane [lane
" Francisco F laborer b 10 Oneko
" Joseph laborer b 153 Belleville av
" Joseph mill hand h 80 Davis
" Joseph F sausage mfr 433 S Second h 41 Briggs
" Joseph P laborer h 3 Mitchell
" Joseph S laborer h 3 Mitchell

Rezendes
" Manuel laborer b 50 Dean [ell
" Manuel E watchman h 39 Mitch-
" Manuel F laborer b 98 Oneko lane [lane
" Manuel T operative b 8 Oneko
" Maria Mrs h 173 Coggeshall
Rheumme Joseph D shoemaker h 910 S Water
" Oscar laborer h 204 Sawyer
RHODE ISLAND DETECTIVE AGENCY The 395 Westminster Providence R I See page 37
Rhodes Addie widow Henry W h 536 Purchase
" George H (Rhodes, Woodward & Co) 45 William h at N Y city
" John B asst treas and general mgr 123 Front h at Newport
" John C h 412 County [Front
" J C & Co Inc shoe eyelets 123
" Lavinia h 536 Purchase
" Nellie F h 536 Purchase
" William weaver h 191 Brock av
" Woodward & Co (G H Rhodes and Francis and Thomas Woodward Jr) cotton 45 William [Reynolds
Riach Charles electrician h 37
Ribchester Francis B died Nov 22 1910 [280 Bowditch
" John overseer Quisett Mill h
Ribeiro Antonio J speeder tender h 27 Dunbar
" Mary Mrs h 205 Bonney
Riber Nicholi rem from city
Ribourg Albert Rev pastor French Baptist church h 45 Willis
Ricard Alphonse mason's supplies 142 Nye h 79 Holly
" Arsene carpenter h 69 Hathaway
" John B carpenter h 118 Whitman
RICARD LEVI sawing and planing mill 142 Nye and (Ricard & Marsh) liquors 410 N Front h 91 Holly See page 765
" Napoleon grocer 126 Bowditch h 128 do
" Pierre carpenter h 358 N Front
" & Marsh (Levi Ricard and James Marsh) wholesale liquors 410 N Front
Rice Adoniram J baker h 171 Washington [av
" Antone weaver h 150 W French
" Arthur W conductor h 595 Union

CHARLES A. CROSHERE
38 FOURTH ST. Bell Phone 1964-23
SIGN PAINTING
GLASS LETTERING
ELECTRIC SIGNS
SHOW CARDS

Rice
" Damon W clerk to supt N B W W 40 Masonic bldg b 75 Sycamore [ison
" Elmo T glasscutter bds 24 Mad-
" Emeline G prepared foods h 118 Arnold [359 Park
" Hallett L foreman 123 Front h
" J Harry glasscutter h 24 Madison
Rich Solomon L painter h 286 Cedar
Richard Adelard clerk 1510 Acushnet av rms 364 N Front
" Albert clerk 61 County bds 27 Roosevelt
" Albert shoecutter h 180 Austin
" Albert C bridge builder h 109 Tallman
" Alfred E physician 78 Nye h do
" Alphonse boarding house 60 Bullard h do
" Angilena type machinist operator 101 Kenyon b 78 Nye
" Arthur operative h 28 Katharine
" Calixte second hand h 178 Phillips av [man
" Calixte stonecutter h 88 Tall-
" Clement operative bds 43 Holly
" Cyril twister b 2740 Acushnet av
" Delphis driller h 473 N Front
" Denise weaver h 52 Ashley
" Didier truckman b 28 Holly
" Edmonde operative b 16 Hicks
" Edmonde third hand b 395 Belleville av
" Edward shoecutter b 180 Austin
" Emery fixer h 681 Purchase [man
" Emma widow Arthur b 88 Tall-
" Euclid weaver h 115 Nash rd
" Eugene lather b 33 Holly
" Eugene weaver b 289 Coffin av
" Fred laborer b 15 Margin
" Gilbert h 28 Holly
" Henry fisherman h 154 Eugenia
" Henry third hand b 70 Ruth
" Herminie clerk 1009 Acushnet av bds 1060 do [chase
" Horace carpenter b 1191 Pur-
" James painter h 6 Bonneau court
" Jean fisherman h 477 N Front
" John carpenter h 177 Dean
" John fisherman b 12 Nye [R I
" John (twister) rem to Georgeville
" Joseph carder h 237 Coffin av
" Joseph mill hand h 487 N Front

Richard
" Joseph painter h 319 Belleville av
" Joseph weaver h 76 Blackmer
" Joseph weaver b 88 Tallman
" Joseph A loom fixer b 88 Tallman [shuet av
" Joseph C restaurant 1185 Acu-
" Louis spinner h 29 Ashley
" Marie T corsets 487 N Front bds do [145 Bullard
" Mary widow Alfred operative h
" Napoleon weaver h 53 Ruth
" Narcisse laborer b 15 Margin
" Noe grocer 383 Belleville av h 179 Earle [chase
" Norman operative bds 273 Pur-
" Odilon carpenter b 61 Dean
" Oliva carpenter h 293 Sawyer
" Oliver operative h 127 Whitman
" Onesime carpenter h 126 Tallman
" Philias clerk h 395 Belleville av
" Philias fisherman b 16 Hicks
" Philip cook h 268 N Front
" Pierre laborer h 15 Margin
" Pierre weaver h 27 Roosevelt
" Pierre Jr laborer h 15 Margin
" William operative b 28 Holly
Richards Charles laborer b 101 Bullard
" Emily L h 15 Warren
" Ernest painter h 195 Crapo
" Ernest V janitor h 128 Fourth
" George painter and baker 40 W French av h 38 do
" George D sporting goods 249 Union rms 14 S Sixth
" George L physician 97 William rm 307 h at Fall River
" Henry D h 101 Bullard
" John laborer h 39 Tallman
" John rem from city
" John H clerk rms 3 Park place
" John R weaver h 156 Holly
" Joseph (Richards & Marshall) b 16 Griffin [nut
" Joseph C conductor h 242 Chest-
" Laura J widow Edward R h 58 Sycamore
" Lillian h 156 Smith [Fourth
" Louise widow Charles h 128
" Paul barber 1107 Acushnet av
" William D stable 19 S Second h 77 Bedford
" & Marshall (Joseph Richards and Antone Marshall) grocers 44 Howland

J. G. NICHOLSON
LUMBER, SASH, DOORS and BLINDS
BOWDITCH STREET, NEW BEDFORD, MASS.

Richards
" Thornton M rem from city
" see Richard [53 Oak
Richardson Ada E widow Morton b
" Clifford G clerk h 27 Maitland
" Deborah widow John h 271 Austin
" Edith M student b 271 Austin
" Florence H supervisor 57 N Second bds 281 Park
" Fred spinner b 113 Division
" George C installer 57 N Second h 219 Cedar
" Guy B beamer h 53 Oak [thorn
" Harry F salesman h 197 Haw-
" James A spinner h 173 David
" John died May 4 1911
" John laborer h 504 Maxfield
" John twister h 18 Abbott
" John H machinist h 945 S Water
" John W spinner h 91 Brock av
" Jonas b Rockdale av cor Winterville road [Belleville av
" Joshua master mariner h 882
" Laura M h 305 Cedar
" Louis E inspector of plumbing 52 Pleasant h 69 Chestnut
" Marion L clerk b 281 Park
" Mary Mrs h 504 Maxfield
" Mary E Mrs h 25 Cannon
" Roy electrician b 881 Belleville av
" Thomas spinner h 113 Division
" William H salesman h 281 Park
Richer Averiste widow h 3 Harmony
" Henry painter 1117 Acushnet av h do
" Rodolphe painter h 290 Collette
" Slivio painter b 98 Beetle
Richman Morris shoe repairer 26 Delano h 917 S Water
Richmond Carrie b 130 Clinton
RICHMOND CHARLES N conveyancer 54 Pleasant h 352 Union See page 94
" Elizabeth E widow George B bds 352 Union
" Frederick slasher h 296 Tinkham
" Henry baker 372 Kempton h 1 Washington square
" Lizzie Mrs h 218 Purchase [av
" Rufus operative h 15 E French
" Samuel P h 49 Walnut [av
" William operative h 72 Acushnet
RICHMOND & CO (James F Devoll) bakers 255 Union and 425 S Water See foot lines
Rickerby Gabriella widow Thomas D h 185 S Second [96 Elm
Ricketson Adelaide Mrs housekeeper
" Alfred C foreman carpenter 100 Fifth h 104 S Sixth
" Anna h 10 Anthony
" Annie C bds 67 Allen
" Arthur h 72 Orchard (S)
" Arthur driver bds 6 Park pl
" Cecile C and Henlen B h 369 County
" Charles L express 108 School h do
" Clifford N salesman City Mfg Co h 27 Buttonwood [pl
" Elias M master mariner h 6 Park
" Elmer bookkeeper 185 Union bds 146 State [Arnold
" Ernest clerk 271 Cedar bds 248
" Estella G bookkeeper 382 Acushnet av b 27 Buttonwood
" Estella G teacher Benton's Business school bds 146 State
" Florence school nurse b 6 Park pl
" Frank M carpenter 161 Clinton h 248 Arnold [High
" Frederick E capt Engine 4 h 111
" Harrison D sergeant police station 3 h 367 Reed [Washington
" Herbert R timekeeper h 182
" James M florist 247 Shawmut av h 243 do
" Katherine W clerk b 6 Park pl
" Levi special police h 182 Washington [mond
" Maria widow William b 2 Rich-
" Mildred Mrs b 189 Park [State
" Orion plumber 47 Delano h 146
" Silas T express h 87 Walden
" Susan S widow Charles W h 67 Allen
" Walton **sculptor 10** Anthony h do
Riddock John printer b 24 Shore
" Peter weaver h 24 Shore
Rideout Otis weaver h 617 Purchase
Rider Carrie E clerk b 82 Morgan
" Ethel bds 82 Morgan [Morgan
" Eugene A instructor H C h 82
" see Ryder [to Fall River
Ridgeway Hartley A Rev removed

Steiger-Dudgeon Co.
"The WOMAN'S Store."
Tel. Bell 82 & 83, Branches connecting all depts.
" " 160 For Office only. Auto. 1211

SUMPTIONS, ASSORTMENTS AT ALL TIMES OF DEPENDABLE DRY GOODS

Riding Albert E fireman h 86 Myrtle
" Alice Mrs h 336 Pinkham
" Harry bookbinder b 305 Davis
" Harry machinist b 86 Myrtle
" James removed to Providence R I
" Joseph weaver h 305 Davis
" Samuel copper worker h 133 Ruth
Ridings Thomas H janitor Abraham Lincoln school h 1627 Acushnet avenue
" William grinder h 163 Frederick
Ridyard Marion Mrs h 18 Ashley
Rieff John weaver h 161 Hathaway
Riel Frank E rem from city
" Joseph weaver h 50 Blackmer
Rielly Joseph P plumber 46 Linden h 9 Richmond
Reindeau Benjamin fixer h 143 Collette [Water
" Dieudonne boarding house 831 S
" Gilbert driver h r 198 State [do
" Louis pool 638 Acushnet av h
" Louis trimmer h 936 County
" Louis weaver h 307 Coggeshall
" Michael weaver bds 4 Fulton
" Miszael operative h 4 Fulton ct
" Ozias blacksmith 52 Acushnet av h Point [h 42 Ashley
" Ozias horseshoer 435 S Second
Rigby Christopher E conductor h 109 Durfee [vell
" George W patternmaker h 88 Co-
" James H spinner h 253 Collette
" John tinsmith h 444 Rivet
" John W clerk 131 Coggeshall h 145 do [av
" Richard conductor h 364 Coffin
" Water removed to Columbus Ga
Riha Charles spinner b 190 Nash rd
" James weaver h 190 Nash rd
Riisinger Frank loom fixer h 199 Brock av
Riley Albert designer b 336 Davis
" Alice A stenographer b 17 Robeson
" Annie F b 109 Austin [lantic
" Annie S widow William h 46 At-
" Bridget widow Thomas h 109 Austin [Thomas
" Catherine A widow Dennis h 60
" Charles N gardener h 606 Allen
" Edward F clerk 515 Kempton b 21 Shawmut av
" Edwin M driver h 190 Elm

Riley
" Elizabeth A stenographer 52 Adams b 21 Shawmut av
" Ellen widow Cornelius h 364 Pleasant
" Francis b 9 Studley
" Francis J asst engineer h 30 Ashland place [162 Chancery
" Frank R cooper 144 S Water b
" George (963 Purchase) rem from city
" George (33 Oak) rem from city
" George reed fixer h 71 Brock av
" Herbert spinner b 299 Collette
" James H laborer h 403 Pleasant
" James H (104 Austin) rem to Oswego N Y
" James S watchman h 214 Fourth
" John overseer Beacon Mfg Co h 162 Dean
" John overseer h 299 Collette
" John twister b 36 McGurk
" John E drillworker b 347 Orchard (S) [Corp h 355 Cedar
" John E overseer Dartmouth Mfg
" John F engineer Hathaway Mfg Co h 17 Robeson [Shawmut av
" John F grocer 515 Kempton h 21
" John H comp 112 Union bds 17 Robeson [city
" John H (570 S Second) rem from
" John H overseer h 329 Shawmut avenue
" John H warper h 79 Linden
" John J laborer h 395 Elm (W)
" John S ropemaker h 162 Chancery [lard
" John W second hand h 126 Bul-
" Joseph clerk 182 Union b 403 Pleasant
" Katherine V Mrs h 558 Cottage
" Margaret widow John W h 36 Atlantic
" Martin bartender 31 Delano
" Martin weaver b 67 Coffin av
" Martin weaver b 837 First
" Mary C teacher John H Clifford school b 21 Shawmut av
" Michael J chef 240 Purchase rms 72 Maxfield
" Michael Jr bartender 1670 Acushuet av h 9 Studley
" Michael A engineer h 120 Fourth
" Miles porter 84 Union b 177 Fourth

PELEG H. SHERMAN 506 COUNTY ST.
FUNERAL DIRECTOR AND EMBALMER
OFFICE PHONES. Bell 690-13. Auto. 1305.
RESIDENCE PHONES. Bell 690-12. Auto. 1306.

Riley
" Norris spinner b 299 Collette
" Patrick motorman rms 781 Purchase [Cottage
" Peter J shoes 147 Union h 527
" Richard G supt Gosnold Mills h S Orchard cor Rockdale av
" Robert carpenter b 36 Atlantic
" Theresa W widow Patrick b 135 Arnold [b 109 Austin
" Thomas engineer N B Theatre
" Thomas laborer b 437 Purchase
" Thomas laborer b 488 Purchase
" Thomas piper h 71 Bates
" Thomas weaver h 22 Roosevelt
" Thomas P piper h 101 Nye
" William b 17 Robeson
" William carder b 800 First
" William operative h 12 Salisbury
" William C treer b 60 Thomas
" William F salesman 156 Purchase b 9 Studley
" William H elevatorman 97 William rms 299 Acushnet av
" William J clerk h 47 Atlantic
" William L salesman b 109 Austin
" see Reilly [Holly
Rimmer Alice widow Edward b 125
" John weaver h 12 Mt Pleasant lane [ant lane
" William E weaver b 12 Mt Pleas-
Ring Daniel stoker h 734 Kempton
" Edward blacksmith b 2 Topham
" Jeremiah chauffeur h 48 Ocean
Riopel Ezra weaver h 141 Collette
" Louis driver h 142 Phillips av
Riopelle Delia widow Nicholas h 54 Holly [h 177 Fourth
Riordan Catherine widow Timothy
Rioux Charles contractor Bowditch c Glennon h 154 Belleville road
" Dominique speeder tender h 59 Brock av [rd
" Ermel painter h 197 Belleville
" Paul carpenter h 47 Belleville rd
" Paul clerk 62 Purchase rms 209 do
" Paul weaver h 47 Hersom [fin av
" Rose widow mill hand h 143 Cof-
Ripa Augusta shoe repairer 103 William and grocer 4 Pearl h do
Ripley Chester S apprentice Standard b 145 Campbell
" Fred painter b 125 Webster ct

Ripley
" Gamalier chauffeur h 154 Tinkham
" George W bricklayer h 38 Shore
" Harry operative h 138 Davis
" Harry M shoecutter h 102 Parker
" Kate Mrs h r 533 Acushnet av
" Lydia M widow Samuel S h 124 Willis [man
" Robert paper hanger h 114 Whit-
" Thomas lineman 43 William
" Thomas H rem to Detroit Mich
" William V lunch S Water cor Commercial h 156 S Second
Rishton John T mule spinner h 24 Viall
Rita Mary Mrs h 3 Maiden lane
Ritchie Ann widow J David h 326 Cedar [Campbell
" David F supt 152 N Water h 162
" Rachel clerk b 326 Cedar
" William treas and mgr 152 N Water h 83 Mill
Rivard Achille carpenter h 13 Hicks
" Albini pedlar b 68 Dean
" Edward mgr 358 Acushnet av
" Ephraim apprentice b 24 Myrtle
" Francois shoemaker h 883 Purchase
" Henry laborer b 70 Phillips av
" Isadore weaver h 58 Salisbury
" Ludger weaver h 91 Eugenia
" Moise laborer h 9 Bentley
" Pierre carpenter h 63 Hicks
Rivers George A clerk 119 Fourth h 120 Robeson
" George E salesman 339 Acushnet av h 256 Fourth [dle (W)
" Josephine shoeworker b 404 Mid-
Rivet Alfred operative h 32 Bentley
" Mary Mrs h 700 Purchase
" Peter carpenter h 908 Acushnet avenue [22 Bullock
Roach Catherine widow Owen J h
" Frederick T electrician 22 William h 253 Palmer
" Henry weaver b 22 Bullock
" John D operative b 25 Elm
" Martin F weaver h 68 Crapo
" Richard E clerk 1413 Acushnet av h at Fall River [chase
" William motorman b 237 Pur-
" William variety 632 Purchase h do
" see Roche and Rotch

F. T. AKIN & CO. FORCE FACTORY FURNACE FAMILY COAL

Robbins Amelia K h 45 North
" Arthur E grocer 770 Purchase b Baylies street [h 99 School
" Charles H supt Manomet Mills
" Edmond machinist b 63 Mechanics lane
" Edward B h 72 North [do
" Elmer E physician 101 School h
" Elmer E Jr student b 101 School
" Emily F widow Henry h 102 Middle [h do
" E Stanley physician 17 S Sixth
" Frank B poultry 1715 Acushnet av h do [lane
" George laborer h 60 Mechanics
" George E Jr salesman 103 William h 59 Foster
" George O clerk h 59 Foster
" Henry A insurance agent 41 William h 263 Purchase
" Henry F second hand h 52 Swift
" James teamster b 63 Mechanics lane [field
" Jennie widow John F h 43 Max-
" John H laborer rms 230 Union
" Lucy E widow Moses b 21 Homer
" Marian L Mrs h 78 Elm
" Phoebe widow Albert b 73 Hillman [County
" Sarah E widow William S h 626
" Thomas C letter carrier h 486 Cottage [lin
" Walter R R engineer b 15 Frank-
Robello Joseph laborer 215 Mt Pleasant b do
" Manuel teamster h 85 Prospect
Robenolt Edward A student b 23 Sycamore [more
" Edward S gardener h 23 Syca-
" Ella A clerk 55 Mechanics lane bds 648 County [County
" Ella A widow Eugene R bds 648
" Ethel L stenographer 307 Times bldg b 23 Sycamore
" J Calvin gardener h 648 County
Roberge Arsene weaver h 134 Nash road
" Arthur carpenter b 391 Bowditch
" Camille carpenter h 391 Bowditch
" Camille operative b 452 Belleville avenue
" Donat carpenter b 391 Bowditch
" Honore laundry worker h 1205 Acushnet avenue

Roberge
" Mederic weaver h 107 Coffin av
" Victor removed from city
Robert Albert teamster h 124 N Front
" Albert Jr weaver b 124 N Front
" Aldea R bookkeeper b 28 Ashley
" Alfred weaver b 86 Davis
" Arthur weaver h 180 Sawyer
" Eddie clerk 79 Austin b 74 Hicks
" Edmonde laborer h 74 Hicks [Nye
" Elphege grocer 80 Tallman b 136
" Ernest painter b 56 Dean
" Hector hairdresser 1266 Acushnet avenue h 136 Nye
" Hector teamster b 417 N Front
" Homer vocalist b Weld Sq Hotel
" Hormidal wine clerk 821 First
" Hormidas weaver h 12 Harmony
" John B glass cutter b 28 Ashley
" Joseph M mgr 878 Purchase h 881 County
" Joseph carpenter h Hawes
" J Ulderic carpenter h 92 Tallman
" Levi barber 1266 Acushnet av b 136 Nye
" Mary widow h 226 N Second
" Napoleon weaver h 112 Collette
" Oliver twister tender h 191 State
" Olivine Mrs h 28 Ashley
" Omar clerk rms 847 Purchase
" Philias hairdresser 120 Cove h 15 Welcome
" Theophile loom fixer h 33 Viall
" William G hairdresser 29 Delano h 519 S Second
" William P b 72 Delano
" Zephir J hairdresser 29 Delano h 85 Jouvett [ard
Roberts Abraham spinner h 57 How-
" Albert fixer h 22 Rockland
" Alfred machinist b 15 Ruth
" Annie M teacher J H Clifford school rms 106 S Seventh
" Antonio M insurance agent 120 Purchase rm 403 h 103 Fifth
" Armidos helper b 148 Tinkham av
" C Franklin ice cream 88 Shawmut av h 76 do
" Edward carpenter h 132 Bullard
" Edward variety 704 Ruth h 39 Ashley
" Edward Jr weaver b 39 Ashley

Don't dream of what you are going to do! Go and do it.
Kinyon's Short-hand School
Odd Fellows Bldg., Cor. William and Pleasant Sts., New Bedford, Mass.

Roberts
" Edward E operative b 36 Independent [tin
" Elizabeth widow John b 168 Aus-
" Ephraim J removed from city
" Ernest C operative h 65 Howard
" Frank bds 212 Weld
" Frank boxmaker b 322 Cedar
" Fred C driver h 178 Dean
" Fred W weaver h 25 E French av
" Gedeon sawyer b 148 Tinkham av
" Gerrian box maker b 322 Cedar
" Henry dentist's assistant 1356 Acushnet av rms 291 Collette
" Hormidas drill worker h 322 Cedar [av
" James twister bds 25 East French
" Jennie widow William h 62 Blackmer
" John laborer b 40 N Water
" John weaver h 395 Bowditch
" John B operative h 28 Ashley
" John E carpenter h 166 Nash road
" John W poloist rms 40 Fifth
" Joseph second hand b 23 Kenyon
" Joseph spinner h 322 Bowditch
" Joseph teamster b 72 Walden
" Joseph twister b 38 Ashley
" Joseph A teamster h 16 Woodlawn avenue [h do
" Joseph D real estate 40 Walnut
" Lawrence M insurance agent 120 Purchase rm 403 b 103 Fifth
" Leonard laborer b 168 Tinkham
" Leroy barber 302 Cedar rms 319 Elm [Cedar
" Pagelia widow Gerrian bds 322
" Philias hairdresser 1035 S Water h 15 Welcome [mouth
" Rita widow John h 128 Dart-
" Robert carpenter h 932 S Water
" Telesphore weaver b 157 Davis
" Thomas carpenter h 15 Ruth
" Thomas operative h 15 Ruth
" Thomas spinner h 212 Weld
" Thomas spinner b 203 Dean
" Thomas H overseer Acushnet Mill Corp h 16 Stapleton
" William spinner h 675 Cottage
" William spinner b 212 Weld
Robertson Arthur clerk b 55 Walnut
" Charles E tillerman ladder 2 bds 238 Pleasant

Robertson
" James W machinist h 233 Fourth
" John C grocer 282 Allen h 185 County [County
" John G clerk 282 Allen bds 185
" Joseph W h 238 Pleasant
" Samuel clerk 84 Union h 29 Emerson (S) [lumbia
" Sarah J widow William b 13 Co-
" William engineer h 120 Rodney
" William F adjustor h 13 Columbia
Robeson William weaver b 85 Tallman
Robichaud Benjamin overseer Holmes Mfg Co h 364 N Front
" Daniel lineman 43 William h 495 N Front
" Donald operative h 4 Jean
" Emilie weaver b 186 Cove
" Fidel weaver b 417 N Front
" Gilbert G silverplater h 32 Tallman
" Hector driver b 364 N Front
" Isadore laborer h 66 Penniman
" Joseph laborer h 92 Bowditch
" Samuel third hand h 123 Ruth
" Thaddee operative h 86 Beetle
Robida Arthur operative h 109 Bullard
" Dolor rem to Fall River
" Eugene mill hand b 107 Davis
" Frank laborer h 492 N Front
" Joseph weaver h 107 Davis
" Joseph A sales stable 45 Spring h 56 Rotch
" Ludger weaver b 107 Davis
" Zephire widow Narcisse bds 109 Bullard [Hathaway
Robidoux Adelard teamster bds 91
" Arthur laborer b 493 Belleville avenue
" Belzemere Mrs h 91 Hathaway
" Eliodor salesman Morris & Co b 473 N Front [ville av
" Joseph mill hand h 493 Belle-
" Theodore second hand h 344 N Front
" Victor weaver h 27 Kenyon
Robidovitz Julius pedlar h 458 S Water [Dean
Robie Fred driver 437 Purchase h
" William Z clerk 11 Purchase b 127 Nye [Earle
Robillard Charles hairdresser h 190

Bread, Cake, Pastry
RICHMOND & COMPANY 255-257 UNION STREET
Bell 993 Automatic 1022

Robillard
" Jacques carpenter h 207 Bowditch
" Peter h 323 Tinkham
" Victor fixer b 323 Tinkham
" Victor operative b 78 Tallman
" William laborer b 323 Tinkham
" William weaver h 57 Merrimac
Robin Alex windor fixer b 89 Ruth
" Arthur weaver h 153 Whitman
" Edmonde blacksmith b 173 State
" Martial operative b 89 Ruth
Robinowitch Charles plasterer h 62 Washburn
" Mary h 62 Washburn
Robinson Alice R teacher sewing public schools b at Fairhaven
" Annie clerk b 98 Park
" Annie A Mrs b 360 Reed
" Anthony cigar mfr 117 Union h 239 Fourth
" Arthur J clerk Nonquitt Spinning Co b 55 Walnut
" Arthur P clerk 156 Weld h 158 Reynolds [b 49 State
" Bessie P bookkeeper 38 N Second
" Bros (James F and Frank J Robinson) variety 106 Rivet
" Catherine widow James h 135 County
" Charles A chauffeur h 34 Wing
" Charles H shoemaker h 105 Tremont [Summit
" Phear C widow William h 28
ROBINSON DANIEL grocer 156 Weld h 66 Mt Pleasant See page 772
" David J electrician 158 Purchase
" Edward joiner b 13 Salisbury
" Edward A clerk b 239 Fourth
" Edward B machinist h 191 Chancery
" Elizabeth widow Robert h 442 N Front [Middle
" Elizabeth A widow Anson h 337
" Ellen widow George h 98 Park
" Ernest carpenter h 132 Clark
" Frank J (Robinson Bros) and overseer h 84 Swift
" Fred H physician 2 Arcade blk h at Acushnet [do
" Frederick clerk 156 Weld h 213
" Frederick L cigars 169 Purchase rms 164 do [(S)
" Frederick S lineman h 21 Ash

Robinson
" Greenwood operative h 283 County [County
" Harry clerk 182 Union bds 283
" Harry glassworker b 137 Acushnet av
" Henry laborer b 71 Rivet
" Herbert foreman h 96 Park
" Herbert mill hand h 192 Collette
" Ida L sewer 40 Purchase b 51 Cottage
" Jacob H (New Bedford Paper & Supply Co) 71 Union h 209 Court
" James laborer h 81 Dunbar
" James laborer b 88 Cove
" James weaver b 15 McGurk
" James weaver b 137 Acushnet av
" James F (Robinson Bros) h 135 County
" John electrician rms 74 School
" John eyeletmaker h 49 State
" John mill hand h 24 Ashley
" John operative h 23 Cleveland
" John weaver b 13 McGurk
" John wine clerk 821 First
" John B carpenter h 17 Oak
" John James laborer h 4 Bethel
" John K bartender h 13 McGurk
" John L cigar maker 117 Union h 51 Cottage
" John S laborer b 12 Cleveland
" John T engineer h 42 Morton ct
" Joseph joiner b 13 Salisbury
" Joseph laborer h 18 Wing
" Julia widow Benjamin b 191 Chancery
" Lewis carpenter rms 22 Mill
" Mary weaver h 7 E Durfee
" Mary widow William h 293 Earle
" Mary A clerk 40 Purchase b 51 Cottage
" Mary A weaver h 189 Hathaway
" Mary E bookkeeper 123 Front b 98 Park [bury
" Mary J widow Edward h 13 Salis-
" Matilda G clerk 40 Purchase b 51 Cottage
" Peter comber h 32 Salisbury [ct
" Peter A machinist b 42 Morton
" Ralph R shoemaker h 337 Purchase [av
" Reuben mill hand h 188 Coffin av
" Roakley b 178 Grinnell
" Simon salesman 71 Union rms 209 Purchase

GLOBE DYE HOUSE 220 SHAWMUT AVE.
J. N. J. LONHOLDT, PROP. Telephone Connections Goods called for and Delivered
Down town Office. 52 Pleasant St., Room 1 North End Office, 1014 Acushnet Ave.

Robinson
" Thomas ins agent 120 Purchase rm 403 rms 760 do
" William ins agent 37 Purchase rm 23 b 283 County [non
" William ins agent h 127 Mt Ver-
" William teamster b 160 Crapo
" William A (W A Robinson & Co) h 84 Hawthorn
" William A Jr (W A Robinson & Co) h 39 Grove
" William C died May 4 1911
" William H clerk 306 Cedar h 153 Myrtle [rd h do
" William H milk 638 Hathaway
" W A & Co (Wm A Robinson Wm A Robinson Jr and Edmond L Wilde) oil refiners 144 S Water
Robitaille Alphonse musician b 150 Collette [h 91 Bullard
" Arthur barber 1210 Acushnet av
" Emile (Vera & Robitaille) mill comb repairing r 213 Coffin av h 129 Tallman
" Etienne carpenter b 150 Collette
" Honorius carpenter h 206 Hathaway
" Jere laborer h 280 Orchard (S)
" Louis carpenter h 206 Hathaway
" Michael carpenter h 150 Collette
ROBITAILLE OVILA contractor 200 Collette h do See page 764
" P George optician 1307 Acushnet av b 1293 do [442 Bolton
Robuk Joseph weaver h 13 Rotch blk
Roby Fred mason h 127 Nye
" William waiter b 127 Nye
Rocco Peter shoe repairer 75 William b 505 Acushnet av [Oak
Rocha Casimir freight handler h 48
" Joaquim barber 34 Dartmouth b 171 Grinnell
" John operative h 120 Dartmouth
" John V clerk h 148 Rockland
" Joseph M hairdresser 34 Dartmouth b 171 Grinnell
Roche George laborer b 277 Park
" Hector tailor b 171 Grinnell
" John oiler h 150 Durfee
" John J heeler h 12 Atlantic
" see Roach [ver
Rocheleau Alexis weaver h 203 Saw-
" Alfred conductor b 18 Hazard ct
" Alfred lunch 1168½ Acushnet av

Rocheleau
" Alphonse driver 1 Hicks b 276 Earle [ard ct
" Araline widow Joseph h 18 Haz-
" Arthur clerk 835½ S Front b 203 Sawyer [yer
" Frederick operative b 203 Saw-
" George fixer h 427 Pleasant
" George operative b 427 Pleasant
" Henri weaver h 36 McGurk
" Hubert carpenter h 276 Earle
Rochell Alexander R barber 503 Purchase h do [Dean
Rochford Eddie third hand bds 85
Rock Alfred died Sept 25 1910
" Charles removed from city
" Christina dressmaker 616 Purchase b 488 do
" Emma widow Alfred b 18 Jean
" Fred H twister b 40 Cove
" George H watchman h 40 Cove
" Grace waitress h 76 Maxfield
" Hannah widow James h 743 S Water
" John B b 160 Earle [Water
" John F clerk 163 Union h 743 S
" Joseph laborer h 1159 Purchase
" Lawrence clerk b 743 S Water
" Lemina widow Joseph h 488 Purchase
" Louis laborer h 488 Purchase
" Louis second hand h 495 N Front
" Napoleon barber h 488 Purchase
" Napoleon hostler 486 Rivet h 68 Nelson
" Oliver laborer h 72 Belleville road
" Oliver Jr doffer b 72 Belleville rd
" Owner operative b 72 Belleville rd
" Parmenie milliner 1354 Acushnet av b 488 Purchase
" Philips hairdresser 833 Purchase h 410 Pleasant
" Rosa operative h 76 Maxfield
" Zepherin doffer b 4 Austin ct
Rockefeller Clarence E clerk b 173 Park
" James B compositor h 144 Mill
Rocklin Hyman clerk 1026 Acushnet av h 234 Coggeshall
" Kesler tailor 1026 Acushnet av h 234 Coggeshall
" William tailor 1026 Acushnet av b 234 Coggeshall

GREENE & WOOD Every Kind of LUMBER AND MILL WORK
PINE STREET, off So. WATER STREET, NEW BEDFORD

Rocklin
" William & Co liquors Second cor Middle h 332 S Second [court
Rocla Antonio mill hand b 7 Bonneau
Rocray Florent J clerk b 16 Hicks
" Joseph operative h 16 Hicks
Rodalewicz Marjan baker h 484 Coggeshall [Orchard (S)
Rode William sausage maker b 354
Roderick Anthony removed to Provincetown
" Anthony J student b 99 Oak
" Bernard city employer h 7 Stanton court
" Frank J carpenter h 99 Oak
" John S fish h 55 Crapo
" Manuel laborer h 61 Acushnet av
" Manuel undertaker 98 Phillips av h 382 N Front
" Manuel Jr twister h 47 Covell
" Peter clerk 1100 Acushnet av b 382 N Front [pendent
Rodericks Frank laborer h 44 Inde-
Rodericque Amelia widow h 66 Middle
" Antone barber 252 Coggeshall
" Antone chauffeur h 66 Middle
" Antone laborer h 65 Prospect
" Antonio J chauffeur 15 Fourth
" Charles clerk 165 S Second h 87 Acushnet avenue
" Charles laborer h 406 S Water
" Edmund laborer h 25 Howland
" Frank city laborer h 224 S Front
" Howeral operative 510 Acushnet avenue
" Jesse F twister h 301 S Front
" Joseph carder h 301 S Front
" Joseph foundryman h 267 Field ct
" Joseph mariner h 33 Babbitt
" Joseph operative h 243 S Front
" Joseph operative h 375 S Front
" Leon h 5 Howland
" Louis laborer h 224 S Front
" Manuel clerk h 6 Howland
" Manuel laborer h 64 Acushnet av
" Manuel laborer h 188 Thompson
" Manuel operative h 65 Borden
Roderigues Antone J mill hand h 204 Coffin avenue [h 82 Nelson
Roderique Angeline widow August
" Antone Mrs h 6 Howland
" Antone fisherman h 305 S Front
" Charles twister b 5 Howland

Roderique
" John laborer h 350 Allen
" Joseph carder h 82 Nelson
" Joseph laborer 144 S Water
" Michael painter h 90 Howland
" Napoleon clerk 62 Purchase b 82 Nelson [Nelson
" Odise traveling salesman b 82
" Peter laborer h 530 First
" Philomena widow Manuel h 206 Rockland
" Robert chauffeur h 327 S Water
Roderiques Clara sewer 40 Purchase b 206 Rockland [dent
" Francisco operative h 44 Indepen-
" Joseph mill hand h 208 Dartmouth
" Manuel h 202 Belleville av
" Manuel laborer b 49 Hemlock
" Manuel operative h 14 Cotter
" Mary J fitter 40 Purchase b 206 Rockland
Rodger Mary h 110 Whitman
RODGERS ANTONIO M steamship agent 177 Acushnet av h at Padanaram See page 25
" Hypolito J barber 394 S Water h do
" Martin mason h 60 Liberty
" see Rogers
Rodier Anthony operative h 198 State
Rodil Arthur mill hand h 57 Grinnell
Rodman Edith M teacher Hosea M Knowlton school b 104 Bonney
" Florence C bookkeeper 131 Acushnet av b 104 Bonney
" Frank P weigher foot of Coffin av h 104 Bonney
" Julia W h 106 Spring
" Samuel T carpenter b 104 Bonney
Rodrick Peter clerk b 382 N Front
" William M laborer h 26 Jouvett
Rodriques Antone died May 20 1911
" Antone operative h 162 Crapo
Roebuck Edith clerk 183 Purchase b 561 Cottage [Cottage
" Ernest jeweler 183 Purchase b 561
" Herbert (H Roebuck & Son) h 561 Cottage
" H & Son (Herbert and Joseph) jewelers 183 Purchase [ska
" Joseph laborer bds 109 Potom-
" Joseph (H Roebuck & Son) bds 561 Cottage

BONNEY, FOLSTER & CO.,
The North End's Shopping Centre
Dry Goods and Men's Furnishings
945-947 Acushnet Ave., New Bedford, Mass.

Roemer George A Rev rem from city
Roger Henrietta widow b 12 McGurk
Rogers Abiatha granite 86 Topham h do [Middle
" Addie N widow Merrill D b 217
" Albert R (Rogers Bros) 86 Topham b do
" Alfred C mariner h 189 Elm
" Anna C b 69 Borden
" Annie Mrs h 35 Prospect
" Annie widow John b 69 Borden
" Antone laborer h 265 Fourth
" Arthur rem to Middleboro
" Arthur J at Public Library bds 120 Grinnell
" August laborer h 75 Delano [dle
" Benjamin C engineer b 102 Mid-
" Betsey P died Jan 23 1911 [tic
" Bridget widow John b 47 Atlan-
" Bros (Fred L, Edward H and Albert R) milk 86 Topham
" Caroline widow Zenas b 247 Palmer [chase rm 14 b 65 Borden
" Catherine stenographer 37 Pur-
" Charles laborer b 52 Washburn
" Charles I laborer bds Mrs Prudence Briggs, Plainville rd
" Charles W carpenter h 123 Campbell
" Constance Mrs h 335 S Water
" Deborah R Mrs h 27 Collins
" Delia A widow Charles L bds Frank B Poole's Plainville rd
" Edward conductor rms 602 Purchase [burn
" Edward operative h 52 Wash-
" Edward C musician b 48 Mill
" Edward H (Rogers Bros) milk b 86 Topham [do
" Edward L ice 252 Brownell h
" Elizabeth L widow William K housekeeper 128 School [ence
" Elsworth B clerk bds 84 Flor-
" Emma P telephone operator 57 N Second b 119 Tremont
" Ethel telephone operator Parker House b 119 Tremont [Crapo
" Eunice cashier 145 Union bds 55
" Eva Mrs h 43 Hemlock
" E Herbert clerk 97 William rm 306 b 120 Grinnell [ral
" Frances widow Manuel h 13 Ru-
" Frank h 63 S Sixth [av
" Frank city laborer h 476 Rockdale

Rogers
" Frank conductor rms 602 Purchase [ond
" Frank machinist h 381 S Sec-
" Frank mill hand h 38 Howland Village
" Frank A silverworker h 48 Mill
" Frank D driver 311 S Water h 64 School
" Frank L lawyer 5 Masonic bldg and (Rogers & Sylvia) h 69 Borden [dle
" Frank R longshoreman h 66 Mid-
" Frank S second hand h 26 Hall
" Fred L (Rogers Bros) milk bds 86 Topham [162 Smith
" George F teamster 70 Union h
" Gertrude Mrs h Winterville rd cor Rockdale av
" Harrison A h 102 Dartmouth
" Harry C laborer b 102 Dartmouth
" Hattie D widow Harrison b 224 Allen [Second b 27 Collins
" Helen L C district cashier 57 N
" Henry B bds 55 Pierce [Kempton
" Henry I driver 14 N Sixth h 740
" Herbert T salesman 385 Acushnet av h 140 Shawmut av
" Isaac T gardener h 85 Bonney
" James laborer h 119 Tremont
" James weaver bds 65 Washburn
" James A drillworker b 120 Grinnell [Shawmut avenue
" Jane widow Benjamin F bds 91
" Joe laborer h 88 Mosher
" John b 480 Bolton [av
" John engineer h 149 Acushnet
" John fireman b 232 N Second
" John fireman U St Ry Co power station h 550 First [son
" John glasscutter h 174 Thomp-
" John laborer h 682 Acushnet av
" John mill hand h 283 S Second
" John operative 8 Hazard's lane b 96 Dartmouth
" John ropeworker h 204 Crapo
" John tinsmith b 269 Palmer
" John A laborer h 52 Washburn
" John A machinist b 47 Briggs
" John D b 137 Acushnet av
" John E removed from city
" John J glasscutter h 370 Orchard (S) [net av
" John M shoemaker h 140 Acush-

Painters Supplies Wall Papers Room Mouldings Ladders
M. P. B. Silva & Son BRUSHES
157 ACUSHNET AVENUE Both Phones NEW BEDFORD

Rogers
" Joseph barber 78 William h Briggs street
" Joseph bicycle repairer 36 Purchase h 174 Thompson
" Joseph carpenter h 49 Nye
" Joseph clerk 135 Acushnet av h 188 Thompson
" Joseph fisherman b 712 Water
" Joseph mariner h 328 S Front
" Joseph mason h 304 Collette
" Joseph operative h r 4 Marvin
" Joseph operative b 13 Rural
" Joseph salesman 50 Union h 65 Short
" Joseph E woodworker h 118 Mott
" Joseph M 2nd engineer h 149 Acushnet av
" Joseph P barber h r 187 Bonney
" Joseph P fireman h 157 Crapo
" Joseph R variety 73 Hemlock h 174 Thompson [Newton
" Josephine L widow Wilson b 169
" Lillian Mrs b 208 Thompson [av
" Manuel laborer h 103 Acushnet
" Manuel teamster h 76 Sidney
" Manuel watchman h 411 Allen
" Manuel S bicycle repairer 36 Purchase b 174 Thompson
" Manuel V carpenter h 269 Palmer
" Mary Mrs h 35 County
" Mary Mrs h 60 Independent
" Mary widow Manuel h 104 Potomska
" Mary E Mrs h 120 Grinnell
" Mary J rms 69 Hathaway
" Michael laborer h 150 Hathaway
" Michael laborer h 400 Elm (W)
" Nellie clerk Wamsutta Mills
" Patrick H buffer 1 Waverly pl
" Peter laborer h 265 Fourth
" Samuel E mariner h 57 Ash (N)
" Terrence spinner h 47 Briggs
" Thomas carder h 10 McMurray terrace
" Thomas operative h 7 LaFrance
" Walter A glass cutter h 497 Acushnet avenue
" Walter S laborer h 840 County
" William clerk b 47 Nye
" William machinist h 712 S Water
" William H drill maker b 120 Grinnell [net av
" William H laborer h 512 Acush-

Rogers
" William H piper h 51 Page
" William T shipper b 124 Bonney
" Winsor P removed from city
" & Sylvia (Frank L Rogers and Antonio A Sylvia) undertakers 100 Potomska
" see Rodgers and Rodericque
Rogerson Reginald E machinist h 7 Stackhouse
" Robert h 916 County
" Robert Jr weaver h 141 Davis
Roggermossee Joseph weaver b 172 Bonney [lette
Rogissart Joseph mill hand h 269 Col-
ROGLER PHILIP restaurant 72-74 William h at Fairhaven See page 772
Roketa Mary Mrs h 20 Hampton ct
Roleau William A cable splicer 57 N Second h 113 Fourth [130 Fair
Rollins John J salesman 99 Front h
" Manuel J driver 149 Purchase h 55 Hemlock
" see Raulino [ion
Rolly Thomas carpenter rms 394 Un-
Roman Orace fireman h r 56 Clark
" Vincenzo removed from city
Romanow Hyman (Eastern Supply Co) b 114 Clark
Romanowicz Adam operative h r 42 Washburn [.Merrimac
Romanzi Santa laborer h 30 East
Romeo Concetto V mason 151 Coffin av h do
Ronan Edward J weaver b 28 Viall
" James H janitor 955 S Water h 28 Viall [501 S Second
" James V bartender 37 Delano h
" Maurice operative b 28 Viall
" William J painter h 28 Viall
Rondeau Aime operative b 32 Nye
" Arthur carpenter h 24 Tallman
" Clores widow b 52 Dean
" Damasse wood 32 Nye h do
" Delphis hostler h 58 Bullard
" Fred driver bds 32 Nye
" Joseph weaver h 52 Dean
" Joseph A removed from city
" Louis driver bds 32 Nye
" Pierre carpenter h 19 Thatcher
" Theodore carpenter h 145 Bullard
Rongo Charles laborer h 8 Seneca

Steiger-Dudgeon Co.
"The WOMAN'S Store."
Tel. Bell 82 & 83, Branches connecting all depts.
" " 160 For Office only. Auto. 1211

SUMPTIONS, ASSORTMENTS AT ALL TIMES OF DEPENDABLE DRY GOODS

Rooks Albert H police h 83 Fifth
" Charles A painter h 15 Elm
" John C police h 4 Washington
" William A steam fitter b 4 Washington
Rooney Anne E teacher William H Taylor school b r 93 Bedford
" Daniel T fitter h 172 Ashland
" Edward bds 72 Winsor
" Frederick laborer b 94 Parker
" James clerk b 72 Winsor
" James J city laborer h 94 Parker
" John watchman h 72 Winsor
" John Jr machinist b 72 Winsor
" John L machinist b 39 Shawmut avenue [93 Bedford
" John P gardener 379 County h r
" Lawrence eyelet maker b 94 Parker [150 Merrimac
" Luke H overseer Manomet Mill h
" William janitor Rivet cor First b 72 Winsor
Roos Adolph laborer h 19 Jean [lette
" Ludwig A brakeman h 284 Col-
Root Thomas clerk rms 7 N Second
Rooth Ella F Mrs variety 174 Acushnet av h 172 do [b do
" Harriet E music teacher 31 Fifth
" H Bartol clerk b 172 Acushnet av
Rosa Amelia h 201 Coggeshall
" Antone M tailor 167 Fourth h do
" Balbini mill hand h 80 Davis
" H Antonio physician 112 Grinnell h do
" Manuel fisherman h 21 Mitchell
" Manuel laborer h 53 Rivet [av
" Manuel P laborer b 202 Belleville
" Maria Mrs h 12 Howland
" Mary widow h 112 Grinnell
" see Rose and Ross
Roscoe Albert J supt silver dept T P Corp h 225 Fourth
" Arthur laborer h 58 Mott
" William E police sergeant Station 5 h 691 Cottage [yon
Roscovitski John operative h 54 Ken-
Roscovitz Joseph tailor h 515 S Water [259 Bowditch
Roscow Frederick H bookkeeper h
Rose Adelaide Mrs h 168 S Second
" Alfred P plasterer h 50 Short
" Anacleto E laborer h 325 S Front
" Anna widow Manuel h 586 Allen

Rose
" Anthony E grocer 57 Howland h r 61 do
" Antone laborer h 55 Crapo
" Antone laborer h 65 Delano
" Antone mill hand h 618 S Water
" Antone E laborer h 51 Hemlock
" Antone F laborer h 81 Prospect
" Antone G laborer h 273 S Front
" Antone P h 156 Acushnet av
" Antonio F city laborer h 407 Alleu [h 58 Fair
" Arthur J shoes 86 Acushnet av
" Charles P clerk City Mfg Co b 323 County
" Enos freight handler h 56 First
" Evora B clerk b 273 Orchard (S)
" Felissiano laborer h 276 S Front
" Francisco P farmer h 111 Field
" Frank b 695 Cottage
" Frank city laborer h 163 Grape
" Frank laborer h 399 S Second
" Frank E teamster h 26 Hall
" Frank G laborer N B W W 41 Larch h do
" Frank P laborer h 323 County
" Frank P operative h 53 Katharine
" Frank P Jr clerk h 259 S Second
" George operative b 56 Ashley
" George weaver h 192 Division
" Gideon operative b 18 Cannon
" Henry asst supt 97 William rm 310 h 25 Griffin [(S)
" Jason laborer h 277 Orchard
" Joe fireman h 77 Katharine
" Joe laborer h 88 Mosher
" John clerk b 35 Thompson
" John helper 55 N Water h at Fairhaven
" John mill hand h 60 Mosher
" John C painter h 62 Middle
" John G city laborer h 616 S Water
" John J laborer h 134 N Second
" John P inspector 43 William b 323 County
" Joseph (Francis & Rose) 599 S Water h 118 Bonney
" Joseph farmer h 16 Independent
" Joseph laborer h 63 Prospect
" Joseph laborer h 64 Acushnet av
" Joseph laborer h 113 Swift
" Joseph laborer h 225 N Second
" Joseph laborer h 288 S Second
" Joseph mill hand b 2 Blackburn

PELEG H. SHERMAN 506 COUNTY ST.
FUNERAL DIRECTOR AND EMBALMER
OFFICE PHONES. Bell 690-13. Auto. 1305.
RESIDENCE PHONES. Bell 690-12. Auto. 1306.

Rose
" Joseph operative h 269 S Second
" Joseph Jr mill hand b 113 Swift
" Joseph S drillworker b 560 Allen
" Manuel carpenter h 53 Rivet
" Manuel driver 437 Purchase h 468 Union
" Manuel laborer h 2 Hyacinth
" Manuel laborer h 63 Grinnell
" Manuel laborer h 97 Sydney
" Manuel laborer h 99 Potomska
" Manuel C carpenter h 107 Cove road
" Manuel D glassblower h 41 Howland
" Manuel F h 23 Bourne
" Manuel F laborer h 94 Acushnet av
" Manuel F laborer h 154 Acushnet av
" Manuel G laborer h 99 Hemlock
" Marguerita widow Joseph h 35 Thompson
" Maria B dressmaker 273 Orchard (S) h do
" Mary Mrs h 531 First
" Mary widow h 396 S Second
" Mary A Mrs h 1 Maiden lane
" Samuel speeder tender h 32½ Acushnet av
" Sarah widow Joseph P h 11 Hickory
" Valentine mariner h 128 S Second
" Victor egg candler h 123 S Second
" William insurance agent 41 William b 107 Beetle
" William operative h 114 Division
" see Rosa and Ross
Rosen Joseph clerk 286 Acushnet av
" Louis Hebrew teacher h 352 First
Rosenberg Solomon (Tracy, Rosenberg & McGurk) 108 Union rm 1 h 117 Fourth
Rosenblumt Max pedlar h 82 Penniman
Rosensweig Abraham pressman 40 Purchase h 286 S Front
Rosenthal Abraham rem from city
" Harry mgr Bay State Chair Co h 113 Acushnet av
" Joseph umbrella repairer 58 Howland h do
" Myer h 827 Purchase
Roshkowich Joseph tailor 50 Howland h 515 S Water
Roshur George F chauffeur 15 Fourth

Roshur
" Rosa W widow Frank E h 114 Seventh
Ross Abbie A widow George h 411 Chancery
" Alexander bricklayer b American House Arcade bldg
" Alexander removed from city
" Alma bookkeeper 73 William bds 245 Sawyer
" Alphonse fixer b 19 Bentley
" Anna Mrs milliner h 245 Sawyer
" Carrie A Mrs b r 35 Smith
" Charles driver h 811 County
" Charles H electrician h 225 Court
" Della B milliner b 243 Sawyer
" Elizabeth widow William H h 97 Parker
" Ferdinand machinist h 145 Sawyer
" Florence milliner b 245 Sawyer
" Franklin C salesman 358 Acushnet av h 52 Cottage
" George N case maker h 51 Shawmut av
" George T clerk 127 Union b 35 Smith st ct
" Grace Mrs h 110 Cedar
" Herbert E inspector 43 William
" James spinner b 97 Parker
" James A laborer h 746 Purchase
" John lunch Purchase cor Elm h 53 Florence
" John mule spinner h 297 Cedar
" Joseph foreman city yard h 38 Keene
" J Conrad physician 1283 Acushnet av h do
" Leander P teamster 28 Union h 28 Hillman
" Lester F b rear 35 Smith
" Mary S Mrs clerk h 225 Court
" M Louise milliner 243 Sawyer h 245 do
" Napoleon lather h 19 Bentley
" Peter O second hand h 820 First
" Rose milliner b 245 Sawyer
" Sadie M mgr rm 3 Arcade bds 97 Parker street
" Samuel laborer h 38 Keene
" Samuel (Ross & Sisson) and sec Mule Spinner's Union h 68 Willis
" Walter B removed from city
" William A b 97 Parker
" William D operative b 746 Purchase
" William H died July 15 1911

F. T. AKIN & CO. PAINTERS AND DECORATORS

Ross
" Worth G Capt (retired) h 75 Madison [S Second
" Zenon repairman 55 Spring b 608
" & Setton (Samuel Ross and Ezra M Setton) clothing 348 Acushnet avenue
" see Roos, Rose and Rosa
Rossi Giovanni director Y M C A band h 158 Mill
" Paul laborer h 30 Spring
" William clerk Standard
Rossijnol Albert weaver h 10 McGurk
Rossiter James third hand h 423 Bowditch [Hampton ct
Rostotsky Roman operative h 13
Rostron Frank weaver h 293 Davis
" George builder h 38 Ashley
" James folder bds 38 Ashley
" John mule spinner h 280 Coggeshall
" Thomas laborer h 35 Jouvett
" William J spinner h 151 Tallman
" see Rawstron
Roswell Fred h 52 Jenny Lind
Rotch Casimiro clerk ft Willis h 48 Oak [County
" Clara M widow William J h 427
" Dept N E Cotton Yarn Co (dept 7-8) Orchard (S) beyond Rivet
" Josephine widow Morgan h 19 Irving
" Mary R b 427 County
ROTCH & POTTER (Paul and Dixon) 97 William rm 303 See front cover
Rothchild Abraham removed to Providence R I
Rothera David h 24 W French av [av
" Ernest A painter b 24 W French
" James R removed to Detroit Mich
" Percy drill worker b 24 W French av [shall h Belleville avenue
Rotheracs Antone barber 252 Cogge-
Rothkop Isaac umbrella maker h 739 Water
" Isaac (J Rubin & Son) 421 S Water bds 479 First [bott
Rothwell Abraham weaver h 3 Ab-
" Abraham Jr weaver b 3 Abbott
" Christopher city laborer h 207 Weld
" Fred weaver h 10 Acushnet av

Rothwell
" George spinner h 55 Brock av
" Henry weaver b 154 Tallman
" John operative h 154 Tallman
" John A loom fixer h 81 Durfee
" Robert removed to Fairhaven
" Susanna widow James b 63 Mt Pleasant
" Walter loom fixer h 39 Valentine
Rotin Louis weaver h 93 Perry
Rotman Morris pedlar h 41 Mitchell
Roudreau George H operative h 91 Kenyon [h 324 Cedar Grove
Rouillier Domina clerk 809 Purchase
" Gideon bartender 946 S Water h 950 do [Linden
" Joseph clerk 485 N Front b 43
" Joseph teamster h 43 Linden
" Moise 809 Purchase h 30 Adams
Rouke Edward T foreman 396 Cottage h 187 Middle
Rouleau Octave h 57 Reginald
Rounds Abbie B widow Russell b 59 Mechanics lane
" Andrew h 244 Arnold
" Emily M widow John h 493 Mill
Rounsevell Charity bookkeeper 100 William h at E Freetown
" Edna A bookkeeper 17 Pleasant b 101 Sycamore
" Ethel E bookkeeper 72 N Water bds 116 Robeson [104 Fourth
" Harry G clerk Manomet Mill h
" John L stenographer 350 S Second b 87 S Sixth
" Joseph piano tuner 18 Purchase h at Wareham [son
" Luman D drill packer h 116 Robe-
" Mildred S rem to Rochester N Y
" Silas H foreman 22 Fourth h at Fairhaven
" Waldo chauffeur rms 38 Walnut
Rourke Andrew W carpenter h 236 North [North
" Andrew W Jr carpenter bds 236
" Edward spinner h 223 Sawyer
" Edward J painter h 103 Ashland
" Francis A clerk Smith Bros h 87 Hazard
" Fred W h 236 North [County
" Frederick J shoemaker h 864
" John R laborer b 233 Sawyer
" Julia h 2 Irvington court
" Mary A bookbinder h 81 Ash (N)

Bookkeeping, Shorthand, Typewriting, Penmanship, etc. Taught thoroughly at
Kinyon's Commercial School
Odd Fellows Bldg., Cor. William and Pleasant Sts., New Bedford, Mass.

Rourke
" Thomas fixer h 186 Dean
" William P laborer h 230 State
" see O'Rourke and Rouke
Rourque Mabel M clerk 129 Rivet b 94 Kenyon [fee
Rouse Minnie Mrs h 28 Durfee
" Stanley W motorman b 28 Durfee
Roush Casmir operative h 63 S Water [159 Holly
Rousseau Adelard wood turner h
" Albert rem to Providence R I
" Albert third hand h 109 Hathaway
" Alfred loom fixer h 12 Harmony
" Alfred helper 91 N Water b 159 Holly
" Alfred piper b 159 Bowditch [av
" Alphonse weaver h 82 Phillips
" Amie loom fixer h 141 Phillips av
" Arsene J waiter 62 Purchase h 44 Sycamore
" Arthur carpenter h 159 Bowditch
" Aurore clerk 1009 Acushnet av b 1498 do
" Celestin laborer h 79 Holly
" Cyprien conductor h 22 Bullard
" Elphage driver h 197 Rivet
" Ferdinand plumber's helper b 159 Holly [shnet av
" Frank operative bds 872 Acu-
" Frank G agent h 975 S Water
" Hector grocer 695 Belleville av h 65 Hatch
" John mason b 553 N Front [dent
" Joseph operative h 78 Indepen-
" Joseph weaver b 478 Coggeshall
" Louis h 1498 Acushnet av
" Louis baker 55 Mechanics lane b 12 Harmony
" Louis mason 3893 Acushnet av
" Louis mason h 61 County
" Louis driver b 330 N Front
" Mary Mrs weaver b 11 Nye
" Napoleon teamster h 330 N Front
" Odilon second hand h 197 Rivet
" Philomen h 975 S Water
" Toussaint bds 11 Nye
" see Brooks [Collette
Rousselle Edward third hand b 178
" Emile weaver b 418 N Front
" see Russell [Nash rd
Roussin William shoemaker bds 113
Rowan James foreman 1 Mill h 73 Dean [County
Rowand Addie C widow h 252
" John O engineer Rotch Mill h 523 Cottage
" William H engineer Dartmouth Mfg Corp h 111 South
Rowbottom George H weaver b 970 County [ty
" Olive widow William b 970 Coun-
" Wright died Jan 18 1911
Rowe Calvin laborer h 68 School
" Daniel asst editor Times h 129 Elm [North
" Myra H widow George T h 56
" Samuel B clerk b 351 Pleasant
" William H painter b 351 Pleasant
Rowland William fixer h 187 Davis
Roy Albert carpenter b 113 Belleville road
" Alice clerk bds 1111 S Water
" Alfred doffer h r 57 Dean
" Alphonse hostler h 23 Hillman
" Alphonse weaver h 775 First
" Amede laborer h 11 Holly
" Andre spindle setter b 21 Salisbury
" Anselme carpenter h 287 Coffin av
" Antoinette h 113 Belleville rd
" Archille chauffeur b 194 Belleville avenue
" Arsene A & Co plumbers 671 Purchase h 108 Austin
" Arthur weaver b 812 First
" Arthur carpenter h 23 Thatcher
" Arthur Mrs h 194 Belleville av
" Caroline Mrs h 812 First
" Donat rem from city
" D Alfred real estate 37 Purchase rm 25 b 464 County
" Edmonde mill hand b 23 Holly
" Edmonde weaver b 101 Coffin av
" Edward rem from city
" Emillie fixer h 1415 Acushnet av
" Ernest laborer b 23 Holly
" Euclid driver h 1086 County
" George carpenter h Oliver off Tarkiln Hill rd
" George mason h 1111 Water
" George M weaver h 88 Holly
" Hector weaver b 154 Cedar Grove
" Henry carpenter b 154 Cedar Grove
" Henry weaver b 15 Phillips av
" Henry M removed from city

Bread, Cake, Pastry
RICHMOND & COMPANY 255-257 UNIUN STREET
Bell 993 Automatic 1022

Roy
" Irenee mill hand b 23 Holly
" John laborer h 9 Felton
" John mill hand b 383 N Front
" John second hand h 52 Collette
" John weaver h 48 Nelson
" John B operative h 24 Clark
" John B removed from city
" John V yard boss Neild M Corp b 33 Tallman
" Joseph carpenter h 403 Pleasant
" Joseph third hand b 215 Church
" Joseph weaver h 53 Salisbury
" Joseph weaver h 55 Hope
" Joseph weaver h 101 Coffin av
" Joseph weaver b 19 Hicks
" Joseph weaver b 883 Purchase
" Joseph C prop Nash Road Wet Wash Laundry h 448 N Front
" Joseph H A fish 30 Delano h 612 S Second
" Joseph O weaver b 59 Brock av
" Leo mill hand b 173 Collette
" Leopold D tailor 1042 Acushnet av h do [av
" Louis bricklayer b 1781 Acushnet
" Louis mill hand h 180 Blackmer
" Louis C carder h 55 Willard
" Louis M baker 35 Peckham h do
" Mary C milliner b 154 Cedar Grove [Cedar Grove
" Mary C widow Joseph H b 154
" Matilda Mrs mill hand h 173 Collette
" Maxim laborer h 14 Beetle
" Maxime carpenter h 23 Holly
" Moise weaver h 19 Hicks
" Narcisse clerk h 89 Collette
" Onsime h 59 Brock av [Jean
" Rea clerk 1039 Acushnet av h 8
" Remi operative h 199 N Front
" Romuald rem to Pawtucket R I
" Romuald yardmaster h 215 Church
" Sadie D clerk 1100 Acushnet av
" Thomas carpenter h 232 State
" Thomas carpenter b 314 N Front
" Uldric carpenter b 203 Belleville avenue
" Ulric weaver h 109 David [rimac
" Virginia widow Louis h r 41 Mer-
" Vital carpenter b 51 Tallman
" Wenceslas clerk 126 Bowditch h 8 Jean
" Willie laborer h 23 Holly
" Willie mill hand h 23 Holly

Roy
" Zenon weaver b 812 First
" Zoel (Langlois & Roy) 945 South Water b 35 Peckham
" see Roi and King [S Water
Royal Theatre Oza Tessier prop 991
Roye Frank laborer h 267 Field
Royer David carpenter h 183 Dean
" Louis laborer b 183 Dean
Roylance Harold tinsmith h 1 Thatcher [Morton court
" Samuel restaurant 116 Cove h 8
Royland Frank painter h 7 Linden ct
Royle David drill maker h 29 East French av [Water
Roza Aurilo mill hand h 509 South
Rubenstein David pedlar h 63 Spruce
Rubin Eva sewer 40 Purchase b 479 S First [479 S First
" Jacob S clerk 407 S Water bds
" Joseph removed from city [First
" Joseph mattress maker h 479
" Joseph & Son (Lewis) mattress mfrs 421 S Water
" Lewis (Joseph Rubin & Son) b 480 S Water
Ruddell John weaver h 105 Nash rd
" Julius spinner b 105 Nash rd
" Richard spinner b 105 Nash rd
Ruddock Albert A chauffeur b 64 Fifth
Ruddy Martin J weaver h 53 Locust
Rudish John removed from city
Rudolph P M Mrs h 535 Acushnet av
Ruel Fred iceman h 155 Shawmut av
Ruffley John baker 55 Mechanics lane h 401 Pleasant [Spring
Rugg Mary P widow Charles R h 101
Ruggles John A Jr h 78 Chestnut
" Sarah N bookkeeper N B Cordage Co h 145 Summer [Summer
" Susan R widow John A h 145
Rumney Chris spinner b 186 County
" John C spinner h 309 Earl
" Joseph spinner h 194 Davis
Rupka Adam shoe operative h 132 Cedar Grove
Rush Annie Mrs h 58 Fair
" Bertha E clerk b 173 Park
" Herbert L at P Corp h 285 Acushnet av
" Louis student b 173 Park
" Maynard F carpenter h 173 Park
" Urike widow Joseph h 81 School

GLOBE DYE HOUSE 220 SHAWMUT AVE.
J. N. J. LONHOLDT, PROP. Telephone Connections Goods called for and Delivered
Down town Office. 52 Pleasant St., Room 1 North End Office, 1014 Acushnet Ave.

Rush
" William J clerk 41 Purchase b 81 School
" see Reusch [field
Rushton Frank H mason h 157 Max-
" Henry removed from city
" William H clerk Cottage c Durfee h 267 Weld [lette
Rushworth Albert N fixer h 321 Col-
" George weaver h 1643 Acushnet avenue
" Joshua weaver h 402 Sawyer
Rusitzky Harris pedlar h 113 Fifth
" Julius mgr 232 Union b 113 Fifth
" Samuel drill worker b 113 Fifth
Russ Charles H painter h 29 Union
" Sarah A principal Thomas R Rodman school b 16 Fifth
Russell Abbie A Mrs b 90 Bedford
" Addison F telephone inspector 57 N Second h 34 Jenney
" Albert M bookkeeper Hathaway M Corp h 23 Sherman [fin av
" Albert W watchmaker h 215 Cof-
" Alfred laborer h 2 Bowditch
" Alice A widow William A h 77 State [net av
" Allen Jr bank clerk b 2559 Acush-
" Alonzo W laborer h 65 Spruce
" Annette B music teacher bds 44 Summer [laundress h 143 Mill
" Annie B widow Frederick H
" Arthur L laborer b 65 Spruce
" Augustus S h 16 Cottage
" Brothers Inc butter 70 William 884 and 888 S Water and 1061 Acushnet av [Parker
" Catherine M widow James A h 37
" Charles A advt solicitor Standard h 424 Union [Linden
" Charles A repairman 55 Spring b
" Charles A wheelwright h 93 Billingtou [ory
" Charles D drill worker h 22 Hick-
" Charles G salesman 198 Union h 75 Maxfield [man h 44 Summer
" David J parquetry floors 11 Rod-
" Edgar W (Parsons Steam Laundry) 270 Acushnet av h 34 S Sixth
" Edmond bicycle repairer 228 Purchase b 127 State
" Edna F Mrs clerk 48 Pleasant h 178 Kempton
" Edward third hand b 178 Collette

Russell
" Edward E painter h 106 Ash (N)
" Edward K b Edward K Russell Jr Plainville rd [ville road
" Edward K Jr blacksmith h Plain-
" Edward S driver 14 N Sixth b 40 Shawmut av
" Edward S painter h 115 Park
" Edward T carpenter h 854 Rockdale av [Union h do
" Ellen M employment office 245
" Elsie M telephone operator 57 N Second b at Westport [Hickory
" Emma L clerk 100 Fifth b 22
" Eugene F wagonman police dept h 43 Rounds [Kempton
" Fannie B widow Carl H h 284
" Fannie L Mrs removed from city
" Florence plumber 26 N Second h at Padanaram [Rockdale av
" Florence L stenographer bds 1107
" Fred A removed from city [do
" Fred T barber 144 Purchase h 209
" Frederick J physician b 37 Parker
" Frederick J planer h 518 Cottage
" Frederick R clerk 98 Purchase b 143 Mill
" George laborer b 2 Bowditch
" George W G Jr electrician h 202 State
" Gladys C clerk b 44 Summer
" Glenn glass worker h 194 Davis
" Grace A nurse b 44 Summer
" Harry E clerk 98 Allen b 56 Walnut
" Henry C city weigher h 305 Mill
" Herbert C (Kinyon & Russell) 76 Pleasant rm 21 h at Pawtucket R I
" James H b 31 Parker
" Jason D salesman h 37 Atlantic
" John A farmer h 2559 Acushnet avenue
" John E stenographer registry of deeds and music teacher 61 Maple h do [ville av
" Joseph carpenter h 297 Belle-
" Joseph A overseer Hathaway Mfg Co h 186 County
" Joseph G carpenter h 66 Dean
" Leonora E widow George h 53 Kempton [284 Kempton
" Lillian M operative 43 William b
" Lloyd C clerk First National Bank b 23 Sherman

GREENE & WOOD Every Kind of LUMBER AND MILL WORK
PINE STREET, off So. WATER STREET, NEW BEDFORD

Russell
" Louis laborer b 53 Kenyon
" Luther driver 255 Union h 373 Court [Parker h do
" Mabel E Mrs music teacher 121
" Mary A housekeeper 424 Union h do
" Mary V h 65 Walnut
" Nathaniel D h 31 Parker
" Oliver removed from city
" Pardon ice h 1107 Rockdale av
" Philip C officer H of C b 424 Union [ence
" Phoebe H widow Perry b 51 Flor-
" Richard overseer Nashawena Mill h 40 Wood
" Thomas bartender h 22 Reynolds
" Thomas removed from city
" Wallace E polisher 18 Market b 43 Rounds [115 Park
" Walter V clerk 1145 Kempton b
" William E baggageman h 596 Hathaway rd [Kempton
" William E hairdresser h 178
" William J painter h 51 James
" William T mariner b 305 Mill
Russoto Barnard A (Collateral Loan Co) 67 Union and Hub Loan Co 27 Weld h 18 Bedford
Rust Fred A sawyer h 27 Elm [Hicks
Rutkowski Joseph weaver h 27 Hicks
Rutledge James R rope maker h Tarkiln Hill rd cor Bowditch
Ryan Ambrose yard overseer Kilburn Mill h 73 Dudley
" Ann Mrs h 149 State
" Annie S Mrs h 267 Austin
" Catherine Mrs h 508 Cottage
" Edward carpenter h 53 Hillman
" Elizabeth M widow John J h 246 Brownell [Linden court
" Ellen F widow Timothy F h 4
" Francis P sub clerk P O bds 94 County
" Henry operative b 194 Blackmer
" Hugh J laborer h 370 Kempton
" James bookkeeper b 58 Locust
" John H sealer of weights and measures Odd Fellows bldg h 563 Cottage
" John H Jr asst inspector bldgs 307 Municipal bldg h 174 Maxfield [press b 4 Linden court
" John J conductor Electric Ex-

Ryan
" Joseph H died Dec 13 1910 [do
" Kate dressmaker 51 Hillman b 53
" Margaret widow Thomas h 408 Chancery
" Martin h 259 N Front
" Martin laborer h 89 Austin
" Mary E widow Patrick J variety 96 County h 94 do [av
" Michael carpenter h 908 Acushnet
" Patrick F spinner b 275 Bowditch
" Patrick J salesman bds 263 Purchase [lumbia
" Peter J clerk 43 Bedford h 7 Co-
" Spencer Mrs h 18 Bullock
" Thomas B engineer h 219 Brownell [State
" William A mule spinner bds 149
" William M chauffeur police ambulance h 170 Fourth
Rycroft John died April 15 1911
" John R clerk 1625 Acushnet av b 296 Davis [Davis
" Margaret widow John h 296
Ryder Charles E cigars and pool 134 Purchase h 68 Foster
" David C salesman N B Fish Co h 51 Maitland
" Deborah S died Sept 30 1910
" Ella F h 36 Ash (S)
" Etta rms 508 County
" Herbert H N laborer 350 S Second b 14 Columbia
" Idella M widow Charles F clerk 24 Pleasant h 88 High
" James C student b 429 Union
" James H boss comber h 96 Scott
" John molder b 65 Washburn
" John Q clerk 100 Fifth h 429 Union [ond rms 56 Walnut
" Joseph H bookkeeper 159 N Sec-
" Marcus M glass engraver h 82 Atlantic
" Philip H student b 429 Union
" Thomas packer b 25 Bentley
" Walter third hand b 34 Stapleton
" Walter weaver h 34 Stapleton
" Walter C machinist h 174½ Grinnell
" William J died March 23 1911
" see Rider

Saba Joseph h 559 Acushnet av [ton
Sabin Robert shoemaker h 419 Kemp-
Sabina Emilio S buffer b 222 Allen

BONNEY, FOLSTER & CO.,
The North End's Shopping Centre
Dry Goods and Men's Furnishings
945-947 Acushnet Ave., New Bedford, Mass.

Sabina
" Lauriana A widow John A h 222 Allen [non
" George P gardener h 34 Mt Ver-
Sabins Ellsworth L foreman C S Knowles h 120 Florence [place
" Job E clerk 98 Allen rms 3 Park
" Joseph laborer h 589 S Water
" Robert B driver h 415 Chancery
Sablon Frank teamster h 228 North Second
" William teamster b 228 N Second
Sabola Stanislaw laborer h 54 Phillips av [Collette
Sabourin Edmond operative bds 93
Sachs Albert (Taylor & Sachs) h 43 Thompson [bard
Sadanho Santos laborer h 76 Lom-
Sadler Edward P gilder h 51 Emerson (S) [Clifford school
" Edward T N principal John H
" Frank clerk b 580 Kempton
" George H laborer h 9 Bay
" Grace F housekeeper 580 Kempton [Pleasant
" Hattie clerk 70 Purchase b 129
" Irene E teacher Abraham Lincoln school b 50 Thompson
" Mabel clerk b 580 Kempton
" Rose Mrs dressmaker 1616 Acushnet av h do [av
" Thomas weaver h 1616 Acushnet
" Walter E trimmer h 580 Kempton
" William G h 129 Pleasant [av
" William J laborer h 899 Rockdale
" William T asst supt N B Cordage Co h 54 Thompson [av
Safa Jervet laborer h 191 Belleville
Sage Louis jeweler 49 William rm 2 h 134 Acushnet av [ham av
Sager James weaver bds 159 Tink-
" John W machine operator b 28 W French av [174 Clifford
" William baker 437 Purchase bds
Saillant Ezra clerk 44 Dartmouth h 103 Fair
St Armand Telesphore blacksmith 268 Sawyer h 109 Bowditch
St Aubin Arthur laborer h 17 Beetle
" Arthur rem from city
" Arthur weaver b 76 County
" Emil doffer b 35 Ingraham
" Francis weaver b 85 Holly
" Francois fireman h 80 Beetle

St Aubin
" Henry carpenter h 85 Holly
" Joseph carpenter h 55 Tallman
" Joseph painter h 18 Peckham
" Oliva carpenter h 115 Nash rd
" Reme laborer b 80 Beetle
" Treffle loom fixer h 76 County
" see Aubin
St Charles Philomeno widow Francois X h 93 Hathaway
" William driver 185 Union bds 93 Hathaway [chase
St Clair Bruno laborer h 772 Pur-
" Louis spinner b 772 Purchase
" Philip quarryman b 772 Purchase
St Dennis Joseph A picker h 124 Rivet [105 Bullard
" Vincent clerk 350 N Front h
St Don Emil hostler h 51 Mill rd
St Gelais Adelard mill hand b 8 Tallman
" Charles weaver b 32 Tallman
" Eugene mill hand h 8 Tallman
" Leontine mill hand h 8 Tallman
" Stanislas weaver h 32 Tallman
St George Archibald physician 92½ Purchase h at Fall River
" George weaver b 563 N Front
St Germain Adelard weaver h 799 First [road
" Alfred engineer h 191 Belleville
" Alfred teaming 47 Covell h do
" Alfred weaver b 227 State
" Belle cashier b 24 Bentley
" Bert foreman h 197 Belleville rd
" Eliza bookkeeper 410½ N Front h 208 Coffin av
" Elphege weaver h 338 N Front
" Emily widow Narcisse h 87 Potomska
" Eva bookkeeper bds 24 Bentley
" Felix h 208 Coffin av
" George musician b 102 Bowditch
" Gilbert teamster h 24 Bentley
" Hector fixer h 553 N Front
" Joseph clerk h 13 Bowditch
" Joseph O driver r 28 Larch h 23 Independent [rms do
" Joseph P physician 13 S Sixth
" Julia widow Damase h 52 Hicks
" Narcisse operative h 102 Bowditch
" Thomas weaver h 227 State
" William electrician h 25 Mosher
St German Joseph lather b 975½ S Water

M. P. B. Silva & Son BUILDERS
Estimates Furnished on all Kinds of Work
157 ACUSHNET AVENUE Both Phones NEW BEDFORD

St Hilaire Bruno died April 5 1911
" Louis spinner b 772 Purchase
" Philip quarryman b 772 Purchase
St Jacques Arthur L cable splicer 57 N Second b 160 Ashland
" Emile machinist h 131 Webster court [fin av
" Ferdinand blacksmith h 289 Cof-
" Joseph carpenter h 160 Ashland
ST JAMES CO-OPERATIVE SALES and Community Houses 66-68 Linden See page 48
St Jean Adolph loom fixer b 89 Collette
" Albert weaver b 1101 County
" Alfred A mgr h 269 Coffin av
" Arthur clerk 32 Purchase b 205 Fourth
" Arthur fixer h 30 Nye
" Dennis operative b 76 Cove
" Joseph weaver h 430 N Front
" Odele widow Joseph h 23 Acushnet av [67 Hathaway
St John Mary J Mrs mill hand h
" William F laborer h 624 Maxfield
St Laurent Charles carpenter h 171 Bowditch
" Paul carder h 49 Nelson
St Lawrence Bertha Mrs h 36 George
" Paul Jr ice 440 Rivet h do
St Louis Alfred laborer b 2 Bowditch
" Alma milliner 129 Rivet b 16 Nelson
" Amedee stonecutter h 16 Nelson
" Edmond carpenter 7 Leonard h 51 County
" Emma milliner b 16 Nelson
" George laborer b 2 Bowditch
" Henry carpenter h 2 Bowditch
" Henry painter 19 N Water b 300 Acushnet avenue
" Napoleon h 16 Nelson
" Oddlin h 51 County
" Ulric teamster b 16 Nelson
St Luke's Hospital Page cor Allen
St Marie Horace overseer h 9 West French avenue
" Joseph teamster h 71 Peckham
" Wilfred carpenter h 51 Ashley
" William operative h 9 Cleveland
St Martin Louis mill hand h 135 Nash road

St Martin
" Peter carpenter b 644 Purchase
St Mary's Home 593 Kempton cor Liberty [518 Kempton
St Montario Emma widow Philip h
St Onge Albert barber h 65 Jouvett
" Alphonse h 171 Tinkham
" Amedee driver 12 School h 211 S Second [h 24 Adams
" Edmund P overseer Oneko Mills
" Frank weaver h 282 N Front
" John mill hand h 475 N Front
" Moise fixer h 553 N Front
" Paul mill hand b 475 N Front
" Philip laborer b 1098 Acushnet av
" Philip spinner h 157 Davis
" Victor laborer h 216 N Second
" Vinnie Mrs h 195 N Second [yer
St Pierre Armedos clerk b 216 Saw-
" Arthur carpenter h 291 Belleville avenue
" Averist teamster h 110 Cove
" Charles carder h 4 Blackburn
" Charles operative h 4 Howland Village [lage
" Charles weaver h 7 Howland Vil-
" Cyprien removed to Fall River
" Eugene operative b 28 Howard
" Eusebe carpenter h 164 Sawyer
" Hormidas clerk 507 N Front bds 216 Sawyer
" Israel mill hand h 80 Hope
" John B carder h 70 Phillips av
" John B operative bds 3 Howland Village [rd
" Joseph carpenter b 113 Belleville
" Joseph fitter bds 47 Covell
" Joseph loom fixer h 59 County
" Joseph shoe maker h 3 Howland Village
" Joseph spinner h 239 Sawyer
" Louis bds 4 Blackburn
" Louis lather h 26 Holly
" Louis second hand h 111 Beetle
" Luc removed from city
" Ludger teamster b 582 First
" Napoleon carpenter b 74 Eugenia
" Narcisse carpenter h 216 Sawyer
" Norbet A painter h 216 Sawyer
" Omer operative b 21 Morton court
" Romeo clerk 1032 Acushnet av b 216 Sawyer [ton ct
St Roach Androise weaver h 21 Mor-

Steiger-Dudgeon Co.
"The WOMAN'S Store."
Tel. Bell 82 & 83, Branches connecting all depts.
" " 160 For Office only. Auto. 1211
SUMPTIONS, ASSORTMENTS AT ALL TIMES OF DEPENDABLE DRY GOODS

St Roach
" Omer mill hand b 21 Morton ct
St Sauveur Henri operative b 93 Collette
" Hormidas removed to Shawmut
" Joseph carder h 93 Collette
St Sauvier Joseph removed to Manville R I
St Silvia Jacinth laborer b 783 Water
Sale John second hand h 291 Collette
Saliba Handawa A H Mrs h 36 Myrtle
Salim Asim mill hand b 48 Davis
Saliotoski Wlaiystat operative h 5 Fulton court
Salisbury Herbert driver 159 Mill
" Herbert florist rms 228 Pleasant
" John operative b 44 W French av
" Lydia C bookkeeper 201 Purchase bds 75 Kempton
" Susan T bds 648 Cottage
" Thomas weaver h 206 Brook
" Walter weaver b 44 W French av
Salles Antone machinist b 59 Grinnell
" Emma M clerk 41 Purchase b 59 Grinnell [Grinnell
" Fred M clerk 601 Water bds 59
" John M carpenter h 59 Grinnell
" John M Jr student b 59 Grinnell
" Joseph driver h 146 Rockland
" Joseph M clerk 601 S Water h 291 Second
Salley George E h 257 Palmer
Salmon Dennis J shoes 796 Purchase h 256 Chestnut [avenue
" Emile weaver bds 399 Belleville
" John H twister b 209 State
" Mary Mrs died April 9 1910
" Samuel cook 1278 Acushnet av b 113 Bullard [Sept 10 1910
Salter Mary D widow William H died
" Robert drill worker h 545 Rivet
" William F insurance agent 37 Purchase rm 23 h 126 Grinnell
Saltonstall Philip L (Tucker Anthony & Co) h at Boston
Saltus George H cigar maker 183 Acushnet av h 662 Kempton
Salusky Nathan laborer h 58 Kenyon
Salvado Joseph removed to Dartmouth [Rivet
Salvador Antone J fisherman h 526
Salvail Joseph mill hand b 530 North Front

Salvail
" Oswald driver h 530 N Front
" Pierre h 350 N Front
" Romolus weaver b 530 N Front
Salvas Thomas doffer b 113 Nash rd
Salvati Gioechino chef Parker House h 104 Morgan [b 104 Morgan
" John asst steward Parker House
Salvation Army Barracks 279 Acushnet avenue [sell
Salves James drill worker bds 40 Rus-
Samansky Jacob h 515 S Water
Samaros Domingos G laborer b 202 Belleville avenue
Samoisette John B h 16 Thatcher
Sample Antone tailor b 86 Nash rd
Sampson Allen E driver h 63 Chancery [ond b do
" A Blanche dressmaker 12 S Sec-
" Betsey widow Frederick H bds 67 Chancery [Mills h 35 Bay
" Charles A overseer Potmska
" C Arthur salesman 43 William rm 3 h 113 Bedford
" Edward laborer b r 371 Hillman
" Edward (weaver) rem from city
" Frederick H died Feb 9 1911
" George driver 64 Dartmouth h Maxfield street [Chancery
" George W drill polisher h 67
" George W teamster h rear 371 Hillman
" Isaac D (Howland & Sampson) 27 Front h 201 Park
" John G laborer h 6 Felton
" Joseph spinner h 1 Edward
" Keziah R widow Warren W b 143 North
" Manuel laborer h 257 Fourth
" Peter operative h 52 Hicks
" Sarah J C Mrs h 82 Forest
" Stella W supt St Luke's Hospital b do [Maxfield st
" William driver 64 Dartmouth h
" William B teamster h r 371 Hillman
Samson Onesime laborer h 64 Hicks
" Syprien carpenter h 126 Perry
Samuelson Louis sorter h 15 Howland
Sanborn Allan P rem from city
" Ida shoeworker h 143 Hillman
" Lawrence spinner h 348 Davis

PELEG H. SHERMAN 506 COUNTY ST.
FUNERAL DIRECTOR AND EMBALMER
OFFICE PHONES. Bell 690-13 Auto 1305.
RESIDENCE PHONES. Bell 690-12. Auto. 1306.

Sanbourin John B mill hand h 31 Beetle [Washburn
Sancif Alix copperworker h 25
Sanderholm Charles G drillworker b 101 Fifth [(N)
Sanders Caesar mill hand h 63 Ash
" Edward W clerk 2 Union h at Fairhaven [h 56 Morgan
" Henry V real estate 166 Purchase
" James machinist rms 110 Middle
" John carpenter h 86 Hathaway
" Joseph A machinist h 39 Shawmut av
" William soldiers aid agent 210 Municipal bldg b 342 Union
" see Saunders [Bolton
Sanderson Cora bookkeeper b 530
" Flora clerk 98 Allen b 530 Bolton
" George H weaver h 5 Howland Village [chase
" Guy B copperworker h 610 Pur-
" James watchman b 530 Bolton
" James Jr clerk 446 Rivet b 530 Bolton
" Joseph clerk rms 25 William
" Joseph waiter 62 Purchase rms 25 William [Cottage
" Mary S widow Robert J h 405
" Thomas b 40 Beech [40 Beech
" Thomas H salesman 211 Union h
" William b 79 Clark
" William bartender 243 Purchase h 239 Fourth
Sando Joseph cook h 12 Bethel
Sanford Addie F widow Charles H b 48 Summer [b 18 Homer
" Edward M clerk Electric Express
" Eliza H h 112 Fourth [son
" Elizabeth widow Thomas b 208 Thompson [Cross b 18 Homer
" Ethel C bookkeeper Leonard cor
" Frank P mariner h 18 Homer
" Gardner T (Sanford & Kelley) banker and broker 20 Market h 98 Spring [Mill
" Lucy C widow Barnabas h 274
" Mary A clerk b 85 Hillman
" Sarah widow Stephen b 87 Locust
" Susie B clerk bds 85 Hillman
SANFORD & KELLEY (Gardner T Sanford and Charles S Kelley) bankers brokers and stock auctioneers 20 Market See front cover
Sanopulus Athan G (National Ice Cream Co) 580 N Front bds 124 Belleville rd
Sanson Pierre operative 64 Hicks
Sansoucy Edward fixer h 131 Nash road
" Elphege clerk b 119 Tallman
" Ludger shoemaker b 92 Holly
Santana Manuel (Pereira & Santana) h 8 Beetle [shnet av
" Manuel P carder h r 2619 Acu-
Santes Antonio grocer 228 Coggeshall [non
Santo Christiana operative h 18 Can-
" Manuel fisherman h 226 Rivet
Santos Anabo removed to Dartmouth
" Antone fireman h 369 Coggeshall
" Antone (operative) rem from city
" Antone B grocer 419 S Water h r 111 Fifth
" Antone F speeder b Farnam st
" Antone G mill hand h 55 Mitchell [mouth h 80 Sidney
" Antonio blacksmith 108 Dart-
" Antonio laborer rem to Fairhaven
" Antonio C wood 469 First h do
" Augustine Rev asst pastor Mt Carmel R C church h 230 Bonney [127 Fair
" Augustus shoes 132 County h
" Caesar C mill hand b 67 N Ash
" Caesar M mill hand h 412 S Water [net av
" Casemere fisherman h 88 Acush-
" Frank clerk h 254 S Second
" Frank operative h 155 Belleville av [ond
" Gabriel boat builder h 371 S Sec-
" Jessie Mrs h 195 Durfee [av
" Joaquim laborer h 325 Acushnet
" John operative b 195 Durfee
" Jose P doffer h 14 Highland
" Joseph cook 62 Purchase b 12 Bethel
" Joseph laborer h 4 Stanton ct
" Joseph laborer b 7 Stanton ct
" Joseph operative h 514 Rivet
" Joseph 132 S Second b 129 do
" Joseph A laborer h 70 Lindsey
" Louder operative h 128 S Second
" Manuel clerk 329 Rivet b 127 Fair
" Manuel driver b 127 Fair
" Manuel rope maker b 195 Durfee
" Manuel F grocer 132 S Second h 129 do

COAL AND WOOD HAY AND STRAW F. T. AKIN & COMPANY WALNUT, COR. WATER, 84 PLEASANT ST., 25 WELD SQ. 129 COVE STREET WHF. FOOT OF COFFIN STREET

Santos
" Manuel P steam fitter 99 Acushnet avenue h 329 South Front
" Manuel S mariner h 33 Oak
" Mary widow Almond h 258 S Second
" Mello Mrs h 56 Grinnell
" Peter gardener bds 195 Durfee
" Satinnino B mill hand b r 111 Fifth [b 76 Hicks
Sanwill Dora clerk 1097 Acushnet av
Saporto Philo mill hand h 926 South Water [erson (S)
Saqueria Manuel laborer h 46 Em-
Saragas Kostas rms 72 Division
Sarasin Albert twister h 32 Woodlawn avenue
Sarda Andrew weaver b 101 Davis
Sardif Arjem mill hand bds 54 Davis
Sardinha Manuel hairdresser h 148 Belleville av [Pleasant rms do
Sargent Clara B Mrs millinery 270
" Daniel removed to Boston
" Fred H electro plating 90 Pleasant rms 270 do
" James mill hand h 91 Eugenia
" James E piper 125 Middle h 25 Richmond
" John apprentice rms 270 Pleasant
" John weaver b 39 Tallman
" Joseph twister h 862 First
" Lydia M widow William teacher High school h 437 Union
" Peter removed to Taftville Conn
" Ruth E teacher Parker st school b at Fairhaven
" William weaver h 383 N Front
" William A watchman h 169 Ashland [Ashland
" William H roll coverer b. 169
Sarmento Frank P fish 559 S Water h 555 do [city
Sasonsky Benjamin, removed from
Sasscer William B died Oct 30 1910
Sasseville Alfred F laborer b 396 N Front
" Ernest operative h 24 Nye
" Fred removed from city
Sater John J mariner h 52 Park
Saucier Leon carpenter h Hawes st
" Paul mason h 121 Whitman
" see Soucy [20 Holly
Saulnier Adolph driver 255 State b

Saulnier
" Adolph laborer bds 20 Holly
" Alexis carpenter h Acushnet av n Brooklawn park [Pleasant
" Alphonse J B clerk 3 Weld b 345
" Clement removed from city
" Clodorise widow Joseph h 345 Pleasant
" Clovis removed from city
" Joseph tailor 28 Delano b 950 S Water
" Marcille laborer h 950 S Water
" Oliver carpenter h 15 Scott
" Theothime carpenter h 178 Phillips avenue
" Thomas laborer b 22 Holly
Saum Afdew pedler h 167 N Front
" Joseph baker 48 Pleasant h 475 Coggeshall [h 100 Pierce
Saunders Horace E shuttle finisher
" Jennie widow Hiram mill hand bds 116 Phillips avenue [velt
" Joseph H operative h 63 Roose-
Sauve Alfred machinist b 52 Fifth
" Arzelia L 92 High [Middle
" Edward glass worker rms 110
" Hector slasher tender b 102 Beetle
" Joseph fireman h 102 Beetle
" Victor slasher b 102 Beetle
Savage Abraham W machinist b 680 Purchase
" Gilbert weaver h 33 Tallman
" James W police h 14 Tremont
" John M variety 688 Purchase h 680 do
" Joseph O died June 27 1911
" Mary A widow Joseph O h 297 Allen
" William J electrician h 24 Myrtle
Savany Ernest chief usher 958 Acushnet av b 55 Bullard [av
Savaria Alexis carpenter h 75 Brock
" Charles weaver h 477 S Front
" Laurenzo removed from city
" Rudolph weaver h 154 Belleville road [Salisbury
Savarie Florida and Martine h 54
Savarier Joseph laborer h 202 State
" Joseph Jr laborer h 202 State
Savery Charles W salesman 46 Purchase b 333 Union
" George H carpenter h 809 County
" John M contract agent 57 N Second h at E Wareham

There's room at the top for young men and women who can do things right.
Kinyon's Commercial School
Odd Fellows Bldg., Cor. William and Pleasant Sts., New Bedford, Mass.

Savoie Albert operative b 300 Earle
" Arthur Rev removed to Attleboro
" Caliste operative h 300 Earle
" Clement U carpenter h 434 North Front [av b 434 N Front
" Edmond bookkeeper 870 Acushnet
" Emma widow George b 82 Independent
" Fidele carpenter h 287 N Front
" Hercule died Oct 19 1910
" Joseph barber 110 William b 209 Purchase
" Peter carpenter h 52 Phillips av
" Sarah confectionery 1561 Acushnet av b 434 N Front
" Wilfred operative b 300 Earle
Savoy Hotel Sullivan & Desmond props 343 Acushnet avenue
" Theatre 162 Union
SAWIN GEORGE F building mover 343 Purchase bds do See page 783
Sawtelle Frank C asst treas Sharp Mfg Co h 34 Eighth [Hillman
Sawyer Albert H motorman h 134
" Albert H Jr tackmaker h 1679 Acushnet av [Smith
" Annie F clerk 58 Adams b 146
" Charles P clerk of committees 206 Municipal bldg h 162 Arnold [nut
" Charles S glasscutter h 235 Chest-
" Clara M teacher Abraham Lincoln school b 146 Smith
" Fred painter b 233 Sawyer
" Fred L engineer h 175 Phillips av
" Frederick G brakeman h 55 Maxfield [Smith
" Frederick T watchman h 146
" Helen J Mrs stenographer 99 William h 235 Chestnut
" Henry A fitter 125 Middle h 47 Sycamore
" James C rem to Howard R I
" Joseph carpenter b 195 Collette
" Mary A clerk 182 Union b 266 Orchard
" Mary L stenographer 15 Masonic bldg h 45 Sycamore [av
" Reuben L carpenter h 174 Phillips
" Rilla D dressmaker 39 High h do [Sawyer
" Rosanna widow Policap h 233

Sawyer
" Stephen P stoves and tinworker 79 N Second h 21 Willis
" William K b 21 Willis [more
" William W watchman h 45 Syca-
Saxon Annie E died May 8 1911
" Charles E agent h 390 Kempton
" George Elias justice h 628 Purchase [ham
" George W operative h 165 Tink-
" Herbert spinner h 448 Sawyer
" Lillian musician b 390 Kempton
" Wright mill hand h 53 Collette
Sayer Caroline W widow Charles C h 77 Fourth
" Thomas S Rev pastor South Baptist church h 72 Hillman
Sayles Charles B draw tender Fairhaven bridge h 154 Summer
" Clarence E armature winder U St Ry Co h at Fairhaven
" Harry D salesman 75 William b 154 Summer
" Joseph G operative h 5 Ashland terrace [County
" William steam fitter rms 833
Scala John weaver b 157 Coffin av
Scales Bessie widow Robert h 293 Allen [city
" Elisha widow Joseph rem from
" John J B second hand h 27 Dunbar
" Robert H carpenter b 293 Allen
" Thomas A printer Times h 293 Allen [131 Robeson
Scammons Joseph H gardener h
Scarborough Elizabeth W widow Henry A h 156 Cedar
" Henry A driver 48 Pleasant bds 156 Cedar [161 Campbell
Schabel Joseph tinsmith 87 Union h
Schaff Joseph b 110 Rockland
Schambier Arthur painter bds 1098 Acushnet av [Austin
Schaper Louise widow Henry b 206
Schaubinger Fridrich laborer rms 1142 Acushnet av [75 Emma
Schaves Josiah fish 319 S Water h
Shellenberg Albert mill hand b 168 Tinkham [av b 10 McGurk
Schelter Bernard clerk 34 W French
" Evangeline widow Henry Jr h 10 Viall [av
" Henry operative h 21 Brock
" Henry Jr died Jan 18 1911
" Mary widow George h 10 McGurk

HASKELL BROS. DEALERS IN
ICE
400 COURT STREET TELEPHONE CONNECTION NEW BEDFORD, MASS.

Scherzer John weaver h 158 Rockland [ditch
Schestak Charles mill hand h 45 Bow-
" Frank operative h 166 Hathaway
" Joe bds 45 Bowditch
Schick John weaver h 819 S Wa-
Schiebel Florien weaver b 284 Cedar Grove [Grove
" Mary widow Frank h 284 Cedar
Schiersohn Joseph B Rev Hebrew teacher h 6 Wing
Schlinansky William R clerk 182 Union b 170 Acushnet av
Schiolino Gaetano (Pirroni & Schiolino) 352 Acushnet av b 20 Wing
Schlais Frank iceman h Phillips rd
" Paul M lastcutter h Phillips rd
Schlam Emile weaver h 723 First
Schmid William chauffeur 170 Purchase b 38 Bentley
Schmidt Auguste weaver h 161 Dean
" Charles motorman h 4 Penniman
" Emile weaver h 367 Earle
" Hugh E (H E Schmidt & Co) b 57 Washburn
" H E & Co (Hugh E Schmidt and Hermann S Tetzner) reed mfrs 116 Front [ond h 108 South
" Jacob H sausage mfr 424 S Sec-
" John removed from city [burn
" Mary widow Joseph b 63 Wash-
" William H clerk b 108 South
Schneider Gustave mill hand h 200 Coffin avenue
" Jacob removed from city
" Raoul O clerk 182 Union b 200 Coffin avenue
Schnitzler Jacob removed from city
Schnur Abraham junk collector h 5 Turner ct [land
Schobek Anton weaver h 28 Cleve-
Schoech Andreas boarding house 57 Washburn
Schoene John weaver h 481 Coggeshall [h 481 Coggeshall
" Theodore shoemaker 76 Purchase
Schofield Albert weaver b 96 Cove
" Alfred watchman h 322 Sawyer
" Alfred tripe dresser h 48 Bourne
" Ellen bookkeeper b 130 Mill
" George T motorman h 9 Linden ct
" James spinner h 231 North

Schofield
" John box maker h 154 Tallman
" John weaver b 27 Viall
" John A operative h 16 George
" John W twister h 76 Hathaway
" Joseph overseer h 120 S Sixth
" Joseph H solderer h 49 Dartmouth
" Joseph W operative b 120 S Sixth
" Mary widow mill hand b 199 Collette [189 Orchard (S)
" Robert agent Sharp Mfg Co h
" Thomas loom fixer h 478 N Front
" Wilbraham plumber 28 N Water b 62 Roosevelt [ond
Scbole George chauffeur rms 7 N Sec-
Scholes John spinner h 12 Cleveland
Schott Albert removed to Olean N Y
SCHOTT GEORGE A auto repairer and metal ceilings 1467 Acushnet avenue h 210 Coffin av See page 753
Schrader James teamster h 98 Austin
SCHULER BROTHERS (George and Jacques) shoe mfrs and dealers 76-78 Purchase See page 24
" George (Schuler Bros) h 55 Campbell
" George T clerk city treasurers office bds 187 Chancery
" Jacques (Schuler Bros) h 33 Sycamore [198 Cottage
" Louis N salesman 76 Purchase h
Schultz Angelina telephone operator 57 N Second b 60 Robeson
" Gabriel foreman h 183 Rockland
" Hugo, U S A bds 60 Robeson
" Mary Mrs h 60 Robeson
" Otto C glass worker h 91 Tremont
Schumm George brew master Smith Bros brewery b 350 Sawyer
Schuster Bros (Solomon and Louis) wholsale fruit 24-26 Union
" Harry junk h 499 First [S Water
" Haskell salesman 26 Union h 371
" Heiman pedler h 17 Morgan's lane [S Water
" Heiman salesman 24 Union h 371
" Hyman H variety 497 S Water h 17 Morgan's lane
" Julius clerk 493 South Water h 363 First [h 139 Acushnet av
" Louis (Schuster Bros) 24 Union
" Louis pedler h 508 S Water

J. F. CROSSLEY 223 MILL STREET COR. EMERSON PHONE
STEAM and HOT WATER HEATING
GAS FITTING and FIXTURES

Schuster
" Michael salesman 24 Union b 371 S Water
" Morris ragman h 700 S Water
" Nathan dry goods 430 S Water h do [125½ Fourth
" Simon pawnbroker 92 Union h
" Solomon (Schuster Bros) 24 Union h 139 Acushnet av
Schwall James B clerk 1 Purchase h 25 Bonney
" Mary Eva principal George H Dunbar school h 37 Allen
" Sarah bookkeeper Standard b 37 Allen
Schwalm Emil S weaver b 723 First
Schwartz Jacob brewer h 1076 County
" Morris shoemaker h 7 North
" Morris L variety 534 S Water h do
" T gas fitter bds 263 Acushnet av
" Wolf second hand furniture 451 S Water h 455 do [ton ct
Schweigart John spinner h 13 Ful-
Schwenker William H weaver b 258 Coffin avenue [avenue
Scott Alfred weaver h 32 W French
" Andrew operative b 273 Purchase
" Annie E widow Joseph M h 169 Emerson (N)
" Arthur E weaver h 69 Crapo
" Betsey died Oct 2 1910
" Charles M iceman h 1360 Rockdale av [church h 18 Cedar
" Dennis Rev pastor A M E Zion
" Edward spinner h 4 Penniman
" Fannie housekeeper b 48 Willard
" Henry H stevedore h 66 Middle
" James A clerk 765 Purchase h 182 Weld
" John E boarding h 44 Beetle
" John T weaver h 34 Willow
" Martha operative h 445½ Pleasant
" Mildred clerk 70 Purchase bds 1360 Rockdale av [av
" Patrick laborer b 1098 Acushnet
" Peter overseer engineer dept foot Rodman h do [h do
" Robert violin teacher 211 Fourth
" Robert P weaver b 69 Crapo
" Thomas P mill hand b 34 Willow
" William operative h 202 Brook
Scowcroft James rem to Woonsocket R I

Scowcroft
" Maud Mrs (Harrison & Scowcroft) 51½ Brock av h 22 Warren
Scranton Clara N widow William N special commisioner 71 William rms 143 North
" House Mrs Ellen MacLane prop 5-7 N Second [school b 39 Arch
Scribner Katherine B teacher High
" Cynthia widow Merritt h 62 Summer [Summer
" Harry A cotton broker bds 62
Scullen Mary M clerk 185 Union b 27 Thompson [son
" Michael A bartender h 27 Thomp-
Sculley John P second hand h 685 Cottage [Front
Schutzch Willie mill hand h 93 N
Seaburg Paul shoemaker bds 147 Rounds
Seabury Arthur G mgr N B Shuttle Co 6 Elm h at Fairhaven
" Caroline O and Sarah E h 398 County
" Horace H machinist h 55 Durfee
" Mary B and Helen H h 414 County [Fifth
" Sarah W widow Charles P h 47
Seals Charles F driver b 316 Middle
" Harrison J cook h 316 Middle
Seaman Charles W clerk 17 N Sixth b 466 Union [Hazard
" George driver 100 William b 99
" John H mgr 64 Purchase h at Fairhaven
" Nellie nurse rms 321 Union
" Thomas teamster bds 99 Hazard
" Walter J clerk 127 Union b 466 do [do
" William grocer 464 Union h 466
Searell Allen J plumber 26 N Second h 7 Jenny Lind
" Mary J widow William A h 54 Summer [54 Summer
" William E salesman 47 School h
Searle Charles H motorman h 620 Union
" Josephine E Mrs confectionery Rockdale av cor Court and dry goods 853 Kempton h 620 Union
Searles Edmund D teacher High school h 19 Maple View ter
Sears Amelia B h 350 County
" Betsey widow Nathan h 91 High

CHARLES A. CROSHERE CARRIAGE AND AUTO
38 FOURTH ST. Bell Phone 1964-23 **PAINTING**

Sears
" Charles clerk 67 Howland b 92 Grinnell [Kempton
" Edward painter 70 High h 74
" Edward H clerk 630 Purchase h 15 Smith [Union
" Eliza F widow John P bds 402
" Estelle teacher Abraham Lincoln school b 181 Summer
" Frank J insurance agent b 11 Columbia [bia
" Frank M watchman h 11 Colum-
" Harrison G O carpenter h 92 Tremont [av
" John teamster rms 390 Acushnet
" Joseph painter h r 64 Spruce
" John J drillworker h 11 Columbia
" Joseph M fireman h 17 Studley
" Katherine B widow Anthony F h 49 Oak
" Louis A foreman b 49 Oak
" Lucie H teacher I W Benjamin school b 159 Washington
" Manuel mill hand h 100 Blackmer
" Mary Mrs h 46 School
" Nathan drillmaker b 91 High
" Sarah E h 350 County
" William H carpenter h 337 Pleasant [liam
Seaver Edwin P tutor bds 179 Wil-
" Edwin P Jr physician 179 William h 32 Eighth
" Gladys E drapery sewer 36 Purchase h 157 Middle
" Manuel laborer b 104 Mosher
Seavor Alice Mrs milliner h 133 Clark [h 607 Cottage
Secour Joseph janitor Wamsutta Club
" Joseph W barber 94 Weld and coal and wood 379 Mt Pleasant h do
" William finisher b 607 Cottage
Seddon George card grinder h 300 Davis
" Percy carpenter b 350 Coffin av
" William weaver h 350 Coffin av
Sederholm Bessie Mrs widow 7139 Acushnet av [Weld
Seed Ada Mrs fish 337 Earle h 260
" Christopher weaver h 303 Brock av [net av h 264 Weld
Sede Thurston R clerk 1623 Acush-
Seely Izah Mrs stenographer Manomet Mill h at Mattapoisett
Seguer Alfred weaver h 66 Ruth
" Charles weaver h 46 Ashley
Sequin Alexander blacksmith h 171 Bowditch
" Andrea telephone operator Parker House rms 493 County
" August painter b 1729 Acushnet av [42 Davis
" Frank blacksmith 944 County h
" Henri weaver b 12 Morton ct
" Isaac blacksmith 944 County h 42 Davis [Coffin av
" Joseph insurance agent bds 345
" Jules weaver h 12 Morton ct
" Louis carpenter h 1729 Acushnet avenue [h 8 Penniman
" Peter blacksmith 558 Purchase
" Stanislas operative h 125 N Front
" Thomas carriage painter r 1279 Acushnet av h 42 Davis
Seidel John weaver h 190 Nash rd
" Marianna widow Joseph b 190 Nash road [ond
Seifert John machinist h 438 S Sec-
Seiferth Otto F finisher h 122 Hathaway [Union
Seip Lydia widow Charles L h 299
Seligson Louis pedlar h 134 Tallman
" Mendi pedlar h 134 Tallman
Selleck Ellen widow William h 8 Clark
" William teamster h 136 N Front
Sellers James fixer h 245 Sawyer
" Thomas weaver h 125 Holly
Selley Fred baker 1528 Acushnet av h 253 Coffin av [h 204 Earle
" George baker 1528 Acushnet av
" Helen bookkeeper b 204 Earle
" Mary clerk 1528 Acushnet av b 204 Earle
" Mary widow Fred h 204 Earle
" William H overseer Whitman Mill h 253 Collette [Earle
Semanica John F fisherman h 72
Semas Manuel oiler h 9 Winsor
Semino Joseph shoemaker b 148 Arnold
Sempis Christ bootblack 816 Purchase h 359 Coggeshall
Senecal Ernest lunch 1493 Acushnet av h 204 Davis
" Lorenzo clerk b 204 Davis

J. G. NICHOLSON
LUMBER, SASH, DOORS and BLINDS
BOWDITCH STREET, NEW BEDFORD, MASS.

Senecal
" Raymond clerk 1493 Acushnet av bds 204 Davis
" Tancride rem from city
Senesac Archibald N physician 1018 S Water h do [av
" Harvey salesman h 964 Acushnet
" Hugh collector h 348 Sawyer
" Genatan actor b 348 Sawyer
Senez William carpenter h 302 Sawyer [av h 101 Nye
Senft Fred variety 1549 Acushnet
" Henry baker b 101 Nye
Senglais Alfred mill hand h 117 Collette [ham
Senior Allen spinner h 151 Tink-
Senna Antone H visitor overseer of poor h 173 Allen
" Charles actor h 152 Grinnell
" Joseph laborer h 330 First
" Louisa widow Manuel b 173 Allen
" Manuel J grocer 90 S Second b 85 do
" Manuel J prop and mgr Pastime Theatre h 152 Grinnell
Senra John L D grocer 113 County h 20 Winsor [Rockdale av
Sequeira Antonio J farmer h 1019
" Harry salesman b 1067 Rockdale av
" John laborer h 117 Mott [av
" John A laborer b 1067 Rockdale
" Joseph F farmer h 1067 Rockdale avenue [avenue
" Manuel J laborer b 1019 Rockdale
" Myrtilla G teacher Fifth street school b 247 North
" Victor J gilt mat board mfr 92 Newton h 247 North [bury
Sequer Henri weaver h 20 Salis-
Sequin Felix C agent Boston American h 69 Spruce
" Hector painter b 42 Davis
" John B laborer h 15 Jenney
Serafino Tereni grocer 436 Purchase h do [Coggeshall
Seredzinski John operative h 484
Sergent Thomas rem from city
Serle John R bricklayer h 159 David
Serpa Charles A salesman 157 Union rms 16 Fifth [rms 165 Middle
" Charles N lawyer 6 Masonic bldg
" Joseph laborer h 389 S Second
" Manuel rem from city
" Manuel laborer h 109 Dunbar

Serpa
" Manuel whitewasher h 273 S Second
" Manuel P laborer h 252 Hillman
" Manuel R operative h r 111 Fifth
" William shoeworker b 243 South Front [shnet block
Serra Trefflay loom fixer h 11 Acu-
Serrantes John operative b 127 Belleville av [vision
Servai Antone carpenter h 129 Di-
Servais August sign painter 76 William and (Baron, Servais & Co) h 84 Whitman [man
" Irene sign painter b 84 Whit-
" Jules painter 76 William bds 84 Whitman
" Mary died Jan 1 1911 [R I
Servan Charles removed to Bristol
" Napoleon removed to Bristol R I
Sesketh Henry mill hand b 1137 Acushnet av
Sestak Barbara F Mrs h 296 Earle
Setera Andrew operative h 12 Fulton court [Ruth
Settele Harry photographer h 66
Setton Ezra M (Ross & Setton) h 209 Court [Orchard
Severance Isabelle R Mrs h 70
Severino Joseph E carpenter h 40 Hemlock
Sevigney Alphonse rem from city
" Ernest usher b 58 Bullard
" Ludger carpenter b 60 Bullard
" Maxime fitter h 113 Belleville rd
Sevigny Alfred weaver h 113 Belleville road
" George weaver h 45 Beetle
" Joseph operative h 113 Nash rd
" Joseph N plumber h 193 Bowditch [Hicks
Seymour Edmond pitman bds 13
" Fred barber b 119 Phillips av
" Henry N carpenter h 214 Coffin av
" Louis mason b 566 First
" Peter pitman b 13 Hicks
" Sophia widow Thomas housekeeper 13 Hicks [Durfee
Shaddock Robert bricklayer h 154
Shafter Harriet L teacher Harrington school b 156 Chestnut
Shakit Arbed mill hand b 42 Davis
SHAMBOW SHUTTLE CO 307 N Main Woonsocket R I See page 30

Steiger-Dudgeon Co.
"The WOMAN'S Store."
Tel. Bell 82 & 83, Branches connecting all depts.
" " 160 For Office only. Auto. 1211

SUMPTIONS, ASSORTMENTS AT ALL TIMES OF DEPENDABLE DRY GOODS

Shandonnair Alfred slasher h 83 Rivet [ton h do
Shanks Charles physician 645 Kemp-
" James (Shanks & Tripp) and (American Steam Laundry) 659 Purchase h 654 Kempton
" James Jr bookkeeper 659 Purchase b 654 Kempton
" K Mabel Mrs h 295 Hillman
" Robert h 633 Cottage
" Robert I shoe repairer 380 Kempton h 288 Palmer
" & Tripp (James Shanks and Charles H Tripp) liquors 214 to 216 Union [Belleville av
Shannahan Hugh operative h 181
Shannon John I theatrical mgr h 270 Hawthorn
" Nancy h 97 Fourth
Shapiro Barnet shoemaker 76 Purchase h 26 Hillman
" Bros (Herman and Israel Shapiro) clothing 907 S Water
" Herman (Shapiro Bros) h 54 Fair
" Hyman auto repairer b 340 First
" Hyman clothing h 54 Fair
" Ida clerk 973 S Water b 424 do
" Isaac kitchen furnishing goods 424 S Water h do
" Israel (Shapiro Bros) h at Lewiston Me
" Joseph Hebrew teacher h 455 S Water [340 First
" Morris lunch 481 S Water h
Shappy Ambrose fireman h 143 Coffin av [vet
Shard Samuel T machinist h 546 Ri-
Sharkey Hattie housekeeper 666 First
" James h r 188 Middle
" Jane housekeeper r 188 Middle
" Joseph glasscutter h 1 Warwick
" Samuel fixer h 226 Fourth
Sharon Joseph boss picker h 871 Purchase [chase
" Joseph F operative b 871 Pur-
Sharp Ann widow Isaac h 36 McGurk
" Arthur R treas Sharp Mfg Co h at Taunton
" Cornelius rem from city [away
" George S second hand h 70 Hath-
" John machinist bds 70 Hathaway
" John weaver h 570 S Second
" Joseph weaver h 12 Morton ct
" Mfg Co cotton goods Dartmouth c Rockdale av

Sharp
" Stanley engineer Beacon Mfg Co
Sharpe Floyd H fireman b 586 Mt Pleasant
" John M clerk 57 N Second b 586 Mt Pleasant [dle h do
" Kate Mrs dressmaker 101 Mid-
" Stanley W engineer Beacon Mfg Co h 586 Mt Pleasant
Sharples Aaron fixer h 128 Clark
" Adam weaver 76 Delano
" Albert weaver h 29 Howland Village
" Alfred weaver h 17 Salisbury
" Alice widow James boarding 258 Coffin av h do [h do
" Anna Mrs dressmaker 60 Beetle
" Annie Mrs h 348 Sawyer
" Arthur (Sharples & Sons) 1378 Acushnet av h 201 Tinkham
" Arthur W salesman 120 Purchase h 106 Chestnut
" Charles H (Sharples & Sons) 1378 Acushnet av h 3 Clifford
" David confectionery h 229 Bowditch
" Ellen widow John T h 85 James
" Fred clerk h 258 Chestnut
" Hugh teamster b 621 First
" James liquors 1290 Acushnet av h 1296 do
" James weaver h 7 Cornell place
" James Jr auto repairer b 1296 Acushnet av
" John h 61 Hathaway rd
" John laborer b 307 Collette
" John spinner b 258 Coffin av
" John weaver h 37 Ashley
" Mabel died Jan 2 1910
" Martha A Mrs (Sharples & Sons) confectionery 1378 Acushnet av h 229 Bowditch [rd
" Robert T weaver b 61 Hathaway
" Rufus weaver h 304 Tinkham
" Smith T police h 30 James
" T Thomas laborer h 56 Thompson
" William fixer h 27 Juniper
" William furniture polisher 170 Purchase b 287 Bowditch
" William loom fixer h 5 Jean
" William weaver b 24 W French avenue [ditch
" William D carpenter b 287 Bow-
" William H weaver h 76 Delano

PELEG H. SHERMAN 506 COUNTY ST.
FUNERAL DIRECTOR AND EMBALMER
OFFICE PHONES. Bell 690.13. Auto. 1305.
RESIDENCE PHONES. Bell 690.12. Auto. 1306.

Sharples
" William H A chauffeur bds 258 Coffin av [yer
" William J brakeman b 348 Saw-
" & Sons (Mrs Martha A, Charles H and Arthur) confectionery 1378 Acushnet av [Hazard
Sharrett Harry L second hand b 6
" Jennie Mrs h 6 Hazard
Sharrock Albert G clerk b 109 Collette [Howard
Sharrocks Robert weaver h 53
Sharves Joseph operative h 165 Grinnell [dar Grove
Shattuck Stanley operative b 211 Ce-
Shaughnessy Ellen Mrs h 269 Collette
" Jeremiah road master U St Ry Co h 399 Cedar Grove
Shaw Ada Mrs h 200 Hathaway
" Adam foreman 2 Union h 637 do
" Albert E rem from city
" Alice G stenographer 97 William rm 304 b 30 Collins
" Allen G clerk Page Mfg Co b 10 Thompson [Walnut
" Almira E widow Franklin b 55
" Arthur engineer b 88 Eugenia
" B Summer mason h 219 Chancery [Morgan
" Charles E clerk 145 Union b 100
" Charles F h 395 Purchase
" Chauncy L Jr clerk R R yard master's office h 72 Foster
" Edward E letter carrier h 443 Chancery
" Edwin mill hand h 191 Campbell
" Elizabeth speeder bds 168 Division [68 Ash (S)
" Elmer H (E H Shaw & Co) h
" Emma K teacher High school h 3 Morgan ter [Chestnut
" Etta H widow Chauncy L h 120
" E A & Co cotton buyers 108 Union
" E H & Co (E H Shaw) kitchen furnishings 24 Pleasant
" Fannie h 4 Morgan terrace
" Frank shoemaker b 283 Cedar
" Fred weaver b 12 Ashley
" George E weaver h 224 County
" George J laborer h 142 Bullard
" Grace cloth inspector b 14 Willow [away
" Hannah widow John b 114 Hath-

Shaw
" Harry operative b 36 Howard
" Hazel clerk 227 Cedar bds 443 Chancery [rms 129 do
" Harvey G engineer 128 Pleasant
" Henry copperworker b 191 Dean
" Henry operative h 36 Howard
" Hugh spinner h 40 Winsor
" James loom fixer h 12 Ashley
" James operative h 26 Holly
" James F glassworker b 48 Rockland
" John operative h 190 Earle
" John E circulation mgr Times h 10 Thompson [Rockland
" John H glassworker bds 48
" John S real estate h 114 Hathaway [ning Co h 206 Eugenia
" John T overseer Nonquitt Spin-

J E NORTON SHAW
Attorney and Counsellor at Law
Examiner of Titles for
the Land Court
4 Masonic Building
Pleasant Street
Bell Telephone 929

Shaw J E Norton lawyer 4 Masonic bldg h at Mattapoisett
" Louise B rem to Vineyard Haven
" Mary A widow Hugh h 168 Division [ant h 54 Chestnut
" Philip R shoecutter 76 Pleas-
" Richard gardener h 97 Park
" Samuel coachman h 64 Ash (S)
" Sarah F widow Albert T h 70 Sycamore
" Susan Mrs h 30 Collins
" Thomas hostler h 91 Tremont
" Thomas laborer b 315 Earle
" Thomas spinner h 48 Rockland
" William mill hand h 158 Central avenue
" William A S clerk 22 Fourth h 194 Kempton [wanse Ill
" William H Rev removed to Ke-

PAINTERS' SUPPLIES
Walnut, Cor. Water, 84 Pleasant St. 25 WELD SQ., 129 COVE ST.
F. T. AKIN & COMPANY

Shaw
" William H Jr artist Times b 10 Thompson [Cottage
" William R officer H of C h 523
" see Shore
Shay Dennis H liquors 6 W French av h 285 Middle
Shea Bridget h 100 Clark
" Daniel salesman 46 Purchase h 75 Atlantic
" Daniel Jr died Feb 7 1910
" Dennis gardener 385 County h 58 Borden [Union
" Dennis A letter carrier h 564
" Edward chauffeur 148 Court bds 659 First [S First
" Edward driver 281 Sawyer b 559
" Henry machinist b 17 Trinity
" Henry J b 488 First
" Joanna h 333 First
" Joseph mason b 2138 Acushnet av
" Mary E died Dec 19 1910
" Melvina E Mrs h 659 First
" Michael b 488 First
" Michael laborer b 51 Howland Village
" Michael stone cutter h 61 Durfee
" Timothy F carpenter b 58 Borden
Sheard Thomas conductor h 99 Hazard [rey h 710 County
Shearman Rebecca P widow Humph-
Shedd Clarence P rem to Worcester
Sheedy James removed from city
" Patrick glass cutter b 79 Fifth
Sheehan Alice A widow Michael J h 206 State [River
" Daniel mgr 145 Union h at Fall
" Daniel J clerk b 206 State
" Frank clerk 58 Linden b 206 State
" Jeremiah laborer b 29 Winsor
" John laborer b 232 N Second
" John J mgr 70 William h 375 Kempton [Clark
" Mary variety 273 State h 29
" Michael mason h 91 Beetle
" Michael second hand h 206 State
" Michael J died Dec 25 1910
" Patrick city teamster h 247 Mill
" William J laborer b 444 Pleasant
Sheehy William Clinton physician 249 Chestnut h do
Sheerin James J electrician 27 William b 482 Cottage
" Michael mason 482 Cottage h do

Sheerin
" Patrick A clerk 248 Purchase b 482 Cottage [Shawmut av
Sheffield John P watchman h 103
" Vesta M bookkeeper 47 William b 103 Shawmut av
Shefton Andrew W chef h 127 Smith
Sheible Michael operative h 321 Earle
Sheiff Barnett baker h 353 First
Sheknoff Acy (Sheknoff & Tublin) 779 Water h at Fall River
" & Tublin (Acy Sheknoff and Solomon Tublin) dry goods 779 Water
Sheldon The Mrs T H Soule prop 169 Union [burn
" Thomas picker tender h 24 Wash-
Shelford James operative b 163 Coggeshall
" Samuel h 163 Coggeshall
Shelmerdine Wilfred doffer h 20 Peckham [rms 3 Park place
Shelton George H mgr 60 Purchase
Shenhoun Elias fruit 1092 Acushnet av h do
Shennan William granite Court cor Ash (N) h 551 Union
Shepard Belvedera widow b 474 Kempton
" Edward blacksmith h 371 Hillman
" Georgianna widow Joseph C died
Shepardson Donn (Crossman & Shepardson) **grocer 111 Durfee h** 265 Hillman
Shephardson Edwin G supt Kilburn Mill h 2 Sears [T h 4 Crapo
Shepherd Annie J widow Nathaniel
" Annie L widow David J b 160 Fair
" Cecelia A Mrs h 17 Lincoln
" David W coachman 191 Hawthorn h 95 Maple [91 Walden
" Frank B clerk 143 Purchase h
" Isabella H teacher Thomas Donaghy school b 17 Lincoln
" I Frank messenger 14 N Sixth rms 187 Purchase
" Joseph weaver h 35 Howard
" Lizzie A widow Caleb h 91 High
" Lucy P widow John h 629 County
" Percey spinner h 1 Baylies
" Stephen H with Standard b 136 Cottage
Shepley Enoch spinner h 345 Collette

Kinyon's Commercial School Will furnish your office help free } **Odd Fellows Building COR. WILLIAM and PLEASANT STS. NEW BEDFORD, MASS.**

Shepley
" George L pres Old Colony Box Co h at Providence R I [ham
" James E loom fixer h 92 Top-
" John William weaver h 143 Belleville rd
" William fixer b 48 Parker
Sher Abraham pedler h 37 S Second
" Bernard driver b 37 S Second
" Bessie sewer b 37 S Second
" David chauffeur 15 Fourth b 37 S Second [26 Sycamore
" Israel horses 404 Acushnet av h
" Jules gasfitter b 37 S Second
" Philip clerk 358 Acushnet av h 147 Elm [139 Fair
Sheridan Philip H glass blower h
Sherin Morris umbrella and shoe repairer 980 Acushnet av h 303 Sawyer [ty
Sherley Edward weaver h 893 Coun-
Sherlock Annie M h 118 Kempton
Sherman Abner P gardener h 155 Fair
SHERMAN ALBERT C stable 50 Elm h 155 William See page 770
" Albert C Jr student bds 155 William
" Annie E Mrs matron H C h 7 Ash (S) [51 Park
" Arthur B city editor Standard h
" Charles A S foreman 125 Middle h 28 Borden [Kempton
" Charles C asst janitor bds 286
" Charles F b 98 Fourth
SHERMAN CHARLES H contractor and builder 20 N Second h at Fall River See page 15
" Charles T machinist b 3 Green
" Clara E teacher High school b 248 County [h 248 County
" Clarence R (R A Sherman & Son)
" Clifford P lawyer 33 Masonic bldg h 73 Sycamore
" C Russell rem to Plainville Conn
" Daniel clerk h 20 Mill
" David A mgr 47 S Second h 85 Oak [Acushnet av
" David W Jr stone cutter h 2825
" Edward D (I C Sherman & Son) 70-76 Union h 362 County
" Edward R clerk Potomska Mills h 10 Rounds [61 Cottage
" Edward W salesman 70 Union h

Sherman
" Edwin D helper 55 N Water b 157 Grinnell
" Elijah L mgr h 385 Cottage
" Eliza R widow Robert A h 248 County [b at Fairhaven
" Ella F teacher Jireh Swift school
" Ella M clerk Nonquitt Spinning Co b 28 Borden
" Ernest L inspector h 21 Page
" Eva G Mrs dressmaker 157 Smith h do [706 County
" Everett B (E B Sherman Co) h
" E Clifton (E B Sherman Co) b 706 County
" E B Co (Everett B and E Clifton) liquors 62 Purchase
" Francis P photographer 74 Purchase h 86 Mill [ion h 160 Mill
" Frederick W compositor 112 Un-
" Grace D asst Public Library b 248 County
" G Arthur police h 402 Union
" Harry A driver 8 Hamilton h 157 Smith
" Harry H driver b 170 Rounds
" Hattie C Mrs h 81 Forest
" Henry A blacksmith helper h 51 Russell
" Henry A Mrs millinery and circulating library 51 Russell h do
" Henry S teacher h 223 Smith
" Herbert H b 322 Pleasant
" Horace G tinsmith b 27 Vine
" H Abner died Aug 9 1910
" Isaac H (Sherman & Aiberski) 161 N Front h 40 Fifth
" Isaac H Jr chauffeur b 40 Fifth
" I C & Son (E D Sherman) wholesale produce 70-76 Union
" James H captain h 158 Middle
SHERMAN JAMES H plumbing 50-52 Union h 192 Middle See page 767
SHERMAN JAMES L lumber 194 N Water h 43 Mill See page 765 [103 School
" James L 2nd clerk 100 Fifth b
" Jesse T mgr N B Tow Boat Co h 98 Arnold [school h 27 Vine
" John D janitor Thos R Rodman
" John D Jr (Sherman & McQuillan) b 27 Vine

Bread, Cake, Pastry
RICHMOND & COMPANY **255-257 UNION STREET**
Bell 993 Automatic 1022

Sherman
" Julia E widow Charles R h 325 Cottage [rms do
" J Harrington janitor 76 Pleasant
" Julia I telephone operator 57 N Second b 214 North
" J Clifford secretary overseers of poor h 185 Fourth
" J Warren test man 57 N Second b 7 Ash (S) [Borden
" Katherine W bookkeeper b 28
" Ladora A widow Charles H b 185 Fourth
" Leonard E laborer b 223 Smith
" Maria C Mrs h 25 William
" Patience J clerk city clerk's office rms 66 S Sixth
SHERMAN PELEG H undertaker and embalmer 506 County h 98 Fourth See foot lines
" Philip J clerk U St Ry bds 28 Borden [h 185 Fourth
" Phoebe S widow James Harvey
" Pliney B printer h 160 Mill
" Reuben P steamfitter h 771 Kempton [County
" Robert C salesman 70 Union h 356
" Robert E fireman h 158 Central av
" Robert R h 2047 Acushnet av
" Ruth R teacher J H Clifford school b 38 Borden
" Ruth S Mrs clerk city clerk's office h 2 Pope's Island
" R A & Son (Clarence R) carpenters 7 Leonard
" Walter C salesman Kilburn Mill h at Fairhaven [Middle
" Wilbur G letter carrier h 158
" William C engineer h 1982 Acushnet av
" William H h 87 School
" William N eyeletmaker h 48 Sycamore
SHERMAN & McQUILLAN (John D Sherman Jr and Peter F McQuillan) plumbers 250 Purchase See page 781
" see Shearman
Sherratt George mach oper h 75 Brock av [Morton court
Sherrington Daniel carder b 55
" James h 55 Morton ct
" James Jr weaver b 55 Morton ct
Shevlin M Theresa teacher Cedar Grove st school b 94 Fourth
Shide Alfred student rms 248 Pleasant [Chancery
Shiels James J drill worker b 49
" John P bartender 5 N Second h 49 Chancery [ty
" Mary widow Charles h 222 Coun-
" Nancy widow James b 49 Chancery [49 Chancery
" Thomas H helper 26 N Water b
" see Sheils
Shields John operative h 90 Brook av
Shine Margaret A widow William H removed to Fall River
Shkolnick Abraham laborer h 638 S Water [h 638 do
" Anna Mrs variety 640 S Water
" Charles tailor 62½ Purchase h 483 Acushnet av [638 do
" Joseph clerk 640 S Water bds
Shockley Abraham L dentist 45 Purchase rm 4½ h 501 County
Sholes Herbert L gardener h 160 Hillman [Purchase
Sholovitz Etta widow George h 557
Shope Charles G bookkeeper 99 Front b 60 Tremont [bott
Shore James bricklayer rms 16 Ab-
" John third hand h 122 David
Shores Alden L draughtsman 57 N Second b at Fairhaven
" Alton F student b 119 Maxfield
" Frederick A grocer 875 Kempton h 119 Maxfield
Shorey Milford bds 372 Cottage
Shorrock A Viola telephone operator 57 N Second b at Padanaram
" Edward h 212 Shawmut av
" Elias mule spinner h 119 David
" John removed to Dartmouth
" Joseph weaver h 15 Ashley
" Walter clerk h 212 Shawmut av
Shortall Anna E clerk 474 Acushnet av b 57 Parker
" Margaret widow James h 57 Parker [ker
" Mary clerk 182 Union b 57 Par-
" Maud G clerk b 57 Parker
" Patrick J carpenter b 57 Parker
Shovelin James copper worker h 978 County [Allen
Showell George E coachman h 398
Shrader Sarah Mrs h 557 Purchase
Shugrue James operative b 45 Winsor

GLOBE DYE HOUSE 220 SHAWMUT AVE.
J. N. J. LONHOLDT, PROP. Telephone Connections Goods called for and Delivered
Down Town Office, 52 Pleasant St., Room 1 North End Office, 1014 Acushnet Ave.

Shuker Thomas overseer h 123 Smith
Shumaniski Felix machinist h 12 McGurk [Brewery b 350 Sawyer
Shumm George B supt Smith Bros
Shumway Earl motorman h 198 Cedar
" Frank H supt Acushnet Mills h 306 Arnold
" Myron J mechanic h 18 Bedford
Shurtleff Bertha A stenographer 30 Purchase b 252 County
" Betsy W died April 7 1911
" Charles E clerk Nashawena Mills h at Fairhaven
" Charles W dentist 1017 Acushnet av h at Fairhaven
" Eliza C h 78 N Second
" Frank driver rms 382 Kempton
" Frederick A clerk 195 Fourth h 343 Orchard [h 252 County
" Israel H druggist 195 Fourth
" Leona housekeeper 265 Pope
" Lewis T supt paper dept T P Corp h at Fairhaven
" Lisbeth Mrs nurse b 281 Allen
" Marian C stenographer 97 William rm 406 b 371 Park [lane
Shuster Abram junk h 17 Morgan
" Hyman junk b 17 Morgan lane
" Moise junk h 700 S Water
" see Schuster [Y M C A
Shute Alfred foreman T P Corp rms
Shuttleworth John fixer h 26 Cleveland [man
Shutz Edward operative h 109 Tall-
" Teresa Mrs h 109 Tallman
Shuy Fong Co (Charlie Yohn) restaurant 68 William
Shyler Joseph laborer b 40 Mosher
Sibley John driver b 535 Acushnet avenue
Sihor Joseph h 113 Tallman
" Robert clerk Dartmouth M Co b 113 Tallman [mer
Sicard Philip fixer h 188 Black-
Sickel Arthur mgr 65 Purchase rms 56 Walnut [b 158 Thompson
Siddall Clarence O clerk 158 Purchase
" Joseph rem to Fairhaven [son
" J Herbert clerk h 158 Thomp-
Siddell Edward laborer h 621 First
Sieckoski Joseph operative h 184 Cedar Grove
Siegal Bros (Joseph and Harry) house furnishings 565 S Water

Siegal
" Harry (Siegal Bros) 565 S Water h do [ter h do
" Joseph (Siegal Bros) 565 S Wa-
Siemnuiski Franciscek operative h 59 Washburn [h 80 do
Siever Hughes L chemist 100 Fifth
Siguer Emil weaver h 98½ Ruth
" Jules weaver b 49 Salisbury
Silk John machinist h 68 Acushnet av
Sillery Alice clerk b 73 Forest
" Elizabeth Mrs h 73 Forest
" John H salesman 16 N Second b 73 Forest [h 10 Green
Silsbee H Arthur foreman T P Corp
" John A rodman 303 Municipal bldg h 10 Green [22 Peckham
Silson Herbert mgr 143 Purchase h
Silva Aldina widow Joseph R h 132 Thompson
" Alfred blacksmith h 139 Fourth
" Alva engineer h 453 Belleville avenue [Fair
" Anna clerk 182 Union bds 121
" Antone fisherman h 79 Prospect
" Antone fisherman h 330 S Front
" Antone laborer h 176 Durfee
" Antone laborer h r 567 First
" Antone mill hand h 90 Acushnet avenue
" Antone mill hand h 336 S Front
" Antone mill hand h Mt Pleasant n Kings Highway
" Antone pedlar h 22 Wing
" Antone roper b 219 S Front
" Antone sawyer b 83 Howard
" Antone A laborer h 324 S Second
" Antone A weaver h 80 Sidney
" Antone C fireman h 263 S Second [h do
" Antone E variety 105 Potomska
" Antone F operative h 223 S Front [Briggs
" Antone I tailor 96 Grinnell h 56
" Antone J driver h 419 First
" Antone J operative h 410 S Front
" Antone J Mrs h 39 Rivet
" Antone P laborer h 41 Columbia
" Antone V fisherman b 259 S Front
" Antonio h 45 Babbitt
" Antonio laborer h 74 Liberty
" Antonio laborer h 137 Field
" Antonio G hairdresser 6 Fifth h 483 Union
" Antonio G painter h 209 Allen

GREENE & WOOD Every Kind of LUMBER AND MILL WORK
PINE STREET, off So. WATER STREET, NEW BEDFORD

Silva
" Antonio P laborer h 136 Field
" Antonio R operative h 79 Hemlock
" Antonio S laborer h 11 Hickory
" August laborer h 17 Margin
" Augustus mason h 396 S Second
" Ayres laborer b 618 S Water
" Bartholomew fisherman h 329 S Front
" Bartholomew weaver h 48 Hemlock
" Caroline S teacher Acushnet av school h 8 Anthony
" Carrie clerk b 46 Howland
" Carrie operative b 48 Parker
" Charles doffer h 441 Mosher
" Claude second hand h 297 South Front
" Delphine R widow John h 297 S Front
" Domingos T real estate 359 Orchard (S) h do
" Edward A G hostler 173½ Acushnet av b 108 Rockland
" Fannie tailoress 129 Union b 154 Allen
" Francis laborer h 399 S Second
" Francis C B Rev pastor Portugese Baptist Mission h 184 Thompson
" Frank city employee h 129 Field
" Frank clerk 100 William b 39 Thompson
" Frank driver h 658 Acushnet av
" Frank fireman h 105 Potomska
" Frank foreman h 245 Tinkham
" Frank laborer h 6 Turners ct
" Frank laborer h 35 Mitchell
" Frank laborer h 132 Field
" Frank laborer h 216 S Front
" Frank mill hand h 7 Holly
" Frank mill hand b 45 Hollyhock
" Frank mill hand bds 103 Davis
" Frank operative h 67 Nash road
" Frank O laborer h r 216 S Front
" Frank P mason h 30 Hollyhock
" Frank S elevatorman h 40 Mosher
" Frank S operative h 299 S Front
" Frank U salesman 67 William b 94 S Sixth
" Gabriel laborer h 252 Field
" Gabriel removed to Fairhaven
" Gregorio fisherman h 17 Margin
" Guilherme mill hand h 25 Babbitt

Silva
" Gustiano laborer h 75 Prospect
" Harry clerk 878 Purchase rms 871 do
SILVA HENRY decorator 63 Fifth h do See page 761
" Henry mill hand b 123 Dartmouth
" Henry shoemaker h 254 S Second
" Isabelle Mrs tailoress 211 Union h 250 Fourth
" Jacinth laborer h r 238 S Second
" Jeremiah clerk b 36 Acushnet av
" Jessie L (M P B Silva & Son) b 155 Acushnet avenue
" Joaquim laborer h 58 S Second
" John baker h 115 Fifth
" John clerk h Potomska cor Water
" John clerk b 122 Dartmouth
" John laborer b 148 Tallman
" John laborer b 180 North
" John mill hand h 5 Bonneau ct
" John mill hand b 139 Coffin av
" John operative h 87 Prospect
" John teamster 8 Union h do
" John C rope worker h 24 Katharine
" John D grocer 153 Tremont h do
" John F operative h 452 S Second
" John L laborer h 150 Field
" John M baker 255 Union
" John M foreman carpenter Acushnet Mill Corp h 39 Thompson
" John S laborer h 341 S Front
" John S operative h 868 County
" Joseph barber 110 William b 48 Nelson
" Joseph carpenter h 14 Edison
" Joseph comb maker 22 Fourth
" Joseph engineer h 48 Briggs
" Joseph laborer h 25 Howland
" Joseph laborer h 46 N Water
" Joseph laborer h 225 S Front
" Joseph laborer h 230 S Front
" Joseph laborer h 680 S Water
" Joseph laborer h 775 S Water
" Joseph mill hand h 8 Grandfield
" Joseph mill hand h 45 Hollyhock
" Joseph mill hand b 160 Belleville avenue
" Joseph operative h 46 Crapo
" Joseph operative h 618 S Water
" Joseph painter h 286 Fourth
" Joseph painter b 373 S Second

BONNEY, FOLSTER & CO.,
The North End's Shopping Centre
Dry Goods and Men's Furnishings
945-947 Acushnet Ave., New Bedford, Mass.

Silva
" Joseph weaver h 73 Briggs
" Joseph A silver plater h 35 Thompson [av
" Joseph B laborer h 102 Acushnet
" Joseph D driver h 171 Acushnet avenue [more
" Joseph De mill hand bds 30 Saga-
" Joseph F died April 16 1911
" Joseph I operative h 36 County
" Joseph I operative h 40 Mosher
" Joseph J barber h 443 Kempton
" Joseph L teamster h 540 Rivet
" Joseph M fish 100½ Potomska h 244 Rivet
" Joseph O laborer h 88 Potomska
" Joseph P city laborer h 477 Mill
" Joseph P machinist h 499 First
" Joseph P mason h 30 Kane
" Joseph S carpenter h 122 Dartmouth [sant
" Joseph S farmer h 644 Mt Plea-
" Joseph T carpenter h 218 Rockland [away road
" Joseph V ice maker b 679 Hath-
" Julius carpenter h 123 Crapo
" Louis engineer h 44 Sherman
" Louis machinist h 274 Nash road
" Louis mill hand b 274 Nash road
" Mach spinner h 316 S Front
" Manuel h 39 Mosher
" Manuel h 314 Coggeshall
" Manuel bricklayer h 396 S Second
" Manuel fish 122 County h 124 do
" Manuel fireman h Bank st
" Manuel fireman h 110 Rockland
" Manuel fish 43 Howland h 69 do
" Manuel fisherman h 20 Belleville avenue
" Manuel laborer h 30 Acushnet av
" Manuel laborer h 103 Acushnet av
" Manuel laborer h 133 Jenny Lind
" Manuel laborer h 399 S Second
" Manuel laborer h 505 S Second
" Manuel mill hand b 136 Thompson
" Manuel millworker h 560 S Water
" Manuel oiler st dept h 356 S First [mac
" Manuel operative h 20 E Merri-
" Manuel operative h 46 Crapo
" Manuel operative h 82 Grinnell
" Manuel operative h 166 Belleville avenue

Silva
" Manuel operative 301 S Front
" Manuel operative h 421 S Water
" Manuel operative h 751 S Water
" Manuel painter h 76 Lombard
" Manuel repairer h 503 Bolton
" Manuel A carpenter h 65 Acushnet av [sey
" Manuel A city laborer h 58 Lind-
" Manuel A Rev pastor St John the Baptist church h 94 S Sixth
" Manuel B operative h 440 S Second [ter
" Manuel B operative h 646 S Wa-
" Manuel C h 116 Fifth
" Manuel C hairdresser Dartmouth Club h 121 Fair [land Village
" Manuel C mill hand b 16 How-
" Manuel E carpenter h 62 Independent
" Manuel F carpenter h 164 Bonney
" Manuel F carpenter h 260 Fourth
" Manuel F laborer h 45 Main
" Manuel F mariner h 74 Acushnet av [h 36 Acushnet av
" Manuel F variety 191 Blackmer
" Manuel J fisherman h 103 Acushuet av
" Manuel J laborer h 30 Kane
" Manuel J laborer h 356 S First
" Manuel L laborer h 295 S Front
" Manuel M operative h 324 S Front [ond
" Manuel P laborer r 500 S Sec-
" Manuel P rem from city
" Manuel P shoemaker h 9 Willow
" Manuel P B (M P B Silva & Sons) h 155 Acushnet av
" Manuel S da mason's tender h 37 Columbia [Front
" Manuel V fisherman h 259 South
" Manuel V grocer 683 Hathaway road h 679 do
" Mariano laborer h 616 S Water
" Marie widow Joseph h 48 South
" Mary h 94 County
" Mary nurse 194 Purchase b do
" Mary Mrs h 8 Coffin av
" Mary Mrs h 52 Independent
" Mary Mrs h 359 First
" Mary Mrs h 692½ S Water
" Mary widow h 33 S Second
" Mary widow h 62 Middle
" Mary widow h 75 Acushnet av
" Mary widow h 492 Rivet

M. P. B. Silva & Son Paints, Oils and Glass
Sole Agents for Lucas Tinted Gloss Paints
157 ACUSHNET AVENUE Both Phones NEW BEDFORD

Silva
" Mary Ann widow Manuel h 76 Acushnet av
" Mary A Mrs h 223 Shawmut [av
" Mary C widow Joseph h 410 S Front
" Mary N widow William h 400 Or- [chard (S)
" Mary P widow Manuel P h 46 Howland
" Matthew plumber 903 County b 679 Hathaway rd
" Michael grocer 90 S Second h [do
" Michael shoemaker h 399 S Second
SILVA M P B & SON (Manuel P B and Jesse L) carpenters builders hardware and painters 155 Acushnet av **See foot lines**
" Paul laborer h 101 Fourth
" Phuribus J laborer h 510 Acushnet av
" Rose Mrs h 123 Dartmouth
" Seraphine P mill hand h 114 Larch
" Stephen N builder 263 Field ct [h do
" Theresa widow h 65 School
" Thiotonio P mill hand h 106 Thompson
" Thiotonio P Jr mill hand h 106 [Thompson
" Thomas laborer h 10 Winter
" Thomas mill hand h 411 Allen
" Timothy mill hand b 56 Briggs
" William mill hand b 692½ S Water
" see Silvia and Sylvia
Silveira Antone weaver h 75 Win- [sor
" Antone G rem from city
" Antonio J carpenter h 289 Orchard (S)
" Edward driver b 864 County
" Frank P carpenter 487 Allen h do
" Henry P carpenter b 487 Allen
" Joaquin grocer 495 Rivet h 492 do
" John B mill hand bds 245 Tink- [ham
" Jose D grocer h 156 Acushnet av
" Joseph h 265 S Front
" Joseph D h 25 Lombard
" Joseph M fisherman h 61 Fifth
" Joseph M laborer h 32 Acushnet avenue
" Manuel D at P Corp h 134 [Fourth
" Manuel D watchman h 100 Potomska
" Manuel G weaver b 130 Rock- [land

Silveira
" Manuel J Jr clerk b 86 Larch
" Manuel K mason h 86 Larch
" Manuel L da variety 130 Thompson h 9 Briggs
" Maria L da Mrs h 126 Thomp- [son
" Mary Mrs h 209 Allen
" Nestor M barber h 10 Winter
" Philbert I machinist h 503 Bolton
Silver David picture framer h 120 Acushnet av
" Eugene laborer h 207 Rivet
" Fred W salesman h 653 Kempton
" John city laborer h 183 Mill
" John fish dealer h 314 Coggeshall
" John mill hand h 53 Crapo
" Max tailor 831 Purchase h 567 Acushnet av
" William fireman 36 Purchase h at [Fairhaven
Silverstein Bernard dry goods 937 S Water h do
Silvia Adolph shoemaker h 49 Crapo
" Ann P variety 418 S Water h do
" Antone C laborer h 661 Mt Pleasant
" August pedlar h 390 S Second
" Charles J steam fitter h 74 Penniman
" David M carpenter h 99 Willis
" Joaquim operative h 418 S Water
" John carpenter b 81 Sidney
" John clerk 45 School h 53 do
" John S truant officer h 126 Campbell
" Joseph P operative h 20 Roose- [velt
" Manuel C shoes and clothing 160 Acushnet av h 116 Fifth
" Manuel J musical instrument maker 428 S Water h 82 Crapo
" Nicholas operative h 323 S Second
" Wallace C salesman 669 Purchase [b 151 Hillman
" see Silvo and Sylvia
Silvya Joseph G mill hand h 17 Hall
Simard Alfred weaver b 119 Phillips avenue
Simas Antone laborer h 102 Acush- [net av
" Antone operative h 20 Independent
" Antone operative h 302 Cogge- [shall
" Charles cone cutter h 119 South
" Frank at P Corp b 93 Rockland
" John mill hand h 17 Mitchell
" John F laborer h 81 Grinnell

Steiger-Dudgeon Co.
"The WOMAN'S Store."
Tel. Bell 82 & 83, Branches connecting all depts.
" " 160 For Office only. Auto. 1211

SUMPTIONS, ASSORTMENTS AT ALL TIMES OF DEPENDABLE DRY GOODS

Simas
" Joseph operative h 79 Thompson
" Joseph C laborer h 177 Allen
" Jule operative h 175 Belleville av
" Jules operative h 20 Independent
" Manuel farm hand b 4299 Acushavenue
" Manuel mill hand h 183 Bonney
" Manuel mill hand b 148 Belleville avenue
" Manuel C operative h 14 Cotter
" Manuel D city laborer h 203 Division [Rockland
" Rita widow Manuel tailoress h 93
" Rose L widow h 50 Sherman
" see Simmons
Simi Hannibal plasterer h 109 Holly
" Joseph plasterer b 109 Holly
Simiansky Aaron mgr 813 S Water h 815 do
" Abram junk h S Second cor Rivet
" Eliza Mrs dry goods 813 S Water h 815 do
" Jacob pool 685 S Water h 515 do
" Lena widow Joseph h 19 Walnut
Simieski Joseph operative h 125 Collette [North
Simister Frances widow Henry b 255
" Louise Mrs h 42 Ash (N)
" William clerk 372 Cedar h 91 Robeson [205 Maple
Simmons Abbie L widow Allen S h
" Adeline widow William H h 15 Potter
" Antone laborer h 350 S Second
" Arthur L foreman 100 Fifth h at Fairhaven
" Charles C h 61 Walden
" Charles H president 97 William rm 312 b 75 Hillman
" **Clarence O auto repairer 55 Spring h at Westport**
" Edmund T died
" Eunice E F bds 72 Durfee
" Francisco F h 319 S Front
" George clerk 207 Coggeshall b 16 Cotter
" George laborer b 871 Purchase
" George A glass cutter b 95 Grinnell
" George A painter b 273 Cottage
" George W painter h 95 Grinnell

Simmons
" Harold L stenographer 24 Clifford bldg b 31 Sycamore
" Harry J clerk 97 Front h 31 Sycamore
" James mgr h 71 Kenyon
" James E R laborer h 339 Pleasant
" James bds 192 Arnold
" Jeremiah W foreman teamster P Corp h 43 Pierce
" John laborer h 66 Acushnet av
" John E salesman 99 Front b 118 Bates avenue
" John F clerk h 30 South [(S)
" John J teamster h 443 Orchard
" Joseph clerk 1051 Acushnet av rm 40
" Joseph mariner h 350 S Front
" Lemuel carriage trimmer 112 Pleasant h 75 Hillman
" Lewis teamster h 314 S Second
" Louisa Mrs h 271 Rivet
" **Louisa Mrs operative rms 309 Kempton**
" Louise L telephone operator 57 N Second bds 13 Lindsey
" Manuel fisherman h 259 S Front
" Manuel laborer h 61 Katharine
" Manuel laborer h 118 Bates av
" Manuel laborer b 90 Winsor
" Manuel tailor 144 Union b 579 First [h 193 Allen
" Manuel E cooper 350 S Second
" Manuel P operative h 62 Briggs
" Manuel P stuffer h 33 Winsor
" Mary M Mrs h 114 Fourth
" May R Mrs h 20 Bethel
" Orrington mill hand b 383 Cedar
" Otis bricklayer h 144 Willis
" Richard weaver h 63 Roosevelt
" Samuel A painter h 383 Cedar
" S Bartlett carpenter h 307 Summer
" Thomas E teamster h 290 Cedar
" Vergino F grocer 66 Durfee h 180 Richmond [chase
" Walter T teamster rms 340 Purchase
" William B iron molder h 169 Middle
" William H machinist b 43 Pierce
" see Symons and Simas
Simms Joseph M retired capt U S R C S h 210 Summer

PELEG H. SHERMAN 506 COUNTY ST.
FUNERAL DIRECTOR AND EMBALMER
OFFICE PHONES. Bell 690-13. Auto. 1305.
RESIDENCE PHONES. Bell 690-12. Auto. 1306.

Simms
" Mary widow Richard operative h 291 N Front
Simoes Jose F jeweler b 73 Briggs
" Manuel F h 73 Briggs [lette
Simon Alphonse teamster h 104 Col-
" Eugene weaver h 363 Earle
" Vincent C dentist 45 Purchase rm 4½ rms 8 Park place
Simoneau Rose widow Isadore h 27 Bullard [Fifth
Simons Antone fisherman h 104
" Manuel L machinist h 13 Lindsey
" Manuel P laborer h 33 Winsor
" Margaret widow Frank bds 303 Sawyer
" Mary Mrs h 281 Hillman
Simpkin David operative b 12 Blackburn
" Jesse weaver h 12 Blackburn
" William operative b 12 Blackburn [shnet av
" William H spinner b 195 Acu-
Simpkins John T second hand h 78 Jouvett
Simplioiso John seaman h 97 S Second [175 County
Simpson Andrew A watchman h
" August operative h 99 Hazard
" Augustus clerk h 241 Pope
" Bertha S cashier 1081 Acushnet av b 171 Summer
" Charles S (Snell & Simpson) 58 Adams h 127 Kempton
" Ellen widow James h 13 Mill rd
" Ellen A (M & E A Simpson) h at Fairhaven
" Florence L stenographer N B Cotton Mills Corp b 41 Parker
" James G auto repairer 55 Spring h 502 Bolton
" James H carder h 164 David
" Joseph loom fixer h 30 Viall
" Levi D bds 241 Pope
" Margaret (M & E A Simpson) h at Fairhaven
" Mark A inspector h 136 Holly
" M & E A (Margaret and Ellen A) fancy goods 952 S Water
" Orton S glass inspector h 42 Bay
" Percy B silversmith b 42 Bay
" Robert spinner b 39 Tallman
" Thomas O h 47 Hemlock

Simpson
" Warren A engineer h 171 Summer [road
" Wilfred carpenter h 158 Nash
" William A printer 34 N Second
" William T weaver b 138 Holly
Sinark Stanistnow operative h 162 Cedar Grove [S Water
Sinclair Josephine Turner Mrs h 179
Singer Abraham h 14 Howland
" Harry painter h 9 Howland
" Robert removed to Taunton
" Sewing Machine Co sewing machines 73 William [Holly
Singewalt Gustaf weaver bds 103
Singleton Christopher fisherman b 116 Middle [lage
" Henry fixer h 34 Howland Vil-
" Joseph fixer h 98 Brock av
" Thomas brick layer h 129 Reynolds
" Thomas fixer h 46 Ashley
" William clerk h 247 Bowditch
Sisco Gertude b 269 Middle [dle
Sisson Charles A clerk b 187 Mid-
" Charles D h 42 Hill
" Charles H driver 255 Union h 432 Court [b 51 Bonney
" Edward A clerk 35 Commercial
" Edward R foreman 14 Bedford h 29 Borden
" Edward R physician h 15 Eighth
" Eliza R h 27 Keene
" Ella F widow Daniel W h 3906 Acushnet av [Chestnut
" Emma B widow William H h 44
" Frank E clerk h 448 Middle
" Frank E salesman b 2143 Acushnet av
" Franklin K salesman h 265 Mill
" Hannah A widow Arnold B bds 308 County
" Hattie A artist 44 Chestnut b do
" James B watchman h 744 Belleville avenue
" James M b 42 Hill
" Jasper L carpenter h 201 Grinnell
" John F b 104 Bonney [Bonney
" Lucretia H widow Charles A h 51
" Minerva bookkeeper rms 107 Elm
" Otis A grocer, hay and grain 3913 Acushnet av b 3906 do [Bonney
" Ralph clerk 31 Comercial bds 51
" Rexford L glass cutter h 73 Elm

F. T. AKIN & CO. FORGE FACTORY FURNACE FAMILY COAL

Sisson
" Rhoda A widow Joseph D L h 187 Middle [Middle
" Samuel S M glass cutter bds 187
" Sarah I widow Benjamin P h 371 Court [Acushnet av
" Thomas pressman Mercury b 282
" William financial agent 97 William rm 404 h 182 Fourth
" William H bottler b 3906 Acushnet avenue [ty h do
" William H A draperies 308 Coun-
" William H H laborer h 83 Locust
Sistare Esther L bookkeeper 111 Willis b 138 do [h 138 Wiliis
" Frank B (Frank B Sistare & Son)
SISTARE FRANK B & SON (Frank B and George H Sistare) carpenters and builders 111 Willis See page 762
" George H (Frank B Sistare & Son) h 54 Shawmut av
Sister Felix superioress 261 Pleasant
" Loretto principal St Mary's school h 59 Rockland
" Marie de St Elizabeth superioress 18 Hyacinth
" Mary Edigna superioress St Mary's Home 593 Kempton
Sisters of Mercy h 261 Pleasant and 59 Rockland
" of St Francis Kempton cor Liberty
" of the Holy Cross Sacred Heart Convent 45 Robeson and 18 Hyacinth
" of the Holy Cross St Anthony's French Convent 120 Bullard
Sivigny Norman G salesman 36 Purchase h at Acushnet
" Wilfred laborer h 7 Blackburn
Sivois J E Rev h 163 County
Siwick Adam mill hand h 55 Mitchell
Skeels Orrin H clerk rms 282 Acushnet avenue [Elm (W)
Skiff Abby widow William E h 338
" Albert C farmer h Phillips road
" John T mason b A C Skiff's Phillips road
" Mary J widow h 121 Austin [nell
" William H inspector h 173 Grin-
Skinner Arthur weaver h 38 Reynolds

Skinner
" Thomas C janitor 15 Bethel rms 43 N Sixth
Skufis George operative b 7 Marvin
Slack N Emma teacher Fifth street school h 52 Washington
Slade George W (Allen Slade & Co) 1 William h at Fall River
" Henry M secretary 37 Purchase rm 27 rms do
" Nancy M teacher Abraham Lincoln school b 24 Cedar [Grove
Slater Bertha N weaver b 399 Cedar
" Fred joiner bds 150 Hathaway
" Hannah widow Thomas operative h 1627 Acushnet avenue
" Herbert messenger Standard
" James decorator h 66 Willis
" John warp twister h 31 Austin
" Mary E widow Samuel h 399 Cedar Grove [Austin
" N Elsie clerk 276 Union bds 31
" Peter F operative b 35 Acushnet avenue
" Rothwell second hand h 78 Linden
" Thomas spinner h 150 Hathaway
" Thomas spinner h 168 Brock av
" Thomas weaver h 16 McGurk
" Verena widow Peter h 35 Acushnet avenue
" Victor O B fixer b 35 Acushnet av
" Walter K printer b 31 Austin
Slattery John P spinner h 6 Acushnet blk [ond
" Timothy T loom fixer h 379 S Sec-
Sleger Antone shoe repairer 75 William h 199 Dean [Front
Slegier Bonney operative h 177 North
Sleight Edward W clerk 92½ Purchase h 202 County
" John H loom fixer h 114 South
" Ludger mill hand h 12 Rodney
" Wilfred weaver b 32 County
" William teamster h 158 Whitman
" William weaver h 61 Rivet
Slinger Eli picture operator h 71 Dartmouth
Slivowski Rose Mrs h 259 N Front
Sloane Ann widow Arthur h 12 McMurray terrace [ray ter
" Michael E engineer h 12 McMur-
" William molder 229 N Water h 103 Durfee

Remember to investigate our methods before taking up a business course.
Kinyon's Commercial School
Odd Fellows Bldg., Cor. William and Pleasant Sts., New Bedford, Mass.

Slocomb Annie F widow bds 52 Rivet
" Parker F dentist 52 Rivet h do
Slocum Abbie A widow Andrew b 82 Forest
" Addie T bds 274 Mill
" Alice A widow George bds 560 Hathaway road
" Andrew M laborer bds 467 Allen
" Charles R salesman 27 N Water h 24 Homer
" Edna G G telephone operator Standard b 274 Mill
" Edward M draughtsman 303 Municipal bldg h 18 Sherman
" Elizabeth S widow Charles dressmaker 65 Elm b do
" Giles P (Slocum & Kilburn) 23 N Water h 96 Bedford
" Harold second hand h 160 Summer [h 67 Atlantic
" Holder engineer 214 S Water
" H Elsie milliner 274 Mill b do
" John O Jr conductor b 523 Cottage [County
" Joseph R master mariner h 597
" Mary E clerk 223 N Second h at Fairhaven
" William A salesman b 361 County
" William L salesman Greene & Wood h 106 S Second
" William L Jr teamster Greene & Wood b 106 S Second
SLOCUM & KILBURN (Giles P Slocum) mill supplies 23-27 N Water See page 766
Sloper Albert supt Pierce Bros Ltd h 92 State [ant
Slosson Henry C laborer h 142 Pleas-
Small Edna widow Hezekiah rms 90 Elm
" Grace W b 75 Thomas [Hillman
" Luthera M widow David S h 123
" Samuel H cooper h 69 Mill
" Stephen Jr helper b 954 S Water
" Stephen P plumber h 954 S Water [123 Hillman
" Susan J clerk 52 Pleasant bds
Smalla Gotleib baker h 88 Tallman
Smalley Ann widow h 113 Mott
" Arthur weaver h 176 Brock av
" Edwin twister h 26 Willard
" Harry teamster h 43 Jouvett
" Henry twister h 39 Valentine

Smalley
" Herbert E teamster N B Tallow Co h 63 Mt Pleasant [lard
" James clerk 144 Union b 26 Wil-
" James drillmaker b 61 Myrtle
" John h 61 Myrtle
" Joseph dipper h 5 Howland
" Luther I helper b 61 Myrtle
" Samuel salesman 99 Front rms 167 Mill
" Walter third hand b 3 Clay
" William overseer Acushnet Mill Corp h 159 Brock av
" William R weaver h 61 Salisbury
Smart Ann H rms 35 Eighth
" William F storekeeper 57 N Second h 283 Court
Smead Edward B hostler 50 Elm b 895 Rockdale av
" Jonathan H letter carrier h 895 Rockdale av [Acushnet av
Smethurst Albert D twister b 1105
" Charles spinner b 19 Howland Village [ditch
" Chester mill hand bds 285 Bow-
" Fred electrician h 211 Brock av
" George h 19 Howland Village
" Harry driver r 28 Larch b 37 Hickory [Forest
" James driver r 28 Larch h 85
" John T spinner b 26 Viall
" Mary H Mrs h 285 Bowditch
" Samuel spinner h 26 Viall
" Walter A student b 285 Bowditch
" Wilfred H fixer h 218 Whitman
" William spinner h 72 Larch
Smiley Frederick G clerk 125 Middle h 141 Willis
Smith Abbott M clerk Quissett Mill bds 20 Hawthorn
" Abbott P Smith (Cook & Smith) 37 Purchase h 95 Hawthorn
" Agnes J h 100 S Second
" Albert spinner h 20 Reynolds
" Albert R page public library b 20 Reynolds
" Alexander h 229 State
" Alexander T salesman 81 Front h at Acushnet
" Alfred drillworker h 52 Fruit
" Alfred rem from city
" Alfred E glassware decorator h 27 Chestnut [87 Hathaway
" Alice widow Arthur mill hand h

HASKELL BROS. DEALERS IN
ICE
400 COURT STREET TELEPHONE CONNECTION NEW BEDFORD, MASS.

Smith
" Alice C stenographer Nashawena Mill b 98 State [h 265 Pope
" Alphonso H salesman 23 N Water
" Alvin J rem from city
" Andrew weaver h 690 Purchase
" Andrew J police h 91 Willis
" Ann operative b 19 Ashley
" Ann E and Ella M h 303 Cedar
" Anna B h 70 Forest
" Anna L clerk registry of deeds b 525 Cottage
" Anna L Mrs b 151 Fair
" Annie widow Joseph h 143 Belleville rd [nut b do
" Annie A music teacher 130 Chest-
" Annie F h 130 Chestnut
" Arthur teamster b 53 Prospect
" Arthur A mariner h 93 Rockland
" Arthur C electrician and locksmith 27 William h 39 Bedford [Sycamore
" Arthur L glasscutter bds 121
" Augustus plumber h 126 Fair
" Augustus Mrs rem to San Francisco Cal
" Benjamin plumber b 303 Fourth
" Benjamin spinner b 38 Bowditch
SMITH BENJAMIN F CONSTRUCTION CO The contractors and builders Five Cents Savings Bank bldg and 22 Mason Pawtucket R I See page 18
" Bernard P (B P Smith & Co) b 196 Hawthorn
" Bertrand J salesman b 67 Larch
" Betsy widow Francis b 285 Park
" Blanche A clerk 372 Kempton b 154 Mill
" Bradford h 83 Willis
SMITH BROS Inc Joseph T Smith pres, James F Smith treas ice mfrs 777-785 Purchase, brewery Coggeshall and at R R See page 779
" Burton F eyeletmaker h 400 Pleasant
SMITH B F & CO Inc artesian wells 38 Oliver Boston See page 31
" B P & Co (Bernard P Smith and James F Cotter) liquors 31-37 Delano
" Carlton W clerk 60 Dartmouth b 232 Acushnet av [Larch
" Catherine M widow Oliver h 67

Smith
" Charles clerk b 225 N Second
" Charles crossing tender b 1668 Acushnet av [mut av
" Charles D gardener b 35 Shaw-
" Charles F police h 174 Summer
" Charles H clerk h 25 Bedford
" Charles H shoe nailer h 249 Hillman [ton h 367 do
" Charles L hairdresser 365 Kemp-
" Charles N compositor Standard rms 205 Pleasant
" Charles R drillmaker h 729 Allen
" Charles T druggist 721 S Water h 202 Orchard [73 Willis
" Charles W baker 92 Walden h
" Charles W draughtsman h 1 Bay
" Charles W laborer 144 S Water h 140 Shawmut av [County
" Charlotte widow John rms 493
" Chrissie telephone operator 57 N Second b 100 Chestnut
" Clara T bookkeeper 14 Clifford bldg b 525 Cottage [cery
" Clarence carpenter h 68 Chan-
" Clarence Sydney master mechanic h 355 County
" Claude C boys' sec Y M C A b 41 Pierce [mouth
" Clifton E student bds 6 Dart-
" Daniel fireman h 303 Sawyer
" Daniel teamster h 6 Walnut
" Daniel H foreman h 56 Fourth
" David A polisher h 35 Shawmut avenue
" David J rem from city
" David J Mrs b 22 W Trinity
" David L laborer b 63 Oak
" D Harrison clerk 100 William h 130 Willis
" Ebenezer weaver h 194 Nash rd
" Edith dressmaker b 45 Emerson (S) [chase b 63 Pleasant
" Edith S stenographer 36 Pur-
" Edmund spinner h 51 Collette
" Edward bricklayer h 38 Fifth
" Edward spinner b 52 Morton ct
" Edward weaver h 87 Dunbar
" Edward B h 213 Orchard
" Edward F salesman 106 Front b 345 Cottage
" Edward M salesman Greene & Wood h at S Dartmouth
" Edward T driver h 23 Ash (S)

J. F. CROSSLEY 223 MILL STREET COR. EMERSON PHONE
STEAM and HOT WATER HEATING
GAS FITTING and FIXTURES

Smith
" Edward T mgr 80 Purchase rms 128 N Second [345 Cottage
" Elias G salesman 188 N Water h
" Elias G Jr machinist b 90 Walden
" Elizabeth h 219 Acushnet av
" Elizabeth asst at public library b 372 Cottage [den
" Elizabeth widow Jesse h 83 Wal-
" Elizabeth widow William h 194 Rockland [161 Middle
" Elizabeth E Mrs dresmaker h
" Elizabeth J h 89 Bedford
" Ella C widow Charles F h 55½ Fifth [shnet av
" Ellen widow Urban h 229 Acu-
" Ellen widow William J h 154 Mill
" Ellen M h 89 Bedford
" Emma widow John K h 1505 Acushnet av
" Everett L clerk b 400 Pleasant
" Florence sec Y W C A rms 195 Cottage
" Everett H skiver b 47 Durfee
" Francis J twister b 93 Belleville road
" Francis N G chief clerk 57 N Second h 68 Parker [Crapo
" Frank clerk 630 Purchase b 69
" Frank foreman b 186 Grinnell
" Frank rem from city [North
" Frank salesman 46 Purchase h 233
" Frank Jr blacksmith 411 Bolton h 532 Rivet
" Frank A rem from city
" Frank C h 64 Hillman
" Frank C plumber 28 N Water h at Dartmouth
" Frank E iron molder h 9 Bedford
" Frank E mariner b 263 Purchase
" Franklin W variety 203 Acushnet av h do [Grove
" Fred operative h 131 Cedar
" Fred E polisher b 35 Shawmut av
" George rms 7 N Second
" George baker rms 34 High
" George fixer b 143 Belleville rd
" George hostler N B Driving Club h 277 Middle [h 299 Brock av
" George overseer Dartmouth Mill
" George teamster h 194 Rockland
" George (watchman) rem from city
" George weaver h 203 Weld

Smith
" George weaver h 437 Orchard (S) [shnet av
" George A conductor b 233 Acu-
" George H bookkeeper Quissett Mill b 184 Washington
" George H drillworker b 44 Briggs
" George K weaver b 545 Cottage
" George T gas fitter 125 Middle h 107 Cedar [h 76 Mt Pleasant
" George W inspector U St Ry Co
" Gertrude nurse bds 208 County
" Gladys Mrs clerk 372 Kempton b 52 Ash (N)
" Gordon C baker h 36 Linden
" Grace D bookkeeper b 27 Chestnut
" Hannah A h 89 Bedford
" Hannah F widow Frank h 263 Acushnet avenue [yer
" Harriet widow James h 290 Saw-
" Harry A foreman st dept h 150 North
" Hartley drill worker h 30 Clark
" Hattie Mrs h 6 Bonneau ct
" Helen widow Henry W h 27 Seventh [school b 27 Chestnut
" Helen H teacher Harrington
" Helen J telephone operator 57 N Second bds 73 Willis
" Helena E telephone operator 57 N Second b 83 Walden
" Henrietta B h 8 Dartmouth
" Henry h 130 Crapo
" Henry fireman h 56 Merrimac
" Henry iceman h 541 Acushnet av
" Henry liquors 572 N Front h 140 Davis
" Henry truant officer h 372 Cottage [ington
" Henry H watchman h 184 Wash-
" Henry M steward h 5 Fifth
" Henry P shoe worker b 137 Perry
" Hensley McB removed from city
" Herbert clerk 98 Allen h 152 Washington
" Herbert deck hand h 160 State
" Herbert laborer b 69 Crapo
" Herbert third hand h 36 Winsor
" Herbert weaver h 30 McGurk
" Herbert E shoemaker b 14 Studley
" Hilda mill hand b 44 Briggs
" Hiram letter carrier h 553 Union

CHARLES A. CROSHERE
38 FOURTH ST. Bell Phone 1964-23
SIGN PAINTING
GLASS LETTERING
ELECTRIC SIGNS
SHOW CARDS

Smith
" Holland clerk 855 Purchase h 203 Weld
" Howard clerk b r 729 Allen
" Howard weaver h 32 Ashley
" Howard T foreman 128 Pleasant h 27 Chestnut
" Howard U h 148 Arnold
" Howarth weaver h 28 Holly
" Hoyland died Jan 19 1911 [Union
" Hoyland (estate) bicycles 248
" Ida M Mrs stenographer First National Bank b 83 Sycamore
" Ira Allen B h 163 Cottage
" Isabella Mrs mill hand h 6 Bonneau court [ry
" Isabella widow Alfred b 137 Per-
" James (Cassidy & Smith) 1271 Acushnet av b 208 Nash road
" James fixer h 238 Sawyer
" James machinist 15 Fourth b 83 Walden [Fourth
" James metal supinner h 225
" James operative b 494 Coggeshall
" James sexton St Mary's church b 33 Reynolds
" James spinner h 299 Brock av
" James teamster 214 S Water bds 954 do
" James F h 196 Hawthorn
" Jane P widow David h 22 West Trinity
" Janet Mrs h 303 Fourth
" Jessie widow Ralph b 95 Linden
" John machinist 8 Seneca b 142½ Purchase
" John mule spinner h 440 Rivet
" John spinner bds 146 Holly
" John weaver h 276 Coggeshall
" John weaver b 85 Tallman
" John A teaming 86 Bay h do
" John Howard salesman 111 William b rear 729 Allen [Grinnell
" John H clerk 50 N Second h 202
" John H laborer h 610 Purchase
" John L carpenter b 67 Coffin av
" John P laborer h 62 Peckham
" John R clerk P O h 42 Pierce
" John S gardener h 14 Studley
" John S Jr removed to Haverhill
" Joseph bds 19 Ashley
" Joseph b 13 Hampton ct

Smith
" Joseph B overseer Whitman Mills h 143 State
" Joseph H h 164 Durfee
" Joseph T president 779 Purchase h 717 County
" Joseph V fixer h 69 Crapo
" Josephine C widow Henry h 340 Middle [b 213 Orchard (S)
" Julia R teacher Parker st school
" Julius farm hand b r 729 Allen
" J Henry advertising solicitor rms 2 Seventh
" J Herbert clerk Mechanics National Bank h 209 Maple [mont
" Leonora A Mrs nurse h 55 Tre-
" Lewis weaver bds 69 Crapo
" Lottie Mrs h 59 S Second
" Louisa R widow John h 140 N Second
" Lucius D h 98 State
" Lucretia N teacher High school b 500 Cottage [Pleasant
" Lydia E widow Sydney h 334
" Lyman R agent 186 Purchase rms 14 High [av
" Manuel painter h 205 Acushnet
" Margaret V milliner 185 Union b 67 Larch [ville rd
" Maria widow William h 26 Belle-
" Maria A widow Royal bds 419 Kempton
" Mary Mrs weaver h 164 Davis
" Mary widow h 102 Potomska
" **Mary** A h 494 Coggeshall
" Mary A dressmaker 45 Emerson (S) h do [geshall
" Mary A Mrs h Myrtle n Cog-
" Mary A widow Edward h 45 Emerson (S) [Dean
" Mary A widow Joseph B h 187
" Mary A widow Michael E h 525 Cottage
" Mary B Mrs b 126 Hawthorn
" Mary E widow Joseph B h 464 S Second [do
" Mary E milliner 172 Fourth b
" Mary K widow Almanzo M h 47 Durfee [North h do
" Mary Louise music teacher 79
" Mary L Mrs h 219 S Front
" Mary P widow Philip h 93 Belleville road [Grinnell
" Mary W widow Theophilas h 202

J. G. NICHOLSON
LUMBER, SASH, DOORS and BLINDS
BOWDITCH STREET, NEW BEDFORD, MASS.

Smith
" Michael bartender h 189 Hathaway [Shawmut av
" Minnie E widow Maurice h 208
" Mitchell city teamster h 384 Court
" Nat C architect 97 William rms 400-401 h Seventh cor Cherry
" Omar driver 238 State h 229 do
" Patrick laborer h 598 Cottage
" Patrick rem from city
" Patrick Jr carpenter b 598 Cottage [340 Middle
" Percy bell boy Parker House bds
" Peter watchman h 747 Belleville av [ton h 740 do
" Peter B watchman 1145 Kemp-
" Philip twister b 206 State
" Preston farmer b 121 Willow
" Rhodes loom fixer h 68 Hathaway
" Richard clerk R R depot h 1086 Acushnet av
" Richard fixer h 296 Tinkham
" Richard weaver h 190 Brock av
" Robert clerk 556 Kempton b 384 Court [nut
" Russell operative bds 109 Chest-
" Sam spinner h 24 Pearl
" Samuel fixer h 84 Covell
" Samuel A variety 1096 Acushnet av h 1090 do
" Samuel J (Burke & Smith) grocers 556 Kempton h 219 North
" Sarah F widow Levi h 75 Sycamore
" Sarah L Mrs b 114 Seventh
" Shubael D h 81 Mill [Chestnut
" Sidney F clerk 201 Union b 27
" Sophia Mrs operative h r 61 Belleville rd [County
" Stephen W bookkeeper h 355
" Susan nurse b 208 County
" Susan widow Alden h 400 Pleasant [nolds
" Sydney clerk 113 Union b 20 Rey-
" Thomas fixer b 257 Coffin av
" Thomas laborer h 295 Hillman
" Thomas mule spinner h 88 Covell
" Thomas twister tender h 24 Myrtle
" Thomas weaver h r 533 Rivet
" Thomas E sampler Wamsutta Mill b 93 Belleville rd
" Timothy P laborer b 980 County
" Tully C motorman h 412 Cedar

Smith
" Victor W carpenter 191 Clinton h 52 Ash (N)
" Walter C driver b 345 Cottage
" Walter E second hand h 25 George [Mills h 585 Union
" Walter K bookkeeper Whitman
" Walter O electrician b 6 Dartmouth
" Wilfred carpenter b 344 Davis
" Willard N foreman N B C C & R Works h 436 Sawyer
" William changer over b 194 Nash road
" William fixer h 276 Fourth
" William laborer b 30 McGurk
" William machinist b 35 Ingraham
" William machinist b 164 David
" William porter 100 William b 384 Court [av h do
" William real estate 1668 Acushnet
" William spinner b 258 Coffin av
" William spinning principal N B T school h 100 Chestnut
" William second hand h 44 Briggs
" William weaver b 25 Viall
" William weaver b 189 Hathaway
" William A L liquors 124 Purchase h 20 Emerson (S) [Fifth
" William Borden glasscutter h 55½
" William B lawyer 1 Masonic bldg h 6 Dartmouth [Richmond
" William C H letter carrier h 81
" William E h 278 Palmer
" William E (N B Steam Dye House) 53 William h 29 Arch
" William H foreman st dept h 310 Park [mut av
" William H shoemaker b 35 Shaw-
" William H twister h 29 E French avenue [h 40 Ash (S)
" William J asst supt The Common
" William M operative rms 384 Court [net av
" William P solderer b 137 Acush-
" William S died
" Willis P photographic supplies 134 Pleasant b 91 Willis
" Wilson clerk 1130 Acushnet av h 187 Dean [len
" Winchester R foreman h r 729 Al-
" see Schmidt, Smyth and Smythe

Smithson Tom foreman h 121 Hathaway

Steiger-Dudgeon Co.
"The WOMAN'S Store."
Tel. Bell 82 & 83, Branches connecting all depts.
" " 160 For Office only. Auto. 1211

SUMPTIONS, ASSORTMENTS AT ALL TIMES OF DEPENDABLE DRY GOODS

Smolec John tailor h 410 Purchase
Smolla Frank mill hand h 11 Nye
" Powell carder h 11 Fulton ct
" Stella Mrs h 34 Penniman
Smyth Fred R overseer h 68 Willis
" Hugh J Rev pastor St Lawrence Catholic church h 110 Summer
Smythe Frederick C overseer Nashawena Mill [53 Rounds
Snailham Walter W letter carrier h
Snape Margaret widow James h 315 Earle
Snedden George master mechanic Grinnell Mfg Corp h 759 County [County
" Jennie W stenographer bds 759
" May S stenographer Old Colony Box Co bds 759 County
Snell Charles H shipper 14 Wall h at S Dartmouth
" David A h 215 Mt Pleasant
" Ernest L apothecary 133 Ruth and clerk P O station 15 h 131 County [bard
" Frederick A carpenter h 59 Lom-
" George A Jr conductor h 10 Collins [County
" Julia A widow Moses L h 131
" Myra G clerk 125 Middle b 101 Mt Pleasant [sant
" Walter R vocalist b 101 Mt Plea-
" William G (Snell & Simpson) 58 Adams h 101 Mt Pleasant
" William I insurance agent 37 Purchase rm 23 h 59 Foster
" & Simpson (W G Snell and C S Simpson) biscuit mfrs 58 Adams
Snow Alban C h 56 Elm [Fair
" Arthur A shipping clerk h 118
" Charles H clerk 100 Fifth h 512 Kempton [bds 42 S Sixth
" Charles H clerk 213 Acushnet av
" Charlie M carpenter 3 E Pope h at Fairhaven [chard (S)
" Constance and Agatha b 115 Or-
" Daniel H teamster h 25 Elm
" Edwin inspector rms 49 William
" Frederick L (Driscoll, Church & Hall) 84 Union h 287 Kempton
" George H clerk 145 Union h 57 S Second [Maple
" Henry K mgr 350 S Second h 52

Snow
" James S conductor h 390 Maxfield
" John A h 192 Washington
" Joshua T bds 68 Parker
" Lester W removed from city
" Loum merchant 37 Purchase rm 7 and president N B Five Cents Savings Bank h 168 Hawthorn
" Loum Jr auditor 37 Purchase rm 7 h 581 Union
" Mary W teacher H A Kempton school bds 68 Parker [ford
" Olive H widow Andrew h 81 Bed-
" Otis B bds 135 Locust
" Rhoda A chiropodist 82 Elm h do
" Sarah Hunt widow Robert h 115 Orchard (S) [137 Hawthorn
" Susan S, Isabel M, Helen T, h
" William J clerk h 33 Katharine
Snyder Andrew weaver h 153 Collette
" Byron P (Blaisdell & Snyder) 956 Acushnet av h 71 Willis
" Charles restaurant 81 Weld h 46 Richmond [Richmond
" Charles S clerk 81 Weld bds 46
" Edith B telephone operator b 300 County [179 Fourth
" Peter H foreman 100 Fifth h
" William loom fixer bds 43 Beetle
" see Schneider
Soares Antone laborer h 17 Bullard
" Antone seaman h 472 S Water
" Bernard laborer h 93 Grinnell
" Eugene harnessmaker h 14 Griffin [avenue
" Eugene M carpenter b 194 Coffin
" Fanny Mrs h 420 First
" Frank operative 41 Winsor
" Joaquim laborer h 139 Coffin av
" Joaquina Mrs h 230 S Second
" John laborer b 185 N Front
" John operative b 186 Cove
" John F clerk 45 School h 53 do
" Joseph carpenter h 36 Sagamore
" Joseph fireman h 544 S Water
" Joseph laborer h 20 County
" Joseph laborer h 185 N Front
" Joseph V mason h 473 First
" Manuel mill hand h 8 Mulberry
" Manuel shoes 259 Coggeshall and 1478 Acushnet av h 387 Belleville av (S) [shall
" Manuel S operative h 381 Cogge-

PELEG H. SHERMAN 506 COUNTY ST.
FUNERAL DIRECTOR AND EMBALMER
OFFICE PHONES. Bell 690-13. Auto. 1305.
RESIDENCE PHONES. Bell 690-12. Auto. 1306.

Soares
" Urben weaver h 61 Lexington
" Victorino J hairdresser 509 County h 32 Grant [Grove h do
Sobil Sadie Mrs fruit 292 Cedar
Socolllos Barin operative h 7 Marvin
Soddy William operative h 203 Dean
Soforenco Jake tailor 17 Arcade blk h 25 Adams [Coffin av
Sola William mill hand b 67 Coffin av
Solanti Louis laborer h r 615 Purchase [ond h do
Soliveia Joseph hairdresser 80 S Sec-
Solomon James laborer h 82 Cedar
Soltas Charles mill hand b 84 Covell
" James h 84 Covell [Covell
" James Jr mill hand bds 84
Sommers Frank W h 89 N Second
" William A shoeworker b 89 N Second
" see Summers [ton
Soper Christine Mrs b 900 Kemp-
" Esther widow b 125 Rivet
Sorelle Adelard grocer h 2311 Acushnet av [av
" Donald carpenter b 149 Philips
" Joseph carpenter 149 Phillips av h do
" Joseph b 200 Collette
" Lucy A bookkeeper 1516 Acushnet av b 149 Phillips av [Fruit
Sorensen Peter S glasscutter h 87
Sorto Manuel S laborer h 564 S Water [Water
" Manuel S Jr engineer b 564 S
Sossenville David rem from city
" George operative b 154 Cedar Grove [dar Grove
" Lemina widow Joseph h 154 Ce-
Sotnick John weaver h 11 Merrill
" Peter weaver b 11 Merrill
" Stephen weaver b 11 Merrill
Soucy Alexander carpenter h 88 Ruth [shnet av
" Andre R R foreman h 2471 Acu-
" Arthur shoemaker b 108 Austin
" Arthur weaver b 320 N Front
" Clovis operative b 2473 Acushnet av
" Eugene operative b 326 N Front
" Harvey doffer b 326 N Front
" John B second hand h 1016 Acushnet av
" Joseph spinner h 108 Austin

Soucy
" Odion operative b 257 Belleville avenue
" Oliver carpenter h 326 N Front
" Omer spinner b 347 N Front
" Valmar spinner h 347 N Front
" Wilfred doffer h 37 Nye
" see Saucier
Sougnez Laurent weaver h 172 Dean
Soulard Arthur baker h 3 Cornell pl
Soule Ernest L molder h 71 Walden [ion
" Etta M stenographer b 169 Un-
" George A teamster h 147 Cedar
" George A Jr teamster N B Tallow Co b 147 Cedar
" Herbert L chauffeur h 72 Atlantic
" Herbert T agent h 273 Purchase
" Herman A usher 162 Union b 169 do [man b do
" Lydia W dressmaker 111 Hill-
" Maranda D widow Abel b 121 Locust [Acushnet av
" Mary L widow Stephen H h 3277
" Mill cotton goods manufacturers foot of Sawyer [Hillman
" Rebecca widow William bds 134
" Robert F farmer h 36 Liberty
" Rufus A coll of customs office Custom House and pres Soule Mill, Nield Mfg Corp and pres City Mfg Co h 12 Eighth [h do
" Thomas H decorator 169 Union
" T H Mrs prop The Sheldon 169 Union
" William A carpenter h 63 Foster
" see Sowle
Soules Phillip stationery b 118½ Cove
Souliere Alfred speeder tender b 530 N Front
" Joseph painter b 530 N Front
" Matilda widow Desire h 350 N Front
Soulis Joe weaver h 475 S Front
Sousa Frank carder b 98 Blackmer
" Joseph mill hand b 39 Mitchell
South Dartmouth Express office N Sixth also Bridge S Dartmouth
" End Social Club 42 Rivet
Southern Mass Telephone Co (The) 57 N Second auditing dept 160 Purchase [ton
Southwick Henry T rem to Brock-

F. T. AKIN & CO. PAINTERS AND DECORATORS

Southwick
" William removed to Brockton
Southwood James operative b 9 Grandfield [Brock av
Southworth Albert operative h 16
" Alice A widow Mark h 151 David
" Amanda M Mrs h 155 Purchase
" Christopher operative b 151 David
" Eli weaver h 167 Richmond
" George fixer h 171 Richmond [vid
" Gilbert mule spinner h 151 Da-
" Isabell stenographer b 151 David
" James laborer b 9 Grandfield
" Richard spinner h 176 Bowditch
" Robert operative h 337 Earle
" Samuel mule spinner h 91 Brock av
" Simeon fixer h 1631 Acushnet av
" William loom fixer h 180 Brock av
Souty Eugene laborer b 954 S Water
Souza Alfred cooper W F Nye h at Dartmouth [av
" Alfred mill hand b 148 Belleville
" Amelia dressmaker 143 Mill h do
" Antone died Nov 17 1910
" Antone engineer h 104 South
" Antone fisherman h 104 Mosher
" Antone fisherman h 117 Swift
" Antone fixer h 509 Rivet
" Antone freight handler h 93 Grinnell
" Antone laborer h 67 Winsor
" Antone laborer h 95 Bellevue [av
" Antone laborer h 184 Belleville
" Antone laborer h 199 Fourth
" Antone laborer h 205 N Second
" Antone laborer h 507 S Second
" Antone laborer h 623 S Water
" Antone mill hand b 84 Earle
" Antone operative h 4 Maiden lane
" Antone operative h 329 First
" Antone A laborer h 71 Delano
" Antone B mill hand h 109 Fruit
" Antone B operative h 24 Katharine
" Antone M operative h 49 Crapo
" Antone R grocer 9 Mitchell h 21 do
" Antonio operative b 15 Clay
" Arthur boat builder h 97 Hull
" Arthur E fireman hose 2 h 785 County

Souza
" August carpenter h 2½ Hyacinth
" August spinner h 127 Belleville av [310 h at Fairhaven
" Augusto agent 97 William rm
" Domingos A drill maker h 50 Lombard
" Emma h 143 Mill
" Eva clerk h 260 Fourth [ville av
" Fortunata operative h 59 Crapo
" Francisco laborer h 1147 Purchase
" Francisco mill hand h 202 Belle-
" Frank fisherman h 56 Nelson
" Frank laborer h 26 Elm
" Frank laborer h 66 Independent
" Frank laborer h 70 Nelson
" Frank laborer h 174 S Second
" Frank laborer h 473 First
" Frank mill hand h 80 Hope
" Frank operative h 85 Winsor
" Frank operative h 346 First
" Frank shoemaker 76 Purchase
" Frank A rope worker h 74 Liberty
" Frank E b 575 S Water
" Frank N mill hand b 82 Belleville rd
" Frank S weaver h 299 S Front
" Henry fisherman h 80 Sagamore
" James carpenter h 171 Bonney
" James R clerk b 194 Bonney
" John fisherman h 75 Prospect
" John laborer h 3 Hyacinth
" John laborer h 42 Division
" John laundryman h 268 S Front
" John mill hand b 72 Earle
" John mill hand b 84 Earle
" John oiler U St Ry Co power station b 42 Division
" John operative h 49 Larch
" John operative h 162 Bonney [av
" John operative b 148 Belleville
" John painter h 264 S Second
" John shoemaker h 637 S Water
" John teamster h 254 Fourth
" John teamster h 544 S Water
" John E operative h 62 Howland
" John J laborer h 9 Stapleton
" John J plumber 91 N Water h 38 Park [Orchard (S)
" John M mason's tender h 281
" John M painter h 109 Fruit
" Jose carpenter h 103 Davis [av
" Jose operative h 127 Belleville

To do things right you must be taught. Our instructors can do it.
Kinyon's Commercial School
Odd Fellows Bldg., Cor. William and Pleasant Sts., New Bedford, Mass.

Souza
" Joseph carder h 85 Cove rd
" Joseph driver 12 School b 104 Mosher [County
" Joseph grocer 243 State h 924
" Joseph laborer h 3 Mitchell
" Joseph laborer h 111 N Water
" Joseph laborer h 115 Field [av
" Joseph laborer h 202 Belleville
" Joseph laborer h 273 S Front
" Joseph laborer h 584 S Water
" Joseph laborer h 715 S Water
" Joseph mill hand h 82 Belleville rd
" Joseph mill hand h 84 Fruit
" Joseph mill hand h 237 Coggeshall
" Joseph mill hand b 39 Mitchell
" Joseph mill hand b 181 Bonney
" Joseph overseer h 79 Katharine
" Joseph teamster 99 Front
" Joseph B rms 78 Swift [av
" Joseph G laborer h 75 Acushnet
" Joseph J mill hand h 87 Briggs
" Joseph L liquors 37 Howland h 9 Thompson [Scott
" Joseph M fish 139 Crapo h 42
" Joseph M mill hand 446 S Second [h 199 Allen
" Joseph M de compositor Standard
" Joseph S drill worker h 84 Fruit
" Joseph V paper maker h 56 Nelson
" Julio operative h 219 Coggeshall
" Julius operative h 218 Acushnet av [Orchard (S)
" Lawrence de emp P Co h 443
" Louisa widow Antone L h 402 S Front
" Manuel carpenter b 75 Emma
" Manuel driver 108 Grape h Dunbar
" Manuel fireman h 52 Nelson
" Manuel fisherman h 20 County
" Manuel laborer h 5 Mitchell
" Manuel laborer h 7 Margin [av
" Manuel laborer h 127 Belleville
" Manuel laborer h 149 Field
" Manuel laborer h 165 Grinnell
" Manuel laborer h 381 S Second
" Manuel laborer h 475 First
" Manuel laborer h 531 First
" Manuel laborer b 27 Mitchell
" Manuel laborer b 72 Acushnet av
" Manuel mariner h 445 S Water

Souza
" Manuel mill hand b 86 Nash rd
" Manuel mill hand b 103 Hemlock
" Manuel mill hand b 195 Coggeshall
" Manuel operative h 17 Sylvia
" Manuel operative h 39 Hollyhock
" Manuel operative h 142 Division
" Manuel operative h 407 S Water
" Manuel speeder h 97 Coffin av
" Manuel A operative h 381 Coggeshall
" Manuel F h 504 Bolton
" Manuel F laborer h 87 Larch
" Manuel G cooper 353 S Second h 53 Fair [av b 161 do
" Manuel L bowling 162 Acushnet
" Manuel M grocer 214 Belleville av h 204 do [ville rd
" Manuel N mill hand b 82 Belle-
" Manuel R painter h 146 Rockland [shall
" Manuel V operative b 301 Cogge-
" Marion C operative h 103 Mosher
" Martin laborer h 113 Rockland
" Mary Mrs h 29 Katharine
" Mary Mrs h 161 S Second
" Mary tailoress 1014 Acushnet av b at Fairhaven
" Mary widow Frank h 190 Bonney
" Mary A teacher Harrington school b 233 Fourth
" Mary A widow D A h 105 Fifth
" Mary P Mrs h 575 S Water
" Mary T Mrs h 68 S Second
" Mathias fish h 475 S Water
" Matthew laborer h 631 S Water
" Michael fireman h 46 Scott
" Paul N laborer h r 288 S Second
" Phebe widow h 15 Clay
" Prima mill hand h 50 Dean
" Rauly M clerk 176 Rockland b 87 Larch
" Virginio operative h 329 First
" Virginio A h Farnham
" William laborer h 41 Page
" William H mill hand h 66 Acushnet av
" William S operative h 57 Crapo
Sowerbutts Jane widow John h 29 Salisbury [h 70 Lombard
Sowle Albert W at Pairpoint Corp
" Ann M widow Benjamin F h 86 Hillman
" Clifton L grinder h 93 S Sixth

Bread, Cake, Pastry
RICHMOND & COMPANY 255-257 UNION STREET
Bell 993 Automatic 1022

Sowle
" Edwin P h 276 Kempton
" Everett W harness maker h 501 Purchase [180 Newton
" Frank W clerk 123 Purchase b
" Fred A clerk b 501 Purchase
" Fred A mgr 1110 Acushnet av b 501 Purchase
" Frederick D teas 360 Kempton h 313 Orchard (S)
" Frederick H florist's asst 327 Coffin av b 325 do
" Frederick L hardware 123 Purchase h 180 Newton [av
" Harry V carpenter b 325 Coffin
" Hattie L tack packer rms 3 Park pl [h 325 do
" Herbert V florist 327 Coffin av
" Isaac N teamster h 330 Cedar
" Laura A widow Frederick A b 32 Eighth (S)
" Lillian S clerk h 313 Orchard
" Lincoln G night editor Mercury h 371 Park
" Myra B checker b 51 Maitland
" Nathaniel P glass and mantles 51 William h 80 Morgan
" Rachel C widow Albert b 70 Lombard
" Sarah F rms 3 Park pl [land
" Theodore B teamster h 51 Mait-
" Walter E shoemaker b 186 North
" William H driver h 186 North
" see Soule
Spachman John machinist h 487 Coggeshall
Spade Ada I nurse rms 150 Middle
Spaden Elizabeth A h 410 Kempton
Spafford Frank C motorman b 494 Acushnet av
" Lila housekeeper 42 Weld
Spanoodis Anthony E (Caperonis Spanoodis & Co) rms 1117 Acushnet av [chard (S)
Spare Arthur F student b 183 Or-
" Chester V salesman 41 Purchase b 183 Orchard (S)
" John V treasurer 41 Purchase h 183 Orchard (S) [Purchase
" J V Dry Goods Co (The) 41
" Romeyn A b 183 Orchard (S)
Spark Alma b 157 Elm
Sparks Esther Ann widow Charles h 324 Cedar Grove [David
Sparling Archibald machinist b 151

Sparling
" Thomas removed from city
" William D clerk h 151 David

FRANK M SPARROW
Counsellor at Law
30 Purchase St
New Bedford, Mass
Telephone Connection

Sparrow Frank M lawyer 30 Purchase h at Mattapoisett
" Hiram E machinist 8 Hazard lane h 25 Buttonwood
Speak James plumber b 679 Purchase
" Margaret Mrs h 679 Purchase
Specialty Shoe Store (Dennis & Ellis) 6 Purchase [h do
Specter Barney tailor 1 Cornell pl
" David cigars 1020 Acushnet av h 1036 do
" Louis mgr b 1 Cornell pl [vell
Spedding Thomas weaver b 12 Co-
Speight Arthur molder h 10 Salisbury
" Robert A molder h 10 Salisbury
Speir John glass cutter b 40 Russell
Spellman Nelson P electrician h 273 Cedar [Ry Co h 31 Richmond
" Nelson T electrician Union St
Spence Ernest bartender 98 Cove h 161 Crapo [land
Spencer Albert operative h 26 Cleve-
" Annette b 90 Davis [Middle
" Antone freight handler h 343
" Barbara widow James b 451 Rivet
" Daisey Mrs h 221 S Water
" Edmund overseer Grinnell Mfg Co h 115 Willow
" Edward helper b 850 First
" Edward K master mariner h 42 Borden
" Ernest spinner h 161 Crapo
" Ezra b J W Spencer's Tarkiln Hill rd [Purchase h do
" Frederick J wood and coal 999
" George h 2 E Durfee
" Hannah widow James b 359 Park

GLOBE DYE HOUSE 220 SHAWMUT AVE.
J. N. J. LONHOLDT, PROP. Telephone Connections Goods called for and Delivered
Down town Office. 52 Pleasant St., Room 1 North End Office, 1014 Acushnet Ave.

Spencer
" Hartley comp Standard h 14 Parker [Mt Vernon
" Hartley 2nd letter carrier h 55
" James lodging house 976 Acushnet av h do
" John W overseer Soule Mill h Tarkiln Hill rd cor Bowditch
" Joseph spinner h 23 Potter
" Joseph N shuttle maker b 280 Cedar
" Louis P foreman h 280 Cedar
" Mary A died Dec 19 1910
" Priscilla widow William h 1140 Acushnet av [velt
" Richard drill maker h 47 Roose-
" Samuel h 221 S Water [Park
" Samuel R clerk Mercury h 359
" Sarah M widow Orin C h 377 Kempton
" Thomas lather b 310 Orchard
" Thomas weaver h 186 Hathaway
" Walter G weigher City Coal Co h 40 Keene [net av
" William H joiner b 1140 Acush-
Sperry & Hutchinson Co (The) trading stamps 13 Pleasant [Water
Sphrian Joseph mill hand h 550 S
Spicer Ambrose laborer h 161 Campbell [lantic
" Benjamin F die maker h 32 At-
" Fred G eyelet maker b 152 Smith
" Lizzie L widow William G h 152 Smith
" Mary C h 142 Arnold [Smith
" Winnifred boxmaker b 152
Spigal John third hand b 260 Coggeshall [39 Hemlock
Spindola Fannie clerk 70 Purchase b
" Manuel J buffer h 39 Hemlock
Spinner Annie E Mrs clerk b 324 Cedar [Second
" Joseph speeder tender h 476
Spinnett John P operative h 163 Rockland
Spinney Anna G bookkeeper 929 Acushnet av h 324 Cedar
Spirlet Adonise widow Louis b 260 Tinkham
" Alphonse weaver h 205 Clifford
" Eugene operative h 336 Nash rd
" Henry fixer h 1671 Acushnet av
" Joseph loom fixer h 278 Nash rd
" Jules weaver h 310 Earle
" Louis machinist h 260 Tinkham

Spirlet
" Nicholas mason h 126 Holly
" Paul weaver b 126 Holly
Spiva Julien S jewelry 70 William h 431 Mill [ty
Splaine John H engineer b 863 Coun-
" Mary widow James h 863 County
Sponner Walter engineer Smith Bros Brewery [Maitland
Spooner Abbie L widow J W b 55
" Albert F carpenter h 3304 Acushnet av [183 Pleasant
" Alonzo repairman 18 Market b
" Alonzo W inspector N B W W h 3233 Acushnet av
" Arthur C constable 1 Municipal bldg h 182 Chancery [lis
" Betsy W widow Caleb h 132 Wil-
" Charles A silver fitter b 323 Maxfield
" Charles F musical instruments 18 Purchase h 1 Park pl
" Charles F Jr teaming 2981 Acushnet av h do
" Charles S packer h 82 Thomas
" Charles W overseer N B C Co h 323 Maxfield [Reed
" Charles W paper hanger h 389
" Clayton T clerk 97 Front b 3278 Acushnet av
" Clifton W plumber 903 County b 3278 Acushnet av
" Daniel A letter carrier 3913 Acushnet av h 3249 do
" Edward C teamster b 63 Mechanics lane
" Edward F ice 682 Kempton h do
" Edward O farmer h 682 Kempton [Morgan
" Edwin E clerk 100 William h 96
" Elizabeth widow C H Jr periodicals 650 Purchase h 652 do
" Ella F h 17 Maitland
" Florence M bookkeeper 20 N Sixth h 17 Maitland [North
" Frank painter 34 Union h 366
" Frank teamster rms 73 Elm
" Frank W carpenter h 75 Vine
" Frederick S picture framer h 117 Grinnell [b at E Fairhaven
" George H driver 14 N Second
" Hannah E widow John A h 2949 Acushnet av [223 River rd
" Harriet B widow Joseph S h
" Harry driver rms 149 Middle

GREENE & WOOD Every Kind of LUMBER AND MILL WORK
PINE STREET, off So. WATER STREET, NEW BEDFORD

Spooner
" Harry L removed to Fairhaven
" Hattie A bookkeeper 255 Union b 682 Kempton [rd
" Herbert M foreman h 209 River
" James died Dec 5 1910 [net av
" James L farmer h 3167 Acush-
" Jenny widow Rufus A removed to Fairhaven
" Job ice dealer h Phillips rd
" John Augustus carpenter h 3278 Acushnet av
" John C police b 183 Pleasant[av
" Lewis G mason h 3195 Acushnet
" Lester F inspector N B W W b 3278 Acushnet av
" Lucy A Mrs clerk 41 Purchase b 69 Summer [Acushnet av
" Lucy A widow Charles F h 2924
" Lucy P died April 10 1911
" Mabel B cashier 87 Union b 36 North [Maitland
" Mary B widow Frederick P h 17
" Oliver G farmer b 3167 Acushnet av
" Ralph b 140 Shawmut av
" Roswell farmer b 2924 Acushnet av [Acushnet av
" Roswell 2nd farmer h 2924
" Sarah A widow Charles H h 208 Shawmut av
" Thomas A clerk rms 43 N Sixth
" Walter R deputy sheriff 31 Masonic bldg h at Acushnet
" William A engineer N Y N H & H R R h 15 Richmond
" William A machinist b 183 Pleasant [Kempton
" William Blackman farmer b 682
SPOONER WILLIAM E real estate Bates & Kirby bldg 52 Pleasant tel 1497-5 h 183 do See page 27 [Nye
Spoor William speeder tender h 11
Spot Cash Furniture Co (F M Weeden) 384 Acushnet av [olds
Spragg Arthur weaver h 11 Reyn-
" Joseph spinner h 99 Beetle
Sprague G Leroy h 315 Pleasant
" Henry M bakery 2161 Acushnet av h 920 Belleville av
" John third hand h 67 Emma
" & Poirier (Henry M Sprague and Joseph Poirier) bakers 2161 Acushnet av

Spranger John laborer h 67 Emma
" Joseph W draughtsman 303 Times bldg b 319 Union
Spratt Mary widow housekeeper 4 N Oak [h 20 Shawmut av
Springer Mercy A widow George W
" Temperance B widow Cornelius h 238 County [h do
Sprott George M mason 132 Cedar
" William B laborer h 290 Orchard (S) [Front
Squarl William operative 205 N
Squire John P & Co pork products 47 S Second [William
Squires Annie M milliner b 172
" Finley H clerk 397 Kempton b 39 Cedar
" Florence b 10 Spruce
" George T carpenter 191 Clinton h 172 William
" John A carpenter h 17 Ash (S)
" Lillian I clerk 185 Union b 172 William
" Mary E Mrs h 172 William
" William C carpenter 191 Clinton h 39 Cedar [dar
" William W electrician b 39 Ce-
Stables John W painter h 40 McGurk [Fair
Stadler William glass cutter h 54
Stafford George B grocer 60 Shawmut av h 58 do [av b 58 do
" Helen D bookkeeper 60 Shawmut
" Joseph driver b 404 Pleasant
" Maud E teacher Phillips av school b 58 Shawmut av
Stageter Charles weaver h 17 Princeton av [h Reed
Stagg John W installer 57 N Second
Stanbridge Hiram C rem from city
" Katie B Mrs h 114 Grinnell
STANDARD CONSTRUCTION CO J R Painchaud proprietor plumbers 281½ Sawyer See page 783
" Evening The Pleasant cor Market
" Oil Co of New York Robert E Doyle mgr Fish Island
" Ring Traveler Co Geo H Hedges mgr 6 Elm
Stanhope Ann widow b 31 Brock av
" Herbert J laborer b 31 Brock av
Standish Rose h 20 S Sixth
" Susan C widow Davis T b 38 Bay

BONNEY, FOLSTER & CO.,
The North End's Shopping Centre
Dry Goods and Men's Furnishings
945-947 Acushnet Ave., New Bedford, Mass.

Stanley Arthur B teacher High school rms 35 Eighth [land
" Charles A machinist b 131 Rock-
" Fred machinist h 327 County
" John B glass cutter h 131 Rockland [Whitman
" John H insurance solicitor h 218
" Martin K helper b 131 Rockland
" Ned A dentist 3 Pleasant h 80 State [Court
" Tobias A agent 73 William h 84
Stansfield Alfred operative b 10 Morton ct
" Eliza widow Paul h 10 Morton ct
" Harry doffer b 112 Mott
" Henry doffer b 113 Division
Stanton Ann widow Michael h 61 Spruce [Park
" Charity C widow Henry C h 350
" Edward laborer h 885 County
" Eugene engineer b 61 Spruce
" Frederick S music teacher 62 State h do
" James engineer b 61 Spruce
" James E Jr treas Acushnet Mill Corp and Hathaway Mfg Co h at Padanaram
" John laborer h 123 Hemlock
" John twister b 885 Counay
" John weaver h 141 Collette
" John E removed to Westport
" Joseph rem to Woonsocket R I
" Martin J repairman U St Ry Co h 885 County
Staples Charles E machinist h 64 Forest
" Clarissa S h 163 Maxfield
" Emma G Mrs h 17 Arch
" John W painter h 40 McGurk
" Mary F teacher Acushnet av school b 16 Fifth
" Thomas S foreman h 179 Collette
" Walter C motorman h 159 Hillman [Rounds
" Willard F clerk Butler Mill b 62
" Willard P removed from city
" William E letter carrier h 62 Rounds
Stapleton Michael h 255 County
Star Clothing Co (Isaac Margolis) 1262 Acushnet av
Stark John H operative b 290 Davis
" Mary A widow John h 290 Davis
Starkie Fred removed from city
" John electrician b 79 Clark

Starkie
" John William painter h 77 Mt Pleasant
" Thomas C clerk h 105 Hazard
" William weaver h 24 Howland Village [nell
Starr Frank M Jr roofer h 61 Grin-
Stavely Fannie mill hand b 76 Dean
Stead Robert hostler rms 23 Ash (S)
Stearns Robert W twister h 30 Dudley
Stebbins Pierre carpenter h 94 Nye
Steben Charles weaver b 168 Tinkham
" Edward laborer b 168 Tinkham
" Isadore mill hand h 910 S Water
" Joseph roofer h 168 Tinkham
" Nazaire roofer b 168 Tinkham
" Virgine widow Joseph h 168
Steckewich Charles J shoemaker 249 Cedar h 125 Willis
Stedman Edna Mrs dressmaker 197 Grinnell b do
Steele James E dyer h 379 Hillman
" John horse clipper h 279 Pleasant
" Percy laborer h 25 Bethel
" Percy twister b 234 Phillips av
Steere Robert E master mechanic Nashawena Mill [Belleville av
Stefanik Wojciech mill hand b 269
Steffin Albert designer P Corp h 162 Butler
Steiblin J weaver h 157 Hathaway
Steiger Albert pres 185 Union h at Holyoke
STEIGER DUDGEON CO dry goods 185-187 Union and 9 to19 Purchase See foot lines
" Ralph 185 Union h at Springfield
STEINERT M & SONS CO pianos and organs 109 William and 162 Boylston Boston See page 23
Steinhof Michael hairdresser 157 N Front h Washburn
Stenson Catharine and Harriet h 124 Hemlock [Winsor
" Thomas laborer N B W W h 24
Stepan Joseph carder h 87 N Front
Stepheniack Mike operative b 184 Cedar Grove
Stephens Henry A janitor Hosea M Knowlton school h 1195 Rockdale av

Painters Supplies Wall Papers Room Mouldings Ladders
M. P. B. Silva & Son BRUSHES
157 ACUSHNET AVENUE Both Phones NEW BEDFORD

Stephens
" Leroy A clerk b 1185 Rockdale av
" Percy overseer b 104 Bowditch
" Thomas operative h 104 Bowditch
" Winston dentist 12 S Sixth h do
Stephenson Alice bookkeeper b 58 Washington
" Annie Mrs h 58 Washington
" Daniel C second hand h 293 Brock av
" David spinner h 84 S Sixth
" Eliza widow Robert h 173 Arnold
" Elizabeth b 173 Arnold [tic
" Ella clerk 182 Union b 22 Atlan-
" Ella widow Thomas h 22 Atlantic
" Emma L clerk 253 Union b 173 Arnold
" Henry machinist h 118 David
" James M clerk b 173 Arnold
" Jesse loom fixer h 240 Tinkham
" John R twister b 68 Hall
" Joseph baker b 58 Washington
" Margaret S nurse rms 378 County rms 256 Union [ham
" Sarah C widow John h 240 Tink-
" Thomas clerk 168 S Water h 127 Summer [ington
" Thomas W spinner b 58 Wash-
" William bookkeeper b 6 Blackburn
" William laborer b 131 Whitman
" William B twister h 104 Rockland
" see Stevenson [Cedar Grove
Stepupalski Stephen barber b 165
Ster Optical Co (Thomas P Payne) opticians 224 Purchase [net av
Stergianos George cook 1136 Acush-
Sterling Alfred designer Dartmouth M Co h 11 Briggs
" Reuben W overseer Kilburn Mill h 219 Orchard
" Walter second hand h 13 Social
Stern Isador operative h 15 Howland
" William h 118 Acushnet av
Sterns Henry clerk 1065 Acushnet av bds 87 Tallman
" Samuel B died August 10 1910
Steroff Dimitri mill hand b 11 Nye
Stetson Charles F oiler h 740 Kempton [Ash (S) opposite Grove
" Edward M b Thomas M Stetson

Stetson
" Eliot D (Stetson & Stetson) lawyer 34 Masonic bldg and speciel justice Third District Court of Bristol h 81 Cottage [do
" Frank E physician 334 Union h
" Frederick D (Stetson & Stetson) lawyer 34 Masonic bldg h 42 Grove
" George R president N B Co-operative Bank and 125 Middle h 7 Anthony
" Helen L h 37 Campbell
" James A civil engineer 214 South Water b 4 Anthony
" John N cutter h 10 Margin
" Maud dressmaker 355 Cottage b do [at Mattapoisett
" Nellie S bookkeeper 6 Campbell b
" Thomas M (Stetson & Stetson) 34 Masonic bldg h Ash (S) opp Grove

---

OFFICES OF T M STETSON
STETSON & STETSON
Councellors at Law
34 Masonic Building
Pleasant Street, New Bedford
Telephone Connection
T M Stetson E D Stetson
Frederick D Stetson
Gerrett Geils Jr

Stetson & Stetson (Eliot D, Frederick D and T M Stetson and Gerrett Geils Jr) lawyers 34 Masonic bldg [b 280 Mill
Stevens Charles carpenter 161 Clinton
" Charles A C h 167 Mill
" Charles H N carpenter b 280 Mill
" Dennis L carpenter h 2 Norton ct
" Edward B cook h 28 Elm
" Edward B waiter Parker House h 11 Elm [263 Palmer
" Edwy E electrician 125 Middle h
" Florence Mrs shoe worker rms 42 Hill

Steiger-Dudgeon Co.
"The WOMAN'S Store."
Tel. Bell 82 & 83, Branches connecting all depts.
" " 160 For Office only. Auto. 1211

SUMPTIONS, ASSORTMENTS AT ALL TIMES OF DEPENDABLE DRY GOODS

Stevens
" Frank drill worker b 40 Russell
" Frank O foreman h 49 Rounds
" George (Stevens & Dukas) rms 20 Mill
" George rms 300 Acushnet av
" George teamster h 190 Acushnet avenue [h 5 Elm
" George A clerk 508 Acushnet av
" George E painter h 280 Mill
" George E Jr painter b 280 Middle
" George F h 11 Elm [h do
" Harry L physician 129 Purchase
" Henry h 129 Purchase [Briggs ct
" Henry F metal worker h 10
" Hiram W third hand b 42 Stowell
" Isaac machinist h 160 Crapo
" John H hostler h 11 Elm
" Mary A widow William H b 501 Acushnet avenue
" Michael h 74 Washington
" Ray drill worker b 40 Russell
" Sidney F helper b 190 Acushnet avenue [net av
" William E teamster h 501 Acush-
" William F cook h 29 S Second
" William O painter 24 N Water h 42 Stowell
" & Dukas (George Stevens and Christophe Dukas) restaurant 125 Union
Stevenson Harry laborer b 88 Cove
" Henry operative h 67 Ruth
" James A twister h 22 Peckham
" Richard weaver h 156 Reynolds
" Thomas glass cutter h 223 Acushnet avenue [net avenue
" Thomas J polisher bds 223 Acush-
" William A vulcanizer b 223 Acushnet avenue
" see Stephenson [h 241 Court
Steward Leon H clerk 251 Purchase
Stewardson William engineer b 554 North Front
Stewart Albert Culler b 21 Jouvett
" Charles clerk 96 Brock av h 152 David [burn
" Charles E painter h 21r Wash-
" George laborer bds 158 Crapo
" George A helper b 140 Florence
" James cabinet maker h 90 Clark
" James spinner h 21 Jouvett

Stewart
" John weaver h 19 Ashley [David
" Munroe L C, U S Army h 159
" Thomas egg tester Anthony Swift & Co h 152 David
Stiles Ardell Mrs h 136 Florence
" Curtis H bookkeeper Manomet Mill h 61 Rounds
" Gilbert mold maker h 212 Grinnell [b 212 Grinnell
" Walter G clerk Taber Mill Corp
Stiller Carl baker h 165 Hathaway
Stillman H Howard mgr 70 Purchase h at Fairhaven
Stilson Mary A widow Horace h 112 Fourth [eca
Stin Antonio laborer h rear 8 Sen-
Stinson John E chauffeur 18 Market h at Marion
Stirrett Chester S student b 24 James
" James h 104 Ash (N)
" Mary C Mrs h 24 James
Stitt John A (Babbitt Steam Specialty Co) h 162 North
" Maude S bookkeeper b 162 North
" William glass cutter b 162 North
Stockdale Benjamin h 89 Winsor
" William spinner bds 89 Winsor
Stokoe Charles W L salesman 36 Purchase h 450 Union [ington
" George A carpenter h 183 Wash-
" Mary J dressmaker 183 Washington h do
Stolle Alfred W designer h 69 Clifford [Kempton
Stone Albert P conductor bds 343
" Alonzo P teamster U St Ry Co h 121 Bates avenue
" Augustin operative h 92 Grinnell
" Bertha R teacher J H Clifford school bds 141 Bonney [do
" David carpenter 343 Kempton h
" Edward operative h 15 Willard
" Edward salesman h 220 Grinnell
" Ernest R salesman h 173 Campbell
" Felix carpenter h 589 S Water
" Francis H h 39 Arnold
" Francis H Jr student b 39 Arnold
" George laborer b 11 Howland Village
" George T shoemaker h 141 Bonney
" Henry weaver h 78 Penniman

PELEG H. SHERMAN 506 COUNTY ST.
FUNERAL DIRECTOR AND EMBALMER
OFFICE PHONES. Bell 690-13. Auto 1305.
RESIDENCE PHONES. Bell 690-12. Auto. 1306.

Stone
" John weaver 205 N Front
" Joseph operative h 58 Hazard
" Manuel operative h Cove road
" Mary E carder h 189 Hathaway
" Matilda widow Napoleon J h 11 Howland Village
" Mitchell stone cutter h Toby Lane
" Napoleon J mill hand b 11 Howland Village [do
" Nelson J hostler 52 Adams h 45
" Samuel jeweler 509 S Water h at Fall River [ney
" Thomas superintendent h 141 Bon-
" William laborer b 11 Howland Village [erson
" William H machinist h 189 Em-
" see Laroche
Stopford Ira h 10 McGurk
" Ira Jr machinist h 72 Division
" James h 36 Peckham
Storan Margaret h 13 Studley
Storominsky Rosie Mrs h 34 Penniman [Nash road
Stott Albert E mill hand bds 162
" Daniel h 244 Phillips avenue
" Delia widow mill hand h 84 Earle
" James weaver b 161 Brook
" John T loom fixer h 161 Brook
Stow Harry D police inspector h 77 Smith [b 77 Smith
" Lizzie M teacher Middle st school
Stowell Addie M cashier 70 Purchase bds 213 Middle
" Asa T shoe cutter h 596 Maxfield
" Benjamin F (B F Stowell & Co) bds 213 Middle
" Benjamin I h 596 Elm
" Bertram F bookkeeper Nashawena Mill h at Fairhaven
" B F & Co (Benjamin F Sowell) rubber stamps and stencils 76 William [avenue
" Charles A buffer h 814 Rockdale
" C Willard rubber stamp maker 76 William bds 213 Middle
" Daniel H machinist 235 N Water h 904 Rockdale avenue
" Flora E Mrs h 63 Oak
" Frederick A driver S F E 7 h 25 Ashland place [dale
" George R drill maker b 814 Rock-
" Harry C clerk b 213 Middle

Stowell
" Herbert B shipper h 641 Maxfield
" Jerome iron cleaner 229 N Water bds 63 Oak [Hillman
" Lester plumber 26 N Sixth b 417
" Lottie M glove cleaner bds 814 Rockdale avenue [Rockdale av
" Mary A widow Alexander T h 814
" Mercy Mrs h 455 Mill
" Richard P laborer h 990 Kempton
" Sidney H driver 55 Mechanics lane h 39 Newton
" Walter E painter h 11 Briggs ct
" William F engineer h 213 Middle
" ——— teamster rms 7 N Second
Strachocki John weaver h 87 Mosher
Strack Alex clerk 101 Clark b 223 N Front [Kempton
Strange Ruth clerk 36 Purchase b 194
" William L engineer Smith Bros brewery h 194 Kempton
Strasil Frank mill hand b 89 Hathaway [123 State
Stratton Caroline E bookkeeper b
" Charles S master mechanic Quissett Mill h 123 State
" Clara J nurse h 123 State
" Edward W assistant superintendent Bennett Mill h 440 Sawyer
" George h 16 Homer
" John P machinist h 314 Summer
" Lucy A widow Robert B, C S practitioner h 124 Maxfield
" Richard painter h 195 Crapo
" Robert B died March 31 1911
" Walter S engineer h 17 Richmond [Rivet
Straughn Matthew city laborer h 315
Straw F E engineer 68 Adams b Sherman House [Grove
Strazpek Konstanty F h 157 Cedar
Streeter Florus L pastor Allen St M E church h 347 County
Strella Benjamin operative rms 132 S Second [Merrimac
Stringer Charles freight checker h 56
Strittmatter Peter weaver h 1129 Purchase [field
Strojny Ignacz mill hand h 16 Grand-
" Welenty operative h 2 Fulton ct
Strome Alfred mariner h 140 State

COAL AND WOOD F. T. AKIN & COMPANY
HAY AND STRAW
WALNUT, COR. WATER, 84 PLEASANT ST., 25 WELD SQ.
129 COVE STREET WHF. FOOT OF COFFIN STREET

Strong Chester D foreman 748 Purchase h 32 Ashland [shall
" Libbie widow Hubert h 495 Cogge-
" Napoleon carpenter h 1085 County [Ashland
" Rhoda M widow Edward L b 32
Strongman John B treasurer Gosnold Mills Co h 2 Grove
Strony John weaver h 13 Fulton ct
Strowbridge William G painter rms 40 Liberty [429 Union
Struhs Eva B clerk 13 Pleasant b
Stuart Abraham fruit 478 S Water bds 340 First [Seventh
" Benjamin C E chauffeur h 35
" Josephine B supervisor of primary grades public schools h 34 S Sixth [sion
" Mary widow David h 126 Divi-
" Max junk h 340 First
Stubbs Adelbert C eyelet maker b 62 Mechanics lane [lane
" Emma R Mrs h 62 Mechanics
" Flora E widow John B b 33 Willis
" Fred clerk 339 Rivet b 317 do
" George D depot baggage master h 67 Merrimac
" John overseer h 40 Fair
" John B died May 6 1911
" Joseph carder b 317 Rivet
" Joseph E operative h 317 Rivet
Stucker John laborer h r 226 State
Studley Alfred G bookkeeper 81 Front h 80 Mill [dar
" Ephraim L shoemaker h 301 Ce-
" Frank A auto repairer 14 Ward h 95 Bonney
" Jethro S died Dec 6 1910 [Front
Stuempeck Frank weaver h 205½ N
Stuke Christian bottler h 350 Sawyer
Stupnitzky Hyman pedlar h 9 Cornell place
Sturgis Almon P h 18 Robeson
" George H clerk b 18 Robeson
" Leroy A clerk 100 Fifth h 2115 Acushnet av
Sturtevant Alice nurse b 392 Reed
" Angelina Mrs h 136 N Second
STURTEVANT BENJAMIN S (Sturtevant & Hook) 224 N Water and agent Ford automobiles 14 Ward h do See page 748 [ant
" Charles B machinist h 209 Pleas-

Sturtevant
" Charles G salesman 81 Front h at Padanaram [Morgan
" Clara B widow Arthur C h 83
" Clara S teacher b 392 Reed
" Dellphene E widow George A h 392 Reed
" Elmer laborer b Tarkiln Hill rd
" Elwood M milk 789 Belleville av h do
" Ernest G engineer b 99 Perry
" Grace F winder b 99 Perry
" Lottie F teacher Thos R Rodman school b 392 Reed
" Harold T bookkeeper First Nat Bank b 14 Ward
" Mary E h 218 Summer [av
" Samuel engineer h r 30 Howard
" Samuel L carpenter h 99 Perry
" Wayland L salesman 14 Ward b do
STURTEVANT WILLIAM F painter 70 High rms 72 do See page 25
" & Hook (B S Sturtevant and G E Hook) concrete blocks 224 N Water and pulp plaster 202 do [Belleville rd
Sucales John 580 N Front b 124
Suffern George electrician h 1005 County
" William J bartender 1449 Acushnet av h 70 Penniman [Grove
Suh Wgrieh operative h r 126 Cedar
Sulaman Samuel mill hand b 37 Phillips av
Sullavou Emanuel lawyer 37 Purchase rm 4 h 223 Park
Sullaway Abraham variety 939 S Water b do [Middle
Sullings Hannah H Mrs rms 181
Sullivan Agnes clerk 878 Purchase b 165 Ashland
" Agnes G teacher Thomas A Greene school b 378 Cedar
" Alice M teacher Abraham Lincoln school b 378 Cedar
" Ann widow Timothy b 90 Parker
" Anna C clerk registry of deeds b 378 Cedar [Cedar Grove
" Annie M widow Patrick H h 344
" Bridget widow Thomas h 63 Forest [Russell
" Carrie F widow John D h 62
" Catherine widow John h 200 Weld

Don't dream of what you are going to do! Go and do it.
Kinyon's Short-hand School
Odd Fellows Bldg., Cor. William and Pleasant Sts., New Bedford, Mass.

Sullivan
" Catherine D teacher b 129 Willis
" Catherine E widow John B h 529 Cottage
" Catherine T h 230 County
" Charles H undertaker 431 Purchase b 433 do
" Cornelius B mariner h 129 Willis
" Cornelius D mgr 343 Acushnet av bds do
" Cornelius F h 614 Purchase
" Cornelius J driver b 1098 Acushnet avenue [ty
" Cornelius J laborer h 886 Coun-
" Cornelius S clerk ft Willis b 129 do [12 Ash (S)
" Daniel F floorman 100 S Water h
" Daniel J died Feb 19 1911
" Daniel J jeweler 130 Union h 65 South Sixth
" Daniel J overseer Wamsutta h 666 Cottage
" Daniel J (estate) pianos and organs 228 Union
" Daniel J teas h 100 Hillman
" Daniel L painter 75 Weld b 56 Reynolds [son
" Daniel P second hand h 42 Robe-
" Daniel R mason h 267 Austin
" Dennis laborer h 62 Myrtle
" Dennis D laborer h 208 State
" Dennis F laborer b 208 State
" Dennis J mill hand h 388 Purchase [County
" Dennis L mgr 99 Front h 603
" Edward A operative b 129 Willis
" Edward J laborer h 56 Linden
" Edward M h 620 Cottage
" Edward M shoe worker and (Sullivan & Brand) 31 Ashland h 620 Cottage
" Elizabeth clerk b 165 Ashland
" Elizabeth widow Daniel J h 215 Maxfield
" Ellen widow James h 211 Weld
" Ellen widow John h 46 Robeson
" Ellen widow John h 345 Orchard (S)
" Etta Mrs h 229 N Second
" Eugene motorman b 781 Purchase

Sullivan
" Eugene H organist St Lawrence church and music teacher 44 Chestnut h do [Chestnut
" Eugene H baggage master h 213
" Eugene H Jr student b 44 Chestnut
" Eugene J conductor h 278 Austin
" Eugene P driver b 287 Arnold
" Florence laborer b 37 Washburn
" Frances A b 251 Hawthorn
" Frances C dressmaker 138 Bedford h do [145 State
" Frances M clerk 160 Purchase b
" Francis B foreman J B Sullivan & Co b 529 Cottage
" Frank mill hand b 56 Linden
" Frank S clerk b 328 Cedar
" Gertrude L teacher Clark street school b 94 Fourth [Purchase
" Hannah widow Jeremiah D h 433
" James b 251 Hawthorn
" James bookkeeper rms 84 Court
" James bricklayer h 200 Weld
" James laborer b 211 Weld
" James laborer b 232 N Second
" James weaver b 257 Cedar Grove
" James A, U S immigrant insepctor Custom House h 479 Cottage
" James D laborer b 287 Arnold
" James F bookkeeper Morris & Co bds 84 Fourth [Court
" James F clerk 40 Purchase b 84
" James F operative b 88 Covell
" James F physician 185 Middle h do
" James H laborer b 44 Stowell
" James H police station 2 h 8 Clay
" James M druggist h 508 Cottage
" Jeremiah drug clerk b 46 Robeson
" Jeremiah laborer b 20 Weld
" Jeremiah Jr teamster h 601 Acushnet avenue [431 Purchase
" Jeremiah D (estate) undertaker
" Jeremiah E died August 18 1910
" Jeremiah F undertaker 594 Purchase h 678 Cottage
" Jeremiah T clerk b 222 State
" Joanna inspector b 100 Clark

HASKELL BROS. DEALERS IN
. ' . ICE . ' .
400 COURT STREET TELEPHONE CONNECTION NEW BEDFORD, MASS.

Sullivan
" Johannah H widow Timothy h 37 Washburn [Hawthorn
" John agent Taber Mill h 251
" John fireman h 296 Cedar Grove
" John laborer b 837 First
" John removed from city [State
" John Jr wraper tender bds 222
" John B & Son (Mark E) stone quarry Hathaway rd n Shawmut avenue
" John C laborer b 211 Weld
" John E clerk rms 137 Kempton
" John E fixer h 10 Abbott
" John E (367 Sawyer) died Sept 16 1910 [Purchase h 413 do
" John E second hand goods 411
" John F clerk b 191 N Second
" John H laborer b 433 Pleasant
" John J bookkeeper J B Sullivan & Son bds 165 Ashland
" John J clerk b 378 Cedar [son
" John J clerk 58 Linden b 46 Robe-
" John J hostler b 601 Acushnet av
" John J laborer h 368 Allen
" John J, R R section foreman h 222 State
" John J teamster h 191 N Second
" John L laborer b 83 Topham
" John L laborer N B W W h 44 Stowell
" John L operative h 56 Linden
" John L stoker h 165 Ashland
" John N salesman 22 Pleasant bds 129 Willis
" John T operative b 222 State
" Joseph barber b 345 Orchard (S)
" Joseph A blacksmith b 8 Clark
" Joseph A (J A Sullivan & Co) b 257 Cedar Grove
" Joseph F clerk 773 Kempton bds 603 County [145 State
" Joseph H foreman street dept h
" Julia E h 230 County
" J A & Co (Joseph A and Stephen H) liquors 1130 Acushnet av [contractors 560 Cottage
" J B & Son (Mark E Sullivan)
" Kate operative h 116 Middle
" Katherine A clerk 40 Purchase b 544 do [st school b 129 Willis
" Kathryn D teacher Cedar Grove

Sullivan
" Lawrence D plumber h 478 Coggeshall
" Lydia widow Peter h 10 Winsor
" Margaret h 433 Pleasant
" Margaret Mrs h 201 Eugenia
" Margaret widow Thomas b 103 Hemlock [560 Cottage
" Mark E (J B Sullivan & Son) h
SULLIVAN MARTIN H contractor and builder 168 N Second h 78 North See page 760
" Mary bookkeeper 1064 Acushnet av h 24 Myrtle
" Mary widow b 837 First [County
" Mary widow Cornelius h 863
" Mary A b 388 Purchase
" Mary A bookkeeper 1056 Acushnet avenue b 62 Myrtle [do
" Mary A clerk 65 Purchase b 614
" Mary A widow John E h 74 Belleville rd [rm 305 h 138 Bedford
" Mary B bookkeeper 97 William
" Mary E widow bds 298 Cedar
" Mary M teacher I W Benjamin school b 78 North
" Mary M widow John G boarding 257 Cedar Grove [Orchard (S)
" Matthew police Station 2 b 345
" Michael city employee b 48 High
" Michael laborer b 48 High
" Michael overseer Hathaway Mfg Co h 837 First
" Michael C h 56 Reynolds [er
" Michael F steam fitter h 57 Park-
" Michael H clerk h 17 Trinity
" Michael J steam fitter h 318 Court
" Michael J (Sullivan & Crocker) 128 Union rms 79 School
" Minnie clerk 251 Summer b 213 Chestnut [Fairhaven
" Nonie G clerk 228 Union h at
" Patrick laborer b 53 Prospect
" Patrick laborer b 200 Weld
" Patrick operative h 88 Covell
" Patrick F bricklayer h 209 James
" Patrick H died January 22 1911
" Patrick H died Feb 7 1911
" Patrick H engineer city yard
" Patrick H fireman h 394 Cedar
" Patrick H operative b r 56 Linden
" Patrick J h 785 County
" Patrick J mason h 218 State

J. F. CROSSLEY 223 MILL STREET COR. EMERSON PHONE
STEAM and HOT WATER HEATING
GAS FITTING and FIXTURES

Sullivan
" Patrick X clerk 124 Union h 290 Acushnet avenue [Cedar
" Peter F clerk 105 William h 328
" Philip watchman b 4 N Oak
" Richard removed from city
" Richard J mason b 56 Reynolds
" Robert J clerk 739 Purchase h 11 Reynolds
" Roger laborer b 388 Purchase
" Sarah widow Patrick b 89 Austin
" Stephen H (J A Sullivan & Co) b 257 Cedar Grove
" Thomas conductor Electric Express h 345 Orchard (S)
" Thomas weaver h 206 Hathaway
" Thomas A bookkeeper D Duff & Son h 244 Pleasant
" Thomas F driver b 345 S Orchard
" Timothy died Aug 25 1910
" Timothy laborer N B W W h 2 Washington avenue [Cedar
" Timothy police station 4 h 378
" Timothy J bar tender h 27 Cedar
" Timothy J laborer h 83 Linden
" Timothy J mill hand b 88 Covell
" Timothy J third hand b 56 Linden
" Walter driver h 162 State
" William bottler b 430 Pleasant
" William F electrician b 57 Parker
" William H clerk b 191 N Second
" William H clerk b 430 Pleasant
" William H yard overseer Acushnet Mill Corp h 91 Willard
" William M foreman Smith Brothers h 5 Jean
" & Brand (Edward Sullivan William H Brand) variety 31 Ashland [bookbinders 128 Union
" & Croker (Michael J Sullivan)
" & Desmond props Savoy Hotel 343 Acushnet avenue
" see O'Sullivan
Sulu Aslan mill hand b 48 Davis
Sulvay Joseph whitener h end Summer st ct [96 Cove
Summer Margaret widow James h
• Summers Mary widow Patrick b 146 State
" Thomas J buffer h 146 State
Sumner Charles hostler rms 236 Kempton
" Club Cedar corner Kempton

Sumner
" Elizabeth D Mrs clerk 40 Purchase b 60 Fourth
" George spinner b 133 Bullard
" James died January 7 1911
" Samuel second hand h 1642 Acushnet avenue
" Thomas h 133 Bullard
" Thomas B spinner b 133 Bullard
" Wilfred spinner b 133 Bullard
Sumpter Felix L coal 185 Summer h do
" George laborer h 422 Purchase
" Rose A milliner 185 Summer b do
Sunderland Abraham removed to Fairhaven
" John removed to Fairhaven
" John E clerk 163 Union bds 2 Cove road
" John W machinist h 246 Nash rd
Sundin Carl A police Station 2 h 283 Court [51 Emerson (S)
" Henry steam fitter 5 Atlantic bds
" Hjalmer clerk 112 Union b 51 Emerson (S) [(S)
" Johan E fireman h 51 Emerson
" John A died Jan 1 1911
Supcezk Frank speeder tender h 2 Hampton court [Hicks
Superenack Salabasti operative h 69
Supreanna Manuel mill hand h 418 First
Suprenant Minnie ticket seller 958 Acushnet av b 334 Bowditch
Supry Arthur spinner h 124 Hathaway
Surette Alex janitor b 45 Hicks
" Edward carder b 644 Purchase
" Lena widow h 45 Hicks
Surprenant Alfred operative h 3 Blackburn [h 135 Whitman
" Alphea shoe repairer 538 N Front
" Amedee second hand h 384 North Front
" Antonio spinner b 344 N Front
" Arthur asst supt 120 Purchase rm 403 h 200 Collette
" Arthur hairdresser 116 Union h 312 Davis
" Arthur removed from city
" Dominic lunch 960 Acushnet av h 95 Kenyon
" Emeline baker h 1159 Purchase

CHARLES A. CROSHERE **CARRIAGE AND AUTO**
38 FOURTH ST. Bell Phone 1964-23 **PAINTING**

Surprenant
" Germaine milliner 1024 Acushnet av b 236 Bowditch
" John spinner h 37 Bullard
" John B clerk 960 Acushnet av h 336 Bowditch [Front
" Marcel second hand h 344 North
" Nelson J salesman 788 Purchase h 208 Cedar Grove [ditch
" Odile widow Gilbert b 334 Bow-
" Philias carpenter h 159 Frederick
" Zeph laborer h 12 Covell
Surprise Clothing Co (H Bloomindale) 156 Purchase
Susini Octave (Ailery & Susini) 78 William and hairdresser 110 do and 131 Purchase h 149 Middle [len
Sutcliffe Adam operative h 394 Al-
" Albert twister h 179 Collette
" Arthur comber h 93 Hemlock
" Benjamin spinner h 296 Davis
" Elizabeth Mrs mill hand bds 392 Belleville avenue
" Fred mule spinner h 13 Harmony
" Horace removed from city
" John carpenter 1 Norton ct
" Montague h 27 Bullard
" William weaver b 186 Dean
Sutherland Leslie H principal Jireh Swift school h 675 Cottage
" Waldo A mgr 43 Purchase h 236 Pleasant
" William painter b 126 Holly
Sutter James designer h 15 Warren
Sutton Abram P clerk h 195 Acushnet av [net av
" Herbert W clerk b 195 Acush-
" William J laborer h 1316 Rockdale avenue [Centre
Svendsen Edward M laborer h 21
Swain Asias R h 149 Elm [Seventh
" Delphina D widow Lloyd h 36
" Frank laborer h 92 Thompson
" Free School of Design 391 County
" George J stock broker 45 Purchase rm 4 and 967 Acushnet av h 55 Fifth
" Henry S carpenter h 69 Maple
" Lloyd S died Nov 13 1910
" Louisa widow Frank h 92 Thomp-
" Margaret widow William rms 53 son [Walnut

Swain
" Mary P h 382 County
" Sarah h 43 Ash (S)
" Thomas W laborer h 25 Stowell
" Walter stock broker b 55 Fifth
" Walter E telephone operator 970 Acushnet av b 55 Fifth
Swainbank James A weaver bds 158 Hathaway [way
Swales George weaver h 189 Hatha-
Swallow James weaver h 407 Bolton
" Joshua conductor b 1498 Acushnet avenue [net av
" Robert operative h 1498 Acush-
" Samuel mill hand h 88 Eugenia
Swan Allen W music teacher 97 William rm 308 rms 29 Buttonwood [Fourth
" Caroline B widow Edwin h 110
" Edith A dressmaker 303 Middle b do [Bowditch
" Harry E advt mgr Times h 423
" Rodolphus A reporter Mercury b 110 Fourth [303 Middle
" Walter A gilder 362 Purchase h
" William mill hand h 84 Willis
" William spinner h 150 David
Swanberg M Louise teacher Rockdale school b 1372 Rockdale av
Swansey George E glass cutter h 109 Fifth [school rms 94 Fourth
" Katharine J teacher Fifth st
Swanton John D shoemaker h 568 County
" William H 105 Hillman
Swarts Joseph laborer h 265 S Front
Swasey Antone removed from city
" Charles A G commission merchant N Y h 58 Maple
" Marion H principal Sylvia Ann Howland school b 58 Maple
" Matthew J h 214 North
" Noami W widow George M h 29 Rockland
" see Swezey [County b do
Sweeney Alice Maud dressmaker 110
" Arthur F b 110 County
" Daniel J dentist 1603 Acushnet av h do [County
" Daniel P police station 5 h 980
" Dennis J operative b 68 Hatch
" Ellen C teacher Cedar Grove st school h at S Dartmouth

J. G. NICHOLSON
LUMBER, SASH, DOORS and BLINDS
BOWDITCH STREET, NEW BEDFORD, MASS.

Sweeney
" Ellen G teacher J H Clifford school b 129 Acushnet av
" George teamster b 195 N Second
" George A watchman H C h 14 Spruce
" James roofer b 137 Acushnet av
" Johanna teacher H A Kempton school b at Dartmouth
" John operative b 68 Hatch [rd
" John watchman h 631 Hathaway
" John J (Thompson & Sweeney) 101 N Second h at Fairhaven
" Margaret Mrs h 787 S Water
" Margaret C stenographer 201 Merchants Nat Bank bldg b 980 County
" Maria Mrs h 141 Dartmouth
" Michael carpenter b 137 Acushnet av [net av
" Michael operative b 1603 Acush-
" Michael D overseer Beacon Mfg Co h 1603 Acushnet av
" Miles laborer P & R C & I Co h 129 Acushnet av
" Patrick supt 8 Hazards lane h at S Dartmouth [ty
" Sophia T housekeeper 980 Coun-
" Thomas laborer b 837 First
" William C loom fixer h 110 County [Acushnet av h 232 Collette
" William J hairdresser 1608
" see McSweeney
Sweet Carrie C Mrs mgr 32 Masonic bldg b 80 Bedford
" Emily J died March 11 1911
" George A clerk h 599 Cottage
" Julien A roll coverer h 134 State
" Lewis B second hand b 103 Perry
" May H P stenographer 54 Pleasant h at S Dartmouth
" Melvina Mrs h 13 Madison
" Nannie P widow Job h 287 Kempton
" O Preston removed from city
" Samuel N clerk h 15 Ocean
" Sarah widow William h 3 Mt Pleasant lane [lane
" Thomas lather b 3 Mt Pleasant
" William teamster 10 Spring b 13 Madison [Phillips av
Sweetzer Truman H carpenter h 11
Swender Frank operative h 210 Cedar Grove
Swenson James P paint grinder 14 Wall h 129 Sycamore
" John L motorman h 126 Shawmut av [Clay
" Mary A clerk 61 William b 7
Swetland Forrest F millwright h 4½ Jenney [Mill rms 124 Mill
Swett Warren L clerk Nashawena
Swezey Nancy M widow Stephen b 154 North
Swift Albert H salesman h 91 State
" Alice V Mrs dressmaker 34 Ash (S) h do [Campbell
" Anderson H carriage maker h 98
" A Clinton clerk A M Carp h 10 Maple [Hillman
" Arthur D letter carrier h 76
" Avis H widow Andrew b 38 Willis [Davis
" Bartholomew J operative b 157
" Benjamin h engineer h 204 Arnold [Walnut
" Betsy J widow Robert b 55
" Caroline clerk b 65 S Sixth
" Charles P chauffeur 98 Pleasant b 35 Cedar [ilton b 402 Cedar
" Charles R cotton broker 17 Ham-
" Clarence B died April 6 1911
" Clifford R clerk b 96 South
" Clifford S clerk 28 Union bds 65 South Sixth
" Edith teacher B b 65 S Sixth
" Edward B h 38 Willis
" Elizabeth A Mrs h 131 Sycamore
" Elizabeth P (M C Swift & Son) h 278 Union
" Elsie h 199 Orchard
" Elizabeth h 56 Fifth
" Elizabeth H rms 24 S Sixth
" Elizabeth S widow Ezra J h 18 Campbell [h 630 County
" E Stanley clerk 1 Municipal bldg
" Francis H b 199 Pleasant
" Frank laborer h 185 Mill
" Frank H collector h 35 Cedar
" Frank W H advertising agent h 492 Kempton [Locust
" George A clerk 103 William h 51
" George D Jr waiter 224½ Union h 3 Lincoln
" Helen Mrs h 72 Willis
" Henry student b 378 County
" Herbert A tailor h 245 Union

Steiger-Dudgeon Co.
"The WOMAN'S Store."
Tel. Bell 82 & 83, Branches connecting all depts.
" " 160 For Office only. Auto. 1211

SUMPTIONS,
ASSORTMENTS
AT ALL TIMES
OF DEPENDABLE
DRY GOODS

Swift
" Horace W salesman 72 Union h 65 S Sixth [26 Seventh
" Humphrey H Jr clerk 100 Fifth b
" Isabel L teacher Thomas R Rodman school b 76 Hillman
" Jireh Jr cotton agent 97 William rm 306 h 29 Clinton
" Josephine bookkeeper 61 William bds at Fairhaven [Foster
" Josephine F widow Edward h 42
" Lillian M Mrs clerk 7 Purchase h 492 Kempton [do
" Martin shoemaker 206 Division h
" Merton W bookkeeper 100 William h at S Dartmouth
" M C & Son (Elizabeth P Swift) clothing and tailors 157 Union
" Obed N (Gatenby & Swift) 33 N Water h 137 Chestnut
" Orville V musician h 34 Ash (S)
" Ralph K shoe cutter b 202 Kempton
" Reuben E cashier P O h 56 Fifth
" Rusha W nurse h 7 Crapo
" Sarah L h 7 Crapo [North
" Susan C widow Leander H h 75
" Thatcher S stable 118 Grinnell h 118 S Sixth [rms 35 Eighth
" Thornton S paymaster Soule Mill
" Walter C city laborer h 4 Shawmut avenue
" Waymon B salesman Anthony Swift & Co h 413 Purchase
" William J died March 11 1911
" William N physician 378 County h do [Butler
Swigney Ludger carpenter bds 45
Swindle James H steam fitter h 447 Coggeshall [Richmond
Swindlehurst John operative h 167
" William operative h 271 Weld
Swirad Maggie operative h 205½ N Front
Swire Ernest E weaver h 59 Howland
" Isabella widow Hezekiah b 59 Howard [ct
Swistak Joseph carder h 18 Fulton
Swithinbank Edwin machinist h 84 Rodney [Sixth
Swords Thomas F lodgings 36 North
Sycko Victor operative b 27 Hicks
Sykes Benjamin mason 17 Highland h do
" Charles twister h 67 Roosevelt
" Clarence W B clerk P O h 199 Cedar
" George mason b 19 Collins
" George twister h 56 Ashley
" George T copper worker h 379 Coggshall
" Gledhill second hand h 183 David
" Herbert operative b 14 Harmony
" John mason b 17 Highland
" John mason h 157 Hathaway
" John (Sykes & Sons) h 19 Collins
" John & Sons (John Sykes) masons 19 Collins
" Joseph mill hand b 19 Collins
" Joseph operative h 14 Harmony
" Leonard driver b 17 Highland
" Lucy A widow bds 199 Cedar
" Thomas operative b 64 Ruth
" William engineer h 14 Harmony
" William mason b 19 Collins
" William spinner bds 183 David
" William H laborer h 39 Bowditch
Sylva Antoni fitter h 74 Liberty
Sylvaia John laborer h 100 Potomska
" Manuel h 235 Rivet
Sylvan Grove Stable (F J Braley) Acushnet av beyond Braley rd
Sylvare John electrician h 10 Salisbury
Sylvaria Benjamin G painter 24 N Water h 480 Acushnet avenue
" Edmund pedlar b 864 County
" Joseph h 156 Acushnet avenue
" Joseph Mrs h 288 Fourth
Sylvester Adolph third hand h 154 Eugenia
" Alpheus E removed to Taunton
" Louis h 109 Collette
" Rebecca widow David b 132 Willis [169 Emerson (N)
" Robert R restaurant 83 Union h
" Thomas laborer b 109 Collette
" see Silvester
Sylvia Adolph weaver b 21 Margin
" Aldina widow Joseph R h 132 Thompson
" Alex P dentist 193 Fourth h do
" Alfred J clerk U St Ry Co b 122 Fair

PELEG H. SHERMAN 506 COUNTY ST.
FUNERAL DIRECTOR AND EMBALMER
OFFICE PHONES. Bell 690-13. Auto. 1305.
RESIDENCE PHONES. Bell 690-12. Auto 1306.

Sylvia
" Alton driver 108 Grape h at Dartmouth [ter
" Amador machinist h 535 S Wa-
" Anthony L coat maker 89 Howland h 38 Sherman
" Antone carpenter h 73 Wash
" Antone carpenter h 164 Rockland
" Antone cooper 350 S Second
" Antone laborer h 411 First
" Antone laborer b 24 County
" Antone painter b 122 Fair
" Antone police h 102 Newton [do
" Antone restaurant 52 Howland h
" Antone B carpenter h 89 Briggs
" Antone D city teamster h 73 Bates av [Mill h 80 Earle
" Antone L merchant 37 Purchase rm 7 and (T C Allen & Co) City Pier No 2 h 89 S Sixth
" Antone L operative h 411 First
" Antone L yard master Manomet Mill h 80 Earle [Front
" Antone M mill hand h 286 S
" Antone M painter h 76 Liberty
" Antonio car cleaner U St Ry Co h 7 South
" Antonio A h 279 County
" Antonio A stable 388 S Second and (Rogers & Sylvia) 100 Potomska h 50 Dartmouth
" Antonio S laborer h 12 Dartmouth
" Archie glass blower b 13 Rivet
" Bella K widow Antonio K dressmaker 55 Katharine h do
" Bros (George Sylvia and Joseph A Andre) grocers 122 Dartmouth [First
" Candido C rope maker h 502
" Caroline h 161 S Second
" Charles L salesman 70 Union h 88 Chancery [110 South
" Charles L traveling salesman b
" Clarence C salesman Anthony Swift & Co b 110 South
" Constantine freight handler b 56 First
" Constantine A mason h 248 Field
" Constantine M grocer 277 Kempton h 178 Chancery
" Constantine M Jr shipping clerk 170 Purchase h 246 Tremont

Sylvia
" Edward C helper b 300 Allen
" Ellen F widow Clarence h 300 Allen
" Emanuel V h 110 South
" Enos mill hand h 35 Prospect
" E F driver 14 N Sixth
" Florence fitter 40 Purchase b 36 Acushnet av [Borden
" Florence B stenographer b 25
" Frank laborer h 103 Dunbar
" Frank mill hand h 45 Babbitt
" Frank mill hand h 71 Nash rd
" Frank mill hand h 248 Acushnet avenue
" Frank operative h 8 weaver
" Frank paver h 115 Dunbar
" Frank E clerk 448 S Water b 7 Waverly
" Frank E laborer 350 S Second h 7 Waverly [h 199 Fourth
" Frank F hairdresser 157 County
" Frank F hairdresser 191 Court rms 85 Fourth
" Frank L salesman b 859 S Water
" Frank W police inspector h 25 Borden
" George clerk b 178 Chancery
" George (Sylvia Bros) b 111 Larch
" George D clerk 57 N Second b 167 County [at Fairhaven
" George E salesman 36 Purchase h
" George F clerk 448 S Water h Rivet [James
" George G (Sylvia & Brown) b 90
" George H salesman h 100 Bedford
" George P pressman 350 S Second b 167 County [cery
" Georgiana operative h 213 Chan-
" Isabella widow Joseph M h 43 Babbitt [h at Fairhaven
" Isabelle L stenographer 42 Front
" Jacinth mill hand h 27 Swift
" James cook h 8 Cleveland
" James M tea and coffee h 141 Dartmouth
" Joaquim laborer h 19 Bourne
" Joaquim laborer h 79 Crapo
" Joaquim R clerk 173 Rockland b 79 Hemlock
" John h 120 Grinnell
" John b 25 Babbitt

PAINTERS' SUPPLIES
Walnut, Cor. Water, 84 Pleasant St. 25 WELD SQ., 129 COVE ST.
F. T. AKIN & COMPANY

Sylvia
" John clerk 77 Grinnell h 92 Acushnet av [Larch
" John clerk 122 Dartmouth b 111
" John comb maker b r 203 Blackmer [do
" John flour 199 Acushnet av b 67
" John laborer h 71 Mosher
" John mill hand h 122 Sixth
" John operative h 8 Grandfield
" John operative h 55 Hemlock
" John operative h 81 Howland
" John operative bds 14½ Cannon
" John shoemaker h 397 S Second
" John tack maker h 145 Bonney
" John watchman Acushnet Mill Corp h 586 S Water
" John A electrician b 193 Division
" John A glass blower h 13 Rivet
" John A third hand b 28 Viall
" John B farmer Almshouse b do
" John B insurance agent 120 Purchase rm 403 b 255 Allen [way
" John B mill hand h 157 Hatha-
" John E liquors 71 Howland h 209 County
" John F laborer h 100 Hall
" John F weaver h 4 Spooner
" John G weaver h 363 Dartmouth
" John J farmer Almshouse h 167 County
" John J salesman h r 18 Hall
" John L prov 262 Purchase h 127 Fair
" John M mill hand b 86 Nash rd
" John P h 249 Allen
" John P operative b 95 N Second
" John P shoemaker h 368 S Second
" John R teamster h 146 Armour
" Jose F prop Idle Hour Theatre h 15 Griffin
" Joseph driver 12 School
" Joseph glass blower b 13 Rivet
" Joseph laborer h 10 Howland
" Joseph laborer h 16 Jenney
" Joseph laborer h 24 Dartmouth
" Joseph laborer 450 S Second
" Joseph mill hand h 715 S Water
" Joseph mill hand b 525 N Front
" Joseph operative h 5½ Harrison
" Joseph weaver h 98 Thompson
" Joseph weaver bds 122 Fair

Sylvia
" Joseph A clerk 604 S Water b 329 S Front
" Joseph A teamster h 75 Cedar
" Joseph C grinder h 271 Park
" Joseph de G laborer h 90 James
" Joseph E shoemaker h 349 Belleville av [house
" Joseph E teamster h 42 Stack-
" Joseph F mill hand h 100 Hall
" Joseph F prop Idle Hour Theatre 62 Acushnet av h 15 Griffin
" Joseph G baker 293 Brock av
" Joseph M second hand h 16 Columbia
" Joseph P actor h 39 Norton ct
" Joseph P mason h 39 Norton ct
" Joseph P mill hand b 46 Howland Village
" Julius laborer h 162 S Second
" Julius mgr b 82 Thompson
" Julius C blacksmith 108 Dartmouth h 5 Clay [mouth b do
" Katharine dressmaker 25 Dart-
" Laura bookkeeper 211 Union b 208 Rockland [South
" Laura T clerk 182 Union b 110
" Lillian M stenographer 386 Acushnet av b 110 South
" Louisa widow Joseph B h r 203 Blackmer
" Lysander mariner h 78 Middle
" Lysander operative b 9 North
" Manuel baker Almshouse h 124 County
" Manuel barber rms 54 Fourth
" Manuel carpenter h 303 S Front
" Manuel drill worker h 284 Fourth [do
" Manuel fish 211 Coggeshall h 314
" Manuel furniture mover 94½ Dartmouth h do
" Manuel laborer h 14 Jenney
" Manuel laborer h 18 Griffin
" Manuel laborer h 69 Howland
" Manuel mill hand h 465 Rivet
" Manuel operative h 19 Peckham
" Manuel operative h 77 Howland
" Manuel twister b 78 Middle
" Manuel weaver b 109 Davis
" Manuel A carriage painting 112 Pleasant rms 149 Middle [do
" Manuel B florist 70 Dartmouth h
" Manuel B laborer h 346 Cedar Grove

Bookkeeping, Shorthand, Typewriting, Penmanship, etc. Taught thoroughly at
Kinyon's Commercial School
Odd Fellows Bldg., Cor. William and Pleasant Sts., New Bedford, Mass.

Sylvia
" Manuel C teamster h 259 Acushnet av
" Manuel E boat builder foot Potomska h 62 Independence
" Manuel E machine operative 269 Sawyer h 88 Acushnet av
" Manuel E photographer h 79 Crapo
" Manuel E twister b 7 Waverly
" Manuel F driver h 73 Mt Pleasant
" Manuel F laborer h 418 S Second
" Manuel J operative h 7 Stanton
" Manuel J paper maker b 25 Dartmouth
" Manuel J shoemaker h 4 Warwick [h 82 Crapo
" Manuel J variety 428 S Water
" Manuel L glass cutter h 133 Bonney
" Manuel L hardware 781 S Water 1147 Acushnet av h at Dartmouth [Margin
" Manuel M stable 49 Delano h 24
" Manuel P doffer b 39 Morton ct
" Manuel P iceman b 195 Durfee
" Manuel P operative h 48 Howland Village [land Village
" Manuel P Jr mill hand b 46 How-
" Manuel R fish 43 Howland h 69 do
" Manuel S drill worker h 43 Hemlock [mouth
" Manuel T drill worker h 88 Dart-
" Manuel V physician 34 Wing h do
" Marie L nurse 194 Purchase b do
" Mary h 47 Hemlock
" Mary Mrs h 25 Babbitt
" Mary Mrs h 25 Howland
" Mary Mrs h 122 S Sixth
" Mary widow Joseph L b 49 Short
" Mary C teacher Harrington school b 223 Brownell
" Mary E clerk 41 Purchase b 123 Rockland [mouth h do
" Mary E dressmaker 25 Dart-
" Mary E widow Manuel h 25 Dartmouth
" Mary G Mrs h 122 Fair
" Mary G Mrs h Sylvias ct [gin
" Mary G widow Frank J h 21 Mar-

Sylvia
" Mary L widow Frank A h 169 County [Rockland
" Mary L widow Lawrence h 194
" Michael L h 106 Acushnet av
" Philomena Mrs h 47 Hemlock [do
" Ralph R real estate 111 County b
" Richard M b 4 Warwick
" Rosa Mrs h 267 S Second
" Samuel J paper worker h 153 Acushnet av
" Theodore J carpenter h 15 Clay
" Thomas A carpenter h 168 Fourth
" Thomas A constable h 125 N Second
" Thomas J h 45 Thompson
" Thomas J h 51 Thompson
" Walter clerk b 110 South
" William h 97½ Fourth
" William F motorman Elec Exp h 402 Purchase [son
" William K salesman h 98 Thomp-
" William T glass cutter h 208 Rockland
" & Brown (George G Sylvia and Daniel W Brown) fruit 25 Purchase
" see Silva, Silvia and Silver
Symes Joseph W third hand h 53 Collette
Symkowicz Thomas baker b 11 Nye
Symonds Lewis L salesman 67 William h 50 Summer
Symons Frederick R glass cntter h 480 Acushnet av
Sypek Albert weaver h 30 McGurk
" Stanislaus weaver h 12 McGurk
Szeliga Frank A carder h 17 Holly
Szczepan Stanislow mill hand h 269 Belleville av
Szezur Adam operative h 10 Fulton ct
Szubargo Frank weaver h 648 First.
" Henry removed from city
Szundler John weaver h 648 First
Szymanski Frank grocer 436 S Front h do [burn
" John agent 73 William h Wash-

Tabbas Joseph (National Theatre) 269 Sawyer h 163 Grinnell
Tabele Louise M clerk 160 Purchase b 394 Cedar [Cedar
" William H city teamster h 394

Bread, Cake, Pastry
RICHMOND & COMPANY 255-257 UNION STREET
Bell 993 Automatic 1022

Taber Abbie F widow William G h 543 County
" Abraham teamster b 309 Kempton
" Abraham Mrs h 21 Lincoln
" Adline widow Richmond M h 185 Cedar [h 221 Pleasant
" Albert M Jr salesman 157 Union
" Alexander D variety 187 Acushnet av h at Dartmouth
" Alice elec needle specialist h 144 Summer [mut av
" Arthur F conductor h 47 Shaw-
" Arthur K salesman 71 William h 101 Hillman [42 Nash (N)
" Arthur W hostler 304 Kempton h
" Benjamin J insurance b 5 Walnut
" Bessie L widow Albert M rms 18 Seventh
" Charles b 409 Elm (W)
" Charles G blacksmith 18 S Water h 137 Campbell [b 375 do
" Charles H F clerk 418 Kempton
" Charles M h 39 Lincoln
" Chester H meterman 125 Middle h at Fairhaven [1005 County
" Clara bookkeeper 240 Union b
" Confectionery Co wholesale confectionery 9 N Second [av
" Cora bookkeeper b 249 Acushnet
" Cyrus E h 119 Sycamore
" Daniel O drill maker h 65 Forest
" Edgar F asst treas Holmes Mfg Co b 42 Campbell
" Edith M B teacher H A Kempton school h 82 Walden
" Edmund h 84 Ash (S)
" Edward C b 77 Morgan
" Edward H driver 97 Front h 469 Acushnet av
" Edward S Mrs h 5 Anthony
" Eliza telephone operator 57 N Second b 126 Fair
" Elizabeth R C died Jan 13 1911
" Elliot C cashier 17 Pleasant h 578 Union [Morgan
" Ellis chauffeur 428 County h 77
" Emma Mrs clerk 139 Union b 517 Kempton [nell
" Francis T operative h 178 Grin-
" Frank G (Wright & Taber) 131 Acushnet av h 5 weaver
" Frank R clerk Adams Ex Co Depot h 233 Maxfield

Taber
" Fred C teamster h 94 Middle
" Frederick pres N B S D & T Co and pres Taber Mill also treas N B Storage Warehouse Co h 78 Hawthorn
" Frederick H (Cook, Brownell & Taber) 1 Masonic bldg h 126 Cottage
" George h 15 Franklin
" George A carpenter b 4½ Jenney
" George C machinist U St Ry Co b 20 Shawmut av [ton
" George F tool maker h 209 Kemp-
" George L overseer Wamsutta Mill h 33 Locust [h 15 Franklin
" George L troubleman 57 N Second
" George S buffer b 13 Madison
" George S provisions and fish 17-21 N Sixth b 21 S Sixth
" George W (O R Taber & Son) h 223 Chancery
" Gifford driver rms 309 Kempton
" Gifton hostler 304 Kempton rms do
" Harry A b 124 Hillman
" Hattie E Mrs b 21 Chestnut
" Henry C h 228 Pleasant
" Henry G machinist h 28 Keene
" Henry W cashier Merchants Nat Bank h 578 Union
" Henry W photographer 26 Fifth h 10 Emerson (S)
" Horace B fish rms 18 Seventh
" Jane widow Henry P h 53 Hill
" Jeremiah B carpenter U St Ry Co h 20 Shawmut av [Sycamore
" Jeremiah M police Sta 2 h 117
" John D trader h 192 Cedar
" John G h 8 Jenney [13 Madison
" John H engineer A W Holmes h
" Joseph laborer b 341 North
" Joseph A comp h 42 Campbell
" Lavinia b 144 Summer
" Lillian F Mrs forelady 1145 Kempton h 94 Middle
" Louis B chauffeur h 483 Union
" Louisa M widow Charles G h 6 Foster [Middle
" Lucy E widow Charles H h 197
" Lucy E widow Noel W h 1071 Rockdale av [Elm (W)
" Lydia C widow Moses H h 409

GLOBE DYE HOUSE 220 SHAWMUT AVE.
J. N. J. LONHOLDT, PROP. Telephone Connections Goods called for and Delivered
Down town Office, 52 Pleasant St., Room 1 North End Office, 1014 Acushnet Ave.

Taber
" Mary Kempton and Sally Gordon h 543 County [Richmond
" Melintha G widow James T b 19
" Mill cotton and silk goods mfrs Coffin av c Church [ley
" Milton clerk 125 Middle h 6 Stud-
" Olive C widow Marcus W h 90 Ashland [223 Chancery
" Oliver R (O R Taber & Son) h
" Ophelia widow Walter matron H C h 7 Ash (S)
" O R & Son (Oliver R and George W) grocers 457 Kempton
" Philip A gardener h 170 Chancery [Emerson (S)
" Philip J clerk 26 Fifth bds 10
" Ray B clerk 17 N Sixth b 21 S Sixth
" Ray H student bds 74 Morgan
" Rebecca widow John R bds 13 Eighth [h 1005 County
" Reuben capt Hose No 2 Weld
" Richard S h 176 Court [do
" Robert A mason 101 Hillman h
" Robert W stationer 28 Pleasant
" Russell S clerk 131 Acushnet av b 5 Weaver [tage
" Ruth A widow Albert b 143 Cot-
" Ruth F stenographer Electric Express b 7 Ash (S) [141 Page
" Sarah A widow William C h
" Sarah F h 624 Kempton
" Sarah S widow William H bds 52 Locust
" Silas cooper h 198 Pleasant
" Silas S supt of mails P O h 74 Morgan [nell
" Thomas P student h 178 Grin-
" Thomas J teamster h 72 Linden
" Thomas J Jr warper b 72 Linden
" Wallace L h 185 Cedar
" Walter F ropeworker b 60 Durfee
" Walter J clerk 457 Kempton bds 223 Chancery [ter
" William operative h 16 McMurray
" William Gamaliel (Taber & Gay) h 524 Cottage
" William H laborer h 60 Durfee
" William W florist b 60 Durfee
" & Gay (William G Taber and Elmer B Gay) teamsters 421 Purchase

Tablas Joseph mgr Dominique Theatre 269 Sawyer h 162 Grinnell

Tablas
" Joseph shoemaker h 162 Acushnet avenue
" Joseph Jr h 162 Grinnell
" Michael H drillworker b 162 Acushnet av [net av
" Samuel drillworker b 162 Acush-

Tackney Philip laborer h 107 Willis

Taffe Francis M sailmaker 35 Commercial h 8 Franklin
" Joseph P weaver b 794 County
" Patrick flagman h 794 County
" Thomas J stonecutter bds 794 County

Taford Alphonse h 19 George

Taft Daniel H second hand h 129 Austin
" George E teamster b 125 Clark
" Hannah Mrs h 596 Cottage [Clark
" Thomas J capt police h 125

Tague William mill hand b 39 Tallman [Padanarum

Talbot Aristides (Talbot & Co) h at
" Celina Mrs h 55 Brock av
" Emma Mrs weaver h 28 Stapleton
" Francis X loom fixer h 11 Hazard court [ond
" Frank hostler rms 60 N Sec-
" Herbert C (Talbot & Co) h at Boston
" James carpenter h 12 Bourne
" Joseph teamster h 111 Eugenia
" Jules weaver h 71 Ruth
" Mary A vocalist b 28 Stapleton
" Samuel spinner h 138 Davis
" Thomas operative h 158 Reynolds
" William clerk Savoy Hotel b do
" William B b 459 Mill
" & Co (Aristides and Herbert C Talbot) clothing 44 to 48 Purchase [isbury

Taletowicz Adam weaver h 24 Sal-

Talley Edward laborer b 80 Ash (W)

Tallman Albert R asst 294 Purchase h 6 Spruce

TALLMAN ARTHUR S livery stable 135 Grinnell h 173 do See page 771
" Caroline A widow William K b 198 Middle
" Edward G bookkeeper 26 Masonic bldg h at Fairhaven
" Edwin S janitor T Donaghy school h 115 South
" Franklin S asst foreman Standard h 223 North

GREENE & WOOD Every Kind of LUMBER AND MILL WORK
PINE STREET, off So. WATER STREET, NEW BEDFORD

Tallman
" James H accountant 26 Masonic bldg h 120 Mill
" see Tolman
Talmage Archibald A reporter Standard b 162 Park
" Charles H insurance agent 41 William h 162 Park
" Nellie C teacher Harrington school b 162 Park
Tanguay Damasse b 11 Desautels
" Damasse Jr mill hand h 11 Desautels
" Omer carpenter h 102 Eugenia
Tangue Manuel P laborer b 202 Belleville av [32 Priscilla
Tanner Charles clerk 201 Union bds
" Edwin Jr asst supt Bennett Mill h 74 Dean
" Ethel L clerk 185 Union b 9 Arch
" Harriet L widow William E h 9 Arch
" John fixer h 270 Tinkham
" Walter E S bookkeeper b 9 Arch
" William C salesman 18 Market b 9 Arch [Kempton
Taper Abraham window cleaner h 286
Tarasko Jan carder h 6 Hampton ct
Tarbox Louise K Mrs h rear 167 Mill
Tardie Alpohnse weaver h 17 Clark
Tardif Jules carpenter h 101 Nye
Tardy John filer h 311 Belleville rd
Tarlecki Frank grocer 659 S First h 70 Delano [587 First
Tarpey Catherine widow Charles h
" Daniel operative b 587 First
Tarr Abijah J carpet layer 76 William h 64 North
" Albert H gardener h 154 Durfee
" James S b 64 North
" Kate M awningmaker 76 William b 64 North [Durfee
" William A H millworker b 154
Tarte A agent 73 William b Hicks st
Tasker Adah M teacher High school b 151 Maple
" Charles N dist plant chief 57 N Second h 289 Palmer
" Edward S salesman 188 N Water h 209 Pleasant [View ter
" John E salesman h 24 Maple
" Joshua B grocer 145 Arnold h 151 Maple
" J Wilder student b 151 Maple

Tassica Peter mule spinner b 20 Ashley [James
Tate Andrew glass cutter h 79
" Bridget widow Robert h 19 High
Tatro Arthur weaver b 329 N Front
" Elmer fixer b 329 N Front
" Frederick roofer h 299 Tinkham
" Ida Mrs h 329 N Front
" Joseph J operative b 14 Armour
Tattersall Alice waitress rms 25 William [away
" Farrow mule spinner h 76 Hath-
" Thomas restaurant 968 Acushnet av h 125 Holly
" Warren bookkeeper 40 Masonic bldg h 29 Buttonwood
" William engineer h 26 Salisbury
TAUNTON-NEW BEDFORD COPPER CO Clarence A Cook vice pres and agent N Front See page 34
Tavares Alfred shoemaker h r 308 S Front [Bolton
" Antone clerk 98 Allen bds 507
" Antone A weaver h 22 Hemlock
" August B weaver h 5 Katharine
" Benjamin laborer h 47 First
" Charles D operative h 706 S Water [ney
" Jason C carpenter h 184 Bon-
" Joaquim laborer h 219 S Front
" Joaquim laborer h 502 First
" John h 202 Belleville av
" John agent 186 Purchase
" John carpenter h 600 South
" John fireman h 458 First [Fifth
" John shoes 63 Howland h 63
" Joseph h 229 S Front
" Joseph drillworker b 45 Short
" Joseph hairdresser h 502 First
" Joseph mill hand h 81 Mosher
" Joseph teamster r 182 N Water b r 154 N Second
" Joseph L mill hand h 55 Mitchell
" Louis hairdresser cor Grinnell
" Lydia Mrs h 298 Cottage
" Manuel cigarmaker h 65 Howland
" Manuel fisherman h 49 Mitchell
" Manuel laborer h 305 S Front
" Manuel operative h 47 Howland Village [av
" Manuel C laborer h 143 Coffin
" Marguerita L widow Jacintho h 118 Fair [ter
" Marianno mill hand h 614 S Wa-

BONNEY, FOLSTER & CO.,
The North End's Shopping Centre
Dry Goods and Men's Furnishings
945-947 Acushnet Ave., New Bedford, Mass.

Tavares
" Victorine laborer h 316 S Front
" William S laborer h 67 Nash rd
" see Travers
Taveira Augusto J Rev pastor Church of Immaculate Conception h 1238 Acushnet av [Campbell
Tavis John W salesman h 145
Taylor Abbie H clerk b 260 Summer
" Abbie W widow Henry W h 84 Elm
" Abraham carder h 344 Davis
" Albert M painter h 695 Cottage
" Alexander shearer h 125 David
" Alexander weaver h 172 Division
" Alfred motorman b 56 Willow
" Alfred rem from city
" Alica A teacher Acushnet av school b 83 Fifth
" Alice boarding house 301 Fourth
" Alice M Mrs b 208 Weld
" Arnold h 234 Phillips av
" Benjamin W painter h 188 North
" Bertha M milliner 84 Elm b do
" Caroline Mrs b 173 David
" Caroline R b 63 Dartmouth
" Charles variety 311 Rivet h 54 Katharine
" Charles weaver h 54 Katharine
" Charles W box mfr h 34 Lindsey
" Clayton clerk 143 Purchase b 125 David
" Clifford laundryman h 44 W French av [Oak st ct
" Daniel S foreman 3 E Pope h 3
" Edith H widow Charles L h 52 Court
" Edmund laborer b 199 S Water
" Edward oiler h 78 Mott
" Edward F overseer Bennett Mill h 79 Linden
" Elizabeth Mrs h 12 Salisbury
" E E Co shoe mfrs 474 Acushnet av [ney
" Frank mule spinner h 171 Bon-
TAYLOR FRANK C general contractor at Fairhaven h 190 Kempton See page 48
" Fred rem from city
" Fred spinner h 47½ Bowditch
" F Stanley b 3 Oak st ct [shnet av
" George harnessmaker h 1458 Acu-
" George D helper b 260 Summer
" George E bookkeeper Anthony Swift & Co h 220 Brownell

Taylor
" George F foreman carpenter r 113 Willis h 242 Maxfield
" George H janitor h 260 Summer
" George S fireman h r 338 Kempton [Pleasant
" George S switchman h 552 Mt
" George W second hand h 695 Cottage [tage
" Harriet widow Newton h 675 Cot-
" Harriet A teacher Cedar st school b 242 Maxfield
" Harry clerk b 187 David
" Hartlay laborer b 78 Belleville av
" Henry h 182 County
" Henry clerk b 187 David
" Henry painter h 74 Eugenia
" Henry W (Taylor & Burke) 146 Pleasant
" James h 72 Hazard
" James carder b 156 Reynolds
" James joiner b 50 Princeton
" James variety 319 Rivet h 440 Orchard (N)
" James weaver h 301 Fourth
" James weaver b 259 Bowditch
" James E spinner h 301 Earle
" James H overseer Grinnell Mfg Corp h 256 Brock av [ant
" Jane widow George h 405 Pelas-
" Jasper C h 39 Mill [Pleasant
" Jerome M fixer bds 552 Mt
" John laborer b 99 Linden
" John operative h 86 Clifford
" John weaver h 122 Nash rd
" John weaver h 124 Collette
" John A steel hardener h 11 Dartmouth
" John C farmer h 160 Grinnell
" John H weaver h 50 Princeton
" John H Jr third hand b 50 Princeton [h 61 Robeson
" John J grocer 1001 Acushnet av
" John J laborer b 232 N Second
" John M teamster h 269 Middle
" John T operative h 1283 Acushnet av [net av
" John W machinist h 195 Acush-
" John W died Jan 9 1911
" Joseph harnessmaker 860 Acushnet av h 1458 do
" Joseph operative h 18 Hazard ct
" Joseph second hand h 191 Brock avenue [h 187 David
" Joseph shoe repairer 198 Rivet

M. P. B. Silva & Son BUILDERS
Estimates Furnished on all Kinds of Work
157 ACUSHNET AVENUE Both Phones NEW BEDFORD

Taylor
" Joseph slasher tender b 102 Nash road [R I
" J Arthur Jr rem to Pawtucket
" Margaret Mrs h 195 Elm
" Mary and Sarah h 96 Ruth
" Mary A widow John P h 63 Dartmouth
" Mary J Mrs h 123 State
" Mary L h 230 County
" Mary M widow George A b 223 Grinnell [3 Oak ct
" Penelope E cashier 211 Union b
" Richard copperworker bds 1039 County [come
" Richard operative bds 20 Wel-
" Robert fixer h 27 Stapleton
" Robert spinner b 191 Brock av
" Robert (William Taylor & Son) b 191 Brock av
" Ralph S carpenter h 114 Fourth
" Roger third hand h 24 Woodlawn avenue [1637 Acushnet av
" Samuel fireman Whitman Mill h
" Samuel supt Soule Mill h 61 Parker
" Samuel O laborer b 260 Summer
" Saul (Taylor & Sachs) h 43 Thompson
" Stanley clerk b 3 Oak st ct
" Stephen H commercial traveler h 643 County
" Susan A nurse h 101 School
" Susie A bookkeeper bds 552 Mt Pleasant [av
" Thomas laborer b 1283 Acushnet
" Thomas operative b 39 Mill
" Thomas G coremaker b 380 N Front [Brock av
" Thomas J loom fixer bds 256
" Wallace N (W N Taylor & Co) 63 Union rms 25 William
" Walter Mrs variety 131 Coggeshall h 145 do
" Walter clerk h 145 Coggeshall
" Walter laborer h 398 S Front
" Walter piper h 398 S Front
" Walter spinner h 87½ Hathaway
" Walter J hatter 310 Acushnet av h at Providence R I
" William assistant b 678 Cottage
" William engineer city yard h 242 Chancery [mer
" William letter carrier h 249 Pal-

Taylor
" William mill hand h 33 Katharine
" William spinner h 28 Winsor
" William weaver h 56 Willow
" William weaver b 172 Division
" William (Wm Taylor & Son) h 19 Winsor
" William & Son (W and R Taylor) liquors 821 First [burn
" William E second hand h 1 Black-
" William H clerk 594 Purchase b 678 Cottage
" William H machinist b 81 Forest
" William H molder 229 N Water h at Fairhaven [223 Grinnell
" William H C glass decorator h
" William T clerk ft Willis h 124 Hillman [(S)
" Wright twister h 440 Orchard liquors 63 Union
" W N & Co (Wallace N Taylor)
" & Burke (Henry W Taylor and Walter M Burke) wall paper 146 Pleasant
" & Sachs (Saul Taylor, Albert Sachs) mattresses Hyacinth cor Thompson
Tchors Alliezik operative h 16 Fulton
Teachman Albert G chauffeur 148 Court h 143 Rounds
" Clifford H carpenter h 379 Reed
" Ernest G S driver No 3 h 608 W Elm
" George E mason h 50 Borden
Teamoh Mary A h 60 Spruce
Teasdale George M dentist 9 W French av b do
Tebbutt James spinner h 28 Viall
" Samuel yard master Butler Mill h 22 Viall [Briggs
Trefke Frank glass worker h 35
" Frank G glass worker h 9 W French av [man
Teilliere Frank spinner h 125 Tall-
Teixeira Alexander E rem from city
" Alfred clerk 293 Purchase b 187 North
" Antone comber h 106 Rivet
" Caesar mill hand b 86 Nash rd
" Claudino carpenter h 203 S Second
" Domingos laborer h 8 Beetle
" Germano C printer b 187 North

Steiger-Dudgeon Co.
"The WOMAN'S Store."
Tel. Bell 82 & 83, Branches connecting all depts.
" " 160 For Office only. Auto. 1211

SUMPTIONS, ASSORTMENTS AT ALL TIMES OF DEPENDABLE DRY GOODS

Teixeira
" Isabelle widow Jason h 31 Page
" John machinist b 31 Page
" John mill hand h 100 Phillips av
" John mill hand b 116 Phillips av
" John mill hand b 180 Belleville av
" Joseph carpenter b 31 Page [do
" Joseph clerk 197 Coggeshall h 201
" Joseph laborer h 411 Allen
" Joseph operative h 14 Cotter
" Manuel blacksmith b 31 Page
" Manuel fireman h 237 Coggeshall
" Manuel fish 153½ Coffin av h 143 do [av
" Manuel mill hand h 180 Belleville
" Manuel oiler U St Ry Co h at Fairhaven
" Mary widow Joseph h 50 Lombard
Telles Augustus fireman N B E Co n Fifth n Wing [ney
Tellier Jeremie loom fixer h 21 Rod-
" John operative h 145 Tallman
" Louis A teamster h 20 Bentley
" Pierre operative b 145 Tallman
" Wilfred weaver h 92 Jouvett
Temar Godetz laborer b 73 S Second
" John laborer h 73 S Second
Temberton Harry shearer h 136 Holly
Temple William F Jr physician St Luke's Hospital b do
Temeira Maria Mrs h 531 First
Tencsar John operative h r 42 Washburn [land
Tenxeira August C clerk h 58 How-
Tercheira Manuel fireman h 761 Water [Purchase b 50 Russell
Terpenny Arthur shade maker 36
" Ella J saleswoman h 50 Russell
" Jane clerk 36 Purchase b 50 Russell
Terra Frank drill worker h 121½ Fourth
" Joaquim h 60 Hall
" Mary J Mrs h 115 Fifth
Terriberry Josephine Mrs b 53 Hill
Terry Alice F widow Lemuel T h 63 Morgan [school b 89 State
" Alice P teacher Cedar Grove st
" Catherine widow Wallace b 970 County [chase h 245 Chestnut
" Charles A V bookkeeper 421 Pur-

Terry
" Clifford B student b 63 Morgan
" Edith M b 63 Morgan [nut
" Eflie P stenographer b 245 Chest-
" Eudora F h 195 Cottage
" Harry G spinner h 98 Brock av
" K Clifton b 89 State [son
" Manuel asst engineer h 6 Thomp-
" Myron H clerk Nield M Corp b 89 State [h 26 Bullock
" Nellie Mrs clerk 861 S Water
" Rachel S clerk P Corp b 89 State
" Robert A lawyer 108 Union rm 6 h 164 Maxfield [nut b do
" Ruth E music teacher 245 Chest-
" Susan A widow Elias h 89 State
" Susan E bookkeeper T-N B Copper Co b 89 State
Terwillegar Anna widow Egbert B h 60 Robeson [Newton
" Frederick W machinist h 159
" Harry R asst mgr 98 Purchase h 149 Washington [Washington
" Jay J manager 98 Purchase h 149
Tessert Henry weaver h 101 Holly
Tessier Alfred clerk b 76 Forest
" Conrad C dentist 56 Pleasant rms 78 Ashland
" Delphis rem from city
" George weaver h 803 First
" Joseph carpenter h 85 Beetle
" Joseph carpenter h 98 Nye
" Joseph rem from city
" Joseph weaver bds 67 Coffin av
" J Napoleon physician 993 S Water h do [Arnold
" Lizzie P widow Joseph A h 106
" Napoleon horseshoer 435 S Second h 128 Mott
" Oza prop Royal Theatre 991 S Water h 76 Forest
" Oza Jr mgr 991 S Water h 76 Forest [shnet av
Tetlow James machinist b 1089 Acu-
" Jane Mrs h 181 State
Tetrault Henri operative h 126 Mott
Tetreault Adelaide widow Benjamin h 20 Austin court
" Adelard painter h 38 Dudley
" Adelard laborer h 5 Bowditch
" Adelard painter b 12 Covell
" Adelord J barber 78 William b 190 Division
" Alfred driver h 3 McDonald ct

PELEG H. SHERMAN 506 COUNTY ST.
FUNERAL DIRECTOR AND EMBALMER
OFFICE PHONES. Bell 690-13. Auto 1305.
RESIDENCE PHONES. Bell 690-12. Auto. 1306.

Tetreault
" Alphee barber 221 Purchase h 31 Bullock [shall
" Alpohnse carpenter h 478 Cogge-
" Amedee fixer h 61 Bullard
" Amedee spinner h 76 Division
" Archille carpenter b 74 Hicks
" Arthur hairdresser 256 Purchase h 31 Bullock
" Arthur mason 151 Coffin av h do
" Audilie Mrs operative b 66 Washburn
" Baloni painter h 669 First [ard
" Delphine widow Jere h 31 Haz-
" Delphis weaver b 190 State
" Edias carpenter b 417 N Front
" Edward operative h 219 Rivet
" Eli weaver h 286 N Front
" Elsie widow h 27 Kenyon
" Emilie barber h 164 N Front
" Felix clerk 103 Rivet h 40 Independent [40 Independent
" Felix H provisions 103 Rivet bds
" Frank weaver h 857 First
" Frank G mason b 38 Dudley
" Frederick carpenter h 417 N Front
" George fixer h 151 Tallman
" George painter 34 Union h 658 Purchase
" George weaver b 196 Collette
" Hector carpenter b 417 N Front
" Henri mason b 38 Dudley
" Henri overseer b 359 Bowditch
" Joseph carder h 221 Sawyer
" Joseph carpenter b 359 Bowditch
" Joseph watchman b 171 Tinkham
" Joseph weaver h 497 S Second
" Joseph weaver b 20 McGurk
" Joseph J teamster b 14 Armour
" Leon weaver h 25 Welcome
" Louis laborer b 190 State
" Louis spinner h 25 Nye
" Louis watchman b 171 Tinkham
" Louis watchman U St Ry Co h 359 Bowditch [ditch
" Louis Jr concreter b 359 Bow-
" Mederice widow Joseph bds 31 Princeton
" Octave rem to Fairhaven
" Odelon teamster h 23 Cedar Grove
" Ovila carpenter b 417 N Front
" Paul rem from city
" Pierre carpenter b 79 Bullard
" Rock machinist h 31 Princeton

Tetreault
" Rose Mrs dressmaker 43 Dean b do
" Wilfred weaver b 76 Division
" William laborer h r 63 Tallman
" William rem from city [av
" William spinner h 399 Belleville
" Zephir died Mar 21 1911
Tettrault Ludger weaver b 587 First
Tetzner Herman S (H E Schmidt & Co) 116 Front rms 20 Beetle
Tew Charles D laborer h 281 Hillman
" William H carpenter h 123 Kempton
Tewksbury John W (Hawes Tewksbury & Co) Masonic bldg h at Boston
Texas Co The oil foot Ark lane
Texeira Isadore laborer b 58 S Second
" Manuel seaman h 58 S Second
Textile Union offices 138 Pleasant
Thacher Mary A widow Albert D h 57 Campbell
" Warren H bds 54 Chestnut
Thacker Teresa dressmaker 72 State h do [dle b 271 Austin
Thackeray Alfred R clerk 125 Mid-
" Charles F clerk 372 Cedar b 55 Maitland [b 55 Maitland
" Lillian E bookkeeper 47 S Second
Thatcher David C Rev rem to Providence R I [Fourth
" Edith stenographer bds 115
" Frank tinsmith 216 Acushnet av h at Fairhaven
" Grace nurse rms 19 Seventh
" Matilda E Mrs dressmaker 96 Middle h do
" Michael laborer h 95 Cove rd
" Richard glassfinisher 223 N Second h at Fairhaven
Thautbau Gasser operative h 21 Jean
Thauvette Albert mill hand h 389 Bolton
Thayer Lottie clerk 185 Union b at Fairhaven [enth h do
" W Hewins physician 25 Sev-
Theberge Arthur doffer b 59 Mosher
" August operative h 20 Roosevelt
" John clerk 103 Rivet b 59 Mosher
" Jonah operative h 68 Kenyon
" Jonas Jr teamster b 68 Kenyon
" Joseph laborer h 43 King
" Wilfred electrician 158 Purchase

F. T. AKIN & CO. FORGE FACTORY FURNACE FAMILY COAL

Theophilo Jose de Braga roofer h 480 S Second [205 State
Therien Admene widow Narcisse h
" Anna E widow Gideon h 110 Clark [av
" Edmund carpenter h 121 Coffin
" Frederick G clerk b 110 Clark
" Joseph fixer h 1848 Acushnet av
" Lillian A clerk city clerk's office b 110 Clark
" Rosalie widow Austin h 417 N Front [Collette
Theroux Alfred carpenter bds 203
Therrault Arthur weaver h 16 Viall
Therreault Alexander carpenter h 16 Bowditch
Therriault Peter weaver h 9 Viall
Therrien Albert boss grinder h 98 Nye
" Aldea rem from city
" Alfred spinner h 140 Tallman
" Alphonse (13 Hicks) died Dec 5 1910 [Front
" Alphonse mill hand bds 417 N
" Arthur helper 351 Kempton rms 279 Cottage
" Arthur student b 269 Coggeshall
" Charles H clerk 122 N Front bds 161 Davis
" Edmund laborer h 98 Collette
" Edmund teamster h 35 Linden
" Edward mill hand b 417 N Front
" Eusebe liquors 267 Coggeshall h 269 do
" George stevedore h 28 Maxfield
" George A lather b 161 Davis
" Gideon M operative b 1671 Acushnet av [av h 1265 do
" Henry hairdresser 1269 Acushnet
" Henry L gas fixtures 77 Holly h 347 Bowditch
" Herbert carder h 98 Nye [av
" Hilaire weaver h 1671 Acushnet
" Hilaire (Normandin & Co) pharmacist 122 N Front h 161 Davis
" Isadore elevatorman h 619 Acushnet avenue
THERRIEN JOHN painter 82 Tallman b 98 Kenyon See page 752
" John B weaver b 162 Whitman
" Joseph teamster N B Fish Co h 543 Acushnet av [av
" Joseph warper h 623 Acushnet
" Louis carpenter h 315 Sawyer

Therrien
" Napoleon teamster h opp 2521 Acushnet av
" Nasse b 7 Bowditch [Hicks
" Onesphore A clerk 3 Weld h 76
" Phellmin widow Louis boarding house 1022 Acushnet av
" Philias lineman 43 William
" Philias operative b 907 County
" Philias slasher b 701 Purchase
" Philias weaver h 35 Independent
" Philip clerk 1263 Acushnet av b 1265 do
" Pierre rem from city
" Wilfred carpenter b 219 Eugenia
Thibeault Arthur mill hand b 90 Davis
" Edward carpenter h 23 Covell
" Fred W loom fixer h 82 Nelson
" George teamster h 15 Nye
" Isadore weaver h 90 Davis
" James barber b 131 Nye
" Joseph laborer b 93 Holly
" Joseph weaver h 675 First
" Joseph W clerk 100 Ruth h 29 Ashley
" Louis weaver h 168 Tinkham
" Ludger J overseer Nonquitt Spinning Co h 150 Phillips av
" Nicholas carpenter h 131 Nye
Thibodeau Eugene shoe repairer 452 Belleville av h do
" George G buyer h 62 Tremont
" Harry rem from city
" Leon weaver b 455 Belleville av
Thilo Edna bookkeeper b 208 Davis
" Frederick E copperworker h 208 Davis [208 Davis
" Mabel stenographer 2 Union bds
Thimisthicos Peter mill hand h 3 McDonald court
Thing Caroline Mrs rem from city
Third District Court of Bristol County William c N Second
Thivierge Annie clerk 1100 Acushnet av b 194 Dean
" Eugene weaver h 82 Ruth
Thmous Samuel operative h 126 Cedar Grove [Bay
Thoen Andrew glass blower h 9
Thoendel Gustave weaver h 115 Reynolds
Thomas Abraham clerk 399 Purchase rms 577 Acushnet av
" Adolphus shoe repairer 314 Acushnet av h 205 North

There's room at the top for young men and women who can do things right.
Kinyon's Commercial School
Odd Fellows Bldg., Cor. William and Pleasant Sts., New Bedford, Mass.

Thomas
" Anna T teacher Harrington school b 212 North [net av
" Antoine cigarmaker h 145 Acush-
" Antone laborer h 47 Crapo
" Antonio J h 130 Rockland
" Ariel C supt Grinnell Mfg Corp b Parker House [Park
" Carlton F clerk 201 Union b 232
" Charles clerk rms 269 Purchase
" Charles painter rms 68 Mechanics lane
" Charles E carpenter h 212 North
" Charles F letter carrier h 59 Fifth [Washington
" Charles Henry operative h 173
" Charles Herbert asst foreman T P Corp b 173 Washington
" Charles H roll coverer h 663 Cottage [bldg b 663 Cottage
" Charles H Jr clerk 6 Masonic
" David A mason rms 428 Kempton
" Edward J h 56 Willow
" Edward J Jr city teamster h 182 North [Acushnet av
" Eleanor H widow Isaac W h 285
" Emily widow Joseph h 141 Division [ton
" Frank clerk 98 Allen h 507 Bol-
" Frank laborer h 107 Swift
" Frank operative b 586 Allen
" Frederick roll coverer h 160 Rockland
" George janitor h 76 Bay
" George E asst undertaker 7 S Sixth h 83 Parker
" Grace F clerk 18 Purchase bds 285 Acushnet av [31 Maitland
" Halbertian L driver foot North h
" Harriet H widow Henry F h 726 County [man h do
" Harriet W dressmaker 73 Hill-
" Hurlbut E asst supt cemeteries h 177 Shawmut av
" John watchman h 33 Lexington
" Joseph dry goods 281 Rivet h 191 Bonney
" Joseph laborer h 586 Allen [1911
" Joseph (141 Division) died July 1
" Joseph C elevatorman h 67 Mechanic's lane [281 Rivet
" Joseph S fruit 399 Purchase h
" Leander F machinist h 232 Park

Thomas
" Lillian L Mrs teacher Parker st school h 38 Park [Village
" Louis mill hand h 45 Howland
" Manuel mill hand h 25 Mitchell
" Manuel F operative h 44 Ash (N)
" Maria and Jane h 239 Arnold
" Mary Mrs clerk 182 Union h 114 S Sixth
" Mary widow Antonio h 244 Rivet
" Minnie widow h 577 Acushnet av
" Peter h 176 Cedar Grove
" S Alice Mrs h 122 Perry [Mill rd
" Virginia A Mrs housekeeper 9
" Walter fixer h 143 Belleville rd
" Walter M asst shipper h 54 Liberty [Parker
" Walter N teamster 68 Adams b 83
" Walter S student b 285 Acushnet av [69 Dean
" William liquors 244 N Front h
" William F iceman h 6 Mt Pleasant lane [150 Summer
" William H clerk 161 Purchase h
Thomasset Alfred weaver b 64 Hicks
Thomber Ebenezer clerk b 77 Hathaway [Acushnet av
Thompson Abraham weaver bds 137
" Alonzo C electrician 141 Purchase b 105 Fourth
" Ann h r 337 Pleasant [ville av
" Arthur loom fixer h 147 Belle-
" Blanche E Mrs milliner 224 Pleasant b do [b 130 Hatch
" Browning S foreman N B E Co
" Clara E clerk 14 Bedford bds 8 Beech [164 Summer h do
" Charles painter and paper hanger
" Charles B clerk 100 Fifth h 1 Anthouy
" Charles B stable foreman 168 S Water h 74 Fourth [do
" Charles G carpenter 485 Mill h
" Christopher weaver h 13 Jean.
" David mill hand h 144 Acushnet av
" David K machinist h 211 State
" Edward died Jan 7 1911
" Edward operative b 211 State
" Edward weaver h 161 Bates av
" Elizabeth W S widow John A h 8 Beech
" Ellen M Mrs h 151 Middle
" Elmer C asst foreman T P Corp h 177 Grinnell

HASKELL BROS. DEALERS IN
ICE
400 COURT STREET TELEPHONE CONNECTION NEW BEDFORD, MASS.

Thompson
" F Gertrude teacher Acushnet av school b 33 Keene
" George teamster b 268 N Front
" George F inspector h 21 Hunter
" George F junk 125 N Water h 448 Acushnet av
" George H rem to Brockton
" George L janitor public schools h 300 Maxfield [Hawthorn
" Gilbert T agent 108 Union h 191
" Grace M teacher Parker st school bds 73 Russell [Front
" Harriet widow Robert h 554 N
" Herbert I driver 14 N Sixth h 414 Park
" Isabelle Mrs h 71 S Second
" James h 151 Cedar [Reynolds
" James freight handler h 113
" James laborer b 105 Fourth
" James A asst janitor High school h 159 Bonney [h 48 Maple
" James E supt 295 Phillips avenue
" James H fixer h 680 Purchase
" James O Jr supt N B Cotton Mills Corp h 48 Maple
" Jane C Mrs h 153 Grinnell
" Jane F widow Samuel nurse h 300 Maxfield
" John boarding house 307 Collette h do
" John mill hand h 510 N Front
" John plumber 903 County h 183 Coffin av
" John weaver b 207 Weld
" John E carpenter h 346 Reed
" John E weaver h 16 McGurk
" John P painter 19 N Water h 100 Morgan [av
" Joseph laborer b 28 W French
" Leroy b 338 Cedar [269 Middle
" Margaretta C widow Charles bds
" Maria J nurse h 73 Dartmouth
" Martha C clerk 160 Purchase b 300 Maxfield [Pleasant
" Mary widow Edward h rear 441
" Mary widow Hugh h 28 Rockland
" Mary L widow Edwin A b 380 Hillman
" Michael laborer h 872 Purchase
" Nellie widow Mark b 1 Jennings court [Park
" Reinard cutter 157 Union h 96
" Richard car repairer U St Ry Co b 13 Jean

Thompson
" Richard weaver b 16 McGurk
" Samuel tackmaker b 101 Middle
" Samuel weaver h 38 Myrtle
" Samuel weaver h 206 Brook
" Samuel weaver b 69 Dean
" Sarah h 145 Chestnut
" Theodore shoemaker 76 Purchase
" Thomas marble and granite 25 Fourth h 105 do
" Thomas weaver h 186 Davis
" Thomas M spinner bds 991 Purchase
" William b 14 S Sixth
" William carpenter h 133 Bullard
" William conductor b 974 County
" William fixer h 554 N Front
" William rem from city
" William (Thompson & Sweeney) h 93 Middle [h 527 Cottage
" William A overseer Quissett Mill
" William E teamster h 974 County
" W B Mrs clerk 40 Purchase b 55 Howard av
" & Sweeney (W Thompson and J J Sweeney) grocers 101 N Second [Keene
Thomson Albert T machinist bds 23
" Asa T boat builder h 23 Keene
" David glassblower h 144 Acushnet av
" Pardon G h 10 S Sixth
" William baker h 856 First [av
Thoresz Miklos weaver h 67 Phillips
Thorley Francis carpenter 515 Rivet h do
" Francis H carpenter b 467 Allen
" George W painter 515 Rivet h do
" Thomas carpenter h 467 Allen
Thorn James H h 337 Tinkham
Thornber Ebenezer weaver h 77 Hathaway
" Elizabeth A Mrs h 233 N Front
" John filling carrier b 11 Harmony
Thorndike Henry A barrels 6 Spring Fairhaven rms 150 Middle
Thorne Caledonia widow Edward dressmaker 72 Ash (N) h do
" Edward F machinist b 72 Ash (N) [Blackmer
Thornhill Thomas asst engineer h 88
Thornley James weaver h 353 Coggeshall [shall
" James L doffer bds 353 Cogge-
" Thomas weaver h 194 Davis
" Walter loom fixer h 315 Tinkham

J. F. CROSSLEY 223 MILL STREET COR. EMERSON PHONE
STEAM and HOT WATER HEATING
GAS FITTING and FIXTURES

Thornley
" Wilbraham spinner b 194 Davis
Thornton Alfred bookkeeper Mechanics National Bank h 28 James
" John H laborer h 2 Pope
" Lester teamster h 16 Clark
" Mabel clerk Mechanics National Bank h 86 Court
" Natalie teacher b 28 James
" Ray foreman 272 S Water h 278 Mill
" Rebecca h 86 Court
" Robert weaver h 286 Coggeshall
" Thomas jeweler h 63 Roosevelt
" Thomas A h 114 Hawthorn
" William laborer h 140 Davis
Thorpe Charlotte widow James h 10 Richmond
" Fred Mrs h 386 Pleasant
" Harriet J teacher Clark st school b 10 Richmond [mond b do
" James H upholsterer 10 Rich-
" John clerk b 191 Collette
" John operator b 839 Purchase
" Mary E clerk N B I for Savings bds 10 Richmond
THORPE RICHARD H kindling wood 1786 Acushnet av h do See page 765
" Thomas loom fixer h 191 Collette
" Thomas William (Tripp & Thorpe) 183 N Water h 19 Richmond
Thorup Oscar rem to Boston
" William M bookkeeper N B S D & T Co h 9 Parker
Thrasher Harrison S clerk N B C M Corp b at Fairhaven
Thuman Agnes G widow John h 56 S Sixth [b 56 S Sixth
" Jane E asst at public library
Thuot Henry L pianos 808 Purchase h at Fall River
" John V physician 938 Acushnet av h do [Bethel h do
Thurber Charles S Rev chaplain 15
" Wesley E clerk pub library b 15 Bethel [Co h 17 Viall
Thursby Asa overseer Hathaway Mfg
Thurston Leland W photographer h 6 Chestnut [89 Chancery
Ticehurst Laura A widow Frank h
Tichon Joseph E foreman 100 Fifth h 43 Shawmut av
" Levi loom fixer h 14 McGurk

Tiernan Andrew A trimmer h 50 North
" Andrew J clerk b 50 North
" Harold M chauffeur 18 Market b 50 North
" Patrick weaver h 5 Katharine
Tierney William hostler rms 12 Rounds [h 139 Orchard (S)
Tiffany Henry L treas Kilburn Mill
" Herbert H engineer h 184 Thompson [Briggs Plainville rd
" Mary J Mrs b at Mrs Prudence
Tighe Catherine widow Patrick h 86 Myrtle
" Francis teamster b 86 Myrtle
" James H clerk 136 County b 462 Bolton [Park
" James J clerk 132 Union b 277
" John F loom fixer h 138 Division
" Martin clerk 130 Union b 162 North
Tilden Caroline N clerk the Pairpoint Corp b 65 Fifth [dar
" Emma J widow John J h 346 Ce-
" George A foreman 152 N Water h 675 County [52 Locust
" John F bookkeeper 58 Adams h
" Louis W clerk Mechanics Nat Bank h 419 Union [Fifth
" Lydia A widow Horace h 65
" Sarah h 10 Mechanics lane
Tilghman Charles F harness cleaner h 163 William
" Hiram I died March 27 1911
" Mary A widow Hiram I h 238 Chancery [L h 12 Borden
Tillinghast Blanche R widow Frank
" Charles weaver h 730 S Water
" Edwin L asst auditor 4 Municipal bldg h 108 Fourth
" Edwin L Jr died April 3 1911
" Elizabeth L widow John T b 288 Union [Fourth h do
" Eugenia H Mrs dressmaker 108
" Sadie C widow William A h 61 Walnut
" Theodore F h 37 Eighth
" Thomas clerk b 61 Walnut
Tillman Sedonia widow Thomas H h 276 Middle [vid
Tillotson Arthur weaver h 119 Da-
" Herbert blacksmith h 20 Cove
Tillson Clifton W clerk 100 Fifth

CHARLES A. CROSHERE
38 FOURTH ST. Bell Phone 1964-23
SIGN PAINTING
GLASS LETTERING
ELECTRIC SIGNS
SHOW CARDS

Tillson
" George M variety 423 Kempton h 334 Middle [Washington
" Lydia C widow Henry H h 118
" William H bookkeeper 645 Purchase h 101 State
" Charles C real estate Merchants Bank Bldg rm 301 b 396 Purchase
Tilton Annie Mrs h 268 Acushnet av
" Edwin M h 396 Purchase
" Ernest L carpenter h 163 Middle
" Hannah housekeeper 38 Madison
" Henry J carpenter b 56 Fourth
" James A master mariner h 51 S Sixth [ney
" Mary J Mrs housekeeper 4½ Jen-
" Wallace C janitor Clark st school h 13 Bannister [chase
" William J caretaker b 396 Pur-
Timber Aaron choreman h 243 Chancery
" Charles W choreman h 80 Cedar
Times Newspaper Co 120 Purchase
Timms Thomas J tailor h 20 Warren
Timon Margaret widow Patrick h 49 Ash (N) [Corp h 287 Allen
Timperley Joseph T Jr clerk P
" William H hairdresser 101 Allen b 35 Crapo
Tinkham Allen W foreman h 5 Smith
" Charlotte A widow George b 89 Chestnut [Campbell
" Clara H widow John M h 168
" David W molder 229 N Water b 80 Park
" Edith A bookkeeper b 512 County
" Ellen A teacher Thomas Donaghy school b 80 Park [do
" Emma L clerk 526 County b 512
" Everett N plumber b 5 Smith
" George H clerk b 80 Park
" Hannah A bookkeeper 145 Arnold b 80 Park
" Harriet T Mrs h 512 County
" John F carpenter h 472 Cottage
" Mary A Mrs shoe stitcher h 234 North
" Mary F nurse b 55 Bonney
" Nellie M b 234 North
" Robert D agent b 80 Park
" Robert N molder 229 N Water h 80 Park [80 Park

Tinkham
" William Nelson piano tuner b 80
Tinney John weaver h 91 Beetle
Tioflo Carriva fish 103 County h County cor Independent
Tipping Laurence weaver h 320 Tinkham [Austin
Tipton James D motorman h 292
Tirrell Abbie M Mrs h 49 Emerson
" Wallace rem to Fairhaven
Tisdelle Anthoine b 148 Central av
Titcomb A Isabel teacher h 143 Hillman
Titus Ada L Mrs h 603 Cottage
" Sarah A widow Eugene seamstress h 199 Purchase
Toares John mill hand b 439 Belleville av [ter
Tobaski Paul weaver b 819 S Wa-
Tobey Charles W (Giles & Tobey) 44 Middle h at Fairhaven
" Henry H city laborer h 362 Kempton [Purchase h 52 Mill
" Joseph T sporting goods 125
" Sadie A Mrs h 142 Pleasant
" Warren P rem from city
" Warren P clerk 84 Union b 209 Maple
" William H A h 163 River road
Tobin Clarence weaver h 561 Acushnet av [net av
" Joseph D shoemaker b 561 Acush-
" Mary E widow h 306 N Front
" William E glassworker bds 561 Acushnet av [Cedar
Todd Agnes widow Mathew bds 414
" Arthur S teacher High school b 641 County [way
" Herbert laborer b 76 Hatha-
" Mary housekeeper 149 Summer
Todsen Christian H h 114 South
" Ida M clerk 41 William b 114 South [ond
Toledo Frank laborer h 464 S Sec-
Tolley George clerk 35 Parker b 945 County
Tolman Ellsworth B student b 658 County [County h do
" Elmer E violin teacher 658
Tomasik Jan weaver b 12 McGurk
Tomb Abraham shoe operative h 53 Washburn [399 Belleville av
Tomkowicz Wladyslaw operative h
Tomlin Richard fixer b 28 Viall

J. G. NICHOLSON
LUMBER, SASH, DOORS and BLINDS
BOWDITCH STREET, NEW BEDFORD, MASS.

Tomlinson Arthur weaver h 423 S Second [way
" Arthur E engineer h 153 Hatha-
" Austin slasher tender h 297 Coffin av [av
" Austin weaver bds 322 Coffin
" David weaver h 25 Winsor
" David H machinist b 25 Winsor
" Edwin copperworker h 8 Marvin
" George weaver b 336 Tinkham
" George L weaver b 32 Ashley
" James machinist b 447 Coggeshall
" Michael city laborer h 6 Acushnet block [b 1505 do
" Peter liquors 1499 Acushnet av
" Samuel plumber 1545 Acushnet av bds 273 Coggeshall
" Walter painter b 20 Ashley
" William loom fixer h 468 Rivet
Tompkins Clara L h 114 Park
Toner Matilda R widow Alexander b 109 Fifth
Tonge James baker bds 31 Cleveland
" John T weaver h 31 Cleveland
" Mathew designer h 60 Hathaway [way rd
Tool John A coachman h 61 Hatha-
Toole George O spinner h 158 Collette
Toolis Patrick laborer h 71 Rivet
Toombs Emma J Mrs b 156 William
Toomey Dennis H clerk h r 36 Linden [Linden
" John J clerk Whitman Mill b r 36
" John J weather strips h 66 Myrtle [den
" Joseph D doffer bds r 36 Lin-
Tooney Kenneth rem from city
Tootte James fixer h 196 Division
Topham Alvin R plumber 55 N Water h 23 North [Oak
" Jennie L widow Philip M bds 22
" Leland b 23 North
" Nannie E Mrs music teacher 55 Rounds h do
" Robert R bds 55 Rounds
" William B clerk h 55 Rounds
" William H died Feb 18 1911
Topholm Margaret F widow Peter H h 64 Bedford [ham
Topping Edwin weaver h 165 Tink-
" Frederick clerk 151 Cove b 75 Brock av [av
" William laborer h 47 Acushnet

Toros Francisco P brick layer h 11 Margin [Knowlton school
Torreson Ida E teacher Hosea M
Tosse Margaret b 204 Eugenia
Totman Charles helper b 1142 Acushnet av
" Charles piper b 59 Bullard
Touchette Blanche 1119 Acushnet av bds 53 Reynolds
" Eugene fixer h 150 Nash rd
" Frederick loom fixer h r 53 Reynolds [Hemlock
" Henry painter 14 Jean h 106
" H Edmonde police Station 5 h r 53 Reynolds [Hillman
" Israel barber 78 William h 85
" J Frederick painter h 53 Reynolds
" Paul barber 131 Purchase h 94 Middle
Toundas Charles lunch 218 Coggeshall h 126 Cedar Grove
Toupin Charles H clerk 2173 Acushnet av b 2155 do
" Hector C druggist 2173 Acushnet av h 2155 do
Tourjee Orrin L pilot h 110 Middle
Tourtellot William E laundry 270 Kempton h 65 Walden
Toussant Gilbert blacksmith 214 Cedar Grove h 302 Coggeshall
" Joseph blacksmith b 302 Coggeshall [91 Tallman
" Louis helper 542 N Front bds
" Lucien blacksmith U St Ry Co h 91 Tallman
" Ludovic plumber b 91 Tallman
Tower Hobart h 8 Studley
Towers Henry machine operator bds 25 Salisbury [velt
" Joseph carpenter h 47 Roose-
" Mary Ann widow Thomas h 25 Salisbury
" Thomas fireman h 20 Margin
" Thomas loom fixer h 16 McGurk
" William laborer b 25 Salisbury
Towle Frank rem from city
Town Carlton G clerk 128 Purchase b 84 Court
Towne Annie Mrs h 383 Purchase
" Antoinette Mrs dressmaker 38 Reynolds h do
Townend Robert engineer Whitman Mill Co h 252 Coffin av
Townley Alice widow Richard housekeeper 16 Robeson

Steiger-Dudgeon Co.
"The WOMAN'S Store."
Tel. Bell 82 & 83, Branches connecting all depts.
" " 160 For Office only. Auto. 1211

SUMPTIONS, ASSORTMENTS AT ALL TIMES OF DEPENDABLE DRY GOODS

Townley
" John D laborer h 858 First
" Joseph S second hand h 289 Davis
Townsend Bessie E clerk 160 Purchase b 116 Chancery
" Carrie M Mrs h 151 Campbell
" Christopher L steam fitter h 123 Maple
" George E machinist h 2 Howland Village
" Idella P bookkeeper 19 Linden b 123 Maple
" Job h 4 N Oak
" Johanna widow Charles F h 430 Pleasant
" Minerva J widow Lewis H h 132 Mill
" Rachel widow Silas h r 900 Belleville av
" Robert E designer Page Mfg Co h 803 Kempton
" Susie I nurse b 123 Maple
TOWNSEND THOMAS cotton combs 157 Orange Providence R I See page 16
" Thomas E pianist b Weld Square Hotel
" Walter R watch repairer 28 Purchase h 116 Chancery
" William C foreman 1 Mill h 150 N Second
" William F b 83 Morgan
Toyfair Joseph motorman h 843 Purchase
Tracy Edward D clerk 295 Purchase b 509 do
" John B (Tracy, Rosenberg & McGurk) 108 Union rm 1 h at Taunton
" Michael baker 1070 County h 30 Adams
" Rosenberg & McGurk (J B Tracy, Solomon Rosenberg and C J McGurk) lawyers 108 Union rm 1
Trafford Orin I bookkeeper h 48 S Sixth
" William shoemaker rms 270 Pleasant
Trafton Harry P traveling salesman b 1 Cottage
Trahan Alfred carpenter h 69 Clifford
" Arsene teamster b 154 Cedar Grove
" Camille engineer N Y N H & H h Whitlow street
" Charles weaver h 142 Phillips av
" Emile carpenter b 69 Clifford
" Gregoir blacksmith 454 Pleasant bds 86 Davis
" Honorias weaver b 86 Davis
" Isaac mill hand h 88 Earle

Trahan
" Jean operative h 154 Cedar Grove
" Jean B b 553 N Front
" Joseph died Feb 4 1911
" Joseph carpenter h 219 Rivet
" Joseph grocer 363 Belleville av h 35 Dean
" Napoleon carpenter b 158 Hathaway
" Narcisse weaver h end of Shaw
" Nathalie widow Israel h 553 N Front
" Ovila carpenter b 158 Whitman
" Ovila mill hand b 88 Earle
" Philadore shoe repairer 83 Collette h 86 Davis
" Polydore grocer 471 N Front h do
" see Trehan
Tramblay Arthur barber h 47 Delano
" see Tremblay
Tranmer James Rev removed from city
Trapenier Paul weaver bds 153 Blackmer
Trapp Henry J steward h 74 Mill
Trask Eugene W assistant engineer h 2 Irvington court
" Helen Mrs operative rms 401 Purchase
" Mary E vice principal Harrington school h 352 Union
" Robert shoeworker h 66 Spruce
Trautwein Paul shoemaker bds 147 Rounds
Travassos Manuel de Souza Rev removed to Taunton
Travers Alfred mill hand b 45 South
" Antone laborer h 106 Fifth
" Antone laborer h 505 Rivet
" Antone mill hand h 45 South
" August B weaver h 3 Acushnet block
" Benjamin laborer h Bank street
" Charles I h 18 Parker
" Frank paver b 51 Howland Village
" Fred laborer h 74 Belleville road
" John operative h 41 Winsor
" John F salesman h 63 Fifth
" Jose L mill hand b 73 Briggs
" Joseph laborer h 308 S Front
" Joseph M laborer h 54 Rivet
" Manuel fireman h 114 Fifth
" Manuel fireman h 305 S Front
" Manuel laborer h 61 Lexington
" Manuel third hand h 73 Briggs
" Mary widow Antone h 11 Rural

PELEG H. SHERMAN 506 COUNTY ST.
FUNERAL DIRECTOR AND EMBALMER
OFFICE PHONES. Bell 690-13. Auto. 1305.
RESIDENCE PHONES. Bell 690-12. Auto. 1306.

Travers
" Susan dressmaker b 7 Cottage
" see Tavares [h 214 North
Treadup Elmore M clerk 240 Union
" Frederick A laborer 144 S Water
h 35 Cedar [Lindsey
" Frederick A Jr machinist h 28
" Matthew C clerk 240 Union h 35
Cedar [Smith
Treadwell William fisherman b 211
Treant Louis teamster h 14 Beetle
Treearchis Constantinos mgr rms 153
Maxfield
Trella John weaver h 277 S Second
Tremblay Adeline Mrs h 1139 Acushnet avenue [av
" Albert bricklayer b 271 Phillips
" Alcide J overseer Grinnell Mill h
159 Ashland
" Arthur mill hand b 3 Desautels
" Arthur plasterer h 826 County
" August carpenter b 89 Ruth
" Catherine widow b 9 Morton ct
" Celio twister h 831 Acushnet av
" Edward h 194 Dean
" Eli mill hand h 202 State
" Emilia Mrs h 89 Ruth [av
" Frank operative b 872 Acushnet
" Frank weaver b 101 Bowditch
" Godfrois h 101 Bowditch
" Hormidas weaver b 47 Holly
" Israel carpenter h 1042 Acushnet
avenue
" Jeremiah h 12 Austin ct
" Jeremiah Jr salesman 1064 Acushnet av h 72 Kenyon
" John died Sept 22 1910
" John removed from city
" Joe teamster h 47 Delano
" Joseph bds 101 Bowditch
" Joseph boss grinder h 275 North
Front [avenue
" Joseph mill hand h 455 Belleville
" Julius teamster h r 36 Hicks
" J E Wilfred second hand store
342 Purchase h 435 Pleasant
" Leo N comber b 1139 Acushnet av
" Louis third hand h 154 Hathaway
" Louis removed from city
" Malcome weaver h 187 Earle
" Mary widow John h 40 Tallman

Tremblay
" Napoleon operative h 297 Coffin
avenue
" Philip laborer b 200 Collette
" Pierre carpenter b 89 Ruth
" Pierre weaver h 37 Bullard
" Rawe mason bds Bristol av opp
2746 Acushnet av
" Romuald provisions 806 Purchase
h 435 Pleasant
" Zephir teamster h 36 Washburn
Trenette Lucien weaver h 47 Delano
Tremont Cafe (Audette C Chapdelain props) 1214 Acushnet av
Trepainier Alfred carpenter h 24
Woodlawn avenue
" Anthony weaver b 153 Blackmer
" Antonio doffer b 153 Blackmer
" Henry twist driller b 153 Blackmer
" Hermidas weaver h 154 Blackmer
" Hormidas J weaver h 64 Division
Tresham Ellen variety 52 Grinnell h
do
" Ellen Mrs h 240 County
" Julia V teacher J H Clifford
school bds 609 Union
" Mary nurse b 609 Union
" Patrick Mrs h 370 Middle
" Peter J city teamster h 609 Union
Tresman John removed from city
Trett William insurance agent 41
William h 38 McGurk
Tribe Dorothy A bookkeeper 71 William rm 10 b at Fairhaven
" Reginald reporter Standard h at
Fairhaven
" Thomas h 15 Cook
Tribou David H foreman E E T Co
h 169 Merrimac
Trigueiro John E druggist 94-98 N
Second and 233 Coggeshall h
95 Ashland
" Joseph machinist h 407 Allen
" Joseph E clerk 233 Coggeshall
h 45 Beetle
" Manuel F night watchman R R
depot h 485 Allen
" Manuel J h 233 S Front
Trimble Eva widow b 113 Mott
" William fixer h 113 Mott
Trindad John weaver b 151 County
" Mariana widow h 151 County
Trinder Thomas rem to Boston

F. T. AKIN & CO. PAINTERS AND DECORATORS

Trinity Antonio h r 33 Wing
" Bertha Mrs housekeeper b 43 Bay
" Manuel mariner b r 33 Wing
Trinklin Gustave operative h 367 Earle
Tripp Abner S h 107 Dartmouth
" Ada widow Arthur h 174 Kempton [Russell
" Ada and Annie drillworkers h 50
" Adna F Mrs h 596 Purchase
" Albert teamster b 62 North
" Alexander A asst supt 37 Purchase rm 23 h 33 Sycamore
" Alexander A teamster 108 Grape h do
" Alfred R h 258 Reed
" Allen S boats to let City Pier No 1 h 59 Bedford [lantic
" Allison O steam fitter h 16 At-
" Almanza engineer h Tarkiln Hill road [ter h 83 Sycamore
" Almedus G W molder 229 N Wa-
" Almira T widow Adoniram h 342 Cedar
" Alton B clerk N Bedford Storage Warehouse h at Acushnet
" Ambrose F salesman 133 Union b 6 Sears [117 Fifth
" Ambrose H janitor 174 Union h
" Andrew E musician h 232 North
" Andrew N steam fitter 5 Atlantic h 17 do [fee
" Andrew W shoemaker h 45 Dur-
" Annie Mrs h 1458 Acushnet av
" Annie C Mrs h 343 Cottage
" Annie E Mrs h 202 Elm
" Arthur bds 341 North
" Arthur Clifford foreman 44 Middle h 74 Pierce [mouth
" Arthur C machinist b 107 Dart-
" Arthur F laborer 144 S Water h at Dartmouth
" Augustus C died Mar 10 1911
" Barjona D 2nd h 76 S Sixth
" Bartlett G clerk P Corp bds 40 Dartmouth [116 North
" Benjamin A mgr 17 Pleasant h
TRIPP BENJAMIN C builder 161 Clinton h 145 do See page 762
" Bessie widow Ebenezer R h 240 Kempton
" Bradford D operative h 7 Crapo
" B Frank conductor h 49 Maitland [h 467 Union
" Caroline E widow Almanza nurse

Tripp
" Carrie E Mrs manicure 133 Cedar h do [chase
" Charles laundryman h 557 Pur-
" Charles E teamster 62 Dartmouth b 31 Babbitt [26 Ward
" Charles F driver 34 Pleasant h
" Charles G (Bates, Kirby & Co) 48 Pleasant h 194 Court
" Charles H (Shanks & Tripp) 214 Union h 328 Cedar [land pl
" Charles H city laborer h 14 Ash-
" Charles S drillworker b 26 Ward
" Charles W die sinker h 123 Hillman [h 86 Ashland
" Chester L police sergt Station 3
" Christopher B h 12 Sherman
" Clara L h 66 State [Chancery
" Clarence L clerk 13 N Sixth b 103
" Clifton F foreman h 43 Cedar
" Daniel A h 341 North
" David Kempton bowling 351 Kempton h 279 Cottage [ty
" David L motorman h 1005 Coun-
" Delia F stenographer 100 Fifth b 158 Arnold
" Desmond W yard boss Whitman Mills h 277 Bowditch [Mill
" Edgar C grocer 47 Foster h 267
" Edith clerk 198 Union b r 205½ Acushnet av
" Edith E Mrs h 748 First
" Edna clerk 48 Pleasant b 137 Sycamore [139 Willis
" Edward C clerk 36 Purchase h
" Edward G laborer h 199 Pleasant
" Edwin F foreman Adams Express R R depot h 473 Kempton
" Edwin I salesman 188 N Water h 99 Florence
" Elias J machinist h 186 Elm
" Eliphalet A (Home Washing Co) 111 Myrtle h 95 Mt Pleasant
" Eliot S driver 48 Pleasant h 175 Park
" Eliza h 44 Allen
" Elizabeth B teacher James B Congdon school b at Fairhaven
" Elizabeth H clerk 40 Purchase b 26 Ward
" Ella B bookkeeper 474 Acushnet av b 83 Sycamore [Reed
" Ella E clerk 160 Purchase b 358
" Ellen M clerk b 229 North
" Elmer H teamster b 64 Spruce

Kinyon's Commercial School Will furnish your office help free
Odd Fellows Building COR. WILLIAM and PLEASANT STS. NEW BEDFORD, MASS.

Tripp
" Elsie M clerk 100 Fifth b 208 Grinnell [ton b 167 Merrimac
" Emerald A bookkeeper 8 Hamil-
" Emma E widow Alexander A b 415 Cottage
" Ernest B buffer b 1199 Kempton
" Etta E widow James H h 31 Babbitt
" Etta M h 25 Thompson
" Everett laborer h 144 S Water
" Everett C clerk N B Five Cents Savings Bank b 55½ Fourth
" E Alton student b 167 Merrimac
" Flora A clerk Mer Nat Bank h at Acushnet [North
" Flora E clerk 159 Mill h 229
" Frances widow Philip M nurse h 173 Arnold
" Francis H h 6½ Sears [Sears
" Francis H Jr whitener bds 6½
" Frank G painter h 137 Sycamore
TRIPP FRANK G prop N B Steam Laundry 128-130 Pleasant h 192 Cottage See front cover
" Frank M machinist h 8 Rounds
" Frank S machinist 235 N Water h 91 Mill [Union
" Frank W (Tripp & Hanley) h 399
" Franklin C salesman h 71 Willis
" Frederick A asst shipper h 200 Elm
" Frederick C color grinder 146 Front h 43 Cedar
" Frederick E teamster h 1188 Kempton [Elm
" Frederick H drillworker h 32 Thompson
" Frederick P foreman 100 Fifth h 33 Borden [Dartmouth
" George driver 108 Grape h at
" George A b 54 Summer
" George E carpenter h 66 Lindsey
" George E surveyor h 326 Tinkham [h 229 North
" George Frederick carriagemaker
" George F city teamster bds 305 Mill
" George F shoemaker h 15 Spruce
" George F teamster h 101 Middle
" George H librarian public library h at Fairhaven
" George L carpenter h 332 Kempton [Cove h 34 Hunter
" George R (Chadwick & Tripp) 84

Tripp
" Hannah A widow Edgar F h 415 Cottage
" Hannah D died June 12 1911
" Harriet E widow Charles M h 7 N Orchard [Maxfield
" Harriet L widow James bds 410
" Harry B drillworker h 102 Fourth
" Harry C clerk 62 Pleasant bds 102 Fourth
" Harry H (New Bedford Welding Co) 177 N Water h 100 Willis
" Henry laborer h 1285 Rockdale av
" Henry C teamster h 31 High
" Henry W h 158 Arnold
" Herbert C driver b 703 Kempton
" Herbert J mgr 8 Hamilton h 167 Merrimac [Linden
" Herbert L city teamster bds 99½
" Hiram C mason 144 Campbell h do
" Holder B motorman b 7 Crapo
" Ida Mrs b 83 Sycamore [Park
" Ida E clerk 40 Purchase h 43
" Ida L clerk b 175 Park [nut
" Ira L freight checker b 131 Chest-
" Irving M electrician 120 Middle h 120 S Sixth [86 Ashland
" Isabella F widow Augustus C h
" Jabez D laborer h r 205 Acushnet av
" James B clerk b 410 Maxfield
" James E blacksmith h 17 Devoll
" James H b 86 Ashland
" James M engraver h 94 South
" James T carpenter 52 Grape h do
" John A chauffeur 181 Hawthorn h 78 S Sixth
" John L F driver h 166 North
" John W clerk 60 Shawmut av h 160 Parker [Palmer
" Joseph F drill straightener h 286
" Joseph J cotton sampler Bennett dept N E Cotton Yarn Co h 25 Keene
" Joseph M h Plainville road
" Katherine M bds 64 Hillman
" Lemuel driver 14 N Sixth rms 382 Kempton [h 180 do
" Leonard B chauffeur 22 Fourth
" Leroy G janitor Middle st school h 131 Chestnut
" Lester A foreman h 358 Reed
" Lester G teamster h 130 Purchase

Bread, Cake, Pastry
RICHMOND & COMPANY 255-257 UNION STREET
Bell 993 Automatic 1022

Tripp
" Lewis A laborer 144 S Water h 1199 Kempton
" Lewis L clerk b 358 Reed
" Lillian A widow John bds 227 Chancery
" Louis teamster bds 62 Kenyon
" Lydia Mrs h 60 Mechanic's lane
" Lydia A widow Orlando J h 267 Mill [Chancery
" Lydia A widow Wilson M h 446
" Lydia M Mrs h 227 Chancery
" Lyman W S glass decorator h 208 Grinnell [b at Acushnet
" Marion clerk 474 Acushnet av
" Mary C widow John E h 109 Smith [Cottage
" Mary F cashier 48 Pleasant b 47
" Mary H teacher Harrington school
" Mary J Mrs h 100 Willis
" Marshall H clerk b 485 Purchase
" Millie L widow Arthur C b 233 Rivet [school
" Myra C teacher Harrington st
" Myron E (Home Washing Co) 111 Myrtle h 449 Cottage
" Nancy widow Marshall h 495 Purchase
" Nancy E bds 78 Hillman
" Nathaniel A paint grinder George Kirby Jr Paint Co h 5 Foster
" Nathaniel C h 40 Dartmouth
" Norris H sec and treas 87 Union h 239 Pope [avenue
" Oliver P operative h 44 Shawmut
" Oscar clerk 240 Union b 103 Chancery [Fairhaven
" Oscar engineer 8 Campbell h at
" Oscar teamster b 31 Babbitt
" Peleg A h 427 Mill
" Rebecca B widow Charles T nurse h 103 Chancery [Chestnut
" Rebecca R widow James M b 79
" Richmond J (Tripp & Thorpe) 183 N Water h 203 Chestnut
" Roxana C widow George A h 330 Cottage [school b 71 Willis
" Ruby M teacher Thomas Donaghy
" Rufus B motorman b 45 Durfee
" Ruth E clerk 48 Pleasant b 175 Park [641 County
" Ruth M teacher Cedar st school b

Tripp
" Sarah S widow Nicholas G h 78 South Sixth [Coffin av
" Saviah C widow Thomas h 180
" Stephen driver 128 Pleasant
" Thomas A mgr The Pairpoint Corp h at Fairhaven
" Thomas B vice president U St Ry Co and real estate 413 County h do
" Thomas H fixer h 208 Eugenia
" Walter E helper 185 Acushnet av bds 160 Parker
" Walter F died Feb 27 1911
" Walter H city laborer h 7 Summit
" Warren Alexander chauffeur h 71 Ash (S) [69 Tremont
" Warren A clerk 168 S Water bds
" Wilhemina Mrs bds 54 Ash (N)
" William carpenter b 512 County
" William driver 108 Grape h 252 Field
" William A clerk b 5 Foster
" William A master mechanic h 42 Keene [chase
" William A machinist b 596 Pur-
" William B engineer 512 County
" William C mgr 109 S Sixth h 212 Fourth [mouth
" William E glass cutter h 66 Dart-
" William E mason h 224 Arnold
" William H bookkeper First National Bank b 117 Fifth [field
" William H foreman h 412 Max-
" William W collector b 64 Hillman
" William T teamster h 252 Field
" Zoeth plumber 202 County b do
" & Haney (Frank W Tripp and William G Haney) blacksmiths Mechanics lane

TRIPP & THORPE (R J Tripp and T W Thorpe) stair builders 183 N Water See page 764
Trodden Mary A h 16 Harmony
Tromblay Clara Mrs ladies tailor 338 Purchase h do [h 239 State
Tromley Edward washer 1066 County
Trotter James weaver b 20 Morton court [court
" Mary widow James h 20 Morton
" Michael weaver h 12 Morton ct
" William weaver b 20 Morton ct

GLOBE DYE HOUSE 220 SHAWMUT AVE.
J. N. J. LONHOLDT, PROP. Telephone Connections Goods called for and Delivered
Down town Office, 52 Pleasant St., Room 1 North End Office, 1014 Acushnet Ave.

Trought William carpenter h 19 Ashley [ford
Truax Sarah W Mrs removed to Med-
Trubak Thomas mill hand h 108 Phillips avenue
Truchon Frank carpenter h 82 Mott
Trudeau Cleophas hairdresser 972 Acushnet av h 4 Kenyon
" Cleophas J barber 972 Acushnet av h 4 Kenyon
" Charles operative h 126 Nash road
" Joseph S barber 110 William h 220 Phillips avenue
" W Antoine bds 4 Kenyon
Trudel Allie mill hand b 452 Belleville avenue [av
" Dolphis carpenter h 452 Belleville
" E L Mrs clerk 40 Purchasee b 25 Fair [bds 427 Pleasant
" Henry J clerk 1112 Acushnet av
" Joseph P clerk 598 Purchase h 427 Pleasant
" Leo weaver b 26 Bullard
" Louis weaver h 26 Bullard
Trudelle Ambrose painter h Church beyond Tarkiln Hill road [rd
" Clarence doffer b Tarkiln Hill
" Leo painter h 771 Purchase
Trueman Hilbert S Rev pastor Evangelical church h 152 Sycamore
Trull Charles F shoe repairer 207 Purchase h 149 River rd
" Charles F Jr shoes 207 Purchase h 124 Hillman
Truman Robert brewer b 57 Washburn [et
Trznadel Frank weaver h 1 Riv-
Tschaen Joseph weaver h 28 Ashley
Tucke Samuel grocer 187 N Front h 178 do [net av
Tucker Annie M Mrs h 300 Acush-
TUCKER, ANTHONY & CO bankers and brokers 17 Pleasant See page 6
" Arthur L cotton broker 25 N Water h 5 Maple
" Charles rigger h 62 Middle
" Charles N rem from city
" Dora L barber 131 Purchase b 97 Sidney [ant h do
" Edward T physician 258 Pleas-
" Edith H b 80 Mill [do
" Laura A dressmaker 198 Elm h
" Robert E b 258 Pleasant

Tucker
" William A h 31 Seventh
" William A (Tucker, Anthony & Co) 17 Pleasant h at Boston
Tueit Bridget widow h 670 First
" Edward P third hand bds 670 First
" John P operative b 670 First
" Thomas operative b 670 First
Tuell Borden clerk b 123 Rotch
" Charles A clerk h 27 Sherman
" Charles D h 1046 S Water
" Clifton P salesman 43 Purchase h 341 S Orchard
" Edward A F clerk 145 Arnold h at Fairhaven
" Frank P P h 28 Sherman
" Helen L clerk 160 Purchase b 28 Sherman [h do
" Joseph B C express 123 Rotch
Tuma Manuel glasscutter h 90 Tallman [99 Bedford
Tupper Amanda J widow Volney b
" Margaret A widow William h 111 Clark [b 238 Tremont
Tura Alphonso overseer 131 Court
Turcotte Aurore bookkeeper 507 N Front b 125 Bates av
" Donat carpenter h 110 Nash rd
" Edward clerk 507 N Front h Whitman cor Diman
" Emile loom fixer h 22 Nelson
" George laborer h 109 Princeton
" George operative h 34 Bullard
" Jean Baptiste carpenter h 83 Howard
" Jerry carpenter h 126 Nash rd
" Louis H grocer 507 N Front h 125 Bates av [Whitman
" Sevarin widow Cyprian h 110
Turenne Alice Mrs h 46 Belleville rd
" Clovis rem to Dartmouth
" Joseph weaver h 158 Whitman
" Louis weaver h 158 Whitman
Tures Frank mill hand b 175 Belleville av
Turgeon Alfred h 9 Felton
" Alfred twister b 70 Ruth
" Alfred J shoecutter h 237 Hillman
" Antoine grocer 155 Coffin av and lunch 1510 Acushnet av b 64 Bullard [net av b 49 do
" Arthur R blacksmith 51 Acush-
" Francois X Jr real estate 535 N Front h do
" F Xavier h 64 Bullard

GREENE & WOOD Every Kind of LUMBER AND MILL WORK
PINE STREET, off So. WATER STREET, NEW BEDFORD

Turgeon
" Moise carpenter h 70 Ruth
" Joseph V police Station 5 h 1791 Acushnet av
Turiel Duriel laborer h 8 Scott
Turkian Kerop shoemaker b 614 County
Turle Morris blacksmith b 45 Winsor [ant
Turner Abraham laborer h 400 Pleas-
" Ada shoeworker rms 19 Seventh
" Alice teacher Fifth street school rms 390 Union
" Alice Mrs operative 31 Commercial b 46 Belleville rd
" Amos spinner h 243 Bowditch
" Andrew R clerk 132 Union b 4 Shawmut av [rd
" Arthur C farmer b 818 Hathaway
" Benjamin R laborer b 36 Chancery
" Bessie M Mrs h 74 Mill
" Charles W jeweler 2167 Acushnet av h 2163 do
" Chester A optician 837 Purchase h 159 Ashland [Chancery
" Cordelia M widow Wilson h 36
" D Frank driver 64 Dartmouth
" Edith clerk 182 Union bds 266 Fourth [mouth
" Edward J loom fixer h 88 Dart-
" Elmira Mrs h 61 Acushnet av
" George E foreman The P Corp h 101 Campbell
" Harriet widow Thomas h 128 Bowditch [ney
" Henry clerk 685 First h 19 Sid-
" Herbert R teamster N B W W
" James fixer b 128 Bowditch
" James laborer h 70 Earle
" James Jr mill hand bds 70 Earle
" James H caterer 115 Tremont h do [dle (W)
" James H Jr teamster h 375 Mid-
" John carpenter h 87 Clifford
" John H teamster h 317½ Hillman
" John W fixer h 101 Nye
" Jonathan h 337 Pleasant
" Josephine A Mrs h 41 Ashley
" Kendall L helper b 446 Kempton
" Louis weaver h 226 Clifford
" Martha G widow Andrew R b 87 Locust
" Olive S housekeeper 446 Kempton
" Reuben fireman h 29 Collins

Turner
" Richard h 330 First
" Robert fixer bds 183 David
" Samuel janitor h 833 County
" Samuel Jr boss weaver Whitman Mill h 8 Studley
" Sarah Mrs h 351 Coggeshall
" Thomas blacksmith b 1039 County
" Walter E shipper b 343 Bowditch
" William gardener h 446 Kempton
" William spinner h 436 Rivet
" William F teller N B Five Cents Savings Bank h 324 Cottage
" William H janitor b 36 Chancery
" William K physician 1105 Acushnet av h do
" William S laborer h 7 Spruce
" Willis B h 818 Hathaway road
Tuttle Francis L Dr agent h 3½ Green
Tweedie Thomas laborer b 153 Hathaway av
Tweedy Bridget widow Robert b 253 Hathaway [b 129 Allen
Twiss Benjamin A commission agent
" William A supt Kilburn Mills h 129 Allen
TYER RUBBER CO 50 Bromfield Boston See page 743
Tyler Caleb B wire chief 57 N Second h 13 Bay
" Charles E removed to Salem
" Julia Mrs cook h 127 Smith
" Marion N clerk 57 N Second bds 13 Bay [Bay
" Ursula B widow Chaplin G bds 13
" William G testman 57 N Second bds 13 Bay
Tynan Catherine A b 335 Cedar
" John J car inspector U St Ry Co h 98 Durfee
" John J Jr shoemaker b 98 Durfee
" Sarah J dressmaker 335 Cedar h do [Bowditch
Tyrer Elizabeth widow Thomas h 341
" George weaver b 341 Bowditch
Tyrrell Ida widow Joseph h 140 Hathaway
" Joseph joiner bds 140 Hathaway
" Robert conductor b 140 Hathaway
Tyson George H teamster 160 North Water b 275 Bowditch [chase
" James J watchman h 621 Pur-
" Joseph eyelet maker b 621 Purchase

BONNEY, FOLSTER & CO.,
The North End's Shopping Centre
Dry Goods and Men's Furnishings
945-947 Acushnet Ave., New Bedford, Mass.

Ubertie James designer Whitman Mill
Uka Henry baker 437 Purchase h Nye
Uleroicz Adam grocer 140 Blackmer 106 Cross
Uliwicz Joseph weaver h 819 Water
Ullrich August baker 1190 Acushnet av bds 284 Earle
Ulric Joseph agent h 258 Cedar Grove
Ulrich Edward fixer h 28 Durfee
Uminski Edward A Rev pastor Church of Our Lady of Perpetual Help h 66 Howard
Underdown Walter H treasurer New Bedford Cotton Mills Corp h 16 Arch
Underwood Arthur C clerk b 48 Mill
" Arthur P treas 11 N Sixth h 48 Mill [Willis
" Drusilla widow George P h 77
" Gertrude M music teacher r 334 Kempton b do [48 Mill
" James F clerk Wamsutta Mills h
" Mary L Mrs bookkeeper 80 Purchase h 48 Sycamore
" Waldo E inspector 100 Fifth h 48 Sycamore [Pleasant
" Willis C police sergeant h 167
Union for Good Works 12 Market
" Shoe Co 120 Purchase
UNION STREET RAILWAY CO The office Purchase cor William car barn Purchase cor Weld See page 21
United Cigar Stores Co (N Y) 94 Purchase [Pleasant rm 39
" States Army Recruiting Office 76
Unwin Charles E watchmaker 183 Purchase h 25 James
" George P machinist h 25 James
Upham John H Jr shoemaker h 50 Rounds
" William foreman 130 Union h 64 Newton [lane
" William O T farmer h Upham
Upjohn James Jr stable foreman 304 Kempton h 140 Mill [Middle
" Maria T widow Aaron h 152
" Sophia H bds 140 Mill
" William R painter h 121 State
Uppstrom Charles blacksmith b 1089 Acushnet av [vell
Upton Louis steamfitter bds 20 Cov-
Urban Jan mill hand 97 N Front
Urquhart Henrietta widow Daniel G h 208 Weld
Uttley Arthur bakery (Velvet Ice Cream Co) 349 Kempton h 91 Shawmut av

Vaillancourt Alfred loom fixer h 47 Ashley
" Edmond weaver b 1103 S Water
" Stanislaus weaver b 1103 S Water [Coffin av
Valecka Adolph back boy bds 350
" Emanuel weaver h 350 Coffin av
Valent Humberto janitor b 1238 Acushnet av [Bowditch
Valentine Daniel operative bds 369
" Freeman city laborer h 71 Cedar
" Jennie J teacher Hosea M Knowlton school b at Fairhaven
" John chief engineer Nonquitt Spinning Co h 369 Bowditch
" John A engineer Manomet Mills h 347 Bowditch
" Joseph weaver h 208 Eugenia
" Robert eyeletmaker h 32 Myrtle
" Thomas conductor rms 602 Purchase
" Thomas laborer b 6 Cove rd
" William weaver b 208 Eugenia
Valerien Emile weaver h 35 Nye
Valadoa Alvaro carpenter b 191 Arnold
" Candida mill hand h 326 First
" Frank gearcutter bds 191 Arnold
" Maria G widow Frank h 191 Arnold [Holly
Vallancort Hormidas printer h 159
Valles John variety 191 S Water h do
Valley Adelard machinist b 5 Fifth
" Henry teamster b 535 Acushnet avenue
" John A third hand h 177 State
" Noel blacksmith 332 Purchase
Valliere Albert operative h 17 Cotter
" Edward weaver h 117 Bullard
" Euclid operative b 216 Sawyer
" Henry weaver h 121 Webster ct
" Hormidas operative h 5 Bonneau court
" James weaver b 25 Bentley
" Lucy widow Raphael h 194 Dean
" Octave operative h 216 Sawyer
" Wilfred operative b 216 Sawyer
Valloza Joseph operative h 86 Crapo

M. P. B. Silva & Son **Paints, Oils and Glass**
Sole Agents for Lucas Tinted Gloss Paints
157 ACUSHNET AVENUE Both Phones NEW BEDFORD

Valois Armand D chauffeur 57 N Second h 24 Ash (N)
" Edward painter 347 Kempton
" Omer Rev pastor St Ann R C church h 60 Brock av
Valoura Domingas F barber 191 Court b 180 Belleville av
Valvoline Oil Co W D Ellis pres foot North
Valway Albert carpenter h 30 Nye
" Henry mill hand bds 30 Nye
Vanasse Alexandre operative h 456 Belleville av
" Joseph operative h 7 Bowditch
" Louis weaver h 37 Scott
" Noe carder b 863 Purchase
" Peter b 456 Belleville av
" Xavier F overseer Wamsutta Mill h 67 Austin [coln
Van Campen Hiram Mrs rms 21 Lin-
VANCE BERT A garage automobile storage and supplies 24 Sycamore h do See page 42
Vancoure George laborer h 129 Eugenia
" Henry weaver bds 129 Eugenia
" **Stanley weaver b 129** Eugenia
Vandal Napoleon F barber bds 60 Cove [295 N Front
Vandamme E Edmond weaver h
Vandenbergh Joseph operative b 271 Shaw
Vanden**bossche Adele** widow Cyrille dressmaker 71 Chancery h do
Van Doorne Leopold weaver h Plainville road cor Shawmut av
Vandreau Wilfred fixer bds 909 S Water [188 Summer
Van Flatern Ernest F insurance h
Vanni Sarah nurse bds 238 Tremont
" Vincent mason 238 Tremont h do
" Vincent J mason bds 238 Tremon [Second
Vanocia Manuel S laborer h 286 S
Vanstone William I motorman h 33 Richmond [Collette
Vantiero Manuel mill hand h 125
Vanzini Frank clerk h 144 Chancery
Varcellone John laborer h r 567 Acushnet av [Rockland h do
Vargas Flora K Mrs dressmaker 123
" Joseph laborer h 197 Elm [av
" Joseph operative b 32 Acushnet
" Joseph King h 123 Rockland

Vargas
" Philomena E clerk 185 Union bds 123 Rockland [S Second
Vargers Manuel F watchman h 503
Varieur Alfred weaver h 205 State
Varley John engineeer h r 35 Smith
Varney Emma widow Arthur h 3 Seneca
" Isaac weaver h 178 Phillips av
" Louis carpenter h 158 Nash road
Varnum Albert H salesman Anthony Swift & Co h 237 Tremont
" Charles W overseer h 204 Earle
" Leon removed to Newtonville
Varville John twister h 1088 S Water
Vasco Joe laborer h 500 S Second
Vasconcelles Antone ropemaker h 470 Union [Union
" Joseph 2nd rope maker bds 470
Vasconcellos Joseph F C canvasser h 380 Purchase [County
" Julio salesman 211 Union h 240
Vaslett Elmer E Mrs b 183 Fourth
Vasolino Giuseppe laborer h 2 Turner's court [away
Vasser John weaver h 158 Hath-
Vaughan Arthur C clerk 23 Borden b do [Mattapoisett
" Arthur S asst 298 Purchase h at
" Charles E mgr 294 Purchase h 650 County
" Frederick J cook rms 91 Waldron

HARRY C VAUGHAN
Real Estate Agent, Auctioneer, Appraiser and Justice of the Peace
Care of Estates a Specialty
Office and Residence
23 Borden Street
Telephone Connection

Vaughan Harry C real estate 23 Borden h do [& Co h 124 Florence
" James bookkeeper Anthony Swift

Steiger-Dudgeon Co.
"The WOMAN'S Store."
Tel. Bell 82 & 83, Branches connecting all depts.
" " 160 For Office only. Auto. 1211

SUMPTIONS, ASSORTMENTS AT ALL TIMES OF DEPENDABLE DRY GOODS

Vaughan
" Joseph D bookkeeper h 613 Cottage [den
" Mary E widow Albert C b 23 Bor-
" Samuel A variety 302 Acushnet av rms do
VAUGHAN UNDERTAKING CO Inc 294 Purchase See advt opp Undertakers in Business Directory
" Weston C 2nd clerk 288 Purchase bds 294 do
" Weston C Jr president Vaughan Undertaking Co Inc 294 Purchase h 92 Hillman
" William H h 101 Willow [side av
Vautour Albert operative h 4 River-
" Cyrille weaver b 96 Davis
" Joseph operative h 96 Davis
Vazde Miranda Ernest freight handler b 56 First
Veara Etta milliner 101½ Fifth b do
" Frank bds 101½ Fifth
" Frank J engineer h 101½ Fifth
" Jesse laborer h 174 S Second
Veary Martin teamster b 303 Austin
" William spinner h 303 Austin
" William Jr doffer b 303 Austin
Veeder Frank J drill cutter h 39 Bay
" Isabel bookkeeper 151 Union rms 33 Fifth
Veeney Julia Mrs h 15 Cannon
Vega Nunes C mill hand h 25 Babbitt
Vegas Antone laborer h 74 Independent [chase
Vegerie Frank engineer rms 781 Pur-
Veil Manuel operative h 126 r Cedar Grove
Veira Alfred laborer h 45 Stowell
" Amelia telephone operator 57 N Second b 21 Winsor
" Annie Mrs h 86 Howland
" Antone laborer h 30 Lombard
" Antonio C Rev printer 250 S Second h 248 do [av
" Armede laborer h 122 Acushnet
" August mill hand h Mt Pleasant near Kings Highway [ska
" Fernandes fisherman h 104 Potom-
" Frank carpenter bds 21 Winsor
" Frank laborer h 63 Grinnell
" Frank L operative b 177 David

Veira
" James machinist h 147 Acushnet avenue
" John h 9 Stapleton
" John laborer h 4 Stanton court
" John laborer h 95 Prospect
" John mill hand h 116 Phillips av
" John operative b 260 S Second
" John C grocer 601 S Water h 30 Cove
" Joseph blacksmith h 49 Chancery
" Joseph clerk 268 Fourth b 48 Oak
" Joseph engineer Anthony Swift & Co h at Fairhaven
" Joseph fisherman h 16 Cotter [av
" Joseph fisherman h 122 Acushnet
" Joseph glass worker h 5434 Acushnet avenue
" Joseph laborer h 282 S Second
" Joseph laborer b 276 Nash road
" Joseph mill hand h 332 S Front
" Joseph operative h 79 Katharine
" Joseph operative b 122 Acushnet avenue
" Louis fireman h 33 Winsor
" Lorie laborer h 12 Scott [av
" Manuel fisherman h 24 Acushnet
" Manuel laborer h 12 Bethel
" Manuel laborer h r 216 S Front
" Manuel mariner h 56 S Water
" Manuel mill hand h 104 Phillips av
" Manuel G h 5 Maiden lane
" Manuel M h 248 S Second
" Manuel M carpenter h 299 S Front
" Mary h 241 S Front [sor
" Mary C widow Manuel h 21 Win-
" Nellie Mrs h 3 E Durfee
" see Vera
Velho Augustus F police h 6 Warwick
" Frank G driver h 285 Davis
Veli Hassan laborer h 191 Belleville avenue [lips av
Velicha Rapo mill hand b 37 Phil-
Vellose Jose shoe repairer 281 Rivet h 86 Crapo [ct
Velois Amedee painter b 13 Austin
" Frank weaver h 13 Austin ct
Velsor Charles W died June 13 1911
Velvet Ice Cream Co (Arthur Uttley) 349 Kempton
Venables Albert rem from city
" George laborer b 25 E French av

PELEG H. SHERMAN 506 COUNTY ST.
FUNERAL DIRECTOR AND EMBALMER
OFFICE PHONES. Bell 690-13. Auto. 1305.
RESIDENCE PHONES. Bell 690-12. Auto. 1306.

Ventor Manuel laborer h 9 Howland
Ventura Antone laborer h 48 South
" Antonio J carpenter h 122 Dartmouth
" Charles laborer h 429 First
" Charles mill hand b 122 Dartmouth [ond
" Frank mill hand h 337 S Sec-
" Frank laborer h 79 Cove rd
" John laborer h 62 South
" Joseph fireman b 631 S Water
" Jules laborer b 122 Dartmouth
" Julio F wood 57 Crapo h do
" Manuel laborer h 464 S Water
" Manuel operative h 59 Cove rd
Vera Annie E widow h 86 Howland
" August fisherman h 328 S Front
" Catherine Mrs h 150 Acushnet av
" Charles R operative h 280 Orchard (S)
" Clara Mrs h 96 Jouvett
" Frank h 58 Fifth
" Frank b 44 Lindsev
" Frank laborer h 79 Cove road
" Frank mariner h 109 Dunbar
" Frank porter 84 Union
" Frank Jr clerk Third District Court h 58 Fifth [ton
" Frank E machinist h 151 Kemp-
" Frank J engineer 270 Acushnet av b 103 Fifth [mouth h do
" Frank L contractor 249 Dart-
" Frank P mariner h 86 Howland
" Frederick machinist h 306 Court
" John R (Vera & Robitaille) rear 213 Coffin av h 312 Davis
" Joseph drillmaker h 340 Allen
" Joseph driver b 127 Dartmouth
" Joseph R died Nov 8 1910
" Lawrence janitor h 53 Swift
" Manuel fisherman h 127 Dartmouth [428 do
" Manuel hostler 430 Purchase bds
" Manuel A gardener h 44 Lindsey
" Mary Mrs h 60 Hall
" Rose Mrs h 127 Dartmouth
" Stella stenographer 5 Beetle lane b at Mattapoisett [Fourth
" William R Vera & Curry h 269
" & Curry props New England Comb works 120 S Sixth
" & Robitaille (John R Vera and Emile Robitaille) cotton comb re-needling r 213 Coffin av

Vera
" see Veira [Acushnet av
Vercelone Giovanni laborer h 694
" Peter laborer h 694 Acushnet av
Vergnia Manuel operative h 205 N Front
Veria Joseph h 49 Chancery [Front
Verner Harry mill hand h 483 South
Vernon John pool 628½ First h 630 do [N Front
Verranault Ephraim doffer h 252
" Francois X laborer h 333 N Front
" Frank X painter h 109 Brook
Verrier Amos carpenter h 201 Austin
Verronneau Frederick clerk bds 161 State
" Joseph weaver h 161 State
Vertefeuille John barber b 89 Beetle
" Joseph weaver h 89 Beetle
" Joseph Jr weaver b 89 Beetle
" Oliver weaver h 1060 County
" Oliver Jr weaver h 1060 County
" Zepherin barber 912 Acushnet av rms 89 Beetle [ton
Vertente John carpenter h 7 Fel-
Verville Arthur second hand h 170 N Front [Bowditch
" Cleopher grocer 223 State b 113
" Joseph C blacksmith 1180 Acushnet av h 113 Bowditch
" Philippe teamster h Hawes st
Vetorina Joseph E (Vetorina & Lemos) h 1353 Rockdale avenue
" Manuel baker h 131 Mt Vernon
" & Lemos (J E Vetorina and F S Lemos) market gardeners 1379 Rockdale avenue [shall
Vetterline William bds 307 Cogge-
Vezina George real estate and insurance 1223 Acushnet av h 99 Holly [niman
Vialo Joseph hod carrier bds 5 Pen-
Viator Edith J widow Antone h 63 Briggs [ty
Viau Rugina widow h 840 Coun-
Vicars Ellen b 132 Mill [h do
" Margaret C dressmaker 132 Mill
Vickers Tamar Mrs mill hand bds 102 Nash road
Victoria Frank baker h 397 Cedar
" Maria Mrs h 242 S Front [Fourth
Victorino Joseph M laborer bds 156
Viegas John fireman h 341 First

COAL AND WOOD
HAY AND STRAW
F. T. AKIN & COMPANY
WALNUT, COR. WATER, 84 PLEASANT ST., 25 WELD SQ.
129 COVE STREET WHF. FOOT OF COFFIN STREET

Vieira Antone mill hand bds 188 Thompson
" Antonio P Rev pastor Mt Carmel R C church h 230 Bonney
" A C publisher O'Independent 250 South Second
" Claudino shoemaker h 5½ Harrison
" Felix laborer h 194 Blackmer
" Frank laborer h 912 County
" John C gardener h 89 High
" Joseph b 148 Belleville avenue
" Joseph mariner b 153 Bonney
" Joseph mill hand h 103 Hemlock
" Joseph P physician 317 Rivet h 230 Bonney
" Julio weaver h 45 Nelson
" Laura clerk b 67 Dartmouth
" Lorenz laborer bds 103 Hemlock
" Manuel fireman h 411 Orchard (S)
" Manuel mill hand b 35 Mitchell
" Manuel mill hand b 153 Belleville avenue [avenue
" Manuel mill hand b 191 Belleville
" Manuel G laborer h 205 Bonney
" Manuel G Jr registry clerk P O h 199 Bonney [h 248 S Second
" Manuel M variety 79 Howland
" Mariano tender h 81 Cove road
" Mary R Mrs h 115 Bonney
" Melaina widow h 55 Independent
" Nicholas R mariner h 153 Bonney
" see Veira [atre h at Lowell
Vien Cordelia Mrs prop Vien's The-
" Edmond teamster b 219 Sawyer
" Elmer teamster b 29 Bullard
" Eugene M mgr 1159 Acushnet av and liquors 1162 Acushnet av h 1166 do
" Frank b 1871 Acushnet avenue
" George shoemaker rms 300 Acushnet avenue
" Gideon fixer h 102 David
" Henry laborer h 219 Sawyer
" William G third hand b 102 David
Vienna Hair and Corset Shop Lulu M Merrill 96 Purchase
Viens Claudia clerk 1131 Acushnet av bds 214 Sawyer
" George P agent bds 82 Valentine
" Henry J fixer h 250 Bowditch
" Joseph teamster h 287 N Front

Viens
" Theatre moving pictures 1159 Acushnet avenue
Vient Abraham fixer h 86 Beetle
" Abraham Jr fixer h 86 Beetle
" Arthur X h 120 Clark [ley
" Frederick second hand h 26 Ash-
" Henry fixer bds 86 Beetle
" Wilfred fixer h 86 Beetle
Viera Antone F carder h 45 Mitchell
" Augusto R spinner h 644 Mt Pleasant
" Francis mill worker h 912 County
" Joseph C clerk h 48 Oak
" Julio laborer h 18 Edison [do
" Virginio fish 523 S Water h 481
Viereck Louis machinist b 111 Grinnell [sor
Vieria Joseph drill maker h 48 Win-
Vierick Mary S housekeeper 73 Russell
Vierton Peter laborer h 648 First
Vigeant Joseph A removed to Acushnet [ditch
" Joseph H operative bds 94 Bow-
" Mederic milk 595 Mt Pleasant h do
" Pierre b 595 Mt Pleasant
" William weaver h 220 Phillips av
Viger Joseph Jr carpenter h 12 Harmony
" Philip laborer h 114 Mott
Vigneault Arthur grocer 1525 Acushnet av h 1527 do
" Cora milliner 1354 Acushnet av bds 95 Bullard
" Stanislas (Vigneault & Laplante) liquors 273 Sawyer h 95 Bullard
" Telesphore died May 12 1911
" Ulric carpenter b 23 Covell
" Urbain h 171 Bowditch
" & Laplante (Stanislas Vigneault and Pierre Laplante) liquors 273 Sawyer
Vigue Mary Mrs weaver h 128 Cove
Villandre Bartholomew doffer b 319 Belleville avenue
" Delphis laborer b 319 Belleville av
" Ernest teamster h 59 Bullard
" Simon laborer b 319 Belleville av

Remember to investigate our methods before taking up a business course.
Kinyon's Commercial School
Odd Fellows Bldg., Cor. William and Pleasant Sts., New Bedford, Mass.

Villemure Henry engineer 235 N Water h 336 Pleasant [bury
Villeneuve Alex carpenter h 40 Salis-
Villeux Louis carpenter h 103 Ruth
Vinal Andrew bds 136 Florence
" Charles H linotype machinist Standard h 9 Rounds
" Charles H registrar 125 Middle h 103 Summer [h 90 Bedford
" Elizabeth C widow Frederick H
" Franklin H Mrs h 145 Kempton
" Herbert R clerk 357 Court h 35 Jenny Lind . [Davis
Vincent Aime shoecutter bds 282
" Andrew h 45 Babbitt
" Antoine b 2062 Acushnet av
" Antone operative h 88 Rockland
" Arthur operative rms 69 Fourth
" Charles H foreman U St Ry Co h 133 Reynolds
" Charles H student b 64 State
" Clara S teacher Middle st school h 233 Middle [net av
" Emile paper cutter h 2062 Acush-
" Frank H machinist h 212 Grinnell
" Frank X operative b 358 N Front
" Fred engineer h 205 Acushnet av
" Fred painter 394 N Front h 196 Bowditch
" Joseph carpenter b 358 N Front
" Joseph grocer 282 Tinkham h 280 do
" Joseph C blacksmith h 206 State
" Joseph C Jr operative b 51 Howland Village [Acushnet av
" Joseph S clerk 781 S Water h 72
" Leonard J reeler b 206 State
" Manuel P operative h 608 S Water
" Mark T (DeWolf & Vincent) hardware 111 William h 77 North
" Mary Mrs h 129 Grinnell
" Perry b 77 North
" Firsera carder h 280 Cedar Grove
" Ulric contractor and builder 77 Bullard h do [271 Phillips av
" Wilfred mgr 1755 Acushnet av h
" William H clerk 190 Weld b 282 Davis
Vinet Arsene weaver b 69 Nelson
Vining Charles W Jr salesman h 27 Fifth [Kempton
" Martha widow Charles W bds 86
Viola Joseph laborer h 7 Penniman
Virtue John hairdresser 162 Purchase rms 142 Pleasant
Visco Albert A rem to Hyannis
" Harry rem to Hyannis
" Peter shoemaker b 183 Bowditch
Vishnefsky Abraham fruit 795 S Water h do
Vital Manuel F reed fixer h 368 First
Vitinty Adanowiecz weaver h 659 First
Viveiros Arthur furniture repairer 170 Purchase h 37 Nelson
" Joseph baker 654 S Water h do
" Julius carpenter h 269 S Second
" Manuel spinner h 69 Katharine
Vlach George mill hand h 81 Davis
Vlvil Hector hostler rms 283 Sawyer
Vogel Caroline widow George h 71 Lindsey
" Ellery L clerk Merchants National Bank b 56 Rounds
" George F painter bds 71 Lindsey
" Robert R police h 56 Rounds
Voghel Hilaire clerk 78 Hicks h 112 Bates av [Princeton
" Hormidas grocer 78 Hicks h 109
" Joseph janitor 70 Hicks bds 63 do
" Sylvina Mrs b 74 Hicks
Vohnoutka Charles weaver h 12 Oneko lane
Voisin Alfred laborer h 199 State
" Alfred Mrs variety 199 State h do [Acushnet av h 313 do
Vokes William W restaurant 315
Von Flatern Elizabeth C teacher J H Clifford school b 184 Summer
" Ernest F clerk 303 Merchants Bank bldg h 184 Summer
" Malvina L instructor N B Industrial school b 184 Summer
Vose Lottie M teacher Thomas A Greene b 1 Park place
" William H driver h 52 Smith
Vossler Carl weaver b 337 Davis
" Martin operative h 337 Davis
" Martin Jr carpenter b 337 Davis
Vouture Adelle widow Bazil h 51 Tallman [ter
Voyer Alphonse fixer h 892 S Wa-
" Mary Mrs operative h 164 State
" William loom fixer h 59 County
" William L mill hand b 164 State

HASKELL BROS. DEALERS IN
ICE
400 COURT STREET TELEPHONE CONNECTION NEW BEDFORD, MASS.

Wach Michael operative b 6 Fulton court [Austin
Waddacor Elizabeth A widow b 121
Waddington James weaver h 111 Tallman
" James R rem from city
" John J ice h 61 Salisbury
" Richard weaver h 56 Thompson
" Ronald electrician bds 32 Viall
" Thomas weaver h 32 Viall
" William E master mechanic Potomska Mills b 21 Crapo
Wade Albert L tinsmith h 100 Crape
" Bernard C clerk Potomska Mills b 20 Howard av
" Charles E engineer Dartmouth Mfg Corp h 18 Willis
" Clifford L draughtsman 303 Municipal bldg bds 18 Willis
" Howarth fixer h 125 Nash rd
" John P plumber 46 Linden h 173 Shawmut av
" John W twister h 259 Bowditch
" Lester tinsmith 185 Acushnet av b 100 Grape [562 Union
" Melville R baker 306 Arnold h
" Patrick J machinist h 178 Weld
" Robert fireman N B E Co h 190 N Front [Front
" Robert drillworker h 190 North
" William E laborer b 21 Rural
Wadsworth Edward foreman h 30 Cottage
" John engineer h 7 Salisbury
" Louise h 28 Kempton
" William H clerk P & R Coal & Iron Co b 227 Union
Wady Arnold B b 107 S Sixth
" Mary E widow Arnold B h 107 S Sixth
Wagner B Franklin laborer h 193 Elm [ant
" Eugene machinist h 438 Pleas-
" Frank weaver b 850 First [cas
" Harry J sergeant U S A h 10 Lu-
" Isaiah C mechanical supt Times h 11 Ocean [tle
" Joseph D motorman h 35 Myr-
" Lillian Mrs b 117 Tremont
" William K collector 57 N Second h 39 Rotch
Wahlgren Herman designer Dartmouth Mfg Corp h 275 Hawthorn
Waiman Fred agent rms 36 N Sixth
Wainer Alfred D laborer bds 256 Chancery [195 Elm
" Charles S plumber 26 N Second b
" Edward farm hand b 195 Elm
" Frederick D city laborer h 270 Mill
" Henry pedlar h 120 S Second
" Lucy housekeeper 195 Elm
" Lucy J widow Thomas J b 80 Cedar
" Lydia A widow David h 195 Elm
" Maurice T laborer h 317 Hillman
" Paul F driver b 80 Cedar
" Walter L teamster h 80 Cedar
Wainscott Jonathan weaver h 29 Social [chase h 231 North
Wainwright Joseph waiter 62 Pur-
" Mary clerk 185 Union b 231 North [do
" Richard H clerk 107 Cove b 109
" Robert grocer 107 Cove h 109 do
" Samuel machinist h 252 Coffin av
Waite B H & Co (Oliver F Brown) carpeting 71 William [Spruce
" Carlton helper 48 Pleasant h 65
" David H rem from city
" Elsie R clerk 182 Union b 249 Hillman
" Florence L b 139 Cottage
" Leon C clerk N Bedford Storage & Warehouse h 143 Reynolds
" Rebecca Mrs h 249 Hillman
" Stephen E furniture 87 N Second h 89 do [Oil Co
Wakeman George V yardman Texas
" Harwood L mgr Texas Oil Co
Walda Frank weaver h 156 Tallman
" Joseph weaver h 156 Tallamn
Walder Juda Hewbrew teacher 10 Grandfield h do
Waldron Ann M h 214 Rivet
" Elizabeth F stenographer 16 Elm b 38 Russell
" Fred C machinist 235 N Water h 288 Acushnet av [net av h do
" F C Mrs dressmaker 288 Acush-
" James mule spinner h 122 Thompson
" John J h 36 Mosher
" John R carder b 36 Mosher
" Joseph F sub letter carrier bds 122 Thompson
" Joseph W gardener b 214 Rivet
" Katherine b 214 Rivet [Russell
" Lydia A widow L Franklin h 38

J. F. CROSSLEY 223 MILL STREET COR. EMERSON PHONE
STEAM and HOT WATER HEATING
GAS FITTING and FIXTURES

Waldron
" Margaret h 214 Rivet
" Margaret operative b 36 Mosher
" Margaret A widow John h 84 Acushnet av
" Thomas laborer h 12 Warren
" Thomas mule spinner h 122 Thompson [son
" Thomas J operative b 122 Thomp-
" William F glass blower bds 122 Thomposn [Willis
" William R, R R engineer h 17
Walecka Charles weaver h 199 Dean
Walkden Alice Mrs h 82 Dartmouth
" James weaver b 32 Cove
" Thomas laborer h 21 Ashley
" Walter b 82 Dartmouth
Walker Ada b 288 Acushnet av
" Albert W spinner b 625 Purchase
" Anna W widow John C cashier 41 William h 284 Pleasant
" Bradford H clerk 100 Fifth bds at S Dartmouth [Purchase
" Catherine widow Henry h 625
" Charlotte E h 49 Maxfield
" Clinton I sub letter carrier h 176 Coffin av [15 Chestnut
" Edith F teacher High school b
" Elmer draughtsman 3 E Pope
" Esther clerk b 1283 Acushnet av
" Frank E tinsmith h 248 Rivet
" Fred spinner b 1283 Acushnet av
" George spinner h 122 Tinkham
" George H spinner h 270 Austin
" Harry V mgr 60 Pleasant h 71 Maple [Fairhaven
" Harold compositor Mercury h at
" Isabelle Mrs h 288 Acushnet av
" Joseph spinner h 297 Belleville av
" Mary Wheeler osteopathic physician 288 Union h do
" Nellie S bookkeeper 160 Purchase b 87 School [Acushnet av
" Plesents widow William h 1283
" Robert I osteopathic physician 288 Union h do
" Samuel R weaver b 291 Collette
" Thomas rem from city
" William died April 16 1911
" William H weaver h 94 Rodney
Wall Annie R rms 20 Seventh
" Charles A janitor Unitarian church bds 52 Park [Robeson
" Elizabeth clerk 40 Purchase b 12

Wall
" Hannah chiropodist 12 Robeson h do [Park
" Hannah C widow John A h 52
" James h 12 Robeson
" James operative h 61 Washington
" James J shoemaker 105 William h 120 Clark [bds do
" Margaret dressmaker 12 Robeson
" Marrie A milliner h 172 Fourth
" Mary M widow Michael D shoemaker and bootblack 105 Union h 98 Clark
" Michael D died January 2 1911
" Richard shoe repairer 149 Purchase h 37 Florence [av
" Thomas H laborer h 900 Rockdale
Wallace Albert P removed from city
" Alexander eyelet maker h 410 Pleasant
" Edmund painter h 190 Dean [do
" Elizabeth Mrs variety 28 Cove h
" Emory W bookkeeper h 238 Chestnut [from city
" Hannah L widow Henry M rem
" James A cloth inspector b 49 Fair
" James P bds 238 Chestnut
" John card maker h Cove rd near Rockdale avenue
" Mary J housekeeper 28 Cove
" Mary L widow James b 80 Thompson [410 Pleasant
" William clerk 830 Purchase bds
" William painter bds 28 Cove
" William J drill maker h 207 Rivet
Wallbank Alice widow James h cor Middle and Ash
" Ignatius T removed to Fall River
" Patrick E clerk 416 Kempton h 348 Middle
Waller Arol removed from city
" Myron D chauffeur h 9 Arch
Walley Edward spinner b 16 McMurray terrace
Wallingford Clarence mail carrier h Shawmut av near Plainville rd
Wallison Hammond clerk 977 S Water h 9 Willis [net av h 190 Davis
Wallner Anna Mrs baker 1233 Acush-
" Anna M clerk 40 Purchase b 190 Davis [190 Davis
" Anton baker 1233 Acushnet av h

CHARLES A. CROSHERE CARRIAGE AND AUTO
38 FOURTH ST. Bell Phone 1964-23 PAINTING.

Wallner
" Helen J stenographer 40 Purchase b 190 Davis
" Thomas J machinist b 190 Davis
Wallworth Richard spinner h 158 Reynolds
Walmsley Albert clerk 1001 Acushnet avenue bds 305 Davis
" Arthur W removed to Boca del Toro Panama
" Carrie Mrs bds 155 Cedar
" Clara Mrs removed from city
" Elmer apprentice Standard
" Herbert assistant superintendent Wamsutta Mill bds 43 Arnold
" Herbert E agent Wamsutta Mill h 43 Arnold
" James h 305 Davis
" James weaver h 5 Fern
" John electrician h 305 Davis
" John weaver bds 12 Salisbury
" John R second hand h 5 Reynolds
" Mary A widow James h 256 Weld
" Richard baker h 12 Salisbury
" Robert painter 303 Collette h do
" Thomas clerk 1625 Acushnet av h 158 Davis
" Thomas weaver bds 305 Davis
" William operative b 19 Ashley
Walne Henry weaver h 62 Dean
Walsh Agnes mill hand h 28 Belleville road
" Albert box maker b 156 Church
" Ann widow James F h 19 Division
" Annie M widow P Charles h 41 Briggs
" Arthur G died March 19 1910
" Arthur L druggist 1263 Acushnet av bds 163 Myrtle [avenue
" Bernard pianist h 182 Acushnet
" Catherine widow James h 139 Reynold [Thompson
" Dennis overseer Page Mfg Co h 52
" Dennis J Jr b 52 Thompson
" Eliza mill hand h 28 Belleville rd
" Fielding H carpenter h 34 Bullock
" Francis H salesman h 58 Borden
" Fred weaver h 36 Howard
" Gertrude milliner 956 S Water b rear 1025 do
" Henry weaver h 284 Earle
" James h 32 McGurk
" James h 175 Fourth

Walsh
" James fireman h 30 St John
" James weaver b 1 Clark
" James L clerk P O b 587 Purchase
" John carder b 19 Division
" John conductor h 55 Gifford
" John driver bds 27 Elm
" John operative bds 154 Tallman
" John weaver h 67 Nash road
" John weaver h 289 Fourth
" John E driver 386 Acushnet av rms 31 Elm [chase
" John H city laborer h 587 Pur-
" John R engineer Steamer No 2 h 400 Elm (W)
" John W packer h 73 Hathaway
" Joseph carder h 135 Bullard
" Joseph (Lowney & Walsh) 2 Masonic bldg h 266 Hawthorn
" Joseph mill hand h 289 Fourth
" Kathleen telephone operator 57 N Second b 255 North Front
" Kathryn bookkeeper b 5 Weaver
" Margaret and Nellie weavers h 57 Reynolds
" Margaret T teacher Thomas Donaghy school bds 52 Thompson
" Martin E operative b 176 State
" Mary J widow Arthur G h 166 Grinnell [school b 52 Thompson
" Mary M teacher I W Benjamin
" Michael W engineer b 108 Cove
" Patrick weaver h 291 Fourth
" Patrick weaver h r 1025 S Water
" Patrick Jr grinder b 19 Division
" P Charles died Feb 12 1911
" Robert spinner h 739 Belleville av
" Robert J weaver h 97 Division
" Sarah Mrs mill hand h 61 Dean
" Sarah widow Robert b 172 Belleville road [165 Shawmut av
" Susannah widow William T bds
" Thomas fitter h 94 Hemlock [av
" Thomas salesman h 165 Shawmut
" Walter operative h 136 Tallman
" William laborer h 201 Eugenia
" William weaver h 97 Division
" William A wood worker h 156 Church
" William M student b 52 Thompson
" see Welsh and Welch
Walten Stephen twister h 11 Welcome

J. G. NICHOLSON
LUMBER, SASH, DOORS and BLINDS
BOWDITCH STREET, NEW BEDFORD, MASS.

Walter Myer collector b 1139 Acushnet avenue
Walton Frederick D weaver h 98 Linden
" James operative h 337 Earle
" William loom fixer b 332 Sawyer
Wambolt Robie teamster b 116 Rounds
·Wamsutta Club 435 County
" Mills E T Pierce treasurer cotton goods Acushnet av cor Wamsutta
" Pharmacy 1 Pleasant [Durfee
Wannacott John D wood worker h 78
Wantman Harry clerk 565 S Water h do
" Ida dry goods 565 S Water h do
Warburton Henry C carver bds 195 Shawmut avenue
" Herbert laborer h 275 Phillips av
" Joseph spinner h 57 Howard
" Richard twister h 76 Hathaway
" Thomas S overseer Page Mfg Co h 195 Shawmut av [Tallman
Ward Caroline Mrs weaver h 152
" Catherine A widow h 534 N Front
" David foreman mailing dept Standard b 1007 Purchase
" Ernest butcher h 989 County
" Eva Mrs operative b 87 Hathaway
" Francis J machinist h 184 Belleville road [ville road
" Francis J Jr printer b 184 Belle-
" Francis R hostler h 57 Church
" Frank b 259 N Front
" Frank master mechanic Neild M Corp h 280 Sawyer [County
" Hanay clerk 704 Purchase h 989
" Harry weaver h 32 Durfee
" Harry weaver h 174 Phillips av
" Henry weaver h 21 Ashland pl
" Herbert weaver h 21 Ashland pl
" James laborer b 87 Fruit
" James variety 879 Purchase h 1007 Purchase
" James H mill hand h 63 Nash rd
" James J machinist h 335 Sawyer
" Jane A widow Noah L b 2157 Acushnet av [Front
" John mill hand bds 534 North
" John weaver h 152 Tallman
" John weaver h 277 Davis

Ward
" John J piper 125 Middle h 171 Bonney [273 Fourth
" John T machinist 42 Front h
" John W weaver h 27 E French avenue
" Joseph J rem to Taunton
" Kate Mrs h 534 N Front
" Loron chauffeur 18 Market bds 19 N Sixth
" Mary waitress rms 41 High
" Mary D h 10 Spruce [Sixth
" Olive P widow Frank E h 13 S
" Owen weaver b 20 Morton ct
" Peter J jeweler h 277 Davis
" Samuel optician 837 Purchase h 251 Chestnut
" Six Furniture Co (Everett B MacLeod) 1020 S Water
" Thomas mill hand b 534 N Front
" Thomas weaver h 436 Sawyer
" Thomas M back boy bds 534 N Front [rd
" Willard D teamster b 126 River
" William machinist b 19 Ashley
" William weaver h 10 Harmony
" William R teamster U St Ry Co h 36 Main [Cedar
Wardell Frank B mill wright b 325
" Lionell clerk 1218 Acushnet av h at N Dartmouth [velt
Warden Robert weaver h 59 Roose-
Wardick John laborer h 28 Penniman
" John H laborer h 28 Penniman
Wardwell Charles rem from city
Warefield John H P janitor Trinitarian Congregational church h 80 Cedar [ard
Wareing Albert L pressman Stand-
" John weaver h 31 McGurk
" Joseph weaver h 431 S Front
" Margaret widow George h 305 Mill
" Richard h 8 Woodlawn av
" Robert weaver h 34 Jouvett
" Thomas plumber 1545 Acushnet av b 305 Mill
" William fixer b 151 Belleville rd
Warfield Sarah widow James h 60 Spruce [ham
Warhurst John W painter h 26 Peck-
Waring John W weaver h 117 Austin
" Walter weaver b 307 Collette
" William loom fixer h 155 Belleville rd

Steiger-Dudgeon Co.
"The WOMAN'S Store."
Tel. Bell 82 & 83, Branches connecting all depts.
" " 160 For Office only. Auto. 1211

SUMPTIONS, ASSORTMENTS AT ALL TIMES OF DEPENDABLE DRY GOODS

Warner John grocer h 22 Jouvett
" Richard E (Household Furnishing Co) 170 Purchase h at Taunton
Warnot Thomas carder h 659 First
Warren Arthur L rem to Fall River
" Benjamin F rem to Dartmouth
WARREN CHEMICAL & MFG CO 49 Federal Boston See advt opposite Business Directory
" David stable 255 State h 131 Merrimac [Merrimac
" Edward E mgr 255 State b 131
" Emily widow Benjamin C h 108 Norman
" Isabelle widow h 7 Cottage
" James A rem from city
" James H roofer h 64½ Dartmouth
" Joseph second hand h 190 Dean
" Joseph C (Warren's Agency) h at S Dartmouth
WARREN'S AGENCY (Joseph C Warren and James F Griffiths) real estate 1063 S Water See back binding and page 789
Warrington William fixer h 168 Cove
Warry Louis weaver b 843 Acushnet av
Warsoski Bruno h 16 Marvin
Warwick Richard Jr laborer b 20 Warren [Coggeshall
Warzele August carpenter bds 487
Wasbutsky Esther Mrs h 335 S Water
Washburn Alanson R grocer 739-741 Purchase h 338 Cedar
" Annie M h 153 Clinton
" Arthur A motorman b 180 Austin
" Bessie h 125 Belleville rd
" Charles C cotton broker 108 Union h 56 State [rd
" Emogene I Mrs b 125 Belleville
" Ernest gardener h 168 Smith
" Francis P carpenter 2443 Acushnet av h do
" Frank Everett carpenter N B W W b 2443 Acushnet av
" Fred C (Lettice R Washburn & Son) h 190 Pleasant [Kempton
" Frederick A asst assessor h 75
" George E general mechanic h 2421 Acushnet av [tage
" George L carpenter h 23 Cot-
" Harold A clerk 100 William bds 2421 Acushnet av

Washburn
" Lettice R (Lettice R Washburn & Son) h 190 Pleasant
" Lettice R & Son (Lettice R and Fred C) cabinetmakers 226 N Water [Maple
" Mary J widow Frederick A h 10
" Newton B foreman rms 218 Pleasant
" Olive A b 2421 Acushnet av
" Oswald A mill hand b 2421 Acushnet av
WASHBURN WILLIAM R stable Nonquitt Mass See page 770
" Winfred R clerk h 402 Cedar
Washkiewic Joseph carder h 642 First [field
Washington Fanny Mrs h 22 Max-
" Fannie M widow John F h 268 Middle [268 Middle
" Lewis F driver 108 William bds
" Social and Musical Club West French av cor Cove [man
Wassner Powell weaver h 135 Tall-
Waterhouse Alice widow William T h 837 First
" Daniel machinist h 837 First
" Fred back boy b 837 First
" James W weaver h 155 Tallman
" John B L shoemaker 76 Purchase dry goods 447 Rivet h 451 do
" William T died April 5 1911
Waterman Frank E bookkeeper Butler Mill h at Fairhaven
" William H b 3 Lincoln
Waters Lena Mrs h 82 Liberty
" Michael laborer b 303 Austin
Waterworth Benjamin weaver h 5 Abbott
" James weaver h 158 Bates av
" Rawson twister h 25 William
Watkins Annie L dressmaker 197 Cedar h do
" Charles F custom shoemaker 90 Pleasant h 209 Chestnut
" Emma C h 71 Hawthorn
" James B h 80 Allen
" Otis H clerk h 3 Weaver
" Sarah T G widow Taylor h 270 Middle [h 187 North
" Thomas M chauffeur 18 Market
Watkinson Hannah h 441 Pleasant
" John T janitor h 441 Pleasant
Watling Fred glasscutter b 35 Larch
" James carpenter b 35 Larch
" John carpenter b 35 Larch

PELEG H. SHERMAN 506 COUNTY ST.
FUNERAL DIRECTOR AND EMBALMER
OFFICE PHONES, Bell 690-13. Auto. 1305.
RESIDENCE PHONES, Bell 690-12. Auto. 1306.

WATLING WILLIAM carpenter and builder 35 Larch h do See page 757
" William Jr carpenter b 35 Larch
Watson Albert carpenter h 77 Hemlock
" Alfred E meter reader 125 Middle h 125 Rivet [Belleville rd
" Alice widow Nathan D b 26
" Benjamin W fixer h 12 Woodlawn avenue
" Bros (William E Jr and Samuel 2nd) fish 108 William
" Charles (Watson & Boardman) 765 Kempton h 560 Elm
" Clara B h 37 Fifth [b 103 School
" Edwin M electrician 158 Purchase
" Elizabeth h 75 Madison
" Emma A Mrs dressmaker 67 Washington h do
" Frank blacksmith b 154 Ashland
" Frank blacksmith 447 Kempton h 137 Arnold
" Fred weaver b 83 Ruth
" Garnett teamster 81 Front rms 154 Ashland
" Helen E h 75 Madison
" Henry fixer h 154 Ashland [Oak
" Henry J pres 2 Rodman h 123
" James teamster b 637 Union
" James D salesman b 154 Ashland
" John city laborer h 799 S Water
" John weaver b 41 Rivet
" John weaver b 137 Acushnet av
" John H coachman T M Stetson Ash (S) b do [32 Ashland
" John H liquors 812 Purchase h
" Luella B lodging 273 Cottage
" Lynn rem from city
" Margaret h 989 County
" Mary h 82 Mott
" Mary janitress public library
" Mary B weaver h 18 Salisbury
" Paul machinist h 198 Blackmer
" Pennell Corp plumbing supplies 2 Rodman [av
" Robert twister b 24 W French
" Samuel 2nd (Watson Bros) h 103 School
" Sidney rem from city [den
" Susanna widow Thomas b 92 Lin-
" Thomas fitter b 850 First
" Thomas weaver h 141 Davis

Watson
" Walter weaver h 20 Warren
" William weaver b 1098 Acushnet avenue [cor Beetle
" William weaver h Acushnet av
" William E Jr (Watson Brothers) h 103 School
" & Boardman (Charles Watson and Arthur G Boardman) druggists 765 Kempton
Watt Abbie F widow h 118 Fourth
Watterson Alice M stenographer 97 William rm 203 b at Fairhaven
Watts Charlotte L P widow Daniel A h 301 Court
" John M bds 301 Court
WATUPPA AUTO CO N Westport Mass See page 750
Watzlavick Antone fixer b 385 Davis
" Joachim weaver h 385 Davis [ham
Waugh David collector h 168 Tink-
" John removed from city
Waybrant Edward L machinist 235 N Water bds 46 Summer [ton
Wayne George third hand h 18 Staple-
" Robert removed from city
" Thomas spinner b 18 Stapleton
Weakley Frank E died March 31 1911
Weatherbie John A cab maker rms 172 William
Weaver Elizabeth B widow George bds 1007 Rockdale avenue
" Elizabeth T bds 13 Weaver
" Ethel A housekeeper 97 Newton
" Frank V music teacher bds 218 North [h do
" Harry V physician 161 William
" Milton T mill hand b 168 Merrimac [Merrimac
" Olive E widow Charles F b 168
" Robert S bookbinder h 168 Merrimac [Weaver
" Sophia A widow William H h 13
" Stephen V foreman city painter h 218 North
" Walter P teamster h 97 Newton
" William L weaver b 28 Viall
Webb Cornelius A watchman h 474 Kempton
" Edward O driver h 423 S Second
" Elijah janitor h 209 Park
" Fred L tailor 239 Sawyer

PAINTERS' SUPPLIES
Walnut, Cor. Water, 84 Pleasant St. 25 WELD SQ., 129 COVE ST.
F. T. AKIN & COMPANY

Webb
" Harriet A widow Hiram bds 20 Seventh [3 Jenny
" Henry B tinsmith 55 N Water h
" Hezekiah died March 3 1911 [nell
" John R glass cutter h 186 Grin-
" Martha D h 211 Park [dle
" Nancy widow Hezekiah h 284 Mid-
Webber Alfred F shoemaker h 22 Mc-Gurk
" Amos P physician 250 Union h do
" Emma Mrs h 10 Coffin av ct
" Harvey H capt S S New York h 45 Chestnut
" Henry drill worker h 446 Allen
" James A foreman U St Ry Co h 9 Richmond
" James William proof reader Standard h 386 Maxfield
WEBBER LUMBER & SUPPLY CO The 172 N Water See page 761
" Mary Mrs h 1042 Acushnet av
Weber Martin weaver h 8 Warwick
Webert Charles L removed from city
Webster Annie W nurse rms 321 Union
" Charles slasher tender h 10 Jean
" Elizabeth h 126 Crapo
" Fred machinist h 414 Orchard (S)
" Gertrude F assistant superintendent St Luke's Hospital b do
" Horatio G teamster h 295 Cottage
" John clerk 108 Cedar b 658 Kempton [Tallman
" John clerk 630 Purchase h 134
" John V student b 341 Cottage
" Joseph S ice cream maker 201 Union h 169 Emerson (N)
" Joseph V bone setter 341 Cottage h do [Corp h 75 Thomas
" Joseph W treas Grinnell Mfg
" Martha rms 394 Union
" Mary M stenographer 5 Masonic bldg b 341 Cottage
Wedege Eva clerk 1081 Acushnet av
Weedall Lillian M weaver b 627 Purchase [h 627 do
" Samuel restaurant 629 Purchase
" Samuel Jr slasher tender b 627 Purchase [14 S Sixth
Weeden Abbie H widow William N h

Weeden
" Carrie E widow William W h 63 Hillman [Court
" Elizabeth A widow Edward h 312
" Everett L drill maker h 109 Rounds
" Fred M, N B Furniture Co 43-45 Weld and Spot-Cash Furniture Co 384 Acushnet av h 47 Willis
" George F deputy sheriff 31 Masonic bldg h 18 Wood [County
" Lizzie B widow Charles L h 622
" Mfg Co toy steam engines 152 N Water
" William W plumber h 306 Middle
Weeks Allen T h 3 Maple [65 Foster
" Amy F widow Capt Charles E h
" Arthur R clerk N B W W 40 Masonic bldg h 241 Middle
" Bessie R telephone operator 57 N Second b 549 Cottage
" Charlotte E widow Henry T bds 268 Palmer
" Edmund mill hand h 39 Hemlock
" Frederick L clerk 100 William b 47 State [ton
" George P T caulker h 1254 Kemp-
" George H painter h 47 State
" George H C draughtsman 97 William rm 211 b 65 Foster
" Henry R milk 1270 Kempton h do [Cottage
" Isabelle G widow H F h 549
" John L clerk h 97 State
" J Frank physician 2193 Acushnet av h do
" Lili B b 268 Palmer
" Lucretia H died Sept 6 1910
" Luella F h 641 County
" Mary A died July 20 1911
" Mary C clerk 57 N Second b 549 Cottage
" Mary W Mrs b 268 Palmer
" Nathan C T laborer h 220 Palmer
" Rebecca H widow John C h 51 Parker [h 294 Cedar
" Stephen S repairman U St Ry
Wefer Elliot insurance agent 95 Elm h do [Washburn
Wegizyniak John operative h 42
Wegniak Frank weaver h 9 Bullard [vis
Wegscheider John weaver h 305 Da-

To do things right you must be taught. Our instructors can do it.
Kinyon's Commercial School
Odd Fellows Bldg., Cor. William and Pleasant Sts., New Bedford, Mass.

Wehoskey Everett drillworker b r 95 Fourth [Fourth
" Herbert C glasscutter h r 95
" John operative h 177 N Front
Weigel Jean B fixer h 310 Earle
" Joseph weaver b 310 Earle
WEIHL JACOB agent Narragansett Brewery 21½ and 23½ N Second rms 92 High See page 779
Weik Eleonora M proof reader Times b 562 Kempton [Kempton
" Mary A widow Michael h 562
Weiman J A agent 37 Purchase rm 19 h at Fall River
Weimert Robert shoemaker h 25 Arch
Weinberger Leo variety 846 Purchase h 434 Pleasant [shnet av h do
Weiner Harris shoe repairer 273 Acu-
" Henry salesman 2 S Water h 120 S Second [183 Coffin av
Weir Annie widow mill hand bds
" Michael laborer h 15 Welcome
Weisberg Abraham produce pedlar h 1030 Acushnet av
" Markus h 1082 County
Weiss Antone operative h 150 West French av
Weitzman David second hand furniture 617 S Water h do
Wejtuszewski Mijk grocer 19 Belleville av h do [h 69 Sycamore
Welch Albert C salesman 157 Union
" Amelia clerk 214 Purchase b 405 Pleasant
" Charles O reamer h 16 Bedford
" Ellen widow John h 91 Acushnet av
" Emma h 172 Emerson (S)
" Helen widow Frank h 405 Pleasant [school rms 179 William
" Helen M teacher Jireh Swift
" James E spinner h 451 S Front
" James H engineer h 91 Acushnet av [ion
" James W engineer h 262 Un-
" John W carpenter h 49 Potter
" Joseph boxmaker h 293 Davis
" Joseph Jr boxmaker b 293 Davis
" Mary widow Thomas h 289 Bowditch [ion h do
" Mary A Mrs dressmaker 262 Un-
" Mary F widow James H h 21 Scott

Welch
" Paul boxmaker b 293 Davis [av
" Robert plumber b 137 Acushnet
" see Welsh and Walsh
Welcome Margaret bookkeeper 79 William b 307 Bowditch
Weld Abber E machine operator h 32 Cottage
" George A clerk b 216 North
" Nina asst teacher manual training public schools b 32 Cottage
" Square Hotel Alexander Lavasseur prop 46 Weld
" Square Pharmacy D S Considine prop 3-5 Weld
Welker Margaret widow Frank h 200 Brock av [av
" William H overseer b 200 Brock
Weller Charles V teamster h 275 Mill
" Christie clerk 65 Purchase b 275 Mill
Wellington Charles farmer h Shawmut av n Plainville road
Wellock George twister bds 9 Stapleton [Corp h at Boston
Wells C Minot pres Lambeth Rope
" Edward copperworker h 99 Linden
" Eugene F foreman h 85 Fourth
" Eugene L clerk b 85 Fourth
" John laborer h 139 Division
" Josephine Mrs h 314 Acushnet av
" Royal C electrician h 117 Willis
Welsh Albert E foreman 123 Front b 114 Newton
" Annie F teacher Thomas Donaghy school b 199 County
" Arthur tailor 15 Pleasant h 114 Newton [Mill b 199 County
" Elizabeth C stenographer Soule
" Frederick W glasscuter bds 114 Newton
" James drillworker b 46 Myrtle
" James mule spinner h 86 Mosher
" John doffer bds 86 Mosher
" John engineer h 79 Nash road
" Margaret widow Patrick h 70 Myrtle [County b do
" Margaret J music teacher 199
" Michael W engineer b 6 Cove rd
" Patrick loom fixer h 46 Myrtle
" Richard F motorman b 70 Myrtle
" Robert wholesale provisions h 199 County
" Thomas laborer bds 70 Myrtle

Bread, Cake, Pastry
RICHMOND & COMPANY 255-257 UNION STREET
Bell 993 Automatic 1022

Welsh
" William police bds 70 Myrtle
" William G (N B Publishing Warehouse) h 198 Clinton [8 Jean
" see Welch
Wenceslas Roy clerk 126 Bowditch h
Wentworth Alice B Mrs h 477 Acushnet av [Walnut
" Frank W treas 211 Union h 74
WENTWORTH F W CO clothing and furnishings F W Wentworth treas 211 Union cor Pleasant
See page 768
" Philip C salesman b 87 State
Werner Hannah widow Andrew h 113 Bates avenue
" Harry asst music supervisor public schools b 140 Summer
Weskosky Anthony mill hand h 1085 South Water [dence R I
Wesley Robert removed to Provi-
Wesolowski Peter mill hand b 7 Bonneau ct
" William weaver h 500 S Second
Wesoly Joseph grocer 15 Belleville av h do [81 Ash (N)
Wessiack Antonette M housekeeper
" Joseph baker 255 Union h 81 Ash (N) [(N)
" Joseph Jr machinist bds 81 Ash
West Adelaide h 232 Pleasant
" Andrew D mariner h 54 Durfee
" Bertram C mariner h 372 Kempton
" Charles laborer bds 36 McGurk
" Charles H salesman b 463 Cottage
" Clara A widow William F h 202 Kempton [463 Cottage
" C Harry salesman 16 N Second b
" Eliza S widow Noah sewer 40 Purchase b 71 S Sixth [sant
" Ellen C widow John P h 223 Plea-
" Ellis E insurance agent 37 Purchase rm 23 h 286 Park
" Ernest A capt Light-ship h 297 Acushnet avenue
" Etta P telephone operator 57 N Second b 223 Pleasant
" Florence B clerk 125 Middle h 223 Pleasant [269 Purchase
" Frank B teamster 229 N Water h
" George W mill hand b 522 Bolton

West
" George W overseer City Mfg Co h 128 Bonney
" Henry F boats to let city pier No 3 h 209 S Second
" Henry N clerk of police 9 S Second h 24 Seventh [dle
" James bricklayer rms 116 Mid-
" James clerk b 2 Cove rd [chase
" John H W painter rms 269 Pur-
" Lamira M widow William b 209 S Second [128 Bonney
" Lowren helper 185 Acushnet av b
" Sarah W widow Henry S h 73 Mt Pleasant
" Sylvester hostler rms 20 S Second
" William H hostler 35 Hillman rms 69 Spring
" William R painter 830 Purchase and president Mt Pleasant Banding Co h 96 Madison
Westby Aloysius (Westby & Baker) h 252 Hawthorn
" & Baker (Aloysius Westby and Daniel W Baker) real estate 308-309 Times bldg
Western Union Telegraph & Cable Co 151 Union and R R depot
Westgate Charles E eyelet maker h 261 Middle
" Clara h 3932 Acushnet avenue
" Clarence E teamster h 3932 Acushnet avenue
" Delbert W drill maker h 58 Allen
" Edward toy maker b 380 Middle
" Helen M bookkeeper 23 N Water bds at Fairhaven [net av
" Herbert N teamster h 3932 Acush-
" Maria F widow Joseph W h 88 High [ushnet av
" Richard A teamster h 3217 Ac-
" William B engineer 152 N Water h 380 Middle [35 Beech
" William C clerk 386 Kempton h
" William G salesman 170 Purchase h 651 Kempton [Coffin av
Westhead James twister bds 258
Weston Evelyn dressmaker b 39 Dartmouth [ond
" Everett K teamster h 212 N Sec-
" Herbert R overseer h 70 Brock av

GLOBE DYE HOUSE 220 SHAWMUT AVE.
J. N. J. LONHOLDT, PROP. Telephone Connections Goods called for and Delivered
Down Town Office, 52 Pleasant St., Room 1 North End Office, 1014 Acushnet Ave.

Weston
" Jennie L stenographer Wamsutta Mills bds 604 County [av
" Josephine D clerk h 862 Acushnet
" Leroy G clerk h 241 Chestnut
" Stephen J clerk foot Willis h 604 County
" Stephen J Jr clerk b 604 County
" William H foreman 1 Mill h 38 Foster [554 N Front
Westwood Benjamin watchman h
Wetherbee Ethel C teacher Thompson street school b 333 Keene
" John A woodworker b 172 William
" William rem to Portland Me
Wetzel Cary F fireman h 22 Bullock
" Ferdinand weaver h 11 Cornell place [velt
Wexler Nicholas weaver h 54 Roose-
" Samuel upholsterer 591 Purchase h 60 Merrimac [202 State
Weyeld Joseph barber 329 Kempton h
Whaite Peter operative h 168 North Front [N Front
Whalen Catherine widow John h 363
" Edward at P Co h 59 Merrimac
" Edward F second hand bds 363 N Front [Weld
" James pressman Mercury h 17
" John laborer b 89 Hathaway
" John weaver b r 1025 S Water
" John J clerk 855 Purchase h 46 Ash (S) [Hathaway
" Mary widow William h 89
" Nicholas liquors 855 Purchase h 10 Robeson [363 N Front
" Patrick H clerk 376 Kempton h
" Thomas J warper tender b 363 N Front
" see Whelan and Whalon
Whalley Alexander weaver b 41 Rivet
" Ambrose operative b 193 Tinkham
" Bella rem to Philadelphia Pa
" Edmund J deputy sheriff 49 William rms 3-4 h 161 North
" John overseer Whitman Mill h 26 Peckham [lette
" John F card grinder h 236 Col-
" Joseph fixer h 94 Church
" Joseph Jr fixer b 94 Church
" Robert weaver h 132 Division
" Thomas operative h 193 Tinkham

Whalley
" William H overseer Wamsutta 236 Austin
" see Wholey [Peckham
Whallin John W mule spinner b 26
Whalon John driver b 1025 S Water
" John G grocer 2165 Acushnet av h 906 Belleville av
" see Whelan and Whalen
Wharmsby William mule spinner h 28 W French av
Wharton Edward B brakeman bds 615 Acushnet av [Hathaway
Whatmougle Robert mason h 158
Wheaton Arthur C (Hiram Wheaton & Sons) h 127 Chestnut
" Clara C clerk b 324 Union
" Clarence A foreman 37 School h 127 Chestnut
" Ernest A (Parsons Steam Laundry Co) 270 Acushnet av h 324 Union
WHEATON HIRAM & SONS (Arthur C) soda water bottlers 45-51 School See page 773
" Nathan mason 16 Spruce h do
" Walter F [Wheaton & Co) 64 Mill h do [lishers) 64 Mill
" & Co (Walter F Wheaton) pub-
Wheeldon Edward overseer h 52 Winsor [sor
" Herbert E operative b 52 Win-
Wheeler Albert candymaker h 12 Marvin
" Belle B teacher h 57 Morgan
" Emma H physician 57 Morgan h do [181½ North
" George F overseer N B C Co h
" Harry F machinist b 181½ North
" John N clerk b 266 Fourth
" Joseph H dvirer 20 Fourth h 111 High [Sixth
" Martin V B machinist b 55 S
Wheelwright Charles S pres N B Ext Co h at Providence R I
" Charles K supt N B Ext Co h at Providence R I [ditch
Whelan Andrew J fixer h 395 Bow-
" George H at P Corp h 9 Warwick [129 Fourth
" James J salesman 46 Purchase b
" Mary J widow James h 387 Bowditch [at Dartmouth
" Nicholas salesman 100 S Water h

GREENE & WOOD Every Kind of LUMBER AND MILL WORK
PINE STREET, off So. WATER STREET, NEW BEDFORD

Whelan
" William N hoseman Hose No 1 h 109 Fifth
" see Whalon
Whelden Thomas H painter h 34 Maitland [b 44 Reynolds
Whelley Maria cashier 882 Purchase
Whelly Thomas driver 8 Campbell h 117 Willis
Whepley John R lineman 57 N Second rms 300 Acushnet av
Whewell Elizabeth widow John b 10 Linden ct
" John weaver h 96 Ruth
Whipple George H h 442 Pleasant
" Rebecca E widow Frederick J h 772 Kempton
" Orin E machinist King's Highway h 109 Locust
" William carpenter h 93 S Sixth
Whipps George baker 143 Purchase b 65 Fourth
Whitaker William Jr salesman 1 William h 13 Studley
Whitcomb Edgar B asst supt 41 William rms Elm [ton
White Albert B police h 80 New-
" Albert P (Puritan Tea & Coffee Co) 829 Purchase h 166 Campbell [Campbell
" Albert P Mrs dressmaker h 166
" Almon K eyeletter b 101 Middle
" Annie widow George b 722 Kempton [h 12 Grape
" Arthur C chauffeur 214 S Water
" Augustus T nurseryman h 3526 Acushnet av [h at Fairhaven
" Canvass yardmaster R R station
" Charlotte Mrs h 179 Mill
" Clifford L oiler b 195 Grinnell
" David laborer rms 760 Purchase
" Eagle Bottling Co Potvin ct r 234½ N Front [rd
" George D lamp lighter h Bralley
" George E foreman h 211 Fourth
" George E Jr b 211 Fourth
" Gertrude L clerk b 592 Kempton
" Harold A clerk b 3501 Acushnet av [Reed
" Harry E clerk ft Willis b 372
" Harry K com trav b 63 Foster
" Harry O musician h 3501 Acushnet av
" Henry notions bds 5 Morgan lane
" Hugh driver b 48 Parker

White
" Isabelle widow Solomon h 268 Middle
" John h 49 Ash [av
" Joseph mill hand b 153 Belleville
" Julia Mrs clerk 161 Purchase b 479 Belleville av
" Leannah E H Mrs h 77 Willis
" Lemuel H (White & Fairchild) druggist 322 County h 195 Grinnell
" Lottie Mrs b 179 Mill
" Lucie teacher Jireh Swift school h at Acushnet
" Lucy M teacher R C Ingraham school rms 761 S Sixth
" Mabel W clerk registry of deeds b 592 Kempton
" Mack C teamster h 45 Bethel
" Malachi H carpenter h 53 Shawmut av
" Martha A M widow Adoniram J M h 592 Kempton
" Mary A clerk 98 Allen b 9 Stone
" Myra D widow Henry h 63 Foster
" Nicholas b 140 Hathaway
" Oliver carpenter b 99 Bowditch
" Otis W janitor 198 Union h 314 Orchard (S)
" Pardon G h 254 County
" Patrick lineman 43 William b 65 Penniman
" Pearl J carpenter h 404 Pleasant
" Peter painter rms 20 Bethel
" Sewing Machine Co 186 Purchase
" Stephen E salesman h 23 James
" Strother laborer b 275 Acushnet av [h 554 Kempton
" S Stanley hairdresser 155 Union
" William back boy b 457 Sawyer
" William lineman 43 William h 65 Penniman [Campbell
" William E draughtsman b 166
" William G h 1 Oak
" William H tailor 344 S Water b 5 Morgan lane
" & Fairchild (Lemuel H White and Thomas H Fairchild) druggists 322 County
" see Le Blanc [ar
Whitehead Albert spinner h 29 Ced-
" Alfred L joiner h 163 Holly

BONNEY, FOLSTER & CO.,
The North End's Shopping Centre
Dry Goods and Men's Furnishings
945-947 Acushnet Ave., New Bedford, Mass.

Whitehead
" Arthur clerk 201 Union b 119 Kempton
" Ernest shoemaker b 129 Tallman
" Fred spinner h 343 Bowditch
" Harry loom fixer rms 40 Elm
" Harry spinner h 80 Clark
" Henry twister tender h 251 Bowditch
" James h 178 Blackmer
" James spinner h 157 Richmond
" James L spinner h 163 Holly
" John lunch 624 Purchase h do
" John real estate 211 Collette h do
" John second hand b 163 Holly
" John B clerk h 1588 Acushnet av
" Joseph letter carrier h 25 Rounds
" J Edward b 4 Penniman
" Linie E driver 748 Purchase b 4 Penniman [Ashley
" Nancy and Bettie carders h 21
" Obed chauffeur h 234 River rd
" Samuel collector h 114 Newton
" Thomas H tinsmith b 59 Mt Pleasant
" Walter overseer b 157 Richmond
" William engineer Holmes Mill h 67 Emma [ant
" William weaver h 59 Mt Pleas-
Whiteley Flora B weaver b 130 Division
" Harold fixer h 296 Tinkham
" Jeanette operative b 130 Division
" Jeanette Mrs h 130 Division
" Samuel machinist 23 Rodney
" Sarah Mrs h 431 Pleasant
Whiteside Christiana M b 586 Kempton [70 Ash (N)
" David comber maker 22 Fourth b
" David machinist b 70 Ash (N)
" Elizabeth widow John h 236 Park
" James carpenter b 70 Ash (N)
" James S machinist apprentice b 586 Kempton
" John died April 2 1911
" John weaver h 17 Viall
" John Jr foreman 14 N Sixth b 236 Park
" Rebecca clerk b 70 Ash (N)

Whiteside
" Rebecca L widow David h 70 Ash (N) [ence
" Robert M gardener b 25 Flor-
" Stephen rope maker N B C Co h 586 Kempton
" Thomas L clerk b 70 Ash (N)
Whitford Thomas E instructing machinist N B T school h 137 Bonney
Whitham Francis T apprentice Standard b 380 N Front
" James weaver b 94 Hathaway
" Thomas watchman h 380 N Front
Whithead Fannie and Lydia F h 225 Grinnell
WHITIN MACHINE WORKS Whitinsville Mass See page 20
Whiting Alice B widow Edward B h 140 Cottage
" Harriet W h 162 Clinton
" Louise S Alice H and Susan A h 140 Cottage
" Nathan B purser b 162 Clinton
WHITINSVILLE SPINNING RING CO Whitinsville Mass See advt end of General
Whitlow Rosetta E bookkeeper 7 S Water b 153 Maxfield
" Samuel electrician 7 S Water h 153 Maxfield
" Samuel 2nd electrician 7 S Water h 205 Austin
Whitman Annie A Mrs h 234 North
" Clifford A bookkeeper 161 Clinton b at Fairhaven
" Mills cotton goods ft Coffin av
" Joseph operative b 27 Hicks
" Ralph M mgr 52 N Second h at Providence R I [Brookline
" William pres Manomet Mill h at
Whitmarsh Elmer timekeeper b 3 Lincoln
Whitney Abbie D b 59 Hill [Locust
" Alfred E freight conductor h 47
" Blanche clerk 185 Union b at Acushnet
" Edward G (Whitney Pharmacy Co) 286 Acushnet av and 119 Fourth h 55 Fifth [h do
" Edward M physician 27 S Sixth
" Emma M h 35 Arch
" Henry L solicitor 97 William rm 407 b 89 Mt Pleasant

Painters Supplies Wall Papers Room Mouldings Ladders
M. P. B. Silva & Son BRUSHES
157 ACUSHNET AVENUE Both Phones NEW BEDFORD

Whitney
" Karl T linotype machinist h at Fairhaven [rms 407-409
" Law Corporation 97 William
" Louis C collector 97 William rm 407 b 89 Mt Pleasant
" Louis M treas 97 William rm 407 h 89 Mt Pleasant
" Pharmacy Co (Edward G Whitney) 286 Acushnet av and 119 Fourth [Pleasant
" Tyler A clerk 182 Union h 187
" Vernon H pres 97 William rm 407 b 89 Mt Pleasant
Whiton Chauncey G agent 7 Commercial h 93 School
" see Whitton
Whittaker Abel chauffeur 65 William h at Fairhaven
" Abraham spinner h 61 Reynolds
" Ada widow Arthur h 24 Roosevelt
" Albert fixer b 38 Bowditch
" Benjamin h 254 Chestnut
" Elizabeth widow George h 16 Welcome
" Charles operative b 61 Reynolds
" Frank musician h 69 Forest
" Fred laborer h 31 Covell
" George spinner b 59 Bullard
" George H h 26 Bullock
" Harry barber b 59 Bullard
" Henry h 536 Purchase
" Henry clerk 630 Purchase b 68 Reynolds
" Henry spinner h 59 Bullard
" James bowling 397 Kempton h 112 Willis
" James loom fixer h 35 Austin
" James M salesman 358 Acushnet av b 342 Cedar
" Jesse operative h 62 Ashland
" John T overseer Gosnold Mill h 39 Willard
" Mary Mrs h 16 Welcome
" May C stenographer 65 William b 464 County
" Raymond doffer b 59 Bullard
" Richard died Dec 23 1910
" Robert doffer b 59 Bullard
" Sadie clerk 1190 Acushnet av h 155 Bowditch [nold
" Samuel letter carrier h 254 Ar-
" Samuel weaver h 34 Robeson
" Thomas weaver h 27 Viall

Whittaker
" Thomas weaver h 401 Pleasant
" Thomas W changer over b 79 Willard
" Walter clerk P O h 3 Homer
" William farmer h Plainville rd
" William laborer b 593 Cottage
" William shoe repairer 7 Wamsutta h 8 Linden ct [nolds
" William H bricklayer b 61 Rey-
" William H twister h 12 Studley
" William Jr salesman h 13 Studley
Whittam Edward student b 94 Hathaway [way
" James mill hand h 94 Hatha-
" William watchman h 158 Central av [ard lane b 390 Union
Whitten Helen P bookkeeper 8 Haz-
" Levi H h 151 North
Whittier Stella C telephone operator b 2 Jenny Lind
Whittingcom Ruth h 32 Stapleton
Whittle Annie weaver h 44 Salisbury
" Charles weaver b 25 Warren
" Charles F weaver h 126 Reynolds
" Edward weaver h 13 Salisbury
" Edward weaver h 18 Salisbury
" Henry spinner h 42 Salisbury
" James E weaver h 25 Warren
" Jane widow Lawrence h 87 Potomska
" John mule spinner b 113 Bates av
" John weaver h 25 Warren
" Joseph bookkeeper h 13 Ruth
" Joseph painter b 25 Warren
" Margaret A weaver b 126 David
" Mary widow Edward h 7 E French avenue [avenue
" Thomas back boy b 7 E French
" Thomas spinner h 44 Salisbury
" Thomas J doffer bds 44 Salisbury
" William H doffer h 30 Belleville road [Thompson
Whitty Albert second hand h 26
" Fred G steward h 178 Cedar
Whitworth James machinist h 165 Shawmut av
" Percy machinist h 59 Roosevelt
" Robert carder h 15 E French av
" Robert engineer h 164 David
Wholey George weaver h 62 Katharine
" Thomas driver h 115 Willis
" Thomas laborer h 44 Reynolds

Steiger-Dudgeon Co.
"The WOMAN'S Store."
Tel. Bell 82 & 83, Branches connecting all depts.
" " 160 For Office only. Auto. 1211
SUMPTIONS, ASSORTMENTS AT ALL TIMES OF DEPENDABLE DRY GOODS

Wholey
" Thomas R agent b 44 Mill
" see Woolley [ditch
Whyatt Aleanah janitor h 342 Bow-
" Eli T weaver b 342 Bowditch
" John packer b 342 Bowditch
" Joseph twister h 90 Kenyon
" see Wyatt
Wicha Joseph weaver h 76 Linden
Wickens Sarah J housekeeper 123 Hillman [field
Wickham Lavinia E Mrs h 54 Max-
Wicks Rodolphus D clerk 9 N Water h 63 Jenny Lind [av
Widdall Freind carder h 29 E French
Widmayer Harry Jr rem to Providence R I
Widuch John laborer h 40 Washburn
Wieczoick John mill hand h 97 Collette [liam h 204 North
Wiggins Charles D porter 100 Wil-
" Gertrude E M housekeeper 176 Emerson (S)
" James laborer 432 Kempton
" Lilla M widow William H h 176 Emerson (S)
" Matilda Mrs h 71 Ash (N)
" Walter F washer 8 Campbell h 136 Cedar [ard
Wigley Alfred machinist h 67 How-
Wignall Frederick died Sept 20 1910
" John H S weaver h 30 Salisbury
" Julia widow Fred h 17 Thatcher
" William molder 229 N Water h 160 David [225 Grinnell
Wilber Bessie A clerk 28 Purchase b
" George W city teamster h 39 Bullock [39 Bullock
" George W Jr city laborer bds
" LeRoy W salesman 65 William h 291 Allen
" Lorinda M widow James L h 73 State [Pleasant
" William S clerk 5 S Sixth h 185
Wilbor Albert P bds 745 County
" Alfred G died Feb 20 1911
" Herbert C teller N B S D & T Co h 745 County [Acushnet av
" Louisa A widow Alfred G h 228
Wilbour Lincoln R salesman 21 Purchase rms 158 Middle
Wilbur Adelaide widow N Hervey h 2344 Acushnet av [shnet av
" Arthur T sawyer h 2242 Acu-

Wilbur
" Edward P carpenter h Plainville road
" Everett conductor b 115 Durfee
" Fanny H teacher Harrington school b Plainville road
" Frank S mariner h 167 Mill
" George F stone mason h 1235 Rockdale av [av h do
" George F Jr ice 1384 Rockdale
" Harriet M seamstress b 110 High
" Henry K chauffeur N B W W h 115 Smith
" Howard C student bds Edward P Wilbur's Plainville road
" James A laborer h 39 Mill road
" John B inspector N B W W h 2393 Acushnet av
" Mary W clerk 97 William rm 303 b at N Dartmouth
" Samuel A rem to Dartmouth
" Sarah B widow John T h 420 Union
" Theodore H rem to Boston
" Walter H foreman 34 Brook h 1217 Rockdale av
" William W ropemaker b 204 Weld
Wilcock Annie weaver h 75 Hathaway
" Eliza A h 75 Hathaway
" Herbert machinist b 283 Fourth
" James spinner h 315 Earle
" John (grinder) rem to Fall River
" John spinner h 202 Tinkham
" Joseph fixer h 94 Nash rd
Wilcox Adley painter h 227 Mill
" Albert carpenter h 502 Bolton
" Amos D boxmaker b 16 Warren
" Arlington b 15 Bourne
" Benjamin treas City M Co h at S Dartmouth [School
" Catherine Mrs stenographer b 82
" Charles C glasscutter b 31 Dudley
" Charles Harold salesman h 59 Shawmut av
" Charles Howland died Apr 6 1911
" Charles T foreman 123 Front h 124 Maxfield
" Charles Y teas h 28 Pearl
" Christopher S conductor h 465 Union [506 Acushnet av
" Cynthia B widow Isaiah H h
" C E laundryman h 76 Willis
" David laborer b end Brock av

PELEG H. SHERMAN 506 COUNTY ST.
FUNERAL DIRECTOR AND EMBALMER
OFFICE PHONES. Bell 690-13. Auto. 1305.
RESIDENCE PHONES. Bell 690-12. Auto. 1306.

Wilcox
" David S city teamster h 157 North [Middle
" Delia M widow Allen B b 217
" Edward C foreman 270 Acushnet av h 86 Willis
" Elizabeth C Mrs h 74 Myrtle
" Ethel M asst public library b 59 Chestnut [chase b 192 Arnold
" Florence P bookkeeper 88 Pur-
" Frank S (Wilcox & Cornwell) 97 William rm 209 h 53 S Sixth
" Frederick T h 15 Bourne
" George H glasscutter h 108 Sidney [ton
" George L drillworker h 672 Kemp-
" Hannah widow Edward F h 162 Smith
" Harry toymaker b 380 Middle (W)
" Henry A bds 15 Bourne
" Henry A Jr yard foreman 214 S Water rms 5 Park pl
" Herbert F died Feb 24 1911
" Hodijah b 123 Bedford
" James Herbert collector 125 Middle h 192 Arnold
" John spinner h 16 Ashley
" John H bookkeeper City Mfg Co h at S Dartmouth [Eighth
" John W tool sharpener h 32
" Lawrence carpenter h 123 Mott
" Lemuel T lawyer 49 William h 97 School [b 41 Sycamore
" L Gertrude asst public library
" Mary E h 218 Middle
" Mary E widow Charles S h 41 Sycamore
" Miner C Mrs b 84 Forest
" Minor W mgr 25 N Water bds 64 Hillman
" Otis A motorman b 15 Bourne
" Patty h 65 Clinton
" Richard weaver b 14 Shore
" Richmond L h 59 Chestnut
" Seth A police h 177 Court
" Thomas h 202 Middle
" Thomas B Jr h 97 Hillman
" Warren C drillworker h 82 School
" Willard S salesman b 41 Sycamore [480 Acushnet av
" William F driver 20 Fourth bds
" William H h 31 Dudley [lis
" Willis R eyeletmaker h 131 Wil-

Wilcox
" & Cornwell (Frank S Wilcox and Joseph F Cornwell) cotton brokers 97 William rm 209
Wild Arthur T pork 131 Blackmer h 630 First
" John spinner b 985 S Water
" William T spinner h 80 Katharine
Wilde Andrew baker 55-57 Mechanic's lane h 84 Chancery
" Annie stenographer 57 N Second b 35 Chestnut
" Channing linotype operator Standard h 449 Union
" Cyrus spinner b 103 Coffin av
" Cyrus W died May 4 1911
" Edmond L (W A Robinson & Co) 144 S Water h 73 Borden
" Edwin E music teacher h 181 Shawmut av [away
" Ellen widow mill hand b 72 Hath-
" Elton S general supt U St Ry Co Purchase cor William h 20 Fifth [Chestnut
" Ezra C clerk 84 Union h 35
" Florence widow Cyrus W bds 215 Hathaway rd
" George F operative b 70 Linden
" Harold doffer b r 433 N Front
" James died April 10 1911
" James spinner h 260 Coggeshall
" James E asst supt 41 William and grocer 433 N Front h r do
" James P h 35 Chestnut
" James W doffer b r 433 N Front
" John weaver b 985 S Water
" John W laborer b 52 Morton ct
" Lorenzo Frank rem to Fairhaven
" Ralph T spinner h 15 Morton ct
" Winifred Mrs b 443 Rivet
" William second hand h 172 Cove
" William S variety 526 County rms 483 do [bury
" Wright mule spinner h 14 Salis-
Wilder Robert waiter 435 County rms 15 Elm [15 Elm
" William S driver 17 N Sixth bds
Wilders George bleacher h 177 David
Wilding Benjamin rem from city
" George wool sorter h 258 Tinkham
" Isabella widow b 102 Nash rd
" James W grinder h 22 Warren
" Mary widow Benjamin h 160 Ashland

F. T. AKIN & CO. FORGE FACTORY FURNACE FAMILY COAL

Wilding
" Robert spinner h 102 Nash rd
" Thomas spinner b 258 Coffin av
" William weaver h 63 Holly
Wildman David laborer h 296 Cedar Grove
Wiley Charles oiler h 644 Purchase
" James weaver b 61 Reynolds
" James A laborer h 3½ Cannon
" see Willey [Fair
Wilkie Edward H engineer h 14
Wilkins Columbia A h 204 Cedar
" Rebecca widow Samuel bds 237 Acushnet av
Wilkinson Albert E painter h 282 Cedar [do
" Albert E variety 114 Cove h
" Alfred weaver h 13 Abbott
" Ann B widow Isaac D h 415 Cottage
" Annie E Mrs h 62 Katharine
" Arthur electrician h 66 Lindsey
" Arthur fixer h 250 Coffin av
" Barnard porter 407 Kempton b 32 Elm [cher
" Benjamin loom fixer h 15 That-
" Charles M C machinist h 12 Pope
" Christopher weaver h 142 Crapo
" Co The Inc electricians 158 Purchase
" David weaver h 1035 County
" Ellis molder h 56 Ashley [av
" Fred second hand h 3 Merrimac
" George weaver h 27 Jouvette
" George V hairdresser 245 Cedar Grove h 79 Clark
" Gladys milliner bds 12 Pope
" Hartley weaver h 238 Sawyer
" Henry twister h 8 Olive
" Henry weaver b 119 Brock av
" Henry W laborer b 86 Dartmouth
" Herbert twister b 26 Cove
" Isaac mill hand h 46 Larch
" James driver h 187 Davis
" James weaver h 13 Viall
" James weaver h 56 Ashley
" John bookkeeper b 118 Norman
" John cloth inspector h 95 Brock av
" John h 105 Hemlock
" John weaver h 554 N Front [son
" John T third hand b 208 Thomp-
" Joseph machinist h 269 Palmer
" Joseph weaver b 118 Norman
" Joseph weaver b 56 Ashley

Wilkinson
" Marion F millinery 1035 County h do
" Richard rem to Fairhaven
" Richard weaver h 16 Warren
" Robert weaver h 119 Brock av
" Robert A pressman 40 Purchase h 118 Norman [man
" Robert A Jr weaver h 118 Nor-
" Walter carder b 12 Pope
" William died Aug 17 1910
" William spinner h 199 Collette
" William variety 1760 Acushnet av h do
" William weaver b 56 Ashley
" William weaver b 157 Myrtle
" William H operative h 428 Pleasant [liam h 97 School
Willcox Lemuel T lawyer 49 Wil-
" Sarah H b 97 School
" Susan P b 97 School
Willett Frank laborer h 8 Grand
Willette Napoleon loom fixer h 55 Brock av [34 Bullard
Willey Catherine widow Antone h
" James boilermaker b 42 Atlantic
" Jesse auto repairer 16 Elm h at Fairhaven
" William A fixer b 34 Bullard
Williams Alexander S engineer h 175 Acushnet av [h 101 Campbell
" Alice M bookkeeper 235 N Water
" Andrew J machinist b 1089 Acushnet av
" Angus molder h 126 Nash rd
" Anna widow Joseph h 55 Ward
" Annabel C asst teacher manual training public school bds 156 Chestnut
" Annie Mrs h 268 S Front
" Arthur bell boy Parker House b Chancery street
" Arthur driver h 79 Washington
" Benjamin F laborer h 60 Babbitt
" Benjamin F Jr police h 32 Ash (S)
" Charles helper b 8 Dartmouth
" Charles teamster h 164 S Second
" Charles H police h 84 Rotch
" Charlotte L died Oct 18 1910
" David mill hand b 126 Nash rd
" David rem from city
" Edward J machinist h 178 Smith
" Edward M tinsmith 745 Purchase h 3 Jean [Hillman
" Flora N widow Joseph h 225

Don't dream of what you are going to do! Go and do it.
Kinyon's Short-hand School
Odd Fellows Bldg., Cor. William and Pleasant Sts., New Bedford, Mass.

Williams
" Florence A clerk 201 Union b 225 Hillman
" Frank foreman h 9 Harmony
" Frank S rem from city
" Fred A chief engineer Aenemonie h 283 Union [389 Cottage
" George F chief clerk 2 Union rms
WILLIAMS GEORGE P motor cycles bicycles etc 331 Kempton h 42 Liberty See page 743
" George W rem from city
" G Walter principal High school h 55 Florence
" Harold draughtsman 303 Municipal bldg bds 34 Court
" Hugh carder h 60 Dudley [ley
" Hugh Jr speeder tender b 60 Dud-
" James H box maker h 323 Tinkham
WILLIAMS JOHN architect and builder r 77 Merrimac h do See page 762
" John mariner h 69 Spruce
" John waiter bds 55 Ward
" John F removed to Norwood
" John O drill worker b 60 Babbitt
" John O foreman h 206 North
" John O fruit 169 Union h 17 Fourth [Water
" John T mill hand bds 281 South
" Joseph driver h 51 Hemlock
" Joseph D second hand h 79 Washington
" Joseph S removed from city
" Joseph S undertaker 173½ Acushnet av h 175 do
" Lillian A assistant bookkeeper 100 William bds 225 Hillman
" Louis S assistant 173½ Acushnet av h 182 do [Middle
" Louisa L widow Alexander h r 269
" Manuel clerk 405 S Water h 505 S Second
WILLIAMS MANUEL A real estate 498 Bolton h do See back cover
" Maria E b 106 Spring
" Maria E widow George H h 472 Purchase
" Mary Mrs h 48 Cedar
" Mary Mrs h 131 State [ter
" Mary widow John T h 281 S Wa-

Williams
" Mary A widow Edward h 4 Jenny Lind [64 Oak h 25 Cottage
" Mary E widow Joseph H variety
" Mary H widow Joseph C h 284 Pleasant
" Melleo carpenter h 155 Cedar
" Melos carpenter h 157 Collette
" Moses tack maker b 155 Cedar
" Moses I h 151 Mill
" Nellie weaver b 163 Collette
" Oscar washer 8 Campbell h 206 North
" Richard B printer b 2 Rockland
" Robert L drill worker b 60 Babbitt
" Samuel D bds 4 Jenny Lind
" Sarah F Mrs dressmaker 93 First h do [225 Hillman
" Stephen C clerk 875 Kempton bds
" Thomas (Black & Williams) h 389 Hillman [Ry Co b 34 Court
" Thomas W civil engineeer U St
" Thomas W porter 212 Union h 389 Hillman (W)
" William F city engineer 303 Municipal bldg h 34 Court
" William J liquors 72 Middle h 146 Fourth
" William S collector h 108 Rockland [sion
Williamson Albert barber h 18 Divi-
" Andrew h 8 Waverly
" Andrew W removed from city
" Harold H draughtsman 100 Fifth bds 35 Grape
" Joseph bricklayer h 126 Whitman
" Richard janitor h 80 Brock av
" Richard Jr machinist b 80 Brock avenue
" Sidney drill worker b 35 Grape
" Thomas mill hand h 1283 Acushnet avenue
" Thomas operative b 12 Cleveland
" William bartender 572 N Front h 1498 Acushnet avenue
Willis Alice Mrs h 443 Rivet
" Charles L shoemaker h 76 Atlantic
" Edith bookkeeper b 52 Seventh
" Edward F ticket taker h 162½ North
" Ellis S clerk h 264 Weld

HASKELL BROS. DEALERS IN
ICE
400 COURT STREET TELEPHONE CONNECTION NEW BEDFORD, MASS.

Willis
" Henry P furrier and men's furnishings 22 Pleasant h 52 Seventh
" Lena M Mrs supervisor sewing public schools h 106 Oak
" Mary C widow Rufus H b 411 Cedar [N Water h 272 Palmer
" William H (Plaisler & Willis) 160
Williston Hiram L engineer b 377 Kempton
" Leander carpenter h 11 Chestnut
" Pardon J painter h 65 School
Willoughby Benjamin F salesman 46 Purchase h 157 Grinnell
Wilmett Edmund grocer h 46 Delano
Wilmot Ellen widow b 77 South
" Emma widow Charles h 30 Ashland pl [dent
" George W weaver h 48 Indepen-
" Josephine St Lawrence b 77 South
Wilson Ada widow Luke h 15 McGurk
" Alfred boarding h 67 Fourth
" Alfred B commercial traveler bds 67 Fourth
" Amos L h 101 Cedar
" Annie widow John h 426 N Front
" Annie B sewer 185 Union bds 25 Mill [cery
" Catherine widow John b 78 Chan-
" Charles H roll coverer rms 602 Purchase
" Charles A asst instructor N B Industrial school h at Fairhaven
" Daniel carpenter h 213 Chancery
" Daniel W h 43 Foster
" Edward weaver h 9 Jean
" Edward L painter 61 Durfee h do
" Edward T h 439 County
" Elizabeth widow George h 312 Pleasant
" Fanny Mrs h 113 Newton
" Francis A widow James G bds 555 Kempton
" Frank weaver h 12 Salisbury
" Fred toymaker b 113 Newton
" Frederick G chauffeur rms 35 Eighth [den
" Frederick J foreman h 91 Wal-
" George A shoemaker b 45 North
" George A rem to Providence R I
" George F engineer h 138 State

Wilson
" Grace L stenographer W F Nye Fish Island b 45 North [av
" Harold K janitor b 305 Shawmut
" Harry weaver b 96 Cove
WILSON HENRY P undertaker 80 Pleasant h 152 William See back cover
" Herbert weaver b 58 Mott
" Israel J carpenter h 267 Hathaway rd
" James fireman h 20 Marvin
" James weaver b 30 McGurk
" James H shoemaker b 22 Homer
" Jenny widow William h 326 First
" Jeremiah H brakeman h 62 Durfee
" Job copperworker h 22 Peckham
" John carpenter h 465 Union
" John machinist b 212 Weld
" John weaver bds 95 Beetle
" John D salesman h 79 Court
" John E loom fixer h 177 Arnold
" John J operative b 131 State
" Joseph clerk 368 Kempton b 69 Liberty
" Joseph mill hand b 496 Bolton
" Joseph weaver b 67 Coffin av
" Lily Mrs h 211 Coffin av
" Luke died Dec 17 1910
" Margaret Mrs h 213 Weld [ton
" Mary widow Benjamin h 496 Bol-
" Mary J h 101 Cedar
" Mary S teacher b 439 County
" Mattie L bookkeeper 48 N Water h 584 County
" Maude M Mrs h 163 Pleasant
" Michael steam fitter h 131 State
" Minnie P stenographer bds 113 Grinnell [North
" Nancy J widow Benjamin h 45
" Otis J machinist h 329 Orchard (S)
" Ralph B rem from city
" Raymond second hand bds 1098 Acushnet av
" Robert fireman h 48 Valentine
" Robert operative h 58 Mott
" Robert rem from city
" Robert weaver b 95 Beetle
" Robert J restaurant 220 Union h 48 Ocean
" Samuel H weaver h 16 Franklin
" Thomas carpenter h 146 Florence
" Thomas mill hand h 157 Davis

J. F. CROSSLEY 223 MILL STREET COR. EMERSON PHONE
STEAM and HOT WATER HEATING
GAS FITTING and FIXTURES

Wilson
" Thomas weaver h 157 Davis
" Thomas H housekeeper police dept h 247 Middle
" Thomas H weaver b 15 McGurk
" Thomas J clerk 159 Purchase h 135 Arnold
" Wallace B treas and general mgr Denison Bros Co 32 Pleasant h 54 North
" Walter E rodman 303 Municipal bldg b 60 State
" William laborer h 146 Florence
" William stuccoworker h 52 Mill
" William A driver 645 Purchase h 1071 County [County
" William D letter carrier h 350
" William H bicycle repairer 7 Bedford h 113 Grinnell [David
" William H machinist h 151
" William T clerk 219 Purchase h 202 do [h 22 Homer
" William T clerk 591 Acushnet av
" William W driver rms 62 Russell
Wilucz Frank insurance agent 37 Purchase rm 23 h 54 Phillips av
" Jan weaver b 20 Holly
Wimet Joseph machinist h 1022 Acushnet av
Winborne Annie Mrs h 80 Ash (N)
" Charlotte widow Henry h 84 Ash (N)
" Henry W pressman h 159 Elm
" James P tackmaker h 71 Ash (N)
" Mary housekeeper 84 Ash (N)
" Watson C clothes cleaner 21 Fourth b 80 Ash (N)
" Williston mgr 270 Kempton rms 84 Ash (N)
Winchel Henry weaver h 79 Cove way
Winchester Alice P teacher Cedar Grove street school b at Fairhaven [h at Fairhaven
" Lucy F teacher Middle st school
" Nellie F widow Charles h 427 Acushnet av
" Wilbur ropemaker b 358 Elm
Windinsky Morris clothing 1602 Acushnet av [County
Windle John W fireman h rear 874
Windzberg David canvasser h 181 Bowditch [ditch
" Oscar dry goods bds 181 Bow-
" Samuel L h 181 Bowditch
Winegar Samuel P watchman 58 Adams h 175 Mill
Winfield Elnora G Mrs dressmaker 302 Middle h do [302 Middle
" George H baker 372 Kempton h
Wing Annie H h 31 Walnut
" Avis A clerk A M Corp b 37 Morgan [37 S Sixth
" Charles F pres 36 Purchase h
WING CHARLES F CO The Inc house furnishings 34 to 38 Purchase See page 40
" Charles F Jr director 36 Purchase h 61 Morgan [Morgan
" Charles H clerk 100 William h 37
" Charles S capt telephone operator Central Fire Station h 96 S Sixth
" Edward H director 30 Purchase h 46 Morgan [Pleasant
" Emma P widow John h 129 Mt
" George F h 151 Cedar
" Harold C Mrs h 90 High [Fourth
" Harry B mgr 94 Purchase bds 54
" Horace C salesman b 24 S Sixth
" James M piper 125 Middle b 71 Walden [No 4 h 3 Green
" James T wagon driver Engine
" John h 24 S Sixth
" John Jr salesman b 24 S Sixth
" John C clerk 145 Union b 76 S Sixth [Chestnut
" Joseph B lieut of police h 81
WING J & W R & CO clothing 133 Union See page 768
" Mary L clerk U St Ry Co b 76 S Sixth [Mechanics lane
" Phoebe W widow Edward h 47
" P Thomas overseer Beacon Mfg Co
" Richard rem to Boston
" Sarah R bds 143 Rotch
" Thomas G sheriff h 71 Walden
" Victor removed from city
" William A sec Old Dartmouth Historical Society 37 N Water b 24 S Sixth
" William L rem to Boston
Winn Annie h 63 Independent
" Herbert shoemaker h 26 Adams
" John clerk rms 249 Purchase
" Patrick J painter b 151 Purchase
" Philip J mule spinner h 27 Juniper
" Ruth P bds 100 S Second

CHARLES A. CROSHERE
38 FOURTH ST. Bell Phone 1964-23
SIGN PAINTING
GLASS LETTERING
ELECTRIC SIGNS
SHOW CARDS

Winn
" Thomas P freight conductor h 228 Smith [vet
" Thomas mule spinner h 506 Ri-
Winsberg Oscar dry goods 827 South Water h 181 Bowditch
Winship Estelle G Mrs stenographer 71 William rm 3 h 32 Rockland [land
" Frank A insurance h 32 Rock-
" Fred H Mrs h 50 Ash (S)
" Fred H Jr dentist 3 Pleasant h 81 Walden [North
Winslow Alonzo F driver h 23
" Annie Mrs h 766 Kempton
" Benjamin S physician 1065 S Water h do
" Betsey B h 315 County
" Cornelia G widow Benjamin h 76 Fifth [b 766 Kempton
" Edward W machinist 22 Fourth
" Everett E clerk h 841 Kempton
" George F retired rear admiral U S N h 710 County
" George F housekeeper police Station 3 h 236 Union
" Harold bds 710 County
" Harold reporter Times bds 710 County [Reed
" Harriet H widow William b 345
" Hudson h 90 Ashland
" James H b 315 County
" Lurana L widow Jonathan b 854 Rockdale av
" Mary Mrs bookkeeper 46 Purchase h 149 River rd
" Robert M paper hanger h 208 Acushnet av [Kempton
" Robert K brassworker h 766
" Sarah A teacher Thompson street school b 90 Ashland
" William bds 854 Rockdale av
" William H produce b 854 Rockdale av
Winsor Walter P pres First National Bank h at Fairhaven
Winsper Francis S, City Mfg Co b 280 Fourth
" John B clerk 213 Acushnet av b 280 Fourth [99 Fourth
" Joseph liquors 326 Acushnet av h
" Marie A Mrs clerk h 99 Fourth
" Samuel F supt City Mfg Co h 226 Grinnell
" Thomas helper 745 Purchase

Winsper
" Thomas janitor h 321 Coffin av
" William J laborer h 280 Fourth
" William J Jr b 280 Fourth
Winstanley Edward machinist h 20 Dudley [Dean
" Joseph F second hand h 183
Winter James E clerk S O Co bds 38 Fifth [den
" Richmond C machinist h 10 Bor-
Winterbottom Albert E clerk Potomska Mills h 208 Thompson
" Albert H weaver b 64 Hathaway
" Edward watchman Gosnold Mills Co h 104 Fruit
" Edward Jr operative b 104 Fruit
" Fred plasterer h 64 Hathaway
" George overseer Whitman Mills h 118 Whitman
" John mill hand b 128 Eugenia
" John E spinner h 643 Purchase
" Joseph E overseer Pierce Mfg Corp h 147 Armour
" Robert spinner h 128 Eugenia
Winterburn George H liquors 329 Rivet h 331 do
" Margaret widow bds 331 Rivet
Winterlict George mill hand h Winterville road [Acushnet av
Wintermeyer August sawyer h 150
Winters John F agent h 96 Spring
" Mary J F Mrs dressmaker 96 Spring h do
Winterson Patrick H h 2 Rockland
Winwood John laborer h 27 McGurk
" John Jr spinner b 27 McGurk
Wischnietzky Mania clothing 289 Coggeshall h 126 Cedar Grove
Wishart George overseer Oneko Woolen Mills h 341 Cedar [Adams
Wishnetzky Martha student bds 25
" Michael I h 25 Adams
Wiskos Michael mill hand h 3 Hampton ct [away av
Witham James weaver h 94 Hath-
Withee Frances bds 114 Park
Witherell A Granville teamster h 362 Kempton [lips av
Withey Howard gas fitter h 174 Phil-
Withman George J foreman bds 156 Church [court
Withowicz Leon weaver h 4 Hampton
Witkos John laborer h 112 County
" Mike carder b 3 Hampton ct

J. G. NICHOLSON
LUMBER, SASH, DOORS and BLINDS
BOWDITCH STREET, NEW BEDFORD, MASS.

Wixon James A police h 326 Cottage
Wladinsky Morris clothing 1602 Acushnet av h 10 Bullard
Wladystin Cierpial weaver h 819 S Water [Grove
Wnok John operative h 119 Cedar
Woakya Karimiesi operative h 190 Cedar Grove
Wobecki Charles tinsmith 87 Union
Wobetski Antoine mule spinner h 199 Dean [Dean
" Antoine Jr brakeman bds 199
" Charles spinner h 297 Davis
" John spinner h 297 Davis
" Joseph back boy b 201 Dean
" Joseph spinner h 297 Davis
" Ludwig spinner h 201 Dean
Wodell Sarah Mrs h 106 School
Wojcecki Anthoni weaver b 114 Nash road [lard
Wojtonvicz Felix weaver bds 9 Bul-
Wolan Konstanteien weaver h r 21 Washburn [burn
Wolfe Charles machinist b 57 Wash-
" Charles M tailor 1½ Fifth h 81 Park
" Jacob pedlar h 8 Penniman
" Louis tailor h 371 Reed
" Susie Mrs h 158 Reynolds
Wolff Robert removed from city
Wolfson Fisher clothing 1285 Acushnet av h 1326 do [av h do
Wolison Harry grocer 527 Acushnet
Wollison Israel grocer 404 Purchase h 9 Willis [Front
Wolstencroft John C engineer h 511 N
Wolstenholme John spinner b 6 Warren
" Jonathan weaver h 130 Tallman
" Robert changer over h r 57 Howard
" Sarah J Mrs h 6 Warren
" William foreman 87 Howard av h Tarkiln Hill road
Wong Samuel waiter rms 59 Kempton
Woniak Daniel mill hand b 269 Belleville avenue [County
Wood Addie J widow Isaiah Jr h 298
" Albert K salesman 41 Purchase h 53 Walnut [N Sixth
" Albert T cooper 9 Hamilton h 55

Wood
" Allen F principal Fifth st school h 111 Acushnet avenue
" Ann widow William h E French avenue n Frederick [County
" Anna G widow Henry T h 274
" Annie D dressmaker 22 Cedar h do
" A W clerk rms 168 Middle
WOOD BRIGHTMAN & CO (Thomas F Wood and Henry Howland) stoves tin plate and iron workers and plumbers 47-55 North Water See page 3
" Carolyn D normal teacher Harrington school h 246 Tremont
" Charles clerk h 137 Tremont
" Charles treasurer 32 Commercial bds 280 Arnold
WOOD CHARLES G publisher New Bedford Times 120 Purchase h 60 S Sixth See page 759
" Clarence D clerk 60 Shawmut av h 123 Locust [h 37 Allen
" Clarence E mgr 1218 Acushnet av
" Daniel blacksmith h 161 Bates av
" David S jeweler 130 Union b 65 S Sixth [ant
" David V carpenter rms 279 Pleas-
" Earl H cashier U St Ry Co William corner Purchase rms 161 liam
" Edmund (Greene & Wood) Cross corner Pine h 105 Ash (S)
" Edward F piper 125 Middle h 122 Potomska
" Edwin F baggage master h 65 Linden [Court
" Edwin M drill worker h 396
" Effie Mrs h 78 Durfee [Fifth
" Eliza A B widow Edward F h 67
" Eliza H widow William G h 122 Hawthorn
" Eliza W widow Greenleaf b 37 Allen
" Elizabeth b 358 Union
" Elizabeth A mill hand h 201 Davis [Linden
" Elizabeth C widow William S h 65
" Elizabeth G K widow Albert h 53 Walnut [b do
" Emma J dressmaker 156 Campbell
" Emma L widow Lemuel C dressmaker 15 Shawmut av h do

Steiger-Dudgeon Co.
"The WOMAN'S Store."
Tel. Bell 82 & 83, Branches connecting all depts.
" " 160 For Office only. Auto. 1211

SUMPTIONS,
ASSORTMENTS
AT ALL TIMES
OF DEPENDABLE
DRY GOODS

Wood
" Ethel A bookkeeper b 298 County
" Evelyn S Mrs h 2 Pope's Island
" Francis T shoeworker b 82 Forest [280 Arnold
" Frank clerk 32 Commercial bds
" Frank cotton broker 13 Hamilton h 47 Fifth [53 Cottage
" Frank C compositor Standard h
" Frank E h 45 Richmond
" Frank E (Wood & Lowrie) 50 Union h 614 County
" Frank O chauffeur 159 Purchase b 78 Walden
" Frederick H engineer U St Ry Co power house h at Fairhaven
" F H (Croteau & Wood) h 52 Main
" George machinist h 56 Cove
" George A painter 46 Foster h do
" George A city teamster h 319 Maxfield [Maxfield
" George A Jr drillmaker bds 319
" George F painter h 258 Cedar
" George H photo engraver Times
" George R (Greene & Wood) lumber etc Cross cor Pine h 117 Cottage [Homer
" Hannah B widow Frank L b 16
" Harriet S widow Fred P h 65 Linden [ter b 67 Fifth
" Harry B cotton broker 62 N Wa-
" Hartley weaver h 593 Cottage
" Helen M bookkeeper 160 Purchase b at Fairhaven
" Henry rem to New York city
" Horace h 85 Mill [County
" Howard M clerk 100 Fifth b 298
" James clerk foot Willis h 16 Homer
" James twister h 71 Peckham
" James A armorer Sycamore cor Pleasant h 56 Walnut
" John operative b 19 Hazard ct
" John weaver b 81 Holly
" John E overseer Whitman Mills h 201 Davis [way
" Joseph operative h 118 Hatha-
" Josiah bds 95 Washington
" Loretta stenographer Nashawena Mill b 1637 Acushnet av
" Louisa C widow Joseph S h 156 Campbell [ant
" Luthan A hostler h 163 Pleas-

Wood
" Maria E B widow Lawton C bds 390 Acushnet av [field
" Mary widow Patrick bds 94 Max-
" Mary widow William h 334 Kempton [ly
" Mary A widow William h 81 Hol-
" Mary H Mrs h 1637 Acushnet av
" Mary S and Abbie h 26 Walnut
" Matthew P carpenter h 3 Pope's Island

WOOD MORGAN DETECTIVE AGENCY 61 Court Boston See page 753
" Patrick F pres 32 Commercial h 280 Arnold [field
" Patrick J carpet layer h 94 Max-
" P F Boiler Works 32 Commercial [at Padanaram
" Ralph W driver 128 Pleasant h
" Rebecca B Mrs b 132 School
" Rebecca H widow Isaiah h 358 Union [Wood b 117 Cottage
" Richmond salesman Greene &
" Robert second hand h 14 Ashley
" Robert E salesman 70 Union h 298 Cedar
" Samuel laborer h 56 Cove
" Sarah b 280 Arnold [Court
" Sarah A widow Charles bds 396
" Schofield fixer h 395 Bowditch
" Stanley W musician bds 85 Mill
" Theodore overseer Nonquitt Spinning Co b at Acushnet
" Thomas F (Wood Brightman & Co) 55 N Water h 89 Bonney
" Thomas L C teamster b 390 Acushnet av
" Walter h 274 County
" Walter I hostler h 309 Kempton
" William bricklayer b 113 Austin
" William loom fixer h 56 Beetle
" William operative h 84 Linden
" William picker h 28 Winsor
" William Jr plumber b E French av near Frederick [33 Clover
" William E salesman 70 Union h
" William G foreman 3 E Pope h 117 Parker
" William H h 408 County
" William H A insideman 283 Union b do
" William O corporation clerk 32 Commercial b 280 Arnold

PELEG H. SHERMAN 506 COUNTY ST.
FUNERAL DIRECTOR AND EMBALMER
OFFICE PHONES. Bell 690-13 Auto 1305.
RESIDENCE PHONES. Bell 690-12. Auto 1306.

Wood
" & Lowrie (Frank E Wood and Geo H Lowrie) wholesale provisions and Simpson Spring beverages 40-50 Union
" see Dubois and Woods [chase
Woodacre Albert V baker b 680 Pur-
" James plumber h 439 S Front
" John weaver h 132 Nye
" John E clerk 133 Union b 680 Purchase [do
" Richard stable 270 Purchase h 680
" Richard Jr baker b 680 Purchase
" William baker 704 Purchase b 680 do
Woodard Burton O photographer 1017 Acushnet av h 203 Dean
" Gordon E student bds 203 Dean
" John W b 38 Campbell [Dean
" John W telephone operator b 203
" Sarah L nurse b 38 Campbell
" see Woodward [ter b 92 Tremont
Woodbridge Henry B foreman carpen-
" Isaiah T h 92 Tremont [Madison
" Mary B widow William H h 38
" Walter B dentist 60 Purchase h 269 Arnold [po
Woodcock Alfred fisherman h 124 Cra-
" Frederic L removed to Brooklyn New York [67 S Sixth
" Henry A L supervisor 100 Fifth h
" Kinder M laborer h 82 Katharine
" Thomas P spinner h 109 Division
Woodhouse George twister h 174 Clifford [69 Bay
" Robert H florist Ward cor Allen h
Woodhull Annie E died Jan 13 1911
Woodland E (Boston Supply Co) 765 Purchase h at Fall River
" John grocer 368 and 416 Kempton h 80 Ashland
" Olive M cashier b 78 Campbell
" Percy E clerk 368 Kempton b 78 Ashland
" Robert E (Keyes & Woodland) provisions 108 Cedar h 658 Kempton
" Robert H grocer 1623 Acushnet av and 702 Purchase h 78 Campbell [van
Woodley Robert H teamster h 4 Sulli-
Woodlin Herbert assistant washer 8 Campbell bds 5 Sullivan

Woodlin
" Sarah R Mrs h 5 Sullivan
Woodman Alice L matron 57 N Second bds at Fairhaven
" Nettie B teacher Parker street school bds 156 Chestnut
Woodruff Florence G telephone operator 57 N Second b 146 Arnold
WOODRUFF FORREST T & CO auto school 244 Purchase h 148 Arnold See page 748
" John painter b 169 Grinnell
Woods Edward weaver b 19 Ashley
" George W gardener 396 County h 29 Oak
" Mary A bookkeeper bds 8 Studley
" Rachael widow John h 8 Studley
" Richard removed to Yarmouth
" Richard J removed to Yarmouth
" William operative h 168 Division
" see Wood
Woodsome Benjamin overseer N B C M Corp h 208 Eugenia
" Lena B clerk 185 Union b 49 Wood
" Wallace farmer h 49 Wood
Woodward Adeline widow Dwight b 85 Campbell
" Clara M removed to Lisbon Me
" Emma J widow Solomon h 74 Morgan
" Francis (Rhodes, Woodward & Co) 45 William h 146 N Main Fairhaven

HENRY E WOODWARD
Attorney and Counsellor at Law
Notary Public
Justice of the Peace
Room 14, Five Cents Savings Bank Building
37 Purchase Street
New Bedford, Mass
Telephones: Bell 1720
Automatic 1692
Residence 1384-5
Residence 54 Fourth Street

F. T. AKIN & CO. PAINTERS AND DECORATORS

Woodward Henry E lawyer 37 Purchase rm 14 b 54 Fourth
" Joseph laborer h 50 Hazard
" Thomas Jr (Rhodes, Woodward & Co) 45 William h at Fall River
" William H h 93 First
" see Woodard
Woodworth Charles E jewelry 29 Purchase h 127 Cottage
" Henry A loomfixer h 98 Covell
" Margaret widow Robert b 341 Bowditch [Salisbury
Wooldrige George A carpenter h 18
Wooler Harry spinner b 41 Highland
" James W laborer h 41 Highland
" John helper 28 N Water b 41 Highland
Wooley Albert laborer h 282 Fourth
" Arthur weaver b 12 Warren
" Ernest laborer b 12 Warren
" George D overseer h 83 Ruth
" John mule spinner h 118 Cove
" John A fixer h 40 Woodlawn av
Woolfenden Albert police h 21 Richmond
" John jeweler 69 Dean h do
" L Theodore shoes 788 Purchase h 6 Studley
" Robert Jr rem to Acushnet
" William real estate 1283 Acushnet av b do [ley
Woollam James W spinner h 7 Ash-
" Joseph card grinder h 126 Eugenia
" Joseph Jr carder b 126 Eugenia
" Llewellyn grinder h 126 Eugenia
Woolley Burgoyne overseer Neild M Corp h 23 George [(S)
" Frank glass blower b 414 Orchard
" Frank weaver h 103 Bowditch
" George D overseer Butler Mill h 83 Ruth
" James boilermaker b 42 Atlantic
" John driver Engine No 6 b 80 Brock av
" John fixer h 103 Bowditch
" Kathleen h 42 Ash (N) [(S)
" Thomas glasscutter h 414 Orchard
" Thomas hoseman Steamer No 8 and foreman 223 N Second h 414 Orchard (S) [chard (S)
" Thomas Jr gardener bds 414 Or-

Woolley
" William glasscutter bds 414 Orchard (S)
" see Wholey [Grove
Woolner John spinner h 324 Cedar
Woolridge George A carpenter h 18 Salisbury
Woolworth F W & Co variety 70-72 Purchase and 1081-1083 Acushnet av [Roosevelt
Wootton William carpenter h 24
Wordell Adeline A widow Hiram h 158 Mill
" Allen E agricultural implements 21 William h at Dartmouth
" Allen H h 17 Rounds [Hillman
" Amelia F widow Charles W h 380
" B Franklin cigars 291-293 Purchase h 59 Sycamore
" Clarence E glassworker b 69 Vine
" Cyrus E carpenter h 325 Austin
" Elizabeth R died June 24 1911
" Elmer L clerk b 87 James
" Elvira stenographer 97 William rm 303 b 17 Rounds
" Frank B carpenter b 325 Austin
" Fred S clerk 21 William h 45 Pierce
" Harold carpenter b 69 Vine
" Helen A bookkeeper 293 Purchase b 59 Sycamore [pl
" Howard I clerk bds 22 Arnold
" James b 261 Hillman
" Jonathan operative h 70 Earle
" Joshua N laborer h 87 James
" Philip H salesman h 261 Hillman
" Rachel M teacher H M Knowlton school b 35 Bonney
" Roy chauffeur rms 188 Purchase
" William S h 581 Allen
" Willis R farmer b 17 Rounds
" Wilson I sales agent Garfield & Proctor Coal Co h 22 Arnold place
" see Wardell and Wodell
Worden Charlotte B bookkeeper bds 20 Viall
" Edward weaver h 20 Viall
" George (loom fixer) rem to Wauregan Conn
" Hugh musician b 20 Viall
" John elevatorman h 6 Cove rd
" Olive S bookkeeper b 20 Viall
" Reuben weaver b 32 Cove
" Thomas weaver b 6 Cove rd

Bookkeeping, Shorthand, Typewriting, Penmanship, etc. Taught thoroughly at
Kinyon's Commercial School
Odd Fellows Bldg., Cor. William and Pleasant Sts., New Bedford, Mass.

Worgren Karl mariner h 71 Smith
Working Men's Club 69 Bowditch
" Men's Home 1 Mill [32 Ashland
Worsley Ruth clerk P Corp bds
" Thomas operative h 808 First
" William hatter h 15 Studley
" William weaver h 56 Beetle
" William M salesman 185 Union h at Fairhaven [nister
Worswick John R twister b 13 Ban-
" Joseph h 341 Tinkham
" Mary clerk 1378 Acushnet av b 341 Tinkham
" Mary Mrs h 168 Cove
Worth Henry Barnard lawyer 37 Purchase rm 24 h 15 Washington
" James bricklayer b 184 Davis
" Sarah B h 38 Madison
Worthington Arthur H spinner h 208 Nash road
" Charles H weaver h 62 Durfee
" Dinah Mrs lodgings 602 Purchase
" George operative h 16 Abbott
" Herbert weaver h 31 Ashley
" James laborer b 182 Cove
" Ralph painter h 62 Durfee
Worthy Ernest spinner h 277 Davis
Wright Amos Franklin carpenter h 20 Maitland
" Arthur weaver b 236 N Front
" Arthur W telegrapher Times b 219 Purchase [Chancery
" Caroline E widow John L h 256
" Christopher operative b 36 Howard
" Edgar F carpenter b 20 Maitland
" Edna E bookkeeper 100 S Water bds 199 Pleasant
" Edward E druggist 88 Purchase h 199 Pleasant [nut
" Ella widow Gideon B h 64 Chest-
" Ernest K carpenter b 20 Maitland [Acushnet av
" Esther cloth inspector b 2103
" George laborer h 2103 Acushnet av [sher
" George second hand h 15 Mo-
" George Jr weaver b 2103 Acushnet av
WRIGHT GEORGE F painter 24 N Water h 66 Cottage See page 777
" Harry mgr 22 Fourth h at Fairhaven

Wright
" James third hand h 39 Myrtle
" Jane widow Martin h 269 Middle
" John weaver h 36 Howard
" Jonathan K (Wright & Taber) h 224 Grinnell [27 Jenny Lind
" J Arnold salesman 276 Union h
" J Smithson umbrellas and Japanese goods 276 Union h 27 Jenny Lind [22 Borden
" J Urbon watchmaker 130 Union h
" Lily widow Robert h 90 Linden
" Louis B clerk b 855 Rockdale av
" Marion T B Mrs h 855 Rockdale avenue [shnet av
" May clerk 198 Union b 2103 Acu-
" Nathan janitor b 286 Orchard (S)
" Nellie F teacher Cedar Grove st school b 220 Grinnell
" Richard piper h 27 Roosevelt
" Robert M rem from city
" S Howell rem to Norwood
" Victoria M bookkeeper bds 2103 Acushnet av
" Walter spinner h 121 Willow
" W Henry carpenter h 40 Ash (S)
" & Taber (Jonathan K Wright and Frank G Taber) grocers 131 Acushnet av
Wrigley Thomas prop Hotel Bristol 219 Purchase h 36 North
" William spinner h 201 Belleville road
" William H weaver h 241 State
Wroe Hannah and Alice h 17 Marvin
" William E b 17 Marvin [ty
Wroughton Mary Mrs h 833 Coun-
Wunshell Adam weaver h 172 Bonney
" Albert slasher tender h 88 Sagamore
" Frank weaver b 172 Bonney
" John M overseer Acushnet M Corp h 32 Bourne [mer
" J August loom fixer h 150 Black-
Wyatt Aaron weaver b 47 Fruit
" Joseph S twister h 90 Kenyon
" Linwood E painter b 4 Oak st ct
" William E machinist b 4 Oak st ct
" see Whyatt
Wydra John weaver h 1 Gifford
Wygrzewalski Alfred weaver h r 35 Acushnet av

Bread, Cake, Pastry
RICHMOND & COMPANY **255-257 UNION STREET**
Bell 993 Automatic 1022

Wylie Isobel widow Robert h 90 Clark
Wyman Adolphus F dentist 265 Union h do
" George painter h 399 Elm (W)
Wynaught Charles G rem from city
Wynne Herbert cutter b 26 Adams
Wyse Agnes rem from city
" Annie E rem from city
" Mary J rem from city
" William pedlar h 344 Kempton
Wywiorski Szcepan weaver h 119 Nash rd
Wyzga Joseph weaver h 14 Fulton court
" Stanislaus operative b 14 Fulton court

Xavier Alvin third hand b 87 Grinnell
" Bonaventure shoeworker h 106 S Sixth
" Charles clerk 209 Coggeshall rms 45 Beetle
" Flora E clerk P Corp bds 106 S Sixth
" John laborer b 16 Briggs
" John J salesman Anthony Swift Co h 119 Acushnet avenue
" Joseph B tailor 144 Union h 59 Lombard
" Joseph L shoe worker b 106 S Sixth
" Manuel J h 30 Cove
" Manuel N agent 73 William h 106 S Sixth
" Mary widow b 89 Grinnell

Yacamovitz Vincent teamster h 47 Washburn
Yaeger Alois weaver h 13 Ashland pl
" Antonio widow Julius h 442 North Front
" Clement L asst at public library b 87 Ashland
" Edward weaver b 442 N Front
" Florian died Sept 5 1910
" Hugh F clerk 100 William bds 87 Ashland
" Josephine Mrs h 87 Ashland
" L Robert musician Hathaway's Theatre bds 13 Ashland pl
Yamins Samuel (Yamins & Jacobson) h at Fall River
" & Jacobson (Samuel Yamins and Joseph Jacobson) dry goods 701 S Water
Yanacek Frank weaver h 133 Bullard
Yangkofski Stanltuis operative h 45 Washburn
Yanovsky John fixer h 109 Davis
Yarlef Samuel shoe repairer 79 Weld h 72 Kenyon
Yaryapka Andreas h 686 Acushnet av
Yates Agnes L teacher Harrington school bds 151 Merrimac
" Albert operative h 286 Davis
" Alice clerk 182 Union b 151 Merrimac
" Ann and Emily h 80 Clark
" Benjamin removed to Ashton England
" Edwin T machinist b 151 Merrimac
" Eliza A widow Robert b 22 George
" Elizabeth M teacher Dartmouth st school b 151 Merrimac
" Emma Mrs h 200 Collette
" Gordon G operative b 12 Viall
" Henry L died December 28 1910
" James conductor h 103 Holly
" James removed to Preston England
" James third hand h 26 Viall
" James H weaver h 187 Brock av
" John insurance agent 120 Purchase rm 403 h 171 Richmond
" John E weaver h 126 David
" Josephine C teacher Phillips av school b 151 Merrimac
" Lawrence fixer h 12 Viall
" Mary E milliner 182 Union b 151 Merrimac
" Robert died March 19 1911
" Thomas overseer Gosnold Mill h 10 Jean
" Thomas weaving principal N B Textile school h 151 Merrimac
" William loom fixer h 76 Earle
" William operative h 387 Bowditch
" William watchman bds 379 Reed
" William weaver h r 61 Belleville road
Yazbek Fares pedler h 555 Acushnet av
Yearwood C Hubert Rev pastor Bethel A M E church h 460 Kempton
Yeary John clerk bds 31 High
Yee Yohn Chinese restaurant 68 William h do
Yehle Otto operative h 127 Eugenia
Yell Edmund H slasher tender h 111 Tallman
" Maxim A painter h 1616 Acushnet avenue

GLOBE DYE HOUSE 220 SHAWMUT AVE.
J. N. J. LONHOLDT, PROP. Telephone Connections Goods called for and Delivered
Down town Office, 52 Pleasant St., Room 1 North End Office, 1014 Acushnet Ave.

Yell
" Mary A B bookkeeper b 1616 Acushnet avenue
Yeo James blacksmith bds 76 Cove
Yerid Annie confectionery 802 Purchase h 790 Purchase
Yerovitz Harry dry goods 1676 Acushnet av h 10 Bullard
Ylenev John mill hand h 19 Rotch block 442 Bolton [liam rms do
Yohn Charlie (Shuy Fong Co) 68 Wil-
Yohst Anton glass cutter h 157 Fair
York Alfred H bookkeeper 830 Purchase b 17 Studley [355 Cedar
" Arthur O mgr 205 Times bldg h
" George A (George A York & Co) h 70 Russell
" George A & Co (Geo A York and Jean B Jean) insurance 97 William rm 301
" Irving Le R laborer h 134 Fourth
" Irving S foreman 100 Fifth h 256 Fourth
" James L engineer h 17 Studley
" Waldo student b 70 Russell
" Walter H photographer 134 Purchase h 46 Borden
" William h 123 Cedar
" William E machinist h 3 Clay
" W Everett driver 185 Union b 123 Cedar [Times b at Fairhaven
Young Alexander O compositor N B
" Alfred third hand h 121 Hope
" Annie E widow dressmaker 214 Cedar h do [Fifth
" Bertha M clerk 7 Commercial b 60
" Blake B barber 24 Purchase b 305 Middle [yer
" Charles H rol coverer h 238 Saw-
" David fireman h 19 Ruth [man
" Edward blacksmith h 102 Whit-
" Edward carpenter h 155 Frederick
" Felix L mgr 140 Purchase h 87 Walden
" Frank driver h 829 Acushnet av
" Frank J bds 829 Acushnet av
" Frank L & Kimball oils and candles 350 S Second [Lind
" Franklin A supt h 169 Jenny
" F A agent 186 Purchase
" Henry weaver h 196 Division [ty
" Henry A shoeworker b 508 Coun-
" Henry D driver h 323 Cedar

Young
" Henry G machinist h 2157 Acushnet av [man
" John W fisherman h 427 Hill-
" John W weaver h 8 Acushnet av
" Joseph spinner b 102 Whitman
" Louisa Mrs rem from city
" Margaret J h 72 Maxfield
" Mary E widow Stephen B h 12 W High
" Mary L b 300 County
" May A dressmaker b 214 Cedar
" Men's Christian Association William cor N Sixth [man
" Milton A glasscutter h 33 Sher-
" Moses speeder tender b 102 Whitman
" Nelson weaver b 102 Whitman
" Orville E clerk P & R C & I Co foot Walnut h 246 Palmer
" Percy H engineer h 112½ Fifth
" Philip rem to Fairhaven
" William A second hand h 2061 Acushnet av
" William C conductor h 243 State
" William H gardener b 159 Arnold
" William T hose wagon driver Engine No 1 h 253 Chestnut
" Women's Christian Association 66 to 70 Spring
Younger Robert weaver h 313 Earle
Youngs William A plasterer h 209 Tinkham

Zachs Joseph spinner h 121 Eugenia
Zalkind Alexander (Zalkind and Kessler) h at Providence R I
" Samuel mgr 486 S Water rms Y M C A
" & Kessler (Alexander Zalkind and Joseph Kessler) butter 486 S Water
Zamos Peter mill hand h 7 Grandfield
Zavadski Stanislaus painter h 38 Washburn
Zavas Eddy (Zavas & Co) rms 136 Bowditch
" & Co (Eddy Zavas and Nick Chargaruly) cigars 1209 Acushnet av
Zavros James cook 1136 Acushnet av
" John mill hand b 3 McDonald ct
" Nicohlas mill hand b 3 McDonald court [court
" Simeon mill hand b 3 McDonald

GREENE & WOOD Every Kind of LUMBER AND MILL WORK
PINE STREET, off So. WATER STREET, NEW BEDFORD

Zebi William operative h 41 Washburn
Zego John h 28 Washburn
Zeima Willie weaver h 65 Nash rd
Zeiter Michael weaver h 40 Hemlock
Zeitz Barney pawn broker 90 and 121 Union h 225 Acushnet av
" Charles commercial traveler h 237 Acushnet av [shnet av
" Fannie widow Kopel h 225 Acu-
" Harry salesman 121 Union b 225 Acushnet av [Acushnet av
" Isaac salesman 121 Union b 225
" Jacob b 225 Acushnet av [ct
Zellhuber Karl machinist h 12 Briggs
Zeman Albert laundryman h 717 Kenyon
" Mendel messenger b 81 Kenyon
Zembra Joseph operative b 41 Washburn
Zerbone Antonio goldsmith 23 Griffin h 190 Acushnet av
" Antonio E drillworker h 25 Griffin [Griffin h do
" Antonio E Mrs dresmaker 52
" Arthur J chauffeur h 211 S Second
Zerbone
" Gerald electrician 194 Acushnet av b 190 do [126 Thompson
" Richard (Electric Printing Co) h
Zeses Anton (Zeses & Blucas) pool 1605 Acushnet av rms 162 Davis
" & Blucas (Anton Zeses and Peter Blucas) pool 1605 Acushnet av
Zielenski Adam weaver h 165 Cedar Grove [field
Ziemba Mike operative h 15 Grand-
Zimberlin Protais laborer h 21 Scott
Zimmer David h 353 Davis
" John weaver b 353 Davis
Zimmermann Ernest L student bds 1105 Acushnet avenue
" Fridolin grocer 1103 Acushnet av h 341 Coggeshall [150 Blackmer
Ziomet Franciszek grocer 627 First h
Zurier Jacob shoe repairer 89 S Second h 112 do [McGurk
Zvijvie Stanislaus weaver bds 12
Zygiel Annie Mrs boarding 23 Washburn [23 Washburn
" John liquors 44 Kenyon bds
" Joseph weaver h 23 Washburn
Zylstra William carder b 526 Cottage [Belleville av
Zyskoski Peter mill hand bds 399

BONNEY, FOLSTER & CO.,
The North End's Shopping Centre
Dry Goods and Men's Furnishings
945-947 Acushnet Ave., New Bedford, Mass.

Send for Illustrated Circular and Specimen Program

THE RAVENS

25 MERCHANTS ROW, - BOSTON

Telephone, 1835-2 Richmond

HOWARD & BULLOUGH

American Machine Company, Ltd.

PAWTUCKET, R. I.

COTTON MACHINERY

Hopper Bale Openers
Feeders
Self Feeding Openers
Breaker Intermediate and Finisher Lappers

Revolving Flat Cards
Drawing Frames
Slubbing Frames
Intermediate and Roving Frames

Improved Spinning Frames
Twisters
Cone Winders
Warpers and Slashers

WE INVITE YOUR INVESTIGATION AND COMPARISON

Send for our Descriptive Circulars with list of users

Spinning Ring Specialists for 38 years

Whitinsville Spinning Ring Company

WHITINSVILLE, MASS., U. S. A.

POPULATION OF MASSACHUSETTS.

UNITED STATES CENSUS OF 1910; STATE CENSUS OF 1905.

Total, in 1905, 3,003,680. Total, in 1910, 3,366,416.

* Cities designated by an asterisk. Shire towns in SMALL CAPITALS.

Towns	1910	1905
Barnstable.		
BARNSTABLE	4,676	4,336
Bourne	2,474	1,786
Brewster	631	739
Chatham	1,564	1,634
Dennis	1,919	1,998
Eastham	518	519
Falmouth	3,144	3,241
Harwich	2,115	2,291
Mashpee	270	317
Orleans	1,077	1,052
Provincetown	4,369	4,362
Sandwich	1,688	1,433
Truro	655	743
Wellfleet	1,022	958
Yarmouth	1,420	1,422
	27,542	26,831
Berkshire.		
Adams	13,026	12,486
Alford	275	275
Becket	959	890
Cheshire	1,508	1,281
Clarksburg	1,207	1,200
Dalton	3,568	3,122
Egremont	605	721
Florida	395	424
Great Barrington	5,926	6,152
Hancock	465	434
Hinsdale	1,116	1,452
Lanesboro	947	845
Lee	4,106	3,972
Lenox	3,060	3,058
Monterey	388	444
Mt Washington	110	87
New Ashford	92	100
New Marlboro	1,124	1,209
*North Adams	22,019	22,150
Otis	494	534
Peru	237	268
*PITTSFIELD	32,121	25,001
Richmond	650	601
Sandisfield	566	657
Savoy	503	549
Sheffield	1,817	1,782
Stockbridge	1,933	2,022
Tyringham	382	314
Washington	277	339
West Stockbridge	1,271	1,023
Williamstown	3,708	4,425
Windsor	404	513
	105,259	98,330
Bristol.		
Acushnet	1,692	1,284
Attleboro	16,215	12,702
Berkley	999	931
Dartmouth	4,378	3,793
Dighton	2,235	2,070
Easton	5,139	4,909
Fairhaven	5,122	4,235
*FALL RIVER	119,295	105,762
Freetown	1,471	1,470
Mansfield	5,183	4,245
*NEW BEDFORD	96,652	74,362
North Attleboro	9,562	7,878
Norton	2,544	2,079
Raynham	1,725	1,662
Rehoboth	2,001	1,991
Seekonk	2,397	1,917
Somerset	2,798	2,294
Swansea	1,978	1,839
*TAUNTON	34,259	30,967
Westport	2,928	2,867
	318,573	269,257

Towns	1910	1905
Dukes.		
Chilmark	282	322
EDGARTOWN	1,191	1,175
Gay Head	162	178
Gosnold	152	161
Oak Bluffs	1,084	1,138
Tisbury	1,196	1,120
West Tisbury	437	457
	4,504	4,551
Essex.		
Amesbury	9,894	8,840
Andover	7,301	6,632
*Beverly	18,650	15,223
Boxford	718	665
Danvers	9,407	9,063
Essex	1,621	1,790
Georgetown	1,958	1,840
*Gloucester	24,398	26,011
Groveland	2,253	2,401
Hamilton	1,749	1,646
*Haverhill	44,115	37,830
Ipswich	5,777	5,205
*LAWRENCE	85,892	70,050
*Lynn	89,336	77,042
Lynnfield	911	797
Manchester	2,673	2,618
Marblehead	7,338	7,209
Merrimac	2,202	1,884
Methuen	11,448	8,676
Middleton	1,129	1,068
Nahant	1,184	922
Newbury	1,482	1,480
*NEWBURYPORT	14,949	14,675
North Andover	5,529	4,614
Peabody	15,721	13,098
Rockport	4,211	4,447
Rowley	1,368	1,388
*SALEM	43,697	37,627
Salisbury	1,658	1,622
Saugus	8,047	6,253
Swampscott	6,204	5,141
Topsfield	1,174	1,095
Wenham	1,010	924
West Newbury	1,473	1,405
	436,477	381,181
Franklin.		
Ashfield	959	959
Bernardston	741	769
Buckland	1,573	1,500
Charlemont	1,001	1,002
Colerain	1,741	1,780
Conway	1,230	1,340
Deerfield	2,209	2,112
Erving	1,148	1,094
Gill	942	1,023
GREENFIELD	10,427	9,156
Hawley	424	448
Heath	346	356
Leverett	728	703
Leyden	363	408
Monroe	246	269
Montague	6,866	7,015
New Salem	639	672
Northfield	1,642	2,017
Orange	5,282	5,578
Rowe	456	533
Shelburne	1,498	1,515
Shutesbury	267	374
Sunderland	1,047	910
Warwick	477	527
Wendell	502	480
Whately	846	822
	43,600	43,362

Towns	1910	1905
Hampden.		
Agawam	3,501	2,795
Blandford	717	746
Brimfield	866	894
Chester	1,377	1,366
*Chicopee	25,401	20,191
East Longmeadow	1,553	1,327
Granville	781	865
Hampden	645	561
Holland	145	151
*Holyoke	57,730	49,934
Longmeadow	1,084	964
Ludlow	4,948	3,881
Monson	4,758	4,344
Montgomery	217	259
Palmer	8,610	7,755
Russell	965	1,053
Southwick	1,020	1,048
*SPRINGFIELD	88,926	73,540
Tolland	180	274
Wales	345	645
Westfield	16,044	13,611
West Springfield	9,224	8,101
Wilbraham	2,332	1,708
	231,369	196,013
Hampshire.		
Amherst	5,112	5,313
Belchertown	2,054	2,088
Chesterfield	536	563
Cummington	637	740
Easthampton	8,524	6,808
Enfield	874	973
Goshen	279	277
Granby	761	747
Greenwich	452	475
Hadley	1,999	1,895
Hatfield	1,986	1,779
Huntington	1,473	1,451
Middlefield	354	399
*NORTHAMPTON	19,431	19,957
Pelham	467	460
Plainfield	406	382
Prescott	320	322
Southampton	870	927
South Hadley	4,894	5,054
Ware	8,774	8,594
Westhampton	423	466
Williamsburg	2,132	1,943
Worthington	569	614
	63,327	62,227
Middlesex.		
Acton	2,136	2,089
Arlington	11,187	9,668
Ashby	885	865
Ashland	1,682	1,597
Ayer	2,797	2,386
Bedford	1,231	1,208
Belmont	5,542	4,360
Billerica	2,789	2,843
Boxboro	317	324
Burlington	591	588
*CAMBRIDGE	104,839	97,434
Carlisle	551	523
Chelmsford	5,010	4,254
Concord	6,421	5,421
Dracut	3,461	3,537
Dunstable	408	412
*Everett	33,484	29,111
Framingham	12,948	11,548
Groton	2,155	2,253
Holliston	2,711	2,663
Hopkinton	2,452	2,585
Hudson	6,743	6,217
Lexington	4,918	4,530

Towns	1910	1905
Lincoln	1,175	1,122
Littleton	1,229	1,219
*Lowell	106,294	94,889
*Malden	44,404	38,037
*Marlboro	14,579	14,073
Maynard	6,390	5,811
*Medford	23,150	19,686
*Melrose	15,715	14,295
Natick	9,866	9,609
*Newton	39,806	36,827
North Reading	1,059	903
Pepperell	2,953	3,268
Reading	5,818	5,682
Sherborn	1,428	1,379
Shirley	2,139	1,692
*Somerville	77,236	69,272
Stoneham	7,090	6,332
Stow	1,115	1,027
Sudbury	1,120	1,159
Tewksbury	3,750	4,415
Townsend	1,761	1,772
Tyngsboro	829	768
Wakefield	11,404	10,268
*Waltham	27,834	26,282
Watertown	12,875	11,258
Wayland	2,206	2,220
Westford	2,851	2,413
Weston	2,106	2,091
Wilmington	1,858	1,670
Winchester	9,309	8,242
*Woburn	15,308	14,402
	669,915	608,499

Nantucket.

Towns	1910	1905
Nantucket	2,962	2,930
	2,962	2,930

Norfolk.

Towns	1910	1905
Avon	2,013	1,901
Bellingham	1,696	1,686
Braintree	8,066	6,879
Brookline	27,792	23,436
Canton	4,797	4,702
Cohasset	2,585	2,727
Dedham	9,284	7,774
Dover	798	636
Foxboro	3,863	3,364
Franklin	5,641	5,244
Holbrook	2,816	2,509
Hyde Park	15,507	14,510
Medfield	3,466	3,314
Medway	2,696	2,650
Millis	1,399	1,252
Milton	7,924	7,054
Needham	5,026	4,284
Norfolk	960	1,089
Norwood	8,014	6,731
Plainville	1,385	1,300
*Quincy	32,642	28,076
Randolph	4,301	4,034
Sharon	2,310	2,085
Stoughton	6,316	5,959
Walpole	4,892	4,003
Wellesley	5,413	6,189
Westwood	1,266	1,136
Weymouth	12,895	11,585
Wrentham	1,743	1,428
	187,506	167,537

Plymouth.

Towns	1910	1905
Abington	5,455	5,081
Bridgewater	7,688	6,754
*Brockton	56,878	47,794
Carver	1,663	1,410
Duxbury	1,688	2,028
East Bridgewater	3,363	3,169
Halifax	550	494
Hanover	2,326	2,176
Hanson	1,854	1,490
Hingham	4,965	4,819
Hull	2,103	2,060
Kingston	2,445	2,205
Lakeville	1,141	912
Marion	1,460	1,029
Marshfield	1,738	1,763
Mattapoisett	1,233	1,180
Middleboro	8,214	6,888
Norwell	1,410	1,534
Pembroke	1,336	1,261
Plymouth	12,141	11,119
Plympton	561	514
Rochester	1,090	1,181
Rockland	6,928	6,287
Scituate	2,482	2,597
Wareham	4,102	3,660
West Bridgewater	2,231	2,006
Whitman	7,292	6,521
	144,337	127,932

Suffolk.

Towns	1910	1905
*Boston	670,585	595,380
*Chelsea	32,452	37,289
Revere	18,219	12,659
Winthrop	10,132	7,034
	731,388	652,362

Worcester.

Towns	1910	1905
Ashburnham	2,107	1,851
Athol	8,536	7,197
Auburn	2,420	2,006
Barre	2,957	2,558
Berlin	904	906
Blackstone	5,648	5,786
Bolton	764	762
Boylston	714	649
Brookfield	2,204	2,388
Charlton	2,032	2,089
Clinton	13,075	13,105
Dana	736	763
Douglas	2,152	2,120
Dudley	4,267	3,818
*Fitchburg	37,826	33,021
Gardner	14,699	12,012
Grafton	5,705	5,052
Hardwick	3,524	3,261
Harvard	1,034	1,077
Holden	2,147	2,640
Hopedale	2,188	2,048
Hubbardston	1,073	1,205
Lancaster	2,464	2,406
Leicester	3,237	3,414
Leominster	17,580	14,297
Lunenburg	1,393	1,293
Mendon	880	922
Milford	13,055	12,105
Millbury	4,740	4,631
New Braintree	464	477
Northboro	1,713	1,947
Northbridge	8,807	7,400
North Brookfield	3,075	2,617
Oakham	552	519
Oxford	3,361	2,927
Paxton	416	444
Petersham	757	855
Phillipston	426	442
Princeton	818	907
Royalston	792	903
Rutland	1,743	1,713
Shrewsbury	1,946	1,866
Southboro	1,745	1,931
Southbridge	12,592	11,000
Spencer	6,740	7,121
Sterling	1,359	1,315
Sturbridge	1,957	1,974
Sutton	3,078	3,173
Templeton	3,756	3,783
Upton	2,071	2,024
Uxbridge	4,671	3,881
Warren	4,188	4,300
Webster	11,509	10,018
Westboro	5,446	5,378
West Boylston	1,270	1,571
West Brookfield	1,327	1,384
Westminster	1,353	1,348
Winchendon	5,678	5,933
*Worcester	145,986	128,135
	399,657	362,668

NEW BEDFORD HOUSE DIRECTORY 1911

(Copyright 1911 by W A Greenough & Co)

ABBOTT

3 Edward Osbaldestom
3 Abraham Rothwell
5 Joseph Picard
5 Richard T Fellows
5 Benjamin Waterworth
5 James Brooks
7 Frederick P Jackson
7 Michael Coyne
7 Walter Giles
9 James Pilkington
10 John E Sullivan
10 Benjamin Howard
11 Dominick Mazza
11 Charles Marinelle
13 Alfred Wilkinson
13 Joseph Morris
13 William O'Hearn
14 Charles Murray
14 William Blackshaw
15 Thomas Harrison
16 George Worthington
16 John W Baron
18 John Richardson
18 Luke Park

ACORN

9 Robert Newsham
20 Peter Lord

ACUSHNET AVENUE

Thomas H Delaney
Annie Flannery
6 Mrs J Chaloner
8 John W Young
8 Robert Davis
10 Fred Rothwell
10 Michael Flannery
10 Edward Neenan
19 Frederick Langevin
19 Noe Caouette
20 William J Hart
21 Idala A Lagasse
21 Ephraim Bissonette
21 Charles Blais
21 Louis Napoleon
22 Joseph P Lacerda
22 Joseph P Joaquim
23 Mrs Odele St Jean
23 Louis Ogara
23 Wladyslaw Czechoosk
24 Manuel S Avila
26 Thomas Baldwin
26 Mrs Ruth Kettenell
27 Isadore Lagasse
28 Thomas Brown
28 William Dawber
28 John Reid
28 William S Brown
28r John Feeley
28r John E Baker
29 Louis Chariatt
29½ Henrique O Firme
29½ Arthur Mellor
29a August Punts
29a William Avery
30 Andrew Lomba
30 Mrs Margaret Quinn

Acushnet av—con
30 Manuel Silva
31 Ernest E Amaral
31 Mrs Angeline Avery
31 Joseph Medeiros
32 Joseph M Silveira
32 Arthur Champaigne
32 Charles C Munroe
32r Arsene Dion
32r Louis Beauregard
32½ Samuel Rose
34 Hermidas Fontaine
34 Mrs Ellen Sullivan
35 Mrs Verena Slater
35 Mrs Rose Barnes
35 Mrs Conradina Keck
35r Alfred Wygrzewalski
36 Alfred Makin
36 Manuel F Silva
36 Jeremiah Da Silvia
37 Joseph Demares
37 Joseph Daley
37 Louis S Garon
37 Adolph Dion
40 John B Coderre
47 William Topping
47 Antoine Levasseur
47 Frank Emond
49 Ettiene Martin
49 William F Morris
49 Gerald Jennings
49 Mrs Clara Couet
49 Joseph Marsh
57 Mrs Mary Oliveria
58 Jacintho K Braga
59 Mrs Emily Gomes
59 Manuel J Brazil
61 Mrs Elmira Turner
61 Mrs Frances T Lima
61 Manuel Roderick
61 Daniel Berube
63 George H Morton
63 Frank F Grade
63 George Nisbet
64 Antone C Lima
64 Manuel Rodericque
64 Joseph Rose
64 Frank E Bettincourt
65 Manuel A Silva
65 Robert Nisbett
65 Antone Santos
65 Henry Marcoux
66 Manuel Menes
66 John Simmons
66 William H Souza
67 Manuel S Bulcoa
67 Joseph C Bettencourt
67 Henry Bulcoa
68 Enos P Lopes
68 John Silk
69 Margaret Keene
70 Manuel B Medina
70 Leonard Junier
70 Mrs Rose Morrissey
70 Leonard Junier
71 Mrs Mary Freitas
71 Joseph Machado
72 Joseph Vincent
72 Richard Harlain
72 William Richmond
74 Manuel F Silva
74 Joseph Costa
74 Bridget Brennan
75 Mrs Mary Silva
75 Antone Marshall
75 Joseph G Souza
76 Antone Costa
76 Mrs Mary Ann Silva
79 Thomas W Hynes
83 Joseph Francis
84 Alfred J Nixon M D
84 Mrs Margaret A Waldron
87 Charles Rodericque
87 Stephen J Cassidy
88 Manuel E Sylvia
88 Casemere Santos
89 Mrs Catherine Jackson
89 John L Downey
90 Antone Silva
90 Philip Horenstein
91 Mrs Ellen Welch
91 James H Welch
92 John Gomes
92 John Sylvia
94 Antone G Falcon
94 Manuel F Rose
96 Joseph Des Ruisseau
96 Joseph F Motta
96 Manuel Cardoza
97 Frank M Paes
97r John Mello
97r Rauly Faria
100 Mrs Clifford O Peirce
102 Antone Simas
102 Joseph B Silva
103 Manuel Rogers
103 Mrs Maglina Julia
103 Manuel Silva
103 Joseph J Medeiros
104 Manuel Fraga
104 Seraphim E Lima
106 Mrs Clara Gray

106 Ross Gray
106 Michael L Sylvia
111 Allan F Wood
111 Mrs Mary A French
113 Harry Rosenthal
113 Arthur Cunha
114 Antone Pomber
116 Hans Rasmussen
116 George C Avila
118 William Stern
118 Morris Goldberg
119 Mrs Johanna McDonald
119 John J Xavier
120 Pierre Quinton
120 David Silver
122 Joseph Veira
128 Frank Paul
129 Miles Sweeney
134 Louis Sage
134 Richard A Cartwright
137 Mrs Jane Mills
138 William A Flynn
138 Mrs Bessie Levin
138 Loma Mcnelis
139 Solomon Schuster
139 Louis Schuster
140 William Randall
140 John M Rogers
141 Mrs Mary P Alexander
142 Manuel Coutu
142 Mrs Willmay R Mingo
142 Manuel Costa
143 Joaquim S Oliveira
143 John F Escobar
144 David Thompson
144 Fred C Bucklin
145 Antoine Thomas
145 Joseph Avila
146 Isaac Horvitz
146 Mary J Loring
147 Mrs Mary Prada
147 James Veira
148 William H Hicks Jr
149 John Rogers
149 Joseph M Rogers 2nd
149r Joseph S Marques
149r Stephen K Paul
150 August Wintermeyer
150 Charles Gracia
150 John Gracia
151 August Potello
152 Samuel Colinski
152 Joseph J O'Brien
153 Samuel J Sylvia
153 Frank Bento
153 Mrs Daniel McNeill
153 Daniel McNeil
153r S Ravich
154 Mrs Mabel Andrews
154 Manuel F Rose
154 Mrs Emma Clare
154 F A Frates
155 Manuel P B Silvia
156 Antone P Rose
156 Mrs Regina Dupont
156 Jose D Silveira
159 Manuel G Cruz
161 Frank Lewis
161 Manuel G Cruz
161 Manuel F Quaresma
162 Joseph Tablas
168 Frank Brown
169 Hyman Levin
169 Erick A Carlson
170 William R Schilansky
170 George A Bowman
171 Joseph D Silva
172 Mrs Ella F Rooth
173 Philip S Briggs
173 Mrs Mary E Boone
174 Byron Bradford
175 Alexander S Williams
175 Joseph S Williams
181 Frank Martin
181 Joseph M Bettencourt
182 Louis S Williams
182 Wilfred Balthazar
182 Bernard Walsh
184 Mrs Emma B Magnett
189 Arthur Guay
190 George Stevens
190 Antonio Zerbone
195 Abram P Sutton
195 John W Taylor
200 Hiram E Burding
200 James Queen
203 Franklin W Smith
205 William Boardman
205 Fred Vincent
205 Leon A Mandly
205 Manuel Smith
205r Mrs Lottie C Press
205r Jabez D Tripp
208 Charles Michelson
208 Robert M Winslow
208 Louis Greenstein
209 Simon Margolis
211 William C DeMello
211 George A Colburn
215 Misses Mitchell
215 Zenas H Phinney
218 Charles Perry
218 John Gonsalves
218 Alfred C Fernandes

Acushnet av—con
218 Julius Souza
219 Fred C Burns
219 Elizabeth Smith
219 George E Powell
219 George Brooks
223 Thomas E Davis
223 Thomas J Stevenson
224 William W Levy
224 Albert Cohen
225 Morris Gersten
225 Barney Zeitz
227 Arthur S Covill
228 Mrs Louisa A Wilbor
229 Mrs Ellen Smith
232 Thomas L Jouvette
233 James H Isherwood
234 Mrs Maria Macy
236 Jacob Fleishner
236 Mrs Georgianna Heroud
236 James C Page
237 Charles Zietz
237 Jacob Black
238 Harry Queen
238 Louis Queen
238 Peter J McGregor
239 George D Molleo
239 Mrs Mary Bisbee
242 Mrs Isabella C T Kelley
243 David O Carver
243 Ezekiel Hurwitz
244 August Gonsalves
245 Mrs Lucy P Greene
248 Frank Sylvia
249 Mrs Harriet S Howland
254 Mrs Mary M Ellis
257 Mrs Agnes M Layton
258 Timothy Crowley
259 Manuel C Sylvia
263 Abraham S Novick
263 Mrs Hannah Smith
266 Morris Meltzer
268 Mrs Annie Tilton
268 Morris Meltzer
268 Paul Pintov
269 Alderic Jussaume
271 Mrs Annie Holmes
273 Harris Weiner
275 George E Hatch
275 William J Carter
277 Charles H Crapo
279 David Main
282 Hugh H Lewis
285 Herbert L Rush
285 Mrs Eleanor H Thomas
288 Mrs Isabelle Walker
288 Fred C Waldron
289 Anthony S Francis
289 Harriet Reed
290 Henry S Peach
290 Patrick X Sullivan
291 Mrs Clara C Howland
293 James Clark
297 Capt Ernest A West
297 George S Allen
299 William B Macomber
300 Mrs Annie M Tucker
303 Mrs Emma McGarigle
303 Mrs Mary J Lowe
304 William T Meagher
304 James F Monaghan
305 James A Randall
311 George L Eccleston
312 Mrs Mattie Helme
313 William W Vokes
313 William M McAFee
314 Mrs Josephine Wells
316 Louis Cardonell
319 Mrs Fred S Barrows
321 Alfred A Davis
325 Joaquim Santos
328 Charles D Finni
343 Joseph E Gauthier
389 Mrs Jennie Morrow
390 William A Henning
392 Andrew C Hurley
425 John B Ginnochio
427 Mrs Nellie F Winchester
433 James Eddus
433 Louis Kruger
437 Mrs Elizabeth Bartel
437 Josephine Jordan
437 George Hill
448 George F Thompson
450 Andrew J Ashley
450 Albert S Morse Jr
460 Mary E Coggeshall
467 Frank J Morris
467 L Henry Gibbs
469 Mrs Ellen Francis
469 Edward H Taber
477 Alice B Wentworth
480 Benjamin G Sylvaria
480 Fred R Symons
482 Mrs Nellie Bennett
482 Mrs Mary Killigrew
483 Alphonso L Marsh
483 Charles Shkolnick
483 Samuel Lipman
487 Max Fox
487 Mrs Mary Neville
487 Mrs Nora Griffin
488 Mrs Cora Brouseau
489 Charles P Johnson

490 James S Goulding
490 Peter Linnehan
494 Mrs Mary Perry
494 Mrs Kate Herstoff
496 Alfred G Howland
496 Henry M Mason
497 Walter A Rogers
500 Mrs Hannah Howard
501 Angelo D Onofrio
501 William E Stevens
503 Joseph D'Ardı
504 Benjamın Korobkin
504 Guiseppi Chinello
506 Mrs Cynthia B Wilcox
506 Leonard Canny
506 Albert J Davidian
510 John Lemos
510 Phuribus J Silva
511 William W Braman
511 William J Borden
512 John F Grıffin
512 Wılliam H Rogers
512 Annie Gıldard
513 Mrs Susan M Drew
516 Sabar Diberg
518 Peter Moses
519 George H Lewis
519 Napoleon Duchaineau
520 Yafath Lahood
523 Edward T Jones
523 Manuel Francis
527 Mrs Sarah Atherly
527 Harry Wolıson
531 Mate S Kranzler
533r Mrs Kate Rıpley
533r John J Dowd
535 Mrs Margaret Bessey
535 Damien Desmarais
535 Mrs P M Rudolph
541 Henry Smith
543 Joseph E Jock
543 Alphonse Foisy
543 Joseph Veira
543 Joseph Therrien
545 Mrs M A J Handy
545 John Grace
545 Mrs J Labarre
545 Mrs Lydia A Hart
555 Fares Yazbek
559 Joseph Saba
559 Isaac Gomes
561 Mrs Eliza Hurd
561 Clarence Tobin
561 Daniel D Harrington
563 Secon Correia
563 Mrs Julıa Connell
567 Michael Cory
567 Thomas McGlynn
567 Charles B Ellis
567 Mrs Annie Ostrofsky
567 Max Silver
567r John Varcellone
569 Antonio Devito
569 Timothy Quıll
575 Thomas O'Malley
577 Mrs Minnıe Thomas
577 Ellis Hassey
585 John J Hayward
585 John Mahoney
601 Andrew C Elliot
601 Jeremiah Sullıvan Jr
609 Napoleon Gauthier
609r Manuel B deMedeiros
609r Jean Baptıste
609r Manuel B Medeiros
615 William H Francis
619 Isadore Therrien
623 Arthur Barriteau
623 Edward Forgue
623 Joseph L Barriteau
623 Joseph Therrıen
628 Egildo Ezzemonte
632 Joseph Gauthier
636 Mrs M Mıskelly
638 Louis Rıendeau
648 John Cairns
648r Alexander Fınger
656 Masson David
658 Frank Silva
658 Michael J Jordan
658 Wılliam McGrath
672 Dominick Paste
672 Emilıano Balegno
674 Mrs Sarah Fisher
676 Spadessa Giovanni
676 Frank Angelo
676 Seconde Carrera
682 John Rogers
686 Adolph Gallo
688 Emilo Real
688 Gallot Adolphe
692 John Andreoli
694 Giovanni Vercellone
696 Antonio Malione
696 Mrs Anna Flemming
696 Giovanni Castellina
702 Margaret F Devine
702 James H Kelley
706 Joseph M Enos
708 John Dubera
708 John Mariano
712 Cıgnottı Alexandro
712 Ernest Polverare
712 Fortunato Battistelli
714 David Horovitz
714 Mrs Rose Hyde
716 Frank Capra
716 Dominıck Antonette

Acushnet av—con
829 Francois Lajeunesse
829 Ernest Duval
831 Celio Tremblay
831 George Demars
833 Joseph Dallaire
833 Samuel Nolet
835 Frank Letourneau
835 Charles Dupuis
837 Luger Jabot
837 William Dutton
839 Napoleon Brodeur
839 Mitchell Beaupre
843 Isadore Christophe
845 John Jabot
845 Eugene Aubin
847 Moise Duchainaux
847 Albert Finch
851 Mrs Annie Farrady
862 Josephine D Weston
862 Joseph Chausse
862 Mrs Agnes Mestan
864 Alex Lebeau
868 Joseph Nerbonne
868 Andreas Yaryapka
872 Mrs Agnes Girard
872 Justine Fortin
872 Margaret Holden
872 John Girard
874 Delphis Guillette
874 Leon Fortier
908 Zelis Novinsky
908 Peter Rivet
908 Michael Ryan
920 Zerick Mornsky
922 Arthur Bessette
922 Fred Berout
931 Mrs Ida Dalphon
931 Peter Pusere
931 Dixon Redfearn
935 Patrick O'Leary
938 Dr John V Thuot
964 Harvey J Senec
964 Albert Marsden
964 John Fox
970 Albert Perrenod
973 Frank R Pease
1005 John T O'Connor
1008 Mrs Bozena Hartman
1008 Napoleon Du Pont
1016 Louis Gariepy
1016 John B Soucy
1022 Joseph Wimet
1022 Pheliming Therrien
1028 Francois Bonneau
1030 Abraham Weisberg
1030r Joseph C Nadeau
1030r Frank Chaddonis
1031 Mrs Susie M Naylor
1036 Mrs Mary A Madden
1036 William Cordonier
1036 David Specter
1039 Adelard L Gonneville
1042 Irall Tremblay
1042 Theodorus Katsarakis
1042 Mrs Mary Webber
1042 Leopold D Roy
1060 Ernest Gauvin
1060 Prudent LeBeau
1060 William F Blower
1060 H Ferdinand Caron
1060 Ernest Gauvin
1060 Joseph Lamothe
1060 Ernest Gauvin
1060 Desire Brochu
1082 Herbert Hammond
1082 John S Pye
1089 Peter Barbour
1090 Napoleon Bessette
1090 Samuel A Smith
1092 Elias Shenhoun
1098 Mrs Mary Dalton
1098 John F Murray
1098 William Quirk
1103 Hermann Eglin
1105 Lawrence Posch
1105 Charles F Linney
1105 Dr William K Turner
1108 Henry Forand
1108 Dr Melvin E DeLavel
1117 Mrs Delima Ouimette
1117 Magloire Dion
1117 Henry Richer
1122 John Reid
1122 Benjamin Hall
1132 John Parkinson
1132 Sigmund Finger
1132 Xavier Haggle
1133 Henry J Patnaude
1137 John Carter
1137 Mrs Almira Picard
1139 Mrs Bessie Sederholm
1139 Mrs Adeline Tremblay
1140 James Bradshaw
1140 Peter Caperonis
1140 James Bradshaw
1140 Mrs Priscilla Spencer
1142 Hector LeCuyer
1142 Joseph Gaudreau
1142 Mrs Sophia Magnant
1149 Abram Mendelson
1149 Adjutor Fortin
1160 Eugene H Vien
1176 Hubert Leblanc

1176 Alphonse Racette
1176 Arcade Prarie
1205 Dr Julien E Fortin
1205 Arthur A Audette
1205 Mrs Paul H Maynard
1205 Honore Roberge
1205 Mrs Favila Dulong
1220 Adolor Levesque
1220 Joseph Carrier
1220 Mrs Mary Chatelle
1221 Mrs Adelie Dionne
1221 Octave Couture
1221 Toussaint Fortin
1225 Joseph Gamache
1225 Dieudonne Paquin
1225 Mrs Helen Perrin
1230 Charles Pittle
1230 Augustus Pittl
1230 Antoine Lemaire
1230 Andrew W Johnson
1238 Augusto J Taveira
1264 Mary Kalish
1264 James Ellis
1264 Robert Gore
1264 James H Gore
1264 Isaac Margolis
1265 Henry Therrien
1265 Dr Frank Birdwhistle
1265 John Craig
1268 Samuel Greenwood
1279 Mrs Delphine Buteau
1279 Henry Fournier
1279 Joseph E Brochu
1280 Henry Coulombe
1280 Mrs Sarah Howard
1280 Hubert Brodeur
1280 Paul Forcier
1283 Thomas Williamson
1283 Dr J Conrad Ross
1283 J Thomas Taylor
1283 Edmund A Delano
1283 Mrs Plesents Walker
1293 Mrs Margaret DeLuc
1293 Wesley Burton
1296 Mrs Ellen Dupont
1296 Joseph Langevin
1296 James Sharples
1305 Thomas Davis
1305 Jean B Jean
1306 Dr J Ubalde Paquin
1325 Frederick L Hayes
1326 Fischer Wolfson
1356 Albini S Martel
1356 Alphonse Despres
1356 Emil J Arcand
1356 Joseph C Bourassa
1359 Rev Hormidas Deslauriers
1359 Rev Lucien C Bedard
1359 Rev Charles Clerk
1359 Rev Astisde Magnan
1359 Rev Albert Ahamel
1378 John Cunniff
1382 William Blanchette
1405 Joseph A Gauthier
1405 Ami Renee
1406 Arthur Isabell
1406 Hypolite Choquette
1407 Andrew Gravalides
1415 Thomas Lemieux
1415 Emilie Roy
1416 Mrs Julia Mahoney
1416 John C Dunkerly
1416 Dr Henry Barnes
1430 Ernest A Dunham
1430 Edward L Burdick
1458 Albert S Lamb
1458 George Taylor
1458 John R Pilling
1458 Mrs Annie Tripp
1462 Wallace Reed
1462 Howard Kingsley
1484 Charles W McGonigle
1462 Arthur L Jean
1492 Charles Emil
1498 Dr Dennis J Lowney
1498 Louis Rousseau
1498 Robert Swallow
1498 William Williamson
1505 Mrs Emma Smith
1521 Ernestine M Deslauriers
1521 John Chartier
1524 Joseph Cohen
1527 Arthur Vigneault
1527r Jean B Chartier
1530 Edward J Gildea
1537 Joseph Breby
1537 Charles Nield
1547 Ashworth Cropper
1547 Onat Chausse
1547 William Holt Jr
1547 Oza Bernard
1547 Thomas Gregory
1547 Fred O Payette
1565 Henry Boule
1565 Cyprien A A Collet
1579 Dr George Marsden
1581 George Boardman
1585 Edward Coupe
1587 Samuel L Dean
1588 John B Whitehead
1588 Willard C Hitchcock
1603 Dr Daniel J Sweeney
1602½ George Entwistle
1602½ Mrs Rose A Patnaude
1602½ Wilfred Frennette
1603 Michael D Sweeney
1606 Hannah Fallas
1616 Maxime A Yell

Acushnet av—con
1616 Thomas Sadler
1618 Mrs Hannah Eccles
1618 Albert Crossley
1620 Mrs Kate Loughlin
1627 Burt Nuttall
1627 George E Entwistle
1627 Mrs Hannah Slater
1627 Thomas H Ridings
1631 John J Purcell
1631 Jarvis Counsell
1637 John T Rawstron
1631 Simeon Southworth
1637 Samuel Taylor
1637 Mrs Mary H Wood
1642 Andrew Henshaw
1642 Samuel Summer
1642 Calixte Babineau
1643 George Rushworth
1643 John H Mackay
1643 Mrs Mary A Gurl
1650 John Bradbury
1650 Joseph F Mullins
1650 John B Frennette
1653 John T Marsden
1655 Gilbert Audette
1655 Mrs Albena Frappied
1668 Richard Smith
1668 William Smith
1671 Hillaire Therrien
1671 Henry Spirlet
1671 George Fraser
1671 Joseph B Boucher
1671 Ernest J Pernelet
1672 August Bachman
1679 Albert H Sawyer Jr
1679 Narcisse Adams
1680 Thomas F Healy
1683 Joseph Christie
1683 Thomas Knott
1690 Leon Branchaud
1715 Frank B Robbins
1715 Mrs Clara J Nash
1727 Augustin Berube
1729 August Seguin
1729 Ambrose Dabignon
1733 Eustache Isabel
1733 Napoleon Derosiers
1737 Edwin Franklin
1737 Daniel H Harrington
1757 Napoleon Codaire
1757 Robert H Kenyon
1757 Noe Bessette
1757 William A Payette
1760 William Wilkinson
1765 Matthew Heys
1767 Alfred Holmes
1767 John E Fothergill
1781 Arthur Barre
1786 Richard H Thorpe
1789 Mrs Beattie H Ashley
1791 Joseph V Turgeon
1799 Henry P Jenney
1808 Charles A Hafford
1811 Mrs Eunice Jenney
1812 Edward Boucher
1814 Alphonse J Query
1848 Frank O Covill
1848 Mrs Jane Marshall
1848 Joseph Therien
1871 Mrs Mary Demers
1871 Joseph V Demers
1890 Marie J Gaudreau
1893 Ruben S Cormier
1901 Joseph Poitras
1901 Ambroise Poitras
1917 Joseph Palme
1918 Stanislaus Desautels
1938 Joseph P Hanson
1946 Mrs Sarah Jane Holden
1946 John H Counsell
1974 Cleophas Guertin
1982 William C Sherman
1982 Benjamin J Hindley
2030 Joseph Langlois
2047 Robert R Sherman
2056 Louis Baillargeon
2057 William S Mosher
2061 William A Young
2062 Emile Vincent
2082 Weston J Borden
2095 Charles S Baylies
2103 George Wright
2112 John E Horsfield
2115 Leroy A Sturgis
2135 Rev Henry E Oxnard
2138 Timothy McCrohan
2143 Mrs Mary Hawes
2143 Frank E Sisson
2155 Hector C Topin
2157 Henry G Young
2163 C W Turner
2193 Dr J Frank Weeks
2228 George J Parker
2237 Joseph Poirier
2242 Willard B Bennett
2311 Adelard J Sorel
2331 James F Reynolds
2339 Charles E Cathcart
2339 Harry C Hawes
2344 Mrs Adelaide Wilbur
2355 George W Hawes
2367 Andrew H Bassett
2381 Frederick B Hawes
2389 Sylvester A Dean

2393 John B Wilbur
2405 Charles B Crocker
2405 J C Morse
2416 Albert A Dunbar
2421 George E Washburn
2430 James D Oman
2443 Francis P Washburn
2444 Walter H Darling
2453 Mrs Phedora F Gifford
2469 Pierre C Harnois
2471 Thomas Gamache
2471 Andre Soucy
2476 Alfred K Howard
2481 Everett C Morse
0 Napoleon Therrien
2521 Allen G Briggs
2522 N Therien
2529 Harry Ratcliffe
2559 John A Russell
2588 Herbert W Lawrence
2588 Charles A Haskins
2603 H Langlois
2619r M P Santana
2745 Sydney B DeMoranville
2753 Frederick DeMoranville
2782 Amerase Chamberlain
2784 Anthony Papa
2784 off Gregoire Lebel
2795 E Cote
2825 David W Sherman Jr
2834 David Fraser
2891 Emery Goddard
2904 Everett L Howard
2914 William J Gibbs
2924 Mrs Lucy A Spooner
2924 Roswell Spooner
2925 Frederick W Bowles
2941 John N Hammond
2949 Charles H Place
2949 Mrs Hannah E Spooner
2981 Charles F Spooner Jr
3136 Mrs Ella F DeMoranville
3136r Reuben B Peckham
3136r Abraham Brooks
3167 James L Spooner
3195 Lewis G Spooner
3217 Richard A Westgate
3217 Elmer Pittsley
3233 Alonzo W Spooner
3249 Daniel A Spooner
3253 Mrs Ruby A Hammond
3277 Mrs Mary L Soule
3277 Edward Reynolds
3278 John Augustus Spooner
3304 Albert F Spooner
3322 Alsedar Bonneau
3374 Lambert Adams
3501 Harry O White
3506 Alfred Marsden
3526 Augustus T White
3531 Henry C Lawrence
3572 John W Leonard
3591 Mary I Ashley
3687 Paul Kuchler
3691 John Mastera
3697 Frank Mastera
3699 George Hageloh
3837 James Davis
3842 George W Lawrence
3863 Dominique Boudreau
3883 Mrs Nancy Gibson
3893 Louis Rousseau
3906 Leonard J Hathaway Jr
3906 Mrs Ella F Sisson
3925 Herbert N Westgate
3932 Clara Westgate
3932 Clarence E Westgate
3982 Charles A Chase
3982 James H Chase
4026 Franklin J Gurney
4035 F J Braley
4102 Millard C Ashley
4125 Henry A McAvoy
4215 Edward F Lewis
4228 Henry Hetu
4228 Seraphin Praeda
4299 Frank P Morton
4409 Edward A Hoxie
4449 Christian J Hess

ADAMS

11 Thomas F Quinnan
11 David Deneault
11 James O Callaghan
13 Arthur Huntington
15 Walter Mansley
15 Oscar Lemieux
17 Adelard Desrosier
20 Adore Beaudry
24 Edmond P St Onge
24 Joseph A Desaulniers
24 Joseph Plante
25 Adelard Bourgeois
25 Michael I Wishnetzky
25 Jake Soforenco
26 Henry F Michelson
26 Herbert Winn
28 Dieudunne Harbeck
30 Michael Tracy
40 David Pendleton
41 John G Plante
43 Harry Johnson
44 Felix Lestage
45 Nelson J Stone
63 Thomas G Ould

Adams—con
63 Mrs Matilda Dahl
63 Francis J Gurl

ALEC

0 Mrs Mary E Lewis
0 Thomas Lanagan

ALLEN

30 Antonio Hurd
37 Louis A Hazard
37 Mary E Schwall
44 Robert E Allen
44 Lester D Patt
44 Eliza Tripp
54 Charles A Oman
57 Dr Joao Carlos da Silva Pitta
58 Delbert W Westgate
67 Mrs Susan S Ricketson
81 Mrs Betsey Jennings
80 James B Watkins
84 Jeremiah F Mahoney
88 William R Hoxie
90 John Cunha
93 Joseph G Davoll
94 Mrs Emma J Gifford
94 John A Gifford
105 Fred Padleford
113 Terrence Grant
124 John A McManus
129 William A Twiss
141 A Frank Clark
148 Henry E Chase
149 Charles R Cornell
152 Mrs Mary J Dias
158 Frank G Allen
158 Thomas Fogarty
159 John C DeMello Jr
162 Charles F Chase
167 Walter S Macaulay
168 Edward E Clarke
168 Edmund Foley
173 Thomas J Noonan
173 Anthony H Senna
176 Patrick H Ennis
176 Joseph Ellis
177 Joseph Simas
177 Mrs Mary C Perry
177 Nils P Hansen
180 Mrs Caroline F King
180 N B Reford & Relief Asso
183 Samuel T Rex
191 Mrs Nellie V Felicianno
193 Manuel E Simmons
198 Charles T Hazard
199 Frank A Manha
199 Joseph M deSouza
202 J Franklyn Bertram
206 George E Pedro
207 Mrs Josephine J Dias
208 Mrs Luella A Chase
209 Mrs Mary Silveira
209 Antonio G Silva
210 Archie R Miller
219 Augustus Almeida
219 Manuel J Braga
222 Mrs Lauriana A Sabina
224 Edward C L Goddune
230 William Almond Jr
230 Carl Carlson
230 Robert Cairns
231 Joseph V Pierce
231 James Akin
234 Mrs Frances C Jenney
234 James A Brown
249 John P Sylvia
255 John Benevidez
262 Frank Enos
262 Patrick Powers
267 John Felecianno
270 Edward P Doherty
274 James Flood
278 Mrs Mary Ennis
280 Mrs Mary W Joseph
281 Leon C Deane
283 Arthur W Child
285 A J Potvin
287 Joseph T Timperly
291 LeRoy W Wilber
292 Antonio J Mandly
293 Thomas A Scales
293 Mrs Bessie Scales
297 Mrs Mary A Savage
300 Mrs Ellen F Sylvia
300 Edward H Jennings
300 John W Jennings
305 Frank E Jason
314 Jesse Law
318 Charles F M Bly
318 George D Hayden
340 Joseph Vera
340 Joseph F Morris
340 Roland C Douglass
350 John Roderique
350 Charles F Potter
354 John Anderson
368 Antone Marshall
368 Antone M Lemos
368 John J Sullivan
378 William H Mudge
388 David R Kipp
394 Adam Sutcliffe
394 Bruce Cary
394 Leander Reed
398 George E Showell
398 Frank Cambra
406 George Coleman

407 Joseph Triguerio
407 Antonio F Rose
410 August Nordmark
411 Manuel Rogers
411 Thomas Silva
411 Joseph Teixeira
417 Robert McMahon
421 Frank Mederios
432 John M Frates
436 William A Lindsay
439 Hugh B Neagus
446 Henry Webber
446 Manuel Costa
446 Jose R deMello
446 Mrs Anna Ballman
459 Gilbert M Jennings Jr
459 Frederick C Lovatt
463 Alfred Beardsworth
464 William H Curtis
467 Thomas Thorley
472 Manuel Camara
473 William A E Howland
484 Samuel Astley
485 Manuel F Trigueiro
487 Frank P Silveira
560 Mrs Philomena Camasho
571 Antonio Reis
581 William S Wordell
586 Mrs Anna Rose
586 Frank Thomas
586 Joseph Thomas
597 Peter Marshall
606 Charles N Riley
709 Frederick A Palmer
723 Antonio Gonsalves
729 Charles R Smith
729r Winchester R Smith

ANTHONY

1 Charles B Thompson
1 Mrs Alice Potter
5 Mrs Edward S Taber
7 George R Stetson
8 Caroline S Silva
9 Mrs Jane W Nye
10 Anna Ricketson
10 Walton Ricketson
15 Benjamin H Anthony

ARCH

2 Charles E Brownell
3 John Y Fuller
4 William T Read
5 Edward V Hazzard
5 J Arthur Feather
9 Mrs Harriet L Tanner
9 Myron D Waller
13 Clifford E Hunt
16 Walter H Underdown
17 Mrs Emma G Staples
20 Henry Howard Jr
21 Henry B James
22 William H Hand Jr
24 William S Davenport
25 Robert Weimert
29 William E Smith
33 Emma M Whitney
37 John W Potter
39 Alice C Munsey
41 Daniel S O'Brien
43 Benjamin F Jenny
43 John H Harding

ARMOUR

14 Edgar S Clark
146 John R Silvia
147 Joseph E Winterbottom
149 Robert Leuchsenring

ARNOLD

28 Charles A Bowen
35 Francis H Stone
52 George H Booth
57 Webster A Arey
58 Seth J Bessette
64 John T Hanna Jr
64 Zebina B Davis
68 Mrs Phoebe E Betram
71 Franklin E James
98 Jesse T Sherman
102 Edward G Caster
106 Mrs Lizzie P Tessier
106 George P Brock
112 Sarah E Chase
112 Mrs Mary J Bolles
112 Mary W Leymunion
118 Emeline G Rice
126 Manuel E Pereira
126 Otto W Newman
130 Misses Bliss
133 Percy C James
134 William Bliss
135 Thomas J Wilson
142 Harmon S Colbeth
142 Mary C Spicer
142 Nathan Hooper
147 John G Purington
148 Howard U Smith
148 Archie L I Chase
148 Philbert O Rainville
153 John Hynes
154 Charles M Davenport
158 Henry W Tripp
159 Allen T Kendrick
162 Charles P Sawyer
162 Elmer E Harlow

Arnold—con
163 William R Binkley
168 Thomas Hall
172 James E Reed
173 Mrs Eliza Stephenson
173 Mrs Frances Tripp
177 John E Wilson
177 Peter Priaulx
178 Charles M Carroll
178½ William F Gibbons
179 Charles H Reed
182 George E Howard
182 Mrs Ida Hume
185 Mrs Isabel Burke
185 John Burke
186 Clarence E Holmes
186 Alfred Coderre
186 Harvey J Borden
190 Andrew Chase
191 Mrs Barbara J Mendoza
191 Mrs Maria G Valladoa
191 Dennis Driscoll
192 Andrew M Chartier
192 J Herbert Wilcox
193 Robert Egan
193 Telesphore V Montminy
194 Christian H Heisel
194 Charles E Jones
195 Walter A Luce
198 William L Flynn
199 Arthur E Duffy
204 Benjamin H Swift
204 Alfred J Johnson
215 Robert O Burns
216 Frank W Mosher
219 Mrs Mary Johnson
219 Frederick J Carew
224 Frank X Jalbert
224 William E Tripp
226 Holder D Crapo
227 Edward A Kirby
228 Mrs Sara J Allen
228 William McKay
228 Mrs Susan H Lord
232 Mrs Emily Martin
233 George H Bliss
239 Misses Thomas
239 Mrs Eliza A Maker
243 Charles E Beckman
244 Andrew Rounds
244 William H Reed
248 Mrs Eleanor Cornell
248 Frank M Ricketson
249 Louis J Hutchinson
253 Frederic B Cook
254 Samuel Whittaker
255 Aruna B Crowell
259 Albert R Hill
259 John J Hill
268 Charles F Phillips
268 Benjamin W Johnson
269 Walter B Woodbridge
273 Frank W Deane
279 Edwin B Jourdain
280 Patrick F Wood
287 Mrs Catherine Gray
301 John J Murphy
305 Thomas Kennedy
306 Frank H Shumway
311 Ralph Hamilton
314 John S Bibber
318 Fred W Luscomb
321 Joseph S Maciel
322 Mrs Frances R Cushman
333 Dennis Haworth

ARNOLD PLACE

15 Frederick H Damon
16 Charles R Price
17 George N Alden
22 Wilson I Wordell
23 George H Nye
26 Edmund W Bourne
27 William Frank Potter
29 Charles E E Mosher

ASH (NORTH)

1 Walter H B Remington
3 Edward H Forbes
5 Luigi Morelli
21 William F Purrington
22 Armand D Valois
22 James B Kershaw
24 Mary McDonald
24 Samuel Bottomley
36 Mitchell W Lowther
38 John H Burke
42 Kathleen Woolley
42 Mrs Louis Simister
42 Arthur W Taber
42 Michael Manning
44 Manuel F Thomas
49 John White
49 Mrs Margaret Timon
50 Clarence E Jones
52 Victor W Smith
52 Mrs Gladys Smith
53 Mrs Eliza Harwood
54 Alfred Nerbonne
57 Samuel E Rogers
57 Mrs Lydia Potts
57 Mrs Alice A Miles
63 Thomas F Reardon
63 Caesar Sanders
67 Isaiah King
67 Charles H Drayton
70 John W Carey
70 Mrs Rebecca L Whiteside

71 Mrs Matilda Wiggins
71 James P Winborne
72 Mrs Caledonia Thorne
72 William L Kydd
75 Vincenzo Germano
75 Mrs Mary Betteridge
78 Mrs Florence A Brown
79 Antone Frates
80 Mrs Annie Winborne
81 Mary A Rourke
81 Joseph Wessiack
84 Mrs Charlotte Winborne
102 Thomas Buckley
102 Manuel A Grace
103 George A Brownell
104 James Stirrett
104 Latham T Jennings
106 Edward E Russell
106 V A Hammett
110 Mrs Frances M Frederick
111 John Holland
121 Manuel F Furtado
125 George E Gifford
126 Robert S Magee
128 John J Nichols
162 Thomas O Baker
162 Samuel J Donaghy

ASH (SOUTH)

6 Frederick W Martin
7 Mrs Ophelia Taber
7 Mrs Annie E Sherman
8 George B Hathaway
11 Harry E Borden
12 Benjamin F Besse
12 Daniel F Sullivan
15 John W Durant
15 Lawrence J Murphy
15 James G Cameron
16 Samuel R Clark
16 Lemuel F Besse
17 John Miguel
17 John A Squires
20 Walter T Almy
21 Frederick S Robinson
23 Edward T Smith
23 Mrs Florence L Doran
23 Joseph L Enos
30 James T Head
31 Frederick D Nudd
32 Benjamin F Williams Jr
34 Orville V Swift
35 Stephen Lowe
36 Ella F Ryder
38 Joseph Enos
38 Michael O'Malley
39 Catherine Duffy
40 William J Smith
40 W Henry Wright

43 Sarah Swain
44 Edward H Cronin
44 Mrs Hanora McKiernan
46 John J Whalen
48 William T McAfee
50 Mrs Fred H Winship
56 Ellis D Hammond
56 Isaac L Ashley Jr
56 Sereno G Mitchell
57 Mrs Mary Groves
57 Mrs Mary Kenney
63 Margaret C Lowe
64 Samuel Shaw
68 Elmer Shaw
69 William O Nelson
71 Mrs Caroline E Ashley
71 Warren Alexander Tripp
75 Mrs Mary Hicks
83 Dr Milton H Leonard
83 William E Hatch
84 Edmund Taber
104 Edwin L Barney Jr
105 Edmund Wood
108 Dr Charles D Prescott
0 Thomas M Stetson

ASHLAND

1 Mrs Eunice Braley
1 Cyrill S Larrivee
1 John Lavoie
20 Daniel C Fortin
26 James J Phelan
27 Rev Simon P Lonergan
27 Rev Charles B Gadboury
28 John S Coy
28 Mrs Ellen Lewis
32 John H Watson
32 Chester D Strong
35 Joseph A Dion
35 Dennis Leary
46 Rev Thomas M Bateman
47 Alfred Vaillancourt
53 Charles E Cook
54 George A Kirby
62 Gustave Hurel
62 Jesse Whitaker
65 Thomas J Gifford
77 Jesse A Knight
78 Conrad C Dessier
80 John Woodland
86 Mrs Isabella F Tripp
86 Chester L Tripp
87 Samuel T Lee
87 Josephine Yaeger
87 Nicholas H Fitzimmons
90 Mrs Olive C Taber
90 Hudson Winslow
95 John E Trigueiro
95 Mrs Elizabeth Maley

Ashland—con
96 Andrew J Nichols
96 Wilfred Barriteau
101 George McLean
101 Peter McNulty
103 William Craig
103 Edward J Rourke
104 James C Bates
106 James W Bates
108 Mrs Catherine Evers
126 Edward C Macomber
126 George F Gray Jr
130 James T Francis
130 Henry Davis
133 Albert Fort
133 Jaames McAlpine
133 John McAlpine
134 Kenneth Campbell
134 John E Doyle
137 Fred Jackson
137 Robert W Moore
145 Mrs Elizabeth Hargraves
145 Mrs Isabelle Birch
148 Magloire Dansereau
154 Harry A Chase
154 James Lee
154 Henry Watson
155 Harmidas P Dion
155 Mrs Adel Daley
159 Alcide J Tremblay
159 Albert Hardy
160 Mrs Mary Wilding
160 Joseph St Jacques
160 Theodore Frechette
160 Mrs Sarah A McDaniel
163 John B Archambeault
165 John L Sullivan
167 Rev Elias C Miller
169 William A Sargent
170 Frederick W Docker
170 Thomas Addy
170 Thomas Redfern
172 James F Megan
172 Benjamin A Bradshaw
172 Daniel T Rooney
174 Thomas Linden
174 John J Foran
174 Napoleon J Berard
177 Mrs Nancy Etchells
179 Joseph Dumoulin
179 Jonathan Jones
183 George C Geddis
183 John Hindle
184 John H Murphy
184 George H Murray
184 David Connolly

ASHLAND PLACE

13 Alois Yeager
13 Patrick H Dupuis
14 Charles H Tripp
15 John Ramsden
21 Herbert Ward
21 Mrs Elizabeth Fender
23 Henry C Churchill
25 Frederick A Stowell
26 Roland E Isherwood
26 Andrew A Lafferty
27 William W Hamilton
30 Mrs Emma Wilmot
30 Francis J Riley

ASHLAND TERRACE

5 Joseph G Sayles
5 Thomas W Norris
7 Mrs Mary Lessard
7 Thomas T Laycock

ASHLEY

7 Mrs Jane A Chapman
7 James Aspden
7 James W Woolam
10 Mrs Jane McCue
11 David Alexander
11 Stanislaus Gladu
11 Arthur C Colles
12 Richard Hilton
12 Thomas Nicholson
12 James Shaw
13 James Nisbet
14 Robert Wood
14 Mrs Ellen King
14 William Marginson
15 Asa Caldecott
15 Thomas Rankin
15 Joseph Shorrock
16 James E Metcalf
16 John Wilcox
16 Mrs Rossanna A Cowell
16 Mrs Nancy Gilbert
17 James La Rochelle
17 Harry H Orr
18 Joseph Lanous
18 John Ashburn
18 Mrs Marion Ridyard
19 William Trought
19 Mrs Margaret Cole
19 Mrs Elizabeth Barlow
19 John Stewart
20 Mrs Rose Dubois
20 Octave Blier
20 Alfred Bury
21 John C Gregory

21 Richard Cottam
21 Richard Crook
21 Thomas Walkden
21 Misses Whitehead
22 Rudolph Bienvenue
22 Raymond Methia
23 George H Gendron
23 James Coleman
24 Joseph Berard
24 Mrs Sarah J Hill
24 Arthur Lanous
24 Joseph Polardy
24 John Robinson
25 Ambrose Lapointe
26 Joseph Blier
26 Joseph Piche
26 Frederick Vient
27 Joseph Leclair
27 John LaCroix
27 Arthur Gauthier
27 Philip Marin
27 Napoleon Boucher
28 John B Roberts
28 Mrs Olivine Robert
28 Mrs Joseph P Dansereau
28 Joseph Tschaen
29 Joseph Thibeault
29 Bruno Lizotte
29 Edward Reinieche
29 Louis Richard
29 John G Deane
30 Eugene Potvin
30 Ferdinand Legault
30 George Dubois
31 Simeon Grenier
31 Antoine Desautels
31 Herbert Worthington
31 Albert Lavigne
32 Ernest F Ilsley
32 Charles P Moss
32 Howard Smith
37 Edward Meyer
37 John Sharples
37 Ferdinand Goudreau
37 Louis Charette
38 Joseph Hardman
38 George Rostron
38 Walter W Greaves
38 Edward LeBel
39 Edward Roberts
39 Francois X Girard
41 Mrs Josephine A Turner
41 Levi Lachapelle
42 Ozias Riendeau
43 Bruno LeBeau
43 John Livesey
45 Charles Holmes
45 Charles Paquette
46 John A Neal
46 Thomas Melia
46 George M Burdick
46 Paul Cormier
46 Thomas Singleton
46 Charles Segeur
47 Henry Remi
47 Leon Gachet
50 Adline Normandin
50 George LaFrance
50 Louis LaFleur
50 Henri Charette
51 Antoine Busquet
51 Wilfred Ste Marie
52 Denise Richard
52 Alphe Lamontagne
52 Joseph Berger
52 John Heaton
53 Mrs Pauline Gagnon
53 Joseph Pitre
53 Walter Birdsall
53 Peter Joseph
56 James Wilkinson
56 Austin C Pierce
56 George Sykes
56 Ellis Wilkinson
56 Ernest Blanchard
56 Joseph LaVoie
57 Antonio Bousquet

ATLANTIC

10 Peter F Heaver
10 Philip H Cook
12 Albert Herstoff
12 Paul Finnerty
12 John J Roche
16 Mrs Lucy J Pitman
16 Allison O Tripp
17 John A Johnson Jr
17 Andrew N Tripp
17 Edward Burkle
19 Mrs Theresa B Maciel
19 Alexander Ferguson
22 Mrs Ella Stephenson
22 William Pender
29 John Brown
32 Morris C Chace
32 Benjamin F Spicer
33 Patrick J McCullough
33 Richard F Morrison
36 Mrs Margaret Riley
36 James H McMullen
37 Jason D Russell
41 George H Cushing
42 Andrew Gunning
46 Ansel A B Norton
46 Mrs Annie S Riley
46 Albert S Ramsden
47 Frederick C Fish
47 William J Riley
67 Holder Slocum

Atlantic—con
67 William D Dean
71 Christian C Banks
72 Martin Hoye
72 Herbert L Soule
72 Annie L Hoye
75 Daniel Shea
75 J Lewis Kniffen
75½ Edward J Larkin
76 Herbert A Manchester
76 Charles L Willis
78 Mrs Katherine M Davis
78 Percy C Copeland
82 Marcus M Ryder
82 Mrs Isabella H Moore
83 Jonathan W Reed
83 Mrs Hannah Linden
83 Jennie Johnson
87 Mrs Katherine Degnan
91 Samuel W Doran
93 Theophilus A Benson
96 Misses Baker

AUSTIN

0 Nathan Lagard
3 William Beardsworth
6 Aaron Grimshaw
9 Mrs Elizabeth Breakell
12 John McGrath
13 William J Hoyle
17 John Kennedy
19 Mrs Jane Galligan
19 John W Finley
23 Joseph Poitras
27 Charles Newman
31 John Slater
35 James Whittaker
39 Alfred M Gravel
39 Isaie Magnant
41 Frank Herzog
45 Andre Grenon
49 Philibert Cloutier
51 James H Mannion
55 Dolphis Audette
55 Augustine Bourbeau
59 Edward England
63 Mrs Amanda Fonteneau
67 Xavier F Vanasse
69 William Bourbeau
81 Joseph LaFrance
85 Frederick Reed
85 Hormidas LaFrance
85r Adelard Labarge
85r Albert Crochetiere
88 James J Clynes
88 Mary Hogan
89 Louis N Breault
89 Edwin Mitchell
89 Ahira W Davoll
89 Eador Lavoie
89 Martin Ryan
90 Alfred Norris
90 Patrick Donovan
90 Eli Kenyon
97 Philip DesRuisseau
97 Mrs Inez Henner
98 James L Schrader
98 Mary McGinnis
98 Misses Flanagan
101 Robert McMillan
103 Thomas Hogan
103 Richard J Murphy
103 Mrs Mary Burke
104 Edward Davies
104 Peter Murray
108 Joseph Soucy
108 Arsene A Roy
109 Daniel Hurll
109 Mrs Bridget Riley
113 Charles A Clark
113 Herbert Hammond
113 Thomas Newton
116 Robert C Hutchinson
117 Mrs Mary J Dalrymple
117 John W Waring
121 Mrs Mary J Skiff
121 Ernest Jones
121 Thomas R Done
129 Daniel H Taft
129 Alfred Isherwood
168 Mrs Mary A Mosher
168 Edward F Murphy
168 William Graham
168 Edward McCarthy
172 Michael J Hurley
172 George Moss
172 John Fairclough
179 Henry C Lawton
180 Albert Richard
180 Charles W Jenney
180 Henry R Butts
183 Joseph A Pothier
183 Mrs Myra Dimond
184 John Coughlin
184 Pierre Fournier
184 Mrs Isabella F Ainsworth
187 Francis A Bonneau
188 Joseph B Bonneau
188 Arthur Nutter
193 John Freitas
193 Mrs Elizabeth Miller
198 Charles F Drew
198 Richard Lonergan
201 Henry C Maxim
201 Mrs Mary Foster
201 Ovilier Brousseau
201 Amos Verrier
201 Mrs Mary Foster
204 Stephen F Manchester

204 John W Kenyon
205 Samuel Whitlow 2nd
205 Humphrey Leary
206 Charles A Choquette
210 Samuel Law
210 Hulbert E Card
213 Delphise J Moreau
213 Patrick O'Donnell
234 J Alfred Deschenes
234 John W Lynch
236 William H Whalley
238 James A Adams
249 Walter Lawrence
249 James Downey
257 Robert H Lindley
257 Joshua Gregory
267 Mrs Annie S Ryan
267 Daniel R Sullivan
270 Mrs Kate Coughlin
270 George H Walker
271 Mrs Deborah Richardson
278 Eugene J Sullivan
280 James Davidson
292 James D Tipton
293 Louis Borofsky
296 John Cairns
297 James Kelley
303 William Veary
305 Manuel T deAvelar
305 Richard H Peters
306 William J Morancy
309 Joaquim M Camara
309 Fred C Chandler
313 Alfred J Denault
322 Edward G Crossman
325 Cyrus E Wordell
325 Carl V Hjelm
328 Charles D Norlander

AUSTIN COURT

1 Mrs Elida Pike
1 Mrs Rose A Maynard
2 Elmer E King
3 Oliver Chevalier
3 Mrs Bridget Lackey
4 Ambrose Guay
6 Mrs Catherine M Foley
7 Patrick Murray
7 Mrs Mary McLaughlin
8 Calixte Lefrancois
10 Augustin Millette
11 Joseph Greenwood
12 Jeremiah Tremblay
13 Frank Velois
14 Noel Lamarche
18 Joseph Dumas
20 Mrs Adelaide Tetreault

BABBITT

7 John Livesey
11 Ephraim G Aiken
12 Joseph Reis
12 Joseph Gonsalves
12 Mrs Mary Alves
12 Joseph Reis
18 Manuel C Pacheco
21 Mrs Mary I Funans
22 William F Gomes
22 Joseph M Henrique
25 Guilherme Silva
25 Nunes C Vega
25 Mrs Mary Sylvia
31 John Andrada
31 John Andre
33 Charles H Dunham
43 Mrs Isabella Sylvia
45 Andrew Vincent
45 Frank Sylvia
47 Manuel F King Jr
48 Antonio Silva
48 Joaquim Gonsalves
51 Samuel Madruga
51 Manuel A Neves
55 Joseph Francis
56 Manuel Augustino
56 Frank A Gonsalves Jr
56 Augustine Perry
60 Benjamin F Williams

BANKS

41 Carl Johnson
0 Mrs Alice Carroll
0 Manuel Silva

BANNISTER

3 Adolphe Perreault
7 Jeremiah Harrington
7 Thomas M Chase
7 John Coulthurst
13 Mrs Mary Flood
13 Samuel Gorton
13 Wallace C Tilton

BATES AVENUE

71 Mrs Karin Hansen
71 Thomas Riley
73 Antone R Faria
73 Antone D Sylvia
107 Delphis Guillette
109 Manuel J Pimental
109 Louis F Correia
112 Hilaire Voghel
112 Antone Mello
113 Peter Landry

Bates av—con
113 Mrs Hannah Werner
113 John Lambert
117 Andre Ouillette
117 Louis Bachand
117 Joseph Cox
118 Heliodore Parent
118 Manuel Simmons
118 Mrs Christie McDonald
121 Napoleon Demarche
121 Alonzo P Stone
121 Xavier Bruneau
125 Stanislaw Cote
125 Edward O Asselin
157 Samuel Lees
158 Rodolphe Goodreau
158 James Waterworth
161 Edward Thompson
161 Daniel Wood
162 Joseph LeBlanc
162 Fred Boudreau
162 James Crook
165 William Beck
165 Thomas Noonan
165 Mrs Jane Lees
165 Richard Furness
166 Wilfred Billodeau
166 Mrs Olive Hebert
166 Alfred LeBlanc

BAY

1 Charles W Smith
3 Joseph R Gidley
5 Charles Padelford
9 Andrew Thoen
9 George H Sadler
10 Frank Martins
13 Caleb B Tyler
13 Sands C Chipman
13 Fred Cowden
14 George S Anthony
17 Leon M Huggins
17 Thomas Fay
20 Mrs Anna J Ellis
21 Everett Green
22 George M Dayton
23 Frederick A Howland **Jr**
35 Charles A Sampson
37 Charles C Jenney
37 Frank N Lincoln
38 Mrs Lydia A Kempton
38 Ansel C Morse
39 Frank J Veeder
42 Orton S Simpson
43 John J Morsey
45 Frank E Jennings
46 James T Cairns
57 Michael J Luby
57 John L Martin
59 John Gudgeon
59 Alexander K Liddell
60 Samuel Morris
61 Walter H Merchant **Jr**
63 Michael Clarke
63 Clifford E Hackett
64 Joseph L Greenough
69 Robert H Woodhouse
74 Roland Macy
75 Clarence W Chase
76 George Thomas
79 Louis J Parsons Jr
80 Charles A Jewett
81 Rev John Pearce
82 Etherlinda G Castino
85 Edward E Crompton
85 Humphrey D Howland
86 John A Smith

BAYLIES

1 Gilford Johnson
1 Percy Shepherd

BEDFORD

9 Frank E Smith
9 Samuel Meltzer
10 Jacques Burgo
10 Reuben Cohen
16 Charles O Welch
16 Albert C Johnson
16 Donald K Mackay
18 Barnard A Russotto
18 Myron J Shumway
25 Charles H Smith
25 Mrs Rosetta Jack
32 Mrs Mary Gifford
32 Julia A Howland
39 Arthur C Smith
42 Mrs Sarah B Borden
50 George H V D Cleveland
50 William Blackburn
53 Carrie A Briggs
54 James H Magnett
56 Mrs Annie E Pierce
57 Harry H Kimball
58r Ivar V Nelson
58 William Nelson
58 Charles Durant
59 N Herbert Greene
59 Allen S Tripp
61 John D Lawrence
62 Mrs Phoebe A Jenney
62 Fred L Jason
64 Mrs Margaret F Topholm
66 John R Barbour
67 Dr Charles A Bonney **Jr**
76 James P Doran

76 Dr Lauretta K Doran
76 Mrs Jeremiah L Cavanaugh
76 Arnold C Gardner
77 William D Richards
79 Oscar F Aldrich
80 William F Caswell
81 Mrs Amanda Hamblin
81 Mrs Oliver H Snow
83 Mrs Maria L Kearn
85 Robert E Baylies
86 William Baylies
89 Elizabeth J Smith
89 Frederick S Brightman
89 Misses Smith
90 Mrs Elizabeth C Vinal
90 David E Lawrence
92 Mrs Mary C Baylis
93 Henry J Perry
93r John P Rooney
94 John Baylies
95 Mrs Elizabeth R Lucas
96 Giles P Slocum
99 John C Emery
100 George H Sylvia
113 C Arthur Sampson
113 Stanislas Ennis
113 Francis Nichols
116 Mrs Jane B Chalfin
120 Mrs Sarah A Knowles
122 J Edwin Jones
123 Henry T Allen
124 Sarah A Gifford
129 Samuel L Herman
130 Neil F Monahan
130 Thomas Dahoney
134 David F Covill
136 Reuben T King
138 Misses Sullivan
138 Isabella C Hill
144 Patrick Kennedy
148 Sylvia Jackson

BEECH

8 Mrs Elizabeth W S Thompson
9 Francis H Cook
10 Charles Frye Jr
26 John Cameron
35 William C Westgate
38 Charles S Jennings
38 Charles E Gardner
40 Thomas H Sanderson
49 Isaac Newton
61 John Q A Cobb

BEETLE

7 Antone C Mattos
7 Samuel Fegarsky
7 Louis Fegarsky
7 Manuel Machado
8 Domingos Teixeira
8 Manuel Santana
8 Francisco Pereira
8r Andrew Bilawa
9 Zephir Goodreau
12 Napoleon Benoit
12 Mrs Julia Fortier
12 Napoleon Bilodeau
12 Fred Collette
12 Etienne Duphily
12 Napoleon Hebert
12 Napoleon Morin
12 Adelard Lebeau
14 Magloire Cyr
14 Louis Treant
14 Joseph Hutchinson
14 Maxim Ray
15 Mrs Emma Maher
15 Edward Landry
16 John Levesque
17 Patrick O'Malley
17 Damase Lavalle
17 Adelard Lavalle
17 Arthur St Aubin
22 John Bosquet
22 Mrs Rebecca Goshein
22 Vital Bourgeois
23 Israel Finklestein
23 James Noon
23 Abraham Bernstein
31 Frank Dragon
31 Joseph La Pierre
31 John B Sanbourin
44 Joseph A Bouvier
44 John E Scott
45 Joseph E Triguerio
45 Treffly Comeau
45 George Sevigney
49 Mrs Leda Bourque
49 Joseph Catudal
49 Oliver Devost
49 Narcisse Blanchette
49 Oliver Devaux
56 Richard Howarth
56 William Worsley
56 William Wood
56 Robert Allen
57 Henry Couture
57 John Barber
57 Matthew Houldsworth
60 Mrs Mary Gudgeon
60 Mrs Anna Sharples
60 Daniel Mayor
76 Dr James W Owen
76 Henry LeFaille
80 Romeo Couture
80 Frank Lambert
80 Francois St Aubin
80 Arsene Dionne
81 Paul Query
81 George McClure

Beetle—con
81 Mrs Azilda LaChappelle
85 Joseph Tessier
85 Arthur Gardner
85 Arthur Fortier
85 Arthur Ouimette
86 Thaddee Robichaud
86 Abraham Vient
86 Abraham Vient Jr
89 William Doucette
89 Jean B Choquette
89 Joseph Vertefeuille
91 William Butterworth
91 Michael Sheehan
91 John Tinney
94 George Ouimette
94 Adelard Le Chappelle
94 Walter H Francis
95 Walter L Lawless
95 Mrs Ellen Connelly
95 J Thomas Lawson
95 John F Haran
98 Peter Golin
98 Delphine Billodeau
98 Oliver Forand
98 Charles Pickle
99 Dennis Leary
99 George Cunliffe
99 Joseph Spragg
102 Wilfred Fivett
102 Frank J Phaneuf
102 Joseph Sauve
102 Phillip Pelletier
105 Alderic Gravel
105 Thomas Connor
105 Joseph Platt
105 Joseph Paquette
106 Joseph Bernard
106 Alexandre Goldberg
106 John B Boubeau
106 Henry Alix
107 Arthur Leclair
107 Archille Maia
109 Napoleon Girouard
111 Louis St Pierre
111 Noe Blais
111 Donald McClure

BEETLE LANE

3 Ellery L Peckham

BELAIR ROAD

0 Thomas Y Arendell

BELLEVILLE AVENUE

15 Joseph Welsolv
19 Mjik Weituszewski
19 Antoni Kielka
20 Manuel Pedro
20 John Parlau
20 Manuel Silva
25 Stanislaus Lubeara
25 Andrea Lubeara
26 Cyril Breton
46 Fred Maynard
51 Agnes Benoit
51 Pierre Boucher
53 Nathan Cohen
53 Joseph Laplante
61r Lawrence Maloney
72 John Michael
122 Manuel Frates
123 Omar Plouffe
123 Manuel M Frates
125 Boris Newmark
125 Manuel Ferreira
125 Frank S Rabeilo
127 August Souza
127 Manuel Souza
127 Joseph Medeiros
127 John Medeiros
127 Jose Motto
145 Antone Motta
145 Jacob Bessarabian
148 Antonio T Mello
148 Manuel Jardin
148 Joseph S Cruz
148 Manuel M Almeida
148 Manuel Sardinha
153 Antone Cabral
153 Mrs Jennie Costa
153 Joseph Costa
153 John Duarte
153 John Andrew
153 John Medeiros
153 Antone F Rego
155 Frank Santos
160 Joseph Antone
166 John Pedro
166 Manuel Silva
168 J B Bausquet
171 Enos D Alfres
171 Manuel Bizarro
171 Joseph Duarte
171 Manuel S Morreia
172 Thomas Astley
175 Manuel P Cardoza
175 Manuel Correia
175 Jules Simas
178 Joseph Holland
178 Manuel C Duarte
178 Manuel Moniz
178 Manuel Furtado
179 Manuel Gomes
179 Justin Gonsalves
180 Manuel Pacheco
180 Luiz Paiva

180 Manuel Teixeira
180 Antone Pimental
181 Manuel Praeda
181 Joseph Maher
181 Hugh Shannahan
184 Manuel Agrella
184 Antone Souza
188 Manuel Mello
188 Jose S Miranda
191 Hoso Ferat
191 Jervet Safa
191 Hassan Veli
191 Manuel Costa
191 Alfred St Germain
194 Pascal Gagnon
194 Orvilia La Brecque
194 George Rainville
194 Mrs Arthur Roy
194 Oliva Langlois
195 J Manuel Floria
202 Manuel Roderiques
202 Antonio Cardoza
202 Manuel Ferreira
202 Francisco Souza
202 Joseph Souza
202 John Tavares
202 Victorino Oliveira
202 Simon J Portnoy
203 Peter Bielawstro
203 Justin Gonsalves
204 Manuel Barboza
204 Manuel G Freitas
204 Manuel M Souza
207 Manuel S Almeida
207 Antoni Czestic
213 Jose Antonio
213 Napoleon Le Blanc
213 Joseph Medeiros
213 John Newsham
259 Antone Niech
269 Anthony Chirigotis
269 Stanislaw Szczcpan
291 Maxim Breau
291 Magloire Leblanc
291 Arthur St Pierre
293 James J Govang
297 Elzear Henley
297 Joseph Walker
297 Joseph Russell
297 Leopold Posch
311 John Tardy
319 Charles Le Blanc
319 Joseph Richard
319 Omer Levesque
319 Mrs Philomene Comeau
325 Luca Breault
325 Wojech Kendra
331 Joseph Belleisle
331 Amidas Macot
331 Bruno Caplete
349 Joseph E Sylvia
349 Theodore Bourgeois
382 Manuel V Goulart
382 Joseph Lima
382 Manuel L Pacheco
383 Manuel Pacheco
383 Joseph Amaral
383 Antone M Alves
387 Jose E Oliveira
387 Joseph Furtado
387 Manoel M Soares
392 Mrs Lizzie Evarts
392 Mrs Ida Goudreau
395 Joseph Bonneau
395 Philias Richard
399 Philip L'Oiselle
399 Fred Gamache
399 William Tetreault
399 Wladylow Tomkowicz
399 Woyciech Fuczak
399 Michael Galoska
439 Frank Furtado
439 Mrs Jennie Mello
446 Basil Poirer
452 Dolphis Trudel
452 Camille Boucher
452 Eugene Thibodeau
453 Antone M Fonseca
453 Alva Silva
455 Henry J Bell
455 Joseph Tremblay
455 Arcade Moffit
455 Louis Z Dion
456 Dominique Le Blanc
456 Alexandre Vanasse
479 Cesime Chace
479 William Morris
479 Mrs Julia Hayes
493 Joseph Robidoux
735 Joseph Lambert
735 Henry Benoit
735 Peter Dube
739 Robert Walsh
739 Dominique Boudreau
739 Joseph Frates
739 Mrs Priscilla Duquet
742 Phillip Bonneau
742 Alex Fillioult
744 James B Sisson
747 Peter Smith
786 Hannah C Gifford
789 Elwood M Sturtevant
800 Frederick E Chase
810 Mederic F Maynard

Belleville av—con
810 Thomas R Marshall
814 Ambrose F Merchant
814 George M Bennett
814 Mrs Helen M Croucher
840 Augustus E Chase
882 Joshua Richardson
900 Azarie Bolduc
900r Mrs Rachel Townsend
906 John G Whalon
910 John M Hathaway
910 Walter E Crapo
914 Phillip E Harding
914 Albert R Marshall
920 H M Sprague
920· Horace A Bird
924 John F Parker
924 Mrs Mary J Howland

BELLEVILLE ROAD

22 Magloire Breault
24 John Bent
24 Mrs Elizabeth Davie
26 James H Duffy
26 Mrs Maria Smith
26 William A Ashworth
28 William Pollard
28 Agnes Walsh
28 Mrs Margaret Cowell
30 Mrs Angeline Belliveau
30 Mrs Marguerite Allain
30 William H Whittle
39 Philip Brodeur
39 Joseph Brodeur
46 Mathias P Maloney
46 Mrs Alice Turenne
47 Paul Rioux
47 Mary Dagesse
47 Edward Cournoyer
47 Lucien Bernique
56 Frank Ouillette
56 Frank E Cormier
56 Pierre LaBrecque
56 John Mason
60 Frank Collard
60 Mrs Clarina Levesque
60 Marcelin Lacombe
60 Adelard Pidgeon
61 Mrs Adella Gauthier
61 Hector Gauthier
61r William Yates
61r Mrs S Smith
72 Oliver Rock
72 Charles Gill
72 Cyril Goulet
74 John Caffrey
74 Mrs Mary A Sullivan
74 Fred Travers
74 Stanislol Corylo
82 Theophile Bois
82 Joseph Souza
82 Thomas Abrais
82 James Anderson
86 John P Bradshaw
86 George Gauthier
86 William Rayno
88 Peter A Carting
88 Thomas Johnson
88 William Lord
92 James Devlin
93 Elmer E Bonney
93 Mrs Mary P Smith
94 Benjamin W Kenyon
103 Alfred Gallant
103 Ralph Moreau
103 J B Maillette
113 Albini Blanchette
113 Antoinette Roy
113 Maxime Sevigney
113 Alfred Sevegny
113 Mrs V Berube
120 Mrs Mary A Healey
120 Theobald M Healey
124 John Bromides
125 Bessie Washburn
127 Thomas J Durand
143 Mrs Annie Smith
143 Walter Thomas
143 John W Shepley
147 Arthur Thompson
147 George Parkinson
147 Joseph Key
154 Charles H Gallagher
154 Alfris LeBlanc
154 Domina Rainville
154 Charles Rioux
154 Rudolph Savaria
155 William Waring
155 Clarence W Covill
155 Isaiah Hatfield
168 James A Emerson
168 Henry Barnes
172 Thomas Astley
176 John A Holden
180 Mrs Sarah Cullins
180 George F Bourne
184 Francis J Ward
184 George Clayton
188 Charles Holding
188 George B Norris
189 Thomas Brewer
189 Dennis F Mellor
189 Patrick J Moher
191 Alfred St Germain
191 George S Metcalf
191 William Knowles
197 Burt St Germain
197 Joseph Blouin
197 Ermel Rioux

198 Murtys E Osborne
198 Michel Brunelle
198 John E Peets
201 Ernest A Potter
201 William Wrigley
201 James Ashworth
301 Arthur Bernier

BELLEVUE

15 Antone Souza
95 Louis Costa
97 John V Medeiros
99 Antone Borges
99 Manuel F Cabral

BENTLEY

7 Mrs Josephine McGee
7 Charles Gilmore
9 Moise Rivard
9 Henri Lemaire
9 Frank Marchand
12 Eli Neild
12 Henri Charpentier
15 William Johnson
15 George Ironside
15 William Crowther
16 John B Blanchard
16 Flavien Carreau
16 Joseph Lapointe
19 Lucien LaFond
19 Napoleon Ross
19 Samuel Lewis
19 Frank Kouble
19 Charles Casavant
20 Mrs Celia Lizotte
20 Charles Lajoie
20 Louis A Tellier
23 Jeremiah Bessette
23 John A Curran
23 George Boyer
23 Jeffrey Duquette
24 Azarie Lecompte
24 Michel Lizotte
24 Gilbert St Germain
25 L Philip Ferland
25 Alfred Letourneau
25 Alphonse Perreault
28 Arsene Poirier
28 John A Marchland
31 Peter Arpin
31 Leon Dupre
31 Mrs Victorine Nadeau
32 Alderic Dansereau
32 Alfred Rivet
32 William W Monty
34 Ernest Iltis
34 Joseph Lemaire
34 Moise Allain
35 Ambroise Labonte
35 Pierre Metthe
35 Jacob Breault
36 James Conway
36 Henri Poutre

BETHEL

2 Mrs Mary Martin
4 John James Robinson
6 Fred Jones
6 William E Dutton
7 August Pina
7 Jacinth Ferreira
7 Mrs Annie Gomes
7 Henry Gomes
7 Henry Jesus
8 Peter Bortle
10 Mary E Harlow
12 Manuel Veira
12 John Lima
12 Joseph Sando
12 Domingo Baptista
14 Antone Gonsalves
14 Manuel Pias
15 Rev Charles S Thurber
17 William Baker
20 Mrs May R Simmons
27 Mrs Elizabeth Dealy
41 William H Drummond
41 Nicholas Evangelidis
43 Mrs Carrie Leck
43 Henry F Barnes
43 Mrs Prudence C Allen
45 Mack C White
45 Percy Steele
45 Mrs Rose Francis

BILLINGTON

93 Charles A Russell

BLACKBURN

1 William E Taylor
1 Robert Latimer
1 S George Mangold
1 Mrs Victoria Lacombe
3 Alfred Surprenant
4 Charles St Pierre
4 Frank Guertin
4 Albert Crossman
4 Thomas Ouillette
6 Joseph L O'Reilly
6 Joseph L Baron
7 Wilfred Sivigny

Blackburn—con
7 Max Berman
7 Haime Eidlin
8 Wilfred Beauparlant
8 Deom Nicollo
9 Ernest Messier
9 Laurant Rapa
10 Napoleon L'Homme
10 Arthur Guertin
11 Andrew Jordan
12 Andre Durant
12 Jesse Simpkin
16 Daniel Corbett

BLACKMER

7 Edward Braley
50 Thomas Gervais
50 Joseph Riel
54 Paul Marquis
54 Antone O Martin
54 Zenon Pelisier
58 Thomas Bramwell
58 Patrick Hayes
62 Alfred Furtado
62 Mrs Jennie Roberts
68 Franciso J Medeiros
68 Manuel Fonseca
72 Antone Lima
72 Mrs Anna Nascimento
72 Antone Cabral
72 Manuel Silva
76 Mrs Ellen Cooney
76 Joseph Richara
80 Edward Dubois
84 Mrs Julia Lepire
84 Treffle Langlois
88 Thomas Thornhill
88 Thomas Brown
94 Charles Berube
98 Mrs Emily Medeiros
100 Manuel Sears
108 Adam Perlin
110 Charles Gilbert
129 Leopold Dumianski
129 John Bosok
130 Joseph S Marshall
130 Philias Brais
131 Antone Morcier
136 James Murphy
136 John Barnes
150 J August Wunshell
150 Franciszek Ziomet
153 Hermidas Trepanier
153 Joseph Prince
154 Anthony Dessert
164 Napoleon Dansereau
164 Joseph Barbieri
166 Eugene F **Braley**
166 John Alferes
178 James Whitehead
178 Robert Reid
178 William Donley
180 Delor Millette
180 Adelard Bergeron
180 Louis Roy
188 Philip Sicard
189 William H Marsden
194 Fred Butterworth
194 Napoleon Baillargeon
194 Felix Viera
194 Zennon Pellerin
198 Paul Watson
198 Kate Gordon
198 Annie Caldwell
199 Joseph Mercier
199 A P Lagasse
202 Martin M Bowman
203 Manuel E Silva
203 David Breault
203r Mrs Louisa Sylvia
204 Wladyslaw Buba

BOLTON

389 Israel Olivier
389 John **Norcross**
389 Albert Thauvette
389 Lewis Duckworth
389 Robert Marsden
389 Stephen A Hatch
407 James Swallow
409 Peter Carter
434 Rotch Block
1 Narcisse Normand
2 Manuel Nunes
3 Jose N Borges
4 Augustine Freitas
435 Rotch Block
33 John Machado
34 John Frates
35 Manuel Radix
35 Mary Mendoza
36 Albert Misiolsk
438 Rotch Block
7 Valentine Gajewski
8 Manuel Medeiros
9 John Ferreira
10 Manuel Amarantes
439 Rotch Block
20 Manuel Lucas
26 Andre Miz
27 Joaquim DeReis
28 Antonio Macedo
32 Manuel Dias
442 Rotch Block
12 Jose Cordeira
13 Joseph Robuk

16 John F Lima
19 John Ylenencv
443 Rotch Block
19 Joseph Mizal
22 Joseph Avila
24 Joseph Henser
459 Manuel F Fialho
459 Henry Lumba
459 Alfred Lague
460 Eliza Norton
460 Elijah W Dickson
460 James H Doyle
461 James B Galligan
461 Joseph Medeiros
461 Anthony F Harden
462 Samuel G Davenport
462 Eugene B Fuller
462 Peter P Kinniery
465 Alfred D Brownhill
465 James McGee
465 Michael Kearney
480 Dennis J Mahoney
480 George Clarkson
480 Matthew J Doyle
482 John De Beech
482 Thomas H Cummings
482 Thomas Latham
482 James Cummings
496 Mrs Mary Wilson
496 Margaret Fidler
496 Mrs Manuel Clement
498 Manuel A Williams
502 Albert Wilcox
502 James G Simpson
502 Gus Alves
503 Manuel Silva
503 James T Dow
503 Philbert Silveira
504 Manuel F Souza
507 Joseph S Mello
507 Frank Thomas
507 Theotonio de Cuadros
522 Frank Fernandes
522 Ernest Jackson
522 Joseph Jacinth
526 George Bond
530 James Sanderson
530 Mrs Sabina R Gomes
530 William Harrop

BONNEAU COURT

5 John Goulet
5 Joussaint Hamel
5 John Silva
5 Amedee Valliere
6 Mrs Hattie Smith
6 Isabella Smith
6 Peter Kourafas
6 James Richard
6 George Pillington
6 Mrs Marietta Carter
6 Henry Drolet
6 Mrs Mary Dresner
7 Theodore Chaberik
7 Manuel T Farinka

BONNEY

4 Roland S Dean
4 Edward C Mosher
8 Mrs Mary Ganson
9 James Campbell
15 Anthony Rawcliffe
15 Frank M Bertram
17 Ray L Blanchard
17 George M Gifford
19 Alex S Felton
25 James B Schwall
29 Frederick K Mein
30 Mary A Leonard
32 James W Hathaway
33 Mrs Lydia A Macreading
34 Mrs Sarah B Hinckley
37 W E Cunningham
41 Mrs Lurania Allen
45 Thomas A Lawrence
46 Frank J Morris
51 Joseph H Mover
51 Mrs Lucretia H Sisson
55 Mrs Marianna Devoll
62 Elias H Kershaw
71 John H Backus
83 William E Davis
85 Isaac T Rogers
89 Thomas F Wood
95 Frank A Studley
95 Frank W King
100 William J Gatie
100 Hugh Beveridge
101 Joseph Gatie
101 Augustus M Kennedy
104 Frank P Rodman
105 Mrs Annie Beveridge
105 Walter H Burns
105 Daniel E Duff
108 Mrs Horatio D Greene
109 James F Craft
109 Daniel N O'Brien
111 Edward W O'Neil
112 Mrs Hannah M Murray
112 William J Moore
113 Gustave A Johnson
115 Mrs Mary R Vieira
115 Constantino M Fraga
117 Henry L Hathaway
118 Joseph Rose
121 Mrs Theresa P Leal

Bonney—con
121 Mrs Mary Bresnahan
122 John Kennedy
122 William Hoxie
124 Henry J Cassin
124 John Cantwell
124 William T Manning
125 Herbert Diggle
125 John W Diggle
126 John K Osswald
126 Robert E Ellis
126 Mrs Ellen J Cotter
128 George W West
128 Hjalmer Gunderson
128 Mrs Annie McMahon
129 Charles A Johnson
129 Henry G Matthews
129 Antonio F Dias
133 Manuel L Sylvia
134 Mrs Mary Lent
134 Marcelina Lima
134 Frank F Cardoza
137 Thomas E Whitford
141 Thomas Stone
145 Manuel B Francis
145 John Sylvia
148 Frank Francis
149 Henry J McDonald
150 Frank Funans
152 Mrs Mary Oliver
153 Nicholas R Vieira
158 John Scherzer
159 John Ashton
159 James A Thompson
162 John Souza
162 Alfred C Costa
163 Henry W Raymond
163 Henry L Raymond
163 Henry J Breton
164 Alphonse J Damos
164 Manuel F Silva
164 Patrick Finley
171 Frank Taylor
171 Letita M Hargraves
171 John J Ward
171 James Souza
172 Adam Wunshell
172 Mrs Louisa A Chadwick
172 John Kisbert
181 John T Barrows
181 Frank S Mesquita
183 Manuel Simas
183 Joseph P Cambra
184 Jason C Tavares
186 John Dumec
186 Peter Dumec
187 Thomas Brown
187 Manuel Lopes
187 Manuel Correia
187r Joseph P Rogers
187r Antone Medeiros
190 Joseph Lawrence
190 Mrs Mary Souza
190 Misses Demello
190 Mrs Rosie Cunha
190 Antonio C DeMello
191 Mrs Elizabeth McCabe
191 Joseph Thomas
191 John A Lafferty
194 Antonio Mello
194 Frederick Joseph
195 Richard Grant
195 Joseph Menezes
195 Evens Brooks
198 Jose M G Luiz
198 Anton Mirando
199 Manuel G Vieira Jr
205 Manuel G Vieira
205 Mrs Mary Ribeiro
210 Henry W Hathaway
230 Rev Antonio P Vieira
230 Rev Augustine Santos
252 Mary E Gloria
266 Frank S Avela

BORDEN

7 Joseph M Ashley
8 Mrs Mary E Briggs
9 Jerome B Farnham
10 Walter H Nelson
10 Richmond C Winter
11 William D Garthly
12 Edwin J Reed
12 Blanche R Tillinghast
12 Merton R Davis
14 Edward D Baker
15 John H Deane
15 Lida J Brightman
16 Arthur M Chase
17 Frederick T Colyar
17 Leon Colardeau
19 Mrs Annie H Bolles
19 Clarence E Allen
22 J Urbon Wright
22 William H Hurley
23 Harry C Vaughan
25 Frank W Sylvia
26 Ernest G Bridgham
26 Samuel S Broadbent
27 John T Marley
27 Terry Broadland
28 Charles A S Sherman
29 Edward R Sisson
32 Charles H Kane
33 Frederick P Tripp
36 William Pedro

36 Owen McMahon
38 Michael Keavy
42 Edward K Spencer
45 Joseph F Morris
46 William E York
46 John H Fuller
46 William L Downey
47 Joseph Gracia
48 Wendell Macy
49 Wesley H Acorn
49 Antone Enos
50 George E Teachman
51 Willis S Fuller
53 John J Connors
54 Manuel R Perry
58 Dennis Shea
58 Francis H Walsh
59 Lawrence E Bertram
60 Joseph R Perry
64 Rev George H Howes
64 Charles F F Jones
65 Manuel Rodericque
68 Frederick R Fish
69 Frank L Rogers
70 John S Howland
73 Edmond L Wilde

BOURNE

10 Andrew Bauer
12 James Talbot
14 Seraphin Oliver
15 Frederick T Wilcox
16 Jacintho S Furtado
16 Elizabeth A Hulton
19 Joseph A Brown
19 Joaquim J Sylvia
22 Jule Gomes
23 Manuel F Rose
23 Ernest Lamb
27 Alexander Moore Jr
27 Manuel J Perry
28 John Almeida
28 Manuel Raffael
28 Antonio Marks
32 William R Benoit
32 Edwin W Church
32 John M Wunshell
40 Joseph Anthony Jr
48 Alfred Schofield
48 Samuel Bancroft
56 Frank Guba

BOWDITCH

1 Abraham Girard
1 Jeremiah Cloutier
2 Nelson Prunneau
2 Henry St Louis
2 Alfred Russell
3 Frank Coombs
3 Alfred LaFlamme
4 Everest Dudevoir
4 Adolph Hartel
5 Oliver Lemieux
5 Adelard Tetreault
6 Charles F Clapp
7 Eugene Henner
7 Joseph Vanasse
8 Mrs Mary Dion
8 Victor A Loranger
8 Michael Choquette
9 George Morsette
10 Adelard Metevier
11 Joseph George
11 Alexander Pothier
12 Wilfred Menard
12 Leon Boucher
13 Henry Parent
13 Joseph St Germain
14 Marcus E Clifford
14 Frank Lizzotte
14 Napoleon Aubrey
15 Mrs Zoe Pidgeon
15 Thomas E Gaughan
16 David Monblow
16 John Magnant
16 Alexander Therrault
18 Joseph Cayer
18 Adelard Brule
28 William Machon
30 Jacob Lider
32 Philip Benoit
34 John W McGuire
34 Joseph Bath
36 Andrew P Carter
38 John Morgan
38 Mrs Mary J Colbert
39 Mrs Kate Hanley
39 William H Sykes
40. Loring T Bentley
41 William Cottam
42 George Pepin
42 Josiah Benoit
44 John Mullins
44 Michael Harrington
44 Daniel F Harrington
45 Carl Chestak
45 Charles Schestak
45 Nathan Novinsky
47 Helen Munroe
47 Edward Hosker
47 Arthur Howarth
47½ Fred Taylor
47½ Fred Crossley
49 John Mercer
49 John Brewer
49 Mrs Mary Pomfort
53 Joseph H Leach
53 Joshua Besse
68 Mrs Victoria Arcand

Bowditch—con
68 Rev J Edmond Potvin
69 Joseph E Morris
79 Thomas Banks
87 Joseph Bourbeau
87 Michele Dextras
92 Charles Brillion
92 Martial Desrosiers
92 Joseph Robichaud
94 Jose Cardoza
94 Edeas Brillion
95 John Bardsley Jr
95 Mrs Jane A Gregory
95 Gustave Petijean
99 James Norton
99 Alphonse Lemaire
101 Raphael Lemieux
101 Godfrois Tremblay
102 Joseph Mitron
102 Narcisse St Germain
103 Arthur Patnaude
103 Frank Woolley
104 Narcisse LeBlanc
104 Edson Boyer
106 Philip Beaudoin
106 Xavier Chausse
106 Mrs Lillian Blackburn
109 Dominick J Jarry
109 Joseph G Metthe
109 Telesphore St Armand
113 Ernest Levasseur
113 Arthur Perron
113 Joseph C Verville
128 Onesime Gelinas
128 John W Entwistle
128 Mrs Harriet Turner
128 Napoleon Ricard
132 Edmond Burque
132 Hormidas Duval
132 Fred Magnant
132 Walter Goyette
132 J E Grenache
134 Gotfried Brunner
138 Jeremiah Mullins
138 Mrs Hannah O'Neil
144 Frederick Heran
155 Mrs Herminie Dagesse
155 Sadie Whittaker
156 Mrs Jane Nuttall
156 James S Harrison
156 Peter Broshek
156 Kasper Hanslick
159 Elphege Gaucher
159 Arthur Rousseau
159 Edward W Johnson
160 Emile L Francois
160 Onesphore Bertrand
162 Elie Girouard
171 Charles St Laurent
171 Alex Seguin
171 Urbain Vigneault
171 Alfred Fonteneau
174 Frank Jirasco
174 William Knowles
174 Joseph Bakewell
176 Richard Southworth
176 John Broughton
176 John W Carter
177 L J Oscar Fontaine
178 Mrs Adaline Remi
178 Mrs Nora Dion
178 Alfred Chausse
178 Hormidas Magnant
179 Patrick Melancon
179 Nelson Melancon
179 Joel Remillard
181 Mrs Bertha Laube
181 Oscar Winsberg
181 Adolph Laubi
181 Samuel L Windzberg
183 John Perra
183 Albert Eastwood
183 Mrs Catherine Gray
183 Arthur Garside
185 William H King
189 Aristide La Brecque
189 Joseph Duperry
189 Mrs Matilda Choquette
193 Edward Lyons
193 Louis G Gagnon
193 Joseph N Sevigney
193 Hector Pelletier
193 Pierre Lapointe
195 Mrs Delia Perra
195 Nelson Noel
196 Fred Vincent
197 Oliver A Bourgeois
197 Thomas Holden
199 Benjamin Horne
201 Mrs Exilia Lussier
203 Mrs Delmina Lussier
203 Jerry Caisey
203 William D Bourbo
207 Jacques Robillard
207 Joseph A Goulet
207 John B Codaire
209 Tranquille Gauvin
209 Alphee Gautreau
211 Arthur Demars
211r Charles Hebert
213 George E Gendron
219 Anselme Carrier
219½ Adelard Letendre
219½ Elizabeth LaBrie
219½ Joseph Beaudoin
219½ Louis Beaudoin
223 Pierre Laplante
225 George D Lacroix
229 David Sharples

229 Mrs Martha A Sharples
235 Fred A Phillips
235 Joseph Buteau
247 William Singleton
247 Joseph Clement
248 Joseph Lague
248 Samuel Fortin
248 Cleophis Deslauriers
248 Joseph N Fonsenca
248 Joseph F Nunes
249 Henry Geyer
250 Joseph Brodeur
250 Henry J Viens
250 Franklin M Darling Jr
250 Albert E Dean
251 John H Clark
251 John W Pimblett
251 Henry Whitehead
259 Frederick H Roscow
259 Herbert Green
259 John W Wade
269 Joseph Giguere
269 Adelard Chadanais
275 Mrs Mary Downey
277 Desmond W Tripp
280 John Ribchester
281 Abraham Knowles
282 William R Moore
283 Rev John Oldham
285 Cavig Heys
285 Mrs Mary H Smethurst
285 John L Coholan
287 William C Henry
287 David Harris
289 Ludwig Heuberger
289 John M Lemos
289 Mrs Mary Welch
289 Herbert Green
306 Rev Michael V McDonough
306 Rev James J Brady
307 Patrick J Driscoll
311 John H Finnell
322 Joseph Roberts
322 Robert Greenhalge
326 Jules Menard
328 Mrs Eliza Messier
328 Sidney Boyer
328 Henry Kenten
332 Ludger Legere
332 Stanislas Bedard
332 James Lord
333 Henry Fecteau
334 Joseph W Bordley
335 Richard Harvey
335 Dennis Perrault
336 John B Surprenant
341 William W Francis
341 Philip H Morris
341 Mrs Elizabeth Tyrer
342 Joseph Phaneuf
342 Aleanah Whyatt
342 Charles J Foster
342 Eli Fredette
343 Amos Turner
343 Michael Ratchford
343 Fred Whitehead
344 Ulric Cote
347 John A Valentine
347 John W Allen
347 Henry I Therrien
350 John Bousquet
350 Emanuel Patsy
350 Walter Anderson
357 Gustave Fontaine
357 Andrew Proulx
357 Adelard M Boisvert
357 Elphege Gaucher
359 Pierre LeCroix
359 Delphis Ouimette
359 Louis Tetreault
366 James Moorehouse
369 John Valentine
371 Ernest Neild
373 Horace H Chapard
373 Thomas LaFontaine
373 Pierre A Leduc
373 Jean B Paquette
387 William Yates
387 Joseph Peltier
387 Mrs Mary J Whelen
387 Godfrois Fortier
391 Camille Roberge
391 Napoleon J Poisson
391 Joseph Manseau
395 Andrew J Whelan
395 Larry Dulude
395 John Roberts
395 Schofield Wood
397 Joseph Dulude
423 James Rossiter
423 Harry E Swan
492 Arthur Gladu
505 Joseph Dionne
507 Edward J Powers
507 Michael J Griffin

BRALEY ROAD

0 John Billington
0 Wm B Pittsley
0 Geo D White
0 Otto Krause
0 Charles H Chase

BRIGGS

9 Manuel L da Silveira
11 Alfred J Sterling
13 Antonio E Perry
16 Thomas Cummisky

Briggs—con
16 Jacintho Cabral
16 Manuel Arruda
20 John L Lima
20 Amelia E Cabral
20 James Houghton
30 Manuel Ponte
35 Frank Tefke
35 Joseph Adams
35 Joseph Christian
41 Joseph F Rezendes
41 Alfred E Lemos
41 Mrs Annie M Walsh
44 Wm Smith
44 Mark L Greenleaf
44 Mrs Elizabeth Lightbown
47 Terrence Rogers
47 Edward H Alexander
48 Samuel H Jenkins
48 Joseph Silva
48 John S Furtado
52 Fred Haworth
52 Frank X Houde
52 Oliver Bergeron
53 Marguerita S Gracia
53 Joseph N Grigware
56 Mrs Marianna Gracia
56 Nedhart Amaral
60 Frank P Fonseca
60 G A Broadbent
60 Robert Howard
60 Jacob Etienne
62 Manuel Jason
62 John M Cardozo
62 Manuel P Simmons
63 Frederick J Francis
63 Fred Crowther
63 Mrs Edith J Viator
73 Joseph Silva
73 Manuel Travers
73 Manuel F Simoes
86 Albert Crossley
86 Angelo L Fraga
87 Joseph J Perry
87 Joseph J Souza
87 Edwin L Potter Jr
88 John T Eastwood
88 Alexander J Jones
88 John J Avila
89 Antone P Cordeiro
89 Antone B Sylvia
89 Antonio P Cordeiro

BRIGGS COURT

8 Frederick C Brightman
9 Manuel S Gracia
10 Henry F Stevens
11 Walter Stowell
12 Karl Zellhuber

BRIGHAM

68 Manuel J Lomba
92 Harry A Mosher
99 Max E Fisher

BRIGHTMAN COURT

4 Ellery E Colvin
6 John J Powers

BROCK AVENUE

16 Albert Southworth
17 John Duerden
19 John R Heap
21 Henry Schelter
31 Wm Brierly
31 Philias Coutu
31 Joseph Demers
32 Mrs Mary Curry
32 Arthur G Delacy
32 Thomas Allen
45 Joseph Forant
45 Hughues Desautels
45 Wm Lambert
47 Joseph Desorcy
47 Mary Charett
47 Alex Leboeuf
53 Amedee Beauchemin
53 Ozepie Carriveau
53 Romeo Beachemin
55 Geo Rothwell
55 Mrs Celina Talbot
55 Joseph Dixon
55 Napoleon Willette
55 Wilfred Hartley
55 Wm F Parsons
59 Onesime Roy
59 Doninique Rioux
59 Michael Holihan
60 Rev George J Cain
60 Rev Omer Valois
63 Joseph Gendron
63 Charles A Knapton
63 Alphire Bombardier
65 Arthur Bolduc
66 Napoleon Ouimette
71 Samuel Bussiere
71 Evariste Coache
71 Harry Lucas
71 George Riley
71 Eugene Genereux Jr
72 John Harrison
75 George Sherratt
75 Mrs Catherine Gorner
75 Azarias Beauregard
75 Alexis Savaria
75 Edward S Edge
76 Ferdinand Breault
76 Antonio Cadorette
80 Richard Williamson

80 George E Dexter
80 Herbert R Weston
83 Alphonse LeBoeuf
90 John Shields
91 Henry J Parker
91 John W Richardson
91 Samuel Southworth
95 Thomas Kirkham
95 Mrs Elizabeth J Grimshaw
95 John Wilkinson
96 Harry Jackson
98 Harry G Terry
98 Misses Hill
98 William Bleasdale
98 Joseph Singleton
98 John Middleton
98 Polly Kenyon
99 John Holt
99 Alyn H Platt
99 Isaac Makin
102 P Damien Jarry
103 Hermingilde Lafleur
119 George L Fawcett
119 Albert Beard
119 James H Chant
119 Leonard Howson
119 Robert Wilkinson
119 William Nelson
156 Eli Higginbotham
156 Joseph J Haydock
159 William Smalley
160 Thomas Calderbank
164 Michel Parent
164 Francis Bernard
165½ William A Harriman
167 Robert Dyson
167 Charles H Haggas
168 Thomas Slater
168 Alphe Arcand
171 Edward J King
175 Manuel Alexander
176 Arthur Smalley
180 Charles T Pemberton
180 William Southworth
180 Richard Carroll Jr
187 Joseph J Charnley
187 Mrs Ruth Keelan
187 James Yates
190 Albert Bradley
190 Richard Smith
191 William Rhodes
191 Joseph Taylor
191 James Lees
195 Albert Bradshaw
195 Harry Gill
195 Matthew Conlan
199 Frank Riisinger
199 Henry Bamforth
200 John S Marks
200 William Landry
200 Mrs Margaret Welker
205 Ellis Marshall
205 James Marshall
205 William A Adams
205 Harry L Ray
206 Harold Cooper
207 Mrs Mary E Barrett
207 James Doigl
208 Thomas Kenyon
211 Frederick Melling
211 Frederick Smethurst
211 Frederick Audette
0 James P Cash
229 Joseph A Fernandes
231 Joseph H Lewis
231 Eli Heys
236 Thomas A Loftus
236 John McAlpine
236 Fred Castle
236 John Handron
236 Maxime Cadorette
250 Henry Bowker
250 Paul Connolly
256 James H Taylor
258 August Lutz
264 Vincent Geier
293 William Lace
293 Daniel C Stephenson
293 Joseph G Sylvia
299 George Smith
303 Christopher Seed
303 Ada Kay
330 Charles Grant
330 Mrs Elizabeth Metcalf
0 Emocence R Correia
0 Frederick W Andrews

BROOK

15 Mrs Jane Carr
32 Henry Littler
32 William Green
109 Cleophis Deslandes
109 Frank X Verranault
109 Joseph H Fredette
109 Joseph Jette
161 Thomas C Coates
161 John T Stott
161 Joseph W Davenport
178 Frank Cadieux
178 William Malone
178 Thomas Davis
202 James W Ashworth
202 Honore Martel
202 William Scott
206 Samuel Thompson
206 Daniel Dolan
206 Thomas Salisbury
209 Jules Blouin
210 Ludger Gervais

Brook—con
229 Colin Gleason
299 Fred Farnsworth

BROWNELL

204 Nils Olson
204 John T Carter
204 Benjamin F King Jr
205 Herbert A Braman
210 William Bell
213 Hormidas J Fredette
218 Hugh L Donaghy
219 Thomas B Ryan
220 George Elmer Taylor
220 Ralph A Jennings
223 Francisco V Andrada
226 Joseph S Figueido
227 Antonio C de Mora
241 James E Danzell
245 Mrs Elizabeth Cleary
246 Edward P Kirivin
246 Mrs Elizabeth Ryan
252 Edward L Rogers

BULLARD

5 Samuel D Martin
5 Vincenzo Paratore
5 Mrs Phebe Doucette
9 Alphonse LeBoeuf
9 Frank Wegniak
9 Edmont Hodkowski
10 Edward Bouthillette
10 Morris Wladinsky
10 Harry Yerovitz
12 Alfred Belanger
12 Enoch Pigeon
15 John Kuthan
15 Paul Bittner
15 Charles Blechinger
16 Philias LaPlante
16 Alfred Adamsky
16 Thomas Christo
17 Manuel Fernandes
17 Antone Gonsalves
17 Mrs Rose Mello
17 Antone Soares
18 Hormidas Belisle
18 Arthur Bessette
19 John Gomes
20 Evangelist Casavant
21 Joseph Kobeck
21 Michael Belohlarvek
21 Frank Kral
22 Cyprien Rousseau
22 Francis Fahey
26 Louis Trudel
26 Evangelist Casavant
26 Honoreus Meunier
27 Manuel Medeiros
27 James Dumas
27 Mrs Rose Simoneau
27 Adelard Fleury
27 Montaque Sutcliffe
27 Mrs Clara Couture
29 Henry Maher
29 Emanuel Martel
29 Frank Millette
31 Anselme Boudreau
31 Aristide C W Gelinas
31 Alphee Tetreault
31 Arthur Tetreault
31 Annie Morgan
33 Ovila T Brun
34 Mrs Catherine A Willey
34 Paul Moreau
34 George Turcotte
35 Mrs Malvina Arcand
37 Octave Pothier
37 John Surprenant
37 Oliver Monville
37 Pierre Tremblay
38 Clement Ouillette
38 Joseph Boucher
38 Dennis Leger
40 Joseph M Desrosiers
40 Oliver Bibeau
40 Pierre Bibeau
54 Ernest E Couture
54 Aime Gelinas
54 Joseph E Landry
54 Aime Giguere
54 Pierre Landry
58 Delphis Rondeau
59 Pierre Duchene
59 Mrs Delima Ouillette
59 Henry Whittaker
59 Ernest Villandre
60 Wilfred L Rainville
60 Peter S Rainville
60 Joseph Bois
60 Alphonse Richard
61 Mrs Virginia Beaulieu
61 Amedee Tetreault
61 Arthur Ratte
61 Joseph A Boucher
61 Samuel Manville
64 F Xavier Turgeon
64 Mrs Emerance Morin
64 Mrs Catherine Pyne
77 Adonai Benjamin
77 Ulric Vincent
79 Joseph Lebeau
79 Ephraim Dextraze
81 Jean A Forand
85 Flavien Hamel
87 Aristide C W Gelinas
87 Oscar C Goddu
87 Louis Marchessault
91 Arthur Robitaille

91 Antoine Marion
91 Arthur Coulombe
91 David Charest
95 Stanislas Vigneault
101 Zepherine I Peloquin
101 Elie Racicot
101 Henry D Richards
105 Charles Gautreault
105 Antone J Morris
105 Vincent St Dennis
109 Antoine Brun
109 Henry Belisle
109 Arthur Garry
109 Arthur Robida
113 Hector Garceau
115 Philip Gingras
115 Charles Lavalle
115 James Carriere
115½ Mrs Paulina Gaeng
115½ Edward Bessette
115½ Exlard Desjardins
115½ Achille Laverdiere
115½ Edward Forbes
115½ Alfred Carrier
117 Edward Valliere
117 Mrs Lavina Demers
117 George Chausse
119 Raymond Jansen
126 John W Riley
126 John B Fahey
131 Geremie Lortie
131 Theodore Fortier
131 Norbet Boule
132 Joseph Lizotte
132 Mrs Olivina LaPlante
132 Joseph Lamothe
132 August Clermont
132 Albert Blanchette
132 Joseph Niedzwiechi
132 Joseph LeBlanc
133 William Thompson
133 Thomas Summer
133 Frank Yanacek
135 William H Fenton
135 Percy Austin
135 Joseph Walsh
136 Edward Ossibach
136 Mrs Isabelle Nicholson
136 Joseph H Bibby
139 Frederick J Hodson
139 William H Fletcher
139 Emile Fortin
140 Treffle Messier
140 Fred Pearson
140 Michael Moran
141 Fred LeBlanc
141 William Jamba
141 Cleophas R Loiseau
142 George J Shaw
142 Robert Duckworth
145 Theodore Rondeau
145 Mrs Mary Richard
145 Isaie Boucher
146 Joseph Nolin
146 Antone Kalish
147 James W Millward
147 Mrs Agnes Morin
149 George Brun
149 Charles I LeBlanc

BULLOCK

7 Frank Duffy
17 William Leary
18 Mrs Spencer Ryan
18 John C Hawes
22 Mrs Catherine Roach
22 Katharyn Foley
22 Carl F Wetzel
26 George H Whittaker
26 Mrs Nellie Terry
28 M Clarence Nunes
29 Edward E Manchester
30 Thomas Bullen
34 Fielding H Walsh
37 Thomas Hargraves
39 Andrew F Nichols
39 George W Wilber
142 Harmedos Charpentier

BUTLER

0 Matthew Beanland
40 Mrs Catherine A Borden
51 Irving A Chace
74 Mrs Daniel B Leonard
81 Edgar M Almy
89 Alfred D Bourbo
104 William Bond
105 Mrs Walter S Howland
107 Mrs Janet B Haigh
115 Enoch Mullins
117 Arthur H Mather
162 Albert Steffin
171 Hatton Langshaw

BUTTONWOOD

15 Bernard C Feenan
17 Franklin O Pierce
21 Frank B Kirby
25 Hiram F Sparrow
27 Clifford N Ricketson
29 Warren Tattersall
30 James S Cooke
31 Joseph Adshead
35 William Jones
35 Dr T P Ernest Greene
36 G L Rau

Buttonwood—con
37 Fred A Blossom
38 Albert J Bernard
39 Walter I Hamilton

CAMPBELL

5 George Kamel
5 Abraham Howland
5r Alfred G Mitchell
5r Mrs Eliza Lavoie
7 Mrs Bridget Calnan
9 James H Matthews
9 Hormidas Levesque
10 Mrs Josephine Garrow
10 Fred Enos
10 George Parris
10 Mrs Josephine Garrow
15 Edgar W Darling
17 Dr Fred C Graves
17 Harry C Jenney
18 Mrs Elizabeth S Swift
37 Helen L Stetson
37 H Louise Crocker
38 Mrs Mary Price
41 William A Dunbar
42 Joseph A Taber
42 William H Gidley
46 Jane M Gardner
53 Joseph F Donahue
54 Henry T Corson
55 George Schuler
56 Howard N Dexter
56 Mrs Phoebe C Dexter
57 Walter S Brown
57 Mrs Mary A Thacher
58 Misses Brown
59 Henry S Hutchinson
62 Henry C Hathaway
75 E M Cushman
75 Mrs Joanna Cushman
78 Robert H Woodland
79 George M Conant
85 George Hough
85 Eugene W Lamb
87 James E Moore
89 James L Hathaway
92 Alonzo C Blossom
94 Charles Blossom
98 Anderson H Swift
100 Charles A Cook
101 Mrs Matilda Reed
101 George E Turner
109 Mrs Mary Platt
109 Charles A Howe
111 Ferdinand S Read
113 Frank E Colyar
113 Mrs Agnes Corey
115 Charles E Hewitt
115 Andrew L Estes
117 George N Pitman
123 George H Clark Jr
123 Charles W Rogers
124 George L Howland
125 Samuel R Gay
125 Jeremiah P McCarthy
126 William Salter
126 John S Silva
128 Lawrence S Brightman
128 Horace S Chase
136 Franklin M Dammon
137 Charles G Taber
138 Annie W Carsly
138 Herbert F Butler
139 William T Luce
144 Edmund F Drew
144 Hiram C Tripp
144 Thomas E Luce
145 John W Tavis
145 William V Ripley
151 Mrs Elizabeth Drew
151 Mrs Carrie M Townsend
155 Mrs Mahala S T Negus
156 Mrs Louisa C Wood
161 Joseph Schabel
161 Ambrose Spicer
162 Ella F Braley
162 David F Ritchie
163 Mrs Harriet S Atwood
163 Mrs Amy A Bloomfield
166 Albert P White
168 Mrs Clara H Tinkham
169 Mrs Elsie Liedholm
170 John A French
171 Isabel Davis
171 Mrs Maria L Howland
173 Benjamin Howard
173 Ernest R Stone
183 William J Knox
184 John F Judge
189 Benton Colbert
190 David Jennings
191 Edwin Shaw
197 J Willis Jepson

CANNON

3 John Moniz
3½ James A Wiley
3½ Louis de Almeida
8 John Gracia
8 Joseph Caimbra
8 Joseph F Fortes
9 Max Goldstein
9 Henry Lomba
12 Theophilus Britto

12 Mrs Mary Costa
12 Samuel Ginsburg
13 George M Hill
14 Mrs Nellie Perry
14½ Peter Lopes
14½ Domingo Alves
15 Mrs Julia Veeney
15 William Morgan
15½ Joseph L Frates
16 Manuel Francisco
17 David Miller
17 Mrs Mary Perry
18 Christiano Santo
18 Ceasar Lopes
18 Mrs Lottie Gonsalves
19 Margaret L Marr
25 Mrs Mary E Richardson
25 William Bach
27 Mrs Mary Ann Duarte
27 Mrs Minnie Heroo
27 Mrs Emilin G Calda
27 Mrs Marion R Leighton

CAPITOL

41 Joseph Fregeau
73 Hermengilde Lamoureux
73 Hermengilde Lafrenais

CEDAR

18 Rev Dennis Scott
22 Annie D Wood
23 William J Boyle
23 James Gilmour
24 Jeremiah L Luce
24 Willis H Coggeshall
25 John G Dantsizen
27 Timothy J Sullivan
29 Albert Whitehead
29 James J O'Brien
33 James Irwin
33 Paul A Gast
35 Frank H Swift
35 Frederick A Treadup
36 George McEwen
36 Mrs Sarah W Balloch
38 Mrs Gertrude M Getchell
38 George H Goff
39 William C Squires
43 Clifton F Tripp
43 Mrs Lizzie A Andrews
48 Nellie Jenkins
48 Mary Williams
50 Mrs Martha J James
52 Robert H Houtman
53 Mrs Lavinia Jones
53 William E Nooth
67 William Ferguson
68 Mrs J Arthur Piper
71 Freeman Valentine
71 John W Carter
75 Philip G Howland
75 Joseph A Sylvia
76 Edward Carter
76 Frederick A Abbott
79 Fred Lincourt
80 Walter Wainer
80 John H P Warefield
80 Charles Timber
80 Garrison L Oliver
81 James G Gidley
82 James Solomon
82 Thomas Deshon
82 Walter D Pell
83 Mrs Emma L Freedom
96 Mrs Susannah Henderson
96 Herbert King
101 Mary J Wilson
101 Amos L Wilson
101 Mrs Sarah Goff
106 Mrs Angelin C Parker
107 George T Smith
107 Robert C Munroe
108 John T Mehame
110 John K H Offley
110 Mrs Grace Ross
111 John LeClair
111 Tobias Gross
114 Florence E Cook
114 Isaac R Chumack
115 Mrs Rose M Frawley
117 Frederick C Lemunyon
117 Mrs Ruth A Gifford
120 Edward D Hayden
121 William Lloyd
121 Thomas H Monjohn
123 William York
123 Fred E Oliver
124 Charles Fleetwood
127 John J Holmes
127 Mrs Susan A Peckham
128 Lewis E Bryan
129 Mrs Sarah F Howland
132 George M Sprott
133 Mrs Carrie E Tripp
132 John Puerwinski
133 Mrs Laura Johnson
136 Walter F Wiggins
136 Mrs Carrie E Howland
141 Mrs Anna D Perkins
141 Ulysses G Brownell
143 Edgar F Johnson
143 William W Lewis
144 Agnes G Reilly
146 Michael McCabe
147 George A Soule
148 William F Hathaway
151 Frank W Chace
151 James Thompson

Cedar—con
152 Isaiah C Dade
155 Moses Williams
155 John C Guinn
156 Mrs Elizabeth W Scarborough
157 Albert J Johnson
160 Manuel A Concaicao
167 Mrs Emma Miller
171 Richard H Cook Jr
171 Duncan Belboda
171 Richard H Cook
171 James Harper
173 Mrs Matilda J Payne
173 Fred Arthur
174 Frank W Cannon
174 Alphonse F Potvin
176 Edward M Kelley
177 William B Ellis
178 Fred G Whitty
185 Wallace L Taber
185 James Borden
187 Edward J Cunningham
191 William L G Brown
192 John D Taber
193 Percy Gilmore
197 Clarence Borden
197 Charles F Brown
198 Mrs Mary E Morancy
198 Earl Shumway
199 Clarence W B Sykes
201 Mrs Eliza M Bliss
201 James B Manchester
202 Charles J Becker
204 Mrs Sarah E Harper
204 Columbia A Wilkins
211 William C Ashley
214 Mrs Annie E Young
216 William B Morrill
217 Alexander H Hillman
219 George C Richardson
225 Charles H Gooding Jr
227 Mrs Sarah E Bowen
229 Louis E Bowen
233 Mrs Rhodo E Peckham
238 Mrs Kathleen C M Durfee
239 Harry B Johnson
239 Moses C Drew
245 Isabella Luscomb
246 Manuel Andrada
248 Thomas W Lawrence
258 George F Wood
269 Arthur H Borden
273 Nelson P Spellman
273 Daniel F Murphy
276 Erwin H Chamberlain
278 John R Barrett
279 Edgar B Gifford
280 Louis P Spencer
280 Marion S Maxcy
280 Marvin Maxie
282 Albert E Wilkinson
283 Joshua B Bowman
283 Leonard H Morse Jr
285 Francis A Murphy
285 Samuel Lowe
286 Jesse M Macomber
286 Solomon L Rich
287 Ellen Devaney
287 John H Isherwood
290 Mrs Eva Hellyer
290 Thomas E Simmons
294 Stephen S Weeks
294 Thomas P Murray
295 James McLean
295 Patrick Leonard
297 William L Kelley
297 John Ross
298 Robert E Wood
298 Joseph E Jaques
300 Daniel E J Cleary
300 Mrs Susan Corbett
301 Thomas Cashman
301 Ephraim L Studley
303 Schuyler C Cornell
303 Misses Smith
304 Jeremiah Barry
304 Andrew Murphy
305 Mrs Bridget O'Brien
305 Laura M Richardson
319 John Cottans
319 George H Bonner
321 William W Brownell
321 Mrs Ethel Haskell
322 Hormidas Roberts
323 Henry D Young
323 George W Lapham
324 Anna G Spinney
324 Clarissa C Glasse
324 Mrs Amy A Grinnell
325 Thomas A Potter
325 Frank Perry
326 Mrs Ann J Ritchie
327 George P Reed Jr
327 Merton E Bennett
328 Charles A Tripp
328 Peter F Sullivan
329 Cyrus T Lawrence
330 Joseph P Doyle
330 Isaac N Sowle
331 Mrs Elizabeth Butts
331 Sherod M Brownell
332 Thomas A Murphy
332 Thomas F Dwyer
334 Mrs Bridget McDonnell
335 Sarah J Tynan

337 Charles H Holden
338 Alanson R Washburn
340 John Y Brightman
341 George Wishart
342 Mrs Almira T Tripp
343 Mrs Susie Palmer
343 Southward P Negus
344 Charles F Athearn
344 Mrs Annie L Francis
346 Mrs Emma J Tilden
350 George W Guard
350 Thomas P Pickett
355 Arthur O York
355 John E Riley
358 Mrs Sarah Hoye
358 James McDermott
360 Charles W McDermott
360 Thomas McNulty
361 Ernest A Bennett
363 George A Krumbholz
366 Mrs S Ella Card
370 Bradley D Goldthwait
370 Frank F Gifford
375 Dennis Lyons
375 Mrs Elizabeth G Ashley
378 Timothy Sullivan
379 Mrs Catherine Kelly
379 John Lowney
382 Walter H Athearn
382 Kennedy Brown
383 Samuel A Simmons
383 James B Archer
386 Robert Hall
389 Lewis Gifford
390 James Hickey
394 William H Tabele
394 Patrick H Sullivan
395 George O Hathaway
397 Frank Victoria
397 William H Gifford
400 Edward E Dalrymple
402 Winfred R Washburn
407 Thomas Eccle
408 John P Burke
408 Louis C Dunham
410 William N Arnett
410 Mrs Mary E Kent
411 William E Hathaway
411 Mrs Mary C Willis
412 Tully C Smith
413 George L Chase
413 William H Peets
414 Thomas Hilton
415 James Kenney

CEDAR GROVE

16 William Coury
23 Adelon Tetreault
104 Joseph Beausoleil
104 Joseph Correia
104 Mrs Victoria Poitras
108 Antone Kubacki
108 John Ogarra
108 Jose Linhares
108 Antonio Pechoto
115 Joseph Babola
115 Stanislau Gwozdz
119 John Wnok
126 Samuel Thmous
126 Levi Gaudette
126 Charles Toundas
126 Mania Wischnietzki
126r Ugrieh Suh
126r Charles Gendron
131 Theodore Carl
131 Anna Graham
131 Fred Smith
132 B Moses Bloom
132 Rabbi Isaac Minsky
132 Adam Rupka
137 Selma Benzel
137 Annie Oullery
138 Oliver Lantain
138 Absalom Brousseau
141 Napoleon Martin
141 John Barry
154 Arthias Langlois
154 Armas Langlois
154 Ulderic Demers
154 Arthur J Langlois
154 Jean Trahan
154 Theodore Levesque
154 Lemina Sossenville
156 James Price
157 Konstanty F Strazpek
159 Florien Kataszewski
159 Morris Lekovski
162 Philemon Jesus
162 Stanistnow Simark
162r Manuel Cabral
162r Joseph Gracial
162r John Polan
164 Nelson Normandin
164 Moise Brouillette
164 Joseph Jalbert
164 Joseph Marchessault
165 Adam Zielenski
167 Frank Normandin
167 Hugh J Hackett
176 Peter Thomas
176 Olive LeBeau
180 Stanislaw Kiviatkowski
180 Karimiesi Woayka
180 Annie Baba
180 John Babola

Cedar Grove—con
180 Mrs Bar Mishar
184 Joseph Sieckoski
194 Abraham Edlin
200 Sydney C Maxcy
201 George McConville
201 Mrs Mary Finch
201 Ralph Butterfield
203 Edward McConville
206 Joseph Gauthier
206 Paul Mailloux
208 Prosper Mailloux
208 Ralph Brindle
208 William Mailloux
208 Nelson Suprenant
209 John Murphy
210 Frank Swender
211 Stanislau Alberski
211 Mamert Anthony
212 Michael Pyteraf
212 Joseph Pokopek
216 B Joseph
217 Said Dugally
217 George Parris
221 Mrs Annie Prigoda
221 Solomon Patnaude
247 Charles Lewin
247 Thomas F Lewin
247 Dora Clark
253 James Parkinson
253 Joseph Favreau
254 Napoleon Bessette
254 Richard Green
254 Spencer Green
254 Armand C Poirier
256 John E Perrin
256 William Kearney
257 Mrs Mary M Sullivan
258 Victoria Arcand
258 Joseph Ulric
258 Oscar Harpin
258 Nellie Archaud
274 Mrs Nellie Brinan
274 Domenico Girardo
275 Bertie W Besse
275 Jennie Murphy
275 James Murphy
279 John Blackburn
279 John Colbert
279 Robert Blackburn
279r William Blackburn
280 Martin Keefe
280 Tirsera Vincent
280 Wolf Goldforb
280r Robert McGuire
284 Albion E Bochman
284 Frank Lenhart
284 Mrs Mary Schiebel
288 Arthur Gailbois
288 Victor Barriteau
288 Panteleon Levesque
288 David Allard
288r Henry Belisle
288r Thomas P Haydock
292 Call Kellie
292 Mrs Sadie Sobil
292 Simon Cassis
292 James Houghton
292 Frank Bisheau
296 David Wildman
296 Martin J Dwyer
296 John Sullivan
297r Charles L Leavitt
300 Phebe Keehn
300 Joseph Barselou
324 Domina Rouillier
324 Thomas J Quinn
324 Esther Ann Sparks
324 Jenny Alexander
324 John J Crudden
324 John Woolner
330 John H Boyle
330 Israel Cadieux
330r Mrs Isabelle Godwin
344 Mrs Annie M Sullivan
344 George Long
344 Patrick H Sulivan
346 Manuel B Sylvia
346 Felix Beaudry
350 Joseph Poncelet
350 Mrs Mary Clare
356 William C Gilmore
356 James Gill
366 Mrs Jane Poncelet
373 Mrs Alice Butler
373 Joseph H Bannister
383 Thomas F Hurley
383 John W Boardman
383 Margaret Boardman
396 Manuel Costa
397 Morris H Lipson
399 Jeremiah Shaughnessy
399 Mrs Mary E Slater
399 John H Cahill
404 Louis Choquette

CENTRAL AVENUE

16 Zacharie Houle
16 Antonio Lopes
20 Philebert Martin
148 George Isabell
148 A Donat Labrie
149 Hiram E Raymond
0 Felix Blanchard
158 Wright Chadwick
158 Philias Audette
158 Vital Barsalou

158 Wiliam Whittam
158 William Shaw
158 Robert E Sherman
0 Joseph Boucher
0 Philias Blanchard

CENTRE

21 Edward M Svendsen

CHANCERY

25 Mrs Clara Hicks
31 Joseph T Murphy
36 Mrs Cordelia M Turner
47 Robert A Goss
48 Thomas P Carroll
49 Joseph Veria
49 John P Shields
50 Edward Lyons
61 Mrs Ellen Moran
62 Martin Nokelki
62 Samuel L Doran
63 Allen W Sampson
63 Charles W Christopher
67 Albert F Brownell
67 George W Sampson
68 Clarence Smith
68 Mrs Mary M Carr
71 Mrs Adele Vandenbossche
72 Mrs Frida Carlson
74 Mrs Florence Lowe
77 William Higgins
77 Wilham H Dyer
78 William Donaghy
81 John Q A Bumpus
82 Edward Dutton
82 William T Marshall
84 Andrew Wilde
85 Stephen D Pierce Jr
86 George W Crapo
88 Charles L Sylvia
88 Clarence W Reed
89 Mrs Laura A Ticehurst
89 Mrs Hannah M Hadley
103 Mrs Rebecca B Tripp
103 Lucy A Mather
107 Charles H Coxen
114 Misses McAfee
115 George W Gay
116 Walter R Townsend
117 Isaac C Hicks
118 Clarence H Pierce
119 William E Pierce
142 Carlos T Pina
142 Peter J Houtman
144 Frank Vanzini
150 Edward J Begley
150 Michael Finnerty
152 David H Curtis
157 Fred C Hinds
157 John E W Craig
162 John S Riley
170 William A Dow
170 Philip A Taber
178 Constantine M Sylvia
182 Arthur C Spooner
184 John J Hennessey
187 George T Schuler
187 Theodore P Crowell
188 Arthur J Parry
189 Mrs Ellen Flaherty
191 Joseph S Manning
191 Edward B Robinson
192 Mrs Ida M Howland
192 Catherine McCarthy
193 Joseph L Enos
193 Felix Kane
194 Tanjore T Henry
194 John C Healy
205 Michael J Murray
207 Frank B Chubbuck
210 Addie Anderson
213 Mrs Lydia A Perry
213 Georgiana Sylvia
213 Daniel Wilson
219 B Sumner Shaw
223 Oliver R Taber
223 George W Taber
224 Rhoda A Cobb
226 Richard F Burke
227 Emily F Manchester
227 Mrs Lydia M Tripp
228 Charles E Hoard
235 Hiram I Tilghman
238 Mrs Mary A Tilghman
239 Mrs Emily J Blackwell
240 Leon Lake
240 Thomas R Keach
242 Augustus D Piper
242 William Taylor
243 Aaron Timber
248 William M Fabio
249 Edward J Costello
256 Mrs Caroline E Wright
299 Walter J Gaetz
299 Joseph C Forbes
306 Arthur L Devoll
315 Ransom Frederic
367 Mrs Catherine Higgins
371 John P Buckley
373 Truman A Galley
404 Daniel Boyle
408 Mrs Margaret Ryan
411 Mrs Abbie Ross
415 Robert B Sabins

Chancery—con

419 Patrick Murphy
426 Mrs Laura Marshall
427 Patrick Cannavan
428 Frank M Jenkins
443 Edward E Shaw
445 Hatton Brindle
445 Mrs Celia Hathaway
445 Charles M Mosher
446 Mrs Lydia A Tripp
446 Frank H Landers
456 David T Mendell
459 Timothy J Burns
461 Herbert H Chandler
463 John W Grew
465 Marshall L Cowen

CHESTNUT

6 Leland W Thurston
6 Abraham Epstein
11 Benjamin Jones
11 Leander Williston
15 Jesse F Barlow
17 Charles E Davis
17 William Gifford
21 Jesse Allen
25 Mrs Catherine Hubbard
27 Howard T Smith
27 Alfred E Smith
30 Mrs Julia R Pierce
30 Mrs Julia A Hunt
35 James P Wilde
39 William F Manchester
40 Rev James L Bartholomew
44 Eugene H Sullivan
44 Mrs Emma B Sisson
45 Harvey H Webber
47 Charles W H Potter
47 Fred F Dumas
53 Alfred G Alley Jr
54 Philip R Shaw
54 James E Budlong
55 Egbert G Bullard
59 Richmond L Wilcox
60 Benjamin Lawton
60 William H Pitman
61 Mrs Eva J Griffin
64 Mrs Ella Wright
65 **Rev Frank H Peters**
65 **William J Cochrane**
69 Louis E Richardson
69 Mrs Susan A Jenney
74 William T Laughlin
75 David B Folger
78 John A Ruggles
79 George E Allen
81 Joseph B Wing
82 Sarah S Baker
87 Herbert K Haskins
89 Charles S Howland
95 Elmore P Haskins
95 Mrs Mary F Delano
96 Thatcher B Crocker
100 William Smith
101 Herbert L Fisher
101 James S Kelley Jr
103 John F Marley
103 Robert T Lawton
106 Arthur Sharples
106 Lysander W Davis
107 William Farr
109 Otis L Hitch
116 Mrs G Jenney
120 Mrs Etta H Shaw
120 Thomas H Forbes
126 Nelson T Fuller
127 Clarence A Wheaton
127 Arthur C Wheaton
130 Mrs Elizabeth E Frasier
130 Annie F Smith
131 Leroy G Tripp
131 George A Gardner
133 Charles F Glass
133 William R Geddis
134 John J McAuliffe
135 Fred G Douglass
135 Edgar M Bennett
136 Edward F Allen
136 Eunice S Church
137 Obed N Swift
137 Mrs Asha Maxfield
139 George E Luscomb
139 Arthur S Briggs
141 Charles P Emerson
141 Mrs A E Heap
145 Sarah Thompson
154 Frederick A Mickell
154 Susan E Hathaway
154 Mary F Brown
154 Mary Crowell
156 Edwin R King
164 Patrick J Mahoney
166 Charles F Davis
186 John O'Brien
186 Patrick J Calnan
197 Richard J Malyan
197 George Handy
203 Richmond J Tripp
206 Joseph N Pineault
206 Mrs M Laura Pineault
209 Charles F Watkins
210 Clifton N Hatch
211 Michael Finn
211 Charles M Coffman
213 Eugene H Sullivan
213 James F Hutchinson
235 Charles S Sawyer

238 Samuel Herstoff
238 Emory W Wallace
239 Peter F Dufficy
239 William S Jordan
240 Peleg H S W Allen
241 Leroy G Weston
242 Joseph C Richard
243 Alonzo F Reynolds
244 Samuel T Eldridge
245 Charles A V Terry
248 Edmund Hindle
248 Richard Cowell
249 Dr William Sheehy
250 Charles A Morrison
251 Samuel Ward
252 Joseph L Crowley
253 William H Young
254 Benjamin Whittaker
255 Charles Newman Jr
256 Dennis J Salmon
257 Conrad Drexler
258 Fred Sharples
260 Beecher Burns

CHURCH

57 Francis R Ward
61 Walter Carr
65 Edouard Auger
69 Valentine Alletag
74 Louis P Libby
74 James Kennedy
81 Wenzel Koerber
85 John P Palmer
94 Joseph Whalley
96 Wright Bolton
141 John B Francis
141 John Ouillette
141 Daniel Calnan
141 Franklin Kanuse
144 Mrs Ann Barns
144 Arthur B Magnant
156 Henry Collette
156 William A Walsh
156 Charles Moore
188 Mrs Kate McGoff
190 Zofia Gorka
206 Alexis Lussier
207 Joseph England
211 Oliver Dupont
211 Zepherin Beauregard
211 Zephio Goudreau
215 Romuald Roy
219 Thomas Carr
220 Joseph Desmarais
0 Norbet Davignon
0 Frank Patnaud
0 Ambrose Trudelle

CLARA

126 John Lapre
126 Joseph Laprie
0 James Gleason

CLARK

1 John O Adams
1 Edward O'Hara
1 Joseph M La Brie
1 George Demers
3 Mrs Hugh Finlan
3 Thomas Connell
4 Maragret Mahoney
4 Damina Liberty
5 Egnarte Kashinski
7 Thomas Handy
8 Thomas O'Brien
8r Michael Flannery
11 Mrs Eleanor Lang
11 Stanislaus Kansinski
11 Joseph P Mathieu
12 Frank McMahon
12 John Brogden
12 William Flanagan
16 Lester Thornton
16 Benjamin Goyette
17 Alphonse Chauvin
17 Alphonse Tardif
18 John Glaser
18 Mrs John Hirschman
24 Napoleon Landry
24 John Roy
27 Joseph J Collins
27 Hugh J Collins
27 Mrs Sarah Newsham
28 Mrs Joanna Balderson
29 John McCarthy
29 Mary Sheehan
30 John Cocker
30 Hartley Smith
32 Mrs Flora Gonsalves
32 John Donovan
32 Patrick J Burke
50 John J Doherty
56 John Fernandes
56 Mrs Octave Brisson
56 Mrs Malvina Jalbert
56r Bernard M Ormonde
56r Manuel Enos
56r Orace Roman
59 Mrs Francois Bouchard
59 Sinai Boucher
59 Edward Butler
63 Morris Polonsky
63 James O'Hare
63 Mrs Ellen O'Leary
67 John Beaudray

Clark—con
67 Andrew Munds
67 Michael Moran
75 Arthur McDonald
75 Conrad Blecha
75 John Nicklas
75 John H Parker
76 William Beserosky
78 Hyman Gerstein
78 Simon Beserosky
79 Edward Laferriere
79 Alfred M Bessette
80 Harry Whitehead
80 Misses Yates
80 Thomas Castle
86 Rufus F Morgan
86 Alexander Green
90 Abraham Duxbury
90 James Stewart
90 Mrs Isobel Wylie
94 John Moran
94 Robert Brody
96 James H Mahoney
98 Elton B Alger
98 Mrs Mary M Wall
100 Bridget Shea
100 Robert Bessett
100 James S McGrath
109 William T Morgan
110 Mrs Anna E Therien
111 Hyman Ramanon
111 Mrs Margaret A Tupper
111 John W Cutting
111 James W Calverley
112 John Flynn
112 William Midgley
113 William Boyle
113 John Hurst
114 Nathan Aisenstat
116 Hymen Mendelson
116 John Hartley
117 Gilbert Bouchard
120 Arthur X Vient
120 James J Wall
121 Hugh A Dugan
122 Harry Amey
125 Thomas J Taft
128 Albert Ashton
128 Aaron Sharples
128 Ralph Barber
129 William Gaschka
129 Lawrence J Durant
129 Thomas S Findlay
131 James MacQuarrie
132 Ernest Robinson
133 Alex A Petit
140 Lawrence Cronin
140 James F Crosson

CLAY

3 William E York
5 Julius C Sylvia
7 Irving H Jenney
8 James H Sullivan
10 Mrs Lydia C Chase
10 Edward J Hodson
12 Mrs Mary Clarke
14 Arthur C Davis
15 Mrs Phebe Souza
15 **Manuel F** Perry
15 Theodore J Sylvia
16 Frank A Fernandes
16 William B Gates
16 Charles Goodman

CLEVELAND

7 Mrs Marie R V Gilbert
7 Timothy Gorton
7 Harry Preston
8 James Sylvia
9 William St Marie
9 Joseph Horn
10 Fred F Freitas
10 Antoine Morin
10 William McCormick
11 Aime Peloquin
12 George Kershaw
12 George Hurst
12 James W Newton
12 John Scholes
12 Joseph Prevost
12 Gustave Bourgon
13 William Heaton
14 Richard Hodson
14 Herbert Conway
14 William Pilling
15 Manuel R Dutra
15 Duke Halliwell
15 John Holmes
16 Charles Ratcliff
18 James Gauthier
18 Thomas Prescott
18 George T Eccles
19 Mrs Elizabeth A Gardner
19 John Mendoza
22 Richard Margeson
23 Joseph Hartley
23 John Robinson
23 Paul Permette
25 Thomas Park
26 John P Jackson
26 John Shuttleworth
26 Albert Spencer
27 James Howarth
27 Mrs Sarah Dyson
27 Joseph Parkinson
27 Mrs Mary Folkes
28 Joseph Provost
28 John Haydock

28 Joseph Cusson
28 Anton Schobek
31 Charles Guimont
31 John T Tonge
41 Joseph Peter
43 Albert Bernard

CLIFFORD

3 Charles H Sharples
55 Arthur Masse
59 Thomas Grime
69 Alfred W Stolle
69 Alfred Trahan
84 Moise Biron
86 John Taylor
86 Mrs Olivina Handfield
86 Joseph Rathe
86 Cecil Paradis
86 Philias Fortin
86 Calix Belliveau
87 Ademar Manny
87 Lewis Jacob
87 John Lerch
87 John Turner
87 Joseph Lorek
100 John Hargraves
100 Joseph Marsh
100 Chester Eldridge
103 Mrs Damase Houle
156 Ludger Caron Jr
174 George Woodhouse
174 Joseph Bittar
174 Gustaf Lundin
0 John J Lawrence
0 Chryostone Gallant
0 Antone Lawrence
205 Alphonse Spirlet
226 Louis Turner

CLINTON

29 Jireh Swift Jr
31 Ida M Eliot
57 William B Hinckley
63 George S Perry
65 Miss Pattv Wilcox
67 John W Brennan
77 A W Hadley
98 R Manning Gibbs
99 Ernest V Alley
105 Misses Cleveland
109 Francis J Denby
122 Williston H Collins
123 Alfred S James
129 Thomas W Cook
130 Charles H Lobdell
133 Arthur H Chace
136 George H Hedge
139 Frank L Hoxie
143 John E Donovan
145 Benjamin C Tripp
153 Annie M Washburn
162 Harriet W Whiting
163 George Hibbard
163 John E Hibbard
166 Carl J Olsson
190 Joseph C Kennelty
194 Charles K Eldredge
198 William G Welch
199 Firman Durant
202 C Clifford Peirce
203 Frank E Macy
349 Joseph H Handford
350 Asa L H Allen

CLINTON PLACE

1 Otis Seabury Cook
2 James L Humphrey Jr
3 Edgar R Lewis
4 Albert R Pierce
5 Albert W Holmes
6 Frank A Cummings

CLOVER

27 Paul T Cieurzo
29 Joseph Hardy
31 Peter Hildman
33 William E Wood

COFFIN

8 Mrs Mary Silva

COFFIN AVENUE

6 Frank Glosh
10 Mrs Emma Webber
67 Zenon Lafleur
67 Joseph Duffy
97 Calixte Breault
97 Manuel Souza
97 Luca T Allain
101 Maximillian Le Blanc
101 George Le Blanc
101 Joseph Roy
103 Joseph C Jansen
107 Zotique Quintin
107 Mederic Roberge
107 Henry Christie
107 Mrs Jane Daigle
107 Norbet Guillet
121 Edmund Therien
127 Arthur Godin
127 Moise Langlois
137 Frank Enos
137 Manuel Mello
139 Joaquim Soares

Coffin av—con
139 Frank J Morrice
139 Annie Maria
143 Manuel Teixeira
143 Mrs Rose Rioux
143 Antone Praeda
143 Manuel L Correio
143 Antonio Morris
143 Ambrose Shappy
143 Manuel C Tavares
151 Arthur Tetreault
151 Concetto V Romeo
157 Antonio Del Pazzo
157 Vincenzo Del Pazzo
157 Antonio Luminiello
157 John Scala
171 Louis Langevin
171 David Cormier
171 Maxim Cormier
171 Omer Leroux
171 Clement Cormier
172 Isaac Arsenault
176 John W Quirk
176 Clinton I Walker
180 Mrs Saviah C Tripp
181 Manuel Lorenz
181 Joao V Fagundes
183 Joseph Greaves
183 Elizabeth Entwistle
183 John Thompson
184 Charles J Francis
188 Patrick MacKenzie
188 Reuben Robinson
190 Edmond Lapierre
190 Joseph Morin
190 Thomas Morin
193 William E Cleary
193 James Brown
194 Joseph A Bettencourt
200 Gustaf A Schneider
201 Jeffrey W P LeBlanc
203 Frank C McCann
203 Margaret McMenamin
204 Joseph Fortune
204 Joseph Mello
204 Antone J Roderiques
207 Joseph Dugas
207 Alfred Gagne
208 Felix St Germain
209 Guilherne A D Andrada
210 Patrick O'Malley
210 George A Schott
211 Mrs Lily Wilson
211 John M Macerel
211 Napoleon Gladu
214 Hormidas Baron
214 Alphe LeBlanc
214 Henry N Seymour
214 Philip Levesque
214 Amedee Caron
214 Delphis Cardinal
215 Thomas W Kelleher
215 Egesipe Giroux
215 Albert W Russell
237 Joseph Richard
237 Victor Pelletier
237 Joseph Foisy
241 Ovila Maranda
241 Oscar Crapeau
241 William Fay
241 James Marsh
250 Mrs Deborah B Davis
250 Roland G Pray
250 Arthur Wilkinson
250 Mrs Deborah B Davis
251 Nazaire Chainay
251 Alphonse Ledoux
252 Robert E Townsend
252 Samuel Wainwright
253 Elzear Fournier
253 Raymond Bourque
254 Bourgoyne Fish
257 Mrs Frances Dunkerley
258 Mrs Alice Sharples
269 Alfred A St Jean
283 Henry Paradis
283 Joseph Prejzner
283 Joseph Czaja
287 Euclide Beauchemin
287 Jules Lague
287 Joseph Breton
287 Israel Letendre
287 Joseph Lamothe
287 Anselme Roy
287 Alfred Comeau
289 Mrs Heloise LeClair
289 Alfred Lefebvre
289 James Lowe
289 Ferdinand St Jacques
289 Donat LeClair
293 Joseph A Holden
293 Mrs Mary A Duxbury
293 Vitalis Quintin
293 Rudolph Savaria
297 Napoleon Tremblay
297 Marjorique L'Etoile
297 Alcide Dupuis
297 Alfred Rawson
297 Austin Tomlinson
297 P Aldege LaCroix
301 Owen Dyer
301 Felix C Fezette
301 Eugene Marchesseault
301 Joseph E Lemieux
311 Ernest E Dupuis
311 Joseph LePage
311 Frank Jepson

311 Joseph Lavelle
311 Clement Benjamin
314 Alphonse J Houde
315 Mrs Ellen Holt
315 Mrs Sarah J Marsh
321 Thomas Winsper
321 James Halsall
322 Thomas Dennett
322 Christian E Moessinger
325 Herbert V Sowle
326 Luc Moquin
326 Hyacinth Gallant
328 J Calvin Bessey
332 William J Grimshaw
336 Samuel Grundy
336 Daniel Henson
340 Daniel Landry
341 John Egan
344 John Berry
344 James E Pratt
344 Mrs Margaret Brittain
345 Alfred P Jackson
348 Joshua Fort
348 Alphonse Reidmann
348 Joshua Fort
349 Arthur Haskell
349 Konrad Lehner
350 William Seddon
350 Lawrence W Coupe
350 Wallace Greenhalgh
350 Emanuel Valecka
353 Charles Nemec
353 Mrs Catherine Nemec
354 Irenee Dionne
354 Vincent Dresner
354 Godfried Herzog
357 Ralph Clegg
357 Alfred Cadieux
358 Paul N Girard
358 Sidney McMullen
358 James O'Neil
362 Joseph LaBella
362 Adolphus Christie
362 Mrs Mary Pollitt
362 John Garvey
362 Walter Dickenson
364 Richard Rigby
364 Mrs Mary L Laflamme
364 Pierre A Lefebvre

COFFIN AVENUE COURT

6 Frank Grosl
8 Fred Palme
8 Helmuth Heuberger
10 John Mello

COGGESHALL

115 William L Jenkins
121 Anthony Domingas
127 Lawrence Gallagher
145 John W Rigby
145 Walter Taylor
145 Arthur Houle
158 Joseph Perry
159 Frank Lemaire
159 Joseph Lemoine
159 Edward J McCann
163 Alidia Norton
163 Mrs Margaret Dunkerley
171 William B Craw
171 Mrs Pauline Bourque
173 Jacintho Costa
173 Joseph Isteva
175 Manuel Amaral
175 Manuel Augusto
175 Jacintho Palmeira
175 Peter Amaral
195 Daniel Medeiros
195 Manuel Medeiros
195 Procopio Borges
197 Louis M Chaves
197 Antone Moniz
197 Joao Frank
201 Joseph Teixeira
201 Joao Carvalho
201 Francisco Mello
201 Joseph Regados
201 Henrique Gomes
201 Amelia Rosa
218 Telesphore Vigneault
219 Julio Souza
219 Joseph Agravea
226 John Borbetski
226 Zwad Ogof
234 Francois Beaulieu
234 Hyman Rocklin
234 Kesler Rocklin
234 Adelaide Angier
237 Manuel Teixeira
237 Joseph Souza
237 John S Cabral
237 Frank Bezerre
243 Simon D Cormier
246 Simon J Portnoy
250 Joseph Courry
250 George Barkett
250 Joseph Abraham
250 James Harris
250 Peter Joseph
251 Wladyslaw Przbyzewski
251 Stephen Barron
251 Michael Kocolinakis
251r Charles Patistas
251r Andrew Munds
253 Solomon Epstein
253 Moses Epstein

Coggeshall—con
258 Nagip Makati
260 John Marr
260 James Wilne
260 Mrs James Kidd
269 Alfred N Rainville
269 Joseph Jussuame
269 William Gannon
269 Eusebe Therrien
270 Folk Levin
270 Mrs Alice Greenhalge
273 Henry Magnant
273 Joseph Magnant
273 Charles H Morrice
276 Mrs Bridget Dunn
276 John Smith
279 Mrs Amelia Lemaire
279 William Goldstein
279 Joseph Lemaire
279 Joseph Abraham
279 Christus Patropoulos
280 William Morris
280 John Rostron
280 Phillip Brownley
286 Thomas Eastwood
286 George E Howarth
286 Robert Thornton
295 John Lord
295 James Cameron
301 Eliza Hanlon
301 George Mulligan
302 Antoine Simas
302 Gilbert Touissant
302 Mrs Milly Groves
304 Joseph Macier
307 Louis Riendeau
307 Louis Lattimore
307 Magloire Lemaire
307 Prosper Lamarche
310 Peter Papaioannon
311 Dr Joseph A Bernier
311 John Gregory
311 Hervie Paradis
314 Manuel Sylvia
314 John Silver
341 Wenzel Kussi
341 William Pell
341 Friolin Zimmerman
351 Mrs Sarah Turner
353 John Lamb
353 James Thornley
355 Charles Gregory
355 Lewis Canos
359 John Johnson
359 Antone Collins
359 Nicolas Collins
359 William Denault
359 Apostelos Kapopovolos
359 Aso Koupar
361 Anthony S Raymond
361 Charles Karelcas
361 Joseph Champegny
363 Pierre Denault
363 John R McVicker
363 Joseph Pelletier
363 Charles Lemaire
363 Eugene R Chausse
369 Mrs Elizabeth Le May
369 Antone Pelnara
369 Mrs Mary Preimoure
369 William Read
369 Antone Santos
379 George Brillion
379 John Nicklas Jr
379 George E Sykes
379 Samuel Hamilton
381 Manuel S Soares
381 Manuel A Souza
407 Louis Benoit
443 Leo Kuntz
447 James H Swindle
447 John E Luby
451 Katherine Luby
455 Eli Chagnon
457 Joseph Ouimette
461 William H O'Neil Jr
461 Frank Kopacki
474 Walter S Morton
474 Samuel Hesketh
474 Mark Hartley
475 Julius Lang
475 Katherine R McDonald
475 Joseph Saum
478 Wilfred Lemond
478 Mrs Victoria Boyer
478 Mrs Maggie Landry
478 Alphonse Tetreault
478 Lawrence D Sullivan
480 Archille Provoncher
481 Theodore Schoene
481 John Schoene
484 John Seredzinski
484 Marjan Rodalewicz
485 Robert Klein
485 Cyrille C Barthiaume
486 Philias Lapointe
486 Aime Lapointe
487 Henry Oatner
487 Joseph Spachman
488 Isadore Lapointe
494 Joseph Aumann
494 Mary A Smith
494 Joseph Lord
495 Edmond Blanchard
495 Mrs Libbie Strong

495 Adelard LeClair
499 Oswald P Messier
505 Cleophas Fortier

COLLETTE

24 Manuel Lateira
37 Bert Pearson
51 Stephen Goguen
51 Stanislas Contois
51 Edmond Smith
52 Octave Peloquin
52 Ernest LeBlanc
52 Joseph A Methot
52 Achille Jacques
52 John Roy
53 Wright Saxon
53 Joseph W Symes
59 Joseph Charbonneau
59 Albert Laplante
64 Luiz S Oliveira
64 Manuel DeCosta
89 Ludger Fortier
89 Narcisse Roy
93 Albini Gould
93 Emilien Bussiere
93 Joseph Cote
93 Joseph St Sauveur
93 Joseph Gagnon
97 Ludger Lariviere
97 John Wieczoick
97 Calixte S Cormier
98 Francis Boisvert
98 Louis Parent
98 Edmund Therrien
101 Jan Gwozdz
101 Josef Bienia
102 Clovis Labadie
102 Mrs Mary L Pepin
104 Celestin Cormier
104 Louis Cormier
104 Joseph J Legere
104 Alphonse Simon
104 Louis Leavitt
105 William Petipas
105 Ferdinand B LeBlanc
109 Donat Hamel
109 Louis Sylvester
109 Edward Poirier
112 Napoleon Robert
112 Mrs Marie Preneau
113 Ludger Langevin
113 Amedee Blanchette
114 Ralph Gagnon
114 Napoleon Bergeron
117 Napoleon Carreau
117 Hormidas Carreau
117 Alfred Senglais
117 Michael DeGoff
120 Daniel LeBlanc
120 Mrs Damilde LeBlanc
120 Henry Belair
121 Jan Kurgan
121 Manuel Barboza
121 John Almeida
121 Joseph Oliveira
124 Mrs Annie F Johnson
124 James Cryer
124 John J Laughlin
124 Leon Renaud
124 John Taylor
125 Manuel Vantiero
125 William Miller
125 Pierre Dupont
125 Frank Buraczenski
125 Joseph Buraczenski
125 Joseph Simieski
141 Ezra Riopel
141 Mrs Mary Lamarche
141 Adelbert Gauvin
141 Albert Gauvin
141 John Stanton
141 Joseph Lebeau
141 Desire Beauregard
143 Frank Lapointe
143 Blanche Chausse
143 Mrs Mary Dandurand
143 Benjamin Riendeau
144 William R Croasdale
144 William H Croasdale
146 Henry J Nelson
150 Joseph E Dumas
150 Arthur DesCoteau
150 Michael Robitaille
150 Julian Moquin
150 Alexander Dumas
150 Edmond Generoux
153 Andrew Snyder
153 Alphe Maillette
154 Robert P Bernard
154 Louis Poulette
154 Amedee Bourgeois
157 Melos Williams
157 Rock Chandonet
157 Louis Jalbert
157 Mrs Minnie Lawrence
157 William Moniz
158 John C Armfield
163 Edward Cavanagh
173 Mrs Matilda Roy
173 Eli Bessette
178 Peter Barlow
178 Arcade Lemery
178 Valmore Girard
178 Francois X Girard
179 Thomas S Staples
179 Simeon J Bastien
183 Joseph Hebert
183 Manuel Exelson
183 Damase Leduc

Collette—con
186 Antonio Chausse
186 Wilbram Lemire
186 Arthur J Cadieux
187 Mrs Helen Lesieur
187 Dolor A Houle
188 Annie McMillan
188 Harriet McMillan
188 Joseph Collette
188 J Arthur Gaudette
191 James Munn
191 Thomas Thorpe
192 Alfred Leger
192 Ulric E Collette
192 Richard Dupre
192 Herbert Robinson
195 Arthur Ousley
195 Fabien Boudreau
195 Wilfred LaPalme
195 Mrs Marie LaCroix
196 Mrs Albina LaPlante
196 Joseph Chauvin
196 John Arkwright
196 Crosby Langlois
199 William Wilkinson
199 Albert Driver
199 Levi A Pemberton
200 Mrs Emma Yates
200 J Napoleon Reeves
200 Arthur Surprenant
200 Henry Aicken
203 John Gargan
203 Edward Bacon
203 Ismahel Collette
211 Josephat Manny
211 John Whitehead
211 John Houghton
211 Stanislas A Lamoureux
228 James Ainsworth
228 Albert Fournier
232 William J Sweeney
232 Felix Griffin
232 Michael E Daley
236 John F Whalley
236 Hector Florent
237 Thomas L Kane
240 Mrs Ellen Duerden
240 James Heald
240 John J Buckley
253 William H Selley
253 James H Rigby
269 Mrs Ellen Shaughnessy
269 Joseph Coulombe
269 Joseph Rogissart
275 John H Astley
275 Joseph D Caouette
275 John H Astley
276 Antone Gasse
276 Pierre Gentilhomme
276 Mrs Rosanna Murden
276 Jonathan B Boothman
279 Joseph Alix
279 Willian Jenkinson
279 Isaac M Hibbs
283 Bernard Hopkins
283 James H Knowles
283 Bernard Hopkins
284 Mrs Annice Pearson
284 Alfred Pearson
284 Ludwig A Roos
289 George C Ogden
299 Onesphore Bergeron
289 Thomas K Pickup
289 William Eccles
290 Rodolph Richer
290 James W Holden
291 Martha Headfield
291 John Sale
296 Benjamin Sutcliffe
299 John Riley
299 Bramley Kenworthy
303 Elisha Hallworth
303 Frank Partington
303 Robert Walmsley
303 Edmond Houle
304 Herman I Nulman
304 Joseph Rogers
307 John Thompson
311 James Connor
311 John Dauvell
321 Albert N Rushworth
341 John Greenfield
345 Enoch Shepley

COLLINS

10 Hervey B Peck
10 George A Snell Jr
15 Horace Borden
19 John Sykes
22 George P Palmer
22 Robert Jackson
26 Walter Burns
26 Albert Barber
27 Mrs Deborah R Rogers
29 Reuben Turner
30 E H Coggeshall
30 Mrs Susan Shaw

COLUMBIA

7 Peter J Ryan
11 Mrs Mary Edwards
11 Frank M Sears
11 John F Machado
13 William F Robertson
14 Mrs Ada Allen
15 George A Brownell
16 Joseph M Sylvia
16 Mrs Caroline W Hart

17 Anthony D Peters
19 George F Curry
21 Gilman E Hook
37 Manuel S da Silva
37 Manuel K Miguel
41 Antone P Silva
42 Rev William H Moseley

COOK

15 Thomas Tribe

CORNELL COURT

1 William H O'Rourke
2 Mrs Hannah Borgendahl
3 John Meehan

CORNELL PLACE

1 John Buehr
1 Barney Specter
1 James Bickustaff
2 Joseph L'Heureux
2 Mrs Delia Crapo
3 Louis Kirouack
3 Arthur Soulard
4 Madore Metras
5 Stephen F Neary
5 Joseph Cote
6 Magloire Magnant
7 James Sharples
7 Mrs Elizabeth Boucher
7½ John Hall
8 Ovide Pothier
9 Jozef Dziuba
9 Hyman Stupnitsky
10 Camille Normandin
11 Ferdinand Wetzel

COTTAGE

1 Mrs Mabel L Little
5 James F Devoll
5 Thomas J Chippendale
6 John W Airey
7 Mrs Isabelle Warren
9 Edwin L Potter
13 George W Randall
14 Mrs Mary Benson
14 Elijiah B Gridley
16 Augustus S Russell
21 Frederick J Manchester
22 Francis A Butts
23 George L Washburn
23 Thomas Arnold
24 Timothy C Allen
25 Mrs Mary E Williams
25 Mrs Annie C Kennedy
28 Mrs Alice Morrey
30 Edward Wadsworth
31 Nicholas G Beck
31 Richard R Bennett
32 Abber E Weld
41 Frank J Furnandes
46 Edward E Bean
47 Herbert M Atwood
48 Adeline M Cornell
49 Easton Y Pierce
51 John L Robinson
52 Franklin C Ross
53 Frank C Wood
57 Samuel F Aiken
61 Erskine Pierce
61 Edward W Sherman
65 Fennimore G Bachelor
66 George F Wright
66 Thomas C Holmans
76 Mary R Grinnell
81 Eliot D Stetson
85 Halford H Adams
98 Otis N Pierce
100 Mrs Ellen L Cook
110 Charles S Kelley Jr
112 Henry S Knowles
116 William H Jennings
117 George R Wood
121 Albert B Drake
125 Daniel W Cory
126 Frederick H Taber
127 Charles E Woodworth
128 Arnold C Hopkins
132 Charles E Chamberlain
135 Robert B Gifford
139 Oliver F Brown
140 Mrs Alice B Whiting
140 Mrs Alice B Whiting
143 William H Knowles
150 Frank R Kirby
152 Walter H Langshaw
155 William Huston
156 William C Parker
159 Mrs George F Kingman
160 Henry C Denison
163 Ira Allen B Smith
179 Daniel A Anthony
184 Robert W Bartlett
185 Edwin A Douglass
187 Mrs Mary J Batchelor
188 David L Parker
192 Frank G Tripp
193 George H Batchelor
195 Eudora F Terry
196 Arthur R Brown
197 Charles A Burt
198 Louis N Schuler
201 Mrs Ruth M Bryant
213 Henry J Marshall
217 William P Pierce

Cottage—con
226 James A Drayton Jr
226 William A Henwood
258 Mrs Emma C Allen
261 Patrick J Crane
261 George W Ashley
262 William W Nickerson
265 Louis Bertram
265 Mrs Julia A Gay
267 Brayton W King
267 Mrs Cynthia A Kelley
272 Misses McFarlin
273 Mrs Luella B Watson
279 David Kempton Tripp
279 Mrs Emma R Abbott
283 George A Mitchell
283 Willard P Mosher
295 Mrs Clara A Borden
297 Mrs Mary A Lyon
297 John B Oliver
298 Mrs Lydia Tavares
298 Mrs A M Gordon
309 Charles Hussey
309 Mrs Mary C Kimball
319 Oscar S Hammond
319 William S Bowie
320 Mrs Estelle Peirce
323 Mary H Perry
323 John M Hathaway
324 Mrs Elizabeth M Holcomb
324 William F Turner
325 William P Barstow
325 Mrs Julia E Sherman
326 George T Macomber
326 James Wixon
329 Edward F Fawley
330 Mrs Roxanna C Tripp
330 Mrs Abbie A Aiken
332 Douglas C Betram
332 Robert P Boman
340 Miles F Bixby
341 Joseph V Webster
342 Mrs Maria N Manchester
342 Laura C Ashley
342 James F Hargraves
343 Mrs Eunice E Damon
343 Mrs Annie C Tripp
345 Elias G Smith
346 Arthur G Luce
349 Veneretta Bourne
349 Rebecca J Card
350 Mrs Mary A Lowe
355 Mrs Mary J Grant
363 Thomas M Denham
369 Francis M Kennedy
369 Mrs Adaliza H Harrington
370 Charles F Keene
370 Annie E Pearce
372 Mrs Mary A Brightman
372 Henry Smith
373 Charles Dennison
373 John A Chase
378 Charles N Buchell
378 Franklin B Parker
379 P F Manchester
379 Irene R Gracia
379 Joseph M Lawton
384 Lester A Kane
384 Irving L Bassett
385 David W Caswell
385 Elijah L Sherman
389 Susan Duddy
393 George L Cory
403 Felix W Marrotte
403 Horace M Keene
405 Mrs Mary S Sanderson
415 Mrs Hannah A Tripp
415 Mrs Ann B Wilkinson
433 Edward F Nicholson
433 Nathan B Brooks
434 Mrs Aurilla P Peterson
435 Mrs Almira Bosworth
435 Daniel A Mackenzie
450 B Frank Barnes
453 Ira B Austin
453 Robert F Reid
457 George H McCarthy
457 James O Godfrey
463 Charles S Fossett
463 Samuel E Gabriel
467 Luke J Kilcoin
472 John F Tinkham
473 George T Ferguson
473 Daniel F Driscoll
475 Patrick O Driscoll
477 Elmer E Bennett
479 James A Sullivan
482 Michael Sheerin
486 Thomas C Robbins
498 David L Hathaway
499 Myron E Tripp
500 Joshua J Hatch
508 James M Sullivan
508 Mrs Mary J Mahoney
508 Mrs Catherine Ryan
514 George L Chase
514 Mrs Emma Fury
518 Frederick J Russell
518 Edward A Fuller
523 John O Rowand
523 William R Shaw
524 William G Taber
525 Mrs Mary A Smith
525 Stephen B Arnold
526 Gerrett Geils Jr
526 William H Crocker
527 William A Thompson

527 Peter J Riley
529 Mrs Catherine E Sullivan
530 James W Kane
530 Frederick B Colcord
539 Arthur W Bartle
544 Mrs Nancy M Johnson
545 Joseph Bunney
545 Matthew T Glennon
549 Mrs Helen Dehoney
549 Mrs Isabelle G Weeks
558 John B Lowney
558 Mrs Katherine V Riley
559 Patrick J Connors
559 Nellie Driscoll
560 Mark E Sullivan
561 Herbert Roebuck
561 Ernest Hegele
561½ James Craven
563 John H Ryan
563 Samuel Hague
577 William O'Donnell
577 Patrick F Lynch
577 Thomas Kelley
578 Sarah E Dowling
584 Austin J Cawley
584 Albert E Pailthorpe
588 Charles A Cotter
588 Annie J O'Brien
592 Mrs Julia Dwyer
592 Jeremiah E Dwyer
592 Anthony Newman
592 Thomas Hornby
593 Hartley Wood
593 Leon W Chase
596 Patrick H Mahoney
596 Mrs Mary Mountain
596 Mrs Hannah Taft
598 Patrick Smith
599 George A Sweet
599 Thomas F O'Hara
602 Patrick H O'Brien
602 John R Ashworth
603 Angus W MacKenzie
603 Mrs Ada L Titus
603 Mrs Abbie Judson
606 William H Niles
606 Walter E Mosher
607 William H Bottomley
607 Mrs Kate A Dufour
607 Joseph Secour
613 Joseph D Vaughan
615 William Nerbonne
616 James H Finnell
618 J Simon Paquette
618 Mrs Mary E Moore
620 Edward M Sullivan
620 T J F Donovan
621 Narcisse Bonneau
624 Anna and Mary Canavan
629 Wilfred H Duprie
629 Lucian F Bouchard
633 John J Duggan
633 Robert Shanks
634 Mrs Sarah M Brownell
636 Daniel Collins
637 John Isherwood
657 William T Ainsworth
663 Charles H Thomas
666 Daniel J Sullivan
667 Hary Allen
674 George A Bosworth
675 Leslie H Sutherland
675 William Roberts
675 Mrs Harriet Taylor
678 Jeremiah F Sullivan
679 James R Goddard
682 Thomas W Ramsden
685 James Higginson
685 John P Sculley
690 Benjamin F King
691 Mrs Florence J Collins
691 William E Roscoe
695 George W Taylor
695 James T Acheson

COTTER

14 Joseph Teixera
14 Joseph Quirt
14 Manuel Roderiques
14 Manuel C Simas
14 Joseph Coito
14 Joseph Dias
14 Joseph C Furtado
14 Damasse Correau
14 Manuel Carros
14 Manuel Roderiques
15 Yenocencio Andrada
15 Manuel Ferreau
15 Manuel Pacheco
16 Joseph Veira
16 Manuel Alves
16 Frank Rebello
16 John Betello
16 Manuel Correia
16 Antone Medeiros
17 Albert Valliere
17 Joseph De Mello
19 Samuel Finkelstein
19 John Menies
23 Joseph Cromblehome
23 John Macoliza
24 Louis Beaulieu
24 Flavien Cournoyer
24 Joseph Beaulieu
24 Raphael Beaulieu

COUNTY

20 Joseph Soare
20 Joseph Rego
24 Antone J Alves
24 Manuel Perry
25 Jose Gerome
25 Manuel S Montague
25 Mrs Mary Costa
25 Manuel S Bravo
26 Manuel Souza
26 Manuel B Ramos
28 Manuel Alves
30 Joseph I Silva
30 Antonio Pais
31 Victorine Costa
32 Leo Morancy
32 John Morency
35 Joseph Cardoza
35 Mrs Mary Rogers
40 Joseph Desbiens
40 Frank Perron
42 Louis Dextraze
42 Louis J Dextraze
42 Camille Dextraze
51 Edmond St Louis
51 Oddlon St Louis
51 Louis Lussier
53 Benjamin Gignac
53 Peter Gosselin
53 Edwin Bessette
55 Simon Gregoire
55 Antoine Goyette
55 Guillaume Le Beau
59 Joseph St Peter
59 Adelard Bellanger
59 Albert Mongeron
59 William Voyer
59 Alfred Bergeron
61 Louis Manjeau
61 Louis Rousseau
61 Michale Delaire
63 Edward Carroll
63 Mrs Arthemese LaChappelle
65 Mary Gorman
68 Mrs Eleanor Channing
69 Samuel E Bentley
74 Astil Ducharme
74 Pierre Garand
74 Alphonse Fafard
76 Stanislaus Bergeron
76 Charles W Edwards
76 Oliver Languedoe
76 Treffle St Aubin
79 Manuel J Noia
79 William Miller
80 Pierre Antaya
80 Paul Antaya
80 Napoleon Labau
83 Andrew Leonard
83 Mrs Ann McNabo
91 Mrs Jane McGrath
91 Thomas Henry
91r Henry Millette
91r Mrs Amanda Mont
92 John Leeman
92 Josephine Hyde
92 Daniel E Driscoll
94 Mrs Mary E Ryan
94 Louis Bocard
94 Mary Silva
94 Arthur Pelletier
95 Michael Joyce
99 Mrs Eliza Holgate
109 Joseph Daley
109 William Dean
109 George Matthews
109 Mary Gracia
109 Joseph Pennington
110 William C Sweeney
110 John Flood
111 Mrs Louise W Grant
112 John Wilkos
112 Frank Harding
113 Thomas A Heaver
120 Hugh P Collins
120 James J Duncan
123 Benjamin Addy
123 Mrs Annie F Machado
124 Manuel Silva
124 Jacques Didier
124 Manuel Sylvia
128 Robert T Boardman
130 Thomas Brierly
131 Antonio J Freitas
131 Mrs Julia A Snell
131 Ernest L Lewis
134 Joseph Greene
134 Mark Quinn
135 James F Robinson
135 Mrs Catherine Robinson
139 John Cordeira
140 Oliver Blanchette
143 Robert LaHaye
151 Thomas P Paynes
151 Theophile Gambra
151 Mrs Mariana Trindad
153 Laura Land
155 Joseph Ferris
160 George L Maynard
162 John V Azevedo
163 Rev J E Sirois
163 Rev Antoine Berube
163 Rev Adrien Gauthier
167 John Sylvia
167 Clement M Laussier
167 John J Sylvia
169 Mrs Mary L Sylvia

173 William H Hunter Jr
175 Mrs Isabella Hunter
175 Mrs Caroline H Bardsley
175 Andrew Simpson
181 Manuel M Machado
181 Manuel S Lucas
182 Henry Taylor
182 Francis Livesey
183 Arsene Picard
183 James Hartley
184 Ambrose S King
184 Michael J Collins
185 Mrs Catherine Long
185 John C Robertson
186 William Dean
186 Joseph A Russell
186 Chris Rumney
186 Mrs Elizabeth A Chadwick
191 Leonide Hotte
191 George Hotte
195 Cesaire Hotte
195 William Hotte
195 Arthur Hotte
195 Ovila Grenier
197 Mrs Annie E Black
198 Calvin T Bosworth
199 Robert Welsh
200 William H Broadbent
202 Edward W Sleight
202 Ovide Gelinas
202 Hermidas Benjamin
203 Victor Mello
205 Charles E Greene
205 Henry M Mosher
209 John E Sylvia
211 Joseph A Place
211 Thomas Albert Jr
212 Edward E Langshaw
216 Dr J J H McAllister
222 John Garlington
222 Mrs Mary Shields
222 William A Doyle
230 Misses Sullivan
230 Mary L Taylor
233 Rev Martin Fitzgerald
233 Rev Mortimer Downing
233 Nellie Manning
234 John P Langshaw
236 Mrs Annie Hopkinson
238 David Manuel
238 Mrs Temperance B Springer
239 Mrs Mary M Kerns
240 Mrs Ellen Tresham
240 Julio Vasconcellos
248 Clarence R Sherman
248 Mrs Eliza R Sherman
252 Israel H Shurtleff
252 Mrs Addie C Rowand
254 Pardon G White
255 Michael Stapleton
256 Manuel E Costa
261 George O Baker
264 Frank J Kilburn
265 Joseph C Perry
266 Edward F Penney
271 Joseph F Francis
274 Mrs Anna G Wood
275 Arthur G Durfee
275 Charles F Borden
275½ John Holmstrom
275½ Mrs Lillie Murphy
279 Antone A Sylvia
283 Greenwood Robinson
289 Abraham Levy
293 Susan Kavanagh
296 Harry C Ellis
297 George F Howland
298 Howard M Wood
298 Mrs Addie J Wood
298 Mrs Adeline S Holcombe
299 Charles J Lincoln
299 Mrs Mary M Hitt
300 William E Bradley
300 Samuel U Oliver
301 Jesse Gifford
302 George F Burgess
302 Mrs Marie Douglas
303 Phylander Chace
303 Mrs Annie M Chase
304 Eliza M Allen
304 Mrs Lucy T Jennings
308 William H A Sisson
311 Alfred Budgeon
311 Henry T Phillips
314 C H Murphy
315 Betsey B Winslow
320 Emily W Davis
323 Frank P Rose
327 Fred Stanley
327 James T Pollett
347 Rev Florus L Streeter
350 Misses Sears
350 William D Wilson
351 Edward R Hathaway
351 Arthur C Browning
351 Mrs Lizzie B Briggs
352 Mrs Amelia Frates
354 William H Bonney
354 Mrs Elizabeth A Bonney
355 Clarence Sidney Smith
355 Mrs Nancy W Chadwick
356 Robert C Sherman
359 Charles P Kasmire
359 Charles W Currier
361 Mrs Almy W Davis

County—con
362 Edward D Sherman
365 Mrs Ada B Cornwell
366 E Maud Hume
368 Mrs Herbert F Frost
369 Misses Ricketson
371 Edgar A Barrell
372 Rev Percy Gordon
374 Thomas B Akin
378 William N Swift
379 Mrs Frederick Grinnell
380 Frank H Gifford
382 Mary Swain
385 Mrs Horatio Hathaway
385 Thomas S Hathaway
388 Dr John D Hathaway
391 Swain Free School
396 Mrs Mary L Jones
397 Gilbert N Hall
398 Misses Seabury
399 Mrs Sarah B Delano
401 Mary R Prescott
402 Mrs Thomas H Knowles
402 Mrs Annie Knowles
404 Mrs Clara A Read
405 Edward S Brown
408 William H Wood
411 Benjamin Cummings
412 John C Rhodes
413 Thomas B Tripp
414 Misses Seabury
416 Martha Haskins
427 Mrs Clara M Rotch
428 Dr John T Bullard
439 Edward T Wilson
442 Charles W Read
446 Rev F E Ramsdell
448 Ella F Ivers
451 Annie Loftus
460 Mrs Mary E Marshall
460 Charles Marshall
464 Pink House
464 Misses Hill
465 Henry C W Mosher
470 George M Haskell
474 Dr Charles R Hunt
478 William L Kelley
479 John Duff
482 Mrs Elizabeth H Handy
483 Mrs Mary E Coggeshall
485 Mrs John P Knowles Jr
486 Mrs Sarah M Barrows
490 John S Perry
491 Mrs Clara P Lawton
493 Mrs Josephine W Luce
493 Elizabeth K Pease
493 Mrs Josephine W Luce
494 Lot B Bates
508 Mrs Laura A Anthony
509 Frank T Perry
511 Michael J Hayden
512 Mrs Sarah H Long
512 Mrs Harriet T Tinkham
522 Mrs Julia B Notter
528 Philip A Powers
535 Charles H Adams
542 Dr Garry de Hough
543 Mrs Abbie F Taber
546 Dr William G Potter
549 William O Devoll
550 Thomas Luce
552 Dr Ellen R Canney
553 Mrs Susan H Kempton
556 Mrs Mary A Jenney
560 Mrs Margaret Gibbons
564 Albert J Kelley
564 Katherine C Cotter
568 John D Swanton
570 Leslie A Howard
578 James W Hervey
584 Mattie L Wilson
591 Dr Abraham L Shockley
597 Mrs Alice P Adams
597 Joseph R Slocum
603 Dennis L Sullivan
604 Mrs Mary A Downey
604 Stephen J Weston
606 Mrs Mary E Colburn
606 Chester F Gidley
609 Clifton H Cornish
610 Albert A Crapo
613 Frederick E Allen
613 Lucy M Brightman
614 Frank E Wood
614 Mrs Nina B Marquis
619 Mrs Hannah Lee
619 Jasper W Braley Jr
622 Mrs Lizzie B Weeden
623 Ernest H Hearne
623 Mrs Eliphal S Case
625 Caroline E Hicks
625 Isaac R Case
626 Mrs Sarah E Robbins
629 Reed McCready
629 Mrs Lucy P Shepherd
630 John H Cook
630 James W Lawrence
630 E Stanley Swift
633 Ignace E Michaud
633 George I Macy
634 Misses Comerford
635 George C Hale
638 Burton Lewis
640 John McCue
641 Luella F Weeks

643 John A Neal
643 Stephen H Taylor
648 J Calvin Robenold
650 Charles E Vaughan
654 Seth T Delano
657 Edward L Killigrew
658 Elmer E Tolman
658 Mrs Lucinda C Pease
661 Ezra Holmes
661 Mrs Lydia C Chase
662 Louis Jean
662 Mrs Mary L Gerin
665 Albert F Meyers
665 Cornelius J Cronin
671 Henry C Perry
672 George Kirby Jr
675 Arthur L Blackmer
675 George A Tilden
676 Ernest A Jennings
677 George F Brightman
684 J Henry Herring
688 Mrs Annie M Bartley
689 F William Oesting
691 Thomas F Glennon
692 Walter S Gordon
695 William A Reed
706 Everett B Sherman
709 Mrs Susan Nye
710 George F Winslow
710 Mrs Rebecca P Shearman
716 Rev I C Fortin
716 Mrs Eliza B Irwin
717 Joseph T Smith
718 Rev John J Phelan
720 William A Congdon
721 Thomas J Murphy
726 Mrs Harriet Thomas
729 Mrs Mary J Knowles
731 Mrs Amanda E Pierce
731 Mrs Annie C Howland
732 Charles H Beetle
744 William A MacCord
745 Herbert C Wilbor
759 George Snedden
759 Edward B Gray
762 Mrs Mary Hewins
705 Charles Edward Benton
705 Mrs Harriet J Drown
762 George W Clarke
765 Mrs Harriet J Drown
772 Mrs Catherine Doolan
772 Patrick J Foley
774 George P Macomber
774 William J Redpath
785 Patrick J Sullivan
785 Arthur E Souza
786 Patrick Dufficy
788 Parick Finlon
798 John Connors
792 Damase Caron
794 Patrick Taffe
800 Patrick Hickey
804 Patrick Higgins
806 Mrs Victoria Dupuis
809 George H Savery
809 Oscar Remillard
809 Olivier Boucher
810 Arthur Boulet
811 Mark Hacking
811 Charles Ross
812 Mrs Annie Bancroft
825 Joseph A LaFrance
825 Leon P Braun
825 Philias LaFrance
826 Mrs Fabian Landry
826 Benjamin Potter
826 Joseph F Forand
826 Frank D Dupuis
826 Treffle Bonneau
826 Hervy Daudeline
826 Demas Dupuis
826 Baptiste Duteau
827 Lewis C Martin
827 Adelard Lague
827 Eliza Levins
827 Desire Gaouette
827r Thomas Burgess
827r Octave Bergeron
830 Edmund Parkinson
830 Charles Leonard
831 Peter Pineau
833 Mrs Mary Wroughton
833 Samuel Turner
834 John J Bouchard
834 Mrs Johanna Murphy
840 Walter S Rogers
840 Rugina Viau
842 Frederick E Duckworth
842 Charles R Minor
863 Mrs Catherine Murphy
863 Mrs Mary Sullivan
863 Mrs Mary Splaine
864 Charles Goodfellow
864 Frederick J Rourke
864 Francis A Lang
864 Charles Goodfellow
865 Joseph Howarth
865 Patrick Dolan
868 Mrs Ellen Downey
868 John S Silva
868 Louis Mankin
868 Joseph Maranha
868 Manuel Ferreira
869 Patrick Gannon
869 Alfred Dextradeur
874 Henry A Forgue
874 Charles A Parr
874 James Gilmore
874r Oclide D Jasmin

County — Con
874r Charles Radcliffe
874r John W Windle
878 Patrick J Finnerty
878 Mrs Johanna Finnerty
881 Joseph M Roberts
881 Austin Provost
884 Mrs Julia McCarthy
884 Alfred Barriteau
885 Martin J Stanton
885 Patrick Dolan
885 Edward Stanton
886 Cornelius J Sullivan
886 Bernard McManus
889 Henry J Arkison
893 John Dufficy
893 Catherine Grogan
893 Edward Sherley
893r Onslow Johnson
907 Mrs Elizabeth A Dawe
907 Joseph Lague Jr
907 William H Allen
907 Mrs Annie C Allen
908 Julian Jacob
908 Mrs Bridget Lodge
909 Joseph Brillon
909 Edwin Mitchell Jr
909 Elmer E Gifford
912 Manuel M Pease
812 Manuel Ferreira
912 Francis Ciera
912 Antone Luiz
912 Mrs Gertrude Martin
912 Francis Viera
912 Joseph M Freitas
916 Joseph Clavner
916 Robert Rogerson
916 Fred Fatimia
917 Adelard J Marcille
917 Mrs Melvina Marcille
917 Hector Faucher
917 Albert Boucher
920 Michael O'Brien
920 Edward M Canavan
921 Arthur Pelletier
924 Joseph Souza
924 Antone V de Mello
926 Frank E Mendes
928 Alfred Machado
929 Joseph da Beru
929 James Beauregard
934 Timothy Donovan
934 Matthew J Connolly
934 Mrs Margaret McCarthy
936 Louis Riendeau
936 Antone Pelletier
936 Joseph Lapage
940 Charles Bonin
940 Henry F King
943 William T Bryden
943 Dennis Donovan
944 John Deroche
945 Thomas McCartney
946 Jeremiah Harrington
945 Henry Goodby
945 James Galloway
949 William Bilsborrow
949 Sylvia Deragon
954 Fannie Keil
954 John Bowen
958 Samuel Nolan
959 Robert R Foutter
959 John H Mahoney
966 John Donnolly
966 Richard Barry
969 George Mills
969 Misses Miller
970 Samuel Archer
970 Joseph Moores
971 John B Blais
971 Hugh F Boyle
972 Henry Parkinson
972 Agnes Boyle
972 Thomas Crook
972 Samuel Batty
974 William E Thompson
974 Peter Pieraccim
974 Gioconde Piorascinc
978 James Shovelin
978 Mrs Martha J Clinishaw
978 John W Bryant
980 Paul Duchaine
980 Daniel P Sweeney
989 Ernest Ward
989 Margaret Watson
993 Jesse Bannister
993 Misses Fawcett
1005 Reuben Tabor
1005 George Suffern
1005 David L Tripp
1009 Joseph D Maynard
1009 Horace Desilletts
1009 Manuel Perry
1011 William Barker
1011 Frederick Goulet
1031 James Kay
1031 William J Haigh
1035 David Wilkinson
1039 George Butterworth
1039 Jas Ormerod
1045 Mrs Martha Blackburn
1045 George Hammersmith
1049 Wm G Parkins
1049 Albert H Krapt
1049 Joseph G Hammersmith
1053 Timothy Foley
1053 John Hall
1054 Mrs Rosanna Bock

1054 Robert H Kinney
1054 Tom Lloyd
1056 Tom Lloyd Jr
1057 Mrs Grace A Kiel
1060 Erenne Deller
1060 Eugene Renault
1060 Oliver Vertefeuille
1061 Michael Fisher
1061 Mrs Annie Lehner
1064 Mrs Angelina Lepan
1064 Joseph La France Jr
1065 Pierre J Cote
1065 Mrs Philomene Levique
1069 George Graham
1071 Ernest S Davignon
1071 Wm A Wilson
1075 Stanislaus T Benoit
1076 Mrs Rose Chevalier
1076 Jacob Schwartz
1077 Albert Milotte
1079 Victor B Dion
1081 Mrs Jesse Bellerose
1081 Manuel Marshall
1081 John B Francis
1081 Honorat J Masse
1081 Victor B Dion
1081 Henri Brassard
1082 Marcus Weisberg
1082 Thomas F Lewin
1085 Albert H Martel
1085 Napoleon Strong
1085 Prosper Foisy
1086 William Laycock
1086 Euclid Roy
1086 Wolfgang Herold
1101 Norbert De Roches
1101 Adrian Charon

COURT

30 Wm H Bartlett
34 Wm F Williams
52 Mrs Edith H Taylor
54 Laurent Poisson
55 Isabel Lucas
55 Thomas Brady
58 Orion E Covil
59 Mrs Ella F Allen
59 Geo A Chambers
60 E C Brownell
82 Mrs Jane F Graham
84 Tobias A Stanley
86 Misses Thornton
87 Robert C P Coggeshall
87 Merton L Hathaway
91 Frederic T Browne
95 Frank H Macy
108 Franklin L Hathaway
113 Mrs Melissa B Cuff
117 Frank B Peckham
118 Joseph Draper
119 John A Dunham
158 Axel K Apelquist
171 Edmond E Baudoin
173 Andrew D Paine
176 Richard S Taber
177 Seth A Wilcox
179 Gideon H Allen
184 George E Faisneau Jr
185 Frederick A Braman
188 William Almy
193 Joseph E Mello
193 Manuel Perry
194 Charles G Tripp
201 Stephen Perry
205 E B Danzell
207 Frank A Lewis
208 William S Gatenby
208 Anthro Braley
209 Jacob H Robinson
209 Ezra M Setton
210 Mrs Mary Lucardi
212 John Drafgord
213 Mrs Annie E McIsaac
213 James Manning
225 Charles H Ross
225 Benj F Downs
226 Joseph Pallatroni
229 Elizabeth F Himes
237 Albert A Dunlap
241 Leon H Steward
241 John N Dennis
251 John T Champion
255 Benjamin F Downs
283 Carl A Sundin
283 William F Smart
287 Everett W Cole
287 Olaf J Lindgren
294 George A Lackie
294 Cynthia V Jackson
301 Mrs Charlotte L P Watts
306 Eugene Perry
306 Frederick Vera
307 Joseph A Dobbyn
312 Mrs Elizabeth Weeden
312 James Laughlin
314 Arthur L Dreher
318 Isaiah Elliott
318 Michael J Sullivan
320 Mrs Winifred Blood
327 Mrs Henrietta A Clark
327 William S Backus
340 Mrs Mary A Hart
340 James T Langell
349 William F Howland
351 Thomas M Boomer
351 Clifford S De Moranville
355 Abram Gifford
360 Charles F Braley

Court—con
361 Alexander B Crapo
371 Mrs Sarah I Sisson
371 Sarah Gifford
373 Luther Russell
380 John A Nilson
384 Mitchell Smith
396 Charles F Kennedy
396 Herbert B Pittsley
396 Edwin M Wood
400 Isaac F Haskell
404 Frederick U Nickerson
408 John Foley
408 John M Foley
432 Charles H Sisson
432 Douglas E Gay
461 Robert McCardell

COVE

12 Ernest Bathell
12 Thomas Bowker
12 George Preston
16 George Livesey
16 Joseph Lewis
20 Herbert Tillotson
20 Mrs Ellen Almond
20 Charles Boardman
24 John Langton
24 Ellis Birchall
24 Lord Barker
26 Misses Kenyon
26 George Marvel
26 John T Coakley
26r Mrs Martha Hardacre
28 Louis Gerard
28 Heaton Atkinson
28 Mrs Elizabeth Wallace
30 Charles H Norton
30 Manuel J Xavier
30 John C Veira
30 Benjamin Barrett
32 William Iredale
32 John J Fraga
34 Albert J Allen
36 Mrs Mary Duffy
40 Mrs Margaret M Nolan
40 George H Rock
56 Samuel Wood
56 John Paradis
56 Henry Lafrenais
56 George Wood
60 Charles Dion
60 Pierre Lagasse
60 Hormidas Grenier
60 Hormidas Mathieu
76 William Manghan
76 William Niles
78 Alice Barnes
81 Mariano Vieira
88 Peter Gary
92 Jerry Moots
92 Alphonse Coutemanche
96 Mrs Margaret Sumner
96 Michael J Reddy
106 Edward Adam
106 Alexander Olevitz
108 Joseph Bonner
108 William E Hudson
109 Robert Wainright
110 Averist St Pierre
112 Patrick J Gibson
112 Frank Dargis
114 William Wilkinson
114 Albert E Wilkinson
115 Joseph J Norton
118 William Berenguier
118 Thomas Barker
118½ Harry Goldberg
122½ Euzeb Gamanche
122½ George W Davis
124 Henry Billington
124 Henry Eagan
124 John Maw
125 John Belanger
125 John Jourdain
125 Edward Charette
125 Joseph Keroack
125 Alonzo Martin
128 Louis H Deroches Jr
128 Octave Lariviere
128 Mrs Mary Vigue
128 Louis H Desroches
142 Florence Bossler
161 Peter D Lavoie
161 Edward Mayot
161 John Arseneault
168 Mrs Mary Worswick
168 William Warrington
168 Mrs Kate Carraher
172 William Wilde
176 John E Hoyle
182 William T Howard
186 Eugene April
186 Pierre Dumont
186 Mrs Priscilla Cote
186 Mrs Ovilia Berube
190 Carlos Pais
190 Vasco de Gama Pais

COVE ROAD

4 Roger Farren
2 Mrs Esther Etchells
6 John Worden
8 William R Longworth
18 Adelard Farland
18 Athanase Lavigne
18 Eugene Farland
18 Henri Desuisseau

20 John T Ramalhete
24 James Barlow
26 Peter Krakowska
26 Joseph I Da Terra
56 James Norwood
57 Joseph S Gomes
59 Manuel Ventura
59 Joseph Tavares
60 Francis M Pease
66 Jane E Noble
79 Antone Furtado
79 Henry Winchel
81 Joseph Frates
81 Joseph Frazer
85 Joseph Souza
85 Frank Medeiros
95 Michael Thatcher
107 Manuel C Rose
107 Manuel Perry
107 Joseph Frasier Jr

COVELL

12 Louis Beaullieu Jr
12 Zephir Surprenant
16 Napoleon Duval
16 John H Counsell
16 John Johnson
20 Arthur Desautles
20 Peter Beaulieu
20 Mrs Malvina Goyette
23 Eulege Desiel
23 Edward Thibeault
23 J Edward Clegg
27 Theophile Lefort
27 Peter Pelletier
27 Joseph Pelletier
31 Domingo De Costa
31 Fred Whittaker
31 Joseph Duquette
41 George F Morse
47 Peter Laivmonere
47 Charles Bardsley
47 Alfred St Germain
47 Manuel Roderick
58 Albert Bourque
58 Joseph Belanger
59 James Parkinson
59 Hector A Bayeur
59 James Higham
61 Manuel B Paulo
61 Adelard Gaudreau
69 Aduaran La France
84 James Soltas
84 Samuel Smith
84 Louis Brodeur
88 Thomas Smith
88 Patrick Sullivan
88 George W Rigby
92 Louis A Casavant
92 Joseph M Landry
92 George Lowe
98 Henry A Woodworth
98 David Eastwood
98 William Pegg
98 James Hartley
98 William Galvin
98 George Pilkington

CRAPO

4 William G Pierce
4 Mrs Annie J Shepard
4 Mrs Maria Martin
6 John M Castino
7 Bradford D Tripp
7 Misses Swift
12 John Reynolds
14 Oscar Eger
14 John H Paisley
16 John F Dias
20 Mrs Mary A Corey
21 Fred Holt
21 David F Polycarpo
21 Joseph Frates
22 James T Brooks
22 Henry A Browne
23 Henry Leeming
23 William H Longhill
24 William H Marsden
24 John Bramwell
24 Jacinth Costa
24 William Davidow
25 John Egan
25 Mrs Mary Meaney
26 John Jackson
27 Arthur Buffington
28 Burton G Davoll
28 Joseph S Johnson
30 John C Clarke
31 J Woodcock
31 Dixon Redfearn
32 John H Murphy
32 Elliott J Burt
33 William Pearson
33 Arthur Law
34 Francis Mullaney
34 Edward McWhinnie
35 Patrick Barrett
35 Patrick J King
37 Jethro C Delano
39 John W Donaghy
44 Domingos S Goulart
45 Joseph F Kraihanzel Jr
46 Manuel Silva

Crapo—con
46 Joseph Silva
47 Walter F Brownell
47 Samuel Hathaway
47 Antone Thomas
49 Antone Souza
49 Adolph Silvia
53 John Silver
53 Manuel Gresino
53 John G Chalupa
55 Edward Phaneaf
55 Antone Rose
55 John S Roderick
57 Julio F Venture
57 William S Souza
57 Mrs Sarah Ames
59 Fortunato Souza
59 Joseph Fratado
59 Antone Maria
59 Manuel B de Mello
59 Manuel Bente
59 Philip S Marsala
61 Camille E Mello
63 Miguel F Polycarpo
65 John L Correia
68 William Fitton
68 Thomas Miller
68 Martin F Roach
68 Alfred Abbott
68 William McCarthy
69 William Ahern
69 Joseph V Smith
69 Arthur E Scott
69 James Y Potter
70 Rufino Cacho
72 Saverino Gomes
75 Mrs Alvaro Costa
75 John Medeiros
75 Alvaro Oliveira
75 Antone Costa
75 Manuel C Pacheco
75 Jose M Raposa
75 Antone Oliveira
75 Julius P Oliver
75 Joseph Oliver
75 John Medeiros
79 Joaquim Sylvia
79 Manuel E Silva
82 Mrs Annie Oliver
82 Manuel J Silvia
83 Nassar Joseph
83 Peter Joseph
83 Manuel Dupont
83 Frank Luiz
83 Frank Motta
83 Manuel Medeiros
83 Joseph D'Aranjo
83 Manuel Medeiros
83 William Mansley
86 Antone Andrews
86 Mrs Alvaro Costa
86 Joseph Valloza
123 Mrs Mary Brown
123 Julius Silva
124 John Bowe
124 Alfred Woodcock
124 Caleb Bromley
126 Fred Rawcliffe
126 Elizabeth Webster
126 Thomas Green
130 John Fender
130 Misses McNamara
130 Alexander Moore
130 Thomas Bretherton
130 Samuel Neville
130 Henry Smith
131 John B Moniz
142 Christopher Wilkinson
142 Patrick Farrelly
142 Magloise Balanger
143 Manuel E Mendoza
145 Antone Costa
147 Mrs Betsy J Hubbenett
157 Joseph P Rogers
157 Hugh Gallagher
158 Thomas Holden
158 Joseph R Dutra
159 William McCarthy
159 Albert Harrup
159 Martin Maguire
160 Isaac Stevens
160 Walter Mont
161 Ann Brennen
161 Ernest Spencer
161 Thomas Bremans
162 Peter Choppin
162 Antone Roderiques
163 John Dias
163 Samuel Jackson
178 James Griffin
178 Richard Carroll
178 Edward Maguire
187 Patrick J Joyce
195 Richard Stratton
195 Ernest Richards
204 Frank Martin
204 John Rogers

DARTMOUTH

6 William B Smith
8 Henrietta B Smith
11 John A Taylor
12 Antonio S Sylvia
12 Mrs Mary Avila
22 Frederick Karcher
23 Ann S Eldridge
23 Robert T Matthews

24 Edward F Moran
24 Joseph Sylvia
24 Edward F Moran
25 Mrs Mary E Sylvia
26 Ferdinand D McGee
27 Isaac B Ranagan
29 Percy Batchelder
28 Alexander H Chase
28 Mrs Rebecca Fish
28 George H Phinney
29 Percy Batchelder
30 Frank J Gonsalves
31 Charles F Allen
32 Joseph H Bell
33 Louis Gregson
35 Albert G Mosher
35 Mrs Isabel G Chase
36 Charles A Reed
36 Frank P Moody
37 Benjamin H Kirby
39 Harry W Allen
39 Manuel Alves
40 Nathaniel C Tripp
41 Benjamin P Beers
41 John Banks
42 John L Martin
45 Lauchlan W Murray
47 John F Gile
49 Joseph H Schofield
50 Antonio A Sylvia
51 William P Mitchell
53 John Enos Lemos
60 Alberto L Potter
63 Mrs Mary A Taylor
64½ James H Warren
64½ Marion Reed
66 William E Tripp
66 Fred L Hathaway
67 Thomas Connor
67 Antone S Furtado
67 Joseph E Perry
68 Joseph S Bettencourt
68 George R Lawrence
68 Joseph Mello
70 Manuel B Sylvia
71 Frank A Gracia
71 Thomas H Kendall
71 Eli Slinger
73 Maria J Thompson
73 Manuel M Mendes
82 Frank S Reca
82 Mrs Alice Walkden
82 Michael E McCarthy
86 James H Bruce
86 Arthur Rawcliffe
88 Herbert N Brownell
88 Manuel T Sylvia
88 Edward J Turner
92 Harry W Rex
92½ William H Gamble
92½rJoseph Costa Jr
94 Mrs Annie Heyes
94½ Crawford N Mosher
94½ Manuel Sylvia
96 Loren N Mosher
98 Manuel Francis
100 John Hanson
102 Harrison A Rogers
102 Mrs Carrie Davis
104 Mrs Elizabeth Costa
104 Antonio Marshall
107 Abner S Tripp
107 LeRoy W Wilber
109 Joseph V Garcia
111 Angela F Bowie
112 Russell S Lawton
115 Thomas G Pearson
116 Joseph Andre
117 Thomas Littlewood
118 Mrs Sadie Morrill
118 Oliver Laurient
120 Mrs Mary Oliviera
120 John Rocha
120 Nicholas Cambra
121 Frank Gomes
121 Joseph Gonsalves
122 Joseph S Silva
122 Antonio J Ventura
123 Antonio Gregoria
123 Rose Silva
125 Herbert Machado
126 Joseph Gonsalves
126 John Costa
126 Joseph Gonsalves
127 Manuel Vera
127 Mrs Rose Vera
128 Mrs Rita Roberts
128 Antone Machado
128 Mrs Frances Netto
132 Francis P Medeiros
132 John B Foster
135 Bartholomew Corrie
140 John Foster
141 Mrs Maria Sweeney
141 James M Sylvia
363 Charles F Britton
363 John G Sylvia
363 Antone Moniz
380 John Larma

DAVID

90 Ruth A Ashley
99 Thomas Lavalle
99 Mrs Marie Poirier
99 William LePage
99 Joseph Halle
102 William R Fairweather
102 David Chasseur

David—con
102 Peter Joseph
103 William Cloutier
103 August Miclo
103 Joseph Millette
105 Emile Pilaire
106 Henry Choquette
106 Emery Choquette
107 Leo Calderbank
107 Ernest Plant
107 Joseph Daniel
109 William A Kenyon
109 John Browne
109 Joseph Belanger
109 Uldric Ray
110 John Higgins
110 Squire Marshall
111 John Burke
111 Charles Plante
111 Robert Anderson
111 Joseph Anderson
114 Arthur Garside
114 Henry LeClair
115 Howard E Miner
115 James Morrison
118 Thomas Clitherow
118 Walter Greenwood
118 Henry Stephenson
119 Arthur Tillotson
119 Mrs Elizabeth A Higginson
119 Elias Shorrock
122 Robert Allen
125 Robert Taylor
125 Thomas Crook
125 Thomas Heys
125 Alexander Taylor
126 William J Lister
126 John E Yates
131 Paul Hampson
131 Thomas Hampson
151 William D Sparling
151 Gilbert Southworth
151 William H Wilson
151 Mrs Alice A Southworth
152 James Livesey
152 Charles Stewart
152 Thomas Stewart
156 John Carter
156 Hillery Howman
156 William Swan
159 Monroe L Stewart
159 David Carroll
159 Mrs Rose Chartier
159 James Rainford
159r Albert Koshelba
160 William Wignall
163 Joseph Martel
163 Joseph Belanger
163 Wilfred Normand
164 Mrs Mary Smith
164 Robert Whitworth
164 James H Simpson
165 Mrs Anna LaBonte
165 James McLaughlin
167 Walter Gardner
169 William Hendra
170 Alfred Noblet
170 Robert Arnold
173 James A Richardson
173 John Buckles
173 Richard Howard
176 Walter Draine
177 Philip Laflamme
177 August Menes
177 George Wilders
183 William Maudsley
183 Gledhill Sykes
183 Edward McGowan
187 James Lambert
187 Antone Marwan
187 Joseph Taylor

DAVIS

20 Richard H March
42 Isaac Seguin
42 Artif Armat
42 Thomas Seguin
48 Abdula Adem
48 Mrs Delia Nadeau
54 James Nure
54 Telial Cezim
54 Bactash Duma
71 Joseph Medeiros
77 Manuel P Ponte
77 Charles Argiropoulos
80 Christian J Boetilho
80 Joseph Rezendes
80 Balbini Rosa
81 Patrick Duffy
81 Frederick Heptonstall
81 William Bocotte
81 Mrs Marie Hetu
81 Napoleon Gauthier
81 George Vlach
81 Louise Cardinal
86 George Courtemanche
86 Philadore Trahan
86 Israel Cote
86 Augustin Lariviere
86 Louis Latraverse
90 Emile Bosse
90 Louis Bertrand
90 Isadore Thibeault
96 Wilfred Gallant
96 Joseph Vautour

96 Antonio Coelho
101 Gustave Lelievre
101 Thomas Cote
102 Gideon Vien
102 Wilfred Belanger
102 Wilfred Parkinson
102 Sophia Michaud
102 Roger Preston
103 Manuel E Rebello
103 Joseph Pinault
104 Pierre Leger
105 Joseph Nutter
105 Adelard Gladu
107 Mrs Azelda Guertin
107 Alfred Chabotte
107 Joseph Robida
107 Alex Levesque
109 John Yanovsky
109 Frank De Mello
109 Mrs Maria A Jesus
109 Louis Lavoie
109 Joseph Perry
138 Harry Ripley
138 James H Forrest
138 Samuel Talbot
138 Luke Murphy
138 James McConnell
138 Frederick Heptonstall
140 William Thornton
140 Henry Smith
141 Thomas Watson
141 Robert Rogerson Jr
141 William J Hicks
142 Archie Newton
146 Patrick J Fitzgerald
150 William P Baines
154 Olivine Fontaine
154 Robert Hill
154 Charles La Belle
156 Hugh McMann
157 Octave Gauthier
157 Mrs Melina Gaucher
157 Euclide Duval
157 Pierre Branchaud
157 Philip St Onge
157 Thomas Wilson
158 Thomas Walmsley
161 George E Middleton
161 Robert H Moore
161 Hilaire Therrien
162 Francis La Mothe
162 Manley R Hubbard
167 Claus A Lindberg
167 Charles W Praray
171 Daniel S Considine
175 Mrs Johanna Considine
176 Antonio M Lemos
178 Bernard F McCarthy
178 Charles H Pickles
180 Ovedos Nolin
180 Pierre Nolin
184 Thomas Carman
184 Fred Mercer
184 William Mercier
186 Thomas Thompson
186 John B Lafleur
187 James Marsden
187 James Wilkinson
187 William Rowland
190 Anton Wallner
190 Aime Legere
190 David Landry
191 William Driver
191 William G Hitchcock
191 John T McKay
194 Thomas Thornley
194 Charles W Burgess
194 Joseph Lassey
194 Joseph Rumney
194 Glenn Russell
194 Fred Bowden
195 Joseph Couture
195 Joseph A Demers
195 Pierre Demers
199 Mrs Mary Fox
199 George Davies
199 Samuel Fern
199 Kate McCann
201 Max Couza
201 John Wood
201 Elizabeth A Wood
204 Ernest Senecal
204 Joseph Z Boucher
204 Joseph W Grimshaw
208 Frederick E Thilo
208 Benjamin Lamothe
208 John Kelly
230 Timothy J O'Brien
272 Hector A Michon
272 Joseph Lamaire
272 Albert Goodwin
272 Mrs Emma Hornshaw
276 John Hamer
277 John Ward
277 Ernest Worthy
277 John Malone
277 Peter J Ward
281 Walter Key
281 Charles Key
282 Austin Garvey
282 Camille Laporte
282 Hercule Dionne
285 Albert Chenel
285 Frank G Velho
285 Arthur Cutler

Davis—con
286 Albert Yates
286 Edward Gallant
286 Mrs Georgianna Laplante
286 Albert Yates
289 Matius Cardoza
289 Moise Lord
289 Joseph S Townley
290 Charles E Hanrahan
290 Joseph O Blanchard
290 Mrs Mary A Stark
292 William Gregory
292r John Gregory
293 Mrs Mary Blecha
293 Joseph Welch
293 Frank Rostron
296 Mrs Margaret Rycroft
296 Walter Lethbridge
297 James McKenzie
297 Charles Wobetski
297 Joseph Wobetski
300 George Seddon
301 Leon Pelletier
301 Calixte Henry
301 Peter J Macy
304 Joseph M Freitas
304 Philip L Hamel
305 Joseph Riding
305 John Walmsley
305 John Wegscheider
305 James Walmsley
309 William Pinner
312 John R Vera
312 Arthur Surprenant
315 Mrs Ann Duckworth
316 Michael J Kerrigan
316 Fred M Harder
317 Charles R Goewey
317 Robert McWhinnie
320 Etienne Gauvin
320 Alfred Choquette
320 James Irwin
336 Timothy P Collins
336r Mrs Margaret Kay
337 Vosseler Curl
337 Englebert Eisenbach
340 Alonzo Dutton
341 Thomas Cranshaw
344 Abraham Taylor
344 Mrs Annie Catlon
344 John B Licocq
345 Louis LeBoeuf
345 Thomas Baron
348 John Bjelahlavek
348 Lawrence Sanborn
349 Richard J Barton
349 John W Birdsall
352 Ludger Gaouette
352 Allen Bessey
353 David Zimmer
353 Fred Honeker
353 Edward L Hughes
357 Henry Delisle
357 Arthur Gadbois
361 Norbert Nemec
361 Andrew Greenwood
385 Joachum Watzlavick
389 Antone Knapp

DEAN

35 Alex Plante.
35 Marie L Dragon
35 Eugene Patnaude
35 Mrs Adeline Goulet
35 Joseph Trahan
35 Mrs Delphine Beauregard
36 John Garvenyski
39 Calixte Champagne
39 Stanislas Joly
39 Mrs Delima Patnaude
43 Narcisse Monville
50 Joseph Piva
50 Antone Rezendes
50 Prima Souza
51 Emile Cote
51 John B Audette
51r Albert Holt
52 Joseph Pietras
52 Philias Phaneuf
52 Samuel Goulet
52 Henry Gagnon
52 Joseph Rondeau
56 Misael LeClair
56 Joseph Angers
56 Mrs David Dupre
57 Silvio Caron
57 Marcille Gamache
57r Alfred Roy
61 Camille Dhaze
61 Simon Caissie
61 Mrs Sarah Walsh
61 Joseph Deblois
61r Mrs Euphemie Poirier
61r Hermenegilde Dextras
62 Henry Walne
62 Thomas Chadwick
63 Luke Chadwick
63 Wilfred Cote
63 Louis Goulet
66 Maurice LeBlanc
66 Joseph G Russell
66 Albenie Dupuis
66 Ernest Herbert
66 Napoleon LeBlanc
66 Adelard Daigneault
66 Charles A Belanger
67 Alfred Jepson

67 John J Layland
67 Mrs M Alice Manley
68 Gaudiose Paradis
68 Oliver Landry
68 Mrs Severe Marcotte
68r Joseph Marcotte
69 John Woolfenden
69 William Thomas
72 John T Hamer
73 James Rowan
73 John McCarthy
73 George A Braley
74 Edwin J Tanner
76 David I Bowen
76 Mrs Mary A Duerden
82 Fredric C Dunham
82 William Barnett
85 Elzear Allard
85 Henrietta Carrier
85 Henry Carrier
85 Arthur Landry
85 Olivier Cormier
90 William J Kerwin
161 Napoleon Champagne
161 August Schmidt
162 John Riley
165 John B Halin
166 Wilfred Dufresne
166 Ovide B Pothier
166 Magdale Desmarais
170 Andrew E Bray
170 Arsene Levesque
170 Henry Chausse
171 Harry O LeBell
172 Alfred Blouin
172 Andrew Papas
172 Laurent Sougnez
177 Francois X Charbonneau
177 John Richard
177 George H Menney
177 Alexander Hadfield
178 Edward Carrier
178 Calixte Picard
178 Thomas Ouillette
178 Fred C Roberts
179 John Boehler
179 John Catlow
179 Joseph Donth
179 John Boehler
182 Joseph Bourque
182 Fabien Gagnon
182 Ulderic Hevey
183 Joseph F Winstanley
183 David Rayer
186 Thomas Rourke
186 Napoleon Ouimette
186 Dieudonne Bessette
186 Peter J Gagnon
186 Joseph Morency
187 William Dyer
187 Mrs Mary A Smith
187 Frank Buckley
187 Amedee Perrier
189 Frank F Buckley
189 Jane A Pearson
189 James W Holden
190 Joseph A Dupuis
190 Edmund Wallace
190 Joseph Warren
193 Wenzel Nemec
193 Albert E Hafford
193 Robert Cryer
194 Sinai Cote
194 Isaie Hevey
194 Mrs Lucy Valliere
194 Edward Tremblay
195 Frank Buckley
195 James W Holden
198 Hemenegilde Gagne
198 Archille Benoit
198 Julius Parmentier
199 Antone Sleger
199 Antoine Wobetski
199 George Fink
199 Charles Walecka
200 Robert Bell
201 George Cunningham
201 Alfred Boisvert
201 Ludwig Wobetski
202 Thomas Bury
203 William Soddy
203 John Horacek
204 William Parkinson
234 Adolph Herzog
234 Thomas Crook
234 John J Barlow
234 Harry Bolton
234 James E Hardman

DELANO

4 Damase Larochelle
4 Stephen Larochelle
4 Harry Lipman
8 Jacob Kaliff
8 Harry Levine
8 Samuel Levine
8 Mrs Mary Corbeil
25 Evariste Boisvert
25 William Marquis
33 Joseph Buba
33 Mrs Margaret Beaulieu
46 Treffle Charroux
46 Edmund Wilmet
46 Delphine Ouimette

Delano—con
47 Arthur Tramblay
47 Joe Tremblay
49 Lucien Trenette
52 Jean B Caouette
55 Peter Dubrinski
55 George Dietier
63 Manuel G Medeiros
65 Antone Rose
65 Joseph S Medeiros
67 Mrs Mary Alvila
68 Joseph Prevost
70 Frank Tarlecki
70 Joseph Dubiel
71 Antone A Souza
71 Manuel Joseph
72 William Roberts
75 August Rogers
75 John J Gonsalves
76 Mrs Mary Allison
76 William H Sharples
77 Mrs Louise Mello

DESAUTELS

3 Joseph Loiselle
3 Remi Cote
3 Siffroid T Jendreau
7 William B Murray
11 Damasse Tanguay Jr
22 Robert C Crapo
33 Charles Fisher
34 Emma C Crapo
34 Nicholas Crapo

DEVOLL

3 Joseph S Nunes
10 Frederick J Murdock
11 Erase Anctil
17 James E Tripp

DeWOLFE

2 John B Preneau
3 Mrs Mary Francis

DIMAN

69 John W Knowles
69 Joseph Muhl
95 Philip Goulet
95 Victor Casavant

DIVISION

4 Jeremiah Irvin
9 John Guerin
12 Peter Lamontague
12 Peter Paradis
16 John Hushon
19 William Hodgins
19 Mrs Ann Walsh
20 Michael Martin
20 Thomas Clark
20 Michael Kilmartin
32 Joseph Poirier
32 Ludger Lauthier
32 Emil Durup
38 Dennis Dolan
42 John Souza
42 Manuel Souza
43 Isador Cournoyer
49 Narcisse Cournoyer
64 Patrick H Meany
64 Mary Meaney
64 James Foster
64 Hormidas Trepanier
68 Alphonse Hebert
72 Joachim Cournoyer
72 Andrew Billing
72 Ira Stopford Jr
72 Henry Lavinge
74 Joseph Brunelle
74 Napoleon Nadeau
74 Pierre Cournoyer
74 Henry Bonneau
76 James H England
76 Amedee Tetreault
76 Thomas H Fish
76 John Brimley
96 Philip Lemlin
96 John Kenyon
96 Ancline Desjardins
96 Flavien Lepine
96 Arthur Berube
97 Robert J Walsh
97 William Walsh
108 Samuel Harrison
109 George Moss
109 Thomas P Woodcock
110 Joseph Mangum
110 Thomas Cassidy
113 Thomas Richardson
113 Mrs Susan Cole
113 Mrs Elizabeth Brinley
114 William Rose
115 Timothy J Moriarty
119 Manuel S Beatriz
119 Manuel Louis
120 William Ormerod
120 Robert McLeod
120 James J Dodds
125 Joseph Demaira
125 Joseph Courtemanche
126 Mrs Mary Stuart
126 John Gatenby
126 James Dodds
129 Manuel A Fernandes
129 Frank Moniz
129 Antone Servia
130 Mrs Jeanette Whiteley
130 James Openshaw
131 Henry Cadieux

131 Louis A Bessette
131 Antone Costa
132 Edward Eastwood
132 Robert Whalley
132 Albert Duxbury
134 Mrs Sarah Fawcett
134 Mrs Sarah Greer
134 James Normile
136 Mary Neenan
138 James Farrell
138 John J Tighe
139 Frank Fisher
139 John Wells
141 Hugh Meekin
141 John F O'Connell
141 Joseph Thomas
141 Mrs Emily Thomas
142 Manuel Gomes
142 Manuel Souza
144 James Quale
144 Albert Hunt
144 Peris Powers
152 Margaret Parker
152 Thomas Kelley
156 Thomas Maxham
156 Frederick Kean
156 Walter Ellison
161 Thomas Normile
162 Henry D Cunningham
162 James Crane
162 Eli Marshall
167 Manuel Correia
167 Antonio J Medeiros
167 Gasper Leschna
168 Mary A Shaw
168 William Woods
170 Mrs Rose Jacintho
170 Mrs Mary Mello
170 Joseph Q Costa
171 James Mullen
172 Alexander Taylor
172 William Dawson
172 George Bolton
175 Manuel B Nunes
179 Antonio R Mello
185 James O'Rourke
186 James Cawley
186 Frank Ferreira
186 Mrs Alice McCoombs
187 Catherine Cunningham
187 Patrick Cunningham
188 Andrew G McGee
188 John A Gage
188 Albert Williamson
188 John Feeley
190 Auguste P Gosselin
192 John Mouer
192 Thomas Murty
192 George Rose
192 John N Mercer
193 Joseph G Anthony
195 Frank Costa
195 Manuel Pacheco
196 James Tootte
196 Henry Young
203 Jesse Raphael
203 Manuel D Simas
206 Martin Swift
210 Misses Mullen
210 James Mullen Jr
210 Mrs Margaret Latham
210 Thomas Gallagher

DOVER

6 Mrs Ellen F Redfern
6 Abner J Jones
8 Ellen E Meaney

DUDLEY

16 Peter W Nelson
20 Edward Winstanley
30 Robert W Stearns
30 John S Gill
30 Edward Ostler
31 William H Wilcox
38 Adelard Tetreault
60 Hugh Williams
73 Ambrose Ryan
78 Frank England

DUNBAR

22 William Hewitt
22 Antone Pacheco
27 Antonio J Ribeiro
27 John J B Scales
39 Antonio Ferreira
41 Manuel P Amaral
41 Mrs Mary Furtado
41 John Ferreira
77 Mrs Mary S Gamboa
77 Antone Costa
77 Antonio E Edwards
81 Arthur Bradley
81 Robert Howarth
81 James Robinson
83 Salina Jones
84 Edward DeMello
84 John C Pavao
87 Edward Smith
89 John W Noble
92 John Brierley
92 Joseph H Chadderton
95 Thomas J Murray
96 Herbert Healey
96 Charles A Deloid
103 Manuel L Lima
103 Frank Sylvia
109 Manuel Correia

Dunbar—con
109 Frank Vera
109 Manuel Serpa
115 Frank Sylvia
115 Mrs Lodina Desmarais

DURFEE

2 Frank T Kohn
2 Patrick J Hines
2 John Cheadle
4 Sumner B Hammond
4 Jonathan Covell
15 Philip Lacey
28 Mrs Minnie Rouse
28 Edward Ulrich
29 Theodore N Manchester
29 Nellie F Clagg
29 Mrs Fannie L Jenney
30 John D Manseau
30 Myra Hayden
31 Mrs Mina Ducheineau
31 Patrick J Cotter
32 Harry Ward
33 Edward Prifogle
34 Mrs Maria Merchant
38 Mary McCarty
38 Mrs Julia Ellis
38 John Michelson
42 Mrs George W Gibbs
42 Amos F Aldrich
45 Andrew W Tripp
47 Charles E Anthony
47 Mrs Mary K Smith
50 James J Gordon
50 Mrs Margaret E Culhane
54 Nathaniel H Caswell Jr
54 Mrs Lydia Groves
54 Andrew D West
54 Joseph Lewis
55 Mrs Mary F Hames
55 Horace H Seabury
55 George Mason
60 William H Taber
61 John Borba
61 Michael Shea
61 Edward L Wilson
62 Jeremiah H Wilson
62 John H Galligan
62 Ralph Worthington
63 Albert H Bassett 2nd
65 Edward F Jenney
65½ John W Cross
72 Frank S Enos
72 William Grant
72 Mrs Annie I Prentiss
75 John Crowley
76 Henry W Baldwin
78 John D Wannacott
78 Mrs Effie Wood
81 John A Rothwell
83 Mrs Ellen M Benson
88 Mrs Matilda A Angell
91 Joseph Lemos
91 Manuel S Justley
94 Michael Quinn
97 Simeon Broadmeadow
98 John Tynan
101 John W Gifford
102 George Broadmeadow
102r Mrs Georgianna Randall
103 William Sloane
105 James A Macomber
107 Henry Deneault
107 Ezra A Judson
109 Christopher E Rigby
115 John E Dyer
118 Mrs Cora Manchester
150 John Roche
154 Albert H Tarr
154 Robert Shaddock
155 John W Gibson
156 William Addy
159 Charles O Greenhalgh
160 Dennis McNulty
164 James A Little
164 Joseph Smith
166 George A Holden
175 Severin Gill
176 Antone Silva
195 Manuel Santos
195 Mrs Jessie Santos
207 Manuel J Leal
209 Abraham Ogden
210 Manuel C Gabriel
211 Mrs Rosa Pike

EARLE

69 Napoleon Durocher
70 James Turner
70 Jonathan Wordell
70 Mrs Winnifred McDonald
72 John Amaral
72 John F Semanica
76 William Yates
76 Michael Connors
80 Antone L Sylvia
80 Mrs Rose Berube
84 Mrs Mary Farraday
84 Antone Morris
84 Manuel DeMello
88 Isaac Trahan
88 Jean B Jarry
92 Antone Marcourele
92 John H Bourcier
92 George Jouvin

139 Didier Bourgeois
139 Victor Martin
155 John Kenyon
155 Joseph Newsham
155 Emille Belanger
159 Edward Dandelin
159 Emile Arsenault
159 Thomas Cormier
160 Albert Dickinson
160 Noel Letendre
160 Walter Martin
179 George H Hargraves
179 Noe Richard
179 Joseph Dion
187 Amede Reeves
187 Hyacinthe Mathurin
187 Marcome Tremblay
188 John Lancaster
189 Silvio Fournier
189 Alfred Goulet
190 Joseph Lemay
190 Charles Robillard
190 John Shaw
190 Alice Desrosier
190 Henry Brouillette
190 Peter Lavimoniere
191 Mrs Alice Bellmay
191 Arthur Anderton
191 James E Bolton
195 Joseph A Lawrence
196 George A Fredette
196 Cyril Morin
200 Thomas Lewis
200 Edward Geary
204 Agnes Callaghan
204 Mrs Mary Selley
204 George Selley
204 Charles W Varnum
225 James Burgess
276 Thomas Rayner
276 John K Baty
276 Hubert Rocheleau
277 Walter B Miller
280 Alberic Menard
280 John T Kelley
280 George Cook
284 Henry Walsh
284 Martin Curry
285 John J Anderton
285 Herbert H Hallworth
288 Joseph D McDermott
288 Mrs Harry P Mort
288 Edgerton Butterworth
289 Mrs Esther Cullen
289 Clifford E Reed
293 Louis Lemay
293 Mrs Mary Robinson
296 Mrs Barbara F Sestak
296 Robert Greenwood
297 Herman Landry
300 Marcelin Bureau
300 Frederick W Blundell
300 Caliste Savoie
301 Charles E Fournier
301 Robert Leighton
301 James E Taylor
305 John Kulpa
305 Joseph Pies
306 Henry Lund
306 James Lund
306 John Haggerty
309 Benjamin Bramwell Jr
309 Joseph James
309 John C Rumney
310 Jules Spirlet
310 Jean B Weigel
313 Edward Hetherington
313 Robert Young
313 Robert Houghton
315 Mrs Margaret Snape
315 James Wilcock
321 Michael Sheible
321 Annie and Nellie Morris
323 John Duckworth
323 John Bauer
323 Mary Foote
324 Fred Houserman
324 Francis T Grimshaw
324 Andreas Huber
330 Eugene Frieh
330 Michael Pflug
337 Robert Southworth
337 Thurston R Seed
337 James Walton
354 John J Barton
354 John McGuire
358 John Koroski
362 John G Bear
362 Ferdinand Glaser
363 John Moll
366 John T Carrick
366 Ernest Mercier
367 Albert Pemberton
367 Emile Schmidt
367 Gustave Trinklin
394 John Doehla
397 Walter Morgan
398 Mrs Mary Lenhart
399 Antone Hirshlag
400 Walter F Chace

EAST DURFEE

1 Mrs Mary Ferreira
2 George Spencer
2 Joseph D Murray

East Durfee—con
3 Mrs Nellie Veira
7 Mrs Lizzie Doherty
7 Mrs Marjorie Kenyon
7 Mrs Florence Peel
7 Mrs Mary Cawley
7 Mary Robinson
15 Mrs Elizabeth Peters

EAST FRENCH AVENUE

5 Richard T Fallows
5 William Etherington
5 Florenzi Alexander
5 Richard T Fallows
5r Fred Jackson
7 Mrs Mary Whittle
9 James Kenyon
9 Robert Martin
13 John Hardacre
13 Misses Green
13 William Fish
15 Robert Whitworth
15 Rufus Richmond
15 Mrs Mary J Leary
17 John H Ashton
19 William Oliver
19 Joseph Oliver
19 John Chapman
21 John Hutton
21 James Bates
23 Fred Barrett
23 Henry Bowden
25 Walter Ashworth
25 Manuel Crossley
25 Fred Roberts
27 Joseph Anderton
27 John W Ward
27 John Reynolds
29 David Royle
29 Friend Widdall
29 William H Smith
31 Robert D Burhoe
31 Joseph McAllister
0 Arthur Morse
Charles D Beetle
John H Beetle
Mrs Ann Wood

EAST MERRIMAC

20 Manuel Silva
20 Monticone Giovanni
20 Antone Jacintho
22 Joseph Corando
28 Mrs Mary Furtack
28 Arthur Ansay
30 Joseph Christopher
30 Mrs Mary Adams
30 Benjamin Bloom
30 Santa Romanzi

EDISON

13 William A Walsh
14 Joseph Silva
18 Joseph Costa
18 Armand J Magnant
18 Julio Viera
36 Frank J Masalina
41 Antone Avellar

EDWARD

1 Joseph Sampson
42 Joseph Machado
42 Joseph King
48 Henry Perry
48 Frank C deMello
48 Manuel Picand

EIGHTH

6 Fred W Andrews
8 Mrs Mary E MacKellvey
10 Edmund G Otis
11 Horatio C Allen
12 Rufus A Soule
13 Mrs Emma C Myrick
14 George L Olivier
15 Dr Edward R Sisson
32 Dr Edwin P Seaver Jr
32 John W Wilcox
35 Almy F Gifford
35 A Davis Ashley
36 Vincent Gerardi
37 Theodore F Tillinghast

ELIZABETH

19 Arthur Goulart

ELLEN

57 Armand Fortier
59 James Lawton
59 George Pearson

ELM

5 William H G Leonard
5 George A Stevens
11 George F Stevens
15 Charles A Rooks
15 Philip Jones
17 John N Finnell
24 Jacob Frankel
24 Peter Gordon
25 Daniel H Snow
25 Mrs Annie Cook
26 Frank Souza
26 Ignacio Correio
26 Peter Gomes
26 Peter Borst
27 F E Rust
28 Isaac Brown
28 John A Lemos

28 Edward B Stevens
36 Joseph A Burke
40 Wilfred Quinton
53 Mrs Leonora D Chapman
59 James Lawton
59 Mrs Rose Ledoux
65 James R W Bates
65 Herman L Bliss
73 Archibald Macfarlane
73 Rexford L Sisson
78 Mrs Marian L Robbins
81 George Fichtenmayer
82 Rhoda A Snow
84 Mrs Abbie W Taylor
85 Granville P Hicks
86 Alban C Snow
89 Mrs Charles H Lawton
90 Hezekiah A Manchester Jr
90 Mrs Ida T Coggeshall
92 Mrs M Ellen Anthony
94 Eben C Milliken
95 Mrs Lydia W Hough
95 Elliot H Wefer
96 William W Barry
97 William C Phillips
97 George R Phillips
98 Mrs Mary E Fox
99 Dr Arthur V Pierce
105 Mrs Melancie F Hitch
107 Lavelia V Witchell
109 Alfred W DeWolfe
129 Daniel Rowe
129 Mrs Lydia J Cranston
131 Thomas L Parsons
147 Frank E Pierce
147 Philip Sher
149 Louisa A Hathaway
149 Asias R Swain
149 Lyman K Reed
149 Annie Oliver
153 Charles F Payne
153 William J Gibson
155 Albion R Gidley
156 Charles H McKim
157 Richard Day
157 Albert J Barbour
157 John W Houtman
159 William H Winborne
159 John Markmen
165 Mrs Love P Chamberlain
167 Mrs Lucy F Coles
169 Charles R Burpee
169 John W Offley
169 John R Offley
185 Mrs Emma F Kimball
186 James H Norton
186 Elias J Tripp
187 Charles H Harrison
188 Albert L Johnson
188 John D Osborne
189 Alfred C Rogers
189 Mrs Edward W Jones
190 Edwin M Riley
191 Rose P Dantsizen
191 Antone E DeMora
192 Mrs Elizabeth Lightfoot
193 B Franklin Wagner
195 Mrs Margaret Taylor
195 Mrs Lydia A Wainer
196 Misses Gomley
197 Joseph Vargas
197 John F Cunha
197 Joseph P Jefferson
198 Laura A Tucker
200 Thomas Galligan
200 Frederick A Tripp
202 Mrs Annie E Tripp
334 Antonio Rose Brazil
338 Mrs Abby Skiff
338 Mrs Marv Herlihy
350 Patrick Murphy
351 William P Farrell
355 Michael McGrath
357 Theron G DeMoranville
358 John J Gunning
358 Mrs Clara Eddy
364 Mrs Mary Burke
379 David A Cobb
390 John F Oliver
394 James F Kelley
395 John J Riley
399 James F McKiernan
399 George Wyman
400 Ernest Gifford
400 Michael Rogers
400 John R Walsh
403 Thomas Percy
409 Mrs Lydia C Taber
411 Joseph A Bauer
420 Alexander G Fricker
420 Walter C Davenport
428 Louis Longleux
536 Timothee Dion
536 Mrs Mary E Perry
537 Andrew F Jenks
541 Charles H Douglass
560 Charles Watson
566 John C Brown
567 Charles A Kilburn
570 Otis L Briggs
570 Franklin B Hathaway
571 Augustus M Davenport
584 Edward Casey
584 William J Davis
585 Burgess T King
586 Benjamin I Stowell
594 Charles F Cook
608 Ernest G F Teachman

Elm—con
613 Mrs Ann Cook
615 Charles L Jones

EMERSON

10 Henry W Taber
13 Arthur S Booth
14 Mrs Harriet H Randall
15 George A Caswell
18 James T Murray
19 Mrs Emily A Gifford
20 William A L Smith
21 Joseph E Fay
25 Sylvester Paul
29 Samuel Robertson
34 Misses Connor
34 William H O'Neil
35 Walter S Dillingham
35 Peter C Keith
38 Peter Anthony
42 Joseph P Morrison
45 Mrs Mary A Smith
46 Mrs Mattie A Carr
46 Manuel A Saqueira
49 Edward I Lawrence
49 Frank A Habicht
49 Mrs Abbie M Tirrell
51 Curtis Hardy
51 Johan E Sundin
51 Edward P Sadler
53 George Fredette
53 Joseph Battey
54 Fred A Gardner
56 Henry W Ellison
141 John Almeida
141 Antoni Reis
157 Sarah F Goff
157 Albert H Jackson
161 Mary Davis
161 Isaiah Haskins
163 Lawrence F Jordan
163 Mrs Mary Osborne
164 Samuel Miller
168 Francis H Gray
169 Joseph S Webster
169 Robert R Sylvester
169 Mrs Annie E Scott
172 Ida V Lee
172 Emma Welch
173 Herbert A Crocker
173 Mrs Ella F Crapo
173 Mrs Lena French
176 Mrs Lilla M Wiggins
180 Isaac Griggs
189 William H Stone
317 Jasper M Achorn
317 Fred M Potter
317 Milton Potter
317 Nahan H Delano

EMMA

67 Harry Jordan
67 William Whitehead
67 John Sprague
71 Fortunate Bergeron
71 Joseph Hamel
71 Walter King
71 George H Neale
75 Joseph S Chaves
75 Robert Arnold
75 Joseph Collis
75 Charles W Brennan

EUGENIA

70 Louis Boucher
70 Hormidas Cote
71 Charles Hebert
74 Henry Taylor
74 Samuel Pidgeon
78 George LaFontaine
80 Louis Lebeau
80 Joseph Cormier
82 Onesime Gauvin
82 Emery Millette
82 Louis Cahouette
88 Mrs Kate A Bradshaw
88 Ferdinand LaFrance
88 Samuel Swallow
91 Ludger Rivard
91 James Sargent
102 Eucher Gallant
102 Albert Bourgeois
102 Arthur Belliveau
102 Omer Tanguay
109 Edward Babineau
109 Elzear Pepin
109 Hilaire Pepin
109 Romuald Coutu
109 Edward Fredette
111 Joseph Talbot
113 Alfred Joly
113 Louis Moquin
117 David Knight
117 Henry Newton
117 Peter Bonoyer
121 Joseph Zach
125 Joseph Gaudette
126 Albert E Leaver
126 Joseph Woollam
127 Otto Yehle
128 Henry Dion
128 John Reedy
128 John W Connolly
129 Gabriel Letourneau
129 George Vancoure
129 Frank Berard
130 Donald Dunn
130 Henry Doyle

130 James W Lindley
130 Edmond Dumas
154 Calixte Babineau
154 Mrs Julia Gagnon
154 Henry Richard
154 Adolph Sylvester
154 Mrs Frances Correia
154 Joseph L Hereux
175 Alfred Carreau
175 Phillipe Coache
175 Adelard Boulet
175 Thomas R Goodwin
201 William Hughes
201 William Walsh
201 Oswald H Hughes
201 Mrs Margaret Sullivan
203 Peter T Jeffries
203 Hormidas Langevin
204 Horace H Chapard
206 Alfred Christie
206 John T Shaw
207 Philisa Adam
207 John A Delisle
207 Alfred Levesque
208 Thomas H Tripp
208 Benjamin Woodsome
208 Joseph Valentine
210 James Atwood
210 Alfred Montpetit
210 Mrs Mary L Harkee

FAIR

14 Edward H Wilkie
15 Francis F Bennett
15 Antone Marks
19 Joseph Cardoza
19 Mrs Mary Mattes
23 Frank J Nicklas
23 Timothy J Canty
25 Mrs Ellen Frost
33 Benjamin F McGuinness
33 Mary R Matthews
33 Philip Leen Jr
38 William H McCarty
38 Stephen J McCarty
40 John Stubbs
40 Amedee H Desjardins
42 Fran Gracia
42 Walter A Butler
42 James E Metcalf
49 Frank G Petzold
49 Robert L Broadbent
49 Manuel T Perry
52 Edward Pothier
53 Manuel G Souza
53 Charles Broadbent
53 Joseph F Dias
54 Hyman Shapiro
54 William Stadler
57 James Phalen
58 Joseph V Picanso
58 Arthur J Rose
58 Mrs Annie Rush
62 David Carlaw
81 Joseph T Baldwin
81 Mrs Sarah Gunderson
99 Robert Jackson
99 Robert Gunderson
103 Ezra Saillant
103 Joseph S Cabral
103 Joseph J Fernandes
114 Anson L Beaumont
114 George J Davis
114 Sydney A Cornell
117 William O Buzzell
117 John J Miller
118 Edward McManus
118 Margarita L Tavares
118 Arthur A Snow
121 Manuel C Silva
122 Joseph F King
122 Mary G Sylvia
125 Mrs Rose E Amaral
125 William Jason
125 Manuel Ferreira
126 Augustus Smith
127 John L Sylvia
127 Augustus Santas
126 John Augusto
126 Mrs Annie M Greene
130 George B Breakell
130 John L Enos
130 John J Rollins
131 Charles H Paine
131 Mrs Martha Goodinson
131 George J Morris
131 Mrs A B Mendoza
139 Olympia Caton
139 Alfred E Lemos
139 Philip H Sheridan
142 Antonio Goulart
151 Mrs Eudora F Mosher
152 John H Maxfield
152 George W Mowry
152½ Harrison T Borden
155 John W Barrett
155 George T Davis
155 Abner P Sherman
157 John T Miller
157 Anton Yobst
158 Matthew Lawrence

Fair—con
160 Charles H Babcock
160 John Rex
165 George E Briggs

FARNAM changed to **Lombard**

FARWELL

1 Ann Lamb

FAYETTE

131 Frank Perry

FELTON

5 Anthony Fitting
6 John G Sampson
6 Thomas Jones
6 William J Lomas
7 John Vertente
8 John Pacheco
8 Andrew Moran
8 Arthur G Chase
9 Alfred Turgeon
9 John Roy
10 Enos Nosek
13 Vincent Mrkvicka
13 Alois Docekel
14 Frank Dolecal
14 Adam Docekal
30 James Holt

FERN

James Walmsley
6 Charles P Mattson

FIELD

31 Mrs Myra L Doane
81 John Rapoza
99 Manuel Miguel
99 Manuel Rapoza
111 Francisco P Rose
115 John Arruda
115 Louis Correia
115 Joseph Souza
121 Joseph Hilton
125 Manuel Bent
129 Frank Silva
132 Frank Silva
136 Antonio P Silva
137 Antonio Lorenz
137 Antonio Silva
137 Manuel Pimental
143 Joseph Moniz
143 Manuel Ferreira
145 Joseph E Correia
149 Frank Arruda
149 Manuel Souza
149 Joseph S Bettencourt
150 John L Silva
150 Antone Mello
150 Rose Lenhart
151 Daniel Heyworth
239 Alfred Matthews
239 Mary Matthews
239 Arnold Diggle
239 Frank H Fernandes
252 William H Tripp
252 Gabriel Silva
255 Honorato Pimental
255 Richard A Brownhill
256 Arthur N Harriman
256 Manuel Ladino
263 Stephen N Silva
263 August Dutra
267 Frank Roye
267 Joseph Rodericque
270 John M Perry
270 Antone F Perry

FIFTH

2 Dr Joseph A Frasier
5 Henry M Smith
6½ Mrs Kate P B Jourdain
7 James E Brierly
11 Robert H Luce
16 John B Daffinee
18 Francis H Ellis
20 Elton S Wilde
20 James B Bradley
21 Frank W Francis
21 Samuel B Hathaway
25 Albert F Caldwell Jr
25 William D Raymond
27 Charles W Vining Jr
28 Ida M Hatherley
29 Stephen L Child
29 Mrs Sarah J Hofe
31 Mrs Anna Jones
33 Mrs Mary R Keeney
35 George F Castino
37 Clara B Watson
37 Matthew C Julien
38 Edward Smith
38 Mrs Sarah Moriarty
39 Benjamin D Cleveland
40 Isaac H Sherman
41 Cyrena A Peirce
42 Asa C Pierce
43 Fred Loraine
44 Mrs Edith M Baker
45 Herbert F Brown
45 William J Bullock
46 Wanton M Gladding
47 Frank Wood
47 Mrs Sarah W Seabury
48 Dr Herman Grocshinsky
48 Mrs Ellen N Pollard
49 Dr Frederick L Clark

50 Abraham Herman
51 Thomas W Croacher
52 Josephine M Molway
52 George W Cary
53 Thomas H Fairchild
53 Herbert C Reynolds
54 Cooper Gaw
54 Charles M Miller
55 Edward G Whitney
55 Patrick Connor
55½ William B Smith
55½ Mrs Ella C Smith
56 Albert Almeida
56 Reuben E Swift
57 Mrs Sarah R Bennett
58 Frank Vera
59 Charles D Finni Jr
59 Mrs Azubah N Koehler
59 Charles A Bowen
60 Daniel W Baker
61 Joseph M Silveira
62 William A Nield
63 Henry Silva
63 John Tavares
63 John F Travers
63 Mary A Lima
64 Herbert Peirce
65 Mrs Lydia A Tilden
65 Mrs Clara B Jenney
67 Mrs Eliza A B Wood
68 William S Remington
69 J Franklin Briggs
69 Wanton H S Beauvais
76 Mrs Cornelia G Winslow
76 Herbert E Longley
77 James T Kane
77 Winnie Deane
77 John F Lawlor
78 George P Rexford
79 Oliver S Gurney
79 John Gurney
80 Hughes L Siever
83 Joseph M Lima
83 Albert H Rooks
84 George C Hewins
86 Harvey Cushman
100 Fennimore G Batcheler
101 Henry S Abrams
101½ Mrs Nellie Lewis
101½ Fritjof H Gunderson
101½ Frank J Veara
103 Antonio M Roberts
103 Frank Enos
104 John Pache
104 Mary Marshall
104 Mrs Emma Bradley
104 Antone Simons
105 Mrs Mary A Souza
105 George Lawton
105 Joseph M de Bandarra
105 Francis Dutra
105 Antonio J C Point
106 Antone Travers
107 Fred Marshall
108 Antone F DeChaves
108 Manuel Machado
109 William N Whelan
109 George F Swansey
110 Manuel T Brazil
111 Charles W Brown
111 Manuel R Serpa
111r Antone B Santos
112 Joseph M Fraga
112½ Percy H Young
113 Harris Rusitzky
114 Manuel Travers
114 Mrs Mary E Dutra
114½ Joseph Barnes
114½ Cornelius J McGregor
115 Mrs Mary J Terra
115 John Silva
115½ Manuel V Avellar
115½ Joseph Dias
115½ Manuel J Rea
115r Gilbert N Brunette
116 Manuel C Silva
117 Ambrose H Tripp
117½ Charles H Rennerfelt
117½ Axel Almgren
117½ Stephen J Perry
118 Green B Allen
119 Henry F McConville
119 Sarah E D Jouvette
119 Harriet Pierce
121 James W Mulaney
123 Frank T Bentley
123 Mrs Rose Alexander
123 Lillian Enos
248 Constantine A Sylvia

FIRST

5 Manuel J Martin
5 Antonio Fuller
15 Antonio Marcelli
22 Thomas Donaghy Jr
29 Abbott D McMullen
47 Benjamin Tavares
49 Manuel Baptista
53 Marthinho S Monteiro
53 Domingos Monteiro
54 Mrs Phoebe M Reed
56 Nellie Johnson
56 Neva Ferdandes
56 Enos Rose
63 Paul Gomes
71 Sylvester Lopes
72 Andrew Lawson
73 Nicholas Monty

First—con
74 John Lazaro
74 William Butterworth
74 Joseph Antone
76 Borach Babchick
76 David M Herman
80 Bernard McGuire
80 Samuel Marinoff
85 Mary A Monteiro
86 Mrs Abbie Gann
88 Antonio Pina
93 Mrs Sarah F Williams
93 Mrs Kate Holden
93 William H Woodward
95 Antonio Joseph
303 Joseph DePonte
323 John S Costa
323 Manuel Gois
326 Mrs Jenny Wilson
326 Candida Valladoa
329 Antone Souza
329 Virginio Souza
330 Joseph Senna
331 Frank Furtado
331 Mrs Mary Morris
331 Manuel Furtado
333 Johanna Shea
333 Frank Ponts
334 Joseph A Boteilho
340 Max Stuart
340 Morris Shapiro
341 John Viegas
341 Frank J Oliver
345 Joseph Aspin
346 Frank Souza
346 Manuel Correia
350 Morris Cohen
352 Louis Rosen
353 Julius Schuster
353 Barnet Sheiff
353 Matthew Lopes
356 Frank P Cadoza
356 Manuel J Silva
356 August Camill
359 Antone P Ponte
359 Mrs Mary Silva
359 Joseph Correia
363 Julius Schuster
365 Manuel Costa
365 Manuel Mendoza
365 Antone Rapoza
368 Manuel F Vital
371 Caesar Burgo
371 Louis F Correia
371 Joseph Oliveira
385 Joaquim Aralia
385 August Frazier
398 Charles Paul
399 Manuel Mello
399 Joseph Borges
399 Joaquim Perry
400 Ferdinand Augustus
400 Joseph Jason
405 John V Cabaca
405 Frank Medeiros
405 Manuel C Bolarinho
407 Manuel J Perry
407 Victor Mello
408 Jacinth Philip
408 Vitriano R Fontes
411 Antone L Sylvia
411 Mrs Marie Rapoza
412 Joseph Brier
412 Manuel Perry
412 Daniel Nicholas
417 Enos Oliver
417 Mrs Josephine Morris
418 Mrs Annie Medeiros
418 Manuel Supreanna
419 Antone J Silva
419 John Gracia
420 Mrs Fanny Soares
421 Francisco Martin
428 Joseph Murach
429 Charles Ventura
429 Manuel Andrada
431 Manuel Medeiros
450 John Nicholson
450 Joseph Francis
450 Manuel S Braga
458 Jose Pacheco
458 John Tavares
469 Antone C Santos
469 Joaquim Furtado
470 Manuel Jackson
470 Antonio Dutra
472 Manuel Mello
473 Frank Souza
473 Michael J Lacey
473 Joseph V Soares
475 Manuel Souza
475 Manuel Pacheco
477 Severino Henriques
477 Antone Fragoso
477 Samuel Ginsberg
486 Phillip Goldberg
486 Samuel Kaplan
486 Joseph Jacobson
486 Esidor Corske
488 Mrs Mary Shea
490 Abraham Kaplan
490 William A Kaplan
495 Francis Devlin
495 Manuel Costa
499 Harry Schuster
499 Joseph P Silva

501 Antone Andrews
502 Antone Mendoza
502 Joseph Tavares
502 Candido C Sylvia
502 Joseph Tavares
510 Ibitson Dawson
512 Joe Davris
530 Manuel Arsenio
530 Manuel Avila
530 Peter Rodericque
531 Frank Costa
531 Manuel Souza
531 Manuel A Alves
531 Joseph Machado
531 Mrs Maria Temeira
531 Mrs Mary Rose
537 Manuel J Mello
550 Benardino Gregorio
550 Joseph Martin
550 John Rogers
557 Asher H Levy
557 Joseph Harney
557 Maurice Levy
561 Charles Bramwell
563 Albert Pisi
566 William Franklin
567 Arthur Boudreau
567r Antone Silva
567r James Crane
570 Michael Norton
571 Mrs Margaret A Balderstone
579 Mrs Annie O'Rourke
581 Manuel Boteilho
582 August Ouillette
582 John L'Heureux
582 Frank Houle
582 Ansene Houle
587 Mrs Victoria Lavallee
587 Mrs Catherine Tarpey
591 John Aralia
591 Wilfred Longtin
592 Fred Millette
592 Samuel Hurwitz
592 Fred Millette
592 Joseph A Balthazer
592 Louis Boucher
616 Walenty Adamowitz
617 Mrs Marie Piva
617 Peter Lachance
617 Mrs Marie Piva
620 Mrs Ellen Chenard
621 Edward Siddel
622 John Helm
624 Fred Mendoza
630 Arthur T Wild
630 John Veron
631 Thomas Neenan
637 William Gerrard
642 Louis Brunnelle
642 Archie Arenville
642 Joseph Washkiewic
642 Ambrose Charroux
643 Alcide A Barobe
648 Peter Vierton
648 Frank Szubargo
648 Peter Kolodziey
648 John Bezetta
648 Frank Szubarga
648 John Szundler
649 William Almond
649 K Kulon
658 Mrs Mary Lebeau
658 John McCabe
658 Frank Beauregard
659 Louis Galanska
659 Thomas Warnot
659 Adanowiecz Vitinty
659 Mrs M E Shea
666 Mrs Mary Allen
666 Zeska Naski
666 John McKay
669 Belonie Tetreault
669 Jean B Gladu
669 Frank C Gladu
670 Harry Craig
670 Mrs Bridget Tueit
673 Joseph X Gaudreau
675 Fred Febeo
675 Joseph Thibeault
680 Charley Coblez
683 Peter Cure
690 Emile LeChance
694 Joseph Gillow
696 Samuel McFarland
696 Joseph Des Rochers
699 Daniel McAuliffe
701 John O Reagan
708 Andrew E DeTerra
708 Mrs Alice Grimshaw
721 Remi Lemarche
721 Joseph Lefebvre
721 Joseph Lafavor
723 Edward Lavelle
723 Emile Schlam
723 Mrs Augustina Lambald
723 Edward B Lavalle
723 Celestine Lambalot
733 Thomas Bachand
748 Mrs Edith E Tripp
748 Patrick O'Donnell
755 Rev Charles F Hearsey
773 Arthur Farland
773 Thomas Monty Jr
773 Xavier Lague
775 Emil Huette
775 Narcisse Pcland

First—con
775 Alphonse Roy
775 Joseph Perry
790 Charles R Cash
799 Adelard Baron
799 Henri Berard
799 William L'Heureux
799 Frank Dion
799 Adelard St Germain
800 Hugh A Cunningham
803 Adelard D Bernard
803 Joseph Dupuis
803 William Caron
803 Joseph Laprie
803 George Tessier
806 Jean Claer
806 Napoleon Chabotte
807 Joseph Blein
807 Euclide L'Heureux
807 Jeffrey LaLiberte
808 Thomas Worsley
808 Henry Menard
808 Luis Bassinet
811 Arthur Parent
811 Euclid Lemieux
811 Napoleon Baron
811 Joseph Beauregard
812 Samuel Loey
812 Napoleon Morin
812 Mrs Caroline Roy
815 Joseph Lamothe
815 Joseph Langlois
815 Louis Lapre
815 Alfred Marcoux
815 Joseph Lamothe
820 Peter O Ross
820 John B Kane
835 Timothy Donnelly
837 William T Waterhouse
837 Mrs Annie Collins
837 Michael Sullivan
837 Mrs Alice Waterhouse
850 John A Isherwood
856 William Thompson
856 John J Mills
856 Arthur W Gilmour
857 Senial Dubois
857 Alfred Desmarais
857 Aime LaBonte
857 Henry Lepine
857 Frank Tetreault
857 Alonzo Lambert
857½ James Davis
857½ Mrs Mary Daigle
857½ William Norwood
858 John D Townley
858 Thomas H Fish
858 Peter Edge
858 James Henry
858 William H Lang
862 Edward Bertrand
862 Albert Howarth
862 Alfred Mayall
862 Joseph Sargent
866 Albert Z Blois
866 Thomas E Knowles
866 William Almond
872 Herbert Bach
872 Joseph Brasseur
872 Joseph Corre
872 Edmund Pidgeon
872 Anseline Monty
872 Joseph Corre

FLORENCE

10 Thomas Boomer
15 Samuel Cook
25 James Cook
26 Horace D Bradley
32 Delmont A Miller
37 Richard Wall
39 Selmar Eggers
43 Martin B Foley
49 David M Piper
51 John H Lupton
52 William T Atwood
53 John Ross
55 G Walter Williams
76 Patrick O'Brien
80 Lutham W Mosher
83 Elmer W Brownell
84 Mrs Ella Macomber
84 Charles G Patterson
88 John R Gray
88 Irville L Damon
99 Mrs Mary A Brownell
119 Alfred I Brightman
120 Ellsworth L Sabins
122 George H Devoll
124 Herbert E Negus
124 James Vaughan
126 Frederick W Dalzell
127 Mrs Josephine Johnson
127 William F Kane
130 Mrs Mary H Manchester
136 Mrs Ardell Stiles
137 E Frank Minier
137 Edgar E Cory
140 Joseph Noble
142 George A Marky
146 William Wilson
152 Bernard T Garland
153 Mrs Emily Janorin
173 John Joseph

FOREST

61 Charles A Cushman
61 Frank W Hathaway
62 Andrew A Cory
63 Mrs Bridget Sullivan
64 Charles E Staples
65 Mrs Amanda M Palmer
65 Daniel O Taber
66 Norris P Howland
66 Mrs Caroline E Macomber
68 Mrs Abbie K Church
68 Harold P Lewis
69 Frank Whittaker
69 Mrs Helena A Barker
70 Mary Nicolou
70 Anna B Smith
71 James Ennis
73 Mrs Elizabeth Sillery
73 Mrs Martha W Bennett
75 Gilbert M Jennings
76 Oza Tessier
79 Thomas Morrison
81 Mrs Hattie C Sherman
82 Mrs Sarah J C Sampson
83 Ralph W Case
83 Charles J Francis
84 Ezra F Howland
85 James Smethurst

FOSTER

2 Lynn A Field
4 Zadoc A Cottle
4 Jefferson Davis
5 Nathaniel A Tripp
5 Charles N Burchell
6 Mrs Louisa M Taber
6 George E Braman
37 Augusta W Pittman
38 Benjamin A Larmarine
38 William H Weston
38 Eben F Haskins
38 Mrs Annie Kershaw
39 John M Burgess
42 Josephine F Swift
42 Frank E Fowler
43 Daniel W Wilson
43 Mrs Helen S Dickerman
45 Orin A Pearce
45 George D Meikle
46 George A Wood
49 Andrew Marvine
49 Harry G Edger
55 William E Heron
55 William J Cowing
56 Thomas F Allen
57 Mrs Esther G Gifford
57 William O Gifford
59 William L Snell
59 George O Robbins
62 Daniel Meehan
63 Mrs Myra D White
63 William A Soule
64 Edward M Durfee
64 Clark D Nye
65 Mrs Amy F Weeks
65 Mrs Susie S Mills
67 Charles Knowe
67 Martin J Daly
68 James H Allen
68 Charles E Ryder
69 William C Coon
71 Albert A Crapo Jr
72 Mrs Abbie M Baker
72 Chauncy L Shaw Jr
73 Charles J Allen
73 Charles A De Moranville
73 Phoebe D Howes

FOURTH

17 John O Williams
17 William T Baker
53 Frederick W Reynolds
54 Mrs Eunice M Macomber
54 Mrs L M Hodgkins
56 Daniel H Smith
57 Lemuel D Adams
59 Richard D Chase
60 John K Blair
60 Wilfred L Bacon
66 Henry A Holcomb
67 Alfred Wilson
69 Cyrus H Flanders
69 Mrs Helen F Allen
71 Ednora E Howland
71 Joseph L Gibbs
74 Arthur W Grover
74 Charles B Thompson
76 H August Jahn
76 Albert C Church
77 Mrs Caroline W Sayer
77 Alonzo T Le Baron
77 George R Poor
81 Morgan Barney
85 Elizabeth A Peckham
85 Eugene F Wells
89 Matthew F Barry
89 Ambrose W Bosworth
94 George H Paul
94 Dr C M Atchison
95 James C Page
95 Herbert C Wehoskey
97 Mrs Ella M Bolles
97 Nancy Shannon

Fourth—con
97 George Jackson
97½ Mrs Elizabeth M Lovejoy
97½ William Sylvia
98 Peleg H Sherman
98 Edith Brodhead
98 Emma S Landre
99 Joseph Winsper
99 Martin Martyn
101 Paul Silva
102 Harry B Tripp
104 Harry G Rounsevell
105 Thomas Thompson
106 Charles M Morse
106 John D Elliot
107 John B Eldridge
108 Edwin L Tillinghast
109 Mrs Sarah W Francis
110 Mrs Caroline B Swan
111 David A Miller
112 Edward A Murphy
112 Mary A Stillson
113 Mrs Catherine Lanagan
113 Albert Noel
114 Mrs Mary M Simmons
114 Ralph S Taylor
115 Mrs Mary E Burns
116 Mrs A Emma Cummings
117 Solomon Rosenberg
117 John William Kelley
118 Leslie A Bly
118 Mrs Abbie F Watt
120 Alfred Carlson
120 Michael A Riley
121 Norman S Dyer
121½ Frank Terra
121½ Mrs Matilda Peterson
121½ Mrs Fanny Costa
122 Arthur W Clark
122 James G England
125½ Henry Queen
125½ Simon Schuster
126 Abraham Cohen
126 John Linhares
128 John E Enos Jr
128 Ernest V Richards
129 Peter Lambert
130 Louis F Degagner
131 Joseph E Benoit
133 John E Moriarty
133 Joseph C Babcock
134 I LeR York
134 Antone R Bronco
134 Cassius B Mott
134 Jule Campus
134 Charles A Howland
134 Manuel D Silveira
135 John Medeiros
136½ Mrs Elizabeth A Morgan
137 Minerva Dwight
138 Mrs Margaret E Doran
138 Mrs Maud Markham
139 Alfred Silva
140 George Gardner
146 James Ciaburri
146 William J Williams
150 Mrs Abbie C Rathburn
150 Ernest E Gillum
152 Mrs Charles B Hillman
156 Walter Jenkins
156 Joaquim A Correia
167 Antone M Rosa
168 Thomas A Sylvia
168 John C McBride
169 Marcelino Oliver
170 Grace Carter
170 William M Ryan
171 Edward A Ennis
171 Michael M Conway
172 Mary E Smith
172 Marrie A Wall
173 Manuel A Lawrence Jr
173 Benjamin F Hinckley
174 Mrs Ellen Harrington
174 Frank G Harrington
175 John A Flynn
175 Manuel Marshall
175 James Walsh
176 Oscar Buffington
176 Mrs Hattie B Childs
177 Luis E Grover
177 Mrs Catherine Riordan
178 Patrick Kenney
178 Lester M Austin
179 Peter M Snyder
179 Herman T Karcher 2nd
180 Norris H Tripp
180 Mrs Joanna M Pease
181 William A Gibbs
181 Harry E Phinney
182 William E Sisson
182 Zephaniah W Pease
183 Mrs Margaret G Baker
185 Mrs Hannah W Harrington
185 Mrs Phebe S Sherman
185 J Clifford Sherman
186 Rossa Moriarty
186 William W Grieve
189 Francis Little
189 John C Noyer
193 Alex P Sylvia
199 Manuel P Perry
199 Joao Claudino

199 Frank F Sylvia
199 Antone Souza
201 Manuel Mora
205 Henry J McDonald
205 William C H McAllister
210 Manuel F Cardoza
211 George E White
211 Robert Scott
211 Michael J Donovan
212 William C Tripp
212 Daniel J Humphrey
213 Joseph Dupre
213 John P Kilbride
213 Mrs Mary B Joseph
214 James Riley
214 David Hutchings
215 George L Jennings
216 John F De Silva
216 William J Hunt
218 Patrick J McQuillan
218 Manuel Grace
219 Manuel Alferes
225 Albert J Roscoe
225 James Smith
226 Samuel Sharkey
229 Mrs Emma F Morse
229 Nathaniel Bonney
233 James W Robertson
235 Antone M Praeda
235 Mrs Mary I Catin
235 Antone Menes
235 Mrs Mary Raymond
239 Anthony Robinson
239 William Sanderson
240 John E Kilburn
240 Jeremiah J McCarthy
246 Mrs M Ella Paine
246 Lewis Kelley
246 James A Reed
247 Dr Joseph Pothier
250 Mrs Isabelle Silva
250 Mrs Annie Grenada
253 John G Lange
254 Arthur Bunoit
254 John Souza
256 Irving S York
256 William Phillips
256 George E Rivers
256 Irving S York
257 Virginio Ignavis
257 Manuel Sampson
259 Edward Mills
259 Arthur A Dion
260 Eva Souza
260 Manuel F Silva
262 Antone F Gomes
264 Robert Holliday
265 Antone Rogers
265 Peter Rogers
266 Robert Cooke
266 Newell T Cowan
269 William R Vera
269 William Holland
272 John O'Malley
272 James Carr
273 James McCaffery
273 John T Ward
276 James W Gleason
276 William Smith
276 James W Gleason
280 Joseph Marchi
280 Mrs Jennette Gatenby
280 William J Winsper
281 Herbert C Lawrence
281 Antone Mickell
282 Albert Wooley
283 Manuel Gaspar
283 James Littlefair
284 Manuel Sylvia
284 Manuel A Boim
284 James C Murphy
284 Mrs Jennie Donnelly
286 Joseph Silva
286 Charles Mont
286 Arsene Chartier
288 William Brockelhurst
288 James Kilbride
289 John Walsh
290 Mrs Mary Bilsborrow
291 Patrick Walsh
291 Jacob Philippi
292 Docithe Maynard
292 Henry C Berube
292 Alex Menard
292 Joseph A Gagnon
293 Manuel Medeiros
293 Frank S Rose
297 Thomas W Hudson
298 Joseph Oliveira
301 Walsh Duxbury
301 Alice Taylor
303 Mrs Jennet Smith

FRANKLIN

3 Frederick Dawson
4 Joseph Lapolla
5 John Miller
5 Ida Randall
6 Luke T Keith
6 Sidney S Fisher
7 C A Bearse
7 Mrs M L Austin
8 Edwin Johnson
8 Francis M Taffe
11 Helen M Gordon
14 Mrs Phoebe D Hathaway
15 Mrs Elizabeth Lord
15 George L Taber
15 James O'Connor

Franklin—con
16 Mrs Mary A Harrington
16 Samuel H Wilson
17 Robert H Black
17 Chester A Eaton
27 Mrs Eveline Kirk
29 Gilbert J Hart
32 Matthew Donovan
32 Mrs Rachel Fielding

FREDERICK

155 Edward Young
159 Philias Suprenant
163 Christopher Martin
163 William Ridings

FREMONT

204 Carl E Morde
451 David Liljequist

FRONT

284 Mrs Mary Costa
479 Manuel Machado

FROST

670 Thomas Maguire

FRUIT

29 Cornelius Downey
44 George Booth
44 Alfred Needham
46 Wm Craven
46 Daniel Perrington
52 Alfred Smith
52 Clarence M Potter
53 Mrs Ellen Howarth
55 Wm Cooper
59 Mercer Fielding
71 Joseph Farren
71 Wallace Ashley
73 Wm Melody
74 Thomas Cross Jr
77 John Flores
77 Herbert F Jones
77 Mrs Mary Garlington
84 Manuel Dionizio
84 Herbert N Brock
84 Joseph S Souza
87 Peter S Sorensen
87 Walter Keighley
87 Mrs Virginia Phenix
89 Alfred Owen
90 Mrs Catherine Baptista
94 Jerome J Pedro
99 Zebina B Chase
99 John Devine
100 Edward J McCauley
104 Edward Winterbottom
109 Manuel R Lopes
109 Antone B Souza
110 Thomas Quinn
116 Anthony J Melody
118 John J Flanagan
118 William T Green
130 Ellery E Brightman
132 Albion S Peck

FULTON COURT

2 Walenty Strojny
4 Miszael Riendeau
5 John Olejesz
5 Marcel Kral
5 Wlaivstat Saliotski
6 Mrs Verinita Bolan
7 John Fraser
7 Xavier Breton
8 Wojciech Piekielniak
8 John Kokowski
8 John Groblecki
9 Wladislaw Sabotowski
9 Andrew Kosera
10 Adam Szezur
11 Powell Smolla
11 Patrick J Lyons
12 Andrew Setera
12 Piotz Kuczera
13 John Schweigart
13 John Strony
14 Joseph Wyzga
15 Jan Blyracchyk
15 Charles Gonet
16 Alliezik Tchors
16 Jan Jagedrieziski
17 Wladyslaw Przybyla
17 Adelord Charbonneau
18 Joseph Switsak

GENDRON

194 Joseph Beaudoin

GEORGE

8 John T Miller
8 James Copeland
8 Christopher Cheetham
11 Aaron Burke
11 David Cartwright
15 John W Etchels
16 John A Schofield
16 Joseph Dubois
16 Joseph Lavalle
17 Jabez Newby
19 Alfred Page
19 Alida Cadieux
19 Smith George
19 William H Gervais
19 Joseph Cortu
19 Alphonse Faford Jr
19 James Pearson
20 John T Catterall

20 Thomas Cooper
20 Philip Genensky
20 John Hyland
20 Hector Bolduc
20 Samuel Reeves
22 James Farraday
22 Hector Lucas
23 Burgoyne Woolley
25 Walter E Smith
26 John Halliwell
26 Pierre Caron
28 Daniel Buckley
30 George Noblet
33 John W Duckworth
33 Edward Moss
33 Edward Fitton
35 William Bauman
36 Frank T Healey
36 Mrs Bertha St Lawrence
36 Peter F Clark
36 Edward J McGowan
36 James Littlefair
36 Henry Maynard Jr
71 William Lacharite

GIFFORD

1 Josef Driota
1 Felix Laliberte
1 John Wydra

GLOVER

3 Herbert W Ellis
3 K H Moulton
15 Mrs Jerusha Cannon
15 John Murphy

GRAND

8 Frank Willett
24 Manuel Correio
25 Chas H Peets
45 Charles F Parker
45 Manuel Bant

GRANDFIELD

7 Peter Zamos
7 Abdod Mossis
8 Joseph Silva
8 John Cambra
8 John Sylvia
9 Henry Houghton
10 Manuel Furtado
10 Juda Walder
10 Hyman Lipnik
12 John Correia
12 Antone S Mello
12 Manuel Moniz
15 Jacob Kulick
16 Yusef Amiszczyk
16 Ignacz Strojny
18 Frank Koplitzski

GRANT

22 Candido Frates
22 John Angrella
28 Lindolf De Costa
32 Victorino Soares
39 John Borges
45 Manuel F Martin
46 James E Hallowell
46 Francis Duffy Jr

GRAPE

4 Minnie Cleary
12 Arthur C White
13 Robert W Carr
16 Mrs Sarah A Blackie
16 Mary C Hiscox
17 Michael Dahoney
21 Daniel Mason
22 Philip C Randall
23 Robert Butler
31 Thomas H Hughes
31 E Adolph Gunderson
33 James F Griffith
34 Benjamin P Pease
42 Antonio S Furtado
48 Charles O Redfield
52 James T Tripp
53 Herman K Knechtel
55 Harold S Macomber
67 Frank E Francis
68 Francis V Crumley
71 John Jacinth
74 Jose Pacheco Pleso
100 Albert L Wade
108 Alex A Tripp
163 Frank Rose

GREEN

2 Jas H Miskell
2 Mrs Julia A Almy
3 James T Wing
3 Horatio B Cooke
3½ Dr Francis L Tuttle
3½ Charles E Gardner
4 Wm A Clark
5 George H Atwood
5 Mrs Jabez A Gordon
6 Patrick J Cunningham
7 Chas T Ennis
10 H Arthur Silsbee
12 Mrs Annie S Ramos

GRIFFIN

2 Antone Cruz
4 John Perreira

Griffin—con
7 John Baptiste
7 John Pries
8 Enos Land
8 Sylvester Anton
8½ Joseph Cruz
8½ Peter Baptiste
10 Joseph Ponte
10 Martin A Gomes
10 Levana Lopes
10 Mrs Nellie Reis
10 Joseph Ponte
12 Antone Frates
14 Henry J Barrows
14 Eugene Soares
14½ Antone Frates
14½ Joseph Almeida
14½ John D Leighton
15 Frank V Francis
15 Joseph F Sylvia
15½ Joseph M Morris
16 Frank Couta
16 Mrs John F Dias
17 Manuel Peter
17 Manuel King
18 Frank Oliveira
18 Manuel Madeiros
18 Manuel Sylvia
21 Joseph Matthews
21 Fredk Porth
21 Manuel Cardoza
22 August Perry
22 Frank Pacheco
25 Manuel Allgie
25 Antonio E Zerbone
25 Henry Rose
26 Helen B Aikin

GRINNELL

52 Ellen Tresham
54 Joseph Perry
55 Manuel Goulart
55 Michael Goulart
55 Antone Costa
56 Mary Amaral
56 Antone M Correia
56 Manuel Fells
56 Joseph Furtado
56 Mrs Mello Santos
57 Samuel Kuplisky
57 Amraham Glech
57 Arthur Rodil
58 Manuel Francis
58 Paul S Nunes
58 Jose Medeiros
59 Mrs Nancy Kennedy
59 John M Salles
61 John F Simas
61 Frank M Starr Jr
61 Joseph Cardoza
62 Joseph De Mello
63 Frank Pedro
63 Frank Veira
63 Andre Neves
63 Manuel Rose
63r Manuel B Pereira
66 Marianno Menics
67 Antone Perry
68 Mrs Mary Costa
68 Manuel Correira
75 Fernandez Gonsalves
75 Lichandre Mello
76 John Andrada
76 Joseph G Perry
79 Antone Oliver
79 Mrs Lillian M Briggs
79 Soloman Brick
82 Nathan Levin
82 Manuel Correiro
82 Manuel Silva
83 John E Enos
84 Antonio Barboza
85 Lewis Ladino
86 Levi Hurwitz
86 Joseph M Jacobson
87 Vergino Ponte
89 Antonio De Mello
90 Manuel F Souza
90 Augustin Stone
92 Manuel D Perry
93 Antone Souza
93 Bernard Soares
93 Manuel Frates
94 Lena Bailey
95 Arthur S Head
95 George W Simmons
97 Patrick F Burnes
97 Frank Perry
109 Marcellini C Mello
109 Sergio Dutra
111 Mrs Elizabeth Abrams
111 George H Baylis
112 Mrs Mary Rosa
112 H Antonio Rosa
112 Mrs Emily K Barker
112r Andrew J Kelley
113 Joseph A Norris
113 William H Wilson
114 Fortunato A Arruda
114 Mrs Katie B Stanbridge
114 Joseph A Nickerson
114 Mrs Catherine H Baker
115 Mrs Catherine Downey
115 Mrs Margaret Darcy
117 Fred S Spooner
117 John H McNamee
120 Max Erlbeck
120 Mrs Mary E Rogers

120 John Sylvia
127 Sarah Kane
129 Manuel Consalves
129 James O'Connor
133 Mrs Margaret Monarch
135½ Abel Fachado
151 Joseph C Durfee
151 Mary E Enos
152 Manuel J Senna
153 Robert McGlung
153 Mrs Jane Thompson
154 Manuel Catin
154 Edward J Anderson
155 Charles V Covill
155 Wilfred I Ellis
156 Charles M Gifford
156 Mrs Nancy S Peters
157 Benjamin F Willoughby
157 F R Brightman
158 Mrs Elmira K Barnes
160 John Taylor
161 Arthur W Macy
162 Joseph Tablas
163 Ralph B Leavitt
164 John E Luce Jr
165 Manuel Souza
165 Lawrence J Oliver
165 Joseph Sharves
166 Manuel Lawrence
166 Mrs Mary J Walsh
166½ Manuel Rose
167 Herbert Paulding
167 Catherine M Murphy
167 James F Murphy
168 Charles A Baker
169 Mrs Carrie E Gilman
170 William T Jenney
171 Thomas H Howland
173 William H Skiff
174 William B Jenney
174½ Walter C Ryder
175 Frank C Dunham
175 Louis Cross
176 Herbert R Paulding
176 John B Paulding
177 Mrs Anna B Dillingham
177 Elmer C Thompson
178 Francis R Taber
179 Catherine Carmody
179 Mrs Rose Bettencourt
179 Manuel F Bettencourt
180 Mrs Angelica T Hallet
181 Edgar F Howland
181 Mary L Chadwick
186 John R Webb
192 Rufus Cleveland
195 Lemuel H White
196 William Cole Jr
197 H Eugene Covill
201 Jasper L Sisson
202 Mrs Mary W Smith
202 James H Gray
207 Millage G Besse
207 Frederick P Coe
208 Charles H Malmedie Jr
208 Lyman W S Tripp
211 Willard F Hervey
212 Frank H Vincent
212 Gilbert G Stiles
215 Mrs Joanna O'Shea
216 William E Kern
217 Mrs Barbara Krebs
217 James H Barr
217 Benjamin Barr
220 William N Jewett
220 Edward Stone
223 W H C Taylor
223 George S Bowen
224 Jonathan K Wright
225 Leon S Handy
225 Misses Whitehead
226 Samuel F Winsper
232 Herbert A Miller

GRIT

31 Antone Francis

GROVE

2 John B Strongman
33 George H H Allen
35 Gideon Allen Jr
38 George S Homer
39 William A Robinosn Jr
42 Frederick D Stetson
288c Robert Maguire

HALL

13 Wilbur E Hayford
13 Joseph Enos
13 F Marshall
17 Antonio Machado
17 Joseph G Silvya
18 John G Luiz
18 John J Sylvia
21 George Perry
21 John McGladory
21 Antone E Francis
22 Mrs Mary A Foggarty
25 Antonio Machado Jr
25 Victorino Reizendes
26 Fernando Migeul
26 Frank E Rose
29 Patrick Ford
29 Manuel J Espinola
45 Manuel S Mello
49 Joseph B Fagan
49 Arthur Breault

Hall—con
49 Mary A Lee
51 John W Cunningham
52 Daniel Charlebois
52 Richard Green
56 Walter Almond
60 Mary Vera
60 Joaquim Terra
60 James Duckworth
60 Joseph S Cardozo
68 Manuel C Luiz
69 Edward J Hildman
69 Manuel J Azevedo
70 Manuel Grace
70 Eli Bryant
71 Mary O'Hearn
71 George H Clark
96 Jose F Leonard
96 William A Matthews
96 Manuel Peters
97 Arthur Souza
97 Mrs Theresa King
97 Frank J Garcia
100 John F Leonard
100 Joseph F Sylvia
100 John F Sylvia
100 Frank F Cordoza
100 John F Leonard
101 Manuel J Picanso
101 Fred Fredette
101 Peter Fatulli

HAMPTON COURT

1 Antony Jensky
1 Michael Perboiller
2 Wojsiech Dygos
2 Frank Supcezk
3 Joseph Latusik
3 Mchael Wiskos
4 Leon Withowicz
4 John Jackouvlitch
4 Josef Braun
5 Jusaf Petriska
6 Jan Tarasko
7 Walenty Sunday
7 Frank Bowen
10 Joseph Kounday
13 Czeslaw Baron
13 Roman Rosowski
16 Louis Chouniard
17 Peter Bedan
17 Clemens Nietah
18 Powell Jaskalka
19 Ozga Sylvester
20 Mrs Mary Roketa

HARMONY

1 Omer Carrier
1 Philias Carrier
1 John B Boulieu
1 Mason E Nelson
1 William Clarke
3 Mrs Averiste Richer
3 Joseph Mossie
3 Mrs Melinda Dragon
4 James Orr
4 Mrs Elizabeth Pickering
4 William Baron
4 James Cross
6 William Thomson
6 Daniel F Higgins
7 John Moran
7 John Bauer
8 Collin Barrett
8 Mrs Mary J Nairn
8 John Higgins
9 John Graham
9 Frank Williams
9 Thomas Blacow
10 William Norris
10 William Ward
10 Thomas Lownds
11 Mrs Elizabeth Ashworth
12 Leon Beaudry
12 Joseph Viger Jr
12 Hormidas Robert
12 Alfred Rousseau
13 Samuel Carter
13 John Sutcliffe
13 John Buchanan
14 William Sykes
14 William H Boardman
14 Joseph Sykes
16 Mrs Matilda Hewitt
16 Mary A Trodden

HARRISON

1 John T Parry
1 James D Butts
2 John C Cabral
2 Cornelius J Leary
2 Abbie Hogan
3 Joseph P Cronan
5 Joseph Gonsalves
5½ Claudino Vieira
5½ Joseph Sylvia
6 John B Ray
7 Mrs Annie Dodge
8 Alfred Dumolin
8 Robinson Gregson
9 Mrs Annie O'Brien
9 James Clunie

HATCH

65 Hector Rousseau
65 Frank Hebert
68 George Perault
68 George Courcy

72 Manuel Frates
72 Mrs Maria Augusta
162 John Baptiste Patnaude
162 Samuel Doyon
170 John McCormack
170 Octave Gravel
170 Edward Pepin
172 F Gendron
172 Mrs Adele Goguen
174 Marcella A Dion

HATHAWAY

60 John Crowther
60 Matthew Tonge
60 Stephen Hebden
61 John A Tool
61 John Sharples
64 Richard Mason
64 Moses Dewhurst
64 Fred Winterbottom
65 Abraham Allen
67 Napoleon Girard
67 James A Francis
67 Mrs Mary J St John
67 Thomas Beck Jr
67 Antonio Laliberte
67 Abaraham Allain
68 Albert Bennett
68 Rhodes Smith
69 Aresene Ricard
70 George S Sharp
71 Frank Gauthier
71 Frank Babineau
72 John Baty
72 Mrs Elizabeth Gill
72 Samuel Bowler
73 John W Walsh
73 Anna Phillips
73 Walter J Bryden
73 Joseph Leger
73 Ernest Menard
73 Alphonse Parent
74 Mrs Isabella Foster
74 Thomas Hulme
75 Benjamin Bailey
75 George Johnson
75 John Wilcock
76 John W Schofield
76 William Castle
76 Farrow Tattersall
77 Ebenezer Thornber
77 John C Hatton
77 Walter Ashton
85 Albert Plummer
85 Thomas Fenton
85 David Hogarth
86 Armanda Lemieux
86 Mrs Kate Carr
86 Emile La Page
86 John Sanders
86 John R Ingham
87 Frank McCullough
87 Mrs Alice Smith
87 Ernest Johnson
87 Mary Pollitt
87 Mrs Jennie Bloeser
87½ Michael S Glynn
87½ Walter Taylor
87½ Joseph Lima
88 Adelard Gauthier
88 Didias Gamache
88 Pierre Cournoyer
88 Amedee Auclair
89 Mrs Mary Whalen
89 Joseph Pospisal
89 Charles Dlouhy
90 Mrs Jennie Connelly
90 Patrick McLynch
90 George Pollitt
90 Thomas H Carroll
91 Harold Duffy
91 Mrs Agnes Mailhot
91 John E Duffy
91 Alfred Bessette
91 Adelard Harbeck
93 Calvert George
93 Mrs Philomena St Charles
93 Albini Gallant
93 Louis Morin
93 Alexander La Porte
94 William O Hampson
94 James Whittam
94 Percey Bowden
94r William Brown
95 Andrew Poirier
95 Michael H Grimes
95 William Acker
96 William J Leonard
96 Antoine Arbour
96 Edward Clegg
104 Thomas Stephens
105 Mrs Ellen Jennings
105 George F Chadwick
109 Albert Rousseau
109 John H McMay
109 Benjamin Bailey
110 Richard Blacow
110 Mrs Catherine Noble
110 Isaac C Noble
110 Alphonse G Hebert
113 Mary O'Brien
113½ Herbert Leathers
114 John S Shaw
115 Martin Livesey

Hathaway—con
115 Joseph Picher
116 Samuel A Goodfellow
116 John Pilkington
116 Joseph Harrison
118 James Meeking
118 Mrs Sarah A Kaye
119 Robert Hunt
120 James Meeking
120 Joseph Wood
121 Louis Frates
121 Tom Smithson
121 Joseph Langlois
122 Ootto F Sieferth
122 George Walker
122 Joshua H Goodfellow
123 Joseph O Paquette
123 Richard Kobes
123 John Hargraves
124 Arthur Supry
124 Benjamin B Mills
124 Edward Molloy
127 Oliver Giguere
127 Odelon Giguere
127 Albert E Miller
128 George Myers
132 Hiram Hughes
135 Mrs Mary O'Brien
135 Edward C Crosby
135 John Allcock
139 Oliver Lebeau
140 Mrs Ida Tyrell
140 John Bolton
147 Philip Comeau
147 Alphonse Levesque
149 Joseph M Francis
149 Frank G D'Aguiar
150 Michael Rogers
150 A Ranicar
150 Thomas Slater
153 Arthur E Tomilson
153 John Marwan
153 Margaret Jordan
153 Francis J Boyle
154 Louis Tremblay
154 George Macy
154 Mrs Domidile Cormier
154 Mitchell Glass
154 Mary Germain
155 John Robert Sykes
157 Thomas Lewin
157 John B Sylvia
157 Kasper Feser
157 Thomas Lewin
157 John Punch
157 J Steiblin
158 George O'Toole
158 John T Halligan
158 Andrew M Bush
158 John Vasser
158 Robert Whatmough
161 John Rieff
161 Joseph Heck
162 J A S Guimaraes
162 Azarie Blais
165 Carl Stiller
165 Fred J Brittain
165 John Hoffman
166 Frank Schestak
169 William Hindle
169 Frank Messner
169 Joseph S Harper
173 Alfred Antosch
173 Adam Leupold
173 John Gow
176 Adelard Bourassa
176 Arthur Charles
176 Richard Warburton
182 Mrs Anthenaise Bissot
186 Mrs Anne Hearne
186 Thomas Spencer
186 Alas Brodeur
186 John Gillibrand
186 Theodore Hebert
186 Dan Greenwood
187 Richard Knowles
187 Thomas W Holden
187 Charles Le Clair
189 Mary A Robinson
189 Mary E Stone
189 George Swales
189 Michael Smith
200 Mrs Ada Shaw
203 Antoine Moniz
205 Edmond Lague
206 Michael Dumais
206 Thomas Sullivan
206 Thomas Goodhue
206 Honorius Robitaille
206 Louis Robitaille
208 Mrs Mary Ferreira
210 Charles A Poulin
211 William Champagne
211 Frederick Raistrick
211 Joseph Magee
212 Alphonse Meunier
212 Antone Oliver
212 A M Oleiveria
212 John Harrison
330 Mrs Mary J Hathaway

HATHAWAY ROAD

31 John P Amaral
61 John Sharples
65 Oliver Cormier

201 Zeferino Cardoza
210 Henry W Hathaway
215 David Grew
267 Israel J Wilson
270 William H Lynch
330 Mrs Mary J Hathaway
337 Mrs Amantha B Gammons
485 Antone Fernandes
507 Charles Benjamin
521 John J Armstrong
558 Hervey W Pittsley
558 Fred LaPierre
560 Mrs McLena Nelson
560 Charles Dutton
580 Nathan P Chase
596 William E Russell
631 John Sweeney
638 William H Robinson
672 David G Ashley
679 Manuel V Silva
699 Mrs Anjanette Allen
702 George B Mosher
702 Manuel Peters
803 Mrs Charlotte T Casey
817 Mrs Clara E Hathaway
818 Willis B Turner
868 Ernes L Faulkner
906 George B Faulkner

HAWES

0 Albert Esta
0 Philippe Verville
0 Firmin Bedard
0 John Bisson
0 Joseph Robert
0 Napoleon Fountain
0 Leon Soucier
0 Patrick J Mullen
0 John H Bagley
0 Antone Lemos

HAWES LANE

0 William P Reed
0 James H Cobb
0 George H Reed
8 Mrs Nellie A Gifford

HAWTHORN

20 Julia Delano
71 Emma C Watkins
74 Edward T Pierce
78 Frederick Taber
81 William W Crapo
81 Henry H Crapo
84 William A Robinson
89 Mrs Lydia Grinnell
90 Mrs Mary A Allen
94 Standish Bourne
95 Abbott P Smith
100 James P Francis
109 Joseph W Nicklas
111 Philip E Macy
114 Thomas A Thornton
115 Z Edward Booth
122 Mrs Eliza H Wood
124 William B Gardner
126 Caleb A Hayward
127 Walter Clifford
137 Misses Snow
143 Mrs Mary K Potter
144 Herbert E Cushman
148 Leander A Plummer
149 Alice Russell Howland
150 William S Bourne
150 Dr William G Branscomb
154 Emilie Beaudry
163 William C Hawes
168 Loum Snow
178 Henry M Knowles
181 Joseph F Knowles
191 E Williams Hervey
191 Gilbert T Thompson
196 James F Smith
197 Harry F Richardson
203 John A Fernley
211 William A Carroll
215 Frank C Barrows
219 Albert C Langshaw
240 Mrs Margaret R Damon
244 Mrs Mary Gifford
248 Annie M Potts
251 John Sullivan
252 Aloysius Westby
268 Guy L Murdoch
270 John I Shannon
275 Herman Wahlgren
282 Charles S Ashley Jr

HAWTHORN TERRACE

15 Richmond Gordon

HAZARD

16 John W Hayden
31 Squire Lownds
31 Delphine Tetreault
31 Victor Andrew
32 Pasquale Laurenze
32 Archangelo Arado
34 Victor Dextradeur
36 Annie Laughlin
36 Mrs Lea Bernard
36 Paul M Bochman
36 Thomas Mulroy
40 Mrs M A Jenney
40 Elizabeth Henderson
42 Mrs Martha Moncrieff
50 Joseph Woodward
50 Charles E Marchessault

Hazard—con
54 Thomas Dugan
58 Joseph Stone
58 William A Johns
60 Andrew Magee
64 William Burns
64r Joseph Lemaire
68 Mrs Mary Noonan
68 John T Noonan
69 John J Mitchell
71 Jean B Cloutier
72 James Taylor
87 Francis A Rourke
87 Mrs Julia McCarthy
99 Oscar G Fricker
99 Thomas Sheard
99 August Simpson
103 Thomas Bowers
103 James W Navasey
103 John O'Malley
105 Thomas C Starkie
105 George C Geddis Jr

HAZARD COURT

1 Mrs Aurore Champagne
2 Jules Berube
2 James P Leddy
3 John Bowers
4 Mrs Margaret Doyle
5 Hector Cloutier
6 Mrs Jennie Sharrett
6 Henri Boule
7 Frank Breau
8 Patrick F McGuiggan
8 Frank H Marshall
9 Xavier Gosselin
10 John Foye
10 Patrick H Reardon
10 Charles F Mitchell
11 Frank Talbot
12 Remi Lebeau
13 David Bonin
14 John B Demanche
15 Valentine Cloutier
16 Isidore Clouthier
17 Mrs Sarah A Kilmartin
18 Mrs Araline Rocheleau
18 Joseph Taylor
19 Edward Norris
20 William Hinkley

HEMLOCK

1 Joseph B Perry
1 Samuel J Nelson
19 James E Jackson
19 Manuel Correia
22 Joseph Braga
22 Manuel F Goulart
22 Antone Tavares
34 John Feeney
39 Edmund Weeks
39 Manuel J Spindola
39 Robert Gundberg
40 John Gresser
40 Joseph E Severino
43 Frank S Machado
43 Manuel S Sylvia
43 Manuel S Medeiros
43 Eva Rogers
44 John G Gomes
44 Antone M Lema
44 John S Pavonia
47 Mrs Annie M Howland
47 Mrs Philomena Sylvia
47 Mary Sylvia
47 Thomas O Simpson
48 Mrs Mary G Fernandes
48 Luiz Perry
48 Bartholomew Silva
49 John Gonsalves
49 John Connelly
49 Mary Brown
51 Antone E Rose
51 Joseph Williams
55 Manuel J Rollins
55 John Sylvia
75 Joseph Costa
75 Joseph Praeda
75 Joseph Praeda Jr
77 Joaquim P Ramalhete
77 Albert Watson
79 Manuel Joseph
79 Antonio R Silva
90 Manuel T De Mello
93 Arthur Sutcliffe
94 Thomas Walsh
99 Manuel G Rose
103 Joseph Vieira
103 Manuel S Perry
103 Mrs Martha Dale
104 J Fred Arseneault
104 Harris J Daffinee
104 Mastai Bouthillette
105 John Wilkinson
105 Antone Almeida
105 John M Cabral
106 William J Hathaway
106 Henry Touchette
106 Calixte Boissoneault
120 Thomas J Hart
123 John Brown
123 John Stanton
123 Manuel Medeiros
124 James Cook
124 Misses Stenson
141 Juan Daniels
141 Manuel Marshall
153 Antonio Motta
156 Cephas Higginbottom
156 Joseph Coelho

HERSOM

0 George S Cobb
47 Lous Brodeur
47 Paul Rioux

HICKORY

11 Frederick Dickson
15 Antonio S Silva
22 Charles D Russell
22 Sarah Rose
37 Olaf Erlandson
37 Lawrence A Gillis

HICKS

2 Parelli Bonanentura
2 Alfred Dion
3 Omer Demers
4r Edward Moquin
6 Moise LeBeau
8 William Dabrooski
8 Henry L Galipeau
13 Achille Rivard
13 Mrs Mary Brule
13 John Lafoi
13 Martin Pejko
13 Aurelia Monty
13 Sophia Seymour
13 Adam Rubea
16 Amede Delude
16 Firman Lapointe
16 Joseph Frechette
16 Joseph Rocray
16 Henri Moquin
19 Moise Roy
19 Ludger Gervais
19 Edward Bouchard
19 Mrs Mary Lapalme
21 Joseph Dionne
27 Mrs Annie Kilanowich
27 Laddius Antoncovitch
27 Joseph Rutdkowski
27 Victor Sycko
27 Eran Delaire
27 Mrs August Charbonneaux
31 Edmond Potvin
31 Arthur Deroche
33r Raimund Janak
36 Joseph Laporte
36 Alfred Huard
36 Mrs Elodie Nolin
36 Arthur Laporte
36 Joseph F Parent
36r Edmonde Laporte
36r Augustus LeClair
36r Julius Tremblay
36r Emile Perville
39 Antone Blacha
39 Simon Jabott
43 Edward Bessette
43 George Frechette
45 Henri Delour
45 Mrs Lena Surette
51½ Albert Cassidy
52 Joseph Bariteau
52 Edward Dion
52 Frank Couture
52 Peter Sampson
52 Mrs Mary Dupre
52 Mrs Julia St Germain
53 Eusebe Bouchard
53 Lucien Belanger
59 Philomene Guibeault
59 Edmund J Couture
63 Alexandre Dupre
63 Pierre Rivard
63 John Fregeau
63 Ozebelle Gendron
63 Mrs Nellie Burns
64 Joseph La Brecque
64 Pierre Samson
64 Hugo La Pierre
64 Mrs Brandie Charance
69 Joseph Henzl
69 Peter Kosto
69 Joseph Hezek
69 John Harrison
69 Victor Benoit
69 Michael Koleck
69 Salabasti Superenack
69 Dloule E Louise
69 Thomas Dibb
74 J Arthur Deslaurier
74 Joseph Fortin
74 Edmond Robert
76 Frank Fregeau
76 Onesphore A Therrien
76 Frank Renaud
128 Benson Bruno

HIGH

15 John B Alves
17 Fred C Dwyer
19 Mrs Bridget Tate
19 Mary Dillon
24 Mrs Clara Reed
24 Seth Hatch
28 Mrs Mary Akin
31 Henry C Tripp
31 Julius Lerch
33 Abram H Matthews
33 William L Peirce
34 Thomas E Potter Jr
34 Edward H Bryant
39 Rilla D Sawyer
39 Ruth F Haskins

High—con
41 Emma Lamarine
48 Charles M Crossman
53 Edward Cusson
60 Annie Meaney
72 Mrs Sarah M Murdock
86 Mrs Mattie McIntyre
86 Charles W Allen
88 Mrs Idella M Ryder
88 Mrs Maria F Westgate
89 Edward B Reed
89 John C Vieira
90 Harold L Hoxie
90 Mrs Harold C Wing
91 Mrs Lizzie A Shepherd
91 Mrs Betsey Sears
92 Arzelia L Sauve
92 Albert J Martin
95 Mrs Mary M Mann
95 Mrs Phoebe B Faunce
96 Edwin Buckley
100 Daniel A McKinnon
106 Thomas A McAfee
106 Walter N Brown
110 Alphus A Braley
111 Frederick E Ricketson
111 Joseph H Wheeler
112 Squire H H Lucas
112 Patrick A Mahon
114 Jacob Altman
117 Thomas Hankerson
118 Nelson L Orcutt
118 Elisha Davoll
120 Herbert C Pratt
120 Isaac R Allen
122 Joseph Alleck
124 William A Davis
124 Herbert H Borden

HIGHLAND

9 Mrs Mary J Clark
14 Jose P Santos
14 John Lima
17 Benjamin Sykes
23 Fred Joubert
27 Charles W Crooks
40 Charles A Lincoln
41 James W Wooler
43 Joseph Baron
150 Arthur Bonneau
194 George Melanson
194 John Doyle
196 Andrew Cheetham
205 William Henshaw
215 Mrs Mary Bonneau

HILL

30 Arthur C Lee
30 George D Maxim
37 Mrs Almira C Colby
42 Edwin R Bentley
42 Charles D Sisson
46 Axel G Hanson
46 John H Cunniff
50 Mrs Olive L Benjamin
51 Frank R Delano
53 Lewis D Baldwin
53 Mrs Jane Taber
55 Mrs Almira W Potter
55 Alvin H Paine
56 Charles M Comey
56 Augustus J Moulton
57 Charles H Cragen
58 Mrs Debra Brownell
59 Mrs Angennette Hazzard
59 Joanna K Hayes
61 Edward P Lawrence
61 Norman W Oakes

HILLMAN

1 John Pacheco
23 Alphonse Roy
25 George W Heights
25 Amanda M Pager
26 Bernard Shapiro
26 Rose Dufre
27 Mrs Mary A Francis
27 Frank F Lewis
28 Charles F Landrie
28 Leander P Ross
29 Samuel Barash
32 Charles F Naylor
33 Mrs Eliza Booth
34 Mrs Geogene Dyer
34 Ivan E Armstrong
34 Mrs Emma L Borden
36 Eudora Hayes
36 Emma T Baker
37 Eugene H Godfrey
39 Willard B Hafford
47 Fred C Morse
49 George A Babcock
50 Edmund Labrie
50 Ludger Laliberte
53 James Orcutt
53 Edward Ryan
57 May E Davis
59 Charles W Coggeshall
61 Leland C Peirce
61 Mrs Charles F Folger
62 Mrs Eldoretta Bates
63 Mrs Carrie E Weeden
63 Gertrude S Howland
63 William T Davis
64 Frank C Smith
64 Katherine M Tripp
65 Arthur S Allen
66 Joseph Austin
67 Frederick T Maxfield

67 Lewis E Keyes
68 Chester W Chase
70 Mrs Etta Branceri
71 Clarence J Davoll
71 Charles L Borden
72 Rev Thomas S Sayer
73 Harriet W Thomas
73 Lewis E Milliken
74 Theodore W Cole
75 Lemuel E Simmons
76 Arthur D Swift
78 Rosa Booth
78 Susan M Hathaway
79 Dr H B Hamilton
81 Mrs Flora B Baker
81 Edgar F Randall
83 Frank R Cass
85 Israel Touchette
85 Lizzie R Hazard
85 Robert W Potter
86 Mrs Ann M Sowle
86 Fred T Almy
90 Charles A B Peterson
90 A Bassett Kenyon
92 Weston C Vaughan Jr
94 R Eugene Ashley
94 Emery S Judd
95 Mrs Etta C Lucas
95 William M Bonney
97 Walter P Morton
97 Thomas B Wilcox Jr
98 Edward E Hicks
100 Dan J Sullivan
101 Arthur K Taber
101 Robert A Taber
105 William Swanton
111 Samuel H Perry
111 Mrs Mabel A Coggeshall
113 John L Burton
115 John G Nicholson
117 James A Drescott
119 Samuel Dudgeon
123 David S Small
123 Charles W Tripp
124 William T Taylor
124 Charles F Trull
125 Joseph E Landers
125 Mrs Ellen M Davis
129 Edwin A Gammons
129 Emma J Merrick
134 Albert H Sawyer
138 Daniel Burns
138 William Hall Jr
143 Ida Sanborn
143 A Isabel Titcomb
143 Mrs Sarah A Leach
145 Joseph Deacon
146 Mrs Azubah A Gifford
147 George H K Brownell
148 Joseph Nannery
151 George T Hardwick
155 Charles L Aldrich
155 Alberto S Nickerson
157 Edward C Neagus
159 Walter C Staples
159 Manuel Cunha
166 Herbert L Sholes
217 David A Dexter
221 George W Cunningham
225 Mrs Flora N Williams
229 John P Cunningham
237 William J Albro
237 Alfred J Turgeon
237 Philip H Crandon Jr
246 Sherman Murray
246 Joseph C Murray
249 Mrs Rebecca Waite
249 Charles H Smith
252 Manuel P Serpa
253 Thomas Browning
256 Morgan O'Meara
256r Harry A Gifford
257 Stephen J Burns
260 Michael J Goulding
261 Philip H Wordell
265 Donn Shepardson
267 Justus A Briggs Jr
271 Mrs Clara Pheland
273 Mrs Clarissa E Chadwick
275 Frank B Chadwick
277 Albert A Potter
277 Mrs Isabel M Chace
279 Thomas E Moriarty
281 Charles D Tew
281 Edmund McCoy
281 Mrs Mary Simons
291 Benjamin Dias
291 Manuel Antone
295 Mrs K M Shanks
317 Joseph Francis
317 Maurice T Wainer
317½ John H Turner
371 Charles C Pierce
371 Edward Shepard
371 Mrs Lillian Monty
371r George W Sampson
371r Joseph R Campbell
375 William H Revallion
377 Samuel Barros
379 James E Steele
380 Mrs Amelia F Wordell
380 Ferdinand Phillips
381 Thomas L Butts
389 Mrs Elizabeth Jackson
389 Thomas Williams
395 Mrs Frances E Johnson
416 Andrew T Allen

Hillman—con
417 Fred Flemming
418 Patrick H Lowney
427 John W Young
453 Charles Burke

HILLMAN STREET COURT

2 Robert I Johnson
2 Isadore Gallant
3 Henry McCarthy
3 Mrs Margaret Perry
5 George John

HOLLY

7 Frank Silva
7 Napoleon Gosselin
7 Mrs Margaret Hunter
7 Hormidas Demers
7 Stanley Ceborowski
11 Amedee Roy
11 Jozef Mikolajczyk
11 Joseph Bass
11 Joseph Mekolaczk
11 Albert Bass
14 Mrs Alice Gasse
14 Joseph Jenard
15 Frank Dubois
15 George Dragon
16 Fred Babineau
16 Philias Goguen
16 Theophile Lemaire
17 Amee Bastarache
17 Frank Szcliga
17 James W Potter
18 Joseph Le Blanc
18 Mrs Tomasio Azevedo
18 Joseph Levesque
19 Cyrille Allain
19 Albert Girard
19 Thoedore Lareau
20 Flavien Benjamin
20 Belonie Racine
22 Mrs Jane Nolan
22 Richard Caissie
22 Pierre Bourgeois
23 Henry Hebert
23 Maxime Ray
23 Joseph Ferron
26 James Shaw
26 Louis St Pierre
28 Francois X Normandin
28 Jude Caissie
28 Gilbert Richmond
28 Arthur Adams
28 Mrs Sabin Cote
28 Fred Pollitt
28 John Alevizos
28 Bella Marshall
28 Abraham Binns
28 Howarth Smith
29 Mrs Elizabeth Grime
29 Mrs Euclide Beaudry
29 George Breau
31 Charles Aguros
31 Wilfrd Breault
32 Aime Breault
32 Calixte Charest
32 Mrs Aurelie Chainay
33 Pierre Ledoux
33 Joseph Genard
33 Joseph Pelletier
43 Camille Cote
43 Osias Racine
43 Fidell Allen
43 Leon Cote
47 Benjamin Ellingworth
47 Edouard Lemoine
47 Samuel Pickup
47 Joseph Laflamme
52 William Ingham
54 William Carman
54 Mrs Delia Riopelle
54 Cordelia Normandin
54 Joseph Normandin
57 Exilme R Gravel
63 Peter Kalish
63 William Wifdine
75 Joseph Cartier
75 Joseph M Poulin
75 Henry Hamel
79 Celestin Rousseau
79 Alphonse Ricard
81 Mrs Mary A Wood
81 Elzear Morin
82 Joseph Hamel
82 Stanislaus L'Hereux
85 Henry St Aubin
85 Adelard Brillion
85 Joseph Hardy
85 Wiliam Perryman
88 Henri Fortin
88 George M Roy
88 Flavien Gamache
88 Pierre Boucher
88 Alphonse Giguere
88 Francois X Poulin
91 Levi Ricard
91 Mrs Marie Gagnon
92 Arthur Larose
92 Ludger Sansoucy
92 Wilfred E Gonneville
93 Henry Duchaine
93 Mrs Rose D Fortier
96 Narcisse Remillard

96 Joseph Bolduc
96 Augustus Bessette
99 George Vezina
99 Alcibiade Bessette
99 Theodore Quintin
99 William Mainville
99 Ludger Maheu
100 John Moreau
100 Gedeon Poisson
100 Dosithe Dextras
101 Henry Tessert
101 Alphonse Meunier
101 Hugo Houselhof
101 Joseph O Bessette
101 Arthur J Hughes
103 Joseph Konvalinka
103 James Yates
103 Oliver Gervais
103 Mrs Mary Lee
107 Philmon Leonard
107 Moise Gosselin
107 James Clouthier
107 Henry Gosselin
109 Oliver Drolet
109 Hannibal Simi
109 John Castognoli
113 Charles A Poirier
119 Fred Girouard
119 Orias Cormier
119 Louis Champagne
124 William Hogg
125 Thomas Tattersall
125 Jose P Correia
125 Thomas Sellers
126 Nicholas Spirlet
126 Alfred Fredette
129 Hugo A Gendron
130 James Coates
130 Mrs Mary Brozek
136 Mark A Simpson
136 Harry Temberton
137 Ernest H Boucher
137 Abraham K Casson
137 Philip Gallant
138 Richard Forrest
138 James Milligan
140 Wendell Couza
141 William Lajoie
141 Samuel W Conn
143 Albert Hartley
143 Hardwell Bland
143 Thomas Lonsdale
146 Thomas Oddy
146 Antone Frates
146 Arthur Frates
146 Jonathan Counsell
147 Charles McCarthy
147 Joseph Marsland
151 George Anderton
151 Michael C McCarthy
155 Benjamin Cohen
155 Kopel Cohen
156 Bruno Dinter
156 John R Richards
156 Joseph Ball
156r Joseph Crampton
159 Adelard Rousseau
159 Hormidas Vallancort
163 Alfred L Whitehead
163 William Layland
163 Hubert Desmaris
164 Pierre LeBlanc
164 Mrs Aurelia LeBlanc

HOLLYHOCK

16 Joseph R Damos
18 Mrs Gertrude Machado
18 Joseph Correia
22 Seraphin Mello
22 Antonio Medeiros
22 Louis S Arruda
30 Frank P Silva
30 Frank Gracia
30 Joseph Perry
32 Jacintho Matteus
32 Joseph Dias
32 Frank Bender
35 Frederick Karcher **Jr**
38 Manuel Moniz
38 Antonio J Mello
38 Robert Houghton
38 John Mello
39 Julio J Cabral
39 Manuel Souza
45 Manuel S Moniz
45 Joseph Silva
56 John Arruda
56 Manuel de F Branco
56 Manuel Figueiredo
56 Joseph Arruda
56 Manuel Lima

HOMER

3 Walter Whittaker
7 George Peirce
11 Clifford M Farmer
11 Frederick J Bentley
14 Herbert W Hirst
14 Mrs Lois Hirst
15 Charles E Raymond
15 William S Broadbent
16 George Stratton
16 James Wood
18 Frank P Sanford
18 John Desmond
19 George T Castle
21 Fred Karl

Homer—con
21 Leander Crowell
22 William T Wilson
22 William T Hindle
22 Walter E Crapo
23 Walter M Burke
23 Frank N Allen
24 Charles E Allen
24 Charles R Slocum
25 John Hollihan
25 Frank H Childs

HOPE

0 Albert Rieu
55 Ludger Dessaint
55 Pierre D Lapointe
55 Joseph Roy
80 Israel St Pierre
80 Frank Souza
80 Louis Nault
121 Alex Pidgeon
121 Alfred Young

HOWARD

16 Minnie A Bullard
20 Stanley Poymola
24 Louis Karand
24 Joseph Motil
28 Elizer Gordon
28 Edward Frechette
35 Joseph Shepherd
35 Mrs Mary Little
35 Charles Dewhurst
36 Fred Walsh
36 John Wright
36 Henry Shaw
43 George Breault
49 William Messier
53 Martin Loughlin
53 Robert Sharrocks
53 George Lowe
55 Mrs Susannah Hesford
55 Thomas Pomfort
55 John Lundy
55 Mrs Mary Pomfort
57 Robert M Clunie
57 Abraham Roberts
57 Joseph Warburton
57r George Almond
57r Robert Wolstenholme
59 Ernest E Swire
59 Ralph Hartley
60 William H Johnson
65 Ernest C Roberts
65 Mrs Fanny Harrison
65 John Keelty
66 Rev Edward A Uminski
67 Alfred Wigley
67 John H Hollingworth
67 Charles Horner
70 John Baptiste Balthazer
83 Jana Capthis Turcotte

HOWARD AVENUE

20 Daniel H Parker
20 Robert H Chase
24 Charles F Chase
28 Samuel Sturtevant
30 H B Braley
43 Philip Leger
53 John J Buckley
54 Mrs Hannah E Bennett
55 Mrs Susan Perry
59 William Couza
83 Manuel Frasier

HOWLAND

5 Joseph Smalley
6 Morris Cohen
6 Antone Roderique
6 Manuel Rodericque
8 Joseph Branchini
9 Morris P Greenstone
9 Joseph Correia
9 Morris Herman
9 Harry Singer
10 Joseph Sylvia
12 Mrs Marie Rosa
14 James Pinto
14 Abraham Singer
15 Barnard Basken
15 Phillip Feingold
15 Isador Stern
16 Morris Cohen
16 Joseph Fransis
24 Nathan Levin
25 George Hodson
25 Joseph Silva
25 Edmund Rodericques
25 Mrs Mary A Sylvia
25½ William Caton
41 Henry Frates
41 Manuel D Rose
46 Mrs Mary P Silva
46½ William Fontaine
47 Mrs Mary Peter
47r Manuel Luiz
52 Antone Sylva
55 Mrs Mary Menes
58 Joseph Rosenthal
58 Manuel Coutie
58 August C Tenxeira
58 Antonio L Pereira
59 Mrs Mary Costa
60 Antone L King
60 Mrs Rose P Rays
60r Samuel Lansky

61 Antone Correia
61r Anthony E Rose
61r Joseph D Campos
62 John Enos Souza
69 Manuel R Sylvia
69 Mrs Phebe Marshall
69 Manuel B Davis
69 Manuel Silva
72 John Mederios
75 Domingas Almeida
75 Antonio Avila
76 Manuel Cabral
76 John Almeida
77 Manuel Sylvia
81 Frank Lear
81 Mrs Mary P Francis
81 John Sylvia
86 Frank P Vera
86 Mrs Clara Oliver
86 Antone Cabral
86 John B Mello
86 Mrs Annie Veira
90 Joaquim Enos
90 Antone Cabral
96 Mrs Francis Perry
90 Michael Rodericque

HOWLAND VILLAGE

1 Simeon Gledhill
3 Joseph St Pierre
4 Charles St Pierre
5 George H Sanderson
7 Charles St Pierre
8 Ovide Masse
9 Harry Iddon
10 John Hanley
11 Mrs Matilda Stone
12 John J King
14 Thomas F McGreevey
15 Joaquim Goulart
16 Joseph R Mendes
16 Manuel Andrade
17 Antone C Amaral
18 William Maule
19 George Smethurst
21 Edward A Cunniff
22 Barrett Judson
23 Thomas Murray
24 William Starkie
26 Michael Cawley
28 Joseph Enos
29 Albert Sharples
29r Joseph S L Boardman
30 Joseph Baxendale
31 John J Herron
32 Alexander Duckworth
34 Joseph Ramshead
34 Henry Singleton
35 James H Goldrick
36 John D Gomes
36 Manuel R Mendes
37 Frank Pennington
38 Frank Rogers
39 William H Gelder
41 Peter Brennan
42 Antone Jacinth
44 Manuel Andrada
45 Louis Thomas
45 Jacques Ferreira
46 Manuel Sylvia
47 Manuel Tavares
48 Joseph Medeiros
49 Arthur J Hales
50 Antonio Andrada
51 Howland Hotel
51 Patrick F Mitchell
53 William H McClurg

HUDSON

0 James H Oliver

HUNTER

11 Vernon F Curran
12 Joseph H Days
13 Charles H W Brownell
18 Thomas F Reed
21 George F Thompson
25 George F Gibbs
34 George R Tripp
40 Abram C Lawton
46 Mrs Amelia J M Austin

HYACINTH

1 John C Armfield
1 Joseph Donnelly
2 Manuel Rose
2 Joseph Correio
2½ August Souza
2½ Manuel J Praeda
3 John Souza
10 Manuel P Andrade
11 Wilfred Dessere
11 Mrs Mary J Bannon
12 Antone Medeiros
18 Sisters of the Holy Cross

INDEPENDENT

1 Boaventura J Bettencourt
8 Manuel E Gill
12 John Cartmell
12 William Nary
16 Manuel P Mello
16 Joseph Rose
16 Augusto J Arruda
16 Manuel Machado
20 Anton Simas

Independent—con
20 Jules Simas
21 Mrs Mary E King
21 Hugh Barker
23 David Phaneuf
23 Frobe J Lagasse
23 Joseph O St Germain
24 Mrs Mary Murphy
24 John J Goodwin
24 Misses Hoye
35 Mrs Henrietta Desjardins
35 Philas Therrien
35 Isadore Larue
36 Mrs Matilda Ledoux
36 Mrs Julia Coholan
36 John McConville
39 Agathe Gagnon
40 Felix Tetreault
40 Napoleon Poitras
40 Thomas Collins
44 Antone Lawrence
44 Joseph L Cabral
44 Francisco Rodericques
44 Marianno Medeiros
47 Thomas Egan
48 Joseph Bergeron
48 Walter Bain
48 Rev Alfred K Collett
48 George W Wilmot
48 John Clave
48 Joseph Bergeron
51 Manuel Frates
51 Joaquim Frates
52 Mrs Mary Silva
52 Edmond Cloutier
52 Anthony Alphonse
55 William Meridith
55 Lewis Cotnoir
55 Melania E Vieira
56 Joseph F Lee
56 Giraldo Caton
60 Antonio F Hendriques
60 Joseph Andre
60 Mrs Mary Rogers
60 Mrs Mary Castro
61 James F Gawthorne
62 Manuel E Silva
62 Lawrence Harney
62 John B Hallworth
63 Mrs Josephine Berube
63 John J Garrey
63 Annie Winn
65 Oliver J Raulins
65 Joseph Medeiros
65 Manuel P Leite
66 Mrs Sarah Holden
66 Frank Souza
67 Manuel Reis
70 Manuel Correia
73 Harry Bletcher
73 Zephraim Breault
73 Mrs Adeline Fountain
73 J O Lapointe
74 Antone Vegas
74 Peter J King
78 Antonio DeC Machado
78 Antone Post
78 Domingos Costa
78 Joseph Rousseau
78 Napoleon Larocque
81 Adam Laliberty
81 Edward Larocque
81 Arthur Fecteau
81 Edward Ducharme
81 Louis J Paquette
82 Wincelas Frennette
82 Ubaul Frenette
82 Mary Desjardins
82 Joseph R Neves

INGRAHAM

27 Charles Lizotte
35 Louis Drisdell
35 Athanase Charest
39 James O'Grady
39 Rev Jovite Chagnon
39 Ernest E Cote

IRVING

1 Mrs Elizabeth R Hussey
3 Ellen Clifford
19 Mrs Josephine Rotch

IRVINGTON

2 Eugene W Trask
2 Julia Rourke
2 Samuel L Hand
2 John Cox
8 Misses Dana
136 Philip Fonseca

JACINTO

0 Antonio Andre
0 Joseph Jacintho

JAMES

21 Edward C Earley
23 Stephen E White
24 Mrs Mary C Stirrett
27 Rev Howard C R Gale
28 Mrs Mary W Montague
28 Alfred Thornton
28 Henry H Phinney
30 Smith T Sharples
31 Emery Cushman
32 Louis H Haight
34 George W Paige
36 Frank W Hatch

45 Catherine V Brady
51 William J Russell
51 Mary Fitchiney
55 Joseph C Lisbon
58 Edward Y Baker
58 Arthur E Davis
59 Murdock McDonald
60 Manuel Franklin
60 Lawrence E Perry
63 Joseph Raposa Jr
67 John Nelson
70 Mrs Mary Ellen Ayler
75 Harry R Bourne
75 Charles Clarke
79 Andrew Tate
85 Manuel F Avila
85 Mrs Ellen Sharples
87 Joshua N Wardell
90 Joseph de G Sylvia
91 William MacGregor
91 Henrietta Price
97 Samuel T Madison
109 Louis Balboni
113 Thomas Louis
113 William J Dunn
113 George N Mason
139 John H D Brown
143 Charles H Little
147 John Dunn
181 Orliff R Howland
206 Everett A Lucas
209 Patrick F Sullivan

JEAN

2 Joseph Ste Marie
2 Andrew Henaumount
2 Desire Noel
3 Edward M Williams
4 Donald Robichaud
4 Zenon Dube
4 Henri Dionne
5 William Sharples
5 William M Sullivan
7 Mrs Margaret Hunter
8 Joseph Dube
8 Napoleon Dube
8 Wenceslas Roy
8 Rea Roy
8 Adelard Dube
9 Abraham K Casson
9 Lawrynz Pyteraf
9 Edward Wilson
9 Oliver Gillespie
10 Charles Webster
10 Thomas Yates
11 Joseph Pinel
11 Francois X Dube
11 Silvia Patnaude
13 Alexander Harrison
13 Christopher Thompson
14 Walter Dionne
16 Charles La Liberte
16 Elie La Liberte
18 Joseph McGuinness
18 William F Foley
18 Ben Hesford
18 Albert Foisy
19 Adolph Ross
21 Amende Lajoy
21 Ferdinand Anneham
21 Gasser Thautoau
22 George Dubois
22 Dusithe Dubois
22 Mrs Armina La Croix
22 Nester LaBonte

JENNEY

2 John H Francis
3 Alton B Ellis
3 Henry B Webb
4 William H Hathaway
4½ Forrest F Swetland
5 Joseph Gonsalves
6 Mrs Minnie L Nickerson
6 Daniel H Carney
7 David Higgins
7 Mrs Alice T Davis
8 John G Taber
9a Manuel S Almeida
11 Joseph E Cabral
13 Mrs Mary F Fowler
14 Manuel Silva
15 John E Mitchell
15 John B Sequin
16 Joseph Sylva
20 Mrs Kate Johnston
20 John Benevidez
34 Addison F Russell
36 Antonio C Nunes
38 Robert Burke

JENNINGS COURT

1 Frank M Jennings
2 Manuel Machado

JENNY LIND

2 Israel N Paine
4 Mrs Mary A Williams
5 Charles Erickson
7 Allen J Searell
9 Joseph Eccleston
11 Albert E Mosher
13 Alverdo A Drew
17 Charles L Allen
18 Frederick H Palmer
27 J S Wright

Jenny Lind—con
27 J A Wright
32 William H Davenport
35 Herbert R Vinal
52 F Roswell
52 Frederick Boswell
58 Edward O Higgins
59 Herbert A Manchester
61 John H Bryant
62 Dennis F Mahoney
63 Rodolphus D Wicks
67 Thomas L Coppinger
72 Walter C Fisher
73 James Burcham
74 Charles C Cornell
133 Manuel Silva
133 John J O'Brien
138 Mrs Lillian S Fleming
163 Mrs Martha Greenhalgh
169 Franklin A Young

JOUVETT

17 Lucien Cyr
17 Lucien Couville
17 Adhemar Methe
21 James Stewart
22 John Warner
22 Sydney I Cornell
23 Peter Ditchfield
26 John W Caton
26 William M Rodrick
27 George Wilkinson
27 Mrs Amelia Barker
30 Thomas Kilshaw
30 Alphonse Keroack
31 Harry Fogg
31 John W Lomas
31 Edward Openshaw
34 Robert Wareing
34 James Anderton
35 Thomas Rostron
35 Richard Brimley
36 Toefil La Bel
36 Frank Jackson
36 Onesime Deschaine
36 Emily Ostignay
43 Harry Smalley
43 William Lofthouse
58 John P Slatery
60 Ernest Horsfall
64 Mrs Celia Killeen
65 Napoleon Metras
65 Louis Boeneau
65 Zepherine Cote
65 Albert St Onge
68 Michael Goff
68 Mrs Alice Connulty
68 Frederick McLoughlin
68 John Callaghan
70 John McCarthy
70 Narcisse Methe
70 Ernest Caron
71 John J Pinnington
71 Henri Caron
71 John B Gregory
77 Joseph Monjeau
77 Teles Martel
78 John T Simpkins
78 John Healey
78 Robert Burnes
84 John B Codair
84 Noe La Bonte
84 Samuel Doyon
84 Delphise Moreau
85 Zephir J Robert
85 Arcade Marcoux
85 William Foster
91 Alfred Pelletier
92 Wilfred Tellier
92 Joseph Perreault
92 Hugh Quail
92 Alfred Berube
95 Louis Monjeau
96 Diogene Plouffe
96 James Powers
96 Mrs Clara Vera
99 Adelard Laliberte
100 Hugh Blair
103 Arthur Gagne
104 Dona Goyer
104 Donase Goyer
104 Moise Berube

JOYCE

0 Polidor Barie

JUNIPER

7 John J Cope
7 George J Edwards
7 Mrs Sarah Benn
10 Chrysalogue Beaulieu
10 Uric Lacrourse
10 Frank Gonsalves
23 Casimer S Machado
24 John Norwood
24 Richard Bowers
27 Philip J Winn
27 William Sharples
30 Manuel Mello
30 Charles Regan
31 John C Astley
31 James Jump

KANE

19 David Dow Jr
30 Mrs Mary Joseph

30 Manuel J Silva
30 Joseph P Silva

KATHARINE

5 August B Tavares
5 Daniel Bolton
15 George Archambeault
15 John A Jardine
15 John A Jardine
15 Simon Burgess
16 Patrick Tiernan
16 Antone G Mello
21 Mrs Mary Francis
24 John C Silva
24 Antone B Souza
25 Joseph Lapointe
25 Anton Mecido
28 Arthur Richard
28 Francis Dutra
29 Mrs Mary Souza
29 Manuel F Paiva
32 Francis Dupre
33 Joseph Frasier
33 William Taylor
33 William J Snow
36 Manuel Correia
36 Mrs Catherine McCarthy
40 Antone Botella
40 Joseph Dias
42 Ernest B Almeida
42 Ernest Fernandes
43 Ralph Hill
43 Christina Bain
43 Henry Craig
43 William H Craig
45 Manuel Cardoza
45 Edwin Ganson
45 Mrs Marie Pimental
46 Manuel E Gracia
46 Jose Mattos
49 Paulineo Medeiros
49 Hugh McGregor
49 John F Gomes
50 Antonio S Medeiros
50 John S Medeiros
50 Manuel Martin
53 Patrick McGuire
53 Frank P Rose
54 Fred Marshall
54 Charles Taylor
55 Mrs Belle King
55 Mrs Philomena Francis
55 Joseph Almeida
55 Antone Mederios
58 Patrick Menton
59 Jose de Freitas Grade
59 Vergino N Andrade
61 Manuel Simmons
62 Mrs Annie E Wilkinson
62 George Wholey
64 Amos Horsfall
65 Manuel J Perry
65 Frank Dutra
69 Frank Hall
69 Manuel Viveiros
70 Joseph A Horsfall
70 George Aspin
74 Manuel Cabral
74 Mary King
76 Victorine Ferreira
77 Mrs Margaret Cannon
77 Joe Rose
79 Frank Arruda
79 Joseph Souza
79 Joseph Veira
80 Manuel Mathews
80 William T Wild
80 Edward Farrar
80 Manuel Mattos
82 James Downhill
82 Kinder M Woodcock

KEARSARGE

9 Joseph Lague

KEENE

20 Samuel D McLeod
22 Myron P Howland
23 Asa T Thompson
24 William R Chase
25 Joseph J Tripp
26 Joshua G Baker Jr
27 Eliza R Sisson
28 Henry G Taber
30 Ezra G Farnham
31 Irving A Brown
32 Theodore Ambrose
33 Thomas B Norris
34 Isaac F Holland
35 Edward W Bragg
36 Mrs Caroline Johnson
37 Giles A Gifford
38 Joseph Ross
40 Walter G Spencer
41 Simon N W Chaney
42 William A Tripp
46 Carl O Gustafson

KEMPTON

50 William Bachand
52 Mrs Bridget Donovan
53 Mrs Elizabeth F Murphy
53 William Connell
53 Leonora E Russell
54 John Driver
54 Albert H Pollock
56 W H Reed

Kempton—con
56 John Leary
59 Abraham Herstoff
59 John M Neto
74 Edward Sears
74 Addie F Caswell
75 Frederick A Washburn
83 Addie F Goodrich
83 Mrs Mary L Ames
86 Edward D Francis
86 Harry A Francis
113 George W Mason
113 John E McMullen
118 Annie M Sherlock
118 Mrs Gertrude M Frost
119 Robert W McAfee
119 Mrs Mary E Putnam
123 Mrs Susan C Bennett
123 William H Tew
131 Dr Lurana A Chubbuck
133 Fred W Brightman
137 Mrs Abbie Nickerson
145 Mrs Sophia W Jennings
145 Mrs Franklin H Vinal
151 Walter A Jenney
151 Mrs Mary E Jenney
151 Frank E Vera
157 Misses Driggs
165 Roland H Bliss
165 Andrew Peirce
165 Mrs Elizabeth C Chadwick
171 Robert E Edwards
171 Joseph H Lawrence
174 John Pearson
174 Mrs Ada Tripp
176 John H Gifford
176 Hiram W Look
178 William E Russell
178 Daniel J Berry
183 James E Blake
184 Sarah D Ottiwell
184 Oliver B Davis
190 Joseph G Jenison
190 Frank C Taylor
191 Frederick F Ellis
191 Mrs Joanna P Peirce
194 William A Shaw
194 William L Strange
198 William P Lawton
201 Annie W Lothrop
201 Pardon A Macomber
202 Mrs Clara A West
202 Mrs Laura S Kimball
202 James W Averill
207 Joseph Hois
208 Charles H Kelley
208 Mrs Mary E Borden
209 George F Taber
211 George F Netcner
219 David W Howland
220 William P Briggs
226 J Charles Lamoureux
226 Joseph D Bourque
230 John H McKenna
230 Ephraim T Gammons Jr
236 Mrs Hattie Clifford
240 Mrs Bessie Tripp
275 Peter Perroni
275 Mrs Annie E Becker
276 Mrs Bertha T Hartford
276 Edwin P Soule
279 Samuel Ginsburg
281 Mary Crosby
281 Harry F Chase
281 Louise Wadsworth
282 Fred H Chase
282 George A Brown
284 Mrs Fannie B Russell
286 Abraham Gordon
286 Abraham Taper
287 Frederick L Snow
287 Mrs Nanie P Sweet
296 Rev Henry Mette
304 Mrs C M Peirce
309 Mrs Emma Nelson
309 Walter I Wood
310 Harriet V Dumont
315 Aaron S Allen
317 Charles F Getchell
317 Richard Osborne
324 Richard A Haddock
324 Charles H Jennings
325 William M Norris
325 William E Ellis
328 Albert Morgan
328 Albert Moore
328 Edward Brick
332 George L Tripp
332r Mrs Bertha S Burdick
333 George N Guerin
333 Walter B Cunha
334 Mrs Bertha S Burdick
334 Rev Mrs Mary S Ransom
334 Mrs Mary Wood
335 Allan McAlpine
338 Herbert I Revalion
338r George S Taylor
340 Frederick R Reed
340 Ernest B Nye
343 David Stone
343 Frank S Bullard
344 William Wyse
344 Mariano Aulisio
358 Mrs Anna Hamilton

358 Mrs Louise C Clark
362 Henry H Tobey
362 A Granville Wetherell
362 Joseph P Mitchell
364 Oakes A Coombs
364 C H DeGrasse
367 Charles L Smith
367 Celia College Garnes
367 Clarence L Chaplin
367r William E Gainville
367r Mrs Lucy Cooper
370 George Desrosiers
370 Hugh J Ryan
372 Bertram C West
375 Mrs Mary C Gifford
375 John J Sheehan
377 Mrs Sarah M Spencer
382 Mrs Hattie E Motta
383 Louis Goodman
383 Mrs Mary A Haskins
383r Andrew H Allen
384 Calvin J Benn
384 Herbert Grovell
384 Dr William W Nelson
390 Charles E Saxon
390 Mrs Amelia Owens
396 Harry R Ellis
408 Benjamin A Andress
410 Sarah Esson
410 Elizabeth A Spaden
413 Mrs Sylvia Casey
413 Joseph Perry
419 Robert Sabin
419 Harold R Brownell
428 John Oliver
428 Mrs Mary E Foster
432 James Wiggins
443 George J Silva
446 William Turner
447 Joseph Benoit
460 Rev C Hubert Yearwood
464 John A Gomley
473 Mrs Mary J Allen
473 Edwin F Tripp
474 Cornelius A Webb
475 Julia Crowley
475 Michael McGreevy
483 Mrs Catherine Barrett
483 Anthony J Murray
492 Harry Allen
492 Frank W Swift
501 Mrs Ella F Chace
512 Emma C Austin
514 Frederick T Gardner
512 Charles H Snow
514 Loyde G Pells
517 James Arundale
518 Mrs Emma St Montario
518 Edwin Hunt
525 George F Pierce
525 John F Befuhs
525 Mrs Ursula A Pease
526 Mrs Catherine L Norton
550 Henry B Allen
550 Ira T C Cobb
551 William E Cooper
551 John Gobell
554 Andrew R Douglass
554 S Stanley White
555 William N Freeman
555 Charles F Easton Jr
559 Obed S Cowing
561 Leon Byran
562 Mrs Mary A Weik
567 Mrs Mary E Chase
567 Charles E Harding
567 William A Forsyth
568 William E Carroll
570 Charles T Battey
573 Dominick Finni
573 Ella G Flanders
573 Joseph H Penney
574 Raymond H Brierly
574 William Quesko
580 Charles C Connor
580 Walter E Sadler
586 Stephen Whiteside
592 Mrs Martha A M White
592 Frances H Ransom
593 Rev James Conlon
593 Sister Mary Edigna
624 Sarah F Taber
645 Dr Charles Shanks
647 Ralph Brightman
651 William G Westgate
653 Fred W Silver
654 James Shanks
655 William J Clarke
658 Robert E Woodland
662 George H Saltus
663 Joseph S Martin
672 G L Wilcox
682 Edward O Spooner
682 Edward F Spooner
690 James H Manchester
703 George D Greene
712 Mrs Alferetta Coggeshall
712 John H Reed
712 John F Brown
713 James S Gorner
715 James Meehan
715 Mrs John W McCauley
721 Aaron C Bryant
721 Mrs Alvira Hathaway
722 Mrs Rebecca E Whipple
728 William H Morse
734 Daniel Ring
734 Michael O'Brien
740 Edward A Osgood

Kempton—con
740 Henry C Rogers
740 Peter B Smith
740 Charles Stetson
755 William S Osgood Jr
763 Loring T Parlow
764 Allen Damon
766 Mrs Annie Winslow
766 Charles A Mosher
766 Robert K Winslow
770 William H Hambly
771 Reuben P Sherman
771 Mrs Mary Higgins
782 Ernest B Eno
797 Mrs Josephine G Aiken
803 Robert E Townsend
804 Jacob W Chase
805 George Hatfield
805 James J Hatfield
807 Archer C Gardner
807 Horace L Humphrey
820 Angelo Govoni
820 Geo W Offley
833 Mrs Cynthia Norton
841 Everett E Winslow
851 Leonard R Reed
857 Mary A Barker
859 Andrew J Oliver
948 Arthur G Boardman
950 Charles G Page
952 Mrs Lucretia Coward
966 A J Poulin
969 Richard E Nofftz
975 Samuel C Barrett
973 Joseph F Perry
975 Lawrence J Levins
975 William Haworth
980 Selma Erickson
985 Allen W Haskell
990 Richard P Stowell
991 George H Clough
991 Noah B Davis
1188 Frederick E Tripp
1199 Lewis A Tripp
1254 George B T Weeks
1270 Henry R Weeks

KENYON

4 Atude Pouchard
4 Joseph Goyette
4 Arthur Archambeault
4 Cleophas Trudeau
23 Joseph Dextradeur
23 Robert Forehand
23 John J Marsland
23 Joseph Breton
27 Victor Robidoux
27 Mrs Elsie Tetreault
27 Casmire Kulpinski
27 Mrs Elsie Lajore
27 Louis Boulais
50 William Herbert
52 John Bisi
52 Michal Kokofski
53 Guillaume Davignon
53 Joseph Forgue
53 W Forgue
54 John Roscovitski
57 Alex Le Vasseur
57 Alex Gagnon
57 Philip Benjamin
57 Alphonse Hotte
58 Nathan Salusky
60 Henry Irwin
61 Peter Guay
61 Pierre Guay
61 Edmand Morrissette
62 Solomon Bernstein
62 William E Houston
62 Mitchell Dextradeur
65 Timothy LaRue
65 Mrs Mary Kay
65 Alphonse Bessette
68 Mrs Victoria Dube
68 Jonas Theberge
71 William Esinhart
71 Albert Zeman
71 James Simmons
72 Samuel Yarlef
72 Archille Ferreau
75 Omar Graville
75 Israel Gerstein
75 Alphonse Maillotte
79 Narcisse Dontigny
82 David Cantor
82 Joseph Metivier
83 Mrs Ada W Beaumont
83 Eddy Mechaber
84 Joseph Cyr
84 Mrs Eliza Plante
84 Joseph Goyette
87 Phillip Fortin
87 Hyman Mechaber
88 David Barnard
88 Moses Goldstein
88 Jake Jenesky
90 Henry Etchells
90 Joseph S Wyatt
90 Thomas Aylward
91 George H Boudreau
94 James McHugh
94 John Bazinet
94 Henry Bourque
95 Dominic Surprenant

98 William Hodgson
98 Henry R Blanchette
100 William F Kozorek

KILBURN

1 Dominique Manny
3 James Nelson

KING

43 Joseph Theberge
0 Fred Normandin

KINGCROFT

0 Philiase Dubois

KING'S HIGHWAY

0 Frank A Cornell

LaFRANCE COURT

7 Thomas Rogers
7 Antone Fernandes
12 Felix Gonneville
12 Henri Chausse
12 Frank Fournier
13 Paul Gagne
16 Narcisse L Dragon
16 Joseph H Guenette
20 Etienne Morreau
20 John B Matthews
20 Thomas S Arnold
20 Joseph Dupre
20 Joseph Jodoin
20 Etienne Morin
20 John J Price

LAKE

53 William A Ashley
73 William J Oothout
75 James C Beers
81 Frank L Reed

LARCH

28 John Chicoine
32 Patrick Featherstone
35 William Watling
36 Robinson Laycock
41 Mrs Bridget Clark
41 Frank G Rose
46 John Forrest
46 Isaac Wilkinson
49 John S Dias
49 Antone R Farry
49 Michael J Hurley
49 John Souza
50 Thomas Higham
50 William Ashworth
65 Mrs Diana S Ray
65 Antone Andrews
67 Mrs Catherine M Smith
72 William S Smethurst
72 John I Gifford
73 Antone Costa
80 John J Cordeira
83 Patrick Beehan
86 Manuel King Silveira
87 Manuel F Souza
87r Joseph Cabral
98 William C Barbour
107 Manuel M Correia
107 Antonio Gracia
111 Mrs Mary G Andre
112 Charles Joseph
114 Frank Oliveira
114 John Mello
114 Seraphine P Silva

LEONARD

1 Louis Pease

LEWIS

0 Frank J Freitas

LEXINGTON

21 John Dennis
33 John Thomas
33 James Gorner
35 John DeCosta
61 Manuel Travers
61 Urben Soares

LIBERTY

26 Bernard McCabe
30 Edney A Lapham
32 Emil Johnson
34 Ellsworth M Longfield
36 Robert F Soule
38 Frank Mansur
40 William H Habicht
42 George P Williams
43 Antonio Pallatroni
44 John Carroll
44 Ernest H Balboni
45 Arthur E Davis
50 Mrs Mary A Leahy
54 Walter M Thomas
54 Mrs Bridget Blundell
54 Chester M Hathaway
57 Isaac F Chumack
60 Martin Rogers
60 James Reardon
65 William Befuhs
73 Sarah E Bird
73 Antonio M Lima
74 Antonio Silva
74 Antone Sylva
74 Frank A Souza
76 Atone M Sylvia
76 Mrs Agnes Burns
81 John Reardon

Liberty—con
81 William Akin
82 Frank H Ashley
82 Mrs Lena Waters
86 Joseph Maranaa
86 Manuel Baptista
88 Edward H Ashley
88 Burton L Perry
130 John H Parker

LINCOLN

3 George D Swift Jr
5 Joseph M Read
8 Frank A Milliken
11 William F Read
12 Joseph C Nowell
17 Mrs Cecelia A Sheperd
18 Annie E Bacon
21 Mrs Abraham Taber
25 Charles E Pierce
27 Mrs Helen M Kollock
28 James W Allen
31 Mrs Betsey W Shurtleff
35 Samuel C Hart Jr
39 Charles M Taber

LINDEN

14 Vital Girard
17 Thomas Finnell
18 Mrs Lydia S Adams
18 Dr Alphonse Normandin
23 Dr Edward W Dehn
23 George R Dehn
28 Contantine Hologgotis
28 Alfred F Benoit
35 Mrs Regina Goulet
35 Edmund Therien
35 George Goulet
36 Norman C Lucas
36 Gordon C Smith
36r James Barber
36r Dennis H Toomey
36r James Harwood
37 John Burke
37 Joseph Forcier
37 Martin J Conway
40 Pierre Gauthier
43 Harry A Jameson
43 Joseph Rouillier
43 Moise Brouillette Jr
56 John L Sullivan
56 George A Mahon
65 Edwin F Wood
65 Mrs Harriet S Wood
68 William T Entwistle
68 Misses Chadwick
68r Ella C Adams
69 Walter Begen
69r Elias Marsden
70 Harry Lunn
70 John H Hartley
70r James E Holden
70r John A Quinn
72 Thomas J Taber
73 Frank L Remington
73 William Kimball
76 Joseph Wicha
77 Alfred Leveille
77 Benjamin Noyes
77r Samuel F Gifford
77r John T Joyce
78 Rothwell Slater
79 Edward F Taylor
79 Henry Lang
79 John H Riley
83 Timothy J Sullivan
84 William Wood
90 Edmonde Caya
90 Speridion Lebeau
92 William Bailey
93 Thomas Billington
94 Victor F Bellenoit
95 Joseph A Burt
95 Robert Parkin
96 Mrs Lilly Wright
96 George Dooley
97 Rowell E Bennett
97 Mrs Mary A Bennett
98 Fredrick D Walton
98 James Entwistle
99 Edward Wells
99 James F Ashworth
99½ Peter Loranger
101 James J Foley
101 Mrs Annie Berry

LINDEN COURT

2 Joseph Greenough
2 Bessie Hurley
4 Mrs Ellen F Ryan
5 James E Knott
6 Frank Kemnitzer
7 Peter Boardman
7 Frank Rovland
8 William Whittaker
9 George TSchofiled
9 Joseph Bowler
10 William Fell
10 Richard Ashcroft

LINDSEY

6 Manuel G Neves
9 Henry Curtis
12 Hadley Burt

13 Bernard A McGuinness
13 Manuel L Simmons
16 William F Bergan
16 Dennis J Crowley
24 Arthur F Butler
28 Frederick A Treadup Jr
28 George A Miller
32 Walter Rawcliffe
34 John Frates
34 Charles W Taylor
37 William F Butts
37 John McCormack
44 Manuel J Machado Jr
44 Manuel A Vera
54 Joseph de Costa
58 Manuel A Silva
58 Mrs Deborah A Lake
62 Manuel G Machado
62 Lucy A Pike
66 Arthur Wilkinson
66 George E Tripp
67 James V Kane
70 Joseph A Santos
70 John J Braga
71 Mrs Caroline Vogel
74 Mrs Sarah F Allen
74 Mrs Ruth A Osgood
75 Frank LeB Howes

LOCUST

12 Moses Ashley
14 B Frank Penney
20 Allen P Keith
27 Stephen L Finnell
30 Dennis W Lawrence
30 John O'Brien
33 Charles F Daley
33 George L Taber
39 Philip D Drew
39 Levi R Johnson
42 Camille D Bellenoit
42 John F Oates
43 James B Frizzell
43 Clarence P Jenny
47 Lillian Gifford
47 Alfred E Whitney
50 Mrs Ella R Knight
50 David W Judson
51 Martin McCarthy
51 George A Swift
52 John F Tilden
52 Thomas J Norton
53 John Johnson
53 Martin J Ruddy
56 Herbert N Peck
56 Michael J Glennon
57 Mrs Margaret O'Neill
58 George L Brownson
58 John H Kane
61 Samuel Higham
69 George P Caswell
69 D Edward Bliss
71 Joseph B **Menzer**
74 John E Glennon
74 Joseph R Glennon
75 Horace C Johnson
75 Carleton C Paine
78 Edward Harris
79 Frank C Holmes
79 Charles F Keen
83 William D Gifford
83 William H H Sisson
87 Edward B Card
87 Wallace C Caswell
97 Frank C Howard
97 John H Pollock
104 Frederick Bence
104 Dennis O'Neil
108 Edward Magnant
108 Parick McQuaid
109 Orrin E Whipple
109 Celestin Farland
109 Andrew Gonneville
117 Cornelius J Puckley
118 Ernest Boardman
118 William H Crocker
120 Antone da Souza Maciel
121 Arthur F Howard
123 Felix Poirier
123 Clarence D Wood
123 James P Porter
135 Herbert E Davis
137 George W Gardner
139 Joseph Hindle Jr

LOGAN

11 James Moult
15 Napoleon Peltier
45 Henry J Proulx
47 Albert Cross
47 Eliza Grady
47 William Ainsworth

LOMBARD

21 Henry Lomba
25 Joseph D Silveira
25 Joseph A Barrows
30 John Lopes
30 Antone Veira
30 Manuel H Lopes
37 Julio Borges
45 Manuel F Oliver
47 Ernest W Ogden
50 Mrs Mary Teixeira
50 Domingos A Souza
54 Mrs Magida DeResende
54 David A Mosher
59 Mrs Rosa Medeiros

Lombard—con
59 Frederick A Snell
59 Joseph B Xavier
70 Albert W Sowle
76 Santos Sadanko
76 Edwin Ford
76 Manuel Silva
80 Januario O Amarantes

LOWELL

0 Alphonse Lucier

LUCAS

10 Harry J Wagner
10 Raymond J Hammersley
10 Henri Arseneault
17 Wilbur A Lilly
22 Joseph Garrant
52 Levi Coop

MADISON

9 John B Fernandes
9 Mrs Mary Correia
11 Manuel S Faria
13 John H Taber
13 Mrs Melvina Sweet
14 Mrs Mary Andrada
18 J S Oliver
20 Michael Gomes
21 Mrs Rose Dillon
24 Wilbur Denny
24 J Harry Rice
25 Mrs Louisa Laliberte
29 L Merton Brightman
29 Leander Brightman
31 Mrs Edith B Gifford
33 Alfred Ainsworth
36 Leonard C Lapham
36 Zaccheus C Dunham
37 Isaac N Burbank
37 W H Morse
38 Mrs Mary B Woodbridge
38 Sarah B Worth
75 Misses Watson
75 Capt Worth G Ross
95 Elizabeth K Howland
96 William R West
97 Mrs Sarah P Cook
98 Mrs Celia L Anthony
99 Andrew G Pierce Jr
100 Mrs Sarah M B Potter

MAIDEN LANE

1 William Medeiros
1 Mrs Mary A Rose
2 Martin Raphael
2½ Dionisio Cruz
3 Joseph R Pinheiro
3 Mrs Mary Rita
3 Antone Gracia
4 John Almedia
4 Antone Souza
4 Joe Frates
5 Manuel Veira

MAIN

5 George A Cobb
30 Thomas M Perry
30 Mrs Mirtie Peckham
36 William R Ward
40 Michael Gomes
40 Benjamin Queripel Jr
45 Manuel F Silva
52 F H Wood
58 Napoleon Courtemanche

MAITLAND

16 William J Peters
16 Mrs Eliza Peters
17 Mrs Mary B Spooner
17 John H Ennis
20 Amos F Wright
21 Charles Parsons
21 George L Douglass
26 John F Craw
26 Mrs Sarah E Ashley
26 Horace C Ashley
27 C G Richardson
27 James L Cowen
30 Edward F Pender
30 Amy McCurdy
31 George H Holden
31 Halbertian L Thomas
32 John O'Donnell
34 Thomas H Whelden
39 James H McVicker
40 B Frank Tripp
45 Daniel Herbert Cook
49 Charles L Davis Jr
49 John Barkley
51 Robert G Refuse
51 Theodore Sowle
51 David C Ryder
54 Harry C Crowell
54 Henry H Labrode
54 James Longden
55 Charles X Norton
55 Charles F Thackeray
55 Mrs Mary E Greenwood

MAPLE

3 Allen T Weeks
5 Arthur L Tucker
6 Mrs Jenny G Grinnell
7 Elisha D Anthony
8 Geo M Eddy
9 Misses Church
10 A Clinton Swift
10 Mrs Mary J Washburn

48 James O Thompson Jr
51 Geo H Dailey
51 Robert Hardy
52 Henry K Snow
57 C Augusta Lockwood
58 Chas A G Swasey
61 John E Russell
65 Fred J Pierce
69 Henry S Swain
71 Harry V Walker
77 Mrs Florence McLeod
77 John A McLeod
81 Mrs Lydia E Gaffney
87 Andrew B Chase
95 David W Shepherd
99 Mary Hawes
103 Andrew J Brooks
111 Ward C Batchelder
117 Christopher A Best
123 Christopher Townsend
127 Mrs Sophia E Briggs
151 Joshua B Taska
155 Mrs Annie C Gustafson
171 Malcoln A Mackay
175 Thomas L Andrews
175 Mrs Jennie H Andrews
181 Geo O Gardner
189 Homer W Hervey
205 Mrs Abbie L Simmons
205 Walter J Gilbirt
209 J Herbert Smith
217 Raymond H Cook
235 Frank A Gurney
257 Herbert F Barsow
257 Louis W Macy

MAPLE VIEW TERRACE

11 Geo E Mandell
12 Charles F Lawton
15 Francis R Peabody
16 Austin C Fuller
19 Edmond D Searles
24 John E Tasker

MARGIN

1 Joseph Mello
7 Manuel Souza
10 John N Stetson
10 Wm E Dean
10 Frank P Dean
11 Francisco Menes
11 Francisco P Toros
12 Wm E Arnott
12 Mrs Jane Arnott
15 Pierre Richard
15 John Parkes
15 Pierre Richard Jr
16 Caleb E Ramsbottom
17 Antone Gaspa
17 August Silva
17 Gregorio Silva
17 Mrs Jane Briggs
20 Bent B Mello
20 Thomas Towers
20 Charles Michell
21 Manuel P Lima
21 Mrs Mary G Sylvia
24 Manuel M Sylvia
27 John S Baron
27 Mrs Jane Latham
28 Aldie Fournier
28 James Gray
28 Joseph Paradis
31 Joseph Rably

MARVIN

3 Morris Dargis
3 Henry Chausse
4 Joseph Rogers
4 Stanislaus Blanchette
4 James Morgan
7 Barin Socollos
7 John Pupos
8 Joseph Cohen
8 Sophia LaPorte
8 Edwin Tomlinson
8 Abram Altman
11 Joseph A Bourget
12 John Beard
13 Mrs Elizabeth Duxbury
15 Frank Gregory
15 Thos Howley
15 Frederick Harrington
16 Andrew Kosiba
16 Bruno Warsoski
16 Thomas Morak
16 Joseph Needham
17 John Gilchrist
17 Misses Wroe
20 Joseph W Nichols
20 James Wilson
20r Adelard Brillode
21 Samuel Newton
21 Mrs Jane Burr
21 Edward Morris
24 Patrick Bourgeois
25 Misses Miller
25 Robert Marvel

MAXFIELD

22 Mrs Fanny Washington
22 Clara B Lake
28 George Therrien
28 Henry Gasperella
36 L J Hathaway
37 George Homer
37 Joseph Hurd
37 Joseph B Jordan

Maxfield—con
43 Mrs Jennie Robbins
45 Joseph Pollitt
45 Mrs Margaret Langley
49 Charlotte E Walker
49 Ezra V Barkers
50 Lezime C Chassey
54 Mrs Levina E Wickham
54 Mrs Susan E Lamb
55 Frederick G Sawyer
55 Martin J Cairnes
68 Mrs Elizabeth Chapman
71 James Marquand
71 Elmer E Phillips
72 Margaret Young
74 Mrs P Jane Brady
75 Herbert C Gifford
75 Charles G Russell
76 Mrs Mary Hitch
76 Elliot F Jones
76 Grace Rock
81 Mrs Marry Murphy
81 Thomas Egan
94 Alfred M Gifford
94 Patrick J Wood
96 Mrs Charlotte E Maker
96 Arthur F Packard
97 William A Driscoll
97 Thomas Burke
101 Benjamin Hillman
101 Alfred F James
107 John E Linton
111 Eben S Gilkey
111 Mrs Sarah R Luce
115 Frank A McGrillis
118 Daniel H Gifford
118 George W Baldwin
119 Edward L Cronin
119 Frank A Shores
123 Ronald C McDonald
123 Patrick J McDonald
123 Charles Keehlc
124 Charles T Wilcox
129 Frederick Jameson
135 Louis Meyer
138 John D Martin
139 Elizabeth J Dillingham
139 Mrs Nellie M Booth
147 Carrie J Hunt
148 Hugh A Perry
148 Robert T Hillman
153 Samuel Whitlow
154 Jeremiah J Crowley
157 Frank H Rushton
157 Windsor C Peirce
161 Herbert J Brownell
161 Mrs Lucy H Keith
163 Clarissa S Staples
164 Robert A Terry
174 James C Manchester
185 Hiram T Lambert
186 Richard Barry
189 Mrs Annie L C Nye
190 Timothy J O'Brien
190 Mrs Catherine Brennan
194 Joseph Donaghy
194 Alex Donaghy
199 Ebenezer S Perry
202 Mrs Jennie M Gammons
202 Mrs Harriet Covil
202 Mrs Jennie M Gammons
215 Mrs Elizabeth Sullivan
223 Stephen F Adams
215 Edward L Brawley
223 Stephen F Adams
223 David K Hayes
233 Frank R Taber
233 Nathan G Jenney
236 John C Gidley
236 John H Davis
237 Mrs Alice G Harps
237 Mrs Tabatha G Keen
240 George P Hurll
242 George F Taylor
242 Mrs Fanny J Fearing
242 Louis Gidley
243 Mrs Mary Grew
243 Herbert N Kelley
254 Charles A Pierce
254 Charles T Drum
257 Frederick A Hathaway
257 Ida E Hathaway
293 William H Brown
293 Alfred A Black
300 Mrs Jane F Thompson
301 James M Payne
305 Daniel M Howland
305 C W Oliver
309 Mrs Mary J Dunham
319 George A Wood
323 Charles W Spooner
341 George W Briggs
369 Major J Casey
373 Ernest E Burke
378 Mrs Jane A Mitchell
382 Mrs Martha W Moynan
386 James W Webber
390 John W Pieraccini
390 James S Snow
394 Raphael Pierassini
400 E A Pierce
404 Clement G Francis
410 Anthony Luna Jr
412 William H Tripp
413 Antone Pedro
440 Antone S Avila
440 William E Hillman

456r Ira S Joseph
462 Joao Alves
466 Benjamin Gomes
476 Alfred Barboza
476r Mrs Isolina Pina
484 Joseph Barboza
484 Manuel Perry
488 Aaron C Joseph
488 Waler J Gainville
498 Philip Cruz
504 John Richardson
504 Mrs Mary Richardson
504 Robert Johnson
506 Nehemiah Dawson
520 Mrs Silvia A Johnson
522 Antone Gonsalves
596 Asa T Stowell
597 T Williams Jackson
603 Mrs Mary Marston
622 Jean B Beauparlant
624 Wiliam F S John
641 Herbert G Stowell

McDONALD COURT

1 Joseph Antava
1 Desire Bousquet
1 Vitale Burgess
1 Abraham Kramer
2 Phillis Menir
2 Wladislaw Minkofski
2 Joseph Gosda
3 Philip Cormier
3 Assard Farras
3 Mrs Rose Horvitz
3 Alfred Tetreault
3 Peter Thimisthicos

McGURK

5 Napoleon Lapointe
5 Daniel W Burgess
6 John Bernier
6 Howard Agnes
6 William Costello
6 Mrs Amelia Fielding
6 Christopher Lanous
6 Leo Reaume
7 Arthur Dumaine
8 Joseph Boucher
8 Louis Bourbeau
8 Michel Lajeunesse
10 Wellington Hartley
10 Mrs Mary Schelter
10 Ira Stopford
10 Dana E LeBoeuf
10 Frank Loshink
10 Albert Rossijnol
12 Stanislaus Sypek
12 Fred Perry
12 Felix Shumaniski
13 John K Robinson
13 William N Bramwell
14 Levi Reeves
14 Albini Dichon
14 Frank Millette
14 Levi Tichon
15 Mrs Ada Wilson
16 John E Thompson
16 Thomas Slater
16 Thomas Towers
18 Rosario Carroll
20 Eugene Genereux
22 Alfred LaBarre
22 Alfred F Webber
24 Mrs Catherine Hewitt
25 Marie Mahan
25 Mrs Mary Reardon
27 John Winwood
27 John Malone
28 Louis Morin
28 Joseph Delcourt
28 William Levy
28 George D Raymond
29 Mrs Elizabeth D Barlow
29 Mrs Mary A Gray
29 Nathan Knowles
30 Albert Sypek
30 Thomas Deane
30 Edward McHugh
30 Herbert Smith
31 John Wareing
31 Walter E Hadfield
32 James Walsh
32 Albert J Brule
32 James McNichols
32 Mrs Lena Derosier
33 James Flanagan
33 John McNamee
33 James Gibson
34 Alexander Koss
34 Albert Grindrod
35 A J Rawlins
35 Mrs Emma Peckham
36 Henri Lebeau
36 Henri Rocheleau
36 Louis Dame
36 Mrs Ann Sharp
38 John Giusti
38 William Trett
38 Narcisse Lapointe
40 John W Staples

McMURRAY TERRACE

9 Arthur J Cockshott
9 Joseph Adamson
9 Henry Benac
10 Thomas Rogers
10 Frank J Murray
11 Joseph Reedy
11 Thomas H Parkinson

McMurray ter—con
11 George Bancroft
12 John N Cunningham
12 Mrs Ann Sloane
16 Albert F Matthews
16 William Taber
16 Edward Walley
16 John McCall
18 Mrs Elizabeth J Philips

MECHANICS LANE

10 Sarah Tilden
47 Mrs Phoebe W Wing
49 William H Maxfield
59 Mrs Adeline W Brownell
60 Mrs Lydia Tripp
60 George Robbins
62 Mrs Emma R Stubbs
63 Mrs Mary R Bishop
64 Martin Freundschuh
64 Charles A Johns
66 Charles LaBossiere
67 Joseph S Thomas
68 Thomas K Eldredge
69 Mrs Abby B Howland
69 Mrs Jennie F Groves
71 William A Coe

MERRILL

11 Ida Duffany
11 John Sotnick

MERRIMAC

41 Mrs Ellen Leonard
41 David K Thompson
41 Adam Dupuis
41 Jacob Dupuis
41 Walter Ducharme
41r Joseph Pennell
41r Mrs Virgina Roy
42 Samuel D Fredette
44 Lucien Dupuis
44 Peter Dupre
44 William Mondon
44 Peter Dupre
53 James W Holt
53 Louis A Castino
55 Melvina Correau
55 Carlos M Cram
56 Charles Stringer
56 Henry Smith
57 William J French
57 William Robillard
59 Edward Whalen
60 Zepherin Bergeron
60 Samuel Wexler
61 James Jennings
67 Mary J Halenan
67 Mrs Charlotte W Clifton
69 Henri Lavoie
69 Arthur Phenix
71 John W Hoyle
71 William LeClair
77 Misses Hanlon
77 Mrs Elizabeth Doyle
77 Chester A Freelove
77r John Williams
78 Mrs Catherine McCown
78 Charles E Cox
80 John A Budlong
80 George Malone
84 William H Brown
84 Septimus Marland
90 James H Bamford
90 Walter Partington
91 Ellen Melling
98 Dennis Calnan
98 Mrs Daisy M Cook
102 William M Downey
102 Jeremiah Calnan
106 Mrs Johanna Reardon
106 John A Haurlen
110 Johnson McNally
110 Mayhew Burns
111 Mrs Ohelia J Dantsizen
111 Sarah H Hewins
131 David Warren
131 William J Mills .
135 Percy C Estes
135 John F Butts
138 James F Powers
139 Mrs Mary J Noonan
141 Cyrus J Gidley
142 William T Concrieff
142 Waldo E Cushing
143 William F Desmond
144 James McDonald
147 J Thomas Daley
147 Obediah Butler
150 Mrs Ellen Keenan
150 Luke H Rooney
151 Thomas Yates
154 Martin C Healey
156 Edward F Otis
160 James S Fitts
167 Herbert J Tripp
167 James P Duggan
168 Robert S Weaver
168 Daniel A Harrington
169 David H Tribou
169 C F Hurley
170 Henry F Janell
171 Simon Mechaber
172 Albert H Peters
190 John F Coggins
190 Daniel Deneen

MERRIMAC AVENUE

1 George A Cory
2 Theresa Birtwhistle
3 Fred Wilkinson

MIDDLE

52 Henry Gomes
56 Jeremiah Mahoney
56 Mrs Mary Donnelly
62 John C Rose
62 Joseph Brennan
62 Mrs Mary Silva
62 Charles Tucker
62 Charles R Cash
62 Antone Gonsalves
62 John C Rose
66 Antone Rodericque
66 Manuel I Costa
66 Frank R Rogers
66 Mrs Amelia Rodericque
66 Henry H Scott
66 Charles W Jones
74 Antonio J Edardo
74 Joseph Morris
78 Lysander G Silva
93 William Thompson
93 Mrs A Davis
94 Paul Touchette
94 Fred C Taber
94 Mrs Minnie Goslin
96 Mrs M E Thatcher
97 William E Cook
97 George L Fisher
101 William T Meagher Jr
101 George F Tripp
101 Sidney N Hathaway
101 Mrs Kate Sharpe
102 John Costa
102 Charles W Buttz
102 Earl McFarland
102 Henrietta Gray
102 Thomas F McCauley
102 Mrs Emily F Robbins
102 Sarah Dunbar
110 Orrin L Tourjee
116 Kate Sullivan
116 Mrs Mary Cooper
122 Mrs Mary Putz
135 Therena R Cote
149 Octave Susini
150 Richard L Ellis
150 Mrs Maria S Anthony
150 Mary E Donovan
151 Mrs Ellen M Thompson
151 Charles O Anderson
152 Mrs Maria T Upjohn
157 Dr E Stanley Robbins
157 Gladys E Seaver
158 James H Sherman
161 Mrs Elizabeth E Smith
161 Mrs Julia A Berry
161 Walter Lewis
161 Mrs Edith Babcock
161 Mrs Mary F Johnson
163 Ernest L Tilton
164 Dr William J Nickerson
165 Chester E Davis
169 William B Simons
169 Mrs Amanda J DeWolf
173 William A Kirby
173 Mary E Chace
180 Clifton H Lincoln
180 Albert Goodwin
181 William J Barrett
184 Louis Millette
184 D J Murphy
185 Dr James F Sullivan
187 Mrs Rhoda A Sisson
187 Edward T Rouke
188 James W Mitchell
188 George W Parker
188r James Sharkey
192 James H Sherman
193 Mrs Lucy A Dudley
193 William R Dennis
193 Henry G Dennis
197 Edward K Cowen
197 Mrs Lucy E Taber
198 James H Hathaway
201 Misses Pierce
202 Thomas Wilcox
207 Sidney F Cooper
207 William B Johnson
209 Mrs Hattie R Macomber
212 Nannie M Healy
212 Samuel A Gates
213 Ellsworth C Jacobs
213 William F Stowell
216 Edward A Clark
217 A Herbert Dean
218 Mary E Wilcox
221 Emma A Remington
227 Adley Wilcox
233 Clara S Vincent
237 Frederick J J Abrams
237 William C Card
238 Katherine C Phelan
238 Misses Phelan
240 William L Fitzgerald
241 Arthur R Weeks
247 Thomas H Wilson
257 Frank Benton
257 Mrs Isabel F Pinkham

Middle—con
259 Thomas Brown
261 Charles E Westgate
261 Ellen H Packard
265 Michael Myers
265 John Ray
265 David Barnes
268 Mrs Fannie M Washington
268 Mrs Isabella White
269 Mrs Jane Wright
269 James E Cotton
269 John B Corbin
269r John M Taylor
269r Mrs Ophelia Johnson
269r Mrs Louisa L Williams
270 Mrs Katherine Ellis
270 Mrs Sarah T G Watkins
272 George Groebe
275 Harry Hart
276 Mrs Sedonia Tillman
276 John C Austin
277 George Smith
277 Joseph Delvalle
284 Mrs Nancy Webb
285 Dennis H Shay
290 Edwin Hunt
291 Charles B Jenney
291 John H J Deverell
291 Mrs Mary E Douglass
291 Charles B Jenny
292 Mrs Grace Reed
300 John Munroe
302 William H Hinds
302 George H Winfield
303 Walter A Swan
303 Samuel Fleish
305 Mrs Mary E Jones
305 Mrs Emma J King
305 Mary E Jones
306 William W Weeden
310 Robert S Cobbins
315 M Meyers
316 Harrison J Seals
317 Chester Bennett
319 Alfred G Guinn
325 Mrs Rosa Ames
326 John W Post
326 Horace H Reed
329 John T Casey
329 Lyman E Peters
334 George M Tillson
335 F A Brownell
337 Mrs Elizabeth A Robinson
340 Mrs Louisa Ayler
340 Mrs Josephine C Smith
341 Mrs Ann Cavanaugh
342 George Greer
343 Antone Spencer
343 Charles Brown
343 Mrs Margaret Nelson
345 Mrs Minnie F Henderson
345 Mrs Sarah Dakin
345 Jacintho Mendez
348 Patrick E Wallbank
370 Mrs Patrick Tresham
370 Thomas Crane
374 Mrs Maria G Cannon
374 Abner Mayhew
375 John L Duarte
375 James H Turner Jr
378 James Finnerty
378 Manuel S Medeiros
380 John B Jones
380 William B Westgate
404 Manuel Francis
408 Harry M Frates
410 George H Butler
412 Charles H Mendell
488 Edward B Haskell
491 B W Kendrick

MILFORD

0 Joseph A Duchesneau
0 John B Beauchaine
0 Joseph Moreau

MILL

15 Charles F Jones
15 Mrs Mabel E Maxcy
18 Mrs William J Newcomb
18 Joseph Kenworthy
19 Mrs Susan McGlennon
19 Frank Mont
20 Leonard H Craw
20 Daniel Sherman
22 John Olsen
25 Mrs Mary E Norton
35 James Dowden
35 Melvin J Brown
38 Mrs Abba A Macomber
38 James R Forbes
39 Jasper Taylor
40 William H Bennett
40 Herbert W Brightman
43 George J Dodge
43 James L Sherman
44 Mrs Louisa A Dodge
48 Arthur P Underwood
48 Frank A Rogers
49 Mrs Nancy B Crapo
50 John Lopes
50 Annie M Hathaway
51 Mrs Harriet B Ge Gatt
51 Cologuero Medeiros
51 Thomas Craig
52 Joseph T Tobey
52 William Wilson
56 Joseph B Reynolds

56 Washington A Eldredge
63 Elmir A Jenkins
63 Charles E Lamphear
64 Walter F Wheaton
64 Mrs Eliza J Caswell
66 Peter F McQuillan
67 Manuel D Martine
67 Arthur R McGowan
69 Samuel H Small
69 Fred H Geiles
70 George T Duckworth
70 Theodore E Lawton
74 Mrs Bessie M Turner
74 Henry J Trapp
74 Joseph Relahaunty
75 Charles S Collins
75 Mrs Sarah E Lee
76 Thomas E Day
76 Henry Lamy
78 Michael Noonan
78 John E Phelan
78 Mrs Alice Galligan
79 Charles S Coombs
79 Mrs Emma L Hammond
80 Alfred G Studley
80 Mrs Ellen M Gray
81 Mrs Charlotte N Hillman
81 Shubael D Smith
82 Charles O Brightman
83 William Ritchie
84 William W Mann
85 Horace Wood
86 John Corish
86 Francis P Sherman
87 Edward L Murphy
87 Frederick E Eubanks
90 Isaac W Giles
91 Frank S Tripp
102 Mrs Lucretia Lewis
114 Frederic A Brownell
114 Allison R Dorman
115 Clark W Holcomb
117 Mrs Mary Chadwick
118 Charles E Ellis
118 Charles E Cowen
119 Mayhew R Hitch
120 Andrew E Hathaway
120 James H Tallman
124 Ralph B Parlin
126 Sadie M Drown
126 Edward G Leighton
128 Mrs Susanna Carney
130 Peter Peterson
130 Charles A Gifford
132 Mrs Minerva J Townsend
132 Margaret C Vicars
132 Abner D Lowe
140 James Upjohn Jr
140 Charles A Chase
143 Emma Souza
143 Amelia Souza
143 Mrs Annie B Russell
144 Amos R Caswell
144 James B Rockefeller
147 Ann McGee
150 George F Guild
151 Moses I Williams
154 Ellen Smith
156 Charles H Dowty
158 Giovanni Rossi
158 Mrs Adeline A Wordell
160 George A Harlow
160 Pliney B Sherman
166 Irene M Bassett
166 Allen G Mayhew
167 Charles D Brown
167 Frank S Wilbur
167 Charles A Stevens
167r Mrs Louise K Tarbox
168 Charles A Caswell
169 Mrs Helen A Brown
171 Frederick O Pollock
175 Samuel P Winegar
176 William C Macomber
176 Henry W Besse
179 Mrs Charlotte White
179 Ernest Gillum
180 Clarence E Cowing
181 John H Haynes
181½ Charles H Martin
183 John Silver
185 Frank Swift
186 Mrs Parthenia M Carter
186 Braddock Andress
187 George S Frawley
189 Harry P McGowan
224 John J Meagher
226 John F Gifford
227 Adley Wilcox
228 Edward F Magrath
247 Patrick P Reardon
247 Patrick Sheehan
253 George H Lowther
264 John H Gainville
265 Franklin K Sisson
267 Mrs Lydia C Tripp
267 Edgar C Tripp
269 Michael J Conroy
270 Frederick D Wainer
273 Mrs Lillian Crapo
274 Mrs Lucy C Sanford
275 Charles V Weller
278 Ray Thornton
280 George Stevens
286 Frank E Guillette

Mill—con
286 Joseph Bedon
286 Mrs Myra G Murphy
286 Robert Kendrick
305 Robert Fitzgerald
305 Henry C Russell
305 Mrs Margaret Waring
404 Charles W Lawton
408 Henry J Ackerman
427 Peleg A Tripp
431 Jack Auclair
431 Julius S Spiva
431 C H Murphy
435 Alfred S Dunham
436 Mrs Susan W Bryant
436 Barker H Cushman
437 Eliphalet N Horton
439 Henry Fauteux
455 Mrs Mercy Stowell
456 Harry I Humphrey
456 Ernest A Jennings
458 Belle S Fisher
459 George J Allen
461 George W Munsey
461 George W Munsey Jr
463 Edward E Butts
467 A H Jennings
477 Joseph P Silva
484 Adam C Henderson
485 Charles G Thompson
492 James Cunniff
493 Mrs Julia S Bryant
493 Mrs Emily M Rounds

MILL ROAD

9 James H Paige
13 Mrs Ellen Simpson
13 William J Cathcart
19 Benjamin R Baker
19 Henry A Haskins
30 James A Wilbur
51 Erastus C Pierce
51 Emil St Don
55 John Griffin

MILTON

2 Charles E Crosby

MITCHELL

3 Joseph P Rezendos
3 Antone Medeiros
3 Joseph Souza
5 Manuel Souza
5 Manuel Bardoza
5 Jose Furtado
5 Guito Giard
5 John Correia
13 John Perreira
13 Manuel Olivier
17 Domingos Ponte
17 Antone Moniz
17 Manuel Mauricio
17 Antone M Furtado
17 Manuel Moniz
17 John Simas
17 Antone Boteilho
21 Jose Oliveira
21 Manuel Rosa
21 Antone R Souza
21 Antone Jacintho
23 Joseph Jacinth
23 Frank Amaral
23 Manuel Lima
23 Joseph Pacheco
23 Antonio De Mello
23 Manuel Cashmere
25 Manuel Mello
25 Manuel Thomas
27 Mitchell Green
27 Augustine Correia
31 John Boczek
31 Peter Boczek
35 Frank Silva
35 Joseph A Cardoza
35 Luiz S Martin
35 Jose DeRego
39 Joseph Medeiros
39 Agusto Medeiros
39 Manuel F Rezendes
39 Jacintho Correia
39 Manuel Martin
39 Jules M Ferreira
41 Morris Rotman
41 Louis Koffman
45 Domingos Frates
45 Shaid Coury
45 Antone F Viera
45 Manuel Rapoza
49 Manuel Tavares
49 Joaquim Cabral
49 Joaquim Andrada
55 Manuel J Leandro
55 Joseph Frates
55 Antone Moura
55 Luiz Andrada
55 Manuel Pedro
55 Adam Siwik
55 Joseph L Tavares
55 Jacintho Rapoza
55 Antone G Santos

MOORE

27 Nellie F Fairbrothers

MORELAND TERRACE

0 Charles M Hussey
11 Charles K Knowles
0 Arthur D Delano
25 Walter S Allen

MORGAN

13 Henry M Maine
21 Norman L Almy
37 Charles H Wing
41 Charles W Hurll
45 Mrs Mary T Howland
45 Mrs Hannah Howland
46 Edward H Wing
48 William S Cook
49 Arthur H Jones
52 Harry Bloomingdale
56 Henry V Sanders
57 Emma H Wheeler
57 Carrie E Gifford
61 Charles F Wing Jr
63 Mrs Alice F Terry
70 Emily M Eldridge
71 John W Paul
74 Silas S Taber
74 Mrs Emma J Woodward
77 George A Dunn
77 Ellis Taber
78 Wilfred C Burt
78 Elishup P Allen
79 Robert S Gorham
79 Oscar F Caswell
80 Frank W Davis
80 Nathaniel P Sowle
82 William A Battles
82 Eugene A Rider
83 Mrs Clara B Sturtevant
83 John F Andrews
85 Mrs Elizabeth Davis
85 Mrs Bertha C Burns
86 Mrs Hannah H Nooning
86 James H Gorham
96 John A Lee
96 Edwin E Spooner
100 John P Thompson
100 Mrs Maria K Johnson
101 William C Diamond
101 Pardon B Gifford
103 John Butler
103 Charles Moore
104 Gioechino Salvatti

MORGAN'S LANE

5 Mrs Ida Harris
8 Manuel Ramos
8 Mrs Jennie Gomes
8 Antonio Canto
8 Manuel Raymond
10 Mrs Olympia Gonsalves
11 Heiman Miller
11 Caesar Gomes
15 Verissimo F Britto
17 Abram Shuster
17 Hieman Shuster
17 Harry Drazen
21 Harris Resevitz

MORGAN TERRACE

1 Frank B Chase
3 Charles G Akin
4 Misses Shaw
5 Herbert Parker

MORTON COURT

8 Samuel Roylance
8 James Crook
8 Robert Dewhurst
9 John F Maguire
9 James Henry
10 Mrs Sliza Stansfield
12 Jules Seguin
12 Michael Trotter
12 Joseph Sharpe
12 Mrs Mary E Powers
14 Lawrence Cocking
15 Ralph T Wilde
15 John Munroe
15 Joseph A Burding
16 Mrs Ann Reddy
18 John Denick
18 Joseph Bisoski
20 Mrs Mary Trotter
21 Joseph Melland
21 Emile Perry
21 Androise St Roach
21 Cyrille Gendron
21 John Morin
24 John Gaida
25 Napoleon Larochelle
25 Joseph Bassinett
31 Philip Charette
31 Joseph Lapointe
31 Mrs Mary Derine
35 William H McMahon
35 Edward Fitzgerald
39 Joseph P Sylvia
42 John T Robinson
44 Mrs Mary Hogan
48 Timothy Fournier
52 Mrs Ellen Buckley
55 Octave Carroll
55 James Sherrington

MOSHER

13 Charles H Dugdale
13 Joseph Dube
15 George W Beck
15 Albert Bates
15 George Wright
18 Frank F Lee
21 Joseph P Menard
21 Henry Blanchette
21 Alfred Desjardin

Mosher—con
21 Edgar Bazinet
24 Mary Holt
24 William Bowden
24 George B Bentley
24 Mary Holt
25 Harry Proudfoot
25 William St Germain
25 Paul Cournoyer
28 Mrs Emma Dunce
28 Alexander A Dowty
29 Mrs Tamer Craven
29 Arthur Knowles
29 William Hayhurst
32 Patrick Foy
35 Dennis O'Connell
36 John J Waldron
39 Manuel Silva
40 Seraphin J Gregoria
40 Eva Angelo
40 Joseph I Silva
40 Frank S Silva
41 Virginia Recardo
44 Manuel B de Medeiros
44 Charles Silva
45 James Marvel
52 Amide LaFrance
53 Bridget McLaughlin
53 Edward Mealey
56 William A Kilpatrick
56 Thomas Parker
59 John Avery Jr
59 Mrs Hannah Howard
60 Joseph S Gomes
60 John Rose
60 John Costa
64 Levi Languirand
64 Mrs Margaret Kilpatrick
65 Joseph King
65 Manuel F Estrella
69 James W Kershaw
71 P Melo Emilio
71 Jose A Otins
71 John Sylvia
73 Frank Morrow Jr
73 Jacine Carriere
73 Manuel M Alves
74 John Medeiros
74 Marie de Gloria
75 Manuel Gracia
75 Charles Andrews
75 Antone Gonsalves
81 Joseph Tavares
81 Hermidos Quintin
81 Samuel Harwood
81 William Bramwell
84 Thomas Hushon
85 John Munroe
86 James Welsh
86 Thomas Mullaney
88 Joe Rogers
88 Joe Rose
89 Mrs Mary May
89 James Payton
89 Martin Quinn
102 Antone Rabeilo
102 Antonio DeMello
103 Marion C Souza
103 John Barboza
104 Matthew O'Malley
104 Manuel Seaver
104 Manuel Rabeilo
104 Antone Souza
104 Manuel F Rebello

MOTT

32 Mrs Mary Halliwell
58 Robert Wilson
58 Arthur Roscoe
58 John Coupe
74 Albert Lafrenais
74 Alex Dulieu
78 Edward Taylor
78 Moses Dupuis
82 Mary Watson
82 Frank Truchon
86 Michel Belanger
86 George Isabell
86 Louis Lucier
86 Michel Belanger
86 Mrs Mary McDonald
109 Arthur Finch
109 William Kolasz
110 Andrew Oniski
110 Frank Hlebus
110 Mrs Georgina Blean
112 Camille Derocher
112 F W Meillray
113 William Trimble
113 Mrs Ann Smalley
113 Ernest Finch
114 Philip Viger
117 John Sequeira
117 Samuel McNair
117 Edward Garlington
118 Joseph E Rogers
118 Henry Fontaine
119 Joseph Hendriques
119 August De Mello
119 J Leo Fournier
122 Mrs Selina Hellowell
122 Joseph Lavoie
122 Ludger Bergeron
123 Lawrence Wilcox
123 John Dowbekin
126 Fred Hellowell
126 Henri Tetrault

128 Napoleon Tessier
128 Paul L Forand
130 Walter Melline
130 James E Howarth
130 William W Hittenheine
130 Herbert Melling
143 Mrs Carrie E Hayward
178 Albert H Ashline

MOUNT PLEASANT

3 Joseph Doyle
51 Seth E Bryant Jr
51 Charles B Huxford
55 John C Andrews
55 J Clifford Bates
59 William Whitehead
60 Irod J B Folsom
63 Herbert E Smalley
63 Mrs Susan Colwell
65 John H Moore
65 James Fowler
66 Daniel Robinson
69 Jean B Charpentier
72 George H McCulloch
73 Mrs Sarah W West
73 Manuel F Sylvia
73 Collins S M Gifford
76 George W Smith
77 John W Starkie
78 Jean B Dion
81 Gaspard Lamourex
83 Mrs Annie W Renex
86 William Platt
86 Henry Garon
89 Louis M Whrtney
93 Frank S Bonney
95 Eliphalet A Tripp
96 Joseph F Aubertin
97 Oliver A Brunelle
99 Joseph Poisson
99 Alfred L Poisson
100 Mrs Michel Mathieu
100 William H Hosmer
101 William G Snell
102 Elzear H Chouquette
112 Joseph Hámpson
112 Silvio Ploude
124 Louis E Destremps
126 Joseph Chausse
126 Ovila Chausse
129 Mrs Emma P Wing
129 John W Peake
144 Stephen F Amos
151 George Caldecott
151 John T Caldecott
152 Charles Jubenville
153 Mrs Catherine Price
158 Charles Gubinville
163 Mrs Fannie M Mason
163 Mrs Rebecca E Reed
164 Louis J Bellenoit
174 Samuel C France
215 David A Snell
229 David Levasseur
257 Francis H Pasell
259 Mrs Mary Malonson
259 Dennis J Devlin
260 Mary F Gurl
264 Gorge Paradis
281 Samuel Davis
281 Thomas H Jenkins
318 William F Chase
320 Charles T Brownell
379 Joseph W Secour
379 Charles Chase
379 Joseph Secours
379 Joseph Voknouth
445 William L Cobb
463 Michael J McNulty
480 Mrs Lydia King
531 Henry Hough
552 George S Taylor
578 Arthur Normandeau
578 Fred U Normandeau
586 Stanley W Sharpe
595 Medric Vigeant
640 Vergino Medeiros
640 Joseph S Silva
644 Juan V Pedro
644 Augusto R Viera
647 Frank Frates
661 Nicholas Antone
661 Antone C Silvia
735 James Davis
756 Antone Silva
756 August Veira

MOUNT PLEASANT LANE

3 Mrs Sarah Sweet
5 Patrick Bannon
6 William F Thomas
9 John H Jameson
12 John Rimmer

MOUNT VERNON

34 George P Sabino
35 J F McGuinness
42 Robert P McEwen
44 Albert Jones
55 Hartley Spencer
111 Francis X Bellenoit
124 Charles G Poole
124 Albert K Poole
127 William Robinson

Mount Vernon—con
131 Manuel Vetorina
131 Ernest S Medeiros
137 Edwin F Drown

MULBERRY

1 Joseph Francis
2 Frank Lima
8 Manuel Soares
8 Manuel Cambra
8 Jacques Boissoneault

MYRTLE

18 Benjamin A Clapp
18 Michael Francis
18 William H Breakell
18 Lester W Briggs
18 John Dolan
18 Joseph Holderness
18 Ernest A Hall
24 William J Savage
24 Joseph Z Longpre
24 Mary Sullivan
24 Thomas Smith
25 John J Crompton
29 Mrs Margaret J Hargraves
29 James Kitchen
32 Reuben Isherwood
32 Robert Valentine
35 Mrs Mary H Baldwin
35 Joseph D Wagner
36 Mrs Ann D Canavan
36 Robert Barber
36 Mrs Handawa A H Saliba
38 Samuel Thompson
38 James Kenyon
39 James Wright
45 Herbert L James
46 John Downey
46 Mrs Susie Gammons
46 Patrick Welsh
46 George Buckley
51 James Booth
61 John Smalley
62 Dennis Sullivan
62 Ernest Margeson
65 George H Harrison
66 John J Toomey
66 Maurice Harrington
66 Timothy Manning
69 Joseph Gatley
69 Jonathan Bailey
70 Mrs Margaret Welsh
73 Adam Bury
73 Arthur Partington
73 Clarence E Hodson
73 William Hodson
74 Mrs Elizabeth C Wilcox
74 Matthew T Hood
76 Edwin R Johnson
76 Mrs Joanna Armstrong
77 Richard Bailey
81 Dennis Mahon
82 John B Charbonneau
82 Harry Andrews
82 Jeremiah M Harrington
86 Albert E Riding
86 Mrs Catherine Tighe
148 James Barber
148 William Acomb
149 George Oldham
149 Joseph Oldham
153 William H Robinson
159 Frank M Bradshaw
159 William C Dame
159 Charles Corcoran
0 Mrs Mary A Smith

NASH ROAD

27 Samuel King
31 Mrs Amalda LeClair
63 Joseph Miller
63 James H Ward
65 Willie Zeima
67 Frank Silva
67 John Walsh
67 William S Tavares
67 Gabriel Massola
68 William Cote
68 Seraphin Lemaire
68 Gedeon Gangnier
71 Robert Leeming
71 Frank Sylvia
71 Charles Griffiths
75 Richard Bourgeois
75 John Cooper
79 John Welsh
86 Manuel S Medeiros
86 Joseph C Mello
90 Manuel Jarindi
90 Antone C Mello
90 Manuel Jarindi
94 Ernest Comery
94 John Halkyard
94 Joseph Wilcock
102 William J Bibby
102 Samuel Bradshaw
102 Robert Wilding
105 John Ruddell
109 Octave Lariviere
109 Frank Mercier
109 Theophile Gagne
109 Alcide Groulx
109 Ambrose Landry
110 Donat Turcotte
110 Thomas McManus
110 Edward Fontaine
113 Walter J Chausse

113 Joseph Sevigney
113 Placide A Leger
114 Thomas Morgan
114 John Apolonsky
115 Joseph Dugal
115 Euclid Richard
115 Oliva St Aubin
118 John B Fontaine
118 Eustache Jaillet
118 Philomon Comeau
119 Joseph Bourdua
119 Szcepan Wyiroski
121 Robert Burke
121 John Gilmore
122 Paul Levasseur
122 John O Driesen
122 John Taylor
125 Louis Laperiere
125 Edmund T Gilmore
126 Jerry Turcotte
126 Joseph H Denham
126 Victor Ise
126 Eric Bourque
126 Angus Williams
126 Charles Trudeau
128 Michael Fitzpatrick
128 Edward Blake
128 Cyrille Allain
131 Edward Sansoucy
134 Arsene Roberge
134 Philip Cormier
134 Mrs Olive LaRoche
135 Henry Lagasse
135 Louis St Martin
150 George Nutall
150 Eugene Touchette
150 Lorenzo Pelletier
154 John B Pepin
154 Honore Dagesse
158 Louis Varney
158 Wilfred Simpson
158 James Nolan
161 Lawrence Duckworth
161 Frank G Leonard
162 James Hughes
162 John Gilmore
162 James Lord
166 Joseph Hebert
166 Robert Proctor
166 John E Roberts
190 John Seidel
190 Joseph Barnes
190 Adelard Alax
190 James Riha
190 James Hudson
190 Louis Inne
194 William L Menard
194 Mrs Sarah E Farrow
194 Abraham Jackson
194 Ebenezer Smith
204 Gertrude Mort
204 George E Jones
204 Aldi La France
208 Harold Lee
208 D F Murphy
208 Arthur H Worthington
212 James McLaughlin
212 Samuel Lane
212 Mrs Mary A Butler
213 Philip Poirier
213 Odilon Poirier
242 Joseph Laplante
242 Michael Metiver
242 James Moran
246 John W Sunderland
246 Robert Hartley
246 Victor Cousin
274 Treffle Major
274 Louis Silva
274 Bento Brazil
276 John Costa
278 Mrs Adrienne Bernique
278 Joseph Spirlet
336 Horatio Berry
336 Eugene Spirlet

NELSON

9 Nicholas Dubois
9 Hermidas Mengeau
9 Arthur Bertrand
15 Zenan Berube
15 Alphonse Dautriel
16 Amedee St Louis
16 Napoleon St Louis
16 Telesphore Levesque
19 Edward Berube
19 Joseph Gagnon
22 Emile Turcotte
22 Robert Beckman
22 Joseph Rancourt
23 Manuel R Maderios
26 Sabin Goyer
27 Joseph Costa
28 Joseph Potvin
32 Manuel Pacheco
32 Arthur Viveirios
32 John L Pereira
37 John Almeda
37 Anton Arruda
37 Jess Perry
38 Frank Cordeira
40 Querino G Pepp
45 Manuel R Medeiros
45 Antonio Raposa
45 Julio Vieira
48 Hermidos Letourneau

Nelson—con
48 John Roy
48 John Jodoin
48 Manuel Foster
48 Hormidas Letourneau
48 Edmond Bouley
49 Paul St Laurent
49 Telesphore Doyon
52 Manuel Souza
56 Frank R Lopes
56 Joseph V Souza
56 Frank Souza
57 Alfred Gagne
60 Cyrille Mailloux
61 Marjooricque Boivin
61 Ludger Boivin
61 Mary Borrin
64 Henry Desnoyer
68 Napoleon Rock
69 Ephraim Clement
70 Frank Souza
70 Melvin Coanick
73 Arthur Frechette
73 Henry Pellend
74 Napoleon Gregoire
74 Joseph Lamontague
74 Mrs Valoire Boisclair
74 Pierre Lamontagne
79 Eugene Melancon
79 Mrs Gene Duval
79 Alcide Larriabbee
79 Victor Hudon
82 Mrs Angeline Roderique
82 Joseph Roderique
82 Wilfred Lebeau
82 Benjamin Chovin
82 Fred Thibeault
88 Alexis J Lavalley
88 Mrs Jesse Allen
88 Desire Forant
92 Delphis Parent
93 Manuel Lawrence
100 David Favor
100 Cyrille Monbleau

NEWTON

39 Sidney H Stowell
48 John W Goggin
48 Dennis McAuliffe
64 William Upham
77 Patrick Hart
80 Albert B White
81 Anthony W Felix
84 William F Glennon
85 Joseph M Butts
88 Jessie S Allen
89 Benjamin F Hubbard
96 William C Paddack
97 Walter P Weaver
101 J Wesley Howarth
101 Nathan S Gibbs
102 Mrs Carrie H Howes
102 Antone Sylvia
105 Samuel T Bennett
106 Mrs Rachel Cook
109 Leonard O Curtis
110 Hannah F Leonard
110 Frank Glista
113 Mrs Fanny Wilson
114 Samuel Whitehead
114 Arthur Welsh
140 Charles Lark
145 Stephen A Burt
149 William Keating Brown
152 Michael A Conway
154 Robert Hargreaves
159 Frederick William Terwilegar
169 William H Allen
175 John W Lord
177 James F Howland
181 Leonard H Mellar
184 Charles H Grinnell
187 Fred B Cook
333 Adelard Bussiere

NORMAN

51 James W Judd
67 William Cocker
69 Samuel Middleton
108 Mrs George L Kent
108 Mrs Emily Warren
118 Robert A Wilkinson Jr
130 John J Nicholson
136 Mrs Josephine Bambardier

NORTH

1 Misses Carr
1 Joseph P Hall
5 Patrick Kavanagh
5 Mrs Adelia Lemarine
7 Morris Schwartz
9 Mrs Mary J Gorton
16 Henry T Fowkes
22 Matthew L Green
22 Robert G Brightman
22 Olivia Bates
23 Alonzo F Winslow
23 Alvin Topham
24 Peter M Harrington
36 Thomas Wrigley
36 Zepherin R Pinault
39 Lucy A Church
40 Rodney F Ashley
41 Misses Leeming
43 William B Chase
44 Charlotte Hicks
44 Edwin M Ashley

45 Mrs Nancy J Wilson
45 Amelia K Robbins
48 Oliver H Gardner
49 Leander P Nichols
50 Mrs Sarah J Brightman
50 Mrs Druscilla E Allen
50 Andrew A Tiernan
53 John L G Mason
54 Wallace B Wilson
56 Mrs Myra H Rowe
56 Mrs Almira C Booth
56 Rupert S Allen
57 Mrs Julia M Gurney
58 Thomas A Chadwick
62 Bartlett B Danzell
64 Ahijah J Tarr
64 Mrs Rena A Holberton
66 Edgar B Hammond
68 Mrs Sarah L Brownell
68 Mrs Verona D Hazard
71 Frederick C Clarke
71 Frederick W Davis
72 Edward B Robbins
73 James N Parker
74 John J Howland
75 Mrs Susan C Swift
75 Elbert B Davis
77 Mark T Vincent
78 Martin H Sullivan
79 Mary Louise Smith
81 Herbert C DeMoranville
87 Mrs Emma L Chace
112 Mrs Johanna Peters
116 Edward E Chadwick
116 Benjamin E Tripp
139 Otis M Keith
139 Benjamin Baker
143 Charles C Fisher
150 Harry A Smith
151 Charles C Gifford
151 Levi H Whitten
152 Charles F Jennings
152 Charles F Goff
154 Mrs Ellen M Bates
155 Mrs Esther A Brownell
155 Charles L Davis
157 David S Wilcox
157 Arie A Coffin
159 Ralph Coville
160 Ellery R Bassett
161 Melvin J Macomber
161 Edmund J Whalley
162 Mrs Amanda Kennedy
162 John A Stitt
162½ Edward F Willis
164 John F Edgar
166 John L F Tripp
166 Charles Holm
167 Thomas McKenzie
168 Noah W Morgan
168 Charles W Morgan
178 William D Reynolds
180 Mrs Rose Dabney
181 Winthrop O Howland
181 Peter Carlson
181½ George F Wheeler
182 Edward J Thomas Jr
184 Mrs Alice J Bessey
185 Mrs Olive A Brownell
185 John W Reiter
186 William H Sowle
187 Mrs A P Guinet
187 Daniel W Cronin
188 Benjamin W Taylor
189 Thomas Ferguson
190 Nathaniel Hastings
190 Mrs Olivia Brown
194 Carl Carlson
194 Mrs Phoebe A Pierce
196 William W Atwood
204 Charles D Wiggins
205 Adolphus Thomas
206 Lawrence J Barboza
206 John O Williams
212 Charles E Thomas
212 James H Brown
214 Elmore M Treadup
214 Matthew J Swasey
216 Frank A Mague
218 Stephen V Weaver
219 Irving Barrett
219 Mrs Susan Pedro
219 Samuel J Smith
220 Henry J Ewing
220 Alexander Ewing
221 Melville C Chase
223 Franklin S Tallman
224 Charles E Allen
224 David Murphy
225 Jacob Koster
226 William G Kirschbaum
227 Fred C Gifford
229 George Fred Tripp
231 Joseph Wainwright
231 James Schofield
232 Andrew E Tripp
232 William E Mosher
233 John Kenealy
233 Frank Smith Jr
234 Mrs Mary A Tinkham
235 Charles E Phinney
236 Andrew W Rourke
238 Lewis Moore
247 Victor J Sequira
251 Francis V Crowley
255 John C Parker
341 Daniel A Tripp
341 Harry M Poole

North—con
344 Alexander G Cook
344 Albert B Cook
348 George A Lake
348 Lewis R Gifford
357 Belonie Poirier
359 Edward D Maynard
365 Charles H Gooding
365 Henry K Dexter
366 Frank Spooner
369 J S Hathaway
378 Mrs Evelyn A Cottle
381 George L Adams
382 James Neville
384 Charles H McKenna

NORTH FRONT

85 Letan Bisiadecki
85 Josef Potliz
87 Joseph Stepan
91 P Franiczyk
93 Willie Schutzch
97 John Beal
97 Jan Urban
99 Severence Johnson
99 George Geroux
103 Joseph Plante
103 Manuel Barboza
109 Isaie LaJoie
111 Julian Desroches
124 Albert Robert
124 Francois Breton
124 Antone Longton
125 Stanislas Seguin
125 Joseph Benoit
131 Napoleon Nolin
132 Charles M Baskin
132 John Dionne
135 Mrs Mary DeRoches
135 Isadore F Houde
135 Kazimier Dubrowski
135 John Goodreau
135 Joseph Laperle
136 Mrs Mary Conway
136 William Selleck
137 William Edmonson
141 Abraham Dostaler
149 Walter Ardent
153 Octave Nault
164 Henry Lagasse
164 Emile Tetreault
166 Arthur Marcotte
166 Lamous Lajoie
166 Noel Masseau
167 Stanislas Ducuilk
167 Afdew Saum
167 Felix Deroche
168 Avatole Goulet
168 William Bouchard
168 Peter Whaite
170 Alfred Belanger
170 Arthur Verville
172 John Kulaczenoski
172 John Coulegar
176 Gustave Gervovolski
176 Frank Arglanski
176 George Joseph
177 John Wehoskey
177 Bonney Slegier
177 Joseph Raymond
178 Aldea Derosier
185 Joseph Soares
189 Mikolaiz Kaliss
190 George Brown
190 Robert Wade
190 Charles Cameron
190 Napoleon Courtemanche
191 Alex Golasz
192 Giovanni Massette
193 Edward Mickenofiski
193 Frank Putchlopek
193 Margaret Arseneau
194 George Fournier
194 Alfred Dube
197 Adam Pietrekoz
197 John Filochowski
199 Otto Fass
199 Remi Roy
199 Antonio Plaza
200 William McCann
200 Mrs Ellen Daly
202 Albert Crozman
202 Fred Eastwood
202 Mrs Annie McDonald
204 Patrick Joyce
204 Robert Bassett
205 Manuel Vergnia
205 John Stone
205 William Squarl
205 Anthony Popielasc
205½ Maggie Swirad
205½ Frank Stuempeck
221 John Gallant
222 Manuel Maurice
222 Antonio Mello
222 Manuel Morris
223 Mrs Elizabeth A Thornber
223 Robert Holt
223 James O'Neil
234r Peter Courroulis
234r Wladyslaw Deptula
235 John Fredette
235 Joseph Govin
235 George Perreault
235 Hormidas Poitras
235 Omer Marcotte
236 Andrew W Johnson

241 Oliver Labossiere
247 Joseph Labonte
247 Francois Glasson
247 Pierre Millette
247 George Gadbois
248 Joseph Dragon
252 Ephraim Verranault
252 Come Le Page
255 James Lord
255 Alphonse Breault
255 Edmond Breault
256 Mrs Alexis Cournoyer
256 Charles Carter
256 Adolfe Ducharme
257 Ida Le Boeuf
259 Martin Ryan
259 Stanislaus Ciborowski
259 Mrs Rose Slivowski
259 Alex Bjurstrom
259 Michael Nowakowski
259r Jan Gouet
259r Albert Golin
259r Frank Putchlopek
259r John Pecrar
263 Moise Brouillette
265 Delphis Jarry
268 William Breau
268 Charles Lemaire Jr
268 Ferdinand Paquin
268 Philip Richard
268 Gregoire Leblanc
274 Joseph Ledoux
274 Alfred Cormier
274 Belino Bergeron
274 Peter Babineau
275 Henry Brousseau
275 Joseph Tremblay
275 Henry Phaneuf
275 Hector Beauregard
275 Rebecca Dextraudeur
282 Vital Belliveau
282 Raymond Gallant
282 Edward Branconnier
282 Vital Belliveau
282 Frank St Onge
282 Antoine Le Blanc
282 Pierre Morin
286 Marcellin Le Blanc
286 Eli Tetreault
286 Alida Le Boeuf
287 August Goudreau
287 Joseph Gaudreau
287 Louis Nolan
287 Joseph Viens
287 Fidele Savoie
291 Mrs Mary Simms
291 Homer R Lussier
291 Jules Racine
293 Joseph O Houle
295 E Edmonde Vandamme
297 Alfred Cardin
297 Peter Lemaire
297 Edward A Moran
297 Simeon Duchaine
306 Mrs Mary E Tobin
306 Frank Gagnon
307 Joseph H Desrosiers
307 William Bourque
307 Leon Desrosiers
310 Joseph Cousineau
310 Edmond A La Casse
310 Mrs Georgianna Morreau
310 John B Cote
311 Joseph Dumas
311 John B Lafleur Jr
311 Alpherie Depontbriand
311 Elzear Monette
311 Edmund Leblanc
314 Emile Depault
314 Victor Depault
314 John Balthazer
314 Charles Fournier
314 Alfred Bessette
314 Mrs Phebee Cormier
325 Norbert Menard
325 Mrs Virginia A Langlois
325 Oliver M Cormier
326 William Fontaine
326 Frank Menard
326 Theodore Houde
326 Serville Denault
326 Oliver Soucy
329 Joseph Bessette
329 Philip Lemieux
329 Rock Mondeau
329 Peter Lampara
329 Mrs Ida Tatro
330 Adelard Blanchette
330 Donat Letendre
330 Theodore Bergeron
330 Napoleon Duval
330 Mrs Delia LeClair
330 Napoleon Rousseau
333 Michel Bessette
333 Francois X Verranault
338 Frank Leger
338 Elphege St Germain
338 Ovilla Beaulieu
338 Alphonse Deslaurier
339 Delphis Langlois
339 Mrs Maria Morrell
340 Celina Benoit
340 Mathilda Lalumiere
343 Pierre Boucher

North Front—con
343 Isaie LeBlanc
344 Theodore Robidoux
344 Marcel Surprenant
344 Philip Beaulieu
346 Alfred Larochelle
346 Mizael Magnant
346 Fidele Bourque
347 Mrs Delphine Landry
347 Mrs Mary Allard
347 Valmar Soucy
347 Mrs Delphine Landry
351 Mrs Vitaline Beique
351 Joseph Lizotte
351 Alfred Berry
352 Arthur Dube
352 Napoleon Maver
352 Arthur G Lemerise
352 Michel Leblanc
353 Mrs Catherine A Ward
358 Joseph F Bessette
358 Charles Fuette
358 Pierre Maher
358 P Ricard
358 Mrs Mary Cote
358 Mrs Virginia Lussier
359 Ovilla Cote
359 Joseph Martin
359 Vital Perras
361 Oliver Page
361 Ulric Casault
361 Joseph N Colomb
361 Charles Letourneau
361 J Maxine Gaudette
363 Charles J Dextradeur
363 Mrs Catherine Whalen
364 Gelina Perron
364 Benjamin Robichaud
364 Azaras Couture
364 Archille Couture
369 Edward LeFrancois
374 Richard Heap
374 Frank Buckley
374 Mrs Margaret Powers
380 Thomas Whithan
380 Isaiah Atkinson
382 Manuel Roderick
382r Frank E Cote
382½ Delma Blain
382½ Etienne LeBert
383 William Sargent
383 Hormidas Provencher
383 Stanislaus Leger
384 Amedee Surprenant
384 Mrs Doralice Latimer
384 Rock Masse
385 Mrs Azilda Maranda
385 Arthur Ducharme
386 Arthur Lariviere
387 Donat Maranda
395 Joseph Billodeau
395 Samuel W Quirk
395 Paul Guilbeault
396 Isidore Poirier
396 Joseph A Proulx
396 Alfred F Sossenville
396 Eugene Chausse
407 Leon Ferland
407 Leon Pratt
407 Noe Froment
409 Alexander Baron
409 Frank LeBlanc
409 Adelard Courtemanche.
411 Hyacinthe LaLiberte
412 Lucien Binnette
412 Mrs Lucy Larocque
417 Delphis Langlois
417 Mrs Julia LeBlanc
417 Edward Landry
417 Alfred Daigle
417 Frederick Tetreault
417 Arthur Delombe
417 Mrs Rosalie Therien
418 Manuel Houghton
418 Louis Lagasse
418 Theodore Dupont
418 Ernest Paquin
418 Oscar Papineau
424r Abdo Mosie
426 Mrs Annie Wilson
426 Mrs Mary Kirkham
426 Eusebe LeBeau
429 Henry S Larivere
429 Placide Allain
429 Joseph E Dumas
430 Joseph St Jean
430 Hector Demers
430 Rosalie Forand
433 James E Wilde
434 Joseph Messier
434 Clement U Savoie
434 Alphonse Dube
440 Mrs Margaret Hall
442 Mrs Antonio Yeager
442 Joseph Carr
442 Mrs Elizabeth Robinson
446 Theodore Danisch
446 Mrs Johannah Halloran
446 Louis Leblanc
448 William Bonney
448 Joseph McLean
471 Polydore Trahan
473 Delphis Richard
475 Frank Lemaire
475 John St Onge
475 Moise Gabriault
475 John B Audette
477 Rose Levaseur

477 George Parent
477 Jean Richard
478 Thomas Schofield
478 Thomas Barber
487 John Cowling
483 Charles A Parr
483 Mrs Adeth Hafner
483 Ludger Chartier
487 Rahael Melanson
487 Dennis Melancon
487 Joseph Richard
487 Udari Audette
487 John Lawrence
488 William H Duckworth
491 Elmer Girard
491 Celestine Babineau
492 Henry Frechette
492 Emile Laurendeau
492 Alfred Guilmette
492 Frank Robida
492 William Edwards
492 Pierre Parent
495 Eutroppe Cormiere
495 Daniel Robichand
495 Louis Rock
495 John Martin
505 Philias Breault
505 Joseph Johnson
510 John Deasy
510 John Thompson
510 Owen McQuade
511 John C Wolstencroft
511 Moses Kersner
511 Mrs Tomazia Azevedo
513 Mrs Mary J Braithwaite
513 Thomas Higginbottom
513 Malcolm Norwod
515 David Goldstein
515 Andrew Hall
515 Wilfred Bourque
515 Theophile B Le Blanc
519 Mrs May J McDonald
519 Charles Camire
525 Hector Levasseur
525 Zephir Quintin
525 George Bessette
530 Pierre Salvail
530 Exear Levasseur
530 Mrs Matilda Souliere
530 Delphis Morin
531 Remi Guitin
531 Joseph Arsenault
531 Mrs Mary Martin
531 Hilliare Laurendeau
531 Fred Belvery
534 Harold R Brownell
534 Patrick Gilmour
534 Mrs Kate Ward
535 Francois X Turgeon Jr
535 Edward D Davenport
539 Joseph Bergeron
540 William Goyette
540 John H Lowney
540 Joseph Gratton
540 Alphonse Caya
541 Norbert Duval
541 Hormidas Ledoux
543 Felix Lapointe
546 Joseph Lange
546 Albert Mini
546 Amato Maino
550 B J Mulvey
550 Oliver Niquette
551 Ulric Gagne
553 Hector St Germain
553 Mrs Josephine Martin
553 Moise St Onge
554 William Thompson
554 Benjamin Westwood
554 John Wilkinson
554 Mrs Harriet Thompson
555 Henry Lelievre
563 Samuel Bousquet
563 John Bardsley
563 Mrs Mary Crowther
580 John Bromides

NORTH OAK

2 Edward Duff
3 Michael J McCarthy
3½ John McGlynn
4 Job Townsend
4 Mrs Mary J Gale

NORTH ORCHARD

3 Benjamin B Barney
7 Mrs Harriet E Tripp
9 George R Cherry
11 Dr C F Connor

NORTH SECOND

7 Henry H MacLane
7 Peter Lemaire
17½ Mrs Emma Gonsalves
57 Armand D Valois
60 Mrs Florence Manning
63 R L McLachlan
63 Frank E Lewis
66 Mrs Clara M Eaton
78 Eliza C Shurtleff
89 S E Waite
89 Frank W Sommers
95 Mrs L Katharine Moore
105 John Machado

North Second—con
109 Manuel J Frates
119 Frank E Cooley
119 Mrs Ellen Downey
125 Mary E Fay
125 Sidney Gifford
125 Lawrence P Fay
125 Thomas A Sylvia
128 Manuel Ferris
128 Frank J Breen
129 Mrs Delphine D Dufresne
133 Georgianna Mitchell
133 Ann Murphy
134 John J Rose
134 Manuel Caton
136 Mrs Angelina Sturtevant
140 Mrs Louisa Smith
144r Wiliam F Randall
145 George L Colyar
150 Minor A Belanger
150 William C Townsend
154 Alfred Pachedo
154 Joseph Constantino
154r Antone Jacintho
154r Joseph Peter
185 Peter David
191 Mary Frasier
195 Mrs Vinnie St Onge
195 Mrs Mary McAfee
195 John Millette
199 Daniel Calden
199 Mrs Louisa Pina
199 Fidel Pina
201 Isaac De Chaves
201 Marianna Lopes
205 Antone Souza
205 Joseph Rapoza
212 Manuel Perry
212 Everett K Weston
212 Arthur Lemieux
216 Victor St Onge
216 Joseph Maroon
218 Thomas Maroon
218 James H Murphy
218 Ada Millette
219 Chester L Myrick
222 Edward Mylotte
222 Thomas Doherty
225 Wallace C Hull
225 Joseph Rose
226 Mrs Mary Robert
226 Louis Hebert
226 Hormidas Vallencourt
228 George Brown
228 Napoleon Gravelle
228 Frank Sablon
229 Mrs Etta Sullivan
229 Frank Hollywood
232 William Heath
233 Thomas Parkinson
520 C L Myrick

NORTH SIXTH

19 Dammin Gladu
36 Thomas F Swords
39 Emma Warsden
39 Joseph M Babbitt
43 Mrs Emma Denham
43 Mrs Clara M Murphy
55 Mrs Sarah A Chisholm
55 Albert T Wood
56 Mrs Eliza Bennett
56 Mrs Emmie S Hart
57 Jasper L Cook
58 James Collins Jr
58 William J Edgeton Jr

NORTH WATER

17 Philip Lavoie
40 Martin M Gonsalves
40 Manuel Andrada
46 Benjamin F Drummond
46 Joseph Silva
111 John Bentson
111 Joseph Souza
129 C J Drake
129 Joseph A Correia

NORTON COURT

1 John Sutcliffe
2 Dennis L Stephens
3 Michael A Crowe
4 Joseph S Brown
39 Joseph P Sylvia

NYE

8 Alfred Prince
8½ John H Gilleney
10 Thomas Abrian
10 Romeo Houle
10 Yako Blenko
10 Joseph C Fredette
11 Mrs Celina Bolduc
11 Vanziel Nicola
11 Frank Smolla
11 William Spoor
11 P Rainville
11r Zephir Bessette
11r Joseph Bessette
12 John Papas
12 Mrs Emilien Arseneault
12 Mark Legere
12 Arthur Bissonette
12 John B Blain
12 Israel Breault
12 Omer Lavigne
12 Louis Payette

12 Joseph M Oliver
12 Mary Leger
15 George Thibeault
15 Onesime Chapdelaine
15 Antone Ouillette
19 Frank Moniz
19 Antone Perry
19 Frank Perry
19r Manuel M Mello
20 Napoleon Milotte
20 Frank Bourgeois
20 Paul Latraverse
20 Godfroi Audette
23 Isadore Kazinski
24 Ernest Sasseville
24 Modeste Blain
24 Victor Phaneuf
24 Ernest Sasseville
25 Louis Tetreault
25 John Jarry
25 Joseph Dupre
26 Napoleon Gaouette
26 David Lacroix
27 Joseph Laflamme Jr
27 Clement Cormier
27 John M Chase
28 Cariste Gelinas
28 Mrs Rose Lefebvre
28 Noe Mandeville
28 Eugene Belisle
29 Napoleon Beaulieu
29 Mrs Philomene Beaulieu
30 Albert Valway
30 Arthur St Jean
30 Honore Michaud
31 Ida Barriteau
31 Sylvester Forge
31 Peter Beaulieu
32 George LaForrest Jr
32 Damasse Rondeau
32 Alexis Boisvert
35 Nazaire Cormier
35 Emile Valerien
35 Peter Mailloux
37 Wilfred Doiron
37 Wilfred Soucy
37 Armand Girouard
47 Frank Fahey
47 Anthony Cormier
49 Joseph Bouchard
49 Joseph Rogers
49 Frederick Jarry
50 Alexie Mandeville
50 Mark Arseneault
50 Henry Martin
50 Joseph P Lariviere
50 Theophile Regis
50 Napoleon Brousseau
51 DeForest Provost
51 Odilon Jarry
56 Mrs Josephine Hebert
56 Eugene D Hebert
56 George Levesque
56 Joseph O LeClair
56 Ephraim Desaulniers
60 Edmond F Fredette
60 John Giroux
60 Frank O Duffy
61 Joseph Blecha
63 Mrs Elizabeth Mandeville
63 Mrs Priscilla Crossley
63 Herbert Crossley
78 Alfred E Richard
80 Urlain P Arseneault
82 Joseph E Gendron
82½ Albert H Doyle
82½ Henry Racicot
84 Octave Frigeault
86 Frank Lemaire
86 John B Desroches
88 Damien Oinelle
88 Michel Boucher
88 Francois Boucher
90 Charles Peloquin
90 Mrs Valerie Pelletier
90 E D Pothier
92 Mrs Margaret Hebert
94 Arthur Baillargeon
94 Arthur Racicot
96 Antonio Cusson
96 Edward Martin
98 Joseph Tessier
98 Albert Therrien
98 Herbert Therrien
98 Mrs Mary J Healy
101 Thomas P Riley
101 Albert Inne
101 Fred Senft
101 Richard Grierson
101 Joseph Kolouch
101 Jules Tardif
101 John W Turner
124 Arthur Guillett
126 Ernest Dubois
126 John H Dunn
126 John W Parker
126 Joseph Fournier
127 John Donaldson
127 Henry Poettich
127 Alcide Castonguay
127 Harry Goldberg
127 Achille Carriere
127 Fred Roby
130 Theodule Guillet
131 Mrs Aurelie Guilbeault
131 Rene Gingras
132 John Woodacre
132 Wilbraham Bellend
132 Moses Fournier

Nye—con
135 William H Isherwood
135 Eli Bourassa
136 Hector Robert
136 John F Fullen
136 John Kalisch

OAK

1 Joseph D Frates
1 Frederick R Reed
1 William G White
2 Robert Gillespie
3 Patrick McGlynn
4 John F Harrington
11 Marceline Bettencourt
15 Joseph F Harden
17 John B Robinson
22 Henry W Hammond
23 Owen Brophy
23 Hannibal King
25 George Enos
26 H Percy Arnold
29 George W Woods
30 Henry Marsh
33 Mrs Mary Avila
33 Manuel F Santos
34 Joseph Carney
40 Elizabeth A Boyle
45 Mrs Bridget Dempsey
46 William N Nelson
48 Philip E Jones
48 Simeon P Ashley
48 Joseph C Viera
48 Casimir Rotch
49 Mrs Katherine B Sears
52 William B Brownell
53 Guy B Richardson
53 Ventura C Noyer
54 Manuel Enos Perry
63 Mrs Flora E Stowell
67 John Burns
68 Frank A Reid
68 Albert J Courtney
70 Sarah M Howland
72 Margaret Callanan
75 Edward Leary
75 James Garvin
76 Frank Francis
78 Judson Clough
78 Antone M De Mello
80 Richard A Reed
80 Frank E Gilman
80 William J Haworth
81 John H Mackay
85 David A Sherman
92 John Murphy
96 William Moore
99 Frank J Roderick
100 John F Cook
102 James M McCarthy
103 Adolph J Frederick
106 John Krauss
106 Mrs Lena M Willis
123 Henry J Watson
152 James J Moore

OAK STREET COURT

2 John A Harrington Jr
3 Daniel S Taylor
4 Mrs Emma F Black
0 Nelson L Pike

OAKLAND

3 Robert Gregory

OCEAN

6 Charles T Kidder
9 Mrs Hulda W Nelson
11 Isaiah C Wagner
15 Samuel N Sweet
19 Andrew B Gibson
27 Henry V Davis
39 Charles E Benton
43 Dudley C Hathaway
47 Robert McKenzie
48 Robert J Wilson
48 Elbert W Bartow
48 Jeremiah Ring
61 Benson C Bates
65 John Peterson
68 Henry W Christenson
69 Rev Robert Larson

OLD MARKET SQUARE

10 Jacob H Brown

OLIVE

8 Henry Wilkinson

OLIVER

0 George Roy

ONEKO LANE

6 George Entwistle
8 Antone D Rezendes
8 Manuel F Rezendez
9 Charles Lauermann
10 Antone Rezendes
12 Charles Vohnoutka
12 James Hampton

ORCHARD (SOUTH)

60 Dr Charles A Pratt
61 Dr Stephen W Hayes
70 Mrs Isabell R Severance
71 Albert C J Perrier

72 A Ricketson
78 Charles W Clifford
88 John W Knowles
115 Mrs Sarah H Snow
139 Henry L Tiffany
183 John V Spare
189 Robert Schofield
199 Elsie Swift
213 Edward B Smith
213 Charles D Cundall
217 E Edwin Foster
219 Reuben W Sterling
251 Frank C Brightman
262 William P Howland
262 Manuel M Moniz
262 Antonio Correia
266 James F McMullen
269 Manuel Ramos
269 Antonio Luiz
274 J J Moraes
274 Mrs Philomena G Pinha
277 Jason Rose
277 Annie McDonnell
280 Jeremiah Robetoye
280 Charles R Vera
281 John M Souza
285 Manuel G Da Rosa
286 John T Handy
289 Antonio J Silveira
290 William B Sprott
290 William Boardley
292 Antonio J Fernandes
310 Mrs Jeanette Gatenby
310 Crawford Gatenby
313 Nelson E Jewett
313 Frederick D Sowle
314½ Otis W White
331 Mrs Mabel Hall
331 Jeremiah Coholan
336 Mrs Nellie H Cook
336 Isadore F Eldridge
337 Mrs Charlotte L Barstow
338 Mrs Ada B Chase
338 James T Bonney
341 Adelbert C Ashley
341 Clfton P Tuell
342 John T Currie
343 Charles T Bonney
343 Fred A Shurtleff
344 Mrs Isabel Davis
345 Herbert P Howland
345 Mrs Ellen Sullivan
347 John A Cabral
347 George A Butts
347 John W Bryden
354 Frank Graner
354 Antonio F Francis
355 John F Flarez
358 Domingos T Silva
358 Mary R Hathaway
358 George J Nunes
359 Joseph Medeiros
359 Manuel Caton
359 Peter Cummings
363 Manuel Costa
363 Manuel M Morgado
370 William F Carney
370 John J Rogers
370 John P O'Connell
374 Frederic Bulman
385 Jeremiah McDonald
395 Thurston Campbell
395 Andrew P Doyle
395 George R Holt
398 Philomena Nicholas
398 Antone Martin
398 George E Belyea
400 Mrs Mary N Silva
400 John Gourley
400 Manuel Jacinto
400 Walter Gardner
401 Patrick H Fay
405 Manuel F Mello
405 James A Adams
405 Joseph McGinness
408 Maurice Downey
411 Manuel Vieira
414 Thomas Woolley
414 Fred Webster
414 William E Fortman
415 Thomas Lord
415 Edmund Collinge
415 Joseph Mullarkey
416 Henry Horrocks
416 John Miranda
436 William J Gibbs Jr
436 Joseph Bentley
436 Manuel Corey
437 George Smith
439 George B Davis
440 Thomas Leigh
440 James Taylor
440 Mrs Ann Harrison
440 Wright Taylor
441 Joseph Mendoza
443 Manuel F Miranda
443 Lawrence de Souza
443 John J Simmons
443 John Chester
449 Albert Kennedy
449 James McQuilkin
449 Mrs Mary Onsley
451 John McQuilkin
0 Gosnold House

PAGE

21 James W Grewcock
21 Ernest L Sherman
31 Antone Perry
31 Manuel Baptista
31 Mrs Isabelle Teixeira
41 Carl Gunderson
41 William Souza
42 Adilord Huberdeau
42 Edward Houghton
42 Mrs Annie McBride
45 Manuel V Correia
46 Albion C Johnson
46 William G Ashley
50 Smith M Ide
50 Mary E Fletcher
50 Hubert Knowles
51 William H Rogers
54 Joseph Enos
54 Antone Dutra
54 Manuel Rapoza
55 Joseph Perry
55 Antone F Goulart
55 Bernado J Machado
141 Mrs Sarah A W Taber
147 Misses Allen
157 W Kempton Read
172 George C Hatch Jr
172 Rev Francis B Boyer

PALMER

220 Nathan C T Weeks
233 Joseph M Grace
245 Benjamin Madison
246 Orville E Young
247 Hilliard H Paine
248 George F Gay
249 William Taylor
253 Frederic T Roach
257 George E Salley
261 Willard N Lane
263 Edwy E Stevens
268 Robert A Bartlett
268 Mrs Lottie Weeks
269 Joseph Wilkinson
269 Manuel V Rogers
271 John H Aindow
272 William H Willis
274 Charles E Dexter
275 R Archer Perkins
277 Henry Mandly
278 William E Smith
279 Andrew J Fish
282 Louis Almy
282 Raymond Chase
286 Joseph F Tripp
287 Henry B Parlow
288 Robert J Shanks
288 Henry A Gray
289 Charles N Tasker
290 Leo F McAuliffe
290 George S Kennedy
291 Arthur H Ashley
291 Arthur S Doane
295 James F McLaughlin
299 Robert E Knapp

PARK

38 Mrs Lillian L Thomas
39 Herbert M Braley
42 Frederick L Holt
43 Ida E Tripp
46 Edward P Bigelow
47 Louis R Kerr
51 Arthur B Sherman
52 John J Sater
52 Mrs Hannah C Wall
55 L Alexander Jennings
58 Michael F McKieman
60 George Keyes
64 Fred J Hayward
68 Mrs Jeanette McLeod
69 Francis O Johnson
71 Mrs Michael J Murphy
72 Joseph A Dauphinais
74 Joseph Gleason
78 Charles P Hathaway
80 Robert N Tinkham
81 Charles M Wolf
81 Joseph H Foisy
83 Albert D Brown
85 Michael Leary
85 Arthur E Morrill
86 John G Kennedy
88 George H Reynolds
89 Herbert C Ellis
93 Benson C Bates
93 Frederick R Dodge
96 Reinard Thompson
97 Richard Shaw
98 Mrs Ellen Robinson
98 David Ferguson
101 Moses Moore
105 Robert J Moore
111 Mary McDermott
114 Patrick T Foy
114 Clara L Tompkins
115 Edward S Russell
115 Herbert E Macy
121 Luthan D Allen
121 William M McBride
126 Charles G Griffin
126 Charles E Gelette
127 William McBride
159 James Diamond
162 Charles H Talmage

163 James G Meade
166 Samuel W Beers
167 Thomas O Phillips
170 James A Collins
173 M F Rush
173 Clarence E Rockefeller
175 Eliot S Tripp
179 Thomas Doherty
183 Emile J Hirth
189 Mrs Emily E Jenkins
193 Mrs Elizabeth Austin
194 Jose Gonsalves
201 Isaac D Sampson
201 Charles C Johnson
202 Henry Grace
205 Julia A Morse
206 Matilda Larson
209 Elijah Webb
211 Mrs Martha D Webb
215 Harry Harper
215 Mrs Ann Arthurs
221 Mrs Rosa A Lane
223 Emanuel Sullavou
225 James Ames
226 James J Finn
226 George Hadaeld
232 Leander F Thomas
235 George P Healey
235r Mrs Louisa Coleman
235r J Thomas Holloway
235r John Ponte
236 Mrs Elizabeth Carr
236 Elizabeth Whiteside
239 Henry G Brown
271 Joseph C Sylvia
277 John B Desrosier
277 Bryan Monaghan
281 William H Richardson
285 Mrs Ella F Lewis
286 Ellis E West
286 Edgar V Bradford
291 Robert Lindsay
295 Frederick E Eldridge
310 William H Smith
311 George E Macomber
314 John T Grimshaw
318 Harry McNamee
318 Albert G Hathaway
319 William H Brand
319 Joseph H Chace
323 Herbert M Hammond
324 Mrs Isabel M Nye
349 Mrs Sarah M Kent
349 Percy L Kent
350 Mrs Charity C Stanton
353 Mrs Mary Reed
359 Samuel R Spencer
369 George V Crothers
371 Lincoln G Sowle
414 Herbert S Thompson
415 George F Maxfield
452 Mrs Lena B Hammer
474 Clark W Delano
474 Charles R Gedley

PARK PLACE

1 Mrs Clara S Kilburn
1 Charles F Spooner
3 Mrs Ruth E Borden
5 Peter Nelson
6 Elias M Ricketson
6 Caroline W Hathaway
7 Charles R Halliday
7 A Clifford Hawes
8 Misses Davis

PARKER

9 William M Thorup
14 Hartley Spencer
14 John P Chace
18 Jeremiah J O'Connor
18 Charles I Travers
22 Frederick B Macy
28 George Priestly
29 James P Fenton
31 Nathaniel D Russell
32 Gaudiose Bedard
32 Frank Mason
33 William H Jennings
36 Theophilus Gay
36 Arsen Davidian
37 Mrs Catherine M Russell
39 Leonard Keen Jr
40 Mrs Eliza Parker
40 Ephraim A Landress
41 Winthrop L Dunham
42 J Frank Burbank
43 John W Gilston
44 Gideon F Gray
45 James Dignam
48 Mrs Emma L Boden
49 Mrs Mahaly Arnold
51 Mrs Rebecca H Weeks
56 William F Gamage
57 Mrs Margaret Shortall
57 M F Sullivan
60 Samuel Clark
61 Samuel Taylor
62 Mrs Rebecca Heyer
63 James W Hindle
64 William Connolly
66 Charles F Bliss
66 John H Lawrence
67 Mrs Katherine Hill
67 Mrs Elizabeth C Keen
68 Francis N G Smith

Parker—con
68 John T Burbank
74 Bradford A Hathaway
74 William A Dorr
83 George E Thomas
84 Benjamin W Mendell
87 Henry A Morse
90 Mrs Hannah Downey
90 Nathaniel E Pierce
94 James J Rooney
96 Herbert Robinson
97 Mrs Elizabeth Ross
98 Robert B McEnnis
100 Jacob Howard
101 Samuel Lipschitz
102 William Barker
102 Harry M Ripley
117 William G Wood
117 Edward P Lowrie
118 John S Machado
119 Samuel B Briggs
120 Mrs Mary Ann Higham
120 William Fielding
121 Mrs Mabel E Russell
121 William M Jenks
123 Martin Brenneke
124 Joseph A Carroll
125 Jeremiah E P O'Connor
143 James P Linton
160 John W Tripp
185 Edmund M Cornell

PEARL

4 Augusta Ripa
6 Antonio Di Clement
8 Patrick H O'Malley
8 Mrs Amelia Paquette
24 **Sarah L Greene**
24 Sam Smith
28 Charles Y Wilcox
34 Burt W Flint
36 Charles A Galligan
38 Charles W Barney
40 Mrs Emeline Parson
42 James L Fay
44 Mark B Creed
46 Mrs Alice M Considine

PEASE COURT

1 Mrs Sarah E Hubbard
1 Lyman B Chase
2 Lysander F Howland Jr

PECKHAM

15 Samuel Brierly
15 Thomas Bedard
15 James S Coupe
18 Joseph St Aubin
18 Mrs Ellen A Dalton
18 Mrs Margaret Carr
19 Manuel Sylvia
19 John B Nadeau
20 Charles Kay
20 Thomas Homer
20 Wilfred Shelmerdine
21 Carl F Hayward
21 James K Gregory
22 James A Stevenson
22 Herbert Silson
23 Mrs Jennie Monahan
23 Thomas Eccleston
24 **John T Carter**
24 Albert Gill
26 **Arthur Jennings**
26 John W Warhurst
26 John Whalley
26 Arthur H Jennings
27 Napoleon Belisle
27r James Beswick
30 Eraton Cox
35 Louis Roy
36 James Stopford
51 Thomas H Parkinson
53 Charles E Buckley
53 Mrs Carrie L Clark
54 James R Morris
54 Peter Davis
60 Thomas Bibbery
60 Stephen Dean
60 Thomas Dakin
62 John P Smith
62 Henry Davis
71 Joseph St Marie
71 Delia Gallant
71 James Wood

PENNIMAN

2 Frank N Connell
4 Charles Schmidt
4 Edward Scott
5 Joseph Vialo
5 Antone Giraca
5 Alfred P Bigelow
6 Alexander Lemire
7 Joseph Viola
7 Mrs Caroline Burton
8 Jacob Wolfe
8 Peter Seguin
8 Charles Barriteau
10 Philip Lemire
11 George A Driscoll
11 Napoleon Diou
11r Augustus Monette
15 Louis Morein
15 Joseph A Chartier
15 Mrs Milina Guilbeault
21 Wiliam H Kelly
24 Edward F Foley

24 Mary L Coughlin
27 Michael H Brennan
27 Dulrick Perpensela
28 Patrick McCormick
28 John Wardick
32 Benjamin Perry
32 Albert Perry
32 Arthur Gosseling
33 Harry Hacking
33 Joseph Beckwood
33 John Kenney
34 Gustav Huebner
34 Mrs Stella Smolla
34 Hosheia Naiman
34 Mrs Rosie Storominsky
34 Henry Hahn
61 William Feeney
65 William White
65 Mrs Marie LeBlanc
66 Misses Brown
66 Isadore Rohicaud
66 Elizabeth Murphy
67 Thomas Melanson
70 William J Suffern
70 John Haworth
74 Charles J Silvia
74 Mrs Elizabeth Isherwood
78 James Ellis
78 Henry Stone
78 Fred T Mathews
79 Eugene Melanson
82 Max Rosenblumt
82 Louis Magnant Jr
82 Henry Hesford

PERRY

93 Francis A Demers
93 Louis Potin
93 Edward Berube
97 Joseph Desautels
99 Samuel L Sturtevant
99 Philias Legere
99 Arsene Deneault
99 Albert Legere
103 George Bibeau
103 Joseph Lemieux
107 Remi Millette
107 Frank Rego
107 Mrs Caroline Chartier
118 John F Gifford
122 Mrs S Alice Thomas
126 Mrs Rose Lague
126 French Perry
126 George A Hammond
126 Syprien Samson
129 Henry Allard
129 Louis Jenney
133 Mrs Mary H Luce
137 Harry Mitchell
137 Henry H Lewis
139 Mrs Flora Gonsalves

PHILLIPS AVENUE

7 Octave Gagnon
7 Charles Carrier
7 Joseph Martel
11 Trueman H Sweetser
11 George E Randall
11 Fred Potter
15 Hormidas Langevin
15 Alphonse Clocher
15 Pierre Gagnon
19 Emery Hainault
37 Oscar E Holdridge
37 James Bram
45 Brahim Nano
45 Peter Martin
49 Peter D Labbe
49 Arthur Gobeil
49 Peter Chabot
49 Irinie Laliberte
49 Donat Benjamin
50 Maxim Degauff
52 George Rainville
52 Peter Savoie
54 Stanislaw Sabola
54 Sylvian Gallant
54 John Ardelan
54 Mrs Jennie Boyer
55 Eugene Gamache
57 Autumn Benss
57 Giril Kasab
57 Thomas Carrier
58 Mary Duffy
58 Mary Coauette
62 Alex Christie
62 Godfrois Bessette
66 Eusebe Caron
66 Joseph W Redman
67 Miklos Thoresz
67 Clovis Desrosier
70 Rose Lariviere
70 Emily Lariviere
70 Adelard Chaput
70 Philip Pelletier
70 Albini Langevin
70 Peter Giroux
70 John B St Pierre
82 Alphonse Rousseau
82 Raoul Prouteau
82 Eusebe Benoit
82 John Lauer
82 William Hebert
82 Omer Lavalle

Phillips av—con
93 Manuel Perry
93 Antone Pacheco
100 Manuel J Butler
100 Joseph Abreu
100 John Teixeira
100 John Pacheco
101 John J Pacheco
101 Noel Poirier
101 Emile Langevin
101 Marianno Cardoza
101 Mary Mitchell
101 Oliver Lemerise
103 Manuel C Barros
101 Mrs Sophie L'Oiselle
103 Antone Foster
104 Mrs Rose Mello
104 Manuel Veira
104 Virginia Decate
108 L Walter Conet
108 Joseph Karkowcki
108 Thomas Trubak
109 Joseph Lamaire
109 Archie Bass
109 Edward Marleau
100 Manuel Boteilho
112 Alfred Deneault
112 Basil Karmous
116 Adam Bunting
116 John Veira
116 Joseph Lemerise
119 Alfred Maurice
121 Mrs Helen Chase
121 Joseph Hainault
121 Joseph Chase
125 Hormidas Boisvert
125 John B Giguire
125 Joseph Devost
133 Theodore A Davignon
137 Joseph Gobeil
141 M Melancon
141 Aime Rousseau
141 Edward Bernard
142 Donat Gelinas
142 Narcisse Letourneau
142 Charles Trahan
142 Bernard Lebrun
149 Louis Ducharme
149 Joseph Desmarais
149 Joseph Sorelle
150 Solime Lebreau
150 Edward A Gallant
150 Louis Chartier
150 Ludger J Thibeault
154 Simon Duchene
174 Harry Ward
174 Ludger Lambert
174 Reuben L Sawyer
174 Honore Lachance
174 Howard Withey
175 Honore Comeau
175 James Gill
175 Antonio Cloutier
175 Fred L Sawyer
178 Oscar Nadeau
178 Oscar Anarda
178 Calixte Richard
178 Theothime Saulnier
178 Isaac Varney
178 Philip Coulombe
178 Joseph Courchaine
178 Ambrose Belleveau
183 Eugene A Allain
183 John Breault
183 Richard Poirier
183 Alfred LeBeau
184 Leon Ducharme
184 Damasse Poitras
184 William Finch
184 Mrs Marie L Dagenais
184 Mrs Admire Messier
185 Theophile Lebeau
187 Mrs Josephine Ouimette
192 Joseph Levesque
193 William Little
194 Etienne Levesque
195 Joseph Gobeille
195 Ludger Labbe
195 Joseph Quintin
195 Mrs Emma Gobeille
195 Antone Bourque
195 Delphis Gosselin
199 Thomas Fleury
199 Edmonde Beauregard
199 Donat Gallipeau
199 Honore Payette
199 Emile Belanger
217 William S Frates
217 Frank N Cleveland
217 Mrs Mary Clark
217 Mrs Delia Frates
220 Paul Duval
220 Thomas F Brazeil
220 Joseph S Trudeau
220 Alfred Langis
224 Herman Landry
224 Joseph Comeau
224 Onesime Landry
224 Louis B Landry
225 Edward Lachance
225 Joseph Quintin
226 Joseph Alix
234 Arnold Taylor
234 Adelard Loranger
238 Theodore Loranger

240 Henri Marchesseault
240 Charles Rawson
240 Joseph Lagrenade
244 George H Bellamy
244 Daniel Stott
249 Nathan Fowler
251 Mrs Mary Dvorak
251 Mrs Elmire Folster
251 Albert Blecha
260r John Krupka
260r Thomas Mitchell
263 John Hilton
263 Isaac Fawcett
263 Frederick P Macedo
271 Wilfred Vincent
271 Henry Fernandes
274 John W Powell
274 Charles F Levalley
275 Herbert Warburton
275 William Bottomley
275 George Garlick
278 William Ogden
278 Arthur Ogden
278 Charles Banks
278 Charles B Hart
282 William Margeson
282 William Fazackerly
282 Francis McDonald
287r Leopold Reusch
289 Ralph Clegg
291 William Krouzek
297 Gotthot Mayer

PHILLIPS ROAD

0 James T Hancock
0 Frank Schlais
0 John Hilton
0 Albert C Skiff
0 Edwin F Morton
0 Job Spooner
0 Frank Schlais
0 Benjamin F Howe

PIERCE

35 Charles A Cunningham
38 Harry M Gray
39 Frank L Nelson
41 Manuel Brown
42 John R Smith
43 Jeremiah W Simmons
45 Fred S Wordell
45 Harriet Hathaway
46 Mrs Fannie M Bonney
50 William L Flynn
50 Mrs Catherine Frey
54 Harold M Coxen
55 S Frank Andrews
55 Thomas Renihan
58 Roger T Fay
59 Harry Olsen
63 Abram L Hayden
64 Mrs Clara M Jansen
68 James A Irwin
74 Arthur C Tripp
77 Frederick A Keith
77 Joseph De Costa Jr
79 Sherman G Chamberlain
80 Simeon B Eldridge
82 Lars Anderson
87 Louis Parenti
88 Albert Anderson
91 J L Poole
94 Nathan J Knight
96 I E Potter
99 Joseph F O'Connell Jr
100 Albert A Kershaw
100 Horace E Saunders
103 Antone Foster
105 Lloyd C Lamprey
105 Andrew B Chase Jr
108 Edward H Colwell
112 Seth B Hammett

PINE

4 Mrs Emma E Brown

PLAINVILLE ROAD

0 Edward P Wilbur
0 Joseph Rainville
0 Joseph G Rainville
0 Joseph M Tripp
0 Edward K Russell Jr
0 Frederick J Deardon
0 Arthur T Poole
0 Philip S Poole
0 John H O'Neil
0 Joseph Amarantes
0 John E Poole
0 Annie E Hatch
0 Frank Poole
0 Mrs Prudence Briggs
0 Charles H Brownell
0 Thomas J Ashley
0 William Whittaker
0 Levi Hartley
0 Mrs Annie Hatch
0 Ralph Emmett
0 Daniel H Allen
0 Charles B Phillips
0 Thomas Broughton
0 Leopold Van Doorne
0 Walter Pelczer
0 John Ashworth
0 John Palacz
0 Joseph Amarantes
0 John E Poole

Plainville road—con
0 Albert Reynolds
0 Thomas Broughton

PLEASANT

129 Stephen E Demoranville
129 William G Sadler
142 Mrs Sadie Tobey
142 Henry C Slosson
163 Arthur D Munroe
163 Mrs Maude M Wilson
163 Luthan A Wood
163 Charles R Chapman
167 Willis C Underwood
170 Mrs Rena D Nickerson
170 Philip S Colyar
170 Austin T Howland
176 Mrs Jennie W Gibbs
181 Dr Clifton D Briggs
183 A Edwin Clarke
183 William E Spooner
185 Wiliam S Wilber
185 Arthur B Case
186 James M Bonnar
187 Francis R Boston
187 Tyler A Whitney
190 Fred C Washburn
190 Lettice R Washburn
193 John F Hatch
194 Mrs eJnnie A Bancroft
198 Silas Taber
199 Edward E Wright
199 Edward G Tripp
200 John B Demers
200 Joseph M Daigneault
201 Daniel J Kelleher
201 Charles H Gardner
203 Adeline R Gorham
205 Samuel J Lowe
205 George H Allen
206 Charles S Calhoon
206 Andrew J W McAvoy
208 Edmund D Ashley
208 Edward Allen
209 Charles B Sturtevant
209 Edward S Tasker
210 Edward G Reynolds
218 Mrs Annie E Butts
221 Albert M Taber Jr
221 Lydia A Phinney
222 Mrs Amelia B Hatch
223 Mrs Ellen C West
224 Martin F Kavanaugh
224 Mrs Annie McMann
228 Lewis D F Negus
228 Henry S Taber
232 William L Ashley
232 Adelaide West
236 Edmund F Maxfield
236 Waldo A Sutherland
238 Joseph W Lavers
238 Joseph W Robertson
242 Manuel G Lobo
242 Mrs Sarah G Coon
244 Thomas A Sullivan
248 Charles H Hastings
252 Parkman M Lund
258 Dr Edward T Tucker
261 Sisters of Mercy
264 Mrs Delia Goggin
270 J Abajian
270 Charles S Irish
271 Mrs Nora McIsaac
274 Samuel Percy
274 Nicholas E Howland
279 John Steele
280 Henry Howland
281 Frederick W Besse
284 Mrs Anna Walker
284 George H Bowen
285 Mrs Maria K Bacon
285 Dela E Patry
286 Edward H Field
287 Mrs Harriet J Milliken
287 Charles E Hewitt
290 Charles F Nickerson
290 Henry McClusky
291 Mrs Lydia B Gifford
311 John Featherstone
312 Mrs Elizabeth Wilson
315 Otis M Dunham
315 G Lerow Sprague
316 George Maloney
316 Caroline A Hutchins
317 Joseph R Furnans
318 Gilbert K Nickerson
320 Joseph F Favreau
320 James Harrington
320 William Peers
321 Samuel Peers
322 Edward F A Cowen
327 Mrs Anna E Hall
332 Mrs Maria A Hafford
334 Mrs L E Smith
334 Joseph Lamothe
335 Thomas F Kavanagh
336 Henry Villemure
337 Williams H Sears
337 Jonathan Turner
337r Ann Thompson
338 Fred Johnson
338 George F Caswell
339 James E R Simmons
339 Leonard B Field
342 Noel H Charpentier
342 Mrs Betsey J Howard

344 John Boruque
344 Alex Johnson
345 Mrs Clodorise Saulnier
345 Mrs F E Paine
351 Mrs Mary Coughlin
351 Daniel H Curtis
355 Mrs M A Galligan
355 Henry Cooper
356r Henry Allby
359 William H Mulberry
359 Allen B Currie
359r Peter H Dowd
359r George F Bliven
360 David Gardner
360 Ellis Hesford
362 John F Hayes
362 Herbert P Ames
362 Thomas P Ames
363 John Paquette
364 John E Higgins
364 Mrs Ellen Riley
364 Edward J Feeley
365 Robert H Mather
365 Mrs Eliza A Caldwell
365 Peter V Cummings
366 George H Lapham
366 Mrs Valentine Dinter
367 John Hobin
367 Mrs Emma Marchessault
371 Zepherin Beaudoin
373 Henry Proulx
375 Mrs Alice Mulholland
377 Joseph Brothers
379 Thomas Kelley
380 George Dubois
381 Joseph Papillion
382 Aldei J Labrode
383 James A McGrath
384 Similean Provost
385 Arthur Bonneau
386 Mrs Fred Thorpe
387 Alfred Crossley
388 Joseph Petit
389 Charles Hebert
389 Thomas R Gilman
390 Bernard Muruin
399 Holden A Heap
399 Edmund Duckett
399 George H Lord
400 Burton F Smith
400 Abraham Turner
400 Benjamin F Cosgrove
400 William H Greenwood
400 Mrs Susan Smith
401 Thomas Whittaker
401 William Haworth
402 John Frasier
402 Victor Lemieux
403 James H Riley
403 Joseph Roy
404 Pearl J White
405 Mrs Helen Welch
405 Mrs Jane Taylor
409 Margaret E Harrington
410 Alexander Wallace
410 Philip Rock
411 Thomas Madigan
411 Thomas Farley
415 Dr C J Leary
415 Michael J Burke
426 Lawrence Horton
426 Alfred A Fletcher
426 Arthur Cooper
427 Joseph P Trudel
427 Omar Charpentier
428 James Armitage
428 William H Wilkinson
429 Timothy C Calnan
430 Mrs Johanna Townsend
430 Andrew H Johnson
431 Mrs Catherine A Mahoney
431 Mrs Sarah Whiteley
431 Joseph Desaulniers
432 Henry Holden
432 Michael M Leary
433 Margaret Sullivan
433 John F Daley
434 Gilbert Brunnette
434 Leo Weinberger
434 Victor Galipeau
434 John B Lavoie
434 Richard Remillard
435 J E W Tremblay
435 Joseph Caouette
435 Joseph Caya
435 Treffle Bonneau
438 Alfred J Forand
438 Eugene Wagner
438 Thomas F Green
440 Arthur Betell
440 John Morris
441 John T Watkinson
441 William Bolton
441r Mrs Winifred Grogan
441r Mrs Mary Thompson
442 William Dacy
442 George H Whipple
443 Mrs Frances Barker
443 James H Harrison
443 Thomas Potter
444 David Sheehan
444 Honore Boule
445 Mrs Mary Moran
445 Henry McCarthy
445 Michael F Balderson
445½ Peter Kelley
445½ Martha Scott
446 Isaac W Greenup
446 William H Gifford

Pleasant—con
446 Mrs Jane McLeod
447 Paul R Leistritz
447 Mrs Ellen Breen
447 William Ogden
447½ Frederick W Holt
447½ Mrs Margaret Hicks
449 Mrs Hannah McCarthy
449 Charles A McKenna
451 Charles McDermot

PONTIAC

0 Elmer J Cayer

POPE

2 John H Thornton
2 Mrs Barbara Murphy
9 Benjamin Dawson
11 Harry W Bly
12 C M C Wilkinson
13 Charles L Faunce
14 William P Covell
15 James F Hoye
22 William Kelly
221 George W Baker
227 John P Moore
231 Frederick G Hillman
235 John Morris
239 Norris H Tripp
241 Augustus Simpson
261 Joshua Addy
261 Sidney C Atwood
265 Alphonso H Smith
266 Walter F Potter
267 James L Lemos
267 Eliza Ellis
270 Walter J Case
270 Joseph Ferns
274 Daniel J Murphy
274 Benjamin Braley
274 Robert Brittain
275 Edward H Carter

POPE'S ISLAND

1 Samuel Bryden
2 Mrs Evelyn S Wood
3 Matthew P Wood
4 James S Howard

POTOMSKA

51 Martin Hogan
51 Michael Boyle
51 George Bolton
51 Fergus Bolton
51 Henry Bolton
55 Henry Jordan
55 Thomas O'Donnell
55 Foster Hirst
55 Edward Curry
55 Margaret Foy
69 John Gracia
69 Joaquin Gregoire
69 John Correia
76 Miles Costello
80 Louisa Fordham
80 Joseph Pacheco
82 Severino P Mello
87 Mrs Emily St Germain
87 Mrs Jane Whittle
88 Joseph O Silva
88 John Martin
89 Charles Jenney
92 Joseph Francis
92 Mrs Constantia Foster
93 James E Jackson
93 Mrs Margaret Jackson
94 John Ponte
94 Antone Escobar
99 Mrs Sarah Pepin
99 Manuel Rose
100 John Sylvaia
100 Louisa Forham
101 Jacinth Ferreia
101 Henry Rainey
101 Augustus Neves
102 Joseph Fagan
102 Mrs Mary Smith
104 Joaquin Jesus
104 Fernandes Veira
104 Joseph T Correia
104 Mrs Mary Rogers
105 Antone E Silva
105 Frank Silva
106 Manuel D Silveira
106 Joseph M Andrada
106 Antone Gracia
109 John T Perry
109 Patrick J McDonald
109 Frank J Alves
118 Joseph Currier
118 Octave Carrier
118 Felix Brierly
122 Mrs Julia McManus
122 Edward F Wood
122 Mrs Margaret Dugan

POTTER

11 Joseph Burgess
12 Robert J Felton
12 John Hindle
15 Mrs Adeline Simmons
23 Joseph Spencer
29 James H Jones
30 George T Bennett
49 John W Welch

PRINCETON

13 George Farley
13 Francis Lemay
13 Ovela Leclaire
13 Joseph Burgess
13 Ferdinand Lafleur
17 Richard Bachman
17 Henry Kallinger
17 Charles Stageter
31 Rock Tetreault
50 Charles L Lawrence
50 F Ramsbottom
106 Louis Fivett
109 Hormidas Voghel
109 George Turcotte
126 Albert Bovyn
126 Euclide Fissette
126 Simeon La France
155 James T Cowley
155 Carl O Anderson
155 Michael Mahoney
0 Jeremiah Gagne
0 Rudolph Grenier

PRISCILLA

7 James O'Brien
23 Samuel McVey
32 Alfred Bradley

PROSPECT

35 Enos Sylvia
35 Hyman Matz
35 Andrew Perry
37 Mrs Rebecca Baskin
37 Manuel Dutra
37 Max Fine
53 Charles Crossley
55 Manuel J Menes
55 John Moriarty
57 Michael O'Donnell
57 John Pina
63 Manuel O Baganlia
63 Joseph Rose
65 Antone Roderick
65½ John Cosmo
65½ John Lima
65½ Manuel Menes
67 Joseph M Mendoza
69 Mrs Mary A Silva
71 Manuel Medeiros
71 Manuel Correia
73 Antone Ferris
75 Gustiano Silva
75 John Souza
79 Antone Silva
79 Mrs Sarah Curran
81 Antone F Rose
85 Manuel Robello
85 Manuel J Ferreira
87 John Silva
87 John Marl
87r Manuel Costa
87r Manuel C Gullio
93 Manuel Avila
93 Joseph Luiz
95 Antone S Medeiros
95 John Veira

PURCHASE

12 Mrs Nettie L Bowen
14 Fred P Grimshaw
25 Bert E Longwood
126 Simeon Folsom
126 Harry L Stevens
129 Henry Stevens
130 Lester G Tripp
130 Mrs Annie L Johns
139 H I Nulman
142½ Mrs Emma L Conneff
151 Arthur Guillett
152 Frank C Eldridge
155 Mrs Amanda M Southworth
155 Douglas Patterson
157 Misses Kent
163 John H Matthews
164 S W McKenzie
187 Hettie H Lewton
188 Mrs Annie W Raymond
188 Henry Ladue
188 Edward T Clarke
194 Charles A Derby
199 Mrs Sarah A Titus
202 William T Wilson
202 Joseph Lawrence
203 Emma Pomeroy
203 Edward H Martin
205 Mrs Nellie E Gibson
209 Fred T Russell
212 Andrew P Kirby
212 Mrs Dora Nye
218 Sidney Gifford
218 Annie Forrester
218 Joseph Benoit
218 Mrs Lizzie Richmond
218 Albert E Chase
218 Annie Forester
221 Mrs Lena Deneault
226 Mrs Corrillia De Amaral
230 Abraham Cohen
237 Mrs Clara J Haskins
245 Edward J O'Donnell
249 Mrs Mary A Hoyle
254 Alice Julien
263 Harry A Robbins

Purchase—con
266 Benjamin Fox
269 Frank B West
269 Mrs Minnie Magoon
270 Joseph M Chaput
273 Herbert T Soule
273 Walter Buckley
273 Addie F Caswell
276 Charles McLeod
276 Joseph Moran
285 Wilfred Guerin
289 Joseph Durantt
289 George W Auger
290 William T Luce Jr
292 James Dowling
300 Misses McCullough
300 Mrs Mary A Kelleher
337 Ralph R Robinson
337 William C Burbank
343 Mrs Lydia L Kirby
343 Mrs Mary A Nansett
346 Mrs Sarah Kelley
346 John Leigh
346 Thomas J Geary
347 Edgar O Grenier
347 Mrs Adie B Fuller
347 William H Merrill
350 Mrs Annie M Braywood
352 Mrs Etta K Church
354 Gruide Durant
355 Henry A Morse 2nd
358 James W Owen Jr
363 Mrs Nellie M Case
366 Frank T Merrill
366 Thomas Blackburn
366r Mary Craig
367 Mrs Anna E Cole
369 Mrs Cecil LeBlanc
373 William McMurray
379 Louis S Edwards
379 Mark Davidson
380 Joseph F C Vasconcellos
380 Charles F DeWolf
383 Alton Dunbar
383 Mrs Sarah Piper
383 Mrs Annie M Towne
384 Mrs Mary J Leathers
388 Frank C King
388 Dennis Sullivan
388 Wilfred Radcliffe
390 Charles Flowers
395 Joseph H Cullen
395 Charles F Shaw
396 Edward M Tilton
401 Henry Meagher
402 William F Sylvia
410 Joseph Jacob
410 John Lompos
410 John Smolec
413 Waymon B Swift
413 John E Sullivan
414 Patrick F Healey
418 Antonio Grossi
419 Mrs Margaret Ellis
422 George Sumpter
427 Charles A Gray Jr
428 Joseph Foster
431 Stephen E Cassidy
433 Mrs Hannah Sullivan
434 Mrs Amelia G Yanni
434 Amilia I Grossi
436 Tereni Serafino
437 Athea Lussier
442 James C Doherty
472 Mrs Maria Williams
488 Napoleon Rock
488 Mrs Katherine E Hibbard
495 John H Galligan
495 Mrs Nancy Tripp
496 Walter B Chase
499 Mrs M L Hunt
501 Everett W Soule
503 Alexander W Rochell
506 Joseph P Herbert
509 Dennis Mansfield
509r H W Drayton
512 Ernest H Crowell
512 Daniel Honeker
514 John G Burns
514 Mrs Anne Duquette
519 Antonio Billani
526 William F Hathaway
526 Edward Kinney
527 George H Denham
527 George W Haskins
535 Thomas Moore
535 E Thomas Denham
536 James L Haskins
536 Henry Whittaker
536 Mrs Addie Rhodes
541 Pierre Frechette
542 George Greenwell
543 Herbert Dawson
557 Franklin H Haskell
557 Mrs Etta Sholovitz
557 Harris Barash
557 Herman Nisson
557 Mrs Sarah Shrader
557 Charles Tripp
559r Abram Lederman
564 Paul Pielho
565 Israel Green
565 Arthur Merrill
570 Mrs Lydia T Browning
573 James G Hellyer
580 Edwin E Browning

581 Joseph Havard
581 Hartley Eastwood
586 Dr Lewis Z Normandin
587 John Walsh
587 Mrs Sarah A Arigan
595 Theodore O Breton
595 Felix McKay
596 Mrs Delina Plomondon
596 Emerson Havard
596 Mrs Adna F Tripp
596 Romeo J Normandin
602 Dina Worthington
610 Peter J Bertrand
610 John H Smith
610 Joseph Hurl
610 Guy B Sanderson
610 Fabien Chicoine
611 Max Marden
614 Cornelius F Sullivan
615r Louis Solanite
617 Otis Rideout
619 George Banfield
619 Louis Beserosky
620 Margaret Edwards
620 Mrs Mary Bentley
621 James J Tyson
624 John Whitehead
625 William O Halliwell
625 Mrs Catherine Walker
627 Samuel Weedall
628 George E Saxon
632 William Roach
637 Thomas P Knowles
542 Shaken Lahood
643 Mrs Anne Heap
643 Joseph LaFrance
643 Thos J Clynes
643 John E Winterbottom
644 Chas Wiley
644 Mrs Melvina Bessete
652 Mrs E Spooner
652 Frederick W Holt
652 Silas E Ashley
658 George Tetreault
662 Arthur Dumas
662 Mrs Kate Murray
662 Arthur Carodeau
666 Marcus E Clifford
666 John W Bowen
672 John Costa
672 Salime Bedord
679 Mrs Margaret Speak
679r Wilfred Lemay
679r Arthur Dumas
680 Wallace Hornby
680 Richard Woodacre
680 James H Thompson
680 John M Savage
681 Emery Richard
688 Joseph Descheneau
690 Andrew Smith
691 Jean Baptiste Bourassa
695 Noe Demers
696 Joseph Mitchell
696 Henry Delauries
696 Joseph Brun
696 Mrs Grace Morley
700 Edward F McGarigle
700 Thomas O'Leary
700 Edward McGarigle
700 Mrs Mary Rivet
701 Manuel Laberge
703 Alfred Forand
740 Alex Fihault
740 Simon Beserosky
746 James A Ross
746 Joseph Heroux
760 Hector A Proulx
760 Mrs Mary Morrill
760 Mrs Emma Gauthier
763 Mrs Henriette Aubin
771 Leo Trudelle
772 Bruno St Clair
772 William Henry
775 Louis Beaubien
775 John Pennell
777 William Henry
778 H Clara Poliquin
778 Walter Isherwood
781 Patrick J Cafferty
790 Dr Joseph A Chausse
790 Antonio Bonneau
790 Alex H Huard
790 Annie Yerid
798 Philip Arcand
798 Arthur Delauriers
798 Joseph Gagnon
804 Isaac Barber
804 Harry T Covell
807 Alphonse Laplante
814 Romuld Dupuis
814 Peter Dupuis
815 Frank Benjamin
815 Joseph A Davignon
821 Philip D Bourque
827 Myer Rosenthal
827 Morris Hait
839 Joseph Lagesse
839 Adelard Breton
843 Joseph Neveux
843 Joseph Toyfair
846 Iver Nelson
847 Joseph Frawley
847 Edward J Begley
857 James S Bowen
863 E Frank Hathaway
863 Joseph S Gendron
863 Napoleon Goudreau
863 Oliver Bonneau

Purchase—con
863 Mrs Ellen Dupuis
863r Narcisse Perry
863r Amedee Fortin
864 Alfred Cross
864 Dr William O Lord
866 James Lord
871 Joseph Sharon
871 T La Blanc
871 Josepha Des Roches
871 A Bourgault
871 Arthur Bachand
872 Mrs M Carney
872 William McCarney
872 J Alphonse Milotte
880 Thomas Brouseau
880 Mrs Azelda Bessette
883 Oliver Bosquet
883 Clement Lemoine
883 Thomas Heywood
883 John Phaneuf
883 Francois Rivard
955 Ellen Fitzgerald
955 Mrs Catherine Devlin
963 John Moriarty
963 John Higgins Jr
963 Thomas Alexander
963 Patrick Gordon
981 George P Norton
991 Timothy Coughlin
991 Mrs Ellen M Brennan
999 Frederick J Spencer
1007 James Ward
1007 James T Maiden Jr
1013 Max Berman
1013 Mrs Annie Gurry
1017 Josiah Benoit
1017 Ferdinand Breton
1129 Amede Moratte
1129 Peter Strittmatter
1129 Alexander Gardner
1147 Francisco Souza
1159 Alfred Emmons
1159 Emelien Surprenant
1159 Edward Fregeau
1159 Joseph Rock
1159 R W Hornby
1183 James Newcomb
1183 Alfred Beauregard
1187 Manuel Pedro
1187 Marciel Caron
1187 Existe Lamarche
1191 Victor Ledoux
1191 Damina Bisaillion
1191 Louis Lemire
1201 C Monest
1203 Herman D Dupuis
1340 Francis Look

REED

323 George H Comstock
339 George W Dyer
345 Lucy P Hathaway
346 John E Thompson
349 Harlie B Jennings
355 Hillard M Macomber
356 Samuel B Davenport
357 Fred A Stowell
357 Clark H Jennings
358 Alfred R Tripp
358 Lester A Tripp
360 Mrs Elizabeth B Hathaway
360 Charles Gardner
367 Harrison D Ricketson
367 Byron B Hambly
371 Louis Wolfe
372 Gilbert K Brownell
372 Milford I Buker
377 Wilbur A Chase
379 Clifford H Teachman
385 Clarence E Chace
388 George T Fuller
389 Robert B King
389 Charles W Spooner
392 Mrs Dellphene E Sturtevant

REED'S COURT

1 Lemuel Bowman
1 Mrs Margaret Murphy

REYNOLDS

5 John R Walmsley
5 Joseph S Doucet
5 Edward Murphy
7 John Crossley
11 Timothy O'Brien
11 Arthur Spragg
11 Robert J Sullivan
12 Charles E Jennings
14 Mrs Jessie Downey
14 Mrs Annie Delano
17 John H Harrington
17 A P Milotte
18 James F Cotter
20 Albert Smith
20 William A Duprey
20 Mrs Francis Lees
21 Hartley Pollard
21 James Bennett
21 James Marshall
22 Alfred Caton
22 Thomas Russell
25 Robert Howarth
25 William Foley

25 John C Gorner
26 Moise Perreault
27 Mrs Margaret Gilchrist
27 Mrs Mary Hindle
27 Joseph Casey
28 Frank Jenkins
28 John W Holmes
28 Fred Middlebrook
33 Mrs Bridget Lyons
33 Mrs Jane Byrne
34 Joseph Dixon
34 Joseph P Banks
34 Joseph Acton
37 Charles Riach
37 Mrs Ellen Dwyer
37 Herbert Reece
38 Mrs Antoinette Towne
38 Arthur Skinner
38 Mrs Catherine P Gifford
39 John McCann
41 Mrs Harriett Daley
43 Thomas Hamlet
43 Fred Reece
44 John Lyons
44 Thomas Wholey
46 Timothy Harrington
46 John Fitzgerald
46 John O'Neil
47 Antoine Goyette
47 James F Halloran
47 Joseph Dupuis
53 Joshua Forgue
53 Mrs Rosanna Jodoin
53 J Frederick Touchette
53r H Edmonde Touchette
56 Michael C Sullivan
56 Michael E Ahearn
57 Richard Manning
57 Octave Rouleau
57 Misses Walsh
61 Samuel Goldis
61 Abraham Whitaker
61 Fred S King
113 Edward J Foisy
113 James Thompson
113 Walter Baldwin
115 Gustave Thoendel
115 Henry Butler
115 Conrad Berong
119 Samuel Braudy
119 William Coates
119 Joseph Bender
125 John F Puntschuh
125 Vincent Kubicek
125 John Dakin
126 Charles F Casidy
126 Charles F Whittle
126 Patrick J Aylward
127 Thomas Hartley
127 Archie Cryer
128 Mrs Anne Bowker
128 John Harrison
128 John H Ashworth
129 Thomas Singleton
131 James Miller
133 Charles H Vincent
133 Richard Grinnell
135 Edward Coyle
135 Peter Millette
137 John E Coyle
137 William Furness
139 Mrs Catherine Walsh
141 Alfred Boardman
141 William S Morley
143 James H Canghey
143 Leon C Waite
143 John F Haran
156 Mrs Ellen McKillop
156 Alphonse Cross
156 Richard Stevenson
158 Peter Doolan
158 Thomas Talbot
158 Robert F Cosgrove
158 Arthur P Robinson
158 Mrs Susie Wolf
158 Richard Wallworth

RICHMOND

2 Mrs John E Gill
5 Walter Clifford
5 Albert Broadbent
9 James A Webber
9 J P Reilly
10 Mrs Charlotte Thorpe
14 Henry Butts
14 Robert B Chase
15 William A Spooner
15 Walter Dixon
16 Frank J Raphael
16 Thomas W Comstock
17 Walter S Stratton
17 Mrs Lydia A Philips
18 William Raphael
18 James Kiernan
19 Thomas William Thorpe
20 Nathaniel F McCulley
21 Albert Woolfenden
21 Mrs Annie M Burns
22 George S P Gifford
25 James E Sargent
25 Felix A LeClair
25 John O'Hara
28 Mrs Margaret C Dahill
31 Nelson T Spelman
32 Martin Barry
33 William J Vanstone
34 Antone Losianno
37 Reuben T Algar

Richmond—con
45 Robert T Refuse
45 Joseph W S Ellis
45 Frank E Wood
46 Charles Snyder
48 Thomas A Morrison
50 William Mason
50 William Martin
59 W L G Parker
79 John H Hollihan
81 William C H Smith
137 Paul C Bochman
137 Fred F Manchester
144 John T Budd
144 Charles Lindley
146 Lawrence Charnley
157 George Pemberton
157 Stanislaus Quintin
157 James Whitehead
161 Harry A Kenworthy
161 Joseph Child
161 Robinson Peel
167 John Swindlehurst
167 Eli Southworth
171 George Southworth
171 John Yates
175 John Jackson
175 James J Gordon Jr
175 Alfred Cockshutt
180 Vergino F Simmons
185 Solomon M Baker
185 Edward W Gifford
200 Treffly Daigneault

RIVER ROAD

108 Joseph Florent
112 Arsene Allen
122 Hugh Corlett
130 Maxim Breault
136 Leander Perry
137 Cyrille Mailloux
143 M Chester Claudino
143 Manuel S Claudino
149 Mrs Mary Winslow
149 Charles F Trull
161 R Teel
163 William H A Tobey
169 Charles M Horton
178 Edmond Laporte
186 George F Brightman
191 Mrs Abbie J Brooks
203 Job T Haskins
209 Herbert M Spooner
217 Albert H Bismore
223 Mrs H B Spooner
226 Jason F Pierce
231 Dr Joel P Bradford
234 Obed Whitehead

RIVERSIDE AVENUE

1 Furman Laine
1 John Bolek
1 Oliver Girard
2 Narcisse Houle
2 Calixte Martin
3 Joseph Hebert
3 Delphis LaChapelle
4 Mederic Gaumond
4 Albert Vautour
4 Mrs Minnie Curley
4 Henry Daigle
5 Romeo Byron
5 Jean B Brisson
6 Henry Giguere
6 Ernest Pepin

RIVET

1 Frank Trznadel
13 Manuel Francis
13 John A Sylvia
13 Manuel Raposa
39 Mrs Antone J Silva
41 Jennie Lafferty
42 Manuel P Daniels
49 Joseph Piva
49 Antone Medeiros
49 Joseph Pripa
52 John Frayes
52 Parker F Slocomb
53 Henrietta Costa
53 Manuel Rose
53 Henry Millette
53 Manuel Rosa
54 Elinor Palnaude
54 Joseph M Travers
57 Remi Lavoie
57 Louis Poirier
58 Manuel Cunha
58 John Medeiros
61 Edward Koenig
61 William Sleight
67 John Ramos
67 Manuel Frates
71 Mrs Mary Graham
71 Patrick Toolis
83 Alfred Chandonnair
83 Pierre Ostignay
85 Rosalie Remillard
87 Edmund Cote
87 Louis Peloquin
87 Xavier Jeffrey
91 Ferdinand Delarge
97 Antone P Amaral
106 Ferdinand Desjardins Jr
106 Antone Teixeira
106 Louis Erseneau

106 Grusca Kelter
106 Ferdinand Delarge
106 John Hall
107 Henry Chenette
107 Andrew Gagnon
109 Amos Davineau
112 Mrs Carrie H Cole
113 Mrs Mary H Aspin
116 Mrs Mary O'Brien
116 John F McDonnell
119 Joseph Machado
124 Samuel Dupuis
124 Joseph A St Denis
124 Arsene Dupre
124 Henry Harbeck
124 Alfred Levasseur
125 Alfred E Watson
125 Ferdinand Desjardin
125 Dr David S Belanger
128 Adolph Dion
128 Isaac Benoit
128 Orme Campbell
128 Frank De Ganger
128 William Brockelhurst Jr
166 Edward Ducharme
170 Mrs Marie L Morrison
170 Mrs Clothile Lefebvre
170 Sifroyd Belanger
172 Alphonse Dion
172 Oliver Dion
172 John Donnelly
172 Eugene Hernan
190 Theodore Fourier
190 Ancline Desiardins
190 Louis Caver
190 Mrs Alice Dilworth
195 James Henthorn
195 Patrick Griffin
195 James Ainsworth
195 Manuel Cambria
195 James Henthorn
196 Silva Desjardins
197 James Hemenway
197 Elphage Rousseau
197 Odilon Rousseau
197 Melvin A Longtin
200 Antonio A Fernades
207 Eugene Silver
207 Joseph Hemenway
207 William J Wallace
208 Joseph Marshall
208 Mrs Frances Alexander
208 John S Alexander
211 Jose S Dutra
214 Ann M Waldron
219 Edward Tetreault
219 Joseph Trahan
219 Frank McArdle
219 James E Howarth
225 James Duchaine
226 John Mason
226 Manuel Santo
226 Mrs Canstantina Caton
232 Mrs Annie Perry
232 Antonio King
232 Marion De Mello
233 Marshall S Greene
235 Manuel S Sylvia
235 Manuel Lopes
238 Emanuel Frates
238 Henry Cooper
238 Manuel Mello
244 Joseph M Silva
244 Mrs Mary Mendauca
244 Joseph Pacheco
244 Mrs Mary Thomas
248 Joseph Deslandes
248 Frank E Walker
248 Louis A Lambert
261 George A M Brier
261 Joseph Dias
261 Joseph Pimental
271 Mrs Louisa Simmons
283 John Bletcher
283 Louis Meal
287 Stanislas Gallipeau
287 Manuel Jessie
291 Stanilas Benjamin
291 John P Hargrave
315 Matthew Straughn
317 Dr Joseph P Vierra
317 Rose H Azevedo
317 Joseph E Stubbs
321 John Leigh
331 George H Winterburn
331 David Mitchell
339 Ode Guillette
339 Mrs Ann Barry
347 John Enos
347 Edward Raymond
371 Joseph Enos
391 Frank Medeiros
391 John Costa
391 Mrs Marie Piva
391 Joseph Perry
397 Manuel Ferreira
397 Peter Dufresne
397 Adolph Dufresne
397 George Collins
411 George Racine
411 John B Moran
415 Mrs Alice Butler
417 Francisco Pimental
417 Mrs Mary E Mulkearns

Rivet—con
419 Maurice Downey
431 John Connors
436 Harry Kenyon
436 John Kenyon
436 William Turner
436 Mrs Sarah Jameson
439 Mrs Annie Power
439 Charles Durfee
440 John Smith
440 Paul St Lawrence Jr
441 Thomas Jones
443 Mrs Alice Willis
444 John Rigby
444 Mrs Susanna Cooper
448 James Haworth
448 John Jackson
448 F Ducharme
451 Thomas M Burhoe
451 John B L Waterhouse
457 John S Nunes
457 Joseph P Martin
465 Jacob Forman
465 Manuel Sylvia
465 Reuben Forman
468 Joseph Francis
468 William Tomlinson
473 William K Lees
475 Peter Forand
477 Joseph Etchells
481 Thomas Mills
481 John W Collinge
481 John Quinn
486 Joseph McQuade
486 William Dickson
492 Mrs Mary Silva
492 Joaquin Silveira
492 Manuel P Daniel
494 Manuel M Ferreira
494 John P Cabral
494 Antone P Daniels
499 John Lucas
499 Frank Brown
505 Jacinth Mello
505 Antone Travers
505 Manuel Mello
506 Chadwick Hulton
506 Thomas Winn
509 Antone Souza
509 John Farrell
509 Joseph Benevides
514 Manuel Cunha
514 Joseph Santos
514 Frank Dobson
515 Francis Thorley
515 George W Thorley
518 Frank Joseph Cambia
518 Mrs Louise Leal
518 Antone Gaspa
519 William E Gleason
526 Antone J Salvador
526 Joseph Lema
531 William S Holmes
531 Dennis Regan
532 William H Anglin
532 Frank Smith
532 Antonio Arruda
533 John H Holden
533 Alfred Allen
533r Thomas Smith
540 Joseph L Silva
544 Robinson Ogden
544 Rauly Faria
544 Joseph Cooper
545 Robert Salter
546 Samuel T Shard
546 James Furbey
552 Charles Frank
552 Joseph B Madruga

ROBESON

8 John Northcott
10 Nicholas Whalen
11 Edward F Dahill
12 James Wall
17 John F Riley
17 Clara Pierce
18 Almon P Sturgis
22 Henry S Foster
23 Rev James R Burns
23 Rev James M Coffey
27 William J Haggerty
27 Arthur S Babbitt
34 Samuel Whittaker
34 John Dawson
34 Mrs Mary Entwistle
38 John Kenney
38 Michael J Gorham
42 Daniel P Sullivan
42 Edward D Kenney Jr
45 Sisters of Holy Cross
46 Mrs Ellen Sullivan
46 Thomas F Murray
52 John Medeiros
60 Mrs Anna Terwilgar
60 Mrs Mary Schultz
63 Robert E Wood
63 Thomas H Lyons
64 August Bertholet
66 Mrs Mary Boucher
66 Wilfred Deslandes
79 James S Gatenby
82 Clarence L Damon
82 William J Hall

85 Albert B MacKinstry
85 James Harding
86 Mrs Rose Burke
86 James Le Claire
88 John Leary
89 Terrence Clark
89 Philiza La France
90 Edward I La France
90 Joseph Nolet
90 Mrs Cora E Manchester
91 George Grew
91 William Simister
92 Edmund Johnson
101 John N O'Brien
101 Isaac N Cory
107 Percy W Caswell
107 Charles A Merrow
109 David M Cheny
109 James J Moore
116 Luman D Rounsevell
116 Daniel T Murphy
116 William Crabtree
117 H B Remington
120 George A Rivers
120 Hollis M Reed
120 George Peirce
124 William H Cleary
127 Charles G Allen
130 Delphis Gauthier
130 Joseph Christophe
131 J H Scammons

ROCKDALE AVENUE

230 George Howarth
230r William De Mello
0 Joseph Almeida
389 Frank Jacintho
389 Manuel Perry
391 Manuel Arruda
476 Frank Rogers
806 William J Murray
814 Mrs Mary A Stowell
845 Chester K Borden
854 Sylvester Almy
854 Edward T Russell
855 Mrs Marion T B Wright
855 William Ferguson
859 Anthony Loftus
860 William H Humphrey
866 Thomas F Breakell
868 Andrew T Cory
874 William G Cook
876 Arthur H Bennett
887 G B Borden Jr
888 Joseph H Allison
889 Hubert Kerrigan
895 Jonathan H Smead
900 Thomas H Wall
904 Daniel H Stowell
915 William J Sadler
987 George G Cory
1007 Charles T Reed
1019 Antonio G Sequeira
1038 John Enos
1038 Frank Oliver
1067 Joseph F Sequeira
1071 William P Perry
1071 Mrs Lucy E Taber
1093 William H Flynn
1094 Mrs Martha A Cory
1107 Pardon Russell
1143 William T Cole
1159 William A Coggeshall
1171 Samuel Churchill
1187 Frank Grohde
1194 Willard E Bosworth
1194 Frank Bragga
1195 Henry A Stephens
1212 Harrison R Cook
1213 David Brown
1213 Herman J Feldgen
1213 Henry E James
1217 Walter H Wilbur
1235 George F Wilbur
1248 James Baron
1267 Charles M Andrews
1267 Fredrick Chadwick
1267r Abner A Howland
1272 F H Mellor
1276 Mrs Sarah Mellor
1285 George B Borden
1285 Henry Tripp
1285 Mrs Mary A Hyde
1316 William J Sutton
1353 Joseph Enos Vetorino
1360 Charles M Scott
1360 John L Galpin
1372 Charles H Mosher
1379 Frank S Lemos
1384 George F Wilbur Jr

ROCKLAND

2 James F Evans
2 Patrick H Winterson
4 William J Moore
22 Mrs Katherine Oesting
22 John Boswell
22 Albert Roberts
28 Mrs Mary Thompson
28 Harry Makin
29 Mrs Emma E Baker
29 Mrs Noami W Swasey
32 Frank A Winship
32 Mrs Estelle G Winship

Rockland—con
32 Michael W Gilmartin
48 Daniel V McAvoy
48 Thomas Shaw
52 Jireh P Jennings
52 Joaquin P Lopes
56 Michael A Hickey
56 Mrs Bridget L Hickey
59 Sisters of Mercy
60 Mrs Mary A Cameron
60 John A Chadwick
64 Mrs Mary Alves
64 Manuel Paulino
66 Antonio G Mello
70 Frank Perry
70 Patrick D Malley
70 Mrs Margaret Dodd
71 Joseph Jacintho,
71 John Jacinth
74 Joseph T Moriarty
74 Mrs Nancy Higton
75 Mrs Mary Durfey
75 John W Pike
79 Thomas F Hoye
79 Charles J McGurk
80 James McKenna
83 Hannah N Bogie
83 Antonio L Correia
84 Mrs Mary M Bonney
84 Alexander G Perry
87 Mrs Mary Frates
87 Mrs Mary de Mello
87 Manuel C de Mello
88 Antone Vincent
88 Samuel Alsop
90 James P Hayes
92 Manuel J Falcon
92 Frank Frey
93 Samuel N Fairbrother
93 Mrs Rita Simas
93 Arthur A Smith
94 Mrs Mary Avellar
94 George Best
94 George M Chase
94 Mrs Mary G da Terra
94 Joseph I da Terra
100 Joseph F Kraihanzel
101 Walter Clark
103 Lloyd S Delano
108 William S Williams
104 William B Stephenson
107 William Lopes
107 William Rankin
108 Joseph Claudino
108 Mrs Barbara Marshall
110 Joseph Schaff
110 Joseph S Goulart
110 Manuel Silva
110r Joseph Chaves
111 Mrs Alice S Murphy
113 Martin Souza
114 Timothy S Farrell
123 Joseph K Vargas
125 Robert Copeland
125 Joseph Brockelhurst
130 Antonio J Thomas
131 Joseph Houth
131 John B Stanley
131 James H Almond
137 Mrs Mary J Pimental
137 Manuel L Noia
137 John M Morgado
146 Joseph Salles
146 Manuel R Souza
146 Nelson Dumas
147 Fred Costa
147 Manuel Moniz
147 Manuel Piva
147 Joseph Menezes
148 Manuel J Espinola
148 Philip H Levesque
148 John V Rocha
151 Joseph Correia
151 Joseph P Ponte
151 Henry L Burding
151 Angelo L Frago
154 John Marshall
154 Josephine Bouthilette
159 John B Marshall
159 George S De Sota
159 William O Fuller
160 Frederick Thomas
160 Louis Z Allen
160 Joseph Antone Jr
163 John J Morris
163 Antonio Frates
163 John P Spinnett
164 Antone Sylvia
164 Benjamin Dratch
169 John Barros
169 Mrs Ann Baldwin
169 Joseph A Enos
178 Antone B Gracia
178 Seraphin Mello
178 Frank Mello
183 Antonio F Spindola
183 Gabriel Schultz
183 William Durfee
184 Dallus Brown
184 Mrs Louisa Clark
194 Mrs Elizabeth Smith
194 Mrs Mary L Sylva
198 Anthony Moniz
198 Charles C Nourse

202 John H Lindblom
206 Manuel F Medeiros
206 Joseph Roderique
206 Alexander B Mercer
208 William T Sylvia
208 Antonio C Morris
212 John L McManus
216 William C Murray
216 Frank T Mosher
218 Frank Frates
218 Joseph T Silva
218 Manuel Baptiste

RODNEY

12 Albert Morrissette
12 Ludger Sleight
16 John J Medeiros
16 James Cordingley
16 John W Needham
16 Mary McCarthy
19 Felix Brunelle
19 Adelard Dupuis
20 Mrs Jennie Miller
21 Jerome Tellier
22 Treffle Daniels
23 D Porrier
23 Samuel Whiteley
23 William Braidwood
30 Joseph Baldwin
30 Malcolm Hibbert
30 Mrs Isabelle Knowles
75 Rocco Escola
75 Virginio Enos
76 Peter A Hill
79 Thomas Brown
79 James Eastham
79 Matthew Merrick
84 Edwin Swithinbank
84 James E Connelly
84 John Butterworth
84 Arthur Egan
84 Charles Foster
94 William H Walker
94 Aurele J Banville
105 Theophile Boudreau
107 Robert Hartley
107 Thomas Carter
107 John J Carter
120 William Roberston
122 George M Bogie

ROOSEVELT

6 Joseph Hosp
12 Levi Bonvoulior
12 John W Emmett
12 John Chatburn
16 Emil Mathieu
16 Cyrill Catieux
16 Joseph Ehret
16 Joseph Metevier
18 Harry Gregson
18 Michel Lamothe
18 Nector Burnnette
20 Edmonde Lamiele
20 Joseph P Silvia
20 Mrs Rose B Galipeau
20 Edward Harrison
20 August Theberge
22 Asa Caldercott
22 Peter Deane
22 Thomas Lizotte
22 William P Brindle
22 Thomas Riley
22 Thomas Bradbury
24 Mrs Mary Copeland
24 Mrs Ada Whittaker
24 William Wooton
26 Arthur Gent
26 William Morrow
26 William Atkinson
27 Mrs Azilda Desmarais
27 Richard Wright
27 Pierre Richard
28 Euclide Phaneuf
28 John Hingham
28 Arthur Cote
29 Oliver Gauthier
29 Edmond Miour
39 Albert Bibby
39 James Middleton
39 Emil Lambalot
39 Eli B Ogie
39 Louis Proulx
40 Emil Begue
40 Emile Reinieche
40 Arsene Boisvert
42 Thomas E Bassett
42 Harry Green
42 Harry Ingham
44 Robert Chadwick
44 John W Regan
44 Elizabeth Lomas
46 John A Heap
46 Joseph Emmett
47 George Kilshaw
47 Richard Spencer
47 Joseph Towers
49 Samuel Johnson
49 Priscilla Gibson
49 Thomas Fairclough
54 Adelphine Chappius
54 William Knowles
54 Nicholas Wexler
58 Sidney Osbaldestom

Roosevelt—con
58 Samuel Coates
58 Mrs Mary Eller
59 Percy Whitworth
59 Robert Warden
59 James Howarth
62 James McNealey
62 Richard Harrison
62 Mrs Eliza Cleveland
62 Frederick Greenwood
62 William C Holden
63 Richard Simmons
63 Joseph Saunders
63 Thomas Thornton
66 Mrs Alice Fairclough
67 Charles Sykes
67 Modest Correau

ROTCH

39 William K Wagner
43 Edward A Carter
45 Stanley G Akin
47 Frederick Brand
50 George H Lawrence
55 George H Brittain
56 Joseph A Robida
63 Charles F Heap
71 David P Jennings
72 Herbert W Bliss
77 Andrew M Bush
79 John T Champion
82 Alton H Bailey
84 Charles H Williams
114 Howard M Gibbs
119 Frank L Sylvia
123 Joseph B C Tuell
127 Lavon T Ames
138 Gertrude A B Bruce
148 John Greer
154 Michael F May
154 Murdock Mackay
155 Lester E Hawes

ROUNDS

8 Frank M Tripp
9 Charles H Vinal
10 Edward R Sherman
11 Charles T Allen
12 James McMahon
17 A H Wordell
22 Mrs Mira J Perkins
25 Joseph Whitehead
26 Edgar H Gifford
29 Edward Macomber
32 Joseph McGowan
33 Mrs Nancy A Davis
38 William Quesko
38 John E Moores
42 James S Macomber
43 Eugene F Russell
49 Frank O Stevens
50 John H Upham
52 Alexander McLeod
53 Walter W Snailham
55 William B Topham
56 Robert F Vogel
61 Curtis Stiles
62 William E Staples
109 Everett L Weeden
109 Frederick W Coon
109 Clarence Bowman
113 George S Perry
114 John A Davis Jr
116 George A Pike
141 James J Earley
143 Albert G Teachman
147 Albert E Clarke
170 Mrs Mary F Leonard
176 Joseph J Azevedo

RURAL

11 Mrs Mary Travers
11 Daniel Falcon
13 Mrs Frances Rogers
13 Manuel Ferreira
14 Oscar E Findeisen
20 Samuel Cowling
21 John Dutton

RUSSELL

38 Roswell K Gammons
38 Mrs Lydia A Waldron
40 George D Herron
50 Misses Tripp
50 Ella Terpeny
51 Henry A Sherman
51 Clarence Cushman
52 Theodore C Hoffman
54 Mrs Carrie Howland
61 Henry B Howland
62 Mrs Carrie F Sullivan
64 Mrs Eliza A Lewis
65 Fred W Greene Jr
66 Harry A Neyland
67 William J Abrams
69 Samuel Genensky
69 James E Jackson
70 George A York
71 Marshall F Lewis
73 George L Habicht

RUTH

13 Joseph Whittle
13 Ernest Le Page

13 Agnes Atherton
15 Thomas Roberts
15 Wilfred Jukes
17 David Young
19 Margaret Reidy
19 Alfred Green
53 George Bernier
53 Horace Francis
53 Napoleon Richard
53 Gilbert Brault
53 Mrs Olivine Brodeur
59 Francois Dion
59 Daniel Clancy
59 Gasper Pepin
62 Richard Kilshaw
63 Alpherie Lague
63 Charles F McGarrity
64 John Moss
66 Harry Settele
66 Alfred Seguer
67 Henry Stevenson
67 John L Brodeur
67 Michele LaLiberte
67 Ward Hindle
67 Eleodore Brouillette
68 Richard Kilshaw
70 Ferdinand Dumont
70 Charles Lambert
70 Ernest Dupre
70 Moise Turgeon
71 Walter B Griswold
71 Jules Talbot
71 Austin Conway Jr
71 Jules Couture
71 Napoleon Lebeau
72 James Mangham
72 William Crawshaw
72 Daniel Chapman
72 Samuel Firth
82 Andrew Kucharski
82 Henri Gauthier
82 Eugene Thivierge
82 August Dautriel
83 George D Wooley
83 Mrs Delia Moriarty
88 George R Millet
88 Alexander Soucy
88 Gustave Goudreau
88 Eli Desbiens
89 Joseph Bicher
89 Edmond Debrosse
89 Mrs Emilia Tremblay
92 Albert Lefleur
96 John Whewell
96 Misses Taylor
98½ Philias Charron
98½ Emile Siguer
102 Napoleon Potvin
102 Adolphus Lariviere
102 Alexander Norwood
103 Louis Villeux
103 Thomas H Gibson
103 Mrs Georgianna Bolduc
103 August Gussaume
103 Noe Henner
103 Charles A Blanchette
106 Philemon Hotte
106 Pierre Levasseur
106 John Boucher
115 Bryan Doyle
115 Hormidas Letourneau
115 Alfred Kuntz
117 Louis Lavoie
119 George A J Lagasse
123 James Gilbert
123 Samuel Robichaud
123 Antoine Montigney
127 Francis X Faford
127 Mrs Katherine Frohmater
129 George H Parker
133 Charles Billington
133 Richard Hartley
133 Samuel Riding

RYAN

43 Alexandre Brown
47 James Dean

SAGAMORE

30 John De S Cabral
36 Antone S Medeiros
36 Joseph Soares
80 Mrs Mary Medeiros
80 Henry Souza
80 Joseph F Cambra
88 Albert Wunshell
88 John Beaur

ST JOHN

30 James Walsh

SALISBURY

7 Mrs Lucien LaFrance
7 John Bryson
7 Michael Cioper
7 John Wadsworth
7 Louis Dion
9 Emile Berthiaume
9 William Dennin
9 Noel Desrosier
9 William Dawes
10 John Sylvare
10 Alexander Lavalle

Salisbury —con
10 Robert Arthur Speight
12 Mrs Ellen Dyer
12 William Riley
12 Mrs Elizabeth Taylor
12 Frank Wilson
12 Richard Walmsley
13 Elizabeth Pullen
13 Nellie Almond
13 Edward Norris
13 Misses Brindle
13 Mrs Mary J Robinson
13 Edward Whittle
13 Joseph Briggs
14 Wright Wilde
14 Percy Lees
14 Adelbert A Chapman
14 Rene Lemarcher
16 Henry Poirier
16 Emile Marchal
17 Jules Reinieche
17 Alfred Sharples
18 Mary B Watson
18 George A Wooldridge
18 Edward Whittle
19 George Dietz
20 Henri Seguer
20 Mrs Sarah J Clarkson
20 Napoleon Dubois
20 Rock Racette
21 James Eatough
21 Thomas Bradley
22 Thomas McCue
22 Emile Martin
22 Eugenie L Forrester
23 Enoch Gardner
23 Fred W Greenhalge
23 Mrs Mary A Towers
24 Adam Taletowicz
25 Gilbert Henner
26 William Margeson
26 John Fairhurst
26 William Tattersall
27 James Howard
28 Alveris Pare
29 Mrs Jane Sowerbutts
29 James Hemmings
30 John H S Wignall
30 Richard Hayhurst
30 Alex Hargraves
31 Napoleon Caron
32 Peter Robinson
40 Alex Villeneuve
42 Henry Whittle
42 William Gordon
44 Annie Whittle
44 Thomas Whittle
46 Alphonse Cadieux
46 Wilfred Desnoyer
48 Philidor Benjamin
48 Octave Benjamin
49 George Perry
49 Clement Bernard
49 Louis Pelletier
50 Charles Morin
50 Louis Bertrand
51 David Howard
51 Thomas Fletcher
53 George Fournier
53 Joseph Roy
54 Mrs Florida Savarie
54 Amedee Doplaise
56 John T Davis
56 Edward Cadieux
58 Isadore Rivard
58 William H Generoux
58 Herculan Gaumont
60 Matthew Pollard
60 Mrs Maria Burgess
60 George A Collier
61 William R Smalley
61 John Waddington
90 Thomas Ball

SAWYER

109 Courtois Leoder
109 Napoleon Gerad
162r Edmonde Charbonneau
164 Eugene Cote
164 Eusebe St Pierre
175 Mrs Mary A Quinnin
180 Arthur Robert
180 Armand Belanger
180 Alma Belanger
180 Belonie Belliveau
184 Joseph Jovin
184 Francois Pluff
184 Benjamin Le Blanc
192 Mrs Melvina Demers
192 Ferdinand Fortin
192 Alphege Bonneau
192 Mrs Catherine Cameron
201 Clara Chouinard
201 Cleophas Poulette
201 Anselme Houle
201 Edward Coupe
203 Albert Rainville
203 Alexis Rocheleau
203 Hermangilde Preneau
204 Gilbert Audette
204 Joseph La Brecque
204 Oscar Rheaume
204 Digene Bouley
207 Thomas Anderson

207 Alfred Dechene
214 Arthur Ostiguay
214 Alfred Caron .
214 Mrs Adeline Belisle
214 Edmond Deroche
216 Norbet A St Pierre
216 Frank Pheneuf
216 Octave Valliere
216 Mrs Damase Houle
219 Adelard Pinell
219 Henry Vien
221 Joseph Tetreault
221 Mrs Minnie Desautels
223 Edward Rourke
226 Zephir Lemieux
226 Antoine A Poirier
226 Adelard Bousquet
229 Dr Edwin B Denham
229 Benjamin Nolan
229 Arthur Barton
229 Thomas Lessard
232 Augustin Allen
232 Patrick Hurley
233 Elie Fournier
233 Mrs Rosanna Sawyer
235 Thomas Hartley
235 Joseph T Burgeois
235 Ademor A Normandin
238 Charles H Young
'238 James Smith
238 Hartley Wilkinson
239 Peter Marinis
238 Oscar Messier
239 Fred L Webb
239 Frederick Meny
239 Joseph Nadeau
239 Peter Burton
239 Wesley Burton
239 Levi DePalteau
242 Mrs Martha Geddis
242 John F Fanning
245 Mrs Anna Ross
245 James Morris
245 Ferdinand Ross
245 James Sellers
253 Adolphe Florent
257 Joseph Goguen
274 John E W Hanford
280 Frank Ward
280 Henry Etchells
280 John F Nelson
283 Arsene Cyr
283 J R Painchaud
284 Thomas Connors
284 James Green
285 Joseph Gadreau
287 Louis Fredette
287 Edmonde Ethier
290 James W Green
290 Mrs Harriet Smith
290 Joseph Furlong
291 Eli LaBonte
291 Emil Breault
291r Charles Leclair
293 Joseph Breault
293 Oliva Richard
294 Edward Lamonthe
200 Pierre Nault
300 Calixte Nault
300 George Neagus
301 Mrs Matilda Fredette
301 Ely Gonneville
301 Joseph Barrette
302 Edmond Larochelle
302 Napoleon Renaud
302 William Senez
303 Joseph J Forgue
303 Daniel Smith
303 Morris Sherin
310 Sigfroid Poirier
310 Asa Auger
315 David Labonte
315 Lewis Therrien
319 William Jones
319 George Brindle
319 August Heilmann
322 Alfred Schofield
322 Edward Demanche
327 Edward Deslaurier
322 Charles Fanton
327 Victoria Berube
327 Lora Barselou
328 Jonathan Hargraves
328 Alphonse Allaire
328 Sidney Fryer
332 William H Fredette
332 Jack Barsley
332 Hormidas Jabott
332 Mrs Sarah J Platt
335 James J Ward
335 Walter Greenwood
335 Mrs Margaret Duckworth
335 Robert Leatherbarrow
336 William Hand
336 Oliver Hubert
336 John C Holt
345 Prime Malo
345 Walter Duxbury
345 James E McGoff
346 Stanislaus A Bonneau
346 James Lynch
346 Vital Hentis
348 Vincent LaFrance
348 Hugh Senesac

Sawyer—con
348 Mrs Annie Sharples
350 N Rosalphee Lussier
350 John Connell Jr
350 Christian Stuke
351 William Brougnton
351 Wilfred Nutall
351 Dennis McGoff
367 Victor Jacques
402 James Hesford
402 Joshua Rushworth
436 Willard N Smith
436 John Haslam
436 Thomas Ward
440 Gideon Plante
440 Edward W Stratton
441 Edward Brophy
442 James Alick
442 Honore Grenier
447 Dennis E Noonan
448 Francis X Grenier
448 Herbert Saxon
448 Joseph Grundy
448 Ralph Ratcliffe
451 Mrs Jane Hill
454 John P Gilmore
454 Louis A Paquette
457 John Norton
460 Michael J Norton
461 Joseph LaFrance

SCHOOL

37 Isabel S Dean
41 Clark Green
46 Mrs Mary Sears
46 Mary Gomes
46 Philip Almeida
46 Frank Partes
46 Mrs Annie Pina
50 Arthur Bentley
50 Charles H DeWolf
52 Mrs Mary Brightman
53 John F Soares
53 John Silvia
55 Antone Morris
57 William J Lemos
57 Joseph Leighton
59 Isaac S Crocker
59 Mrs Jessie Loring
63 John T Cantwell
63 William O'Malley
64 Frank D Rogers
65 Pardon J Williston
65 Irvin Adams
65 Mrs Theresa Silva
66 Mrs Doris Peterson
66 William R Cavalier
67 Hiram Howarth
72 Ruth Percival
74 Thomas J Hudson
81 Mrs Ulrike Rush
81 Dr Barker C Howland
82 Lawrence Kruse
82 William Duddy
82 Warren C Wilcox
83 Helen R Chadwick
83 L Auburt Kelley
84 Misses Donaghy
87 Mrs Mary J Barrows
87 William H Sherman
91 Frank R Dearborn
91 Mrs Edith S Perry
93 Chauncey G Whiton
93 Charles F Briggs
95 Lizabeth L Jay
96 Mrs Angie Armstrong
97 Lemuel T Willcox
99 Charles H Robbins
101 Dr Elmer E Robbins
101 Susan A Taylor
103 Samuel Watson
103 William E Watson
106 Mrs Sarah Wodell
106 Chester P Rexford
108 Charles L Ricketson
128 George A Covell Jr
128 Edward Denham
130 George M Kingman
132 Mrs George B Merrill

SCOTT

8 Duriel Turiel
12 Lorie Veira
15 Oliver Saulner
17 Mary J Rawstron
21 Mrs Mary F Welch
21 Potrais Zimberlin
21 James Gartside
23 Antone Medeiros
23 Joseph Careiro
37 Joseph Fournier
37 Damase Hanger
42 Joseph M Souza
46 Manuel Bento
46 Michael Souza
46 John Cabral
46 Harry Kolifas
46 Pedro Oliver
59 David Bourgeois
63 Frencisco Medeiros
96 James H Ryder

SEARS

2 Edwin G Shepardson
2 William Butler

4 Bartholomew Otheman
6 Mrs Elizabeth C Parsons
6½ Francis H Tripp
8 William F F Coe

SENECA

3 Mrs Emma Varney
3 E Jerry Chimussi
3 John Baldeau
5 Innocence Castellina
5 Peter Lavetto
8 Charles Rongo
8r Dominick Capra
8r Antonito Stin
154 Arthur Bishop

SEVENTH

1 Mary A Brown
2 Mrs Elizabeth E Haverstock
17 Dr William C Macy
18 George R Pearce
19 Andrew Boucher
20 Mrs Helen W Cromwell
23 George L Dunham
23 Mrs Florence E Danforth
24 Henry N West
25 Dr W Hewins Thayer
26 Roland A Leonard
27 Mrs Helen Smith
29 Elizabeth Gifford
30 Herbert P Bryant
31 William A Tucker
33 Mrs Matilda J Bourne
34 Arthur E Coffin
35 Benjamin C E Stuart
36 Frederick S Fuller
36 Mrs Delphina D Swain
43 Nathaniel B Kerr
47 Joseph Dias
51 Samuel J Nowell
52 Henry P Willis
0 Nat C Smith
106 William H Perry
111 Alonzo V Jason
114 Ann R Fletcher
114 Mrs Rosa W Roshur

SHAW

163 George Dawson
213 Henry Dupont
213 Charles E McMurray
255 Fred Hampson
255 Sophia Fortin
271 Arthur Bovyn
271 Donat Pepin
283 Damase Pelletier
335 Joseph Beaudoin
0 Pierre Cournoyer
0 Narcis Trahan

SHAWMUT AVENUE

1 Mrs Maria Lund
1 George E Look
2 Antonio P Cardoza
4 Walter C Swift
6 William J Edgerton
7 James E Bailey
8 Carl A Johnson
15 Mrs Emma L Wood
19 Frederick G Bowman
19 George L Bowman
20 Mrs Mercy A Springer
20 Jeremiah B Taber
21 John F Riley
28 Walter B Peck
31 Frederick C Baker
31 Mrs Alice R Church
32 Clifford J Hedges
39 Samuel Holt
39 Joseph A Sanders
40 Joseph Dyer
43 Joseph E Tichon
44 Oliver P Tripp
47 Arthur F Taber
51 John Colwell
51 George N Ross
52 Joseph S Longfield
53 Malachi H White
54 George H Sistare
57 George W Pasell
58 George B Stafford
58 Mrs Maria Lonsdale
59 Mrs Lucinda C Gibbs
59 Charles H Wilcox
62 Oliver W Burgess
62 John S Harrington
67 Benjamin W Jones
72 T Franklin Gay
73 Mrs Addie H Jennings
75 James C McNulty
76 C Franklin Roberts
76 D Edwin Allen
77 Walter D Hathaway
85 William H Potter
85 Collins Chase
89 Asa W Jenney
89 Allen W Peters
91 Arthur Uttley
101 Henry H Buckley
103 John P Sheffield
117 Mrs Jennie Gifford
118 Francis J Glasgow
119 Matthew T Furlong
120 David Grew Jr
121 Mrs J Erica Coford
121 William T Nye

Shawmut av—con
122 Charles Manchester
122 Mrs Ida M King
124 Joseph P Kennedy
125 Archibald R Peters
126 Manuel Perry
126 John L Swenson
128 John H Cockshoot
128 William J Cowen
140 Walter Fowler
140 Charles W Smith
140 Herbert T Rogers
148 Mrs Anna M Canavan
155 Dennis S Mason
155 William L Gibbs
155 Fred Ruel
159 Mrs Mary D Lawrence
159 John A Heap
165 James Whitworth
165 Thomas Walsh
165 John E O'Brien
168 Eugene G Crapo
168 George G Crapo
169 Arthur L Parker
169 Charles Norlander
170 Thomas C Lowe
172 Edward F Gero
173 John P Wade
173 Earl Butts
175 William G Flower
177 Hurlburt E Thomas
181 Edwin E Wilde
184 James F Goldrick
188 William A Lake
188 Benjamin F Ellis
190 George P Grant
192 Philip O Allen
192 Mrs Mildred Clough
193 Peleg Bosworth
195 Thomas S Warburton
195 Edward G Davis
202 Robert Bradley
205 Richard Parkinson
208 Mrs Sarah A Spooner
208 Mrs Minnie E Smith
212 Edward Shorrock
215 Walter Barnes
215 Henry Grindrod
216 James Reed
219 James Byrne
220 John N J Londholdt
221 Thomas F DeCourcey
221 Seth T McVicker
222 Benjamin S Brownell
223 Antone DeMello
223 Nathan Burgess
223 Mrs Mary A Silva
226 George Barnes
232 Willard G Poole
232 Edwin T Judson
233 Beriah G Howland
234 Alexander A Brainerd
235 William Bassett
241 David H Mitchell
243 Joseph S Kimber
243 James M Ricketson
249 Henri M Crotteau
250 Thomas D Kenney
251 Mrs A T Colwell
257 Edward Aspinwall
291 Charles T W Gifford
295 Rebecca W Gifford
305 Lloyd W Austin
327 George E Reed
327 Julius F Herman
329 John H Riley
333 Theophile Proulx
0 Paul Puchala
0 Xavier Millette
0 Ralph Emmett
0 William J Brownell
0 Clarence Wallingford
0 Charles Wellington
0 William T Gifford
0 Joseph Booker

SHERMAN

12 Christopher B Tripp
15 Joseph P Kennedy
18 Edward M Slocum
19 Mrs Calista A Macomber
23 Albert M Russell
24 Mrs Susan J Doan
27 Charles A Tuell
28 Frank P P Tuell
28 Mrs Emily F Peckham
30 William S Cushing
33 Milton A Young
33 Hannah B Hunt
34 William E Armitage
38 Anthony L Sylvia
42 Antonio F Frasier
43 Frederick S Nelson
44 Louis Silva
50 Manuel J Clement
50 Frank P Lenhart
50 Mrs Rose L Simas
51 Patrick Henry
51 Manuel Eugenio
52 William A Davis
53 William Gordon
58 Mrs Annie D Mendoza
58 Alton DeMoranville
58 Manuel F King
59 Joseph Lardner,
62 Matthew R Goulet

SHORE

5 Simon Gudgeon
8 Patrick Carolan
14 Mrs Martha Crockett
24 Peter Riddock
24 Lawrence H Dalton
24 J Albert Davenport
26 Joseph McGowan
26 Elizabeth Kenyon
38 George W Ripley

SHORT

45 Mrs Maria Bernard
45 Joseph Fernandes
45 Joseph Perry
49 Harry Elgeschewitz
49 Harry Ellis
49 Frank Enos
49 Mary Mello
50 Philip F Murphy
50 Alfred P Rose
50 Joseph S Amaral
51 Manuel Miguel
51 Joseph Perry
53 Louis V Macedo
53 Manuel Lopes
58 John C Costa
65 Joseph R Borges
65 Antone King

SIDNEY

19 Henry Turner
76 Manuel M Raymundo
76 Manuel Rogers
76 Theatonil Gonsalves
80 Mrs Sylvina Enos
80 Manuel Mello
80 Antone A Silva
80 Frank L Medeiros
81 Jose M G Luiz
81 Arthur Ramos
90 Antonio Bento
90 Joseph A Perreira
97 Manuel Rose
97 Dora L Tucker
97 Jacintho E Correia
97 John Bowser
104 August Naegele
108 George H Wilcox
108 Thomas W Hatch

SLOCUM

23 Adelard Boucher

SMITH

2 Chester B Hammond
4 John I Paulding
4 William T Davis
5 Allen W Tinkham
9 Charles L McBay
15 Edward H Sears
15 Mrs Abby D Davenport
35 Clifton Hopkins
35 Alexander Forsyth
35r John Varley
35r Samuel McKim
39 Martin Blanchard Jr
39 George A Brightman
45 Michael McDermott
45 Hannah Hurley
48 Thomas N Meyer
48 Mrs Annie F McDonnell
49 Luther R Gifford
50 William G Brown
52 William H Vose
52 Elizabeth Buist
55 Abram H Durfee
55 David S R Durfee
57 William Edy
66 Orlando I Nye
71 Mrs Annie Furtado
71 Karl Worgren
72 Albert Faunce
77 Harry D Stow
78 Peleg C Macy Jr
92 Edward F Conary
101 Charles F Edwards
104 Calvin Raymond Jr
104 Edward J Bly
109 Mrs Mary C Tripp
109 Dennis Finlan
111 Henry A Mosher
115 Henry K Wilbur
123 Thomas Shuker
127 Andrew W Shefton
127 Mrs Julia Tyler
137 Frederick A Dammon
146 Frederick T Sawyer
147 Charles H Onley
147 Mrs Mary S Hudson
152 Lizzie L Spicer
152 Mrs Sarah McNeil
153 A T Peterson
153 Richard Gallop
156 Charles E Marshall
156 Lillian Richards
157 Mrs Eva G Sherman
161 Thomas A Crapo
161 Mrs Patience A Case
161r Mrs Mary Manuel
162 Mrs Hannah N Wilcox
162 George F Rogers
164 John H Davidson
164 Fred W Colson
167 William H Madden

Smith—.con
167 Marion D Caton
168 Ernest Washburn
168 Mary Equi
171 Daniel R Allen
173 Henry P Harriman
174 Mrs Mary Champlin
174 William H Hayden
176 Josephine V Guinn
176 Mrs Gertrude Borden
178 Edward J Williams
181 Eben F Andrews
181 Frederick M Murphy
186 Albert H Jackson
186 Frank Colvin
195 Mrs Mary M Allen
198 Mary Alice Jackson
198 Mrs Emma Oliver
199 Louis Matthews
203 Mrs Margaret Allen
208 Mrs Sarah Johnson
209 Mrs Mary V Marr
209 Mrs Rosanna Cornell
211 Frank H Allen
211 Mrs Etta H Green
212 Mrs Bridget Brennan
217 Joshua B Johnson
223 Joseph Lewis
223 Henry S Sherman
224 Robert G Heyliger
228 Thomas P Winn
228 James E Andrews

SMITH STREET COURT

1 Manuel F de Terra
3 Mary Cypres
4 Catherine McCann

SOCIAL

1 Mrs Jane A Crabtree
3 Mrs Alice Baldwin
3 Adams Hettinger
4 Angus Genaw
4 Francis Francotte Jr
4 Alphonse Bourbeau
8 Konstanti Mroz
8 Valenty Karmarch
9 Theodore C Ball
10 Robert Henderson
10 Thomas Alcock
10 William F Mason
13 Walter Sterling
17 George Billington
17 James A Alcock
21 Joseph F Crowell
25 Robert Nightingale
29 Jonathan Wainscott
31 John Fielden
31 John T Griffin
32 John Delyen
32 Albert Lewis
32 Benedict J Harrison
32 John Morrell
32 Herbert Lewis
32 Eugene Plante

SOUTH

7 Antonio Pacheco
7 Antone Sylvia
9 Manuel Costa
9 Frank Pacheco
29 Marianna Martin
29 Frank P Ponte
29 Antone P Ponte
30 Antone Ponte
30 John F Simmons
30 Angello Rebello
30 Antonio Mello
31 Manuel Costa
31 Frank Piva
32 Joseph Rafel
32 Manuel F Perry
32 Manuel V Fiatti
34 Manuel Moreira
34 Joseph Alves
45 Antone Travers
46 Joseph Pacheco
46 Frank V Ferreira
46 Joseph Pacheco
47 John DeArbo
47 Antone Mello
48 Antone Ventura
48 Mrs Maria Silva
51 Antone Grace
51 Frank M Paiva
62 Louis Ventura
62 John S Machado
64 Elizabeth Bailey
69 Mrs Bridget P Mullaney
69 Robert J Curry
74 William S King
77 Ezra Horvitz
77 Paul Champigny
94 James M Tripp
96 Thomas W Buckley
97 James F Avery
98 William Davenport
99 Mrs Mary A Hervey
100 John Marvel
101 Jacob A Horvitz
102 Richard M Kuechler
103 John Greenwood
104 Joseph B Foster
104 Antone Souza
104 Sanford K Read
105 Julius Berkowitz
106 John T Broadbent
106 Mrs Flora Diaz

107 Charles O Bennett
108 Jacob H Schmidt
109 Walter S Hunt
110 Emanuel V Sylvia
111 Herbert L Bragdon
111 William H Rowand
112 Michael Phelan
113 Albert F Hammond
114 Christian H Todsen
114 John H Sleight
115 Edwin S Tallman
116 Everett C Pierce
116 John R Himes
117 Elwood E Booth
118 Mrs Ida Marcotte
118 William M Green
119 Charles Sinias
119 Edward G Burke

SOUTH FRONT

185 Antone M George
206 Harry Finkle
206 Mrs Fannie Gomes
206 Antone Duarte
207 Mrs Adelina Frates
207 Manuel Mello
207r Manuel Frates
207r Amos Carmos
210 Manuel C Pinda
212 Jacintho F Medeiros
213 Ferdinand L Martin
213½ Raulino Frates
214 John F Lema
215 Mrs Rita A Marshall
216 Antone Correia
216 Manuel Tavares
216 Frank Costa
216 Antone Correia
216 Frank O Silva
216 Andrea Domingos
216 John Mello
216 Manuel Fonce
216r Manuel Veira
216r Joseph Barboza
219 Joaquim Avaral
219 Joachim Tavares
219 Mrs Mary S Smith
219r Mrs Clara Perry
219r Joseph Amaral
223 M Bendaras
223 Antone F Silva
224 Louis Rodericque
224 Frank Rodericque
225 Joseph Silva
226 Manuel Davis
227 Frank Luiz
229 Joseph Pedro
229 Joseph Tavares
229 Antone Perreira
230 Joseph Silva
230r John Demoral
230r Joseph Cardoza
232 Manuel Francis
233 Antone Ferreira
233 Manuel J Triguerio
233 Antone S Povong
234 Domingo Francis
234 Henry Foster
236 Manuel Medeiros
236 Manuel Pacheco
240 Manuel G Lorenz
240 Jose D Medeiros
241 John Joseph Pacheco
241 Frank Joseph
241 Mary Veira
242 Frank Lopez
242 Mrs Maria Victoria
243 Manuel J Pacheco
243 Peter A Cabral
247 Joseph M Ramon
247 Manuel Costa
247 Joseph M Raymond
259 Manuel Simmons
259 Manuel T Silva
260 John Medeiros
260 Manuel Costa
262 Augustus Medeiros
265 Joseph Oliver
265 Dennis Oliver
265 Joseph Swarts
265 Joseph Silveira
267 Joseph P Amaral
267 Albert Costa
267 Manuel Correia
268 Joseph D Medeiros
268 John Souza
268 Mrs Annie Williams
271 Mrs Mary D Francis
272 Joseph Cruz
272 John Lima
272 Joseph Pedro
272r Joseph Cabral
272r Manuel Furtado
273 Joseph Souza
273 Peter Keating
273 Manuel P Medeiros
273 Antone Clifford
273 Joseph Holmes
276 Antone G Rose
276 Felissiano Rose
277 Joseph Raposa
284 Joseph E Amaral
286 Abraham Rosensweig
286 Antone M Sylvia
286 Abraham Braude
295 Manuel L Silva
297 John Lewis
297 Claude Silva

South Front—con
297 Mrs Delphine R Silva
299 Mrs Mary King
299 Manuel M Veira
299 Frank S Souza
301 Jesse Rodericque
301 Joseph Rodericque
301 Manuel Silva
303 Edward D Francis
303 Joseph Ponte
303 Manuel Sylvia
303 Manuel V Perry
305 Manuel Tavares
305 Antone Costa
305 Antone Rodericque
307 Mrs Francis King
308 Antone Mello
308 Joseph Travers
308r Mrs Marie Joaquina
308r Alfred Tavares
310 Ferdinand Dutra
310 Joseph P Ferreira
316 ——— Silva
316 Victohine Tavares
317 Joseph C Barboza
317 Marianno Bandarra
318 John Medina
319 Joseph F De Mello
319 Francisco F Simmons
319 Mrs Mado Macedo
322 Joseph Neto
323 Joseph Menes
324 Manuel M Silva
325 Joseph Furtade Jr
325 Frank W Fialho
325 Anacleto E Rose
328 August Vera
328 Joseph Rogers
329 Bartholomew Silva
329 Manuel Enos
329 Manuel P Santos
332 Mrs Kate Furtado
332 Joseph Veira
333 William Parkes
334 Antone Nunes
335 Domingas Lorenze
335 Joseph Gonsalves
336 Antone Silva
338 Henry Perry
341 John S Silva
342 Felix McKay
350 Joseph Simmons
375 Joseph Rodericque
398 Walter Taylor
402 Mrs Louisa Souza
402 Thomas Monty
402 Joseph Hamel
402 Alipo C Bartholo
406 James Carr
406 Alfred Boucher
410 Antone J Silva
410 Antone Pacheco
410 Mrs Mary C Silva
410 Joseph Marques

ACUSHNET BLOCK

1 Ovide A Downie
2 James Kelley
3 August B Travers
3 Joseph Newton
4 Antone Perreira
6 John P Slattery
6 Michael Tomlinson
7 Manuel P Dutra
7 Vitriano Fontes
9 Antone F Mello
10 Manuel Praeda
11 George Grenier
11 Trefflay Serra
428 Joseph Murach
429 Samuel Connor
431 Joseph Wareing
435 Mrs Ann Lord
436 Frank Szymanski
436 Alex Petit
439 Mrs Mary J Brown
439 James Woodacre
445 Peter Dwaszko
449 Antone Kratachville
451 James E Welch
475 Joe Soulis
475 Peter Boucher
477 Osease Leduc
479 Telesphore Larochelle
483 Henry Verner
487 Anty Purtkieurk
489 Christopher Corrigan
492 Manuel F Marshall
493 Arcand Cote

SOUTH SECOND

12 Isaac D Sampson
15 Joseph Martin
15 Thomas Flaherty
20 Sam Mickelson
20 Mrs Sarah Brown
29 Frank Lopez
29 William Stevens
31 Joseph Gonsalves
33 Joaquim Almeida
33 Mrs Mary Silva
33r Misses Morrison
37 Abraham Sher
37 Dr Edward D Osborne
49 Edgar A Long
49 Mrs Jeanette M Larner
50 Martin Johnson
53 Martin Manley
54 Mrs Ellen Morrissey
57 John Carroll

57 George H Snow
58 Manuel Texeira
58 Joaquim de Silva
59 Lottie Smith
50 John M Cabral
62 Matthew Ramos
62 James Maguire
63 Joseph Gomes
63 Chrales Freeman
64 Daniel Farrell
64 Fred Walter Fish
67 Mrs Ann Conway
68 Mrs Mary T Souza
70 Virginio Pimental
71 Mrs Cecelia Jones
71 Isabell Thompson
71 Annie Britto
72 Max Ginsberg
72 Morris Gordon
73 Leander Fernandes
73 John Temar
73 Elias S Morgan
78 Thomas Larner
85 Carall Ramos
85 Manuel F Canaca
86 Mrs Mary A Abrams
87 Manuel Gomes
90 Michael Silva
93 Mrs Domingas Pives
93 Mrs Polly Almeida
93 Mrs Dominca Peres
94 Antoin Britto
94 Josephine Gomes
96 Jule Lopes
97 John Simpliciso
97 Frank Ramos
97 Benjamin Alves
98 David Peter
100 Fannie Flaherty
100 Agnes J Smith
101 Manuel Morris
105 Mrs Minnie Pina
106 William L Slocum
106 Charles O DeWolfe
107 Henry Costa
112 Jacob Zurier
117 Benjamin Barber
117 Frank Gomes
118 Seraphim Almeida
120 Henry Weiner
123 Victor Rose
123 Daniel Conners
123 Joseph Correire
128 Louder Santos
128 Valentine Rose
129 Mrs Hermina A Pives
130 Mrs Mary Dugan
131 Frank Morrell
131 Mrs Mary Allen
137 John Lomba
137 Antoine Foote
137 John Gracia
137 Charles Gilbert
137 Mrs Mary Lyng
138 Fred J Lyng
141 Joseph C Fields
145 Theophilus Correia
145 John Baptiste
148 Manuel Gomes
149 F A Michaels
149 Mrs Rose Almeida
150 Henry Gomes
152 Jule Razario
152 John Edwards
152 John Duarte
154 Daniel Eldridge
154 Henry Bryll
156 William V Ripley
157 Francis T Payne
161 Charles Williams
161 Mrs Mary Souza
161 Caroline Sylvia
162 William De Mello
162 John H Gillick
162 Julius Sylvia
162 John Jackson
168 Mrs Adelaide Rose
170 Thomas H Francis
170 Mrs Isabel Martin
172 Nicholas Duarte
174 Frank Souza
174 James Ferreira
174 Jesse Veara
180 Joseph Freeman
189 Alexander Alves
185 Margaret A Mann
185 Mrs Gabriella Rickerby
191 W Henry Clare
191 Antone Rapoza
195 Mrs Isabelle McDonald
203 Claudino Teixeira
211 Thomas H Johnson
211 Arthur J Zerbonne
211 Amedee St Onge
230 Frank Magellen
230 Mrs Joaquina Soares
230 Joseph Da Villa
231 Mrs James F Moore
235 Manuel Frates
238 Jacinth Silva
238 Joseph Neves
238 Joseph Galph
238 Joseph F Avila
248 Manuel M Vieira
248 Joseph Lawrence
248 Rev A C Veira
249 Frank Cabral
249 John Almeida
254 Mrs Mary L Bettencourt
254 Henry Silva

South Second—con
254 Frank Santos
255 Joseph Alma
255 Frank J Francis
257 Mrs Mary Francis
257 Joseph Enos
258 Mrs Mary Santos
258 Fernando Noon
259 Frank P Rose Jr
259 Joseph R Perry
259 John Enos
260 Antone Lima
260 John Veira
262 Louis Marshall
263 Antone Oliveira
263 Joseph L Ferreira
263 Manuel J Paul
263 Manuel Cunha
263 Antone C Silva
264 Frank Boteilho
264 John Souza
266 Antone Pacheco
267 Mrs Rose Sylvia
267 Mrs Clara Oliver
268 Mrs Anna Williams
269 Joseph Rose
269 Julius Viveiros
269 Mrs Mary Mello
261 Manuel Corr
272 Joseph Marks
273 Manuel Serpa
273 Alex Mello
273 Emilio Avellar
274 William Friedberg
275 Joseph Brown
277 John Trella
278 Joseph Medeiros
278 Michel Enos
281 Louis Leite
281 David Furtado
282 Joseph Veira
283 John Rogers
283 Mrs Annie Perry
284 Joseph Pacheco
284 Antone P Silva
284r Mrs Isabella Frates
285 Fred Machado
286 Manuel S Vanocia
288 Joseph Rose
288 Joseph Mello
288r Paul Souza
289 Joaquim Medeiros
291 Max Horenstein
291 Mrs Mary A Frates
291 Joseph M Salles
291 Joseph Murray
291½ Frank M Ponte
305 Joseph D Perry
305 Thomas Lord Jr
305r Manuel Silva
306 John Costa
306 Manuel Correll
306 John Enos
307 Joseph Costa
307 Frank August
309 Manuel Silva
310 Manuel De Mello
310 Antone De Mello
313 Jacinth Pacheco
314 Lewis Simmons
314 Manuel Medeiros
320 Manuel Menes
323 Nicholas Silvia
324 Antone Cabral
324 Antone A Silva
326 John Meadeiros
326 Manuel Goulart
327 Manuel B Perry
329 Mrs Mary C Nunes
329 Harry Gordon
332 Philip Katzman
336 Mrs Loretta S Palmer
337 Kurt R Kuechler
337 Frank Ventura
339 Mrs Mary Caton
366 Israel Herman
368 John P Sylvia
371 Joseph Marshall
371 Mrs Mary Perry
371 Gabriel Santos
371 Marriano A Cabral
373 Manuel Perry
374 Arthur Borges
374 Manuel J Boteilho
375 Joseph Rodericque
375 Manuel Perry
377 Frank Pacheco
377 Frank B Medeiros
379 Timothy T Slattery
379 Christopher Correia
379 Mrs Mary A Pimental
381 Constantine Gonsalves
381 Manuel Souza
381 Frank Rogers
383 Mrs Mary Baxter
383 Joseph H Fernandez
383 Antone Rego
389 Antone Pacheco
389 Manuel Almeida
389 Joseph Serpa
390 Edmund Caron
390 August Silvia
390 Archer Benjamin
390½ Mrs Mary Costa

390½ Frank Jose
390½ Manuel Ninze
391 Joseph Costa
391 Joseph D Perry
396 August Silva
396 Mrs Mary Rose
396 Manuel Mello
396 Antone Marshall
396 Joseph Rego
396 Manuel Silva
397 John Sylvia
399 Joe Cunha
399 Francis Silva
399 Michael Silva
399 Frank Rose
400 Pierre Paquette
403 Manuel Andrada
403 George B Coleman
412 Nicola Ramos
418 Manuel F Sylvia
418 Peter Curley
419 John Lemos
419 John Moniz
422 Henry Stephenson
422 Joseph Perry
422 Manuel Raposa
423 Athur Tomlinson
423 Edward O Webb
423 John J Chadwick
426 Manuel P Arruda
434 Samuel Goldstein
434 Bonet Goldstein
434 Mrs Mary Perry
434 Mrs Maria Allen
438 John Seifert
438 William Makin
438r William Gregory
438r John Clayton
440 Manuel B Silva
440 Mrs Margaret McKee
446 Joseph Souza
446 Antone Paes
448 Mrs Emily Costa
450 Mrs Mary Hall
452 John F Silva
452 Patrick McGowan
0 Abram Simiansky
464 Mrs Mary E Smith
464 Frank Toledo
472 Joseph Medeiros
472 Frank Menez
476 Mrs Mary Joyce
476 Joseph Spinner
480 Manuel Nichols
480 Jose de Theophilo
480 Michael Macdonald
490 W N Morosse
493 Harry Wilcox
493 Eugene Martin
496 Joseph Cushing
496 George Bernier
496 Louis Belanger
497 Joseph Tetreault
498 Robert Harney
498 Mrs Matilda Fuller
500 William Wesolowski
500r Joe Vasco
500r Manuel P Silva
501 George Dedads
501 James V Ronan
503 Manuel F Vargers
504 Louis Constant
505 Manuel Williams
507 Antone Souza
507 David Labelle
507 John Aradia
509 Mrs Elizabeth Durant
509 Thomas Crook
510 Manuel Mello
510 Antone Geraia
511 Edward Jarvis
514 Manuel Rego
514 John Costa
514 Manuel Costa
516 Patrick Benoit
519 Anthony J Armour
519 Joseph J Ray
519 William G Robert
519 Israel L Carrier
519 John Platt
525 Joseph Masse
531 Cyrille Mombleau
531 Clement Languedoc
531 Joseph Beche
533 Mrs Marceline Quinton
533 Adam Kersec
533 Annie Prince
533 Calixte Hebert
533 Mrs William Brouillette
539 Frank Govisky
539 Adam Kersez
558 Yosef Golezynski
559 Joseph Marques
559 John Devine
560 Timothy Carey
560 John Devine
560 Charles Doyle
564 Manuel Mello
566 Thomas Martin
570 James Sharp
577 Napoleon J Fourneau
577 Rev S Basinski
581 Louis Desnoyer
596 Fred H Bellmore
596 James McDonald
596 Joseph Charrette
596 Samuel Charette
600 Wilfred Benoit

South Second—con
600 Mrs Mary Quintin
600 Joseph Oliver
604 W M Baudette
604 Mrs Pauline Denjoux
604 Zepherin Mailloux
604 John B Gregoire
604 Elzear Guerette
608 Herbert Z Fournier
608 William Mathieu
608 Joseph Mello
608 Philias Gregoire
612 Abbot Clark
612 Joseph H A Roy
612 Paul Desjardens
612 Elzear Lenderville
616 Louis Bourassa
616 Silas Langlois
616 Treffle Berube Jr
622 Alphonse Lacourse

SOUTH SIXTH

10 Pardon G Thompson
12 Dr Winston Stephens
13 Mrs Olive P Ward
14 Mrs Abbie H Weeden
17 E Stanley Robbins
20 Rose Standish
21 Mrs Annie F Davis
22 Mrs Helen K Milliken
24 John Wing
26 Mrs A Martin Pierce
27 Dr Edward M Whitney
33 Albert C Kirby
34 Edgar W Russell
34 Ludger Poisson
37 Charles F Wing
38 John McCullough
39 Francis T Aikin
42 Isaac L Ashley
46 Charles H Church
47 Rev William G Geoghegan
48 Oren I Trafford
51 James A Tilton
53 Frank S Wilcox
54 Gedeon Poisson
55 Thomas Croacher
56 Agnes G Thuman
57 Robert G Bennett
58 Henry T Bulman
60 Charles G Woods
61 Harry Chapman
63 Frank Rogers
67 Herbert Jones
65 Daniel J Sullivan
65 Horace W Swift
66 Della M Butler
67 Henry A L Woodcock
68 George W Burgess
69 Joseph T Edwards
70 Robert H Crawford
71 Albert N Brown
71 Mrs Elizabeth C Fisher
72 Max Levy
73 Mrs Elizabeth E Merry
76 Charles S Wing
76 Barjona D Tripp
78 Moise D Prevost
78 Mrs Sarah S Tripp
78 John A Tripp
80 James McWeeney
84 Joseph Chase Jr
84 David Stephenson
85 C A Paul
85 Mrs Ella Ballou
85 Edward Ballou
86 Howard Ensen
86 Mrs Hermine Le Rocque
87 Mrs Mary A Handy
87 George L Durfee
87 David B Caswell
87½ Annie J Muspratt
88 Mrs Elsie M Chase
88 Mrs Priscilla C Delano
89 Antone L Sylvia
93 William Whipple
93 Clifton L Sowle
94 Rev Joaquim Cardoza
94 Rev Fortunato Neves
94 Rev Manuel A Silva
95 Leander C Courtwright
95 William J O'Brien
96 William J Best
96 Mrs Jane Manning
97 Charles Joseph
97 John E Joseph
98 Franciscan Missionary of Mar.
100 Hendrique Silva
100 Thomas Bainbridge
100 Nelson Reid
101 Misses Kirwin
103 George L Briggs
103 Frank L Pope
104 Alfred C Ricketson
105 Dr Edmond F Cody
106 Manuel N Xavier
107 Neil Gallagher
107 Mrs Mary Wady
110 Manuel Goulart
112 Edward F McAloon
112 Frank McLaughlin
114 Lewis Mallick
114 Mrs Ida Cohen
116 Tracy Marks
116 Arthur R Howland

116 William H Crook
118 Thatcher S Swift
118 Mrs Susan K Cornell
120 Irving M Tripp
120 Joseph Schofield
120 Mrs Eliza A Chartier
120 Joseph H Diamond
122 John Sylvia
122 Frederic Lewis
122 Alexander Lewis
122 John Lewis
531 Henry Boardman

SOUTH WATER

9 Alves Gomes
13 Oliver Hart
19 Frederick C Allen
56 Manuel Veira
62 Isaac Gomes
63 Casimer Roush
90 Manuel Peters
127 Manuel A Gomes
129 Joseph Correia
141 Rose Gonsalves
141 Daniel F Hannibal
144 Frank Perry
141 Marie Hall
144 Everett Tripp
175 Antonio N Leyton
177 Joseph de Barros
179 Mrs Josephine Turner Sinclair
181 John L Valles
191 Manuel Andrada
191 Rosa Sylvia
199 James A Drayton
205 Joseph A Duarte
205 Charles A Helme
221 Lawrence Barros
221 Samuel Spencer
221 Mrs Louisa Odams
221 Mrs Daisy Spencer
225 Juan Almeida
281 Mrs Mary Williams
281 Manuel Canneca
285 Antonio Lopes
285 John Monteiro
287 Joseph Perry
291 Joseph Alves
291 Antone Brodrick
316 Mrs Nellie Andra
316 Joseph Lomba
317 Joseph Gomes
317 Louis Gomes
317 Mrs Manuel Dias
317 Manuel Duarte
317 Louis Andra
320 Antone Gomes
327 Joseph Kaplan
327 Robert Roderique
328 Joseph Enos
335 Henry Costa
335 Joseph Ferreira
335 Esther Wasbutsky
335 Mrs Constance Rogers
343 Simon Davidson
348 John Britto
348 Hector R DeCosta
349 Mrs Phoebe Duarte
349 Mary Calder
353 Manuel Pina
353 John Comeau
356 Manuel F Pina
356 John Fonseca
356 John A Pinto
356 Henry Perry
356 Alfred Monteiro
371 Mrs Mary C Duvals
371 Heiman Schuster
371 Hyman Fishman
379 Mrs Kate Lomba
385 Joseph Mackler
395 Mrs Julia Lopes
395 Fredelle De Barros
395 Joseph Perry
401 Hendrick W Morse
401 Vetrine Pina
402 Leando Barros
402 John A Duarte
406 Millett Galvin
406 Charles Rodericque
407 Antone Ramos
407 Frank Costa
407 Manuel Souza
409 Nathan Alpert
410 Harry Cohen
412 Caesar M Santos
412 John Ramos
412 Peter Cruz
412 Nicolo Rainos
417 Florentine Fermine
418 Boa Centura Barros
418 Joaquim Silvia
421 Manuel Silva
422 Manuel Gomes
424 Isaac Shapiro
426 Samuel Cohen
426 Simon Cohen
426 Samuel Plotnick
426 Samuel Forman
427 Manuel Frazier
428 Abraham Feingold
429 Antonio Luiz
429 Ernest Costa
430 Nathan Schuster
435 John Ramos
435 John Hart
435 Mrs Mary Oliver

South Water—con
435r John Nunes
437r Sebastien Almeida
437r Antone Alfama
438 Joseph Lopez
438 Mrs Justa Gomes
440 Manuel Cabral
440 Mrs Mary De Costa
440 Manuel Martin
445 Manuel Souza
445 Greggore Martin
455 Samuel Ostroff
455 Samuel Masaninoff
455 Wolfe Schwartz
455 Joseph Shapiro
455 Morris Cohen
456 Philip Leen
456 Manuel Costa
456 Frank Costa
456 Manuel Croney
458 Julius Robidovitz
458 Antone Enos
458 Mrs Mary Robidovitch
464 Frank Marks
464 Jules Andrada
464 Manuel Ventura
467 Robert Benjamin
472 Julius Goodman
472 Antone Soares
472 Harry Drazen
474 Maurice Polonsky
474 Louis Nisson
475 Mathias Souza
475 Hyman Goodman
477 Charles Savarid
480 Abraham Kroudvird
480 Lewis Rubin
480 Mrs Rosa Garmansky
481 Virginio Viera
483 Abram Cohen
486 John Oliver
487 John Marshall
490 Harry Davis
494 Louis Lansky
497 Hyman Cohen
498 Joseph Herman
500 Israel Mirsky
505 Avelviro A Oliver
505 Mrs Annie Fernandes
505 Haskell Horenstein
508 Louis Shuster
508 Max Burstein
509 Aurilo Roza
509 Max Ambash
512 Joseph Cohen
512 Mrs Martha Frifield
513 Manuel Cabral
515 Joseph Roscovitz
515 Jacob Simiansky
516 Morris Cohen
516 Hyman Cohen
521 Harris Edelstein
521 Mrs Gertrude Finklestein
525 Manuel S Grace
526 David Alpert
528 Joaquim Fartado
528 Mrs Rose Falk
534 Morris L Schwartz
535 Amador Sylvia
535 Manuel L Grace
536 Joaquim Dias
536 Manuel Medeiros
536 Joseph Miranda
543 Austin L Pierce
544 John Souza
544 Joseph Soares
544 Joseph Francis
544 Mrs Jessie Campus
550 Manuel Alvas
550 Manuel Correia
550 Manuel Silva
550 Joseph Sphrain
550 Joseph Amaral
555 Frank P Sarmento
556 Max Bronshpigel
556 Manuel Amaral
559 Frank Perry
560 Manuel Silva
562 John Alphonse
564 Manuel S Sorto
564 Joseph A Lima
569 Barnard Greenstein
570 Harvey L Delano
570 Owen O'Donnell
570 Lewis Pacheco
570 Mrs Emily Holmes
573 John L Carvalho
573r Manuel Almeida
574 Manuel Morgado
575 Mrs Mary P Souza
584 Joseph Souza
584 Antone E Christo
585 Julio Afonce
586 John Sylvia
589 Felix Stone
589 Wolf Gleckman
589 Joseph Sabins
595 John Lima
595 Manuel Sylvia
595 Francisco Mello
600 Max Levenson
600 Harry Ragin
600 John Tavares
608 Manuel P Vincent
608 Domingos J Espinolo
614 Marianno Tavares
614 Mary Nunes
616 Manuel Dwarte

616 John G Rose
616 Mariano Silva
617 David Weitzman
618 Joseph Medeiros
618 Antone Rose
618 Joseph Silva
623 Antone Souza
623 John Medeiros
624 Manuel Antone Jr
630 Mrs Emiline Enos
630 John Barboza
630 Frank Enos
630 Antone Pereira
631 Joseph Costa
631 Matthew Souza
637 John Souza
638 Abraham Shkolnick
638 Mary Frates
641 Manuel King
641 Joaquim Pacheco
642 Louis Levovsky
646 Manuel B Silva
646 Joseph Mello
646 Manuel G Brown
654 Manuel Viveiros
654 John Perreira
658 Joseph Jerome
660 Manuel Dourte
661 Joseph S Machado
664 Michael Menes
664 John Joseph
672 Frank Jules
679 August Medeiros
680 Manuel Pacheco
680 Joseph Silva
680 Manuel P Alexander
689 Antone Carvalho
685 Manuel Mello
686 Joseph Ferreira
692 Manuel J Baptiste
692 Louis Pimental
692½ Joaquim Leandro
692½ Mrs Mary Silva
699 Joaquin Duarte
700 Morris Schuster
700 Abraham Berkowitz
700 Samuel Cudish
700r Manuel Avila
701 Manuel Linhares
706 Frank Medeiros
706 Charles D Tavares
712 Delor Martin
712 William Rogers
715 Joseph Souza
715 John J Perry
715 Joseph Sylvia
723 Manuel Correia
723 John Mello
730 John Fish
730 Charles Tillinghast
739 Mrs Maria Baptiste
739 Isaac Rothkop
743 Mrs Hannah Rock
751 Philip Munroe
751 Mary Bonneau
751 Manuel Silva
761 Manuel Tercheira
775 Jack Rapoza
775 Joseph Silva
783 Joseph V Medeiros
785 Isaac Alpert
787 Mrs Margaret Sweeney
795 John Derby
795 Abraham Vishnefsky
799 John Watson
805 Patrick Carney
806 Manuel Correia
815 Aaron Simiansky
819 Joseph Schick
819 Michael Costeria
819 Alex Hajkoc
819 Joseph Olevitz
819 Cierpial Wladystin
819 Joseph Uliwicz
819 John Olevitz
839 John H Hope
841 Mrs Ellen O'Brien
841 Annie Golden
845 John Boteilho
855 Eugene Brunnelle
859 Louis Lavault
863 Desire Dupont
868 Isadore Bouchard
870 Clovis Menard
871 Bernard Luminasky
874 Mrs Elizabeth Hartley
874 Thomas Grimshaw
877 Pilot Dawnorwitz
877 Matthew Quinlan
878 Edward H Gregory
878 John B Jackson
878 William Abrams
882 Eusebe Morrisette
882 William Cadaretto
883 Samuel Murphy
883 Robert Charnock
892 Alphonse Voyer
892 Treffle Lanier
893 Emanuel Kestenbaum
901 Jerome Cayouette
905 James M Dunlop
907 Joseph Raymond
909 Lois Brazeau
909 Homer Boisvert
910 Phoebe Gagneau
910 Levi Locherhell

South Water—con
910 Isadore Steben
911 James Charperles
917 Morris Richman
921 Mrs Mary E Ryan
926 Joseph Rabideau
926 Napoleon Guertin
926 Richard Martin
926 Philo Saporto
926 Henry Martin
927 Barnard Abrams
932 Meyer Levine
932 Annie Costa
932 Robert Roberts
939 Abraham Sullaway
945 John H Richardson
947 Amedee Delwyn
950 Gideon Rouillier
950 Marcille Saulnier
954 Stephen P Small
954 Charles Gilbert
954 Louis Beaumont
954 Gilbert Joly
954 David Joly
960 Alec Menard
968 Peter Letarte
968 Vitel Cote
968 Amedee Desmarais
968 Joseph Boucher
968 Mrs Nathalie Lajeunesse
975 Philomen Rousseau
975 Jean B Larochelle
975 Mrs Carrie Beaudette
975 Mrs Josephine Bartalow
985 Henry Duchaine
985 Joseph Enos
993 Dr J Napoleon Tessier
993 George E Fisher
993 Joseph Foye
995 Leon Goldstein
995 Henry Daudelin
1012 Henry Bonville
1012 Philip Prevost
1018 Eugene Charpentier
1018 Dr D A N Senesac
1020 Joseph Benjamin
1025r Patrick Walsh
1026 Fred Larch
1026 Frank J Lach
1026 Louis Morin
1039 Owen J Dowd
1043 L J Friedman
1043 I Friedman
1046 Charles D Tuell
1046 Mrs Catherine McFarland
1049 Mrs Ann Derby
1049 John J Bilsbarrow
1058 Joseph Pedro
1058 James Railton
1065 Dr Benjamin S Winslow
1073 Victor E Dupre
1073 Colin Barret Jr
1073 Alfred Gooselin
1074 Mrs Marceline Quintin
1081 Richard Feldon
1083 Mrs Octaive Dorey
1085 Stanley Morach
1085 Anthony Weskosky
1086 Joseph H Lebrun
1086 Ettiene Quintin
1088 John Varville
1092 Charles O Andrews
1101 Meyer Lipson
1101 Nelson Labombard
1103 Alphonse Fortin
1103 William Morey
1103 Joseph LeBlanc
1111 Samuel Bennett
1111 Dr Arthur R Adam
1111 George Roy

SPOONER

3 Benjamin H Clifford
4 John F Sylvia
4 Samuel V Madruga
5 Duleterio Cardoza
5 Mrs Marv Golden
8 Manuel Mello
9 Marion S Reed
9 John F Johnson
12 Robert H Murdy
19 Frank S Marks
21 Gabriel De Camp
21 William B Murray
21 Raul Perry
23 Joseph Boteilho
23 Manuel Bettencourt

SPRING

0 Abbott D McMullen
9 Mrs Lucy Carpenter
13 Willard C Flaherty
28 John Flahertv
28 Robert G Helme
30 Joseph Lopez
30 Paul Rossi
51 Charles J Griffin
56 Mrs Nora F Howland
56 Nancy B Fuller
60 Mrs Nancy P Burbank
72 F M Metcalf
84 Eloise A Hafford
93 Mrs Emily M Almy
96 John F Winters
98 Gardner T Sanford
101 Mrs Mary P Rugg

102 Mrs Emma T Church
103 Mrs Andrew G Pierce
106 Julia W Rodman

SPRUCE

1 Judith C Pierce
2 Herbert A Brown
2 Thomas A McGowan
3 Mrs Maria Aiken
5 Mrs Emma L Lee
6 Albert R Tallman
6 William R Parry
7 George H Miggins
7 Rev Nathaniel A Marriott
7 William Turner
8 Richard Fisher
8 Mrs Mary A Codding
10 Mary D Ward
10 Joseph F Greene
11 Frederick P Clark
11 Emerald A Remington
12 Delia A Gilmore
12 Samuel Entin
12 Frank W Bumpus
12 Emma Penney
13 Mrs Minnie A Borden
13 Mrs Emma Cornell
14 George A Sweeney
15 George F Tripp
16 Nathan Wheaton
17 Arthur Linden
19 Mrs Mary McCarthy
58 Mrs Hope A Carpenter
58 Willard F Raymond
59 Charles F Pierce
60 Mary A Teamoh
60 Mrs Sarah Warfield
61 Mrs Anna Stanton
63 Jerome Gonsalves
63 David Ruberstein
64 John T Drew
64 Peter Lyons
64r Joseph Sears
65 Alonza W Russell
65 Carl Dwight
65 Carlton Waite
66 Robert Trask
68 John A Perkins
69 Felix C Seguin
69 John Williams
70 Edward Francis
70 George W Perry
71 James McFarlin
72 William H Lincoln
72 Wilfred F Manchester
74 Alonzo V Jason Jr
74 Herbert E Davis

STACKHOUSE

0 John Frasier
7 Reginald E Rogerson
12 Manuel Mello
27 Nicholas Gonsalves
31 Antonio J Correia
42 Joseph E Sylvia
49 Jacintho M Davis

STANTON COURT

1 Manuel R Frates
3 Douglass Crossley
4 John Veira
4 Frank E Francis
4 Joseph Santos
4 Victor Mello
4 Joseph Francis
5 Thomas Osswald
7 Bernard Roderick
7 Manuel Sylvia

STAPLETON

9 Joao Barron
9 John J Souza
9 Benjamin Heyes
9 Joseph Lima
9 John Veira
16 Delphis Lebeau
16 Marianno Pacheco
16 Thomas H Roberts
18 George Wayne
18 Francis McDonnell
18 Richard Gilmore
20 John Bayreuther
21 Joseph R DePorto
23 John Brindle
27 Ralph Crosydale
27 Robert Taylor
28 Michael Quinn
28 Mrs Emma Talbot
32 Ruth Whittingcom
32 Doctor Gorner
32 Mrs Elizabeth Billington
34 Robert E Hindle
34 Walter Ryder
34 Rcland Reed
34 Mrs Sarah Hardman

STATE

21 Mrs Honorah Mahoney
43 Mrs Amanda Ginnochio
44 T Merritt Gifford
45 M Joseph Crowley
46 Mrs Fonshonetta H Hussey
46 William F Farrar
47 George H Weeks
47 Arthur B Brightman

State—con
48 Henry S Chase
48 George H Lowrie
49 James Ferguson
49 John Robinson
51 John Neild
54 Frank I Neild
54 Edward H Cook
55 Henry Field
56 Charles S Washburn
56 Joseph A Cronin
57 Henry W Nichols
60 Henry Howard
60 Eusebe Gosselin
62 James G Harding
62 Fred S Stanton
63 Alfred M Gifford
63 James T Heron
64 George Coffin
64 Elliott P Harris
66 Clara L Tripp
66 Wellington A Francis
68 Harry C Brightman
68 Mrs Clara O Hathaway
72 Edmund F Kelley
72 Teresa Thacker
73 Mrs Lorinda M Wilbur
73 Henry H Dews
74 William B Macomber
77 Mrs Alice A Russell
80 Dr Ned Stanley
81 Mrs Susan A McPherson
81 Misses Ashley
82 Rev Lester M Conrow
84 Mrs Sarah S Dixon
87 Mrs Mary M Lawton
87 Olin S Paine
89 Willard O Clark
89 Mrs Susan A Terry
91 Paul Howland
91 Albert H Swift
92 Albert Sloper
93 Charles S Ashley
94 J Frank Kirk
96 Mrs Marv H Barney
97 John L Weeks
98 L Lucius D Smith
98 William L McDavitt
100 Benjamin F Horr
101 William H Tillson
102 Robert G McKinley
102 Mary F Rafferty
104 Peter Couroussi
121 Arthur F Caswell
121 William F Upjohn
123 Mrs Mary J Taylor
123 Clara Stratton
124 Joseph Dawson
127 Louis Rasscette
128 James A Dorrigan
131 Michael Wilson
131 Mrs Mary Williams
131 Mrs Isabella Ray
131 Patrick Reddy
132 Patrick H O'Brien
133 Timothy Donahue
133 Edward S Harrington
133 Daniel Ratcliffe
134 Julian A Sweet
134 Mrs Isadore G Deming
138 George F Wilson
138 William Oldfield
140 Ferdinand Loreau
140 Alfred Strome
140r Claus F Forsblom
143 George R Hooper
143 Joseph B Smith
144 Patrick J Doyle
144 Azarie Chaille
145 George E Bellenoit
145 Joseph H Sullivan
146 Thomas J Summers
146 Orion Ricketson
147 Jeffrey Gibbons
147 Joseph H Provost
149 Alfred Beaucaire
149 Mrs Ann Ryan
160 Herbert Smith
161 Albert Dubois
161 Joseph Verronneau
162 John T Jefferson
162 Walter Sullivan
163 Mrs Alice Narv
163 Mrs Sarah J Mazoh
164 Mrs Mary Voyer
164 William Miller
169 Harrv Lewis
169 Mrs Matilda Lewis
172 Lawrence Rettinger
172 William Godere
173 Mrs Josephine Archambeault
174 Horace Allie
175 Beloni Bessette
176 Mary Kilmartin
176 Isadore Coderer
177 John A Valley
178 Mrs Melvina Lizotte
178 Mrs Mary Booth
179 Delene Deneault
180 Mrs Mary L Gould
180 Moise Gallant
181 John B Dupuis Jr
181 Joseph Charpentier
181 Melvina Carreau
181 Mrs Jane Tetlow

182 John J Grimes
182 Patrick Gannon
183 Mrs Johanna Downey
184 Mrs Mary E O'Brien
185 William Charpentier
186 Henry Barrett
187 Stephen W Downey
187 Napoleon Patnaude
188 John Bourbeau
189 Anatole England
189 Louis England
190 Aldei Breault
190 Mrs Henriette Puplessis
191 Oliver Robert
191 Mrs Hanora Kelley
198 David Breault
198 Olivier Gauthier
198 Alfred Martel
198 Baptiste Comeau
198 David Langlois
198 Arthur Poudrier
198 Anthony Rodier
198r David Duncan
198r James McSally
198r Joseph LeBlanc
198r Gilbert Reindeau
198r Edward Gilbert
198r Eugene O'Leary
198r Daniel Lewis
199 Alfred Voesin
199 Napoleon Duval Jr
202 Joseph Savarier Jr
202 George W G Russell Jr
202 Joseph Bergeron
202 George Weyeld
202 Stanislas Plante
202 Thomas Alexander
202 Elie Tremblay
202 Joseph E Savarier
202 Zephir Cyr
202 Pierre Mailloux
205 Mrs Admene Therian
205 Mrs Ellen Callahan
205 Alfred Varieur
206 Daniel J Sheehan
206 Joseph C Vincent
207 Susan T Harrington
207 John Edmond Birch
207 William J Packard
207½ Thomas F Donahue
207½ Wilfred Lorette
207½ Dolor Gauthier
208 Dennis J Sullivan
208 Francis Sweeney
209 Adolphus LeClair
211 Samuel Beaumont
211 David K Thompson
212 Hector Roullier
212 Fortunate Gosselin
213 Mrs Catherine Crapo
216 Joaquim Plomondon
216 Charlotte Dalas
218 Timothy Hourihan
218 Patrick J Sullivan
219 Ann Fitzsimmons
219 John Gavaghan
219 Mrs Catherine Burns
219 Thomas McLee
220 Timothy Lowney
220 John J Durkin
222 Thomas Laughlin
222 John J Sullivan
222 Francis H Johnson
223 David Metthe
224 John E Lawrence
225 Joseph Pelardy
226 Clovis Lague
226 William Hall
226 Francis X Houle
226 Charles A Leonard
266r John Stucker
226r E A Prichette
227 Adelard Bonneau
227 John Reynolds
227 Thomas St Germain
228 William Bowker
228 Antone E Cardoza
228 J Patrick Reddy
228r Lawrence Peterson
229 Omar Smith
229 Charles A Quill
229 Alexander Smith
229 Mark Anthony
229 Isaac Gotlieb
229 Michael Gousie
229 Emery Langlois
230 William P Rourke
230 Paul Courtemarche
230 Hyman Kravetz
232 Thomas Roy
237 John O'Neil
237 Edward Quinn
239 Timothy Calnen
239 Edward Tromley
240 Zephir Bessette
240 Joseph I Boucher
241 William H Wrigley
241 Edward Boyer
241 Thomas Keenan
242 Michael McGrath
242 Mrs Mary Pinkham
243 William C Young
243 Daniel A Calnen
244 Misses Kane
244 William D Burns
244½ Mrs E Brierly
245 Hormidas L'Homme
246 Moise Bariteau

State—con
247 Frederick Fisher
247 Joseph A Labrode
247 Mrs Mary Lomba
249 Prosper Foisy Jr
249 Fred Lemaire
251 Amasa R Fissell
251 Pierre Breault
251 Christopher Denham
275 Mrs Mary Perry
275 Omer E Belair
275 John L Blanchard
366 Moses Deneault
366 T Arthur Deneault
366 Lucien Beauregard
370 Frank P Briggs
370 Daniel Connolly
371 Mary Mrs Bourget
371 Henry Hacking
371 George Patten

STEPHEN

39 Caesar Gonsalves
48 Manuel King
54 Jacintho Barboza
59 John Correia
59 Adrianno Camara

STONE

5 Thomas J Borden
7 Antone A Marshall
9 Henry O'Leary
10 James T Lanagan
12 William H Lanagan

STOWELL

25 Edward J Gamble
25 Antonio Gonsalves
35 Manuel A Mendoza
38 Henry Hobson
39 Jacintho E Medeiros
39 Mark Dias
42 William O Stevens
44 John L Sullivan
44 Mrs Mary Enos
44 Mrs Claudina Moniz
48 Alfred Veira
55 Frank Medeiros
55 Manuel Bent Jr

STUDLEY

6 Milton Taber
6 Charles Castle
6 Lawrence T Woolfenden
8 Mrs Rachael Woods
8 Samuel Turner Jr
8 Hobart Tower
9 John Cryer
9 Michael Riley Jr
9 James W Gillett
10 John Ogden
10 Edward Chippendale
10 Mrs Eliza Leach
11 Jeremiah Marsden
11 William B Carr
11 Charles Chadwick
12 James O Heap
12 Thomas McPeak
12 William H Whittaker
13 Isaac Livesley Jr
13 William Whittaker Jr
13 Margaret Storan
14 Oliver La Berge
14 Mark Gorham
14 John S Smith
15 Herbert Atkinson
15 William Worsley
16 Francis M Hatch
16 Edmund Dalbec
17 James L York
17 Joseph M Sears
18 George E Raymond
18 Richard Clifford

SULLIVAN

1 Frederick I Morse
2 Elder Howard L Chase
3 Gentil Pina
4 R H Woodley
5 Mrs Sarah Woodlin
7 Mrs Isabella Pugh

SUMMER

42 Harriet L Miller
44 David J Russell
46 F Lewin Pope Jr
48 Lot B Bates
50 Lewis L Symonds
54 William E Searell
54 Mrs Mary J Searell
58 James C Ashley
62 Charles J Johnson
62 Mrs Cynthia Scribner
65 Mary Crapo
65 Mrs Mary B Jenney
66 Edward L Paull
66 John F Grade Jr
68 John Connelly
68 Joseph C Forand
69 Henry T Chase
69 Mrs Annie A Gray
72 Mrs Rebecca R Peirce
72 Margaret J Heighton
81 Charles S Paisler

81 Mrs Emma A Hadley
83 Thomas Nickerson
83 Arthur W Forbes
100 Edward E F Potter
103 Charles H Vinal
105 Laurence S Perry
107 Frank H Purington
110 Rev Michael J Owens
110 Rev Hugh J Smyth
110 Rev Joseph P Lyons
111 Mrs Amanda M Blackler
115 Misses Davis
115 Mrs Robie A Emerson
127 Joseph Hargraves
127 Thomas Stephenson
128 Edward Meaney
130 Mrs Harland C Chadwick
130 Louisa Emery
130 Joseph G Boucher
130½ Frank L Mulcahey
131 Franklin C Bennett
131 Thomas Greene
136 Mrs Cordelia M Quimby
137 George W Paine
137 Fred Butterfield
140 Charles E Hardy
141 Isaiah P Pratt
141 Mrs Esther Bennett
141 Daniel T Hillman
144 Mrs Harriet L Fish
145 Mrs Susan Ruggles
148 Mrs Josiah A Dexter
149 George Pickens
149 Vesta E Hussey
150 William H Thomas
154 Charles B Sayles
155 Samuel R Brownell
158 Daniel L Connor
160 Harold D Slocum
162 Joseph N Gage
164 Charles Thompson
167 Mrs George F Brown
170 George F Bosworth
171 Warren A Simpson
174 Charles F Smith
177 Martin Gerraughty
177 George C Bumpus
184 Michael McAuley
184 Ernest F Von Flatern
185 Felix L Sumpter
190 Mrs Caroline B M Hussey
190 Charles H Bartlett
191 Robert T Bradshaw
193 George N Dyer
194 Mrs Annie E Dayton
197 Hiram Higham
198 Mrs Elizabeth Crowell
198 Otis H Almy
205 William Bryant
209 William O Martin
210 Capt Joseph M Simms
211 Charles M Bly
213 Fred F Moulton
216 Mrs Mattie V Clarke
218 Simeon B Livesley
218 Mary E Sturtevant
220 Mrs Annie Murphy
233 William T Caswell
237 William H Killigrew
241 Albert J Barney Jr
242 Charles E King
250 James F Mannion
252 William J Glasgow
256 Thomas A Raymond
260 Hormidas Masse
260 George H Taylor
267 Hayden Coggeshall
285 Ellen A Harrington
286 John Lowe
287 Edward T Bannon
288 Misses Lee
289 William Cottrell Jr
289 William H Miller
290 Arthur S Ashley
290 William Hawkins
294 William F Murray
294 John Connors
299 Isaac W Phelps
303 William J Burrows
304 Walter S McPhail
304 Daniel J Curtis
307 S Bartlett Simmons
310 Thomas J Hennigan
311 George E Jepson
314 John P Stratton
316 William Armitage

SUMMER STREET COURT

0 Joseph Sulvay

SUMMIT

2 Frederick W Chase
4 John Budd
6 George M Dayton
6 George M Dayton Jr
7 Walter H Tripp
7 Mrs Caroline Brownell
28 Mrs Elizabeth Percy
29 Mrs Adelaide I Jones
31 Edgar M L Jackson
32 Charles N Broadbent
38 Mrs Annie J Lawes

SUTTON

1 John Corrigan

SWIFT

18 Mary Mello
18 Martin McDonald
22 Marion J DeCosta

Swift—con
22 Michael J Deady
22 Manuel J Floris
27 Jacinth Sylvia
27 Augustine Raposa
30 Charles J Bauer
33 Manuel Reis
33 Joseph L Costa
51 Mrs Mary Cruz
51 Francisco T Paiva
51 John Gracia
51 Frank G Cunha
52 Henry F Robbins
52 Mrs Rosa A Pickering
52 Manuel Lemos
53 Lawrence Vera
53 Manuel Lewis
68 Manuel Perry
69 Manuel Bento
69 Raul Medeiros
76 Walter L Matters
78 John P Martin
80 William Haworth
82 John Adams
84 Frank J Robinson
99 Henry Dutra
105 John Clegg
107 Frank Thomas
113 Joseph Rose
115 Frank F Correia
117 Antone Souza
119 Frank Arruda

SYCAMORE

21 Mrs Emily H Damon
22 Rev William F Davis
23 Nathan Jennings
23 Edward S Robenolt
24 Bert A Vance
25 Augustus H Mandell
26 Israel Sher
27 John L Gibbs
31 Mrs Jane Brightman
31 Harry J Simmons
32 Clifton C Chambers
32 John T Hathaway
33 A A Tripp
33 Jacques Schuler
36 John S Cabal
37 George R Deane
39 Frank Milliken
41 Mrs Mary E Wilcox
43 Andrew H Donaghy
44 Armour J Grenier
44 Arsene J Rousseau
45 Michael F McKiernan
45 William W Sawyer
46 Mary J Halloran
46 Rose McCormick
47 Henry A Sawyer
48 Waldo E Underwood
48 William N Sherman
49 Addie W Poole
52 Margaret Marsden
57 Loranus C Fish
58 Mrs Laura J Richards
58 Mrs Addie H Davon
59 Walter H Parsons
59 Benjamin F Wordell
60 Charles B Allen
60 William Hawes
63 Miss K V Brennan
69 Lemuel W Hayes
69 Albert C Welch
70 Mrs Sarah F Shaw
70 George Drew
71 Thomas H Fuller
72 Joseph M Lobo
73 Clifford P Sherman
74 Anna L Jennings
75 Mrs Sarah F Smith
75 William H H Leach
80 Joseph Nelson
83 Almedus G W Tripp
83 Charles Raymond
85 Walter S Potter
85 Mrs Mary F Davis
88 John Bauer
88 Otto Fichtenmayer
101 Walter G Hamlen
103 Mrs Ruth H Reed
104 Herbert F Mosher
105 Frank M Fisher
106 Ezelia Burke
107 Mrs Sylvia S Haskins
108 Frank V Mecado
108 James Carr
108 Joseph Gero
108 Mrs Mary E McGurty
113 Mrs Annie Marble
114 Alfred E Rainford
115 Charles C Lee
116 Sumner Peirce
117 Ashbury A Mayo
117 Jeremiah M Taber
119 Cyrus E Taber
119r Abraham Luscomb
120 Joshua G Doane
121 Oscar E Johnson
123 Edmund J Barry
129 James P Swenson
131 Mrs Sarah A Dennison
131 James E Maloy
135 George E Davenport
137 Frank G Tripp
148 Thomas Bradbury
150 Charles S Cory

150 Mrs Adeline Briggs
154 Edgar B Crosby

SYLVIA

12 Mrs Marion Davignon
17 Manuel Souza
28 Elias H Reynolds
60 Ozee Breault

SYLVIA'S COURT

0 Louis Gracia
0 Mary G Sylvia

TABER

57 Anthony S Lewis
57 Manuel Andrews
77 Joseph M Attaide
77 Robert T Borden

TALLMAN

8 Vital Allain
8 Henry Cournoyer
8 Eugene St Gelais
8 Wilfred Belisle
8 Napoleon Bertrand
12 Jude Leger
12 Oliver Babineau
16 Francois Duval
16 Mrs Victorio Durand
16 Joseph Blanchard
16 Joseph Gagnon
20 Martin Le Blanc
20 August Messier
20 Eudore Croteau
24 Odille La Palne
24 Victor Boucher
24 Arthur Rondeau
24 Placide Maillotte
28 Michel Bessette
28 Fred Lemieux
28 T William Buteau
28 Adolphus Paquin
28 George Borden
28 Peter Fletcher
28 Alexis Govette
32 Gilbert G Robichaud
32 Stanislas St Gelais
32 Patrick Kelley
33 John D Gaudette
33 Joseph Dubois
33 Gilbert Savage
33 Edward H Cormier
39 Pierre Bourgeois
39 Henry Goguen
39 John Richards
39 Henry Mevins
45 Melos Allaine
45 Joseph Michaud
45 Bartholomew Gobeille
50 Mrs Mary Tremblay
50 Donat Depault
50 Frank Lambert
50 Donat Monette
51 Francois X Plante
51 Phileas Jodoin
51 James Buckley
51 Mrs Adelle Vouture
51 Jean B Jaillet
54 Ludger Caron
55 Joseph St Aubin
55 Pierre Hebert
55 Joseph Chicoine
55 William Charron
59 Eliza Boardman
59 Arthur P Cloutier
60 Albert Dumas
60 Omer L'Heureux
60 Alma Perisier
60 Alfred Chagnon
63 Joseph Ouillette
63 William Tetreault
64 Paul Godere
64 Antoine Deschaine
64 Didia Cyr
64 Joseph P Blais
64 Eugene Isabell
66 Leopold Bellemare
68 Joseph Gagnon
68 Napoleon Duval
72 Charles Laplante
78 Henry Larose
78 Honore Payette
78 Percy Cottle
78 Saul Pothier
80 Elphege Robert
85 Lewis Hamer
87 Mrs Virginie Coulombe
87 William Bolduc
88 Philip Auclair
88 Calixte Richard
88 Gotleib Smalla
88 Oliver Baron
90 Edwin J Healy
90 William Martin
90 Manuel Tuma
91 Lucien Toussant
92 J Uldric Robert
92 Charles Kobza
93 Mrs Mary Murphy
93 Remi J Payette
95 Wilhelm Moser
95 Max F Boehler
95 Mrs Louise Boehler
98 Edwin Ashworth
100 Ernest Lemieux
104 Pierre Cloutier
104 Isaie Lussier
104 Raphael Beloin

Tallman—con
106 Joseph P Pelletier
109 Edward Shutz
109 Albert C Richard
109 Joseph Caron
109 Mrs Teresa Shutz
110 Leon Pelletier
111 Edmund H Yell
111 James Waddington
111 Peter Ledoux
113 Annis Cejka
113 Joseph Sibor
113 Mrs Clara Jacques
119 William D Hamel
119 Cleophas Pelletier
119 Mrs Melina Dubuque
120 Arthur Bourque
120 Frank Hey
125 Alexander Messier
125 Frank Teilliere
125 Joseph Lussier
126 Everett Hawes
126 John Myer
126 Lawrence Gauthreau
126 Onesime Richard
129 Ernest Whitehead
129 Joseph Mason
129 Ojeda Gignac
130 William Majndle
130 Jonathan Wolstenholme
131 Arthur N Bessette
131 Anthony Entwistle
131 Fred Barber
131 Martin Jennings
131 Robert Latham
131 Romeo Lemire
132 Remi Pombriend
132 Charles Maynard
132 Honore Bergeron
132 Thomas Harwood
134 Mrs Caroline McGregor
134 Louis Seligson
134 Alphonse Gaucher
134 Mendi Seligson
134 John Webster
135 Powell Wassner
135 Joseph F Kraihanzel Jr
136 Venzel Kares
136 Mrs Lucy Hawkswell
136 Walter Walsh
137 Thomas Parkinson
137 Esdras J Lavoie
137 Samuel Allain
140 Alfred Therrien
140 David Boucher
140 Zepherin Deslauriers
141 Mrs Rose Malige
141 Frederick Lussier
141 Willard E Reynolds
144 M Metcalf
144 William Garrity
144 Frank Halma
145 Hormidas Bergeron
145 John Telliere
147 Joseph McDuff
147 Alfred Levesque
148 Manuel Pacheco
148 Henry J Fournier
148 Joseph Barber
150 Eugene Lemire
150 Jean B Lafaille
150 Patrick H Powers
150 James Carter
151 Stephen Dion
151 Charles Duhamel
151 George Tetreault
151 William J Rostron
152 Mrs Caroline Ward
152 John Ward
152 John Oddy
152 Franz Prihoda
154 Thomas Kershaw
154 John Schofield
154 John Rothwell
154 James A Ivey
155 Elizabeth Reilly
155 William Hunter
155 John A Miller
155 James W Waterhouse
156 Harry Martin
156 Joseph Walda
156 William Nuttall
159 Hermenegilde Castonguay
159 Alphonse Castonguay
159 Alphonse Gasse
159 Joseph Lizotte
159 Napoleon Gregoire
159 Raoul Gasse

TALLMAN'S LANE

4 Joseph S Marques

TARKILN HILL ROAD

0 Clarence E Lawrence
0 Mrs Anna L Hathaway
0 Henry Marcotte
0 Philip Gray
0 Constantine Frates
0 Mrs Martha J W Andrews
0 Maxime Daigle
0 Armand LaCroix
0 William Wolstenholme
0 Mrs Henrietta T Reed
0 Isaac Reed
0 Charles H Manchester
0 Stephen F Manchester
0 Christopher Lackenmacher
0 Edwin F Davis
0 Avery O Parker

0 John W Spencer
0 James R Rutkowski
0 Almanza Tripp
0 Damase Leduc
0 Henry J Ladieu
0 Elmer L Burchill
0 Mrs Charlotte E Evans
0 Mrs Emma P Doyle

THATCHER

1 Harold Roylance
2 Damasse Desmarais
2 Esdras Chicoine
5 William Luchraft
7 William Gallagher
7 Mrs Rachel Crone
15 Benjamin Wilkinson
16 Andre Brien
16 John B Samoissette
16 James Daly
17 Mrs Julia Wignall
19 Eugene Brunnelle
19 Pierre Rondeau
23 Alfred Lavoie
23 Walter Lees
23 Arthur Roy
23 Edgar Dube

THOMAS

17 James Dwyer
59 Martin S Nelson
60 Mrs Annie Buckley
60 Mrs Catherine A Riley
62 Charles E Pierce
62 William B Perry
63 Abner B Pope
64 John H Barrows
64 Mrs Laura A Allan
72 Whitney E Bates
75 Wilfrid L Houle
75 Joseph W Webster
77 Mrs Mary E Lilley
78 James Purcell
81 James E Card
81 Mrs Annie Morris
82 Frank Post
82 Charles S Spooner
83 D Herbert DeMoranville
85 Misses Chaney
85 Caroline S Parlow

THOMPSON

Peter Healey
Joseph S Perry
Manuel Terry
John Edmonson
6 Joseph L Souza
10 John E Shaw
25 Mrs Rose Lemaire
25 Frank Catelli
25 Etta M Tripp
26 Albert Cornell
26 Enos C Paul
26 Albert Whitty
27 Carl B Carlsen
27 Michael A Scullen
30 John A Jason
30 John Meader
30 Arthur Michon
30 John Medeiros
30 Frank J Perry
32 Matthew J Hart
32 William Campbell
32 Frederick H Tripp
35 Joseph A Silva
35 Peter P Kinniery
35 Mrs Marguerita Rose
36 Manuel Jacintho
36 John De Mello
39 John M Silva
39 Daniel T Hanley
42 Antone Joseph
43 Saul Taylor
43 Albert Sachs
43 William King
45 Thomas J Sylvia
46 Mrs Lillian M Kelley
46 Otis W Pease
47 Martin Mulkearn
47 Manuel Matise
47 Mrs Elizabeth Hammond
48 Antone Monteiro
48 Frank S Fogler
48 Frank S Fogler Jr
50 Agnes Larkin
50 William T Sadler
51 Thomas J Sylvia
52 Dennis Walsh
56 Thomas Sharples
56 Mrs Mary Callahan
56 Richard Waddington
79 Joseph Simas
79 Frank Perreira
80 Angelo E Morris
80 Joseph Alexander
80 Harry Cook
81 Joseph M Faria
81 Jacintho Domingos
81 Susanna Forrest
82 Antone J Moniz
84 Douglas J Girvan
84 Joseph Dufficy
84 Sylvester Carroll
84 Joseph Dufficy
88 John R Bragg Jr
88 Marion J Costa
88 Fernando Pimental
92 Joseph Donaghy Jr

Thompson—con
92 Mrs Louisa Swain
96 Joseph Pacheco
96 Joseph Ferreira
96 Mary Boisvert
98 Joseph Sylvia
98 William K Sylvia
98 Manuel S Mello
99 John C DeMello
103 Fred Cunha
103 Manuel Costa
103 Cosmo C Jilo
104 Frank Perry
104 John Oliver
105 Patrick Downey
106 William A McHugh
106 Thiotonio P Silva Jr
106 Antonio J Raulino
112 Maria Howarth
112 Agnello D'Aragao
112 Michael McHugh
114 Condito Paulino
115 John Hayes
115 Timothy Donovan
122 Thomas Waldron
122 Robert Hall
122 Joseph Gorman
126 Mrs Maria L Silveira
126 Manuel Corey
126 Richard Zerbone
126 John Hendricks
126 Sarah Bullock
126 Mary Farren
132 Joseph Frates
132 Frank Enos
132 Aldina Sylvia
135 Henry S Davis
136 Joseph Faria
136 Manuel Costa
136 Mrs Marianna Goulart
136 Manuel Baptista
136 Manuel Freitas
136 Antoine P Arruda
137 Mrs Maria S Almeida
137 William Fawcett
152 Antone Jason
152 Joseph Correia
154 Frank Nelson
154 Mary Oliver
158 John J Harney
158 J Herbert Siddall
158 Charles H Benoit
162 James H Higgins
170 Mrs Elizabeth A Milnes
173 Manuel R Lopes
173 Domingas A Medeiros
173 Albert Dubord
174 John Rogers
176 Alfred Emmons
176 Francisco A Frates
177 Marrianno Medeiros
177 Amos Morris
177 Manuel Perry
178 Andrew P Lang
183 Manuel S Perry
184 John Joseph
184 Herbert H Tiffany
184 Rev Frank C B Silva
188 Manuel Martin
188 Manuel Rodericque
188 Antonio Boteilho
188 Joseph Rogers
208 Mrs Louisa Kempton
208 James Blanchflower
208 Albert E Winterbottom

TILTON

2 Thomas LaRoche
5 Timothy J Dorgan
6 William M Drew
8 John S Heywood

TINKHAM

148 Sylvian Hebert
148 Emilien Cormier
148 Philias Cyr
149 Emilien Cormier
149 John Allen
149 Albini Hebert
151 Charles Bourdon
151 Allen Senior
154 Gelasse Chagnon
154 Simeon Boudreau
154 Gamalier Ripley
158 Franklin Grinnell
159 Maximillian Belliveau
159 Robert Heyworth
159 Arthur Comery
162 Ansemme Cormier
162 Joseph S Lecuyer
162 Henri Charette
163 Donat Cormier
163 Harry Brogden
163 John Dewhurst
163 Alfert Mailhot
164 Philip LeBlanc
164 Joseph A Lamore
165 Edwin Topping
165 Edward Dennette
165 George W Saxon
168 Mrs Virginie Steben
168 Louis Thibeault
168 Rosario Chausse
168 Joseph Steben
168 David Waugh
171 Alphonse St Onge

171 Frank Boucaire
171 Arthur Lussier
189 Philip Dupuis
189 Joseph Belliveau
189 Oliva Methe
190 William Bloomer
190 Owen McDermott
190 Anthony Bloomer
193 Oswald Descheneaux
193 Constant Aillerie
193 Thomas Whalley
197 Richard Livesey
197 James A Foley
198 Thomas B Blais
198 Theophile Dextradeur
198 Nathalie Farley
201 Arthur Sharples
201 William A Bessette
202 Charles L'Oiselle
202 John Wilcock
203 Mrs Margaret E Murray
203½ Thomas F Quigley
206 Harry Duxbury
206 Robert Chandler
206 Ernest Miville
209 William A Youngs
209 John W Gibbs
210 Adam V Ferriere
210 John Law
210 Edmund Hindle
217 Frederick Higgins
218 Matilda Mahoney
218 Misses Daley
237 John Chambers
237 Manuel J Lemos
240 Bramwell Bulcock
240 Charles Gendron
240 Mrs Sarah C Stephenson
241 William LeClair
244 Donat Bourassa
244 Fred E Hunt
244 Wilfred Henry
245 Mrs Mary Perry
245 Manuel Furtado
245 Frank Silva
249 John Mauer
249 William Ohnesorge
253 Augustus Herzog
254 Henry A Langevin
254 Eugene E Barthelmy
254 Leonard Nowell
257 L Frederick Rainville
257 Charles A Gammons
257 C Phenix
258 Albert J Levalley
258 George Wilding
258 Edward Gorman
260 Louis Spirlet
261 Joel Bancroft
261 Mrs Mary J Hindle
261 James Gardner
268 Adam Lafferiere
268 Joseph Lafferiere
268 Prosper Martel
270 Jerry Jarvais
270 Mrs Harriet L Tanner
271 Carl F Huberger
270 Omer Bergeron
271 Joseph Alber
271 Arthur Ashworth
278 John Furtade
280 Thomas Lunday
280 Joseph Vincent
282 Charles Garant
296 Henry Preston
296 George Dewhurst
296 Michael Pickup
296 Richard Smith
296 Frederick Richmond
296 Harold Whiteley
299 Frederick Tatro
299 Wilbert Morrow
299 Xavier F Petijean
299 Frank Moreau
301 Alexis Hubert
303 Thomas Hargraves
304 Rufus Sharples
305 John Lyon
306 Harvey R Eldredge
306 Mrs Albert Towden
310 Frank Holden
310 Frederick Langhorn
310 Ernest Colclough
310 John J Hargreaves
315 Walter Thornley
319 Mrs Louisa Laprade
319 Alexander MacNeil
320 Lawrence Tipping
323 Peter Robillard
323 James H Williams
326 George H Tripp
327 Malam Cottam
327 Mrs Annie Barrett
327 Robert Heys
331 Alfred Bolton
337 James Dearden
337 James H Thorn
337 Charles H Buckley
341 Sandy McNeil
341 Joseph Worswick

TOPHAM

2 Mrs Addie Hines
14 Henry I Dickens
83 John Quapp
85 Jules Raulet
86 Abiatha Rogers
92 James E Shepley

TREMONT

14 James W Savage
15 Leonard Johnson
21 Eugene M Barrows
25 Georgge F Kirby
29 John C Brown
35 Lot P Besse
35 Isaac C Howland
46 Henry W Benson
54 Charles E Kelley
55 Mrs Leonora A Smith
60 Arthur L Buffington
62 George G Thibodeau
62 Edgar Archambeault
69 George A Eggars
69 Thomas Aiken
91 Otto C Schultz
91 Thomas Shaw
91 John Aque
92 Isaiah T Woodbridge
92 Harrison G O Sears
95 Margaret J Quirk
96 Eldad E Moore
96 F Russell Moore
99 Bernard Anderson
99 William R Manuel
101 Mrs Elsie G Carter
105 Charles H Robinson
105 Charles W Johnson
115 James H Turner
117 Thomas Blake
119 James Rogers
137 Charles Wood
137 Adolphus Dreher
141 Robert Arnett
147 Walter E Dreher
147 Timothy J Driscoll
153 John D Silva
179 Arthur F Fisher
179 Edgar E Head
179 Alexander H Adams
200 William MacKenzie
204 Carl E Morde
208 Roy M French
221 George A Burt
221 Mrs Jennie R Burt
228 Leo Beech
237 Albert H Varnum
238 Fred G Barker
238 Vincent Vanni
240 Arthur M Lucas
241 Gildo Lucardi
245 Arod B Holloway
246 Carolyn D Wood

TRINITY

6 Alphonse L La France
10 Alexander Goldthrop
10 John J Goldthrop
12 Nathaniel Dewhurst
17 James F Collins
17 Michael H Sullivan
18 William M Anglum
18 Lawrence H Powers
25 Joseph Booth
25 Joseph H O'Neil

TURNER'S COURT

2 Antone Carretto
2 Guiseppo Vasolino
4 Vinano Brassi
5 Abraham Schnur
6 Frank Silva
6 Mrs Maglione Antonio

UNION

27 Rufina Pina
27 Mrs Mary Barros
29 Charles H Russ
29 John Cosmo
41 James Monteiro
41 Frederick Garcia
69 Louisa M Arrick
77 Horatio J Edinborough
96 Mrs Eliza Cardoza
109 James F McAdams
169 Thomas H Soule
185 Philomena E Vargas
226 Mrs Margaret Barker
230 Mrs Mary E Baker
236 Charles S Moynan
236 Mrs Mary Chase
236 Joseph S Coates
236 George F Winslow
245 Ellen M Russell
245 Herbert A Swift
250 Dr Amos P Webber
256 John E O'Neil
262 James W Welch
265 Adolphus F Wyman
270 Charles S Kelley
271 Mrs Grace M Brownell
277 Clarence A Cook
278 Elizabeth P Swift
278 Dr Lester F Potter
283 Fred A Williams
283 Mrs Sarah C Lawrence
284 Mrs S Lilla Parker

284 Ezra Howland
288 Mary W Walker
288 Robert I Walker
298 Mary E Galvin
299 Mrs Lydia Seip
299 Mrs Caroline P Chase
318 Louis Aillery
319 Mrs Susan R Perry
320 John A Johnson
321 Rebecca Chittick
324 Ernest A Wheaton
330 D P O'Brien
331 Norman B Nesbett
333 Stephen R Potter
334 Dr Frank E Stetson
342 Mrs Lucretia C Cannon
345 Mrs Louisa B Haskell
347 Walter H Bassett
350 Charles O Dexter
352 Mary E Trask
352 Charles N Richmond
355 Henry P Burt
358 Mrs Rebecca H Wood
362 Mrs Caroline M Knowles
386 Richard J Davis
386 Henry W Taber
390 Charles H Hathaway
390 Cora A Newton
394 Frederick H Morse
397 Misses Kane
397 John S King
399 Edward B Gray
399 Frank W Tripp
400 William H Bly
400 William O Devoll Jr
402 G Arthur Sherman
402 Ellis W Holmes
403 Edgar Lord
404 Catherine M Hines
405 Herman A Brightman
406 William G Lamb
407 Winifred Ellis
411 Misses Hathaway
411 Elisha H Fisher
416 Edward P Canny
416 William B Fanning
417 William Deacon
417 Lucy B Fish
417 Henry Harlow
418 Walter F Preston
418 Lynton M Buffington
419 Mrs Ruth A Manchester
419 Louis W Tilden
420 Mrs Sarah B Wilbur
420 J Arthur Luther
421 Walter F Hathaway
421 Samuel J Ferguson
424 Charles Russell
424 Roswell L Brightman
426 Charles F Cushing
429 John Q Ryder
429 Seth W Godfrey
437 Mrs Lydia Sargent
439 George Esslinger
449 Channing Wilde
449 William Gordon
450 Joseph Ferguson
450 Charles W L Stokoe
457 Oscar Belmore
457 Oscar H Belmore
457 Michael McGough
461 Joseph F O'Connell
463 Mrs Sadie McKenzie
465 George H Kenney
465 John Wilson
465 Christopher S Wilcox
466 William Seaman
466 Frank S Macedo
467 Mrs Caroline E Tripp
468 Charles Harwood
468 Manuel Rose
470 Antone Vasconselles
470 James N Conway
478 William Foster
480 Richard Hall
483 Mrs Elmina H Para
483 Antonio G Silva
483 Louis B Taber
488 Everett H Hinckley
490 William A Hamer
490 Sydney B Burrell
495 Ruel S Francis
499 Bertram Gray
499 Florence E McCarthy
511 William D Hoyt
549 Alfred Anderson
551 William Shennan
553 Hiram Smith
555 William A Burt
561 William F McClure
562 Melville R Wade
563 Daniel H Ferguson
564 Dennis A Shea
568 H Karl
574 Joseph S Lewis Jr
574 John W Dennis
578 Henry W Taber
581 Loum Snow Jr
585 Walter K Smith
585 Albert C Braley
595 Arthur W Rice
596 John A Perry
609 Peter J Tresham
616 John M Brightman
616 Bror O Ekholm
620 William Brown
620 Charles H Searle
633 Fred William Butz

Union—con
637 Frederic W May
637 Adam Shaw

UPHAM'S LANE

0 William O T Upham

VALENTINE

9 Patrick Croften
9 Mrs Bridget Loftus
13 Percy Miller
13 George H Bessette
14 William Heyes
15 John Catterell
21 Adamson Mills
23 Jeremiah T Haggerty
27 George Blocksage
29 Thomas E Broadbent
31 Frank McKenna
39 William Moss
39 Henry Smalley
39 Walter Rothwell
41 James McGovern
48 James Cinnamard
48 Robert Wilson
49 John Correia
51 Patrick Quinn
56 John Hannigan
56 David Beanland
60 Joseph Blackledge
60 Edward A Hynes
61 George H Black
67 George England
71 Thomas Butler
78 James Cree
80 Mrs Mary L Acornley
82 Louisa M Caizergues

VIALL

7 Ludger Ouimette
7 Ernest Ouimette
8 Edmond Fournier
8 William Hogan
9 Mary Boyle
9 Isadore Belanger
9 Mrs Elizabeth Farrell
9 Mrs John Edwards
9 Thomas Atkinson
9 Peter Therriauld
10 Mrs Philamone Bessette
10 Mrs Evangline Schelter
10 Joseph Dalbec Jr
12 William Greenwood
12 Lawrence Yates
12 Mary Mason
13 Arthur Dionne
13 Alex Domperre
13 James Wilkinson
14 Alfred Pye
14 John McKenna
14 Howarth Greenwood
16 Frederick Brie
16 Arthur Therrault
16 William Barlow
16 Mrs Celina Gamache
17 Asa Thursby
17 John Whiteside
18 Richard Howarth
18 James Martin
18 Abraham Oldfield
19 Dominick Horan
20 Edward Warden
20 Louis N Fredette
20 Joseph Dessert
22 Richard Bury
22 Samuel Tebutt
23 Paul Brunnette
23 John Lepire Jr
23 Michael Clare
23 Albert Clerc
23 Emile Clerc
23 Jules Crommenschlager
24 John T Rishton
24 Robert Astley
25 Thomas Crook
25 Mrs Ellen Livesey
25 Thomas Elder
25 George Brogden
26 James Yates
26 Samuel Smethurst
26 James A Pettey
27 Thomas Whittaker
27 Thomas Duckworth
27 Andrew E DeTerra
27 Albert Finch
27 Alfred Owen
28 James Tebbutt
28 James H Ronan
29 Joseph Hettinger
29 William Hettinger
29 Fred Hettinger
30 Mrs Mary A Campion
30 Joseph A Babb
30 Misses Cronin
30 Joseph Simpson
31 Omer Pepin
31 Herbert Noble
32 Robert Marsden
32 Joseph Barnes
32 Thomas Waddington
33 Mrs Mathilda Lamoureux
33 Eugene D Dupin
33 Mrs Anna Lavoie
33 Theophile Robert

VINE

2 Edward H Booth
2 Arthur C Drew
18 Mrs Susan F Atwood
23 George A Lapham
24 Harry G Nichols
27 John D Sherman
34 William Booker
34 Clifton Nichols
40 Eugene F Kane
41 John Connolly
45 William Ratcliffe
48 Joseph Booker
49 A Alfred Buhl
52 Antone Losette
56 William Hill
62 James Gregory
69 Lester Mosher
69 Thomas O'Grady
75 Frank W Spooner
75 Frank Herzog

WALDEN

61 Charles C Simmons
61 John M Heath
65 William Tourtellot
68 Harry L Ellis
69 Ralph Jowett
70 Edwin B Powers
71 Ernest L Soule
71 Thomas G Wing
72 Willliam A Brightman
78 William A Perry
81 Fred H Winship Jr
81 Mrs Verona H Perkins
81 Ira B Brush
82 Edith M B Taber
83 Mrs Elizabeth Smith
83 Fred E Hathaway
84 Michael J Osborne
84 Arthur Boden
85 Israel Blume
85 Ludger Lavoilette
86 Thomas J Davis
87 Silas T Ricketson
88 John Franks
88 William Fowler
90 Luke T Haran
91 Frederick Wilson
91 Frank B Shepherd
93 James Hankerson Jr
93 Mrs Emma M Ekdahl
95 Herbert Harper

WALL

1 George Bertignono
3 Frank Fernandes
3 Antone Fernandez
4 Victorio Ragazi
6 Louis Cottino
6 Giovanni Bessone
8 Antonio Bono
8 Joseph Castellina
12 Giovanni Gianetto
12 Mrs Joanna Donovan
12 John Donovan
12 Angelo Paoni
12 Antone Rappolo

WALNUT

1 Anthony S Francis
2 Joseph Pina
2 Frank Almeida
2a Henry N Leyton
4 Peter Martin
5 Benjamin Taber
5 Joseph J Gomes
6 Harold Dombovand
6 Daniel Smith
8 William R Green
8 James H Hoyt
9 John F Centeio
9 Romano Duffoncea
12 Edward S Fowler
17 Leander A Borden
17 Thomas Larner
19 Lena Simiansky
19 Manuel Ramos
23 Albert W Lawton
23 Gregory Monteiro
26 Charles Henry Gifford
26 Misses Wood
27 Mrs Sarah L Pope
29 Paul Pintof
30 Isaiah S Ellis
30 William S Jenney
31 Annie H Wing
36 Joseph Davis
38 Frank E Nickerson
40 Joseph D Roberts
48 Joshua G Lapham
49 Samuel P Richmond
50 Norman P Hayes
52 H I Jamieson
53 Albert K Wood
53 Mrs Elizabeth G K Wood
55 James H Murkland
61 Mrs Sadie C Tillinghast
65 Mary V Russell
68 Mrs Sarah Hicks
74 Frank W Wentworth
75 Mrs Cornelia A Cook
76 Dr George F Lewis
77 William A Mackie
81 Charles E Davis

WAMSUTTA

3 Emilio Petrino
3 Henry McMahon

Wamsutta—con
4 James Gallagher
4 Joseph Noonan
5 John Connell
5 Mrs Lizzie Boyd
5r Antone Frandes

WARD

8 William Keith
12 Fred W Palmer
14 Benjamin S Sturtevant
24 Charles J King
24 Antone R Perry
26 Charles F Tripp
42 Mrs Katherine McGurk
55 Mrs Anna Williams
55 George Dunham
62 Herbert Cooper
62 Anthony T Martin
62 Leonard E Johnson
65 Aurile Carroll
66 John Perry
68 Axel Olson
68 August J Borges

WARREN

6 L Arthur Beauchemin
6 Dallas B Hathaway
6 Thomas E McGaughey
6 Mrs Sarah J Wolstenholme
6 Henry Morris
6 Richard Houghton
10 Edwin Bardsley Jr
10 Mrs Ann Gilham
10 David Reidy
11 George P Hansom
12 Manuel Pedro
12 Thomas Waldron
12 Mrs Ann Dyson
15 Emily L Richards
15 James Sutter
15 Clarence A Hutchinson
16 Mrs Eva Lougnez
16 Anton Podgorski
16 Richard Wilkinson
20 Walter Watson
20 Thomas J Timms
20 Henry T Lambert
22 Albert Harrison
22 James W Wilding
22 Mrs Maud Scowcroft
24 Philip Normand
24 Ovila Fontaine
25 William H Chadwick
25 Mrs Mary Atwood
25 John Whittle

WARWICK

1 Joseph A Boardman
1 Horace Coupe
1 Joseph Sharkey
1½ Joseph Armstrong
2 Etta Matthews
2 James H McNulty
3 Sylvester L Manning
4 Manuel J Sylvia
4 Christ H Hill
5 William D Flagg
5 Antone Pacheco
6 Augustus F Velho
6 Altone Almeida
7 Michael Downey
7 John H McDermott
8 Martin Weber
8 William E Gibson
9 Misses Keating
9 George H Whelan

WASHBURN

2 Philip Hahn
6 Frank Monty
12 Peter O'Gara
12 Thomas O'Gara
12 Peter Ogorra
12 Thomas Ogorra
14 Anton Feibeger
15 Mederick Allard
15 Frank S Reisch
15 Peter Kulik
16 Edmund Dick
16 Joseph Huard
16 Philias Phaneuf
18 Dennis Jussaume
18 Toni Meskresiewrki
18 Alderic Jussaume
18 Dennis Jussaume
19 George Hartman
20 Voycher Karfer
20 Vilon Golin
20 Albert Bredeau
21 Alfred Langelier
21 Wolin Konstance
21 Joseph Dextras
21r Michael Fife
21r Konstarteren Wolan
21r Charles E Stewart
22 Joseph Dombrowski
22 Peter Jaros
22 Felix Glinski
22r Frank Gero
23 Joseph Zygiel
24 Agutor Patnaude
24 Thomas Sheldon
25 Alix Sancif

26 Lawrence Giotski
27 Gibbs Germaine
27 Napoleon La Croix
28 John Zego
28 William Lake
31 Emerie Martin
31 Alphonse Patnaude
31 Adolphe Ducharme
32 Paul Lemoine
32 Arthur Prebe
33 John Boos
33 Thomas Marrick
34 Michael Breder
34 Peter Mioski
34 John Mickoy
37 Mrs Johanna H Sullivan
37 Catherine McLeod
37r Walenty Galuszka
38 Albert Britton
38 Ally Bergovitz
38 Stanilaus Zavadski
39 Frank Presnor
40 Jan Widuch
41 William Zebi
42 John Wegrzyniak
42r John Tencsav
42r Adam Romanowicz
42r Frank Polak
42r Roman Kucefski
42r Walenty Banas
42r Mike Kolouck
43 Frank Govstylov
43 John Glowaski
43 Antone Polchlopek
43 Mike Peteroff
44 Victor Forcier
44 John O'Brien
44 Victor Boucher
45 Stanltuis Yangkofski
45 Ashimer Paquet
46 John Przastek
46r Felix Kava
47 William Jachemowicz
47 Alex Babecki
47 Vincent Yacamovitz
47 Charles Goodovitch
47 Barbara Bertuska
47 Gustaf Hahn
47 Kostonti Jurczykowski
50 Jacob Faber
50 Mrs Leopoldine Reul
50 Frank Choquette
51 Rock Faradofski
52 John A Rogers
52 George F Murray
53 Leodor Colte
53 Patrick Dwyer
53 Abraham Tomb
54 Patrick Herlihy
55 August F Weaver
56 Arthur Boucher
56 Misses Herlihy
57 Andreas Schoech
58 Joseph Palme
59 Franciscek Siemnuiski
59 Ignaci Pruistas
60 John Pisowcryk
60 Mrs Nellie Reagan
60r John Goskovitch
60r Mrs Bridget McQuade
60r Mrs Mary J Bradley
61 Wolkas Gorsetsa
62 Charles Robinowitch
62 Edward Reynolds
63 Charles Martin
65 Mansfirth Duckworth
66 John Growatski
66 Exist Puhamel
66 Napoleon Potnier
66 Mrs Mary LaCroix
68 Mrs Victorline Daigle
70 Louis Fealteau

WASHINGTON

4 John C Rooks
4 Maria A Bettencourt
9 Mrs Sabra E Healey
10 Thomas Davies
12 Manuel A Pedrozo
15 William A Baker
15 Henry Barnard Worth
15 Frank Reisch
16 Samuel Horvitz
19 Arthur Knowles
23 J J Cunningham
48 William Higginson
52 Alex H Hillman
52 Percival Le R Lamb
53 James C Briggs
58 Mrs Annie Stephenson
60½ Mrs Minnie Leavitt
61 Patrick Downey
61 James Wall
62½ Harry D Millett
64 Mrs Mary J Nunes
64 Louisa E Perry
66 Joseph A Brady
66 George Chase
67 Mrs Emma A Watson
70 Terrence F Galligan
73 Antone Sylvia
73 Joseph Barboza
74 Michael Stevens
74 John Greenhalge
79 Arthur D Williams
79 Joseph D Williams
80 Joseph E Dupre
81 William H Bliven

Washington—con
81 Harrison Cambia
83 William N Burkle
84 Harris Goldstein
84 Mrs Mary Gracia
87 William D H Butts
87 James H Downey
88 Edmund A Reed
89 Myron S Briggs
89 James J Donaghy
92 Mary A Albert
92 William P Kirby
95 Josiah Wood
95 Walter F Jenney
96 Patrick H Fagan
96 Richard Harvey
106 Herman L Grumbt
117 Eugene S Hayes
118 Mrs Lydia C Tillson
119 Guy Couch
124 Isaac H Coe Jr
132 Mrs Corrinne H Gardner
133 Mrs Andrew P Brownell
143 William W Cranston
143 Joseph W Chadwick
149 Jay J Terwillegar
149 Manuel A Andrews
152 Herbert Smith
152 Sarah F Reddy
155 Frank C Hoxie
156 William Gilmore
166 John P Neagus
166 William W Holmes
167 Clarence W Arey
171 Adoniram J Rice
173 Charles H Thomas
174 Charles J McQuillan
174 Mrs Hannah E Meaney
179 Walter W Guthrie
179 Thomas A Mullaney
181 Mrs E Fannie Martin
182 Herbert R Ricketson
182 Levi Ricketson
183 Charles A Bennett
183 George A Stokoe
184 Henry H Smith
184 Charles J Matthews
188 Amos Gee
191 Guy Couch
191 John Lanagan
191 Edwin L Law
192 John A Snow
192 John J Rawlins
196 Frank A Hanna

WASHINGTON AVENUE

1 Francis Marrotte
2 Timothy Sullivan

WASHINGTON SQUARE

1 Henry Richmond

WATER

See North and South Water

WATSON

2 Harry Reeves
4 Sidney B Chase
0 Mrs Mary A Cornell

WAVERLY

3 Mrs Margaret Kane
4 Albert M Johnson
6 Charles Hayes
7 Frank E Sylvia
7 Albert Perry
8 Andrew Williamson
9 Michael J McCarthy

WAVERLY PLACE

1 Patrick H Rogers
2 Manuel Oliver

WEAVER

1 Aquila A Healey
2 Mrs Isabelle Bowie
3 Otis H Watkins
5 Frank G Taber
8 Manuel Gracia
10 A P Howland
13 Mrs Sophia A Weaver

WEBSTER COURT

121 Henry Valliere
121 Stanislas Davignon
125 Henry Kenyon
125 Arthur Bilodeau
129 George J B Lamontagne
131 Joseph LaPlante
131 Emile St Jacques
131 Abel Bourgeois

WELCH

2 Richard Hopwood

WELCOME

2 Louis Carroll
4 Joseph Pitt
4 Edouard Lajeunesse
4 Michael J Brennan
8 Abraham Earnshaw
8 James Lepine
8 John Prior
11 Stephen Walters
11 Joseph Krenmager
11 Albert Pfeninger

15 Michael Weir
15 John Doherty
15 Philias Roberts
16 Mrs Mary Whittaker
16 Arthur Hargraves
19 Nelson Bonin
19 Patrick Kelley
19 James J Farrell
20 Mrs Mary A Hartley
23 John Reynolds
24 Robert Critchley
24 George Hinchcliff
25 Mrs Jane McAvoy
25 Leon Tetreault
29 John Milberger
29 James Livesey
30 Thomas Michaud
30 Tony Neglia
30 John Michaud
30 Thomas Moffett

WELD

1 Joseph Boucher
1 Peter Lavalle
2 Adolp Beland
17 William Hood
52 Celina Duckworth
54 Henry D Hunter
130 Pierre Plouffe
130 Ben Goyette
130 Joseph Doyle
159 Mrs Isabella Lafferty
159 Andrew A Lafferty
159 Margaret O'Donnell
163 Wilfred Desroches
163 Arthur Labelle
165 Mrs Margaret Garvin
171 Frank Curran
171 Joseph Desaulniers
171 Thomas Lord
171 George Dumas
171 Arthur Langlois
171 Louis Dube
177 Frobisher M Choquette
177 John M Maynard
177 John H Balderson
178 William O'Brien
178 John W H Buckley
178 Patrick J Wade
179 Napoleon LaFlamme
179 Dennis Casey
182 John Reel
182 F Real
182 John Read
182 J Henry Gosselin
182 Mrs Julia Gosselin
182 Edward Mitchell
182 Arthur Pion
182 James A Scott
185 John McKay
185 Louis Hall
185 Harry L Marsh
188 Napoleon Jette
188 Adalord Lareau
188 Adelard C Hebert
193 Simon F Lynch
193 Mrs Maria McFadden
193 Noel H Charpentier
197 Michael Driscoll
197 Mrs Mary Costello
197 Luther H Gifford
200 James Sullivan
200 Charles J Callahan
200 Mrs Margaret Berry
203 Patrick Hunt
203 James Herrity
203 Howland Smith
203 George Smith
204 John J Murray
204 Thomas B Martin
207 William Cross
207 Christopher Rothwell
207 John Mather
207 Robert H Boardman
208 William Reed
208 John William Hancock
208 Mrs Henrietta Urquhart
211 Mrs Ellen Sullivan
211 Hartley Hollingsworth
211 Alexander Couza
212 William Mattocks
212 Mrs Mary Broadbent
212 Thomas Roberts
213 Mrs Margaret Wilson
213 William T Garlick
213 Frederick Robinson
215 Mrs Catherine E Hebblewaite
215 Joseph Kirk
255 Thomas J Quinlan
256 Robert Gillis
256 James H Livesey
256 Mrs Mary A Walmsley
259 John F Keane
259 Joseph Codin
259 Edwin H Burt
260 Mrs Ada Seed
260 Mrs Helmina Lelaidier
260 Ralph C Parris
260 Donat Chausse
264 John J Doherty
264 Mrs Mary Lenhart
264 Ellis S Willis
264 Thurston R Sede
267 William H Harrison
267 William H Rushton
268 Joseph Nolin Jr
268 Oliver H Benoit
270 William Fowler

Weld—con
271 Humphrey Hunchcliffe
271 William Hall
271 William Swindlehurst
272 William H H S King
273 Joseph Livingstone
274 Orrin Cornelius
284 William H Pickering

WELD AVENUE

2 William Mullen
2 Walter Orzechowski

WELD SQUARE

1 Cyril Burke

WEST

11 Philip F Ready
15 Lawrence Matthews
17 George H Higgins
19 Alfred K Aiken
69 Manuel S Pina
69 John M Gracia

WEST FRENCH AVENUE

9 P Hormidas Dandurand
9 Horace Ste Marie
9 Frank G Tefke
9 Stephen Bennett
9 Delphis P Dufesne
13 Edward Lajeunesse
13 George Pilling
22 Joseph Gladu
22 Pierre Dandurand Jr
24 David Rothera
28 William Wharmsby
28 Samuel Derbyshire
32 Joseph Munroe
32 Alfred Scott
38 Robert S Burns
38 George Almond
38 John B Jordan
38 George Richards
38 Thomas Garrity
44 Joseph Chadwick
44 Clifford Taylor
44 John Hall Jr
44 Ernest Kemp
46 Thomas Finlay
46 Mary Fitzpatrick
46 John F Madden
57 Fred Marsden
57 Gregory Brennan
57 Patrick Kennedy
64 Michael J Fagan
76 Mrs Katherine Farrell
78 Fergus Bolton
90 Elisha F Clark
114 Margaret Blanchard
114 Winsor B Redman
116 George Gosseler
116 Napoleon Dubois
116 Mrs Emille Boudreau
116 Joseph Ironfield
116 Eli Bazinet
150 Antone Muller
150 Anton Weiss
150 Antone Rice
190 Thomas Cuddy
192 Pierre Desmarais
206 Edward P Duffy
208 Frank Dowd

WEST HIGH

5 Zachariah Caldwell
7 Ella Cooper
7 Mrs Sarah Bankitt
8 Walter Lewis
9 James McDonald
10 Isaac D Maddox
12 Mrs Mary E Young
14 Edward Harris
16 Mrs Annie E Galloway
16 Frederick N Jones

WEST MORGAN

343 Edward E Pierce
343 Clarence R Bowman

WEST TRINITY

19 Alfred J Kennedy
22 Mrs Jane P Smith
23 Joseph Carreau
27 Leander V Parker
30 Mrs Sarah Collins

WEST WILLOW

18 Frank A Judson

WHITLOW

0 Camille Trahan

WHITMAN

25 Aristide J Gauthier
84 Charles Bariteau
84 Joseph Talbot
84 William Servais
84 Levi Labrade
87 Louis G La Fontaine
90 Joseph C Fredette
90 Theodore Denesha
102 Edward Young
102 Pierre Longpre
104 Philias Jordanis
0 Edward Turcotte
106 Philip Jordanis

106 Edward Lajeunesse
110 Antoine Hetu
110 Mary Rodger
110 Mrs Sevarin Turcotte
114 Thomas H Cooper
114 Robert Ripley
118 George Winterbottom
118 John B Ricard
118 Thomas Inglesou
121 Paul Saucier
121 Hermine Duval
122 Samuel Gooselin
123 William J Clark
124 Annie Fletcher
124 George H Hancock
124 Lees Bardsley
124r John Meal
126 Joseph Williamson
126 Thomas Heyes
127 Charles H Hardy
127 Joseph Momarquette
127 Oliver Richards
127 Gedeon D Patnaude
129 Amedee Arseneault
131 Samuel L Fairbanks
131 Arthur Martin
131 Archille Codaire
132 John Gogan
133 K William Henke
135 John Belanger
135 Wilfred Laplante
135 Alphea Suprenant
152 Felix Bandry
152 Joseph Desroches
152 Mrs Adaline Lauzon
152 Edward Blanchaud
153 Arthur Robin
153 Alfred Bessette
154 Jean B Desjeunesse
154 Henry A Fauteux
154 Benjamin Blakely
155 Everett L Borden
155 Homer Branchaud
158 Louis Turenne
158 William Sleight
159 Josephine Maynard
162 Joseph A Bessette
162 Joseph Fouquette
211 Toussant Girard
211 Vital Gamache
211 Leonidas Houle
218 Thomas S Ashton
218 Willie LaCroix
218 John W Harrison
218 Wilfred H Smethurst
218 John H Stanley
318 John Harrison

WILLARD

7 Walter Giles
15 Edward Stone
15 Robert Catterall
15 John Morey
22 Edmonde Dalbec
22 Remi Caouette
26 Edwin Smalley
26 David Dixon
26 Matthew Curry
26 Edward Rayner
27 Thomas Rawcliffe
30 Luc Gagnon
35 Sherman S Covey
38 Thomas Henderson
44 James Booth
46 Manuel Freitas
55 Louis C Roy
55 John Booth
55 Alphonse Lafrenais
59 Thomas Murray
59 William Graham
59 William J Harnish
79 John T Whittaker
91 William H Sullivan
95 Alfred E Clarkson
99 H Norwood
103 Mrs Sophia Boisclaire

WILLIAM

18 Mrs Annie Putz
25 Mrs Catherine T Murphy
25 Walter Perry
25 Rawson Waterworth
25 Joseph Bernandini
25 Mrs Mary Feeney
25 George H Clough
25 Mrs Maria C Sherman
43 Frederick W Besse
70½ William F Fitzgerald
82 Mrs Lucy Lewis
152 Henry P Wilson
155 Albert C Sherman
156 Dr Henry L Dwight
160 Charles E Drake
161 William L R Doane
161 Dr Harry V Weaver
163 Thompson Hill
163 Charles F Tilghman
172 George T Squires
175 Charles H Barstow
179 Edwin P Seaver
190 Mrs Clara G Bartlett

WILLIS

2½ Mrs Catherine McCluskey
2½ Mrs Delia Foquette
2½ Robert Armstrong
3 Daniel A Harrington

Willis—con
4 Daniel F Lynch
4 Rosario Quartarone
7 Charles W Field
7 John T Gaughan
9 Harry A Kenyon
9 Israel Wollison
10 Arthur Harpin
10 Felix Raphael
10 Denis Mahoney
17 William R Waldron
18 Thomas J Crowley
18 Charles E Wade
21 Mrs Esther B Chappell
21 Stephen B Sawyer
25 William H Lyng
29 Horace M Plummer
33 Charles A Croshere
33 Mrs Carrie L Higgins
34 Timothly Hennessey
38 Edward B Swift
41 Henry Breault
43 James H Nuttall
45 Rev Albert Ribourg
45 Misses Butts
47 Fred M Weeden
47 John P Holmes
49 Maurice W Paige
51 Augustine F Childs
53 Henry W Mason
64 Otis G Beale
64 Mrs Eliza Casavant
66 James Slater
67 N Ernest Ford
68 Fred R Smyth
68 Samuel Ross
69 Mark H McIntyr
70 William Higham
71 Franklin C Tripp
72 Helen Swift
72 Edward T Brightman
73 Charles W Smith
73 Frank G Carpenter
74 Warren C Foote
74 Mrs Susan A Ingalls
74 W Cleveland Foote
75 James W Arnett
75 Dexter W Lewis
76 Mrs Sarah Bowker
76 C E Wilcox
77 Mrs L E H White
77 Mrs Drusilla Underwood
78 Edward S Lanagan
80 William A Halliday
80 William E James
83 Bradford Smith
84 William Swan
84 John P Ferns
86 Edward C Wilcox
87 Mrs Sarah E Knight
87 David M Ashley
88 William L Sayer
91 Chester L Freeman
91 Andrew J Smith
93 Mrs Catherine Irving
93 Mrs Susan M Howland
93 Clarence E Braley
95 Richard Jackson
95 Philip R King
96 Edwin J Bates
96 Edward W Hunt
97 Ellery Pierce
97 James E Balloch
98 Charles Hadfield
99 David M Silvia
99 Mrs Ann Mowry
100 Mrs Mary J Tripp
100 Harry H Tripp
107 Joseph B Lenz
107 Philip Tackney
108 James M Masson
109 Herbert M Dingwell
109 William M Darling
110 Bradford L Church
112 Albert C Neagus
112 James Whittaker
113 William H Crowther
113 Charles W Gelette
114 Harry Mitchell
114 Shirley E Cunningham
115 Byron A Briggs
115 Thomas Wholey
116 William H Fisher
117 Arthur P Brown
117 Royal C Wells
117 Thomas Whelly
117 Arthur P Brown
121 William G Onley
123 John C Mendez
124 Abraham G Hathaway
124 Mrs Lydia M Ripley
125 Edward H Gifford
125 Charles J Steckewick
126 Edward T Almy
129 Cornelius B Sullivan
130 Fred C Luce
130 Daniel H Smith
131 Mrs Susan Caswell
131 Willis R Wilcox
132 Mrs Betsey W Spooner
132 Robert A Gooding
133 Antone M Francis
133 Jeptha Reed
134 Misses Burgess
135 Charles H Kean
136 Jonathan D Faulkner
138 Frank B Sistare
139 Edward C Tripp

141 Frederick G Smiley
143 James P Fitzgerald
144 Otis Simmons

WILLOW

9 Manuel P Silva
9 James S McCarthy
14 Fred K Alty
14 John I Petty
16 Mrs Alice Labrode
16 Mrs Margaret Reid
16 J B Munroe
17 Frederick E Damon
17 Edward Brittain
25 Edwin S Broadbent
25 Charles H Brown
28 James Greenhalg
30 George W Mahon
34 John T Scott
48 Edward Burton
52 John King
52 John H Mathewson
56 William Taylor
57 Richard Geary
59 James Norris
59 Harry Halsall
59 Henry S Gorner
59 Walter Greenhalgh
61 Caleb L Ellis
66 Mrs Mary M Perry
66 Clarence E Lawton
66 Edward J Thomas
73 Cyrille Bernier
101 William Vaughan
115 Edmond Spencer
121 Walter Wright

WILSON

Changed to Richmond

WING

6 Joseph B Shiresohn
8 Dr Sylvester E Donovan
12 Mary Mattos
12 Mrs Maria DeCosta
16 Mrs Mary J Cruz
16 Antone Lewis
18 Joseph Robinson
18 Joe Madeiros
20r John DeMello
24 John Baptiste
26 Samuel Goldberg
28 Frank Lima
28 Joe Costa
32 William H Fuller
33 John J Debem
33 Joseph V Dias
33r Antone S Trinity
33r C M Fragosa
34 Manuel V Sylvia
34 Charles A Robinson
41 John W Keane
41 James T Mosher
44 Mrs Maud Collins

WINSOR

9 Manuel Semas
10 Mrs Lydia Sullivan
10 Mrs Emma Fay
14 James D Meakin
14 Thomas Blanchflower
19 George H Guest
19 William Taylor
20 John L D Senra
20 Felix Correa
20 Virginio Frates
21 John B Almeida
21 Mrs Mary C Veira
21 James Britten
24 Thomas Stenson
24 Hubert Hall
25 David Tomlinson
25 William Nisbet
25 Joseph L Cotnoir
28 John T Bee
28 William Taylor
28 William Wood
29 Thomas O'Malley
29 Joseph S Ferreia
32 James Bleasdale
32 Fred C S Edmonson
32 Thomas S Edmonson
33 Manuel P Simons
33 Louis Veira
33 Manuel Souza Mello
36 Henry Drinkwater
36 Herbert Smith
36 Thomas Carroll
39 Antonio J Bettencourt
40 Hugh Shaw
41 Manuel Cabral
41 John Travers
41 Frank Soares
44 William E G Battey
44 John King
45 John Doyle
45 Thomas Barker
45 Thomas McDonald
48 Joseph Vieria
48 John Nicholson
49 Misses Mahon
49 Mrs Margaret O'Malley
52 John Lees
52 Edward Wheelden
53 Manuel Medeiros
53 John Frendes
53 Frank Mello

Winsor— con
53 John Pointe
57 Fred Fremon
59 John Costa
64 James Powers
64 John Murphy
67 Henry Beckett
67 Antone Souza
69 John Isherwood
69 Mrs Mary J Harvey
70 Manuel Praeda
70 Manuel Medeiros
72 John Rooney
73 Frank Cabral
73 Antone Cabral
73 John O Correia
75 Philippe S Affonso
75 Antone Silveira
75 Manuel Dutra
76 Frank P Medeiros
76 Antone Dupont
76 Antone J Cunha
80 Antone Costa
83 John S Neves
83 Patrick Lally
85 Joseph Correira
85 Manuel Andrews
85 Frank Souza
85 Manuel Andrada
89 David Coates
89 Annie Montgomery
89 Mary Frew
89 Benjamin Stockdale
90 Mrs Helna Amaral
90 Manuel Simmons

WINTER

3 William Gartside
10 Nestor M Silveira
10 Mrs Francis Correia
10 Thomas Silva

WINTERVILLE ROAD

0 George Winterlict
0 Manuel F Morris
0 John Jacintho
0 William E Jacintho
0 Mrs Gertrude Rogers
0 James Houghton
0 Roland G Devoll
0 Antone Jerome
0 John Cassidy
0 John Cordeira
0 Manuel F Martin
0 Manuel S Bettencourt
0 Manuel Costa
0 Mrs Anna Gonsalves

WOOD

18 George F Weeden
34 Albert H Horne
40 Richard Russell
46 Thomas Denton
49 Wallace Woodsome
51 James Lafield
69 Charles B Hazard
81 Peter Dufault

WOODLAWN AVENUE

8 Richard Wareing
12 Ernest Barrett
12 James W Marvel
12 Benjamin W Watson
12 Joseph Bridge
16 Joseph A Roberts
16 Mrs Agnes Cross
20 James Leva
20 Abraham Birch
20 Pasqualle Fradipeteo
23 William Newton
23 William Burrows
23 Albert W Norris
23 William Middleton
23 Robert I Hope
24 Roger Taylor
24 Alfred Trepanier
28 John Allen
29 Henry O Crowell
32 Paul Raymond
32 Francois Forand
32 Albert Sarasin
36 Angus MacLeod
36 Mary A Loftus
40 John A Wooley
40 Thomas Blades
40 George Johnson
41 Herbert Griffiths
41 Matthews Perry
44 William J Clark
44 Thomas Hill
48 Joseph Hindley
48 Cyrus Arnold
48 Joseph Hindley
53 Albert Lees
54 August Mello

1855 1912

Get the best. Use

WARREN'S ANCHOR BRAND NATURAL ASPHALT

ROOFING

Superior to all others

250,000,000 square feet in use giving entire satisfaction

"PARIA" Brand Roofing Felt and Cement.

ANCHOR BRAND Mastic (For floors)

ANCHOR BRAND Paving Cement for Streets and Sidewalks.

Refined Asphalt (hard) for Crossings, etc.

Asphalt Varnish — Asphalt Roof Coating

Asphalt 2 ply Ready Roofing—Lasts Indefinitely

Warren Chemical & Mfg. Co.

17 Battery Place
New York

49 Federal St., Boston
New John Hancock Building

1855 1912

COAL TAR

WARREN'S L. L. and CRESCENT
Brands of FELT and PITCH
FOR
ROOFING and PAVING

WALRUS ROOFING	**PERMANOID ROOFING**

SMOOTH SURFACE

MINERALITE ROOFING
Complete in Itself
Needs No Painting

ROOFING SLAG

Warren Chemical & Mfg. Co.

17 Battery Place
New York

49 Federal Street
Boston

NEW BEDFORD BUSINESS DIRECTORY 1911

Of all Trades, Professions and Pursuits in NEW BEDFORD for the year 1911

(Copyright 1911 by W A Greenough & Co.)

Accountants

BENTON CHARLES E 97 William See map
Francis J P 27 Masonic bldg
Fuller F S 37 Purchase
GUNN, RICHARDS & CO Tremont bldg Boston Mass See page 40

Advertising Bulletin Signs

BLAIR SIGN & ADVERTISING CO 60 Fourth See page 754

Advertising Specialties

Purrington Frank H 107 Summer

Agricultural Implements

DeWOLF & VINCENT 111 William See page 44
Wordell A E 21 William

Akron Drain Pipe

BORDEN & REMINGTON CO 115 Annawan Fall River See page 11

Alterations

GERARDI V V 36 Eighth See page 769

Anchor Brand Roofing

WARREN CHEMICAL & MFG CO 49 Federal Boston See opposite

Antique Stores

Eldred L D 12 William
Foster A P 38 N Second
Fuller A C 18 N Water

Appraisers

ASHTON & MURPHY 1109 S Water See page 48
DRISCOLL R F 14 Clifford bldg See front cover
MACY PELEG S 78 Smith See advt Real Estate
SPOONER WILLIAM E 52 Pleasant See page 27
VAUGHAN H C 23 Borden
WARREN'S AGENCY 1063 Water See back binding and page 789

Architects

Athearn W H 382 Cedar
Bullard E G 76 Pleasant rm 30
Destremps L E 251 Union
Hammond C & Son 179 N Water
Hand W H Jr (naval) 108 Union
PRARAY C W 303 Times bldg See page 42
Smith Nat C 97 William
WILLIAMS JOHN r 77 Merrimac See page 762

Art Goods

Peckham Elizabeth A 85 Fourth

Art Monuments

REX MONUMENTAL WORKS 90 Dartmouth See back cover

Artesian Wells

Hopkins H C 23 N Water
SMITH B F CO 38 Oliver Boston See page 31

Artists

Alden Charles E 7 William
Braley Clarence E 25 N Second
Breton T C 595 Purchase
Colyar P M Mrs 113 Campbell
Grinnell A G 89 Hawthorn
Hesse E 189 Purchase
LeBlanc John 456 Belleville av
Plummer L A 148 Hawthorn
Sisson Hattie A 44 Chestnut

Artists' Materials

AKIN F T & CO 84 Pleasant See foot lines

Asphalt

WARREN CHEMICAL & MFG CO 49 Federal Boston See opposite page *583

Asphalt Materials

BARRETT MFG CO 297 Franklin Boston See front cover
WARREN CHEMICAL & MFG CO 49 Federal Boston See opposite page *583

Asphalt Paint

WARREN CHEMICAL & MFG CO 49 Federal Boston See opposite page *583

Auctioneers

ASHTON & MURPHY 1109 S Water See page 48
Bourne Standish & Son 50 N Second
DESAUTELS S 269 Sawyer See page 758
DRISCOLL D F 14 Clifford bldg See front cover
GREEN FRED W JR 21 Clifford bldg See page 758
Hathaway H C 350 Acushnet av
SANFORD & KELLEY (stock) Clifford bldg See front cover
VAUGHAN H C 23 Borden
WARREN'S AGENCY 1063 Water See back binding and page 789

Auditors

GUNN, RICHARDS & CO Tremont bldg Boston See page 40

Automobile Accessories

McNEAR GEORGE W 26-30 Cambria Boston See page 748

Automobile Bodies

McNEAR GEORGE W 26-30 Cambria Boston See page 748

Automobile Gears & Supplies

BAKER MACHINE CO 8 Seneca See page 744

Automobile Instruction

WOODRUFF F T & CO 244 Purchase See page 748

Automobile Machinists

BAKER MACHINE CO 8 Seneca See page 744
GILES & TOBEY 44 Middle See page 744
HATHAWAY CHESTER F 107 N Water See page 743
NORTH END GARAGE 115-117 Bowditch See page 741
O'NEILL MURRAY 55-57 Spring See page 746
SCHOTT GEORGE A 1467 Acushnet avenue See page 753
VANCE BERT A 24 Sycamore See page 42

Automobile Painters

BOURGEOIS DAVID 105 Bowditch See page 744
CROSHERE C A 38 Fourth See foot lines
HATHAWAY L J 7 Elm See page 771
LINTON JOHN R & SONS 105 Maxfield See page 33
McNEAR GEORGE W 26-30 Cambria Boston See page 748

Automobile Repairs & Supplies

AUTO SELLING & SUPPLY CO 15 Fourth See page 741
BAKER MACHINE CO 8 Seneca See page 744
BORDEN HARRY E CO The 86-98 Pleasant See page 746
Gifford S E Auto Co 131 Pleasant
GILES & TOBEY 44 Middle See page 744
GREEN EVERETT 185 Acushnet av See page 780
HANDY JONATHAN CO 28 William See page 766
HATHAWAY CHESTER F 107 N Water See page 743

HATHAWAY L J 7 Elm See page 771
HILLMAN F G 669 Purchase See page 26
JEWETT HARDWARE CO 108 Middle and 415 Acushnet av See page **784**
LENOX MOTOR CAR CO Inc 3368 Washington Jamaica Plain Mass See page 739
NEW BEDFORD AUTO CO 16 Elm See page 741
NORTH END GARAGE 115-117 Bowditch See page 741
O'NEILL MURRAY 55-57 Spring See page 746
PARKER D L & CO 18 Market See page 746
SCHOTT GEORGE A 1467 Acushnet av See page 753
STURTEVANT BENJAMIN S 14 Ward See page 748
VANCE BERT A 24 Sycamore See page 42
WATUPPA AUTO CO at The Narrows N Westport Mass See page 750
WILLIAMS GEORGE P 331 Kempton See page 743

Automobile Stations

AUTO SELLING & SUPPLY CO 15 Fourth See page 741
BAKER MACHINE CO 8 Seneca See page 744
Chamberlain Charles E 156 Clinton and 148 Court
GILES & TOBEY 44 Middle See page 744
LOWE S C SUPPLY CO 22 Fourth See page 745
NEW BEDFORD AUTO CO 16 Elm See page 741
NORTH END GARAGE 115-117 Bowditch See page 741
PARKER D L & CO 18 Market See page 746
SCHOTT GEORGE A 1467 Acushnet av See page 753
STUTEVANT BENJAMIN S 14 Ward See page 748
VANCE BERT A 24 Sycamore See page 42

Automobile Teaching

WOODRUFF F T & CO 244 Purchase See page **748**

Automobile Tops

McNEAR GEORGE W 26-30 Cambria Boston See page 748

Automobile Tubes

TYER RUBBER CO 50 Bromfield Boston See page 743

Automobile Upholstering

McNEAR GEORGE W 26-30 Cambria Boston See page 748

Automobiles

AUTO SELLING & SUPPLY CO (Buick) 15 Fourth See page 741
BAKER MACHINE CO 8 Seneca See page 744
BORDEN HARRY E CO The 86-98 Pleasant See page 746
GILES & TOBEY 44 Middle See page 744
LENOX MOTOR CAR CO Inc 3368 Washington Jamaica Plain Mass See page 739
LOWE S C SUPPLY CO 22 Fourth See page 745
NEW BEDFORD AUTO CO 16 Elm See page 741
NORTH END GARAGE 115-117 Bowditch See page 741
O'NEILL MURRAY 55-57 Spring See page 746
PARKER D L & CO 18 Market See page 746
Peirce Stephen D Jr 101 William
Powers R W 99 William
SCHOTT GEORGE A 1467 Acushnet av See page 753
STURTEVANT BENJAMIN S 14 Ward See page 748
STURTEVANT BENJAMIN S 14 page 42
WATUPPA AUTO CO at The Narrows N Wesport Mass See page 750

Awnings

BRIGGS & BECKMAN 31-35 Commercial See page 785
Hitch O L 76 William
Newman O W 126 Arnold

Bail Commissioner

BARNEY BENJAMIN B Masonic bldg rms 11-12 See page **117**

Bakers

Allen A J 38 Cove
Allmond William 18 Harmony
Barker L 24 Cove
Barabe A A 643 First
Bates Kirby & Co 46-52 Pleasant
Boucher Joseph A 59 Bullard
Boucher Joseph I 238 State
Cardoza J E 33 South
Cleveland G H V D 14 Bedford
Cockshott Arthur J 39 Linden
Cooke F T 125 Potomska
Crowther William 1190 Acushnet av
Del Pazzo Antonio r157 Coffin av
DION HARMIDAS P 1070 County See page 773
Fisher M E 97 Allen
Garon L S 37 Acushnet avenue
Gifford & Magee 214 Purchase
Gill & Billsborrow 704 Purchase
Giusti & Co 861 S Water
Gomley John A 468 Kempton
Gracia A B, Bolton corner Rockland
Hadfield Alexander A 175 Dean
Harrison & Scowcroft 51½ Brock av
Hartley E Mrs 911 S Water
Holden James E 861 Purchase
JARRY D J 107 Bowditch See page 25
Keehn Phebe 913 Acushnet avenue
Keith C H 11 and 437 Purchase
Kovstylov Frank 43 Washburn
Krouvird R 480 S Water
Lane Rosa A Mrs 221 Park
Langlois & Roy 945 S Water
Lees Samuel 959 Acushnet avenue
Loose-Wiles 385 Acushnet av
Marsden John T 1653 Acushnet av
Martin J O 537 First
Melling & Sons 977 S Water
Milliken Eben C 166 Purchase
Milliken Frank 92 Walden
Murray Mary 292 Cedar
Noble Jane E 68 Cove
National Biscuit Co 16 N Second
Richards George 40 W French av
Richmond Henry 372 Kempton
RICHMOND & CO (wholesale) 255 Union and 425 S Water See foot lines
Roy Louis 35 Peckham
Selley George 1528 Acushnet av
Snell & Simpson (wholesale) 58 Adams
Sprague H M 2161 Acushnet av
Uttley Arthur 349 Kempton
Viveiros J 654 S Water
Wallner Anna Mrs 1233 Acushnet av
Wilde Andrew 55 Mechanics lane
Woodacre William 704 Purchase

Bakers' & Confectioners' Supplies

American Supply Co 19 Commercial
HATHAWAY & MACKENZIE GRAIN CO 748 Purchase See advt Grain
O'Grady Thomas 69 Vine

Bands & Orchestras

Gray's 5 S Sixth
Parry's 188 Chancery
Y M C A, William cor N Sixth

Banjo Mfrs

Silvia Manuel J 428 S Water

Bankers & Brokers

HAWES TEWKSBURY & CO Masonic bldg See page 7
SANFORD & KELLEY Clifford bldg See front cover
TUCKER, ANTHONY & CO 17 Pleasant See page 6

Banks

(See Co-operative Banks also Savings Banks)

FIRST NATIONAL BANK 110 Union See page 7
MECHANICS' NATIONAL BANK The 47 Purchase cor William See page 6
MERCHANTS' NATIONAL BANK William cor Purchase See page 4
NATIONAL BANK OF FAIRHAVEN 42 Main Fairhaven See advt in Fairhaven Department
NEW BEDFORD SAFE DEPOSITE & TRUST CO The 61 William See page 8

Baths

Ideal Turkish Baths, N Front near Beetle

Bedding

HOUSEHOLD FURNISHING CO 170 Purchase See page 94
WING CHARLES F CO The Inc 34-38 Purchase See page 40

Belting & Belt Hooks

BABBITT STEAM SPECIALTY CO 57 S Water See page 29
HILLMAN F G 669 Purchase See page 26
SLOCUM & KILBURN 23 N Water See page 766

Bicycles & Bicycles Repairers

Allen J S 92 Newton
AUGER G W & CO 228 Purchase See page 782
Cassidy & Smith 1271 Acushnet av
Covill H E 199 Grinnell
Curry Bros 123 Holly
Hathaway Walter D 132 Purchase
Hazzard Alton L 136 Pleasant
Hoxie W R 88 Allen
Lapolla J 543 Purchase
Leigh John 321 Rivet
Rogers Manuel S 36 Purchase
Smith Hoyland estate of 248 Union
WILLIAMS GEORGE P 331 Kempton See page 743
Wilson W H 7 Bedford
WING CHARLES F CO The Inc 34-38 Purchase See page 40
WOOD BRIGHTMAN & CO 47-55 N Water See page 3

Billiards & Pool

Andrew J A 207 S Water
Benjamin S 337 Rivet
Breault Alphonse 41 Beetle
Enos John 349 Rivet
Gaudreau J X 634 First
Grace Manuel S 538 S Water
Gracia F 75 Potomska
Harps Edward F 244 Cedar
Herrity John W 9 Linden
Mills A A 82 Purchase
Patistas John 245 Coggeshall
Perry Henry 269 Rivet
Plouffe F 236 Purchase
Riendeau Louis 638 Acushnet av
Simiansky J 685 S Water
Vernon John 634 First
Zeses & Blucas 1605 Acushnet av

Bill Poster

Hathaway A E 90 Purchase

Blacksmiths V Horseshoers
(See also Horse Shoers)

Bissonette M Felix 13 Beetle
Bocotte William 27 Hathaway
Bonneau F A 1180 Acushnet av
Boucher L 230 N Front
Braley H B 40 Spring
Butler John 8 Pine
Caswell Nathaniel H 8 Pine
Charbonneau Bros 454 Pleasant
Charest C 854 Acushnet av
Chicoine Esdras 52 Dartmouth
Collette Ulrich E 105 Bowditch
Desrosier John B 200 Mill
Donaghy H L 447 Kempton
Duddy William 11 Walnut
Durfee E M 30 Bethel
Fichtenmayer Martin P 326 S Water
Fuller N T 16 First
Goldstein S 431 S Second
Herbolt W H 124 N Front
Larochelle Alfred 162 N Front
Lawton Henry C 332 Purchase
McGowan F M 100 Pleasant
Parker L V 174 Shawmut av
Refuse R T 391 Acushnet avenue
St Armand T 268 Sawyer
Seguin Isaac 944 County
Seguin Peter 558 Purchase
Smith Frank Jr 411 Bolton
Sylvia J C 108 Dartmouth
Taber C G 18 S Water
Tessier Napoleon 435 S Second
Toussant Gilbert 214 Cedar Grove
Tripp & Haney Mechanics lane
Turgeon A R 51 Acushnet avenue

Blacksmiths' and Carriage Makers' Tools

CONGDON CARPENTER & CO 56-58 Fourth Fall River See page 10

Blacksmiths' Supplies

HANDY JONATHAN CO 28 William See page 766
JEWETT HARDWARE CO 108 Middle and 415 Acushnet av See page 784

Blank Book Mfrs

BRIGHTMAN F S CO Inc 127 Union See page 769
COLLINS WILLISTON H & CO 34-40 N Second See page 23

Boarding and *Lodging Houses

American House 1089 Acushnet a
*Arrick Louise M 69 Union
Baker M E Mrs 230 Union
Bessette Azilda Mrs 880 Purchase
Bonneau F Mrs 1028 Acushnet av
*Borden Ruth E Mrs 3 Park pl
*Bortle S A Mrs 8 Bethel
*Brown Sarah Mrs 20 S Second
*Burbank N P Mrs 60 Spring
Crossman A E Mrs 48 High
Davis A F 21 S Sixth
*DeWolf Charles F 380 Purchase
Duckworth Mansfirth 65 Washburn
Eaton C M Mrs 66 N Second
*Eldridge C M Mrs 152 Purchase
Farage Kalil 261 Coggeshall
Fortuna S 86 N Second

Boarding & *Lodging Houses—con
Francis E Mrs 469 Acushnet av
Francis S W Mrs 109 Fourth
Gauthier A Mrs 61 Belleville road
Gauthier Henry Mrs 84 Davis
Gladu D 19 N Sixth
Goyotte Malvina 20 Covell
Grady Eliza 47 Logan
Hatch Mercy Mrs 24 High
Hatherley Ida M 28 Fifth
Heath Margaret Mrs 232 N Second
Hervey M A Mrs 99 South
Hitt Mary M Mrs 299 County
Howarth Hiram 67 School
Howland Hotel 51 Howland Village
Isherwood James H Mrs 233 Acushnet avenue
Lafferty Jennie 41 Rivet
Lamarine Emma 41 High
Langlois Joseph 815 First
*Lawton H H 187 Purchase
*Leathers Mary J Mrs 384 Purchase
LeClair H Mrs 289 Coffin av
*LeDuc M Mrs 1293 Acushnet av
Lefleur Zenon 67 Coffin av
Luce Robert H 11 Fifth
Luiz John G 18 Hall
*Macomber W B 299 Acushnet av
*Mariners' Home 15 Bethel
McGarigle Emma Mrs 303 Acushnet
McKay Mary Mrs 236 N Front
Mevins Henry 39 Tallman
Michaud A 880 Purchase
Miller Catherine 111 Fourth
Mills Jane Mrs 137 Acushnet av
Moriarty D Mrs 83 Ruth
Moult James 11 Logan
*Murdock S M Mrs 72 High
Nolan Jane Mrs 22 Holly
Nolin N Mrs 131 N Front
Pink House 464 County
Plymouth House 245 Purchase
Prospect House 82 William
*Putz M Mrs 122 Middle
*Raymond A W Mrs 188 Purchase
Richard Alphonse 60 Bullard
Riendeau Dieudonne 831 S Water
*Schoech A 57 Washburn
Scott J E 44 Beetle
Scranton House 5 N Second
Sharples Alice Mrs 258 Coffin av
*Sheldon The 169 Union
Spencer James 976 Acushnet av
Sullivan M M Mrs 257 Cedar Grove
Swords T F 36 N Sixth
Watson L B Mrs 273 Cottage
Wilson Alfred 67 Fourth
Working Men's Home 1 Mill
Worthington D Mrs 602 Purchase
Zygiel A Mrs 23 Washburn

Boat Builder

Beetle Charles D E French av

Boats to Let

Jenney E R ft Grinnell
Tripp Allen S City pier No 1
West H F City pier No 3

Boiler Makers

GUNNING BOILER & MACHINE CO 67 S Water See page 31
New Bedford Boiler & Machine Co 42 Front

Boiler Testing

GUNNING BOILER & MACHINE CO 67 S Water See page 31

Bonds

RICHMOND CHARLES N (surety) 54 Pleasant See page 94

Bonesetting

Webster Joseph V 341 Cottage

Book Binders

COLLINS WILLISTON H & CO 32-40 North Second See page 23
Sullivan & Crocker 128 Union

Bookkeeping

KINYON'S COMMERCIAL SCHOOL 76 Pleasant rms 21-24 See foot lines

Books and Stationery

(See Stationery also Periodicals and Newspapers)
BRIGGS GEORGE L 161 Purchase See back cover

Booksellers and Directory Publishers

GREENOUGH W A & CO 65 Broad B (write for list published)

Boot Mfrs

SCHULER BROS 76-78 Purchase See page 24

Boot & Shoe Dealers

Allen Shoe Co 118 Union
Barnet David 1219 Acushnet av
Berkowitz J 889 S Water

Boisvert A 107 Ruth
Brochu Joseph E 1275 Acushnet av
Champegny & Le Blanc 1071 Acushnet av 123 Union and 947 S Water
Costa Antone 103 County
Davis J & Co 165 Union
Demers P & Son 1019 Acushnet av
Devoll Pardon & Son est 32 Purchase
Downey M 419 Rivet
Dupuis Ernest E 1351 Acushnet av
Fernandes M A & F A 126 Dartmouth
Genereux E 1107 S Water
Glennon D A 241 Purchase
Goldberg H 277 Fourth
Goldberg M 733 S Water
Goldberg S 22 Wing
Harrison Samuel 43 Rivet
Healy T F 1084 Acushnet av
Horvitz A J 883 S Water
Horvitz Julius A 64 Union
Horvitz S 64 Union
Kaplan Abraham 136 Washington
Kaplan Joseph 327 and 463 S Water
King Walter 204 Brock av
Lacroix G D 1138 Acushnet av
Lang F A 1059 Acushnet av
Leen P Jr 449 S Water
Lipman H 943 S Water
Lipson M 1101 S Water
Lipson M H 967 Acushnet av
Long R H 75 William
Lucas Shoe Co 43 Purchase
Mayor Daniel 1559 Acushnet av
Nichols & Damon 103 William
Perry Joseph 107 County
Perry J E 111 Rivet
Riley P J 147 Union
Rose Arthur J 86 Acushnet av
ST JAMES CO-OPERATIVE SALES 68 Linden See page 48
Salmon D J 796 Purchase
Santos A 132 County
SCHULER BROS 76-78 Purchase See page 24
Silvia M C 160 Acushnet av
Specialty Shoe Store 6 Purchase
Tavares J 63 Howland
Trull C F Jr 207 Purchase
Union Shoe Company 120 Purchase
Woolfenden L T 788 Purchase

Boot & Shoe Findings

Battles W A 126 Union
Dahill E F 667 Purchase

Boot & Shoemakers & Repairers

Abel Fachado 153½ Grinnell
Almeida D, S Second c Howland
Almeida J 225 S Water
Aulisio Marino 45 Ash (S)
Barnes George 226 Shawmut av
Baskin C M 980 Acushnet av
Benedictis Bros 406 Purchase
Bernstein Solomon 910 Acushnet av
Bettencourt M F 136 Washington
Boetilho Christian J Belleville av c Dean
Bonanentura P 57½ Hillman
Brick Harry 342 Kempton
Brick Philip 807 S Water
Brick S 33 Rivet
Budgen Arthur 64 Dartmouth
Burgeois Didier 391 N Front
Carver D O 204 Acushnet av
Cayouette Jerome 901 S Water
Cormier O M 312 N Front
Correia J L 65 Crapo
Costa A G 103 County
Dansereau M 87 Ruth
Davidian A J 265 Purchase
Davidian Arsene 163 Summer
Delarge F 91 Rivet
Demers Joseph 42 W French av
Desmarais Joseph 42 W French av
Dickson E W 321 County
Dionne A 266 Sawyer
Drisdell Louis 2169 Acushnet av
Duarte Jose 64 Grinnell
Durant F 58 Chancery
Durfee J C 151 Grinnell
Elgeschewitz E 9 Oak
Ellis Harry 9 Oak
Ellis Sam 420 Purchase
Ellis Washington P 348 Cedar
Feldon Richard 1081 S Water
Fraga J J 32 Cove
Frazier M 427 S Water
Freundschuh Martin 41 Bedford
Gleek Abraham 123 Potomska
Goldberg Samuel 22 Wing
Gould P T 766 Purchase
Hartley Albert 1679 Acushnet av
Hoffman John 165 Hathaway
Houle H & Son 786 Purchase
Jackson A H 170 Cedar
Kravetz Hyman 597 Purchase
LeBou Alex 864 Acushnet av
Leonardo Joseph F 10 Dartmouth
Lonsdale T 158 Union
Martin Joseph P 455 Rivet
Martin William r 1136 Acushnet av
Mayor Daniel 1551 Acushnet av
Medeiros Jose C 31½ Acushnet av
Messier Louis 141 Bowditch

Boot & Shoe Makers & Repairers—con
Mitchell J P Jr 730 Kempton
Moore R J 4 Fifth
Nicholas Daniel 413 S Water
Nichols A J 96 Ashland
Nisson H 517 Purchase
Pilders M 1027 S Water
Pimental Antone 145 Dartmouth
Pimental Francesco 421 Rivet
Potnier Napoleon 66 Washburn
Red Cross Shoe Co The 864 and 1494 Acushnet av
Renault Eugene 1053 County
Reusch Leopold r 287 Phillips av
Richman M 26 Delano
Santos Augustus 132 County
Shauks Robert J 380 Kempton
Sherin M 980 Acushnet av
Soares Manuel M 1478 Acushnet av and 259 Coggeshall
Souza John 637 S Water
Steckwich Charles J 249 Cedar
Surprenant A 538 N Front
Swift Martin 206 Division
Taylor Joseph 198 Rivet
Thibodeau Eugene 452 Belleville av
Thomas A 314 Acushnet av
Trahan Philadore 83 Collette
Velloso Jose 281 Rivet
Wall M M Mrs 105 Union
Wall R 149 Purchase
Watkins C F (custom) 92 Pleasant
Weiner H 273 Acushnet av
Whittaker W 7 Wamsutta
Yarlef S 79 Weld
Zurier Jacob 89 S Second

Bootblacks

Caralaka Kosta 92 Purchase
Dedopoulos Bros 881 S Water
George James 1504 Acushnet av
Gravalides Andrew 1407 Acushnet av
Keches G 58 Pleasant
Matsos Charlie 1063 Acushnet av
Pifko Alexander 71 Washburn
Sempis Christ 816 Purchase

Bottlers (Tonic & Cider)

Heyworth Daniel 151 Field
Isherwood John 69 Winsor
Neves Joseph 277 S Second
New Bedford Bottling Co 32 Morton court
SMITH BROS Inc 777 Purchase See page 779
WHEATON HIRAM & SONS 45 to 51 School See page 773
White Eagle Bottling Co Potvin ct rear 234½ N Front

Bowling

Elm Bowling Alleys 34 Elm
McAuliffe D 40 Delano
Nowell Leonard 1497 Acushnet av
Potomska Bowling Alleys 705 S Water
Souza Manuel L 162 Acushnet av
Tripp D K 351 Kempton
Whittaker James 397 Kempton

Box Mfrs

COFFIN BROS paper and cigar boxes 38 Middle See page 782
Old Colony Box Co (wood) Nash rd cor Church

Braid Mfrs

LaFontaine Braiding Co 85 and 87 Whitman

Brass Composition Castings

FOSTER ROBERT W BRASS FOUNDRY 115 N Water See page 781

Brass Founders

FOSTER R W BRASS FOUNDRY 115 N Water See page 781

Brass & Iron Pipe & Fittings

BRAMAN DOW & CO 239 Causeway Boston See page 38

Bread

RICHMOND & CO 255 Union and 425 S Water See foot lines

Brewers

Dawson & Son 645 Purchase and 34 Brook
SMITH BROS Inc Coggeshall near R R tracks and 777 Purchase See page 779
WEIHL JACOB agent Narraganset Brewery 21½ and 23½ N Second See page 779

Bricks

PAINE S S & BRO 139 Front See page 776
PAISLER & WILLIS 160 N Water See page 774

Brokers

(COTTON)

Almy William & Co 62 N Water
Amory I & Co 49 William
Andrews & Horton 25 N Water
Barry Thayer & Co 43 William rm 3
Choremi Benachi & Co 108 Union

Congdon A & Co 50 N Second
Cooper & Brush 97 William rm 306
Gifford Frank H 17 Hamilton
Hazard Cotton Co 52 N Second
Headley P C 56 N Water
Heineman M & Co 60 Pleasant
Hurley & Brady Co 62 N Water
Knowles E O 15 Clifford bldg
Malloch John & Co 97 William rm 306
McFadden George H & Bros 29 N Water
Mohr & Fenderl 97 William rm 306
Plummer L A Jr 15 Hamilton
Rhodes Woodward & Co 45 William
Shaw E A & Co 108 Union
Swift C R 17 Hamilton
Swift J Jr 97 William rm 306
Tucker Arthur L 25 N Water
Washburn C S 108 Union
Wilcox & Cornwell 97 William
Wood F 13 Hamilton

(REAL ESTATE)

WARREN'S AGENCY 1063 S Water See back binding and page 789

(STOCK)

(See also Bankers and Brokers)

HAWES TEWKSBURY & CO 22 Pleasant See page 7
Hodkins G H & Co 71 William
SANFORD & KELLEY Clifford bldg See front cover
Swain G J 45 Purchase
TUCKER ANTHONY & CO 17 Pleasant See page 6

Bronze Castings

FOSTER ROBERT W BRASS FOUNDRY 115 N Water See page 781

Broom Mfrs

Bowen George S & Co 44 Union
Lapointe Pierre D 199 Chestnut

Brush Dealers

DeWOLFE & VINCENT 111 William See page 44
MORIARTY T J 184 Fourth See page 49
SILVA M P B & SON 155 Acushnet avenue See foot lines

Builders

(See also Carpenters and Builders)

BISHOP J W CO 410 Times bldg and 417 Butler Exchange Providence R I and 107 Foster Worcester See page 19
BRIGHTMAN CHARLES O 72 N Water See page 95
BUFFINGTON ARTHUR E 1 Crapo See page 788
COOK & McQUADE 45 Maitland See page 763
DAVIS Z B CORP 668 Acushnet av See page 762
DESAUTELS HUGHUES 45 Brock av See page 760
FAFORD F X W French avenue and 127 Ruth See page 763
FAUNCE CHARLES L 138 N Second See page 765
HAZARD C B 69 Wood See page 764
JAMES F E 169 Clinton See back binding and page 761
LORANGER THEODORE 238 Phillips avenue See page 763
MOORE F R 96 Tremont See page 760
ROBITAILLE OVILA 200 Collette See page 764
SHERMAN CHARLES H 20 N Second See page 15
SILVA M P B & SON 157 Acushnet av See foot lines
SISTARE F B & SON 111 Willis See page 762
SMITH B F CONSTRUCTION CO The 37 Purchase and 22 Mason Pawtucket R I See page 18
SULLIVAN MARTIN H 168 N Second See page 760
TRIPP BENJAMIN C 161 Clinton See page 762
WATLING WILLIAM 35 Larch See page 757
WILLIAMS JOHN 77 Merrimac See page 762

Builders' Hardware

DeWOLFE & VINCENT 111 William See page 44
HILLMAN F G 669 Purchase See page 26
LAWRENCE J A 1032-1034 Acushnet av See page 784

Builders' Supplies

Blossom Bros 1659 N Second
BORDEN & REMINGTON CO 115 Annawan Fall River See page 11
DAVIS Z B CORP 668 Acushnet av See page 762
PAINE S S & BRO 139 Front See page 776

Builders' Supplies—con
PAISLER & WILLIS 160 N Water See page 774
QUINTIN H N 1223 Acushnet av See page 767

Building Moving

Hathaway Franklin B 570 Elm (W)
SAWIN GEORGE F 343 Purchase See page 783

Building Papers

BARRETT MFG CO 297 Franklin Boston See front cover

Bulbs

MOSHER WILLIAM E 325 Hillman See page 40

Burial Vaults

MASON J L G (Lockwood) 51 Foster See page 774

Business School

BENTON BUSINESS SCHOOL 97 William See map

Butter Cheese & Eggs

Ames S K 128 Purchase
BRIGHTMAN E T 248 Purchase See advt Grocers
Humphrey J L Jr (wholesale) 95-97 Front
NEW YORK MARKET 251 Purchase See page 772
ROBINSON DANIEL 156 Weld See page 772
Russell Bros Inc 70 William, 864 S Water and 1061 Acushnet av
Zalkind & Kessler 486 S Water

Button Mfrs

Hedge-Lewis Mfg Co 6 Elm

Cabinet Makers

CROOKER CO 230 Weybosset Providence R I See page 754
DANTSIZEN JOHN G 214 Court See back cover
JONES & DODGE 202 N Water See page 764
Keene C F 17 Centre
Perry J 287 S Water
TRIPP & THORPE 183 N Water See page 764
Washburn Lettice R & Son 226 N Water

Canned Goods

DRISCOL, CHURCH & HALL (wholesale) 84 Union See page 13
POTTER WILLIAM F & CO 81 to 85 Front and 3 to 11 Union See page 30

Card Clothing

HOWARD BROS MFG CO 44 to 46 Vine Worcester See page 14

Carpenters & Builders

Arruda F O 165 Rockland
Arseneault Urbain P 80 Nye
Beauregard James 929 County
Benoit S G 188 Dean
Bergeron Honore 132 Tallman
Bergeron Theodore 330 N Front
Bosworth G A 676 Cottage
Boudreau Dominique 3863 Acushnet av
Branchaud Leon 29 Hathaway
Braley George A 73 Dean
Briggs H A 204 Rockdale av
BRIGHTMAN CHARLES O 72 N Water See page 95
Brownell George A 197 Ash (N)
Bulman Frederic 374 Orchard (S)
Butts Joseph M 85 Newton
Cadorette Maxime 236 Brock av
Caron Silvio 57 Dean
Chainay Nazaire 251 Coffin av
Chase Charles F 24 Howard av
Daley Michael E 232 Collette
Dalrymple E E 189 N Water
DAVIS Z B CORP 668 Acushnet av See page 762
DeGagner L F 130 Fourth
DESAUTELS HUGHUES 45 Brock av See page 760
Dion Louis Z 455 Belleville av
Dulude J 397 Bowditch
FAFORD F X W French av and 127 Ruth See page 763
FAUNCE CHARLES L 138 N Second See page 765
Fisher Herbert L 101 Chestnut
Fournier N 577 S Second
Gay G W 115 Chancery
Gay T Franklin 72 Shawmut av
Greenhalgh Willard E 163 Jenny Lind
Hammond O S 177 N Water
Hathaway D L & Son 27 Centre
HAZARD C B 69 Wood See page 864
Houle L 211 Whitman
JAMES F E 169 Clinton See back binding and page 761

JONES & DODGE 202 N Water See page 764
Judson Bros 50 Locust
Judson Frank A 18 Willow
Lafleur H 103 Brock av
Lambert Frank 50 Tallman
Langlois Authier & Co 2030 Acushnet av
Lefrancois Emile 160 Bowditch
Levesque Adolor 1220 Acushnet av
LORANGER THEODORE 238 Phillips av See page 763
Lucas E A 206 James
Lumbard Charles E 19 Bethel
MacKay Malcom A 171 Maple
MacKenzie Daniel A 445 Kempton
Martin Samuel D 5 Bullard
Miller Herbert A 232 Grinnell
Monjeau Louis 61 County
MOORE F RUSSELL 96 Tremont See page 760
Moore James J 125 Oak
Morsey Joseph J 43 Bay
Nolin Pierre 180 Davis
Peekham E L 3 Beetle lane
Perry Joseph R 60 Borden
Pierce & Kilburn ft Leonard
PINEAULT J N 682 Purchase See page 761
Poirier Dephis 23 Rodney
Poole L W & Son 42 Spring
Poulette Louis 154 Collette
Poulin Albert F 90 Nye
Poulin Philbert 82 Holly
Randall G W 13 Cottage
ROBITAILLE OVILA 200 Collette See page 764
SHERMAN CHARLES H 20 N Second See page 15
Sherman R A & Son 7 Leonard
SILVA M P B & SON 157 Acushnet av See foot lines
Silva S N 263 Field ct
Silveira F P 487 Allen
SISTAIRE FRANK B & SON 111 Willis See page 762
Squires George T 191 Clinton
SULLIVAN MARTIN H 168 N Second See page 760
Thompson C G 485 Mill
Thorley F 515 Rivet
TRIPP BENJAMIN C 161 Clinton See page 762
Tripp James T 52 Grape
Vincent Ulric 77 Bullard
WATLING WILLIAM 35 Larch See page 757
Washburn F P 2443 Acushnet av
WILLIAMS JOHN 77 Merrimac See page 762

Carpet Cleaning

N B STEAM CARPET BEATING AND RUG CO H M Maine prop North cor N Water See front cover

Carpets & Oilcloths

GALLIGAN C A 1516 Acushnet av See page 37
HOUSEHOLD FURNISHING CO 170-174 Purchase See page 94
Waite B H & Co 71 William
WING CHARLES F CO The Inc 34-38 Purchase See page 40

Carriage Dealers & Mfrs

HATHAWAY L J 7 and 9 Elm See page 771
LINTON JOHN R & SONS 105 Maxfield See page 33

Carriage Painters

Baron Servais & Co 1188 Acushnet av
BOURGEOIS DAVID 105 Bowditch See page 774
CROSHERE C A 38 Fourth See foot lines
Forbes J R 33 Elm
HATHAWAY L J 7 Elm See page 771
Hazzard Edward V 1 Spring
LINTON JOHN R & SONS 105 Maxfield See page 33
Mellor Frank H 1272 Rockdale av
Sylvia Manuel A 112 Pleasant

Carriagesmiths

(See Blacksmiths)

Carriage Stock

CONGDON CARPENTER & CO 58-60 Fourth Fall River See page 10
HANDY JONATHAN CO 28 William See page 766
HATHAWAY L J 7 Elm See page 771
JEWETT HARDWARE CO 108 Middle and 415 Acushnet av See page 784

Carriage Trimmers

Boomer A 38 Fourth
Briggs Philip S 173 Acushnet av
Simmons L E 112 Pleasant

Cash Registers
National Cash Register Co 37 Purchase

Castings
FOSTER ROBERT W BRASS FOUNDRY 115 N Water See page 781

Caterers
CROWN CONFECTIONERY STORE 56 Purchase See page 783
Turner James H 115 Tremont

Catholic Goods
FOREST F & CO 1041 Acushnet av See page 778

Caulkers
Drew G H 155 Front

Ceilings
BERGER MFG CO of Massachusetts 286 Devonshire Boston See page 753
DEXTRADEUR CHARLES J 363 N Front See page 754

Cement Blocks
FAFORD F X W French av and 127 Ruth See page 763

Cement Lime & Brick
BORDEN & REMINGTON CO 115 Annawan Fall River See page 11
CITY COAL CO Front foot Middle branches 114 William and 1026 Acushnet av See page 3
PAINE S S & BRO 139 Front See page 776
PAISLER & WILLIS 160 N Water See page 774

Cement Work
SILVA HENRY 63 Fifth See page 761

Certified Public Accountant
COOLEY MORGAN L, C P A mgr Gunn, Richards & Co Tremont bldg Boston See page 40

Chair Mfrs
Bay State Chair Co factory Prospect
Johnson J S (reseated) 28 Crapo

Charcoal
AKIN F T & CO 168 S Water cor Walnut and 1218 Acushnet av See foot lines

Charitable Organizations
ST JAMES CO-OPERATIVE SALES 68 Linden See page 48

Chemical Works
Davis H V Chemical Works 147 Chancery

Chiropodists & Manicurists
Davis May E 71 William
Dodd M A Mrs 120 Purchase rm 206
Duffy Dora D 34 Purchase
Hopkins Ivy G 76 Pleasant rm 25
Johnson M F Mrs 161 Middle
Miller Harriet L 42 Summer
Mosher Mary E 24 Purchase
Pierce L Mrs 163 Purchase
Razoux H A 74 Purchase
Snow Rhoda A 82 Elm
Wall Hannah 12 Robeson

Christian Science Practitioners
Brierly J E 7 Fifth
Lowell Fannie C 8 Borden
Macy Louise R 74 Gay
Stratton L A Mrs 124 Maxfield

Cigars & Tobacco
*Manufacturers and Wholesale)
*Acushnet Mfr The 20 Arcade
*Bessarabian Jacob 225 Coggeshall
BROWNE PHARMACY The 197 to 203 Union See back cover
Cabral J 79 Howland
Chapman E T & Co 358 Acushnet av
CHURCH CHARLES H 122 Purchase See page 25
*Cleary J F 183 Acushnet av
Cotnoir J L 105 County
Ellis C E (wholesale) 48 N Water
*Francis F W Cigar and Tobacco Co The 164 Union
Hebert Charles 1217 Acushnet av
Howard L A 570 County
Hutchinson Robert 836 Purchase
Kearns T H 218 Union
LAWTON C H & H A CO 1 and 52 Purchase and 113 Union See advt Drugs
*Moss J 225 Coggeshall
*Racicot E 101 Bullard
*Robinson A 117 Union
Robinson Fred L 169 Purchase
Ryder C E 134 Purchase
Specter D 1020 Acushnet av
United Cigar Stores Co 94 Purchase
Wordell B F 291-293 Purchase
Zavas & Co 1209 Acushnet av

Cleansing Your Clothes

YOU want your cleansing done promptly—*we will return your garments within the week.* You want your cleansing done carefully and skillfully—*we will give each of your garments individual attention, and the benefit of modern methods and sanitary conditions.*—Our work is *the best* because our facilities are superior. Test us with a trial order.

"The best Glove Cleansing in New England"

"No matter where you live—our mail order service is at your door"

WRITE or telephone for our team to call, or send your garments by express. We pay express charges both ways in greater Boston—One way to any point in New England.

GOWNS, SUITS, WRAPS, FEATHERS, GLOVES, CURTAINS, BLANKETS, RUGS

CLEANSED

WRITE FOR COMPLETE PRICE LIST

THE C. G. HOWES COMPANY

Address Mail Order Dept. D. ALLSTON, MASS.

See Other Side

Cleanse Your Gloves and Feathers by Mail

NO matter where you live, you get your gloves, feathers, gowns, etc. cleansed as promptly as if you lived next door to our works.

GLOVES returned to you within 12 hours

We pay return charges on all work

WRAP your soiled gloves in a package or envelope, enclosing fifteen cents for each pair, in stamps or coin, and drop in the mail.

"The Best Glove Cleansing in New England"

HIGH-GRADE CLEANSING

OF GARMENTS, LACES, FEATHERS, ETC.

THE C. G. HOWES COMPANY

Address Mail Order Dept. D. ALLSTON, MASS.

See Other Side

Civil Engineers & Surveyors

DAHILL & KIRBY 11 Clifford bldg See page 42

DRAKE ALBERT B 164 William See front cover and bottom edge

FRANK M METCALF
Civil Engineer and Surveyor
211 Merchants Bank Building
Auto Tel 1276 Bell Tel 431-2
Residence 378 Cottage Street
Bell Tel 767-5

Williams W F (City) 303 Municipal bldg

Clairvoyants

Cosmos Mary Agnes Mrs 332 Kempton
Peltier Isabel H 24 Purchase
Rena Madam 135 Middle

Cleansers

HOWES C G & CO Allston Mass See opposite

Cleansing & Dyeing

BUSH A M & CO 47 William and 19 Jenny Lind See page 786
CRONIN EDWARD H 504 County See page 769
GLOBE DYE HOUSE 220 Shawmut av and 52 Pleasant rm 1 and 1014 Acushnet av See foot lines
NEW BEDFORD STEAM DYE HOUSE 53 William See page 768
Winborne W C 21 Fourth

Clergymen

Ahamel Albert (R C) 1359 Acushnet av
Bartholomew James I (M E) 40 Chestnut
Basinski S (R C) 577 S Second
Bateman T M (P M) 46 Ashland
Bedard Lucien C (R C) 1359 Acushnet av
Berube A (R C) 163 County
Blanchette L N (R C) 60 Brock av
Boyer Francis B (Epis) 172 Page
Brady J J (R C) 306 Bowditch
Burns James R 23 Robeson
Burstein Max (Hebrew) 508 S Water
Cardozo Joaquim (R C) 94 S Sixth
Chagnon Jovita (R C) 39 Ingraham
Clerk Charles (R C) 1359 Acushnet avenue
Coffey James M (R C) 23 Robeson
Collett Alfred K (P M) 48 Independent
Conlon James (R C) 593 Kempton
Conrow L M (Pres) 82 State
Deslauriers H (R C) 1359 Acushnet avenue
Domina Frederick W 83 Atlantic
Downing Mortimer (R C) 233 County
Felton Harry (M E) 257 Palmer
Fortin Ivan C (Epis) 716 County
Gadboury Charles P (R C) 27 Ashland
Gale Howard C R (Univ) 27 James
Ganter M (Epis) 21 S Sixth
Geohegan W B (Unit) 37 S Sixth
Gordon P (Epis) 372 County
Hersey C F (Cong) 755 First
Howes G H (Univ) 64 Borden
Jacobson J M (Hebrew) 86 Grinnell
Julien M C (Cong) 37 Fifth
Larson Robert (Bap) 69 Ocean
Lemieux Charles F (R C) 1415 Acushnet av
Longergan S P (R C) 27 Ashland
Lyons J P (R C) 110 Summer
Maddox I D (M E) 10 W High
Marriott Nathaniel A (Bap) 7 Spruce
McDonough M V (R C) 306 Bowditch
McNamara J L (R C) 233 County
Mette H (Luth) 296 Kempton
Miller E C (Bap) 167 Ashland
Moseley William H (P M E) 42 Columbia
Neves Fortunato (R C) 94 S Sixth
Oldham John (M E) 283 Bowditch
Owens M J (R C) 110 Summer
Oxnard Henry E (Cong) 2135 Acushnet av
Pearce John (M E) 81 Bay
Peters Frank H (Christ) 65 Chestnut
Phelan J J (Bap) 718 County
Potvin J Edmond (R C) 68 Bowditch
Purington O B (Epis) 93 State
Ramsdell F E (Cong) 446 County
Ransom Mary S 334 Kempton
Ribourg Albert (Bap) 45 Willis
Santos Augustine (R C) 230 Bonney
Sayer T S (Bap) 72 Hillman
Scott D (A M E) 18 Cedar

Clergymen—con
Silva F C B (Bap) 184 Thompson
Silva Manuel A (R C) 94 S Sixth
Smyth H J (R C) 110 Summer
Streeter F L (M E) 347 County
Taveira Augusto J (R C) 1238 Acushnet av
Thurber Charles S 15 Bethel
Trueman H S (Evang) 152 Sycamore
Uminski E A (R C) 66 Howard
Valois O (R C) 60 Brock av
Veira A P (R C) 230 Bonney
Yearwood C Hubert (A M E) 460 Kempton

Cloaks & Garments

Boston Specialty Shop 24 Purchase
Cherry & Co 40 Purchase
Cohen & Son 829 Purchase
New York Cloak Store 1097 Acushnet av
Paris Cloak Co 1031 Acushnet av
ST JAMES CO-OPERATIVE SALES 68 Linden See page 48

Clothes Wringers

DeWOLF & VINCENT 111 William See page 44

Clothing

Adelsohn Isaac 517 S Water
American Clothing Co 1029 Acushnet av and 915 S Water
Bargain Clothing Co The 956 Acushnet av
Benoit Bourassa Co 1249 Acushnet av
Blaisdell & Snyder Inc 956 Acushnet av
Brightman Leander 55 William
Charpentier C Henri 1055 Acushnet av
Choquette Elzear H 80 William
Cohen Bros 1088 Acushnet av
Empire Clothing Co 88 Purchase
Furnans Bros 144 Union
Genesky P 841 S Water
Globe Credit Co 140 Purchase
Gothieb Isaac 776 Purchase
Goodman Hyman 321 S Water
Goodman Julius 475 S Water
Herman A 493 S Water
Hurwitz Samuel 789 S Water
IDEAL CREDIT CLOTHING HOUSE 7 Purchase See page 33
Levine M 934 S Water
Lumiansky B & Son 871-873 S Water
MacLeod Credit Co 92½ Purchase
Markovitz Samuel 739 S Water
Mechaber S 849 Purchase
Mendelson A & Son 1135 Acushnet av
Paris Store Co 1031 Acushnet av
Peoples Credit Co 80 Purchase
Poisson Bros 1064 Acushnet av
Poisson G & L 912 S Water
Power & Desmond 67 William
Ross & Sisson 348 Acushnet av
Silvia M C 160 Acushnet av
ST JAMES CO-OPERATIVE SALES 68 Linden See page 48
Star Clothing Co 1262 Acushnet av
Surprise Clothing Co 156 Purchase
Swift M C & Son 157-159 Union
Talbot & Co 44-48 Purchase
WENTWORTH F W CO 211 Union cor Pleasant See page 768
WING J & W R & CO 133 Union See page 768
Wischnietzksy M 289 Coggeshall
Wladinsky Morris 1602 Acushnet av
Wolfson Fisher 1285 Acushnet av

Coal & Wood

(See also Wood & Coal)

AKIN F T & CO 168 S Water cor Walnut 84 Pleasant 9 N Water 1218 Acushnet av See foot lines
Borden H T 62 Dartmouth
CITY COAL CO Front cor Middle branches 114 William and 1026 Acushnet av and 1109 S Water See page 3
CONNOR PATRICK 486 Rivet See page 783
DENISON BROS CO 32 Pleasant foot Hillman and 77 Rivet See front edge
DUFF DAVID & SON 105 William 73 Weld and Fish Island See front cover
Garfield & Proctor Coal Co foot of Hillman
HOLMES ALBERT W (wholesale and retail) 201 Purchase and Holmes wharf foot of Cannon See back cover
Philadelphia & Reading Coal & Iron Co foot Walnut
Secour Joseph W 379 Mt Pleasant
THORPE R H 1786 Acushnet av See page 765

Coal Tar Products

BARRETT MFG CO 297 Franklin Boston See front cover
WARREN CHEMICAL & MFG CO 49 Federal Boston See opp *583

Coat Apron & Towel Supplies
HOWLAND S D & CO 86 Chancery See page 786

Coffee Roasters
ALLEN SLADE & CO 1 William and 18-26-30 Third Fall River See page 12

Cold Storage
BOSWORTH W E 1194 Rockdale av See page 785

Collections
Merchants Law Exchange Inc The 97 William rm 312
Whitney Law Corp 97 William

Comber Needling & Supplies
TOWNSEND THOMAS 157 Orange Providence R I See page 16
Vera & Robitaille r 211 Coffin av

Commercial Printers
BUDLONG J E PRESS The 38 Middle See page 778

Commercial School
KINYON'S COMMERCIAL SCHOOL 76 Pleasant rms 21-24 See foot lines

Commission Merchants
Bartlett Robert W 97 William rm 302
WING J & W R & CO 133 Union See page 768

Commissioners (To Qualify Civil Officers)
GOODSPEED ALEX. McL 37 Purchase
HITCH MAYHEW R 37 Masonic bldg
(FOR OTHER STATES)
BARNEY BENJAMIN B (R I) Masonic bldg rms 11 and 12
CRAPO HENRY H (Mich) Masonic bldg rm 6
MacCORD WILLIAM A (Quebec) 37 Purchase
STETSON ELIOT D (New York) Masonic bldg rm 34
(SPECIAL
Scranton C N Mrs 71 William

Concrete Blocks
Branchaud Leon 29 Hathaway

Concrete Composition
WARREN CHEMICAL & MFG CO 49 Federal Boston See opp *583

Concrete Pitch
WARREN CHEMICAL & MFG CO 49 Federal Boston See opp *583

Concrete Walks & Driveways
PERKINS A W & CO 167 Hillman See page 789

Concrete Work
CROTEAU & WOOD 249 Shawmut av See page 776
PROUTEAU RAOUL 82 Phillaps av See page 760

Confectionery
Annis Bros 817 S Water
Bates Kirby & Co 48 Pleasant
BROWNE PHARMACY The 197-203 Union See back cover
Christopher & Mellen 749 S Water
CHURCH CHARLES H 122 Purchase See page 25
Couroussi P & Co 774 Purchase and 953 Acushnet av
CROWN CONFECTIONERY STORE 56 Purchase See page 783
Duckworth William H 488½ N Front
Fallas Hannah 1606 Acushnet av
Fatulli Peter 123 Fourth
Greenwood Samuel 1268 Acushnet av
Krivoff Hyman 497 S Water
Lessard Thomas 250 N Front
Mackler Joseph 179½ Belleville av
McGill David Co (wholesale) 193 Blackmer
Mellen C 138 Purchase
Peters & Conos 1295 Acushnet av
Savoie Sarah 1561 Acushnet av
Searle Josephine E Mrs Rockdale av cor Court
Sharples & Son 1378 Acushnet av
Taber Confectionery Co (wholesale) 9 N Second

Contractors & Builders
Bennett F C 131 Summer
BISHOP J W CO Times bldg and 417 Butler Exchange Providence R I and 107 Foster Worcester See page 19
Blier Joseph 26 Ashley
BRIGHTMAN CHARLES O 72 N Water See page 95
BUFFINGTON A E 1 Crapo See page 788

Contractors—con
COOK & McQUADE 45 Maitland See page 763
CROTEAU & WOOD 249 Shawmut av See page 776
DAVIS C B CORP 668 Acushnet av See page 762
DESAUTELS HUGHUES 45 Brock av See page 760
FAFORD F X 127 Ruth and W French av See page 763
FAUNCE CHARLES L 138 N Second See page 765
Goodreau D 9 Beetle
HAZARD C B 69 Wood See page 764
Labrode Henry H 54 Maitland
LEBEAU THEOPHILE 410½ N Front See page 33
LOFTUS & DUGAN (granolithic) 121 Clark See page 776
LORANGER THEODORE 238 Phillips av See page 763
MAHER PIERRE 358 N Front See page 763
MASON J L G (mason) 51 Foster See page 774
Miller H A 232 Grinnell
MOORE F RUSSELL 96 Tremont See page 760
PROUTEAU RAOUL 82 Phillips av See page 760
Rioux Charles Bowditch cor Glennon
ROBITAILLE O 200 Collette See page 764
SHERMAN CHARLES H 20 N Second See page 15
SILVA HENRY 63 Fifth See page 761
SILVA M P B & SON 157 Acushnet av See foot lines
SISTARE F B & SON 111 Willis See page 762
SMITH B F CONSTRUCTION CO The 37 Purchase and 22 Mason Pawtucket R I See page 18
Sullivan J B & Son 560 Cottage
SULLIVAN MARTIN H 168 N Second See page 760
TRIPP BENJAMIN C 161 Clinton See page 762
WARREN AGENCY 1063 S Water See page 789 and back binding
WATLING WILLIAM 35 Larch See page 757
WILLIAMS JOHN 77 Merrimac See page 762

Contratctors (Sand & Gravel)

CONNELL JOHN JR 350 Sawyer See page 774
Vera Frank L 249 Dartmouth

Contratctors (Teaming)

CONNELL JOHN JR 350 Sawyer See page 774
DUFF DAVID & SON 73 Weld See front cover
PERKINS A W & CO 167 Hillman See page 789

Conveyancer

RICHMOND CHARLES N 54 Pleasant See page 94

Cooked Meats

Davidson J & Son 280 Austin

Co-operative Banks

(See also Banks and Savings Banks)
Acushnet 125 Middle
New Bedford 125 Middle

Coopers

Souza Manuel G 353 S Second
Wood A T 9 Hamilton

Copper Mnfrs

TAUNTON-NEW BEDFORD COPPER CO N Front between Wamsutta and Logan See page 734

Copper Paint

AKIN F T & CO 168 S Water 84 Pleasant and 1218 Acushnet av See foot lines

Cordage

Allen T C & Co City pier No 2
HILLMAN F G 669 Purchase See page 26
Lambeth Rope Corp Tarkiln Hill rd
McEwen Robert (cotton) 140 Durfee
New Bedford Cordage Co 131 Court

Cornices

PERRA JOHN 19 Linden See page 766

Corsets

Richard Marie T 487 N Front

Cotton Goods Mfrs

(See Mfg Companies)

Cotton Machinery

DRAPER CO Hopedale Mass See page 2
MASON MACHINE WORKS Taunton Mass See page 39
WHITIN MACHINE WORKS Whitinsville Mass See page 20

Cotton Waste

New Bedford Waste Co 58 Middle

Court & General Reporting

DAVOL CLARENCE H 23 Clifford bldg See page 755

Credit Clothing

IDEAL CREDIT CLOTHING HOUSE 7 Purchase See page 33

Crockery China & Glass Ware

Horvitz A J 541 S Water
HOUSEHOLD FURNISHING CO 170 to 174 Purchase See page 94
Kesterbaum Emanuel 801 S Water
WING CHARLES F CO The Inc 34 to 38 Purchase See page 40

Curtains & Curtain Fixtures

HOUSEHOLD FURNISHING CO 170 to 174 Purchase See page 94
STEIGER DUDGEON CO 185 to 187 Union and 9 to 19 Purchase See foot lines
WING CHARLES F CO The Inc 34 to 38 Purchase See page 40

Cutlery

Christensen Henry M 190 Purchase
DeWOLF & VINCENT 111 William See page 44
LAWRENCE J A 1032 Acushnet av See page 784
QUINTIN H N 1223 Acushnet av See page 767

Decorators

AKIN F T & CO 168 S Water, 84 Pleasant and 9 N Water See foot lines
ALLEN MARCUS M 15 to 19 N Water See page 777
BERTRAND O 160 Bowditch See page 754
BLAIR SIGN & ADVERTISING CO (hall & street) 60 Fourth See page 754
CASWELL WILLIAM T 34 to 38 Union See page 94
CORMIER & DUBE 394 N Front See page 776
DIONNE WALTER 14 Jean See page 752
DROLET & MILOTTE 109 Holly See page 775
GALLOP R G & CO 55 Hillman See page 752
JENKINS ELMIR A 431 Acushnet av See page 752
MORIARTY T J 184 Fourth See page 49
PELLETIER HENRI 86 Hathaway See page 37
PHILLIPS THOMAS O 167 Park See page 44
SILVA HENRY 53 Fifth See page 761
Soule T H 169 Union
THERRIEN JOHN 82 Tallman See page 752
WRIGHT GEORGE F 24 N Water See page 777

Dentists

Adam A R 1111 S Water
ARCAND EMILE J 1356 Acushnet av See page 27
Ashley Frederick M 30 Purchase
Austin Joseph 163 Purchase
Bannister L A 250 Union
Birtwistle Frank 1265 Acushnet av
Browning E E 570 Purchase
Caron H F 1060 Acushnet av
Dufresne D P 9 W French av
Finie Joseph N 1105 Acushnet av
Gilbert E A 60 Purchase
Gravel Arthur H 1043 Acushnet av
Gilmartin C W 910 S Water
Greene T P E 208 Times bldg
Hennessey John L 74 Purchase
Hollihan John H 5 Arcade block
Irish George O 34 Purchase
Jalbert F X (mechanical) 301 Times bldg
Jean Arthur L 1452 Acushnet av
Kennedy F M 139 Purchase
King Dental Co 24 Purchase
Lima Joseph M 83 Fifth
Logwood B E 25 Purchase
Macy William C 17 Seventh
Mann W W 174½ Purchase
McKenna JJ 149 Middle
McQuillan E J 218 Fourth
Neal C A 155 Union
Nesbett Norman B 331 Union
Pease James E 1 Bedford
Perrier Albert C J 5 Pleasant
Perry S D 132 Pleasant
Peters William L 185 Purchase

Dentists—con
Pierce F E 97 William
Shockley A L 45 Purchase
Shurtleff C 1017 Acushnet av
Simon V C 45 Purchase
Slocomb P F 52 Rivet
Stanley Ned A 3 Pleasant
Stephens Winston 12 S Sixth
Sweeney Daniel J 1603 Acushnet av
Sylvia A P 193 Fourth
Tessier C C 56 Pleasant
Winship F H Jr 3 Pleasant
Woodbridge W B 60 Purchase
Wyman A F 265 Union

Detective Agencies

NATIONAL DETECTIVE AGENCY The 49 Westminster Providence R I See page 28
RHODE ISLAND DETECTIVE AGENCY The 395 Westminster Providence R I See page 37
WOOD-MORGAN DETECTIVE AGENCY 61 Court Boston See page 753

Detectives

BURNS DETECTIVE BUREAU 1 Beacon Boston See opposite page 161
RHODE ISLAND DETECTIVE AGENCY The 395 Westminster Providence R I See page 37

Dining Rooms
(See Restaurants)

Directory Publishers

GREENOUGH W A & CO 65 Broad Boston (write for list published)

Disinfectants

BARRETT MFG CO 297 Franklin Boston See front cover

Doors Sash & Blinds
(See also Sash, Doors and Blinds)

GREENE & WOOD Pine street See foot lines
NICHOLSON JOHN G 27 to 35 Bowditch See foot lines

Drain Pipe

PAINE S S & BRO 139 Front See page 776
PAISLER & WILLIS 160 N Water See page 774

Draperies

HOUSEHOLD FURNISHING CO 170 to 174 Purchase See page 94
Sisson William H A 308 County
WING CHARLES F CO The Inc 34 to 38 Purchase See page 40

Dressmakers

Albert Mary A 92 Washington
Alexander A G Mrs 80 Thompson
Allen Eliza M 304 County
Allen J S Mrs 88 Newton
Almy Helen R 2 Green
Ashley Elizabeth G 375 Cedar
Baker Lydia R 96 Atlantic
Bannon Misses 11 Hyacinth
Barker Mary A Mrs 857 Kempton
Barnes E K Mrs 158 Grinnell
Barrett Elizabeth A 181 Middle
Bartlett Elizabeth R 108 Seventh
Bateman Estella G 46 Ashland
Bellerose J Mrs 1081 County
Bessette Eulalie Mrs 65 Kenyon
Birch Theresa C 207 State
Blanchette R Mrs 103 Ruth
Boisclair Marion 21 Acushnet av
Bonneau Mary 751 S Water
Bonney Kate 354 County
Boone Eliza C 173 Acushnet av
Booth S Lizzie 56 North
Bourget M Mrs 11 Marvin
Bowers Clara 103 Hazard
Brierly Jane Mrs 118 Potomska
Brightman Ida M 133 Kempton
Brochu Annie Mrs 1279 Acushnet av
Brownson Helen S 58 Locust
Buffington J A Mrs 107 Chancery
Burbank I N Mrs 37 Madison
Burke Ezelia M 106 Sycamore
Cambra Mary J 518 Rivet
Carr Cornelia 68 Chancery
Catin Annie 235 Fourth
Caton Virginia 226 Rivet
Chaney Emma E 85 Thomas
Charbonneau Phoebe 82 Myrtle
Chatelle Mary Mrs 1220 Acushnet av
Cleveland Alice M 50 Bedford
Conville L Mrs 17 Jouvette
Cornell Adaline M 48 Cottage
Cotnoir Rose A 55 Independent
Davis D B Mrs 250 Coffin av
Dias Josephine 152 Allen
Dion R O 1117 Acushnet av
Doutigny Flora 79 Kenyon
Duffy Catherine D 39 Ash (S)
Dufour Kate A Mrs 607 Cottage
Eaton Annabelle 248 Hawthorn
Edwards Lillian 238 Sawyer
Ellis Mary S 270 Middle

Epstein Uel 972 and 345 Acushnet av
Esson Sarah 410 Kempton
Evans A A Mrs 22 North
Felecianno Mary 267 Allen
Finley T A Mrs 46 W French av
Fleury Celestine 199 Phillips av
Francis A M Mrs 133 Willis
Frates H M Mrs 408 Middle (W)
Freeman W N Mrs 555 Kempton
Galligan Kate A 78 Mill
Gallipeau S Mrs 287 Rivet
Gauthier Georgianna 40 Linden
GERARDI V V 36 Eighth See page 769
Gerraughty Mary E 177 Summer
Gifford A G 176 Kempton
Gifford Mary C Mrs 375 Kempton
Gilmore Delia A 12 Spruce
Gingras S Mrs 15 Holly
Groves J F Mrs 69 Mechanics lane
Guinet A Porsch Mrs 187 North
Hadfield Martha 291 Collette
Harrington Kathryn R 946 County
Hathaway Ida F 257 Maxfield
Hathaway Sarah L 411 Union
Havard D H Mrs 92 Weld
Henning N A Mrs 390 Acushnet av
Hines Catherine M 404 Union
Holmes C E Mrs 186 Arnold
Hopkins Margaret E 48 Cottage
Howarth Elsie P Mrs 865 County
Hunter Ellen 55 N Sixth
Jay Lizbeth L 95 School
Jeuks Lizzie H Mrs 96 Bonney
Johnson Laura L 50 Mill
Jourdain A E Mrs 279 Arnold
Keith C F Mrs 55 Walnut
Kelley James S Mrs 101 Chestnut
Kirwin Mary J 101 S Sixth
Langlois Virginia A 325 N Front
Larocque Lucy Mrs 412 N Front
Lavoie Josephine 117 Ruth
LeBlanc Jennie E 369 Purchase
LeBlanc Lea 268 N Front
Leonard Mary A 30 Bonney
Lima Mary A 53 Fifth
Little Mabel L Mrs 1 Cottage
Manter Bessie N 22 Cedar
Marshall B Mrs 108 Rockland
Mason George N Mrs 113 James
Mason Mary F 79 Bedford
Mattos Mary 12 Wing
Maxfield Maria E 137 Chestnut
McAvoy Elizabeth M 206 Pleasant
McAvoy Martha A 206 Pleasant
McCarthy C 192 Chancery
McCarthy Helen T 51 Locust
McGee Josephine 7 Bentley
Meikle E E Mrs 45 Foster
Murphy Anna 304 Cedar
Murphy E Mrs 354 Kempton
Peckham Georgianna 127 Cedar
Pelletier Joseph Mrs 33 Holly
Perry Mary C 183 Thompson
Phelan Katherine C 283 Middle
Plouffe D Mrs 96 Jouvett
Potts Annie M 253 Union
Ransom Frances H 592 Kempton
Remillard Rosalie 85 Rivet
Reynolds Nettie L 56 Mill
Rock Christiana 616 Purchase
Rose Maria B 273 Orchard (S)
Ryan Kate 51 Hillman
Sadler Rose 1616 Acushnet av
Sampson A Blanche 12 S Second
Sawyer Rilla D 39 High
Sharpe K Mrs 101 Middle
Sharples Anna 60 Beetle
Sherman Eva G 157 Smith
Slocum E S Mrs 65 Elm
Smith Mary A 45 Emerson (S)
Soule Lydia W 111 Hillman
Souza Amelia 143 Mill
Stedman Edna 197 Grinnell
Stokoe Mary J 183 Wash
Sullivan Frances 138 Bedford
Swan Edith A 303 Middle
Sweeney A Maude 110 County
Swift Alice V34 Ash (S)
Sylvia Katharine 25 Dartmouth
Sylvia K B Mrs 55 Katharine
Sylvia Mary E 25 Dartmouth
Tetreault Rose 43 Dean
Thacker Teresa 72 State
Thatcher M E Mrs 96 Middle
Thorne Caledonia 72 Ash (N)
Tillinghast E H Mrs 108 Fourth
Towne A Mrs 38 Reynolds
Tucker Laura A 198 Elm
Tynan Sarah J 335 Cedar
Vandenbossche Adele 71 Chancery
Vargas F K Mrs 123 Rockland
Vickars Margaret C 132 Mill
Waldron F C Mrs 288 Acushnet av
Wall Margaret 12 Robeson
Watkins Annie L 197 Cedar
Watson E A Mrs 67 Wash
Welch M A Mrs 262 Union
White A P Mrs 166 Campbell
William S F Mrs 93 First
Winfield E G Mrs 302 Middle
Winters M J F Mrs 96 Spring
Wood Annie D 22 Cedar
Wood Emma J 156 Campbell

C. H. & H. A. LAWTON CO.
Prescription Work Our Specialty
Accurate Composition
Druggists
Pure Drugs
Best Service in the City
Established 1822
THE THREE BIG STORES
Cor. Union and Purchase Sts. Cor. Union and Second Sts. Cor. William and Purchase Sts.
NEW BEDFORD, MASS.
THE REXALL STORES

Wood E L Mrs 15 Shawmut av
Young A E Mrs 214 Cedar
Zerbone A E Mrs 25 Griffin

Drill Mnfrs

MORSE TWIST DRILL & MACHINE CO 100 Fifth See page 15

Driven Wells

SMITH B F CO 38 Oliver Boston See page 31

Druggists

Aillery Joseph L 190 Weld
Anthony, Guinn & Co 396 Kempton
Beauvais Fortunato M 1881-1883 Acushnet av
Berard & Co 274 Cedar
Blackmer H A 165-167 Purchase
Boston Drug Co 155 Blackmer
Bosworth C T & Co 133 County
Bourne & Damon Co 131 Belleville rd
Brown C W 452 S Water
Brown John C 209 Coggeshall
BROWNE PHARMACY The 197-203 Union See back cover
Bullock W J 268 Fourth
Chartier Charles O, W French av cor Cove
CHURCH CHARLES H 122 Purchase See page 25
Church & Hammond 115 William
Cobb John A 849 Kempton
Collet Cyprien A A 1567 Acushnet av
Corson Henry T 639 County
Cote Ernest E 1972 Acushnet av
Cundall C D 44 Dartmouth
Dartmouth Pharmacy The 246 Union
Davignon T A 420 N Front
Dion V B 1201 Acushnet av
Drummond W H 75 N Second
Fontaine A D 1115 S Water
Giguere Olivier 161 Coffin av
Giguere O & Co 1669 Acushnet av
Goddu Oscar C 1401 Acushnet av
Healey M C & Co Cottage cor Durfee
Higham William M & Co 212 Union and 403 Purchase
Holly Drug Co 1263 Acushnet av
Janson Raymond 1301 Acusnhet av
Kelleher J M 215 Purchase and 513 County
Lamoureux G 1104 Acushnet av
Lamoureux S A 1598 Acushnet av
LAWTON C H & H A CO 1 and 52 Purchase and 113 Union See page above
Lussier N R 1189 Acushnet av
Lussier & Lagasse 125 Rivet
Mahoney-Edward T 45 Linden
McManus John A 122 Allen
Mello Joseph 195 Court
Murphy James A 409 Rivet
Nolan J J 862 Purchase
Normandin A & Co 122 N Front
Normandin L Z 598 Purchase
Nuttall James H 146 Arnold
Otis E F 377 Cedar
Pease Frank R 977 Acushnet av
Pease & Dandurand 913 S Water
Perry M P 91 Grinnell
Petit A A 888 Purchase
Querry Ernest H 352 Kempton
Red Cross Pharmacy 116 Dartmouth
Reilly Florence M 396 Union
Shurtleff Israel H 195 Fourth
Smith C T 721 S Water
Snell E L 133 Ruth
Toupin H C 2173 Acushnet av
Trigueiro John E 94-98 N Second and 233 Coggeshall

Wamsutta Pharmacy 1 Pleasant
Watson & Boardman 765 Kempton
Weld Square Pharmacy 3-5 Weld
White & Fairchild 322 County
Whitney Pharmacy Co 286 Acushnet av and 119 Fourth
Wright E E 88 Purchase

Drugs

BORDEN & REMINGTON CO 115 Annawan Fall River See page 11
LAWTON C H & H A CO 1 and 52 Purchase and 113 Union See above

Dry Goods

Abrams W 890 S Water
Ambash M 541 S Water
Au Bon Marche 139 Union
BONNEY, FOLSTER & CO 945 Acushnet av See foot lines
Boucher Joseph Z 419 N Front
Bowen Sarah E Mrs 227 Cedar
Braude A 725 S Water
Burdick A M Mrs 1647 Acushnet av
Campbell James 11 Bonney
Clynes H M Mrs 656 Purchase
Cohen Albert 242 Coggeshall
Cohen J 267 S Water
David Peter 185 Second
Davidow Sarah Mrs 831 S Water
Davidson S 343 S Water
Deneault R B Mrs 931 County
Deslauriers Ernestine M 1521 Acushnet av
Edlin A 840 Purchase
Egan & Boudreau 957 S Water
Epstein S & Sons 253 Coggeshall
Epstein Uel 1097 and 1345 Acushnet avenue
Faford & Nerbonne 49 Brock av
Forand Henry 1235 Acushnet av
Forman Jacob 426 S Water
Fortin Azeline 17 Weld
Gaudreau Marie J 1890 Acushnet av
Gendron J E 1115 and 1119 Acushnet avenue
Girard Eugene 1239 Acushnet av
Goldstein Moses 33 Weld
Goodman E Mrs 384 Kempton
Gotlieb Isaac 776 Purchase
Grant W T Co 65 Purchase
Holgate Eliza 99 County
Horsfield John E 1500 Acushnet av
Jacob J 410 Purchase
Joseph Nassar & Bro 259 Rivet
Kaplan A 731 S Water
Kramer A 234 N Front
Leduc Delima 1291 Acushnet av
Levin F 266 Coggeshall
Levine Bros 725 S Water
Mailloux Mary Mrs 1239 Acushnet avenue
Mechaber R & Sons 1050 Acushnet avenue
Mitchell Joseph 694 Purchase
Morse W H 1049½ Acushnet av
Mosie Abdo 424 N Front
New Bedford Dry Goods Co 182 Union
Paquette Oda Mrs 2147 Acushnet av
Patnaude & Co 1604 Acushnet av
Perron Cordelia 354 N Front
Peter David 98 S Second
Schuster N 430 S Water
Searle Josephine E 853 Kempton
Seligerson Louis 21 Arcade bldg
Silverstein B 937 S Water
Simiamsky E Mrs 813 Water
Spare J V Dry Coods Co The 41 Purchase
STEIGER DUDGEON CO 185 to 187 Union and 9 to 19 Purchase See foot lines
Stetson Maud 355 Cottage
Thomas Joseph 281 Rivet
Wantman Ida 565 S Water
Waterhouse J B L 447 Rivet
Winsberg Oscar 827 S Water
Yamins & Jacobson 701 S Water
Yerovitz Harry 1676 Acushnet av

Dyeing & Cleansing

BUSH A M & CO 47 William See page 768
CRONIN EDWARD H 504 County See page 769
GLOBE DYE HOUSE 220 Shawmut avenue and 52 Pleasant See foot lines
NEW BEDFORD STEAM DYE HOUSE 53 William See page 768
Novinsky Zelis 920 Acushnet av

Efficiency Engineers

GUNN, RICHARDS & CO Tremont bldg Boston See page 40

Electric Bells

JAMES F E 169 Clinton See page 761 and back binding

Electric Contractor

HOWARTH ERNEST 120 Middle See page 784

Electric Globes

PAIRPOINT CORP The Prospect cor Howland See page 23

WM. P. BRIGGS

Electrician and Locksmith

Private Telephone Systems

Dealer in Guns, Ammunition, Sporting Goods, Fishing Tackle

141 PURCHASE STREET

Electric Lights and Bells Installed and Repaired **Connected by Telephones**

Electric Lighting

New Bedford Gas and Edison Light Co 125 Middle and 214 S Water

Electrical Supplies

BRIGGS WILLIAM P 141 Purchase See above

HOWARTH E 120 Middle See page 784

Electrical Work of All Kinds

HOWARTH E 120 Middle See page 784

Electricians

BRIGGS WILLIAM P 141 Purchase See above

Chrarron Joseph O 33 Holly

Eastern Electric Co 22 William

Fitch Horace A 109 Union

Gatenby & Swift 33 N Water

HOWARTH ERNEST 120 Middle See page 784

Lord Peter 104 Union

Payette Fred O 1539 Acushnet av

Smith Arthur C 27 William

Whitlow S 7 S Water

Wilkinson C The Inc 158 Purchase

Electrolysis

Maxim Agatha L 568 County

O'Brien M V 230 Davis

Electro Plater

Sargent Fred H 92 Pleasant

Embalmers

BENNETT ROBERT G 7 S Sixth See Undertakers

CHAUSSE ALDEGE 388 N Front See page 772

SHERMAN P H 506 County See foot lines

VAUGHAN UNDERTAKING CO Inc 321 Purchase See Undertakers

WILSON H P 80 Pleasant See back cover

Embroidery & Stamping

Bowen N L Mrs 12 Purchase

Oxford Shop 97 William rm 403

Emery Wheels

BABBITT STEAM SPECIALTY CO 57 S Water See page 29

SLOCUM & KILBURN 23 N Water See page 766

Employment Offices

Palmer Mary J 345 Orchard (S)

Russell Ellen M 245 Union

Enamel Colors

AKIN F T & CO 168 S Water, 84 Pleasant and 1218 Acushnet av See foot lines

Engineers

GUNN, RICHARDS & CO Tremont bldg Boston See page 40

Engineers' Supplies

BABBITT STEAM SPECIALTY CO 57 S Water See page 29

SLOCUM & KILBURN 23 N Water See page 766

Expresses

Adams Express Co 14 N Sixth and Pearl street station

Allen's Express Co 149 Purchase branch office 414 N Front

A. F. CHILDS, President J. P. HOLMES, Vice-President BENJ. BAKER, Treasurer

NEW BEDFORD FISH CO.

INCORPORATED

WHOLESALE AND COMMISSION DEALERS IN

ROTCH'S WHARF FISH MERRILL'S WHARF

SCALLOPS

Telephone Connection P. O. Box 385

NEW BEDFORD

Andress Benjamin A 408 Kempton
Boston, Providence & Fall River Express Co 386 Acushnet av
DeMORANVILLE D H 83 Thomas See page 787
Eagle Express Co 45 School
Electric Express N Water cor Elm
MACY JOHN S 21 S Second See page 775
New Bedford Despatch Express 4 N Second
Ricketson Charles L 108 School
South Dartmouth Express N Sixth
Tuell J B C 123 Rotch

Extracts

Harper X L Mfg Co 5 Willis

Eyelet Makers

Rhodes J C & Co Inc 123 Front

Fancy Goods

BONNEY, FOLSTER & CO 945 Acushnet av See foot lines
Chadwick Lillie A 58 North
Donovan Mary E 133 Purchase
Keene Margaret 69 Acushnet av
STEIGER DUDGEON CO 185 to 187 Union and 9 to 19 Purchase See foot lines
Simpson M & E A 952 S Water

Farms for Sale

WILLIAMS M A 498 Bolton See back cover

Feather Cleansers

HOWES C G CO Allston Mass See opposite Cleansers

Ferry

Fairhaven foot Union

Fertilizers

HERSOM THOMAS & CO 11 Commercial See page 24
New Bedford Extractor works Shawmut avenue beyond Hathaway road

Fireproof Materials

BERGER MFG CO of Massachusetts 286 Devonshire Boston See page 753
DEXTRADEUR CHARLES J 363 N Front See page 754

Fish (Wholesale)

NEW BEDFORD FISH CO Inc City pier No 4 and Merrill's wharf See above

Fish & Oysters

Allen C G (shrimp) Nye's wharf
Athearn C E 345 Cedar
Barrett C Jr 1085 S Water
Bassett William A Co 193 Purchase
Boisclair A 1106 S Water
BRIGHTMAN E T 109 S Sixth, 248 Purchase and 306 Cedar See advt Grocers
Chadwick Charles 674 Purchase
Costa J 513 S Water
Dean's Oyster Market 17 N Second
Ferreira J 67 Howland
Gonsalves Domingos 211 Coggeshall
Goul Manuel 207 Coggeshall
Humphrey H J 253 Purchase
Joseph C 108 Larch
Leighton Manuel 523 S Water
Luce W T 131 Smith
Magnant Louis Jr 277 Coggeshall
Manchester John A 274 Kempton
McAvoy C A 633 First
McDermott Charles W 39 Weld and 1518 Acushnet av
Medeiros Manuel 135 Crapo
Mello Manuel 221 Rivet
NEW BEDFORD FISH CO Inc City pier No 4 and end Merrill's wharf See page *605
Normandin A A 248 Sawyer
Pacheco J 689 S Water
Potter Albert A 400 Kempton
Roy J H 30 Delano
Sarmento F P 559 S Water
Schaves Joseph 319 S Water
Seed Ada Mrs 337 Earle
Silva J M 100½ Potomska
Silva M 122 County
Souza J M 512 S Second
Sylvia M 43 Howland
Sylvia M 211 Coggeshall
Taber George S 17-21 N Sixth
Teixeira Manuel 153½ Coffin av
Tioflo C 103 County
Watson Bros 108 William

Fishing Tackle

BRIGGS WILLIAM P 141 Purchase See advt Electricians

Flags

BRIGGS & BECKMAN 31-35 Commercial See page 785

Floral Work

MOSHER WILLIAM E 325 Hillman See page 40

Florists

Brown William L G 191 Cedar
Chamberlin E H 4 Purchase
Davenport W H 35 Purchase
Davis E G 191 Shawmut av
Donaghy S J 162 Ash (N)
Hathaway A B 146 Court
Howland H P Mrs 473 Allen
Jahn H A 290 Brock av
Malanson M & Son 255 Mt Pleasant
MOSHER WILLIAM E 325 Hillman See page 40
Nofftz Richard E 106 William and 961 Kempton
Peirce Easton Y 49 Cottage
Peirce William P 232 Union
Ricketson J M 247 Shawmut av
Sowle Herbert V 327 Coffin av
Sylvia Manuel B 70 Dartmouth
Woodhouse R H, Ward cor Allen

Flour & Grain

(See also Hay Straw and Grain)
ALLEN SLADE & CO (wholesale) 1 William and 18-26-30 Third Fall River See page 12
Baylies William 8-16 Union
DION HORMIDAS P 1070 County See page 773
DRISCOLL, CHURCH & HALL (wholesale) 82 Union See page 13
HATHAWAY & MacKENZIE GRAIN CO The 748 Purchase See opposite Grain
JARRY D J 107 Bowditch See page 25
KIRK J FRANK 374 Purchase See page 775
PLUMMER & JENNINGS GRAIN CO 100 S Water See page 775
Sylvia John 199 Acushnet av
POTTER WILLIAM F & CO 81-85 Front and 3-11 Union See page 30

Founders (Iron)

ACUSHNET IRON CO 229 N Water See page 788

Fruit (*Wholesale)

Abraham Joseph 1484 Acushnet av
Adem Abdula 1282 Acushnet av
Daprato Antonio 1610 Acushnet av
Davidson H B 197 Purchase
Deprato L 983 S Water
Elioperlos & Panos 82 Purchase
Finni D, Union cor Purchase
George J 11 Cotter
Kapopoulos George 1051 Acushnet av
Kiviatkowski Stanislaw 232 N Front

Koffman Louis 41 Mitchell
Lansky Julius 614 S Water
Lansky S r 60 Howland
LeBoeuf E Mrs 27 Delano
Lucchesi Luigi 884 Purchase
Maimaris D 32 Pleasant
Mihati Nagip 258 Coggeshall
Morelli L 98 Union
Nardini G, Union cor Pleasant
NEW YORK MARKET 251 Purchase See page 772
Onofrio A D 263 Purchase
Pallatroni A 114 Purchase
*Pease F W Co Union cor N Water
Pieraccini F Jr 392 Kempton
Poulos S 1150 Acushnet av
*Schuster Bros 24 to 26 Union
Shemhoun Elias 1092 Acushnet av
*Sherman I C & Son 70 to 76 Union
Sobil Sadie 292 Cedar Grove
Stuart A 478 S Water
Sylvia & Brown 25 Purchase
Thomas J S 399 Purchase
Vishnefsky A 795 S Water
Williams John O 169 Union

Funeral Directors

BENNETT ROBERT G 7 S Sixth See advt Undertakers
CHAUSSE ALDEGE 388 N Front See page 772
SHERMAN P H 506 County See foot lines
VAUGHAN UNDERTAKING CO Inc 294 Purchase See advt Undertakers
WILSON H P 80 Pleasant See back cover

Furnaces Ranges & Stoves

ALLEN GEORGE J & CO 91 N Water See page 26
BAILEY W P 216 Acushnet av See page 766
HIRST E P CO 28 to 32 N Water See advt Plumbers
HOUSEHOLD FURNISHING CO 170 to 174 Purchase See page 94
LOWE S C SUPPLY CO 87 Union See page 740
MAXFIELD CHARLES A 26 N Second See page 769
SHERMAN & McQUILLAN 250 Purchase See page 781
WOOD BHIGHTMAN & CO 47 to 55 N Water See page 3

Furniture Cleansers

HOWES C G CO Allston Mass See opposite Cleansers

Furniture Dealers
(*Second Hand)

*Alpert I 787 S Water
*Alpert Nathan 409 S Water
Ashley A Davis (antique) rm 14 Arcade bldg
*Bedord Salime 665 Purchase
Bettencourt B J 147 County
Bigelow E P 292 Acushnet av
Boston Furniture Co 953 S Water
Boston Supply Co 765 Purchase
Bourbo Alfred D 1112 Acushnet av
Burns Bros 950 S Water
Caouette J B 50 Delano
Chicago Furniture Co 1228 Acushnet avenue
Cohen Morris 637 S Water
Continental Furniture Co 1065 Acushnet avenue
Duggan J P 133 Acushnet av
Feingold A 399 S Water
GALLIGAN C A 1516 and 1522 Acushnet av See page 37
Galligan John H 497 Purchase
Gauthier D H 867 Purchase
*Gleckman W 577 S Water
*Green Israel 567 Purchase
Gregoire John B 924 S Water
Grimshaw T 874 S Water
Gubinville C 961 Acushnet av
Hartman B Mrs 1004 Acushnet av
HOUSEHOLD FURNISHING CO 170-174 Purchase See page 94
Jubenville C 961 Acushnet av
Levinson M 548 and 600 S Water
Magnant J & Son 275 Coggeshall
Marshall F 89 Howland
*Moon J 71 Delano
New Bedford Furniture Co 43 to 45 Weld
New York Furniture Store 180 Acushnet av
North End Hardware & Furniture Co 1147 Acushnet av
*Ouimette D 639 First
Ouimette Phoebe 665 Purchase
Peirce Herbert S 661 S Water
*Portnov Isaac 212 Coggeshall
Resevitz & Rabinovitz 315 S Water
Schwartz Wold 575 S Water
Spot Cash Furniture Co 384 Acushnet av
Wait S E 87 N Second
Ward Six Furniture Co 1020 S Water
*Weitzman David 617 S Water
WING CHARLES F CO The Inc 34 to 38 Purchase See page 40

Furniture Repairers

Bennett Merton E 277 Purchase
DANTSIZEN JOHN G 214 Court See back cover
Macy Roland 11 Bedford
Rae & Osborne 27 Fifth

Furniture Storage

NEW BEDFORD STORAGE WAREHOUSE CO 352-378 Sawyer See back binding and page 35

Furniture & Piano Movers

Bergeron Napoleon 114 Collette
DeMORANVILLE D H 83 Thomas See page 787
Driscoll W A 97 Maxfield
Frawley Joseph 847 Purchase
Grindrod Harry 215 Shawmut av
Jennings Addie H 73 Shawmut av
McAfee Bros 41 Spring
Morin Thomas 190 Coffin av
Poitras H 235 N Front
Sylvia Manuel 94½ Dartmouth

Furrier

Cook Mattie W 57 N Sixth

Garage

WATUPPA AUTO CO at The Narrows N Westport See page 750

Garden Seeds

DeWOLF & VINCENT 111 William See page 44

Gas Company

New Bedford Gas & Electric Light Co 125 Middle works 214 S Water

Gas Fitters & Fixtures

BOLDUC AZARIE 115 Bowditch See page 780
Brown & Cobb 158 Purchase
BURKE J P 903 County See page 782
King & Begley 978 Acushnet av
LEVESQUE WILFRED 211 Coffin av See page 787
Madison S T 312 Kempton
New Process Gas & Supply Co 211 Purchase
Therrien H L 77 Holly
WOOD BRIGHTMAN & CO 47 to 55 N Water See page 3

Gas Mantels

MARANDA DONAT 393 N Front See page 757

Gas Piping

SHERMAN JAMES H 50 to 52 Union See page 767

Gas & Steam Fitters

ALLEN GEORGE J & CO 91 N Water See page 26
BACON W L 514 County See top edge
CEJKA GEORGE 1480 Acushnet av See page 785
CROSSLEY JOHN F & CO 223 Mill See foot lines
GREEN EVERETT 185 Acushnet avenue See page 780
GREGORY EDWARD H 880 S Water See page 780
Norton J J 115 Cove
PERRA JOHN 19 Linden See page 766
STANDARD CONSTRUCTION CO 281½ Sawyer See page 783

Gas & Water Pipe Mfrs

BRAMAN DOW & CO 239 Causeway Boston See page 38

Gasoline Engines

HATHAWAY CHESTER F (repairs) 107 N Water See page 743
RANKIN & ARNOLD 19 N Second See page 780

Gilt Mat Board Mfr

Sequeira V J 92 Newton

Glass Cutters

Blackmer Cut Glass Co The 223 N Second
PAIRPOINT CORP The Prospect cor Howland See page 23

Glass Dealers

AKIN F T & CO 168 S Water cor Walnut, 84 Pleasant and 1218 Acushnet av See foot lines
GREENE & WOOD Pine street See foot lines
MORIARTY T J 184 Fourth See page 49
Sowle Nat P 51 William

Glass Tubing & Rods

PAIRPOINT CORP The Prospect cor Howland See page 23

Glaziers & Grainers

AKIN F T & CO 168 S Water cor Walnut, 84 Pleasant and 1218 Acushuet av See foot lines

CORMIER & DUBE 394 N Front See page 776
JENKINS ELMIR A 431 Acushnet av See page 752
LEBEAU J 141 Collette See page 785
MORIARTY T J 184 Fourth See page 49
New Bedford Stained Glass & Crystal Window Co 164 County

QUALITY

OATS

HAY GRAIN

SALT FLOUR

The Hathaway & Mackenzie Grain Co.

748 Purchase St., New Bedford, Mass.

BellPhone 550 Auto. 2034

Dartmouth See also [illegible]
Rogers A 86 Topham
Shennan William, Court cor Ash (N)
Thompson Thomas 25 Fourth

Granolithic Sidewalks

LOFTUS & DUGAN 121 Clark See page 776

Gravel & Sand

CONNELL JOHN JR 350 Sawyer See page 774

Grindstones

DeWOLF & VINCENT 111 William See page 44

Grocers
(WHOLESALE)

ALLEN SLADE & CO 1 William and 18-30 Third Fall River See page 12
Archambeault Arthur, N Front cor [illegible]

Benjamin O 962 S Water
Bertrand Ellen Mrs 475 Belleville av
Bessette L A 61 County
Billington Thomas 85 Linden
Boardman R T 128 County
Bolduc Joseph 225 Sawyer
Bonneau Alphege 174 Sawyer
Borden A H 271 Cedar
Bouchard William 263 Coggeshall
Braley C F 357 Court
Braley J W Jr 645 County
Braley & Duckworth 81 N Second

Furniture Repairers

Bennett Merton E 277 Purchase
DANTSIZEN JOHN G 214 Court See back cover
Macy Roland 11 Bedford
Rae & Osborne 27 Fifth

Furniture Storage

NEW BEDFORD STORAGE WARE-

LEVESQUE WILFRED 211 Coffin av See page 787
Madison S T 312 Kempton
New Process Gas & Supply Co 211 Purchase
Therrien H L 77 Holly
WOOD BRIGHTMAN & CO 47 to 55 N Water See page 3

Gas Mantels

MARANDA DONAT 393 N Front See page 757

Gas Piping

SHERMAN JAMES H 50 to 52 Union See page 767

Gas & Steam Fitters

ALLEN GEORGE J & CO 91 N Water See page 26
BACON W L 514 County See top edge

foot lines
MORIARTY T J 184 Fourth See page 49
Sowle Nat P 51 William

Glass Tubing & Rods

PAIRPOINT CORP The Prospect cor Howland See page 23

Glaziers & Grainers

AKIN F T & CO 168 S Water cor Walnut, 84 Pleasant and 1218 Acushnet av See foot lines

QUALITY
OATS
HAY GRAIN
SALT FLOUR
The Hathaway & Mackenzie Grain Co.
748 Purchase St., New Bedford, Mass.
BellPhone 550 Auto. 2034

CORMIER & DUBE 394 N Front See page 776
JENKINS ELMIR A 431 Acushnet av See page 752
LEBEAU J 141 Collette See page 785
MORIARTY T J 184 Fourth See page 49
New Bedford Stained Glass & Crystal Window Co 164 County
PHILLIPS THOMAS O 167 Park See page 44

Glove Cleansers

HOWES C G CO Allston Mass See opposite Cleansers

Grain

Abram Altman 75 Beetle
GUAY BROS 846-848 Acushnet av See page 773
HATHAWAY & MACKENZIE GRAIN CO The 748 Purchase See opposite
Horvitz Grain Co 106 Dartmouth
KIRK J FRANK 374 Purchase See page 775
PLUMMER & JENNINGS GRAIN CO 100 S Water See page 775

Granite Cutters & Dealers

Allen F E 18 N Second
Beaulieu C 10 Juniper
BUFFINGTON ARTHUR E 1 Crapo See page 788
Cole Theodore W 20 William
Foley John, Court cor Jenney
GURL FRANCIS J Sawyer cor Ashland See opposite Undertakers
Herlihy Patrick 54 Washburn
Lawlor John F 1256 Kempton
Markey George A end Robeson
McCue John 6 to 12 Smith
POTHIER JOSEPH A 305 Mt Pleasant See page 29
REX MONUMENTAL WORKS 90 Dartmouth See back cover
Rogers A 86 Topham
Shennan William, Court cor Ash (N)
Thompson Thomas 25 Fourth

Granolithic Sidewalks

LOFTUS & DUGAN 121 Clark See page 776

Gravel & Sand

CONNELL JOHN JR 350 Sawyer See page 774

Grindstones

DeWOLF & VINCENT 111 William See page 44

Grocers

(WHOLESALE)

ALLEN SLADE & CO 1 William and 18-30 Third Fall River See page 12
Archambeault Arthur, N Front cor Kenyon
Bates Lot B 423 Acushnet av
Cobb Aldrich & Co 111 Front
DRISCOL, CHURCH & HALL 82 and 84 Union See page 13
DUPUIS H D & CO 1201 Purchase See page 757
POTTER WILLIAM F & CO 1-11 Union and 81-85 Front See page 30

(RETAIL)

Acushnet Co-operative Association 213 Acushnet avenue
Adams George L 855 Kempton
Adamsky Alfred 16 Bullard
Alcock J A 2 Harmony
Alferes Enos D 153 Belleville av
Alferes M 279 Fourth
Allen D Edwin 76 Shawmut av
Allen Mary 19 S Water
Almeida Joseph 320 S Water
Alpert David 438 S Water
Amaranthes J O 48 S Second
Andrews M A 81 Acushnet av
Angelo Frank 676 Acushnet av
Anthony & Gregory 281 Coggeshall
Archer J B 393a Cedar
Armitage William 819 Purchase
Ashworth John Plainville road cor Shawmut avenue
Barbieri Joseph 164 Blackmer
Barboza Manuel 439 Belleville av
Barrows Rose 179 Bonney
Bartel E Mrs 437 Acushnet av
Bates J W Co 104 Ashland
Baylies William (cereals) 1460 Acushet av
Belthazar Joseph 1 Hicks
Benjamin O 962 S Water
Bertrand Ellen Mrs 475 Belleville av
Bessette L A 61 County
Billington Thomas 85 Linden
Boardman R T 128 County
Bolduc Joseph 225 Sawyer
Bonneau Alphege 174 Sawyer
Borden A H 271 Cedar
Bouchard William 263 Coggeshall
Braley C F 357 Court
Braley J W Jr 645 County
Braley & Duckworth 81 N Second

E. T. BRIGHTMAN

Meats and Groceries

We make a Specialty of **CORNED BEEF** and you always obtain a good piece at our store

3 STORES

248 Purchase Street **109 So. Sixth Street**

306 Cedar Street

Grocers—con
BRIGHTMAN E T 248 Purchase, 306 Cedar and 109 S Sixth See above
Brousseau M L Mrs 201 Austin
Burgess James 1625 Acushnet av
Burke Ernest E 546 Kempton
Burke & Smith 556 Kempton
Butler Alice Mrs 415 Rivet
Casavant & Landry 1892 Acushnet av
Casey John T 329 Middle
Central Union Store Inc 11 N Sixth
Chadwick & Co 238-240 Union
Chaney S N W 196 Pleasant
Chartier Ludger 485 N Front
CHAUSSE ALDEGE 398 N Front See page 772
Chausse Joseph 11 Weld
Chaves L M 197 Coggeshall
Cohen H 410 S Water
Colwell George R 261 Arnold
Consolidated Meat & Grocery Co 132 and 163 Union, 64 and 143 Purchase, 1141 Acushnet av and First cor Cove
Cook John H 127 Maxfield
Cook Harry 136 County
Copeland P C 178 Arnold
Correia J 219 N Second
Cote Pierre 1065 County
Cote S M 76 Church
Crompton John J 101 Clark
Crossman & Shepardson 111 Durfee
Cruz P 498 Maxfield
Cummings & Cummings 98 to 104 William
Cushman Bros 141 Fourth and 726 Kempton
Dammon F A 137 Smith
De Mello Antino 162½ Crapo
Darling Edgar W 385 Purchase
Dehn G R 70 Cove
De Mello A C 144 Belleville av and 88 Nash rd
Dion Alfred 2 Hicks
De Mello Antone 20 Wing
Dixon John W 214 Weld
Donaghy S N 205 Brownell
Dragon Frank 246 N Front
Dourte M 84 Potomska
Dragon M L Mrs 3 Harmony
Duboski Koza 2 Hicks
Dugally Bros 308 Coggeshall
Dunkerley M Mrs 163 Coggeshall
Duphily Maglorie Clifford n Bowditch
Dutra Manuel R 104 County
Duval Hermmie 47 Belleville rd
Dwyer Thomas F 600 Cottage
Dyer & Co 195 Shawmut av
Entwistle Elizabeth 183 Coffin av
Erickson Bros 39 Jenny Lind
Espinola Antonio F 562 S Water
Espinola D J 602 S Water
Fahey John B 302 N Front
Fahey & Beaulieu 1284 Acushnet av
Falk R M rs 528 S Water
Farras & Joseph 283 Coggeshall
Felianno John 261 Allen
Felianno N V Mrs 189 Allen
Fernandes Alfred 360 S Water
Fernandes Amos 11 S Water
Fernandes Antonio A 200 Rivet
Fernandes A 145 Belleville av
Finklestein G Mrs 521 S Water
Fischer S Mrs 674 Acushnet av
Fish L C 59½ L Sycamore
Folger David 140-142 Union
Fox John 293 Coggeshall
Frankel J 69 N Second
Frates Joseph D 77 Dartmouth
Frates Manuel 145 Belleville av

Frenette J B 415 N Front
Frey C Jr 386 Kempton
Frifield Martha 512 S Water
Galligan Edward W 70 Wash
Garcia J V 121 Dartmouth
Garmansky R Mrs 480 S Water
Gauthier J 634 Acusnnet av
Gerin Henry 187 Weld
Gaudette Joseph 555 N Front
Goewey Charles R 327 Davis
Gomes M A 129 S Water
Gonneville Felix 936 County
Gonsalves Justin 186 Belleville av
Gorka Zophia 190 Church
Goshein Rebecca 28 Beetle
Gratton Joseph 538 N Front
Gray G F 46 Parker
Great Atlantic & Pacific Tea Co The 98 Purchase
Guillett Bros 1347 Acushnet av
Gustafson Carl O 46 Keene
Hahn Henry 277 State
Hambley Albert R 40 Main
Hampson P 133 David
Harrison John 85 County
Haworth & Sons 446 Rivet
Herbert Adelard 223 State
Hirst Herbert W 630 Purchase
Hodziewich George 32 Delano
Hotte Bros 48 Rivet
Houde A J 314 Coffin av
Hughes H 1592-1594 Acushnet av
Hurd Frank 26 Wing
Hyde Rose Mrs 714 Acushnet av
Jackson Harry 96 Brock av
Jackson J B 876 S Water
Jeglinski Frank 159 N Front
Jenney W F 138-140 Washington
Jennings C L 1645 Acushnet av
Jesus J 99 Potomska
Joseph J & H 666 SWater
Kilshaw E Mrs 62 Ruth
Korobkin B 504 Acushnet av
Koster Jacob 252 Cedar
Kraihanzel J F Crapo cor Rockland
Kranzler M 505 Acushnet av
Kwiatkowski S 232 N Front
LaBrecque Pierre 79 Belleville rd
Labroski W 2 Hicks
LaCroix A 2177 Acushnet av
LaCroix Pierre 261 Bowditch
LaFrance Bros 79 Austin
Lajeunesse E 15 W French av
Landry A 335 N Front
Langevin Henry A 326 Bowditch
Langevin J 357 N Front
Lapointe Isadore 488 Coggeshall
Larochelle Edmond 41 Bentley
Lapolla J 543 Purchase
Lavoie Louis 109 Davis
Lazaro J 78 First
LeBoeuf Valerie 345 Davis
Lee F F 145 County
Leduc Philodore N County cor Sawyer
Levy A 916 S Water
Lewis Fred 124 S Sixth
Loo Manuel F 145 Belleville av
Lopes J P 78 Acushnet av
Lussier Bros 166 Brock av
Lussier Exilia 201 Bowditch
Manchester James H 688 Kempton
Manny H 200 Belleville av
Marcoux Arcade 61 County
Marder Max 607 Purchase
Martin N 175 N Front
McAllister Joseph Mrs 31 E French av
McCartney Thomas 35 Parker
McConville H F 329 County
McDonald Michael 372 Cedar
McHugh J A 904 Acushnet av
McMahon Robert 417 Allen
Medeiros Francis P 130 Dartmouth
Medeiros J V 448 S Water
Mello Antone C 144 Belleville av
Mello Bros 176 Rockland
Mello C E 61 Crapo
Mello J 66 Howland
Mello Manuel, S Second cor Delano
Mello S P 80 Potomska
Menes M 322 S Second
Messier Oswald P 134 Reynolds
Methe A 75 County
Methe Oliva 1681 Acushnet av
Mikati Najib & Bro 274 Coggeshall
Milliken L E & Co 98 to 104 Allen
Miranda Jose S 229 Coggeshall
Moncrieff W T 44 Hazard
Moniz J B 133 Crapo
Morency J P 167 Cove
Mott Gertrude 1612 Acushnet av
Mullen James 171 Division
Murphy Thomas J 58 Linden
NEW YORK MARKET 251 Purchase See page 772
Nisson L 474 S Water
Noia M L 135 Rockland
Normandin J E 1404 Acushnet av
Nye Frederick L 156 North
Oliva Methe 1681 Acushnet av
Oliveira & Rebello 175 Sawyer
Oliver F J 341 First
Owen Alfred 89 Fruit
Palme Joseph 1120 Acushnet av
Pacheco G M 263 Coggeshall

Grocers—con
Pacheco Manuel 679 S Water
Pacheco & Cardoza 428 N Front
Papaioannou Peter 308 Coggeshall
Paquette Serville 2012 Acushnet av
Patistas Charles 241 Coggeshall
Pelletier A 490 S Second
Pelletier Joseph 1541 Acushnet av
Pereira & Santana 195 Belleville av
Perron Gelina 350 N Front
Perry Antone 65 Grinnell
Phenix Charles 292 Sawyer
Phillips Charles B Plainville road
Piche J 100 Ruth
Pina L Mrs 201 N Second
Pomper Antone 114½ Acushnet av
Ponte Antone P 359 First
Ponte & Andrews 91 Grinnell
Potter Edwin L 69 Dartmouth
Quintin Z 189 Belleville av
Rapoza M C & Co 133 Dartmouth
Raymond M 339 S Water
Raymond W F 62 Spruce
Real Emilo 688 Acushnet av
Ricard N 126 Bowditch
Richard Noe 383 Belleville av
Richards & Marshall 44 Howland
Riley John F 515 Kempton
Ripa A 4 Pearl
Robbins A E 770 Purchase
Robertson John C 282 Allen
ROBINSON DANIEL 156 Weld See page 772
Rose A E 57 Howland
Rousseau H 695 Belleville av
Santa Maria Cash Store 124 Thompson
Santos A B 419 S Water
Santos M F 132 S Second
Seaman W 464 Union
Senna Manuel J 90 S Second
Senra J L D 113 County
Serafino T 436 Purchase
Silva John D 153 Tremont
Silva Manuel V 683 Hathaway rd
Silva M 90 S Second
Silveira J 495 Rivet
Simmons Vergino F 66 Durfee
Sisson Otis 3913 Acushnet av
Souza Antone R 9 Mitchell
Souza Joseph 243 State
Souza Manuel M 274 Belleville av
Stafford G B 60 Shawmut av
Stern W 407 S Water
Sylvia Bros 122 Dartmouth
Sylvia C M 277 Kempton
Szymanski F 436 S Front
Tabor O R & Son 457 Kempton
Tarleski Frank 650 S First
Tasker J B 145 Arnold
Taylor J J 1001 Acushnet av
Tetreault Felix 103 Rivet
Thompson T Sweeney 101 N Second
Trahan Joseph 363 Belleville av
Trahan Polydore 471 N Front
Trembly R 806 Purchase
Tripp Edgar C 47 Foster
Tuche Samuel 178 N Front
Turcotte L H 507 N Front
Turgeon Antoine 155 Coffin av
Ceira J C 601 S Water
Ulewicz A 140 Blackmer
Vigneault Arthur 1525 Acushnet av
Vincent Joseph 282 Tinkham
Voghel Hormidas 78 Hicks
Wainwright R 107 Cove
Washburn A R 739-741 Purchase
Wejeszewski M 19 Belleville av
Wesalosky Joseph 15 Belleville av
Whalon J G 2165 Acushnet av
Wilde James 433 N Front
Wollison H 527 Acushnet av
Wollison Israel 404 Purchase
Woodland John 702 Purchase, 378 and 416 Kempton
Woodland R 702 Purchase and 1623 Acushnet av
Wright & Taber 131 Acushnet av
Zimmerman F 1103 Acushnet av
Ziomak Frank 627 First

Guns & Ammunition

BRIGGS WILLIAM P 141 Purchase See advt Electricians

Hair Goods

Noble Catherine 1049 Acushnet av
Vienna Hair & Corset Shop 96 Purchase

Hairdressers

Abbott F A 82 Cedar
Adams Narcisse 413 N Front
Aillery & Susine 78 William
Amaral A P 95 Rivet
Amaral M P 279 Rivet
Aranjo Julio S 114 S Second
Avila Antonio 119 N Second
Avila George C 245 S Second
Avila J J 74 Grinnell
Bandarra J de M 444 S Water
Baptista J 24 Wing
Bathelho Antonio 267 Fourth
Benac Joseph 1124 Acushnet av
Blanchard J 81 William
Blanchette Stanislaus 1040 Acushnet avenue
Bonneau A Jr 204 Sawyer

Bonneau S A 912 Acushnet av
Bouchard J J 866 Purchase
Bouchard Lucien F 771 Purchase
Breault Edmond 41 Beetle
Caron Napoleon 20 Harmony
Caya Alphonse 578 N Front
Chamberlain A 2782 Acushnet av
Chausse H 1107 Acushnet av
Cheuel Albert 271 Sawyer
Claudino John 323 Acushnet av
Cohen H 516 S Water
Cormier D C 931 S Water
Costa M 678 S Water
Cunha John 90 Allen
DeBarros Joseph 177 S Water
Dessert J 1110 S Water
Dowd O J 1039 Water
Duart M J 84 Potomska
Dumas Arthur 692 Purchase
Easton C F Jr 553 Kempton
Edinborough H J 77 Union
Ellis Harry R 24 Purchase
Ferris M, Parker House
Fontaine William 46½ Howland
Gauthier Napoleon 617 Acushnet av
Gilmore A 835 S Water
Gilmore Edmund T 1673 Acushnet av
Gilmore Levy 397 N Front
Godin J 1601 Acushnet av
Gomes J A 10 N Second
Gonsalves A M & Son 136 Dartmouth
Goulart A 586 S Water
Gregoire N 145 Cove
Guerin George N 329 Kempton
Guerin W 285 Purchase
Harpin Arthur 42 Elm
Hayes Charles 482 S Second
Healey P F 416 Purchase
Henning W A 336 Acushnet av
Henriques Severino 230 S Second
Huard A H 33 Elm
Hudon Joseph E 150 Arnold
Isabell E 1148 Acushnet av
Jardin Manuel 199 Coggeshall
Jason John A 533 S Water
Katsarakis T 251 Coggeshall and 1749 Acushnet av
Lemos Joseph 137 Grinnell
Lewis A 323 Acushnet av
Limieux Joseph 2172 Acushnet av
Lobo Manuel G 259 Purchase
Louis T W 240 Cedar
Mailhot Adelphis 1408 Acushnet av
Marchado Urbano 271 Rivet
Martin M J 86 Union
McAvoy D V 47 Delano
McGreevey J F 39½ Rivet
Medeiros John 393 Rivet
Medieros John 623 S Water
Medeiros M 5 Bedford
Menard Clovis 870 S Water
Miller Granville A 395 Kempton
Mills T 489 Rivet
Minton Frank 133 Smith
Monjohn T H 54 Ash (S)
Montrand Leo 387 S Water
Monty Philip 662 Purchase
Moquin Henri 1526 Acushnet av
Morris William 102½ Bowditch
Motta Antone 252 Coggeshall
Nerbonne William 152 Union
Neves Manuel A 1 Oak
Noble Joseph 711 Kempton
Noyer J C 137 Grinnell
Offley & Son 150 Purchase
Onley William G 57 Smith
Ostroff Sam 461 S Water
Pacheco M 275 Rivet
Pare A 28 Salisbury
Parkinson John 1126 Acushnet av
Pell John F M 98 Ashland
Perlin A 108 Blackmer
Pirroni & Schiolino 352 Acusnhet av
Poirier Belonie 111 Union
Racine Jules 1210 Acushnet av
Raphael F 407 Purchase
Raymond H W 405 Rivet
Rego J 232 Coggeshall
Robert Hector 1266 Acushnet av
Robert P 1035 S Water
Robert W G 29 Delano
Rocha Joseph M 34 Dartmouth
Rochell Alexander R 503 Purchase
Rock Philip 833 Purchase
Rodgers H J 394 S Water
Russell Bros 888 S Water
Secours J 94 Weld
Silva A G 6 Fifth
Smith Charles L 365 Kempton
Soares V J 509 County
Surprenant Arthur 116 Union
Susini O 131 Purchase and 110 William
Sylvia Frank F 157 County
Sweeney William J 1608 Acushnet av
Sylvia Frank F 191 Court
Taveres John 68 Howland
Tetreault Alphee 221 Purchase
Tetreault Arthur 256 Purchase
Therrien H 1269 Acushnet av
Timperley William H 101 Allen
Trudeau C J 972 Acushnet av
Virtue J 162 Purchase
White S Stanley 155 Union
Wilkinson George V 245 Cedar

Hairdressers (Ladies)

Braywood A M Mrs 350 Purchase
Bush B M Mrs 77 Rotch
Garnes Celia College 367 Kempton
Heighton Margaret J 72 Summer
Jourdain K P B Mrs 6½ Fifth
LeBlanc Regina 174½ Purchase
Lee C C Mrs 15 Sycamore
McMahon Eliza E 97 William rm 309
Piper C B Mrs 383 Purchase

Hardware and Cutlery

Butler William P & Sons 801 South Water
Cobb George A 2172 Acushnet av
CONGDON CARPENTER & CO 58-68 Fourth Fall River See page 10
Cote Ulric 1543 Acushnet av
Dawe W C & Co 844 Purchase
DeWOLF & VINCENT 111 William See page 44
Dunham Crawford L 745 Purchase
FREDETTE & COLLETTE 1023 and 1025 S Water
Gregoire J B 924 S Water
HANDY JONATHAN CO (heavy) 28 William See page 766
Hathaway & Co 516 Purchase
Hayes N P 65 William
Jenney P P & Son 146 Pleasant
JEWETT HARDWARE CO 108 Middle and 415 Acushnet av See page 784
LAWRENCE J A 1032-1034 Acushnet av See page 784
Lemlin & Gosselin 7 W French av
Levesque Arsen J 1360 Acushnet av
LOWE S C SUPPLY CO 87 Union See page 745
Manufacturers Supply Co 382 Acushnet av
MORIARTY T J 184 Fourth See page 49
QUINTIN H N 1223 Acushnet av See page 767
Reca F S 84 Dartmouth
SILVA M P B & SON 157 Acushnet av See foot lines
Sowle F L 123 Purchase
Sylvia Manuel L 781 S Water 372 First and 1147 Acushnet av

Harness and Horse Clothing

CONGDON CARPENTER & CO 58-68 Fourth Fall River See page 10

Harness Mfrs, Dealers and Repairers

Allen Jesse 156 Union
Allen Jesse S 92 Newton
Bachand Charles 247 Sawyer
Collette Fred 7 Beetle
Cronin William & Co 54 Elm
Cushing C F 34 Pleasant
Dibb T 860 Acushnet av
Frates Frank A 154 Acushnet av
Gage J N 144 Pleasant
Mendell D P 646 Purchase

Hat Repairers

Taylor W J 310 Acushnet av

Hats, Caps and Furs

Reilly F L 21 Purchase
WENTWORTH F W CO 211 Union corner Pleasant See page 768
WING J & W R & CO 133 Union See page 768

Hay, Straw and Grain

AKIN F T & CO 168 S Water cor Walnut and 1218 Acushnet av See foot lines
Altman Abram 75 Beetle
Altman J 518 County
Bouvier J A
DESAUTELS HUGHUES 45 Brock av See page 760
Foisy P 380 Sawyer
Greenstone M P 551 S Water
GUAY BROS 846-848 Acushnet av See page 773
HATHAWAY & MACKENZIE GRAIN CO The 748 Purchase See opp Grain
HOLMES ALBERT W 201 Purchase and Holmes wharf foot of Cannon See back cover
KIRK J FRANK 370-374 Purchase See page 775
Phaneuf & Son 188 Rivet
PLUMMER & JENNINGS GRAIN CO 100 S Water See page 775

Heel Mfr

Paulding J B 176 Grinnell

Horse Dealers

Jones P 13 Elm
Sher Israel 404 Acushnet avenue

Horses and Carriages to Let

WASHBURN WILLIAM R Noquitt Mass See page 770

Hosiery & Gloves

WING J & W R & CO 133 Union See page 768

Hospitals

New Bedford Emergency Hospital 194 Purchase
St Joseph's Hospital 261 Pleasant
St Luke's Page corner Allen

Hot Water Heating

ALLEN GEORGE J & CO 91 North Water See page 26
BACON W L 514 County See top edge
BAILEY W P 216 Acushnet av See page 766
BOLDUC AZARIE 115 Bowditch See page 780
BURKE J P 903 County See page 782
CEJKA GEORGE 1480 Acushnet av See page 785
COHOLAN J 703 S Water See page 767
ELLIOT JOHN D 106 Fourth See page 45
GREGORY EDWARD H 880 South Water See page 780
HIRST E P **CO** 28-32 N Water See advt Plumbers
LOWE S C SUPPLY CO 87 Union See page 740
MUDGE & FRANCIS 157 Acushnet av See page 781
PERRA JOHN 19 Linden See page 766
SHERMAN & McQUILLAN 250 Purchase See page 781
STANDARD CONSTRUCTION CO 281½ Sawyer See page 783

Hotels

Hotel Bristol 219 Purchase
Hotel Waverley 1162 Acushnet av
Mansion House 109 Union
Parker House 110 Purchase
Savoy Hotel 343 Acushnet av
Weld Square Hotel 46 Weld

House Furnishings

GALLIGAN C A 1516 and 1522 Acushnet av See page 37
HOUSEHOLD FURNISHING CO 170-174 Purchase See page 94
Siegel Bros 565 S Water
WING CHARLES F CO The Inc 34-38 Purchase See page 40

House Movers

SAWIN GEORGE F & CO 343 Purchase See page 783

Ice Cream

CROWN CONFECTIONERY STORE (mfrs) 56 Purchase See page 783
Dawson & Son 645 Purchase
Howland A P 10 Weaver
Macomber George E (wholesale and retail) 159 Mill
Maine Ice Cream Co 535 Kempton
National Ice Cream Co 580 N Front
Roberts Charles H 88 Shawmut av
Velvet Ice Cream Co 349 Kempton

Ice Dealers

Buckley Jonh J 53 Howard av
Chadwick Arnold 63 Dean
Dawson & Son 645 Purchase
Donaghy William 78 Chancery
Dyer John 115 Durfee
FAIRHAVEN ICE CO 428 Washington **Fairhaven** See page 684
Gilmore R 18 Stapleton
Greene George D 703 Kempton
HASKELL BROS 400 Court See foot lines
Hathaway J S 369 North
Mellor Frank H 1276 Rockdale av
Mosher C H 1372 Rockdale av
NEW BEDFORD ICE CO George H Paul treas office 2 School See page 773
O'Connor D J 431 Rivet
Reed C A 36 Dartmouth
Rogers E L 252 Brownell
St Lawrence P Jr 440 Rivet
SMITH BROS Inc (artificial) 777 Purchase See page 779
Spooner Job, Phillips road
Spooner E F 682 Kempton
Wilbur G F Jr 1384 Rockdale av

Ice Plants

BOSWORTH W E 1194 Rockdale av See page 785

Importer

Edwards J T 112 William

Industrial Engineers

GUNN, RICHARDS & CO Tremont bldg Boston Mass See page 40

Information

BURNS DETECTIVE BUREAU 1 Beacon Boston See opp page 161
WOOD-MORGAN DETECTIVE AGENCY 61 Court Boston See page 753

Injectors

BABBITT STEAM SPECIALTY CO 57 S Water See page 29
BRAMAN DOW & CO 239 Causeway Boston See page 38

Instalment House

HOUSEHOLD FURNISHING CO 170-174 Purchase See page 94

Insurance Agents

Aindow John H 37 Purchase rm 16
ALDEN GEORGE N 205 Merchants Bank bldg 97 William See back cover
ASHLEY C S JR & CO 62 Pleasant See page 43
ASHTON & MURPHY 1109 S Water See page 48
Bly W H 97 William rm 301
Chase William R 97 William rm 302
Cook Jasper S 97 William rm 206
CORNISH CLIFTON H 12 Clifford bldg See page 778
DAVOL CLARENCE H 23 Clifford bldg See page 755
Francis J B Jr 97 William
GREENE FRED W JR 21 Clifford bldg See page 758
HOYE JAMES F 305 Merchants Bank bldg 97 William See page 44
James Alfred S 97 William rm 201
JAMES THOMAS M & CO 305 Merchants Bank bldg See page 36
Knapp Lina L 10 Masonic bldg
Knapp R E & Co 13 Masonic bldg
Laliberte Michel 67 Ruth
McCann William 35 Arcade bldg
PARLOW & GODDARD (general) 97 William rm 206 See page 782
PAUL & DIXON 97 William rm 303 See front cover
Peirce Leland C 10 Masonic bldg
ROTCH & POTTER 97 William rm 303 See front cover
Vesina George 1223 Acushnet av
Wefer E R (life) 95 Elm
York G A & Co 97 William rm 301

Insurance Companies

Boston Mutual Life Ins Co 97 William rm 311
General Accident Fire and Life Assurance Co Ltd 97 William rm 300
John Hancock Mutual Life Ins Co Times bldg rms 401-407
Mass Accident Co 23 Clifford bldg
Metropolitan Life Ins Co of New York 37 Purchase rm 23
Prudential Ins Co The of America 41 William

Interior Decorators

CROOKER CO 230 Weybosset Providence R I See page 754

Investigation Experts

BURNS DETECTIVE BUREAU 1 Beacon See opp page 161
WOOD-MORGAN DETECTIVE AGENCY 61 Court Boston See page 753

Iron Founders

ACUSHNET IRON CO 229 N Water See page 788

Iron Pipe (Galvanized, Plain and Wrought)

BRAMAN DOW & CO 239 Causeway Boston See page 38

Iron and Steel

CONGDON CARPENTER & CO 58 to 68 Fourth Fall River See page 10
HANDY JONATHAN CO 28 William See page 766
JEWETT HARDWARE CO 108 Middle and 415 Acushnet av See page 784

Jewelry

(See Watches, Jewelry etc)

Job Printing

BUDLONG J E PRESS The 38 Middle See page 778

Job Wagons

(See also Teamsters and Truckmen)
Brown J H 31 Spring
Duckworth Mansfirth 65 Washburn
DUFF DAVID & SON 105 William Merchants Bank bldg 73 Weld and Fish Island See front cover

Gosselin Moise 107 Holly
Lagasse Henri 164 N Front
McFarlin James 71 Spruce
O'Brien John 44 Washburn
Paira F M 51 South
Santos Antonio C 469 First
Percy T, Spring cor First

Junk

Fox Max 135 S Water
Katzman P 94 Front
McCullough John 98 Front
Mirsky I 500 S Water
Munroe John 300 Middle
Schuster A 17 Morgan lane
Thompson G F 125 N Water

Justices of the Peace

(For full list see end of Miscellaneous Department)

BARNEY BENJAMIN B Masonic bldg rms 11 and 12
BRIGGS JUSTUS A JR 18 Masonic bldg
BROWNELL MORRIS R rm 1 Masonic bldg
CLIFFORD CHARLES W 6 Masonic bldg Pleasant street
CLIFFORD JOHN H 6 Masonic bldg
CLIFFORD WALTER 6 Masonic bldg
COOK OTIS S rm 1 Masonic bldg
CRAPO HENRY H 6 Masonic bldg Pleasant street
CRAPO WILLIAM W 6 Masonic bldg Pleasant street
DESAUTELS S 269 Sawyer
DEXTER LEMUEL LeBARON 37 Masonic bldg
DRISCOLL D F 14 Clifford bldg
GARDINER GEORGE N Masonic bldg rm 3
GAUTHIER JOSEPH A 37 Purchase rm 15
GOODSPEED A McL 37 Purchase
HERVEY H W 405 Merchants Bank bldg
HITCH MAYHEW R 37 Masonic bldg
LILLEY GEORGE E 37 Purchase rm 17
LOWNEY JOHN B 2 Masonic bldg
MacCORD WILLIAM A 37 Purchase rm 5
MACY PELEG S 78 Smith
MILLIKEN ALLEN W Masonic bldg rm 3
MITCHELL CHARLES 16 Masonic bldg
MURPHY W H 1109 S Water
PARKER WILLIAM C 30 Masonic bldg
PRESCOTT OLIVER 6 Masonic bldg
RICHMOND CHARLES N 54 Pleasant
SHAW J E NORTON 4 Masonic bldg
SPARROW FRANK M 30 Purchase
STETSON E D, F D & T M rm 34 Masonic bldg
TABER FREDERIC rm 1 Masonic bldg
VAUGHAN H C 23 Borden
WARREN JOSEPH S 1603 Water
WOODWARD HENRY E 37 Purchase rm 14

Kindling Wood

AKIN F T & CO 168 S Water, 84 Pleasant and 1218 Acushnet av See foot lines
THORPE R H 1786 Acushnet av See page 765

Kitchen Furnishing Goods

DeWOLF & VINCENT 111 William See page 44
HOUSEHOLD FURNISHING CO 170 to 174 Purchase See page 94
Leen P 351 S Water
Leen Samuel D 153 Purchase
Shapiro Isaac 424 S Water
Shaw E H & Co 24 Pleasant

Lace Curtain Cleansers

HOWES C G CO Allston Mass See opposite Cleansers

Ladies' & Childrens' Furnishing Goods

BONNEY FOLSTER & CO 945 Acushnet av See foot lines
STEIGER DUDGEON CO 185 and 187 Union and 9 to 10 Purchase See foot lines

Ladies' Tailor

GERADI V V 36 Eighth See page 769

Lamps & Lamp Goods

WING C F CO The Inc 34 Purchase See page 40

Lathing Contractor

DEXTRADEUR CHARLES J 363 N Front See page 754

Laundries

American Steam Laundry 659 Purchase
City Steam Laundry 6 Campbell
CLEAN WET WASH The 76 Shawmut av See page 786
Gem Wet Wash Laundry 18-20 Katharine
Hathaway's Laundry 6-8 Campbell
HOME WASHING CO 111 Myrtle See page 786
HOWLAND S D & CO 86 Chancery See page 786
Ideal Wet Wash Laundry 270 Kempton
Improved Wet Wash Laundry 409 Chancery
LaFrance Joseph 111 Clifford
NASH ROAD WET WASH LAUNDRY 95 Nash road See page 787
NATIONAL WET WASH LAUNDRY CO Audette & Chapdelaine 281 Sawyer See page 787
NEW BEDFORD STEAM LAUNDRY 128 to 130 Pleasant See front cover
NORTH END LAUNDRY CO 1066 County See page 786
PARSONS STEAM LAUNDRY CO The 270 Acushnet av See front cover
Perfection Wet Wash Laundry r 28 Larch
PURITAN LAUNDRY CO 298 Acushnet av

(CHINESE)

Acushnet avenue 220-312½-317-1010-1227-1520-1617
Cedar 296
Coggeshall 306
Fifth 3
Purchase 773
S Second 8
S Water 1079

Lawyers

Auger Asa 37 Purchase rm 25
Bannon E T 15 Masonic bldg
BARNEY BENJAMIN B Masonic bldg rms 11 and 12
BRIGGS JUSTUS A JR 18 Masonic bldg
Clarke A E 183 Pleasant
Clarke E E 30 Masonic bldg
COOK BROWNELL & TABER 1 Masonic bldg
CRAPO, CLIFFORD & PRESCOTT 6 Masonic bldg Pleasant
Cunniff T A 4 Masonic bldg
Dade Isaiah C 37 Purchase
da Terra Joseph I 49 William
Devoll Daniel T 97 William rm 402
DEXTER L LeB 37 Masonic bldg
Doran J P 5 Masonic bldg
Douglass E A 14 Masonic bldg
Fisher M C 37 Masonic bldg
GARDINER & MILLIKEN Masonic bldg rm 3
GAUTHIER JOSEPH A 37 Purchase rm 15
GOODSPEED A McL 37 Purchase rm 13
HERVEY HOMER W 97 William rms 405 and 406
HITCH MAYHEW R 37 Masonic bldg
Holmes E W 37 Purchase rm 5
Jourdain Edwin B 49 William
KENNEY JOSEPH T 97 William
Knowles Henry S 97 William rm 301
Knowles R 6 Masonic bldg
LILLEY GEORGE E 37 Purchase rm 17
LOWNEY & WALSH 2 Masonic bldg
MacCORD WILLIAM A 37 Purchase
Marchant E L 97 William rm 203
Milliken F A 33 Masonic bldg
MITCHELL CHARLES 16 Masonic bldg
Munsey G W Jr 24 Clifford bldg
O'Brien Timothy F 71 William
PARKER WILLIAM C 30 Masonic bldg
Perry, Jenney & Potter 57 William
Perry L S 97 William rm 312
Rogers Frank L 5 Masonic bldg
Serpa C N 6 Masonic bldg
SHAW J E NORTON 4 Masonic bldg Pleasant street
Sherman C P 33 Masonic bldg
Smith William B 1 Masonic bldg
SPARROW FRANK M 30 Purchase
STETSON & STETSON 34 Masonic bldg 12 Pleasant
Sullavou Emanuel 37 Purchase
Terry Robert A 108 Union
Tracy, Rosenberg & McGurk 108 Union
Willcox Lemuel T 49 William
WOODWARD HENRY E 37 Purchase rm 14
Worth H B 37 Purchase rm 24

Lead Pipe & Sheet Lead

CONGDON, CARPENTER & CO 58 to 68 Fourth Fall River See page 10

Leather Belting

BABBITT STEAM SPECIALTY CO 57 S Water See page 29

SLOCUM & KILBURN 23 N Water See page 766

Libraries

Free Public Library Pleasant corner William, branches Blackmer corner S Water and rm 31 Arcade bldg

Young Men's Christian Association William corner N Sixth

Lighting Fixtures

CROOKER CO 230 Weybosset Providence R I See page 754

Lime, Brick and Cement

BORDEN & REMINGTON CO 115 Annawan, Fall River See page 11

CITY COAL CO Front foot Middle branch 114 William See page 3

PAINE S S & BRO 139 Front See page 776

PAISLER & WILLIS 160 N Water See page 774

Liquors, Wines, Etc

(See also Wines, Liquors, etc)

DEXTRAZE CAMILLE 1276 Acushnet av See page 79

SMITH BROS Inc 777 Purchase See page 779

WEIHL JACOB 23½ N Second See page 779

WHEATON HIRAM & SONS 45-51 School See page 773

Livery Stables

(See Stables)

Loans

American Loan Co 120 Purchase rm 6

Chisholm T M 120 Purchase rm 307

Desautels Stanislas 269 Sawyer

Hougham G H Co 76 Pleasant rm 20

Merrimac Loan Co 96 William rm 11

N B Loan Co 37 Purchase rm 25

North End Loan Association 1307 Acushnet av

Locksmiths

BRIGGS WILLIAM P 141 Purchase See advt Electricians

Fine M 39 S Second

HOWARTH E 120 Middle See page 784

James Henry E 1213 Rockdale av

Loom Reed Makers

Horsfall Amos 644 Katherine

Knowles Loom Reed Works Myrtle Penniman

Schmidt H E & Co 116 Front

Looms and Spinning Frames

DRAPER CO Hopedale Mass See page 2

MASON MACHINE WORKS Taunton Mass See page 39

Lost & Found

BURNS DETECTIVE BUREAU 1 Beacon Boston See opp page 161

Lubricating Oils and Greases

AKIN F T & CO 168 S Water corner Walnut 84 Pleasant and 1218 Acushnet av See foot lines

BORDEN & REMINGTON CO 115 Annawan, Fall River Mass See page 11

Lumber Dealers

Acushnet Saw Mills Co Mill road Acushnet

Croacher T W Leonard cor Cross

DAVIS Z B CORP 668 Acushnet av See page 762

GREENE & WOOD Pine near South Water See foot lines

NICHOLSON JOHN G 27-35 Bowditch See foot lines

SHERMAN JAMES L 194 North Water See page 765

WEBBER LUMBER & SUPPLY 172 N Water See page 761

Lunch Rooms

PALACE CAFE 173 Purchase See page 779

ROGLER PHILIP 72-74 William See page 772

Machinery Mfrs

BAKER MACHINE CO 8 Seneca See page 744

Continental Wood Screw Co (Screws) 8 Hazard's lane

Davenport Machine Tool Co 90 South Sixth

DRAPER CO Hopedale Mass See page 2

HOWARD BROS MFG CO Worcester Mass See page 14

HOWARD & BULLOUGH Pawtucket R I See opp 589

Machinery Mfrs—con
MASON MACHINE WORKS Taunton Mass See page 39
MORSE TWIST DRILL & MACHINE CO 100 Fifth See page 15
New Bedford Boiler & Machine Co 42 Front

Machinery Movers

CITY COAL CO Front foot of Middle branch 114 William See page 3

Machinists

ACUSHNET IRON CO 229 N Water See page 788
BAKER MACHINE CO 1 E Pope and 8 Seneca See page 744
GILES & TOBEY 44 Middle See page 744
GUNNING BOILER & MACHINE CO 67 S Water See page 31
HATHAWAY CHESTER F 107 N Water See page 743
Norlander Albert Prospect near Howland
RANKIN & ARNOLD 19 N Second See page 780
Tripp Frank S 235 N Water
Wood P F Boiler Works 32 Commercial

Machinists' Tools

MORSE TWIST DRILL & MACHINE CO 100 Fifth See page 15

Manganese Bronze & Electrical Supplies

TAUNTON-NEW BEDFORD COPPER CO N Front See page 34

Mantel Mfrs

TRIPP & THORPE 183 N Water See page 764

Manufacturing Companies

Acushnet Mill Corp foot Delano
Beacon Mfg Co end Purchase
Blackstone Valley Comb Works 100 Bonney
Booth Mfg Co, E French avenue
Bristol Mfg Corp 198 Coggeshall
Butler Mill, Ruth street.
City Mfg Corp foot Grinnell
Crescent Mfr Co (silks) 1145 Kempton
Dartmouth Mfg Corp, Cove bey Harbor
Gosnold Mills Co, Orchard (S) cor Cove road
Grinnell Mfg Corp, Kilburn cor N Front
Hathaway Mfg Co, Gifford
Holmes Mfg Co, E French av
Kilburn Mill, W French av
Manomet Mills, Riverside av and Manomet
MORSE TWIST DRILL & MACHINE CO 100 Fifth See page 15
Nashawena Mills Co, Belleville av
Neild Mfg Corp, Nash road cor Brook
New Bedford Cordage Co 131 Court
New Bedford Cotton Mills Corp 295 Phillips avenue
New Bedford Textile Co 1 E Pope
New England Cotton Yarn Co, Bennett dept 115 Coggeshall; New Bedford Spinning dept North; Rotch dept Orchard (S) bey Rivet
Nonquitt Spinning Co, 693 Belleville avenue
Oneko Woolen Mills, end Purchase
Page Mfg Co, Cove road cor Bonney
PAIRPOINT CORPORATION The Prospect cor Howland See page 23
Pierce Bros Limited Purchase junc County
Pierce Mfg Corp, Belleville av cor Sawyer
Potomska Mills Corp, 774 S Water
Quissett Mill, Grinnell street
Sharp Mfg Co, Dartmouth cor Rockdale avenue
Soule Mill (cotton goods) end of Sawyer
Taber Mill, Coffin avenue
TAUNTON-NEW BDRFORD COPPER CO N Front rear Wamsutta Mills See page 34
Wamsutta Mills, E T Pierce treas Wamsutta
WARREN CHEMICAL & MFG CO 49 Federal Boston See opp *583
Weeden Mfg Co 152 N Water
Whitman Mills, end Coffin av

Manufacturers' Supplies

BORDEN & REMINGTON CO 115 Annawan Fall River See page 11

Marble & Granite Monuments

POTHIER JOSEPH A 305 Mt Pleasant See page 29
REX MONUMENTAL WORKS 90 Dartmouth See back cover

Marine Hardware Cordage

BRIGGS & BECKMAN 31 to 35 Commercial See page 785
CASWELL WILLIAM T 34 to 38 Union See page 94

Market Gardeners

Brownell C T 320 Mt Pleasant
Vetorino & Lemos 1379 Rockdale av

Masons

Alves Manuel 39 Dartmouth
Barthelemy Eugene E 256 Tinkham
Benoit Louis 407 Coggeshall
Breault F 76 Brock av
BRIGHTMAN CHARLES O 72 N Water See page 95
BUFFINGTON ARTHUR E 1 Crapo See page 788
COOK & McQUADE 45 Maitland See page 763
CROTEAU & WOOD 249 Shawmut av See page 776
DAVIS Z B CORP 668 Acushnet av See page 762
Ducharme Louis 149 Phillips av
Gonsalves Frank J 30 Dartmouth
Greene Marshall S 233 Rivet
Gregoire Napoleon (stone) 159 Tallman
Hook Gilman E 21 Columbia
Kilcoin L J 467 Cottage
LaFrance Vincent 348 Sawyer
Languedoc Clement 531 S Second
MAHER PIERRE 358 N Front See page 763
MASON JOHN L G 51 Foster See page 774
Mendoza M A 35 Stowell
Nelson Bros 316 S Second
Nelson William N 46 Oak
Paine H H 247 Palmer
Parker Charles F (brick) 45 Grand
PROUTEAU RAOUL 82 Phillips av See page 760
Romeo Concetto V 151 Coffin av
Sherrin Michael 482 Cottage
Sprott George M 132 Cedar
Sykes John & Son 19 Collins
Taber Robert A 101 Hillman
Tetreault Arthur 151 Coffin av
Tripp Hiram C 144 Campbell
Vanni V 238 Tremont
Wheaton Nathan 16 Spruce

Masons' Supplies

PAISLER & WILLIS 160 N Water See page 774
Ricard Alphonse 142 Nye

Massage

Chadwick Elizabeth A 44 W French avenue
Garvey Marion R 305 Times bldg
Tripp C Mrs 133 Cedar

Mattings

WING CHARLES F CO The Inc 34-38 Purchase See page 40

Mattresses

Rubin Joseph & Son 421 S Water
Taylor & Sacks, Hyacinth corner Thompson
WING CHARLES F CO The Inc 34-38 Purchase See page 40

Mechanics' Tools

DeWOLF & VINCENT 111 William See page 44
MORIARTY T J 184 Fourth See page 49

Men's Furnishing Goods

Burns T J 127 Purchase
Phinney Nathan D Estate 194 Union
Read & Co 141 Union
WENTWORTH F W CO 211 Union corner Pleasant See page 768
Willis H P 22 Pleasant
WING J & W R & CO 133 Union See page 768

Men's Garments Clensed

HOWES C G CO Allston Mass See opp Cleansers

Mercantile Agencies

Bradstreet's 205 Times bldg
Dun R G & Co 5 Beetle lane

Merchants

(See also Commission Merchants)
Knowles Henry M 37 Purchase rm 30
Lewis E R 15 Hamilton
Snow Loum 37 Purchase rm 7
Sylvia Antone L 37 Purchase rm 7

Metal Ceilings

BERGER MFG CO of Mass 286 Devonshire Boston See page 753
DEXTADEUR CHARLES J 363 N Front See page 754
JONES & DODGE 202 N Water See page 764

Metal Lathing

BERGER MFG CO of Mass 286 Devonshire Boston See page 753
DEXTRADEUR CHARLES J 363 N Front See page 754

Metal Polisher

Burke T 177 N Water

Metal Roofing

BERGER MFG CO of Mass 286 Devonshire Boston See page 753

Metal Siding

BERGER MFG CO of Mass 286 Devonshire Boston See page 753

Milk

Brousseau H 275 N Front
Chace Clarence E 385 Reed
Kenney W D 250 Shawmut av
Laplante Joseph 242 Nash road
Lemerise Albert T 116 Phillips av
Mastera F 3697 Acushnet av
Miguel Manuel 99 Field
Mitchell Robert 241 Shawmut av
Place C H 2949 Acushnet av
Puchala Paul, Shawmut av n Plainville road
Robinson William H 638 Hathaway rd
Rogers Bros 86 Topham
Sturtevant E M 78 Belleville av
Vigeant M 595 Mt Pleasant
Weeks H R 1270 Kempton

Mill Engineer

PRARAY C W 302 Times bldg See page 42

Mill Supplies

BORDEN H E CO 86 Pleasant See page 746
BORDEN REMINGTON CO 115 Annawan Fall River See page 11
BRAMAN DOW & CO 239 Causeway Boston See page 38
HANDY JONATHAN CO 28 William See page 766
HILLMAN F G 669 Purchase See page 26
JEWETT HARDWARE CO 108 Middle and 415 Acushnet av See page 784
LOWE S C SUPPLY CO 87 Union See page 740
Manufacturers' Supply Co 382 Acushnet av
Mt Pleasant Banding Co Hathaway road near Mt Pleasant
RANKIN & ARNOLD 19 N Second See page 780
SLOCUM & KILBURN 23 to 27 N Water See page 766

Mill & Auto Supplies

BABBITT STEAM SPECIALTY CO 57 S Water See page 29
BORDEN HARRY E CO The 92 to 98 Pleasant See page 746

Milliners & Millinery Goods

Baillargeon L Mrs 1077 Acushnet av
Baker Flora B Mrs 81 Hillman
Bettencourt Maria E 4 Washington
Blanchette Celine 364 Kempton
Brunelle O A 8 Purchase and 129 Rivet
Conniff Emma L Mrs 142½ Purchase
Crothers G B P 930 S Water
Downey K J Mrs 46 Borden
Enos George Mrs 25 Oak
Faford & Poitras 51 Brock av
Gibson Bertha M S 205 Purchase
Goldberg Harry 1024 Acushnet av
Goulet R Mrs 35½ Linden
Gray B Mrs 499 Union
Grew Susan E 243 Maxfield
Grimshaw B Mrs 14 Purchase
Gudgeon N Mrs 86 Cove
Hathaway Susan M 78 Hillman
Jones William 956 S Water
King Marietta 7 Purchase
Marshall M E Mrs 460 County
Martel A S & E D 1354 Acushnet av
McGuinness A K Mrs 10 Purchase
Montminy Amanda 865 S Water and 1535 Acushnet av
O'Neill K E 262 Union
Peloquin Z I Mrs 98 Weld
Perry Mary C Mrs 535 S Water
Petit A A 1245 Acushnet av
Pierce E C Mrs 534 S Water
Poirier C R Mrs 1039 Acushnet av
Ross M Louise 243 Sawyer
ST JAMES CO-OPERATIVE SALES 68 Linden See page 48
Sargent C B Mrs 270 Pleasant
Sherman H A Mrs 51 Russell
Slocum H Elsie 274 Mill
Smith Mary E 172 Fourth
Sumpter Rose A 185 Summer
Taylor Bertha M 84 Elm
Thompson Blanche E 224 Pleasant
Veara Etta 101½ Fifth
Wilkinson Marion F 1035 County

Mineralite Roofing

WARREN CHEMICAL & MFG CO 49 Federal Boston See opp *583

Mirrors Resilvered

DANTSIZEN JOHN G 214 Court See back cover

Missing Friends Located

BURNS DETECTIVE BUREAU 1 Beacon Boston See opposite page 161

WOOD-MORGAN DETECTIVE AGENCY 61 Court Boston See page 753

Monuments & Statuary

GURL FRANCIS J Sawyer cor Ashland See opposite Undertakers

POTHIER JOSEPH A 305 Mt Pleasant See page 29

REX MONUMENTAL WORKS 90 Dartmouth See back cover

Mortgages

GREENE FRED W JR 21 Clifford bldg See page 758

Motor Boat Supplies

Allen G H, city pier No 4

CASWELL WILLIAM T 34 to 38 Union See page 94

Motor Cycles

WILLIAMS GEORGE P 331 Kempton See page 743

Mouldings & Window Frames

DAVIS Z B CORP 668 Acushnet av See page 762

GREENE & WOOD Pine near S Water See foot lines

NICHOLSON JOHN G 27 to 35 Bowditch See foot lines

Multigraph Letters

BENTON'S BUSINESS SCHOOL 97 William See map

Music & Musical Instruments

FOREST FELIX & CO 1041 Acushnet av See page 778

Spooner Charles F 18 Purchase

STEINERT M & SONS CO The 109 William See page 23

Naval Brass

TAUNTON-NEW BEDFORD COPPER CO N Front See page 34

Naval Bronze

TAUNTON-NEW BEDFORD COPPER CO N Front See page 34

Naval Stores

AKIN F T & CO 168 S Water cor Walnut See foot lines

News Dealers

(See also Periodicals)

BRIGGS GEORGE L 161 Purchase See back cover

MARANDA DONAT 393 N Front See page 757

Newspapers & Publishers

Catholic Union The Pleasant c Mill

EVENING AND REPUBLICAN STANDARD (daily and weekly) E Anthony & Sons Inc publishers, Pleasant cor Market

LaLiberte 1205 Acushnet av

L'Echo de la Presse 101 Kenyon

LE JOURNAL 267 Sawyer See page 758

MERCURY PUBLISHING CO 112 Union See page 756

NEW BEDFORD DAILY MERCURY 112 Union See page 756

NEW BEDFORD TIMES (Evening and Sunday) 120 Purchase See page 759

O'Correio Portuguez 143 Acushnet avenue

O'Independent, Antonio C Vieira publisher 250 S Second

Notaries Public

(For full list see end of Miscellaneous Department)

BARNEY BENJAMIN B rm 11 and 12 Masonic bldg

BRIGGS JUSTUS A JR 18 Masonic bldg

BROWNELL MORRIS R rm 1 Masonic bldg

CLIFFORD CHARLES W 6 Masonic bldg

CLIFFORD JOHN H 6 Masonic bldg

CLIFFORD WALTER 6 Masonic bldg

COOK OTIS S rm 1 Masonic bldg

CRAPO WILLIAM W 6 Masonic bldg

DEXTER L LeB 37 Masonic bldg

GARDINER GEORGE N Masonic bldg rm 3

GAUTHIER JOSEPH A 37 Purchase rm 15

Notaries Public—con
GOODSPEED A McL 37 Purchase
HERVEY H W 97 William rms 405 and 406
HITCH MAYHEW R 37 Masonic bldg
HOYE JAMES F Merchants Bank bldg rm 305
MacCORD WILLIAM A 37 Purchase rm 5
MITCHELL CHARLES 16 Masonic bldg
PRESCOTT OLIVER rm 6 Masonic bldg
RICHMOND CHARLES N 54 Pleasant
SHAW J E NORTON 4 Masonic bldg
SPARROW FRANK M 30 Purchase
STETSON ELIOT D rm 34 Masonic bldg
TABER FREDERIC rm 1 Masonic bldg
WALSH JOSEPH rm 2 Masonic bldg
WOODWARD HENRY E 37 Purchase

Nurses
(*Trained)

Allen Annie C 907 County
Andrews Martha J W Mrs Tarkiln Hill road
*Baker Harriet C 96 Atlantic
Bertram F M 15 Bonney
Bowman George L 19 Shawmut av
Brawley Maria G 68 Walden
Brown Sally C 58 Campbell
Burt Jennie R 121 Tremont
Carr Mattie A 46 Emerson (S)
*Cavalier Eveyln 57 Maple
Chase C E Mrs 14 Richmond
*Chittick Rebecca 321 Union
Clement Katherine S 149 Summer
Coffin Arie A 157 North
Colwell Annie T Mrs 251 Shawmut avenue
Connor Minnie G 34 Emerson (S)
Crapo Emma 34 Desautels
Davis Mabel R 166 Chestnut
Dexter Elizabeth 914 Belleville av
Diaz Margaret J 106 South
*Donnelly Mary 57 Maple
*Donnelly Mina 57 Maple
Dyer George N 193 Summer
*Dyring Hilma 64 Hillman
Duxbury Elizabeth 13 Marvin
Fogarty Emma F 158 Allen
Francis Annie L 344 Cedar
*Gallivan M Mrs 321 Union
*Gendreau Marie 42 Locust
*Gibson Nettie V 2883 Acushnet av
Gifford Alice 321 Union
Greene Emma F 204 County
Grieve Jessie K 43 Shawmut av
Grinnell Amy A Mrs 324 Cedar
Hannon Sarah F 94 Fourth
Hardy Ellen M Mrs 140 Summer
Hargraves J 242 Sawyer
Hayes Eudora 36 Hillman
Hayward Carrie E 143 North
Hillman Lucy E 152 Fourth
Hogan Abbie 2 Harrison
*Howard Jessie I 22 Arnold place
*Hunt Jessie 256 Union
Hussey Vesta E 149 Summer
Jameson Sarah 436 Rivet
Kimball Emma B 57 Bedford
Larkin Agnes 50 Thompson
Lermond Jennie 15 Mill
*Lockwood S Augusta 57 Maple
*Lowney Catherine F 1498 Acushnet av
*Macdonald C A 41 Morgan
Mack Elizabeth B 25 Sycamore
*McCarthy Dora 9 Smith
McLeod Florence Mrs 77 Maple
McManus Ella 107 Chestnut
Miller Alice 242 Maxfield
*Nichols Rebecca L 17 Richmond
*O'Brien Addie 321 Union
Palmer Susie Mrs 343 Cedar
Penney Emma 12 Spruce
Percy Emma 403 Elm
*Perry Anna B 93 Bedford
Phillips Lydia A Mrs 17 Richmond
Renex A W Mrs 83 Mt Pleasant
*Renex Belle 83 Mt Pleasant
Smith Lenora A Mrs 55 Tremont
*Spade Ada I 150 Middle
*Stephenson Margaret 256 Union
Stratton Clara 123 State
Swift Rusha W 7 Crapo
*Thatcher Grace 19 Seventh
Thompson Jane F 300 Maxfield
Thompson Maria J 73 Dartmouth
Tinkham Mary F 55 Bonney
*Townsend Susie I 123 Maple
Tripp Caroline E Mrs 467 Union
Tripp Frances 173 Arnold
Tripp Rebecca B 103 Chancery
Woodward Sarah L 38 Campbell

Office Supplies

MONARCH TYPEWRITER CO 67 Milk Boston See page 34

Oil Dealers

AKIN F T & CO 168 S Water corner Walnut, 84 Pleasant and 9 N Water and 1218 Acushnet av See foot lines

DRISCOL CHURCH & HALL 80 and 84 Union See page 13
HERSOM THOMAS & CO 11 Commercial See page 24
Marcotte Leo 68 Dean
SLOCUM & KILBURN 23 N Water See page 766
Valvoline Oil Co foot North

Oil Refiners

Nye William F Estate Fish Island
Robinson W A & Co 144 S Water
Standard Oil Co of N Y Fish Island
Texas Co foot Ark lane
Young Frank L & Kimball 350 South Second

Opticians

Almy J T Estate 5 Purchase
Brown Irving A 206 Union
Coakley J T 26 Cove
Hurll Charles W 23 Purchase
Jenkins Frank M 64 Pleasant
Miller G E 24 Brock av
Moncrieff & Co 7 and 9 Arcade blk and 861 S Water
Robitaille P George 1307 Acushnet av
Ster Optical Co 224 Purchase
Ward S 837 Purchase

Oysters

NEW BEDFORD FISH CO City pier No 4 and Merrill's wharf See advt Fish

Packing

BABBITT STEAM SPECIALTY CO 57 S Water See page 29
SLOCUM & KILBURN 23 N Water See page 766

Paint Mfrs

KIRBY GEORGE JR PAINT CO 14-20 Wall See page 33

Painters

(HOUSE, SHIP, SIGN, ORNAMENTAL AND FRESCO)

AKIN F T & CO 168 S Water cor Walnut 9 N Water 84 Pleasant and 1218 Acushnet av See foot lines
ALLEN MARCUS M 15-19 N Water See page 777
Beardsworth Alfred 463 Allen
Benjamin Adonai 77 Bullard
Berard Frank 129 Eugenia
BERTRAND O 160 Bowditch See page 754
Bessette Arthur 18 Bullard
BLAIR SIGN & ADVERTISING CO 60 Fourth See page 754
Bourgeois Albini 91 Bullard
BOURGEOIS DAVID 105 Bowditch See page 744
Bowie W S 498 County
Bowman Martin M 202 Blackmer
BRILLON A 80 Holly See page 777
Brown I 28 Elm
Brownell William B 52 Oak
CASWELL WILLIAM T 34 to 38 Union See page 94
Cobb D A 379 Elm
CORMIER & DUBE 394 N Front See page 776
Cottam John 319 Cedar
CROSHERE C A 38 Fourth See foot lines
Damon Allen 764 Kempton
Dewhurst Charles 35 Howard
DIONNE WALTER 14 Jean See page 752
DROLET & MILOTTE 109 Holly See page 775
Dube Arthur 394 N Front
Ellis & LeClair 520 County
Ennis John H 17 Maitland
Fogarty Philip E 22 Hall
Francis Manuel 404 Middle (W)
GALLOP R G & CO 55 Hillman See page 752
Garrant Joseph 22 Lucas
Geotta Peter 431 First
Gorner James S 713 Kempton
HALLIDAY C R 257 Union See page 777
Hickey M A 151 Blackmer
Hill Co (sign) 257 Union
Hindle James W 10 Homer
Howland G L 124 Campbell
JENKINS ELMIR A 431 Acushnet av See page 752
Johnson Charles C 201 Park
King C E 77 Rivet
LeBeau Alfred 183 Phillips av
LeBEAU JOSEPH 141 Collette See page 785
Lemieux J P Co 329 N Front
Mackay John H 81 Oak
MORIARTY TIMOTHY J 184 Fourth See page 49
PELLETIER HENRI 86 Hathaway See page 37

Painters—con
PHILLIPS THOMAS O 167 Park See page 44
Potter Isaac E 96 Pierce
Remington E A 347 Kempton
Richer H 1117 Acushnet avenue
Seguin Thomas r1279 Acushnet av
Servais A (sign) 76 William
STURTEVANT W F 70 High See page 25
THERRIEN JOHN 82 Tallman See page 752
Thompson Charles 164 Summer
Thorley G W 515 Rivet
Walmsley Robert 303 Collette
West William R 830 Purchase
Wilson Edward L 61 Durfee
Wood G A 46 Foster
WRIGHT GEORGE F 24 N Water See page 777

Painters' Supplies

AKIN F T & CO 168 S Water 84 Pleasant and 1218 Acushnet av See foot lines
ALLEN MARCUS M 15-19 N Water See page 777
BRILLON A 80 Holly See page 777
KIRBY GEORGE JR PAINT CO (mfrs) 14 Wall See page 33
MORIARTY T J 184 Fourth See page 49
STURTEVANT W F 70 High See page 25

Paints Oils & Glass

AKIN F T & CO 168 S Water cor Walnut, 9 N Water, 84 Pleasant and 1218 Acushnet av See foot lines
BORDEN & REMINGTON CO 115 Annawan, Fall River See page 11
Brightman Bros (mfrs) 146 Front
CASWELL WILLIAM T 34 to 38 Union See page 94
DeWOLF & VINCENT 111 William See page 44
GALLOP R G & CO 55 Hillman See page 752
HANDY JONATHAN CO 28 William See page 766
Hickey M A 151 Blackmer
HILLMAN F G 669 Purchase See page 26
JENKINS ELMIR A 431 Acushnet avenue See page 752
JEWETT HARDWARE CO 108 Middle and 415 Acushnet av See page 784
KIRBY GEORGE JR PAINT CO (mfrs) 14 to 20 Wall See page 33
LAWRENCE J A 1032 to 1034 Acushnet av See page 784
MORIARTY T J (wholesale and retail) 184 Fourth See page 49
QUINTIN H N 1223 Acushnet av See page 767
WRIGHT GEORGE F 24 N Water See page 777

Paper Box Mfrs

COFFIN BROS 38 Middle See page 782

Paper Hangers & Hangings
(See Wall Papers)

AKIN F T & CO 168 S Water, 9 N Water, 84 Pleasant and 1218 Acushnet av See foot lines
ALLEN MARCUS M 15 to 19 N Water See page 777
BERTRAND O 160 Bowditch See page 754
BRILLON A 80 Holly See page 777
CASWELL WILLIAM T 34 to 38 Union See page 94
CORMIER & DUBE 394 N Front See page 776
DIONNE WALTER 14 Jean See page 752
DROLET & MILOTTE 109 Holly See page 775
GALLOP R G & CO 55 Hillman See page 752
LEBEAU J 141 Collette See page 755
MORIARTY T J 184 Fourth See page 49
PELLETIER HENRI 86 Hathaway See page 37
PHILLIPS THOMAS O 167 Park See page 44
THERRIEN JOHN 82 Tallman See page 752
WRIGHT GEORGE F 24 N Water See page 777

Paper Tube Mfrs

PAIRPOINT CORP The Prospect c Howland See page 23

Paper & Twine

BRIGHTMAN F S CO Inc 127 Union See page 769
Kennedy & Kirwin 311 S Water
New Bedford Paper & Supply Co 71 Union

Parquetry Floors

Russell David J 11 Rodman

Patent Medicines

BROWNE PHARMACY The 197-203 Union See back cover

LAWTON C H & H A CO 1 and 52 Purchase and 113 Union See advt Drugs

Pattern Makers

ACUSHNET IRON CO 229 N Water See page 788

JONES & DODGE 202 N Water See page 764

Paving Materials

WARREN CHEMICAL & MFG CO 49 Federal Boston See opp *583

Pawnbrokers

Collateral Loan Co 67 Union

Goenensky Rena Mrs 851 Acushnet avenue

Schuster S 92 Union

Periodicals and Newspapers

Berthiaume E P 877 S Water

BRIGGS GEORGE L 161 Purchase See back cover

Brightman F S Co Inc 127 Union

Spooner E Mrs 650 Purchase

Pharmacists

BROWNE PHARMACY The 197-203 Union See back cover

Phonographs

HOUSEHOLD FURNISHING CO 170-174 Purchase See page 94

Perry M E 605 S Water

Zerbone Gerald 194 Acushnet av

Photographers

Azevedo J V 162 County

BROWN F A 88 Purchase See page 778

Ducharme E 166 River

Frennette J C 1 Arcade blk

Frommell Martin H 80 Purchase

Gagne Ulric 551 N Front

Goulart Manuel 110 S Sixth

Griffin C G 71 William

Havard Ella B 92 Weld

Havard Joseph 92 Purchase

Kozorek William F 921 Acushnet av

Maciolsk Charles 234 N Front

Martin J S 49 William

New Bedford Art Studio 25 Purchase

Raymond P 897 S Water

Reed James E 7 Purchase

Pereira Manuel B r 63 Grinnell

Sherman Francis P 74 Purchase

Taber H W 26 Fifth

Photographic Supplies

BROWNE PHARMACY The 197-203 Union See back cover

Redfearn D 853 S Water and 933 Acushnet avenue

Smith William T 134 Pleasant

Physicians and Surgeons

Allen Horatio C 11 Eighth

Atchinson Charles M 94 Fourth

Barnes Henry 1416 Acushnet av

Belanger David S 125 Rivet

Bernier Joseph A 311 Coggeshall

Bonnar J M 186 Pleasant and 173 Campbell

Bonnev C A Jr 67 Bedford

BRADFORD JOEL P 25 Main See page 24

Branscomb William G 150 Hawthorn

Briggs C D (homeo) 181 Pleasant

Brown M J 35 Mill

Bullard John T 428 County

CLARENCE EDWARD BURT
PHYSICIAN
298 Union Street
Office Hours 8 to 9
2 to 4
7 to 8
Residence 298 Union Street

Caldwell Albert F Jr 25 Fifth

Canney Ellen R 552 County

Chausse J A 790 Purchase

Chubbuck Lurana A 133 Kempton

Clark F J (opthalmic) 49 Fifth

Cody Edmond F 105 S Sixth

Connor Charles F 327 Union

Croacher Anna W 51 Fifth

Dehn Edward W 23 Linden

Derby C A 888 Purchase

De Laval M E 1108 Acushnet av

Denham Edwin B (osteo) 229 Sawyer

Donovan S E 8 Wing

Physicians—con
Doran L K Mrs 76 Bedford
Drummond Juan F B 124 Cedar
Dwight H L 156 Middle
Fortin Julien E 1205 Acushnet av
Foster E E 271 Union
Frasier Joseph A 210 Union
Graves Fred C 256 Union
Grocshinsky Herman 48 Fifth
Hale G C 635 County
Hathaway John D 388 County
Hayes Stephen W 61 Orchard
Healey Harrison T 1680 Acushnet av
Hough Garry de N 542 County
Howland B C (homeo) 96 William
Hunt Charles R (homeo) 474 County
Jernegan Walter S 28 Fifth
Johnson E St J 271 Union
Kirby Holder C 33 S Sixth
Lamothe Alexander 519 N Front
Lamoureux Stanislas A 211 Collette
Leary C J 415 Pleasant
Leonard Milton H 83 Ash (S)
Lewis George F 76 Walnut
Lord W O 864 Purchase
Lowney D J 1498 Acushnet av
Mandell A H 25 Sycamore
Marsden George 1579 Acushnet av
McAllister J J H 216 County
Nelson William W 384 Kempton
Nickerson W J 164 Middle
Nield W A 62 Fifth
Nixon Alfred J 84 Acushnet av
Normandin Alphonse 37 Purchase
Normandin Louis Z 584 Purchase
O'Brien D P 330 Union
Osborne E D 37 S Second
Owen James W 76 Beetle
Paquin J Ubalde 1304 Acushnet av
Parker Henry W 13 S Sixth
Parlin Ralph B (osteo) 124 Mill
Pearce Edward 44 Fifth
Perras Louis 359 N Front
Peterson C A 90 Hillman
Pierce A V 99 Elm
Pitta Joao C da Silva 43 Allen
Pothier J C 245 Fourth
Potter Lester F 278 Union
Potter William G 546 County
Pratt Charles A 60 Orchard
Pratt D D 319 Union
Prescott C D 176 William and 108 Ash (S)
Prescott H D 176 William
Ravich S 153 Acushnet av
Richard Alfred E 78 Nye
Richards G L 97 William rm 307
Robbins Elmer E 101 School
Robbins E Stanley 17 S Sixth
Robinson Fred H 2 Arcade block
Rosa H Antonio 112 Grinnell
Ross J Conrad 1283 Acushnet av
St George A 92½ Purchase
St Germain J P 13 S Sixth
Seaver Edwin P Jr 179 William
Senesac A N 1018 S Water
Shanks Charles 645 Kempton
Sheehy William Clinton 249 Chestnut
Sisson Edward R 15 Eighth
Stetson F E 334 Union
Stevens H L 129 Purchase
Sullivan James F 185 Middle
Swift William N 378 County
Sylvia Manuel V 34 Wing
Tessier J N 993 S Water
Thayer W H 25 Seventh
Thuot John V 938 Acushnet av
Tucker E T 258 Pleasant
Turner W K 1105 Acushnet av
Vieira Joseph P 317 Rivet
Walker Mary W (osteo) 288 Union
Walker R I (osteo) 288 Union
Weaver H V 161 William
Webber Amos P 250 Union
Weeks J F 2193 Acushnet av L C
Wheeler Emma H 25 Morgan
Whitney Edward M 27 S Sixth
Winslow B S 1065 S Water

Physicians' Prescriptions

BROWNE PHARMACY The 197 to 203 Union See back cover

Piano Repairers & Tuners

Carter Peter 409 Bolton
Emerson Charles P 141 Chestnut
Paige W H 109 William
Peirce George 7 Homer
Rounsville J 18 Purchase

Piano Movers

DeMORANVILLE D H 83 Thomas See page 787
STEINERT M & SONS CO The 109 William See page 23

Pianos & Organs

(See also Music and Musical Instruments)

Boardman W 201 Acushnet av
Cottelle B F 306 Acushnet av
Forest Felix 1041 Acushnet av
Hallet & Davis Piano Co 99 to 101 William
STEINERT M & SONS CO The 109 William See page 23
Sullivan D J Estate of 228 Union

PLUMBING

MAGEE
Superior { FURNACES HEATERS RANGES
They Save Coal

HIRST, THE PLUMBER
28-32 NO. WATER STREET
North Office, 1230 Acushnet Ave.
It Pays to Patronize the Competent

A1 PLUMBING
First Quality Fixtures
Competent Mechanics
Sheet Metal Work of all kinds

HEATING

E. P. HIRST CO.

Thuot H L 808 Purchase
WING C F CO The Inc 34 Purchase See page 40

Picture Frame Mfrs

Ashworth E 98 Tallman
PINEAULT J N 682 Purchase See page 761

Pictures & Frames

Allen Asa L H 228 Union
Alves M M 25 N Second
Bates Whitney E 72 Thomas
Crowell A B 24 Fifth
Crowell E N (foreign photographs) 20 Seventh
HOUSEHOLD FURNISHING CO 170 to 174 Purchase See page 94
Howland A T 52 Pleasant
Parsons L J Jr 4 Beetle lane
Percy S A 362 Purchase

Pitch (Roofing & Paving)

BARRET MFG CO 297 Franklin Boston See front cover

Planing Mills

DAVIS Z B CORP 668 Acushnet av See page 762
GREENE & WOOD Pine near S Water See foot lines
NICHOLSON J G 27 to 35 Bowditch See foot lines
RICARD LEVI 142 Nye See page 765
WEBBER LUMBER & SUPPLY CO 172 N Water See page 761

Plants

KIRK J FRANK 370 to 374 Purchase See page 565
MOSHER WILLIAM E 325 Hillman See page 40

Plasterers

CROTEAU & WOOD 249 Shawmut avenue See page 776
PROUTEAU RAOUL 82 Phillips av See page 760
SILVA HENRY 63 Fifth See page 761

Plumbers

ALLEN GEORGE J & CO 91 N Water See page 26
BACON W L 514 County See top edge
BAILEY WALTER P 216 Acushnet av See page 766
BOLDUC A 115 Bowditch See page 780
BURKE JOHN P 903 County See page 782
CEJKA GEORGE 1480 Acushnet av See page 785
Clark & Son 503 S Water
COHOLAN J 703 S Water See page 767
CROSSLEY JOHN F & CO 223 Mill See foot lines
ELLIOTT JOHN D 106 Fourth See page 45
Gifford Thomas J & Co 650 Cottage
GREEN EVERETT 185 Acushnet avenue See page 780
GREGORY EDWARD H 880 S Water See page 780
Gregory Plumbing Co 1545 Acushnet avenue
Hamel Flavien 915 Acushnet av
Hargrave J P 293 Rivet
Hellyer James G 575 Purchase
Higgins E O 361 North
HIRST E P CO 28 to 32 N Water See above
Jones A & Co 15 Division
LEVESQUE WILFRED 211 Coffin avenue See page 787

Plumbers—con
LOWE S C SUPPLY CO 87 Union See page 740
Lowney John H 540 N Front
Macaulay A 138 Blackmer
Mahoney J H 957 County
Margeson & Bazinet 542 N Front
Marshall Henry J 126 Acushnet av
MAXFIELD CHARLES A 26 N Second See page 769
McAlpine Allan 339 Kempton
McGoff J E 339 Sawyer
MUDGE & FRANCIS 157 Acushnet avenue See page 781
Penney Edward F 266 County
PERRA JOHN 19 Linden See page 766
Reynolds H C 46 Wing
Ricketson O 47 Delano
Rielly Joseph P 46 Linden
Roy A A & Co 671 Purchase
SHERMAN J H 50-52 Union See page 767
SHERMAN & McQUILLAN 250 Purchase See page 781
STANDARD CONSTRUCTION CO 281½ Sawyer See page 783
WOOD, BRIGHTMAN & CO 47-55 N Water See page 3

Plumbing Supplies
Watson-Pennell Corp 2 Rodman

Pork, Lard and Hams
DRISCOL, CHURCH & HALL (wholesale) 82-84 Union See page 13
Squire J P & Co 447 S Second

Poultry
Bonneau Alsedar 3322 Acushnet av
Robbins Frank B 1715 Acushnet av

Poultry Supplies
DeWOLF & VINCENT 111 William See page 28

Prepared Roofing
WARREN CHEMICAL & MFG CO 49 Federal Boston See opp *583

Pressing
GERARDI V V 36 Eighth See page 769

Printers (Job)
ANTHONY E & SONS Inc Pleasant corner Market
BRIGHTMAN F S CO Inc 127 Union See page 769
Bristol Printing Co 354 Purchase
BUDLONG J E PRESS The 38 Middle See page 778
Catholic Union The Pleasant corner Mill
Coffin A E Press The 69 Purchase
COLLINS WILLISTON H & CO 34-40 N Second See page 23
EVENING AND REPUBLICAN STANDARD Pleasant corner Market
Habicht F A 21 N Second
Haskell Press 555 Purchase
Horton Printing Co 258 Purchase
Howland P Jr 20 Wall
L'Echo Publishing Co 101 Kenyon
Mercury Publishing Co 112 Union
N B Printing Co 25 N Second
Vieira Antonio C 250 S Second

Private Detectives
BURNS DETECTIVE BUREAU 1 Beacon Boston See opp page 161
NATIONAL DETECTIVE AGENCY The 49 Westminster Providence R I See page 28
WOOD-MORGAN DETECTIVE AGENCY 61 Court Boston See page 753

Private School
(See Academies also Teachers Private Schools)
BENTONS BUSINESS SCHOOL 97 William See map

Produce and Fruit
(WHOLESALE)
Campbell J M 860 Acushnet av
Fisher E L Co Inc 2 S Water
Lawrence D E 39 Union
Pease C H & Co 94 Union
Sherman I C & Son 70-76 Union

Production Engineers
GUNN, RICHARDS & CO Tremont bldg Boston Mass See page 40

Provisions Etc
(WHOLESALE)
Anthony Swift & Co Bridge sq
Armour & Co 99 Front
Bannister J W 188 N Water
Bolduc H 65 Brock avenue
BRIGHTMAN E T 248 Purchase, 306 Cedar and 109 S Sixth See advt Grocers

DRISCOL, CHURCH & HALL 82-84 Union See page 13
Holden C H & Co 45-49 Union
Hutchinson George 537 N Front
Marshall & Co 106 Front
Morris & Co Bridge sq
N B Packing Co 224 Cedar Grove
POTTER WILLIAM F & CO (salt) 81-85 Front and 3-11 Union See page 30
Wood & Lowrie 40 to 50 Union

(RETAIL)

Andrews J H Mrs 426 Kempton
Ashley J B Jr 177 Purchase
Baldwin J T 126 Cove
Bay State Market Co 878 Purchase
Bergeron O & J 188 Blackmer
Bolduc Arthur 65 Brock av
Boule Henry 1413 Acushnet av
BRIGHTMAN E T 109 S Sixth, 306 Cedar and 248 Purchase See advt Grocers
Brightman H W 106 Union
Chadwick & Tripp 84 Cove
Cohen Hyman 497 S Water
Cohen M 460 S Water
Consolidated Meat & Grocery Co 132 and 163 Union, 64 and 143 Purchase, 1141 Acushnet av and 149 Cove
Cook H 136 County
Darling Edgar W 385 to 387 Purchase
Fredette H J 213 Brownell
Hettinger J W 34 French av
Hudner M T 145 Union
Jussaume Oliva 305 N Front
Kenyon Theodore F 152 Arnold
Keyes & Woodland 108 Cedar
Lawton C W 773 Kempton
NEW YORK MARKET 251 Purchase See page 772
Oliver J S 113 S Second
Ouimette L 104 Cove
Pare A 28 Salisbury
Perry W A 159 Purchase
Poirier Charles A 1174 Acushnet av
ROBINSON DANIEL 156 Weld See page 772
Sylvia J L 262 Purchase
Taber George S 17 N Sixth
Tremblay Romuald 806 Purchase
Wild Arthur 131 Blackmer

Public Warehousemen

DENISON BROS CO 32 Pleasant foot Hillman and 77 Rivet See front edge
New Bedford Public Warehouse cor School and Water
New Bedford Storage Warehouse Co 352 to 378 Sawyer

Publishers

GREENOUGH W A & CO New Bedford and Fairhaven Directory 65 Broad Boston (write for list published)
Wheaton & Co 64 Mill

Pulleys

BABBITT STEAM SPECIALTY CO 57 S Water See page 29
SLOCUM & KILBURN 23 N Water See page 766

Pumps (Copper & Iron)

BRAMAN DOW & CO 239 Causeway Boston See page 38
WOOD, BRIGHTMAN & CO 55 N Water See page 3

Railroad Companies

Dartmouth & Westport, Purchase cor William
New Bedford & Onset, Purchase cor William
New York, New Haven & Hartford, foot Pearl
UNION STREET RAILWAY CO The Purchase cor William See page 21

Ranges

DeWOLF & VINCENT 100 Williams liam See page 44
WING CHARLES F CO The Inc 34 to 38 Purchase See page 40

Rattan Furniture

HOUSEHOLD FURNISHING CO 170 to 174 Purchase See page 94

Ready Roofings

BARRETT MFG CO 297 Franklin Boston See front cover

P. S. MACY

Appraiser Justice of the Peace Estates Cared for

REAL ESTATE

78 SMITH STREET, NEW BEDFORD

Bell Telephone 1386-5

Real Estate Agents

ASHLEY CHARLES S JR & CO 62 Pleasant See page 43
ASHLEY ROLAND R 40 North See page 755
ASHTON & MURPHY 1109 S Water See page 48
Bentley F T & Son 123 Fifth
Bourgeois Oliver A 197 Bowditch
Brock George P 52 Pleasant
CHAMBERLAIN CHARLES E 132 Cottage cor Arnold See back cover
CHAMBERLAIN & SILVA 132 Cottage See back cover
Cook & Smith 37 Purchase rm 2
DAVOL CLARENCE H 23 Clifford bldg See page 755
DESAUTELS S 269 Sawyer See page 758
Driscoll D E 92 County
DRISCOLL D F 14 Clifford bldg See front cover
Driscoll P J 307 Bowditch
Genensky Samuel 69 Russell
Gibbs H M 114 Rotch
Gifford J N 97 William rm 200
Goldys S 61 Reynolds
GREENE FRED W Jr 21 Clifford bldg See page 758
Haskins H K 87 Chestnut
Haskins & Gibson 66 Pleasant
HERON CHARLES T 114 William See page 27
KENYON A B 120 Purchase rm 209 See page 27
Knott Thomas 1683 Acushnet av
Landry Pierre 54 Bullard
LEBEAU THEOPHILE 410½ N Front See page 33
Luce Frederick C 130 Willis
Macomber George T 326 Cottage
MACY PELEG S 78 Smith See above
MARANDA DONAT 393 N Front See page 757
Motta Antonio 151 Hemlock
Paquette Joseph C 29 Arcade bldg
Parsons Thomas L 131 Elm
Perry Ebenezer S & Son 136 Pleasant
Powers & Luce 37 Purchase rm 3
Prevost M D 120 Purchase rm 307
Queen H 125½ Fourth
Reid Frank A 77 Rivet
Roberts Joseph D 40 Walnut
Roy D A 37 Purchase
Sanders H V 166 Purchase
Silva D T 358 Orchard
Smith William 1668 Acushnet av
SPOONER WILLIAM E 52 Pleasant See page 27
Sylvia Ralph R S 111 County
Tilton C C 97 William rm 301
Turgeon F X Jr 535 N Front

H C VAUGHAN

Real Estate Agent Auctioneer
Appraiser and Justice of the Peace
Care of Estates a Specialty
23 Bordon Street
Telephone Connection

Vezina George 1223 Acushnet av
WARREN'S AGENCY 1063 South Water See foot lines back binding and page 789
Westby & Baker 308 Times bldg
Whitehead John 211 Collette
WILLIAMS MANUEL A 498 Bolton See back cover
Woolfenden William 1283 Acushnet avenue

Reeds Harness Etc (Mill)

N B Reed Co 189 N Water

Refrigerators

BOSWORTH WILLARD E 1194 Rockdale av Se page 785
HOUSEHOLD FURNISHING CO 170-174 Purchase. See page 94

Remnants

Doyle A H 1215 Acushnet av and 1105 S Water

Renovators

(Naphtha and Steam)

DANTSIZEN JOHN G 214 Court See back cover

Restaurants and Lunch

Anthony & Gregory 254 Coggeshall
Audette & Chapdelaine 1214 Acushnet avenue
Bachman A 1674 Acushnet avénue
Barrows Harry 173 Purchase and 345 Acushnet avenue
Barker F G 224½ Union
Bean F B 845 Purchase
Bedard Oliva, N Front corner Coffin avenue
Bernier C 950 S Water
Canton Cafe 949 Acushnet avenue
Caperaonis Spanoodis & Co 1136 Acushnet avenue
Charperles J 958 S Water
Chenette Henry 37 Rivet
Cleveland George H V D 193 Acushnet avenue
Coury William 122 Cove
Cordeira Bros 108 Potomska
Couroussi P 953 Acushnet avenue
Croker Isaac 10 S Second
CROWN CONFECTIONERY STORE 56 Purchase See page 783
Dennis Ellis 150 Union
Dolplaise A Cove corner First
Ellery E M, Acushnet av near Willis
Fitzgerald William F 102 Union
Flannery M 106 Weld
Garlick George 762 Purchase
Gregory Harry 881 Purchase
Hurley Andrew C 15 S Water
Jabott H 265 Sawyer
Janak J 919 Acushnet avenue
La Croix Wilfred J 1278 Acushnet av
Lambert Amos 304 N Front
Law S, Spring cor S Second
LEBEAU THEOPHILE 416 North Front See page 33
Lester James 403 Kempton
Lupo E D 363 Acushnet av and 154 Purchase
Masse Joseph 61 Delano
Matthews J H 240 Purchase
McAfee J 44 Acushnet avenue
McConigle C W 1484 Acushnet av
Mort Gertrude 1612 Acushnet av
Moy Toy Co 354 Acushnet avenue
Nerbonne Joseph cor Purchase and Weld
Nerbonne P 233 Purchase
Nicholson Joseph 423 Rivet
Norris William N 171 Purchase
PALACE CAFE 173 Purchase See page 779
Platt John 110 Rivet
Radcliffe Wilfred 400 Purchase
Puritan Lunch 1027 Acushnet av
Richard J C 1185 Acushnet avenue
Ripley W V, S Water cor Commercial
Rocheleau Alfred 1168½ Acushnet av
ROGLER PHILIP 72-74 William See page 772
Ross John Purchase cor Elm
Roylance S 116 Cove
Senecal Ernest 1493 Acushnet av
Shapiro M 381 S Water
Shuy Fong Co 68 William
Snyder Charles 81 Weld
Surprenant D 960 Acushnet avenue
Sylvester R R 83 Union
Sylvia Antone 52 Howland
Tattersall Thomas 968 Acushnet av
Toundas Christos 218 Coggeshall
Turgeon Antoine 1510 Acushnet av
Vernon John 628½ First
Vokes W W 317 Acushnet avenue
Weedall S 629 Purchase
Whitehead J 624 Purchase
Wilson Robert J 220 Union
Yee Yohn 68 William

Riggers

Black Peter 72 Front
Howland & Sampson 27 Front

Ring Travelers

Standard Ring Traveler Co 6 Elm
WHITINSVILLE SPINNING RING CO Whitinsville Mass Se opp 589

Road Preservatives

BARRETT MFG CO 297 Franklin Boston See front cover

Roof Coating

WARREN CHEMICAL & MFG CO 49 Federal Boston See opp *583

Roofers & Roofing Materials

AKIN F T & CO 168 S Water, 84 Pleasant and 1218 Acushnet av See foot lines
Bertram John & Son 59 Borden
HURLEY C F (gravel and slate) 90 Beetle See page 781
LAWRENCE J A 1032 Acushnet av See page 784
PERKINS A W & CO 167 Hillman See page 789
WARREN CHEMICAL & MFG CO 49 Federal Boston See opp *583

Roofing Pitch

WARREN CHEMICAL & MFG CO 49 Federal Boston See opp *583

Roofing & Paving Materials

BARRETT MFG CO 297 Franklin Boston See front cover

Rope & Twine

BRIGGS & BECKMAN 31-35 Commercial See page 785

Rubber Goods

New Bedford Rubber Co 66 William

Rubber Hose

BABBITT STEAM SPECIALTY CO 57 S Water See page 29
DeWOLF & VINCENT 111 William See page 44
SLOCUM & KILBURN 23 N Water See page 766

Rubber Stamps

Stowell F B & Co 76 William

Rug Mfrs

NEW BEDFORD STEAM CARPET BEATING & RUG CO North cor N Water See front cover

Rug Cleansing

HOWES C G CO Allston Mass See opp Cleansers

Rummage Sales

ST JAMES CO-OPERATIVE SALES 68 Linden See page 48

Safe Deposit Vaults

HAWES TEWKSBURY & CO Masonic bldg See page 7
NEW BEDFORD SAFE DEPOSIT AND TRUST CO 61 William See page 8

Sail Makers

Briggs & Beckman 31-35 Commercial

Salt

HATHAWAY & MACKENZIE GRAIN CO The 748 Purchase See opp Grain

Sand & Gravel

CONNELL JOHN JR 350 Sawyer See page 774

Sanitariums

ACUSHNET SANITARIUM 25 Main L C See page 24

Sash Doors & Blinds

GREENE & WOOD Pine See foot lines
NICHOLSON J G 27-35 Bowditch See foot lines
SHERMAN JAMES L 194 N Water See page 765
WEBBER LUMBER & SUPPLY CO 172 N Water See page 761

Sausage Mfrs

Cameron John 26 Beech
Kuechler Bros 337 S Second
Ladieu H J Tarkiln Hill rd
Schmidt Jacob H 424 S Second

Savings Banks

(See also Co-operative Banks)

NEW BEDFORD FIVE CENTS SAVINGS BANK 37 Purchase See page 5
NEW BEDFORD INSTITUTION FOR SAVINGS 174 to 178 Union cor Fourth See page 9

Sawing & Turning

GREENE & WOOD Pine n S Water See foot lines

JONES & DODGE 202 N Water See page 764
NICHOLSON J G 27 to 35 Bowditch See foot lines
RICARD LEVI 142 Nye See page 765

Scenery Painters

BLAIR SIGN & ADVERTISING CO 60 Fourth See page 754

Schools

(See also Teachers Private Schools)
(COMMERCIAL)

BENTON'S BUSINESS SCHOOL 97 William See map
KINYON'S COMMERCIAL SCHOOL 76 Pleasant rms 21-24 See foot lines

PRIVATE

International Correspondence Schools 23 Clifford bldg
New Bedford Textile School 303-331 Purchase See page 36

Screens (Window & Door)

JAMES FRANKLIN E 169 Clinton See back binding and page 761

Sculptor

Ricketson Walton 10 Anthony

Second Hand Goods

Cullen J H 391 Purchase
Kranzler Mates 533 Acushnet av
Portnoy Isaac 212 Coggeshall
Radciffe W 402 Purchase
ST JAMES CO-OPERATIVE SALES 68 Linden See page 48
Sullivan J E 411 Purchase
Tremblay J E W 342 Purchase

Secret Service Experts

BURNS DETECTIVE BUREAU 1 Beacon Boston See opp page 161

Seeds

LAWTON C H & H A CO 1 Union See advt Drugs

Sewer Pipe

PAISLER & WILLIS 160 N Water See page 774

Sewing Machines and Repairing

Singer Sewing Machine Co 73 William
White Sewing Machine Co 186 Purchase

WING CHARLES F CO The Inc 34-38 Purchase See page 40

Shades

WING CHARLES F CO The Inc 34-38 Purchase See page 40

Shafting Hangers and Pulleys

MASON MACHINE WORKS Taunton Mass See page 39

Sheet Copper

TAUNTON-NEW BEDFORD COPPER CO N Front See page 34

Sheet Iron, Tin Plate and Metals

CONGDON, CARPENTER & CO 58 to 68 Fourth Fall River See page 10

Sheet Metal Work

ALLEN GEORGE J & CO 91 North Water See page 26
BACON W L 514 County See top edge
BAILEY W P 216 Acushnet av See page 766
GREEN EVERETT 185 Acushnet av See page 780
GREGORY EDWARD H 880 South Water See page 780
HIRST E P CO 28-32 N Water See advt Plumbers
HURLEY CORNELIUS F 90 Beetle See page 781
MAXFIELD CHARLES A 26 N Second See page 769
SHERMAN JAMES H 50-52 Union See page 767
SHERMAN & McQUILLAN 250 Purchase See page 781

Sheriffs (Deputy)

Balthazar J A 21 Clifford bldg
Brooks N B 433 Cottage
Oliver J B 37 Purchase rm 28
Spooner W R 31 Masonic bldg
Weeden G F 31 Masonic bldg
Whalley E J 49 William

Shingle Stains

BARRETT MFG CO 297 Franklin Boston See front cover

Ship Agent

(See also Merchants)

Nye P H City pier No 2

Ship Chandlery

AKIN F T & CO 168 S Water cor Walnut 84 Pleasant and 1218 Acushnet av See foot lines
CASWELL W T 34 Union See page 158
DeWOLF & VINCENT 111 William See page 44

Shipsmith

Peters A J 11 Front

Shipwrights

Chace A & Co 12 Merrill's wharf

Shirt Makers

Bourne M J Mrs 3 Seventh
Brown D E 83 Hillman

Shoe Eyelet Mfrs

Rhodes J C & Co Inc 123 Front

Shoe Mfrs

Taylor E E Co 474 Acushnet av

Shorthand & Typewriting

KINYON'S COMMERCIAL SCHOOL 76 Pleasant See foot lines

Shuttles

DUDLEY S A (mfr) 148 Dean Taunton Mass See page 17
N B Shuttle Co 6 Elm
SHAMBOW SHUTTLE CO (mfrs) 307 N Main Woonsocket R I See page 30

Sidewalks (Granolithic)

LOFTUS & DUGAN 121 Clark See page 776

Sign Painters

BLAIR SIGN & ADVERTISING CO 60 Fourth See page 754
BOURGEOIS DAVID 105 Bowditch See page 744

Silk Mfrs

Crescent Mfg Co 1145 Kempton

Silver Plated Ware

PAIRPOINT CORPORATION The Prospect cor Howland See page 23

Skating Rink

Elm Rink 302 Purchase

Slag (Roofing)

WARREN CHEMICAL & MFG CO 49 Federal Boston See opp *583

Slate

BARRETT MFG CO 297 Franklin Boston See front cover

Slaters

HURLEY C F 90 Beetle See page 781
PERKINS A W & CO 167 Hillman See page 789

Soap Mfrs

HERSOM THOMAS & SON 87 Howard av and 11 Commercial See page 24

Soda & Mineral Water

WHEATON HIRAM & SONS 45-51 School See page 773

Spar Mfrs

Howland E F & Son Front next Merrill's Wharf

Spindles & Flyers

DRAPER CO Hopedale Mass See page 2

Spinning Rings

WHITINSVILLE SPINNING RING CO Whitinsville Mass See opp 589

Sporting Goods

Braley A L 103 Union
BRIGGS WILLIAM P 141 Purchase See advt Electricians
Eggars George A 10 William
LAWRENCE JOSEPH A 1032-1034 Acushnet av See page 784
Richards G D 249 Union
Tobey Joseph T 125 Purchase

Stables

(Boarding, Livery and Sale)

Ashley I L 12-20 Fourth
Braley F J Acushnet av bey Braley rd
Brawley E L (sale) 27 Fourth
CHAUSSE A 388 N Front See page 772
Club Stable Corp 34 S Second
Covil O E 33 Elm
Cyr Arsene r 281 Sawyer
Dunlap A A (private) 318 and 319 Union
English James 236 Kempton
Enos John E 83 Grinnell

Foster J A 430 Purchase
Gardner & Gray 861 Kempton
Godfrey E H 35 Hillman
Gravel E R 57 Holly
Lagesse Henry 223 State
Lomba H rear 30 Acushnet av
Monty Frank 6 Washburn
MURPHY C H & SON 40 and 42 Fourth See page 771
Padelford F 5 Briggs ct
PEIRCE W H & L F 304 Kempton See page 770
RAYMOND CHARLES 396 Cottage See page 771
Richards W D 19 S Second
Robida J A (sale) 45 Spring
SHERMAN A C 50 Elm See page 770
Swift Thatcher S 118 Grinnell
Sylvia A A 388 S Second
Sylvia M M 49 Delano
TALLMAN A S 135 Grinnell See page 771
Warren David 255 State
WASHBURN WILLIAM R Nonquitt Mass See page 770
Woodacre R 270 Purchase

Stair Builders

SHERMAN CHARLES H 20 N Second See page 15
TRIPP & THORPE 183 N Water See page 764

Stationers

(See also Periodicals & Newspapers)
Alider Jacob 1007 Acushnet av
BRIGGS GEORGE L 161 Purchase See back cover
BRIGHTMAN F S CO Inc 127 Union See page 769
COLLINS WILLISTON H & CO (mfr) 34-40 N Second See page 23
FOREST FELIX & CO 1041 Acushnet av See page 778
Hutchinson H S & Co 198 Union
Robinson Bros 106 Rivet
Taber Robert W 28 Pleasant

Steam Boiler Mfrs

BRAMAN DOW & CO 239 Causeway Boston See page 38

Steam Carpet Cleaning

N B STEAM CARPET BEATING AND RUG CO North cor N Water See front cover

Steam Engines

Weeden Mfg Co (toy) 148-152 N Water

Steam Fitters' Supplies, Gas and Water Pipe Mfrs Heating Apparatus

BRAMAN DOW & CO 239 Causeway Boston See page 38

Steam Packing

BRAMAN DOW & CO 239 Causeway Boston See page 38

Steam Radiators, Valves & Gauge Cocks

BRAMAN DOW & CO 239 Causeway Boston See page 38

Steam Specialties

BABBITT STEAM SPECIALTY CO 57 S Water See page 29

Steam & Gas Fitters

ALLEN GEORGE J & CO 91 N Water See page 26
BACON W L 514 County See top edge
BOLDUC AZAIRE 115 Bowditch See page 780
BURKE J P 903 County See page 782
COHOLAN J 703 S Water See page 767
Conway James N 470 Union
CROSSLEY JOHN F & CO 223 Mill See foot lines
Damon C L 129 Smith
Earl Griffin & Co 57 S Water
GREEN EVERETT 185 Acusnet av See page 780
GREGORY EDWARD H 880 S Water See page 780
HIRST E P CO 28-32 N Water See advt Plumbers
LEVESQUE WILFRED 211 Coffin av See page 787
PERRA JOHN 19 Linden See page 766
RANKIN & ARNOLD 19 N Second See page 780
Santos M P 99 Acushnet av
SHERMAN & McQUILLAN 250 Purchase See page 781
STANDARD CONSTRUCTION CO 281½ Sawyer See page 783
WOOD BRIGHTMAN & CO 47-55 N Water See page 3

Steam & Gas Fittings

BRAMAN DOW & CO 239 Causeway Boston See page 38
CROSSLEY JOHN F & CO 223 Mill See foot lines

Steam & Hot Water Heating

BAILEY W P 216 Acushnet av See page 766
SHERMAN JAMES H 54 Union See page 767

Steamship Companies & *Agents

*Lemos W M 73 Howland
Murphy T J 235 Purchase
New Bedford Martha's Vineyard & Nantucket Steamboat Co 7 Commercial
N E Navigation Co 2 Union
***RODGERS A M** 177-179 Acushnet av See page 25

Steel Ceilings

BERGER MFG CO of Mass 286 Devonshire Boston See page 753

Steel Lathing

BERGER MFG CO of Mass 286 Devonshire Boston See page 753
DEXTRADEUR CHARLES J 363 N Front See page 754

Steel Pulleys

SLOCUM & KILBURN 23 N Water See page 766

Stenographers

DAVOL CLARENCE H (court) 23 Clifford bldg See page 755
Kendall E V Mrs 97 William rm 210
Monroe Frederick S 49 William

Stocking Mfr

Fish Burgoyne 254 Coffin av

Stocks & Bonds

HAWES TEWKSBURY & CO Masonic bldg See page 7
SANFORD & KELLEY Clifford bldg See front cover
TUCKER, ANTHONY & CO 17 Pleasant See page 6

Stone Cutters & Dealers

GURL FRANCIS J Sawyer cor Ashland See opp Undertakers
POTHIER JOSEPH A 305 Mt Pleasant See page 29
REX MONUMENTAL WORKS 90 Dartmouth See back cover

Storage Warehouse

NEW BEDFORD STORAGE WAREHOUSE CO 352-378 Sawyer See back binding and page 35

Stoves & Ranges

BAILEY W P 216 Acushnet av See page 766
CEJKA G (repaired) 1480 Acushnet av See page 785
DeWOLF & VINCENT 111 William See page 44
GALLIGAN C A 1516 Acushnet av See page 37
Gauthier D H 867 Purchase
HIRST E P CO 28-32 N Water See advt Plumbers
HOUSEHOLD FURNISHING CO 170-174 Purchase See page 94
Knowles T P 635 Purchase
LAWRENCE JOSEPH A 1032-1034 Acushnet av See page 784
MAXFIELD CHARLES A 26 N Second See page 769
MUDGE & FRANCIS (repairing) 157 Acushnet av See page 781
QUINTIN H N 1223 Acushnet av See page 767
Sawyer S P 79 N Second
Sherman & McQuillan 250 Purchase
WING C F CO The Inc 34 Purchase See page 40
WOOD BRIGHTMAN & CO 47 to 55 N Water See page 3

Stripping Cards

MASON BROS MFG CO Worcester See page 14

Stucco Worker

MASON J L G 51 Foster See page 774

Surveyors and Civil Engineers

ASHTON & MURPHY 1109 S Water See page 48
DAHILL & KIRBY 11 Clifford bldg See page 42
DRAKE ALBERT B 164 William See front cover and bottom edge

FRANK M METCALF
Civil Engineer and Surveyor
211 Merchants Bank Building
Auto Tel 1276 Bell 431-2
Residence 378 Cottage Street
Bell Tel 767-5

Systematizers of Accounts

GUNN, RICHARDS & CO Tremont bldg Boston Mass See page 40

Tailors (Merchant)

(See also Clothing Dealers)

Allen George E & Co 120 Union
Balboni Louis 109 James
Barash Bros 258 Purchase
Barnes J 136 Blackmer
Barry M F & Son 129 Union
Becker A 146 Purchase and 326 Acushnet avenue
Bernstein A 1482 Acushnet avenue
Bonnoyer B 1229 Acushnet avenue
Burns Stephen J 184 Purchase
BUSH A M & CO 47 William See page 768
Campbell James 11 Bonney
Cohen Joseph 1524 Acushnet avenue
Conant George M 131 Union
Cook Richard H Jr 326 Kempton
Cyr Magloire 9 Arcade blk
Figueiredo J S 83 Howland
Fish A J 52 Pleasant
Fleischer J I 356 Acushnet av
Gallagher N 89 Fifth
GERARDI V V (ladies) 36 Eighth See page 769
Habicht G L (ladies) 73 Russell
Hait Morris 619 Purchase
Howland Daniel W 303 Maxfield
Hunt E W 137 Union
Jackson E W 85 Cedar
Leary John 76 William
Lecuyer H 1140 Acushnet avenue
Leigh John 346 Purchase
Lipman Bros 45 Purchase
Lipschitz S 239 Purchase
Lipson J 139 Cove
Masse H 131 Union
McIntyre M H 15 Pleasant
Mitchell The Tailor 27 Purchase
Navinsky Nathan 593 Purchase
Novick A S 263 Acushnet av
Nulman H I 139 Purchase
Onley C H 340 Acushnet avenue
Pintov Paul 29 Walnut
Potvin Alphonse F 174 Cedar
Remillard J 1014 Acushnet avenue
Rocklin K & Son 1026 Acushnet av
Roshkowich J 50 Howland
Roy Leopold D 1042 Acushnet av
Saulnier J 28 Delano
Shknolnick C 62½ Purchase
Silva Antone I 96 Grinnell
Silver Max 831 Purchase
Soforenco J 17 Arcade blk
Spectre B 1 Cornell place
Tromblay C Mrs 338 Purchase
Webb F L 239 Sawyer
Wilkinson R A 40 Purchase
Wolfe Charles 1½ Fifth

Talking Machines

STEINERT M & SONS CO The 109 William See page 23
WING C F CO The Inc 34 Purchase See page 40

Tallow

HERSON THOMAS & CO 11 Commercial See page 24
N B Tallow Co r 182 N Water

Tanks & Flues

GUNNING BOILER & MACHINE CO 67 S Water See page 31

Tar

BARRETT MFG CO 297 Franklin Boston See front cover

Teachers

(AUTOMOBILE)

WOODRUFF F T & CO 244 Purchase See page 748

(BOOKKEEPING)

BENTON'S BUSINESS SCHOOL 97 William See map

(DANCING)

Kavanaugh M F 96 William
Pease Otis W 46 Thompson

(LANGUAGES)

Rosen Louis (Hebrew) 352 S First
Walder Juda (Hebrew) 10 Granfield

(MUSIC)

Abrams Alice M 86 N Second
Anthony Alice G 92 Elm
Bamforth H 199 Brock av

Teachers—con
Barrell Edgar A 371 County
Bassett Helen 160 North
Beauchemin A 53 Brock av
Bryant Elsie L 205 Summer
Church Eunice S 136 Chestnut
Cook Alice P 336 Orchard (S)
Covell Addie R (vocal) 14 Pope
Davis Esther S 8 Park pl
Davis Hannah L 22 Sycamore
Demers Alice (violin) 195 Davis
Done Harry (violin) 121 Austin
Ekdahl S E 93 Walden
Fontain L J Oscar 177 Bowditch
Forbes Florence E 67 Hillman
Freedom Flossie M 83 Cedar
Gibbs Florence L 90 Mill
Gifford F L Mrs 57 Foster
Gifford Leonora F 19 Emerson (S)
Gillespie Lillian (piano) 9 Jean
Green M L 22 North
Hawes Sarah C 7 Park pl
Hirth Mary 183 Park
Jackson T W 597 Maxfield
Jones Annie P 31 Fifth
Lord G H 399 Pleasant
Lowther Olive 253 Mill
Mandeville Lea 204 Davis
McNulty Margaret I 360 Cedar
Michelson B Frank 38 Durfee
Monty Frank 6 Washburn
Morse Julia A V 205 Park
O'Brien May 116 Rivet
Otheman Mary (violin) 4 Sears
Paddack Fannie C 96 Newton
Parker Arthur L Mrs 169 Shawmut av
Pierce Cynthia 312 Pleasant
Prentiss Clara M 72 Durfee
Purrington Abbie 87 Mill
Ramsden Thomas W 682 Cottage
Reed Bertha 103 Sycamore
Rooth H E 31 Fifth
Russell J E (mandolin) 61 Maple
Russell Mabel E 121 Parker
Scott Robert (violin) 211 Fourth
Smith Annie A 130 Chestnut
Smith Mary L 79 North
Stanton F S 62 State
Sullivan Eugene H 44 Chestnut
Swan A W 97 William rm 308
Terry Ruth E 245 Chestnut
Tollman E E (violin) 658 County
Topham Nannie E Mrs 55 Rounds
Underwood Gertrude M 334 Kempton
Wilde Edwin E 181 Shawmut av

(PAINTING)
Davis Mabel E 8 Park pl
Monarch Mina E 133 Grinnell

(PRIVATE SCHOOLS)
BENTON'S BUSINESS SCHOOL 97 William See map
Swain Free School of Design 391 County

(SHORTHAND & TYPEWRITING)
BENTON'S BUSINESS SCHOOL 97 William See map
Caswell Emma A School 32 Masonic bldg
KINYON'S COMMERCIAL SCHOOL 76 Pleasant rms 21 to 24 See foot lines

(TEXTILE)
NEW BEDFORD TEXTILE SCHOOL 303-331 Purchase See page 36

Teamsters

(See also Job Wagons)
AKIN F T & CO 168 S Water 84 Pleasant and 1218 Acushnet av See foot lines
Borges Julio 37 Farnum
CITY COAL CO Front foot Middle branch 114 William See page 3
CONNELL JOHN JR 350 Sawyer See page 774
Connors J 431 Rivet
Cook J 124 Hemlock
Crapo G G 168 Shawmut av
DeMORANVILLE D H N Y N H & H depot and 83 Thomas See page 787
Duddy William 116 S Water
DUFF DAVID & SON Fish Island See front cover
Ferguson David 98 Park
Goodreau D 27 Hathaway
McCarthy Mortimer 258 State
McClure George 82 Tallman
McMullen Abbott D 10 Spring
O'Gara Thomas 12 Washburn
PERKINS A W & CO 167 Hillman See page 789
Rose Frank G 41 Larch
St Germain Alfred 47 Covell
Smith John A 86 Bay
Spooner C F Jr 2981 Acushnet av n Phillips rd
Taber & Gay 421 Purchase
Tripp A A 108 Grape

Teas, Coffees & Spices

(See also Grocers)
BRIGHTMAN E T 248 Purchase See advt Grocers

Crescent Tea & Butter Co 1099 Acushnet av
Davis & Hatch Spice Co 28 Union
Direct Importing Co 80 Purchase
Gildea Mary Mrs 1530 Acushnet av
Great Atlantic & Pacific Tea Co The 98 Purchase
Lorraine F 22 Purchase and 1110 Acushnet av
McDonnell James 144 Merrimac
NEW YORK MARKET 251 Purchase See page 772
Orient Distributing Co 60 Purchase
Puritan Tea & Coffee Co 169 Campbell
ROBINSON DANIEL 56 Weld See page 772
Sowle F D 360 Kempton

Telephone & Telegraph Companies

AUTOMATIC TELEPHONE CO of New Bedford 41 William See page 22
Postal Telegraph-Cable Co Acushnet av cor William
Southern Mass Telephone Co The 57 N Second
Western Union 151 Union and R R depot

Telephones Installed for Private Use

BRIGGS WILLIAM P 141 Purchase See advt Electricians

Tents

BRIGGS & BECKMAN 31-35 Commercial See page 785

Test Borings

SMITH B F & CO 38 Oliver Boston See page 31

Textile Fabric Mfrs

New Bedford Textile Co 1 E Pope

Textile School

NEW BEDFORD TEXTILE SCHOOL 303-331 Purchase See page 36

Theatres

Casino Theatre 822 Purchase
Hathaway's 90 Purchase
Idle Hour 62 Acushnet av
National Theatre 269 Sawyer
New Bedford 249-253 Union
Pastime 955 S Water
Royal 991 S Water
Savoy 162 Union
The Comique 958 Acushnet av
Vien's Theatre 1159 Acushnet av

Ticket Agents & Exchange on Europe

RODGERS A M 177 and 179 Acushnet av See page 25

Tile

CROOKER CO 230 Weybosset Providence R I See page 754

Tinplate Copper & Sheet Iron Workers

BACON W L 514 County See top edge
CEJKA GEORGE 1480 Acushnet av See page 785
COHOLAN J 703 S Water See page 767
CROSSLEY JOHN F & CO 223 Mill See foot lines
LOWE S C SUPPLY CO 87 Union See page 740
PERRA JOHN 19 Linden See page 766
WOOD BRIGHTMAN & CO 47 to 55 N Water See page 3

Tinware

HOUSEHOLD FURNISHING CO 170-174 Purchase See page 94

Tool Mfrs

Dean Moses 2 Beetle lane

Top Roll Coverers

Aubertin J F r 96 Mt Pleasant
Lawrence John H & Son 167 N Second

Tow Boats

N B Tow Boat Co Merrill's wharf

Towel Supply

Bouchard L F 771 Purchase
HOWLAND S D & CO 86 Chancery See page 786

Trading Stamp Co

Sperry & Hutchinson Co 13 Pleasant

Transmissions

BABBITT STEAM SPECIALTY CO 57 S Water See page 29

Truckmen
(See also Teamsters)

AKIN F T & CO 168 S Water 84 Pleasant and 1218 Acushnet av See foot lines

DUFF DAVID & SON Fish Island See front cover

Twist Drill Mfrs

MORSE TWIST DRILL & MACHINE CO 100 Fifth See page 15

Typewriter Supplies

MONARCH TYPEWRITER CO 67 Milk Boston See page 34

Typewriters

MONARCH TYPEWRITER CO 67 Milk Boston See page 34

Umbrellas

Rosenthal Joseph 36 Howland
Wright J S 276 Union

Undertakers

BENNETT ROBERT G 7 S Sixth See opp
Carrier Joseph 1220 Acushnet av
CHAUSSE ALDEGE 388 N Front See page 772
Girard Vital 14 Linden
Lagasse Adolph P 201 Blackmer
MacDonald 100 Potomska
Moriarty J E 149 Blackmer
Murphy T J 235 Purchase
Proulx Henry J 45 Logan
Roderick Manuel 98 Phillips avenue
Rogers & Sylvia 100 Potomska
SHERMAN P H 506 County See foot lines
Sullivan Jeremiah D Estate 431 Purchase
Sullivan J F 594 Purchase
VAUGHAN UNDERTAKING CO Inc 288-294 Purchase See opp
Wexler Samuel 591 Purchase
Williams J S 173½ Acushnet avenue
WILSON H P 80 Pleasant See back cover

Upholsterers

DANTSIZEN JOHN G 214 Court See back cover
Fielding R C 71 William
Hitch H 803 Purchase
HOUSEHOLD FURNISHING CO 170-174 Purchase See page 94
Methot J A 504 County
New York Upholstering Co 757 Purchase
Thorpe J H 10 Richmond

Vacuum Cleaners

BERGER MFG CO of Mass 286 Devonshire Boston See page 753
WING C F CO The Inc 34 Purchase See page 40

Variety Stores
(See also Fancy Goods)

Akin E G Dartmouth cor Rockdale avenue
Almeida L de 229 S Water
Aspin Mary H Mrs 113 Rivet
Bailey Lena 94 Grinnell
Barnes Alice 78 Cove
Bell A M Mrs 32 Dartmouth
Benjamin S 295 Rivet
Bernard L Mrs 36 Hazard
Beserosky William 1500 Acushnet av and 740 Purchase
Billington Charles 34 Brock avenue
Bleasdale John 97 County
Boardman J S L r29 Howland Village
Boim M A 284½ Fourth
Boissoneault H 393 Bowditch
Braga J K 58 Acushnet avenue
Branchini Joseph 8 Howland
Brierly Elizabeth Mrs 244½ State
Brierly Thomas 130 County
Britto J 217 N Second
Bruley Lulu 522 S Second
Brun O T 33 Bullard
Bryll Matilda Mrs 156 S Second
Burhoe Thomas Mrs 453 Rivet
Card S E Mrs 366 Cedar
Centeia J F 9 Walnut
Charpentier N H 905 County
Costa Joseph Jr 92½ Dartmouth
Daniel A P 135 Hemlock
Demers Omer 7 Hicks
Derby Ann Mrs 1051 S Water
Dollard Ellen 521 Rivet
Doyle P J 758 Purchase
Dutton Alonzo 1666 Acushnet av
Ellis Julia 36 Durfee
Etchells Joseph 477 Rivet
Ferguson W 67 Cedar
Ferreira Manuel 240 S Second
Ferris Joseph 155 County
Fielding William 208 Cedar
Foley William F 341 Sawyer
Fregeau John 64 Hicks

ROBERT G. BENNETT
Undertaker and Embalmer
7 SOUTH SIXTH STREET
Third Door South of Union Street

Orders Taken Day and Night by Automatic and Bell Telephones
Residence, 57 South Sixth Street

Weston C. Vaughan, Jr., Pres. Established 1871 Chas. E. Vaughan, Mgr.
Vanghan Undertaking Co., Inc.
Funeral Directors and Embalmers
Telephone Connections, Day and Night. Bell 201. Automatic 1207
Office 294 Purchase Street

FRANCIS J. GURL
MONUMENTS
GRANITE CUTTERS
CEMETERY WORK
Sawyer St., cor. Ashland St., - New Bedford

Established 1862
W. A. Greenough & Co.
Compilers, Printers and Publishers of
DIRECTORIES
65 BROAD STREET
BOSTON, MASS.
Telephone, Main 4415-W

Variety Stores—con
Gerrard William 635 First
Glowaski Joseph 16 Hicks
Golden Annie 841 S Water
Goldstein L 1104 S Water
Gorman Mary 65 County
Grossi E J 434 Purchase
Hamilton Samuel 377 Coggeshall
Hancock Samuel A Mrs 273 Rivet
Harriman W A 165 Brock avenue
Hayes Annie M 138 Thompson
Helm John 622 First
Holcroft S H Mrs 87 Ruth
Holden K Mrs 93 First
Hollywood Henry A 251 Summer
Howland George L 122 Campbell
Hoxie William R 88 Allen
Hubbenett B J Mrs 147 Crapo
Hynes T W 79 Acushnet avenue
Jackson E M L 840 Kempton
Jackson Mary A 205 Smith
Janik Raimund 33 Hicks
Jenney Ethel H Mrs 264 Acushnet avenue
Jones E F 382 Kempton
Kenyon V Mrs 210 Brock avenue
Lahood S 642 Purchase
Lajeunesse M 8½ McGurk
Land L Mrs 153 County
Lapointe Dora 543 N Front
Larkin Catherine T 11 W French av
Larkin Sarah J 50½ Thompson
Larma S J Mrs 380 Dartmouth
Laughlin Frank 9 Weld
Lewin C 1087 Acushnet avenue
Lewis John 124 S Sixth
Lewis J 120 S Sixth
Lider Jacob 23 Weld
Lopes S 3 Walnut
Lord John 297 Coggeshall
Loughlin Frank 9 Weld
Luminiello Antonio 153½ Coffin av
Maranda Donat 393 N Front
Meaney Martha 212½ Fourth
Milnes E A Mrs 170 Thompson
Moran Margaret 773 S Water
Mullin James 171 Division
Myers George 319 Bowditch
Newton Archie 142 Davis
Noyer George W 77 County
Oliver Avelino A 487 S Water
Papa Anthony 2784 Acushnet avenue
Pelletier Arthur Mrs 921 County
Pepp Querino G 40 Nelson
Perry H 269 Rivet
Peters Mary Mrs 47 Howland
Pina John F 487 S Water
Pina Philomina 264 Middle
Preston Henry W 1502 Acushnet av
Randall James A 307 Acushnet av
Raulino Antonio J 104½ Thompson
Roach William 632 Purchase
Robinson Bros 106 Rivet
Rogers J R 73 Hemlock
Rooth E F Mrs 174 Acushnet av
Ryan M E Mrs 96 County
Savage J M 688 Purchase
Schuster H H 497 S Water
Senft Fred 1549 Acushnet avenue
Sheehan Mary 273 State
Shkolnick A Mrs 640 S Water
Silva Antone E 105 Potomska
Silva M F 191 Blackmer
Silveira M G da 120 Thompson
Smith F W 203 Acushnet avenue
Smith S A 1096 Acushnet avenue
Suble Sadie 292 Cedar Grove
Sullaway A 930 S Water
Sullivan & Brand 31 Ashland
Sylvia Manuel J 428 S Water
Taber A D 187 Acushnet avenue
Taylor Charles 311 Rivet
Taylor J 319 Rivet
Taylor W Mrs 131 Coggeshall
Tillson G M 423 Kempton
Tresham Ellen 52 Grinnell
Vaughan S A 302 Acushnet av
Vallec John 181 S Water
Vieira Manuel M 79 Howland
Voisin A Mrs 199 State
Wallace E Mrs 28 Cove
Ward James 879 Purchase
Weinberger L 846 Purchase
Wilde W S 526 County
Wilkinson A E 114 Cove
Wilkinson W 1760 Acushnet avenue
Williams Mary E Mrs 64 Oak
Woolworth F W 1081 Acushnet av

Veterinarians

Dews Henry H 73 State
Hamilton H B 134 Pleasant

Visible Typewriters

MONARCH TYPEWRITER CO 67 Milk Boston See page 34

Wall Papers

AKIN F T & CO 1218 Acushnet av See foot lines
Baker Solomon M 559 Purchase
CORMIER & DUBE 394 N Front See page 776

MORIARTY T J 184 Fourth See page 49
SILVA M P B & SON 157 Acushnet avenue See foot lines
Taylor & Burke 146 Pleasant
WING CHARLES F CO The Inc 34-38 Purchase See page 32

Walrus Roofing

WARREN CHEMICAL & MFG CO 49 Federal Boston See opp *583

Washing Powder

HERSOM THOMAS & CO 11 Commercial See page 24

Watches, Jewelry, Etc

Allen David W 199 Acushnet av
Baron Joseph & Son 868 Purchase
Benoit S T 1075 Acushnet av and 143 Cove
Coutu J H 1563 Acushnet avenue
Davidow Bros 831 S Water
Dumas F F 269 Purchase
Finnegan John T 1109 Acushnet av
Gidley C J 23 Purchase
Guimaraes J A S 162 Hathaway av
Hebert A G 1080 Acushnet av
Hodgdon Edward J 45 Purchase
Howland H B 26-28 Purchase
Kelley William L 2 Purchase
Levens Lawrence J 975 Kempton
Maheu L 1021 Acushnet avenue
Michaud Joseph 1307 Acushnet av
Morgado M L 157½ Acushnet avenue
Patnaude J C & Co 102 Weld
Perrenod A & Co 970 Acushnet av
Poor Bros 20 Purchase
Portnoy S J 246 Coggeshall
Roebuck H & Son 183 Purchase
Sage L 149 William rm 2
Spiva J S 79 William
Stone S 509 S Water
Sullivan D J 130 Union
Turner Charles W 2167 Acushnet av
Woodworth C E 29 Purchase
Woofenden John 69 Dean

Waterproof Composition

WARREN CHEMICAL & MFG CO 49 Federal Boston See opp *583

Waterproofing Material

BARRETT MFG CO 297 Franklin Boston See front cover

Wax Mfrs

Knowles C S King's Highway

Welding

New Bedford Welding Co 177 N Water

Wells (Artesian & Driven)

SMITH B F & CO 38 Oliver Boston See page 31

Wet Wash Laundries

CLEAN WET WASH The 76 Shawmut av See page 786
HOME WASHING CO 111 Myrtle See page 786
NASH ROAD WET WASH LAUNDRY 95 Nash rd See page 787
NATIONAL WET WASH LAUNDRY 281 Sawyer See page 787
New Bedford Wet Wash Laundry 179 Acushnet av
NORTH END LAUNDRY CO 1066 County See page 786

Whaling Guns & Lances

Brown Frank E 4 S Water

Wheelwrights

(See Carriage Mfrs also Blacksmiths)

Dion O 222 Mill
HATHAWAY L J 7 Elm See page 771

Whitening & Whitewashing

BRILLON A 80 Holly See page 777
LEBEAU J 141 Collette See page 785
MASON J L G 51 Foster See page 774
MORIARTY T J 184 Fourth See p 49
Tripp F H Jr 6½ Sears

Wholesale Grocer

DUPUIS H D & CO 1201 Purchase See page 757

Window Shades & Fixtures

HOUSEHOLD FURNISHING CO 170 to 174 Purchase See page 94

Window & Door Frames

NICHOLSON J G 27 to 35 Bowditch See foot lines

Window & Door Screens

DAVIS Z B CORP 668 Acushnet av See page 762
HOUSEHOLD FURNISHING CO 170 to 174 Purchase See page 94

Window & Plate Glass

AKIN F T & CO 168 S Water 84 Pleasant and 1218 Acushnet av See foot lines

Wines & Liquors

Allen John 503 N Front
Barrett P J 124 Union
Brier G A M & Co 261 Rivet
Brillon Joseph 809 Purchase
Burke J A 35 Elm
Cardonell Louis 318 Acushnet av
Chausse Alfred & Co 1755 Acushnet av
Chicoine & Co 23 S Second
Christie A & Co 1670 Acushnet av
Corey W S 418 Kempton
Clark E T 133 N Front
Dawson & Son (whol) 645 Purchase
DeMello Antone C 717 S Water
Dextradeur A 1501 Acushnet av
DEXTRAZE CAMILLE 1276 Acushnet av See page 779
Dextraze Louis & Son 590 First
Dias Antonio F 105 S Water
Dias & Chase 540 S Water
Dohoney D J 5 N Second
Dowling 613 Acushnet av
Downey Maurice 407 Rivet
Duffy E P 1116 S Water
Fay James L 962 Acushnet av
Fay R T 25 N Second
Fontaine Pierre 870 Acushnet av
Francis A F & Co 77 Grinnell
Francis A S 165 S Water and 2c Walnut
Francis & Rose 599 S Water
Gagnon & Son 301 N Front
Geary Richard 353 Acushnet av
Ginnochio John B 131 N Water
Greenwood William 98 Cove
Hargreaves & Marshall 407 Kempton
Harney L 821 S Water
Harrington D A 591 Acushnet av
Hunter Henry S 56 Weld
Hindle J Acushnet av cor Elm
Jansen J M 246 N Front
Joyce P J 745 S Water
Kelley John W 243 Purchase
Kelligrew W H & Co 357 Acushnet av
Lebeau T 416 N Front
Markey G E & Co 233 S Water
Marsden Jeremiah 678 Purchase
Marshall James 1200 Acushnet av
Marshall M P 437 S Water
McCarthy & Hurley 346 Acushnet av
Murphy C D 166-168 Coffin av
Murray Anthony 376 Kempton
O'Brien Patrick H 438 Purchase
O'Leary Patrick 925 Acushnet av
Olivier G L & Co (whol) 384 Acushnet av
O'Neil Thomas F 215 Coggeshall
Phelan J 894 S Water
Phelan M 685 First
Pothier E 946 S Water
Query A J 876 Acushnet av
Potter T E & Co 887 Purchase
Ricard & Marsh (whol) 410 N Front
Rocklin William & Co 97 N Second
Russell Francis 874 Purchase
Shanks & Tripp 214 Union
Sharples James 262 Coggeshall
Shay Dennis H 6 W French av
Sherman E B Co 62 Purchase
Sherman & Alberski 161 N Front
SMITH BROS Inc 777 Purchase See page 779
Smith B P & Co 31-37 Delano
Smith Henry 572 N Front
Smith William A L 124 Purchase
Souza J L 37 Howland
Sullivan J A & Co 1130 Acushnet av
Taylor William & Son 821 First
Taylor W N & Co 63 Union
Therien Eusebe 267 Coggeshall
Thomas William 244 N Front
Tomlinson Peter 1499 Acushnet av
Vien Eugene H 1162 Acushnet av
Vigneault & Laplante 273 Sawyer
Watson John H 812 Purchase
WEIHL JACOB 23½ N Second See page 779
Whalen Nicholas 855 Purchase
WHEATON HIRAM & SONS 45-51 School See page 773
Whittaker George H 49 and 51 Hicks
Williams W J 72 Middle
Winterburn George H 331 Rivet
Zygiel & Alberski 44 Kenyon

Wire Heddles

HOWARD BROS MFG CO Worcester Mass See page 14

Women's Garments Cleansed

HOWES C G CO Allston Mass See opposite Cleansers

Wood Floors

CROOKER CO 230 Weybosset Providence R I See page 754

Wood Turning and Sawing

GREENE & WOOD Pine See foot lines
JONES & DODGE 202 N Water See page 764
NICHOLSON J G 27 to 35 Bowditch See foot lines
RICARD LEVI 142 Nye See page 765

Wood Workers

Allen & Booth Co 272 S Water

Wood & Coal

(See also Coal and Wood)

AKIN F T & CO 168 S Water cor Walnut 84 Pleasant 9 N Water and 1218 Acushnet av See foot lines
Benjamin Flavien 20 Holly
Bourque Fidelle 346 N Front
Cabral Manuel 360 S Second
Chauvin Alphonse 15 Clark
CITY COAL CO Front foot Middle branches 114 William, 1026 Acushuet av and 1109 S Water See page 3
City Mission Wood Yard 1 Mill
CONNOR PATRICK 486 Rivet See page 783
Cormier Orias 53 Holly
Delano Jethro C 37 Crapo
DENISON BROS CO 32 Pleasant foot Hillman and Prospect corner Grinnell See front cover
Dionne John 132 N Front
Dowty A A 126 County
DUFF DAVID & SON main office Merchants Bank bldg branch Fish Island See front cover
Figueiredo E J 425 S Second
Gallant Alfred 103 Belleville road
Gifford Lewis R 384 North
Guillet N 107 Coffin avenue
HOLMES ALBERT W 201 Purchase and Homes' wharf foot of Cannon See back cover
Hutchings David, Mosher n County
Laplante Bros 279 Belleville avenue
Lariviere Louis 145 Coggeshall
Lemare Fred 249 State
Mailloux C 53 Nelson
O'Brien John N 32 Linden
Pacheco Jose 458 First
Pedro John Jr 166 Belleville avenue
Peirce J H Estate 425 Kempton
Powers J 64 Winsor
Rondeau D 32 Nye
Santos A C 469 First
Secour J W 379 Mt Pleasant
Spencer Frederick 999 Purchase
THORPE R H 1786 Acushnet av See page 765
Ventura J F 57 Crapo

Wooden Ware

DeWOLF & VINCENT 111 William See page 44
HOUSEHOLD FURNISHING CO 170 to 174 Purchase See page 94

Yeast (Compressed)

The Fleischmann Co 38 Elm

Yellow (Meuntz) Metal Sheets

TAUNTON-NEW BEDFORD COPPER CO N Front See page 34

Send for Illustrated Circular and Specimen Program

THE RAVENS

25 MERCHANTS ROW, - BOSTON

Telephone, 1835-2 Richmond

NEW BEDFORD CITY GOVERNMENT

City Government Organized First Monday in January
City Elections First Tuesday in December

MAYOR

Hon Charles S Ashley, 93 State, Office rm 202 Municipal Building, Office hours 11.30 a m to 12.30 p m except Saturdays; Mayor's Secretary, Laurence H Barney

BOARD OF ALDERMEN

Ward 1—Charles S Baylies
Ward 2—Joseph Chausse
Ward 3—John F Hatch Jr
Ward 4—Frank W Francis
Ward 5—Robert C Sherman
Ward 6—John Hannigan

Regular meetings second and fourth Thursdays of each month at 7.45 p m (temporarily) in Registry of Deeds bldg

MESSENGER TO BOARD OF ALDERMEN

Cornelius B Piper

COMMON COUNCIL

Ward One

James M Hughes
Albert Cassidy
Aldege Chausse
William D Hamel

Ward Two

James F Collins
D Herbert Cook
Albert Leveille
Mortimer McCarthy

Ward Three

Oscar D Kelleher
Samuel A Percy
Charles W Jones

Ward Four

Frederick J J Abrams
Hugh Donaghy
Walter H Peirce
Frederic H Taber

Ward Five

Robert L Baylies
Samuel T Rex
Henry E Woodward
Harry C Vaughan

Ward Six

Arthur Dumaine
Joseph H Fernandes
William H Murphy

Organizations: President, D Herbert Cook; clerk, Charles P Sawyer

Messenger to Common Council—David M Piper

COMMITTEES

Standing Committees of the Board of Mayor and Aldermen

Burial Grounds—Aldermen Chausse (ch), Sherman, Hannigan

Enrollment—Alderman Hatch (ch), Chausse, Baylies

Streets—The Mayor (ch), Aldermen Baylies, Sherman
Licenses—Aldermen Sherman (ch), Francis, Chausse
Police—The Mayor (ch), Aldermen Chausse, Francis
Soldiers' Aid—The Mayor (ch.), Aldermen Hatch, Hannigan

Joint Standing Committees of the City Council

Armories and Military Property—Aldermen Baylies (ch.), and Sherman; Councilmen Livesey, Hughes, Abrams
Audit—Aldermen Hannigan (ch.), Hatch; Councilmen Taber, Livesey, Jones
Bath Houses—Aldermen Hannigan (ch.), Francis; Councilmen Collins, Dumaine
Buildings in the Fire Districts— Aldermen Baylies (ch.), . Sherman; Councilmen Hamel, Peirce, Murphy
Charities, Almshouses and the Poor—Aldermen Baylies (ch), Chausse; Councilmen Leveille, Baylies, Rex
City Property—Aldermen Francis (ch.), Hannigan; Councilmen McCarty, Peirce, Jones
Claims—Aldermen Hatch (ch.), Francis; Councilmen Cassidy, Kelleher, Vaughan
Education—Aldermen Sherman (ch.), Hannigan; Councilmen Cassidy, Leveille, Kelleher
Finance—The Mayor (ch.), Aldermen Hatch; Councilmen Chausse, Cook, Jones, Taber, Woodward, Murphy
Fire Department—Aldermen Chausse (ch.), Baylies; Councilmen McCarty, Donaghy, Baylies
Fuel—The Mayor (ch.), Alderman Hatch; Councilmen Percy, Vaughan, Fernandes
Ordinances—Aldermen Hatch (ch.), Hannigan; Councilmen Hughes, Leveille, Donaghy
PrintingJAlderman Hannigan (ch.); Councilmen Percy, Abrams
Roads, Bridges and Sewers—Aldermen Francis (ch.), Baylies; Councilmen Chausse, Vaughan
Street Lights—Aldermen Chausse (ch.), Sherman; Councilmen Hamel Kelleher, Livesey
Water Works and Water Supply—Aldermen Hannigan (ch.), Chausse Councilmen Percy, Woodward
Wharves—Aldermen Sherman (ch.), Baylies; Councilmen Cassidy, Collins, Fernandes

Standing Committees of the Common Council

Bills in the Second Reading—Councilmen Woodward (ch.), Taber and Murphy
Elections and Returns—Councilmen Baylies (ch.), Rex, Hamel
Enrolled Ordinances — 'Councilmen Fernandes (ch.), Collins, Dumaine

CITY OFFICERS

City Clerk—Walter H B Remington, rm 208 Municipal bldg
Assistant City Clerk—James Dignam, rm 208 Municipal bldg
City Treasurer · and Collector of Taxes—William S Cook rms 1-3 Municipal bldg
Auditor—Charles J McGurk rm 4 Municipal bldg
Assistant City Auditors—Edwn L Tillinghast rm 4 Municipal bldg
City Messenger—Lawrence H Barney 203 Municipal bldg
Clerk of Committees—Charles P Sawyer rm 205 Municipal bldg
City Solicitor—Benjamin B Barney rm 204 Municipal bldg
Engineer—William F Williams rm 303 Municipal bldg
Superintendent of Streets—Charles F Lawton rm 302 Municipal bldg
Superintendent of Sewers—Superintendent of streets ex-officio
City Forester—Superintendent of streets ex-officio
Superintendent of Public Buildings and Buildings in the Fire District—Joseph L Gibbs rm 307 Municipal bldg
Inspector of Buildings—Joseph L Gibbs
Physician—Dr Edmond F Cody
Superintendent of City Clock—Fred F Dumas
Inspector of Milk and Animals—Dr Herbert B Hamilton
Sealer of Weights and Measures—John H Ryan Odd Fellows bldg, Mechanics lane

Harbor Master—Charles H Purrington, Fairhaven Ferry ticket office

Fence Viewers—George A Cobb, Robert E Edwards, John E Russell

Wharfinger—Joseph Donaghy

SINKING FUND COMMISSIONERS

William A Mackie (ch.), Edmond W Bourne, Dr John T Bullard

Sec and Treas—William S Cook, City Treasurer

ASSESSORS

9 Municipal bldg, office hours 9 a m to 4 p m

Joseph H Handford, chairman

John H Finnell, secretary

R Eugene Ashley

ASSISTANT ASSESSORS

Ward 1—Douglass L McGee

Ward 2—William Hall

Ward 3—Frederick A Washburn

Ward 4—Roland A Leonard

Ward 5—William J Abrams

Ward 6—Matthew Quinlan

BOARD OF HEALTH

52 Pleasant, Bates & Kirby bldg 9 a m to 4 p m; Regular meeting 12.30 p m daily except Sunday; Free agency for vaccination 11.30 a m to 12 30 p m

William G Kirshbaum agent; Louis Z Normandin, Francis M Kennedy chairman; Harold Winslow

Clerk—Susan J Small

Health Inspector—Robert N B Doane

Inspectors of Plumbing—Louis E Richardson 7.30 to 9 a m and 12.30 to 2.30 p m; William Deacon

Quarantine Physician—Dr Joseph A Frazier

Bacteriologist—Dr Augustus H Mandell

Medical Inspector—Dr Archibald N Senesac 1018 S Water

Medical School Inspectors—Dr D J Lowney, Dr E St Johnson, Dr J F Weeks, Dr J A Bernier, Dr Charles Shanks, Dr J P St Germain, Dr W A Nield, Dr E P Seaver Jr, Dr A V Pierce, Dr H V Weaver, school examiner

Inspector of Slaughtered Carcasses—Dr H B Hamilton D V S

OVERSEERS OF THE POOR

167 William st— 9 a m to 4 p m Saturdays 9 a m to 12 m

Stanislaus Desautels (ch), Manuel A Andrews

Secretary—J Clifford Sherman

Clerk—Ella F Bucklyn

Visitor—Anthony H Senna

Interpreter—Joseph A Desjardins

Superintendent of Almshouse and Farm— Thomas F Brown, City Farm, Clark's Point

Matron of Almshouse—Mrs Thomas F Brown

Keeper of Wood and Coal Yard—Andrew J Ashley

Physicians to Board—Dr Clarence E Burt, Dr Joseph A Chausse, Dr Edward T Tucker

CEMETERY BOARD

304 Merchants Bank Building 9 a m to 5 p m, Regular meetings Friday at 7.30 p m

Board consists of three members one elected annually in April by city council in convention. Term three years Regular meetings Fridays at 7.30 p m No salary

William M Highman, chairman, Elected April 1909; term expires May 1, 1912

Charles H Vinal, secretary. Elected April 1911; term expires May 1, 1914

John G Nicholson. Elected in April 1910; term expires May 1, 1913

Clerk of Board—Pardon A Macomber

Assistants—Ivah M Hunt, Alice G Shaw

Superintendent of Cemeteries George H Nye, Hurlbert E Thomas

Sexton—Oak Grove, Edmund M Cornell; Rural, Nelson L Pike

Location of Cemeteries—Rural Dartmouth; Oak Grove, Parker; Pine Grove, Tarkiln Hill rd; Griffin Street (closed) corner S Second and Morgan lane

PARK COMMISSIONERS

251 Union Regular meetings Monday 8 p m. Antone L Sylvia; Samuel P Richmond, William F Caswell, William Keith, Obed C Nye

General Superintendent—Thomas W Cook

REGISTRARS OF VOTERS

Office rm 7 Municipal bldg. Meetings when called. Willard N Lane, chairman, John E McBride, Joseph C Patnaude, Walter H B Remington, city clerk ex-officio, clerk

WATER BOARD

40 Masonic Building, Hon Charles S Ashley, mayor, president ex-officio; D Herbert Cook, president of common council ex-officio; William H Pitman, Francis P Washburn, Lettuce R Washburn

Clerk of Board and Superintendent —Robert C P Coggeshall

Clerks Superintendent's Office—Arthur R Weeks, Damon W Rice, E Maud Butts, Etta M Holloway

Water Registrar—Clifford Baylies

Bookkeeper—Warren Tattersall

Inspectors—John B Wilbur, Gilbert B Borden Jr, Alonzo W Spooner, Justin C Perkins, Arthur F Colwell, Lester F Spooner, Thomas Rawcliffe

Distribution and Repaires—Work Shop 213 North Water; General Foreman, John C DeMello, Asst Foreman, Herbert C Gifford

Pumping Stations—Little Quittacas Pond and Purchase; Chief Pumping Engineer, Adoniram S Negus

LICENSING BOARD

207 Municipal bldg Office hours daily 9 to 1 Rodolphus A Swan, chairman and sec, Thomas Donaghy Jr, Samuel Higham

Clerk—Ida B Maxfield

Board of Shellfish Commissioners for the City of New Bedford and the Town of Fairhaven—Hon Charles S Ashley, Francis M Kennedy, Joseph B Peck (Fairhaven), Charles P Maxfield (Fairhaven), Walter H B Remington, sec

POLICE DEPARTMENT

Chief—Henry W Mason

Deputy Chief—John C Parker

Captains—Thomas J Taft (day) Arthur H Jones (night)

Lieutenants—Thomas W Comstock, Thomas Fay, Charles L McBay Joseph B Wing, Charles C Gifford

Court and Committing Officer—Lieutenant Lemuel D Adams

Inspectors—George E Gendron, (chief inspector) Frank W Sylvia, Walter Almond, Harry D Stow

Clerk—Henry N West

Sergeants—William Fowler, William E Roscoe, Willis C Underwood, Jeremiah McCarty, Harrison D Ricketson, Daniel Deneen, George R Lawrence, Chester L Tripp

Matron—Mrs Sarah M Brownell

Number of Patrolmen—103

Reserve officers—28

Station 1—9 S Second

Station 2—S Water and Blackmer

Station 3—Kempton and Cedar

Station 4—Willis west of Purchase

Station 5—Weld corner Bowditch

Police Barn—S Second south of Spring

Police call on fire alarm—2-2-2 Struck four times

FIRE DEPARTMENT

Office (Chief's office) Central Fire station

Regular meeting second Tuesday of each month 7.30 p m

Chief Edward F Dahill, 1st asst James J Donaghy, 2nd asst William E Watson Jr, 3rd asst Frank R Pease, 4th asst Stephen L Finnell; Clerk Joseph P Kennedy; Department Lineman, William H Curtis

STEAMER NO 1

556 Purchase

James L Haskins, capt; Charles H Thomas, 1st lieut; Herbert C Clifford, 2nd lieut; L T Wolfenden clerk; Joseph L Crowley, engineer; Edward F A Cowen, William H Young, William D Flagg, drivers

STEAMER NO 2

Kempton corner Reed

Loring T Parlow, capt; Richard E Burke, 1st lieut; Frank R Riley, 2nd lieut; Harry B Jennings, clerk; John R Walsh, engineer; Ernest G S Teachman, James S Cook, drivers; Thomas F Breakell, hoseman

STEAMER NO 4

Bedford corner Sixth

Frederick E Ricketson, capt; Arthur C Smith, 1st lieut; Fred L Jason, 2nd lieut; Frank C Jennings clerk; Walter H Merchant Jr, eng; William L Durfee, Norman S Dyer, drivers; James T Wing, hosemen

STEAMER NO 5

Hillman corner County

Thomas H Forbes, capt; Samuel E Gabriel, 1st lieut; Ernest L Soule, 2nd lieut; Joseph C Forbes, clerk; Benjamin C Groves, engineer; Martin S Nelson, hoseman; Edward J Bly, Fred B Chadwick, drivers

STEAMER NO 6

Fourth head of Potomska

Robert E Allen, capt; William Butler, 1st lieut; William J Gibbs, 2nd lieut; Fred S Nelson, clerk; Henry Leeming, engineer; John Wooley and N Herbert Greene, drivers

STEAMER NO 7

Durfee corner Cottage

Edward H Coggeshall, capt; Edward H Booth, 1st lieut; John H Ryan, 2nd lieut; John N O'Brien, clerk; James R Goddard, engineer; William H H S King and Fred A Stowell drivers; George Pierce Jr, hoseman

STEAMER NO 8

Acushnet av corner Davis

George H Cook, capt; Daniel S Considine, 1st lieut; Robert McWhinnie, 2nd lieut; William R Moore, eng; Antonio M Lemos and Frank N Cleveland, drivers; Thomas Wooley, hoseman

HANCOCK HAND ENGINE NO 9

2236 Acushnet av

Francis P Washburn, capt; Ambrose Merchant, 1st lieut; John F Parker, 2nd lieut; Albert Crossley, chauffeur

HOOK AND LADDER NO 1

Purchase corner Mechanic's lane

Edward D Francis, capt; David Cobb, clerk; William F McDonald, driver; Isaac R Allen, tillerman

HOOK AND LADDER NO 2

Purchase cor Cedar Grove

Edward M Murphy, capt; Chas H McCarthy, lieut; William Sellick, 2nd lieut; Peter F Sullivan, clerk; George S Allen, drivr; Charles E Robertson, tillerman

HOOK AND LADDER NO 3

Fourth head of Potomska

John W Donaghy, capt; John O'Neil, 1st lieut; Frank Cook, 2nd lieut; John McQuilkin Jr, clerk; Charles E Green, tillerman; William J Moore, driver; James Doran, Henry L Burding, laddermen

CHEMICAL NO 1

Purchase cor Mechanic's lane

Frank A C Greene, capt; Frank A Lewis, lieut; James H Downey, chauffeur; William H Whelan, Peter Lambert, Horace S Bennett, William S Gatenby, hosemen

HOSE NO 2

Purchase cor Cedar Grove

Reuben Taber, capt; James H Mahoney, lieut; Allan Phillips, John J Mahon hosemen

HOSE NO 3

Purchase cor Mechanic's lane

David W Howland, capt; Wilfred L Bacon, clerk; Charles W Allen, driver

HOSE NO 4

Brock av

Jeremiah T Haggerty, capt; Owen J Dowd, 1st lieut; Michael Quinn, 2nd lieut; Charles E McAvoy, clerk; Frederick E Mosher, driver

NEW BEDFORD PROTECTING SOCIETY

Directors, Alfred Thornton, Edward F Penney, Henry S Hutchinson, Thos B Akin, Henry P Burt, Fred M Weeden, Charles S Baylies, Otis P Cook, Edmond L Wilde; sec and treas, Edmond L Wilde

FIRE ALARM BOXES

3 Lund's Corner
4 Mt Pleasant n Reservoir
5 Durfee and Cottage
6 Hazard and State
7 Purchase and Franklin
8 County and Pearl
9 Bowditch and Coffin av
12 Shawmut av and Durfee
13 Howard av and River rd
14 Purchase and Willis
15 Smith and Cedar
16 County and Hillman
17 Maxfield and Acushnet av
18 Purchase and North
19 State and Sycamore
21 Water and North
23 Kempton and Liberty
24 Kempton and Cedar
25 Kempton and County
26 Water and Middle
27 Purchase and Mechanic's lane
28 Court and Cedar
29 Arnold and Ash
31 Acushnet av and Union

32 Union and Eighth
34 Union and Water
35 Fourth and School
36 Walnut and Water
37 Orchard and Clinton
38 Sixth and Bedford
39 Second and Cannon
41 Hawthorn and Page
42 Page and Allen
43 Walnut and Seventh
44 Allen and Dartmouth
46 S Water and Leonard
47 County and Grinnell
48 S Water and South
49 S Water and Howland
51 Dartmouth and Rockland
52 Fourth and Potomska
53 Crapo and Rivet
54 Bolton and Rivet
56 S Water and Rivet
57 County and Mosher
58 S Water and Cove
59 Dartmouth and Dunbar
*61 Union St Ry, Weld
*62 Grinnell Mills
*63 Wamsutta Mills
*64 New Bedford Mfg Co
*65 E E Taylor & Co
*67 N B Cordage Co
*68 N B Copper Works
*69 Dawson's Brewery
*71 Pairpoint Mfg Corp
*72 Young & Kimball's Oil Works
*73 Potomska Mills
*74 Acushnet Mills
*75 Morse Twist Drill Co
*76 City Mfg Co
*78 Dartmouth Mills
*79 Butler Mills
*81 Gosnold Mills
*82 Hathaway Mills
*83 Rotch Mills
*84 Sharp Mill
*85 N B Gas & E Light Co
*86 New England Navigation Co
*91 Bennett Mills
*92 Z B Davis, Pope
*93 Pierce Mills
*94 Freight House, Pearl
*95 Bristol Mfg Co
*96 Columbia Mills
*97 Whitman Mills
113 Sawyer and County
114 Brook and Earl
115 Nash rd and Church
116 Nash rd and Bowditch
117 Holly and N Front
118 Coffin av and N Front
119 Tinham av and N Front
123 Acushnet av and Davis
124 Acushnet av and Sawyer
125 Bowditch and Weld
126 Cedar Grove and N Front
127 Purchase and Linden
128 County and Penniman
129 Purchase and Cedar Grove
131 Acushnet av and Perry
132 Acushnet av and Belleville rd
133 Belleville av and Covell
134 Belleville av and Nye
135 Belleville av and Coggeshall
136 Acushnet av and Bullard
137 Acushnet av south of Coggeshall
138 Belleville road and Hope
139 Belleville av and Davis
*143 A L Blackmer Co
*145 Power Station foot Middle
*146 Car House, Pope's Island
211 Linden and County
212 Merrimac and Summer
213 Cedar and Locust
221 Arnold and Rotch
223 Court and James
224 Kempton and Reed
225 Kempton and Florence
226 Rodman and Front
227 Fish Island
231 Hillman and Ash
321 Union and Park
361 Coffin and S Water
381 Bedford and Borden
512 Orchard and Fair
561 S Water and Division
581 City Almshouse
582 Brock avenue and Butler
583 Brock avenue and Mott
584 Cove and E French avenue
585 Ruth and Salisbury
*611 Neild Mfg Corporation
*612 Snell & Simpson
*613 Beacon Mill
*614 Taber Mill
*615 Old Colony Box Co
*616 Pierce Bros Ltd
*617 New Bedford Cotton Mills Corp
*618 Smith Bros Brewery
*619 N B Storage Warehouse
*712 Quisset Mill
*781 Kilburn Mills
*821 Holmes Mfg Co
*823 Booth Mills
*831 Page Mills
*912 Soule Mill
*931 Nashawena Mill
941 Freight station foot Willis

942 Railroad Engine House
*971 Manomet Mills
*972 Nonquitt Spinning Co

121 struck twice general alarm. All second and third alarms will be given by the chief or members of the board of engineers

Companies responding to second and third alarms will get one round of box before leaving the house

Two blows relief

Two blows in succession struck twice no school signal At 7.30 a m for High school and 8.15 a m and 12.45 p m for all other schools

2-2-2 struck four times police call

Ten blows struck twice military call Battery E 1st Regiment will assemble at Amory

Fifteen blows struck twice military call Co G Naval Brigade will assemble at Amory

*Private boxes for fire on premises only

Alarms to be given from the box nearest the location of the fire

Do not give an alarm for a fire seen at a distance

To give an alarm open the door pull the hook to the bottom of the slot once and let go

Never open a box except to give an alarm

After giving an alarm remain or leave someone at the box to direct the firemen to the fire and see that no one inteferes with the box

Do not pull the hook a second time or allow anyone to do so

FREE PUBLIC LIBRARY

TRUSTEES

The Mayor—Hon Charles S Ashley, the president of the Common Council, D Herbert Cook, chairman of the City Council Committtee on Education, Alderman Robert C Sherman, ex-officio; Rev Matthew C Julien, Otis Seaburk Cook, Frank A Milliken, Francis M Kennedy, Alexander McL Goodspeed, Jireh Swift Jr, president Hon Charles S Ashley; clerk Alex McL Goodspeed; librarian George H Tripp; cataloguer Anna M DeWolf; assts Clement L Yeagher, Jane E Gardner, Josephine A Merrick, Anna W Cleveland, Edith H Cobb, Grace D Sherman, Minerva F Maxfield L Gertrude Wilcox, Jane E Thuman, Caroline E Best, Nellie F Dollard. Elizabeth Smith, Ethel M Wilcox, Edith H Brodhead, Marion Briggs

LIBRARY BUILDING

William corner Pleasant

Established March 3, 1853. 125,000 volumes. Open 9 a m to 9 p m week days; reading room open 1 to 6 and 7 to 9 p m Sundays. New library building occupied Dec 1, 1910. Branch reading rooms and delivery stations; ward room, Weld street; ward room, Blackmer and South Water streets; ward room, corner Kempton and Cedar street; special delivery stations; Lunds corner, Bolton street, Kempton and Hunter streets

PUBLIC SCHOOLS

SCHOOL BOARD

Board room and supt's office 166 William 8.30 a m to 4.30 p m; Saturdays 8.30 to 11 a m 2 to 4 p m Regular meetings of the board first Monday of each month at 7.30 p m except in January, August and September

In January and September meetings Tuesday after first Monday, in August no meeting

Chairman ex-officio, Hon Charles S Ashley, Mayor; vice-chairman Calvin T Bosworth; D Herbert Cook, president of the common council, ex-officio; Allen P Keith, sec and supt

Ward One

Napoleon Beaulieu
Frank R Pease
J Frank Weeks

Ward Two

William A Thompson
Herbert C Wilbor
William T Ainsworth

Ward Three

William R Chase
Herbert C Hammond
William E Jennings

Ward Four

Ernest A Wheaton
Harry M Gay

Ward Five
Francis B Boyer
Charles T Smith
Betsey B Winslow

Ward Six
Calvin T Bosworth
James F Robinson
James W Gleason

Supt, Allen P Keith; asst to supt and supervisor of primary grades, Josephine Stuart; head clerk, Emma M Almy; asst Mary P Chase, Clara S Blake; truant officer, Henry Smith, Francis N Howes, John S Silvia; janitor and messenger, George K Dammon

HIGH SCHOOL

Summer between Mill and North

G Walter Williams, principal; Edmund D Searles, 1st asst; A R Dorman, head commercial dept; Summer E Marvel, head science department; Charles T Bonney, science; M I Buker, science; Arthur B Stanley, science; Arthur S Todd, Walter J Goggin, Lydia J Cranston, Mary E Austin, Lucretia N Smith, Emma K Shaw, Helen L Hadley, Mabel W Cleveland, Gertrude M Cunningham, Adah M Tasker, Lena M Newcastle, Clara E Sherman, Jessie M Barbour, Edith F Walker, Mary F Hitch, Lydia M Sargent, Katherine B Scribner, Tyna Helman, assistants; Edmond E Baudoin, military instructor; Sarah D Ottiwell, librarian; Grace E Hunt, clerk; Phylander Chace, janitor; James A Thompson, asst janitor

NORMAL AND TRAINING SCHOOL

HARRIGTON MEMORIAL

Court corner Liberty

Cora A Newton, principal; Mary E Trask, vice-principal; Carolyn D Wood, normal teacher and nature supervisor in primary grades; assts, Kate Moore, Lulu M Bennett, Jeanette Greer, Grace B Gardner, Lillian G Hunter, Edith A Austin, Harriet L Shafter, Clara M O'Neil; Dennis J McAuliffe, janitor

GRAMMAR SCHOOLS

FIFTH STREET

Fifth corner Russell

Allen F Wood, principal; Lydia A Macreading, N Emma Slack, Grace L Carver, Mary W Leymunion, Sadie M Moulton, May B Jason, Katherine C Swansey, Myrtilla G Sequeira, Alice Lilley, Alice Turner, assts; Henry T Phillips, janitor

HOSEA M KNOWLTON

County near Coggeshall

Edward B Gray, principal; Emma A McAfee, Florence M Ellis, Carrie J Hunt, Alice E Bent, Jennie J Valentine, Hope E Crowell, Alice T Corrigan, Stella McCarthy, Ada G Bruce Alice G Freeman, Edith M Rodman, Ethel M Hilton, Edna E Nason, Rachel M Wordell, Louise M Newhall, Mary E Fury, Ida E Tórreson, assts; Henry A Stephens, janitor

MIDDLE STREET

Summer between Elm and Middle

Elwyn G Campbell, principal; Lucy B Fish, Lucy F Winchester, Etta M Abbott, Elizabeth E Omey, Julia C Gifford, Clara S Vincent, Helen McCoy, Alice T Paull, Margaret T C Murphy, Rhoda A Briggs, Lizzie M Stowe, assts; LeRoy G Tripp, janitor

PARKER STREET

Parker near County

Arthur F Gilbert, principal; Belle W Burt, Grace M Thompson, Daisy M Butts, Helen T Maxfield, Lillian L Thomas, Rose M Meaney, Louise E Hicks, Katherine M O'Malley, Mary L Killigrew, S Agnes Holmes, Nettie B Woodman, Ellen A Hurley, Julia R Smith, Ellen O Holmquist, Agnes M O'Mally, Ruth E Sargent, assts; John H Murphy, janitor

ROBERT C INGRAHAM

Rivet between Acushnet av and S Second

Alice C Munsey, prin; Elizabeth M Briggs, Agnes M James, Annie L Murkland, Cora B Cleveland, Margaret E Phillips, Edna H Dyer, Elizabeth S Boyle, Maude G Carleton, Marion L Mann, Lucy M White, Emily W Davis, Florence Jenks, assts; Philias Gregoire, janitor

MIXED SCHOOLS

JOHN HENRY CLIFFORD

Coggeshall cor Bowditch

Edward A Sadler, prin; Julia V Tresham, Florence E Moore, Mary R Dalton, Ruth R Sherman, Mary C Riley, Elizabeth C Von Flatern, Mary E Herlihy, Bertha R Stone, Ellen G Sweeney, Mary I Ashley, assts

THOMAS R RODMAN

Mill cor Rockdale av

Sarah A Russ, prin; Lottie F Sturtevant, Anna A Cleary, Adelaide J McFarlin, Alice W Lowther, Agnes T McPhee, Isabel L Swift, Florence A Poole, Katherine Haley, assts; John D Sherman, janitor

WILLIAM H TAYLOR

Brock av

Mary E M Duffy, prin; Carrie M Leavitt, Mary Z Dorgan, Elizabeth J Hurley, Helen C Gleason, Adelaide M Cota, Elizabeth C Carter, Ellen T Connorton, Olivia H Norcross, Carrie M Frost, Anne E Rooney, Mary E O'Connor, Elizabeth A Dugdale, Ada D Howland, assts; John Booth, janit-

THOMAS DONAGHY

South bet Fourth and Acushnet av

Walter I Hamilton, prin; Laura M King, Florence L Loring, Annie F Welsh, Grace D Inman, Elsie M Putnam, Sarah F Pratt, Ruby M Tripp, Sarah F Reddy, Ethel M Daley, Marguerite E Budgen, Mary A Kennedy, Isabelle H Shepherd, Mabelle A Moulton, Janet M Livingston, Margaret T Walsh, Ellen A Tinkham, assts; Edwin S Tallman, janitor

JAMES B CONGDON

Hemlock corner Thompson

Raymond H Cook, prin; Jane E Conway, Ada R Holden, Anna B McDiarmid, Marjorie Lewis, Clara L Davis, Annie S Palmer, Mary A Lee, Elizabeth B Tripp, Annie B Lyon, Grace S Dixon, Ann M Gleason, Angela F Bowie, Helen R Leffingwell, Margaret Gleason, Mary A Arey, Catherine F Lynch, assts; John De Beech, janitor

JIREH SWIFT

Acushnet av near Lund's Corner

Leslie H Sutherland, prin; Helen M Welch, Marion H Dexter, Lillian E Page, Louise R Howland, Edna W H Koehler, Ella F Sherman, Lucie White, Rita M Briscoe, Isabel Campbell, assts; Jason F Pierce janitor

ABRAHAM LINCOLN

John W Northcott, prin; Margaret I Kaeton, Rachel R Bailey, Bessie F Nesmith, Nancy M Slade, L Estelle Sears, Georgia M Dignam, Mary E Martin, Lucille C Irving, Clara M Sawyer, Mary K Almond, Irene Sadler, Alice Sullivan, Mabel G Andrews, assts; Thomas H Ridings janitor

PRIMARY SCHOOLS

ACUSHNET AVENUE

Acushnet av near Grinnell

Sarah E Kirwin, prin; Grace A Knowlton, Gertrude L Corish, Mary F Staples, Alice A Taylor, Caroline S Silva, Catherine O'Connell, Eudora K Barry, Harriet L Cornell, F Gertrude Thompson, Elizabeth Downey, assts; Samuel S Broadbent, janitor

I W BENJAMIN

Division between Acushnet av and Second

Jane E Gilmore, prin; Florence M Anthony, Mary E Bannon, Ethel Bliss, Mary G Almy, Lucie H Sears, Sophie T Anthony, Cecelia A Deane, Hannah G Hammond, Mary M Sullivan, Mary A Horan, May F Livingston, Bessie M Noland, Mary M Walsh, Ethel A Baker, Loretta M Creed, assts; William Clark, janitor.

CEDAR STREET

Cedar cor Maxfield

Annie G Brawley, prin; Madeline A Gregg, Mabel L Hathaway, Ruth M Tripp, Irene M Bassett, Harriet A Taylor, assts; Robert Arnett, janitor

CEDAR GROVE STREET

Cedar Grove n Acushnet av

Agnes J Dunlap, prin; Ellen C Sweeney, Alice P Winchester, Margaret J Marshall, Alice P Terry, Lillian P Case, M Theresa Shevlin, Katherine D Sullivan, Lillian F Akerstrom, Nellie F Wright, Grace M Finnell, Mary H French, Edith Hutchinson, Mary A Budgen, Jane M Davis, assts; Frederick O Pollock, janitor

CLARK STREET

Clark cor Myrtle

Alice J Lawrence, prin; Isabella Luscomb, Annie S Ray, Gertrude L Sullivan, Harriet P Brownell, Harriet J Thorpe, Lucy S Leach, Alice B Knight, assts; Wallace C Tilton, janitor

DARTMOUTH STREET

Dartmouth cor Hickory

Isadore F Eldridge, prin; Carrie W Bliss, Mary A McDermott, Elizabeth M Yates, Eliza M Eaton, Laura C McCabe, Nellie L Foster, Mabel Burnham, assts; Henry L Hathaway, janitor

GEORGE H DUNBAR

Dartmouth cor Dunbar

M Eva Schwall, prin; Florence L McNamara, Ruth D Beetle, Annie R Keith, Jane A Murphy, Lizzie A Peirce, Ethel A Reed, Ella C Chandler, Mary H Magnett, assts; Thomas C Holmans, janitor

THOMAS A GREENE

Fourth cor Madison

Anna L Macreading, prin; Bertha C Hathaway, Nellie E Ashley, Isabelle Harwood, Mary E Doyle, Agnes G Sullivan, Grace U Nichols, Margaret M Gibbons, Lottie M Vose, assts; Timothy J Crowley, janitor

SYLVIA ANN HOWLAND

Pleasant between High and Kempton

Marion H Swasey, prin; Jennie M Deacon, Helen J Kirk, Helen L L Corish, Carolyn S Jones, assts; Hiram T Lumbert, janitor

HORATIO A KEMPTON

Shawmut avenue near Maitland

Bessie P Peirce, principal; Edith M B Taber, Johanna Sweeney, Amelia A Murray, Mrs Alice E Jenney, Mary W Snow, assts; Edward I Lawrence, janitor

MERRIMAC STREET

Merrimac corner State

Harriet S Damon, principal; Edna W Hinckley, Grace W Dillingham, Bertha S Brown, Anna I Dexter, Julia A Ellis, assts; Edward H Field, janitor

PHILLIPS AVENUE

Phillips avenue corner Bowditch

Carrie E Footman, principal; Josephine C Yates, Maud E Stafford Helen F Moore, May Bryant, Esther L Cole, Stella Caouette, May O Burrows, Sarah D Barrows, assts; William J Cochrane, janitor

THOMPSON STREET

Thompson corner Crapo

Emma L Gartland, principal; Hannah E Meaney, Catherine A McGuinness, Bertha E Jenney, Nellie H Cook, Sarah A Winslow, Mary E Cunningham, Ethel C Wetherbee, Nancy M Johnson, assts; James T Heron, janitor

MARY B WHITE

Maxfield corner Pleasant

Clara C M Gage, principal; Mary E Bumpus, Annie E Pearce, Helen I Boyd, assts; Thomas A Morrison, janitor

SUBURBAN SCHOOLS

PLAINVILE

Plainville road

Alice M Grant, principal; Annie E Hatch, janitor

ROCKDALE

Hathaway road

Emma G Casey, principal; M Louise Swanburg, asst; Henry O Casey, janitor

ELEMENTARY EVENING

FIFTH STREET

Fifth corner Russell

Elwyn G Campbell, principal

ROBERT C INGRAHAM

Rivet between Acushnet avenue and Second

Leslie H Sutherland, principal

HOSEA M KNOWLTON

Coggeshall corner County

Edward B Gray, principal

PARKER STREET

Parker near County

Arthur F Gilbert, principal

PHILLIPS AVENUE

Phillips avenue corner Bowditch

Raymond H Cook, principal

THOMAS DONAGHY

South between Fourth and Acushnet avenue

Walter I Hamilton, principal

EVENING COMMERCIAL CLASS

In High School building

G Walter Williams, principal

NEW BEDFORD INDUSTRIAL SCHOOL

North Water

Wesley A O'Leary, director of dept of applied science, Lewis H Haight, head of metal working dept. Oliver H Gardner, head of bldg dept; Charles A Wilson, William Law, Charles F Chase, Arthur O Engstrom, instructors

SUPERVISORS AND SPECIAL TEACHERS

Lucy C Bedlow, drawing; Frederick H Butterfield, Harriet G Werner, music; Mabel W Chandler, Gertrude Borden, cooking; Edwin R King, Nina Weld, Annabel C Williams, manual training; Lena M Willis Gertrude H Leonard, Emma S Y Alley, Alice R Robeson, Dora D Parker, sewing; Allison R Dorman, penmanship; Janet Hunter, permanent substitute; Ethel M Minier, Elizabeth G Hayes, primary assts; Florence Ricketson, Margaret J Dias, nurses

SPARE JANITORS

George L Thompson, William H Hayden, George Thomas

PRIVATE SCHOOLS

BENTON'S BUSINESS

97 William

Charles E Benton, principal

FRIEND'S ACADEMY

25 Morgan

MOSHER HOME PREPARATORY

29 Arnold place

Charles E E Mosher, principal

NEW BEDFORD TEXTILE

303 to 331 Purchase

Henry W Nichols, supt

SWAIN FREE SCHOOL OF DESIGN

391 County

PAROCHIAL SCHOOLS

ANGEL GUARDIAN

Acushnet avenue corner Logan

HOLY FAMILY

County near North

Conducted by Sisters of Mercy under the direction of Rev Hugh J Smyth; eight teachers and about 350 pupils

THE SACRED HEART

45 Robeson

Conducted by Sisters of Holy Cross

ST ANTHONY'S

120 Bullard

Conducted by Sisters of Holy Cross

ST HYACINTH

Rivet

Conducted by Sisters of Holy Cross

ST JOHN THE BAPTISTE DE LA SALLE

W French av corner Brock av

Conducted by Sisters of Holy Cross

ST JOSEPH'S

Linden corner State

Conducted by Sisters of Mercy

ST MARY'S

Acushnet avenue corner Wing

Conducted by Sisters of Mercy

BRISTOL COUNTY

Court House, 443 County

Registry of Deeds, N Sixth

County Cities, Fall River, New Bedford and Taunton

COUNTY COMMISSIONERS

Frank M Chace, Fall River; Richard E Warner, Taunton; John I Bryant, Fairhaven

Associate Commissioners—John Thacher, Attleboro; John M Reed, Westport

Times of meeting—At Taunton on Fourth Tuesday of March and September

County Commissioners meet about the fifth of every month

William F Fuller, Taunton, Judge of Probate

Simeon Borden, Fall River, Clerk of Courts

Edwin L Barney Jr, New Bedford, Asst Clerk

Arthur M Alger, Taunton, Register of Probate

Albert B Collins, New Bedford, Register of Deeds, Southern District; Marietta Hammond, Asst Register

George F Pratt, Taunton, County Treasurer

Joseph T Kenney, New Bedford, District Attorney; Frank B Fox Taunton, asst

MEDICAL EXAMINERS

Garry de N Hough; John T Bullard, Associate

JAIL AND HOUSE OF CORRECTION

Ash between Court and Union

Franklin L Hathaway, keeper; John H Cornell, deputy keeper, Wilson E Bannister, clerk

Mrs Ophelia Taber, matron; Mrs Annie E Sherman, Ruth E Hathaway, Mrs Cynthia C Marchant, asst matrons

Seth W Godfrey, Ezra Holmes, Charles H Peck, Albert J Martin, Amos H Dyson, J Thomas Daley, Edward P Canny, Thomas W Buckley, officers

E A DeWolf, Thomas Finnell, William R Shaw, George A Sweeney, Alexander G Crapo, Herman A Brightman, John A Dunham, Philip C Russell, watchmen

Joseph E Fay, Eugene A Rider, William H Flynn, John H Bannon, instructors

Arthur E Davis, steward; Thatcher B Crocker, chief engineer, William Ferguson, engineer

SESSIONS OF COURT IN BRISTOL COUNTY

THIRD DISTRICT COURT OF BRISTOL

New Bedford

William corner N Second

Frank A Milliken, justice; A Edwin Clarke, Eliot D Stetson, special justices; Frank Vera Jr clerk; Elizabeth H Cobb, asst clerk; Lemuel D Adams, court officer; Merton L Hathaway probation officer. The court is held on the morning of every day, Sundays and holidays excepted. Regular term days for the trial of civil cases Mondays and Thursdays at 10 o'clock a m, except July and August

SUPERIOR COURT FOR CIVIL BUSINESS

At Fall River with jury second Monday of January, first Monday of April and third Monday of September; without jury first Monday of January and fourth Monday of March. At New Bedford for Bristol County with jury, first Monday of May and second Monday of December; without jury first Monday of June and December. At Taunton for Bristol County with jury first Monday of March and second Monday of September, without jury first Monday in February and November

SUPERIOR COURT FOR CRIMINAL BUSINESS

At Fall River first Monday in November. At New Bedford for Bristol County first Monday in June. At Taunton for Bristol County first Monday in February

PROBATE COURT FOR 1911 IN NEW BEDFORD

February 5th, March 19th, May 7th, June 18th, August 6th, September 17th, November 5th

SUPREME JUDICIAL COURT

Jury Term

At New Bedford for the counties of Bristol, Nantucket and Dukes, second Tuesday of November. At Taunton for the counties of Bristol, Nantucket and Dukes third Tuesday of April

Law Term

At Taunton for the counties of Bristol, Nantucket and Dukes, on the fourth Monday of October

U S OFFICERS, ETC

CUSTOM HOUSE

North Second corner William

District of New Bedford

Open very day (Sundays, Fourth of July, Christmas, New Year's Day and such other days as may be designated by law excepted) from 9 a m to 4.30 p m. Close Saturdays at 1 p m

Officers—Rufus A Soule, collector Edward P Haskell, special deputy collector; John F Goggin, deputy collector; Arthur E Duffy, deputy collector and inspector; George S Anthouy, Joshua G Lapham, watchmen; Francis J McDonnell, janitor

Acting asst surgeon U S Public Health and Marine Hospital Service —Dr John T Bullard 428 County

IMMIGRATION INSPECTORS

Office Custom House bldg

William B Hinckley, James A Sullivan

INTERNAL REVENUE OFFICER

Albert L Carpenter, deputy collector, office Custom House bldg (Tuesdays only)

SHIPPING COMMISSIONER

H C Hathaway, deputy

REFEREE IN BANKRUPTCY

Clifford P Sherman

COMMISSIONER

Alexander McL Goodspeed

FORT RODMAN
Clark's Point

Roster of officers and N·C S officers

Captain, Godwin Ordway C A C comanding 52nd Co C A C and Post; first lieutenant, Sidney H Guthrie C A C with 52nd Co C A C; first lieutenant, M E Hughes M R C surgeon; Ord Sergt Benjamin C Waite; P Q M Sergt, Albert Kay; Elec Sergt, Joel Rowan; first class Sergt, Algernon Van Aller; Post Commissary Sergt, Harry Klaproth; Sergt Major, W A Biddinger

LIGHTHOUSE KEEPERS

William A Day, Palmer Island Amos C Baker Jr, Butler Flats; William P Howard, Ned Point; Zimri T Robinson, Bird Island; Ernest H Small, Dumpling Rock; George E Kezer, Cuttyhunk; Joshua Richardson, Hen and Chicken Light Vessel; Wallace A Eldredge, Wing Neck; Samuel J Howes, Vineyard Sound Lightship

PORT WARDENS

William E Cooper, Francis C Smith of New Bedford, James F Monahan of Wareham, Howes Norris and William Buckley of Martha's Vineyard

POST OFFICES

NEW BEDFORD

William corner Acushnet av

Frank C Barrows, postmaster; Andrew J McAvoy, asst postmaster; Reuben E Swift, cashier; C H Lobdell, supt of delivery; Frederick T Almy, supt of carriers; S S Taber, supt of mails; Joseph A Doblyn, supt money order division; James P Porter, Stanley G Akin, George E Hatch, Samuel W Doran, Ernest Jones, Ralph B Leavitt, Clarence W B Sykes, Alfred J Isherwood, Frank D Coppinger, Edward E Pierce, James Nelson Jr, John R Smith, Frank Manning, William J Knox, John W Frasier, Albert Morde, Wallace G Hathaway, Walter Whittaker, Edward E Casey, Angelo L Fraga, clerks; Edward J Lyons, Thomas W McAuliffe, Arthur Mellor, John R Plante, Francis P Ryan, Walter T Raymond, Henry W Smith, Wiliam J Frawley, John R Ashworth, sub clerks; Nancy C Foster, Mary T Eldridge, James L Walsh, money order clerks; Manuel G Vieira Jr, Isabel F McDonald, registry clerks; William S Backus, James Booth, Otis L Briggs, William A Burt James T Cairns, Frank P Campbell, Frank R Cass, George T Castle, Geo A Chambers, Frederick A Clark, Wm J Clarke, John J Cunningham, John T Curry, Wilfred Deslandes, Joseph B Downey, Timothy S Downey, William A Doyle, James J Earley, Ernest B Eno, John P Ferns, Joseph B Foster, J Arthur Gaudette, Frederick H Geils, Edward F Gero, John M Harvey, Frank B Kirby, Charles C Lee, Thomas Littlewood, Walter A Luce, John J McAuliffe, James H McNulty, Frank E Macy, John E Moores, Charles S Moynan, Sylvester Paul, Albert H Peters, Alfred E Rainford, Alfred O Raymond, Thomas C Robbins, Edward E Shaw, Dennis A Shea Jr, Wilbur G Sherman, Jonathan H Smead, Hiram Smith, William C H Smith, Walter W Snailham, Hartley Spencer, William E Staples, Arthur D Swift, William Taylor, Charles F Thomas, Joseph Whitehead, Samuel Whittaker, William D Wilson, carriers; Edward R Arnett, Ernest H Balboni, Rufus Cleveland, Francisco T Francis, Levi Hartley, Roland E Isherwood, Aaron Marvel, George A Peters, John A Quinn, George G Sylvia, Thomas H Tripp, Joseph F Waldron, Clinton I Walker, sub carriers

Office hours from 6.45 a m to 9 p m; Sundays 8.30 to 10 am

Lobby open to box holders from 6.45 a m to 11 p m. Sundays 8 a m to 10 p m

Money Order Department open from 9 a m to 6 p m

Registry Department open from 8 a m to 8 p m

Sale of stamps from 6.45 a m to 9 p m

SUB STATIONS

No 1—3 Weld square, Daniel S Considine, clerk

No 2—45 Linden, Catherine L Ryan, clerk

No 3—133 County, Calvin T Bosworth, clerk

No 4—913 S Water, P Damien Jarry, clerk

No 5—122 Allen, John A McManus, clerk

No 6—396 Kempton, John C Guinn, clerk

No 7—403 Purchase, William M Higham, clerk

No 8—Cottage corner Durfee, Martin C Healey, clerk

No 9—1401 Acushnet av, Oscar C Goddu, clerk

No 10—113 Union, Joseph W Nicklas, clerk

No 11—209 Coggeshall, John C Brown, clerk

No 12—274 Cedar, Napoleon Berard Jr, clerk

No 13—639 County, Henry T Corson, clerk

No 14—396 Union, Florence M R Jean, clerk

No 15—133 Ruth, Ernest L Snell, clerk

ACUSHNET POSTAL STATION

Main corner Mill road head of river, A R Hambly, clerk in charge

Mail arrangements—Leaves Acushnet for New Bedford at 8 a m and 1 and 6 p m; arrives from New Bedford at 10.30 a m and 5 and 8.00 p m

Route No 1, William A Gurney, carrier; Route No 2, Abraham L Dillingham, carrier

or

CLIFFORD

3913 Acushnet av

Otis Sisson, postmaster

Mail Arrangements—Leaves Clifford at 7.20 a m and 5,20 p m; arrives from New Bedford at 8.10 a m and 6 20 p m

Rural free delivery, Route No 1, Nelson W Gurney

SHAWMUT

Plainville road near Shawmut av, Plainville

John Ashworth, postmaster

RATES OF POSTAGE DOMESTIC AND FOREIGN

First class—Letters and all matter sealed so that it cannot be examined without breaking the seal. Postage 2 cents per ounce or fraction for United State (including Hawaii, Porto Rico, Guam, Philippine Archipelago, Tutuila and Canal Zone) Mexico, Canada, Cuba and Republic of Panama, also Shanghai. At least one rate (2 cents) must be prepaid to insure forwarding except to Cuba and Republic of Panama. Postal cards, United States, Cuba, Republic of Panama, Mexico and Canada, 1 cent.

Letters and postal cards are forwarded from one postoffice to another without additional postage. Other matter only on prepayment of additional postage.

The use of hand stamps for personal communications, as stamping a receipt or credit on a bill of accounts; price lists with prices in writing, and all matter produced by typewriting constitutes first class matter.

On Postal Cards the left third and on "Post Cards" the left half of the address side as well as the back may be written or printed on, and very thin sheets of paper may be attached to same if they completely adhere thereto.

Second Class—Newspapers and periodicals issued as frequently as four times a year with a legitimate list of subscribers. Postage to other than subscribers, 1 cent for each four ounces.

Third class—Books (printed), circulars, labels, photographs, proof sheets, corrected proof sheets and M S copy accompanying the same, blank checks, drafts, insurance policies and other legal papers, handbills, posters, and all matter of the same general character. Postage 1 cent, for each two ounces or fraction; full prepayment of postage compulsory. Seeds, cuttings, roots, bulbs, etc., may be forwarded in the mails for the U S with postage prepaid at third class rate, but matter of this nature for Canada must be prepaid at fourth class rate. Date of issue, name of addressee and name of sender may be written on a circular or typographical errors corrected without subjecting it to letter postage. Reproductions from Hectograph, Papyrograph, Electric Pen or other similar process may be sent as third class if mailed at post-office and in lots of not less than 20 identical copies. The limit of weight, 4 pounds, except single volumes of books to which there is no limit of weight.

Fourth class — Patterns, address tags, bill heads, letter heads, playing cards, blotting paper printed or unprinter, merchandise, metals, and all other matter not included in the first, second and third classes. Postage 1 cent for each ounce or fraction. Full prepayment compulsory. The limit of weight is 4 pounds. Tags or labels may be attached, marked or numbered for purpose of description.

All mail matter of the third and fourth classes should be securely wrapped but admit of easy inspection. When matter of a lower class is enclosed with matter of a higher class, the whole package is subject to postage at the higher rate.

Liquids (not vinous, spirituous, ardent or malt) and oils, not exceeding four ounces liquid measure, salves, ointments, and articles easily liquefiable and not liable to explode or ignite spontaneously or by shock or jar; also ink-powder, pepper and other powder not explosive or poisonous may be forwarded in the Domestic mails when put up in glass blottles or vials strong enough to stand the shock of handling enclosed in a metal, wooden or papier-mache block or tube, not less than three-sixteenths of an inch thick, impervious to liquids, including oils, lined with a cushion of some absorbent material and fastened with a cover so adjusted to make the block or tube watertight or in tin or metal tubes fastened with a lid and placed securely in a wooden block or tube open only at one end, of same thickness and strength as above. On all such packages the sender may write or print his name and address preceded by the word "From" and also the name of the article enclosed.

Unmailable—All packages containing poisons, explosives, substances exhaling bad odor, liquors (vinous, spirituous, ardent or malt), obscene matter of any description, dunning notices on postal cards, and all articles which from their nature are liable to damage the mails or any person handling them.

Canada—All packages of merchandise not exceeding 4 lbs. 6 oz. weight addressed to Canada, if presented for mailing in such form as to be capable of easy inspection, can be forwarded in the mails to the office of address if postage is fully prepaid at the rate applicable to the same in the Domestic mails. Sealed packages, other than letters in their usual and ordinary form, are not allowed to be despatched to Canada, even if postage is prepaid thereon at full letter rates.

Mexico—Matter addressed to Mexico is subject to same rules and conditions as if it were addressed for delivery in the United States, except that articles of merchandise not sent as bona fide trade samples, should be sent by parcels post. Sealed packages other than letters in their usual and ordinary form are not allowed to be despatched to Mexico even if postage is prepaid thereon at full letter rates.

Commercial papers for Canada and Mexico, 5 cents for first 10 oz. or less and 1 cent each additional 2 oz. or less. Limit of weight 4 pounds, 6 oz. and must be unsealed.

Special Delivery—A Special Stamp of the face value of 10 cents attached to an article of mailable matter, in addition to the lawful postage of such article, entitles it to immediate delivery within the carrier delivery limit of any Free Delivery Post Office and within one mile of any other Post Office in the United States. The law permits the delivery by mail of letters bearing only the Special Delivery Stamp, but the ordinary postage due will be collected of the addressee on delivery. Letters from foreign countries bearing United States Special Delivery Stamps are entitled to Special Delivery. If special Delivery fee is paid by means of ordinary postage stamps, article must be marked "Special Delivery."

The hours within which Special Delivery shall be made in Free Delivery Post Offices, are from 7 a m to 11 p m, unless in special cases otherwise ordered by the Postmaster General. At other post offices the hours are at least from 7 a m to 7 p m and to the arrival of the last mail, not later than 9 o'clock p m.

All letters or packages containing money or valuable articles should be registered to insure their safe delivery. The fee for registration is ten (10) cents additional to regular postage.

Domestic Money Orders—Not exceeding $2.50, 3 cents; exceeding $2.50 and not exceeding $5, 5 cents; exceeding $5 and not exceeding $10, 8 cents; exceeding $10 and not exceeding $20, 10 cents; exceeding $20 and not exceeding $30, 12 cents; exceeding $30 and not exceeding $40, 15 cents; exceeding $40 and not exceeding $50, 18 cents; exceeding $50 and not exceeding $60, 20 cents; exceeding $60 and not exceeding $75, 25 cents; exceeding $75 and not exceeding $100, 30 cents.

Orders payable in Antigua, Bahama Islands, Barbadoes, Bermuda, British Guiana, British Honduras, Canada, Canal Zone, Cuba, Domenica, Grenada, Jamaica, Mexico, Montserrat, Nevis, Newfoundland, Philippine Islands, St Kitts, St Lucia, St Vincent, Trinidad and Virgin Islands, are domestic and the fees are the same as for domestic money orders.

International Money Orders—The fees for international money orders payable in Apia, Austria, Belgium, Bolivia, Cape Colony, Costa Rica, Denmark, Egypt, Germany, Great Britain, Honduras, Hong Kong, Hungary, Italy, Japan, Liberia, Luxemberg, New South Wales, New Zeland, Orange River Colony, Peru, Portugal, Queensland, Russia, Salvador, South Australia, Switzerland, Tasmania, the Transvaal, Uruguay and Victoria, are as follows: 1 cent to $2.50, 10 cents; $2.51 to $5.00, 15 cents; $5.01 to $7.50, 20 cents; $7.51 to $10.00, 25 cents; $10.01 to $15.00, 30 cents; $15.01 to $20.00, 35 cents; $20.01 to $30.00, 40 cents; $30.01 to $40.00, 45 cents; $40 01 to $50.00, 50 cents; $50.01 to $60.00, 60 cents; $60.01 to $70.00, 70 cents; $70.01 to $80.00, 80 cents; $80 01 to $90.00, 90 cents; $90.01 to $100.00, $1.00.

The fees for international money orders payable in Chili, France, Algeria and Tunis, Greece, Netherlands, Norway and Sweden, will be as follows: 1 cent to $10.00, 10 cents; $10.01 to $20.00, 20 cents; $20.01 to $30.00, 30 cents; $30.01 to $40.00, 40 cents; $40.01 to $50.00, 50 cents; $50.01 to $60.00, 60 cents; $60.01 to $70.00, 70 cents; $70.01 to $80.00, 80 cents; $80.01 to $90.00, 90 cents; $90.01 to $100.00, $1.00.

Foreign—Canada, Mexico, Porto Rico, The Philippines, Hawaii, Guam, Tutuila, Shanghai, China, Cuba, Canal Zone, and Republic of Panama, not included. Rates of postage for letters, 5 cents per ounce or less and 3 cents for each additional ounce or fraction; Great Britain, Ireland and Newfoundland 2 cents per ounce or fraction; Germany, 5 cents for first ounce or less and 3 cents for each additional ounce or fraction, if for forwarding via England or France; two cents per ounce or fraction if forwarded by direct sea conveyances; printed matter, 1 cent per 2 oz. or fraction; size of package limited to 18 inch cube, or in form of a roll 30 inches long by 4 inches in diameter; limit of weight, 4 pounds, 6 ounces. Commercial papers (Canada and Mexico included) 5 cents for 10 ounces or fraction and 1 cent for every additional 2 ounces; weight of package limited to 4 pounds, 6 ounces. Admisable bona fide trade samples of merchandise, 2 cents for first 4 ounces or less and 1 cent for each additional 2 ounces or fraction thereof; limit of weight is 12 ounces; limit of length is 12 inches; breadth 8 inches; depth 4 inches.

Postal cards 2 cents; postal cards with paid answer, 4 cents.

Registry fee, 10 cents.

PARCELS POST.

Parcels may be sent by mail accompanied by a Customs Declaration to the following countries:

Australia, Austria, Bahamas, Belgium, Bolivia, Barbadoes, Caicos Islands, Chili, Colombia (U S of), Costa Rica, Danish West Indies, Germany, British Guiana, Dutch Guiana, Guatemala, Honduras (British and Republic of), Hungary, Hong Kong,

Jamaica, Japan, Leeward Islands, Mexico, Nicaragua, Newfoundland, New Zealand, Norway, Sweden, Salvador, Bermuda, Ecuador, Turks Island, Trinidad, Tobago, United Kingdom of Great Britain and Ireland, Venezuela, Winward Islands, Peru, Denmark, France, Italy, Uraguay, Netherlands, China (parts of) and Korea (via Japan).

Rate for one pound or less and each additional pound or fraction 12 cents.

An additional charge of 5 cents or its equivalent is made on the delivery of each package by parcels post from Austria, British Guiana, Bermuda, Ecuador, the Windward Islands, Newfoundland, Trinidad, Chili, Germany, Guatemala, Hungary, Nicaragua, New Zealand, Venezuela, Bolivia, Hong Kong, Japan, Dutch Guiana, Norway, Sweden, Belgium, France, Italy, Netherlands, Uraguay, Honduras (Republic of), Great Britain, Ireland. Australia, Denmark and Peru.

From Danish W I, there is a maximum charge of 10 cents, and from other parcels post countries the delivery charge is 1 cent for each 4 ounces or fraction thereof, minimum charge, 5 cents.

Limit of weight is eleven pounds except to France and to certain places in Mexico, to which it is 4 pounds, 6 ounces.

Limit of size is 3 ft. 6 in. long and 6 ft. length and girth combined, except to U S of Colombia, and Mexico, to which the limit of length is 2 ft. and girth 4 ft.

Value limited for France and Ecuador to $50.

Value limited for Australia. Austria, Belgium, parts of China via Japan, Denmark, Hong Kong, Italy, Japan, Netherlands, Norway and Sweden to $80.

Any person wishing to withdraw a letter after having mailed it should make immediate application to the postmaster, and in case the letter has not been forwarded it will be returned, if the letter has been forwarded, he can request the postmaster to take up the matter of return through the second assistant P M General (Division of Foreign Mails) Washington, D. C., the owner of the letter paying charges incurred. Great Britain and the British Colonies (except Cape Colony, Orange River Colonly, Southern Rhodesia, Antigua, Bahamas, Barbadoes, Ceylon, Gold Coast, British Guiana, Jamaica, Zanzibar and the Australasian Colonies) including Canada and British India; also Haitti, the Dominican Republic, Colombia and the French Establishments in Oceanica do not allow senders of articles to withdraw them from the mails or change their address.

CHURCHES AND MINISTERS

ADVENT

SECOND ADVENT Foster c Kempton—Rev————pastor; Mrs Edna Bennett ,clerk; Samuel T Bennett, treas

SEVENTH DAY ADVENTIST Willow cor Bullock—no settled pastor

BAPTIST

ELIM BAPTIST, Middle near County—pastor supplied

FIRST BAPTIST, William above Sixth—Rev Gibbs Braislin, pastor, Charles S Coombs, treas

FRENCH BAPTIST 186 Cedar Grove—Rev A E Ribourg, pastor

IMMANUEL BAPTIST, Acushnet av corNash rd—Rev J J Phelan, pastor

NORTH BAPTIST, Merrimac c County—Rev Elias C Miller, pastor

PORTUGESE BAPTIST MISSION, Thompson cor Crapo—Rev F C B Silva, pastor

SOUTH BAPTIST, Brock av off Mott—Rev Thomas S Sayer, pastor

UNION BAPTIST, cor Cedar and Court—Rev Nathaniel A Marriott, pastor

CHRISTIAN

NORTH CHRISTIAN, Purchase cor Middle—Rev Frank H Peters, pastor

PLAINVILLE CHRISTIAN—no settled pastor

SOUTH CHRISTIAN, Bonney cor Sherman—no settled pastor

SPRUCE STREET CHRISTIAN, Spruce cor Smith—Rev George A Roemer, pastor

CONGREGATIONAL

FIRST CONGREGATIONAL, Acushnet av, Lund's Corner—Rev H E Oxnard, pastor; Frederick B Hawes, clerk; George A Cobb, treas

NORTH CONGREGATIONAL, Purchase cor Elm—Rev Frank E Ramsdell, pastor; J William Webber, clerk; Charles E Benton, treas parish; Ezra Holmes, treas church

TRINITARIAN, Fourth cor School —Rev M C Julien, pastor; J F Briggs, treas; Harry G Rounsevell, clerk

EPISCOPAL

GRACE, County corner School—Rev Percy Gordon, rector, 372 County

ST ANDREWS, Belleville rd n Acushnet av—Rev Middleton S Barnwell, pastor

ST JAMES, County cor Linden—Rev Ivan C Fortin, pastor

ST MARTIN'S, County cor Rivet —Rev Francis B Boyer, rector; Percy Rawcliffe, clerk; Alfred Bradley, treas

EVANGELICAL

FIRST EVANGELICAL, Mill cor Newton—Rev H S Trueman, pastor

LATTER DAY SAINTS

REORGANIZED CHURCH OF JESUS CHRIST, Bourne cor Thompson—pastor supplied

LUTHERAN

ST JOHN'S GERMAN LUTHERAN, 296 Kempton corner Summer—Rev Henry Mette, pastor; John Quapp, clerk; August Meyer, treas

METHODIST EPISCOPAL

ALLEN STREET METHODIST EPISCOPAL, Allen corner County—Rev Florus L Streeter, pastor; H T Borden, treas

BETHEL AFRICAN METHODIST EPISCOPAL, Kempton opp Chestnut —Rev C Hubert Yearwood, pastor; Rev John R Offley, asst pastor; Daniel R Allen, clerk; John Oliver treas

ZION A M E, Elm next Cottage—Rev Dennis Scott, pastor; Harry Harper, treas; Aaron Timber, clerk

COUNTY STREET METHODIST EPISCOPAL, County corner Elm—Rev James I Bartholomew, pastor

FIRST PORTUGUESE METHODIST EPISCOPAL, Dartmouth cor Rivet—Rev William H Moseley, pastor; Mrs Alice P Moseley, rec steward;

FOURTH STREET METHODIST EPISCOPAL, Fourth south of Walnut—Rev John Pearce, pastor; Jesse Law, treas; Joseph T Timperly, rec steward

HOWARD METHODIST EPISCOPAL, Kempton corner Rockdale av—Rev Harry Felton, pastor

METHODIST EPISCOPAL CHAPEL near 3591 Acushnet—no pastor; Sunday schol 2 p m

PLEASANT STREET METHO- EPISCOPAL, Pleasant cor Sycamore —Rev William F Davis, pastor; George W Paine, clerk and treas

WESLEY METHODIST EPISCOPAL, 1614 Acushnet av—Rev John Oldham, pastor

PRESBYTARIAN

FIRST PRESBYTARIAN, 100 High near County—Rev Lester M Conrow, pastor; John H Hope, clerk; Jeremiah Irwin, clerk of session; Robert McLeod, treas

PRIMATIVE METHODIST

FIRST PRIMATIVE METHODIST Weld near Pleasant—Rev Thomas M Bateman, pastor; Charles Lindley, pres; Rev Thomas M Bateman, sec; William Johnson, treas

SOUTH PRIMATIVE METHODIST, County near Thompson— Rev Alfred K Collett pastor

ROMAN CATHOLIC

CHURCH OF THE IMMACULATE CONCEPTION, 1238 Acushnet av— Rev Agusto J Taveira, pastor

CHURCH OF THE SACRED HEART, Ashland corner Robeson—Rev C P Gadboury, pastor; Rev S P Lonergan, asst

HOLY ROSARY, Acushnet av—Rev Edmund J Potvin, pastor

MT CARMEL, Rivet cor Bonney—Rev Antonio P Vieira, pastor

OUR LADY OF PERPETUAL HELP, N Front near Coggeshall—Rev E A Uminski, pastor

ST ANNE'S Ruth cor Brock av—Rev Omer Valois, pastor; Rev George J Cain, asst pastor

ST ANTHONY, Acushnet av cor Bullard—Rev H Deslauriers, pastor; Rev Charles Clerk, Rev Lucien C Bedard, assts

ST HEDWIGS, Delano cor S Second

ST HYACINTH Rivet near County—Rev Antoine Berube, pastor; Rev Adrien Gauthier, asst

ST JAMES, County cor Rockland—Rev Mortimer Downing, pastor

ST JOHN THE BAPTIST, Fifth corner Wing—Rev Manuel A Silva, pastor, Rev Joaquim G Cardozo, curate; Rev Joao P Damaso, asst

ST JOSEPH'S Acushnet av cor Duncan—Rev Jovite Chagnon, pastor

ST KILLIAN'S, Davis corner Bowditch—Rev James J Brady, pastor; Rev Michael V McDonough, asst

ST LAWRENCE, County corner Hillman—Rev Hugh J Smyth, pastor; Rev Michael J Owens, Rev Joseph P Lyons, assts

ST MARY'S, County corner Studley—Rev James M Coffey, pastor Rev James R Burns, asst

UNITARIAN

FIRST CONGREGATIONAL SOCIETY, Union corner Eighth—Rev William B Geoghegan, pastor

UNIVERSALIST

FIRST UNIVERSALIST, William near Eighth—Rev Howard C R Gale. pastor

MISCELLANEOUS DENOMINATIONS

CANNONVILE CHAPEL, Kempton corner Rockdale av— No settled pastor

CHURCH OF GOD; Saints of Christ, Middle near Cedar—Howard L Chace, elder

CITY MISSION, Dennison Memorial bldg 755 First—Rev C F Hersey, missionary

CLIFFORD UNION CHAPEL ASSOCIATION, Acushnet av near Braley road— No settled pastor

DEUTSH LUTARISCHE KIRCHE Summer corner Kempton—pastor supplied

FIRST CHURCH OF CHRIST (SCIENTIST) 36 Pleasant reading room open daily (except Sunday) from 2 to 5 p m

FIRST SPIRITUAL HARMONY CHURCH, Purchase ft Hazard—Charles H DeGrasse, sec; Mrs Joe Beckwell, treas

HEBREW SYNAGOGUE, 51 Howland

HOME GOSPEL MISSION, r 332 Kempton—Rev Mrs Mary S Ransom, pastor

N B SPIRITUALIST AND PROGRESSIVE LYCEUM, meet at Jenney's Hall, Pleasant and Kempton

PENTICOSTAL CHURCH OF THE NAZARENE—Rev Frederick W Domina, pastor, cor Kempton and Cottage

ROCKDALE FREE CHAPEL ASSOCIATION, Chapel Hathaway road—pastor supplied

SALVATION ARMY, 279 Acushnet av—David Main, adjt

SEAMEN'S BETHEL, 15 Bethel—Rev Charles S Thurber, chaplain

SHAWMUT CHURCH, pastor supplied

SOCIETY OF FRIENDS, Meeting house on Spring between S Sixth and Seventh—William Thompson, Susan C Thompson, Eloise A Hafford, and Alvano C Goddard, ministers; Frederick Taber,78 Hawthorn, clerk; Sarah D Holmes, 14 S Sixth, treas

MASONIC

EUREKA LODGE A F & A M—Edwin R King, W M; Elisha H Fisher, treas; Daniel W Cory, sec; regular communications first Friday of each month at Masonic bldg, Union c Pleasant

STAR IN THE EAST LODGE—George E Allen, W M; William M Thorup, treas; Charles H Vinal, sec; regular communications first Monday of each month at Masonic bldg, Union cor Pleasant

ADONIRAM R A CHAPTER—Merton L Hathaway, M E H P; William Bliss, E K; Henry S Foster,

E S; Zac C Dunham, treas; Damon W Rice, sec; regular convocations first Wednesday of each month at Masonic bldg, Union cor Pleasant

NEW BEDFORD COUNCIL OF ROYAL AND SELECT MASTERS—Philip S Briggs, T I M; Harry M Gay, D M; Channing Wilde, P C of W; E Stanley Swift, treas; Clement L Yaeger, recorder; Regular meetings first Tuesday of each month except July and August, at Masonic bldg, Union cor Pleasant

SUTTON COMMANDERY NO 16 K T—Elton S Wilde, E C; Merton L Hathaway, rec; Zac C Dunham, treas. Regular conclaves first Thursday of each month at Masonic bldg, Union, cor Pleasant

UNION LODGE NO 7 F & A M—Joseph S Webster, W M; David M Piper, S W; Cornelius B Piper, J W; William J Knox, treas; Frederick S Monroe, sec. Regular communications first Monday of each month at 21 N Second

ST MARK'S CHAPTER NO 5 HOLY ROYAL ARCH MASONS—C Augustus Webb, M E H P; Frederick S Monroe, sec; Lewis S Moore, treas; meet third Monday of each month at 21 N Second

THOMAS DALTON COMMANDERY NO 7 K T—meet fourth Monday at Asylum 21 N Second

J W HOOD CHAPTER NO 20—Estelle Knox, W M; Annie Becker, sec; Emma L Wright, treas; meet fourth Friday of each month at 21 N Second

ORDER OF THE EASTERN STAR

DARTMOUTH CHAPTER NO 106—Constituted April 24, 1907; Ellen L Goddard, W M; Marianna Devoll, treas; Helen A Hafford, sec; Meet second and fourth Wednesdays of each month at Odd Fellow's Hall, 76 Pleasant

NEW BEDFORD CHAPTER NO 49—Constituted Nov 20, 1895; Margaret A Smith, W M; Caroline F Austin, sec; Harriet S Potter, treas; Meet second and fourth Tuesdays of each month at Odd Fellow's Hall, 76 Pleasant

LOYAL KNIGHTS AND LADIES

COURT THEMIS NO 6—William L Downey, P R; Lyman W S Tripp, chan; Daniel H Smith, cham; Meet second and fourth Tuesdays of each month at G A R hall Pleasant

ODD FELLOWS

CANTON NEW BEDFORD NO 42 PATRIARCHS MILITANT— Instituted April 22, 1885; Reduced April 22 1891; Clarence L Tripp, com; James H Bamford, clerk; Alanson R Washburn, acct; meet third Wednesday of each month at 76 Pleasant

ANNAWAN ENCAMPMENT NO 8 I O O F—George R Heath, H P; William L Ashley, C P; Anderson H Swift, rec scribe; Nathaniel E McCulley, treas; meet second and fourth Thursdays of each month at 76 Pleasant

UNITY ENCAMPENT NO 38 I O O F— Lewis D Baldwin, C P; Samuel T Rex, R S; Justin C Perkins, treas; meet first and third Tuesdays of each month at Pacific hall, Purchase corner William

ACUSHNET LODGE NO 41, Instituted April 11, 1844; Harry C Vaughan, N G; Amos W Hadley, rec sec; Anderson H Swift, treas; meet every Tuesday evening at 76 Pleasant

VESTA LODGE NO 166— Instituted Feb, 1874 Edward F Otis, N G; Thomas C Holmans, sec; Henry S Swain, treas; meet every Monday evenng in Vest Lodge hall 16 North Sixth

PACIFIC LODGE NO 123— Meet every Wednesday evening at Pacific hall William corner Pleasant

JOSEPH YORK REBECCA I O O F NO 157— Meets second and fourth Fridays of each month at I O O F ball, 76 Pleasant

STELLA LODGE REBEKAH I O O F NO 46—Lizzie V Kelley, N G; Josie W Partington, 90 Merrimac, sec; Marion L Holloway, treas; meet first and third Thursday evenings of each month at Odd Fellows' bldg, 76 Pleasant

USHER LODGE REBEKAH I O O F NO 114—Meet second and fourth Monday evenings of each month at Odd Fellows' hall, 76 Pleasant

I O O L M U

OMEGA LODGE NO 15—Clara Rumney, N G; Mary Kay, 118 Hathaway, P S; Ida E Sutcliffe, treas; meet second and fourth Tuesdays at 16 North Sixth

MANCHESTER UNITY

LOYAL ALPHA LODGE NO 6463—Instituted Oct, 1881; Walter Whithead, N G; Nelson L Pike, sec; Levi Pemberton. treas; meet first and third Fridays of each month at 16 N Sixth

LOYAL PRIDE OF NEW BEDFORD LODGE NO 7019 M U—William J Harnish, N G; Hartley Pollard, sec, 21 Reynolds; Fred Dickson, treas; meet second and fourth Fridays of each month at Weavers' hall

AMERICAN ORDER OF FORESTERS OF AMERICA

COURT LUSITANO NO 215—Joaquim F Portugal, C R; Joseph F Lisboa S C R; F P Rose Jr, fin sec; F Marshall, treas meet second and fourth Tuesdays of each month at Monte Pio hall

COURT NEW BEDFORD NO 69—Organized Feb 17, 1892 Alphonse Fura, C R; John L Rooney, treas; M J Baker, 286 Fourth, fin sec, meet second and fourth Fridays of each month at Red Men's hall 13 Fourth

COURT THOMAS JEFFERSON NO 205—meet second and fourth Wednesdays of each month at Bonaventure hall, 905 Acushnet avenue

COMPANIONS OF THE FOREST

GOOD HOPE CIRCLE NO 492—Mary E Sullivan, C C; Mrs Julia F Sullivan ,213 Cottage, fin sec; Minnie Downey, treas; meet second and fourth Tuesdays of each month at Weaver's hall

ANCIENT ORDER OF HIBERNIANS

DIVISION NO 7—Thomas Hart, pres; Robert Hart, sec; Michael Quinn, treas; meet first and third Sundays at Downey's hall

LADIES AUXILIARY OF DIVISION NO 4—Meet at 403 Rivet

DIVISION NO 9, 803 Purchase—Meet first and third Monday of each month at Dawson bldg, Linden cor Purchase

LADIES AUXILIARY OF DIVISION NO 6, A O H—Nellie Wade, pres; Ellen Duffecy, sec; Clara Rodney, treas meet every Monday evening at A O H hall, Linden

ANCIENT ORDER OF UNITED WORKMEN

CENTURY LODGE NO 101—Fred L Jason, M W; Thomas C Holman, rec; L W S Tripp, treas; meet first and third Thursdays of each month at Odd Fellows' bldg, 76 Pleasant

BENEVOLENT AND PROTECTIVE ORDER OF ELKS

NEW BEDFORD LODGE NO 73—Instituted Nov 22 1887; William H Thayer, E R; Charles S Ashley Jr, E L K; Edward E Wright, sec; Irving A Brown, treas; meet every Tuesday evening from Oct 1st to June 1st at Elks' hall, 88 Purchase

FRATERNAL ORDER OF EAGLES

NEW BEDFORD AERIE NO 647—Walter Peirce, pres; Anthony M Lima Jr, vice-pres; Charles A McAvoy, treas; William A Burt, rec sec, meet first and third Mondays of each month at 138 Pleasant

FRATERNAL ORDER OF TIGERS

NEW BEDFORD JUNGLE NO 25 Andrew Gunning, R T; Geo Fredette, R treas; meet second and fourth Thursdays of each month at Odd Fellow's hall 76 Pleasant

GRAND ARMY OF THE REPUBLIC

WILLIAM LOGAN RODMAN POST NO 1—Organized Oct 4, 1866; Thomas W Cook, com; John H Lawrence, 66 Parker, treas; George H Carpenter, sec; meet every Wednesday evening at Post hall, 132 Pleasant

R A PIERCE POST NO 190—Organized May 28, 1888; William H H Jennings, com; George P Macomber, adjt; James W Hervey, Q M; meet every Monday evening at R A Pierce hall, 57 William

CUMBERLAND NAVAL VETERANS ASS'N NO 20—Organized 1891; Peter Dumac, pres; Theodore E Lawton, sec and treas; meet second Sunday of each month at 6 Green

SONS OF VETERANS

JOHN H CLIFFORD CAMP NO 130—Harry M Gay, pres; Clarence H Davis, sec and treas; meet third Tuesday at 51 William

JOHN A HAWES CAMP NO 35 —Henry W Hammond, com; Chester H Jason, sec; George T Duckworth, treas; meet every Tuesday evening at Temperance hall, 69 Purchase

LADIES AUXILIARY of the John A Hawes Camp No 35 S of V—Meet every Friday evening at Temperance hall, Purchase

WOMAN'S RELIEF CORPS

WILLIAM LOGAN RODMAN CORPS NO 53 Auxiliary to Post No 1, Instituted Sept 11, 1875—Ida R Janell, pres; S Ella Card, sec; Jennie L Topham, treas; meet every Thursday evening at G A R hall 138 Pleasant

R A PIERCE CORP NO 95 Auxiliary to R A Pierce Post No 190, Instituted Jan 13, 1891—Mrs Lydia A Kempton, pres; Mrs Mary M H Washburn, sec; Lydia C Salisbury, treas; meet second and fourth Fridays of each month at R A Pierce Post hall, 57 William

SYLVIA H DELANO'S CIRCLE NO 1 DEPT OF MASS, Incorporated 1896—Eudora R Nye, pres; Lydia A Perry, sec; Mrs Mahala S T Negus, 155 Campbell, treas; meet first and Tuesdays of each month at Temperance hall, 69 Purchase

UNITED SPANISH WAR VETERANS

CAPT CHARLES V GRIDLEY CAMP NO 19—Meet first and third Wednesdays of each month at 196 Union

LADIES SPANISH WAR VETERANS

MOTHER GRIDLEY AUXILIARY NO 11—Mrs Mahola S T Negus, pres; Mrs Anna G Hambly, sec; Mrs Jennie M Pierce, treas; meet first and third Thursdays of each month at S W V hall 196 Union

IMPROVED ORDER OF RED MEN

SIPPICAN TRIBE NO 77, Organized June 28, 1888—Louis A Vierick, sachem; Samuel R Spencer, 359 Park, C of R; F Lewin Pope Jr, K of W; meet Monday evenings at Red Men's hall 153 Union

U O R M

BEETHOVEN STAMM NO 269—meet first and third Monday at 65 Elm

HUMBOLDT LAGER NO 47—Louis Kruger, Prophet; William Butz, Kanzler; G A Schneider, treas; meet first and third Tuesdays of each month at Red Men's hall 81 Elm

POTOMSKA STAMM NO 182—William Butz, chief; Edward Goddune, sec; Martin P Fichtenmayer, treas; meet second, fourth and fifth Tuesdays at 81 Elm

INDEPENDENT ORDER OF BRITH ABRAHAM

NEW BEDFORD LODGE NO 304 —David Stone, pres; David Silver sec; Em Krastenbaum, treas; meet first and third Sundays of each month at Temperance hall Purchase

DAUGHTERS OF THE REVOLUTION

CAPT THOMAS KEMPTON CHAPTER; Abbie L Prichard, Regent; Mrs E J Howland, sec; meets first Tuesday of each month at 21 Arch

DAUGHTERS OF POCAHONTAS

MASS STAMM NO 11 P D—Mrs Mary Wunschell, pres; Mary A Weik, sec; Cathrina Osswald, treas; meet second and fourth Wednesdays of each month at 65 Elm

KNIGHTS OF COLUMBUS

McMAHON COUNCIL NO 151 Instituted Feb 23, 1896—James P Doran, G K; William H Loughlin, D G K; John J McNamee, fin sec; William E Cleary, rec sec; Arthur J Cunningham, treas; meet second and fourth Mondays of each month at Cummings bldg, William corner Purchase

KNIGHTS OF HONOR

NEW BEDFORD LODGE NO 667 Organized June 15, 1887 meet first Thursday of each month at G A R hall 138 Pleasant

KNIGHTS OF MALTA

PURITAN COMMANDERY NO 231 Instituted August 1897— Thomas S Ellis, S K C; William A Burt, 555 Union, S K rec; Charles F Smith, S K treas; meet second and fourth Wednesday evenings of each month at Jenney's hall Pleasant and Kempton

KNIGHTS OF PYTHIAS

BUZZARDS BAY LODGE NO 137, Samuel S Broadbent, C C; John C Clarke, 30 Crapo, K of R and S; Charles A Croshere, M of F; meet second and fourth Friday of each month at G A R hall 13 Fourth

UNION LODGE NO 7, Instituted Jan 20, 1886—Louis Mechaber, C C; C Harry Walker, K of R & S; Fred G Sawyer, M of E; meet first and third Thursdays at 16 N Sixth

FRIENDSHIP LODGE NO 11—Albert J Barbour, C C; D B Gardner, K of R and S; William Reynolds, M of E; meet first and third Thursdays of each month at 137 Union

MASSACHUSETTS CATHOLIC ORDER OF FORESTERS

JOHN BOYLE O'REILLY COURT NO 79, Instituted Jan 1891—Charles A McAvoy, C R; John B Duffy, R S; Timothy J Burns, treas; meet first Wednesday evening of each month at Weaver hall

ST ELALIA COURT NO 164 Instituted August 1899—Meet third Wednesday of each month at Labor Temple

COURT WINDHORST NO 133—Francis A Lang, C R; Charles Zellhuber, 12 Briggs ct, rec sec; Andrew Lang, treas; meet fourth Sunday of each month at Redmen's hall 69 Elm

ST URSULA COURT NO 123—Anna Lynch, C R; Katherine Porter, sec; Alice Sweeney, treas; meet third Tuesday evening of each month at 76 Pleasant

N E O P

BAY STATE LODGE NO 59—Jonathan Tober, warden; Frederick F Ellis, sec, 73 Elm; William H Rankin, treas; meet second and fourth Mondays of each month at Odd Fellows' bldg

O S C

CALEDONIAN LODGE—Robert Lindsay, chief; Louis Cross, rec sec; William T Moncrieff, treas; meet first and third Thursdays of each month at Jenney's hall Kempton corner Pleasant

UNION FRATERNAL LEAGUE

ST ANTOINE NO 227—Azarie Chaille, 144 State, speaker; Joseph Champagne, clerk; Mrs Marie L Chaille, treas; meet second Thursday of each month at C M B A hall, Hacienda bldg, Acushnet av near Cedar Grove

ROYAL ARCANUM

OMEGA COUNCIL NO 683—George L Bronson, regent; John H Barrows, sec; James B Athearn, treas; Frank W Davis, collector; meet second and fourth Thursdays of each month at Vesta Lodge hall 16 N Sixth

SONS OF ST GEORGE

GORDON LODGE NO 172, Instituted March 1885—John Sutcliffe, W pres; William Donley, W sec; 178½ Blackmer; Richard Thatcher, (Fairhaven), W treas; meet first and third Friday of each month at 138 Pleasant

TEMPERANCE SOCIETIES

ACUSHNET DIVISION NO 87 S of T—George S Bowen, sec, 53 Fifth; Mary A Cameron, treas; meet every Tuesday evning at Temperance hall 69 Purchase

CHRISTIAN TEMPERANCE UNION—Samuel McVien, pres; Thomas Sweet, sec; Mattie McIntyre, treas; meets Sundays and Thursdays at 15 Bethel

GOOD WILL TEMPERANCE UNION—Meet Sunday afternoons, Monday and Friday evenings at 85 Cedar

MILITARY ORGANIZATIONS

4th COMPANY COAST ARTILLERY CORPS, M V M—William Stitt, capt; Edward Doane, clerk; John A Stitt, treas; Walter J Gilbert, sergt major; meet every Monday evening at State Armory, Sycamore corner Pleasant

COMPANY G Mass Naval Brigade, Organized Nov 28, 1892—Harold S Bowie, lieut chief of Co; James Stetson, lieut; Omer J Parent, ensign; Patrick A Sheerin, clerk; Joseph A Bertwhistle, treas; meet every Wednesday at State Armory

CLUBS

ALGONQUIN CLUB, 803 Purchase—meet first Monday in January and July rm 4

ARBEITER LIEDENTAFEL SOCIETY, 14 Adams—John Boehler, pres; John Bear, sec; John Puntschuh, treas

CAPE VERDE CLUB, 277 S Water—meet on last Thursday of each month

CLUB AUTONINO LIBERAL, 399 Rivet; Domingos Costa, pres; Guilherme de Rego, sec; Antone Macerda, treas; meet every Monday

COUNTRY CLUB OF NEW BEDFORD MASSACHUSETTS Grounds and Club House, Smith's Mills, North Dartmouth
Incorporated 1902
President—Charles W Clifford
Secretary—Henry S Knowles
Treasurer—Charles F Kelley Jr

Governing Board—John T Bullard, Charles W Gifford, William E Hatch, Charles S Kelley Jr, Henry S Knowles, William A Robinson Jr, Frederick D Stetson, Henry W Taber, William F Williams, Benjamin B Barney, Rodolphus A Swan

Annual meeting last Saturday in October at such place Governing Board shall determine

DARTMOUTH CAFE CLUB 5 S Sixth—Edward L Hathaway, pres; Horace Wood, treas; George J Swain, sec; directors' meeting third Monday of each month

DARTMOUTH CLUB 246½ Union corner Sixth—John Paul, pres; Lawrence H Barney, sec; Edward E Wright, treas; directors meet second Monday of each month

EAST SIDE CLUB 72 Middle

HATHAWAY'S PORTUGUESE CRICKET CLUB 207 S Water—C A Pinto, pres; Manuel Rose, treas; Pedro Teixeira, sec; meet first Sunday of each month

LAURIER CLUB 1448 Acushnet av; Wilfred Brouillette, pres; Alfred M Gravelle, treas; Thomas St Germain, sec; meet at call of pres

LUZITANO CLUB, 100 Acushnet av; John B Francis Jr, pres

MERCHANTS CLUB, 128 Union —Thomas G Wing, sec

MOTHERS' CLUB—meet second and fourth Tuesday of each month

NEW BEDFORD DRIVING CLUB, Plainville rd, Chester R Borden, mgr

NEW BEDFORD FIREMEN'S RELIEF CLUB—Organized April 19, 1892—Frank E Washburn, pres; Joseph C Forbes, sec; Frank R Pease, treas; meet on call at Central Fire Station Purchase

NEW BEDFORD NORTH END CRICKET CLUB Coffin av—Meet every Monday

NEW BEDFORD ORCHESTRAL CLUB—Meet Wednesdays at Cornell hall

NEW BEDFORD YACHT CLUB, New Bedford Harbor, Pandanaram Harbor, organized March 16, 1877; incorporated January 25, 1878; officers for 1911—Henry W Ellison, commodore; Fred M Reed, vice commodore; Mark Vincent, rear commodore; William H Hand Jr, sec; Horace Wood, treas; Harry Jason, measurer; Frank H Masy, fleet captain; Annual meeting first Tuesday of March

NORTH END LITERARY AND SOCIAL CLUB 983 Purchase

NURSES' HOME 321 Union

ODD FELLOWS' RELIEF CLUB NO 1— Meet at Odd Fellows' bldg Pleasant c William; William Bamford, pres; Frank A Habicht, sec; Frederick S Spooner, treas; Annual meeting first Friday in October

PASKAMANSETT GUN CLUB— George A Eggers, sec; 10 William

PLYMOUTH CLUB—21 Masonic bldg Pleasant; James Dignam, pres; Samuel F Winsper, vice-pres; Peter

F Sullivan, treas; Henry J Perry Jr, sec; annual meeting last Thursday of January

POLISH TURNERS ALLIANCE BRANCH 90—Frank J Wilusz, pres; Joseph Baczek, treas; Adam Szczur, sec; meet first Monday of each month at Polish hall, Kenyon

ROCHAMBEAU CLUB 418 S Front—meet first Monday of each month

SOCIAL CLUB — William A Browne, pres; James Tonge, fin sec; meet every Monday evening at Meaney bldg

SOUTH BRISTOL FARMERS CLUB 76 Pleasant—Herbert Wing, pres; Allen Russell Jr, sec; John A Russell treas; annual meeting in Feb

SOUTH END SOCIAL CLUB Rivet corner First

SUMNER CLUB Cedar corner Kempton—Robert H Coblin, pres; Charles W Timber, sec; George Anthony, treas; yearly meeting second Tuesday in January

THISTLE ROAD CLUB—Patrick J Coyne, pres; G G Southworth, rec; William Craig, fin sec; John J McAvoy, treas; meets first and third Mondays at Meaney bldg

WAMSUTTA CLUB 435 County, organized May 28 1866 chartered April 4 1880—Otis S Cook, pres; Clifton W Bartlett, sec; Alfred Thornton, treas; meet last Tuesday of each month

WARD ONE SOCIAL CLUB 422 Pleasant

WASHINGTON SOCIAL AND MUSICAL CLUB, W French av cor Cove—Robert Woods, pres; Joseph H Schofield, sec; Herbert Roebuck, treas; meet third Thursday of each month

WORKINGMEN'S CLUB, 69 Bowditch—Charles H Morris, pres; John Drinkwater, treas; Joseph Branhall, sec; meet third Thursday of each month Directors meet every Tuesday night

SOCIETIES

AMALGAMATED SHEET METAL WORKERS LOCAL 289—meet second and fourth Wednesday at 112 William

AMERICAN FEDERATION OF MUSICIANS—Arthur J Parry, pres; Frank Whittaker, sec; Charles F Trull Jr, treas; meet first Sunday of each month at Labor Temple

BAKERY AND CONFECTIONERY WORKERS LOCAL UNION 95 —meet first and thid Saturday of each month at eWaver's Union bldg

BARTENDERS' LOCAL UNION NO 100—Martin J Cairns, pres; R R Foutter, cor sec; M H Sullivan, fin sec; meet first and third Sundays of each month at Labor Temple

BOHEMIAN SLAVONIAN BENEVOLENT SOCIETY organized 1901 —meet every Monday at 146 Bowditch

BREWERY WORKMEN OF AMERICA, LOCAL NO 197—L B Fields, pres; Joseph Netsch, C of R; William Parkerns, fin treas; meet second and last Monday of every month at 14 Adams

BRICKLAYERS' AND PLASTERERS' UNION NO 39—William Wilson, pres; N H Fitzimons, rec sec; A B Cook, fin sec; James H Murkland, treas; meet every Wednesday evening at 39 Masonic bldg

BOOT AND SHOE WORKERS UNION LOCAL 243—J Edward Johnson, pres; Lizzie McCann, fin sec; Ida Sanborn, treas; meet second Monday of each month at Weaver's hall

CARDERS' UNION—Instituted 1893—meet second and fourth Tuesdays at 61½ Purchase

CARPENTERS' AND JOINERS' UNION NO 1021—P Cooche, pres; Adolore Houle, sec; Donat Turcotte, treas; meet every Monday evening at 39 Masonic bldg

CENTRAL LABOR UNION—Peter Cairns, pres; Henry S Davis, rec; John A Andrews, treas; meet second and fourth Fridays of each month at 138 Pleasant

CHARITY ORGANIZATION SOCIETY OF NEW BEDFORD 12 Market—Rev W B Geoghegan, pres; Frederick H Taber, clerk; Emma R Hall, treas; Dr Florence M Dyer, gen sec; meet fourth Tuesday of each month at 2 Market

GRANITE CUTTERS UNION —meet firstThursday after the 15th of the month at 138 Pleasant

HOISTING AND PORTABLE ENGINERS UNION—meet second and fourth Mondays at 138 Pleasant

INDUSTRIAL WORKERS OF THE WORLD—Textile Workers Industrial Union No 157, meet second and fourth Wednesday of each month at Phelan bldg 45 Delano

IRON MOLDERS UNION NO 363, established 1902—meet fourth Wednesday of each month at St Lawrence Hall, Purchase

JOURNEYMEN BARBERS UNION, LOCAL 447—Joseph S Trudeau, pres; William J Goulet, sec; Emelien Cormier, treas; meet third Monday of each month at 138 Pleasant

JOURNEYMEN PLUMBERS UNION NO 53—James F Murphy, pres; James F Collins, sec; Charles DeLoid, treas; meet second and fourth Wednesdays of each month at 4 Pleasant

LADIES' CATHOLIC BENEFIT ASS'N, BRANCH 407—meet second and fourth Tuesday of each month at Hacienda bldg 947 Acushnet av .

LOOM FIXERS ASS'N—Peter Cairns, pres; John Hobin, sec; Herbert Clark, treas; meet third Friday of each month at 138 Pleasant

MASSACHUSETTS SOCIETY FOR THE PREVENTION OF CRUELTY TO CHILDREN—James P Doran, pres; Mrs Edmond Anthony vice-pres; William Phillips, treas; Rev Charles F Hersey, sec; Meet at 12 Market

MASTER BUILDERS EXCHANGE—F B Sistare, pres; Henry Harlow, sec; Benjamin C Tripp, treas; meet third Monday of each month at Board of Trade Rooms

MAZEPPA HAND ENGINE ASS'N. Organized 1899, Henry L Taber, pres; John F Parker, sec; William M Darling, treas; meet first Monday or each month at Mazeppa hall, Lund's corner

MONTE PIO SOCIETY—Joaquim F Portugal, pres; Theophilo Barcellos, sec; M P B Silva, treas; meet second Monday of each month at Monte Pio hall, 160½ Acushnet av

MULE SPINNERS UNION—Urban Heming, pres; Samuel Ross, sec; John Halliwell, treas; meet third Tuesday of each month at 62½ Purchase

NATIONAL ASS'N OF LETTER CARRIERS BRANCH NO 18—Frederick H Geiles, pres; Frank P Campbell, vice-pres; Joseph F Waldron, sec; John E Moores, treas; Albert H Peters, coll, M B A; meet first Saturday evening of each month at P O

NATIONAL ASS'N OF STATIONARY ENGINEERS MASS NO 7—Joseph Eccleston, pres; C N Potter, sec; John F Butts, treas; meets second and fourth Fridays of each month at Cornell bldg 132 Pleasant

NATIONAL HAYMAKERS ASSOCIATION SIPPICAN NO 77½ —meet last Wednesday of each month at 153 Union

NEW BEDFORD BAR ASS'N Incorporated—Charles W Clifford, pres; Frank A Milliken, sec; Frank M Sparrow, treas; meet annually second Monday in April at the law library, Court House County

NEW BEDFORD BOARD OF TRADE
97 William

President—Frederick B Macy
Secretary—Fred W Greene Jr
Treasurer—George R Philips

NEW BEDFORD CITY EMPLOYEES UNION NO 15 Richard Burke, pres; John F Andrews, sec; John Quinn, treas; meet first and third Tuesdays of each month at Labor Temple hall

NEW BEDFORD CITY MISSION, Organized 1846—Betsy B Winslow, pres; Miss A B Sears, vice-pres; Mrs H K Milliken, sec; Annie C Howland, treas; Mrs Ella R Knight, auditor; Rev C F Hersey, missionary; meet first Wednesday of each month

Office of City Missionary, Dennison Memorial bldg, 755 First

Dispensary at 755 First; open daily except Sunday, from 4 to 5 p m

City Mission Rescue Home for Homeless Men, N Second c Mill

City Mission Wood Yard, N Second C Mill

NEW BEDFORD DAY NURSERY, 16 Howard and 208 County; Elise Swift, pres; Mrs Otis Pierce, vice-pres Alice Wood, sec; Mrs A

W Holmes, treas; meet first Tuesday of each month at home of one of the members

NEW BEDFORD DORCAS SOCIETY, organized Jan 3, 1831—Mrs Esther G Gifford, pres; Mrs A M C Jahn, sec; Mrs Louisa A Wilbor, treas; meet from Oct to May at Union for Good Works bldg

NEW BEDFORD EMERGENCY HOSPITAL, 194 Purchase, established 1902—Dr Charles A Derby, supt; Louise G Quirk, matron

NEW BEDFORD FIREMEN'S MUTUAL AID SOCIETY, organized Sept 17, 1872, incorporated Sept 25, 1895—Alonzo V Jason, pres; Nelson L Pike, treas; Joseph C Forbes, sec; annual meeting first Wednesday after second Monday in January; other meetings upon call of president at the several fire stations

NEW BEDFORD HORTICULTURAL SOCIETY, organized Feb 2, 1903— Frank C Barrows, pres; Jeremiah M Taber, sec; Walter A Luce, treas; meet first Monday of each month at Board of Trade Rooms annual meeting second Tuesday in January

NEW BEDFORD, MASS, POST OFFICE RELIEF ASSOCIATION, Ernest B Eno, pres; Wilfred Deslandes, vice-pres; Stanley G Akin, sec; Hiram Smith, treas; meet last Monday of each month at P O

NEW BEDFORD PORT SOCIETY —For the moral improvement of seamen; chaplain's office at Mariner's Home 15 Bethel; William H Pitman, pres; N C Hathaway, treas; Olive Paine, sec; Rev Charles S Thurber, chaplain; open from 9 a m to 12 m

(LADIES BRANCH)—Mariners' Home, 15 Bethel—Mrs William G Taber, pres; Mrs Frederick Brownell, sec; Mary K Taber, treas; meet first Thursday of each month; annual meeting first Thursday in January

NEW BEDFORD PRINTERS BENEFIT ASSOCIATION, Organized Sept 1883—Frank E Habicht, pres; Fred F Ellis, 191 Kempton, sec; Frank A Habicht, treas; annual meeting for the election of officers held the last Saturday of September, December March and June

NEW BEDFORD PROTECTING SOCIETY—Alfred Thornton, pres; Edmond L Wilde, sec and treas; meet last Monday in January, April, July and October in Board of Trade Rooms 97 William

NEW BEDFORD REFORM AND RELIEF ASSOCIATION, 180 Allen —Betsey B Winslow, pres; Mrs H A Jahn, treas; Mrs S Emma Perry, sec; meet first Tuesday of each month at 180 Allen

NEW BEDFORD TEACHERS BENEFIT ASSOCIATION, organized March 20, 1891, incorporated June 21, 1893 meet on request

NEW BEDFORD TYPOGRAPHICAL UNION NO 267, I T U— Hartley Spencer, pres; A W Bradbury, sec, Channing Wilde, treas, meet third Friday of each month at Labor Temple

NEW BEDFORD VETERAN FIREMEN'S ASSOCIATION COLUMBIAN NO 5—John I Byrant, pres; Robert N B Doane, sec, John H Bryant, fin sec; John A W Burgess, treas meet first Wednesday of each month at Veteran Firemen's hall High cor Foster

NEW BEDFORD HOME FOR AGED, 396 Middle, incorporated, Jan 20, 1902—Elizabeth C Carter, pres; Mrs H A Scarborough, treas; Flossie May Freedom, clerk; meet second Friday of each month at 396 Middle

NEW BEDFORD ORPHANS' HOME, Taber, organized 1842—For Orphans of both sexes; about 40 inmates; Dr Anna W Croacher, pres; Mrs H L Delano, sec; Helen H Allen, treas; Board of mgrs meet last Saturday of each month at 427 County

NORTH END GUILD, established 1888, Wamsutta blk, Hazard—William E Hatch, pres; Augusta Thornton, sec; Mrs Charles D Prescott, treas; meet second Thursday of each month

NURSES HOME AND REGISTRY 321 Union—Rebecca Chituk, head matron

OLD DARTMOUTH HISTORICAL SOCIETY, 37 N Water—Edmund Wood, pres; William A Mackie, treas; William A Wing, sec

POLISH NATIONAL ALLIANCE —Eugene Javorek, pres; John Rymut sec; Mik Bryda, treas; meet first Monday of each month at 67 Washburn

PROVISION CLERKS' BENEFIT ASSOCIATION, incorporatd 1893—Herbert W Davidson, pres; James L Manning, rec sec; John J Crompton, treas; meet first and third Tuesday of each month at 36 Pleasant

ST JOSEPH''S HOSPITAL—Convent of Sisters of Mercy, 261 Pleasant cor Campbell

ST LUKE' HOSPITAL, Page cor Allen, Incorporated 1884—Charles W Clifford, pres; Thomas S Hathaway, vice-pres; James P Francis, treas; Charles M Hussey, sec; Stella Sampson, supt; Gertrude F Webster, asst supt; a private charity established 1884, 108 beds This hospital has a training school of nurses and graduates a class yearly Quarterly meeting second Friday of Feb, May Aug and November

ST MARY'S HOME 594 Kempton corner Liberty, organized 1893 for orphans and the aged of both sexes; about 180 inmates, conducted by the Sisters of St Francis

TEXTILE COUNCIL, 112 William —Peter Cairn, pres; John Hobin, sec; Thomas Moriarty, treas; meet second Monday of each month at 62½ Purchase

THE TEACHERS ANNUITY GUILD—New Bedford Branch—Miss N Emma Slack, pres; Isabella Luscomb, sec; Lucreita N Smith, treas; treas; meet annually at High school during month of February

UNION FOR GOOD WORKS, 12 Market—Oliver Prescott, pres; Morris Brownell, sec; James P Francis, treas

UNITED NATIONAL ASSOCIATION OF POST OFFICE CLERKS, BRANCH 72—Samuel W Doran, pres; Wallace G Hathaway, vice-pres; Ralph G Leavitt, sec; Angelo L Fraga, treas; meet first Sunday of each month at P O

WARP TWISTERS UNION—John J Barton, pres; William Norwood, treas; William Hayhurst, sec; meet first Monday of each month at 138 Pleasant

WEAVERS' UNION, Instituted January 1891—Meet every Wednesday evening at 138 Pleasant

YOUNG MEN'S CHRISTIAN ASSOCIATION, William corner North Sixth; organized 1854, reorganized, 1867, incorporated 1883—Charles Mitchell, pres; Edward G Caster, gen sec; Howard M Wood, clerk; William E James, treas; Charles E Benton, auditor; Harold B Drew, educational sec; Charles B Brown, fin sec; Charles C Smith, boys sec; James Alcock, office sec; George T Ferguson, physical director; meet every Sunday afternoon from October to April; regular monthly meetings of the Board of Directors third Friday evening of each month, annual meeting second Tuesday in May

WOMEN'S AUXILIARY OF Y M C A—Mrs L E Keyes, pres; Mrs Mary E Benton, sec; Mrs Charles G Russell, treas; meet second Tuesday of each month from Sept to June inclusve at Y M C A building

YOUNG WOMEN'S CHRISTIAN ASSOCIATION, 66 Spring—Eloise A Hafford, pres; Mrs Maria Thornton, sec; Mrs Frederick Taber, treas; Florence Smith, gen sec; meeting of the Board of Directors third Tuesday of each month

FRENCH SOCIETIES

ASSOCIATION DE BIENFAISANCE ET SECOUR MUTUEL—Mrs Arthemise Brochu, pres; Mrs Melaine Bellenoit, sec; Mrs Ida Tetreault, treas; meet third Thursday of each month at Hacienda bldg

CERCLE DRAMATIQUE CANADIEN—J E Lemieux, pres; Pierre Mandeville, sec and treas; meet first Tuesday of each month at Sharpshooters' hall Hicks st

COUNCIL BLANCH DE CASTILE —Mrs Bussiere, pres; Mrs Mary L Dionne, sec and treas; meet third Monday of each month at Phelan hall

COUNCIL NO 3 LA LIQUE DES PATRIOTES DE L'UNION ST JEAN BAPTISTE D'AMERIQUE—Honorius Robitaille, pres; Louis J Bellnoit, sec; Ludger Caron, treas; meet fourth Wednesday of each month at Poirier hall

COUNCIL NO 76 STE CECILE DE L'UNION ST JEAN BAPTISTE D'AMERIQUE—R O Dion, pres; Delia J Girard, sec; Mrs Caroline La France, treas; meet second Wednes- of each month at Poirier bldg

COUR BONAVENTURE NO 25 FORESTIERS FRANCO AMERICANS—Joseph P Peletier, C F; Vital M Allain, fin sec; Adelard J Lachappelle, treas; meet first and third Tuesday of each month at Hacienda bldg

FRANCO AMERICAINE CONSEIL NO 1—J B Patnaude, pres; Wilfred Gonneville, sec; E P Berthiaume, treas; meet second and fourth Thursday of each month at Federation hall

FEDERATION FRANCO AMERICAINE GRAND CONSEIL NO 1—Joseph B Patnaude, pres; Wilfrid Gonneville, sec; E P Berthiaume treas; meet second and fourth Thursday of each month at Federation hall

FEDERATION FRANCO AMERICAN CONSEIL NO 2— Noe Caouette, pres; George A J Lagasse, sec; E P Berthiaume, treas; meet second and fourth Wednesday of each month at Phelan's hall

FRANCS TIREURS (FRENCH SHARPSHOOTERS) SUPREME CONSEIL—meet second and fourth Wednesdays of each month at Phelan's hall

FRANCS TIREURS (FRENCH SHARPSHOOTERS) BRANCH NO 1—Edmond Dumas, pres; J M Roberts, sec; Antone Pichetti, treas; meet first and third Wednesday evenings of each month at Francs Tireurs bldg 70 Hicks

FRANCS TIREURS (FRENCH SHARPSHOOTERS) BRANCH NO 2—Odilon Rousseau, pres; Joseph Ménard, sec; M D Prevost, treas; meet second and fourth Thursday evenings at Meaney's hall S Water

LAGARDE DES FRANCS TIREURS—Prudent Coderre, capt; Firmin Lecompte, rec sec; Ernest Lamothe, treas; meet first Thursday of each month at Meaney's hall, South Water

LA GARDE D'HONNEUR—meet at St Anne's church

LA GARDE NATIONALE INDEPENDANTE—Alfred Lague, capt

LES ARTISANS, SUCCURSALE NO 35— Meet second and fourth Tuesdays of each month at Hacienda bldg

L'UNION CHORALE DES FRANCS TIREURS—Meet at 76 Hicks

SOCIETE DE L'ASSOMPTION D'ENTREMONT NO 5—meet second and fourth Mondays of each month at Poirier's hall

INCORPORATED COMPANIES ETC

ACUSHNET CO-OPERATIVE ASSOCIATION 213 Acushnet av

ACUSHNET CO-OPERATIVE BANK 125 Middle

ACUSHNET IRON CO, 229 North Water

ACUSHNET MILL CORP, foot of Delano

ACUSHNET SAW MILLS CO Mill road, Acushnet

AMERICAN CLOTHING CO 1029 Acushnet avenue

E ANTHONY & SONS (INCORPORATED), Pleasant corner Market, newspaper publishers and printers

AUTOMATIC TELEPHONE CO, 43 William

THE BAKER MACHINE CO, E Pope

BEACON MFG CO, end Purchase

BLACKMER CUT GLASS CO, 223 N Second

BOOTH MFG CO, E French av

BRISTOL COUNTY MUTUAL FIRE INSURANCE COMPANY, 205 Merchants Bank bldg Incorporated 1829

BRISTOL MANUFACTURING CORP, office 198 Coggeshall

BUTLER MILL, Ruth cor Cleveland

CENTRAL UNION STORE, 11 N Sixth

CITY COAL COMPANY, Front cor Middle

CITY MFG CORPORATION, foot of Grinnell

CONSOLIDATED MEAT AND GROCERY CO 163 Union

CONTINENTAL WOOD SCREW CO, 8 Hazard's lane

CRESCENT MFG CO, Kempton

DARTMOUTH AND WESTPORT ST RAILWAY CO, Purchase cor William

DARTMOUTH MFG CORP, Cove bey Harbor

DAVIS Z B CORP, 3 E Pope

DENISON BROTHERS COMPANY, foot Hillman
FIRST NATIONAL BANK, 110 Union
THE F W FRANCIS CIGAR AND TOBACCO CO, 164 Union
GARFIELD & PROCTOR COAL CO, foot of Hillman
GATENBY & SWIFT, 33 N Water
GOSNOLD MILLS CO, Orchard (S) cor Cove rd
GRINNELL MANUFACTURING CORPORATION, Kilburn cor N Front
HATHAWAY AND MACKENZIE GRAIN CO The 748 Purchase
HATHAWAY MANUFACTURING CO, S Front near Gifford
HIRST E P CO, 28-32 N Water
HOLMES MANUFACTURING CO, E French av
HOME WASHING CO, 111 Myrtle
KILBURN MILL, W French av
KIRBY GEORGE JR PAINT CO, 10-14 Wall
LA FONTAINE BRAIDING CO, 85 Whitman
LAMBETH ROPE CORPORATION, Tarkiln Hill rd
LOWE S C SUPPLY CO (INC), 87 Union
MANOMET MILLS, Riverside av cor Manomet
THE MECHANICS NATIONAL BANK, 47 Purchase
MERCHANTS NATIONAL BANK, William cor Purchase
MERCURY PUBLISHING CO, 112 Union
MORSE TWIST DRILL AND MACHINE CO, 100 Fifth
MOUNT PLEASANT BANDING CORP, Hathaway rd n Mt Pleasant
NASHAWENA MILLS CO, Belleville av n Belleville rd
NEILD MFG CORP, Nash rd cor Brook
NEW BEDFORD CO-OPERATIVE BANK, 125 Middle
NEW BEDFORD CORDAGE CO, 131 Court
NEW BEDFORD COTTON MILLS CORP, 295 Phillips av
NEW BEDFORD DRY GOODS CO, 182 Union
NEW BEDFORD EMERGENCY HOSPITAL, 194 Purchase
NEW BEDFORD FISH CO, Rotch (North) and Merrill's wharves
NEW BEDFORD FIVE CENTS SAVINGS BANK, 37 Purchase
NEW BEDFORD GAS AND EDISON LIGHT CO, 125 Middle
NEW BEDFORD ICE CO, 12 School
NEW BEDFORD INSTITUTION FOR SAVINGS, 174-178 Union
NEW BEDFORD MARTHA'S VINEYARD & NANTUCKET STEAMBOAT CO, office 7 Commercial
NEW BEDFORD OPERA HOUSE CO, 249-253 Union
THE NEW BEDFORD SAFE DEPOSIT AND TRUST CO, 61 William
THE NEW BEDFORD TEXTILE SCHOOL, 303-331 Purchase
THE NEW BEDFORD TOW BOAT CO, office Merrill's wharf
NEW ENGLAND COTTON YARN CO, mills Bennett, N B Spinning Co and Rotch
NEW BEDFORD & ONSET ST RY CO, office Purchase cor William
NEW BEDFORD SHUTTLE CO, 6 Elm
NEW BEDFORD STORAGE WAREHOUSE, 352 Sawyer
NONQUITT SPINNING CO, Belleville av near Hatch
OLD COLONY BOX CO, Nash rd cor Church
ONEKO WOOLEN MILLS, end Purchase
PAGE MFG CO, Cove rd cor Bonney
THE PAIRPOINT CORPORATION, Prospect cor Howland, Pairpoint Mfg Co, Mt Washington Glass Co, New Bedford Paper Co Consolidated
PIERCE MANUFACTURING CORP, Belleville av cor Sawyer
POTOMSKA MILLS CORP, 774 S Water
PURITAN LAUNDRY CO, 298 Acushnet av
QUISSETT MILL, Grinnell
J C RHODES & CO INC, 123 Front
SHARP MFG CO, Dartmouth c Rockdale av
SMITH BROS INC, 777 Purchase
THE SOUTHERN MASS TELEPHONE CO, 57 N Second
SOULE MILL, end Sawyer
THE J V SPARE DRY GOODS CO, 41 Purchase
STANDARD RING TRAVELER CO, 6 Elm
STEIGER DUDGEON CO, 185-187 Union and 9-19 Purchase

TABER MILL, Coffin av cor Church

TAUNTON-NEW BEDFORD COPPER CO, N Front rear Wamsutta Mills

THE UNION STREET RAILWAY CO, Purchase cor William

.VALVOLINE OIL CO, ft North

UNION SHOE CO, 120 Purchase

VAUGHAN UNDERTAKING CO, 294 Purchase

WAMSUTTA MILLS, Wamsutta

WEEDEN MFG CO, 152 N Water

F W WENTWORTH COMPANY, 211 Union

WHITMAN MILLS, Coffin av at the river

THE WILKINSON CO INC, 158 Purchase

THE CHARLES F WING CO INC, 34-38 Purchase

WOOD P F BOILER WORKS INC, 32 Commercial

RAILROAD

NEW YORK, NEW HAVEN & HARTFORD RAILROAD CO, Old Colony system; station foot Pearl

TEXTILE INDUSTRY INFORMATION

Name.	Location.	No. Mils.	Capital	Spindles.	Looms.	Employees.
Acushnet Mills	South	2	$1,000,000	105,336	3,500	1,280
Beacon Mfg Co	North	1	487,000	6,528	232	340
Booth Mill	South	1	1,250,000	52,000	1,300	500
Bristol Mill	North	1	1,000,000	67,240	1,954	650
Butler Mill	South	1	1,500,000	100,000	2,100	850
City Mfg Co	South	2	750,000	65,312		650
Dartmouth Mfg Co	South	3	1,800,000	202,512	5,600	2,000
Gosnold Mfg Co	South	2	1,650,000	3,250	3,200	1,100
Grinnell Mfg Co	North	2	1,000,000	128,000	3,135	1,100
Hathaway Mfg Co	South	2	800,000	108,976	3,500	1,280
Holmes Mfg Co	South	1	1,200,000	52,164		725
Kilburn Mills	South	2	1,500,000	119,120		1,100
Manomet Mills	North	2	2,000,000	126,288		1,350
Nashawena Mills	North	2	2,500,000	125,000	4,000	1,600
Neild Mfg Co	North	1	800,000	54,400	1,320	600
N B Cotton Mills Co	North	1	1,100,000	65,000	1,400	750
•N E Cotton Yarn Co						
Depts 1-4	North	5		183,892		2,248
Depts 7-8	South	2		51,564		425
Depts 9-10	Centre	2		38,464		527
Nonquitt Spinning Co	North	2	2,400,000	130,000		1,150
Page Mfg Co	South	1	1,000,000	63,000	1,740	650
Pierce Mfg Co	North	2	600,000	116,008	3,592	1,200
Pierce Bros Limited	North	2	700,000	51,440	1,154	325
Potomska Mills	South	2	1,200,000	108,000	2,614	1,200
Quisset Mill	South	1	1,250,000	6,000		800
Sharp Mfg Co	Southwest	1	1,500,000	80,000		650
Soule Mill	North	1	1,260,000	93,000	2,300	950
Taber Mill	North	1	1,300,000	70,720	1,600	800
Wamsutta Mills	North	9	3,000,000	228,000	4,300	2,100
Whitman Mills	North	2	2,000,000	149,500	4,930	1,800
Crescent Mfg Co (silk)	West	1	65,000	1,000	107	75
Totals,		60	$36,612,000	2,764,202	53,378	31,275

•N E Cotton Yarn Co capital not included. This company has $3,900,000 common and $2,000,000 preferred.

JUSTICES OF THE PEACE AND AND *NOTARIES PUBLIC

**Justice of the Peace and also Notary Public
***Justice of the Peace authorized to solemnize Marriages
****Justice of the Peace authorized to solemnize Marriages and also Notary Public

Aindow John H
Alden George N
Allen Walter S
Almy Walter C
Ashley Charles S Jr
Ashley Roland R
Ashley William L
**Auger Asa
Baker Benjamin
Baker Daniel W
**Bannon Edward T
**Barney Benjamin B
Barney Edwin L Jr
Barney Lawrence H
Barrows Frank C
Bassett Charles M
*Boucher Joseph Z
Bourne Standish
**Briggs Justus A Jr
Brock George P
***Brooks Nathan B
Brown Charles W
Brown Edward S
Brown Frederick R
*Brown John C
**Brownell Morris R
**Caswell William F
Chase William R
Chausse Aldege
Clarke A Edwin
Clarke Edward Everett
**Clifford Charles W
**Clifford John H
**Clifford Walter
**Cook Otis S
Cook William S
Cooke Robert
*Cormier Reuben S
*Cory Daniel W
Covell William P
Coxen Harold M
**Crapo Henry H
Crapo William W
*Cruz Manuel G
Cunniff Thomas A
**Dade Isaiah C
*Da Terra Joseph I
*Demers John B
Desautels Stanislas
**Dexter Lemuel LeB
*Dias Joseph 2nd
Dignam James
*Dixon Henry H
**Doran James P
Douglass Edwin A
Driscoll Daniel F
Driscoll Patrick J
*Dudgeon Samuel
England George
Finnell John H
*Fisher Merton C
Fitzgerald William L
**Francis James P
Francis John B Jr
Francis Vincent
Franks John
Fuller Frederick S
**Gardiner George N
**Gauthier Joseph A
**Geils Gerrette Jr
Gibson John
*Goggin John F
Gomes Manuel
**Goodspeed Alex McL
Hadley Eugene J
Hartley John H
*Haskell Edward P
Haskins Elmore P
Hathaway James H
Hawes William C
Healey Thomas F
Heron Charles T
**Hervey Homer W
Hess Christian J
**Hitch Mayhew R
**Holmes Edward W
Holmes Ezra
**Holt James W
Howe Benjamin F
Howland Henry
*Hoye James F
**James Alfred S
**James Clarence H
*James William E
**Jenney Lester W
Jones J Edwin
Jourdain Edwin B
Kelley Charles S

Kelley William E
**Kenney Joseph T
Kirby Albert C
Knapp Robert E
**Knowles Henry S
**Knowles Richard L
*Lemerise Arthur G
**Lewis Edgar R
Lilley George E
Lowney John B
Luce Frederick C
**MacCord William A
Mackie William A
Macomber Pardon A
**MacPhail Walter S
Macy Peleg S
Marchant Everett L
McAuliffe John J
McCann William
McDonnell Michael
McGurk Charles J
Milliken Allen W
**Milliken Frank A
**Mitchell Charles
Murphy William H
**O'Brien Timothy F
**Oliver John B
Owen James W
Paquette Jean B
Paquette Joseph
Paquette Joseph O
Parker William C
Parlow Henry B
Paul John W
Perry Ebenezer S
**Perry Laurence S
Perry William B
Phelps Isaac W
**Philips George R
Pierce Edward T
**Potter George H
Prescott Oliver
*Prevost Moise D
Price Charles R
****Raulino Antonio J
Remington Walter H B
*Richmond Charles N
**Rogers Frank L
Rosenberg S
Ross Samuel
Russell Allen Jr
Russell Henry C
Russell John E
**Sanders Henry V
Sanders William
*Sanford Gardner T
Sawyer Charles P
Saxon George E
**Serpa Charles N
**Shaw J E Norton
**Sherman Clifford P
*Simoes Jose F
**Smith William B
**Sparrow Frank M
**Stetson Eliot D
**Stetson Frederick D
Stetson Thomas M
Sullavou Emanuel
Swift Merton W
*Sylvia William K
**Taber Frederick
Taber Robert W
**Taylor William T
**Terry Robert A
Thompson Thomas
Thomson Pardon G
*Thornton Alfred
*Thorup William M
Turner William F
Vaughan Harry C
Vera Frank Jr
*Walsh Joseph
Warren Joseph C
*Washburn Frederick A
Weeden George F
Whalley Edmund J
Willcox Lemuel T
**Williams Manuel A
**Wolfson Fisher
**Woodward Henry E
**Worth Henry B

National Bank of Fairhaven

INCORPORATED 1831

MAIN, CORNER CENTRE STREET
FAIRHAVEN

Telephone 934-1

LEVI M. SNOW, President GEORGE B. LUTHER, Cashier
EDWARD T. PIERCE, Clerk

CAPITAL = $120,000

DIRECTORS

CHARLES H. MORTON, Chairman
LEVI M. SNOW HENRY H. ROGERS, JR. THOMAS A. TRIPP
GEORGE B. LUTHER EDWARD G. SPOONER

DISCOUNT DAY, MONDAY

Fairhaven Institution for Savings

INCORPORATED 1832

19 Centre Street, Fairhaven

Telephone 934-2

THOMAS A. TRIPP, President WALTER H. JUDD, Vice-President
C. H. MORTON, Treasurer

BOARD OF INVESTMENT

Thomas A. Tripp Lewis E. Bentley Levi M. Snow George B. Luther Walter H. Judd

TRUSTEES

Job C. Tripp, Charles H. Morton, Levi M. Snow, Thomas A. Tripp, Daniel W. Deane, George B. Luther, Arthur C. Wheaton, Elisha S. Whiting, Jr., Samuel S. Bumpus, Walter H. Judd, Joseph Pettee, Jr., Edward G. Spooner, Lewis E. Bentley, Horace K. Nye, Charles D. Waldron, William B. Gardner, David N. Kelley, Lemuel LeBaron Dexter.

ATLAS TACK COMPANY

PLEASANT STREET, FAIRHAVEN Telephone New Bedford 91

The Largest and Oldest Manufacturers of Tacks and Nails in the World.

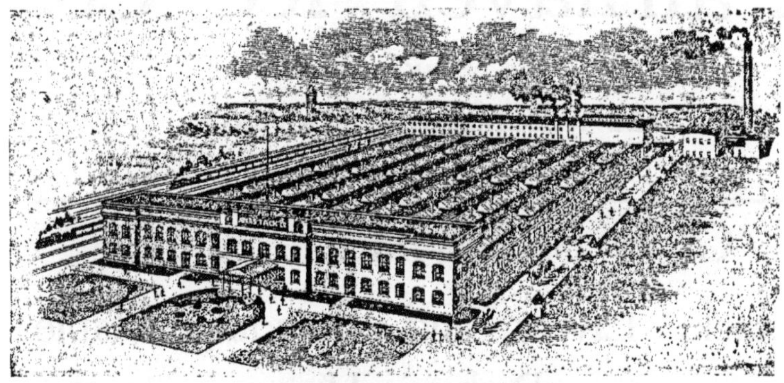

SUCCESSORS TO

B. Hobart, 1810; Albert Field, 1827; Arby Field, 1830; Samuel Loring, 1842; B. Hobart and Son, 1848; Jude Field, 1851; Taunton Tack Co., 1854; Wm. S. Guerineau, 1855; A. Field & Co., 1855; A. Field & Son, 1859; Dunbar, Hobart & Whidden, 1865; Old Colony Rivet Co., 1866; American Tack Co., 1867; Albert Field Tack Co., 1869; Loring and Parks, 1886; Dunbar, Hobart & Co., 1887; Atlas Tack Corp'n., 1891; Atlas Tack Co., 1897

Cable Address, "Tamarind," Fairhaven

Phoenix Poultry Yards

Farms at Fairhaven and Eastham, Mass.

Annual Production 20,000 Chickens

Broilers, Roasters and Eggs

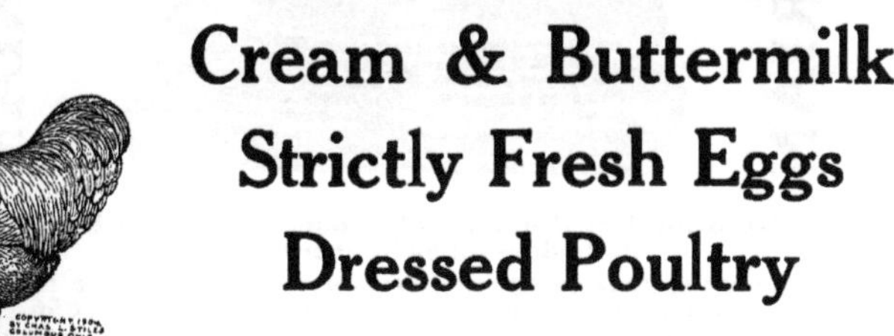

Cream & Buttermilk

Strictly Fresh Eggs

Dressed Poultry

PURE CREAM A SPECIALTY

A. G. & G. F. BRALEY 50 CEDAR STREET, FAIRHAVEN

Tel. 746-5

Established 1842

Fairhaven Ice Co.

L. S. CLARK, Proprietor

428 Washington St., Fairhaven

Telephone, New Bedford, 1484-13

C. F. BROWNELL & CO.

Hack, Livery and Boarding Stable

Dealers in Hay

63 and 65 Main Street, Fairhaven

Telephone Connection First Class Teams Terms Reasonable

MADE IN NEW ENGLAND

TYRIAN AUTOMOBILE INNERTUBES

TYRIAN

TYRIAN

are made from the finest quality of rubber and are strictly first grade up to date tubes in every respect.

Insist upon having your garage man supply you with these tubes. They are fully guaranteed by a house established in 1856.

If you cannot get them at your supply house, write direct to

TYER RUBBER CO.

ANDOVER, MASS., - U. S. A.

FAIRHAVEN STREET DIRECTORY 1911

(Copyright 1911 by W. A. Greenough & Co.)

ADAMS from Spring to 345 Main

1	3	Spring
18		Christian
40	43	Bridge
0		Huttleston avenue
	91	Holcomb
	125	Hicks
146		North
	155	Long road
228	227	Ball
	233	Wilding
240		Briggs
	247	Brown
	259	East Coggeshall
0	265	Main

ALDEN ROAD from Washington opposite Sconticut Neck road to Acushnet line

0	0	Wash
0	0	Bridge
	253	Boston Hill road
0		Long road
0		Morton
0	0	Acushnet line

ALLEN from 67 Fort to 48 Green

ALMY from 109 Bridge

ALPINE AVENUE from Acushnet river to 392 Main

0	0	Acushnet river
0	0	Sycamore
0	0	Main

ATLAS from Farm Field lane to 11 Allen

0	0	Farm Field lane
	10	West Allen
0		East Allen

BALL from Main opposite cemetery to Burgess avenue

0	0	Main
0	0	Adams
0	0	Burgess avenue

BEACH from Howland road to Kendrick avenue

BEACON from end Fort to the beacon

BENNETT HILL on Cedar Island Sconticut Neck road

BLACKBURN from 411 Main

BLOSSOM HILL Washington Weeden and Gelatt road

BOSTON HILL ROAD from 253 Alden road east to Oak Grove lane

0	0	Alden road
0	0	Mill road
0	0	Oak Grove lane

BRIDGE from Acushnet river near N B & F bridge to New Boston road

0	1	Acushnet river
8	7	Middle
16	15	Main
24	25	William
50	49	Green
	61	Mulberry
	69	Jefferson
82	81	Adams
	109	Almy
	119	Delano
126		Holcomb
0	0	Alden road
0	0	Mill road
0	0	New Boston road

BRIGGS from opposite 314 Main to 240 Adams

BROWN from 247 Adams to beyond Burgess avenue Oxford Heights

0 0 Adams
0 11 Spruce
0 0 Burgess avenue

BRYANT from 121 Spring to 144 Washington

BURGESS AVENUE from Ball to beyond Brown

0 0 Ball
0 0 Wilding
0 0 Brown

CEDAR from opposite 25 Fort to Farm Field lane

0 0 Fort
0 Green
0 Laurel
0 Chestnut
65 Oak avenue
0 0 Farm Field lane

CENTRE from Acushnet river at Handy's wharf to Hitch

0 0 Acushnet river
0 0 Water
0 0 Middle
18 19 Main
36 35 William
46 47 Walnut
52 53 Green
64 65 Laurel
74 75 Chestnut
82 83 Pleasant
96 95 Rotch
0 0 Summer
0 0 Hitch

CHERRY from Acushnet river at Point Comfort to Cooke

0 0 Acushnet river
0 0 Pilgrim avenue
0 0 Lafayette
12 13 Oxford
23 North
30 0 Cooke

CHERRY 2nd from Acushnet river to 432 Main Villa Park

0 0 Acushnet river
0 0 Sycamore
0 0 Main

CHESTNUT from opposite 45 Cedar to 53 Spring

0 0 Cedar
0 0 Cottage
0 0 Farm Field lane
0 0 Church
86 85 South
0 0 Union
0 0 Centre
124 123 Washington
140 141 Rodman
0 0 Spring

CHRISTIAN from Green to 18 Adams

0 0 Green
16 17 Mulberry
34 33 Jefferson
0 0 Adams

CHURCH from 1 Main to beyond Pleasant

0 0 Main
0 0 Fort
0 William
0 0 Green
46 47 Laurel
0 0 Chestnut
0 0 Pleasant

CLARK from Harding

COOKE from end Cherry to 222 Main

COTTAGE from 35 Fort to beyond Laurel

0 0 Fort
0 0 Green
0 0 Laurel

COWEN from 83 Middle to 104 Main

DAVIS from Harding

DELANO from 110 Spring to 119 Bridge

DOVER from Main near Maitland to Acushnet river

EAST ALLEN from 57 Pleasant to Atlas

0 0 Pleasant
11 Atlas

EAST GOGGESHALL from 259 Adams

EGYPT LANE from 141 Washington to the cove

ELDRIDGE LANE from 38 Water to Acushnet river

FARM FIELD LANE from 49 Green to the cove

0 0 Green
0 0 Pleasant
0 0 Laurel
0 Atlas
0 0 Chestnut
0 Cedar
0 0 Cove

FERRY from Water to 16 Main

0 R R depot
0 Water
0 Middle
0 0 Main

FORT from Beacon to William
0 Beacon
25 Cedar
35 Cottage
67 Allen
88 89 Church
0 103 South
105 Walnut

GARRISON from 45 Howland road to Kendrick avenue

GELATT ROAD from 623 Washington to Little Bay

GREEN from Cedar near Fort to Huttleston avenue
0 0 Cedar
0 0 Cottage
48 Allen
49 Farm Field lane
70 69 Church
84 83 South
96 97 Union
0 0 Centre
124 123 Washington
141 Rodman
144 145 Spring
0 Christian
190 189 Bridge
0 0 Huttleson avenue

HARDING from 448 Main to beyond Sycamore
0 Clark
0 Davis

HAWTHORN from 427 Main

HEAD OF RIVER ROAD changed to Alden road

HICKS from 125 Adams

HITCH from 113 Washington to the railroad
0 0 Washington
0 0 Centre
0 0 N Y, N H & H R R

HOLCOMB from 126 Bridge to 91 Adams

HOWLAND ROAD from Acushnet river to 330 Main
0 0 Acushnet avenue
0 Beach
0 River avenue
0 Oak
0 0 Sycamore
45 Garrison
55 Orchard
0 0 Main

HUTTLESTON AVENUE from Main opposite N B & F Bridge to Adams
0 0 Main
0 William
0 Green
0 0 Adams

ISLE OF MARSH off Point Comfort Oxford

JACOB'S NECK end Sconticut Neck road

JACOB'S POINT east end Sconticut Neck road

JEFFERSON from 66 Spring to opposite 70 Bridge
2 1 Spring
16 15 Christian
0 0 Bridge

KELLEY'S LANE from 32 Water to the wharf

KENDRICK AVENUE from 298 Main at Riverside cemetery to the Acushnet River
0 0 Main
0 Orchard
0 Garrison
0 Sycamore
0 Oak
0 River avenue
0 Beach
0 0 Acushnet river

LAFAYETTE from opposite 2 West to 198 Main
2 West
16 15 Cherry
36 35 Main

LAUREL from Cedar to 41 Spring
0 0 Cedar
0 0 Cottage
44 0 Farm Field lane
68 71 Church
84 83 South
0 0 N Y, N H & H R R
98 97 Union
0 0 Centre
124 123 Washington
142 141 Rodman
0 0 Spring

LINDEN AVENUE from 163 Main to Linden Park

LINDEN PARK rear 163 Main

LONG ROAD from 155 Adams to Head of River road

MADISON SQUARE junction Spring and Washington

MAGNOLIA AVENUE from Acushnet river to Main opposite Hawthorn
0 0 Acushnet river
0 0 Sycamore
0 0 Main

MAIN from 1 Church through Oxford Village to Acushnet line
1 Church
13 South
16 Ferry
30 31 Union
42 39 Centre
64 65 Washington
73 Spring
92 Pease
104 83 Cowen
116 117 Bridge
130 N B and Fairhaven bridge
131 Huttleston avenue
163 Linden avenue
163r Linden park
192 Pilgrim avenue
198 Lafayette
206 207 Oxford
214 215 North
222 Cooke
248 Taber
256 Wood
0 Riverside cemetery
298 Kendrick avenue
0 Ball
315 Briggs
330 Howland road
345 Adams
368 Winsor
0 0 Morton
0 0 Morgan
392 Alpine avenue
0 Dover
397 Maitland
411 Blackburn
0 Veranda avenue
427 Hawthorn
428 Magnolia avenue
432 Cherry 2nd
448 Harding
0 485 Acushnet line

MAITLAND from 397 Main

MANHATTAN AVENUE from Sconticut Neck road to Pope Beach

MIDDLE from Ferry to N B and Fairhaven bridge
2 1 Ferry
14 15 Union
26 25 Centre
42 41 Washington
72 71 Pease
83 Cowen
98 97 Bridge
0 0 N B & F Bridge

MILL ROAD from 404 Washington to Boston Hill road
0 0 Washington
0 0 Bridge
0 0 Boston Hill road

MORGAN from Acushnet river across Main

MORTON from Sycamore to Alden road
0 0 Sycamore
0 0 Main
0 0 Alden road

MULBERRY from 54 Spring to 61 Bridge
18 19 Christian
0 0 Bridge

NASKATUCKET VILLAGE Washington between Mill road and Weeden road

NEW BOSTON ROAD from Washington at Blossom Hill to Acushnet line
0 0 Washington
0 Bridge
0 0 Acushnet line

NORTH from 23 Cherry to 140 Adams
2 1 Cherry
14 15 Main
84 83 Adams

OAK from Howland road to Kendrick av

OAK AVENUE from 65 Cedar

OAK GROVE LANE from end Boston Hill road to Turkey Grove

ORCHARD from 55 Howland road to Kendrick avenue

OXFORD from Acushnet river at Point Comfort to beyond Main
0 0 Acushnet river
7 West
24 25 Cherry
50 49 Main

OXFORD VILLAGE at Oxford and Lafayette

PEASE from Acushnet river to 92 Main
0 0 Acushnet river
8 9 Middle
0 0 Main

PILGRIM AVENUE from 192 Main to Cherry

PLEASANT from Farm Field lane to Washington
0 0 Farm Field lane
57 Allen
0 0 Church
0 0 South
92 93 Union
102 103 Centre
0 119 Washington

POINT COMFORT foot Lafayette
POPE BEACH Manhattan avenue off Sconticut Neck road
POPE BEACH ROAD from Sconticut Neck road to Little Bay
POTTER'S LANE from Sconticut Neck road below the Union Chapel to Buzzards Bay
RIVER AVENUE from Howland road to Kendrick avenue
RODMAN from 141 Green to beyond Summer
4 5 Green
10 9 Laurel
0 0 Chestnut
0 0 Rotch
49 Summer
ROSELAWN from opposite 196 Washington
ROTCH from 90 Union to Spring opposite Adams
2 Union
0 0 Centre
32 31 Washington
48 49 Rodman
0 89 Spring
SCONTICUT NECK ROAD from opposite Washington down Sconticut Point
0 0 Washington
0 Pope Beach road
0 Manhattan avenue
0 Whitfield lane
0 Potter's lane
0 Jacob's Neck
0 0 Sconticut Point
0 West Island
SOUTH from 13 Main to Pleasant
SPRING from 73 Main to 212 Washington
0 3 Main
10 9 William
17 Walnut
32 31 Green
41 Laurel
53 Chestnut
54 Mulberry
66 Jefferson
84 Adams
0 Rotch
110 Delano
121 Bryant
0 Temple place
0 0 Washington
SPRUCE from 6 Wilding to 11 Brown Oxford Heights
SUMMER from end of Centre to 49 Rodman
0 0 Centre
0 0 Washington
44 45 Rodman
SYCAMORE from Kendrick avenue to Acushnet line
0 0 Kendrick avenue
0 0 Howland road
0 0 Winsor
0 0 Alpine avenue
0 0 Veranda avenue
0 0 Magnolia avenue
0 0 Cherry 2nd
0 161 Harding
0 0 Acushnet line
TABER from 248 Main to Acushnet river
TEMPLE PLACE from 180 Washington to Spring
TURKEY GROVE end Boston Hill road and Oak Grove lane
UNION from Acushnet river at Union wharf to 2 Rotch
0 0 Acushnet river
0 0 Water
0 0 Middle
12 13 Main
28 27 William
32 33 Walnut
42 41 Green
48 49 Laurel
0 0 Chestnut
0 Pleasant
90 Rotch
VERANDA AVENUE from Main opposite Hawthorn to Acushnet river
0 0 Main
0 0 Sycamore
0 0 Acushnet river
VILLA PARK VILLAGE foot Harding next Acushnet line
WALNUT from 105 Fort to 17 Spring
0 1 Fort
0 0 Union
24 23 Centre
0 Washington
58 57 Spring
WASHINGTON from 45 Water to Mattapoisett line
3 Water
8 9 Middle
14 19 Main
0 0 William
34 33 Walnut
48 47 Green
60 61 Laurel
70 71 Chestnut
0 Pleasant
94 93 Rotch

Washington—con
102 101 Summer
113 Hitch
141 Egypt lane
144 Bryant
180 Temple place
0 Roselawn
212 Spring
0 0 Madison square
0 Alden road
0 Sconticut Neck road
404 Mill road
475 Weeden road
0 New Boston road
623 Gelatt road
774 773 Mattapoisett line
WATER from Ferry opposite N Y, N H & H R R depot to 3 Washington
2 0 Ferry
8 0 Granite wharf
0 0 Union
22 City Marine Ry wharf
26 25 Centre
32 Kelley's lane
32r Kelley's wharf
38 Eldredge lane
45 Washington
WEEDEN ROAD from 745 Washington to Little Bay
WEST from Oxford to Acushnet river
0 Lafayette
WEST ALLEN from 10 Atlas to the cove
WEST ISLAND end Sconticut neck off Long Island
WHITEFIELD LANE from Sconticut Neck road to Little Bay
WIGWAM BEACH off Sconticut Neck road
WILDING from 233 Adams to Burgess avenue
0 0 Adams
0 Spruce
0 0 Burgess avenue
WILLIAM from end Fort to Huttleston avenue
2 3 Fort
14 15 Union
24 25 Centre
44 43 Washington
54 55 Spring
0 0 Bridge
0 0 Huttleston avenue
WINSOR from the Acushnet river to 368 Main
0 0 Acushnet river
0 0 Sycamore
0 0 Main
WOOD from 256 Main to Riverside cemetery

CEMETERIES

Naskatucket, Washington opposite Mill road
Riverside, Main between Kendrick avenue and Cooke, Thomas White, superintendent
Woodside, Main corner Morton

WHARVES AND BRIDGES

Atlas Tack Company r 40 Fort
Chace's 22 Water
City Marine Ry 22 Water
Coggeshall st Bridge end Howland road to Coggeshall N B
Delano's foot of Washington
Ellis' 60 Fort
Fairhaven Iron F Co's Water near Ferry
Granite 8 Water
Handy's foot of Centre
Kelley's rear 32 Water
N B and Fairhaven Bridge from Main opposite Huttleston avenue to North Second street N B
N Y, N H & H R R, Ferry
Smith's Boat Landing 80 Middle
Union, foot Union

BLOCKS, BUILDINGS, HALLS PARKS, ETC.

Academy Hall, Main near the bridge
Banquet Hall, Town Hall building
Cooke Memorial Park end Pilgrim av
Cushman Park junction Main, Bridge, Green and Spring
Fort Phoenix end Beacon
Harbor View, Beach end of Farm Field lane
Masonic Building, Main corner Centre
Masonic Hall, Main corner Centre
Millicent Public Library Building Centre corner William
National Bank Building 40-42 Main
Phoenix Block, 41 to 45 Main
Phoenix Hall, 41 Main
Town Hall, Town Hall Building
Town Hall Building, Centre corner Walnut
Veterans' Hall, Union corner Water
Willow Park, Fort corner William

WILLIAM P. SHAW PROPRIETORS JESSE S. GIFFORD

PHOENIX GARAGE

STRICTLY FIREPROOF PUBLIC GARAGE

AUTOMOBILES REPAIRED, STORED, CLEANED AND PAINTED

BEST WORKMANSHIP AND SATISFACTION GUARANTEED

OPEN DAY AND NIGHT

OFF MAIN ST., NORTH OF PHOENIX BLOCK

FAIRHAVEN, MASS.

BELL 1451-2

FAIRHAVEN DIRECTORY

1911

Adams Express Co H D Barker agent 22½ Middle
" John b 99 Pleasant [liam
Adshead Frank machinist h 39 Wil-
Aiken Albert C constable h 78 Centre
Akin Archie C florist P Murray's b 111 Chestnut [b do
" Bartholomew G artist 14 Oxford
" Charles T clerk P O b 14 Oxford
" Durfee D farmer h 474 Washington [Oxford
" Elizabeth E widow Eben Jr h 14
" Ellen H b 10 William
" Fred W molder h 19 Rodman
" Fred W Jr removed to New Bedford
" Henry T carpenter h Mill road
" Ida Mrs tack maker h 111 Chestnut
" John Jr core maker h 34 William
" Mary E manicuring 14 Oxford h do [Mill road
" Prince S carpenter b H T Akin's
Alberghini Frank laborer h Kelley's wharf [wharf
" Philip tack maker b Kelley's
Albiston Roger W farmer h 181 Washington [14 Washington
Alden Clinton W plumber 55 Main h
" George L farmer h 254 Washington
" Gordon shoemaker rms 43 Cedar
" William K laborer h r 50 Spring
Aldrich Mabel Mrs h 46 William
" William N molder h 46 William
Allard Edwin A machinist h 343 Washington
" Joseph h Alden road
" Stephen W shoemaker b 343 Washington
Allen Bartlett 2ud machinist h 11 Lafayette [Neck road
" Charles E farmer h Sconticut
" Elizabeth M, Sarah E and Emily P h 30 Main
" Ella J h 72 Centre
" Fred R clerk Atlas Tack Co b 41 Fort
" George E removed from town
" Harriet nurse b 42 Church
" James M Jr boat builder 21 Oxford h 5 Lafayette
" Joseph H treasurer Nield Mill N B h 8 Walnut
" Lillie B teacher Rogers Annex school b 5 Lafayette [Main
" Mary B widow William H h 30
" Minnie L bookkeeper b 5 Lafayette [Church
" Nathan P boat builder h 42
" Pearson fixer h 11 Wilding
" Stephen M drill maker h 10 Spring
" Warren L carpenter h 52 Cedar
" William M commercial traveler h 30 Main
Allerson Joseph h Alden road [Allen
Allesandra John laborer h 20 West
Allmond Benjamin G molder b 20 Adams

Almeida August laborer h Hitch
Almy George L nightman 56 Main h 153 Green [school h 44 Water
Alton B Joseph janitor Old High.
" William E steamfitter h 44 Water
Alves Joseph eyelet maker h 139 Laurel
" Manuel laborer h Mill road
" Mary widow Joseph F h 139 Laurel [h do
Amaral Manuel D express 3 Spring
Amelia Rosa widow b Sconticut Neck road
Ames Florence S teacher of English High school b 55 William
Amos Joseph operator h 111 Spring
Anderson Albert coachman H H Rogers Jr h 25 Chestnut
" Oscar D engineer F W Co Mill road h do [Middle
" William O clerk Atlas Tack Co b
Andrews Frank laborer h 13 Roselawn [keeper 14 Middle
" Lizzie A widow Walter D house-
Anthony Joseph S mason h 33 Christian [Main
" Sarah C widow Edmund Jr h 192
Arnold Amanda M widow Rhodes h 123 Green [ing road h do
Arseneault Mark M carpenter Hard-
Ashton Herbert spinner h 57 Howland road [h 99 Bridge
Astin Hattie M widow William H
" Herbert H speeder b 99 Bridge
" William H driver b 43 Bridge
Athearn Susan E Mrs china decorator 162 Main h do
ATLAS TACK CO Pleasant near Church See page *683
Atwood Henrietta E died Nov 26 1909
" Lizzie h 27 Union
Audette Ulric farm hand h Oak Grove lane
Auky August weaver h Veranda av
Austin Albert I wood Laurel cor Spring h do [6 Jefferson
" Arthur H janitor Oxford school h
" Emily F widow John F h Sconticut Neck road [ington
" Harry S motorman b 544 Wash-
" Hiram A foreman h 544 Washington [road
" Loring M mason h 167 Alden
" Reuben A carpenter h 544 Washington [Allen
Avilla Frank fisherman h 14 West
Ayer Lefce teacher of German High school rms 3 William

Babbitt Annie A widow Isaac N h 43 Cedar
" Brothers (James M Babbitt) loom crank manufacturers 12 Main
" Elizabeth G widow Isaac N Jr h 85 Fort
" Isaac N steam specialties N B and assessor h 28 Laurel
" James M (Babbitt Brothers) h 35 Green
" Joseph W blacksmith h 25 Green
Babcock Raymond F machinists' apprentice b 141 Green [William
Backus Henry L cotton classer h 51
Baetseher Bernard De assistant pastor Sacred Heart R C church h East Coggeshall near Main
Bagnoche Octave laborer h 26 East Coggeshall [Bedford
Bailey James E removed to New
" William eyelet maker h 171 Adams [road cor Beach h do
Baillargeon Arthur grocer Howland
" Casimer laborer h Beach
" Nelson spinner b Beach
Baker Annie I widow Nehemiah b 70 Washington
" Charles carpenter h Taber
" Clarence J clerk Rotch corner Washington bds 19 Mulberry
" Edward E h 123 Green
" Edwin h Weeden road
" James B metal stripper h 51 Pleasant [21 Mulberry h 19 do
" James E furniture and repairer
" James G manager N B h 2 North
" John J foreman Atlas Tack Co h 103 Fort
" John L fisherman h Weeden road
" Josephine widow William b 51 Pleasant
" Lorenzo D carpenter h 50 Church
" Mary A housekeeper b 50 Cedar
" Samuel J tack worker h 51 Pleasant
" Winifred bookkeeper b 103 Fort
Baldwin Edward G painter h 15 Oxford
" James C 54 West Allen [ington
Ball William E foreman h 514 Wash-
Barlow James A engineer h 23 Middle
Barnes Edward farmer h Spring cor Washington
" Emily removed to New Bedford
Barney Herbert H express 63 Spring bds do
" Herbert W fruit h 63 Spring

Barrows Irving M draftsman b 22 Lafayette [ant
" John A mill operator h 123 Pleas-
" William H h 22 Lafayette
Bartlett Manuel fireman h 141 Laurel
Bassett Eli E removed to San Francisco California
" George A apparatus b Chestnut
" George M machinist h Chestnut
" Nellie removed to Plymouth
" see Bessette
Bates Benjamin M carpenter h 2 Lafayette [174 Adams
" Frank M carpenter 72 Main h
" Otis H carpenter h 218 Main
Battles Benjamin removed to Mvricks
Baudoin Louis N hairdresser 49 Main h 49 Bridge
Bauldry Lyman C foreman P Corporation N B h 27 Spring
Bayer Hyacinthe Rev assistant pastor St Joseph's R C church h 3 Adams
Bearse Mary F widow Elisha B bds 6 Lafayette
Beauregard Osias manager h 82 Union
Beebe Theodore Rev removed to Peabody [Tack Co rms 84 Green
Belding Edgar F sales dept Atlas
Bennett Albert N h Washington near Rotch
" Anna A died Oct 23 1910
" Charles L carpenter h 93 Laurel
" Clara h 199 Main
" Cordelia widow housekeeper 8 Middle [ford
" Eliza A widow Robert h 43 Ox-
" Mary L widow James h 83 Laurel
Benoit Albert L conductor bds 33 Alpine avenue
" Joseph h Alden road
" Joseph carpenter h Magnolia av
" Marshall carpenter h 33 Alpine av
Benson Addie F nurse h 580 Washington [ton
" Charles F farmer h 620 Washing-
Bentley Lewis E selectman and overseer poor h 252 Main
" Milton J b 252 Main
Bento Albert laborer h Hitch
Bernard Bert h 65 Washington
" Stanislas Rev assistant pastor St Joseph's R C church h 3 Adams
Besse Edward L machinist h 10 Cooke
" Eldred E removed from town
" John T farm foreman West Island h do [Middle
" Melissa A widow James T h 6
Bessette Pierre painter h Veranda av
" Pierre third hand h 24 Hicks
Betagh Bessie A stenographer Atlas Tack Co b 50 William
" Robert foreman Atlas Tack Co h 50 William
Bettencourt John E foundryman h 117 Washington
" Joseph engineer h 7 Walnut
Bigelow William H b 44 Summer
Bingham Allen R foreman P Corporation N B h 68 Laurel
" Ralph W box maker b 68 Laurel
Bisbee George H h 27 Middle
" Martin L billiards 25 Centre h 59 Main [Sycamore
Bissonette Ludger mill operator h 153
Black Antone tacker h 24 Middle
" Peter rigger b 52 Washington
Blackburn John A carpenter h Farm Field lane beyond Cedar
" William clerk at N B b Farm Field lane beyond Cedar
Blackwell Benjamin M carpenter b 103 Pleasant
Blackwelle Annie G dressmaker h 209 Main
" Frank L glass cutter h 209 Main
Blakely Charles mule spinner h 156 Sycamore
" John W laborer b 165 Sycamore
Blanchette Elzear oil 45 East Coggeshall h do [Fort
Bliss Alexander F eyelet maker h 41
" A Leonard (Bliss & Upjohn) h 10 Spring
" Malcolm G shoemaker b 41 Fort
" Mary M widow George N h 21 Washington
" & Upjohn (A L Bliss and W F Upjohn) painters 107 Main
Blossom Benjamin F carpenter bds Mrs Paulina Blossom's Bridge
" Franklin A provisions h 583 Washington
" Levi farmer h 565 Washington
" Lewis F milk 565 Washington h do [Bridge
" Paulina widow Charles h end of
Boardman William spinner h 200 Washington
Boisvert George weaver h 33 Brown
Bolles Henry P carpenter h 552 Washington
Bond Adam weaver h 6 Wilding
" Stephen H pattern maker h 65 Bridge [36 Washington
Boodry James D foreman at N B h
Borden Frank driver h 24 Bryant

Borden
" Isaac S driver b 204 Washington
Boucher John variety Main cor Daniel h do [ington
Bourassa Joseph laborer h 289 Wash-
Bourdeau Joseph M barber h 44 Bridge [Bridge
Bourne Henry J tack maker h 43
" Marshall clerk 64 Fort h at New Bedford
Bourque Ovila fisherman h 20 Winsor
Bousquet Patrick carpenter h Hicks
Bowen William bds 11 Cooke
" William fisherman h 46 West Allen [Bedford
Bowman Martin M removed to New
" Pheobe A widow Charles b 93 Pleasant
Bradford Mary E h 10 Fort
" Mary E widow John W h 34 Farm Field lane [William
Bradley Thomas H machinist h 46
Bradshaw Emma E clerk 26 Centre b 92 Main
" James W nail maker h 92 Main
Bradwell George salesman N B h 6 Oak avenue [Chestnut
Brady Nellie widow John bds 131
Braley Albert G (A G & G F Braley) h 50 Cedar
" Albert L salesman h 33 Lafayette
BRALEY A G & G F (Albert G and George F) Phoenix Poultry Yards 50 Cedar See page *683
" Charles F teamster h 15 Cherry
" Eunice Mrs housekeeper 47 Cedar
" George F (A G & G F Braley) h 31 Green [Pleasant
" Isabelle widow William h 51
" Wallace L molder h 137 Green
Braman David P cooper 6 Spring b 41 Water [Green
Brand John S master mechanic h 69
Brant Charles W tacker h r 49 Cedar
Breault Corrine Mrs bds 33 Alpine av
Brierley James gardener h 1 Walnut
Briggs Benjamin bds 49 Cedar
" Charles F motorman h 15 Oxford [Main
" Julia A widow George A h 304
" Otis L laborer h 25 Middle
" Pelig A gateman Fairhaven depot b 15 Middle [cester
Brigham H Prescott removed to Wor-
Brightman Ralph plumber h 33 Centre
Britto Frank fireman h Sycamore near Alden road [Middle
Broadland Adna J glass cutter h 77

Broadland
" John glass cutter h 2 Lafayette
Brotherson Frederick F janitor N B h 50 Spring
Brown Albert teamster h 7 Lafayette
" Allen A laborer h 7 Lafayette
" Andrew G laborer b 2 Oak av
" Antone laborer h Sconticut Neck road [h at Taunton
" Augustus H clerk Atlas Tack Co
" Candy fisherman bds Sconticut Neck road [ford
" Charles D removed to New Bed-
" Domingo carpenter b Sconticut Neck road [Green
" Elizabeth widow Thomas A b 132 Green
" Frank E Mrs 193 Main
" Frederick A photographer h 24 Mulberry [ington
" George D mechanic h 428 Wash-
" James A hairdresser 28 Centre h do [road
" John farmer h Sconticut Neck
" Joseph farmer h Sconticut Neck road [Green
" J Wilson plumber 72 Main h 38
" Manuel farmer h Sconticut Neck road [avenue
" Mary A widow John h 9 Oak
" Mercy D M Mrs h 149 Main [ton
" Roy E salesman b 428 Washing-
" William painter b Tripp
Browne Harry H manager Browne Pharmacy Centre corner Main h 31 Fort
" Pharmacy Harry H Browne manager Centre corner Main
Brownell Ada bookkeeper b 27 Middle
" Algernon F hackman 65 Main h 27 Middle
" Charles F (C F Brownell & Co) 63 Main h 90 Laurel
" Charles H b 42 Rotch
BROWNELL C F & CO (Charles F Brownell and Granville P Hicks) stable 65 Main See page *684
" Edwin student b 27 Middle
" Harriet T nurse b 64 Main
" Malcolm G machinist b 82 Bridge
" Morris R lawyer N B selectman and overseer of poor h 60 Main
" Thomas R machinist h 82 Bridge
Bruckshaw Andrew N physician 23 Walnut h do [Brown
Brunnette Aglaee E dressmaker h 45
" Anthime A bartender h 41 Brown

Brunnette
" Felix carpenter h 45 Brown
Bruso Louis doffer h 29 Sycamore
Bryant Arthur DeW bookkeeper N B h 93 Laurel [Fort
" Delia widow George M nurse h 71
" Elbert L mason h 91 Main
" John I county commissioner h 70 Washington
" May teacher at N B b 71 Fort
" William H laborer h 74 Fort
Bryden Elizabeth widow Ebenezer proprietor Bryden House 35 Main h do [Main h do
" Esther manager Bryden House 35
Buffington Henry C clerk N B h 85 Laurel [32 Lafayette h do
" Nancy H coal and insurance
" Susan F Mrs stenographer Atlas Tack Co h 85 Laurel [ington
Bulger John laborer h r 544 Wash-
Bullen Thomas fixer h 265 Adams
Bumpus Jeremiah B carpenter h New Boston road
" Mary E teacher b 3 Washington
" Samuel S sealer of weights and measures h 3 Washington
" Susan D widow Jeremiah B h New Boston road
" S S Mrs nurse b 3 Washington
Bund Albert Rev assistant pastor St Joseph's R C church h 3 Adams
Burgess David h 260 Main
" Ellsworth M sales manager Atlas Tack Co h Pleasant near Washington
" John A W machinist h 12 Middle
" Leslie F janitor h Mill road near Washington
" William P bds 191 Main
Burgoyne Lindsay J fisherman h 14 Main [h 26 do
Burke Herbert D bicycles 22½ Middle
" Patrick H removed to New Bed ford
" Susan widow Daniel h 26 Middle
Burns Milton tack maker h 36 Water
Burt Clarence E removed to New Bedford [ford
" Stephen A removed to New Bed-
Bushnell Charles F salesman N B h 16 Oak avenue
" Louise clerk superintendent of schools office Town Hall b 16 Oak avenue [land road
Butler Nicholas carpenter h 55 How-
Butman Eleanor widow William T h 106 Washington
Byros Romeo carpenter h Newbury

Cabana Arsene mill operator h 98 Sycamore [amore
" Delphine widow Amedee h 98 Syc-
" George mill operator b 98 Sycamore [more
" Joseph mill operative h 98 Syca-
Cabral Charles M h 60 Spring
" Joseph tacker b 39 Christian
" Lawrence tack cutter h 68 Rotch
" Manuel fisherman h 39 Christian
Caldwell Eliza widow James h 9 Rodman [Tack Co h 135 Chestnut
Calloway Frank S foreman Atlas
Campbell Elwyn G teacher N B h 6 William
Cannon Charles E b 6 East Allen
" James cooper h 4 Lafayette
Caouette Stella F removed from town
Capron Harry clerk h 65 Washington
Card Henry L variety 26 Centre h 96 Middle
" Norman removed to New Bedford
" William C removed to New Bedford [85 Fort
Carleton Ida M widow Charles H b
Carpenter Bert drill worker b 35 Taber
" Charles L carpenter h 35 Taber
" Clayton W shipping clerk bds 35 Taber [do
" George H grocer 36 Lafayette h
" Orrin B clerk bds 36 Lafayette
" William removed to New Bedford
Carrie John J mate h 18 Mulberry
Carroll James C overseer h 10 Cherry 2nd
Carsley Edith S bds Mrs Emily F Austin's Sconticut Neck road
Carvalho Joseph former h Gelatt rd
Casey Ambrose O boatbuilder b Middle
" Major (M J Casey Co) h at N B
" M J Co (Major J Casey Co) boat builders Bridge near Middle
Cash Henry foreman Atlas Tack Co h 43 Green [Co b 43 Green
" Mary J stenographer Atlas Tack
Caswell Abram H died Feb 11, 1911
" Arthur G engineer h 6 Middle
" William H baggage master Fairhaven depot b 30 Spring
Caton Antone carpenter h Roselawn
" Joseph foreman h Roselawn
Chace Abram died Feb 3, 1911

Chace
" Andrew P draughtsman h 4 Cowen [h at N B
" Walter F shipwright 22 Water
" William L foreman 65 Main h 97 Pleasant [Brown
Chadwick George machinist h 11
" Hannah housekeeper 47 Union
Champlin William D draftsman h 64 Green [Field lane
Chandler Azel R laster h 23 Farm
" Chester bookkeeper b 61 Bridge
" Herbert T h 61 Spring
Chapman James C gardener h 83 North
" James E b 83 North
" Rosa C h 63 North
Charbonneau Adelard h 9 Cherry 2nd
" Lewis died Feb 16, 1911
" Lewis Mrs h 12 Blackburn
Charry Alice A h 195 Main
Chase Deborah h 36 Water
" Edward F farmer h Sconticut Neck road [Pleasant
" George H eyelet finisher h 115
" John A h 50 William
" Mary W widow Daniel b 42 Church [lane
Cheever Ernest carpenter h Egypt
Chicoine Antone baker h 285 Alden road [William
Childs Laura A widow William b 14
Choquette Delia widow Alphonse h 10 Wilding
" Elphage carpenter h 51 Maitland
Christopher Christian removed to New Bedford
Church Charles H student b 219 Main
" Frank H drug clerk at N B h 219 Main
" James I h 45 Rotch
" Sarah C h 18 Church
" William F provisions 45 Main h 33Middle
City Marine Ry 22 Water
Clark Amanda h 35 Summer
" Elizabeth A widow Roswell h Sconticut Neck road
" Harry lineman b 45 Cedar
" John chauffeur h 310 Washington
" John L traveling salesman h 33 Main [Main
" John L Jr traveling salesman b 33
CLARK LEIGHTON S proprietor Fairhaven Ice Co 428 Washington h do See page *684
" Lillian manager 24 Centre b 23 Rotch

Clark
" Lottie Mrs h 24 West Allen [mer
" Nathaniel W painter h 35 Sum-
" Stanton B driver h 7 Chestnut
" Stephen H packer h 39 William
" Stephen H Jr shipper h 45 Cedar
" Thomas A painter 87 Main h 70 Fort ,[h 37 Main
Clarke Sara B principal Rogers school
Clay Joseph W clerk h 12 Union
Clifford Frank tinsmith 55 Main h at New Bedford
" Samuel A cook h 105 Fort
Cloutier Henry mill hand b 44 Brown
" Joseph weaver bds 44 Brown
" Joseph weaver h 44 Brown
Cobb Charles W clerk h 63 Main
" John H carpenter h 34 Oxford
Coggeshall Eliza widow Charles W h 21 Rotch
" John E auditor h 5 Cherry
Cole Edward R shipsmith Union cor Water h 36 Middle
" Ella E h 36 Middle
Colgate Frank operative h 25 Oak
Collins Albert B registrar of deeds N B h 6 Washington
" Sybil K teacher b 6 Washington
Colson Ellen M h 184 Alden road
Conant Henry A salesman h 7 Walnut
Connor Charles A salesman bds 162 Main [West Allen
Conway Dennis tack worker h 24
" John stitcher b 48 Centre
Cook Charles W fisherman h Sconticut Neck road [William
" John T mechanical engineer h 45
Coombs C Henry machinist bds 23 Lafayette [Lafayette
" Martha B widow Charles H h 23
Copeland Helen B assistant P O h 18 William [liam
" Mary A widow Elisha h 18 Wil-
Corbett Dennis removed to New Bedford
Corey Edmund S h 31 Green
Corimer Domitila widow Theophile b 23 Alpine avenue
" Urbain loom fixer h 23 Alpine av
Correia Joseph laborer h end Atlas
" Joseph laborer h 35 River av
Correira Frank laborer h Hitch
Corson Everett H chauffeur b 180 Washington
" James A h 180 Washington
" Temple A clerk N B b 180 Washinton [Neck road
Costa Ernest B farmer h Sconticut

Costa
" Frank farm hand bds Ernest B Costa's Sconticut Neck road
" John laborer h. Veranda avenue
" John P mariner h 65 Washington
Cote Aneclet lather h Beach [shall
" Joseph carpenter h 9 East Cogge-
" Paul lather b 9 East Coggeshall
" Stanislaus grocer at N B h 21 Bridge
Cottelle Benjamin F pianos N B h 84 Fort [Bridge
Cottle Lucy S widow Albert b 45
Coupe Thomas H overseer N B h rear 163 Main [Adams
Cowen Benjamin F carpenter h 68
" Edson S clerk Atlas Tack Co h 28 Middle
" George D h 102 Main
" James H tool maker h 11 Cooke
" Percey E removed to New York City
Cox Arthur P h 192 Main [ter
Craig Annie widow Robert h 25 Wa-
" Frank glass cutter b 25 Water
Creelman Sarah widow John b 14 Cooke [dle h 95 do
Crocker Gorham D manager 98 Mid-
Cromwell Charles E marine ry Kelley's wharf h do
Cronin Edward H clothing repairer 29 Centre h at N B
Crossley Charles barber b 23 Mulberry [Main
Crowell Henry P molder h 17
" Myra D principal Oxford school rms 13 William [Main
" Sarah R widow Milton B h 179
Crowther Alfred baker h 314 Main
Croxtall Lillian Mrs h 25 Main
Cummings Albert L master mariner h 175 Green [Main
" Arthur L master mariner h 21
" George W wire worker h 73 Main
Cunniff Frank J glass blower b 173 Green
" George K shoemaker b 85 Middle
" Thomas P laborer h 85 Middle
" William J shoemaker b 85 Middle
Cunningham Frederick plumber 55 Main h at N B
" George W wire worker h 73 Main
Curran Frank painter h Farm Field lane
" Sarah A widow John D h 7 Rodman [Laurel
Cushman Barker H bookkeeper h 25
" Ruth T widow Frederick E h 41 Rotch

Daley Bridget widow John T h 40 Water
" William H tack worker bds 40 Water [h 34 Mulberry
Damas Phelomena widow Francisco
Dammon William F teller First National Bank N B h 155 Chestnut
Damon Herbert b 12 Middle
" Susan bds 7 Middle
Dana Eliza N widow Edward A h 200 Adams [42 Oxford
Danforth Herschel R eyelet maker b
" John H confectioner b 42 Oxford [ford
" Mary F widow Charles h 42 Ox-
Danzell Warren H gardener h Spring cor Washington [Washington
Davidson Harry B fruit N B b 116
Davis Dudley h 60 Oxford
" Frank L foreman Atlas Tack Co h 66 Washington
" Ruel W patternmaker h 71 Fort
" Stephen S engineer h 16 Cooke
" Thomas W carpenter h 163 Main
" Warren L clerk at N B b 177 Main
Day Walter H carpenter h 144 Green
Days Enos E carpenter h Farm Field lane
Dayton Albert h 6 Allen
Dean Daniel W farmer h Sconticut Neck road [51 William
" Everett K clerk Atlas Tack Co h
" Joseph H h 22 Cherry
Deblois Philip carpenter h 23 Alpine avenue
DeCosta Antone carpenter b 68 Rotch
" Frank grocer 21 W Allen h do
" Joaquim mill hand h 96 Sycamore
" Manuel tack feeder h 68 Rotch
Delano Ada E dressmaker 130 Green h do
" Calvin teamster 38 Rotch h do
DELANO CLARENCE F plumber 72 Main h 35 Middle See page 767
" Elizabeth R milliner b 48 Spring
" Elizabeth T artist 91 Pleasant h do [lane
" Emma R Mrs h end Farm Feld
" Emma T h 130 Green [road
" Ephraim Jr farmer h Weeden
" Frances J writer bds 92 Green
" Harry poultry breeder Weeden road h do
" Harry W driver h Weeden road
" Helen N removed to Everett
" Herbert T auto repairer b Mrs E R Delano's Farm Field lane

Delano
" Joseph S fish 48 Main h 64 Laurel [sant
" Joshua H boat builder h 109 Plea-
" Joshua R caulker h 48 Spring
" J Everett cream 91 Centre h do
" Louis A clerk Washington D C bds 109 Pleasant
" Mae stenographer 66 Fort b Mrs E R Delano's Farm Field lane
" Mary R widow Frederick P h 73 Green
" Nancy P h 27 Main
" Wade H carpenter b Mrs E R Delano's Farm Field lane
" Warren Jr (New York) summer residence 39 Walnut
" Warren P florist b Mrs E R Delano's, Farm Field lane
" W Fred h 73 Green
DeMello Harrison fisherman h 5 Hawthorn [bert E b 336 Main
Demoranville Elizabeth S widow Al-
" Luther K carpenter h 372 Washington [ington
" Maurice A foreman b 372 Wash-
Dennie Harold B salesman h 44 Spring [shall
Derosier Joseph fixer h 42 E Cogge-
Desrochiere Joseph third hand h Magnolia av near Sycamore
DeVeigo Martin laborer bds Sconticut Neck road
Devoll Helen V violin teacher and leader 140 Green h do [Green
" Hannah widow Pardon Jr h 140
Dewitt Fred H machinist h 25 Mulberry [New York
Dexter Albert G removed to Corning
" Edwin F engineer Sewerage Pumping station h 41 Water
" Edwin F Mrs nurse h 41 Water
" Walter R machinist 28 Spring b 41 Water [Chestnut
Dillingham Charles F machinist h 138
" Eben J laborer h 89 Main
" Louise D widow Edward H h 89 Main [Chestnut
" William A boilermaker h 138
Disbury Robert polisher h Adams cor Brown [ley's wharf b do
Dixon Herbert F boat repairer Kel-
Dlugg Jacob watchman h 9 Chestnut [ford
Dodd Margaret removed to New Bed-
Dodge Harry E draughtsman b 48 William

Dodge
" Harry E Mrs teacher Latin High school b 48 William [liam
" Sylvia widow Isaac H h 48 Wil-
" William C apprentice b 53 Walnut [Walnut
" Zenas W mason 88½ Main h 53
Dolby James E horseshoer bds 11 Oxford [Field lane
Donovan Patrick laborer b 23 Farm
" William D pres Atlas Tack Co h at Marion
Doran Robert N blacksmith 8 Spring h 87 Laurel
Douglass Ansel G special police and ladders 189 Green h do [sor
Dowd James mill hand h 30 Win-
Downey Patrick J laborer h 49 Green
Drake Charles P tack packer h 19 Middle [136 Adams
Drew Annie widow Benjamin F h
" Benjamin F died July 16, 1911
" Charles Irving carpenter h 27 Green
" Charles LeB carpenter h 58 Fort
Driscoll John variety 16 Main h do
Dudley Hary H widow George H h rear 177 Main
Duffy John H packing dept Atlas Tack Co h 50 Church
" William tackmaker h 24 Middle
" William Jr tacker bds 24 Middle
Dufrane Frank J painter h 122 Chestnut
" Frank J Jr b 122 Chestnut
Dugdale Charles R clerk N B h 145 Chestnut
" Richard clerk N B h Holcomb
Dunbar Ida J died Jan 14 1911
Dunham Crawford L plumber N B h 51 Green [ford
" William H constable h 59 Ox-
Dunn Frank E fisherman h 48 Pleasant [Neck rd
" Howard P poultry h Sconticut
" Nathaniel plumber 72 Main h Weeden road [h 16 Cottage
" Robert gardener H H Rogers Jr
" Samuel P farmer h Sconticut Neck road [Daniel
Dupre Arthur weaver h Main corner
Dupuis Alfred carder bds 30 Oak
" Joseph carpenter h 30 Oak
Duramp Harry farmer h off Sconticut Neck road [b 87 Union
Durfee Elizabeth J widow Seth R
" Leopold J G machinist rear 53 Main h 87 Union [fayette
Dwelley Andrew H mgr h 31 La-

Dwelley
" Edward G farmer b 88 Middle
" William H teaming 88 Middle h 55 William

Eagan Daniel mariner h 74 Cedar
Eames Katherine R teacher Rogers Annex school bds 13 William
Eastham S Derbyshire removed from town [B h 27 Fort
Eaton Clarence W cotton broker N
Eccles Joseph milk Oak Grove lane h do
Ede Hubert R reporter b 65 Green
" James dry goods Masonic bldg h 65 Green [25 Middle
Eldred Albert F painter 26 Water h
" Annie bookkeeper 29 Centre b 25 Middle
" Chester die sinker b 99 Main
" George F h 44 Summer
" Harriet M clerk Masonic bldg b 99 Main
" Myra W h 49 Rotch
" William H carpenter h 99 Main
Eldredge Gulielma P widow William D h 117 Main [45 Bridge
Eldridge Abbie E widow Edward h
" Chester shoemaker h 43 Cedar
" Harmony P widow Capt. Martin L h 110 Green [do
" John L supt 301 Washington h
" Peter V machinist h 31 Rotch
Ellis Abbie F removed to Boston
" Benjamin S plumber 72 Main b 56 Pleasant
" Clarence fisherman b r 90 Farm Field lane
" Clinton E removed to Braintree
" Ebenezer plate roller h 137 Laurel [ant
" Edward M yacht capt h 56 Pleas-
" Edward W h 29 Walnut
" Ellen P widow Benjamin h 33 William
" George A teamster h 14 Spring
" Gertrude M teacher Rogers school bds 29 Walnut
" Henry T carpenter h r 90 Farm Field lane [Field lane
" James H engineer h 90 Farm
" Joan P died Feb 28 1911
" John W driver bds 95 Main
" Louisa widow George H h 95 Main [Rotch
" Philena P widow Hiram B h 42
" Sarah D widow Hiram B h 80 Fort
" William A laborer bds 95 Main

Ellis
" William F laborer h 200 Spring
Emberson Eva stenographer bds 129 Green
" George bookkeeper h 129 Green
" Thomas student bds 129 Green
Enos Joseph fisherman h 31 Water
" Manuel h New Boston road
Escolas Julian sheet metal worker h Sycamore cor Magnolia av
Ettleman Deborah stenographer b 8 Ferry
" Hyman conductor b 8 Ferry
" Minnie Mrs tailoring 8 Ferry h
" Solomon conductor b 8 Ferry
Evans Edward machinist h 97 Main
" Edward W fireman b 97 Main
Ewer Frederick F eyeletmaker h 72 Centre

Fairfield Georgia E secretary Fairhaven High School Association h 38 Middle [ton
Fairhaven Almhouse 301 Washing-
FAIRHAVEN ICE CO L S Clark prop 428 Washington See page *684
FAIRHAVEN INSTITUTION FOR SAVINGS 19 Centre See page *682
" Iron Foundry Co, W H Judd treas 2 Water [Water
" Sewerage Pumping Station 8
FAIRHAVEN STAR The Charles D Waldron prop 20 Main See page 758
" Water Co office Town Hall bldg pumping station Mill rd
Fallows Samuel removed from town
Fell Benjamin operative h 142 Adams
Ferguson Rose Mrs b 23 Oak
Fett Nicolas Rev asst pastor St Joseph's R C church h 3 Adams
Field George L tack maker h 73 Main
" Judith widow William H h 73 Main
" Lewis H removed to Newark N J
Fish Andrew student b Temple place
" Charles F laborer h Temple place
" Mary E Mrs bds 63 Spring
" M Alice h 20 William
Fisher Albert teamster h Egypt lane
" Julia A widow Walter H h 63 Fort
Fitch Elizabeth W h 87 Green
Fitzimons William J electrical engineer Atlas Tack Co h 112 Washington [ams
Fleming Archibald farmer h 141 Ad-

Fletcher Percy I bookkeeper N B h 71 Green [near Mattapoiset line
Florence Joseph weaver h Washington
Fluette Auguste weaver h 9 Cherry 2nd
Folger Reuben mason b 137 Bridge
Fontaine Charles fisherman h Jacob's Neck [89 Middle
Forbes Harriet C widow Charles H h
Forrest Edwin W plumber Bridge near Middle h 8 Cottage
" Walter S clerk N B h 39 Fort
Fortin Lucien fisherman h 79 Fort
Foster Aspah P rattan chairs at N B h 89 Green
" Edwin E Dr summer residence Naskatucket Island Little Bay off Sconticut Neck road [road
" Frank farmer h Sconticut Neck
" Joseph farm hand b Frank Foster's
" Manuel mariner h end Hitch
" Robert W brass foundry N B h 185 Main [West
Foye Charles J granite cutter h 2
Fraga Minnie W Mrs h 103 Main
Francis Charles B removed to New Bedford [Washington
" Edward DeV Jr farm hand h 623
" Humphrey A blacksmith h 78 Laurel
" Isaac P real estate 163 Main h do
" Joseph farmer h 623 Washington
" Rita widow Manuel C h 134 Chestnut [1910
" Sarah L widow John died Nev
" Walter H eyelet maker h 47 Bridge [89 Bridge
Franklin Charlotte widow Edwin b
" Edward P master mariner h 135 Green
Frates Annie Mrs housekeeper F X Paulino Boston Hill road
" Antone h 58 Rotch
" Antone F bowling 26½ Water h 2 Albany [road
" Frank farmer h Sconticut Neck
" Joseph shoemaker h Washington near Mattapoisett line [Middle
Frawley Arthur H brakeman h 3
" David h 3 Middle
Freitas Antone farmer h 50 Adams
" Antone Jr laborer h 50 Adams
" Helen W widow John M h 77 Middle
" Joseph teamster b 77 Middle
" Manuel fisherman h 79 Middle
" Manuel G removed to Newport R I
Frizzelle Samuel molder h 102 Main
Frommell Bertha F Carl physician 44 Green h do [Green
" Martin H photographer N B h 44
Fuller Sarah F widow Thomas B h Laurel near Centre [Spring
Furenteel Michael driller bds 39

Gadu Adelard painter h 48 Hawthorn
Gagnon Frank h Alden road
" Alfred second hand h 44 East Coggeshall [h 99 Pleasant
Galley Truman A express messenger
Galligan Eugene F milk Mill rd h do
Gammons James A painter h 210 Main
" James F glass cutter h 210 Main
Garcia Antone S teamster 26 Rotch h do [70 Green
Gardiner Abby C widow Ezekiel C b
" George N (Gardiner & Milliken) lawyer 3 Masonic bldg New Bedford h 70 Green [Allen
Gardner Alice widow George A h 6
" Andrew M b 6 Allen
Garthley James head gardener H H Rogers Jr h 17 Cedar
Gaucher Charles speeder tender h Newbury [h 54 Church
Gault Frank A baggage master R R
Gauthier Levi doffer h 331 Main
Gautreau Alfred shipper b 21 Bridge
" Olive widow Philip h 21 Bridge
Geddis Henry S watchman h 336 Main
Gelette John grocer 64 Fort h 386 Washington [Boston road h do
" John Jr milk Bridge near New
Gerstlauer Daniel J h 64 Bridge [land
Gervais Ephriam weaver h 110 Mait-
Gething Daniel molder h 337 Main
" Daniel C painter b 337 Main
Ghimoussi Jeremiah laborer h 39 Spring
Gibbs Benjamin M buffer h 22 Main
" Clara E bds 35 Main [Green
" Francis W engineer 8 Water h 127
" Preston H laborer h 23 Adams
" William R poultry dresser h 19 Main [ford
Gifford Albert E shipper h 34 Ox-
" Annie E widow George W dressmaker 209 Main h do
" Daniel W caulker b 104 Main
" Elmer C laborer h 32 Water
" Henry A ship carpenter h 84 Middle
" Herman W tackmaker h 90 Main
" Isabella bds 35 Main [Green
" James M real estate N B h 121

Gifford
" Jesse S (Shaw & Gifford) r 53 Main h 104 do
" Lewis E helper bds 105 Main
" Minnie B widow Frederick N h 37 William
" William C bds 43 Cedar
Gigante Rocco laborer h 2 Delano
Gilbert James Mrs b 48 Centre
Gillingham Dana H chemist b 32 Spring
" James L lawyer h 32 Spring
" James L Jr bds 32 Spring
Girouard John carpenter h Oak st
Gloria Joseph tackmaker h 20 Rotch
Goddard Alvano C Rev insurance at N B h 24 Oxford
" Arthur arctitect bds 24 Oxford
Goggin James gardener h 23 Farm Field lane [let powder 47 Main
Gold Bond Sterilizing Powder Co toi-
Gonsalves August carpenter h 68 Rotch
" Diziderim teamster h 6 Wilding
" John carpenter bds 68 Rotch
Goodale Eula P teacher Rogers school b 57 Main [Oak
Goode Eliza widow Thomas h 23
" Thomas weaver h end Oak
" William mill operative h 23 Oak
Goodnow Alden removed to Lynn
" Jotham clerk P O h 9 Main
Goodrich Willis K carpenter 184 Alden road h do [Bridge
Gothro Olive widow Philip h 21
Goulart Joseph B farmer h Sconticut Neck road [Neck road
" Manuel B farmer h Sconticut
Gould Martha E b 3 Washington
Gourley Helen dry goods 259 Adams h do [ams
" Hugh mill operative h 259 Ad-
Goyette Fred operative h 32 Oak
Gracia Michael laborer h 22 Bryant
Graham Ella J h 37 Main
" Robert S draughtsman bds 76 Washington
Grant Frank A foreman h 38 Main
" Grace M removed from town
Green Ruth M widow John F bds 10 Oxford
" Thomas shoe repairer 53 Main h at N B [257 Adams
Greenhalgh Wallace mule spinner h 257 Adams [h do
Greenwood Thomas milk 122 Bridge
Greenya Robert S clerk N B b 36 Laurel
" William S tacker h 3 Laurel
Gregoire Napoleon farmer h off Sycamore [avenue
" Pierre real estate h 33 Alpine
Grimshaw Joseph L removed to New Bedford
" William H clerk h Beacon street
Grindrod Joseph T hostler h 227 Adams
" Leonard clerk b 227 Adams
Grinnell Ebenezer G h 108 Main
Grunshaw James teamster h 109 Spring
Gubellini Adolphus laborer h 5 Delano
Guilford Edward W carpenter b 152 Main [Main
" Frank F tailor's cutter h 152
" Frank T drillmaker b 152 Main
Guinois Jean farmer h Veranda av
Gunn Harold N bookkeeper b 79 Laurel [Main b 70 Bridge
Gurney Edward H clerk 29 Centre
" Isabel O widow Lysander C h 88 Fort
" Isaiah clerk 25 Centre b 152 Main
" James M carpenter h 46 Bridge
" John F b 88 Fort
" Lysander C died June 30 1911
" William H boat builder h 70 Bridge

Hacker Clifton A supt fire alarm h 20 Fort [den road
Hackett Charles S farmer h 62 Al-
" Margaret A widow James F mgr bds 46 William
Hadfield John weaver h 15 Oak
Hadley Caroline bookkeeper h 304 Main
Hagen Augustine C captain Fairhaven Ferry h 5 Middle
" Frederick machinist bds 5 Middle
" John W clerk b 5 Middle
Hall Drew B removed to Somerville
" Everett E h 40 Laurel
" Harold R florist's helper P Murrey's bds 66 Laurel [station
" Herbert station agent Fairhaven
" Herbert E foreman Atlas Tack Co h 66 Laurel
" James M gardener h 151 Green
" Jesse F district manager S Mass Tel Co h 32 Laurel
Halloran Margaret A Mrs clerk Atlas Tack Co h at Fall River
Hamblin Eben W widow Sylvanus h 8 Washington [nut h do
Hamlin Alice D dressmaker 23 Wal-
Hammond Amelia died

Hammond
" Arthur C farmer h r 544 Washington [Washington
" Charles E clerk 94 Centre h 56
" Charles W grocer 94 Centre h do
" Clarence W carpenter h 115 Washington
" Edward machinist b 18 Middle
" Elizabeth P rem to N Y City
" Francis H Jr farm hand h 18 Middle [Fort
" George D druggist at N B h 93
" Henry Jr fisherman b Weeden rd
" Henry W fisherman h Weeden rd
" Rhoda wid Martin V P h 187 Spring [Washington
" Susan B widow Albert h 292
" William A laborer h 34 Beacon
Handy Frank E salesman h 33 Green
" George B shoemaker h 257 Adams
" Melora B h 85 Chestnut
" Pliny B master mariner h 101 Main [Mulberry
Haney William G blacksmith h 20
Hanna Bessie M music teacher 42 Water h do
" Fred A clerk b 42 Water
" J Herbert electrician b 42 Water
" Martha L widow John T h 42 Water
" Mattie L bookkeeper b 42 Water
" Thomas h 5 Rodman [Bedford
Hargraves Alice removed to New
" John removed to New Bedford
Harring James L superintendent N B h 9 East Coggeshall
" William b 9 East Coggeshall
Harrington Andrew E laborer b 137 Bridge [Bridge
" Arthur H fish 8 Ferry h 137
" Edward G painter b 29 Water
" Henry F clerk b 137 Bridge
" Herbert E tack feeder b 29 Water
" William A clerk 26 Centre h 29 Water [B h 178 Adams
Harvey Emory P foreman P Corp N
Haskell Edward S florist h 35 Rotch
" Emma L widow William F h 193 Main
" Frank C h 36 Huttleston avenue
Haskins Richard H eyelet maker h 46 Bridge
" Urial M removed to Taunton
Hatfield James removed to New Bedford [h Sconticut Neck rd
Hathaway Adiel H rural mail carrier
" Allen G removed to New Bedford
" Catherine D widow Daniel K h 155 Main

Hathaway
" David T machinist h 64 Green
" Herman H painter 87 Main h 155 do [155 do
" Nellie A W bookkeeper 87 Main h
" Thomas h 41 Union
Hawkins Charles E molder b J H Hawkins [park
" John H painter 87 Main h Linden
Haydon Ernest J salesman h 17 Cooke
Hayes Esther bookkeeper N B b 89 Bridge [Middle
" Helen L widow William W h 8
" Ira R overseer N B h 89 Bridge
Hayward Ambrose B eyelet operator h 20 Adams
" Frederick J clerk b 20 Adams
" George A molder h 2 Burgess av
Heath Julia clerk N B b 137 Green
Hebert Joseph fisherman h Oak
Heise Albert R clerk h 10 Oxford
Hendrickson Andrew tug boat captain h 65 Cedar
Henry Robert spinner h 32 Oak
Herbolt William H shipsmith h 11 Oxford [ford
Hibbard John E removed to New Bed-
Hicks Granville P (C F Brownell & Co) stable 63 Main h at N B
Hill Frederick C teacher physical education High school rms 87 Laurel
" G W librarian Millicent Public Library bds 76 Washington
Hiller George L farmer and poultry Sconticut Neck road h do
" George L Jr poultry Sconticut Neck road h do [Marion
" Robert B stable 98 Middle h at
Hillman Ella F Mrs C S practioner h 49 Walnut
Hinchcliffe Bertha E teacher Rogers school b 119 Laurel [berry
Hirst Eben P plumber N B h 3 Mul-
" Herbert W grocer Adams corner Brown h at N B [res 60 Main
Hitch Joseph F (New York) summer
Hoar Mary E widow Patrick A h 12 Cherry [Portland Ore
Hoeg William H Jr removed to
Hoerstedt A Rudolph engineer h 146 Adams [ant
Hoger George tack maker b 69 Pleas-
Holbrook George W R R conductor h 30 Green
Holland Benjamin S foreman Atlas Tack Co h 113 Pleasant
" Ralph student b 113 Pleasant
" Warren E clerk b 113 Pleasant

Holmes Esther Y widow Henry W h 65 Main
" George T carpenter h 92 Middle
" Henry Dean laborer b 65 Main
" Walter T shoemaker h 17 Middle
" William fisherman h 23 Oak
Hope James glass cutter h 210 Main
Howard Abby A K died Dec 30 1910
" Charles F farmer h 590 Washington
" Charlotte h 106 Main
" Edwin J teamster h New Boston road [New Boston road
" Elizabeth widow George F h 28
" Elmer C removed to New Bedford
" Henry machinist b 82 Bridge
" Henry T farmer h New Boston rd
" Idella tack worker b 25 Spring
" John F farm hand h New Boston road [road
" Matthew H farmer h New Boston
" Rebecca D h 51 Walnut
Howe Josiah R machinist h 332 Washington [Washington
Howes Annie widow Gorham B h 399
Howland Abby and Rebecca h 44 William [h 249 Main
" Pardon A janitor High school
" Rachael secretary and treasurer 24 Centre h 44 William
" Ralph S student b 249 Main
" Thomas H canvasser h Garrison
" Walter C farmer h 253 Alden road
" William S milk Oak Grove lane h do [Co h at N B
Howe Isabel stenographer Atlas Tack
Hoxie Earle W shipper Atlas Tack Co h 42 Washington
" Willard L shipping department Atlas Tack Co h 42 Washington
Hoye Alice clerk b 44 Laurel
" Bridget J widow James h 44 Laurel [at N B
" Martin foreman Atlas Tack Co h
" Paul student b 44 Laurel
" Thomas foreman Atlas Tack Co h at N B [Bedford
Hoyt Emma W removed to New
" James (New Bedford) summer resident Sconticut Neck road
" William D removed to New Bedford
Hubbard Alton clerk 30 Centre b G A Hubbard's Oak Grove lane
" George A teamster h Oak Grove lane [rel
Hudson Lucy J housekeeper b 75 Lau-
" William F h 75 Laurel

Huff James laborer b 165 Sycamore
Hughes Frederick T foreman h 43 Green [Brown
" John welder bds Adams corner
Hunter William H h 40 Huttleston avenue [New Bedford
Huppee Louis J helper 6 Spring b at
Hursell Maria M widow William H h 10 Cherry [William h do
Hutchins Sarah F dressmaker 54
Huttleston Sarah T h 47 Union

Irish Frank J Miss h 193 Main [ion
" George O dentist at N B h 49 Un-
Irving Lizzie F widow Charles A h 12 Cherry

Jacinth Jules laborer h 92 Centre
Jackson Albert h 32 Green
" Emma widow George b 27 Green
" Richard laborer h 40 Water
" Samuel B at Atlas Tack Co h 34 Union [more
Jacques Charles laborer h 145 Syca-
Jarvis Rose widow Manuel h 9 Ball
Jenney Adelia T bds 35 Main
" Alice L dressmaker 71 Green b do
" Alton eyelet maker b 8 East Allen
" Andrew J salesman h 45 Summer
" Caleb E clerk N B b 300 Washington [Green
" Caroline A widow Charles h 71
" Elizabeth R widow Levi h 57 Main
" Everett H manager b 398 Washington
" Franklin B freight handler Fairhaven depot b 1 Eldridge lane
" George A b 95 Main
" George Edwin shipper Atlas Tack Co h 8 East Allen
" George H clerk b 58 Main
" Horatio h 58 Main
" Joseph J foreman h 64 Oxford
" Lucy A widow Andrew P h 300 Washington [Washington
" Lucy B widow Simpson h 398
" Rufus B h 1 Eldridge lane
Jennings Alice C Mrs h 34 Walnut
Johnson George A telegrapher b 93 Pleasant
" Thomas fisherman h 8 Pease
Jones Caleb S fisherman h 18 Cherry
" John checker b 16 Adams
" John H laborer h 19 Cherry [ford
" William F removed to New Bed-
Jordan Robert painter b 44 Bridge
" Sarah E widow Charles S b 155 Main

Joseph Manuel laborer h 40 Water
Judd Walter H president and treas F I F Co Water corner Ferry h 114 Green

Karl John shoemaker h 39 Fort
Keen Gideon H S telephone operator N B h 93 Pleasant [fayette
Keene Annie W widow Levi h 32 La-
" Emily B widow rms 31 William
Kelley Achasia P widow Ahira h 40 Walnut [151 Main
" Anderson W bookkeeper N B h
" Daniel D watchman h 16 Centre
" David L salesman D N Kelley's h 149 Chestnut
" David N wholsale salt fish Kelley's wharf h 103 Green
" Frank H clerk N B h 27 Church
" Theron A salesman D N Kelley's h 151 Chestnut
" William laborer h 122 Bridge
Kelly Joseph weaver h 29 Alpine av
Kempton Ann H bookkeeper D N Kelley b 150 Green [150 Green
" John W L mould maker h
Kendall Edith V Mrs typewriting at N B h 22 Lafayette [Main b do
Kendrick Chester F poultry 468
" Daniel W farmer h 468 Main
" Stanley stenographer b 468 Main
Kent George clerk Atlas Tack Co h at N B [dle h 5 Holcomb
Kerns Michael F horse shoer 97 Mid-
" Stephen helper 97 Middle bds 5 Holcomb
Keys Mary Alice Mrs h 16 Adams
Kiff Victoria R widow Marcus R h 52 Washington [ool h 3 William
Kimball Albert B principal High sch-
King Annie E widow Alfred C h 106 Main
" Eliza A housekeeper h 13 Cherry
" Frank laborer b Manuel King's Tripp
" Fred P fixer h 42 Hawthorne
" George W h 141 Green
" John laborer h 109 Bridge
" John W belt repairer h 67 Pleasant [ant
" Laura M teacher N B b 67 Pleas-
" Manuel laborer h 34 Garrison
" Nora stenographer Atlas Tack Co b 67 Pleasant
" Perry S helper b 67 Pleasant
Kingsley Rachel teacher Rogers Annex school b 21 Middle
Knight Julia B housekeeper 110 Green
Knipe Fanny widow Charles O h 54 Church
" Paul clerk N B b 54 Church
Knowles Henry M 2nd h 184 Main
Kolb John D h 6 Allen [Sycamore
Kudgewski Barney meat cutter h 172

La Belle Joseph farmer h end Sconticut Neck road
Labonte Alaire mill operator h Veranda avenue [da avenue
" Albert mill operator b 45 Veran-
" Jules laborer b 45 Veranda avenue
Lagarde Louis J locomotive engineer h 27 Church [North
Lagasse Fred J steam fitter h 7
Lahue Frank H tack maker h 123 Laurel
Lamb Richard F removed from town
Langelier Frank shoemaker h 15 Middle [h do
Langlois Valere milk 15 Alpine av
" Victor fisherman h 41 West Allen
Lannan William M beef h 448 Main
Lapham Herbert poultry b Emily F Austin's Sconticut Neck road
LaRocque Alfred H paymaster Atlas Tack Co h at N B [at N B
Laughlin William clerk 64 Fort h
Lawrence Joseph laborer h Roselawn
Lawton Albert W foreman 6 Spring h at N B
" Charles eyelet maker b 58 Main
" Emma D widow L Sconticut Neck road
" George G died June 23 1911
" George G helper b Sconticut Neck road
" Jessie widow Levi M h 36 Main
" Myra F widow Frederick E h 474 Washington
LeBaron Charles E died June 8 1911
" Sarah A widow Charles E h 140 Green [Water
Lebeau Elizabeth widow William h 35
" Joseph painter h 46 Alpine av
Leblanc Clovis fisherman h 34 Beach
" Elaire carpenter h 14 Beach
" Oliver carpenter h 25 River av
Leclair Mildred widow Alfred A bookkeeper b 27 Middle [Spruce
Lecounte Charles glass cutter h 2
" Eugene weaver h 3 Spruce
" Paul laborer b 2 Spruce
Lee Albert G stripper h 69 Fort
Legault Henry carpenter bds Charles Baker's Taber [Main
Legua Rose widow Godfrois h 402

Leighton Flora H Mrs assistant The Millicent Library h 7 Main
Lemery Adam laborer b 50 Blackburn
" Edward teamster h 50 Blackburn
" Hermidas weaver b 50 Blackburn
" Odias spinner b 50 Blackburn
Lemonde Arthur laborer b Joseph Benoit's Magnolia
Lemos Emily widow Matthew M h 773 Washington
" Walter M steam ship agent b 773 Washington
Leonard Aurilla S h 36 Oxford
" Francelia N h 36 Oxford
" Juliet P h 36 Oxford
" Louise h 36 Oxford
" Reuben W painter h 103 Pleasant
" Sarah T widow Samuel h 36 Oxford
Lester Annie G widow Jackson h 16 Spring
Letendre Aurore housekeeper 33 Alpine avenue
Lewis Antonio D mariner h 60 Spring
" James A ship carpenter h 14 Middle
" John fisherman h 109 Spring
" Joseph laborer h 26 Rotch
" Joseph laborer h 94 Centre
" Joseph F laborer h 3 Eldridge lane
" Lester glass cutter b 18 Lafayette
" Manuel laborer h 11 Holcomb
" Mary widow housekeeper h Rotch
" Percy W fisherman h 6 Cowen
" William A telegrapher h 570 Washington
Libby Idèlla M bds 54 Church
Lilley Alice teacher N B b 229 Adams
" Charles compositor b 229 Adams
" Frank E compositor 20 Main h 229 Adams
" Fred machinist b 229 Adams
" John spinner bds 229 Adams
" James musician h 229 Adams
" James E spinner h 233 Adams
" William clerk b 229 Adams
Lima Antone C removed to New Bedford
Lincoln Alfred E Mrs h 101 Washington
" Bessie P clerk at N B b 101 Washington
" Carlton P traveling salesman b101 Washington
" Deborah B widow Erastus M dressmaker 82 Middle h do
" Harold C shoemaker b 101 Washington
" Hope E bookkeeper Town Hall b 101 Washington

Lincoln
" Percy G electrician b 101 Washington
Livesey James weaver h 134 Sycamore
" John spinner h 24 Winsor
" Oswell U S N b 26 Winsor
" Thomas third hand b 26 Winsor
" William hardware 26 Winsor h do
" William Jr spinner b 26 Winsor
Livesley James milk 375 Washington h do
Lloyd Fred painter 87 Main bds 22 Spring
" George W h Pleasant near Centre
" George W painter h 22 Spring
Long Charles H tack maker h 149 Green
" Gilbert assistant superintendent F W Co h 182 Main
" G E Mrs clerk 19 Centre h 182 Main
" Henry A tacker h 32 Lafayette
" Rebecca S widow Lewis b 182 Main
Longel Avery M shoemaker h 27 Main
" Frank shoeworker h 15 Middle
Longworth Edward spinner h 33 Oak
" Samuel spinner h 33 Oak
Lonsdale Thomas shoe repairer 53 Main h at N B
Loomis James W h 86 Fort
Lopes Antonio farmer h Gelatt road
" Joseph laborer h 35 Water
Lothian James tack maker h 58 Rotch
Lowney John ticket collector steamer Fairhaven h 23 Main
Lumbard Charles E carpenter and builder 19 Bethel New Bedford and 102 Laurel h do
" Ralph E clerk N B b 102 Laurel
" Susan E widow John h 102 Laurel
Luscomb Frederick salesman Atlas Tack Co h at N B
" George A fish cutter h 31 Water
Lussier Joseph land salesman h Sycamore near Alpine avenue
Luther George B cashier National Bank of Fairhaven h 101 Fort
Lynch Henry tack maker b 22 Green
" Peter laborer h 36 Spring
Lyons James P baggage master h 14 Cooke
Lytle James A Rev pastor Fairhaven Congregational church h 23 Walnut

MacDonald John G carpenter h 45 Cedar
Machado Bazilio teamster Phaneuf & Son h 4 Almy
" Joseph S farmer h Sconticut Neck road
" see Marshall

Maciel Joseph farmer h 3 Holcomb
Mack Edna B clerk b 14 North
" Thomas E clerk at N B h 14 North
Mackie Edward B clerk h Sconticut Neck road [school
Macklin Paul M sub master High
MacLeod Everett B clothier N B h 7 Lafayette [h 8 Rotch
Macomber Ada F widow Frederick C
" Edgar T glass engraver h 5 Cottage [ford
" Edward G removed to New Bed-
" Florence B bookkeeper b 8 Rotch
" William P minister Society of Friends h 20 Oxford
Macy Nellie b 21 Main
Madruga John laborer h 395 Main
Magoon Edna Mae b 110 Main
Mahoney Dennis F tack maker h 40 Walnut [Main
Maker Rosanna widow Charles h 156
" Sylvanus engineer h 27 Mulberry
Malaguti Enrico laborer h 22 Middle
Milliet Cora E widow Henry J h 146 Main [Adams
Maloney Michael farm hand b 181
Manchester Edward Jr farmer h Sconticut Neck road
" George removed from town
" Susan B Mrs h 38 Middle
Mangan Joseph weaver h Gelatt road
Manganelli Lewis tack worker h 10 Washington [64 Main
Manter Arthur E P boat builder bds
" Mary L Mrs h 64 Main [Fort
Mantius Abner E clerk 67 Main h 69
" Albert W tacker b 60 Fort
Mara Mav and Rosa h North near Main [road h do
" Joseph M variety Sconticut Neck
" Joseph R fisherman h Sconticut Neck road
March Agnes h 101 Green
" James shoe repairer 12 Ferry h 4 East Coggeshall [ford
" Richard removed to New Bed-
Marchant Fred S bookkeeper N B h 7 Oxford [Union
Marsh Frank M supt of schools h
" Thomas glass cutter h 25 Summer
" William H fixer h 9 Wilding
Marshall Albina h Roselawn
" Frank J laborer h 111 Bridge
" see Machado
Marston James W h 191 Main
" J H Chester reporter h 133 Green

Martin Della widow Cyrus W b 89 Bridge [road
" Joaquin laborer h Sconticut Neck
" Manuel S boat repairer Kelley's wharf b do
" William H weaver h Long road
Martineau Damase laborer h 46 Maitland
Marvel George fixer h 47 Bridge
Mathewson George C fisherman h 111 Main
" William eyelet maker b 111 Main
Matterson Frederic H glass cutter h 70 Fort [38 Walnut
Matthews Emma Mrs housekeeper
" Frank W printer h 75 Cedar
" Mabel A teacher Old High school
Matthewson Frank W student b 404 Washington
" George A h 404 Washington
Maxfield Charles A plumber at N B h 91 Bridge
" Charles P selectmen and overseer of the poor h 85 Bridge
" HelenT teacher at N B b 85 Bridge
" May W artist 36 Lafayette h do
Maynard J Dewolfe Mrs h 5 Delano
Mays Benjamin R removed from town
" Deborah E widow Benjamin h 37 Bridge [Green
McAuliffe John G blacksmith h 177
McCracken Louis C agent N B h 89 Centre [Cedar
McEnerney Dennis J tacker b 38
McGill David wholesale confectionery h 8 Main
" John removed to New Bedford
McGowan Thomas A printer h 22 Mulberry [14 Adams
McLaughlin Patrick farm hand h
McNamee John J bookkeeper Atlas Tack Co h at N B
Meeker Charles H h 24 Green
Meiggs Minnie housekeeper b 48 Green
Mello Angelo laborer h 96 Sycamore
" Joseph laborer h 12 Christian
" Manuel h Alden road [pine av
" Manuel D boss picker h 18 Al-
" Thomas M mill hand 96 Sycamore
Merrill Elizabeth R widow Charles b 84 Green [waukie Wis
Metcalf Harold removed to Mil-
Miles Catherine J widow William R bds 160 Main [Water
Miller Chester A shoemaker h 43
" Eugene W fireman h 41 Summer

Miller
" Mercy E widow Munson h 182 Main
Millette John fixer h 42 Coggeshall
Millicent Public Library (The) Centre corner William [Washington
Mitchell Annie R widow Amos D h 8
" David removed to New Bedford
" George W salesman b 103 Main
" Shirley G clerk b 8 Washington
Mollieux Joseph laborer h Alden road
Momini Joseph third hand h 33 Alpine avenue [avenue
" Mary Mrs housekeeper 33 Alpine
Monastery of the Sacred Heart 3 Adams [ington
Monk Audell W painter h 99 Wash-
Montague George L assessor h 164 Main [Blackburn
Montplaiser Dostillie laborer h 8
Moody Sarah M died April 30 1911
Mooney Martin teamster h 30 Jefferson [Pleasant
Morris Frank C master mariner h 57
Morse Abbie T widow Joseph G h 164 Main [ington
" Chester A apprentice b 538 Wash-
" Emma widow Joseph b 19 Main
" Eunice F widow Thomas N b 107 Fort
" George A laborer h 64 Oxford
" Harry A fisherman b 204 Washington [Washington
" John P farmer and trader h 538
" Levin S iron stripper h 60 Fort
" Merinda E widow Charles L h 204 Washington [Chestnut
Morton Anna teacher Boston b 123
" Charles H treasurer F I for Savings h 123 Chestnut
" Elbridge G machinist h 41 Middle
" Frank teamster h 35 Bridge
" Linneus W plumber 55 Main h do [ian church h 21 Green
Mosgrove Anthony H janitor Unitar-
Mowatt Alex janitor Town Hall bldg h do [Temple pl b do
" Mary bookkeeper Washington cor
Moxon Charles J metal buffer h 22 Main [Bedford
Munroe Arthur R removed to New
" Charles S teamster b 27 Water
" Edward S laborer h 27 Water
" Walter J clerk b 27 Water
Murray Gertrude F widow James G housekeeper 24 Middle
" Peter florist Washington corner Temple place h do

NATIONAL BANK OF FAIRHAVEN Levi M Snow president George B Luther cashier 42 Main See page *682
Needham Arthur E clerk bds George Needham's Sconticut Neck rd
" George poultry h Sconticut Neck road
Nelson John L painter h Tripp
" Mary A widow Martin b 162 Main
Neves Manuel carpenter bds Joseph S Machado's Sconticut Neck road [Middle
Newcomb Ida tack packer b 19
" Sarah A widow Nathaniel L h 19 Middle
Newington John salesman h 25 Main
New York, New Haven & Hartford R R depot Ferry [William
Nickerson Benjamin F express h 33
McGowan Thomas A printer h 22 William
" David W fisherman h 27 Water
" Dean B driver b 27 Water
" Malva telegraph operator Fairhaven department b 93 Fort
Nilson Karna widow Nils bds 50 Washington [ant
Noia Manuel C operative h 57 Pleas-
Nolan Frederick F laborer h 95 Main
Noland Bessie M teacher bds 82 Fort
" Frank restaurant Providence R I h 82 Fort
" Frank E machinist b 82 Fort
" Katherine J nurse b 82 Fort
" Margaret A h 18 Adams
" Margaret M teacher b 82 Fort
" T Hamilton electro plater b 82 Fort [ford
Nolin Benjamin removed to New Bed-
" Nelson driver h 21 East Coggeshall [Lafayette
Morris Arthur H glass cutter b 8
" Israel shell fish 8 Lafayette h do
" Mattie L teacher Rogers school b 8 Lafayette
Nourjian Mark H laborer h 6 Cottage
Nunes Joseph tacker h 53 Cedar
" Martin tack maker h 3 Eldridge lane
Nye Abbie H h 147 Main
" Alfred F student b 84 Green
" Charles G eyelet maker h 98 Main
" Eliza B widow Thomas W h 147
" Harrison G O machinist h 34 Middle [Green
" Horace K grocer 67 Main h 84

Nye
" Joseph K proprietor William F Nye and superintendent F W Co h 142 Main
" Thomas died July 24 1911
" Thomas W Mrs bds 147 Main
" William F (Joseph K Nye prop) oils Fish Island

O'Hara James bds 268 Main
Oldfield Frank jeweler N B bds 32 Main [ferson
O'Leary Cornelius laborer h 14 Jef-
" Humphrey laborer H H Rogers Jr h 81 Cedar
Olivere Antone laborer h 34 Water
Olsson Nicholas H mariner h 50 Washington [12 Cherry
Omev Allie W bookkeeper at N B b
" Joseph C carpenter h 13 Cherry
Ooghe Seraphin Rev assistant pastor St Joseph's church h 3 Adams
Orton John A h 36 Main [ams
Osborne Erville shoemaker h 146 Ad-
" Raida rem to East Orange N J
Ouelette Oscar operative h 401 Main
Owen John W spinner b William Owen's Ball near Main
" William weaver h Ball near Main

Pacheco Antonio mill hand h 26 Alpine avenue
" John C foundryman h Centre
" Manuel operative h 33 Sycamore
" Mariano twister h end Atlas
Packard Arthur W painter h 117 Pleasant [ant
" George L painter h 117 Pleas-
" George L Jr painter b 117 Pleasant [116 Washington
Packwood Harry H glass cutter h
Padelford Arthur D pattern maker h 24 Mulberry [Pleasant
" William Seth clerk 45 Main h 68
Page Lillian E teacher N B h 7 Main
Paine Benjamin fisherman h 5 Bridge
" Sydney S bookkeeper h 131 Green
Palmer Albert W carpenter h 177 Adams
" Edith stenographer b 161 Main
" Harriet A widow Harrison h 76 Main
" Henry electro plater b 161 Main
" Jennie stenographer b 161 Main
" John molder h 2 Lafayette [tage
" John M clerk at N B h 18 Cot-
" Mary widow Dennis B b 65 Green
" Robert engineer h 161 Main

Paquette Charles M painter h 26 Brown
" George T tea h 50 Alpine avenue
" William H painter h 28 Brown
Pardee Bertha T cashier N B bds 12 Cooke
" Lewis O mason 12 Cooke h do
Parker Harry O civil engineer h 48 Centre
" Sarah Mrs h Sycamore
Parkin Eliza widow Sylvester b 31 Rotch [road
" Harry printer h Sconticut Neck
Parkinson Leonard R foreman Atlas Tack Co h 66 Laurel
Patnaude Edmond farmer h 16 Magnolia avenue
" Edmonde h 31 Syiamore [avenue
" Ephriam farmer h 16 Magnolia
" Joseph removed to New Bedford
Paul Benjamin C removed to Tiverton R I [Hill rd
Paulino Frank X farmer h Boston
" Joseph X farm hand h Boston Hill road
Paull Alice T Mrs teacher N G h 92 Green [h do
" Alton B music teacher 91 Green
" A Jennett widow Asa E h 96 Middle [Co h 41 Union
" Elbridge G supt Atlas Tack
" James K molder h 171 Green
" Norman M civil engineer h 41 Union [74 Bridge
Pease Annie E bookkeeper at N B b
" Charles H died April 11 1911
" Frederick A fruit N B h 74 Bridge
" Jeremiah H h 32 Summer
" Robert W h Washington corner Egypt lane [ford
Peck Hervey removed to New Bed-
" Joseph B clerk 27 Centre h 131 Laurel [h 225 Alden rd
Peckham Annetta W widow Jacob S
" George H blacksmith h 45 Bridge
" Rebecca widow Cyrus b 45 Summer
" Samuel S carnation grower and agent Columbus Gas Engines 225 Alden road h do
Peet Frank laborer h 47 Hawthorne
Penington John W laborer h 42 Rotch [ford
Pepin Louis removed to New Bed-
Perkins Bettsey W removed to New Bedford [Spring
" Joseph H master mariner h 14
" Oscar T teamster h 87 Middle

Perry Antone E tacker h 2 Delano
" Caesar Enos laborer h 7 Almy
" Charles F real estate 774 Washington h do
" Charles H V packer h 84 Union
" Eda M assistant The Millicent Library b 57 Main [Centre
" Edward R R conductor rms 48
" Frank R fisherman h 124 Chestnut
" Grace B stenographer b 57 Main
" Hiram L oil 19 Centre h do
" Isabel L widow Benjamin G h 57 Main
" John laborer h 26 Bryant
" John S shoemaker h 141 Laurel
" Joseph laborer h 14 Jefferson
" Joseph F carpenter h 26 Farm Field lane [Field lane
" Joseph M machinist h 26 Farm
" Manuel farmer h Bridge near Mill road [uel King's Tripp
" Manuel machine operator b Man-
" Manuel teamster b 75 Fort
" Manuel F carpenter h 31 Centre
" Manuel R laborer h 18 Rotch
" Mary J widow Antone M b 26 Farm Field lane [Adams
" Phoebe E widow Andrew T h 140
" Susan widow Augustus F h 7 Middle
" Thomas teamster h Temple place
" Thomas D laborer h 24 Bryant
Peters Charles E blacksmith h 245 Adams [Green
" William L dentist at N B h 77
Pettee Joseph Jr sales agent Atlas Tack Co h 24 Fort
Phalen Frank L Rev pastor Unitarian church h 49 Centre
Phaneuf David (Phaneuf & Son) h at N B [N B
" Sylvanie (Phaneuf & Son) h at
" & Son (Sylvanie and David) hay and grain Summer cor Washington [ington
Philips George A laborer h 320 Wash-
" Lizzie M widow Addison b 6 East Allen
PHOENIX GARAGE rear 53 Main See page *691
Pierce Edward T clerk National Bank of Fairhaven b 69 Rotch
" George E machinist h 131 Chestnut [lane
" Henry C teamster h Oak Grove
" Henry N fisherman h Weeden rd
" Herbert W eyelet maker b 69 Rotch

Pierce
" Walter S teamster h Weeden rd
Piermento John farmer h Sconticut Neck road
Piper Nahum C h 9 Cooke
Pirson Marie-Bernard pastor St Joseph's R C church h 3 Adams
Pittsley Joseph laborer h Morgan
" Lester teamster b Morgan
Plaxton Willis E Rev pastor M E church h 31 Middle
Poelman Norbert Rev assistant pastor St Joseph's R C church h 3 Adams
Pollock George H b 70 Green
Poole William h 96 Main
Poor George R jeweler N B h 77 Fort
" Lewis F jeweler N B h 18 Cooke
Pope Harry L clerk N B h 24 Fort
" Martha E widow Frederick S bds 22 Lafayette [42 Spring
" Nathaniel clerk Atlas Tack Co h
Portas Peter A mariner h 121 Laurel
Porter Charles H salesman N B h r 177 Main
" John removed to Middleboro
" Richard fixer h 327 Main
Potter Daniel C landscape gardener h Sconticut Neck road
" James driver 65 Main h at N B
Potvin Arthur mason h 26 Magnolia avenue
" Delphis painter b 39 Brown
" Rose Mrs h 39 Brown
Poulson Bernard clerk h 179 Green
" Frank ship carpenter h 179 Green
Poyant Alexis h 406 Main
" Armand fixer h 406 Main
" Clovis mill operative h 399 Main
" George weaver h 406 Main
Pratt John L fixer h 29 Sycamore
Price Alexander h 10 North
" Alexander Jr painter h 80 Centre
" Katherine M Mrs prop Tabitha Inn, Centre corner Laurel h do
" Ralph K clerk at N B b 10 North

Quintin Adelard laborer b 401 Main
" Theodore hostler h 401 Main
Quirk Frederick J carpenter h 70 Cedar
" George M driver h 23 Cottage
" James H laborer h 32 Cedar
" John P teamster h 32 Cedar
" Margaret widow John h 32 Cedar
" William T carpenter h 33 Green

Rae Edward J chair maker h 89 Laurel [Atlas Tack Co h 101 Fort
Raiche Andrew draughtsman Atlas
" Paul apprentice b 101 Fort
Rainville L Z h Alden road
Ramsdell Frederick commercial traveler h 35 Green [Summer
Rand Frank A eyelet maker h 40
" Leonard L Mrs b 69 Rotch
Randall Fayette h 121 Adams
Ransom George E carpenter 16 Cherry [Boston road near Bridge
Rapoza John A farmer h New
Raycroft A M Miss purchasing agent Atlas Tack Co h 10 Main
Raymond H Annie widow Newell h 44 Water [Farm Field lane
Razoux Henry chiropodist N B b end
Reccord Arthur I grocer 33 Washington h 110 Main [Bridge
Reed Sarah S widow Reuben P h 134
Reeves Charles R blacksmith h 77 Main [ington
" George E teamster h 297 Wash-
Regan Daniel A grocer 335 Main h do
" Jeremiah clerk 335 Main b 258 Adams
" Michael laborer h 258 Adams
" William D car inspector h 49 Green
Reynolds Ambrose H farmer h Sconticut Neck road
" Harold E glass cutter h 32 Green
" Rebecca Mrs h 34 Spring
Rezendes Joseph C died Dec 8 1910
" Manuel hostler 65 Main h 3 Almy
" Manuel laborer h 7 Almy
Rhodes Addie Mrs housekeeper 252 Main
Richard Julien weaver h 15 Beach
" Octave painter h 19 Beach [road
" Peter fisherman h Sconticut Neck
Richards David weaver h 33 Oak
" James weaver h 31 Oak
" William weaver h 32 Oak
" William H fixer h 31 Oak
Richardson Ida removed to Winthrop
" Marion I removed to Winthrop
Ricketson Abbie P h 18 Lafayette
" Charles F clerk 48 Main h 66 Spring [Main
Riedell Annie F widow John H b 198
" Clifford H teacher h 198 Main
Riendeau Isaac laborer h 161 Sycamore
Riley Michael Jr h 124 Main
Rivard Dora milliner 333 Main b 377 Alden road [Alden road
" Flora music teacher, bds 377
" John milk 377 Alden road h do
Roach Frank drill maker b 3 Eldridge lane [Pleasant
" Joseph C tack maker h 55
Robert Joseph plasterer b 33 Alpine avenue
RRobert Joseph plastere bds 33 Alpine avenue
Roberts George A carpenter h Harding
Robinson Alice R vocalist h 35 Oxford
" Annie G housekeeper 43 Oxford
" Charles H hairdrsses 28 Water h do
" Leroy brakeman b 28 Water
" Louise B h 35 Oxford [ian
Rocha Antone V laborer h 14 Christ-
" Antone V laborer h Hitch
Rock John spinner b 23 East Coggeshall [Coggeshall
" Zephirin mill operator 23 East
" Wilfred doffer b 23 East Coggeshall [Allen
Roderiques Antone carpenter h 2 W
" Joseph S fish cutter h 10 Atlas
Rodgers John J h Alden rd cor Boston Hill road [burn
Rodillet Francois laborer h 26 Black-
Roe Eleanor b 32 Green
Rogers Henry H Mrs pres Village Industries 24 Centre h at N Y City
" Henry H Jr secretary and treas Atlas Tack Co h Cedar corner Fort
" James F h 6 Lafayette
" John E carpenter h 112 Bridge
" Prince A wood worker h 6 Lafayette [132 Chestnut
Rogler Philip restaurant at N B h
Rooney Edwin A machinist h 136 Laurel
Rose Anton farmer h Gelatt road
" Antone laborer h 63 Hitch
" Antonio mariner h 60 Spring
" Joaquim fisherman h 44 West Allen
" John laborer h 132 Laurel
" Joseph laborer h end Summer
" Joseph teamster b 60 Spring
" Lucy h 97 Laurel
" Manuel laborer h 38 Hawthorn
" Mary E widow Manuel F h 117 Bridge
Ross Florence clerk N B b 21 Green

Ross
" Laurent hairdresser 28 Centre h 14 Adams
Rothwell Frank weaver b 213 Main
" Frederick M farmer h Mill road
" Henry farm hand b F M Rothwell's Mill road
" John A fixer h 213 Main
" Robert mariner h 213 Main
Rounseville Abbie E widow William h 46 Church
" Clyde student b 8 Cottage
" Fred A assistant sexton Riverside Cemetery b 46 Church
" Silas H auto repairer h 8 Cottage
" William B gardener b 46 Church
Rouse Minnie Mrs removed to New Bedford
" Stanley removed to New Bedford
Royce Frederick H tack worker b 50 Church
" Harry fisherman b 48 Middle
" Jessie Mrs housekeeper 20 Water
" Lucy Mrs b 48 Middle
Rubin Joquin h 16 Water
Ruedinger Bertha R, C S practioner h 86 Middle [h do
" Minnie C dressmaker 86 Middle
Russell Clarence S clerk 118 Main h 22 Spring [ford
Ryder George removed to New Bed-
Ryonson Freeman baker b 18 Middle

St Amand Alphonse removed to New Bedford
" Clement hostler h 331 Main
" Clement Jr h 31 Sycamore
" Henry h Alden road
Sale Mary A S teacher Rogers annex school bds 164 Main
Sampson Elizabeth E widow John h 40 Summer [Washington
Sanborn Allen T watchman h 734
" Jeremiah B fisherman h 82 Centre [tre
" Jeremiah J fisherman b 82 Cen-
" Thomas N master mariner h 141 Chestnut [107 Fort
Sanders Edward W clerk N B h
Santana Joseph farmer h 744 Washington
Santos Antone laborer h 46 Spring
" John laborer h 5 Hawthorn
Sargent Ruth teacher at N B b 36 Main [196 Washington
Saunders Mary A widow Edward h
" Stephen C engineer h Taber
Sawin Frank E h 28 Middle
Sawyer William O janitor Millicent Library [79 Cedar
Sayles Clarence E armature winder h
Schiller Arthur glass cutter h 59 Pleasant [imals h 125 Adams
Schroder William H inspector of an-
" William L carpenter b 125 Adams
Schwigart John operative h 23 Hicks
Scott Alice housekeeper 42 Oxford
Seabury Arthur G shuttle manufacturer N B h 46 Huttleston av
Seaman John H foreman h 41 Oxford
Sears Amanda A F h 179 Main
" Julia A h 179 Main
Sekell Emma A widow William h 2 Cowen
" William W fisherman bds 2 Cowen [Middle
Severence Lizzie H tackmaker h 86
Shapleigh Herman mason rms 44 Water [Washington b at N B
Sharples James machinist Rotch cor
Shaw Emeline A h 25 Water
" Helen M died Sept 30 1910
" William P (Shaw & Gifford) rear 53 Main h 149 do [ant
" William T tackmaker b 51 Pleas-
" & Gifford (William P Shaw, Jesse S Gifford) garage rear 53 Main [Laurel
Sheehan Michael J carpenter h 44
" Paul bds 45 Green [45 Green
" Peter janitor Atlas Tack Co h
Shepard Henry teamster h Davis st
Sherman Ella F teacher N B b 212 Main [William
" Emma J teacher at Acushnet b 13
" Eva M teacher b 212 Main
" Lester T glasscutter h 13 William [Middle
" Phoebe S widow Davis h 94
" Roger h 212 Main
" Walter C salesman Kilburn Mill N B h 30 Huttleston
" William F blacksmith 8 Spring h 13 William [Main
Shooks Andrew J constable h 29
Shores Alden L draftsman bds 19 Rotch
" Walter A tackmaker h 19 Rotch
Shumway Harrison machine operator b 29 Water [tage
Shurtleff Charles E clerk h 23 Cot-
" C Weldon dentist at N B h 83 Green [Green
" Elbert H mill apprentice b 67

Shurtleff
" George H carpenter h 84 Adams h 149 Main
" Herbert P foundryman h 25 Green [Green
" Lewis T manager at N B h 67
" Nelson LeB machinist h 48 Green
" Peter farmer h 48 Green
Sidall Joseph h 321 Main
Silva Anna R widow Joseph P h Sconticut Neck road [dle
" Clarence mill operative b 75 Mid-
" Frank G hostler 65 Main h 99 Centre
" Isabelle widow h 150 Main
" Joseph B laborer h 253 Adams
" Joseph C fisherman h 75 Middle
" Joseph C mariner h 60 Spring
" Joseph F fisherman h 34 Atlas
" Joseph J tackmaker h 5 North
" Joseph P stone mason h Sconticut Neck road
" Louis laborer h 109 Bridge [rd
" Manuel farmer h Sconticut Neck
" Manuel laborer h 36 Bryant
" Manuel C laborer h 737 Washington
" Manuel F clams 66 Fort h do
" Manuel S teamster Phaneuf & Son h Hitch street
" see Sylvia
Silver William engineer h 27 Adams
Simas Elizabeth M bookkeeper N B h 24 Farm Field lane
" Lillian H sec selectmen Town Hall h 24 Farm Field lane
Simmons Adeline M Mrs b 114 Main
" Arthur W machinist h 54 Walnut
" James N machinist h 101 Main
Simpson Elizabeth nurse h 18 Cottage [B h 18 Cottage
" Margaret and Ellen dry goods N
Sisko Edward laborer h 1 Centre
Sisson Charles traveling salesman b 35 Fort [Fort
" Frank W traveling salesman h 35
Sisters of the Sacred Heart 334 Main
Slade Henry M secretary at New Bedford h 138 Laurel
Slocumb Emeline L widow Thomas b 4 Cowen
" George F machinist h 26 Green
" Grace E stenographer N B b 26 Green
" Samuel J steam fitter h 268 Main
" Samuel S steam fitter h 268 Main
" William A painter h 5 Bridge
" William A Jr clerk b 5 Bridge
Smalley Albert weaver h 45 Blackburn [b 110 Green
Smith Abbie A widow Lawrence S
" Charles N clerk N B b 127 Green
" Charles W tackmaker b 13 William [127 Green
" Fannie N A widow Nelson F b
" Frank C boat builder 80 Middle h do [74 Bridge
" John C messenger 53 Main bds
" Samuel J loom fixer h 700 Washington
" William J machinist h 45 Green
Snow Charles M carpenter h 2 Ball
" David K janitor High school h 106 Main
" Guliema H h 3 Spring
" Lehella M teacher h 3 Spring
" Levi M pres National Bank of Fairhaven h 19 Walnut
Soares Joseph farm hand h 29 Alden road
" Louis A farmer h Mill road
" Manuel farm hand b L A Soare's
Sohlgren Abraham R blacksmith h 23 Water [ter
" Charles R fisherman bds 23 Wa-
" Fred W clerk h 37 Bridge
" J Albert fisherman b 23 Water
Southern Mass Telephone Co The pay station Main cor Centre
Souza Antone farmer h Sconticut Neck road
" August laborer h 16 Christian
" Gaspa farmer h Sconticut Neck road
" Manuel C laborer h 113 Spring
Spiller William E machinist bds 7 Rodman [7 North
Spooner Allen R clerk 27 Centre h
" Edward G postmaster h 81 Bridge
" Edward G Jr garage Rotch cor Washington h 130 Green
" Jane widow Rufus A h 93 New Boston road [Pease
Sprague Andrew fisherman h 10
Spurr George M master mechanic h Masonic building Main cor Centre [Water
Staples William H mail carrier h 18
" William S laborer b 18 Water
Stearns Alice L Mrs caterer Beacon street h do [Washington h do
Stetson Charles F teaming 342
" Joel D died March 17 1911
" John H tax collector h 83 Laurel [99 Bridge
" William M grocer 35 Centre h

Stevens Annie K bds 32 Union
" Charity h off Bridge near New Boston road
" Cora A music teacher 65 Main h do [ton
" Elmer C iceman h 374 Washing-
" Eunice W widow George H h 65 Main [road beyond Bridge
" Nelson H farmer h New Boston
" Phoebe widow Dennis bds N H Stevens' [Alden rd
" Seth O watchman N B h 413
Stewart George H tackmaker h 7 William [ant
Stiles Charles W helper h 55 Pleas-
Stillman H Howard manager at N B h 97 Fort
" Nancy A widow Amos b 97 Fort
Stoddard Albert wood turner h 15 Jefferson
" Louise C D h 39 Middle
" Martha widow John h 142 Main
" Susan M h 32 Union
" William C h Sconticut Neck rd
" William C Mrs h 28 Middle
Stone Arthur H farm foreman h 181 Adams
" John B laborer h 20 Middle
" John P weaver h Newbury street
" Moses S farmer h Taber street
Storey Charles H h 92 Main
" W Augustus b 19 Middle
Stowell Bertram F bookkeeper at N B h 89 Fort
" Edwin bds 93 Fort
" Harry C clerk Centre cor Main h at N B
" Joseph Jr electrical engineer H H Rogers Jr h 14 Cedar [dar
" Mary E widow Joseph h 14 Ce-
" Nannie M nurse bds 46 Church
Strom Elias C coachman 109 Green h 125 Laurel
Strong Eunice E teacher High school rms 41 Middle
Stubbs Samuel R h 62 Fort
" Sarah C widow Samuel h 65 Bridge [Washington
Studley Braddock G farmer h 483
" William B farmer h 475 Washington [near Alpine av
Sturgeon Odelon laborer h Sycamore
" Ellen widow John M b 42 Middle
Sullivan Cornelius tackmaker b 22 Green
" Ellen widow John M b 42 Middle
" Jeremiah T storekeeper Atlas Tack Co h at N B
" John F weigher h 9 Cowen
" Michael J granite 42 Middle h do

Sullivan
" Nora G bookkeeper N B b 64 Green [h 22 Green
" Patrick gardener H H Rogers Jr
Surprenant Artemise mill operative bds 397 Main
" Celina widow Moise h 397 Main
" Wilfred mill operative h 20 Winsor
Sutcliffe John T manager Adams cor Brown h 10 E Coggeshall
" Joseph clerk bds 10 E Coggeshall [street
Sutherland Abraham warper h Hicks
Swazier John molder h 23 Mulberry
Sweeney Daniel bds 203 Alden rd
" John J grocer at N B h 203 Alden road
" Mary A h 38 Cedar
Swift Charles F Jr b 65 Bridge
" Charles F town clerk and treas office Town Hall h 65 Bridge
" Eliza W widow Micah L h 57 Walnut
" Harriet F tack packer h 105 Main
" Josephine bookkeeper N B b 57 Walnut
" Le Roy W asst treas Atlas Tack Co h 65 Green
" Philip P wood turner h New Boston road opposite Bridge
Sykes Jeremiah farmer h 32 Bridge
Sylvester Chester helper 72 Main b 92 do
" Horace teamster h 2 West
" Madeline L milliner bds 92 Main
Sylvia George E salesman at N B h 37 Fort
" Jesse M farm hand h Weeden rd
" John laborer h end Centre st
" Manuel P carpenter h Atlas cor Farm Field lane
" Manuel R laborer h 115 Spring
" Peter h 18 Rotch
" see Silva

Taber Bartholomew Jr painter 26 Water h 61 Main [nut
" Celia F widow Francis h 54 Wal-
" Emily h 18 Oxford
" Frederick M janitor Rogers annex school h 25 Rotch [h do
" Helen S dressmaker 18 Oxford
" Horace B quahaugs Middle near Pease h at N B
" H Chester collector b 48 Centre
" Jane S h 5 William
" Jonathan Jr engineer h 25 Spring
" Laura H widow Charles S h 115 Main [tre
" Le Ella widow James H h 48 Cen-
" Lizzie A widow Edgar h 200 Main

Taber
" Nathaniel D b 115 Pleasant
" Rebecca L H h 5 William
" Sarah R widow Nathaniel S h 93 Laurel [Main
" Walter T painter 26 Water h 61
" William H treasurer Phoenix Hall Association Main cor Centre h 33 Centre [Centre cor Laurel
Tabitha Inn, Mrs K M Price prop
Talbot Harold F rivetmaker h 25 Summer
Talford Charles clerk b 173 Green
" Frederick A apprentice b 173 Green [Green
" Margaret E widow John h 173
" Robert shoeworker b 173 Green
Tallman Edward G bookkeeper N B h 92 Green [Green
" Nella K stenographer N B h 92
" William architect B b 92 Green
TAYLOR FRANK C contractor Middle n Washington h at N B See page 48
" Harriet widow Henry J h 31 Main
" John removed to Boston [dle
" Thomas T fisherman h 29 Mid-
" William H molder h 41 Rotch
" William T laborer h 33 Water
Tearr John I laborer h 34 Water
Teixeira Manuel laborer h 7 Ball
Terry Clarence A clerk N B h 74 Centre
" James P farmer h 8 Middle
Tew William H removed to N B
Thacher Thomas N h 29 Middle
Thatcher Charles P glass cutter b 39 Rotch [mer
" Fred S glass cutter h 14 Sum-
" Richard glass finisher h 39 Rotch
" Richard T plumber 55 Main b 39 Rotch
" Robert W spinner h 368 Main
" Samuel b 308 Main [Main
Thayer Claude L drillmaker h 152
Thibeault Henry weaver h 391 Main
Thibodeau Henry carpenter h 21 Bridge
" Henry Jr carpenter b 21 Bridge
Thienpont Julien Rev asst pastor St Joseph's R C church h 3 Adams [land rd
Thomas George printer bds 45 How-
" James drillworker h 45 Howland road
" John carpenter h 16 West Allen
" Sarah E widow Joseph h 48 Pleasant
Thompson Annie asst The Millicent Library h 119 Laurel [tre h do
" Charles E P physician 65 Cen-

Thompson
" Mildred teacher Roger's annex b 119 Laurel [Laurel
" Rhoda A widow Henry J S h 119
Thorndike Henry A barrels 6 Spring h at N B [ams
Thrasher Frank A plumber h 86 Ad-
" Harrison clerk b 86 Adams
Thurston Isaac A stone cutter h 2 Oak avenue
" Thomas H h 81 North
Tilden Louis W removed to N B
Tilton George G tacker h 18 Middle [dle
Tinkham Ebenezer laborer h 15 Mid-
Tirrell Wallace B steam fitter h 41 Bridge
Tobey Charles W (Giles & Tobey) 44 Middle New Bedford h 33 Fort
" Emeline bds 36 Oxford [fayette
Tomes Mary A widow William b 11 Lafayette [Laurel
Townsend Samuel P watchman h 133
Tozier Samuel P eyeletmaker h Summer cor Centre [ford
Trask Robert M removed to New Bed-
Trent Charles W smelter h 16 Spring
Tribe Dorothy A bookkeeper N B b 15 Cooke
" Reginald V reporter b 15 Cooke
" Thomas constructing engineer h 15 Cooke
Tripp Benjamin F laborer h 30 Spring
" Cleveland T eyeletmaker bds 30 Spring [Main
" Elizabeth widow Jerome h 198
" Emily J widow Ephraim h 50 Church [h 33 Union
" George F engineer High school
" George H librarian at N B h 115 Green
" James chauffeur b 50 Church
" James F bds 38 Walnut
" Job C coal and real estate Town Hall bldg h 38 Walnut
" Lester E driver h Mill road n Pumping station
" Maria F h 52 Centre
" Oscar engineer h 18 Blackburn
" Thomas A pres Fairhaven Institution for Savings and mgr P Corporation N B h 74 Green
Trowbridge Anna B music teacher public schools bds 7 Main
" Mary L widow h 7 Main
Tuell Edward A clerk at N B h 200 Main [Green
Turner Francis J rivetmaker b 45
" Samuel M clairvoyant h 30 Cherry

Upjohn William F (Bliss & Upjohn) painter 107 Main h at N B

Valentine George R machinist 28 Spring h do
" G Winston machinist 28 Spring bds do [do
Valley David P builder 297 Main h
Van der Meulan Pachomius G C Rec rem to San Francisco Cal
Van Houtte Paul Rev asst pastor St Joseph's R C church h 3 Adams
Varney Emma widow Arthur b 39 Spring [b 119 Laurel
Verder Bessie C teacher High school
Veins Damase fixer h 45 Howland road [at N B
Verroneau Fred clerk 118 Main h
Village Industries (Lillian Clark manager) variety 24 Centre
Vincent Fred removed to N B
Vitorina Joseph h 4 Almy

Waburton John engineer h 25 Oak
Waite David A electrician h 69 Pleasant
Waldron Charles D editor and prop The Fairhaven Star 20 Main h 24 do [Star h 20 Main
" Henry R reporter The Fairhaven
Walker C Harry assessor h 44 Summer
" Emma H widow Seth h 31 Rotch
" Harold L compositor b 31 Rotch
Walls Roy C fisherman h 67 Pleasant
" W B h Alden road
Walter Dora widow George F bds 36 Main [prop 208 Main
Wamsutta Spring Water H F Wilde
Washburn Alanson R grocer 29 Centre h at N B
" Winfred clerk 29 Centre b at N B
Waterman Frank E bookkeeper N B h 9 Cooke
Waters Martin b 89 Centre [h at N B
Watson John E compositor 20 Main
Watterson Annie Mrs h 40 Spring
" Harry H clerk 35 Centre b 40 Spring
" Samuel F gardener h 132 Green
Weaver Henry P tackmaker h 8 Crown
Webb Hannah A Mrs bds 35 Main
Weeden Henrietta H widow Henry b 404 Washington
Weeks Alice G Mrs h end Oxford
" Arthur W painter bds 54 Washington [ington
" Benjamin J engineer h 54 Wash-
" Julia F widow James D h 76 Washington

Weeks
" Kenneth student b A Week's end Oxford [ington
" Pearl E saleswoman b 54 Wash-
" William B engineer High school h do [Chestnut
Weldon Elma housekeeper 116
Wells Alena S Mrs removed to Los Angeles Cal
Welton Avery shoemaker b 27 Main
West Eunice B widow David O h 10 Lafayette [Boston rd
" Richard A farmer h 125 New
Western Union Telegraph Co Fairhaven depot Ferry
Westgate Andrew Jr foreman Atlas Tack Co h 52 Cedar
" Arthur C machinist h 49 Cedar
" Arthur H shoemaker b 57 Fort
" Charles B painter 87 Main h 5 Cottage
" Charles E foreman D N Kelley and confectionery Washington cor Rotch h 40 do
" Delia M died May 27 1911
" Edward tackmaker b 10 Delano
" Elmer eyeletmaker b 47 Cedar
" George A helper b 50 Cedar
" George F feeder h 10 E Allen
" Helen M bookkeeper N B b 43 William
" Henry B eyelet maker h 57 Fort
" Herbert N tackmaker b 47 Cedar
" Joseph T inspector Atlas Tack Co h 43 William
" Martin S variety Pleasant opposite Allen h 6 E Allen [15 Main
" Mary widow Percy A tackmaker h
" Stephen machinist h 105 Main
" William h Alden road
" William H ship carpenter h 21 Water
" William H tackmaker h 10 Delano
Wheeler Walter b 78 Middle
White Bessie Moses teacher bds 160 Main [Main
" Canvass yardmaster N B h 160
" Eliza C widow Dr Charles W Jr h 14 William
" Ellen Till teacher bds 160 Main
" Rufus B janitor Rogers school h do [Mill road
" Samuel S farmer h Bridge near
" Thomas supt Riverside cemetery Main h do
Whitley Albert removed to New Bedford
" John W machinist b 69 Pleasant
" Thomas twister h 19 Wilding
Whitfield Joseph O carpenter b 11 Cherry [Pease h 11 Cherry
" Marcellus P carpenter Middle cor

Whitfield

" Marcellus P Jr carpenter bds 11 Cherry
" Thomas W manager Lincoln Park and Lunch Beacon h 79 Laurel
" William H carpenter b 11 Cherry
Whiting Elisha S grocer 30 Centre h 35 Lafayette [Main
" Elisha S Jr clerk 30 Centre h 216
" Susan E widow Eliab b 63 Fort
Whitman Clifford A bookkeeper N B bds 63 Fort
Whitney Frank L master mariner h Chestnut [dar
" Karl T linotype operator h 61 Ce-
" William teacher manual education High school h 76 Laurel
Whittaker Henry milk 558 Washington h do
Whittimore Mary L b 62 Centre
Wilbar Arthur H nailer h 114 Main
" Lillian F Mrs stenographer Atlas Tack Co h 114 Main
Wilbur H Nelson general store end of Sconticut Neck road h do
" Irving J foreman R R h 105 Fort
Wilcox Elizabeth A widow Edwin T h 58 Main
" Ella Mrs h 30 Spring [Main
" Harrison M eyelet maker b 58
" Jennie C packer b 58 Main
" Otis h Jacobs Neck
" Sylvanus A died May 11 1911
" see Willcox
Wilde Hiram F grocer 208 Main h 97 do [North
" L Frank clerk 208 Main h 15
" N Thayer salesman 208 Main h 97 do
Wilding Joseph W h 237 Adams
Wilkie Annie N h 69 Rotch
Wilkinson John weaver h 57 Howland road [Chestnut
" Richard Jr cotton inspector h 137
Willard Almira M widow Henry L bds 297 Main [do
" Frank H druggist 344 Main h
Willcox Albert M h 103 Main
" Burgess S gateman Green street h 134 Bridge
" Sarah H removed to New Bedford
" Susan P removed to New Bedford
Willey Jesse machinist h 117 Main
Williams Abbie H clerk Atlas Tack Co h 86 Laurel
" Albert iron molder h 59 Fort
" Anne E teacher Rogers school b 35 Main [Laurel
" Elizabeth A widow E Frank h 86

Williams

" Frederick h 116 Chestnut
" Nellie W 86 Laurel [Cherry
Willis Samuel B fisherman bds 22
Wilson Charles A carpenter h 194 Main [do
" Henry L grocer 118 Main h 230
" Thomas carpenter h 78 Middle
" William W painter h 230 Main
Winchester Alice P teacher at N B rms 49 Walnut [Fort
" Lucy F teacher at N B rms 63
Wing Addison F carpenter h 54 Pleasant
Winsor Allen P student b 109 Green
" Bancroft removed to Acushnet
" Caroline I widow Alexander h 28 Fort [William
" Emma A widow Alexander h 10
" Walter P treasurer F W & Co and president First National Bank N B h 109 Green [Middle
" Zenas carpenter Union wharf h 16
Winter Louise E widow William N clerk Masonic Building b 65 Green [Neck road
Wixon George farmer h Sconticut
Wood Frederick H engineer h 24 Water
" Helen M clerk b 24 Water [do
" H Walton physician 57 Centre h
" Irving D driver b 200 Spring
" James E student b 17 Main
" John E laborer h 245 Adams
" J Augustus carriage maker h 36 New Boston road
" Leroy L helper b 200 Spring
" Luke mill hand h 241 Adams
" Nellie housekeeper rms 17 Main
Woodman Charles H h 260 Main
Woodward Charles E clerk 64 Fort b 14 Main [Main
" Francis cotton broker rms 146
" William B watchman h 14 Main
Worsley William M clerk h 25 Bridge
Worsly Peter fixer h 20 Blackburn
Wright Harry manager h 279 Washington [14 Summer
Wrightington Edward A machinist h
" Henrietta widow Charles h 23 Rotch [Oxford h do
" Thomas W poultry breeder 42
Yale Guerdon W carpenter h 131 Laurel [Co b 52 Rodman
York Eleanor C clerk Atlas Tack
" George B brass stripper h 52 Rodman
Young Frank laborer h 28 Water
" Philip E general manager h 32 Huttleston avenue
" William carpenter 243 Adams

FAIRHAVEN BUSINESS DIRECTORY 1911

Artists

Akin Bartholomew G 14 Oxford
Delano Elizabeth T 91 Pleasant
Maxfield May W 36 Lafayette

Automobile Machinists

PHOENIX GARAGE r 53 Main See page *691

Automobile Repairs & Supplies

PHOENIX GARAGE r 53 Main See page *691

Automobile Stations

PHOENIX GARAGE r 53 Main See page *691

Automobiles

PHOENIX GARAGE r 53 Main See page *691

Banks

FAIRHAVEN INSTITUTION FOR SAVINGS Charles H Morton treas 19 Centre See page *682
NATIONAL BANK OF FAIRHAVEN George B Luther cashier 42 Main See page *682

Barrels

Thorndike Henry A 6 Spring

Baths

Fairhaven Improvement Association Bath House off Fort

Bicycles

Burke H D 22½ Middle

Billiards and Pool

Bisbee Martin L 25 Centre

Blacksmiths and Horseshoers

Doran R N 8 Spring
Kerns M E 97 Middle

Boat Builders

Allen James M Jr 21 Oxford
Casey M J Co Bridge near Middle
Smith Frank C 80 Middle

Boot and Shoe Making and Repairing

Lonsdale Thomas 53 Main
March James 12 Ferry

Bowling

Frates A F 26½ Water

Buttermilk

BRALEY A G & G F 50 Cedar See page *683

Carpenters and Builders

Bates Frank M 72 Main
Goodrich W K 184 Alden road
Lumbard Charles E 102 Laurel
Taylor F C, Middle
Valley D P 297 Main
Whitfield Marcellus P, Middle
Winsor Zenas Union wharf

Caterer

Stearns A L Mrs Beacon

China Decorator

Athearn S E Mrs 162 Main

Christian Scientists

Hillman Ella F Mrs 49 Walnut
Ruedinger Bertha R 86 Middle

Clergymen

Baetselier Bernard De (R C) East Coggeshall near Main
Bayer Hyacinth (R C) 3 Adams
Bernard Stanislas (R C) 3 Adams
Bund Albert (R C) 3 Adams
Fett Nicholas (R C) 3 Adams
Goddard A C (Q) 24 Oxford
Lytle James A (Cong) 23 Walnut
Macomber W P (Q) 20 Oxford
Ooghe Seraphin (R C) 3 Adams
Phalen F L (Unit) 49 Centre
Pirson Marie-Bernard (R C) 3 Adams
Plaxton Willis E (M E) 31 Middle
Poelman Norbert (R C) 3 Adams
Thienpont Julien (R C) 3 Adams
Van Houtte Paul (R C) 3 Adams

Coal

Buffington Nancy H 32 Lafayette
Tripp Job C Town Hall Building

Confectionery

Westgate Charles E Washington cor Rotch

Cream

BRALEY A G & G F 50 Cedar See page *683
Delano J Everett 91 Centre

Dressmakers

Blackwelle A G Mrs 209 Main
Delano Ada E 130 Green
Gifford A E Mrs 209 Main
Hamlin Alice D 23 Walnut
Hutchins Sarah F 54 William
Jenney Alice L 71 Green
Lincoln D B Mrs 82 Middle
Ruedinger Minnie C 86 Middle
Taber Helen S 18 Oxford

Druggists

Browne Pharmacy The Centre corner Main
Willard Frank H 344 Main

Dry Goods

Ede James Masonic Building
Gourley Helen 259 Adams

Expresses

Adams Express Co 22½ Middle
Amaral Manuel D 3 Spring
Barney Herbert H 63 Spring

Ferry

Fairhaven Ferry, Ferry

Fish Clams Quahaugs Etc

Delano Joseph S 48 Main
Harrington A H 8 Ferry
Kelley D N (wholsale) Kelley's wharf
Norris Israel (shell fish) 8 Lafayette
Silva M F 66 Fort
Taber H B Middle near Pease

Florists

Murray Peter Washington cor Temple place
Peckham Samuel S 225 Alden road

Furniture and Repairing

Baker James F 21 Mulberry

Garage

PHOENIX GARAGE r 53 Main See page *691
Spooner E G Jr Rotch corner Washington

Granite

Sullivan Michael J 42 Middle

Groceries and Provisions

Baillargeon A Howland road
Carpenter G H 36 Lafayette
DeCosta Frank 21 West Allen
Gelette John 64 Fort
Hammond C W 94 Centre
Hirst H W Adams corner Brown
Nye Horace K 67 Main
Reccord Arthur I 33 Washington
Regan Daniel A 335 Main
Stetson W M 25 Centre
Washburn Alanson R 29 Centre
Whiting E S 30 Centre
Wilbur H Nelson end Sconticut Neck road
Wilde Hiram F 208 Main
Wilson H L 118 Main

Hairdressers

Baudoin Louis 48 Centre
Brown James A 28 Centre
Robinson Charles H 28 Water
Ross Laurent 28 Centre

Hardware

DELANO CLARENCE F 72 Main See page 767
Livesey William 26 Winsor

Hay and Grain
Phaneuf & Son Washington corner Summer

Hay and Sawdust
BROWNELL C F & CO 65 Main See page *684

Hotels
Bryden House 35 Main
Tabitha Inn, Centre corner Laurel

Ice
FAIRHAVEN ICE CO 428 Washington See page *684

Insurance and Real Estate Agent
Tripp Job C Town Hall

Iron Founders
Fairhaven Iron Foundry Co 2 Water

Ladders
Douglas A G 189 Green

Laundry
Chinese Laundry 51 Main

Lawyers
GARDINER GEORGE N 70 Green

Library
The Millicent Public Library Centre corner William

Loom Crank Mnfrs
Babbitt Brothers 12 Main

Machinist
Valentine G R 28 Spring

Manicuring
Akin Mary E 14 Oxford

Marine Railways
City Marine Railway 22 Water
Chace Walter F 22 Water
Cromwell Charles E Kelley's wharf

Masons
Dodge Z W 88½ Main
Pardee L O 12 Cooke

Milkmen
Blossom L F 565 Washington
Eccles Joseph Oak Grove lane
Galligan Eugene F Mill road
Gelette John Jr Bridge
Greenwood Thomas 122 Bridge
Howland W S Oak Grove lane
Langlois Valere 15 Alpine avenue
Livesley James 375 Washington
Rivard J 377 Alden road
Whittaker H 558 Washington

Milliner
Rivard Dora 333 Main

Newspapers
FAIRHAVENN STAR The 20 Main See page 758

Nurses
(*Trained)
Allen Harriet 42 Church
Benson Addie F 580 Washington
Brownell Harriet T 64 Main
Bryant Delia Mrs 71 Fort
Bumpus S S Mrs 41 Water
*Noland Katherine J 82 Fort
*Simpson Elizabeth 18 Cotage
*Stowell Nannie M 46 Church

Oil
Blanchette Elzear 45 East Coggeshall
Perry Hiram L (illuminating) 19 Centre

Painters (House, Ship, Sign and Fresco)
Bliss & Upjohn 107 Main
Hathaway Herman H 87 Main
Taber B Jr 26 Water

Physicians and Surgeons
Bruckshaw Andrew N 23 Walnut
Frommell Bertha F Carl 44 Green
Thompson Charles E P 65 Centre
Wood H Walton 57 Centre

Plumbers
DELANO CLARENCE F 72 Main See page 767
Forrest E W Bridge near Middle
Morton L W 55 Main

Poultry Breeders, Eggs and Dealers
BRALEY A G & G F 50 Cedar See page *683
Delano Harry, Weeden road
Hiller G L Sconticut Neck road
Hiller G L Jr Sconticut Neck road
Kendrick C F 468 Main
PHOENIX POULTRY YARDS 50 Cedar See page *683
Wrightington T W 42 Oxford

Printers
FAIRHAVEN STAR The 20 Main See page 758

Provisions

Church W F 45 Main

Railroad

N Y, N H & H Railroad depot Ferry

Real Estate

Francis Isaac P 163 Main
Perry Charles F 774 Washington
Wilbur Horatio N (shore lots and cottages) end Sconticut Neck road

Restaurant

Whitfield Thomas W Beacon

Savings Bank

FAIRHAVEN INSTITUTION FOR SAVINGS 19 Centre See page 516

Shipsmiths

Cole E R Union corner Water
Chace A & Co 22 Water

Stable (Sale and Livery)

BROWNELL C F & CO 65 Main See page *684
Hiller R B 98 Middle

Steam and Gas Fitters

DELANO CLARENCE F 72 Main See page 767

Tack Manufacturers

ATLAS TACK CO Pleasant See page *683

Tailor

Ettleman Minnie Mrs 8 Ferry

Teachers

(MUSIC)

Devoll Helen V (violin) 140 Green
Hanna Bessie M 42 Water
Paull Alton B 91 Green
Stevens Cora A 65 Main

Teamsters

Delano Calvin 38 Rotch
Dwelley W H 88 Middle
Garcia Antone S 26 Rotch
Stetson Charles F 342 Washington

Telegraph Company

Western Union Telegraph Co Fairhaven Depot, Ferry

Telephone Company

Southern Mass Telephone Co pay station Main corner Centre

Tinsmiths

DELANO CLARENCE F 72 Main See page 767

Toilet Powder

Gold Bond Sterilizing Powder Co 47 Main

Variety Stores

Boucher John Main cor Daniel
Card H L 26 Centre
Driscoll J 16 Main
Marra Joseph M Sconticut Neck road
Village Industries 24 Centre
Westgate M S Pleasant opp Allen

Vocalists

Robinson Alice R 35 Oxford

Wood

Austin Albert L Laurel corner Spring

FAIRHAVEN TOWN GOVERNMENT 1911

Town Clerk and Treasurer Charles F Swift

Selectmen and Overseers of the Poor— Charles P Maxfeld, chairman; Morris R Brownell, Lewis E Bentley

Assesors—Lillian H Simas, secrettary; George L Montague, chairman; Isaac N Babbitt and C Harry Walker

Tax Colector—John H Stetson

Board of Health—Joseph B Peck, chairman; Dr Bertha Carl-Frommel and Charles W Hammond

Inspector of Animals—William H Schroeder

Sewer Commissioners—Clarence F Delano, chairman; J W Burgess and Jesse S Gifford

Park Commissioners—Lyman C Bauldry, George E Sylvia, Jesse F Hall

Superintendent of Streets—Charles P Maxfield, Henry C Pierce, foreman

Constables—Andrew J Shooks and Albert C Aiken

Auditors—Joseph H Allen, Nathaniel Pope

Registrars of Voters—Henry D Waldron, chairman; William M Allen Charles F Swift and Martin L Bisbee

Fence Viewers—Robert W Pease Clarence W Hammond

Tree Warden—Peter Murray

FIRE DEPARTMENT

Organized May 1 1894

Albert C Aiken, chief engineer· Henry L Wilson, first asst; Clarence W Hammond, second assistant

Forest Fire Warden—Albert C Aikin

HOSE NO 1

Oxford

John Palmer, capt; Joseph Jenney, first asst; William Schroeder, second asst; Allen R Spooner, clerk

CONTEST HOSE NO 2

Spring near Main

Alexander Price Jr, capt; George E Jenney, first asst; Fred Sohlgren, second asst; Clarence A Terry, clerk

HOOK AND LADDER CO

Jesse S Gifford, capt; Jonathan Taber Jr, first asst; Walter T Taber, second asst; Thomas A Clark, clerk

FAIRHAVEN PROTECTING SOCIETY

Wash near Main

Horace K Nye, pres; H L Pope, sec and treas

FIRE ALARM BOXES

No.

28 New Boston rd and Washington
29 Weeden rd and Washington
32 Washington and Mill rd
34 Washington and Sconticut Neck rd
36 Temple pl and Washington
42 Allen cor Pleasant
43 Cedar and Green
45 Green and Church
46 Fort opp Old Tack Works

51 Main and Ferry
52 Main and Washington
53 William and Centre
54 Washington and Rotch
56 Spring and Green
57 Centre and Laurel
72 Main and Oxford
73 Howland rd and Main
82 Main and Bridge
84 Bridge and Adams
1 struck twice "all out"
22 No school
4 struck three times Hose 2 at station
6 struck three times H & L at station

PUBLIC SCHOOLS

HIGH SCHOOL
Main cor Huttleston av

NEW BOSTON SCHOOL
New Boston road

OLD HIGH SCHOOL (GRAMMAR)
Main n N B and F Bridge

OXFORD SCHOOL
Main cor Adams

ROGERS SCHOOL
Centre cor Chestnut

ROGERS ANNEX SCHOOL
Washington cor Walnut

WASHINGTON STREET SCHOOL
Washington cor William

PAROCHIAL SCHOOLS

FAIRHAVEN COLLEGE, 17 Adams; Rev Marie-Bernard Pirson, Superior

ST JOSEPH'S PAROCHIAL SCHOOL, Spring cor Rotch; Sisters of the Sacred Heart; Teachers

ACADEMY OF THE SACRED HEART, 330 Main; Sister Beatrix, superior

THE MILLICENT LIBRARY

Centre between William and Walnut
Opened Feb 1, 1893

Henry H Rogers, pres; Walter P Winsor, treas; Galen W Hill, librarian and sec; Eda M Perry, Mrs Flora H Leighton, Annie Thompson, assts

Number of books, 21,000

CHURCHES

FAIRHAVEN CONGREGATIONAL, Centre cor William; Rev James A Lytle, pastor

FRIENDS MEETING HOUSE, Bridge near Green; W P Macomber, minister; Edward B Hiller, (Mattapoisett) clerk; Edward P Wilbur, (Shawmut) treas

NASKATUCKET CHAPEL, Washington st; no settled pastor

ST ANDREW'S MISSION OF THE GOOD SHEPHERD (Epis), North near Main; no settled pastor

SECOND ADVENT, 52 William no settled pastor

UNITARIAN, Green cor Centre; Rev Frank L Phalen, pastor; Harry L Pope, clerk; H H Hathaway, treas; John H Stetson, coll

UNION CHAPEL, New Boston rd; no settled pastor

UNION CHAPEL, Sconticut Neck rd; no settled pastor

UNION CHAPEL, North; no settled pastor

METHODIST EPISCOPAL, Centre cor Walnut; Rev Willis E Plaxton, pastor; Harold Talbot, rec steward

SACRED HEART, ROMAN CATHOLIC CHURCH, Main opp Morton; Rev Marie-Bernard Pirson, pastor; Bernard De Baetselier, asst

ST JOSEPH'S ROMAN CATHOLIC CHURCH, Spring cor Rotch; and MONASTERY OF THE SACRED HEARTS, 3 Adams; Rev Marie-Bernard Pirson, superior; Rev Stanislas Bernard, Rev Hyacinth Bayer, Rev Albert Bund, Rev Nicholas Fett, Rev Norbert Poelman, Rev Julien Thienpont, Rev Paul Van Houtte, Rev Seraphin Ooghe, assts

MASONIC

GEORGE H TABER LODGE F & A M, Peter Murray, W M; Lauchlan W Murray, S W; L C Bauldry, J W; Benjamin G Almond, M; Rev Frank L Phalen, C; Fred A Keith, sec; David N Kelley, treas; I N Babbitt, S D; George F Braley, J D; Ralph E Lumbard, S S;

E P Thompson, J S; George A Hayward, I S; T A Clark, tyler; meet second Monday of each month at Masonic hall

IMPROVED ORDER OF RED MEN

SCONTICUT TRIBE NO 97, T Hamilton Noland, P; A C Akin, S; Albert Lee, S S; H L Wilson, J S; C S Russell, C of R; Walter A Shores, C of W; William M Stetson, K of W; meet at Phoenix hall Main c Centre every Tuesday from October to May and first and third Tuesday from June to September

ORDER OF THE EASTERN STAR

GIFFORD CHAPTER NO 105; Mrs Eleanor B Luther, W M; Isaac N Babbitt, W P; Mary E Akin, sec; Mrs Abbie L Gardner, treas; meet first and third Thursdays of each month at Phoenix hall

ASSOCIATIONS AND CLUBS

FAIRHAVEN HIGH SCHOOL ASSOCIATION—meet at Town Hall at call of president

FAIRHAVEN IMPROVEMENT ASSOCIATION—Jesse F Hall, pres; Morris Brownell, sec; Edward T Pierce, treas; meet at their rooms Town Hall third Tuesday of each month

FAIRHAVEN MUTUAL AID CORPORATION—Incorp April 23, 1885—Charles D Waldron, pres; Charles F Swift, clerk; George B Luther, treas; meet quarterly in January, April, July and October every second Thursday at National Bank bldg

FAIRHAVEN PUBLICITY COMMITTEE—Isaac N Babbitt, chairman; Henry D Waldron, sec; William F Damon, treas; Jesse F Hall, Lyman C Bauldry, Hugh F Gourly; regular meetings second Saturday evening in each month at office, Town Hall bldg

FAIRHAVEN VETERAN ASSOCIATION—Samuel S Bumpus, pres; Charles F Swift, clerk; Henry P Crowell, treas; meet in Town Hall every Tuesday in April and May

LEIGHTON CLUB— Rev Frank L Phalen, pres; Percy I Fletcher, sec; Horace K Nye, treas; meet Unitarian Parish House first Wednesday of the month

OXFORD IMPROVEMENT ASSOCIATION, 242 Adams—Robert Hamer, pres; Daniel C Gething, sec; Charles Lilley, treas; meet first and third Mondays in each month

PHOENIX HALL ASSOCIATION Main cor Centre, incorporated under the laws of Mass—William H Taber, treas and manager

ROGERS CLUB—Charles E Shurtleff, pres; C Forrest Swift, sec; Ralph Howland, treas

THE NASKATUCKET CEMETERY ASSOCIATION—meet annually in May at Naskatucket Chapel

VILLAGE INDUSTRIES—24 Centre; Mrs Henry H Rogers, pres; Rachel Howland, sec and treas

BANKS

FAIRHAVEN INSTITUTION FOR SAVINGS, 19 Centre; incorporated 1837—Thomas A Tripp, pres; Charles H Morton, clerk and treas

NATIONAL BANK OF FAIRHAVEN, 42 Main, capital stock $120,000, established 1831, reorganized 1864—Levi M Snow, pres; Geo B Luther, cashier

FAIRHAVEN WATER COMPANY

Office, Town Hall—Joseph K Nye, pres and supt; Walter P Winsor, treas

CORPORATIONS

ATLAS TACK CO Pleasant at railroad; established 1810; incorporated 1900; William D Donovan, pres; Ellsworth M Burgess, sales mgr; H H Rogers, sec and treas; Leroy W Swift, asst treas; E G Paull, supt

FAIRHAVEN IRON FOUNDRY COMPANY, Water cor Ferry, incorporated April 1891; capital stock $20,000; W H Judd, pres and treas

JUSTICES OF THE PEACE

Henry T Aiken, James W Loomis, George B Luther, Charles H Morton, Joseph Pettee, Jr, Job C Tripp, Geo N Gardiner, Morris R Brownell

NOTARIES PUBLIC

George N Gardiner, Morris R Brownell, Joseph Pette Jr, Job C Tripp

POST OFFICE

Town Hall bldg, Centre corner William

Edward G Spooner, postmaster; Helen B Copeland, asst posmaster; Charles T Akin, clerk; Jotham A Goodnow, clerk; A H Hathaway rural carrier

MAIL SCHEDULE

New Bedford—Close 9.30 a m; 3.15, 6.00 p m; open 8.00, 10.30 a m; 12 m, 4.30 p m

Boston—Close 7.00, 9.30 a m; 3.15, 6 00 p m; open 8.00, 10.30 a m; 4.30, 7.00 p m

New York—Close 7.00, 9.30 a m; 3.15, 6.00 p m; open 8.00, 10.00, 10.30 a m 4.30, 7.00

Cape Cod—Close 7.00, 9.00 a m; 3.15 p m; open 8.00, 10.30 a m; 4.30, 7.00 p m

Western—Close 7.00, 9.30 a m; 3.15 6.00 p m; open 8.00, 10.00, 10.30 a m; 4.30, 7.00 p m

Southern—Close 7.00, 9.30 a m; 3.15, 6.00 p m; open 8.00, 10.00, 10.30 a m; 4.30, 7.00 p m

SUB STATION NO 1—344 Main; F H Willard, clerk in charge

BUILT IN BOSTON

$1800.00 FULL EQUIPMENT

THE CLASSIEST CAR

QUALITY CAR
THE LATEST DESIGNED CAR
NO AGENTS' PROFITS TO PAY. (We have none)
NO FREIGHT TO PAY
ONE YEAR'S GUARANTEE
FACTORY IN BOSTON
FINANCIAL BACKING A 1

We give you in the construction of the LENOX the 25 per cent discount usually given to agents, and sell direct at a small factory profit.

Investigate before you buy, it means much to you.

LENOX MOTOR CAR CO.

FACTORY

3368 Washington St. Tel. Jam. 1588

BOSTON, MASS.

SALES OFFICE

222 Eliot St. Tel. Ox. 1434

S. C. Lowe Supply Co.

AUTOMOBILES

Agents for the LOCOMOBILE, FRANKLIN, EVERETT, and BAILEY ELECTRICS

Component Parts for Standard Cars

Domestic and Foreign Tires kept in Stock

Special apparatus for Vulcanizing all sizes of outer casings and inner tubes

Electrics and Storage Batteries Charged

Accessories of all kinds

Garage Never Closed--Night Staff

· Cars with Competent Drivers for Hire. Skilled Mechanics

GARAGE, Spring and Fourth Sts., Bell 1203

AUTO LIST

Aiken Thomas 25 Everitt 8235
Allen Arthur S 10 Stanley 24345
Allen Charles R 10 Stanley 9131
Allen George J 40 Thomas 29487
Allen Green B 10 Stanley 11858
Allen Horatio C 28 Cadillac 10762
10 Cadillac 10766
Allen James W 34 Peerless 10379
57 Peerless 10380
Allen Thomas F 22 Buick 9821
Allen Walter S 43 Thomas 1193
Almy Edgar M 10 Stanley 14094
Alden George N Jr 38 Peer 13372
Almy Walter T 12 Maxwell 11892
Andre Bros 22 Ford 27099
Andrews Thos L 25 Everitt 13378
Arsenault William T 40 Pack 9513
Ashley A Davis 25 Reo 11303
Ashley Henry T 16 Pope 16201
Atchison Charles M 22 Buick 7218
Auger Asa 27 Olds 11697
Auger Fred J 3 Stanley 27381
Bailey Jonathan 12 Autocar 25071
Baker Benjamin 32 Cadillac 19276
Baker Daniel W 10 Stanley 14604
Ballargeon Louis 24 Carter 22654
Bannister John W 36 Olds 9602
Barahe Alcide A 36 Thomas 22220
Barlow Jesse F 16 Earl 12375
Barney Edwin L Jr 28 White 20627
Barnes Henry 27 Regal 21045
Barrett John R 27 Pope 16668

NORTH END GARAGE

ARTHUR E. PERRON, Proprietor

Dealers in New and Second-Hand Automobiles

Auto Tires and Sundries Always on hand

Automobiles to Let by the Day or Hour

Agent for Norwark "40" Car

MACHINE SHOP AND REPAIRING

115-117 BOWDITCH STREET **Tel. Con.**

GUY L. MURDOCK H. L. DWIGHT

NEW BEDFORD AUTO COMPANY

Agents for WHITE STEAMERS, GAS CARS & TRUCKS

E. M. F. "30" FLANDERS "20"

Automobile and Gas Engines of all kinds repaired by skillfull and competent mechanics. Tire work in all its branches. A complete line of accessories constantly on hand. Garage never closed. Automobiles rented. Competent chauffers furnished.

GARAGE, 16 ELM STREET, Two blocks below Purchase Street

Bassett Gardner C 16 Frank 23638
Batchelor George H 16 Hupp 642
Bates Otis H 10 Stanley 3007
Bayliss Charles S 46 Amer 20179
Beardsworth Alfred 25 Mit 26665
Bedard Lucien C 22 Buick 28502
Begley Edward J 12 Mitchell 9935
Bellmore Frederick 22 Ford 15649
Bennett Frank C 25 Everitt 7989
18 Reo 10046
Bennett Willard B 22 Ford 11354
Benoit Louis 16 Buick 19274
Bentley Milton J 29 Pope 13146
Bentley Samuel E 36 Olds 2961
Bernier Joseph A 22 Buick 11169
Bertram Lawrence E 28 Over 20532
Beruge Alfred 27 P Hartford 26372
Berube Antoine 18 Reo 17373
Binkley William R 26 Wayne 1961
Blackmer Arthur L 16 Buick 10085
Bliss Charles F 25 Regal 24950
Bodluc Joseph 28 Norwalk 25627
Bonneau F A 25 Paterson 19108
Bonner James M 22 Ford 11351

Bonney Charles A Jr 16 Max 8458
Bonney Frank S 28 Cadillac 28833
Booth Edward H 22 Loco 7944
Booth Zachariah E 43 Stevens 5910
Borden Charles F 18 Olds 13763
Bourne Edmund W 32 Cad 8971
Bourne William S 40 Speed 4505
Bouvier Joseph A 18 Motor 319
Bosworth Calvin T 25 Everitt 10526
Boyer Francis B 54 Olds 18947
Bradford Joel P 22 Ford 24462
Bradshaw Frank M 14 Brown 24579
Braley Jasper W Jr 25 Over 10106
Branscomb George L 40 Speed 20688
Breault Ferdinand 25 Mitch 13159
Breault Henry 6 Stanley 13145
Briggs Allen G 12 Maxwell 4262
Briggs Clifton D 22 Ford 3195
Briggs William P 22 Ford 25503
Brightman Charles O 32 Inter 7465
Brightman Edward T 9 Reo 8471
18 Reo 22661
Brightman Fred S 28 Prem 12176
Brightman George F 8 Stanley 25603
Brightman K H 16 Buick 16916
Brittain George H 22 Hudson 12679
Brochu Joseph E 8 Stanley 19738
Brooks Lawrence 28 Overland 8725
Brown Arthur R 22 Ford 8527
Brown Charles W 22 Ford 12618
22 Ford 12718
Brown Ida M 28 Overland 27889
Brown Irving A 22 Overland 10947
Brown John C 22 Buick 11489
Brownell Clarence H 16 Frank 2506
Brownell E C 25 E M F 7002
Brownell Ulysses G 25 Over 27489
Brownell William B 22 Ford 16282
Brunello Oliver A 24 Carter 10939
22 Buick 10940
Bullard Egbert G 12 Max 10340
Bullard John T 22 Overland 10651
29 Pope 7014
Bullock William J 34 Welch 800
Bumpus Frank W 10 Stanley 15064
Burton John L 25 Everitt 16287
Butler Obadiah 18 Franklin 10518
Cadorette Maxime 28 Loco 18953
Carney Ellen R 16 Maxwell 29269
Caswell Amos R 25 Everitt 15530
Chainay Nazaire 34 Olin 11851
Chamberlain C E 28 Cad 6579
32 Buick 10790
Chapman Harry M 40 Thomas 25765
Chase Arthur G 16 Buick 27600
Chase Charles F 22 Ford 16280
Chausse Aldege 22 Buick 15821
Cheny George R 38 Peerless 12821
Church William F 18 Franklin 185
Clark A Frank 40 Packard 14836
Clark Frederick L 10 Stanley 8960
Clifford Harriet R 36 Olds 35901
Coffin James H 20 White 16782
Collette Ulric E 28 Ohio 16447
Collins Williston H 24 Packard 9728
Congdon Charles K 22 Ford 23295
Congdon William A 43 Stev 16661
Connor Charles F 18 Reo 12905
Cook Clarence A 54 Stevens 9092
Cook Sarah P 32 Locomobile 2550
Cook William S 25 Hudson 14076
Cooke Frank T 22 Buick 17762
Corrveau Peter 22 Autocar 19461
Corson Henry T 32 Buick 8866
Couch George L 43 Stevens 20687
Cushing Charles F 36 Stevens 10506
Cowen George D 16 Maxwell 2995
Croacher Anna W 18 Franklin 29443
Crocker Thomas 18 Franklin 2935
Croed Mark B 18 Franklin 10929
Cronin Joseph A 25 Regal 22116
Dahill Edward F 32 Loco 20593
Damon Joseph 40 Pierce 11233
Dandurand Pierre J 22 Buick 1969
Dantsizen John G 16 Maxwell 12174
Davies George 12 Maxwell 13855
Delano Arthur D 22 Hudson 11270
Delano Sarah S B 3 Pope 1971
40 Packard 1972
Denison Bros Co 18 Reo 7036
Deno Henry H 25 Chalmers 28408
Dufresene Delphis P 20 Stan 26813
Desautels Stanislas 18 Motor 10700
27 Norwalk 16907
Deslauries Hormisdos 32 Cad 29236
DesRosiers Arthur R 32 Loco 28907
Destremps Louis E 32 Olds 11298
Desault Moses 22 Ford 20339
Devell Daniel T 22 Hudson 8685
Dews Henry H 25 Chalmers 28007
Dinnigan Daniel G 25 Everitt 10094
Dodge Zenos W 28 Johnson 11718
Donovan Sylvester E 28 Cad 3256
Douglass Edwin A 10 Cadillac 11936
Downing Mortimer 28 Buick 10791
Drake Edward 10 Stanley 7932
Drew Arthur C 16 Buick 4766
Duckworth Mencsfurth 9 Reo 29271
Duff John 40 Packard 2321
28 Moore 2381
Duffy John L 22 Maxwell 27546
Dumaine Arthur 36 P A M C 28888
22 Buick 14357
Durand Thomas J 25 Loco 24668
Eggen George A 25 Everitt 10321

MADE IN NEW ENGLAND

TYRIAN AUTOMOBILE
INNERTUBES

TYRIAN TYRIAN

are made from the finest quality of rubber and are strictly first grade up to date tubes in every respect.
Insist upon having your garage man supply you with these tubes. They are fully guaranteed by a house established in 1856.
If you cannot get them at your supply house, write direct to

TYER RUBBER CO.
ANDOVER, MASS., - U. S. A.

Millwrighting Gasolene Engineering

CHESTER F. HATHAWAY

MACHINE WORK, AUTO. REPAIRS, MARINE WORK

COR. NORTH WATER AND ELM STS.
NEW BEDFORD, MASS.

Machinery Engines

HIGH GRADE ENGINE OILS, GREASES AND GRAPHITE

GEORGE P. WILLIAMS

MOTOR CYCLES, BICYCLES,
TIRES AND SUNDRIES

Auto Soap, Metal Polish, Horns, Lamps,
Motor Clothing, Repairing and Overhauling.
AUTOMOBILE SUPPLIES

Tel. Connection 331 KEMPTON STREET

THE BAKER MACHINE CO.

General Machinists

STEEL ROLLS RE-NECKED AND FLUTED — AUTOMOBILE REPAIRERS

Mill Work a Specialty

Heavy Brazing, Etc.

Automobile Gears Cut and Made to Order — Steel or Phosphorus Bronze

8 Seneca St., and East Pope St., New Bedford, Mass.

DAVID BOURGEOIS

Automobile,
Carriage
and Sign Painting

Prices Reasonable

105 BOWDITCH STREET — NEW BEDFORD, MASS.

ISAAC W. GILES — Bell Telephone 1120 — CHAS. W. TOBEY

GILES & TOBEY

AUTOMOBILE REPAIRING A SPECIALTY

Automobile Supplies — Machine Work and Brazing — Oils and Greases

ESPECIALLY EQUIPPED FOR

CHARGING IGNITION STORAGE BATTERIES

44 MIDDLE STREET, NEW BEDFORD, MASS.

Ellis Winifred 32 Oldsmobile 18025
Faford F Xavier 28 G West 22767
Fahey Wilfrid T 10 Stanley 17325
Faunce Charles L 22 Buick 9688
Fernandes Frank J 22 Buick 20131
Fernandez Antonio A 21 Ever 24040
Fernley John A 16 Franklin 7899
Folsom Simeon 22 Ford 22665
Ferd Ernest N 25 Everitt 27342
Foster Charles O 16 Hupp 17952
Foster E Edwin 25 Chalmers 8883
Fouriner Hubert Z 22 Ford 10107
Fouriner Napoleon J 24 Cart 15310
Francis John B Jr 25 Metzger 10565
Francis Vincent 25 E M F A 1147
Francis Wellington A 21 Ever 11444
Frasier Joseph A 22 Buick 17100
Gardner Frederick A 16 Auto 17860
Gardner William B 22 Hudson 16081
Garrant Joseph 16 Franklin 26114
Gay T Franklin 25 Cadillac 28914
Gendron George E 28 Buick 16099
Genensky Samuel 21 E M F 27901
Gibbs Nathaniel F 32 Buick 17355
Grant George P 18 White 17093
Graves Fred C 12 Maxwell 12772
Gregory Thomas 28 Buick 9156
Gray Gideon F 20 Buckeye 24545
Grinnell Mary B 25 Renault 26208
Grinsell Mary B 48 D Belle 28256
Grenier Honore 32 Bartholo 27062
Groeshinsky Herman 16 Hupp 10013
Grumbt Herman L 22 Ford 12353
12355
Goddard James R 11 Autocar 4661
Goodreau Dolor 32 Loco 22240
Gordon Walter S 52 Thomas 22007
Gorham James H 25 Hudson 18200
Gorner Arthur 12 Maxwell 14128
Guiwaraes J A S 10 Stan 24286
Hagan Joseph 22 Hudson 25622
Hamel Flavion 54 Olds 10143
Hankerson Thomas N 9 Auto 25904
Harrington William E 10 Stan 27995
Haskell Frank C 25 E M F 12783
Hatch John R Jr 25 Everitt 24017
Hathaway Frank B 22 Ford 7738
13760
Hathaway Herman H 22 Will 9807
Hathaway John G 40 Packard 16561
Hathaway Savory C 12 Max 8894
Hathaway Thomas S 40 Pack 3085
40 Pack 4440
Hathaway Wallace W 25 Chal 12721
25 Chal 12621
Havard Emerson E 36 Win 10850
Hawes William C 54 Olds 11213
Hayes Fred L 22 Ford 26801
Hayes Norman P 16 Buick 14828
28 Cad 14829
Haynes Stephen W 25 Autocar 5656
Hayward Caleb A 28 Cadillac 11195
Hazard Edward V 22 Buick 25592
Headley Daisy M 32 Buick 13134
Headley Phineas C 28 Buick 3029
Healy Grace G 24 Regal 10189
Hebert Peter 16 Peerless 24586
Hedge George H 43 Thomas 22617
Hedge Lydia L L 28 Cadillac 13001
Henner Noe 22 Buick 26715
Herring J Henry 43 Stevens 665
16 Hupp 11155
Hervey Homer W 22 Ford 6604
Higham William H 32 Cad 6079
Hill William 22 Buick 14631
Hirst E P Co 12 Autocar 22806
Hitch Allerton D 25 Cadillac 27251
Hindle James W 18 Franklin 9733
Hitchcock Willard C 22 Ford 15905
Hicks Granville P 25 Everitt 28900
Holcomb Clark W 4 Baker 26601
Holden Charles H 22 Ford 22677
Holmes Charles M 28 Autocar 7056
Holmes John P 32 Cadillac 19277
Homer George S 40 Packard 20552
Hopkins Arnold C 28 John 10648
Hook Gilman E 22 Ford 8456
Hough Garry de N 16 Buick 4561
Houghton George H 18 Frank 6239
Howland Henry B 28 Marion 12738
Howland John S 28 Cadillac 7826
Howland Mary T 40 Peerless 24675
Huberdeau Adelard 16 Pope 14831
Humphrey J C 3 Waverly 29467
3 Pope 11693
Hunt Annie V 25 Cadillac 817
Hunt Charles R 28 Cadillac 4622
Hutchinson F B 28 Pierce 24322
38 Pierce 2164
Hutchinson Henry S 16 Hupp 8590
Ingersoll Amory & Co 22 Max 12187
James Herbert L 12 Loco 27444
Jarry D J 20 Carter Co 26149
Jason Harry H 27 Peerless 4654
Jean Arthur L 22 Buick 1195
Jean Jean B 24 Carter Co 13068
Jenkins Frank M 18 Reo 6694
12 Autocar 6695
Jennings Edward H 22 Ford 23070
Jennings G M Jr 22 Ford 22934
Jennings Samuel W 40 Thos 18699
Jenney Harry C 32 Buick 11921
Jenney Walter A 36 Penn 16441
Jenney William B 22 Buick 17264
Johnson Erik St John 10 Cad 11122
Johnson Leonard 25 Chalmers 10973
Johnson William B 12 Max 14073

The HARRY E. BORDEN COMPANY

MILL and MECHANICAL SUPPLIES,

AUTOMOBILES and ACCESSORIES

MOTOR TRUCKS and EXPRESS WAGONS

Agents BONNER & BARNEWELL PERFECTION OAK TANNED and AM. LAMINATED BELTING CO. LAPLESS LAMINATED BELT

Fire and Garden Hose, Lubricating Oils and Greases, Tires, Batteries, Etc.

Estimates and Quotations Furnished

86-98 PLEASANT STREET NEW BEDFORD

WE ARE PRICE SPECIALISTS

D. L. PARKER & CO.

Automobile Station

18 MARKET STREET, opp. Library Building and 225 UNION STREET

Bell and Automatic Phones

Cars Stored, Let, Repaired and Sold

MURRAY O'NEILL AUTO. CO.

Agents for MOON CARS

Special attention to Automobile repairs on all makes either domestic or foreign.

Supplies of all kinds
Tires and Tubes
Oils and Sundries

55 and 57 SPRING ST. NEW BEDFORD, MASS

Telephone Connection

Jones William 22 Ford 15751
Keith Allen P 25 Everitt 7919
Keith Lucy K 32 Buick 14892
Kelleher John W 25 Hudson 24665
Kelley Charles S 22 Buick 14388
25 E M F 11759
Kelley Charles S Jr 22 Regal 22907
Kennedy Joseph P 28 Moore 29195
Kenney Joseph T 40 Amer 17177
Kenyon Albert B 25 Reo 7051
Kerr Louis R 36 Olds 6096
Kerr Nathaniel B 18 Franklin 8134
King Mary F 16 Buick 26231
Kirby Holder C 36 Olds 13416
Knechler Kent R 25 Everitt 11701
Knechler R M 25 E M F 11795
Knight Jesse A 25 Reo 10665
Knowles Annie S 43 Stevens 196
Knowles Edward O 32 Colum 10787
Knowles George B 32 Cad 7720
Knowles Henry M 22 Hudson 3002
Knowles John W 22 Buick 12249
Knowles Joseph F 22 White 10065
Knowles Joseph W 36 Stevens 9504
Knowles May B 25 Chalmers 24200
Knowles Richard 32 Olds 23324
Knowles Thomas C 40 Pack 14287
Knowles William H 32 Buick 12432
Ladieu Henry J 19 Emerson 4644
Lamorre Anthime 10 Olds 20468
Lamoureaux Gaspard 27 Reg 22647
Landry Arthur 28 Johnson 12365
Landry Joseph M 16 Buick 24093
Landry Pierre 28 Johnson 17782
Langlois Joseph 24 Cartercar 15216
Langshaw Edward E 25 Chal 21594
Langshaw Hatton 32 Loco 11335
Langshaw Walter H 38 Peer 18291
38 Peerless 18292
Lapham Leonard C 28 Moon 25937
Lawrence Cyrus T 22 Ford 14816
Lawrence John H 32 Cad 13639
22 Over 13640
Leary Chrysostom J 22 Buick 4678
Lebeau Prudent 28 Carter 9476
Lebeau Theophile 28 Buick 28935
Lee Samuel T 24 Cartercar 14897
Lees Samuel 9 Reo 16904
Lemieux Jean P 6 Pope 28896
Leonard Milton H 10 Cadillac 9068
Lepre Louis 21 Everitt 27959
Levasseur Alfred 12 Maxwell 4470
Lewis Edgar R 52 Thomas 1038
40 Thomas 164
Lewis Frank A 10 Pierce 19317
Lewis George F 24 Thomas 12746
Loranga Theodore 28 Parry 10969
Lord Peter 10 Cadillac 8841
Lord William O 22 Ford 8144
Lowney Dennis J 28 Pope 8558
Lussier Clement M 22 Buick 28804
Macomber George E 19 Over 23941
Macomber William B 6 Stan 20375
20 Stan 20389
Macy Frederick B 1 Electric 14378
16 Buick 11152
Macy George I 16 Buick 12850
Madden William H 16 Frank 15203
Manchester William 25 Ever 27350
Mandell Augustus H 28 Over 9686
Marcille Adelard J 12 Auto 25600
Marsden George 28 Parry 12217
Marsh Henry 32 Oakland 11432
Marshall Frank 22 Ford 28824
Marshall Frank 22 Locomobile 29129
Martin John L 24 Carter Car 25077
Matheson George A 40 Pierce 6644
Mawhinney Chas S 16 Buick 16509
McCarthy Bernard F 32 Barth 17263
McFadden Peter J 7 Olds 16283
McGuinness John F 32 Pope 29333
Meaney Mary 22 White 13524
Miller Charles M 12 Maxwell 13844
Moncrieff John C 16 Hupp 12334
Moncrieff William T 22 Ford 11931
Moore James J 28 Johnson 16135
Morris John 32 Buick 14721
Morse Everett C 20 Jackson 16700
Morse George F 13 Lewis 29303
Mosher Frank T 14 Pope 24589
Mosher Henry C W 40 White 22239
Mosher Thomas L 116 Franklin 9822
Murphy S Henry Jr 46 Amer 20034
Murphy Thomas J 25 Everitt 27279
Nason Albert G 22 Maxwell 14747
Nelson Walter B 11 Autocar 20249
N B St Dept 18 Franklin 3662
3667
N E C Y Co 36 Stevens 11214
Nichols Henry W 32 Olds 14997
Nicholson John G 28 Moon 17918
54 Olds 8659
Nicklas Joseph W 36 Spring 4779
Nield William A 25 Mitchell 8130
Nolan Honoriam 32 Ohio 11392
Normandin Alfred J 27 Pope 1576
27 Over 1577
Nye George H 10 Stanley 429
Nye Joseph K 25 Cole 3963

FORREST T. WOODRUFF & CO.

PRACTICAL AUTO INSTRUCTORS

INDIVIDUAL INSTRUCTION

DAY OR NIGHT

244 PURCHASE ST., - NEW BEDFORD, MASS.

Bell Phone, 2017

STURTEVANT'S GARAGE

B. S. STURTEVANT, Prop.

Storage and Accessories

Repairing of Ford Cars a Specialty

14 WARD STREET, - New Bedford, Mass.

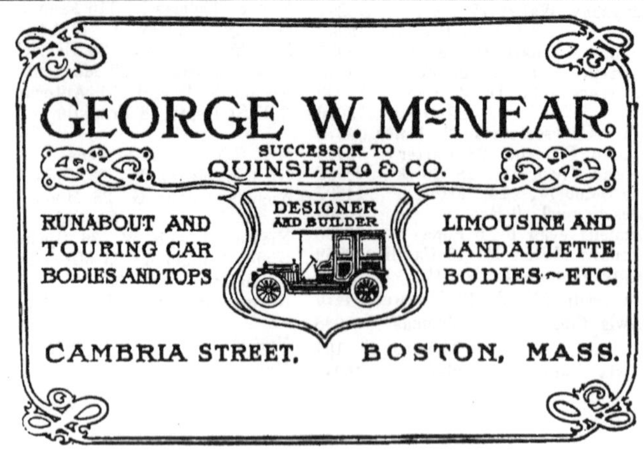

O'Brien Daniel P Hupp 10813

O'Brien Timothy F 32 Buick 25136

Old Colony Box Co 28 Marion 8779

28 Main 8799

O'Leary Wesley A 22 Buick 16724

Otis Alice G 22 Hudson 22992

Owen Alfred 18 Reo 15096

Parker Calista H 29 Pope 13913

Parker Ellis 6 Kresmobile 28296

Patnaude Joseph C 28 Mitch 14266

Patten William F 10 Stanley 10820

Payette Remi J 24 Carter 24018

Pease Annie E 22 Buick 9818

Pease Benjamin F 10 Stanley 25912

Pease Frank R 22 Overland 11245

Pease James E 22 Regal 26226

Perkins John A 28 Overland 27497

Perra John 25 Everitt 14052

Perry Henry C 16 Maxwell 8482

Perry Joseph R 18 Reo 1561

Perry William A 25 E M F 22776

Petit Alexander A 25 Over 28166

Phaneuf Sylvania J 29 Schac 27965

Pierce Albert R 4 Pope 10186

Pierce Andrew G Jr 40 Loco 3451

24 Elm 3452

32 Loco 3453

Pierce Caroline L 42 Royal 8339

Pierce Edward G 36 Penn 1233

Pierce Edward T 32 Loco 17804

Pierce Elmer A 24 Pierce 9778

Pierce Lewis F 28 Buick 24555

Pierce Mary T 3 Bailey 3118

Pierce Otis N 40 Simplex 8983

Pitta John C 22 Ford 10630

Plummer Leander A 21 E M F 10580

Poisson Alfred L 32 Loco 3382

Poisson Gedeon 32 Buick 4255

Poisson Joseph 22 Buick 4069

Poisson Ludger 22 Buick 4256

Pope Abner P 10 Stanley 1364

Pothier Joseph C 22 Ford 11311

Potter Lester F 18 Franklin 12703

Potter Sarah N B 38 Pierce 5701

Pratt Charles A 25 Chalmers 10544

Pratt David D 22 Buick 10505

Pravay Charles W 28 Johnston 6086

Prescott Charles D 11 Autocar 4788

24 Stevens 4789

3 Bailey 11688

Prescott Henry D 24 Stevens 11680

8 Autocar 38

Prescott Oliver 28 Pierce 1862

40 Packard 4339

Price Elizabeth T 3 Anderson 5855

Randall Sarah S 28 Franklin 3592

Razoux Henry A 9 Reo 10039

Read Charles W 43 Stevens 7222

Read Clara A 54 Stevens 1711

Read Everett P 36 Olds 3964

Read Joseph M 25 Chalmers 9727

Read William F 43 Stevens 5909

Reed Cynthia A 3 Studebaker 26711

Reynolds Fred W 28 Buick 14108

Rhodes John C 40 Packard 24284

26 Packard 24285

Ricard Alphonse 24 Cart Car 13620

Ricard Arson 24 Carter Car 13319

Ricard John 24 Carter Car 26471

Ricard Napoleon 24 Motor 18475

Richard Malvina 22 Maxwell 17869

Richmond Samuel P 25 Ever 30730

Robbins Elmer E Jr 32 Loco 4647

Robbins Myra F 22 Ford 4642

Robinson William A 40 Pack 3225

Robinson Wm A Jr 22 Regal 16389

Robitaille Ovilla 28 Parry 12572

Roebuck H & Son 18 Reo 15908

Rogers Manuel S 16 Hupp 7556

Rosa Mary 25 E M F 18232

Ross Ferdinand 19 Winton 23305

Ross J Conrad 20 Jackson 18204

Rowand John O 22 Buick 25083

Roy D Alfred 16 Maxwell 13624

Russell Arthur L 8 Auto 26619

Russell Edgar W 38 Peerless 4102

Schmidt Jacob H 32 Olds 9783

Schott George A 32 Jeffrey 18357

Schum George B 36 Winton 17963

Seaver Edwin P Jr 14534

Senasac Hugh 28 Buick 25375

Senna Manuel J 25 Chalmers 8221

Senseac Archibald N 25 Over 21694

Shaw E A & Co 25 Everitt 4905

Shea Israel 32 Cole 27482

Shepardson Donn C 16 Hupp 8963

Shepardson Edwin C 10 Stanley 256

Sherman Everett B 40 Packard 3864

Sherman Jesse T 28 Maxwell 3500

Shockley Abraham L 22 Ford1308

Sisson Jasper L 16 Buick 1542

Sisson Mary D 22 Overland 19900

Sistare Frank B 20 Maxwell 10880

Sloper Caro I 12 Maxwell 9730

Smith Abbott P 28 Autocar 10343

28 Cadillac 10344

40 Packard 10345

Smith Bernard P 22 Buick 851

Smith B F Con Co 25 Over 26028

Smith Willis P 12 Autocar 28945

Snow Henry K 28 Buick 1928

Sorel Adelard 36 Thomas 28265

Sparrow Frank M 48 Hayes 4858

Sprague Henry M 12 Autocar 22744

Spencer Hartley 25 Cole 12407

"A WISE CHOICE"

is what every owner claims, who selected the

Crawford Car

Strictly High Grade
Low Cost of Maintenance
and
Price as Low as many inferior cars

WATUPPA AUTO CO.

"At the Narrows" P. O. Box 590
Bell Phone Fall River, Mass.
Write or Phone for Demonstration
Byron W. Cottle, Mgr. of Sales

Sterling R William 20 Jack 12184
Stetson Fred'k D 40 Packard 2516
Strongman John B 10 Cad 15449
Stuart Laura V 38 Peerless 12346
Sullivan Daniel J 22 Ford 21033
Sullivan James F 27576
Sullivan James H 22 Ford 10324
Sullivan James M 22 Overland 9471
Sullivan John 22 Ford 9762
40 Packard 9763
Sullivan Mark E 28 Moon 10057
36 Moon 10058
16 Buick 12560
Swift Francis H 36 Olds 3402
Swift William N 28 Penn 769
Sykes John 14 Pierce 28456
Sylvia Alexander 12 Autocar 25275
Sylvia Frank L 22 Buick 11402
Sylvia George H 32 Buick 11542
Sylvia Jose F 22 Ford 14154
Sylvia Manuel V 32 Loco 8678
Taber Frederic 40 Packard 16418
Taber Richard S 22 Ford 28460
Tablas Joseph Jr 25 Everitt 8220
Taft Thomas J 13 Sears 16129
Taylor Edward G 28 Olds 29382
Taylor Frank C 27 Pope 12809
Taylor Samuel 25 Franklin 8968
Tessier Joseph N 22 Buick 12612
Tessier Napoleon 20 White 24437
Thayer William H 24 Dayton 11159
Thompson Charles 28 Haynes 17595
Thompson Gilbert T 28 Buick 7665
Thompson J C Jr 18 Franklin 4314
Thorley Thomas 22 Ford 19201
Thorpe Thomas W 25 Reo 12847
Thuot John V 22 Buick 13326
48 Premier 13327
Tiffany Henry L 22 Hudson 3241
54 Olds 3910
Tinkham William N 12 Max 17863
Tournjee Orrin L 25 Everitt 19909
Tripp Alexander A 18 Reo 21872
Tripp Benjamin C 22 Loco 4742
24 Elmore 12413
Tripp Frank W 16 Franklin 11938
Tripp Harry N 12 Autocar 8901
Tripp Henry W 22 Maxwell 8997
Tripp Thomas A 24 Stevens 10708
Tripp Thomas B 54 Stevens 167
Tucker Arthur L 28 Johnson 1962
Turgeon F X Jr 22 Overland 14718
Underdown W H 18 Frank 7516
Vaughan Arthur C 16 Buick 7033
Vera Frank L 12 Maxwell 19479
Vincent Wilfred H 25 Mora 28626
Vogel Robert F 24 Thomas 14270
Walmsley Herbert 36 Stearns 3557
Washburn Charles S 22 Ford 17114
Washburn Lettice R 32 Pull 3682
Washburn Letice R 32 Pullman 3682
Watkins Emma C 32 Loco 3157
Watson Charles 28 Pope 27977
Webber Amos V 25 Warren 12089
Weeks Alice S 3 Anderson 17458
Weeks Allen T 28 Cadillac 9084
Weeks Joshua F 32 Cadillac 25742
25 Everitt 7015
Welsh William G 48 Ford 28257
Wentworth Frank W 36 Olds 9748
Wentworth Philip C 28 Cad 5618
Wheaton Ernest A 40 Loco 8434
White Lemuel H 22 Ford 21142
Whitney Edward M 12 Max 23485
Whitney Louis M 25 Everitt 13078
Wilbor Herbert C 16 Buick 19334
Wilcox Charlotte W 3 Wav 24666
Wilcox Flora P 12 Maxwell 22726
Wilcox Patty 28 Cadillac 5853
Wilde Edmond L 40 Packard 6678
Wilkinson Co The 12 Ford 14405
Wilson D W 25 D W Wilson 20646
Wing Charles F Jr 28 Mitchell 8542
Wing Grace C 43 Mitchell 8539
Wood Edmund 40 Packard 9795
3 Electric 9796
Wood Ethel A 16 Hupp 3606
Wood George R 25 Peerless 18013
Wood Matthew P 29 Pope 19819
Wood P F Boiler Wks 30 Cad 17862
Woodland John 16 Buick 12668
Woodruff F T & Co 19 Auto 7519
27 Pope 22584
Woodworth Charles E 22 Ford 8665
Wyman Adolphus F 10 Durea 10386
Zerbone Joyna A 18 Max 20943

Estimates Given Terms Cash

R. G. GALLOP & CO.

Paper Hangers, Painters, Grainers and Decorators

Dealers in

Wall Papers, Mouldings, Paints, Etc.

309 Acushnet Ave., - - New Bedford, Mass.

Auto Phone, 1455

WALTER DIONNE

Successor to J. E. DIONNE

Painter and Decorator

General Repairing

Honest Work at an Honest Price

14 JEAN ST., - - NEW BEDFORD, MASS.

AUTO. TEL. 2418

JOHN THERRIEN

Painter and Paper Hanger

REPAIRING OF ALL KINDS

82 Tallman Street - - New Bedford, Mass.

Residence, 98 Kenyon St.

ELMIR A. JENKINS

Painter and Decorator

FIRST CLASS WORK

Dealer in Painters' Supplies

431 ACUSHNET AVE., NEW BEDFORD, MASS.

BELL TELEPHONE 718-2

GEORGE A. SCHOTT

AUTOMOBILES

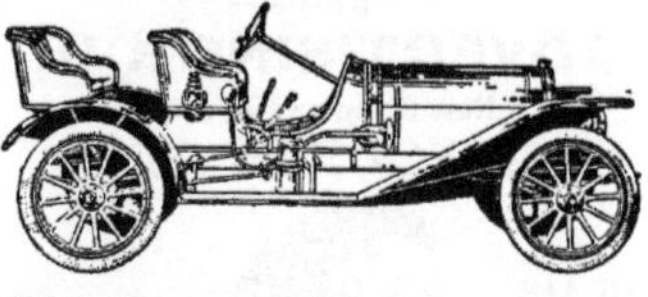

AUTO SUPPLIES
REPAIRING and
MACHINE WORK

Agent Berger Mfg. Co.
Metal Ceilings and Roofings

1467 Acushnet Ave., - - New Bedford

THE BERGER MANUFACTURING COMPANY OF MASS.

286 Devonshire St., Boston, Mass.

"CLASSIK" METAL CEILINGS AND WALLS

BERGER'S

Sheet Metal Building Materials; Roofing, Siding, etc., Expanded Metal Lath, Expanded Floor Metal, Corner Beads, "Raydiant" (Pat.) Reinforced System of Vault and Sidewalk Lights, for Sidewalks, Skylights, Vaults, Areaways, Floors, Roofs, Courts, Etc.

METAL LUMBER.

For Garages, Bungalows and Cottages, Fireproof Floors, Etc.

NEW ENGLAND AGENTS.

"Tuec" Stationary Air or Vacuum Cleaning Systems.
Estimates and Drawings Furnished on All Branches of Work.
We carry the Largest Stock of Metal Ceilings in New England.

LOCAL AGENTS.

Metal ceilings, metal roofing, etc.,	Metal Lath, metal fireproofing materials.
GEORGE A. SCHOTT	CHARLES DEXTRADEUR
1467 Acushnet Av.	363 North Front St.

James R. Wood, Jr. Pres., 687 Somerville — James L. Ripley, Supt. TELEPHONES Office Fort Hill 2022 — H. W. Morgan, Mgr. Everett 580

The Wood-Morgan Detective Agency Inc.

LICENSED AND BONDED

This Agency with correspondents in all parts of the world, is prepared to undertake all legitimate detective business for Corporations, Companies or Individuals.

Detectives furnished for Weddings, Banquets, Receptions, Etc.

61 COURT STREET, - BOSTON, MASS.
Scollay Square

Also succeeding the JAMES R. WOOD DETECTIVE AGENCY Established 1879

BLAIR SIGN

—and—

ADVERTISING CO.

New Shop and Office

60 FOURTH ST.

SIGNS
BULLETIN ADVERTISING
FLAG DECORATING

"We are the Leaders"

☞ CALL AT

O. BERTRAND

All kinds of

INSIDE REPAIRING

160 BOWDITCH ST.

New Bedford, Mass.

CROOKER COMPANY

Interior Decorators

—DEALERS IN—

Wall Paper, Draperies, Upholstery Goods, Parquetry Floors, Gas and Electric Fixtures, Tiles, Metal Ceilings, Wood and Tile Mantels

LARGEST PERMANENT EXHIBIT OF THIS CLASS OF MATERIAL IN NEW ENGLAND

230-232 WEYBOSSET STREET, PROVIDENCE, R. I.

FACTORY, 14 GLOBE STREET

CHARLES J. DEXTRADEUR

Lathing Contractor

AGENTS FOR

BERGER MFG. CO'S

METAL LATH and FIREPROOFING MATERIALS

363 NORTH FRONT ST., - NEW BEDFORD

WM. L. ASHLEY

ESTABLISHED 1853

REAL ESTATE

Residence, 40 NORTH STREET

Telephone Connection

C. H. DAVOL

Insurance and Real Estate

PUBLIC STENOGRAPHER

Court and General Reporter

23 Clifford Bldg., - - New Bedford, Mass.

Bell Telephone in Office and Residence

HOLT & BEEBEE CO.

Manufacturers of

Automobile Lamps

and

Electric Specialties

Repairers of

Lamps, Horns, Radiators, Etc.

NEW PARTS FURNISHED

Silver, Brass & Nickel Plating

BLACK ENAMEL, GUN METAL FINISH

Electric Motor Boat Search Light

Electric Limousine Lamp

40 SUDBURY ST., Tel. Hay. 1191 BOSTON, MASS.

The

Morning Mercury

THE ONLY

DAILY MORNING PAPER

IN NEW BEDFORD

AN UP TO DATE NEWSPAPER WITH FULL

ASSOCIATED PRESS SERVICE

AND SPECIAL CORRESPONDENTS

CARRIER DELIVERY SYSTEM

to all parts of the city in time for the reading at the breakfast table.

Terms $6.00 per year

On sale at all newsdealers

Advertising rates upon application.

If you advertise in this territory you need

THE MERCURY

Published by

MERCURY PUBLISHING CO.

112 and 114 Union Street New Bedford, Mass.

H. D. DUPUIS & CO.

MFRS. OF HARMAN WATER

Wholesale Grocers

Ketchup, Mustard, Pickles, Vinegar, Maple Syrup, Maple Sugar, Ammonia and Blueing.

Full line of Stickney and Poor and Colburn's Spices.

1201-1203 Purchase Street **New Bedford, Mass.**

Auto. Tel. 2224

WILLIAM WATLING

CARPENTER AND BUILDER

Jobbing a Specialty Estimates Furnished

35 LARCH ST., - NEW BEDFORD, MASS.

Auto. Tel. 2639

DONAT MARANDA

REAL ESTATE

Call here for your Books, Daily and Sunday Papers, Postal Cards, Gas Mantles, Candies, Tobacco and Cigars, Knife and Saw Sharpening.

393 North Front Street

FRED W. GREENE, JR.

REAL ESTATE AUCTIONEER
INSURANCE DEPUTY SHERIFF

NEW BEDFORD AGENCY EQUITABLE LIFE

21 CLIFFORD BUILDING NEW BEDFORD, MASS.

BOTH TELEPHONES

Le JOURNAL

The only daily eight page French paper published in New Bedford

Stanislas Desautels, mgr.
Gustave Hurel, editor in chief
Eugène Dupin, city editor
Eugene Breault, advertising agent
J. A. Desaulniers, book keeper
Ephrem Godin, circulation manager

Tel. Auto. 2397 Editorial Rooms
" " 2398 Counting Room
Bell Tel. 379

267 SAWYER ST., - - NEW BEDFORD

S. DESAUTELS

AUCTIONEER, REAL ESTATE BROKER, APPRAISER, JUSTICE OF THE PEACE
ALSO COAL DEALER.

MONEY TO LOAN

OFFICE HOURS:

9 a. m. to 12 m. and 2 to 4 p. m. 7 to 9 on Friday and Saturday Nights

Office Telephone: Automatic 2664
House " " 4298

269 SAWYER ST., - - NEW BEDFORD

Established 1879 Population 5122

The Fairhaven Star

C. D. WALDRON, Proprietor

PUBLISHED SATURDAYS

Star Building, 20 Main Street, Fairhaven

STEAM JOB PRINTING ROOMS

New Bedford Times

Times Building

Contains over 40,000 square feet, the largest newspaper structure south of Boston.

The Times is the only paper in New Bedford that owns the building it occupies.

The remarkable growth in population and increase in property values the last ten years in New Bedford is due largely to the persistent and aggressive and progressive support given by the New Bedford Times.

When people are made to realize the advantages of their own city, they readily recognize the importance of building it up.

Facts about New Bedford

Population 1911, 104,000

LEADS COUNTRY in the Manufacture of Fine Cotton Goods. Makes 1⅜ Miles of Cotton Cloth a Minute.

Number of Mills	67
Capital invested	$36,415,100.00
Number skilled operatives	30,995
Spindleage	3,000,000
Looms	53,000
Product, miles of cloth daily	750
Gain in capital, 1910	$6,990,600.00
Gain in bonds, 1910	750,000.00
Gain in capital, 1909	9,922,500.00
Gain for two years	17,663,100.00
Average dividend, 1910	9.59
Total dividends, 1910	3,057,800.50
Total dividends, 1909	2,993,062.50

Important shipping port of entry for daily New York steamers, Nantucket and Martha's Vineyard line, and whaling fleet. Nearest port to Cape Cod canal.

Pay Roll over $35,000,000 a Year

F. RUSSELL MOORE

Contractor and Builder

Jobbing Promptly Attended to

96 TREMONT STREET NEW BEDFORD, MASS.

Planing Mill, 49 Ocean Street

Bell and Auto. Phones

HUGUES DESAUTELS

Carpenter and Builder

Hay AND Grain

45 BROCK AVENUE, - NEW BEDFORD, MASS.

Tel. Auto. 3886

RAOUL PROTEAU

CONTRACTOR

Mason Work and Plastering

Also Repairing

82 Phillips Ave., - New Bedford, Mass.

Auto. Phone, 4263

MARTIN H. SULLIVAN

General Contractor and Builder

Shop, 168 No. Second St., New Bedford, Mass.

Residence, 78 North Street

Telephone Connection

FRANKLIN E. JAMES
Carpenter and Builder
Jobbing Promptly Attended to
169 CLINTON STREET, - NEW BEDFORD
Residence, 71 Arnold Street
TELEPHONE CONNECTION

WEBBER LUMBER AND SUPPLY COMPANY
Office: 182 NORTH WATER STREET NEW BEDFORD, MASS.
(Main Office, Fitchburg, Mass.)

J. N. PINEAULT
CARPENTER AND JOBBER
Picture Framing to Order
682 PURCHASE ST.
Auto Phone 1595
New Bedford, Mass. Bell Phone 973-5
Residence
39 Locust St.
Auto. 1559

ORNAMENTAL PLASTER
INTERIOR and EXTERIOR
ORNAMENTAL PORTLAND
and KEEN CEMENT WORK
HENRY SILVA
CONTRACTOR
For Lathing and Plastering
Artificial Marble
Jobbing Promptly Attended to in All Branches
63 Fifth St., = New Bedford, Mass.
Telephone Connection

FRANK B. SISTARE & SON

CONTRACTORS and BUILDERS

Jobbing Promptly Attended to

Lumber Yard, Planing Mill and Office, 111 Willis St., New Bedford, Mass.

Residence, No. 138 Willis Street — Bell Phone at Office and Residence

Z. B. Davis Corporation

Builders and Retail Lumber Dealers

Spruce, Hemlock, Shingles, Etc.
Kiln Dried Hardwood, and Builders Finish

668 Acushnet Ave., Cor. East Pope Street — New Bedford, Mass.

Bell and Automatic Telephones

BENJAMIN C. TRIPP

MEMBER OF BUILDERS' EXCHANGE

BUILDER

161 Clinton Street New Bedford, Mass.

BELL TELEPHONES { Shop 1122-13 / Res. 1122-12 }

Successor to HENRY W. TRIPP

JOHN WILLIAMS

ARCHITECT

CARPENTER and BUILDER — **Plans and Specifications Promptly Furnished**

Rear, 77 MERRIMAC STREET, NEW BEDFORD

Auto. Telephone 1533

THEODORE LORANGER

General Contractor and Builder

Repairing of all kinds

238 Phillips Avenue - New Bedford, Mass.

Auto. Phone 2206

PIERRE MAHER

CONTRACTOR AND MASON

STONE WORK OF ALL KINDS

358 North Front St. New Bedford, Mass.

F. X. FAFORD

Special Designs Made

CONTRACTOR AND BUILDER

We do not use 2 mixings

MANUFACTURER OF

Chimney Caps and Window Sills

Concrete Blocks

Our Blocks look just like Granite Stone

Factory, Dudley Street & W. French Avenue, Auto 3308 Res. 127 Ruth St. Auto 2714

NEW BEDFORD, MASS.

COOK & McQUADE

CONTRACTOR AND BUILDER

All kinds of MASON WORK, promptly attended to.

FANCY TILING and FIREPLACE WORK a specialty

ESTIMATES GIVEN

45 Maitland Street - New Bedford, Mass.

'Phone Connection

C. W. JONES G. J. DODGE

JONES & DODGE

Sawing, Planing, Turning, Pattern Making, Cabinet Work

Furniture Repairing, Screens, Screen Doors, Metal Ceilings and General Jobbing

Orders Promptly attended to

202 North Water St. New Bedford

Bell Telephone 1757-2

OVILA ROBITAILLE

General Contractor

200 COLLETTE STREET, NEW BEDFORD

Telephone Connection

TRIPP & THORPE

Established 1872

Stair Builders

CABINET MAKING LIGHT MILL WORK WOOD TURNING

Posts, Rails, and Balusters for Sale Estimates Given on All Kinds of Stair Work

Grills and Colonades made to order

183 NORTH WATER STREET - NEW BEDFORD

Bell Tel. 120

CHARLES B. HAZARD

CONTRACTOR AND BUILDER

Wood and Vernon Sts., New Bedford, Mass.

Auto. Telephone 4361 Let Me Estimate

JAMES L. SHERMAN

DEALER IN EASTERN SPRUCE

Lumber and Shingles

Office, North Water Street, New Bedford

BELL AND AUTO. TELEPHONES

LEVI RICARD

Wood Work Interior Finish

Porch Columns, Balusters, Trimmings, Stair Balusters

91-93 Holly Street, New Bedford, Mass.

Mill, Nye Street, west of Bowditch Automatic Telephone 2027

We Give 20 Bushels

Kiln Dried Kindling Wood, from the Old Colony Box Co. Saw Mill. 20 Bushels for One Dollar.

R. H. THORPE, 1786 ACUSHNET AV.

BOTH PHONES

CHARLES L. FAUNCE

Contractor and Builder

Plans and Estimates furnished as Desired

138 North Second Street Residence, 13 Pope Street

Bell Telephone 885-1

SLOCUM & KILBURN

G. P. SLOCUM

MILL SUPPLIES

Oils, Steam Packing, Leather and Rubber Belting, Emery Wheels and Engineers Supplies. Agents for American All Wrought Steel Pulleys and Asbestine Weatherproof Paint. Fiber Roving Cans and Boxes.

23-27 North Water Street, New Bedford, Mass.

Bell Telephone 263-3 Automatic 1162

JOHN PERRA

Steam, Gas and Hot Water Fitting

Tin and Sheet Iron Work and all kinds of Boiler Repairing

Gas Chandeliers a Specialty. Plumbing

19 Linden Street - New Bedford, Mass.

Telephone, Auto. 2094 Bell 1783

WALTER P. BAILEY

HEATING AND PLUMBING, SHEET METAL WORK

Furnaces, Ranges and Pumps. Jobbing of all kinds

All Work Given Personal Supervision

216 Acushnet Ave., cor. Cannon St., New Bedford, Mass.

Residence, So. Dartmouth, Mass. TEL. CON.

ESTABLISHED 1833

JONATHAN HANDY CO.

CHAS. A. JEWETT, Mgr.

Wholesale and Retail Dealers in

Iron, Steel, Blacksmiths Supplies, Carriage Woodwork, Paints and Varnish. Auto Supplies.

28-30 WILLIAM STREET

BELL AND AUTOMATIC TELEPHONES

J. H. SHERMAN

Established 1872

Plumbing, Sheet Metal Work

Steam and Hot Water Heating

52, 54, 56 UNION STREET Telephone 959

H. N. QUINTIN

Hardware, Paints, Oils

CUTLERY, TINWARE

BUILDERS SUPPLIES

1223 ACUSHNET AVENUE 1223

AUTOMATIC 2082

C. F. DELANO

Plumbing, Hardware

Tinning and Heating

Orders Given Prompt Attention Telephone Connection

SHOE FACTORY BUILDING

72 MAIN STREET FAIRHAVEN, MASS.

Bell Telephone 654-1 Automatic 2573

JEREMIAH COHOLAN

(Successor to JOHN V. O'NEIL)

Sanitary Plumber and Metal Worker

HOT WATER and WARM AIR HEATING

703-705 So. Water Street, New Bedtord, Mass.

J. & W. R. WING & CO.

THE GOOD CLOTHES STORE

Hatters and Men's Furnishings

133 UNION STREET - NEW BEDFORD

Bell Telephone 142 Automatic 1136

F. W. WENTWORTH CO.

Clothiers, Furnishers and Hatters

Union corner Pleasant Street, NEW BEDFORD

W. E. SMITH Established May 17, 1886

NEW BEDFORD STEAM DYE HOUSE

Dyeing and Cleansing of Every Description

AT SHORT NOTICE

Dry Cleaning a Specialty

53 WILLIAM STREET - NEW BEDFORD

A. M. BUSH & CO.

Merchant Tailors

LADIES' TAILORING

47 WILLIAM STREET, opp. Custom House, New Bedford

Clothing Cleaned, Dyed, Pressed and Repaired. Goods called for and returned to any part of the City. Satisfaction guaranteed

Telephone Connection

Naphtha cleaning with the disagreeable odor eliminated

F. S. BRIGHTMAN CO. Inc.
Wholesale Stationers
DEALERS IN
Blank Books, Wrapping Papers, Paper Bags, Twines, etc.
Mill Wrapping, Packing, Toilet and Baling Papers a specialty.
127-129 UNION STREET, NEW BEDFORD, MASS.
TEL. AUTO. 1134 TEL. BELL 1050

For accommodation of my patrons I have a special department for alteration and pressing.

Formerly of Paris and New York
36 EIGHTH STREET
NEW BEDFORD, MASS.
114 BROADWAY
NEWPORT, R. I.
Bell Telephone 805-5

NEW BEDFORD
504 County St., Cor. High
- - TWO STORES - -
FAIRHAVEN
29 Centre Street
E. H. CRONIN
(Formerly with A. M. Bush & Co.)
Ladies' and Gents' Clothing
Cleaned, Pressed, Repaired and Altered
All Work Guaranteed
Furs of all Kinds Sealed and Protected from Moths and all other Insects. Gloves Cleaned.

CHARLES A. MAXFIELD
Successor to COGGESHALL, MAXFIELD & CO.
PRACTICAL - SANITARY
PLUMBERS
Tin and Sheet Iron Workers
Glenwood Hot Air Furnaces, Stoves, Ranges, Etc.
26 North Second Street - - New Bedford, Mass.

ALBERT C. SHERMAN ESTABLISHED 1880

ALBERT C. SHERMAN

Hack, Livery and Boarding Stable

LANDAUS, BERLIN COACHES, BROUGHAMS, ROCKAWAYS and COUPES
FURNISHED at SHORT NOTICE Carriages for funerals and Weddings a Specialty

50 ELM STREET - NEW BEDFORD

Bell Telephone 320 Automatic Telephone 1261

WALTER H. PEIRCE LEWIS F. PEIRCE

W. H. & L. F. PEIRCE

Livery, Sale and Boarding Stable

PIANOS AND FURNITURE MOVED. HACKS AND CABS TO LET.
PLEASURE PARTIES ACCOMMODATED WITH BARGES AND OTHER VEHICLES

HOUSEHOLD FURNITURE MOVED FROM ONE CITY TO ANOTHER
TELEPHONE CONNECTION

304 KEMPTON ST., near Summer, NEW BEDFORD

ESTABLISHED 1878

William R. Washburn

Fine Horses and Carriages to let at Reasonable Prices

NONQUITT

Telephone New Bedford 1476-13

ARTHUR S. TALLMAN

Livery, Hack and Boarding Stable

Cor. Sixth and Grinnell Street NEW BEDFORD, MASS.

Bell Telephone 901-5

Raymond's Boarding & Livery Stable

Chas. Raymond, Prop.

Carriages Furnished for Funerals, Weddings, Etc.

396 COTTAGE STREET

Bell Phone 2189-2

Telephone Connection

C. H. MURPHY & SON

Hack, Livery and Boarding Stables

Hacks furnished for Funerals, Weddings and Parties
Good Horses and Carriages to let at reasonable prices

Cor. Spring and Second Sts., and 42 Fourth St. New Bedford

L. J. HATHAWAY

MANUFACTURER OF

Carriages of all Descriptions
and Dealer in Carriage Stock

Repairing Promptly Attended to

Automobile Repairing and Painting

7 and 9 ELM STREET NEW BEDFORD

ROGLER'S CAFE

PHILIP ROGLER, Proprietor

72-74 WILLIAM STREET

NEW BEDFORD, MASS.

BELL TELEPHONE

DANIEL ROBINSON

DEALER IN

Fine Groceries

Meats, Provisions, Spices, Canned Goods, Teas and Coffees

156 WELD STREET - NEW BEDFORD

NEW YORK MARKET

EDWARD A. HOXIE, Proprietor

Groceries and Provisions

Meats and Vegetables

FOREIGN and DOMESTIC FRUIT

251 Purchase Street, New Bedford Telephone 412

ALDEGE CHAUSSE

JUSTICE OF THE PEACE

Meats, Groceries and Provisions

Livery Stable, Hacks for Weddings and Funerals. Automatic Phone 2151. Bell Phone 2163

Cor. North Front and Coffin Ave., New Bedford, Mass.

GUAY BROS.

(Successors to J. A. Bouvier)

— Dealers in —

Hay, Straw, Grain, Feed, Etc.

Hay by Carload a Specialty

846-848 ACUSHNET AVE. Auto. Tel. 2161

"THE OLD and RELIABLE FAMILY WINE MERCHANTS"

Carry in stock always (both Imported and Domestic) the best brands of

Whiskey, Wine, Brandy, Gin, Rum, Champagne, Claret, Cocktails, Cordials, Bitters, Alcohol, Ale, Porter, Lager Beer, Malt Extracts, Champagne Cider, Mineral Water, Ginger Ale, Soda Water, Etc.

Your order will be given prompt attention and satisfaction is guaranteed or your money will be cheerfully refunded.

HIRAM WHEATON & SONS

45, 47, 49, 51 SCHOOL STREET - NEW BEDFORD, MASS.

Established January 1, 1853.

NEW BEDFORD ICE COMPANY

Wholesale and Retail Dealers in

..ICE..

GEORGE H. PAUL
Treasurer

Telephone Connection

12 SCHOOL STREET

H. P. DION

BAKER AND FLOUR DEALER

1070 County St., foot Adams St., New Bedford

Automatic Telephone

JOHN CONNELL, Jr.

Sand and Gravel

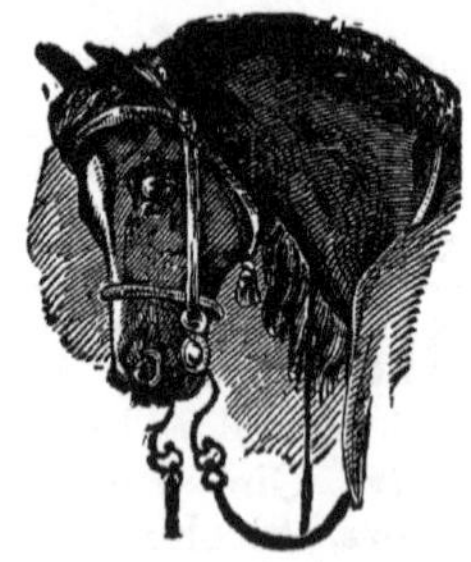

General Teamster

CONTRACTOR

Automatic 2323 350 SAWYER STREET

PAISLER & WILLIS

Masons Building Materials

LIME, CEMENT, BRICK, FLAG-STONES, GRANITE CURBING, DRAIN PIPE, ETC.

Plain, Encaustic and Glazed Tiles for Hearths, Mantel Facings and Vestibules

160 North Water Street, New Bedford

RESIDENCE, 53 North Street BELL TELEPHONE YARD, 51 and 54 Foster Street

JOHN L. G. MASON

Contractor and Jobber in All Kinds of Mason Work

PARTICULAR ATTENTION PAID TO JOBBING

Stucco Work, Tiles Set, Fire Places and Brick Mantels Built to Order. Granolithic, Kilolithic, Anthralithic, Rock Granite and Portland Cement Walks and Drives with Rough or Polished Surfaces as desired. Try works for Whaling Ships, Casting Furnaces, Oven and Boiler Work,

A Specialty made of Whitewashing, Whitening and Tinting in Plastico, Muresco and Neolith

Masons' Stock kept constantly on hand, for Summer and Winter use. Fire Clay Stove Pipe with Fancy Tops for Chimneys. Terra Cotta Chimney Tops and Wind Guards. Expert on Smoky and Slow Draft Chimneys. **Agent for Lockwood Burial Vault.**

Established 1852

J. FRANK KIRK

HAY, STRAW, FLOUR,
GRAIN, FEED, SEED
AND PLANTS

370, 372, 374 Purchase Street
Bell 424-2 Auto. 1255

PLUMMER & JENNINGS GRAIN CO.

CORPORATION
W. H. JENNINGS, Treas.

Flour, Grain, Hay and Straw

100 SOUTH WATER STREET
Telephone, Bell 898 and Automatic 1157

J. S. MACY

EXPRESSING AND JOBBING

Goods Delivered to and from Electric Express
Order Slate at Electric Express Office

Express Office, 21 SO. SECOND, Corner SPRING STREET

TELEPHONE CONNECTION

O. DROLET
109 HOLLY STREET
AUTO. TEL. 2228

A. P. MILOTTE
17 REYNOLDS STREET
AUTO. TEL. 2189

DROLET & MILOTTE

HOUSE PAINTERS

Paper Hangers and Decorators

Estimates Cheerfully Given. Work Guaranteed.

109 HOLLY STREET - NEW BEDFORD, MASS.

George W. Paine Olin S. Paine

S. S. PAINE & BRO.

Established 1836

Lime, Cement, Brick, Drain Pipe

Fire Brick, Fire Clay and Flue Lining

139 FRONT STREET Bell 1212-4, Automatic 1214

Residence, 859 Rockdale Ave. Phone 3476

Residence, 121 Clark St. Phone 2378

LOFTUS & DUGAN

GRANOLITHIC WORK

Sidewalks Driveways Cellars, Etc.

NEW BEDFORD

H. M. CROTEAU 249 Shawmut Ave.

F. H. WOOD 52 Main St.

CROTEAU & WOOD

MASONS

BRICK, PLASTERING, STONE AND CONCRETE WORK OF ALL KINDS

NEW BEDFORD, MASS.

Auto Phone Connections

CORMIER & DUBE

DEALERS IN

PAINTS, OILS and VARNISHES, also PAPER HANGERS and WHITEWASHERS

394 No. Front St., - New Bedford, Mass.

Auto Phone, 2353

HILL CO.

..SIGNS..

FIRST CLASS WORK, PROMPT SERVICE,CORRECT PRICES. CALL UP CHARLES (THE LONG FELLOW) FORMERLY WITH THE BLAIR SIGN CO.

Both Telephones 257 UNION STREET

MARCUS M. ALLEN

Painting and Decorating

Painters' Supplies

15 to 19 North Water Street New Bedford, Mass.

Telephone Connection

GEORGE F. WRIGHT

HOUSE, SIGN AND ORNAMENTAL PAINTING

GRAINER, PAPER HANGER AND FRESCO PAINTER

Sole Proprietor for New Bedford for the PA CRUSTA DECORATION.

24 North Water St. New Bedford, Mass.

ADELARD BRILLON

House and Sign Painter

PAINTERS SUPPLIES

Paper Hanging and Whitewashing

80 HOLLY ST. Auto Tel. 2086 New Bedford, Mass.

F. FOREST & CO.

MUSIC AND MUSICAL INSTRUMENTS
STATIONERY AND FANCY ART GOODS
PICTURES AND FRAMES
A FULL LINE OF CATHOLIC GOODS
JEWELRY & SILVERWARE

1041 ACUSHNET AVENUE, NEW BEDFORD, MASS.

Frederick A. Brown

PHOTOGRAPHER

88 PURCHASE ST., NEW BEDFORD, MASS.

Telephone Connection

CLIFTON H. CORNISH

INSURANCE

Room 12, Clifford Building

Market and Sixth Streets, New Bedford, Mass.

THE J. E. BUDLONG PRESS

PRINTERS

A THOROUGHLY EQUIPPED PRINTING OFFICE
WHEREIN IS DONE THE HIGHEST CLASS
OF WORK.

38 MIDDLE ST., - NEW BEDFORD, MASS.

AUTO PHONE 1544 BELL TEL. 1890

SMITH BROS.

Brewers, Bottlers and Wholesale Liquor Dealers

MANUFACTURERS OF ICE

Office and Warehouse, 777-785 PURCHASE STREET

Brewery, Ice Houses and Bottling Works } **COGGESHALL ST., NEW BEDFORD**

TELEPHONES

Office, Bell 919, Automatic 2123 — Brewery, Automatic 2115, Bell 1768-4

C. DEXTRAZE

Liquor Dealer

Auto Telephone 2137 — **1276 ACUSHNET AVENUE**

NEW BEDFORD, MASS.

Bell Phone 1600 — Auto Phone 1654

JACOB WEIHL

Wholesale and Retail

Liquor Dealer

Also Distributer For

The Famous Narragansett Beers

21½ to 23½ No. Second Street — **New Bedford, Mass.**

THE PALACE

Is intended to fill a demand of the public for a place to obtain a light down-town breakfast or mid-day lunch of wholesome delicious food, nicely prepared and served quickly at a moderate cost. The best of everything, including our famous Coffee.

173 Purchase Street

New Bedford, Mass.

Automatic Telephone 1605

W. H. RANKIN H. PERCY ARNOLD

RANKIN & ARNOLD

Successors to W. A. Rankin

General Machinists and Steam Fitters

Gasoline Engine Repairing

19 NO. SECOND ST., NEW BEDFORD, MASS.

EVERETT GREEN

Lead Burning, Sheet Melal Worker and Plumber

CORNICE MAKER and BLOWER WORK MILL WORK A SPECIALTY

NAPHTHA and WATER TANKS AUTOMOBILE REPAIRING

Jobbing Promptly Attended To. Open Evenings

185 Acushnet Avenue, Cor. Bedford St., New Bedford, Mass.

Auto. Tel. 1013 Bell Tel. 1350

Auto. Tel., 2526

EDWARD H. GREGORY

SANITARY PLUMBER

HIGH GRADE WORK A SPECIALTY

878-880 So. Water Street, New Bedford, Mass.

A. BOLDUC

PLUMBING, TINNING, PIPING and GAS FIXTURES

109 BOWDITCH STREET, NEW BEDFORD, MASS.

AUTO. AND BELL TELEPHONES

C. F. HURLEY

SLATE AND GRAVEL ROOFER

Sheet Metal Work

Special Attention Given to the Repairing of Slate and Gravel Roofs.

Offices and Yard, 90 BEETLE ST., NEW BEDFORD, MASS.

Telephone Connection

Robert W. Foster Brass Foundry

Brass Composition, Phos. Bronze, Copper, Nickel Bronze, Nickel Silver Casting.

BRASS AND TOBIN BRONZE ROD

115 No. Water St., - New Bedford, Mass.

Telephone 647

W. H. Mudge, 378 Allen St. 2143-3 Bell Phones 1145-51 C. J. Francis, 83 Forest St.

MUDGE & FRANCIS

Sanitary Plumbing, Hot Waler and Hot Air Healing

Stove and Furnace Repairs. Lead Burning.

We install Gas Automatic Heaters, also Water Systems for country places. Wind Mill work.

157 Acushnet Ave., - New Bedford, Mass.

815-2 Bell and Automatic Telephones 1194

SHERMAN & McQUILLAN

Successors to George E. Hatch

Plumbing, Tinning, Healing

AND DEALERS IN

Stoves, Ranges and Furnaces

250 PURCHASE ST., - NEW BEDFORD, MASS.

AUTO. TEL. 1124 BELL TEL. 794-2

COFFIN BROTHERS

MANUFACTURERS OF

PAPER BOXES

38 MIDDLE ST., NEW BEDFORD

BELL AND AUTOMATIC TELEPHONES

H. B. PARLOW A. C. GODDARD

PARLOW & GODDARD

ALL KINDS OF

INSURANCE

Room 206, Merchants Bank Building
New Bedford, Mass.

G. W. AUGER & CO.

DEALERS IN

Bicycles and Sundries

HEADQUARTERS FOR OIL-PROOF TIRES
AUTOMOBILE TIRE VULCANIZING

Auto. Telephone 1430

228 PURCHASE ST., NEW BEDFORD, MASS.

Estimates Cheerfully Given. Auto. Tel.

JOHN P. BURKE

SANITARY PLUMBING

HOT WATER AND GAS FITTER

COUNTY and WELD STS., NEW BEDFORD, MASS.

GEORGE F. SAWIN & CO.

BUILDING MOVERS

Teamsters and Contractors

343 PURCHASE STREET
New Bedford, Mass.

PATRICK CONNOR

DEALER IN

WOOD and COAL

486 Rivet Street, New Bedford

Telephone, Bell 354-2, Auto. 3672

Residence, 55 Fifth Street

PARANDELIS & DANGELAS

PROPRIETORS

Crown Confectionery Store

RESTAURANT AND ICE CREAM PARLOR

ICE CREAM MANUFACTURERS AND CATERERS

56 PURCHASE STREET - NEW BEDFORD

TELEPHONE CONNECTION

Standard Construction Co.

J. R. PAINCHAUD, Prop.

PLUMBING, HEATING

—— AND ——

GAS PIPING

281½ SAWYER STREET, - NEW BEDFORD, MASS.

Automatic Phone 2049

ERNEST HOWARTH
ELECTRICAL CONTRACTOR

Electric Light Wirings   Private Telephone Systems

REPAIRS OF ALL KINDS

120 Middle St., (Opposite Gas Co.) - New Bedford, Mass.

Telephone Connection

JOSEPH A. LAWRENCE

DEALER IN

Builders' Hardware

Stoves, Sporting Goods, Roofing Materials, Cutlery, Builders' Supplies, Paints, Varnish, Stains, Glass, etc.

1032 - 1034 ACUSHNET AVENUE

Auto. Phone 2063

Jewett Hardware Co.

Iron, Steel, Bolts, Heavy Hardware, Carriage Woodwork, Blacksmith, Railroad, Mill, Machine Shop, and Contractors Supplies

Cor. Middle St. and Acushnet Ave., - New Bedford, Mass.

Telephone, AUTO 1595   Telephone, BELL 2354

Established 1862

W. A. Greenough & Co.

Compilers, Printers and Publishers of

DIRECTORIES

65 BROAD STREET

BOSTON, MASS.

Telephone, Main 4415-W

W. E. BOSWORTH

Inventor and Manufacturer of

New Plan Refrigerator

Old Refrigerators Altered into the "New Plan" and Warranted Not to Sweat.

Cold Storage of All Kinds a Specialty.

An Improvement on "Lyman Patent"

1194 Rockdale Avenue Auto. Telephone New Bedford, Mass.

GEORGE CEJKA

Plumbing and Gas Fitting

STOVE REPAIRS A SPECIALTY

TIN AND SHEET METAL WORK OF ALL KINDS

STEAM, HOT WATER AND FURNACE HEATING

1480 Acushnet Avenue - New Bedford, Mass.

Auto. Phone 2301

JOSEPH LEBEAU

House Painter and Decorator

SIGN PAINTING

Paper Hanger, Whitewasher and Grainer

141 COLLETTE STREET

Telephone Connection

AWNINGS, TENTS, FLAGS & SAILS

We are jobbers and retailers of the

BEST

in Marine Hardware

"Everything for the Boat"

BRIGGS & BECKMAN

31 - 35 COMMERCIAL ST.

S. D. HOWLAND K. H. BRIGHTMAN

S. D. HOWLAND & CO.

Coat, Apron and Towel Supply

We supply the largest and best towel cabinet, with six large clean towels per week, and all other articles necessary for a first class towel cabinet for the small sum of $1.00 per month

86 Chancery Street, New Bedford, M

Telephone 729-2

Your Washing Done For Fifty C

HOME WASHING

Wet Washes

FIFTY CENTS A BASKET

PENNIMAN, Corner MYRTLE ST. Bell 1787, if busy call 2292-4 Auto. 2107.

NORTH END LAUNDRY CO.

1066 County St., New Bedford, Mass.

Pay the driver, otherwise do not blame him if he does not leave your bundle. Our terms are strictly cash.

Not responsible for woolens. Not responsible in case of fire

Extra Charge for over 60 pieces.

THE CLEAN WET WASH

D. E. ALLEN, Proprietor

Family Washing

Cleaning Woolens a Specialty

76 Shawmut Avenue - - New Bedford, Mass.

Bell Telephone 440
Auto. " 1552

National Wet Wash Laundry Co.

AUDETTE & CHAPDELAINE, Props.

Baskets Called for and Delivered

Automatic 2003 **281 SAWYER STREET**

W. LEVESQUE

PLUMBING, JOBBING
AND
ELECTRICAL WORK

211 COFFIN AVENUE - NEW BEDFORD, MASS.

Automatic Phone, 2065

HOUSEHOLD GOODS MOVED TO AND FROM ADJOINING CITIES
Pianos and Furniture Moved with Care and Despatch

D. H. DeMORANVILLE
GENERAL TEAMSTER

We Do Moving Jobs Over the Road at Right Prices
Railroad Freight Promptly Delivered **Trunks Called for and Delivered**
TELEPHONES: Bell, 978-23. Automatic, 1382 and 1031

Res., 83 Thomas St. Office, N. Y., N. H. & H. Depot, No. 4 Door
NEW BEDFORD, MASS.

Nash Road Wet Wash Laundry

J. C. ROY, Proprietor

THE MOST MODERN LAUNDRY WITH ALL THE LATEST EQUIPMENTS.

We guarantee perfect satisfaction to all who may try our washing.

Diman Street and Nash Road - New Bedford, Mass.
Auto. Tel. 2312 Bell Tel. 1841
Residence Phone, Auto. 4329

ARTHUR E. BUFFINGTON

Mason, Contractor and Builder

All Kinds of Mason Work Done to Order

Office, 1 CRAPO STREET NEW BEDFORD

TELEPHONE CONNECTION

Established by Augustus Swift 1879

ACUSHNET IRON COMPANY

Foundry, Pattern and Machine Shop

Iron Castings of Every Description Made to Order

Corner North and Water Streets

NEW BEDFORD MASS.

AUGUSTUS SWIFT

J. A. PERKINS ULYSSES G. BROWNELL

A. W. PERKINS & CO.

Slate and Gravel Roofers

Concrete Driveways and Sidewalks
Laid in the Best Manner

Special Attention Given to Repairing
Slate and Gravel Roofs

GENERAL TEAMING

Bell and Automatic Telephone P. O. Box 394.

Office, 167 HILLMAN STREET NEW BEDFORD

WARREN'S AGENCY

WARREN & GRIFFITHS

Real Estate

AUCTIONEERS

PROPERTY BOUGHT, SOLD AND EXCHANGED OR CARED FOR.

JUSTICE OF THE PEACE

1063 SO. WATER ST. - NEW BEDFORD, MASS.

TELEPHONE CONNECTION

George L. Briggs NEWSDEALER and STATIONER 161 PURCHA
Office Supplies Wholesale and Retail Bell 996, Au

N C. DANTSIZEN
UPHOLSTERER and FURNITURE REPAIRER
214 Court Street
Bell Telephone

HENRY P. WILSON

Undertaker and Embalmer

Bell 179-13 Automatic 1202 Night 1139 RESIDENCE, 152 WILLIAM STRE

80 PLEASANT STREET, Odd Fellows' Build

ALBERT W. HOLME

COAL

Main Office and Wh
Ft. Cannon S
Branch Office
201 Purchase

Bell and Automatic Telephones

INSURANCE

Fire, Plate Glass, St
Boiler Liability, Acci
Automobile Insurance

Only first-class American and English Companies represented

Business solicited

GEO. N. ALDEN

Office, Room 205, Second Floor, Merchants Bank Building, cor. William and Purchase

NEW BEDFORD, MASS.

The Browne Pharmacy

197-199-201-203 UNION STREET

The Largest and Handsomest
Pharmacy in New England

MASS.

Lightning Source UK Ltd.
Milton Keynes UK
UKHW010955201118
332647UK00013B/1260/P

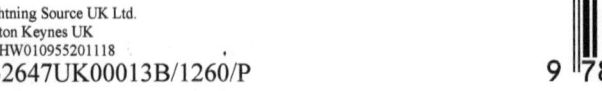

9 781528 013604